PSYCHOLOGICAL SCIENCE

W. W. Norton & Company
New York . London

PSYCHOLOGICAL SCIENCE

MIND, BRAIN, AND BEHAVIOR

Michael S. Gazzaniga
DARTMOUTH COLLEGE

Todd F. Heatherton
DARTMOUTH COLLEGE

Editor: Jon Durbin
Assistant Editor: Aaron Javsicas
Developmental Editor: Joanne Tinsley
Associate Managing Editor: Jane Carter
Project Editor: Kim Yi
Copy Editor: Kate Lovelady
Director of Manufacturing—College: Roy Tedoff
Book Designer: Rubina Yeh
Photo Researchers: Neil Hoos, June Whitworth
Illustrations: Frank Forney
Layout Artist: Brad Walrod

The text of this book is composed in Filosofia with display set in Tarzana
Composition by UG / GGS Information Services, Inc.
Manufacturing by Courier, Kendallville

Library of Congress Cataloging-in Publication Data
Gazzaniga, Michael S.
    Psychological science: the mind, brain, and behavior/Michael S. Gazzaniga, Todd F. Heatherton.
        p. cm
    Includes bibliographical references and index.

    ISBN 0-393-97587-8

    1. Psychology. I. Heatherton, Todd F. II. Title.
BF121 .G393 2002
150—dc21
                                                                    2002026321
W. W. Norton & Company, Inc. 500 Fifth Avenue, New York, N. Y. 10110
www.wwnorton.com
W. W. Norton & Company Ltd., Castle House, 75/76 Wells Street, London WIT 3QT

1 2 3 4 5 6 7 8 9 0

ABOUT THE AUTHORS

MICHAEL S. GAZZANIGA (Ph.D., California Institute of Technology) is the David T. McLaughlin Distinguished Professor at Dartmouth College. He founded and presides over the Cognitive Neuroscience Institute and is editor-in-chief of the *Journal of Cognitive Neuroscience*. His research focuses on split-brain patients. He has held positions at the University of California, Santa Barbara; New York University; the State University of New York, Stony Brook; Cornell University Medical College; and the University of California, Davis.

TODD F. HEATHERTON (Ph.D., University of Toronto) is the Champion Professor of Psychological and Brain Sciences at Dartmouth College. His primary research examines the situational, individual, motivational, and affective processes that interfere with self-regulation. He has been on the executive committees of the Society of Personality and Social Psychology, the Association of Researchers in Personality, and the International Society of Self and Identity and has served on the editorial boards of the *Journal of Abnormal Psychology*, the *Journal of Personality and Social Psychology*, and the *Review of General Psychology*. He has served as Head Tutor and chair of the undergraduate program in Psychology at Harvard University and chair of the graduate program at Dartmouth College. He received the Petra Shattuck Award for Teaching Excellence from the Harvard Extension School in 1994.

CONTENTS IN BRIEF

CONTENTS

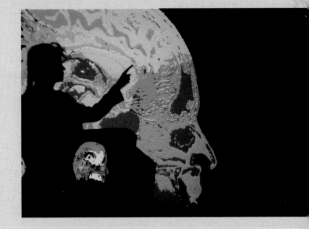

5 SENSATION, PERCEPTION, AND ATTENTION 122

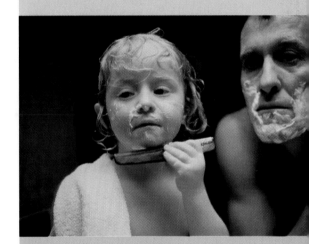

6 LEARNING AND REWARD 162

8 COGNITION 238

13 SELF AND SOCIAL COGNITION 414

14 INTERPERSONAL PROCESSES 448

FREE COPY FREE COPY FREE COPY FREE COI

15 PERSONALITY 484

16 DISORDERS OF MIND AND BODY 518

17 TREATING DISORDERS OF MIND AND BODY 556

PSYCHOLOGICAL SCIENCE FEATURE BOXES

PREFACE

THE INSPIRATION AND GOALS

The idea to write this textbook emerged about five years ago during a series of casual conversations between two colleagues, one a brain scientist, the other a social/personality psychologist. In many psychology departments, these sorts of conversations are rare, as increasing specialization within subfields of psychological science has produced less and less common ground for discussion. As we talked, we discovered that we had a great deal to learn from one another—brain science uses exciting and innovative methods to explore the biological basis of the working mind; social psychology studies problems central to everyday human existence. As our regular conversations continued, it became clear that the perceived chasm between us was not so great and that we could begin to bridge the gap. Over time, we witnessed the common ground between us expanding, providing new insights that would not have been possible without integrating the biological with the social. We were energized by our discussions, as we came to realize that this was a model approach for twenty-first century psychological science.

Our most important point of agreement was that without cross-disciplinary interaction and communication among scientists there could be no full understanding of the workings of the human mind. For instance, social, personality, clinical, and developmental psychologists have developed elaborate theories and models of behavior, but most of these theories fail to consider underlying neurobiological functions or structures. At the same time, neuroscientists have made tremendous gains in understanding the link between brain and behavior, but too often these findings are not informed by the social and cultural contexts that shape and guide human lives. We believe that it is becoming increasingly important for so-

cial psychologists to recognize that brain mechanisms are involved in producing social behaviors, while neuroscientists must begin to appreciate that brains interact in social contexts, in which cultural values and beliefs shape the way that people perceive the world. We further believe that crossing traditional boundaries to consider the biological with the social will energize both approaches and provide new perspectives and ideas. This textbook presents our areas on equal footing, because both are indispensable to developing a rich and integrated understanding of the mind, brain, and behavior.

One of our early discussions focused on teaching introductory psychology. We are committed to providing students with material that invigorates as it informs, and we believe that students should learn about exciting new advances in psychological science. Yet, the traditional approach to teaching introductory psychology fails to reflect fully the dramatic changes that have occurred within the discipline. The field of psychology is undergoing a revolution. It now incorporates a much greater biological perspective within its scope. In this exciting time, traditional psychological questions are being examined by a rich mixture of scientists, including evolutionary biologists, cognitive scientists, neuroscientists, and computer scientists. We have found, as have many of our colleagues, that it is rewarding to introduce these new ideas to psychology students, who are fascinated with the workings of the human mind as it navigates a complex, social world.

One of the challenges in teaching this new approach to psychology is that few if any of the traditional texts available for introductory college courses present this paradigm shift and its accompanying interdisciplinary synthesis. There is pressing need for a book tailored to delve into the rigorous sciences that comprise the essence of psychological thought. Books on the cutting edge in the 1970s (with their focus on information processing) and the 1980s (with their focus on cognition) do not reflect the field that emerged during this "decade of the brain." The emphasis on brain mechanisms is reinvigorating research on classic questions as well as shaping the problems that psychologists are addressing. This emphasis can be seen throughout psychological science. For instance, many social and personality psychologists are now interested in the neuroscientific basis of person-perception, social cognition, and interpersonal behavior. At the same time, researchers in the brain sciences have gained a greater understanding of the neural basis of social cognition, emotion, and personality. The enthusiasm for these new perspectives is clear in the best psychological journals and in the priorities of granting agencies, but it is less well represented in traditional books that introduce students to psychology.

We therefore decided to try to produce an introductory text that would satisfy the goals we identified as the most important: to be scientific, integrative, fun to read, succinct, and less detailed. We have focused on theory and research that crosses various levels of analysis, considering each of psychology's topic areas from multiple levels. Throughout the history of psychology, researchers have typically worked at one level of analysis, and they pursue their questions independently of researchers working at other levels. It is only recently that explanations for behavior are commonly reported in terms of several levels of analysis. It is this crossing of levels that many of us find so captivating. We believe that students benefit from considering research topics from multiple perspectives and dimensions.

In our attempt to write a concise rather than encyclopedic textbook, we chose to focus on the principles of psychological science that provide students with sufficient knowledge to understand research findings across areas of psychology, without inundating them with qualifications, exceptions, and complexities that are of greater interest to scholars conducting psychological research, graduate students completing their dissertations, or advanced psychology majors. It is challenging enough to consider the main areas of psychology within a quarter, semester, or even a full year, let alone to gain a comprehensive understanding of the entire field. Indeed, throughout writing this book we have continued to find that the greatest challenge is in deciding what *not* to include. There is so much fascinating research taking place around the globe that difficult choices had to be made in each section. Of course, we expect that instructors will supplement the text with more in-depth discussion of topics they find personally interesting and important, which in our experience brings vitality to the teaching of psychology.

We wrote this textbook first and foremost for the benefit of students. Like many instructors, we have had difficulty finding a rigorously written text pitched perfectly for the typical undergraduate student. Most of today's books are at too high or too low a level, too soft or too hard. In writing this text, therefore, we tried to strike the right balance. We made every effort to describe material that is occasionally technical and complex in terms that students can understand, believing that it is most important for introductory students to appreciate the basics before tackling the subtleties. As a rule, we tie behavioral examples and applications to the neuroscientific discussion throughout the text. We also tried to avoid jargon as much as possible, and to minimize the number of key terms that require formal definition, believing that the ideas are more important than the particular words used to describe them. Moreover, we chose to write in a declarative style, focusing on providing answers to the important questions within the topic areas of psychology. Our "ask and answer" approach serves as the pedagogical foundation for the book. Each chapter consists of a series of "big questions" that are answered in subsequent sections. Our use of declarative headings reflects our belief that psychological scientists have made headway in providing answers to these questions—perhaps not the final answers, as new research helps shape our thinking, but answers that summarize what psychological scientists have discovered about mind, brain, and behavior.

In writing this book for students, we also made a conscious decision to limit the number of citations in the text. We have talked with many of our colleagues who also teach introductory psychology. There is a growing consensus that, in teaching general psychology, long citation lists detract from the narrative and may well reinforce students' natural tendency to memorize rather than comprehend ideas and concepts. We formulated a middle ground in which we cite specific studies, major controversies, and classic papers, without overloading the text with additional research citations. Students will find sufficient information to conduct literature searches on topics they find interesting. Especially with the growth in electronic resources available to many students, we believe that students who are captivated by specific topics will be able to find additional information from their libraries or the World Wide Web. Finally, in our attempt to reflect the past accurately, we cite the most relevant rather than the most recent examples of research findings. Even as we appreciate the value of providing the most up-to-date information on each issue, we believe that there is also value in keeping true to the historical record.

Our textbook is intended for both students who wish to pursue careers in psychology and those for whom this course will be their only exposure to psychology as a science. Students using this text will gain an integrated grounding in traditional psychology as well as an introduction to new approaches within psychological science. The material is by nature intellectually challenging, but we have tried to make it accessible and enjoyable to undergraduates as well as directly applicable to their lives. Students will satisfy their curiosity about psychological phenomena and will learn to think critically about issues and themes in psychological science. Students also will develop greater self-understanding and understanding of others.

Four themes that characterize psychological science run through the chapters. (1) Psychological science is cumulative, in that principles are established based on incremental advances in knowledge obtained through research. (2) A biological revolution has been energizing psychological research. Increasing knowledge of the neurochemistry of mental disorders, the mapping of the human genome, and the invention of imaging technologies that allow researchers to observe the working brain in action have provided psychological scientists with the methods to examine how the brain enables the mind. (3) The mind is adaptive. The brain has evolved to solve everyday problems, and evolutionary psychology has had an increasing impact on the field in recent years. (4) Crossing the levels of analysis shows the various ways in which psychological scientists work on the same problem or issue, but from different levels of analysis and perspectives, from the molecular to the societal.

Although our book introduces a somewhat radical change in the scope of material, we did not want to sacrifice the rich tradition of psychological theory and research. We wanted to introduce students to the central themes and issues that have shaped the field's development, such as the questions of nature versus nurture, structure and function, determinism versus free will, and person versus situation. Thus, the organization of the textbook will be familiar to most psychology instructors, even if they do not teach the material in the specific order it is presented.

One of the joys of writing this book is that it provided a great reason to continue our ongoing conversations. We met regularly to discuss each section and we sought to make sure that we both contributed to each chapter, at a minimum providing commentary and suggestions for what ought to be included and where topics were most effectively discussed. Sometimes this meant presenting certain topics in chapters other than where they typically appear in introductory textbooks. Again, crossing the levels of analysis means that certain topics could conceivably appear in any number of chapters.

As the book started to take shape, we paused to reflect that it had shaped us as well. No longer pure brain scientist and pure social/personality psychologist, we now meet as psychological scientists. Indeed, we began collaborating on interdisciplinary research, such as examining the neural correlates of self using brain imaging and split-brain patients. We have taken to heart the message of our text that greater scientific progress will be made from crossing the levels of analysis. We hope that our textbook helps narrow the gaps between areas in other departments, as psychological scientists come together to understand mind, brain, and behavior.

TOUR OF *PSYCHOLOGICAL SCIENCE*

Chapter 1 ("Introduction to Psychological Science") sets the stage for the book. We introduce students to psychological science by providing engaging examples of psychological questions that address central themes in psychology, and we briefly trace the historical background of psychological research to answer those questions. The overall orientation stresses the importance of considering the mind as an evolved mechanism for solving adaptive problems. To understand the mind, the student needs to understand how the brain works, how the mind interprets the environment, and how social environments and culture shape behavior. We end this provocative chapter with a section on potential careers in psychology and a discussion of the importance of critical thinking for consumers of psychological research.

Chapter 2 ("Research Methodology") covers the major methods in sufficient detail so that students understand the techniques and strategies used by psychological scientists to examine the working mind and its social consequences. We make the important point that the research question dictates the methods used to answer the question. In addition to basic experimental design, we introduce students to methods used to examine the brain, from neuropsychological assessment to new methods of brain imaging. This information serves as the foundation for understanding research findings and the importance of using empirical methods to assess brain and behavior. We also include a brief description of statistical techniques, here rather than in the appendix, because it is important for students to appreciate how researchers are able to draw conclusions based on their analysis of data.

Chapters 3 and 4 focus on genetic and biological foundations of psychological science. Many introductory textbooks try to cover all of this information in one chapter, presenting laundry lists of important anatomical and functional terms. By providing more information in two medium-length chapters, we give students more time to learn the material. Whereas most general psychology books leave the biological underpinnings of behavior behind after one chapter, *Psychological Science* draws on this foundational information in every chapter. Chapter 3 ("Genetic and Biological Foundations") provides students with an introduction to genetics and the basic processes of the nervous system. We enliven the discussion of the nervous system by focusing on neurotransmitter receptors and their influence on emotions and behavior. We emphasize that all psychological activity results from the integration of billions of connections between nerve cells in different regions of the brain and body. We discuss how neurons form selective networks that underlie all psychological activity and serve the working mind. The interaction of the nervous system and endocrine system is also discussed. Chapter 4 ("The Brain") introduces students to functional neuroanatomy, beginning with an historical view of brain function and dysfunction and progressing to the central issue of whether brain function is localized or distributed throughout the brain. The student is then introduced to gross anatomical and functional subdivisions of the brain. The emphasis, however, is on how the brain works rather than on what the various parts are called. We are not exhaustive with labels but rather introduce students to brain systems and regions that are important for understanding the mind. Considerable attention is given to cerebral lateralization and specialization, with vivid examples from split-brain patients. Common neurological impairments are also discussed.

Chapter 5 ("Sensation, Perception, and Attention") provides a foundation for understanding how the brain senses and perceives the world. Following a discussion of historical approaches to understanding the basis of human knowledge, essential issues in sensation and perception are presented, with an emphasis on how the brain has evolved to make sense of the world. We then discuss how each of the senses work and describe typical dysfunctions within each sense. Finally, we consider how attentional processes influence people's perceptions of the world.

Chapters 6 and 7 ("Learning and Reward" and "Memory") discuss the foundations of learning and memory. Learning theory has a rich tradition in psychological science and is important for understanding most psychological phenomena. We consider the historical record in sufficient detail to provide students with the vocabulary necessary to understand the basic principles of classical and operant conditioning, and then we explore the way that contemporary cognitive neuroscience explains learning. We include a detailed discussion of the biological basis of reward in chapter 6 (rather than in the motivation chapter) in order for students to consider what it means for something to be reinforcing. We also consider recent evidence of the neuronal basis of conditioning. Finally, we consider examples of observational learning, including an in-depth discussion of the effects of media on aggressive and health behaviors. We should also note that various contemporary theories and findings involving learning can be found in chapters throughout the book, which reflects the universal quality of this fundamental behavioral phenomena. The memory chapter re-

views the many new and exciting approaches to understanding memory. Following a brief historical discussion of stages of memory, we explore the distinction between implicit and explicit memory. A central focus of the chapter is the neurological and neuronal basis of memory, with classic and contemporary examples of how brain injury interferes with explicit recall. We discuss false memories, including evidence suggesting that such memories are differentiable from authentic memories using brain-imaging techniques. We also consider the practical aspects of human memory, such as the ability to serve as eyewitnesses and the role of motivation and social context in shaping what we remember.

Chapter 8 ("Cognition") considers how people think, including what it means to think intelligently. The cognitive sciences have advanced our basic understanding of how people acquire and use knowledge. Although rooted in psychological science, the study of cognition is central to the interests of philosophers, computer scientists, evolutionary biologists, and statisticians, among others. This chapter introduces students to the central themes that reflect how the mind thinks and solves adaptive problems. We discuss a variety of obstacles and shortcuts involved in problem solving, such as mental-set and heuristic processing, and we consider whether human decision making is rational or adaptive. We also discuss what is meant by the term *intelligence*, including a discussion of alternative conceptions of what it means to be smart.

Chapter 9 ("Motivation") presents an overview of the factors that motivate behavior. This chapter demonstrates the need to consider biological, cognitive, and social factors in order to develop a satisfactory understanding of why people "choose" to engage in specific behaviors. We consider motivation in its adaptive context, with an interpretation based on evolutionary principles. This chapter also introduces the idea that societal and cultural preferences shape what is valued and dictate the goals that people pursue. This chapter examines human self-regulation and achievement motivation in a way that encourages students to think about their short-term and long-term goals. Eating and sleep are considered in detail, as they provide excellent examples of various aspects of motivation.

Chapter 10 ("Emotions, Stress, and Coping") considers the foundations of emotional processes, as well as how people succeed and fail in coping with the stress of daily living. There has been an explosion of research in emotion over the past decade, and this chapter summarizes what has been learned, emphasizing cognitive neuroscience and evolutionary adaptiveness. We start by considering the functional nature of emotions, both the short-term functions for the person and long-term adaptiveness for the species. For instance, social emotions such as guilt are viewed as adaptive mechanisms that strengthen social bonds and satisfy a fundamental need to belong. Most textbooks ignore guilt, even though most people report guilt as a major source of motivation and displeasure in their lives. This section encourages students to consider why negative interpersonal motives might have evolved. We then review classic theories of emotion with a thorough discussion of cognitive appraisal models. We also describe the physiology and neurochemistry of emotional experience, with an emphasis on the integration of cognition and emotion in the limbic system. Finally, we consider contemporary approaches to understanding stress and coping, including some provocative ideas about gender differences in coping with stress.

Chapters 11 and 12 ("Cognitive and Language Development" and "Social Development and Gender") look at how humans develop. We begin by examining the foundations of cognitive development and language. Chapter 11 focuses on the skills that exist at different times in development, without rigidly adhering to the notion of stages. Following a discussion of the capacities of newborns, we review what is known about cognitive development within specific domains. Such an approach is faithful to the research efforts of contemporary developmental psychologists. One of the most important developments in childhood is the capacity for language, and this topic receives careful consideration. Our focus is on how language facilitates communication rather than on lexical content. Finally, we consider how cognitive processes change during adolescence and aging. Chapter 12 begins our discussion of humans as social animals. We start with the assumption that evolution has adapted a fundamental need to belong. We consider the role of caregivers and discuss the influence of parenting styles while considering issues of temperament and genetics. We then spend considerable time discussing the scientific basis of friendships, a topic that is of utmost importance to undergraduates, but virtually ignored in most introductory textbooks. Finally, we consider the role of biology and culture in sex and gender differences. We review current evidence of cross-cultural consistency in sex differences while explaining how cultural expectations shape gender roles.

Chapters 13 and 14 ("Self and Social Cognition" and "Interpersonal Processes") focus on topics related to social psychology. These issues are some of the most interesting to undergraduates, especially because of the wonderful creativity associated with classic social psychology studies. The first of the two chapters focuses on how individuals perceive their social worlds. It begins with an examination of the personal sense of

self, including self-awareness and self-esteem. We discuss the literature demonstrating that humans have self-serving motivational biases and the possible negative interpersonal consequences of such biases. We also examine the influence of impression management and culture on self-concept. We then expand from attitudes about the self to attitudes about objects and other people. For instance, we examine possible reasons for racism and prejudice and discuss how they might be reduced. We include new perspectives on social psychological phenomena that share common theories and methods with cognitive neuroscience. Whereas Chapter 13 focuses on how individuals perceive their social worlds, Chapter 14 looks at interactions between individuals. This chapter emphasizes the important point that humans have evolved as social animals and that much of human behavior and experience is shaped by social contacts. This chapter is an in-depth look at social interaction and includes discussion of nonverbal communication and interpersonal relationships. We also consider how the need to belong to groups leaves people susceptible to influence from others and can lead to their acting in obedient and conforming ways. The essential theme is that human survival has long depended on group living, and therefore people are motivated to maintain their affiliation and status within the group.

Chapter 15 ("Personality") is a somewhat radical departure from historical treatments of personality. Most textbooks describe personality as it was conceived of more than 40 years ago, with an emphasis on unconscious Freudian processes and social-learning experiences. Yet, recent research has provided compelling evidence that human personality is determined to a large extent by genetic and physiological mechanisms. This chapter focuses on research by contemporary psychologists who have made considerable strides in understanding the development and structure of human personality. We cover traditional topics, such as Freudian and trait theory, but we emphasize a neuroscience approach to personality, examining genetic, biological, and cognitive factors. Finally, we consider whether people can change their basic personalities.

Chapters 16 and 17 consider mental disorders and their treatment. Chapter 16 ("Disorders of Mind and Body") introduces students to well-known and reasonably common forms of psychopathology. We begin by discussing and critiquing various philosophical, statistical, and functional approaches to characterizing mental illness. We then describe the essential features of each disorder and discuss various etiological theories. Vivid case studies are used to illustrate symptoms and assessment. We include expanded coverage of childhood disorders, as they are typically ignored in introductory textbooks and it is our experience that students find these disorders especially interesting. The final chapter ("Treating Disorders of Mind and Body") examines the theoretical basis of psychotherapy, as well as typical treatments and outcomes. Following a discussion of treatment goals, we introduce students to the most common types of therapy. Although we mention classic psychological treatments, we emphasize the types of treatments most widely used by contemporary therapists. We consider treatments for anxiety disorders, depression, and schizophrenia in detail, with special attention to the empirical evidence for successful outcomes. We also consider evidence that social context and familial influences play a major role in therapeutic success.

A PEDAGOGICAL PROGRAM THAT REINFORCES *PSYCHOLOGICAL SCIENCE'S* CORE PRINCIPLES

I. OVERVIEW

Psychological Science's chapters are built around major principles, which are addressed through the "ask and answer" approach. Each chapter focuses on approximately 4–6 major principles, which are first raised in the form of questions ("ask"). Each major section in a chapter then discusses one of these questions ("answer").

Outlining the Principles: This pedagogical feature at one level serves as a simple outline or road map for the chapter. At another level, it clarifies what major principles will be covered in the chapter. Major heads are questions. Minor heads are declarative statements that reveal the current state of knowledge about the larger principles and concepts.

Chapter Timelines: *Psychological Science* is built on cumulative knowledge and experience. This is one of the major themes of the text. Basic principles, both new and old, inspire and guide thinking and research in the field. The timelines highlight major developments within the various domains of psychology.

Research Questions for Studying. . . : *Psychological Science* captures the excitement of contemporary ideas and research driving the field today. The research questions highlighted in the opening pages of every chapter suggest the kinds of questions that researchers are exploring. These questions reappear in the margins throughout a given chapter to alert students when the relevant issues are being discussed. This is another dimension to the "ask and answer" approach.

"Ask and Answer" Running Heads: *Psychological Science*'s left-hand running heads emphasize the greater topics, as the right-hand running heads repeat the questions that are explored in each section. The heads help students stay focused on the larger issue as they try to see the forest for the trees.

Reviewing the Principles: These boxes are a critical component to the "ask and answer" approach and appear at the end of each major section. They repeat the question that governed the section and provide a basic answer that highlights key points for students to remember.

Defining the Principles: *Psychological Science* has a marginal glossary running throughout each chapter as well as a glossary at the end of the book and on the companion Web site. Many books highlight an overabundance of key terms for students to memorize. In keeping with this book's focus on core principles and concepts, *Psychological Science* highlights approximately 30 key terms per chapter.

Summarizing the Principles: This is the last key component to the "ask and answer" approach. *Psychological Science*'s brief chapter conclusions highlight the big ideas and concepts covered and remind students how the book's four key themes wove their way through the chapter. After reading the chapter conclusion, students may want to reread the "Reviewing the Principle" sections to emphasize what they have learned and what they haven't.

II. *PSYCHOLOGICAL SCIENCE'S* USE OF ART AND CITATIONS

A Dynamic Art Program: The visual materials in *Psychological Science* add substantially to the students' experience. The book contains a variety of visual materials, from photographs to tables and charts to drawn art. The emphasis in *Psychological Science*, however, is clearly on the drawn art. Having used many general psychology books ourselves, we wanted to take our text in a new direction. By featuring drawn art, *Psychological Science* is able to convey precisely, accurately, and meaningfully what the students need to gain from every image. This high level of precision can't be gained from the use of the stock photographs common in many texts.

Selective Use of Citations: *Psychological Science* embraces the notion that students should be introduced to material in a narrative style that focuses on ideas, concepts, and empirical findings rather than on specific researchers. At the same time, the text includes sufficient citations so that students can pursue topics of interest and so that they appreciate that psychological science is based on published empirical research. We have selected essential citations that we hope most teachers would agree are central to a first-year student's exploration of psychological science, and we have cited them in a way that should not distract from the narrative voice.

III. *PSYCHOLOGICAL SCIENCE'S* SPECIAL FEATURE BOXES

Every chapter following the introduction contains one of each of the following feature boxes, which are designed to amplify the text's basic strengths:

Studying the Mind feature boxes highlight examples of psychological phenomena that fascinate as well as inform. These often describe case studies that reveal intriguing aspects of the biological basis of the mind, such as the effect of brain injury on motivation, emotion, and personality.

Using Psychological Science feature boxes address questions relevant to students. For example, Is there such a thing as photographic memory? Why do New Year's resolutions often fail? What is the effect of birth order on personality?

Crossing the Levels of Analysis feature boxes explain how significant advances in our understanding of complex psychological phenomena have emerged from research that crosses interdisciplinary boundaries. We explore how psychological scientists are approaching each topic from molecular to societal levels, and how interdisciplinary teams of scientists are providing compelling new insights based on this synthesis.

PSYCHOLOGICAL SCIENCE'S ANCILLARIES REINFORCE THE TEXT'S BASIC STRENGTHS

STUDY GUIDE TO ACCOMPANY *PSYCHOLOGICAL SCIENCE* BY BRETT BECK (BLOOMBURG UNIVERSITY) AND JEFF HENRIQUES (UNIVERSITY OF WISCONSIN-MADISON)

Created by two highly successful instructors of large lecture classes, this carefully crafted study aid offers a guide to the reading with helpful study advice, completion questions, key figure exercises, multiple-choice self-tests, and thought questions.

STUDENT WEB SITE TO ACCOMPANY *PSYCHOLOGICAL SCIENCE:* WWW.WWNORTON.COM/PSYCHSCI

Designed to help students learn the basic principles of psychological science, this highly interactive Web site offers a rich array of exercises and opportunities to explore human behavior. Access is free to every student.

For every chapter there is
- an animated timeline that highlights research milestones
- a guide to the reading that offers helpful advice
- a list of key terms linked to an on-line glossary
- a crossword puzzle that tests recall for new vocabulary
- multiple-choice tests with answer feedback
- a rich collection of activities that features animations of hard-to-visualize concepts, media-enhanced essays with assignable thought questions, on-line labs, and topics for further reading.

INSTRUCTOR'S RESOURCE MANUAL TO ACCOMPANY *PSYCHOLOGICAL SCIENCE* BY GEORGE SPILICH (WASHINGTON COLLEGE)

Prepared by a master teacher from a small liberal arts college who cultivates an active learning environment. Available to all adopters.

Each chapter of the *Instructor's Resource Manual* includes the following:
  I. Chapter Objectives
 II. Key Concepts and Theories
III. Lecture Resources
    a. Ticket In/Ticket Out Assignments
    b. Five-Minute Lecture Launchers
    c. Classroom Demonstrations
    d. Topics for Classroom Discussion
    e. Link Library
 IV. Index of Norton Media Resources (see description below).
  V. Additional Resources (resources, citations, suggested films and readings).

NORTON TESTMAKER TO ACCOMPANY *PSYCHOLOGICAL SCIENCE* BY KATHLEEN VOHS (UNIVERSITY OF UTAH).

This carefully crafted test-item file includes over 2,000 multiple-choice questions of varying degrees of difficulty. The Norton TestMaker allows instructors to add and edit their own questions, control test design and layout, print several versions of the same test, and create optional on-line testing modules. Available to all adopters.

NORTON MEDIA LIBRARY

This collection of PowerPoint slides for instructors includes lecture outlines, line art from the text, classroom demonstration resources, and animations optimized for classroom display. Available to all adopters.

TRANSPARENCIES TO ACCOMPANY *PSYCHOLOGICAL SCIENCE*

These full-color acetates reproduce a wide selection of the drawn art that appears throughout the text.

STUDYING THE MIND: INTERVIEWS TO ACCOMPANY *PSYCHOLOGICAL SCIENCE* (VHS)

Filmed at Dartmouth College's Summer Institute for Cognitive Neuroscience, and featuring original footage exclusive of Norton, this guest lecturer series was developed to help bring examples of current brain-science research into the introductory psychology lecture. These five to seven minute segments feature well known neuroscientific researchers like Marcus Raichle · Robert Knight · Mark D'Esposito · Mike Gazzaniga · John Gabrieli · Elizabeth Phelps · Marcia Johnson · Morris Moscovitch · Helen Neville · Denise Parks · Patricia Reuter-Lorenz. Available October 2002. Free to qualified adopters.

NORTON RESOURCE LIBRARY (HTTP://WWW.WWNORTON.COM/NRL)

An on-line site designed to house all available electronic *Psychological Science* resources from the test bank to PowerPoint slides to video clips. All of these resources are readily uploadable into WebCT and Blackboard environments. Available to all adopters.

NORTON VIDEO LIBRARY

A collection of first-rate documentary films focusing on psychological science drawn from the *Films for Sciences and Humanities* catalog and other fine video collections. Available to qualifying adopters.

ACKNOWLEDGMENTS

Writing this textbook has been both demanding and rewarding. Perhaps the most apt analogy is raising children, an all-consuming labor of love in which daily effort, occasional frustration, and frequent sacrifices yield to the joys of parental pride, as we watch in amazement as our children blossom and grow. This book is dedicated to our children, who have given us the strength and motivation to persevere. We are putting the final touches on this preface on a spectacular Sunday morning in New England, a time that is typically reserved for family. Our wives, Charlotte Gazzaniga and Patricia Heatherton, are, as ever, understanding of our absence. We begin by thanking them for their support, composure, and good humor. Both have advanced degrees in psychology and have listened patiently and provided helpful commentary when we have struggled to explain technical details in a manner comprehensible for students. Both are insightful and pragmatic, and the textbook has benefited greatly from their participation in the writing process.

We are grateful recipients of phenomenal support from our colleagues during all phases of writing this textbook. Many people were particularly helpful in developing and organizing the content of specific chapters. We especially wish to thank Margaret Funnell, Todd Handy, Paul Corballis, Kathleen Vohs, Ian Wickersham, Abigail Baird, and Marin Gazzaniga. Many of our colleagues in the Department of Psychological and Brain Sciences at Dartmouth read sections, gave advice, or provided expert commentary, notably Ann Clark, William Kelley, George Wolford, Robert Leaton, Jay Hull, Howard Hughes, and especially Laura Ann Petitto. We are grateful to them for their expertise. We also benefited from the astute guidance of Endel Tulving, Steve Marcus, Michael Ullman, Steven Pinker, Roy Baumeister, Thomas Joiner, David Funder, Jane Gillette, Mikki Hebl, Peter Ruscitti, George Spilich, and many others who were willing to discuss their teaching goals for introductory psychology and their beliefs about what works and what doesn't work in introductory textbooks. We are also grateful to our exceptionally talented supplements authors: George Spilich (Washington College) who authored the Instructor's Resource Manual and developed activities for the companion Web site, Brett Beck (Bloomsburg University) and Jeff Henriques (University of Wisconsin-Madison) who authored the Study Guide, with George and Kathleen Vohs (University of Utah) who created the test item files. We are grateful to Bobbi Walling for pulling together materials for the glossaries, and Lisa Jones and Tina Wilcox for helping to keep us organized. We especially applaud the contributions of Rebecca Townsend, who not only administers the Center for Cognitive Neuroscience, but also happens to be an amazing proofreader.

There are many people at W.W. Norton who served critical roles in bringing this textbook to realization. First and foremost, we thank Jon Durbin, our editor and friend. Jon was a true believer from the earliest days of the book and has been essential at every step of the process. Jon walks a fine line between motivating and mercilessly badgering his authors, but he does so because he is committed to moving his authors to the highest levels they can attain. Jon pushed us to consider, reconsider, and reconsider again nearly every section of the textbook. His unflagging encouragement and frequent pep talks helped us stay true to the mission of producing a cutting-edge textbook that reflects the excitement of contemporary psychological science. The book would not have been possible without him and the inspiring energy and enthusiasm he brings to his work.

Our developmental editor, Joanne Tinsley, was superb. Every chapter benefited from her exceptional ability to understand the big picture and organize the material in the best possible fashion. She was brutal with us when she needed to be and she galvanized us to push the limits of traditional texts as we sought to achieve our goals. The copy editor, Kate Lovelady, made sure that not a single word was in the textbook that did not need to be there. Her ability to tighten text is stunning. Kim Yi, the project editor, kept the entire manuscript on track with her truly spectacular organizational skills and good humor. Aaron Javsicas performed essential editorial and production duties flawlessly. Neil Hoos and his photo research team did an exceptional job conceiving of an integrated art program composed of the highest quality photography for the book. Rubina Yeh receives the highest credit for a lively and gorgeous book design that graphically serves both as the pattern and as the fabric that ties together all its individual components. We are also grateful to Frank Forney for his incredible art. His drawings are some of the finest to appear in any science textbook, and he managed to create many of these from vague ideas provided by the authors. As all general psychology instructors know, the quality of the supplements and media package play an ever-more-important role in the success of a textbook. We give special thanks to April Lange for all her creative talents and her ability to put together a high-quality team of front-line instructors to create a package that reinforces and builds upon the book's strengths. In each case, the final product is just what we wanted—first rate. Finally, we thank Roby Harrington, director of the College Division, and Drake McFeely, president of W.W. Norton, for their faith in us.

PSYCHOLOGICAL SCIENCE CONSULTANTS

Alan Baddeley, Bristol University
Lori Badura, State University of New York, Buffalo
Mahzarin Banaji, Harvard University
Colin Blakemore, Oxford University
Randy Buckner, Washington University
Tara Callaghan, St. Francis Xavier University
Jennifer Campbell, University of British Columbia
Jonathan Cheek, Wellesley College
Dennis Cogan, Texas Tech University
Martin Conway, Bristol University
Michael Corballis, University of Auckland
James Enns, University of British Columbia
Raymond Fancher, York University
Fernanda Ferreira, Michigan State University
Vic Ferreira, University of California, San Diego
Christine Gancarz, Southern Methodist University
Wendi Gardner, Northwestern University
Rick O. Gilmore, Penn State University
James Gross, Stanford University
John Hallonquist, University of the Cariboo
Mikki Hebl, Rice University
Mark Henn, University of New Hampshire
Don Hoffman, University of California, Irvine
James Hoffman, University of Delaware
Jake Jacobs, University of Arizona
Thomas Joiner, Florida State University
Dacher Keltner, University of California, Berkeley
Mark Leary, Wake Forest University
Monica Luciana, University of Minnesota
Neil Macrae, Bristol University/Dartmouth College
Julie Norem, Wellesley College
Lauretta Reeves, Rowan University

Jennifer Richeson, Dartmouth College
Paul Rozin, University of Pennsylvania
Constantine Sedikides, University of Southhampton
Allison Sekuler, McMaster University
Andrew Shatte, University of Pennsylvania
Dianne Tice, Case Western Reserve University
David Uttal, Northwestern University
Elaine Walker, Emory University

PSYCHOLOGICAL SCIENCE REVIEWERS

Gordon A. Allen, Miami University of Ohio
Ron Apland, Malaspina University-College
John P. Broida, University of Southern Maine
Katherine Cameron, Washington College
Timothy Cannon, University of Scranton
Charles Carver, University of Miami
Stephen Clark, Keene State College
Joseph Dien, Tulane University
Jack Dovidio, Colgate University
Margaret Forgie, University of Lethbridge
David Funder, University of California, Riverside
Peter Gerhardstein, Binghamton University
Peter Graf, University of British Columbia
Leonard Green, Washington University
Norman Henderson, Oberlin College
Terence Hines, Pace University
Sara Hodges, University of Oregon
Mike Kerchner, Washington College
Rondall Khoo, Western Connecticut State University
Charles Leith, Northern Michigan University
Margaret Lynch, San Fransisco State University
Dale McAdam, University of Rochester
Dan McAdams, Northwestern University
Doug McCann, York University
Bill McKeachie, University of Michigan
Judy Miller, Oberlin College
Zehra Peynircioglu, The American University
Brady Phelps, South Dakota State University
Alex Rothman, University of Minnesota
Juan Salinas, University of Texas, Austin
Margaret Sereno, University of Oregon
Arthur Shimamura, University of California, Berkeley
Rebecca Shiner, Colgate University
Reid Skeel, Central Michigan University
Dennison Smith, Oberlin College
Mark Snyder, University of Minnesota
George Taylor, University of Missouri
Robin R. Vallacher, Florida Atlantic University
Benjamin Walker, Georgetown University
Brian Wandell, Stanford University
Kevin Weinfurt, Duke University
Doug Whitman, Wayne State University
Maxine Gallander Wintre, York University
Claire Wiseman, Trinity College

PREFACE FOR STUDENTS

DEAR STUDENT:

Our most important overarching goal for this textbook was to write it first and foremost for you, the student reader. We know that many of you are drawn to psychology to find out more about what makes you and those you know tick. We also know from our own teaching experiences in recent years, that many of you are highly interested in learning more about how the human mind works and what that means for you in everyday life. Thus, as you search for insights into the human experience, we have made every effort to focus on core psychological principles and ideas to provide a starting point (and sometimes the end point) for your quest. Our focus on principles is reinforced by the "ask and answer" approach that serves as the pedagogical foundation for the book. Each chapter consists of a series of "big questions" that focus on major psychological principles and concepts. These questions are answered in subsequent sections. Our use of declarative headings reflects our belief that psychological scientists have made headway in providing answers to these questions—perhaps not the final answers, as new research helps shape our thinking, but answers that summarize what psychological scientists have discovered about mind, brain, and behavior.

Psychological Science is intended for both those of you who wish to pursue careers in psychology and those for whom this course will be your only exposure to psychology as a science. While using this text, you will gain an integrated grounding in traditional psychology as well as an introduction to new approaches within psychological science. The material is by nature intellectually challenging, but we have tried to make it accessible and enjoyable to you as well as directly applicable to your life. We hope that *Psychological Science* spurs on your curiosity about psychological phenomena and that you will learn to think critically about issues and themes in psychological science. In the end (or the beginning!), we hope that you will also develop greater self-understanding and understanding of others.

Before you begin to read the first chapter, please take a few minutes to study the following pages so that you can gain a full understanding of how to get the most out of reading *Psychological Science*.

GUIDED CHAPTER TOUR FOR STUDENTS

1 **OVERVIEW** *Psychological Science's* chapters are built around core principles. The "ask and answer" approach serves as the structure and foundation for every chapter and is designed to reinforce these principles. Each chapter focuses on approximately 4–6 major principles, which are first raised in the form of questions ("ask"). Each major section in a chapter then looks to "answer" one of these questions. Here is how it works in action.

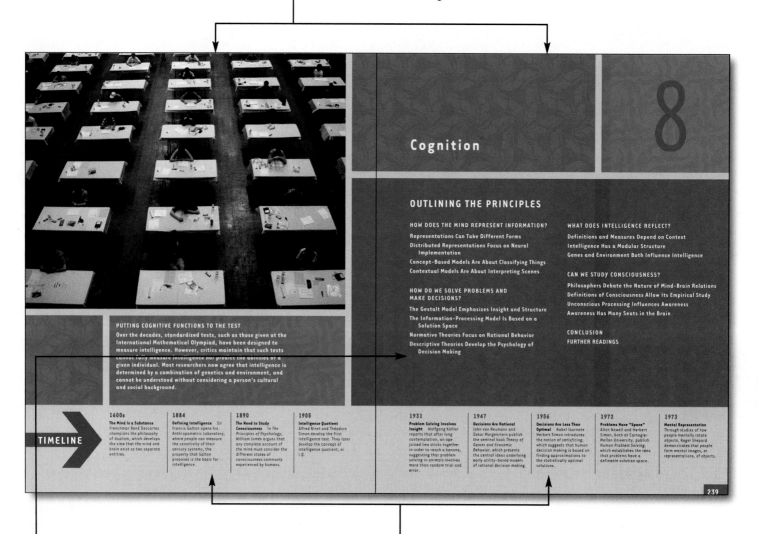

2 **OUTLINING THE PRINCIPLES** appears on the second page of every chapter. This pedagogical feature at one level serves as a simple outline or road map for the chapter. At another level, it reveals what major principles will be discussed in the chapter. By studying the major headings, you can see which major questions ("ask") will drive the chapter. It's also important to note that the subheadings appear in the form of declarative statements ("answer") that reveal our current state of knowledge about the question.

3 **CHAPTER TIMELINES** appear on the bottom of the first three pages of every chapter. *Psychological Science* is built on cumulative knowledge and experience. This is one of the major themes of the text. Basic principles, both new and old, inspire and guide thinking and research in the field. The timelines highlight major developments within the various domains of psychology. By studying them, you will see more clearly how various principles have been established, challenged, and modified.

4 **CHAPTER OPENING VIGNETTES** lead off each chapter. The vignettes are drawn from a variety of sources, including news media, research journals, and history. They highlight a major theme, issue, or tension point that will be discussed throughout a given chapter.

6 **"ASK AND ANSWER" RUNNING HEADS** are designed to reinforce the basic principles. The running heads that appear on each right-hand page repeat the question that is explored in each section. These innovative running heads will help you see the forest for the trees as you read through the chapters.

---

240 | CHAPTER 8 Cognition

In his book *An Anthropologist on Mars* (1995), neurologist Oliver Sacks tells the story of one of his more remarkable patients, a man in his fifties named Virgil. When Virgil was five years old, he developed a severe case of cataracts, which rendered him blind. Virgil soon adapted to a life without vision, and as the years passed by, his childhood memories of what it had been like to see faded from awareness.

When Virgil was in his fifties, he fell in love and got married. As a wedding gift, Virgil's fiancée offered to pay for corneal transplant surgery to restore his vision. Apprehensive but hopeful, Virgil agreed to the operation.

One of the cataracts was removed, and a new lens was transplanted. A day later the bandages were removed, and for the first time in nearly 45 years, light fell unimpaired upon Virgil's retina. What did he see? How did he react? Sacks tells the story best:

Virgil told me later that in this first moment he had no idea what he was seeing. There was light, there was movement, there was color, all mixed up, all meaningless, a blur. Then out of the blur came a voice that said, "Well?" Then, and only then, he said, did he finally realize that this chaos of light and shadow was a face—and, indeed, the face of his surgeon. (p. 114)

Virgil saw a kaleidoscope of color and light that had no connection with the world as he had known it. The sudden addition of "vision" felt confusing and awkward, and the joy that he and his wife had hoped for failed to materialize. As time went on, Virgil grew increasingly frustrated by his inability to adapt to this new aspect of his awareness. Only with the return of blindness due to other causes did Virgil find the peace he had had before the operation.

What went wrong? Why did Virgil fail to gain happiness from being able to see? Those who have vision have spent a lifetime learning how to use and understand visual information. We know that

RESEARCH QUESTIONS ???

for Studying Cognition

Do mental representations exist in different forms?

How do we solve problems?

To what extent is human decision making rational?

How do our decisions deviate from statistically optimal choices?

On what aspects of mind is intelligence based?

To what degree is intelligence influenced by our genes?

What are the elementary properties of consciousness?

How does the brain give rise to phenomenal awareness?

1979	1982	1983	1990s	2000
Decisions Are Relative Daniel Kahneman and Amos Tversky propose prospect theory, which models the tendency of decision makers (1) to use points of reference, and (2) to give more weight to potential losses than to potential gains.	**We Try to Avoid Regret** David Bell, Graham Loomes, and Robert Sugden independently propose that making decisions about uncertain events is based on anticipating possible regret regarding the different possibilities.	**Multiple Intelligence** Howard Gardner expands the traditional definition of intelligence to recognize that people can excel, or show intelligence, in different ways.	**Evolved Decision Making** Gerd Gigerenzer argues that decision making is best understood by considering how humans have solved problems over the course of evolution.	**The Seat of General Intelligence** Using brain imaging, researchers led by John Duncan report that "general intelligence" may be tied to the functioning of the frontal cortex.

looming objects are moving toward us and that shrinking objects are moving away, and that people's moods can be gleaned from their faces. Those with vision are so practiced at using it that seeing seems absolutely effortless and automatic.

If Virgil's difficulties stemmed from a lack of knowledge, what does it mean to have this knowledge? How do we represent it in our minds—and in our brains? Moreover, what would it be like to suddenly have an entirely new sensory experience enter our consciousness? This chapter explores such questions, first by considering the nature of mental representations. Building on this foundation, we then ask a series of questions: How do we represent and organize knowledge, and how do we use it in our thinking? Does intelligence stem only from our knowledge-based reasoning, or does it include a broader selection of mental capacities? Finally, what is consciousness? How does the brain give rise to the awareness of the world that we associate with being conscious?

HOW DOES THE MIND REPRESENT INFORMATION?

Cognitive psychology was originally predicated on the notion that the brain *represents* information, and that the act of thinking—that is, *cognition*—is directly associated with manipulating these representations. While these ideas were central to breaking the behaviorist zeitgeist that had dominated American psychology in the first half of the twentieth century, they immediately gave rise to an important new question: What is the nature of these representations? In the following section, we consider the different ways in which mental representations are characterized. The biological revolution has led to the development of new approaches that now allow us to study these representations empirically.

Over the last several decades, one of the more heated debates in cognitive psychology has been over the nature of mental representations: Are they like pictures, or are they based on more verbal-like descriptions? The topic is important because the representation of knowledge in the brain forms the basis of cognition, intelligence, and ultimately consciousness. As is often the case, the opposing views in this debate are not mutually exclusive.

REPRESENTATIONS CAN TAKE DIFFERENT FORMS

The popular view that mental representations are analogous to pictures holds much intuitive appeal in that, in our mind's eye, we often appear to *see* visual images. For instance, it is difficult to think about a "lemon" without having some sort of image come to mind that resembles an actual lemon, with its yellow and somewhat waxy, dimpled skin.

Not surprisingly, several lines of evidence strongly suggest that representations can indeed take on such picturelike qualities. First, in a famous set of

Do mental representations exist in different forms?

---

5 **RESEARCH QUESTIONS FOR STUDYING. . .** *Psychological Science* captures the excitement of contemporary ideas and research driving the field today. The research questions highlighted on the third page of every chapter suggest the kinds of questions that researchers are exploring. Many of these questions may be directly related to your own questions. These questions reappear in the margins throughout a given chapter to alert you when the relevant issues are being discussed. This is another dimension to the basic "ask and answer" approach.

7 DEFINING THE PRINCIPLES describes the marginal glossary that runs throughout each chapter. Many books highlight an overabundance of key terms for you to memorize. *Psychological Science* highlights approximately 30 key terms per chapter. This should be an excellent review tool, as are the glossaries at the end of the book and on the companion Web site.

9 REVIEWING THE PRINCIPLE boxes are a key element in the "ask and answer" approach and appear at the end of each major section. They repeat the question that governed the section and provide a basic answer. The answer provided won't give you everything you need to understand the question, but it will highlight key points to remember.

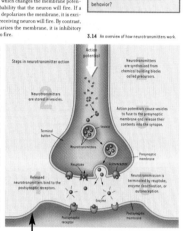

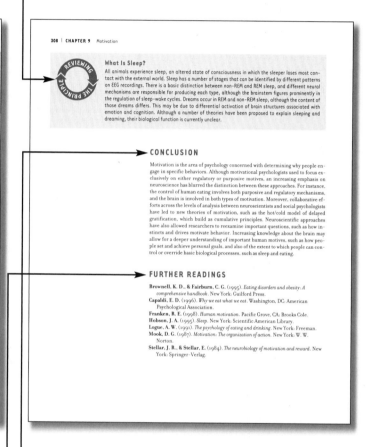

8 A DYNAMIC ART PROGRAM The visual materials in *Psychological Science* should add substantially to your reading experience. The text contains a variety of visual materials, from photographs to tables and charts to drawn art. The emphasis in *Psychological Science*, however, is clearly on the drawn art. Having used many general psychology books ourselves, we wanted to take our text in a new direction. By featuring drawn art, *Psychological Science* is able to convey precisely, accurately, and meaningfully what you need to gain from every image. This high level of precision can't be gained from the use of stock photographs, which are common in many texts.

10 SUMMARIZING THE PRINCIPLES is the last key component of the "ask and answer" approach. *Psychological Science*'s brief chapter conclusions highlight the big ideas and concepts and remind you how the book's four key themes wove their way through the chapter. After reading the chapter conclusion, you may want to reread the "Reviewing the Principles" sections to check what you have learned and what you haven't.

11 FURTHER READINGS represent psychological writing at its best. If any of the topics in a given chapter interested you, we encourage you to followup with one of the suggested reading titles. There are many wonderful popular psychology books that provide keen insights and pleasurable excursions into human behavior.

12 **SPECIAL FEATURE BOXES** highlight the text's basic strengths. Every chapter contains one of each of the following:

- **STUDYING THE MIND** feature boxes highlight examples of psychological phenomena that fascinate as well as inform. These often describe case studies that reveal intriguing aspects of the biological basis of the mind, such as the effect of brain injury on motivation, emotion, and personality.

- **USING PSYCHOLOGICAL SCIENCE** feature boxes address questions directly relevant to students. For example, Is there such a thing as photographic memory? Why do New Year's resolutions often fail? How is the mind a subjective interpreter?

- **CROSSING THE LEVELS OF ANALYSIS** feature boxes explain how significant advances in our understanding of complex psychological phenomena have emerged from research that crosses interdisciplinary boundaries. We explore how psychological scientists are approaching each topic from molecular to societal levels, and how interdisciplinary teams of scientists are providing compelling new insights based on this synthesis.

Studying the Mind

PHINEAS GAGE

Perhaps the most famous historical example of brain damage is the case of Phineas Gage. In 1848, Gage was a 25-year-old foreman on the construction of Vermont's Rutland and Burlington Railroad. One day he dropped his tamping iron on a rock, which ignited some blasting powder. The resulting explosion drove the iron rod—over a yard long and an inch in diameter—into his cheek, through his frontal lobes, and out through the top of his head (Figure 4.4). Gage was still conscious as he was hurried back to town on a cart. Able to walk, with assistance, upstairs to his hotel bed, he wryly remarked to the awaiting physician, "Doctor, here is business enough for you" and said he expected to return to work in a few days. In fact, Gage lapsed into a stupor for two weeks. His condition steadily improved subsequently, though, and he recovered remarkably well.

Unfortunately, the accident had caused some personality changes. Whereas before Gage had been regarded by his employers as "the most efficient and capable" of workers, the new Gage was not. As one of his doctors later wrote: "The equilibrium or balance, so to speak, between his intellectual faculties and animal propensities seems to have been destroyed. He is fitful, irreverent, indulging at times in the grossest profanity . . . impatient of restraint or advice when it conflicts with his desires . . . A child in his intellectual capacity and manifestations, he has the animal passions of a strong man." In sum, Gage was "no longer Gage."

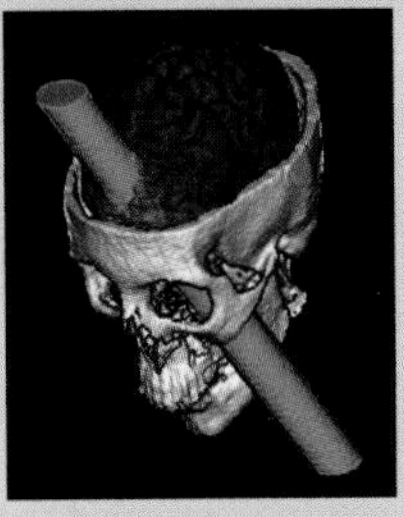

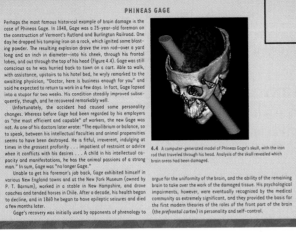

4.4 A computer-generated model of Phineas Gage's skull, with the iron rod that traveled through his head. Analysis of the skull revealed which brain areas had been damaged.

Unable to get his foreman's job back, Gage exhibited himself in various New England towns and at the New York Museum (owned by P. T. Barnum), worked in a stable in New Hampshire, and drove coaches and tended horses in Chile. After a decade, his health began to decline, and in 1860 he began to have epileptic seizures and died a few months later.

Gage's recovery was initially used by opponents of phrenology to argue for the uniformity of the brain, and the ability of the remaining brain to take over the work of the damaged tissue. His psychological impairments, however, were eventually recognized by the medical community as extremely significant, and they provided the basis for the first modern theories of the roles of the front part of the brain (the *prefrontal cortex*) in personality and self-control.

and it has since been repeatedly confirmed to be crucial for the production of language. This was the first of the nineteenth-century localizations to have survived the test of time.

THE BRAIN IS NOW KNOWN TO BE SPECIALIZED

RESEARCH QUESTION

Is function distributed throughout the brain or specialized in different regions?

It is now known that the brain's surface, far from being a uniform structure, is a patchwork of many highly specialized areas. However, instead of being neatly divided into regions corresponding to complex personality traits, as the phrenologists argued, brain areas are actually specialized for far more rudimentary components of perception, behavior, and mental life. A large area of the brain is devoted to different aspects of vision, for example, and another to generating rudimentary movements.

However, the notion that the brain, or at least the *cerebral cortex*, is uniform persisted well into the twentieth century. In the 1920s, physiologist Karl Lashley trained rats to run mazes and then systematically removed pieces of their brains in an effort to determine the location of their maze-navigating memories. To his

Using Psychological Science

THE MIND IS A SUBJECTIVE INTERPRETER

Another interesting dimension to the relationship between the brain's hemispheres is how they work together to reconstruct our experiences. This can be demonstrated by asking a disconnected left hemisphere what it thinks about previous behavior that has been produced by the right hemisphere. In one such experiment, different images are flashed simultaneously to the left and right visual fields and the patient is asked to point *with both hands* to pictures that seem most related to the images on the screen (Figure 4.22). As one example, a picture of a chicken claw was flashed to the left hemisphere and a picture of a snow scene to the right hemisphere. In response, the left hemisphere directed the right hand to point to a picture of a chicken head, and the right hemisphere pointed the left hand at a snow shovel. The participant was then asked why he chose those items. Clearly, the speaking left hemisphere could have no idea what the right hemisphere had seen. However, the patient (or rather his left hemisphere) calmly replied, "Oh, that's simple. The chicken claw goes with the chicken, and you need a shovel to clean out the chicken shed." The left hemisphere had evidently interpreted the left hand's response in a manner consistent with the left brain's knowledge. This left-hemispheric tendency to construct a world that makes sense is called the "interpreter."

This interpreter strongly influences the way we view and remember the world. Shown a series of pictures that form a story and asked later to choose which of another group of pictures had been seen previously, normal participants have a strong tendency to falsely "recognize" pictures that are consistent with the theme of the original series, whereas those that are inconsistent with the theme are easily rejected. The left brain, then, tends to "compress" its experiences into a comprehensible story and reconstructs remembered details on the basis of that story. The right brain seems to simply experience the world and remembers things in a manner less distorted by narrative interpretation. Given the finite capacity of the brain, the advantages of compression seem clear, though it appears that the right brain may check the left brain's unwarranted speculations.

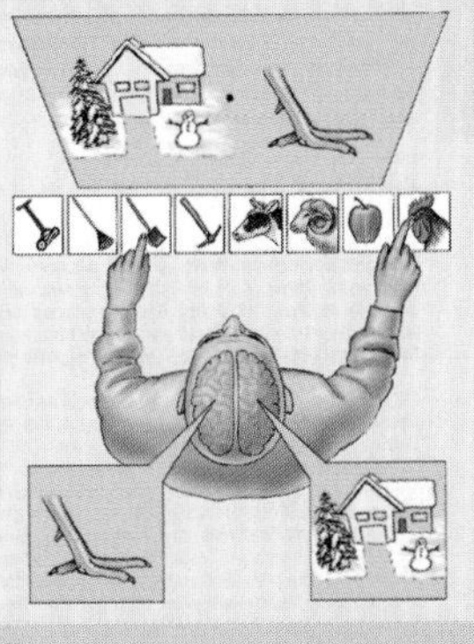

4.22 The left brain interpreter mechanism. The left hemisphere attempts to explain the behavior of the right hemisphere on the basis of limited information.

HOW DOES THE BRAIN CHANGE?

RESEARCH QUESTION

Are there critical periods during brain development?

Despite the great precision and specificity of its connections, the brain is extremely malleable. Over the course of development, after injury, and throughout our constant stream of experience, the brain is continually changing, a property known as **plasticity**. Determining the nature of these changes, and the rules that they follow, is providing major insights into the mind, and is a direct outgrowth of the biological revolution that is energizing the field.

The brain follows a predictable development pattern, with different structures and abilities progressing at different rates and maturing at different points in

82 | CHAPTER 3 Genetic and Biological Foundations

dopamine A monoamine neurotransmitter that is involved in reward, motivation, and motor control.

search for food to satisfy immediate energy needs. The link between arousal and feeding is a good example of how various brain mechanisms work together to facilitate survival.

Dopamine **Dopamine** serves many significant brain functions, especially motivation and motor control. Many theorists believe dopamine is the primary neurotransmitter that communicates which activities may be rewarding. Eating when hungry, drinking when thirsty, or having sex when aroused all lead to activation of dopamine receptors and therefore are experienced as pleasurable. At the same time, dopamine activation is involved in motor control and planning, thereby guiding behavior toward objects and experiences that will lead to additional reward. One theory of drug addiction is that certain drugs are dopamine agonists;

Crossing the Levels of Analysis

PARKINSON'S DISEASE

The actor Michael J. Fox has recently become as well known for his unfortunate medical condition as his acting ability. He is one among many famous people who have developed the neurodegenerative disorder Parkinson's disease, first identified by physician James Parkinson (1755–1828) in 1817. Parkinson's disease affects about 1 in every 200 older adults and occurs in all known cultures. Although most Parkinson's patients do not experience symptoms until after age 50, the case of Fox makes it clear that the disease can occur earlier. Symptoms include muscular rigidity, involuntary movements, and very specific tremors of the hand known as "pill rolling," because it looks as though the individual is rolling a small pill between the thumb and forefinger. As the disorder progresses, Parkinson's patients often develop a masklike facial expression and blink very little. At later stages people suffer from cognitive and mood disturbances. Parkinson's is a slow and degenerative disease that eventually leads to death.

Research in the past few decades has demonstrated that dopamine depletion in an area of the brain known as the substantia nigra is implicated in Parkinson's (Figure 3.16). The substantia nigra is a key area for the synthesis and transmission of dopamine throughout the brain; axons that extend from neurons in the substantia nigra to other regions of the brain have been implicated in the control of movement. With Parkinson's disease, the dopamine-producing neurons in the substantia nigra slowly die off.

What causes Parkinson's disease? At this time the answer is not clear. Some evidence of genetic involvement exists, especially the early-onset forms of the disease, but other evidence points to brain injury or even exposure to environmental toxins. Evidence for the toxin argument is based on the general finding that increasing numbers of young people are afflicted with Parkinson's and that it is more common in industrialized nations than in developing countries.

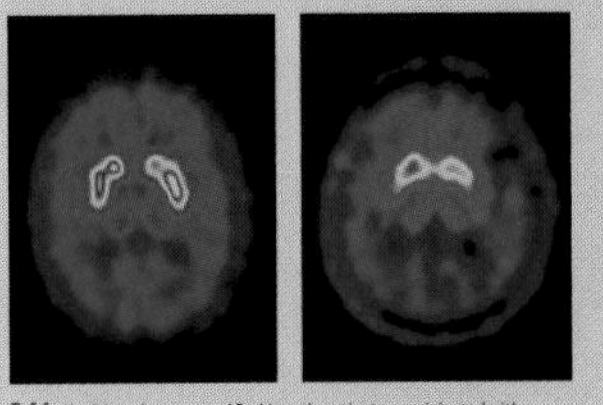

3.16 Healthy volunteers and Parkinson's patients were injected with a radioactive tracer, which allowed researchers to map the distribution of dopamine in the brain. Brighter colors indicate greater amounts of dopamine originating in the substantia nigra. You can see that healthy volunteers (left) have much more dopamine than those with Parkinson's disease (right).

Moreover, in 1982 it was found that a synthetic version of heroin (called MPTP) caused symptoms much like those associated with Parkinson's. Heroin addicts who unwittingly took MPTP all developed severe paralysis and frozen facial expressions (Figure 3.17). It later was found that chemists who had worked with MPTP early in their careers had also developed Parkinson's disease. These findings have led to the use of MPTP in animal research to study the course and treatment of Parkinson's disease.

From a treatment standpoint, drugs that enhance dopamine production can compensate for the lack of dopamine-producing neu-

PSYCHOLOGICAL SCIENCE'S STUDENT SUPPLEMENTS WILL HELP YOU SUCCEED

STUDY GUIDE TO ACCOMPANY *PSYCHOLOGICAL SCIENCE* BY BRETT BECK (BLOOMSBURG UNIVERSITY) AND JEFF HENRIQUES (UNIVERSITY OF WISCOSIN-MADISON)

Created by two highly successful instructors of large lectures classes, this carefully crafted study aid offers a guide to the reading with helpful study advice, completion questions, key figure exercises, multiple-choice self-tests, and thought questions.

STUDENT WEB SITE TO ACCOMPANY *PSYCHOLOGICAL SCIENCE*: WWW.WWNORTON.COM/PSYCHSCI

Designed to help you learn the basic principles of psychological science, this highly interactive Web site offers a rich array of exercises and opportunities to explore human behavior. Access is free to every student.

For every chapter there is

- an animated timeline that highlights research milestones
- a guide to the reading that offers helpful advice
- a list of key terms linked to an on-line glossary
- a crossword puzzle that tests recall for new vocabulary
- multiple-choice tests with answer feedback
- a rich collection of activities that features animations of hard-to-visualize concepts, media-enhanced essays with assignable thought questions, on-line labs, and topics for further reading.

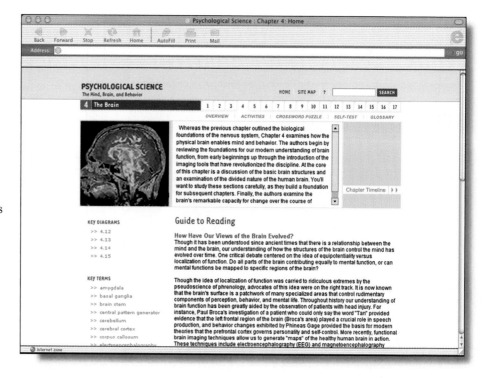

PSYCHOLOGICAL SCIENCE

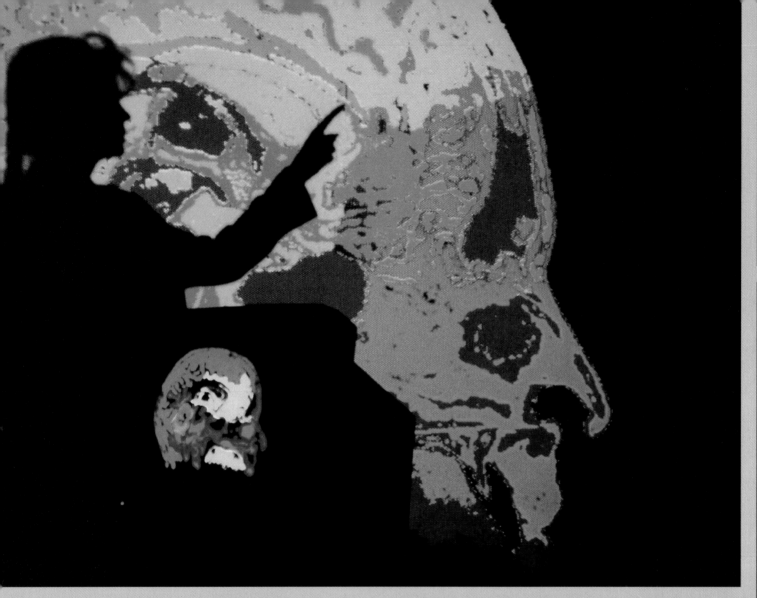

EXPLORING THE MIND AND BRAIN

To understand the mind, psychological scientists need to understand how the brain works, how the mind interprets the environment, and how social environments and culture shape behavior. Advances in brain imaging technology have provided valuable new investigative tools to help pursue these goals.

TIMELINE

1637

Cartesian Dualism René Descartes proposes that mind and body are interrelated but separate entities, with each affecting the other. This idea challenges the long-held belief that the mind, or soul, is master of the body.

1859

The Mind Evolved Charles Darwin's groundbreaking theory of natural selection lays the foundation for a biological basis of behavior and the notion that the human mind has evolved along with physical characteristics and behaviors.

1879

Psychology Adopts the Tools of Science Wilhelm Wundt sets up the first psychological laboratory in Leipzig and starts to measure behavior. His first methods involve asking people to reflect on their mental experiences.

1890

Principles of Psychology Influenced by Darwin's theory, William James argues in his groundbreaking *Principles of Psychology* that there is a need to understand the adaptive functions of behavior.

Introduction to Psychological Science

1

OUTLINING THE PRINCIPLES

WHAT ARE THE THEMES OF PSYCHOLOGICAL SCIENCE?

The Principles of Psychological Science Are Cumulative

A Biological Revolution Is Energizing Research

The Mind Is Adaptive

Psychological Science Crosses Levels of Analysis

WHAT ARE THE ORIGINS OF PSYCHOLOGICAL SCIENCE?

The Nature-Nurture Debate Considers the Impact of Biology and Environment

The Mind-Body Problem Has Challenged Philosophers and Psychologists

Evolutionary Theory Introduces Natural Selection

HOW DID THE FOUNDATIONS OF PSYCHOLOGICAL SCIENCE DEVELOP?

Modern Experimental Psychology Begins with Structuralism

Functionalism Addresses the Purpose of Behavior

Gestalt Psychology Emphasizes Patterns and Context in Learning

The Unconscious Influences Everyday Mental Life

Most Behavior Can Be Modified by Reward and Punishment

How People Think Affects Behavior

Social Situations Shape Behavior

WHAT ARE THE PROFESSIONS OF PSYCHOLOGICAL SCIENCE?

Subdisciplines Focus on Different Levels of Analysis

Psychological Knowledge Is Used in Many Professions

People Are Intuitive Psychological Scientists

CONCLUSION
FURTHER READINGS

1900

The Role of the Unconscious Sigmund Freud introduces the idea of the unconscious and the role it plays in our everyday mental life. His theory of psychoanalysis captures clinicians and scientists alike for almost half a century.

1912

Gestalt Psychology German psychologist Max Wertheimer proposes that perception is a subjective experience that cannot be understood by looking at its elementary components. That is, the whole is greater than the sum of its parts.

1925

Behaviorism John B. Watson and later B. F. Skinner argue that all behaviors can be understood as a result of learning, and that to predict behavior one has to look at environmental forces.

1940s

Physiological Psychology Karl Lashley and Roger Sperry conduct systematic brain research using animals as a way to gain insight into how the human mind works.

1944

Social Dynamics Kurt Lewin introduces field theory, in which he argues that situational dynamics play an important role in predicting human behavior.

A round midnight on February 4, 1999, four members of a special police Street Crime Unit drove down Wheeler Avenue in the Bronx, looking for a rape suspect. They saw 22-year-old Amadou Diallo (Figure 1.1), a West African immigrant, standing in the doorway to his apartment building. The officers say they told Diallo to "freeze" but then saw him reach into his pants' pocket. The officers, believing that Diallo was reaching for a weapon, opened fire. Within approximately 5 seconds, the four officers fired a total of 41 shots at the unarmed Diallo, 19 of which struck him. Diallo died at the scene. Neighbors say that Diallo probably didn't understand the word "freeze," since English was not his first language. Others suggest that Diallo might have been reaching for his wallet to prove his identity. No one will ever know. The four officers were tried for murder, and all were acquitted.

Psychologists are interested in understanding how people perceive, think, and act in a wide range of situations. A situation such as the killing of Amadou Diallo is especially interesting to psychologists because it allows them to consider thought and behavior in the context of a real-life event. The Diallo case involves psychological phenomena such as emotion, memory, visual perception, decision making, social interaction, cultural differences, prejudice, group behavior, and mental trauma. Within this menu of topics, psychologists would be interested in knowing, for example, how the emotional state of the officers affected their decision making at the scene. They would also want to study the accuracy of the defendants' and eyewitnesses' accounts of the shooting. In addition, they would want to examine group behavior. Did the fact that many officers arrived at the scene simultaneously affect individual behavior? Did the high-profile demonstrations outside the courthouse influence the trial? Finally, psychologists would also want to know if prejudice played a role. Did prejudice affect the way the officers identified and approached the suspect? Did prejudice affect the jury's decision? Many Bronx residents charged that the Diallo shooting was moti-

RESEARCH QUESTIONS ???

for Studying Psychological Science

How can we study mental processes that cannot be directly observed?

What role does genetics play in mind and behavior?

Why is evolution important to understanding mental activity?

How can the mind and behavior be studied at different levels of analysis?

How do we disentangle nature and nurture?

How do we use knowledge acquired from psychological science?

1957

The Cognitive Revolution George A. Miller launches the field of cognitive psychology at Harvard University, which will later be formalized by Ulric Neisser in his integrative 1967 book, *Cognitive Psychology*.

1960s

Biology of Mental Disorders Advances in drug-treatment trials support theories of a biological basis for many types of mental disorders. Disorders such as depression and schizophrenia are linked to neurochemical abnormalities.

1980s–1990s

The Return of Darwin David Buss, Leda Cosmides, John Tooby, and Steve Pinker are among those who develop evolutionary psychology, which reintroduces Darwinian thinking into understanding mind and behavior.

1982–2000s

The Brain Enables Mind A number of fields including neuroscience, cognitive psychology, computer science, and neurology forge a new interdisciplinary field, cognitive neuroscience—the cutting edge of psychological science.

vated by racism. The defense lawyers asserted that race had little to do with the shooting. How can we know?

Studying the factors underlying racial attitudes is difficult, since most people deny holding beliefs that are not socially acceptable. How, then, can we "peek inside" the mind to discover what people are thinking?

1.1 Amadou Diallo, a native of West Africa, was shot 41 times by police officers who were searching for a serial rapist. The innocent Diallo died at the scene. Did racism play a part in this tragic death?

A number of important developments over the past few years have opened new doors for studying mental life. We now have methods for observing the working brain in action. A collection of techniques known as *brain imaging* involves assessing changes in metabolic activity in the brain, such as noting where blood flows as people process information. These changes in blood flow represent changes in brain activity that indicate which parts of the brain are involved in certain behaviors or mental activities. For instance, cognitive neuroscientist Elizabeth Phelps and social psychologist Mahzarin Banaji and their colleagues used brain imaging to study racial attitudes. They showed white college students pictures of familiar and unfamiliar black and white faces while they used a technique known as *functional magnetic resonance imaging (fMRI)* to scan the brain (Phelps et al., 2000). For some of the research participants, the unfamiliar black faces activated a structure in the brain called the *amygdala*, which is involved in detecting threat; it indicates a fear response. This does not mean that the white students who responded in this way are necessarily afraid of unfamiliar black people, but it does indicate that those faces activate the brain region that detects threat.

It is important to point out that this response did not occur in all student participants. Rather, it only occurred in those who also showed signs of holding negative attitudes about blacks, as measured by a computer program called the *implicit attitudes test (IAT)*. This test indirectly assesses how people associate positive and negative words with certain groups of people. Those who were found to hold negative attitudes on the computer test were the most likely to show activation of the amygdala when observing unfamiliar black faces (Figure 1.2). In a second study, the researchers showed a new group of white students pictures of familiar black and white faces; this time activation of the amygdala did not occur. This is encouraging news. It suggests that increasing familiarity reduces the fear response, which may indicate a reduction in the likelihood of prejudice and discrimination.

The research just described reveals a great deal about the current state of psychology and touches on a number of issues that are central to this book. Psychology has formally been around for just over 100 years, and in that time we've learned a great deal about such basic mental processes as learning, memory, emotion, and perception. Psychologists have documented changes in individuals from birth to old age and have developed elaborate theories about how humans do things such as acquire language and solve difficult problems. They have explored the importance of the social world in which we live, such as how people are influenced by the presence of others and the circumstances that lead them to prefer some types of people to others. Psychologists have also examined how the environment helps shape each person in a unique way that produces what we call "personality." You will learn what has been discovered about each of these topics in the chapters of this book. You will learn too about how genes and biology influ-

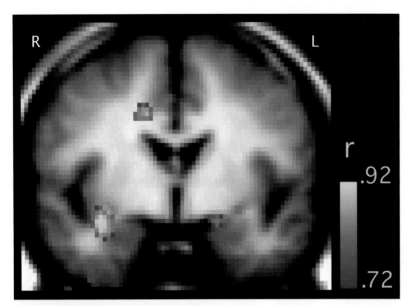

1.2 Composite maps displaying brain regions in which greater activation in response to black versus white faces is associated with an indirect measure of racial attitudes. The areas indicate activation of the amygdala on both the right and left halves of the brain, as well as another area, the anterior cingulate, that is also associated with emotional responses.

ence human mental life, an area of research that has energized psychology over the last few years.

Psychologists using new technologies and refined research methods have been providing amazing insights into the biological dimensions of mental life. On a daily basis, we learn more exciting details about how the brain works. In particular, we've learned what parts of the brain are involved when we perform certain tasks and interact with our social worlds. For instance, did you know that your brain chemistry is being altered with each concept or story that you remember while reading this chapter? Every time we remember a story or a joke or feel an intense emotion, that experience is processed and stored in our brains. The challenge for psychologists is to figure out what brain (neural) mechanisms are involved when we interact with our environment, as well as how the environment influences our neural mechanisms. The new psychological and brain sciences working together have revolutionized our understanding of our behavior, our minds, and our brains. This book is about that new science. It is the psychological science of the twenty-first century.

Psychological science is the study of mind, brain, and behavior. Let's explore each of these terms. **Mind** refers to mental activity, such as your thoughts and feelings. The perceptual experiences that you have while interacting with the world (that is, sight, smell, taste, hearing, and touch) are examples of the mind in action, as are memories, thinking about what you want to have for lunch, and how you feel about kissing someone you find attractive. Mental activity results from biological processes within the **brain,** such as the action of nerve cells and associated chemical reactions. You will read below about the long-standing controversy among scholars about the nature of the relationship between the brain and the mind. For now it is sufficient to note that the "mind is what the brain does" (Kosslyn & Koenig, 1995, p. 4). In other words, it is the physical brain that enables the mind.

Behavior refers to observable actions: body movements, purposeful actions such as eating or drinking, and facial expressions such as smiling. The term *behavior* is used to describe a wide variety of physical actions, from the subtle to the complex, that occur in organisms from ants to humans. For many years psychologists tended to focus mainly on behavior rather than on mental states. They did this in large part because they had few objective techniques for assessing the mind. The advent of technology to observe the working brain in action has allowed psychological scientists to study mental states such as consciousness.

WHAT ARE THE THEMES OF PSYCHOLOGICAL SCIENCE?

For as long as people have been thinking, they've been thinking about other people. We have a strong desire to figure out other people, to understand their motives, thoughts, desires, intentions, moods, actions, and so on. We want to know why they remember some details and conveniently forget others, or why they engage in behaviors that are self-destructive. We want to know whether others are friend or foe, leaders or followers, likely to spurn us or fall in love with us. Our social interactions require us to use our impressions of others to categorize them, to make predictions about their intentions and actions. Essentially, people are constantly trying to figure out what makes other people tick. People who do this for a living are known as *psychological scientists*. They use the methods of science to understand how people think, feel, and act. Four major themes have emerged to define the theory and research of psychological science in the beginning of the twenty-first century. These themes guide and direct the way psychological scientists study the mind, brain, and behavior.

THE PRINCIPLES OF PSYCHOLOGICAL SCIENCE ARE CUMULATIVE

The first theme is that research on mind, brain, and behavior has accumulated over time to produce the *principles* of psychological science. Throughout history there have been occasional leaps in scientific knowledge, such as the recognition of gravitational forces, the discovery of penicillin, and the recent mapping of the human genome. But, more typically, science progresses in smaller, incremental steps, as knowledge accumulates based on systematic study of questions raised by that which is already known. In this way, science builds on the foundation of shared knowledge.

So that you can appreciate the questions that are driving contemporary research, we will describe the basic principles that make up the foundation of psychological knowledge. In doing so, we focus on what is *known* in psychological science. For example, the behavioral properties of memory are quite well known, and today no psychologist has to demonstrate that it is easier to *recognize* old information than it is to *recall* old information. We've known that for more than half a century; it is one of the many principles we will use in this book. As scientists expand the outer edge of knowledge, their search for the unknown is still rooted in the basic principles of psychological science. To demonstrate this, we will describe cutting-edge research that is building on these principles, focusing on the research that we believe will establish the future foundations of psychological science.

One consequence of focusing on principles is that it can at times make things seem simpler than they really are. Most psychological phenomena involve complexities that we do not have the space to discuss. Complexity is inherent in science as ideas and theories are modified by new information that describes the conditions under which phenomena exist. Consider gravity, a basic force that has been recognized for hundreds of years. Gravity does not work in a uniform fashion; its force depends on the properties of the earth itself, such as there being greater centrifugal force near the equator. On earth if you drop an apple, it falls to the ground. That is the principle. Likewise, when we say that recognition is easier than recall, there are certainly conditions under which this is not true. But these complexities are of greater interest to the scientific researcher than to the student learning the material for the first time. For now, it is time to focus on the principles.

A BIOLOGICAL REVOLUTION IS ENERGIZING RESEARCH

The second theme is this: A biological revolution of profound significance is in progress at the dawn of the twenty-first century, bringing with it some of the greatest achievements in psychological science. Since antiquity philosophers and other scholars have asked questions about basic psychological phenomena, but

psychological science The study of mind, brain, and behavior.

mind Mental activity, such as thoughts, feelings, and subjective experience.

brain An organ located in the skull that produces mental activity.

behavior Any observable action or response.

RESEARCH QUESTION ?.?.?

How can we study mental processes that cannot be directly observed?

they lacked the methods to examine many of these fundamental questions, such as, *What is consciousness? Where does emotion come from and how does it affect cognitive processes? How are memories stored in the brain?* In the last 20 years or so there has been a tremendous growth in understanding of the biological bases of these mental activities. This interest in biology permeates all areas of psychological science, from locating the neural, or brain, correlates of how we identify friends to discovering the neurochemical problems that produce various psychological disorders. Three developments have set the stage for a biological revolution in explaining psychological phenomena.

Brain chemistry The first major development in the biological revolution is an understanding of brain chemistry. The brain works through the actions of chemicals known as *neurotransmitters*, which communicate messages between nerve cells. Over the last 30 years psychological scientists have made tremendous progress in identifying these chemicals and their functions. Although it was long believed that no more than a handful of neurotransmitters were involved in brain activity, it is now known that hundreds of different substances play critical roles in mental activity and behavior. For instance, behaviors that are rewarding are associated with the actions of a neurotransmitter called *dopamine* in a specific area of the brain known as the *nucleus accumbens*. The extent to which a drug influences this process determines how easily people become addicted to it; the more dopamine action, the more addictive the substance. Likewise, we now know that people have better memories for events that happen when they are aroused than when they are calm, because chemicals involved in responding to stimuli influence the neural mechanisms involved in memory. Understanding the chemical processes of the brain has provided many new insights into mental activity and behavior and has also been useful for developing treatments to help people with various psychological disorders.

RESEARCH QUESTION ?.?.?

What role does genetics play in mind and behavior?

The human genome The second development that has revolutionized psychological science is the enormous progress in understanding the influence of genetic processes. Not only have scientists been able to map out the *human genome*, the basic genetic code or blueprint for the human body, but they have developed various techniques that allow them to discover the link between genes and behavior. For instance, to study the effects of a gene on memory, researchers have been able to breed mice that either lack a specific gene or have new genes inserted. These mice subsequently show either impaired memory or improved memory, respectively. By identifying the genes that are involved in memory, researchers may soon be able to develop therapies based on genetic manipulation that will assist people who have memory problems, such as those who have Alzheimer's disease.

Of course, the idea that a single gene causes a specific behavior is overly simplistic. Almost all psychological and biological activity is affected by the actions of multiple genes. There isn't a specific gene that is solely responsible for memory, or racist attitudes, or shyness. Nonetheless, evidence is accumulating that genes are involved in many of these various processes. You will see in Chapter 3 that many physical and mental characteristics are to some degree inherited. Mapping the human genome has provided scientists with the foundational knowledge to study how specific genes affect thoughts, actions, feelings, and various disorders. Although many of the fantastic possibilities for correcting genetic defects are decades away, the methods used by scientists to study the influence of genetic processes have provided fresh insights into mental activity.

Watching the working brain   The development of methods for assessing the brain in action has provided the third major impetus to the biological revolution in psychology. The principles of how cells operate in the brain to influence behavior have been studied with increased effectiveness for more than a century, but it is only since the late 1980s that researchers have been able to study the working brain as it performs its vital psychological functions. Using the methods of brain science, or *neuroscience*, psychological scientists have been able to address some of the most central questions of human experience, such as how different brain regions interact to produce perceptual experience, how various types of memory are similar or different, and how conscious experience involves changes in brain activity.

Knowing where in the brain something happens doesn't by itself tell you very much, but knowing that there are consistent patterns of brain activation associated with specific cognitive tasks provides evidence that the two are connected. Indeed, for more than 100 years scientists have disagreed about whether psychological processes are located in specific parts of the brain or distributed throughout the brain. We now know that there is some *localization* of function, but that many different brain regions participate to produce behavior and mental activity. The use of brain imaging has allowed psychological scientists to make tremendous strides in understanding mental states such as volition and attention, both of which have been central to psychology for more than a century (Posner & DiGirolamo, 2000). The progress in understanding the neural basis of mental life has been rapid and dramatic. This new knowledge is being used throughout psychology; for example, as demonstrated in the opening paragraphs of this chapter, social psychologists have been able to identify and better understand the neural correlates of racism. The 1990s were labeled the decade of the brain, for good reason.

THE MIND IS ADAPTIVE

The third theme of psychological science is that the mind has been shaped by evolution. From an **evolutionary theory** perspective, the brain is an organ that has evolved over millions of years to solve problems related to survival and reproduction. During the course of human evolution, those ancestors who were able to solve survival problems and adapt to their environments were most likely to reproduce and pass along their genes. That is, those who inherited characteristics that helped them survive in their particular environments had a selective advantage over those who did not, which is the basis of the process of **natural selection.** Random gene mutations endowed some of our ancestors with physical characteristics, skills, and abilities, known as **adaptations,** that increased their chances of survival and reproduction, which means that their genes were passed along to future generations. Of course, if the environment changes what once was adaptive might become maladaptive. The ability to store fat in the body may have been adaptive when the food supply was scarce, but it may be maladaptive when food is abundant. Further complexities in the process of natural selection are discussed in Chapter 3.

Modern evolutionary theory has driven the field of biology for years. Only recently, however, have psychologists taken it up. But evolutionary theory has been

evolutionary theory An approach to psychological science that emphasizes the inherited, adaptive value of behavior and mental activity throughout the entire history of a species.

natural selection Darwin's theory that those who inherit characteristics that help them adapt to their particular environment have a selective advantage over those who do not.

adaptations In evolutionary theory, the physical characteristics, skills, or abilities that increase the chances of reproduction or survival and are therefore likely to be passed along to future generations.

RESEARCH QUESTION
?·?·?

Why is evolution important to understanding mental activity?

quickly accepted as crucial for understanding mind and behavior, and it now serves as a guiding principle for psychological science (Buss, 1999). Rather than being a specific area of scientific inquiry, evolutionary theory represents a way of thinking that can be used to understand many different aspects of mind and behavior. Two aspects of evolutionary theory are particularly helpful in this regard.

Solving adaptive problems Over the last five million years that humans have been evolving, adaptive behaviors have been built into our bodies and brains. A corollary to this notion is the idea that the body contains specialized mechanisms that have evolved to solve problems that required adaptation. For instance, a mechanism that produces calluses has evolved to protect the skin from the abuses of hard work, and these calluses are useful when humans need to engage in physical labor to survive. Likewise, the brain has evolved specialized circuits or structures that solve adaptive problems (Cosmides & Tooby, 2001).

Evolutionary theory is especially useful for thinking about adaptive problems that occur regularly and have the potential to affect whether one survives and reproduces, such as mechanisms for eating, sex, language and communication, emotions, and aggression. Accordingly, the evolutionary approach is particularly relevant to social behavior. Although situational and cultural contexts are influential in the development of social behavior and attitudes, evidence is accumulating that many of these behaviors have evolved to solve adaptive problems. For example, humans have a fundamental need to belong to their group, and therefore behaviors that lead to possible social exclusion are discouraged in all societies (Baumeister & Leary, 1995). People who lie, cheat, or steal drain group resources and thereby possibly decrease survival and reproduction for other group members. Some evolutionary psychologists believe that humans have "cheater detectors" that are on the lookout for this sort of behavior in others (Cosmides & Tooby, 2000).

Evolutionary theory can also be applied to nonsocial areas. The capacity to see well, remember where food was abundant, recognize dangerous objects, understand the basic laws of physics (such as the effects of gravity if one walks off a cliff), and so on were also critical to survival and therefore can be considered from an evolutionary perspective. According to evolutionary theory, solutions to these adaptive problems are built into the brain and therefore require no special training. Young infants develop a fear of heights at about the same time they learn to crawl, even though they have little personal experience with heights or gravity (Figure 1.3). Such built-in mechanisms assist in solving recurring problems that faced our ancestors over the course of human evolution.

Modern minds in stone-age skulls According to evolutionary theory, we must seek to understand the challenges that faced our early ancestors to understand much of our current behavior, whether adaptive or maladaptive. To provide perspective on this, consider the following: The human brain evolved slowly over millions of years, and many of the adaptive problems faced by early humans no longer exist, or at least no longer present the threat that they once did. Humans began evolving about 5 million years ago, but modern humans (Homo sapiens) can only be traced back about 100,000 years, to the Pleistocene era. If we compare the history of the earth to a 24-hour timescale, the arrival of humans has occurred in the last 30 seconds. The fact that the human brain adapted to accommodate the needs of Pleistocene hunter-gatherers means we should be looking at what life

1.3 Although there is a glass covering the visual cliff, infants will not crawl onto the glass, even if encouraged by their mothers. Infants become wary of heights at about the same age they learn to crawl.

was like then, and look to understand how the brain works within the context of the environmental pressures that the brains of Pleistocene-era humans faced. For instance, people like sweet foods, especially those that are high in fat. These foods are highly caloric and eating them would have provided substantial survival value in prehistoric times. In other words, a preference for fatty-sweet foods would have been adaptive. Today, many societies have an abundance of foods that are high in fat and sugar. That we still enjoy them and eat them, sometimes to excess, may now be maladaptive, in that it can produce obesity. Nonetheless, our evolutionary heritage encourages us to eat foods that had survival value when food was relatively scarce.

Many of our current behaviors, of course, do not reflect our evolutionary heritage. Reading books, driving cars, using computers, talking on telephones, and watching television are behaviors that have only very recently become part of human experience. Rather than being adaptations, such behaviors can be considered *by-products* of adaptive solutions to earlier adaptive problems.

The evolutionary approach has provided new insights into long-standing psychological questions. As we enter the next millennium, the evolutionary perspective will undoubtedly continue to inform our understanding of mind, brain, and behavior.

PSYCHOLOGICAL SCIENCE CROSSES LEVELS OF ANALYSIS

The fourth theme of psychological science is that the mind and behavior can be studied on many levels of analysis. As we'll see throughout this book, researchers working on the same problem often ask different questions and work at different levels. Indeed, many times psychologists collaborate with researchers from other sciences, such as biology, computer science, physics, anthropology, and sociology. This *interdisciplinary* effort shares the common goal of understanding how the mind works, but the level at which these researchers approach this question differs depending on their particular theoretical orientation.

How can the mind and behavior be studied at different levels of analysis?

LEVELS	What is studied?
Genetic	Gene mechanisms, heritability, twin and adoption studies
Neurochemical	Neurotransmitters and hormones, animal studies, drug studies
Brain systems	Neuroanatomical structures, animal studies, brain imaging
Behavioral	Observable actions, responses, physical movements
Perceptual and cognitive	Thinking, decision making, language, memory, beliefs
Individual	Personality traits, sex differences, developmental age changes
Social and cultural	Situations, context, cultural norms

1.4 Psychological scientists study behavior and mental life at seven basic levels.

Seven levels of analysis will be evident throughout this book (Figure 1.4): (1) the genetic level, (2) the neurochemical level, (3) the brain systems level, (4) the behavioral level, (5) the perceptual and cognitive level, (6) the individual level, and (7) the social and cultural level.

To understand each of these levels, let's look at the study of sexual behavior. The mating habits of various animal species are of interest to many psychological scientists. Of course, fundamental to mating, at least among mammals, is that there are two genetically determined sexes. At the *genetic level*, researchers have focused not only on the genes that determine sex, but also on how certain genes seem to turn on to produce sexual behaviors. Genes also control the development of the secondary sexual characteristics, such as breasts and pubic hair, that are associated with adolescence and the rise of interest in sexuality. Other researchers have looked at questions such as whether there is a genetic basis to homosexuality.

At the *neurochemical level*, sexual behavior is controlled by specific actions of chemicals that are spread throughout the brain and body, namely, hormones and neurotransmitters. These chemical compounds can all be measured during sexual behavior and their presence or absence can define what is going on at the chemical level. Thus, male rats that have had their testes removed will not engage in sexual behavior unless they are injected with a male sex hormone, *testosterone*, which leads them to perform appropriately when placed in an eliciting situation. Scientists who work at this level are interested in the processes by which the chemicals influence behavior. Thus, they look at which parts of the brain or body the chemicals affect, they examine the amounts of the various chemicals that influence behavior, and they see whether they can block sexual behaviors by using other chemicals that interfere with the actions of the sex-producing chemicals.

In the same manner, at the *brain-systems level*, researchers might study specific brain structures associated with sexual behaviors. For example, in animal studies, lesions to these structures might result in changes in the animal's behavior. It is well established that damage to certain brain regions, particularly to the *hypothalamus*, causes a reduction in sexual behavior, whereas damage to the *anterior temporal lobes* leads to hypersexuality. The nucleus accumbens, mentioned earlier, is also involved in sexual behavior.

At the *behavioral level*, researchers might study the observable actions involved in all phases of mating, from courtship to copulation. Some animals engage in very specific actions that are designed to arouse potential mates, such as the peacock's bold display. Among rodents, the female elicits male attention by darting around and wiggling her ears. She then assumes a particular body posture, known as *lordosis*, which facilitates male sexual behavior. Researchers who study humans have catalogued the frequency of various types of sexual activities, mostly by interviewing people about their sexual lives.

At the *perceptual and cognitive level*, the particular sensations involved in sexual acts are an important component of sexual pleasure. People perceive the physical attractiveness of others, which is an important contributor to sexual arousal. They also spend a great deal of time thinking about sex, including fantasizing. How people think about sex can affect their performance. For instance, thinking too much about how one is performing during sex often interferes with performance. A certain lack of inhibition and self-awareness during sex is important for humans, but it is likely irrelevant for other animals.

At the *individual level*, some people are more likely to engage in sex than are others. Thus, some researchers are interested in individual differences in frequency and variety of sexual practices, as well as individual differences in how much people enjoy sex. Some people feel guilty about having sex and this interferes with their sexual enjoyment. It turns out that personality is a strong predictor of sexual activity. People who are high in the personality traits of *extraversion* and *sensation seeking* are especially likely to have active sexual lives.

Of course, at the *social and cultural level*, people learn which types of sexual behavior are appropriate in which contexts. Young children need to be taught not to indulge in self-stimulation in public. Simple physical desires and needs of individuals are moderated by social influences. Social forces also inform young men and women about the acceptability of sexual practices, such as whether casual sex is permissible. One argument has recently been made that men and women differ in how sensitive they are to those social forces, with women being much more affected than are men (Baumeister, 2000). Rules about sex vary in different societies, with some being more permissive than others.

More recently, researchers have crossed levels of analysis to gain a greater understanding of sexual behavior. Thus, certain personality types may be most likely to have sex, but personality traits are themselves heavily influenced by genetic influence and are associated with differences in hormone level and responsiveness to neurotransmitters. Moreover, these personality differences are reflected in differential patterns of brain activation, which in turn reflect underlying metabolic and chemical action. Of course, each of the seven levels can be pursued and studied independent of the others. Throughout the history of psychology, this has been the favored approach. It is only relatively recently that an explanation of a behavior is more commonly reported in terms of several levels of analysis. It is this crossing of the levels of analysis that modern-day psychological scientists find so captivating and exciting.

What Are the Themes of Psychological Science?

Psychological science is the study of mind, brain, and behavior. Four themes characterize psychological science. (1) It is cumulative, in that principles are established on the basis of incremental advances in knowledge obtained through research. (2) A biological revolution has been energizing psychological research. Increasing knowledge of the neurochemistry of mental disorders, the mapping of the human genome, and the invention of imaging technologies that allow researchers to observe the working brain in action have provided psychological scientists with the methods to examine how the brain enables the mind. (3) Psychological science has also been heavily influenced in recent years by evolutionary psychology, which argues that the brain has evolved to solve adaptive problems. (4) Finally, although psychological scientists share the common goal of understanding mind, brain, and behavior, they do so by focusing on the same problems at different levels of analysis.

WHAT ARE THE ORIGINS OF PSYCHOLOGICAL SCIENCE?

Psychology is a young science that addresses questions that have challenged great minds for millennia. Many of these issues reflect long-standing philosophical questions about the nature of human experience. Psychology's roots are in philosophy and medicine, and many of the earliest psychologists were trained in one of these disciplines. In this section we will consider some of the "grand" questions and issues that have shaped psychological debate over centuries.

THE NATURE-NURTURE DEBATE CONSIDERS THE IMPACT OF BIOLOGY AND ENVIRONMENT

RESEARCH QUESTION

How do we disentangle nature and nurture?

From the time of the ancient Greeks, there has been a debate about whether psychological characteristics are more due to *nature* or *nurture*, that is, whether they are biologically innate or acquired through education, experience, or culture. **Culture** refers to the beliefs, values, rules, and customs that exist within a group of people who share a common language and environment, the assumption being that the various aspects of culture are transmitted from one generation to the next through learning. For instance, musical and food preferences, ways of expressing emotion, tolerance of body odors, and so on are strongly affected by the culture in which one is raised. The **nature-nurture debate** has existed in one form or another throughout psychology's history and will likely continue as researchers explore how thoughts, feelings, and behaviors are influenced by genes and the culture or society in which one lives. It is now widely recognized that both nature and nurture are important, but more significantly, recent advances in scientific knowledge have allowed researchers to specify *when* either nature and nurture are important, as well as how they interact. It is the relative importance of nature and nurture in determining mind and behavior that captivates the interest of psychological scientists.

As an example of the changing influences of nature and nurture, consider just two mental disorders—schizophrenia and bipolar disorder (you will read much more about them in Chapter 16). *Schizophrenia* is a disorder in which people have unusual thoughts, such as believing they are God, or experience unusual sensations, such as hearing voices. In *bipolar disorder* a person has dramatic mood swings, from feeling extremely sad (depressed) to feeling euphoric (manic). Prior to the 1950s, it was generally believed that these two mental disorders, among others, resulted from bad parenting or other environmental circumstances—that is, the causes were all nurture. But in the late 1950s and 1960s a variety of drugs were discovered that could alleviate the symptoms of these disorders; more recent research showed that these conditions are also heritable. Psychological scientists now believe that many mental disorders result as much from the way the brain is "wired" (nature) as from the way people are treated (nurture). Rapid advancements in understanding the biological basis of mental disorders have led to effective treatments that allow people to live normal lives. So is it all nature rather than nurture? Of course not. Both schizophrenia and bipolar disorder are more likely in certain environments, suggesting that they can be triggered by the situation. Many mental disorders result from events that happen in people's lives, such as combat soldiers who develop *post-traumatic stress disorder* (*PTSD*), in which people have intrusive and unwanted memories of their traumatic experiences. But recent research also indicates that some people inherit a genetic predisposition to develop PTSD, and so nurture activates nature. Thus, nature and nurture are tightly interwoven and inseparable. Psychological science depends on understanding both the genetic basis of human nature and the environment that shapes it.

culture The beliefs, values, rules, and customs that exist within a group of people who share a common language and environment, that are transmitted through learning from one generation to the next.

nature-nurture debate The arguments concerning whether psychological activity is biologically innate or acquired through education, experience, and culture.

mind-body problem A fundamental psychological issue that considers whether mind and body are separate and distinct or whether the mind is simply the subjective experience of the physical brain.

THE MIND-BODY PROBLEM HAS CHALLENGED PHILOSOPHERS AND PSYCHOLOGISTS

Close your eyes and think about yourself for a second. Where do your thoughts reside? If you are like most people, you have a subjective sense that your mind is floating somewhere around your head, perhaps a few inches inside your skull, or perhaps even a few inches above or in front of your forehead. But why do you feel like your mind is in your head? The mind has been viewed throughout history as residing in many organs of the body, especially the liver and heart. What is the relationship between the mental activity of your mind and the physical workings of your body? The **mind-body problem** is perhaps the quintessential psychological issue: whether the mind and body are separate and distinct, or whether the mind is simply the subjective experience of the physical brain.

For most of human history, scholars have believed that the mind and body are separate entities, with the mind very much in control of the body. This belief was held, in part, because of strong theological beliefs that the existence of a *divine and immortal soul* is what separates humans from animals. Even early theorists who challenged church doctrine were careful to avoid being too controversial. Leonardo da Vinci conducted experiments around 1500 to make his anatomical drawings more accurate, which offended the church because they violated the presumed sanctity of the human body. His dissections led him to many conclusions about the workings of the brain, including the idea that all sensory messages, such as vision, touch, and smell, arrived at one location in the brain (Figure 1.5), the

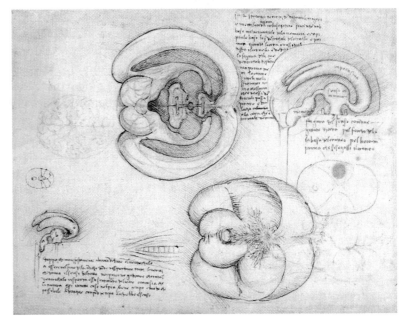

1.5 This drawing by Leonardo da Vinci dates from around 1506. He used a wax cast to study the brain. He found that the various nerves arrived in the middle region of the brain, which he referred to as the *sensus communis*, or common sense.

dualism The philosophical idea that the mind exists separately from the physical body.

sensus communis, which he believed to be the home of thought and judgment. (This is possibly why we call using good judgment *common sense* [Blakemore, 1983].)

It was René Descartes (1596–1650), the great French philosopher, who promoted the first infuential theory that mind and body were separate yet intertwined (the theory known as **dualism**). The notion that the mind and body were separate was not novel, of course, but how Descartes connected them was at the time quite radical. The body, he argued, was nothing more than an organic machine, governed by "reflex," which Descartes defined as a "unit of mechanical, predictable, deterministic action (Figure 1.6)." His idea was inspired by the small clockwork statues in the French Royal Gardens, which moved about and played music when a passerby stepped on a trigger. For Descartes, many mental functions, such as memory and imagination, were the result of bodily functions. Linking some mental states with the body was a fundamental departure from the earlier views of dualism, in which all mental states were separate from bodily functions. In keeping with prevailing religious beliefs, however, Descartes concluded that the rational mind, which controlled volitional action, was divine and separate from the body. Thus, his view of dualism kept the distinction between mind and body, but he accorded to the body many of the mental functions previously considered the sovereign domain of the mind.

Descartes's most radical idea was to suggest that although the mind could affect the body, the body could also affect the mind. For instance, he believed that passions such as love, hate, and sadness arose from the body and influenced mental states, although the body acted on these passions through its own mechanisms. In this way, Descartes brought mind and body closer together by focusing on their interactions.

1.6 A woodcut illustrating Descartes's "reflex" theory of biological function.

EVOLUTIONARY THEORY INTRODUCES NATURAL SELECTION

One of the major intellectual events that shaped the future of psychological science was the publication of Charles Darwin's (1809–1882; Figure 1.7) *On the Origin of Species* in 1859. In the book he outlined a theory of evolution that relied on the process of natural selection (as described above). Earlier naturalists and philosophers, including his own grandfather Erasmus Darwin, had all discussed the possibility that species might evolve, but it wasn't until Charles Darwin came along that the mechanism of evolution became clear. How did Darwin develop his theory of natural selection?

Charles Darwin attended Cambridge and traveled as a naturalist aboard the *Beagle* from 1832 to 1837, collecting information about finches on the Galapagos Islands. When he later analyzed this information, he discovered that each island had slightly different species of finches (Figure 1.8). It seemed clear to him that these different finches must have descended from the same species, but he wondered what could account for the small variations. His famous notebooks from this era trace his thinking about how this must have occurred. He found a suitable explanation in Thomas Malthus's Essay on Population:

1.7 Charles Darwin's theory of natural selection has had a huge impact on how psychologists think about the mind. This portrait is reported to be his favorite picture of himself.

I happened to read for amusement "Malthus on population," and being well prepared to appreciate the struggle for existence which everywhere goes on from long-continued observation of the habits of animals and plants, it at once struck me that under these circumstances

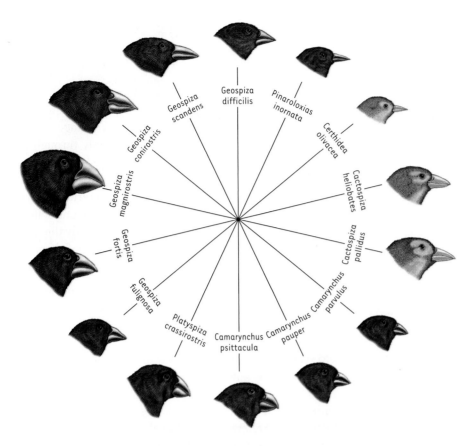

1.8 Different species of finches on the Galapagos Islands. The variation in these finches was powerful evidence for some kind of selection process working on a common ancestor.

favourable variations would tend to be preserved and unfavourable ones to be destroyed. The result of this would be the formation of a new species. (from Darwin's autobiography)

Darwin called this mechanism for evolution *natural selection*, the process by which random mutations in organisms that are adaptive are passed along and mutations that hinder reproduction are not. Thus as species struggle to survive, those that are better adapted to their environment will leave more offspring, and those offspring will produce more offspring, and so on (i.e., the notion of *survival of the fittest*).

A further implication of Darwin's theory was that inheritable *individual differences* provide the basis of evolutionary development. This idea was seized upon by his cousin Francis Galton (1822–1911), who proposed that some differences were psychological in nature (e.g., intelligence), and that they could be measured and tested. The *mental testing movement* followed in Galton's wake. Ultimately, the idea of natural selection has had a profound impact on science, philosophy, and society.

What Are the Origins of Psychological Science?

The origins of psychological science can be found in the major philosophical questions that have endured for centuries. For instance, the nature-nurture debate involves determining the extent to which mind and behavior are predetermined by biology or are developed and shaped by environment. The mind-body problem tackles the question of how mental activity is related to brain functioning. Darwin's theory of evolution set the stage for a new understanding of the origins of mind and behavior.

HOW DID THE FOUNDATIONS OF PSYCHOLOGICAL SCIENCE DEVELOP?

In 1843, John Stuart Mill published *System of Logic*, in which he declared that psychology should leave the realm of speculation and philosophy and become a science of observation and experiment. Indeed, he defined psychology as "the science of the elementary laws of the mind" and argued that only through the methods of science would the processes of the mind be understood. Early scientists, in their own way and perhaps unintentionally, tried to fulfill his predictions. Each had a view of what psychology was to become, and each was determined to be right. As a result, psychology in its early days was characterized by strong schools of thought with passionately held positions regarding how best to study the mind and behavior. Although these schools no longer exist, their basic beliefs have influenced the development of many contemporary trends in psychological science.

MODERN EXPERIMENTAL PSYCHOLOGY BEGINS WITH STRUCTURALISM

Imagine you are living 150 years ago and decide one day to study the human mind. How would you begin to think about how the mind works? Great scientific advances had occurred by then but the scientific method had not been applied rigorously to studying the human mind.

In the mid 1800s, it was widely believed that although psychological phenomena could be described and discussed, they could not be studied experimentally; that is, they could not be measured or systematically manipulated in the laboratory. This assumption was disproven when scientists such as Hermann Helmholtz showed how changes in sensation and perception could be tied to events in the nervous system, and Gustav Fechner showed how a "just noticeable difference" in stimulus intensity could be used as a measuring unit for a psychological variable. In the 1860s, a young assistant to Helmholtz named Wilhelm Wundt (1832–1920; Figure 1.9) came to believe that such studies could form the basis of a new discipline of experimental psychology. He wrote the first textbook in the field in 1874, to describe such a psychology. In 1879 he established the first psychology laboratory and institute in Leipzig, to which students could go to earn higher degrees in the new discipline. Accordingly, Wundt is widely regarded as the founder of experimental psychology as an academic discipline.

Through his training, Wundt realized that psychological processes, as the products of physiological actions in the brain, take time to occur. Thus, to study the mind he would present a subject with two psychological tasks: one that was simple and one that was more complex. He would then measure the speed at which subjects completed the tasks. By subtracting the easier task from the complex task, Wundt could infer how much time a particular mental event took to occur. In other studies he required people to compare their subjective experiences as they contemplated a series of objects, such as by stating which one they found more

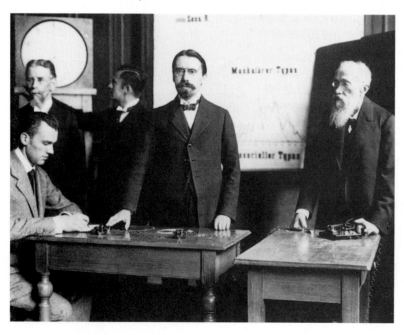

1.9 Wilhelm Wundt (far right), the founder of modern experimental psychology, at work with his collaborators in his later years.

pleasant. Another method that he developed was **introspection**, a systematic examination of subjective mental experiences that required people to inspect and report on the content of their thoughts, such as describing the "blueness" of the sky. Wundt eventually concluded that introspection was too subjective and therefore did not meet the needs of his scientific approach to studying the mind.

Many of the pioneers of psychology trained with Wundt in Leipzig and then established their own research laboratories in the United States, Canada, and Europe. One of his students, Edward Titchener (1867–1927), extended Wundt's approach into what he called *structuralism*. The basic idea of **structuralism** is that conscious experience can be broken down into its underlying components or elements. Just as when you know the ingredients and recipe you can bake a cake, Titchener believed that understanding the basic elements of consciousness would provide the scientific basis for understanding the mind. Titchener seized upon the method of introspection to analyze the mind. He argued that one could take a stimulus such as a musical tone and by introspection analyze its "quality," "intensity," "duration," and "clarity." Although Wundt had rejected this particular use of introspection, Titchener relied on the method throughout his career. Unfortunately, the problem with this approach is that experience is subjective. Each person brings to introspection a unique perceptual system, and it is difficult to determine if subjects are using the criteria in a similar way. Accordingly, introspection was largely abandoned in psychology. Nonetheless, Wundt, Titchener, and other structuralists were important because of their goal of developing a pure science of psychology with its own self-contained vocabulary and set of rules.

introspection A systematic examination of subjective mental experiences that requires people to inspect and report on the content of their thoughts.

structuralism An approach to psychology based on the idea that conscious experience can be broken down into its basic underlying components or elements.

stream of consciousness A phrase coined by William James to describe one's continuous series of ever-changing thoughts.

FUNCTIONALISM ADDRESSES THE PURPOSE OF BEHAVIOR

One of the main critics of structuralism was William James (1842–1910), a brilliant scholar whose work has had an enormous, enduring impact on psychology (Figure 1.10). James abandoned a career in medicine to teach physiology at Harvard University in 1873. He was an excellent lecturer and was among the first professors at Harvard to openly welcome questions from students. His personal interests were more philosophical than physiological; he was captivated by the nature of conscious experience. He gave his first lecture on psychology in 1875, which he later quipped was also the first lecture on psychology he had ever heard. James's charm and brilliance were best expressed in his classic *Principles of Psychology*, published in 1890. Good genes perhaps contributed to his writing skills; his brother was the famous novelist Henry James. James's *Principles* was an immediate hit with students and became, without doubt, the most influential book in the early history of psychology. To this day psychologists find rich delight in reading James's penetrating analysis of the human mind; it is amazing how many of his central ideas have held up over time.

James criticized structuralism's failure to capture the most important aspects of mental experience. He believed that the mind could not be broken down into its elements because the mind was much more complex than its elements. For instance, he noted that the mind consisted of a continuous series of thoughts that are ever-changing. This **stream of consciousness** could not be frozen in time, according to James, and so the strategies used by the structuralists were sterile and artificial. He likened the structural approach to someone who tried to understand

1.10 William James was highly influenced by Darwin and is credited with "naturalizing" the mind. His book *The Principles of Psychology* remains a classic.

a house by studying each of its bricks individually. What was more important to James was that the bricks worked together to form a house, and that a house has a particular function. James stressed that the important point was not the elements that made up the mind, but rather the mind's usefulness to people.

James was heavily influenced by Darwinian thinking, and he argued that psychologists ought to examine the *functions* served by the mind. His approach to psychology, which became known as **functionalism,** was more concerned with how the mind operates than what the mind contains. According to functionalism, the mind came into existence over the course of human evolution, and it works the way it does because it is useful for preserving life and passing along genes to future generations. In other words, it helps organisms adapt to environmental demands. In terms of the mind-body problem, most functionalists viewed mental states as resulting from the biological actions of the brain, and therefore mind was itself a physiological mechanism.

Many of the functionalists were concerned with applying psychological research to the real world. After all, if behavior served a purpose, the purpose ought to be reflected in daily human life. Thus, for example, John Dewey tested functionalist theories in his classrooms, where he stressed teaching students according to how the mind processed information rather than simply through repetitive drill learning. This *progressive* approach to education emphasized divergent thinking and creativity rather than rote learning of conventional knowledge that might be incorrect anyway (Hothersall, 1995). William James was also interested in applying the functional approach to the study of real-world phenomena, such as the nature of religious experience. Yet the broad-ranging subjects to which functionalism was applied led to criticism that it was not sufficiently rigorous, and therefore functionalism slowly lost steam as a movement within psychology. However, the functional approach has returned to psychological science within the past two decades, as more and more researchers consider the adaptiveness of the behaviors and mental processes they study.

GESTALT PSYCHOLOGY EMPHASIZES PATTERNS AND CONTEXT IN LEARNING

Another of the schools of thought that arose in opposition to structuralism was the *Gestalt* school, founded by Max Wertheimer (1880–1943) and further expanded by Wolfgang Köhler (1887–1967), among others. According to **Gestalt theory,** the whole of personal experience is much greater than simply the sum of its constituent elements, or *the whole is greater than the sum of the parts.* If you show people a triangle, they see a triangle, not three lines on a piece of paper, as would be the case for the trained observers in one of Titchener's structuralist experiments. So, for instance, look at Figure 1.11. What do you see? The elements of the picture are organized by the mind, automatically and with little effort, to produce the percept of a dog sniffing the ground. The picture is processed and experienced as a unified whole. Experimentally, the Gestalt psychologists relied not on trained observers but on the observations of ordinary people in investigating subjective experience. This unstructured reporting of experience was called the *phenomenological* approach, referring to the totality of subjective experience.

The Gestalt movement reflected an important idea that was at the heart of criticisms of structuralism: the perception of objects is subjective and dependent on context. Two people can look at an object and see different things. Indeed, one

functionalism An approach to psychology concerned with the adaptive purpose, or function, of mind and behavior.

Gestalt theory A theory based on the idea that the whole of personal experience is much greater than simply the sum of its constituent elements.

unconscious A term that identifies mental processes that operate below the level of conscious awareness.

1.11 What do you see? If you look carefully, you will see that these fragments make up a picture of a dog.

person can look at an object and see it in completely different ways, as in Figure 1.12. Note that you can alternate between seeing the face, the profiles, or the candlestick, but that it is difficult to perceive the image in all three ways at the same time. Thus, your mind organizes the scene into a perceptual whole, so that you see the picture in a specific way. The important lesson of Gestalt psychology is that the mind perceives the world in an organized fashion that cannot be broken down into its constituent elements.

THE UNCONSCIOUS INFLUENCES EVERYDAY MENTAL LIFE

Twentieth century psychology was profoundly influenced by one of its most famous thinkers, Sigmund Freud (1856–1939; Figure 1.13). Freud was trained in medicine and began his career working with people who had neurological disorders, such as paralysis of various body parts. He found that many of his patients had few medical reasons for their paralysis, and he soon came to believe that their conditions were caused by psychological factors.

At the time, the structuralists and functionalists were focusing on conscious experience, but Freud made the deduction that much of human behavior is determined by mental processes that operate below the level of conscious awareness, at the level of the **unconscious.** Freud believed that these unconscious mental forces

1.12 This drawing by Stanford psychologist Roger Shepard can be viewed as either an obscured face behind a candlestick or the profiles of two separate women.

1.13 Sigmund Freud, the father of psychoanalytic theory, had a huge influence in the early days of psychology. Today, his theories have largely been abandoned.

were often in conflict, which produced psychological discomfort and in some cases even apparent psychological disorders.

Based on his theories, Freud developed the therapeutic method of **psychoanalysis**, which involved trying to bring the contents of the unconscious into conscious awareness so that conflicts could be dealt with in a constructive manner. For example, he analyzed the apparent symbolic content in his patients' dreams in search of hidden conflicts. He also used a technique called *free association* in which people would simply talk about whatever they wanted to for as long as they wanted to. Freud believed that through free association people would eventually reveal the unconscious conflicts that were causing them problems. Freud eventually extended his theories to account for general psychological functioning.

Freud's influence was considerable, not only on the psychologists who followed him but also on the public's view of psychology. Many people unfamiliar with psychology imagine that most psychologists have patients lie on couches and probe their innermost thoughts. In fact, today relatively few psychologists follow Freudian thinking. The basic problem with many of Freud's original ideas, such as the meaning of dreams, is that they are extremely difficult to test using the methods of science (as you will see in the next chapter). And although Freud's idea that mental processes occur below the level of conscious awareness is now widely accepted in psychological science, the unconscious processes studied by contemporary scientists share only a passing resemblance to the unconscious sexual conflicts that permeated Freudian theorizing.

1.14 John B. Watson, who spent most of his adult life in advertising, was a proponent of behaviorism. His views were amplified by thousands of psychologists, including B. F. Skinner.

MOST BEHAVIOR CAN BE MODIFIED BY REWARD AND PUNISHMENT

The focus on mental processes was soon challenged as inherently unscientific by John B. Watson (1878–1958; Figure 1.14), an American psychologist who developed the approach known as **behaviorism**, which emphasizes the role that environmental forces have on producing behavior. Watson believed that if psychology was to be a science, it had to stop trying to study mental events that could not be directly observed, and he therefore was scornful of methods such as introspection and free association. For Watson, the mind, if it existed at all, was irrelevant to understanding behavior. In a sense, Watson dealt with the mind-body problem by dispatching it beyond the interests of scientists. He agreed with Descartes on the essential dualism of mind and body, but he felt the mind was simply an ethereal by-product of the workings of the complex human nervous system.

The intellectual question that was more central to Watson and his followers was the nature-nurture question. For Watson and other behaviorists, it was all nurture. Heavily influenced by the work of Russian physiologist Ivan Pavlov, Watson believed that all behavior was caused by environmental factors: understanding the environmental *stimuli*, or triggers, was all one needed to predict a behavioral *response*. Watson's behaviorism was mainly concerned with how animals acquired new behaviors, which is known as learning (discussed in Chapter 6). Psychologists greeted Watson's approach with great enthusiasm. Many had grown dissatisfied with the ambiguous methods used by those studying mental processes; they longed to be taken more seriously as scientists, which they believed would happen if they focused on studying only observable behaviors.

It was B. F. Skinner (1904–1990) who became famous for taking up the mantle of behaviorism. Skinner's version of how learning took place differed slightly from Watson's and was more consistent with the functionalistic properties of behavior. Skinner was interested in how repeated behaviors were shaped or influenced by the events or consequences that followed them. For instance, an animal would learn to perform a behavior if doing so in the past had led to a positive outcome, such as receiving food. Like Watson, Skinner denied the existence of mental states, writing in his provocative *Beyond Freedom and Dignity* (1971) that concepts referring to mental processes were of no scientific value for explaining behavior. Rather, Skinner believed that mental states were nothing more than an illusion.

Behaviorism dominated psychological research well into the early 1960s. In many ways, these were extremely productive times for psychologists. Many of the basic principles established by behaviorists continue to be viewed as critical to understanding the mind, brain, and behavior. At the same time, sufficient evidence has accumulated to show that thought processes do influence outcomes, and few psychologists today describe themselves as strict behaviorists.

HOW PEOPLE THINK AFFECTS BEHAVIOR

During the first half of the twentieth century, evidence slowly emerged showing that how situations were perceived could influence behavior and that learning was not as simple as the behaviorists believed. In the late 1920s, Gestalt theorist Wolfgang Köhler found that chimpanzees could problem solve in their efforts to reach a banana. The chimpanzees had to figure out how to connect two sticks, which would then allow them to reach the banana and draw it close. The animals tried various things until suddenly they seemed to have insight, as evidenced by their reaching the banana and using the strategy perfectly on subsequent tasks. At around the same time, learning theorists such as Edward Tolman were showing that animals could learn by observation, which made little sense (according to behaviorist theory) given that the observing animals were not being rewarded—it was all going on in their heads. Other psychologists conducting research on memory, language, and child development showed that the simple laws of behaviorism could not explain such things as why cultural influences alter how people remember a story, why grammar develops in a systematic fashion, and why children go through stages of development in which they interpret the world in different ways. All of this suggested that mental functions were important for understanding behavior.

In 1957, George A. Miller (Figure 1.15) and colleagues established the Center for Cognitive Studies at Harvard University and launched the *cognitive revolution* in psychology. Ulric Neisser integrated a wide range of cognitive phenomena in his classic 1967 book that named and defined the field. *Cognitive psychology* is concerned with higher-order mental functions, such as intelligence, thinking, language, memory, and decision making (you will read more about cognitive psychology in Chapter 8). Cognitive research has shown that the way people think about things influences their behavior. A number of events occurring in the 1950s set the stage for the rise of cognitive science, with perhaps the growing use of

psychoanalysis A method developed by Sigmund Freud that attempts to bring the contents of the unconscious into conscious awareness so that conflicts can be revealed.

behaviorism A psychological approach that emphasizes the role of environmental forces in producing behavior.

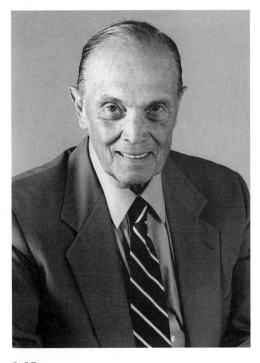

1.15 George A. Miller launched the cognitive revolution by establishing the Center for Cognitive Science at Harvard University in 1957.

computers leading the way. Computers operate according to software programs, which dictate rules for how information is processed. Cognitive psychologists such as Alan Newell and Nobel laureate Herbert Simon applied this process to their explanation for how the mind works. These *information processing* theories of cognition viewed the brain as the hardware that ran the mind as software; the brain takes in information as a code, processes it, stores relevant sections, and retrieves stored information as required. As such, there was an early recognition that the brain was important to cognition, but many cognitive psychologists preferred to focus exclusively on the software, with little interest in the specific brain mechanisms involved.

In the early 1980s, cognitive psychologists joined forces with neuroscientists, computer scientists, and philosophers to develop an integrated view of mind and brain. The field of *cognitive neuroscience* emerged during the 1990s as one of the most exciting fields of science. The basis of this field is that the brain enables the mind and allows for cognitive activity such as thought, language, and memory. Techniques such as brain imaging have provided empirical evidence that mental states are indeed open to scientific investigation. The basic goals of cognitive neuroscience have spread throughout psychology and are now attracting a wide variety of other scientists, including biologists, physicists, and engineers, who are interested in addressing the timeless question of how the mind and body are related.

SOCIAL SITUATIONS SHAPE BEHAVIOR

While tracing the origins of the field of psychology, we have focused a great deal on the relationship between the mind and the brain, and the role of evolution and learning on human behavior. After World War II, psychologists broadened their efforts to better understand human behavior in the real world. In particular, the atrocities committed in World War II led a number of psychologists and thinkers to begin researching topics such as authority, obedience, and group behavior. These topics are the province of *social psychology*, which focuses on the power of situation and how people are shaped through their interactions with others.

In 1962 Adolf Eichmann, one of Hitler's chief lieutenants, was hanged for "causing the killing of millions of Jews." Shortly before his death, Eichmann claimed, "I am not the monster I am made out to be. I am the victim of a fallacy." The atrocities committed in Nazi Germany compelled psychologists to consider whether evil is an integral part of human nature. Why had apparently normal Germans willingly participated in the murder of innocent men, women, and children? Researchers, many influenced by Freudian ideas, initially sought to understand what type of people would commit evil acts, and it was concluded that certain types, especially those raised by unusually strict parents, did display a slightly greater willingness to follow orders. But social psychology shows that almost all people are strongly influenced by social situations. Indeed, as you will read in Chapter 14, people will send painful electric shocks to innocent others if directed to do so by someone in apparent authority. Although it does not excuse anything, Eichmann was correct that people were overlooking the power of the situation in explaining his heinous actions.

Kurt Lewin (1890–1947; Figure 1.16), who was trained as a Gestalt psychologist, was one of the pioneers of contemporary social psychology. His *field theory* emphasized the interplay between people—their biology, habits, and beliefs—and the environment, such as social situations and group dynamics. This perspective

1.16 Kurt Lewin is the founder of modern social psychology. He pioneered the use of theory, using experimentation to test hypotheses.

allowed psychologists to begin examining some of the most complex forms of human mental activity, such as how people's attitudes shape behavior, why they are prejudiced against other groups, how they are influenced by other people, and why they are attracted to some people and repelled by others. The human mind navigates through the social world, and psychological science recognizes the importance of fully considering the situation in order to predict and understand behavior.

How Did the Foundations of Psychological Science Develop?

Early psychologists included some who believed it necessary to reduce mental processes into their constituent, "structural" parts, and others who argued that it was more important to understand how the mind functions than what it contains. During this early period, most research was aimed at understanding the subjective mind, such as Freud's emphasis on the unconscious and the Gestalt movement's focus on perception. It was the behaviorists who claimed that the study of mind was too subjective and therefore unscientific. Accordingly, for the first half of the twentieth century most psychologists studied only observable behaviors. The cognitive revolution in the 1960s returned the mind to center stage, and research on mental processes such as memory, language, and decision making blossomed. Throughout the last century, some psychologists have emphasized the social context of behavior and mental activity.

WHAT ARE THE PROFESSIONS OF PSYCHOLOGICAL SCIENCE?

As you will discover, psychological science covers broad ground. Many different types of researchers study the mind, brain, and behavior at different conceptual levels. This diversity means that psychological scientists pursue research on topics that touch all aspects of human life.

SUBDISCIPLINES FOCUS ON DIFFERENT LEVELS OF ANALYSIS

The term *psychologist* is used broadly to describe people whose careers involve predicting behavior or understanding mental life (Figure 1.17). We use the term **psychological scientist** to refer to those who use the methods of science to study the interplay among brain, mind, and behavior and how the social environment affects these processes. Psychological scientists work in many settings, such as clinics, schools, businesses, universities, and colleges. There are also **psychological practitioners**, who apply the findings of psychological science in order to do such things as help people in need of psychological treatment, design safe and pleasant working environments, counsel people on career paths, or help teachers design better classroom curricula. The distinction between science and practice can be fuzzy, since many psychological scientists are also practitioners. For example, many *clinical psychologists* both study and treat people with psychological disorders.

Psychological scientists pursue their research interests at different levels of analysis, as we described earlier, which tend to be associated with different

psychological scientist Refers to those who use the methods of science to study the interplay between brain, mind, and behavior and how the social environment impacts these processes.

psychological practitioners Refers to those who apply the findings from psychological science in order to assist people in their daily lives.

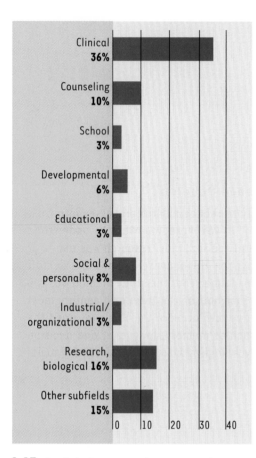

1.17 Psychologists pursue their interests by studying a variety of topics within different settings.

subdisciplines. For example, *cognitive psychology* is concerned with mental processes such as thinking, remembering, and decision making, while *social psychology* focuses on the influence that other people have on how we act, think, and feel. In addition, traditional areas include *developmental psychology*, which addresses changes in mind and behavior over the life span, *physiological psychology*, which typically uses animal models to study the biological mechanisms responsible for behavior, *personality psychology*, which studies individual differences, and *experimental psychopathology*, which studies abnormal or disordered behavior. Many of the chapters of this book reflect the different subdisciplines of psychological science.

Let's apply these levels of analysis to our example of sexual behavior from earlier in the chapter. Many scientists focus on the nuts and bolts of reproduction, such as genetic transmission. Others, who are interested in trying to deal with unwanted pregnancies among teenagers, study why it is that teenagers have impulsive and unprotected sex. They examine the cultural and societal norms that encourage casual sex, and they study the psychological barriers that prevent people from using condoms and following other safe-sex procedures. At the same time, clinical psychologists and pharmaceutical companies focus on sexual dysfunction, such as impotence, that prevents otherwise healthy people from engaging in consensual sex. The different particular interests of psychological scientists reflect the fact that most behaviors can be viewed from many different levels of analysis. The choice of which level to study is based on the scientists' particular interests, as well as their general theoretical approaches and how they were trained.

As a result, the distinctions between areas of psychological science are now often blurred, with many researchers crossing traditional boundaries to collaborate with researchers from other areas. Recall that one of our themes is that there has been a biological revolution within psychological science, with new methods such as brain imaging providing opportunities to address long-standing questions related to mental states and processes such as consciousness and memory. At the same time, not all psychological phenomena are best considered at the brain level. As such, throughout this book you will read about new understandings of how culture shapes the mind and behavior, how social situations compel people to behave in certain ways, and how environmental factors can reward or punish specific actions, making them more or less likely to occur. But, more and more, psychological science emphasizes examining behavior across multiple levels in an integrated fashion. Thus, psychologists interested in understanding the hormonal basis of obesity interact with geneticists who explore the heritability of obesity, as well as social psychologists who study the influences of human beliefs about eating. Crossing the different levels of analysis provides more insights than working within one level. The Gestalt psychologists were right in asserting that the whole is greater than the sum of its parts. Throughout this book you will find the multilevel approach has led to breakthroughs in understanding psychological activity.

PSYCHOLOGICAL KNOWLEDGE IS USED IN MANY PROFESSIONS

Psychology is one of the most popular majors in many colleges. Not only is the subject material fascinating and personally relevant, but psychological science serves as excellent training for many professions. For instance, physicians need to know a lot more than anatomy and chemistry. They need to know how to relate to their patients, how the patients' behaviors are linked to health, and what motivates or discourages patients from seeking medical care or following treatment protocols. Understanding the aging brain and how it affects visual perception, memory, and motor movement is vital for those who treat elderly patients. Psychological scientists make major contributions to research on human physical and mental health, which is why the National Institute of Health funds research in the field. Much of the psychological research you read about in this book is being used today to make people's lives better.

Psychological science is equally useful for anyone whose career involves needing to understand people. In order to persuade jurors, lawyers need to know how groups make decisions. Advertisers need to know how attitudes are formed or changed, and to what extent people's attitudes predict their behavior. Politicians use psychological science techniques of impression management to make themselves attractive to voters. The general usefulness of understanding mental activity may also explain psychology's popularity on campuses. It can help you understand your motives, your personality, even why you remember some things and forget others.

Of course, some of you will be so fascinated by psychological science that you will devote your lives to studying how the brain enables the mind and how mental activity is related to behavior. We, the authors, understand how you feel. There is tremendous excitement in psychological science, as we unravel the very nature of what is means to be a human being. Although the foundations of psychological science are growing and established scientific principles of mind, brain, and behavior exist, there is still a tremendous amount to learn about issues such as how nature and nurture interact, and how the brain enables the mind. Indeed, contemporary psychological science is providing new insights into problems and issues grappled with by the great scholars of the past.

PEOPLE ARE INTUITIVE PSYCHOLOGICAL SCIENTISTS

By their very nature, humans are intuitive psychological scientists who develop hypotheses about and try to predict the behavior of others. People choose marriage partners who they expect will best meet their emotional, sexual, and support needs. Defensive driving relies on an intuitive understanding of when other people are likely to make mistakes while driving. People are also pretty good at predicting whether others are kind, would make good teachers, or are trustworthy. But people can't intuitively know if taking certain herbs will increase memory, or whether playing music to newborns makes them more intelligent, or whether mental illness results from too much or too little of a certain brain chemical.

One of the most important goals of our textbook is to provide a basic education about the methods of psychological science for those students whose only exposure to psychology is through this introductory course. Although psychologists make important contributions to understanding and treating mental illness, most of psychological science has little to do with couches or dreams. Instead, it has everything to do with understanding mental activity, social interactions, and how people acquire behaviors. To understand what makes you tick, and what makes other people tick, you will need to be introduced to the basic operating manual for the human mind. This is found in the psychological sciences.

You will also be consumers of psychological science throughout your lives, and you will need to be skeptical of overblown media accounts of "brand new" findings obtained by "groundbreaking" research. For instance, a very modest study conducted by a cognitive psychologist found that playing Mozart to research

RESEARCH QUESTION

How do we use knowledge acquired from psychological science?

participants led them to score slightly higher on a test that is loosely related to intelligence. The media jumped onto the so-called Mozart effect with abandon; the result has been that many parents are determinedly playing Mozart to young infants, and even to developing fetuses. Unfortunately, subsequent research failed to replicate the findings. Following a careful review of the studies testing the Mozart effect, Christopher Chabris and his colleagues have concluded that the effect of listening to Mozart is quite trivial and certainly unlikely to increase intelligence among listeners (Chabris et al., 1999). John Bruer, in his important book *The Myth of the First Three Years*, notes that people have taken leaps past the data in suggesting that experiences during the first three years shape or alter the developing brain in any meaningful or permanent way.

One of the hallmarks of science is skepticism. You should be skeptical of dramatic new findings reported in science until you have convincing evidence to support the claims. Science progresses carefully and often slowly, and good science takes time. Throughout this book you will learn how to separate the believable from the incredible. You will learn to spot badly designed experiments, and you will develop the skills necessary to critically evaluate claims made in the popular media. The information provided in this book will also provide a state-of-the-art background in psychological science so that you will know whether a claim is consistent with what we know about psychology or not. Reading this book will make you a much more sophisticated consumer of research about mental activities and behavior.

What Are the Professions of Psychological Science?

Psychological scientists study the mind, brain, and behavior across different levels of analysis and often identify themselves within various subdisciplines of psychology. However, there is a growing tendency for researchers to cross traditional areas to collaborate with researchers from different subdisciplines. This is especially true for those who are increasingly interested in how the brain enables the mind, and how the mind was shaped through the evolution of humans in a social world.

The content of psychological science is of interest and value to many professions, which may explain why psychology is one of the most popular majors on most college campuses. At the same time, understanding the methods of psychological science is useful for evaluating research that is reported in popular media.

CONCLUSION

The rich history of psychology is clear. Its founders grappled with the most important and interesting issues there are to be found in life. Who are we? How does the brain get the job done? How much of us is predetermined by our genes? How does our personality affect our lives? What are the social forces that influence our personal decisions?

As Darwin predicted, the concept of natural selection is becoming an integral part of psychological science. In general terms, psychologists have come to appreciate that to understand something, they first must understand what it is *for*. Namely, we need to stop asking, "How does this aspect of the brain work?" and ask instead, "What is this aspect of the brain for? Did it solve a problem for our human ancestors?" The current biological revolution in psychological science seeks to answer exactly these sorts of questions. At the same time, the human brain has evolved in a social world, and so much of the psychological enterprise is concerned with how people interact with one another. Research across the multiple levels of analysis is invigorating psychological science and providing new insights into age-old questions. In the chapters ahead you will learn not only how psychological science operates, but also many remarkable discoveries about the mind, brain, and behavior. It might just be one of the most fascinating explorations of your life.

FURTHER READINGS

Aronson, E. (1998). *The social animal*. New York: W. H. Freeman.

Darwin, C. (1964). *On the origin of species*. Cambridge, MA: Harvard University Press. (Original work published 1859)

Gazzaniga, M. S. (1998). *The mind's past*. Berkeley, CA: University of California Press.

Hothersall, D. (1995). *History of psychology*. Boston, MA: McGraw-Hill.

James, W. (1983). *Principles of psychology*. Cambridge, MA: Harvard University Press. (Original work published 1890)

CREATIVE APPROACHES TO PSYCHOLOGICAL RESEARCH

To test whether people sometimes misattribute the source of their emotions, researchers D. G. Dutton and A. P. Aron conducted a clever field study involving the 230-feet high Capilano Suspension Bridge (pictured here). Compared with men who crossed a safer, more stable bridge, men who were interviewed during their heart-pounding journey across the Capilano bridge responded with greater sexual imagery and were more likely to ask the female interviewer on a date, indicating that they may have confused the source of their arousal.

TIMELINE

1879

Reaction Times Wilhelm Wundt and others at the University of Leipzig use reaction-time measures to study mental processes. These measures assume the time it takes to respond to a stimulus corresponds to the time it takes for mental activity.

1880

Case of Anna O. Josef Breuer, a Viennese physician, treats a young patient who is suffering from a psychological affliction. Sigmund Freud, develops many of his ideas about psychoanalysis by analyzing the case of Anna O.

1896

Correlation Coefficient Karl Pearson, an English statistician, builds on Galton's ideas and develops the correlation coefficient, which is a statistic that measures the degree of association between two variables still widely used in psychological science.

1897

Social Facilitation The first observational study of social behavior is undertaken by Norman Triplett, who discovers that bicycle racers pedal more quickly in the presence of other cyclists than when on their own.

Research Methodology

2

OUTLINING THE PRINCIPLES

1924

The Electrical Brain Hans Berger records the first electrical signals of the brain from the intact skull of a human. The electroencephalogram is used to measure the activity of the brain during mental processes.

1925

The Foundation of Experimental Design Sir Ronald Fisher publishes *Statistical Methods for Research Workers*, which establishes the foundation for contemporary experimental design.

1933

Testing Hypotheses Jerzy Neyman and Egon Pearson, the son of Karl Pearson, detail the central concepts behind statistical hypothesis testing in a paper presented to the Cambridge Philosophical Society.

1950s

Recording Individual Neurons Experimenting on cats, David Hubel and Torsten Wiesel make the first recordings from individual neurons in the cerebral cortex.

1960s

Experimenter Expectancy Robert Rosenthal shows that the outcome of an experiment can be influenced by the researcher's beliefs or expectancies, and others develop techniques to minimize bias in research.

In the late 1800s, the Italian physiologist Angelo Mosso began studying the relationship between mind and brain by examining how mental activity affects the flow of blood to the brain. He was working on the assumption that—because the brain is the organ responsible for generating thoughts, feelings, and emotions—mental activity should affect how the brain functions. In one interesting experiment, Mosso had his subject lie on a table, which in turn was carefully balanced upon a fulcrum. Remarkably, as soon as the subject engaged in emotional or intellectual activity, such as being afraid or doing mental arithmetic, the table began to tilt down toward the head end! Mosso concluded that because mental activity increases the physiological activity of the brain, the tilt in the table was due to an increase in the amount of blood that was flowing into the subject's brain.

Mosso's experiment was a harbinger of the modern experimental techniques that allow us today to visually image mental activity. For example, by injecting subjects with small doses of radioactively labeled water, scientists can now track changes in the flow of blood in the brain during mental tasks, such as trying to remember what you ate for breakfast or looking at a picture of someone who is afraid.

Although dramatic improvements have been made in the research technology relative to Mosso's table, his study does share many of the goals of modern psychological research. Research always begins with a question that intrigues the researcher, who then designs and conducts a study to answer the question. Whether the study provides a useful answer depends on whether it is well designed. In this chapter we will examine the different ways researchers study the questions of psychological science. You will learn the qualities that separate good studies from bad, as well as the types of questions that can be addressed through psychological research.

During the last century psychologists have made a number of important discoveries about the mind, brain, and behavior. These discoveries have emerged

RESEARCH QUESTIONS

for Studying Psychological Science Methodology

What defines an empirical question?

How does an experiment differ from a descriptive study?

What are the different methods used in psychological science?

How do ethical issues constrain psychological research?

How do we ensure that our measures are accurate?

What kinds of statistics are used to analyze data?

What is the basis for evaluating research?

1969

Identifying Cognitive Operations Saul Sternberg updates how to use reaction-time measures to infer the sequence of cognitive processing stages employed during a task, laying the groundwork for human brain-mapping techniques.

1970s

Understanding Relationships Elaine Hatfield and Ellen Berscheid pioneer the scientific study of love. Their research provides important insights into the study of interpersonal relationships.

1986–Present

Linking Brain and Mind Peter Fox and others lay out the theoretical foundation for tracking changes in blood flow in the brain. This leads to the development of brain-imaging technologies that associate brain regions with specific mental processes.

is to understand what level of analysis a particular question is addressing. Recall from Chapter 1 the seven different levels of analysis: (1) genetic, (2) neurochemical, (3) brain systems, (4) behavioral, (5) perceptual/cognitive, (6) individual/personality, and (7) social/cultural. You then select data collection methods that are appropriate for questions at that level. An example of how this works is discussed in "Crossing the Levels of Analysis: Studying Musical Experience."

Researchers studying different levels of analysis tend to use different types of methods to collect data. For instance, at the social, individual, and behavioral levels, researchers have collected data by observing people or asking them questions. This can be done with groups or with individuals. By contrast, at the cognitive/perceptual level researchers have used indirect assessments, such as seeing how fast participants respond to a particular question or whether they accurately discriminate between different sizes of objects. At the brain systems and neurochemistry levels, researchers have used techniques to measure bodily and brain processes in animals or humans. For instance, a drug might be injected into a rat to see what effect it has on behavior. Let's turn now to the major methods used to collect data to study the mind, brain, and behavior.

OBSERVING IS AN UNOBTRUSIVE STRATEGY

Observational techniques involve systematic assessment and coding of overt behavior, such as watching people's gestures during social interaction or coding the eating or sexual behavior of animals that are injected with drugs that affect brain function. As the name implies, these techniques are the major data collection method for descriptive studies, but they can be used in experiments and correlational designs as well.

Using observational techniques to collect data requires that at least three decisions be made. First, should the study be conducted in the laboratory or in the natural environment? At issue is the extent to which you are interested in behavior as it occurs in the real world, and the possibility that the laboratory setting will lead to artificial behavior (Figure 2.3).

Second, how should the data actually be collected—as a written description of what was seen, or as a running tally of prespecified categories of behavior? For example, suppose you have a theory that people greet friends and family more effusively at the airport than at the train station. You could operationally define different categories of "effusive" greetings, such as "hugging," "kissing," "hand-shaking," and the like, and then as each episode of greeting is observed at the gate or platform, the proper categories could be marked down on a tally sheet. Using preestablished categories is usually preferred for more objectivity. However, badly chosen categories may mean that you miss important behavior. Furthermore, the choice of which type of description is preferable may not always be clear.

Third, should the observer be visible? The concern here is that observation might alter the behavior being observed. This

naturalistic observation A passive descriptive study in which observers do not change or alter ongoing behavior.

participant observation A type of descriptive study in which the researcher is actively involved in the situation.

observational techniques A research method of careful and systematic assessment and coding of overt behavior.

2.3 Primate behavior is often observed in natural settings. Here Dr. Jane Goodall observes a family of chimpanzees. Animals are more likely to act naturally when they are in their native habitat, relative to animals in captivity.

Crossing the Levels of Analysis

STUDYING MUSICAL EXPERIENCE

What type of music do you like? The enjoyment of music is a fascinating aspect of human life. There are many questions to be asked about the musical experience, such as how preferences vary across individuals and across cultures, how music affects emotional state and thought processes, and even how the brain perceives sound as music rather than noise. As is indicated throughout this chapter, the specific question dictates the type of method that is used to answer it. For instance, suppose you wanted to know how often people listen to music. You could develop a questionnaire and administer it to your sample of interest. This method was recently used to study the attitudes of 2,465 adolescents at schools in England. On average, they reported listening to 2.45 hours of music each day, and they said that they did so because it allowed them to project a desired "image" to the world and helped them to satisfy emotional needs (North et al., 2000). Thus, at the individual level, questionnaires reveal musical tastes. Questionnaires can also be used to study music at other levels, such as the genetic level. For example, a study of attitudes in 800 British twins (Martin et al., 1986) revealed that about half the variability in the liking of jazz music is determined by genetic influence. Thus, strategies such as observational learning or asking-based methods can provide information about the quantity and type of music that people listen to, as well as the types of people doing the listening.

What effect does listening to music have on people? Researchers have used laboratory experiments to study the effects of music at the cognitive level on mood, memory, decision making, and a variety of other cognitive processes. In these studies, one group of research participants might listen to one piece of music and another group might listen to a different piece of music, and then the groups' emotional or cognitive reactions would be compared. This research has found that music can have dramatic effects on mental experiences. For instance, "Russia under the Mongolian Yoke" from Prokofiev's *Field of the Dead*, played at half speed, reliably puts people into negative moods. Not only may the tempo of the music affect mood, but also whether it is in major or minor mode. At least for Western music, major mode is typically associated with positive moods and minor mode is associated with sad moods. This emotional response appears to be learned rather than innate, since very young children do not discriminate between modes, but by age seven or eight, children can reliably distinguish the mood effects of major and minor modes (Gregory et al., 1996). The latter example also demonstrates the method of stimulus judgments, which are widely used in music research, such as studying whether people can differentiate different musical chords. Why does music affect mood? One way to study this is to look at the effect of music on brain chemistry at the neurochemical level of analysis. Indeed, it appears that pleasant music may be associated with increased activation of one brain chemical, serotonin, that is known to be relevant to mood (Evers & Suhr, 2000).

Finally, researchers can look at this question from a brain-systems level of analysis. Does perceiving music use the same brain circuits as, say, perceiving the sound of automobiles or spoken language? It turns out that the processing of musical information operates in a similar fashion to general auditory processing, but it likely also uses different brain mechanisms. Case reports of patients with certain types of brain injury indicate that some people lose the ability to hear tones and melody but not speech or environmental sounds. One 35-year-old woman who had temporal-lobe damage lost the ability to recognize even familiar tunes and songs, a condition known as *amusia*, even though other aspects of her memory and language systems were intact (Peretz, 1996). There are also case studies of so-called musical savants, who can play piano concertos by ear or sing elaborate songs, but who otherwise show gross intellectual impairments, such as being unable to communicate with others or even respond to their own names. Such findings suggest that there are specific brain regions responsible for the processing of music. Researchers are also using methods such as brain imaging to understand which parts of the brain are involved in perceiving and enjoying music, and how this might differ from the perception of other sounds. The important point is that different levels of analysis can be used to examine different questions about the relationship between mood and music.

---

effect is known as **reactivity.** For instance, people may feel compelled to try to make a positive impression. A classic example of this happened when researchers tried to investigate the effects of workplace conditions, such as lighting, on productivity at the Hawthorne electric plant in Cicero, Illinois, between 1924 and 1932. The workers, who knew they were being observed, increased productivity to impress the researchers and their supervisors, thereby obliterating the effect of interest to the researchers. The *Hawthorne effect* refers to changes in behavior that occur when people know that others are observing them. In general, observation should be as unobtrusive as possible and behavior should be allowed to flow naturally.

Observer bias   In conducting observation research, it is important to be aware of the possibility of **observer bias**, which refers to systematic errors in observation that occur due to an observer's expectations. For instance, if observers are coding the facial expressions of men and women, they may be more likely to rate female expressions as indicating sadness because they believe that men don't show sadness. Likewise, the same level of assertiveness may be rated more strongly for females than males because it might not conform to expectations about how men and women typically behave. There is even evidence that observer bias can lead to actual changes in the behavior of the people or animals being observed, which is known as the **experimenter expectancy effect.** For example, in one classic study conducted in the 1960s by Robert Rosenthal (Figure 2.4), college students trained rats to run a maze. Half of the students were told, in advance, that their rats were genetically bred to be really good at running mazes, whereas the other group was not given this expectation. In reality, there were no initial differences between the groups of rats. Nonetheless, the ones trained by the students who believed that their rats were bred to be fast learners actually did learn the task more quickly. Thus, the students' expectations might have altered how they treated their rats, which in turn influenced the speed at which the rats learned. To protect against experimenter expectancy effects, it is best if the person running the study is *blind*, or unaware, of the hypotheses of the study. It is also desirable to have multiple observers to protect against idiosyncratic coding. However, the significant challenge with multiple observers is to minimize variability in how each observer catalogs or interprets the behaviors encountered during observation.

2.4 Social psychologist Robert Rosenthal's studies of experimenter expectancy effects showed that subtle cues given off by the experimenter can affect how research participants behave.

ASKING TAKES A MORE ACTIVE APPROACH

If observation is an unobtrusive approach for studying behavior, *asking* people about themselves—what they think, why they act, and how they feel—is a much more interactive way in which to collect data. Asking-based methods include surveys, interviews, questionnaires, and self-reports; all are aimed at getting people to divulge information about themselves. The type of information sought ranges from demographic facts (e.g., ethnicity, religious affiliation) to past behaviors, personal attitudes, beliefs, and so on. Have you ever used an illegal drug? Were you in favor of the court-ordered decision to stop the vote recount in Florida during the 2000 election? Are you comfortable sending food back to the kitchen in a restaurant when there is a problem? These questions require people to recall certain events from their lives or reflect on their mental or emotional states.

A critical issue in asking-based research concerns how to frame the questions used in the study, as there are several different options. *Open-ended questions* allow respondents to answer in as much detail as they feel is appropriate. In contrast, *closed-ended questions* require respondents to select among a fixed number of options, such as in a multiple-choice exam (Figure 2.5). Ultimately, the researcher decides what style of question to use in relation to what will provide the most appropriate information for the hypothesis.

Asking-based methods have a number of strengths and weaknesses, but they depend on whether respondents are simply given a questionnaire or survey to fill out, or whether each person in the study is actually interviewed by a researcher. On the one hand, **self-report methods** such as questionnaires can be used to gather data from a large number of people. They can be mailed out to the population of interest or handed out in appropriate locations. They are easy to administer, relatively cheap and cost-efficient, and they can collect a great deal of data in a relatively short period of time. At the same time, researchers have to be careful that people pay attention when they are completing long questionnaires. Sometimes people can fall into the habit of simply selecting the same response for each

reactivity The knowledge that one is being observed alters the behavior being observed.

observer bias Systematic errors in observation that occur due to an observer's expectations.

experimenter expectancy effects When observer bias leads to actual changes in the behavior of the people or animals being observed.

self-report method A method of data collection in which people are asked to provide information about themselves, such as in questionnaires or surveys.

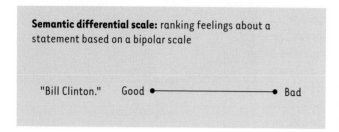

2.5 Examples of two different ways to quantify people's responses by offering a fixed number of options.

item, which is known as *response set*. To counteract these problems, a good questionnaire might use *reverse wording* on some questions to make sure the participant is fully thinking about each item. In contrast to self-reports, interviews can be used with great success for groups that cannot be studied via surveys. Furthermore, interviewing people gives the researcher the opportunity to explore new lines of questioning, as the answers a respondent gives to initial questions may inspire avenues of inquiry that were not originally planned.

An important issue to be considered in both self-reports and interviews is how to select people for inclusion in the study. Psychological scientists typically want to know that their findings *generalize*, or apply, to people beyond those individuals who are in the study. For instance, they might wish to know that their results generalize to all women, or to all college students, or to students who belong to sororities and fraternities, or to everyone. The group of interest is known as the *population*, whereas the subset of people who are studied are known as the *sample*. *Sampling* is the process by which people are selected from the population to be members of the sample. Because it is desirable that the sample be representative of the population, researchers often use *random sampling*, in which each member of the population has an equal chance of being chosen to participate.

Self-report bias   A problem common to all asking-based methods is that people often introduce biases into their answers. In particular, people may be hesitant to reveal personal information that casts them in a negative light. Consider the question, "How many times have you lied in order to get something that you wanted?" Although most people have lied at some point in their lives to obtain a desired outcome or object, few of us want to admit this to total strangers. At issue is the extent to which questions produce **socially desirable responding**, or "faking good," in which the person responds in a way that is most socially acceptable. Imagine having a middle-aged interviewer ask you to describe intimate aspects of your sexual life. Many of us would find talking about this quite embarrassing and therefore would not be very forthcoming. Moreover, even when respondents may not be purposefully answering incorrectly, their answers may reflect less-than-accurate self-perceptions. In other words, research has shown that people have the tendency to describe themselves in especially positive ways, and in many cases this occurs because people believe things about themselves that might not actually be true. For instance, most people believe they are better-than-average drivers.

CASE STUDIES EXAMINE INDIVIDUAL LIVES

A **case study** involves the intensive examination of one person, typically one who is unusual, for good or bad reasons. In psychology, case studies are most commonly conducted on those who have a brain injury or psychological disorder. Case studies of those with brain injuries have provided a wealth of evidence about which parts of the brain are involved in various psychological processes. In one case, a man who was accidentally stabbed through the middle part of the brain with a fencing foil lost the ability to store new memories, whereas case histories of individuals with damage to the front portions of their brains reveal consistent difficulties with inhibiting impulsive behaviors. One famous case study in clinical psychology involved "Sybil," who apparently had *multiple personality disorder*, a rare condition in which a person appears to have more than one distinct personality. These multiple personalities were viewed as Sybil's way of coping with severe abuse she experienced during childhood.

The major problem with clinical case studies such as Sybil's is that it is difficult to know if the researcher's hypothesis about the cause of the psychological disorder is correct. The researcher has no control over the person's life and is forced to make assumptions about the effects of various life events. Thus, the interpretation of case studies is often very subjective. Similarly, understanding the effects of brain injury or disease requires the assumption that apparent mental deficits were caused by the damage to the brain. Although many times such conclusions seem reasonable, especially if friends or family report that the person was different before the brain damage, the lack of control over the situation makes it difficult to draw firm conclusions. For instance, in 1966 a man named Charles Whitman climbed a tower at the University of Texas and began firing a rifle at passersby, killing 14 and wounding many more in a 90-minute spree. The night before he had killed his wife and mother and had composed a letter trying to explain his actions. His case history, including his visits to a psychiatrist and the letter he wrote, indicate that Whitman might have had a brain tumor, and an autopsy did turn up evidence consistent with this assessment. But was a brain tumor responsible for Whitman's murderous actions? We will never know.

RESPONSE PERFORMANCE MEASURES STIMULUS PROCESSING

The typical goal of measuring **response performance** is to quantify how a perceptual or cognitive process responds to a specific stimulus. Specifically, researchers infer how a stimulus is processed from how a person responds to it. Response performance is quantified in three basic ways. First, a researcher can measure **reaction time**, the speed of a response—which has been the workhorse method of cognitive psychology. The interpretation of reaction times is based on the idea that processing in the brain takes time; the more processing a stimulus requires, the longer the reaction time to that stimulus will be. By manipulating what a subject has to do with a stimulus and measuring reaction times, researchers can gain much information regarding the different operations involved in stimulus processing. For example, suppose you have a theory that it takes longer to determine the shape of an object than it does to determine its size. Your theory generates the hypothesis that reaction times should be longer when people are asked to discriminate the shape of an object, relative to when they have to discriminate the size of the object. Why? The assumption is that the longer the process takes, the longer the corresponding reaction time will be. An example of a reaction-time task is presented in Figure 2.6.

Researchers can also measure *response accuracy*, which usually concerns how well a stimulus was perceived. For example, does paying attention to a stimulus actually improve its perception? One way to study this in the visual domain would be to ask participants to pay attention to just one side of a computer screen while keeping their eyes focused on the center of the screen. We can then present a stimulus requiring a discrimination response (to a question such as, Was the shape a hexagon or an octagon?) to either the attended or the unattended side of the

socially desirable responding When people respond to a question in a way that is most socially acceptable or that makes them look good.

case study A research method that involves the intensive examination of one person.

response performance A research method in which researchers quantify perceptual or cognitive processes in response to a specific stimulus.

reaction time A quantification of performance behavior that measures the speed of a response.

2.6 Quickly name the color of ink that each of these words is printed in. Name the color for each word in the row as quickly as you can.

Notice how it took you longer to name the colors for the last row. This is called the Stroop Effect, in which it takes longer to name the color of words printed in a conflicting color. The interference from your automatic reading of the word slows you down.

red blue green red blue yellow red blue

blue red green yellow red blue green red

green yellow red yellow blue red green blue

2.7 A common method for studying questions at the cognitive/perceptual level is to ask participants to make judgments about stimuli. In this case, the participant is required to decide whether the two letters on the screen are the same or different.

psychophysiological assessment A research method that examines how changes in bodily functions are associated with behavior or mental state.

electrophysiology A method of data collection that measures electrical activity in the brain.

Institutional Review Boards (IRBs) Groups of people responsible for reviewing proposed research to ensure that it meets the accepted standards of science and provides for the physical and emotional well being of research participants.

screen. If the accuracy of responses is greater for stimuli presented on the attended side, then the implication is that attention is improving the perception of the stimulus.

Finally, researchers can measure response performance by asking people to make *stimulus judgments* regarding the different stimuli with which they are presented. Typical examples would be asking subjects to indicate whether or not a faint stimulus was noticed, or asking them to compare two objects and judge whether or not they are the same on some parameter, such as color, size, or shape (Figure 2.7). The benefit of using response performance as a methodology is that it can be a relatively simple way in which to study cognition and perception.

BODY AND BRAIN ACTIVITY CAN BE DIRECTLY MEASURED

The activity of the body and the brain can be directly measured in different ways. For instance, it is now well established that certain emotional states influence the body in predictable ways. When people are frightened their muscles become tense and their hearts start beating faster. Other bodily systems influenced by mood and mental states include blood pressure, blood temperature, rate of perspiration, pupil size, breathing rates, and so on. These various measures are examples of **psychophysiological assessment**, in which researchers examine how changes in bodily functions are associated with behavior or mental state. For example, police investigators often use *polygraphs*, or lie detectors, that assess these bodily states, under the assumption that people who are lying are experiencing more arousal and therefore are more likely to show physical signs of stress. It should be noted that there is not a perfect correspondence between bodily response and mental state. For instance, some stressful events lead to increased heart rate whereas others lead to reduced heart rate. Nonetheless, these methods allow researchers to study bodily responses that circumvent the problems inherent in self-report, such as people being unwilling or unable to report on their thoughts or feelings.

Electrophysiology Electrophysiology is a method of data collection that measures electrical activity in the brain to see how it is related to cognitive and perceptual tasks. To do this, a researcher fits electrodes onto the participant's scalp; they act almost like small microphones to pick up the electrical activity of the brain (Figure 2.8). Electrophysiology can be used to assess brain activity even during sleep, and it has revealed that the brain is very active when the body is at rest, especially during dreams.

Another electrophysiological method measures the activity of single neurons in the brains of experimental animals. It has helped us begin to uncover the different kinds of information single neurons code in different parts of the brain, something that can't be done by recording from the scalp. Recall the study by Hubel and Wiesel in which the stuck slide led to the serendipitous finding that cells in a cat's primary visual cortex respond to moving lines. Without being able to directly measure the activity of single neurons in animals, the questions raised by Hubel and Wiesel could not have been answered.

Brain imaging The electrical activity of the brain is associated with changes in the flow of blood, as oxygen and nutrients are carried to the active brain regions. Brain-imaging methods such as *positron emission tomography* (*PET*) and *functional* *magnetic resonance imaging (fMRI)* are based on measuring changes in the flow of blood in the brain. Although the specifics of these methods are discussed in Chapter 4, the basic idea is that by keeping track of these changes in blood flow, researchers can monitor which brain areas are active during a study. Imaging is a powerful tool for uncovering where different systems reside in the brain and the manner in which different brain areas interact in order to process information. For example, research has shown consistent patterns of activation with various cognitive tasks, such as memory, problem solving, and attention.

The value of directly measuring brain activity is that clear links can be made between actual activity in the brain and aspects of personality, social behavior, cognition, and the like. Thus, many different types of researchers are now using brain imaging. For instance, both cognitive and social psychologists have used fMRI to study how people interpret facial expressions. Brain imaging is also widely used to help diagnose psychological disorders, especially those that may result from brain injury or disease. However, research in this domain can be prohibitively expensive—the cost of imaging machines, their upkeep, and their attendant personnel runs in the millions of dollars.

2.8 The relatively small electrical responses to specific events can only be observed by averaging the EEG traces over a series of trials. The large background oscillations of the EEG trace make it impossible to detect the evoked response to the sensory stimulus from a single trial. However, by averaging across tens or hundreds of trials, the background EEG is removed, leaving the event-related potential (called ERP).

THERE ARE ETHICAL ISSUES TO CONSIDER

When selecting a method of research, it is imperative that decisions be made with full knowledge of the ethical issues involved. Are the participants being asked to do something unreasonable? Is there a risk of physical or emotional fallout from the study? Some ethical concerns are specific to the kind of method used, while other concerns apply across all methods. Therefore, in order to ensure the well-being of study participants, all colleges and universities have strict guidelines in place regarding both human- and animal-based research. **Institutional Review Boards (IRBs)** consisting of trained scholars, administrators, and legal advisers are given the task of reviewing proposed research to ensure that it meets the accepted standards of science.

One of the more prominent ethical concerns with research is the reasonable expectation of *privacy*. If behavior is going to be observed, is it okay to observe people without their knowledge? This question obviously depends on what sorts of behaviors one might be looking at. If the behaviors occur in public, then the concerns may be less than if one is interested in behaviors that are considered more private. For example, it would be okay to observe the behavior of couples saying goodbye in an airport, as this is a public domain, but it would be inappropriate to examine the private mating behaviors of couples—at least without their knowledge. The concern over privacy is compounded by the growing technology available for remotely monitoring people. Although someone might like to compare the behavior of men and women in public bathrooms, would it be okay to install a discreet video camera to monitor people in restrooms? Likely not. However, sometimes it may be necessary to invade privacy to understand genuine

RESEARCH QUESTION

How do ethical issues constrain psychological research?

Studying the Mind

MUNCHAUSEN SYNDROME BY PROXY

When is it okay to risk invading people's privacy in order to observe their behavior? Consider the difficulties presented to health care workers and law enforcement officials by the mental illness known as *Munchausen Syndrome by Proxy (MSBP)*. MSBP is a particularly sinister form of child abuse in which the guardian of a child (typically, the mother) induces an actual illness in a child, claims that the child has an illness so that unnecessary medical treatments will be given, or both. The problem in recognizing and diagnosing cases of MSBP is that most guardians afflicted with the disease are highly familiar with the medical environment, and they are quite skilled at hiding their abuse. In the best-case scenario, MSBP is eventually diagnosed, but the difficulties in making a diagnosis extend the duration of child abuse. In the worst-case scenario, MSBP is never recognized, and the child abuse continues unabated, perhaps until the child dies.

To combat these problems, David Hall and colleagues at Emory University in Atlanta established a protocol for covertly monitoring hospitalized children in suspected cases of MSBP. The rooms of these patients were outfitted with multiple hidden video cameras to observe guardian behavior, and with microphones in order to listen to the guardians' conversations with the child and other family members. The decision to allow this monitoring was made by a multidisciplinary team, including physicians, nurses, social workers, and risk-management professionals. Consent to covert monitoring was included in the admission forms signed by the guardians, and signs at the entrance to the hospital indicated that the remote surveillance of patients was used for educational and clinical purposes. Security officers monitored the patients' and guardians' activities on a 24-hour basis and were educated beforehand in the nature of MSBP.

In a report published in the journal *Pediatrics*, the findings from a 4-year study of suspected MSBP cases revealed startling results (Hall et al., 2000). Of 41 patients monitored, 23 were classified as "certain" cases of MSBP. Of these 23 cases, covert monitoring had led to a diagnosis in 56 percent. What evidence was found supporting these diagnoses? One mother who claimed her child was ill was overheard telling family members that the child was having seizures, yet none had actually occurred. Another told family members that the doctors wanted to operate on the child, but that she would not allow it. In fact, the doctors had been trying to convince her that there was nothing wrong with her child. The evidence was much more disturbing for guardians who induced illnesses. In one case, a mother was seen placing a strong sedative into the child's feeding tube.

The value of the covert-surveillance approach to diagnosing MSBP becomes apparent when compared to how diagnoses are made without such evidence. MSBP patients are often characterized as being overly friendly with the doctors treating their child, overly familiar with the terms and jargon used by medical professionals, and frequently sympathetic when doctors can make no firm diagnosis of the child's ailment. However, Hall and colleagues point out that this description fit only half of the 23 guardians who were ultimately diagnosed with MSBP. Not only does this suggest that more traditional methods of diagnosis may frequently be inadequate for identifying cases of MSBP, but also that the use of video surveillance may increase the rate of diagnosis by up to 50 percent.

mental disorders. Such a situation is considered in "Studying the Mind: Munchausen Syndrome by Proxy."

When asking people for information, are there topics that should not be raised because they may be insensitive or inappropriate? For example, many researchers would like to understand how physical and emotional trauma affects people in the months and years after a traumatic event. While exploring such issues is necessary to develop strategies for overcoming anguishing and difficult experiences, researchers exploring such topics must *always* remain sensitive to how their line of questioning is affecting the individuals they are studying, especially when using an interview format.

No matter what kind of method is employed, it is critical to consider who will have access to the data that have been collected. Participant *confidentiality* should always be carefully guarded so that personal information is not publicly linked to the behavioral findings of the study. Often the quality and accuracy of data directly depend on how confident the subjects are that their responses will be kept confidential, especially when dealing with emotionally or legally sensitive topics. For extremely sensitive topics, it is preferable that the participants' responses be anonymous.

Informed consent Research with human participants is a partnership based on mutual respect and trust. People who volunteer for psychological research, whether compensated or not, have the right to know what will happen to them during the course of the study. Ethical standards require providing people with all relevant information that would affect their willingness to become participants. This **informed consent** means that participants make a knowledgeable decision to participate. Typically, informed consent is obtained in writing; in the case of observational studies of public behavior, to protect privacy, individuals are treated anonymously. Minors, the intellectually incapacitated, and the mentally ill cannot legally provide informed consent, and therefore the permission of a legal guardian is necessary.

It is not always possible to fully inform participants about details of a study. Sometimes researchers must use *deception*, which involves either misleading participants about the goals of the study or not fully revealing what will take place, because knowing the specific goals of the study may alter the participants' behavior, thereby rendering the results meaningless. Deception is used only when other methods are not appropriate, when the goals of the research are important, or when the deception does not involve situations that would strongly affect the people's willingness to participate. If deception is used, a careful *debriefing*, or explanation of the study after its completion, must take place to fully inform participants of the goals of the study and the need for deception, and to eliminate or counteract any negative effects produced by the deception.

Relative risks of participation   Another ethical issue is the **relative risk** to mental or physical health. Researchers must always be aware of what they are asking participants to do in the name of data collection. People cannot be asked to endure unreasonable amounts of pain or discomfort, either from stimuli or from the manner in which data measurements are taken. Fortunately, for the vast majority of research being conducted, these types of concerns are not an issue. However, although risk is low, researchers have to think carefully about the potential for risk to specific participants. For example, fMRI involves placing participants in powerful magnetic fields. As a result, participants must be carefully screened to ensure they have no metal in or on their bodies, even if it's only a tattoo with metal-based inks. Again, it is important to note that all research now conducted at colleges and universities must be approved by an IRB that is familiar with the various rules and regulations that protect research participants from possible physical or psychological harm. Most IRBs look at the relative trade-off between risk and benefit. There is much to be gained from the scientific enterprise, and sometimes it requires asking participants to expose themselves to some risk in order to obtain important findings. The *risk-benefit ratio* asks whether the research is important enough to warrant placing participants at risk. Poorly designed studies have little benefit to science, and therefore no element of risk is justified by them. Thus, scientists have an ethical obligation to conduct carefully designed research.

Research with animals   Many of the major medical and scientific discoveries of the past century have involved the use of animals as research subjects. The use of animals allows researchers to examine biological mechanisms that cannot be studied in humans. Obviously, animal research should be undertaken only when the potential benefits outweigh the costs and when the studies are well designed. In addition, researchers have a responsibility to treat the animals as humanely as possible. Indeed, government regulations require a careful monitoring of animals used in research, and potential animal studies are screened for problems before

informed consent   A process in which people are given full information about a study, which allows them to make a knowledgeable decision about whether to participate.

relative risk   An important component of the ethical review in which the potential for possible harm to the participant is considered.

they are conducted. Fortunately, the majority of those who conduct animal research are compassionate and do their best to minimize stress or discomfort in the animals they study.

What Are the Data Collection Methods of Psychological Science?

There are four basic data collection methods in psychological science; the choice of which to use is generally dictated by the research question. First, we can observe behavior as it is taking place and either write down general descriptions of the behaviors or check off a tally sheet of prespecified behavior categories. Second, we can ask people for information about their thoughts, feelings, and preferences by using surveys, questionnaires, interviews, and self-reports. Third, we can measure how quickly and accurately people respond to a stimulus. Finally, we can directly measure electrical activity and blood flow in the brain, techniques that are increasingly being combined with the other three methods. Regardless of the method chosen, it is essential to always consider the ethical consequences associated with the method of data collection; the participant's well-being must always be guaranteed.

HOW ARE DATA ANALYZED AND EVALUATED?

How do we ensure that our measures are accurate?

Up to this point, we have examined the essential elements of scientific inquiry in psychology. In particular, we have examined how to frame an empirical question within the realm of theories, hypotheses, and research; what type of study to run; and the different methods of collecting data. This section focuses more closely on the issue of data, such as the characteristics that make for good data and the statistical procedures that are used to analyze them.

GOOD RESEARCH REQUIRES VALID, RELIABLE, AND ACCURATE DATA

validity The extent to which the data collected address the research hypothesis in the way they were intended.

reliability The extent to which a measure is stable and consistent over time in similar conditions.

accuracy The extent to which an experimental measure is free from error.

central tendency A measure that represents the typical behavior of the group as a whole.

mean A measure of central tendency that is the arithmetic average of a set of numbers.

If data are to properly answer a hypothesis, they must actually address it. **Validity** refers to whether or not the data you collect address your question; valid data provide clear and unambiguous information from which to evaluate the theory or hypothesis. Suppose a theory predicts that children who are physically abused by their parents are more likely than nonabused children to use drugs in high school. The obvious hypothesis generated by this theory is that if we compare the childhoods of high school drug users and non–drug users, we should find that a greater percentage of the drug users were abused by their parents. In this case, examining the medical records of all the students might be one way to document if abuse had occurred. Whether or not the hypothesis was supported, the data would be considered valid on the reasonable assumption that in children abuse often leads to suspicious medical problems. The key here is that the validity of data depends on the question being studied. Data that might be invalid for one question may be perfectly valid for a different question.

Another important aspect of data is **reliability,** or the stability and consistency of a measure over time. If the measurement is reliable, the data collected will not vary because of changes over time in the measurement device. Suppose that you have a theory that people in their twenties are more likely to channel surf than are people in their fifties. To test your theory you would need to study television-watching behavior and, in particular, the average length of time people stay tuned to each station. One option for measuring the duration of each channel stay would be to have an observer use a handheld stopwatch. However, there will likely be some variability in when the stopwatch is started and stopped, relative to when the surfer actually changes channels. As a consequence, the data in this scenario would be relatively unreliable in comparison to data collected by a computer that was linked to the television remote.

Actual correct time

Random error: notice that the final average is correct

A third and final characteristic of good data is **accuracy**, or the extent to which the measure is free from *error*. While this may seem obvious, the problem is that although a measure may be both valid and reliable, this does not guarantee that the measure is *accurate*. The way psychological scientists think about this problem is by turning it on its head and asking, How do errors creep into a measure? There are two basic types of error, *random* and *systematic*. Take the channel-surfing study. The problem with using a stopwatch to measure the duration of each channel stay is that each measurement will tend to either overestimate or underestimate the actual duration (because of human error). This is known as a *random error*, because although an error is introduced into each measurement, the actual value of the error is different each time. But suppose that the stopwatch has a glitch, such that it always overstates the actual time measured by two seconds. This is known as a *systematic error*, because the amount of error introduced into each measure is a constant. Generally, systematic error is more problematic than random error because the latter tends to average out over time and therefore is less likely to lead to inaccurate results (Figure 2.9).

Systematic error: notice that the final average is incorrect

2.9 Systematic errors occur when the measurement has the same degree of error on each occasion, whereas random errors occur when the degree of error varies each time.

DESCRIPTIVE STATISTICS PROVIDE A SUMMARY

The first step in evaluating data is simply to inspect the raw values. This allows researchers to familiarize themselves with the data and to detect possible errors in data recording. For instance, you would assess whether any of the responses seemed especially unlikely, such as finding someone with a blood alcohol content of 50 percent. Once you are satisfied that the data make sense, you summarize the basic patterns using *descriptive statistics*, which provide an overall sense of the results of the study, such as how people performed in one condition compared to another. The simplest descriptive statistic is the **central tendency**, which is a single value that describes a typical response, or the behavior of the group as a whole. Perhaps the most intuitive measure of central tendency is the **mean**, which is the arithmetic average of a set of numbers. The class average on an exam is an example of a mean score. Consider the hypothetical study of alcohol and driving performance. A basic way to summarize the data would be to calculate the mean

What kinds of statistics are used to analyze data?

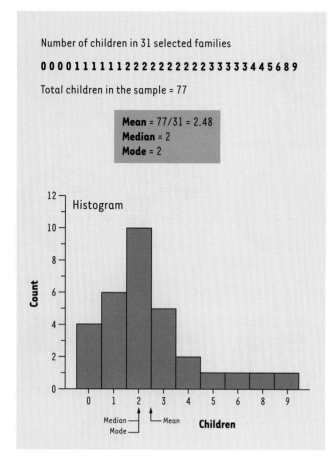

Number of children in 31 selected families

0 0 0 0 1 1 1 1 1 1 2 2 2 2 2 2 2 2 2 2 2 3 3 3 3 3 4 4 5 6 8 9

Total children in the sample = 77

Mean = 77/31 = 2.48
Median = 2
Mode = 2

Histogram

2.10 The mean, median, and mode are different measures of central tendency that reveal an important average for a set of numbers. The graphs here show that for some data sets, all three measures can be the same; however, for other data sets, the values may be quite different.

median A measure of central tendency that is the value in a set of numbers that falls exactly in the half-way point between the lowest and highest values.

mode A measure of central tendency that is the most frequent score or value in a set of numbers.

variability In a set of numbers, how widely dispersed the values are from each other and from the mean.

driving performance across all participants for when they were (1) sober and (2) intoxicated. If alcohol affects driving, then we would expect to see a difference in the mean between sober and intoxicated driving performance.

A second measure of central tendency is the **median,** which is the value in a set of numbers that falls exactly halfway between the lowest and highest values. For instance, if you received the median score on a test, then half the people in your class scored lower than you and half the people in the class scored higher. Sometimes researchers will summarize data using medians instead of means because if one or two numbers in the set are dramatically larger or smaller than all the others, the mean will give either an inflated or deflated summary of the actual "average." This occurs when one tries to examine average income. Perhaps only 50 percent of Americans make more than $30,000 per year, but some make so much more that the *mean* income is much higher. The median provides a better estimate of how much money the average person makes.

A third measure of central tendency encountered in psychological research is the **mode,** or the most frequent score or value in a set of numbers. For instance, the modal number of children in a family is two, which means that most families have two children. Examples of all three central tendency measures are shown in Figure 2.10.

In addition to measures of central tendency, another important characteristic of data is the **variability** in a set of numbers, or how widely dispersed the values are about the mean. For instance, the *range* tells you the distance between the largest and smallest value, which is often not of much use because it only uses two scores. The most common measure of variability is the **standard deviation,** which refers to how far away each value is, on average, from the mean. For instance, if the mean of an exam is 75 percent and the standard deviation is 5, this tells you that most people scored between 70 and 80 percent on the exam.

CORRELATIONS DESCRIBE THE RELATIONSHIPS BETWEEN VARIABLES

The descriptive statistics discussed thus far pertain to summarizing the central tendency and variability in a set of numbers. Descriptive statistics can also be used to summarize how two variables relate to each other. As shown in Figure 2.11, the first step in comparing two variables is to create a graph known as a *scatterplot,* which provides a convenient picture of the data. A scatterplot represents each participant's measure on two different variables, in this case the level of intoxication on an eight-point scale (with higher numbers meaning more intoxicated) and the ability to balance on one leg as measured in seconds. By looking at the scatterplot we can then determine that the people who were more intoxicated also were less able to maintain balance.

In analyzing the relationship between two dependent variables, researchers are not limited to creating a scatterplot. They can also compute a **correlation,** which is a descriptive statistic that provides a numerical value (between +1.0 and −1.0) indicating the strength of the relationship between two variables. If two variables have a strong relationship, knowing how a person measures on one variable becomes a good predictor of how they might measure on the other variable.

What signifies a strong relationship? Consider the different scatterplots in Figure 2.12. Two variables have a *negative correlation* when as one *increases* in value, the other *decreases* in value. For example, as people become more intoxicated, they are less able to balance on one foot. In terms of values, a correlation of −1.0 indicates a perfect negative correlation. Two variables can also have a *positive correlation*, in which the variables increase or decrease together—for example, taller people often weigh more than shorter people. In this case, the correlation is positive, and a perfect positive correlation is indicated by a value of +1.0. If two variables show no apparent relationship, then the value of the correlation will be a number close to zero.

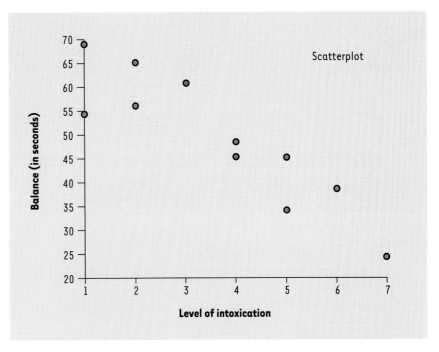

INFERENTIAL STATISTICS PREDICT CHANCE RESULTS

While descriptive statistics are used to summarize data sets, **inferential statistics** are used to decide whether differences actually exist between different sets of numbers. For instance, suppose you find that the mean driving performance for intoxicated drivers is lower than the mean driving performance for sober drivers. How different do these two means need to be in order for you to conclude that drinking alcohol does in fact reduce peoples' ability to drive?

To answer this kind of question, you can use inferential statistics to compute the probability that a difference between means was actually due to chance rather than a causal effect of one variable on another. How does this work? Pretend for a moment that intoxication doesn't influence driving performance. Even so, if you go out and measure the driving performance of sober and drunken drivers, just by chance there will be some degree of variability in the mean performance of the two groups. Most of the time the difference in means will be small, but sometimes the difference may happen to be large. The key is that if alcohol does not actually affect driving performance, then the *probability* of showing a large difference between the two means is relatively small. The principle is the same as for how many heads are obtained when flipping a coin ten times: on average, the number will usually be five or close to it, but every now and then we may get either no heads or ten heads, just by chance.

Therefore, when comparing two means, inferential statistics tell you how probable the outcome would be if in fact there were no actual difference between the variables measured. If the probability is small enough, then you can feel reasonably certain that your result was more likely due to an actual difference (or an effect of one variable on another), rather than simply due to chance. How small is small enough? Although the question has long been contentious, a 5 percent chance of concluding there is a difference, when there is really not, tends to be the most liberal value encountered in psychological research. Regardless, the critical thing when deciding to use inferential statistics is to determine beforehand what probability level will be accepted as "small enough." If the results of the study fall below this predetermined probability value, then the difference in means can be labeled as *statistically significant*. If not, the alternative is to report

2.11 Scatterplots illustrate the relationship between two variables. Note that it appears that the more intoxicated people are, the fewer seconds they can maintain their balance.

standard deviation A statistical measure of how far away each value is on average from the mean.

correlation A statistical procedure that provides a numerical value, between +1 and −1, indicating the strength and direction of the relation between two variables.

inferential statistics A set of procedures used to make judgments about whether differences actually exist between sets of numbers.

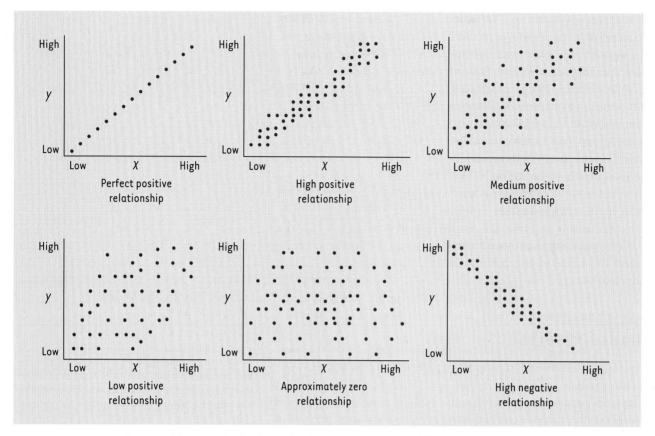

2.12 Correlations can have different values, which in turn reveal different kinds of relationships between two variables. The greater the scatter of values, the lower the correlation. A perfect correlation occurs when all of the values fall on a straight line.

What is the basis for evaluating research?

the effect as *nonsignificant*, meaning that it is likely that the observed difference is due to chance.

EVALUATION IS BASED ON UNDERSTANDING GOOD SCIENCE

Throughout this chapter we have been emphasizing the major issues involved in designing and conducting research in psychological science. However, the ideas that have been discussed have another important application as well: evaluating research. Understanding the quality of research is important whether you go on to conduct experiments yourself or not. Each day the media report some new major finding, such as the link discussed in "Using Psychological Science: Marijuana and Cardiac Health Risks." Should you believe a report and perhaps change how you lead your daily life as a result, or should you ignore new and potentially important data, because they came from a flawed study? To make educated decisions in this domain requires understanding how good psychological science is performed.

So what determines good science? There are a number of factors that need to be considered. Is there a theoretical basis for the work? Was the method and level of analysis appropriate for the question of interest? Does the study have adequate operational definitions of the variables involved? Are the researchers presenting their results as showing a causal relationship between two variables even though an experiment was not performed? If an experiment was performed, was it carefully designed and well controlled, or are there potential confounds that might have been overlooked? Do the results of the study apply to everyone or just the

Using Psychological Science

MARIJUANA AND CARDIAC HEALTH RISKS

Today we are faced with an ever-increasing bombardment of scientific information about ourselves and the world in which we live. Understanding how to evaluate such information has become an indispensable skill. What should we believe and what should we ignore? The question is critical because important decisions and choices we make for ourselves and for our society are often made in direct response to the conclusions drawn from science-based research. The practical benefit of understanding the methods of psychological science is that it provides an invaluable basis for being an informed consumer of scientific information.

For example, whether or not to legalize the medical use of marijuana has been increasingly debated in the United States. Moral stances aside, the opinions many people hold on this issue depend to a large degree on interpreting the available scientific information about marijuana—both its positive *and* negative aspects. In one high-visibility case on March 3, 2000, the *New York Times* published an article that began: "In what is believed to be the first documented link between smoking marijuana and heart attacks, a study has found that a middle-age person's risk of heart attack rises nearly fivefold in the first hour after smoking marijuana." The conclusion is clear: middle-aged people are at an increased risk for a heart attack if they smoke marijuana. But is the conclusion valid?

According to the details provided in the article, the researchers who conducted the study took brief case histories from 3,882 middle-aged patients who had survived a heart attack. Of these, 124 were found to have been regular users of marijuana. Out of these 124 patients, 37 had smoked within the 24 hours preceding their attack, and 9 had smoked within the actual hour. Based on this evidence, the researchers were quoted as suggesting that there is a significantly increased risk of heart attack within the first several hours after smoking marijuana. However, there are several important issues to consider regarding the validity of these data—and the conclusions that can be validly drawn.

First, the study only looked at people who had had heart attacks, which is a nonrandomized sampling technique. As a result, the findings of the study really don't pertain to *all* middle-aged people. Rather, the results only generalize to those middle-aged people who have had heart attacks *and* who smoke marijuana. In order to assess the risk of marijuana-induced heart attacks in all middle-aged people, we would need to compare the rate of heart attacks between the middle-aged population that smokes marijuana and the middle-aged population that doesn't. If the smoking population shows a greater rate of heart attacks, *then* we should advise middle-aged people to think twice before lighting up. But even then, this would be a correlational rather than a true experimental design, and therefore causality could not be assumed.

Second, we need to consider whether factors other than marijuana may have been influencing the rate of heart attacks for marijuana smokers. For example, did these subjects do anything else near the time of the heart attack that may have contributed to—or fully caused—the cardiac event? One possibility is that the heart attack victims might have gotten high prior to engaging in sex or exercise, two key factors that can contribute to the occurrence of attacks. These possible confounds are examples of third-variable problems that again prevent any conclusions about causality. However, the *Times* article does not make it clear if or how the researchers treated this concern. As a result, we are left without critical information to consider—and, in the eyes of the informed reader, the validity of the results remains in serious doubt.

population (e.g., the elderly, teenage males) that was actually studied? These fundamental questions underscore the necessity of being a critical, well-informed research evaluator. If you can't answer these questions when reading about a study, then you can't properly evaluate whether you should believe the results or how those results have been interpreted.

How Are Data Analyzed and Evaluated?

Data analysis begins with descriptive statistics, which summarize the data. Measures of central tendency indicate statistical averages across sets of numbers, while standard deviations and variances indicate how widely numbers in a set are distributed about an average. Correlations in turn are used to describe the relationship between two variables: positive, negative, or none. Inferential statistics are used to decide whether the results of a study were due to an effect of one variable on another or whether the results were more likely due to chance. Finally, the key to evaluating research claims is to understand the basic principles guiding psychological research; if you know how to conduct good research, then you have the conceptual tools necessary to critically judge research as well.

CONCLUSION

Quality research stems from both sound methodology *and* good questions. What defines a good question? Although it may be a subjective issue, there are certainly things to think about. Does the question address something fundamental or something relatively minor? If you obtain the results you predict, what impact will it have on the specific field of study? Will the results establish new understanding between different levels of analysis, or will they simply confirm a minor aspect of an old and arcane theory? We can't all be doing research that places us in the running for a Nobel prize, but at the same time, we shouldn't shy away from focusing our efforts on important rather than trivial issues.

FURTHER READINGS

Fossey, D. (1988). *Gorillas in the mist*. New York: Houghton Mifflin.

Huff, D. (1993). *How to lie with statistics*. New York: W. W. Norton.

Martin, P., & Bateson, P. (1993). *Measuring behaviour: An introductory guide*. New York: Cambridge.

Stanovich, K. E. (2001). *How to think straight about psychology* (6th ed.). Boston: Allyn & Bacon.

Zechmeister, J. S., Zechmeister, E. B., & Shaughnessy, J. J. (2001). *Essentials of research methods in psychology*. Boston, MA: McGraw-Hill.

INVESTIGATING OUR GENETIC HERITAGE

DNA evidence has revealed that Adrian Targett, a schoolteacher who lives in England, is the direct descendant of the Stone Age human "Cheddar Man," whose 9,000-year-old skeleton was discovered near Targett's home (Targett, at right, is shown here with a reconstruction based on the skeleton). Recent research has helped improve our understanding of the genetic and physiological foundations of many aspects of human character, including our psychological activity.

TIMELINE

1817
Parkinson's Disease
Physician James Parkinson identifies this major neurological disorder, which affects muscular control and results from depletion of the dopamine system.

1866
Mendel's Peas Gregor Mendel, a monk, conducts studies on heredity in pea plants. His results provide the basis of genetics, including the idea of dominant and recessive genes.

1870s
Golgi Stain Italian physician Camillo Golgi invents what becomes known as the "Golgi stain," a method of tissue preparation that allows the examination of single neurons.

1880s
Neuron Doctrine Spanish anatomist Santiago Ramon y Cajal uses the Golgi stain to chart the microscopic anatomy of different regions of the brain. He correctly argues that the nervous system is composed of distinct cells.

Genetic and Biological Foundations

3

OUTLINING THE PRINCIPLES

1897

The Synapse Sir Charles Sherrington proposes that neurons communicate with each other across the synapse through electrical means. A few years later, Thomas Renton Elliott suggests that synapses are chemical rather than electrical.

1921

Neurotransmission Is Chemical Otto Loewi shows that neurons communicate through the release of neurotransmitters, chemicals released from one neuron that signal other neurons. He is awarded a Nobel prize.

1936

First Neurotransmitter Identified Sir Henry Dale identifies acetylcholine as the neurotransmitter that operates in the control of muscles.

1950s

Sodium-Potassium Pump Alan Hodgkin and Andrew Huxley show that there are active components within the neuron that stabilize the concentration of sodium and potassium, the main chemicals involved in action potentials.

1950s

Pharmacology Researchers show that chemicals that bind to neurotransmitter receptors can be used in therapies for various forms of mental illness, setting the stage for modern-day drug therapy.

The first sign that Lenore Wexler had a problem was when a policeman observed her stumbling across the street and asked her why she was drinking so early in the day. However, she wasn't drunk; she was showing the first symptoms of Huntington's chorea, a genetic neurological disorder that results in mental deterioration and abnormal body movements. The disease is named after George Huntington (1850–1916), who wrote the first complete description of it in 1872 when he was 22 years old. He first observed the disorder at age 8 while driving with his father in his native New York. Two women were twisting and grimacing as they walked along the road, and the sight so affected him that he decided to become a physician to study the disorder.

The first symptoms of Huntington's chorea, also known as Huntington's disease, strike when people are middle-aged, typically around 40, but sometimes much earlier. The first signs are restless and involuntary movements of whole limbs or major portions of limbs. The afflicted person begins to walk in a jerky fashion, often stumbling, and eventually loses control of all movement including the ability to walk, write, or speak. The individual also experiences emotional and personality changes, such as extreme anxiety and depression. Suicide is not uncommon among those in the early stages of the disease. Autopsies of those with Huntington's show damage to many regions of the brain, possibly caused by too much of the chemical dopamine in the brain. No cure for Huntington's has been found. All those who have the disease die within ten years or so after its onset.

George Huntington noticed that the disorder tends to run in families, and recent research has confirmed that it is indeed a genetic disorder. If a parent has it, a child has a 50–50 chance of also developing the disorder. Because symptoms of the disease are not evident until the victim is around 40, many of those with Huntington's have children before they realize they have a genetic disorder. Those who have relatives with Huntington's spend a good part of their lives wondering whether they will develop symptoms and whether it is safe for them to have children.

RESEARCH QUESTIONS ?? for Studying Genetic and Biological Foundations

How do genes affect behavior?

What determines genetic variation?

How do nerve cells operate?

How do nerve cells communicate with each other to influence mind and behavior?

How are specific chemicals linked to particular mental processes and behaviors?

How does the brain communicate with the body?

1974
Endogenous Opiates Scottish researchers Hans Kosterlitz and John Hughes discover that endorphins are important for reward and for the natural control of pain.

1977
Releasing Hormones Roger Guillemin, Andrew Shally, and Rosalyn Yalow share a Nobel prize for their work showing the existence of releasing factors that regulate hormonal function.

1980s
Behavioral Genetics of Personality Researchers at the University of Minnesota study identical twins who have been raised apart, demonstrating that genetics plays an important role in human personality.

1990s
Human Genome Project An international collaboration of genetics researchers map the basic gene sequence of human DNA, setting the stage for the more complex task of figuring out how genes interact to produce illness and influence behavior.

Following the death of her mother, Lenore, from Huntington's in 1978, Nancy Wexler (Figure 3.1), formerly a clinical psychologist, dedicated herself to finding a genetic marker for the disorder. Thanks to Wexler and her colleagues, relatives of those with Huntington's can now take a genetic test to determine whether they are going to develop the disease. Of course, the decision to have the test is a difficult one, since there is still no cure for Huntington's. Moreover, there are ethical issues related to genetic testing, such as whether the information should be available to employers and insurance companies. There are personal issues, too. If you tested positive when you were 20, how might the knowledge affect your future occupational and relationship goals?

3.1 Nancy Wexler is seen here working with a patient. After her mother's death from Huntington's disease, Wexler helped develop a genetic test to determine if people are at risk for developing the disease.

Interestingly, although she played an integral role in developing the genetic test, Nancy Wexler decided not to take it. Now in her mid-fifties, Wexler shows no signs of the disease, and her chances of developing it are dropping each year.

In this chapter, we will examine the basis for understanding the genetic transmission of diseases such as Huntington's, as well as how neurological diseases affect the brain and the body. To understand such disorders we must learn how communication occurs in the nervous system. Beginning with the basic ideas of genetic influence, this chapter is concerned with understanding how basic physiological processes affect behavior, thought, and emotion.

Over the past three decades, scientific understanding of the genetic and physiological foundations of psychological activity has increased dramatically. As technology has advanced, sophisticated tools have been developed to explore the biological bases of mind and behavior. Researchers can now examine DNA to predict who will develop specific disorders and to understand how certain diseases are passed from one generation to the next. Research at the genetic, neurochemical, and brain-systems levels of analysis has led to great strides in understanding the biological processes that occur within the brain and body to produce experience, thought, emotion, memory, and behavior. By building across the levels of analysis, our plan is to demonstrate how psychological scientists conduct research to understand different questions related to mind, brain, and behavior. This chapter examines psychological activity at the genetic and neurochemical levels; in Chapter 4 we will describe the functions of various brain regions at the brain-systems level of analysis.

WHAT IS THE GENETIC BASIS OF PSYCHOLOGICAL SCIENCE?

One of the major outgrowths of the biological revolution occurred in February 2001, when two groups of scientists published separate articles detailing the results of the first phase of the *Human Genome Project*, an international research effort to map out the entire structure of human genetic material. This achievement represents the coordinated efforts of hundreds of scientists around the globe. To understand their goals it is important to have a basic understanding of genetic processes.

Within each cell is the *genome* for making the entire organism; it is the master blueprint that gives specific instructions for everything from hair color to how to make a gallbladder. The study of how characteristics are passed along through inheritance is called *genetics.* Through sexual reproduction, people receive half of their genetic makeup from each parent in the form of *genes*, the basic units of heredity, which subsequently determine things such as hair color, height, and weight.

Within each cell are **chromosomes**, which are structures made up of genes. The typical human has 23 pairs of chromosomes, half of each pair coming from each parent (Figure 3.2). Genes in turn are made up of a substance called *DNA (deoxyribonucleic acid)*, which consists of two intertwined strands of molecules of sugar, phosphate, and nitrogen. The precise sequence of these molecules along the DNA strand specifies an exact instruction, through the production of *RNA (ribonucleic acid)*, to manufacture distinct proteins. Proteins, of which there are thousands of different types, are the basic chemicals that make up the structure of cells and direct their activities. A **gene**, then, is a segment of DNA that provides a blueprint for the creation of proteins that carry out specific tasks, and that eventually make up a unique organism through these actions. Each cell in the human body contains the same DNA, but cells are specialized for different tasks. Whether the cell becomes a nerve cell, pancreas cell, or hair cell depends on the instructions provided by DNA.

The first step of the Human Genome Project was to map out the entire structure of DNA—in other words, to identify the precise order of molecules that makes up each of the thousands of genes on each of the 23 pairs of human chromosomes. One of the most striking findings from the Human Genome Project is that there are only around 30,000 genes, not many more

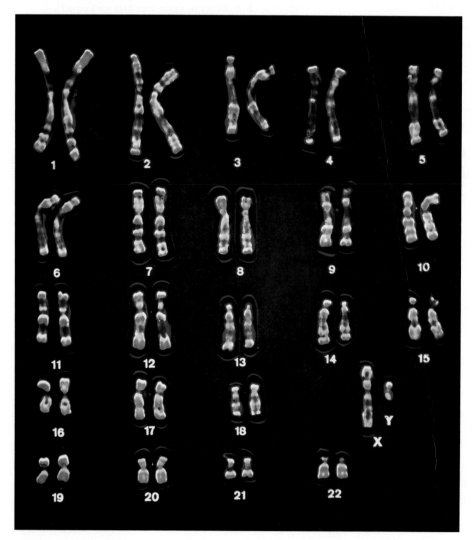

3.2 Each person has 23 pairs of chromosomes. Each parent contributes one chromosome to each pair. Males and females differ on the 23rd chromosome pair, with males having an X and Y chromosome (shown) and females having two X chromosomes (not shown).

than are found in a fly (13,000), a worm (18,000), or even a plant (26,000). This suggests that the complexity of humans is not due simply to our possessing a large number of genes, but more likely due to subtleties in the way that genes are expressed and regulated (Baltimore, 2001). Now that the initial map of the human genome is almost complete, scientists are directing their efforts to understanding how genes influence mind and behavior. The eventual goal of the project is to understand how genes interact with each other to produce illness. By understanding how genes work, researchers can develop methods to alter gene function to cure various ailments. At the same time, genetic research is providing a compelling new understanding of the biological basis of psychological activity.

HEREDITY INVOLVES PASSING ALONG GENES THROUGH REPRODUCTION

The first clues to the mechanisms responsible for heredity were discovered by the monk Gregor Mendel (1823–1884) around 1866. Mendel developed an experimental technique called *selective breeding* for studying genetics. At the monastery where Mendel lived, the study of plants had a long history. By using selective breeding, Mendel was able to have strict control over which plants were bred with which other plants.

Consider a simple study by Mendel. He chose peas that had either only purple flowers or only white flowers. Mendel then cross-pollinated the two types of plants to see which color flowers would be produced. Mendel found that the first generation of pea offspring tended to be completely white or completely purple. If he had stopped there, he would never have discovered the basis of heredity; fortunately, he then allowed the plants to self-pollinate into a second generation. This second generation revealed an interesting pattern. Of the hundreds of pea plants, around 75 percent had purple flowers and 25 percent had white flowers. This three-to-one ratio repeated itself in additional studies, and it also turned out to be true for other characteristics, such as pod shape. From this pattern, Mendel deduced that there must be discrete units, now referred to as genes, that exist in two versions (e.g., white and purple). These two versions of a gene are known as *alleles*. According to Mendel, if the alleles differ (such as in cross-breeding), one of them is dominant and the other is recessive. **Dominant genes** are expressed (become apparent) whenever they are present, whereas **recessive genes** are expressed only when they are matched with a similar gene from the other parent. Thus, because white flowers were recessive, they occurred only when the gene for purple flowers was not present, which happened in only one of the four combinations of white and purple genes (see Figure 3.3).

chromosomes Structures within the cell body made up of genes.

genes The units of heredity that determine a particular characteristic in an organism.

dominant gene A gene that is expressed in the offspring whenever it is present.

recessive gene A gene that is expressed only when it is matched with a similar gene from the other parent.

3.3 In cross-breeding, when purple is the dominant gene (indicated **P**) and white is the recessive gene (indicated p), there are four possible genotypes, but three of the four phenotypes will be purple.

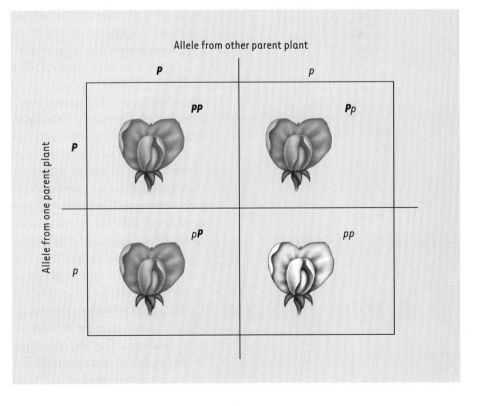

Allele from other parent plant

Allele from one parent plant

genotype The genetic constitution determined at the moment of conception.

phenotype Observable physical characteristics that result from both genetic and environmental influences.

meiosis After fertilization, a process of cell division in which the chromosome pairs are split within each cell and then joined in a random fashion.

mitosis After a zygote is created, a process in which a cell duplicates its chromosome structure and then divides into two new cells that have an identical chromosome structure.

Genotypes and phenotypes The existence of dominant and recessive genes means that not all genes are outwardly expressed. **Genotype** is the genetic constitution of an organism, the actual genetic makeup that is determined at the moment of conception. **Phenotype** is the observable physical characteristics of an organism that result from both genetic and environmental influences. So, for instance, in Mendel's experiments two purple flowers would have the same phenotype, but they might differ in genotype, in that one could have two dominant genes for purple and another could have one dominant purple gene and one recessive white gene. The environment can also affect the phenotype; for instance, good nutrition leads to increased physical size and a suntan changes the color of the skin. An excellent example of environmental influence on the phenotype is *phenylketonuria (PKU)*, a disorder in which infants are unable to break down an enzyme (phenylalanine) contained in dairy and other products, such as the sweetener aspartame. This rare genetic disorder can lead to severe brain damage. Fortunately, providing a bland diet that is low in phenylalanine until the child passes critical stages of neuronal development greatly helps to reduce brain damage. The phenotype, then, is modified by diet.

Polygenic effects Mendel's flower-color experiments dealt with single-gene characteristics. These are traits that appear to be determined by only one gene. But when there is a range of variability within a population for certain characteristics, such as height, this indicates that the characteristic is *polygenic*, that is, influenced by many genes, as well as the environment. Most human traits and diseases are polygenic.

GENOTYPIC VARIATION IS CREATED BY SEXUAL REPRODUCTION

Although they have the same parents, siblings differ from each other in many ways, such as eye color, height, and personality. This occurs because each has a specific combination of genes that differs in part due to random cell division that occurs prior to reproduction. Through a process known as **meiosis**, cells from each parent divide to produce *gametes*, egg and sperm cells, that contain only one half of each pair of chromosomes. The sperm and egg cells then combine during fertilization. One half of each parent's chromosomes join in a random fashion. The fertilized cell, known as a *zygote*, now consists of 23 pairs of chromosomes, one half of each pair from the mother and the other half from the father. The two chromosomes in the 23rd pair are the *sex chromosomes*, denoted *X* and *Y* due to their shape. Females have two X chromosomes, whereas males have one X and one Y chromosome. Calculating all possible combinations of the 23 chromosomes indicates that this can result in some 8 million different outcomes. Further, since both mother and father are themselves one of 8 million possible outcomes, the zygote is one of 64 trillion (8 million × 8 million) possible combinations. The net outcome is that a unique genotype is created at the moment of conception, and this accounts for the genetic variation in the human species.

The zygote grows by a process known as **mitosis**, which is when the chromosome duplicates and then the cell divides into two new cells with an identical chromosome structure. The reproduction of cells through mitosis is the building block of the life cycle and is responsible for growth and development. Sometimes there are errors in this process, which create *mutations*, most of which are benign and have little influence. Occasionally, a genetic mutation may produce a selective advantage or disadvantage in terms of survival or reproduction. The evolutionary significance of these changes in adaptiveness is complex, but mutations that lead to abilities or behaviors that are advantageous to an organism may spread through the gene pool because those who carry the gene are more likely to survive and reproduce. For instance, consider *industrial melanism*, in which areas of the world with heavy soot or smog tend to have moths and butterflies that are darker in color. Prior to industrialization, darker insects were more likely to be spotted against pale backgrounds. Any mutation that led to darker coloring was quickly eliminated through natural selection. But, with industrialization, pollution led to a darkening of trees and buildings, and therefore darker-colored insects became more adaptive.

You may wonder how genetic mutations lead to disease and why they remain in the gene pool. For instance, *sickle-cell disease* is a genetic disorder that mostly affects African Americans and alters how oxygen is processed in the bloodstream; it can lead to pain, physical damage, and anemia. The gene for the disease is recessive, so that most carriers have healthy phenotypes in spite of genotypes that contain the disease. Thus, only those who inherit recessive genes from *both* parents will develop the disease. Recessive genes do not interfere with health in most people, which allows them to survive in the gene pool. In addition, the gene for sickle-cell disease also increases resistance to malaria, and therefore in environments in which malaria is prevalent, such as certain regions in Africa, the sickle-cell gene has some benefit. In contrast to recessive genes, most dominant gene disorders are lethal for most of their carriers and therefore do not last in the gene pool. One notable exception is Huntington's disease, which escapes elimination from the gene pool because it often does not become manifest until after the person has reproduced.

GENES AFFECT BEHAVIOR

What determines the kind of person you are? What factors make you more or less bold, intelligent, or able to read a map? All of these are influenced by the interaction of your genes and the environment in which you were raised. The study of how genes and environment interact to influence psychological activity is known as *behavioral genetics*. Behavioral genetics has also made important contributions to the biological revolution, providing information about the extent to which biology influences mind, brain, and behavior.

Any research that suggests that abilities to perform certain behaviors are based in biology is controversial. Who wants to be told that there are limitations to what you can achieve based on something that is beyond your control, such as your genes? It is easy to accept that genes control physical characteristics such as sex, race, eye color, and predisposition to diseases like cancer, alcoholism, or migraines. But can genes also determine whether or not people will get divorced, how smart they are, or what career they're likely to choose? A concern of psychological scientists is the extent to which all of these characteristics are influenced by nature and nurture, by genetic makeup and the environment. Increasingly, science is indicating that genes lay the groundwork for many human traits. From this perspective, people are born essentially like undeveloped photographs: the image is already captured, but the way it eventually appears can vary based on the development process. However, the basic picture is there from the beginning.

Behavioral genetics methods The fact that siblings are different, even when they are raised in the same household, could be due to the fact that they do not

RESEARCH QUESTION

How do genes affect behavior?

3.4 Shown in the top row are two couples, but their pictures have been randomly arranged. Below are four children. Try to match which child comes from which parents. The answer is revealed at the bottom of the page.*

monozygotic twins Twin siblings who result from one zygote splitting in two, and therefore contain the same genes (i.e., identical twins).

dizygotic twins Twin siblings who result from two separately fertilized eggs (i.e., fraternal twins).

heritability A statistical estimate of the fraction of observed measure of the overall amount of difference among people in a population that is caused by differences in heredity.

*The boy and the girl on either end of the bottom row are children of the parents at the top right. The two girls in the middle of the bottom row are children of the parents at top left.

share identical genes, in that each is one among eight million possible outcomes (Figure 3.4). But there are also subtle differences in the environment, both within and outside the household. Siblings have different birth-order placement, different friends and teachers, and perhaps are treated differently by parents. It is difficult to know what causes the similarities and differences between siblings because some of the genes are the same and often most of the environment is the same. Therefore, behavioral geneticists use two basic methods to assess the degree to which traits are inherited: twin studies and adoption studies.

Twin studies compare similarities between different types of twins to determine the genetic basis of specific traits. **Monozygotic twins**, also called identical twins, are the result of one zygote dividing into two, each having the same chromosomes and the genes they contain. **Dizygotic twins**, sometimes called fraternal twins, are the result of two separately fertilized eggs and are no more related than any other pair of siblings. The processes of meiosis and fertilization occur separately to produce the two zygotes, which then develop independently. To the extent that monozygotic twins are more similar on a given dimension than dizygotic twins, the increased similarity is considered most likely due to genetic influence. Of course, even identical twins do not have the exact same environment (and in rare circumstances might even have different genes due to random mutations), and therefore they have different phenotypes, but they are typically more similar than dizygotic twins, who differ both in genotype and phenotype.

Adoption studies compare the similarities between biological relatives and adoptive relatives. Adopted siblings have similar home environments but different genes. Therefore, the assumption is that similarities between adopted siblings have more to do with environment than genes. Interestingly, it turns out that growing up in the same household has relatively little influence on many traits, such as personality. Indeed, after controlling for their genetic similarity, even biological siblings raised in the same household are no more similar than two strangers plucked at random off the street. This point will be examined in greater detail in the social development and personality chapters, but for now it is sufficient to understand the basic logic of the different types of studies.

Finally, one interesting behavioral genetic study is to compare monozygotic twins who have been *raised together* or *raised apart*. This would seem the ideal way to test the relative contributions of genes and the environment. Examples of twin studies are discussed in "Studying the Mind: Meeting a Long-Lost Twin." Similarities between twins raised apart, who often have never met, can be uncanny. Indeed, some evidence suggests that twins raised apart are more similar than are twins raised together. This would likely occur if parents encouraged individuality in their twins, when they raised them together, by emphasizing different strengths and interests. That is, parents might actively create different environments for the two twins.

Studying the Mind

MEETING A LONG-LOST TWIN

Finding a long-lost twin is a popular plot of books and movies. Although these stories may seem incredible, they are less astounding than some of the actual cases of identical twins separated at birth and reunited later in life. Imagine meeting a stranger who not only looks like you, but whose life path has been eerily similar to yours for the past several decades.

This is what happened to the "Jim twins," boys who were separated just weeks after their birth, adopted by different families, and raised apart. Neither the boys nor their adoptive families knew of the other's existence. When they met at age 39, they discovered that their lives were filled with unbelievable similarities. Not only were the twins both named Jim, but each had married and divorced a woman named Linda, after which each married a woman named Betty. They named their sons James Alan and James Allen, and they both had dogs named Toy. Both were part-time law-enforcement officers who drove Chevrolets and vacationed in Florida. They were the same height and weight, and both chain-smoked the same brand of cigarettes and drank the same brand of beer. Perhaps most strangely, both had built circular white benches around trees in their backyards. Although no one suggests that there are genes for naming dogs Toy or for marrying and divorcing women named Linda, the obvious similarities point to the importance of genetic influences in shaping personality and behavior.

The Jim twins were part of a large study conducted by Thomas Bouchard and his colleagues at the University of Minnesota (Bouchard Jr. et al., 1990). Bouchard and his colleagues have identified more than 100 pairs of identical and nonidentical twins who were either raised together or raised apart (Figure 3.5). They examined a variety of traits and characteristics, including intelligence, personality, sense of well-being, achievement, alienation, and aggression. The general finding was that identical twins were likely to be similar, whether they were raised together or not. Some critics have argued that most of the adopted twins were raised in relatively similar environments, in part because adoption agencies try to match the child to the adoptive

home. However, this argument doesn't explain identical twins Oskar Stohr and Jack Yufe. Oskar was raised a Catholic in Germany and even joined the Nazi Party. Jack was raised as a Jew and lived for a while in Israel. What could be more different? Yet, when they met, they showed up at the interview wearing similar clothes, exhibited similar mannerisms, and had the same odd habits such as flushing the toilet before they used it, dipping their toast in coffee, storing rubber bands on their wrists, and surprising people by sneezing in the elevator. Critics have suggested that nothing more than coincidence is at work in these case studies. Continued research using the methods of behavioral genetics is needed to provide additional insight about the relative influence of heredity and environment on individual behavior.

3.5 Participants of Dr. Bouchard's study, Gerald Levey and Mark Newman are identical twins who were separated at birth. Reunited at age 31, they discovered that they were both firefighters and had similarities in personal traits.

Understanding heritability   *Heredity* is the transmission of characteristics from parents to offspring by means of genes. A term that is often confused with heredity, but that means something else altogether, is **heritability**, which is a statistical estimate of the portion of observed variation in a population that is caused by differences in heredity. *Variation* is the measure of the overall amount of difference among people. Behavioral geneticists calculate the *heritability coefficient* (known as h^2) for specific traits using the following formula: $h^2 = \frac{\text{genetic variance}}{\text{total variance}}$. Genetic variance is estimated based on studies of twins and other methods. The total variance is the extent to which people differ from each other in the real world, which can be ascribed to genetics, the environment, or even measurement error. The calculation is based on an estimate, so it is an approximation used to estimate the degree to which genes and environment contribute to specific traits.

RESEARCH QUESTION

What determines genetic variation?

It is important to understand that heritability refers to differences in a certain trait among individuals, not to the trait itself. If a trait such as height has a heritability of .60, it means that 60 percent of height variation among individuals is genetic, not that you get 60 percent of your height from genetics and 40 percent from your environment. Heritability refers to populations, not to individuals. The heritability for a trait depends on the gene distribution within a population. For instance, almost everyone has two legs, and more people lose legs through accidents than are born without them. Therefore, if you calculate the heritability for having two legs, the total variability is almost zero, and only slightly greater than the genetic variability. Thus, the heritability value for having two legs is nearly zero, in spite of the obvious fact that the human genome contains instructions to grow two legs.

It is also important to point out that the population used to estimate total variation can affect the estimate obtained for heritability. Typically, the more diverse the population, the lower the estimate of heritability. This occurs because of the increased variability that comes from diversity and because the estimates of the genetic variation do not consider such diversity. The important point is that heritability is an estimate that is not precise and that can be affected by a number of factors. Still, it helps behavioral geneticists in understanding the interaction between the environment and genes, so that they can understand the circumstances in which genes operate.

SOCIAL AND ENVIRONMENTAL CONTEXT INFLUENCES GENETIC EXPRESSION

Working across the levels of analysis, John Cacioppo and his colleagues (2000) have argued that social context can influence genetic processes. For instance, African Americans typically have higher rates of hypertension. According to some researchers, the dismal conditions of the slave trade may have led to a change in the genetic constitution of African Americans (Wilson & Grim, 1991). As many as one in four slaves died during transportation, and approximately the same number died within the first few years of arrival in America. Wilson and Grim argue that the horrific conditions imposed a strong selection factor in determining the type of individual who was able to survive. Those slaves who were able to maintain high blood pressure on low levels of salt might have been more likely to survive. In contemporary times, however, with salt readily available, a greater sensitivity to salt may cause African Americans to become salt hypertensive. The theory is provocative and difficult to test, but it highlights one possible way in which social context can affect genetic constitution.

There is also evidence that genes and the social context interact to affect the phenotype. Sandra Scarr (Scarr & McCarthy, 1983) proposed a theory of development that stresses the interactive nature of genes and environment. According to Scarr, early environments influence young children, but children's genes also influence the experiences they receive. For instance, children exposed to the same environment interpret and react to it in different ways. Some children who are teased withdraw; others shrug it off without concern. Similarly, different sorts of children evoke different responses from others. A well-mannered, cuddly child cues more nurturing from parents and others than a baby who is irritable and fussy. Finally, as children become older they can choose their social situations. Some children prefer to spend time outdoors engaged in vigorous physical pursuits; others prefer the tranquility of a good book in a comfortable setting. Thus, genes predispose certain behaviors that elicit different responses, and these subsequent interactions then shape the phenotype. Because genes and social contexts interact, it can be very difficult to separate their independent effects.

What Is the Genetic Basis of Psychological Science?

Much of human behavior is influenced by genetic processes. People inherit both physical characteristics and personality traits from their parents. Only recently have scientists developed the tools to measure genetic processes and the roles that various genes play in psychological activity. The Human Genome Project has succeeded in mapping the basic sequence of DNA, but a great deal more needs to be accomplished before that information can be translated into medical treatments or a greater understanding of individual differences among people. Behavioral geneticists use twin and adoption studies to ascertain the relative contribution of genes and the environment to shaping human behavior.

HOW DOES THE NERVOUS SYSTEM OPERATE?

Many of the genes in the human genome direct the development and ongoing functions of the *nervous system*, a communication network that serves as the foundation for all psychological activity. Comprised of billions of special cells known as nerve cells, the nervous system takes in a variety of information from the external world, evaluates that information, and subsequently produces behaviors or makes bodily adjustments to adapt to the environment. The essence of life—from smelling a rose, to thinking, to moving your big toe—comes down to communication between the billions of nerve cells throughout the body. So how do nerve cells operate? How do they communicate with each other? How do communicating networks function to produce behaviors, thoughts, and feelings? Before we get to the workings of the nervous system as a whole, we begin by describing how cells within this system communicate with each other to produce psychological activity.

NEURONS ARE SPECIALIZED FOR COMMUNICATION

Neurons, the basic units of the nervous system, are cells that specialize in communication. Neurons differ from most other cells because they are excitable: they operate through electrical impulses and communicate with other neurons through chemical signals. They have three functions: to take in information from neighboring neurons (reception), integrate those signals (conduction), and pass signals to other neurons (transmission).

Neurons come in a wide assortment of shapes and sizes, but they typically share four structural regions that represent the neuron's communication functions (Figure 3.6). The first region is the **dendrites**—short outgrowths (sometimes called processes) that increase the neuron's receptive field. These branchlike appendages detect chemical signals from neighboring neurons.

The second region of the neuron is the **cell body**, also known as the *soma*, where information from thousands of other neurons is collected and integrated.

neurons Basic units of the nervous system that operate through electrical impulses, which communicate with other neurons through chemical signals. They receive, integrate, and transmit information in the nervous system.

dendrites Branchlike extensions of the neuron that detect information from other neurons.

cell body The region of the neuron where information from thousands of other neurons is collected and processed.

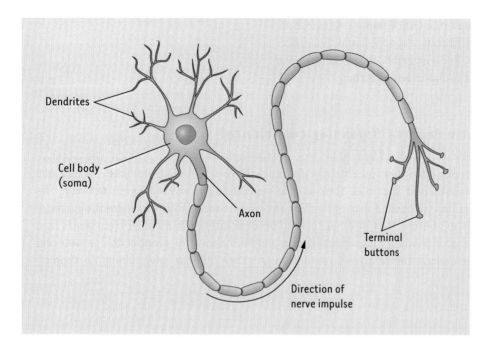

3.6 A neuron. Messages are received by the dendrites, processed in the cell body, transmitted along the axon, and sent to other neurons via substances released from the terminal buttons.

axon A long narrow outgrowth of a neuron by which information is transmitted to other neurons.

terminal buttons Small nodules at the ends of axons, that release chemical signals from the neuron to an area called the synapse.

synapse The site for chemical communication between neurons.

sensory neurons One of the three types of neurons, these afferent neurons detect information from the physical world and pass that information along to the brain.

motor neurons One of the three types of neurons, these efferent neurons direct muscles to contract or relax, thereby producing movement.

interneurons One of the three types of neurons, these neurons communicate only with other neurons, typically within a specific brain region.

The cell body is also the site of metabolism and genetic action. As with all cells in the body, neurons contain DNA, the blueprint for action for the neuron. Once the incoming information has been integrated in the cell body, electrical impulses are transmitted along a long narrow outgrowth known as the **axon**. Axons, the third region of the neuron, vary tremendously in length, from a few millimeters to more than a meter. The longest axons stretch from the spinal cord to the big toe. You have probably heard the term "nerve," as in a pinched nerve. Used in this context, a nerve refers to a bundle of axons that carry information between the brain and the body.

Terminal buttons, small nodules at the ends of axons, represent the fourth region of the neuron. Terminal buttons receive the electrical impulses and release chemical signals from the neuron to an area called the synapse. The **synapse** is the site for chemical communication between neurons. Chemicals leave one neuron, cross the synapse, and then pass signals along to the dendrites of other neurons.

The boundary of a neuron is defined by its membrane, a double layer of fatty molecules called *lipids*. Inside this membrane is an aqueous solution of chemicals and structures known as *intracellular fluid* or *cytoplasm*. As you will see, the membrane plays an important role in communication between neurons by regulating the concentration of electrically charged molecules that are the basis of the neuron's electrical activity.

Types of neurons The three basic types of neurons are *sensory neurons, motor neurons*, and *interneurons*. **Sensory neurons** detect information from the physical world and pass that information along to the brain, usually via the spinal cord. You know from hitting your funny bone that sensory neurons can transmit fast-acting signals that trigger a nearly instantaneous bodily response and sensory experience. Sensory neurons are often called *afferent* neurons, because they send their signals from the body to the brain. Signals that travel from the brain to the body are known as *efferent* (Figure 3.7).

Motor neurons direct muscles to contract or relax, thereby producing movement. Motor neurons are efferent neurons, in that signals *from* the brain are transmitted *to* the body. Large motor neurons originate in the spinal cord; their axons extend through an area of the spinal cord known as the *ventral root*, and then to muscle fibers and internal organs. It is these axons that are involved in the motor disturbances characteristic of Huntington's disease. **Interneurons** communicate within local or short-distance circuits. That is, interneurons integrate neural activity within a single area rather than transmitting information to other brain structures or to the body organs. For this reason, interneurons often have short axons, if any.

Together, sensory and motor neurons control movement. For instance, when you use your pen your brain sends a message via motor neurons to the muscles in your fingers to move in specific ways. Receptors in your skin and muscles send back messages through sensory neurons that help to determine how much pressure is needed to hold the pen. The nerves that provide information from muscles are referred to as *somatosensory*, which is the general term for sensations experienced from within the body.

Even the tiniest actions require the integration and coordination of multiple brain and body systems. Writing requires brain mechanisms that initiate the desire to use the pen, motor messages that direct the arm, hand, and fingers to reach for and hold the pen, and somatosensory messages that provide feedback necessary for successful use of the pen. If any of the components fail to work, you will have great difficulty even writing your name.

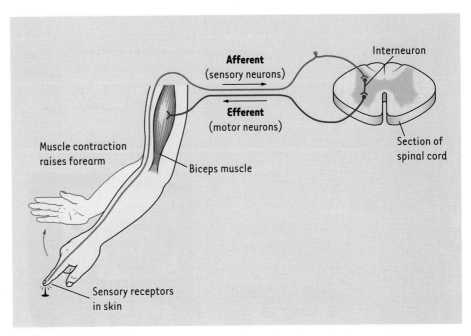

Complex networks of thousands of neurons sending and receiving signals are the functional basis of all psychological activity. Although the actions of single neurons are simple to describe, human complexity is a result of billions of neurons, each making contact with tens of thousands of other neurons. Neurons don't communicate randomly or arbitrarily; they selectively communicate with other neurons to form circuits or *neural networks*. These networks develop through maturation and experience, forming permanent alliances among groups of neurons.

3.7 Receptors in the eye send afferent signals to the brain for processing. An efferent signal is then sent from the brain to the body via the spinal cord to produce a response.

ACTION POTENTIALS CAUSE NEURONAL COMMUNICATION

Neuronal communication depends on the ability of the neuron to respond to incoming stimulation by becoming electrically excited and subsequently passing along signals to other neurons. An **action potential**, also called *neuronal firing*, is the electrical signal that passes along the axon and causes release of chemicals from the terminal buttons. These chemicals then transmit signals to other neurons. To understand how action potentials work, you need to know about certain properties of the neuron's cell membrane.

The resting membrane potential is negatively charged When not active, the inside and outside of a neuron differ electrically because of the balance of *ions* in the intracellular fluid. This electrical difference is referred to as the **resting membrane potential**. As with all salty solutions, the salts in intracellular fluid consist of particles called *ions* that have negative or positive charges. The ratio of negative to positive ions is greater inside the neuron than outside the neuron. Thus, the electrical charge inside the neuron is slightly more negative than that outside the neuron.

A neuron's resting membrane potential is measured by *microelectrodes*, extremely tiny devices that register electric currents, and is displayed on an oscilloscope, a monitor that shows voltage changes over time (Figure 3.8). Placing one microelectrode in the fluid inside the neuron and one microelectrode in the fluid

How do nerve cells operate?

action potential The neural impulse that passes along the axon and subsequently causes the release of chemicals from the terminal buttons.

resting membrane potential The electrical charge of a neuron when it is not active.

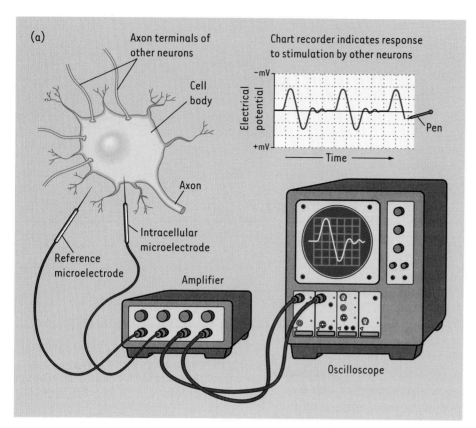

(a)

Axon terminals of other neurons

Cell body

Chart recorder indicates response to stimulation by other neurons

Pen

Time

Axon

Intracellular microelectrode

Reference microelectrode

Amplifier

Oscilloscope

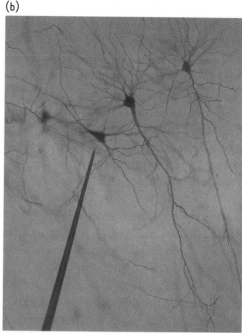

(b)

3.8 (a) The neuron's resting membrane potential can be recorded by placing one microelectrode in the fluid inside the neuron and one microelectrode in the fluid surrounding the neuron and measuring the difference in voltage, approximately -70 millivolts (mV). (b) A microelectrode being placed into a neuron.

sodium-potassium pump A mechanism of the neuron that keeps the resting membrane potential at a constant -70 mV, which sets the stage for electrical action.

surrounding the neuron registers a steady voltage of approximately -70 millivolts (mV). The negative sign indicates that the inside is negative in comparison to the outside, which is arbitrarily defined as zero voltage. This differential electrical charge inside and outside of the neuron is a condition known as *polarization*. It is the polarization across the cell membrane that creates the electrical energy necessary to power the action potential.

The roles of sodium and potassium ions   Two types of ions that contribute to a neuron's resting membrane potential are *sodium ions* (Na^+) and *potassium ions* (K^+). Ions pass through the cell membrane at specialized pores referred to as *ion channels*, each of which is structured to match a specific type of ion. The flow of ions through their channels is controlled by a gating mechanism. When the gate is open, ions flow freely past, but when closed the gate prevents passage of ions through the cell membrane (Figure 3.9). The flow of ions also is affected by the fact that the cell membrane is *selectively permeable*—it allows some types of ions to cross more easily than others. For instance, the cell membrane resists the passage of Na^+ but allows K^+ to pass easily. One explanation for the neuron's resistance to Na^+ is based on the notion that all life-forms evolved from single-celled organisms that probably began in ocean waters. Cell membranes therefore adapted to keep salt water out of the cell body. As a result of the selective permeability of the cell membrane, there is more K^+ inside the neuron than Na^+, which contributes to polarization.

Seminal research by Alan Hodgkin (1914–1998) and Andrew Huxley in the 1950s demonstrated that the neuron moves K^+ into the cell body and Na^+ out of the cell body through a mechanism referred to as the **sodium-potassium pump**, a chemical pump that uses up metabolic resources and is recharged in the cell body by various nutrients and oxygen. This mechanism keeps the resting membrane

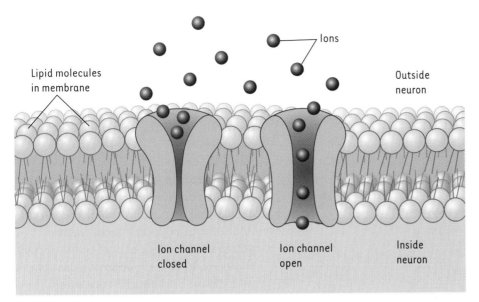

3.9 The cell membrane is selectively permeable. Ions can travel into the neuron when ion channels are open but are blocked when ion channels are closed. The channels are specialized for specific ions. Thus, the Na⁺ channel controls only the passage of Na⁺.

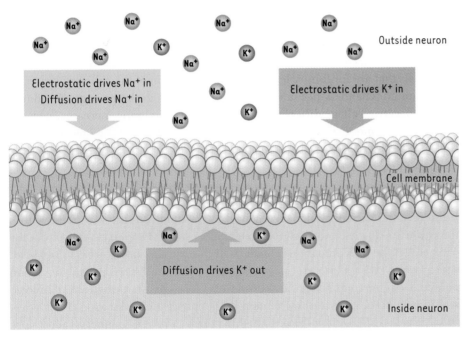

3.10 Electrostatic pressure, diffusion, and the sodium-potassium pump operate to maintain the flow of K⁺ and Na⁺ into and out of the neuron. As a result of these processes there is a greater amount of potassium inside the neuron and sodium outside the neuron, which contributes to the resting membrane potential.

potential at a constant −70 mV, which sets the stage for electrical action (Figure 3.10).

CHANGES IN ELECTRICAL POTENTIAL LEAD TO ACTION

Earlier you read that the dendrites receive chemical signals from nearby neurons, which then signal the neuron to fire or not. "Firing" means passing a signal along the axon and releasing chemicals from the terminal buttons. The signals arrive at the neuron by the thousands and are of two types: *excitatory* or *inhibitory*. Excitatory signals stimulate the neuron to fire, whereas inhibitory signals reduce the likelihood of the neuron firing. Signals work by affecting polarization. Each signal either *depolarizes* or *hyperpolarizes* the cell membrane. *Depolarization* reduces polarity, such that the inside and the outside of the neuron become more similar in electrical charge. *Hyperpolarization* increases polarity by increasing the

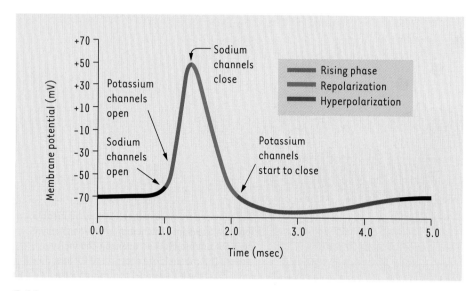

3.11 In the resting state, Na+ ion channels are closed. Depolarization opens the Na+ channels, which allows Na+ to flow into the neuron and changes the electrical charge of the neuron.

electrical difference between the inside and the outside of the neuron. Excitatory signals lead to depolarization, which increases the likelihood that the neuron will fire; inhibitory signals lead to hyperpolarization, which decreases the likelihood that the neuron will fire. Let's look at this in more detail.

Depolarization and hyperpolarization Neurons fire when the cell membrane is depolarized past a threshold, the specific value of which depends on the neuron. Depolarization causes a change in the permeability of the cell membrane, which opens the gates of the sodium channels and allows sodium to rush into the neuron. This influx of Na+, which are positively charged ions, causes the inside of the neuron to become slightly more positively charged than the outside (approximately 50 mV), as shown in Figure 3.11. This change from a negative to a positive charge inside the neuron is the basis of the action potential.

Signals that are inhibitory lead to hyperpolarization of the cell membrane, in which sodium channels become even more resistant to the passage of sodium, and the negative voltage difference across the cell membrane increases, perhaps to −80 mV or more. This hyperpolarization means that it will be more difficult for excitatory signals to cause neuronal firing.

ACTION POTENTIALS SPREAD ALONG THE AXON

Inhibitory and excitatory signals received by the dendrites are integrated within the neuron in an area known as the *axon hillock,* where the axon emerges from the cell body. If the total amount of depolarization surpasses the neuron's threshold, which occurs when there are more excitatory than inhibitory signals, an action potential is generated. When the neuron fires, the signal starts at the axon hillock, and the depolarization of the cell membrane moves along the axon like a wave, which is called *propagation*. Sodium rushing through its ion channels leads to further depolarization, causing adjacent sodium channels to open. Thus, like toppling dominoes, Na+ ion channels open successively along the cell body to the end of the axon. At any point along the axon, the sudden influx of sodium repels the potassium ions, which are forced out of the neuron. This influx of sodium and outflow of potassium continues until a state of near equilibrium is reached, at which point other forces take over to shut the sodium ion channel gates and stop the influx of sodium. All this occurs within about 1/1,000 of a second.

Absolute and relative refractory periods Once the gating mechanism stops the flow of sodium into the neuron, potassium stops leaving. However, this takes 1 to 2 milliseconds, during which a decreased concentration of K+ in the cell body momentarily creates a state of hyperpolarization. During this brief period, known as the *absolute refractory period,* it is impossible for the neuron to fire, which keeps the action potential from repeating up and down the axon in a kind of ripple effect (McCormick, 1999). As each section of the axon depolarizes, the preceding section enters its absolute refractory state. Hence, under natural conditions, action potentials move along the axon in only one direction, from the axon hillock to the terminal buttons. The signal can't travel backward because the preceding axonal section is in its refractory period and its sodium ion channels are blocked.

As potassium stops exiting the neuron and the cell membrane is returning to its resting membrane potential, the neuron can fire, but only in response to an especially strong signal, such as might occur if the neuron were bombarded by excitatory signals. This brief period of time is called the *relative refractory period*. Until the neuron returns to its resting potential, it is somewhat hyperpolarized and requires a stronger signal to become depolarized.

Spatial and temporal summation   Any one signal received by the neuron has little influence on whether it fires. Normally, the neuron is barraged by thousands of inhibitory and excitatory signals, and its firing is determined by the number and frequency of those signals. The firing criterion is the summed electrical voltage produced by the signals at a given time. If the sum of the depolarizations and hyperpolarizations leads to a drop in voltage that exceeds the neuron's firing threshold, then an action potential is generated. It is as if you decided to change your major from English to Psychology because five of the eight friends you asked said to go for it.

The neuron, therefore, is influenced by the *number* of simultaneous excitatory and inhibitory signals, called *spatial summation*, and by the *frequency* of each type of signal, called *temporal summation*. For instance, a signal that depolarizes the cell membrane will have a greater effect if there are several other simultaneous excitatory signals (spatial summation) or if the membrane is already depolarized by other recent excitatory signals (temporal summation). The net effect of the spatial and temporal summation of inhibitory and excitatory signals is referred to as *neural integration*.

The firing of the neuron is all-or-none—a neuron cannot partially fire. What temporal or spatial summation affects is the frequency of the firings. The **all-or-none principle** dictates that a neuron fires with the same potency each time, but at intervals of different frequency depending on the strength of stimulation. Suppose you are playing a video game in which you fire missiles by pressing a button. Every time you press the button, a missile is launched at the same velocity as the last. It makes no difference how hard you press the button. But if you keep your finger on the button, additional missiles fire in rapid succession. Thus, the strong stimulus—your finger holding down the button—controls the firing frequency.

The myelin sheath   The propagation of action potentials along the axon happens quickly, which permits the fast and frequent adjustments required for coordinating motor activity. However, the action potential moving along the axon by depolarizing adjacent sodium channels does not occur rapidly enough to explain the precision of fine motor movements. Signals can travel quickly down the axon because it is insulated by a **myelin sheath**, a fatty material that encases axons (Figure 3.12). Made

all-or-none principle A neuron fires with the same potency each time, although frequency can vary; it either fires or not, it cannot partially fire.

myelin sheath A fatty material, made up of glial cells, that insulates the axon and allows for the rapid movement of electrical impulses along the axon.

3.12 The myelin sheath surrounds the axon, except at the nodes of Ranvier. The electrical signal jumps from node to node.

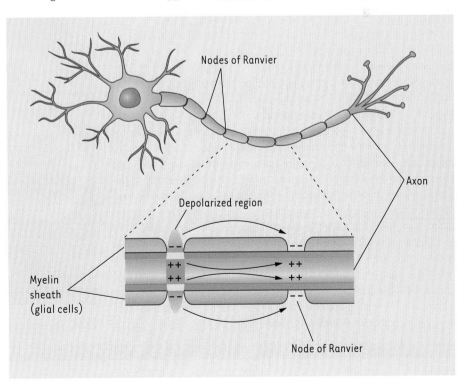

nodes of Ranvier Small gaps of exposed axon, between the segments of myelin sheath, where action potentials are transmitted.

synaptic cleft The small space that exists between neurons that contains extracellular fluid.

up of *glial cells* (Greek, "glue"), myelin, like the plastic tubing around electrical wires in an extension cord, insulates sections of the axon and facilitates the passage of electrical impulses.

As shown in Figure 3.12, the myelin sheath grows along axons in short segments. Between these segments are small gaps of exposed axon known as the **nodes of Ranvier,** named for the researcher who first described them. It is only at these unmyelinated gaps that ion channels can transmit action potentials. Thus, action potentials skip quickly along the axon, pausing only briefly at each node of Ranvier to get recharged. This method of conduction, known as *saltatory conduction* (from Latin, *saltare,* "to jump"), enables signals to move through the nervous system extraordinarily fast. Deterioration of the myelin sheath leads to a breakdown in neural communication, as can be seen in "Using Psychological Science: Multiple Sclerosis Is a Breakdown of the Myelin Sheath."

Using Psychological Science

MULTIPLE SCLEROSIS IS A BREAKDOWN OF THE MYELIN SHEATH

Bill was a vigorous young man in his early twenties. One day while playing squash, his vision seemed a bit off and he was more klutzy than usual. Bill had been working extremely long days and attributed his coordination problems to fatigue. Like most of us would have done, Bill paid little attention to his symptoms until they started to cause more serious problems. In addition to visual disturbances, he began to experience a loss of strength and numbness in one hand. Bill's physician suspected a problem with Bill's nervous system and referred him to a neurologist. Sadly, the neurologist concluded that Bill was in the early stages of multiple sclerosis (MS).

Multiple sclerosis is an especially tragic neurological disorder that mostly affects young adults. The symptoms result from decay of the myelin sheath surrounding axonal projections. The first symptoms are often numbness in the limbs and blurry vision. Since the myelin insulation helps messages move quickly along axons, de-myelination slows down neural impulses. The axons essentially short-circuit and normal neuronal communication is interrupted. Motor actions become jerky and victims lose the ability to coordinate motor movements (called *ataxia*). Over time, movement, sensation, and coordination are severely impaired. As the myelin sheath disintegrates, axons are exposed and may themselves start to break down. The term *sclerosis* means "hardening," which is noticeable from the scarring in the brains of patients with MS, as shown in Figure 3.13.

This progressive disease appears to have both genetic and environmental causes. Evidence for a genetic influence includes that it is more common among identical twins than nonidentical twins and that it is more common among Caucasians than Asians. However, it is also more common in cold climates than in warm climates. It is unclear why cold weather makes MS more likely, although growing up in cold climates seems more relevant than moving to one; moving from a cold climate to a warmer one does not seem to reduce the risk of developing MS. Some theories suggest that MS may be an autoimmune disorder in which the body views myelin as a foreign intruder, triggering an immune reaction that attacks and kills the myelin sheath. This autoimmune disorder may have its origins in some slow-acting infection that occurs early in childhood. There is currently no known cure for multiple sclerosis.

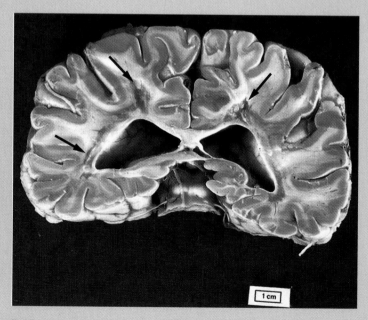

3.13 The brain of an MS patient. The arrows point to areas of sclerosis.

NEUROTRANSMITTERS BIND TO RECEPTORS ACROSS THE SYNAPSE

Neurons do not touch one another; they are separated by a small space known as the **synaptic cleft**, which is the site of chemical communication between neurons. Action potentials cause neurons to release from their terminal buttons chemicals that travel across the synaptic cleft and are received by the dendrites of other neurons. The neuron that sends the signal is called *pre*synaptic and the one that receives the signal is called *post*synaptic.

How do these chemical signals work? Inside the terminal buttons are small packages, or *vesicles*, that contain chemical substances known as neurotransmitters. The term **neurotransmitter** is a generic word used for chemical substances that carry signals across the synaptic cleft. After an action potential travels to the terminal button, it causes the vesicles to spill their neurotransmitters into the synaptic cleft. These neurotransmitters then spread across the synaptic cleft and attach themselves, or *bind*, to receptors on the postsynaptic neuron (Figure 3.14).

Receptors are specialized protein molecules. The binding of neurotransmitter to receptor causes ion channels to open, which changes the membrane potential at that location, thus affecting the probability that the neuron will fire. If a neurotransmitter binds with a receptor and depolarizes the membrane, it is excitatory and increases the likelihood that the receiving neuron will fire. By contrast, if the neurotransmitter's binding hyperpolarizes the membrane, it is inhibitory and makes the receiving neuron less likely to fire.

Ionotropic and metabotropic receptors

Two basic types of receptors are *ionotropic* and *metabotropic*. They differ in the mechanism by which they affect the receiving neuron. *Ionotropic receptors* are fast-acting protein molecules that directly open ion channels. When excitatory neurotransmitters bind with ionotropic receptors, they open sodium channels, increase depolarization, and increase the likelihood that the neuron will fire. When inhibitory neurotransmitters bind with ionotropic receptors they open potassium channels, causing hyperpolarization and decreasing the likelihood that the neuron will fire.

Metabotropic receptors open ion channels indirectly. When a neurotransmitter binds with a metabotropic receptor, a nearby molecule of protein, called a *G protein*, breaks away from the membrane and does one of two things. Either the G protein itself opens relevant ion channels, or it forms a new substance that influences the opening of ion channels. This new substance is known as a "second messenger" (the neurotransmitter is considered the first messenger). It is the influence of the

neurotransmitter Chemical substances that carry signals from one neuron to another.

receptors In neurons, specialized protein molecules on the postsynaptic membrane that neurotransmitters bind to after passing across the synaptic cleft.

RESEARCH QUESTION ???

How do nerve cells communicate with each other to influence mind and behavior?

3.14 An overview of how neurotransmitters work.

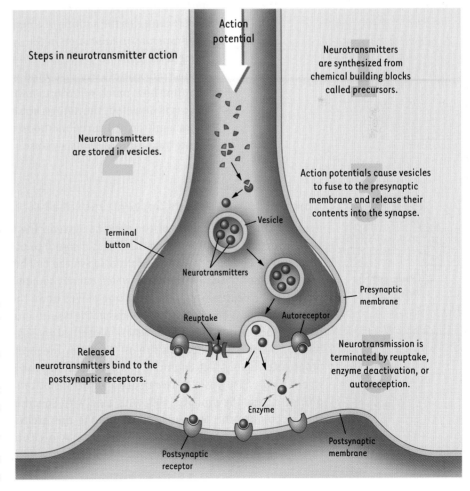

Steps in neurotransmitter action

Action potential

1 Neurotransmitters are synthesized from chemical building blocks called precursors.

2 Neurotransmitters are stored in vesicles.

3 Action potentials cause vesicles to fuse to the presynaptic membrane and release their contents into the synapse.

Terminal button

Vesicle

Neurotransmitters

Presynaptic membrane

Reuptake

Autoreceptor

4 Released neurotransmitters bind to the postsynaptic receptors.

5 Neurotransmission is terminated by reuptake, enzyme deactivation, or autoreception.

Enzyme

Postsynaptic receptor

Postsynaptic membrane

reuptake The process whereby the neurotransmitter is taken back into the presynaptic terminal buttons and repackaged in the vesicles, thereby stopping its activity.

enzyme deactivation The process whereby the neurotransmitter is destroyed by an enzyme, thereby terminating its activity.

autoreceptors A neuron's own neurotransmitter receptors, which regulate the release of the neurotransmitters.

agonist Any drug that enhances the actions of a specific neurotransmitter.

antagonist Any drug that inhibits the action of a specific neurotransmitter.

second messenger that alters ion channels, rather than the direct effect of the neurotransmitter, as is the case with ionotropic receptors. Because metabotropic receptors have an indirect effect on ion channels, they are slower in affecting the postsynaptic neuron.

Relationship between receptors and neurotransmitters Much like a lock opens only with the correct key, each receptor can be influenced by only one type of neurotransmitter. Yet drugs and toxins can mimic neurotransmitters and bind with their receptors as if they were the real thing. Addictive drugs such as heroin and cocaine, for example, have their effects because they are structurally similar to naturally occurring neurotransmitters; the receptors cannot differentiate between the ingested drug and the real neurotransmitter. Through knowledge of how neurotransmitters bind with receptors, researchers have been able to develop effective pharmacological therapies for psychological and medical disorders.

Terminating synaptic transmission The three events that terminate the influence of transmitters in the synaptic cleft are *reuptake, enzyme deactivation,* and *autoreception.* Unless one of these processes occurs, once a neurotransmitter is released into the synaptic cleft it continues to bind with receptors and blocks new signals from getting through. The most common termination process is **reuptake**, when the neurotransmitter molecules are taken back into the presynaptic terminal buttons and repackaged in the vesicles. The cycle of reuptake and release repeats continuously. An action potential prompts vesicles to release the transmitter into the synaptic cleft and then take it back for recycling. Another process that terminates the actions of a neurotransmitter occurs when an enzyme destroys the transmitter substance in the synaptic cleft, which is appropriately called **enzyme deactivation**. Different enzymes break down different neurotransmitters. Neurotransmitters can also bind with their own receptors. These **autoreceptors** monitor how much neurotransmitter has been released into the synapse. When excess is detected, the autoreceptors signal the neuron to stop releasing the neurotransmitter. All three methods of termination serve to regulate the activity of neurotransmitters in the synapse.

How Does the Nervous System Operate?

Neurons are the basic units of the nervous system. The neuron's primary task is to take in information, integrate that information, and pass a signal to other neurons. Neurons receive information at the dendrites and process that information in the cell body. An action potential results from the depolarization of the cell membrane, which causes sodium channels to open and allows sodium ions to rush into the neuron. This depolarization moves down the axon until it reaches the terminal buttons. Whether or not a neuron fires depends on the neural integration of inhibitory and excitatory signals received at the dendrites. Summation of excitatory signals affects the frequency of neuronal firing but not the strength—neurons fire all-or-none. The myelination of axons allows action potentials to propagate rapidly. Action potentials spread along the axon until they reach the terminal buttons, where they cause vesicles to release neurotransmitters into the synaptic cleft. Neurotransmitters diffuse across the synaptic cleft and bind with specific postsynaptic receptors. Neurotransmitters that depolarize the postsynaptic membrane are excitatory, whereas those that hyperpolarize the postsynaptic membrane are inhibitory. These excitatory and inhibitory signals are terminated through reuptake, enzyme deactivation, and autoreception.

HOW DO NEUROTRANSMITTERS INFLUENCE EMOTION, THOUGHT, AND BEHAVIOR?

Before the 1970s, most researchers believed that communication in the brain took place through the actions of just five or so narrowly defined neurotransmitters. Now we know that more than 60 chemicals transmit information in the brain and body, and that different transmitters are responsible for influencing emotion, thought, and behavior. As the numbers of known chemicals have grown, scientists have become more concerned with characterizing the functions of these substances than with identifying and defining them. This change in perspective is largely due to the emergence of new technologies for studying neurochemistry, including new methods in neurobiology and brain imaging that allow researchers to more precisely study function—all of which have furthered the biological revolution.

As you have learned, all neurotransmitters act to enhance or inhibit action potentials, by depolarizing or hyperpolarizing postsynaptic cell membranes. Many substances, such as drugs and toxins, can alter the actions of neurotransmitters in several ways. This fact is important because much of what we know about neurotransmitters has been learned through the systematic study of the effects of drugs and toxins on emotion, thought, and behavior. For instance, drugs and toxins can alter how the neurotransmitter is synthesized, they can raise or lower the amount of neurotransmitter released from the terminal buttons, and they can change the way the neurotransmitter is deactivated in the synaptic cleft by blocking reuptake or preventing enzyme deactivation. Drugs that enhance the actions of neurotransmitters are known as **agonists**; drugs that inhibit action are **antagonists** (see Figure 3.15).

Researchers often inject neurotransmitter agonists or antagonists into the brains of animals to assess the behavioral effects of a neurotransmitter. For instance, researchers can test the hypothesis that a certain neurotransmitter in a specific brain region leads to increased feeding behavior by injecting an agonist into that brain region, which should increase feeding; in contrast, injecting an antagonist should decrease feeding. By understanding agonistic and antagonistic properties of drugs, researchers have developed effective pharmacological treatments for many psychological and medical disorders.

An important point to keep in mind about neurotransmitters is that their effects are not a property of the chemicals themselves, but rather a function of the receptors to which they bind. The same neurotransmitter can be excitatory or inhibitory, or produce radically different effects, depending on the properties of the

How are specific chemicals linked to particular mental processes and behaviors?

3.15 The typical mechanisms of drug action.

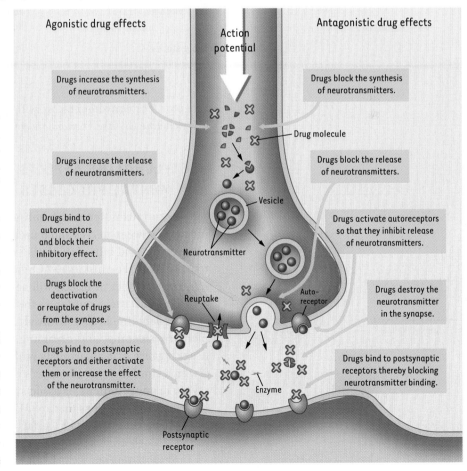

TABLE 3.1	**Common Neurotransmitters and Their Major Functions**
NEUROTRANSMITTER	**FUNCTIONS**
Acetylcholine	Motor control over muscles Learning, memory, sleeping, and dreaming
Monoamines	
Norepinephrine	Arousal and vigilance Eating behavior
Dopamine	Reward and motivation Motor control over voluntary movement
Serotonin	Emotional states and impulsiveness Dreaming
Amino Acids	
GABA	Inhibition of action potentials Anxiety and intoxication
Glutamate	Enhances action potentials Learning and memory
Peptide Modulators	
CCK	Learning and memory Satiety
Endorphins	Pain reduction Reward
Substance P	Pain perception

receptor. For convenience, we will describe neurotransmitters in four categories: *acetylcholine* (by itself), *monoamines*, *amino acids*, and *peptides* (Table 3.1).

ACETYLCHOLINE AFFECTS MOTOR CONTROL AND MENTAL PROCESSES

The neurotransmitter **acetylcholine** (ACh) is responsible for motor control at the junction between nerves and muscles. Terminal buttons release acetylcholine into the synapse, and it binds with the receptors on muscle cells and makes them contract or relax. For instance, ACh both excites skeletal muscles and inhibits heart muscles. Whether its effects will be inhibitory or excitatory depends on the receptors. This difference reinforces the rule that the receptor controls the process.

Acetylcholine is also involved in complex mental processes such as learning, memory, sleeping, and dreaming. Because ACh affects memory and attention, drugs that are ACh antagonists inhibit its activity and can cause temporary amnesia. In a similar way, Alzheimer's disease, a condition characterized primarily by severe memory deficits, is associated with diminished ACh functioning (Geula & Mesulam, 1994). Drugs that are ACh agonists may enhance memory and decrease other symptoms, although so far there has been only marginal success in the pharmacological treatment of Alzheimer's.

Toxins that mimic ACh can bind to its receptors and cause temporary paralysis. For example, curare, an herbal poison used by South American Indians, competes with ACh for receptor binding and inhibits the mechanisms that produce muscle movement. Administration of curare paralyzes the limbs and lungs of its victims, asphyxiating them. Botulism, a form of food poisoning, inhibits the release of ACh from terminal buttons in a similar fashion and leads to trouble with breathing, difficulty in chewing, and often death.

Nicotine   One substance that excites ACh receptors is nicotine, the addictive drug found in tobacco leaves. Given the role of ACh in memory and sleeping, it may not surprise you that the ingestion of nicotine has several cognitive effects. For instance, people who wear the nicotine patch often have extremely vivid dreams, probably because of the activation of ACh neurons known to affect the stage of sleep associated with dreaming. Studies demonstrate that smoking a cigarette can heighten attention, improve problem solving, and facilitate memory (Warburton, 1992). But before you rush out to buy a pack, some evidence suggests that nicotine may produce these effects only for current smokers (Heishman et al., 1994). When nonsmokers are given nicotine gum, they perform more poorly on cognitive tasks, as do former smokers who have not had nicotine for a while. Thus, smoking or chewing tobacco alters how the mind works, and over time users suffer deficits in cognitive performance *unless* they ingest nicotine. This is one of the many reasons why giving up nicotine is so difficult; recent ex-smokers find it hard to think or concentrate.

MONOAMINES ARE INVOLVED IN AFFECT, AROUSAL, AND MOTIVATION

The **monoamines** are a group of neurotransmitters synthesized within the neuron from single amino acids—*mono* means "one." Although the monoamines are involved in a variety of psychological activities, their major functions are to regulate states of arousal and affect (feelings) and to motivate behavior. The four monoamines are *epinephrine, norepinephrine, dopamine,* and *serotonin.*

Epinephrine and norepinephrine   **Epinephrine** is found primarily in the body, although small amounts are in the brain. It was initially called *adrenaline* and is the basis for the phrase "adrenaline rush," a burst of energy caused by its release in the body. **Norepinephrine** is involved in states of arousal and vigilance. In contrast to epinephrine, it has a major influence in the brain, generally acting to inhibit action potentials. Neurons in a region of the brain called the *locus coeruleus* release norepinephrine to several brain regions. The rate of firing in the locus coeruleus is nearly zero when you are sleeping, but it increases dramatically as you awaken. Norepinephrine is especially important for vigilance, a heightened sensitivity to what is going on around you. Norepinephrine appears to be useful for fine-tuning the clarity of attention; it inhibits responsiveness to weak synaptic inputs and it strengthens or maintains responsiveness to strong synaptic inputs. Damage to the locus coeruleus interferes with the ability to ignore distracting stimuli.

There is an interesting link between the firing rate of the locus coeruleus and eating behavior. When an animal awakens, a burst of neurons fires in the locus coeruleus, leading to increased arousal and vigilance. At the same time, there is an infusion of norepinephrine from the locus coeruleus into the hypothalamus, which triggers eating (Leibowitz, 1992). This is an example of a neural network that produces an adaptive behavior. During sleep, energy stores are exhausted; the burst of activity in the locus coeruleus motivates animals to

acetylcholine (ACh) The neurotransmitter responsible for motor control at the junction between nerves and muscles and are also involved in mental processes such as learning, memory, sleeping, and dreaming.

monoamines A group of neurotransmitters synthesized from a single amino acid that are involved in a variety of psychological activities.

epinephrine A monoamine, found primarily in the body, which causes a burst of energy after an exciting event.

norepinephrine A monoamine neurotransmitter involved in states of arousal and vigilance.

dopamine A monoamine neurotransmitter that is involved in reward, motivation, and motor control.

search for food to satisfy immediate energy needs. The link between arousal and feeding is a good example of how various brain mechanisms work together to facilitate survival.

Dopamine Dopamine serves many significant brain functions, especially motivation and motor control. Many theorists believe dopamine is the primary neurotransmitter that communicates which activities may be rewarding. Eating when hungry, drinking when thirsty, or having sex when aroused all lead to activation of dopamine receptors and therefore are experienced as pleasurable. At the same time, dopamine activation is involved in motor control and planning, thereby guiding behavior toward objects and experiences that will lead to additional reward. One theory of drug addiction is that certain drugs are dopamine agonists;

Crossing the Levels of Analysis

PARKINSON'S DISEASE

The actor Michael J. Fox has recently become as well known for his unfortunate medical condition as his acting ability. He is one among many famous people who have developed the neurodegenerative disorder Parkinson's disease, first identified by physician James Parkinson (1755–1828) in 1817. Parkinson's disease affects about 1 in every 200 older adults and occurs in all known cultures. Although most Parkinson's patients do not experience symptoms until after age 50, the case of Fox makes it clear that the disease can occur earlier. Symptoms include muscular rigidity, involuntary movements, and very specific tremors of the hand known as "pill rolling," because it looks as though the individual is rolling a small pill between the thumb and forefinger. As the disorder progresses, Parkinson's patients often develop a masklike facial expression and blink very little. At later stages people suffer from cognitive and mood disturbances. Parkinson's is a slow and degenerative disease that eventually leads to death.

Research in the past few decades has demonstrated that dopamine depletion in an area of the brain known as the substantia nigra is implicated in Parkinson's (Figure 3.16). The substantia nigra is a key area for the synthesis and transmission of dopamine throughout the brain; axons that extend from neurons in the substantia nigra to other regions of the brain have been implicated in the control of movement. With Parkinson's disease, the dopamine-producing neurons in the substantia nigra slowly die off.

What causes Parkinson's disease? At this time the answer is not clear. Some evidence of genetic involvement exists, especially the early-onset forms of the disease, but other evidence points to brain injury or even exposure to environmental toxins. Evidence for the toxin argument is based on the general finding that increasing numbers of young people are afflicted with Parkinson's and that it is more common in industrialized nations than in developing countries.

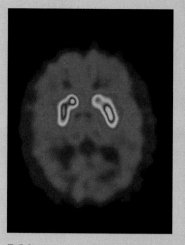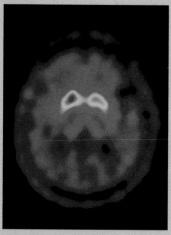

3.16 Healthy volunteers and Parkinson's patients were injected with a radioactive tracer, which allowed researchers to map the distribution of dopamine in the brain. Brighter colors indicate greater amounts of dopamine originating in the substantia nigra. You can see that healthy volunteers (left) have much more dopamine than those with Parkinson's disease (right).

Moreover, in 1982 it was found that a synthetic version of heroin (called MPTP) caused symptoms much like those associated with Parkinson's. Heroin addicts who unwittingly took MPTP all developed severe paralysis and frozen facial expressions (Figure 3.17). It later was found that chemists who had worked with MPTP early in their careers had also developed Parkinson's disease. These findings have led to the use of MPTP in animal research to study the course and treatment of Parkinson's disease.

From a treatment standpoint, drugs that enhance dopamine production can compensate for the lack of dopamine-producing neu-

people self-administer these drugs because they activate dopamine receptors and cause pleasure (Wise & Rompre, 1989). For example, cocaine blocks the reuptake of dopamine into presynaptic vesicles and allows dopamine to have a longer-lasting effect on postsynaptic receptors, leading to heightened arousal and feelings of euphoria. Rats quickly learn to self-administer cocaine, which supports the idea that it has rewarding qualities.

Dopamine also is involved in controlling voluntary muscle movements. Research in the past few decades has demonstrated that dopamine depletion in an area of the brain known as the *substantia nigra* is implicated in **Parkinson's disease**, a neurological disorder marked by muscular rigidity, tremors, and difficulty initiating voluntary action, discussed in "Crossing the Levels of Analysis: Parkinson's Disease."

Parkinson's disease A neurological disorder marked by muscular rigidity, tremors, and difficulty initiating voluntary action, which seems to be caused by dopamine depletion.

3.17 These people developed symptoms of Parkinson's disease after ingesting the substance MPTP, which they mistakenly believed to be a synthetic form of heroin.

rons. For instance, injections of one of the chief building blocks of dopamine, L-DOPA, help the surviving neurons produce more dopamine. L-DOPA is used to treat Parkinson's disease, and often it produces a remarkable, though temporary, recovery, especially when used alongside drugs that block the enzyme that breaks down L-DOPA. However, L-DOPA does nothing to stop the underlying disease that is destroying dopamine neurons in the first place. Fewer and fewer neurons work harder and harder to provide enough dopamine for fine motor movement; eventually, too many neurons die, and L-DOPA's effect diminishes. Other agonistic drugs that enhance the

action of dopamine have also been used to treat Parkinson's, but their effects are temporary, too.

A promising development in Parkinson's research is the procedure to transplant fetal tissue into human brains in the hope that the new fetal cells will produce dopamine. The first studies used MPTP-treated monkeys that had developed symptoms of Parkinson's disease. These studies demonstrated that transplanted fetal substantia nigra cells were successful in reducing the motor symptoms. The first American to undergo fetal neural transplantation, Donald Wilson, regained the ability to walk and was able to return to his hobby of woodworking. Fetal transplants were also used on one of the young people who mistakenly took MPTP. Brain scans using PET imaging showed increased release of dopamine one year following implantation (Figure 3.18). Although there are ethical issues involved in using fetal transplants, they provide new hope to victims of Parkinson's disease.

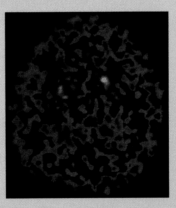
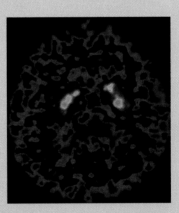

3.18 PET scans showing dopamine activity before (left) and after (right) fetal transplant surgery. This increase suggests that the transplant was successful and that the new neurons are producing dopamine.

Serotonin   Serotonin is a monoamine neurotransmitter involved in many different behaviors; it is especially important for emotional states, impulse control, and dreaming. Low levels of serotonin are associated with sad and anxious moods, food cravings, and aggressive behavior. Drugs that block the reuptake of serotonin are now used to treat a wide array of mental and behavioral disorders, including depression, obsessive-compulsive disorders, eating disorders, and obesity (Tollesfson, 1995).

The drug LSD is structurally similar to the neurotransmitter serotonin; when ingested, LSD enters the brain and binds with serotonin receptors. When LSD binds with serotonin receptors normally involved in dreaming, it causes hallucinations, a dream-like state of mind people experience while they are awake.

AMINO ACIDS ARE GENERAL INHIBITORY AND EXCITATORY TRANSMITTERS IN THE BRAIN

For much of the past century, the monoamines and acetylcholine were considered to be the only neurotransmitters. In the past forty years, however, it has become apparent that many other substances are also involved in neuronal communication. For instance, although the monoamines are made up of amino acids, some amino acids serve as neurotransmitters all by themselves. More recent research has established important roles for amino acids in general levels of inhibition and activation of the nervous system. Here we will look at two amino acids, *GABA* and *glutamate*.

GABA   GABA (gamma-aminobutyric acid) is the primary inhibitory transmitter in the nervous system and works throughout the brain to hyperpolarize post-synaptic membranes. Without the inhibitory effect of GABA, synaptic excitation might get out of control and spread through the brain in a reverberating circuit. Epileptic seizures may happen because of an abnormality in GABA functioning (Upton, 1994).

Drugs that affect the GABA system are widely used to treat anxiety disorders. For instance, people with nervous disorders commonly use benzodiazepines, which include drugs such as Valium. Benzodiazepines assist GABA in binding with one of its primary receptors, an action that inhibits neuronal connections and reduces symptoms of anxiety. These drugs also treat insomnia and other stress-related disorders. Ethyl alcohol—the type that people drink—has similar effects on GABA receptors, which is why alcohol typically is experienced as relaxing. GABA reception also may be the primary mechanism by which alcohol interferes with motor coordination. Drugs that block the effects of alcohol on GABA receptors also prevent alcohol intoxication. However, drugs that prevent the effects of alcohol are not used to treat alcoholics, because reducing the symptoms of being drunk could easily lead to even greater alcohol abuse.

Glutamate   Glutamate is the primary excitatory transmitter in the nervous system and is involved in fast-acting neuronal transmission throughout the brain. It opens sodium gates in postsynaptic membranes (i.e., ionotropic receptors) and causes depolarization. Glutamate receptors aid learning and memory by strengthening synaptic connections.

In addition to being released by neurons, glutamate is also released by *astrocytes*, which are a type of glial cell. Until very recently, it was believed that glial cells played primarily a support role in neuronal communication, such as being

serotonin   A monoamine neurotransmitter that is important for a wide range of psychological activity, including emotional states, impulse control, and dreaming.

GABA (gamma-aminobutyric acid)   The primary inhibitory transmitter in the nervous system.

glutamate   The primary excitatory transmitter in the nervous system.

the building blocks of the myelin sheath. However, within the last few years it has become apparent that astrocytes play an important role in the nervous system. The release of neurotransmitters into the synapse causes a change in the activity of *calcium ions* in astrocytes, which causes the release of glutamate into the synapse. In this way, astrocytes contribute to the activity of neurons, such as by modifying their levels of polarization. Haydon (2001) has described astrocytes as being analogous to stagehands and directors in the theater; they may not be center stage, but they are nonetheless important for the performance. How this alternative mode of communication within the nervous system affects higher brain processes, such as psychological activity, is currently unknown.

PEPTIDES MODULATE NEUROTRANSMISSION

Peptides are chains of two or more amino acids that exist in the brain and the body. Often, neurotransmitters and peptides are released simultaneously into the synaptic cleft, and the peptide modifies the effect of the neurotransmitter with which it is paired. Some peptides, for example, prolong or shorten the action of neurotransmitters, while others influence postsynaptic receptors. An analogy of the effects of peptides on neurotransmitters is the sound controls on a stereo. Peptide *modulation* can turn up or down the volume and alter the tone, but it cannot change the tune. As such, peptides help to explain the vast subtleties and nuances of human experience. There are more than 30 known peptides that act as neurotransmitters or modulators. Three examples are *cholecystokinin (CCK)*, *endorphins*, and *Substance P*.

CCK Cholecystokinin (CCK) is the peptide found in highest concentration in the cerebral cortex. It plays a role in learning and memory, pain transmission, and exploratory behavior. The administration of CCK triggers panic attacks in people who suffer from panic disorder, which creates intense anxiety, a feeling of impending doom, and often feelings of suffocation (Bourin et al., 1998). CCK may also contribute to social anxiety. In one experiment, two rats are placed together in a novel or brightly lit setting. The amount of time they interact, grooming and sniffing, measures their social behavior, which usually declines under stress. Administration of CCK antagonists leads to more social interaction whereas administration of CCK agonists has the opposite effect (Woodruff & Hughes, 1991). CCK is also found in the gastrointestinal system, where it promotes *satiety*, the feeling of fullness that terminates feeding. Administration of CCK before a meal leads people to feel full more quickly and decreases the amount they eat (Woods & Stricker, 1999). As you might imagine, research is currently underway to see whether CCK can be used to help treat human obesity.

Endorphins Endorphins are peptides involved in natural pain reduction and reward. In the early 1970s Candace Pert and Solomon Snyder established that opiate drugs such as heroin and morphine bind to receptors in the brain, which led to the discovery of naturally occurring substances that bind to those sites. These substances were called endorphins (short for "endogenous morphine").

Endorphins are part of the body's natural defense against pain. Pain is useful because it signals that an animal is hurt or in danger and therefore should try to escape or withdraw, but pain can also interfere with adaptive functioning. If pain prevented animals from engaging in behaviors such as eating, competing, and mating they would fail to pass along their genes. The analgesic effects of endorphins help animals perform these behaviors even when they are in pain. In

peptides Chains of two or more amino acids that exist in the brain and the body that can act like classic neurotransmitters or modify the quality of the neurotransmitter with which they are released.

cholecystokinin (CCK) The peptide found in highest concentration in the cerebral cortex and plays a role in learning and memory, pain transmission, and exploratory behavior.

endorphins Peptides involved in natural pain reduction and reward.

substance P A peptide that acts as a neurotransmitter and is involved in pain perception.

humans, administration of drugs that bind with endorphin receptors, such as morphine, reduces the subjective experience of pain. People still feel pain but report detachment; they know about the pain but do not experience it as aversive (Foley, 1993). Apparently morphine alters the way pain is experienced rather than blocks the nerves that transmit pain signals.

Endorphins may account for the *placebo effect*. A placebo is a neutral substance, such as water, that has no pharmacological effect. Yet, people being treated for pain with a placebo might report relief just because they expect relief. In a classic report published in the 1950s, 4 out of 10 surgical patients reported satisfactory relief from pain after the injection of salt water (Lasagna et al., 1954). Placebo effects are real; administration of a placebo leads to such physiological changes as changes in heart rate and digestion. When people take a medication and expect that they will gain relief, mechanisms release endorphins, which confirm their expectations.

Endorphins are associated with euphoric moods, which may explain why drugs such as heroin or morphine, which mimic endorphins by binding with their receptors, are so addictive. Endorphins may also explain "runner's high," the experience that runners get when they push their bodies beyond endurance, and pain turns to pleasure. One theory is that the body produces endorphins to cope with anticipated pain; when pain fails to materialize or is less than expected, the result is pleasure. Skydiving and other high-risk activities may be pleasurable for similar reasons (Jones & Ellis, 1996).

Substance P   Substance P is another peptide that functions as a neurotransmitter and is involved in pain perception. This mysterious-sounding stuff was first identified in 1931 by von Euler and Gaddum, who referred to it in their notes simply by the initial "P," and this simple name stuck. Substance P helps transmit signals about pain along to the brain. Probably the best evidence for it can be found at your local Mexican restaurant, where you can conduct your own experiment. Chili peppers, especially jalapeño peppers, contain a substance known as capsaicin, which releases Substance P. Once released, Substance P makes your tongue and mouth burn, your eyes water, and your hand reach for the nearest pitcher of water—a bad idea, because water spreads capsaicin around and releases more Substance P, which only intensifies the pain.

Over-the-counter liniments also contain capsaicin, which when rubbed on your skin releases Substance P, which transmits pain signals to the brain, causing a burning sensation. Used in sufficient quantity, the capsaicin in these ointments depletes reserves of Substance P, preventing the neurons from transmitting other pain messages to the brain. This analgesic effect lasts until more Substance P is produced.

How Do Neurotransmitters Influence Emotion, Thought, and Behavior?

Neurotransmitters are chemical substances that carry signals across the synaptic cleft and act to enhance or inhibit action potentials by depolarizing or hyperpolarizing postsynaptic cell membranes. Substances that enhance the actions of neurotransmitters are known as agonists; those that inhibit action are antagonists. The number of known substances that act as neurotransmitters is now over 60 and growing. In addition to the classic neurotransmitters, acetylcholine and the monoamines, other amino acids and peptides also serve as neurotransmitters.

HOW ARE NEURAL MESSAGES INTEGRATED INTO COMMUNICATION SYSTEMS?

A number of communication systems operate together to regulate all psychological activity. The most important communication system is the nervous system, which is comprised of networks of neurons throughout the body. The nervous system is divided into two functional units: the **central nervous system** (**CNS**), which consists of the brain and spinal cord, and the **peripheral nervous system** (**PNS**), which consists of all other nerve cells in the body. The two systems are anatomically separate, but their functions are highly interdependent. The PNS transmits a variety of information to the CNS, which organizes and evaluates that information and then directs the PNS to perform specific behaviors or make bodily adjustments. In addition, the CNS receives information from the *endocrine system,* which uses a different mode of communication. This section describes the interaction of the nervous system and endocrine system in the production of psychological activity.

How does the brain communicate with the body?

THE CENTRAL NERVOUS SYSTEM CONSISTS OF THE BRAIN AND SPINAL CORD

Nearly all the functions of the CNS are performed by the brain, and there has recently been dramatic growth in scientific knowledge about how the brain works. For our purposes of understanding how neural messages are integrated into communication systems, it is important to keep in mind that behavior and mental activity are produced within specific locations in the brain. For example, some brain regions are involved with emotional states, others with the ability to see, and others with the ability to speak. The brain has developed specialized mechanisms over millions of years to solve problems related to survival and reproduction. Using methods such as brain imaging, psychological scientists have been able to map out the functions of many structures in the brain, and you will learn about these in the next chapter.

The other part of the CNS is the spinal cord. Although the spinal cord is capable of reflex action, its main job is to receive sensory signals from the body and transmit them to the brain, and to receive signals from the brain and relay them to the body to control muscles, glands, and internal organs. When the spinal cord is damaged, the brain loses both sensory input from and control over the body. The severity of feeling loss and paralysis depends on where the spinal cord is damaged. The higher the damage, the greater the number of nerve connections between the brain and the body that are severed.

The CNS is separated from the rest of the body by the *blood-brain barrier,* which refers to the selectively permeable nature of blood vessels throughout the CNS that prevents certain toxins and poisons in the blood from entering the brain or spinal cord. The extent to which chemical substances have an influence on the brain depends on the ease with which they pass through the blood-brain barrier. Many drugs, such as cocaine and heroin, cross the blood-brain barrier easily and therefore are able to bind with receptors and affect neurotransmitter functioning.

THE PERIPHERAL NERVOUS SYSTEM INCLUDES THE SOMATIC AND AUTONOMIC SYSTEMS

The PNS has two primary components, which themselves are referred to as nervous systems: the *somatic nervous system* and the *autonomic nervous system*

central nervous system (CNS) The brain and spinal cord.

peripheral nervous system (PNS) All nerve cells in the body that are not part of the central nervous system. The PNS includes the somatic and autonomic nervous systems.

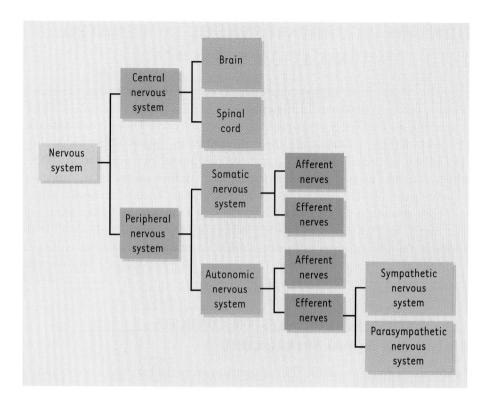

3.19 The major divisions of the nervous system.

(Figure 3.19). The **somatic nervous system** transmits sensory signals to the CNS via nerves (bundles of axons). Specialized receptors in the skin, muscles, and joints send sensory information to the spinal cord, which relays it to the brain. In addition, signals are sent from the CNS to muscles, joints, and skin to initiate, modulate, or inhibit movement.

The second major component of the PNS is the **autonomic nervous system (ANS)**, which regulates the body's internal environment by stimulating glands (such as sweat glands) and by maintaining internal organs such as the heart. Nerves in the ANS carry *somatosensory* signals to the CNS, providing information about, for example, the fullness of your stomach or bladder, and how anxious you feel.

Sympathetic and parasympathetic divisions   Two types of signals travel from the CNS to organs and glands in the PNS. To understand them, imagine that as you are studying, a fire alarm goes off. In the second after hearing the alarm, signals have been sent out to parts of your body to tell it to prepare for action: blood flows to skeletal muscles, epinephrine is released to increase heart rate and blood sugar, your lungs start taking in more oxygen, you stop digesting food to conserve energy, your pupils dilate to maximize visual sensitivity, and you start perspiring to keep cool. These actions are the result of the **sympathetic division** of the autonomic nervous system, which prepares the body for action. Should there be a fire, you will be physically prepared to flee. As often happens, the fire bell is a false alarm. Now your heart returns to its normal beating pattern, your breathing slows, you start digesting food, and you quit perspiring. This return to a normal state results from the action of the **parasympathetic division** of the ANS. Parasympathetic signals return your body to a resting state after sympathetic activation. Most of your internal organs are controlled by inputs from sympathetic and parasympathetic systems. The more aroused you are, the greater the dominance of the sympathetic system (Figure 3.20).

somatic nervous system   A major component of the peripheral nervous system, which transmits sensory signals to the CNS via nerves.

autonomic nervous system (ANS)   A major component of the peripheral nervous system, which regulates the body's internal environment by stimulating glands and by maintaining internal organs such as the heart, gall bladder, and stomach.

sympathetic division of ANS   A division of the autonomic nervous system that prepares the body for action.

parasympathetic division of ANS   A division of the autonomic nervous system that returns the body to its resting state.

endocrine system   A communication system that uses hormones.

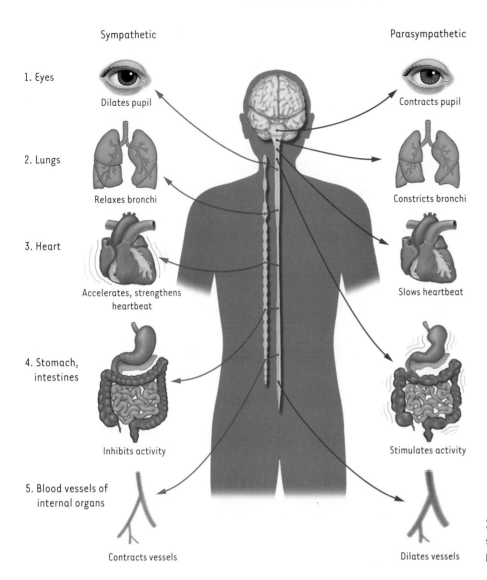

Sympathetic

Parasympathetic

1. Eyes

Dilates pupil

Contracts pupil

2. Lungs

Relaxes bronchi

Constricts bronchi

3. Heart

Accelerates, strengthens heartbeat

Slows heartbeat

4. Stomach, intestines

Inhibits activity

Stimulates activity

5. Blood vessels of internal organs

Contracts vessels

Dilates vessels

3.20 The sympathetic division of the nervous system prepares the body for action, whereas the parasympathetic returns it to a resting state.

It doesn't take a fire alarm to activate your sympathetic nervous system. When you meet someone whom you find attractive, your heart starts beating quickly, you start perspiring, you may start breathing heavily, and although you may not know it, your pupils widen. These are all signs of sexual arousal, which relies on activation of the sympathetic division of the ANS, and they provide nonverbal cues during social interaction.

The sympathetic nervous system is also activated by psychological states such as anxiety or unhappiness. People who worry a great deal or who cannot cope with stress have bodies in a constant state of arousal. Chronic activation of the sympathetic nervous system is associated with medical problems that include ulcers, heart disease, and asthma (Davison & Pennebaker, 1996).

THE ENDOCRINE SYSTEM COMMUNICATES THROUGH HORMONES

Like the nervous system, the **endocrine system** is a communication system that influences thoughts, behaviors, and actions. The main distinction between the two is their mode of communication: the endocrine system uses hormones and

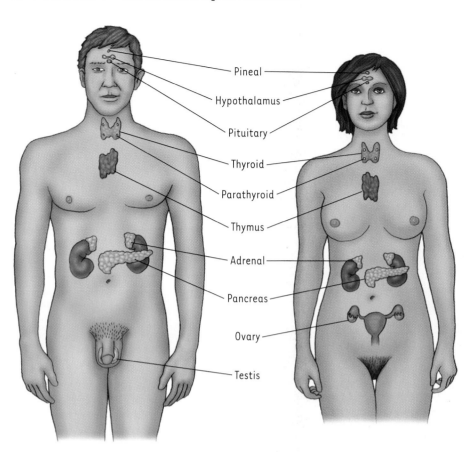

3.21 The major endocrine glands.

the nervous system uses electrochemical signals. **Hormones** are chemical substances released into the bloodstream by *endocrine glands*, ductless glands such as the pancreas, thyroid, and testes or ovaries (Figure 3.21). Other organs (such as the stomach and liver) also secrete hormones but are not usually considered endocrine glands. Once released by a gland or organ, hormones travel through the bloodstream until they reach their target tissues, where they bind to receptor sites and influence the tissue. Because they travel through the bloodstream, hormones can take from seconds to hours to exert their effects; once in the bloodstream, the effects of hormones can last for a long time and affect multiple targets.

The endocrine system and the nervous system work together to regulate psychological activity. For instance, sexual behavior depends on brain centers that assess issues such as whether you are attracted to the person, whether you are inhibited about having sex, and whether the time and circumstances are appropriate. The brain then transmits signals to the endocrine system, which subsequently controls the physiological responses necessary for sexual performance through the release of hormones. Similarly, the brain interprets potential physical threats and directs action in the endocrine system to prepare for battle or to deal with possible injury.

Types of hormones Hormones are of three types: *steroids, amino acids,* and *peptides. Steroid hormones* are synthesized from cholesterol, a fatty molecule manufactured in the body and also found in many foods. Steroid hormones play key roles in growth, tissue repair, and reproduction. Amino acids and peptides, in addition to their role as neurotransmitters, also function as hormones in the PNS. For instance, epinephrine is an amino acid that serves as a neurotransmitter in the CNS and as a hormone in the rest of the body. It is released from the adrenal gland when the sympathetic nervous system is activated. Thus, sometimes hormones function as neurotransmitters and sometimes neurotransmitters function as hormones. One way to clarify matters is to concentrate on the mode of communication rather than on the substance itself.

Consider your computer. A message sent from your computer directly to your printer functions like a neurotransmitter: the message is sent a short distance across a cable linked only to your printer, and it initiates an action. Once the document is printed, the process disappears. By contrast, hormones operate more like messages sent out on the Internet. You might send a message to a newsgroup and anyone who wishes to receive the message has full access to it. The message may linger in cyberspace for a long time and people can read and respond to it as long as it lasts. Moreover, the message can have different effects, depending on who receives the message and how they respond.

Effects of hormones on sexual behavior   An example of hormonal influence is evident in sexual behavior. The main endocrine glands in sexual behavior are the **gonads**, which for males are testes and for females are ovaries. The two major gonadal hormones are identical in males and females, although the quantity differs: *androgens* such as testosterone are more prevalent in males, whereas *estrogens* such as estradiol are more prevalent in females. Gonadal hormones influence both the development of secondary sex characteristics and adult sexual behavior.

For males, successful sexual behavior depends on having at least a minimum amount of testosterone. Surgical removal of the testes diminishes the capacity for developing an erection and lowers sexual interest. Yet a castrated male who receives an injection of testosterone will be able to perform sexually. Do injections of testosterone increase sexual behavior among healthy men? The answer is no, which implies that as long as a minimum amount of testosterone is available, the healthy male will be able to perform and additional testosterone does not seem to have any effect (Sherwin, 1988).

The influence of gonadal hormones on females is much more complex. In many nonhuman animals there is a finite period called *estrus*, when the female is sexually receptive and fertile. During estrus the female displays behaviors designed to attract the male. Surgical removal of the ovaries terminates these behaviors and the female is no longer receptive. However, injections of estrogen reinstate estrus. What does this mean for women? Apparently not very much. The sexual behavior of women is not particularly linked to their menstrual cycle, and surgical removal of the ovaries has a minimal effect on sexual interest or behavior (Dennerstein & Burrows, 1982). Moreover, sexual behavior in women may have more to do with androgens than estrogens (Morris et al., 1987). Women with higher levels of testosterone report greater interest in sex, and injections of testosterone increase sexual interest in women after surgical removal of the uterus (Sherwin, 1994).

ACTIONS OF THE NERVOUS SYSTEM AND ENDOCRINE SYSTEM ARE COORDINATED

Throughout this chapter we have described communication systems that link neurochemical and physiological processes to behaviors, thoughts, and feelings. These systems are fully integrated and interact to facilitate survival. The nervous and endocrine systems use information from the environment to direct behavioral responses that are adaptive. Ultimately, the endocrine system is under the control of the central nervous system. External and internal stimuli are interpreted in the brain and signals are sent from the brain to the endocrine system, which then initiates a variety of effects on the body and on behavior.

Most of central control of the endocrine system is accomplished by a small brain structure called the *hypothalamus*, which is located just above the roof of the mouth. As you will learn in the next chapter, the hypothalamus plays an extremely important role in behaviors related to survival and reproduction, such as feeding and sex. How does this central control work? At the base of the hypothalamus is the **pituitary gland**, which controls the release of hormones from the rest of the endocrine glands. Based on some sort of neural activation, a *releasing factor* is secreted from the hypothalamus. This releasing factor causes the pituitary to release a specific hormone, which then travels to endocrine sites throughout the body.

hormones Chemical substances typically released from endocrine glands, which travel through the bloodstream to targeted tissues, which are subsequently influenced by the hormone.

gonads The main endocrine glands involved in sexual behavior: in males, the testes, in females, the ovaries.

pituitary gland Located at the base of the hypothalamus, the gland that sends hormonal signals that control the release of hormones from endocrine glands.

Once the hormone is at the target sites, it touches off the release of other hormones, which subsequently affect bodily reactions or behavior.

It is fascinating how finely tuned this integration can be. For example, consider the case of physical growth. *Growth hormone (GH)* is an extract from the pituitary gland that affects bone, cartilage, and muscle tissue, helping them to grow or regenerate after injury. External administration of GH can increase body size, something known since the 1930s. A common and effective therapy for children with medical conditions such as dwarfism is a synthetic version of GH. How does it work? To build body tissues, GH requires dietary protein. A lack of protein in the diet is associated with a lack of normal growth.

GH is released in bursts throughout the day. Its release is triggered by the peptide *growth hormone releasing factor (GRF)*. GRF neurons are connected to an area of the hypothalamus that is involved in sleep-wake cycles. Thus, the bursts of GH are controlled by the body's internal clock.

Once GH is available, it needs protein. GRF also plays a role in the control of feeding behavior. Injections of GRF into the area of the brain that controls the body clock increase consumption of protein but not fats or carbohydrates (Dickson & Vaccarino, 1994). Consider the whole picture: GRF selectively stimulates eating protein, perhaps by making protein especially enjoyable. At the same time, it also releases GH, which relies on the higher intake of dietary protein to help build strong bones and muscles. Hence, the CNS, PNS, and endocrine systems are clearly integrated to ensure that behaviors provide the body with substances it needs for survival at the times they are required.

How Are Neural Messages Integrated into Communication Systems?

The central nervous system, consisting of the brain and spinal cord, attends to the body and the environment, initiates actions, and directs the peripheral nervous system and endocrine system to respond appropriately. All three systems use chemicals to transmit their signals, but transmission in the nervous system occurs across synapses whereas transmission in the endocrine system uses hormones that travel through the bloodstream. The hypothalamus controls the endocrine system by directing the pituitary to release specific hormones. The various communication systems are integrated and promote behavior that is adaptive to the environment.

CONCLUSION

The human body is an amazing thing, produced by a genome that has been shaped by millions of years of evolution. Some 30,000 genes provide instructions for producing proteins, and this modest process builds a brain that thinks, feels, and acts. The biological revolution has revealed that these genes not only build the common structures of the human body, but they are also partially responsible for differences between individuals, such as physical appearance, personality, and mental abilities. The complexity of mental life, however, is poorly understood at the genetic level of analysis. Instead, it is the billions of neuronal action potentials occurring each moment, and the subtle variations created by peptide and glial modulation, that profoundly effect behavior, thought, and emotion. There are more neuronal connections in the human brain than there are stars in our galaxy

(Kandel et al., 1995), and the messages that are transmitted are modulated by subtle variations in the actions of dozens of chemicals in the synapses. Moreover, various physiological systems in the body work together in a coordinated fashion to produce solutions to the adaptive problems of human lives. The physiological actions of the brain give rise to the very essence of human experience and enable the minds of scientists to develop new methods and strategies for exploring how it works.

FURTHER READINGS

Carlson, N. R. (2001). *Physiology of behavior* (7th ed.). Needham Heights, MA: Allyn & Bacon.

Feldman, R. S., Meyer, J. S., & Quenzer, L. F. (1997). *Principles of neuropsychopharmacology*. Sunderland, MA: Sinauer Associates.

Gazzaniga, M. S., Ivry, R. B., & Mangun, G. R. (2002). *Cognitive neuroscience: The biology of mind* (2nd ed.). New York: W. W. Norton.

Kandel, E. R., Schwartz, J. H., & Jessell, T. M. (2000). *Principles of neural science* (4th ed.). New York: McGraw-Hill.

Marshall, L. H., & Magoun, H. W. (1998). *Discoveries in the human brain: Neuroscience prehistory, brain structure, and function*. Totowa, NJ: Humana Press.

Pinel, J. P. J. (2000). *Biopsychology* (4th ed.). Needham Heights, MA: Allyn & Bacon.

Restak, S. (1995). *Brainscapes*. New York: Hyperion.

Zigmond, M. J., Bloom, F. E. Landis, S. C. Roberts, J. L., & Squire, L. R. (1999). *Fundamentals of neuroscience*. San Diego, CA: Academic Press.

FOCUSING ON THE PHYSICAL BRAIN

Psychological scientists want to understand how the physical brain enables mind and behavior. The Harvard Brain Tissue Research Center, with a collection of over 5,000 human brains, is the largest repository of its kind in the United States, and provides specimens at no cost to brain researchers.

TIMELINE

Fourth century B.C.E.

Locating the Mind Greek physician Hippocrates describes the brain as the location of the mind. Aristotle later describes the brain as a cooling organ to dissipate excess heat produced by the heart, the location of the mind.

Second century C.E.

Galen's Anatomy Roman physician Galen rejects Aristotle's misconceptions and ascribes mental functions to the brain. Physicians and anatomists accept his writings without question for the next fourteen centuries.

1650s

Mind-Body Dualism French philosopher René Descartes proposes a dualistic theory of the mind and body in which the body's movements are controlled by mechanical reflexes interacting with a nonphysical soul located in the brain's pineal gland.

1800s

Phrenology German physiologist Franz Joseph Gall develops phrenology, arguing that personality traits and mental abilities are housed in distinct areas of the brain, and can be assessed by measuring the external dimensions of the skull.

The Brain

4

OUTLINING THE PRINCIPLES

HOW HAVE OUR VIEWS OF THE BRAIN EVOLVED?

The Link Between Mind and Brain Has Been Suspected
for Centuries

Phrenologists Introduced a Pseudoscience
of Localization

Speech Impairment Provided the First Modern
Localizations

The Brain Is Now Known to Be Specialized

WHAT ARE THE BASIC BRAIN STRUCTURES AND THEIR FUNCTIONS?

The Spinal Cord Is Capable of Autonomous Function

The Brainstem Houses the Basic Programs of Survival

The Cerebellum Is Essential for Movement

The Hypothalamus Controls Elemental Bodily Functions
and Drives

The Cerebral Hemispheres Underlie Higher Cognition,
Memory, and Emotion

HOW IS THE BRAIN DIVIDED?

The Hemispheres Can Be Separated

The Seperate Hemispheres Can Be Tested

The Hemispheres Are Specialized

HOW DOES THE BRAIN CHANGE?

The Interplay of Genes and the Environment Wires
the Brain

The Brain Rewires Itself Throughout Life

The Brain Can Recover from Injury

CONCLUSION

FURTHER READINGS

It was the 1940s, and a patient lay on the operating table, fully conscious, with part of her skull temporarily removed to expose the surface of her brain. Her surgeon at the Montreal Neurological Institute, Dr. Wilder Penfield, delicately touched a small electrode to her brain, and the patient announced that she had the sudden experience *"of being in her kitchen listening to the voice of her little boy who was playing outside in the yard. She was aware of the neighborhood noises, such as passing motor cars, and understood that might mean danger to him."*

The patient suffered from *epilepsy*, the debilitating affliction in which *seizures*, uncontrolled "storms" of electrical activity, begin in some part of the brain and spread throughout much of it, often causing violent, life-threatening convulsions of the entire body. As a last resort, she had agreed to undergo surgery to try to find and remove the part of her brain in which the seizures began.

Penfield was electrically stimulating points on the surface of her brain in an effort to set off the beginning of a seizure, to determine exactly which part of the brain should be excised (Figure 4.1). He was also mapping out the functions of specific brain areas to determine which ones could be removed without damaging the patient's ability to speak. The small electric current interfered with the local area of brain tissue that it flowed through, temporarily deactivating it. If the patient stopped speaking during one of these stimulations, Penfield would know that that area was vital to speech and should not be removed.

Interestingly, the current, while *deactivating* the region in the immediate vicinity of the electrode, *reactivated* more distant brain regions that were connected to neurons in the stimulated area. The result was the vivid reawakening of specific memories in the patient.

Although Penfield repeated this demonstration many times, it is now believed that the specific memory phenomena may have resulted from the patients' disorders, thus not necessarily reflecting a normal brain. However, electrical inductions of experiences, sensations, movements, emotions, and even beliefs, has been reproduced countless times since then. These physical reawakenings of mental events

RESEARCH QUESTIONS ?.?.? for Studying the Brain

How does the brain enable mind?

Is function distributed throughout the brain or specialized in different regions?

Does each half of the brain possess the same capacities?

Are there critical periods during brain development?

Does the brain rewire itself during learning, aging, and repair?

1950s

Recording Neurons David Hubel and Torsten Wiesel make the first recordings from individual neurons in the cerebral cortex, characterizing the response properties of neurons in a cat's primary visual cortex using visual displays.

1953

Patient H.M. During bilateral surgical removal of his hippocampus, Patient H.M. loses all ability to retain new memories for events. Studied by Brenda Milner, H.M. becomes one of the classic case studies of neuropsychology.

1960s

Split-Brains American psychobiologist Roger Sperry and his student Michael Gazzaniga conduct research on patients who have had their cerebral hemispheres disconnected to treat epilepsy. They find that the hemispheres can function independently.

1980s

Brain Imaging Invention of PET imaging and functional MRI enable visualization of the activity of the working human brain.

1990s

Gene Manipulation Molecular biology comes of age, bringing powerful new tools such as transgenic mice and molecular indicators of neuronal activity to bear on the problems of the brain.

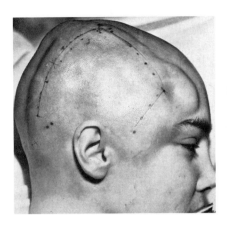 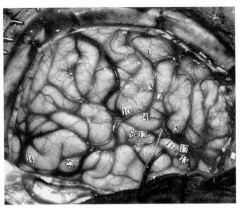

4.1 One of Wilder Penfield's patients undergoing direct stimulation of the brain. Left: the patient immediately before surgery. A local anesthetic has been applied to her scalp; Penfield's patients remained fully conscious throughout the procedures. Right: the exposed surface of her cortex. Numbered tags denote electrically stimulated locations.

demonstrate the physical nature of the mind. Far from existing as an incomprehensible substance distinct from the physical world, the mind is very much a part of it, consisting of the electrical and chemical activity of one of our bodily organs: the brain.

The previous chapter outlined the biological foundations of the nervous system. Mental activities and behaviors are produced by biological processes within the brain, such as the action of nerve cells and associated chemical reactions. This chapter focuses on how the physical brain enables mind and behavior. Scholars have disagreed for centuries about whether psychological processes are located in specific parts of the brain or distributed throughout the brain. This debate continued for so long, in part, because researchers did not have methods for studying ongoing mental activity in the working brain. The invention of brain-imaging methods in the late 1980s changed that swiftly and dramatically. Since that time there has been an explosion of research, cutting across various levels of analysis, linking specific brain areas with particular behaviors and mental processes. This chapter examines what is known about how the brain works. Beginning with an historical view of brain function and dysfunction, which serves as an excellent example of how psychological science has been built on cumulative principles, we will then discuss the major structures and regions of the brain, with an emphasis on the psychological functions associated with each area.

HOW HAVE OUR VIEWS OF THE BRAIN EVOLVED?

It has long been recognized that the brain has some involvement with the mind. At locations from France to Peru, scientists have found prehistoric skulls with manmade holes in the *cranium*, the bony structure that protects the brain. Many of these holes display evidence of healing, indicating that the recipient survived for extended periods after the procedure. The purpose of such surgery, known as *trepanning*, is unknown, but it suggests that ancient peoples ascribed some significance to the brain. In parts of Africa and the Pacific, various groups continued such practices into the twentieth century as treatment for epilepsy, headaches, and, most notably, insanity. It may be that prehistoric trepanning was similarly

RESEARCH QUESTION

How does the brain enable mind?

motivated by notions of a mind-brain connection. In this section we will examine how scholars have viewed this connection through the years.

THE LINK BETWEEN MIND AND BRAIN HAS BEEN SUSPECTED FOR CENTURIES

The brain wasn't always recognized as the home of the mind. The Egyptians, for example, viewed the heart as the seat of the soul; they elaborately embalmed the hearts of their deceased, but the brains they simply threw away. The heart was to be weighed in the afterlife to determine the deceased's fate. The peoples of ancient India and China held similar misconceptions.

In the questioning climate of Greece, however, some alternative ideas flourished. The physician Hippocrates (c. 460–c. 377 B.C.E.) and his followers demonstrated a remarkably modern view in their collective work, the *Corpus Hippocraticum:* "Some people say that the heart is the organ with which we think and that it feels pain and anxiety. But it is not so. Men ought to know that from the brain and from the brain only arise our pleasures, joys, laughter, and tears. Through it, in particular, we think, see, hear and distinguish the ugly from the beautiful, the bad from the good, the pleasant from the unpleasant." Notably, Hippocrates' opinions were shaped in part by his observations of patients with epilepsy. He displayed considerable insight into their condition, writing that it was caused by the brain "when it is not normal."

However, the philosopher Aristotle (384–322 B.C.E.) thought that the heart was the home of the mind. The brain, he espoused, served a cooling function, radiating excess heat produced by the mental exertions of the heart.

It is instructive that Hippocrates was so much closer to the mark than Aristotle. Throughout history, those who have directly witnessed the results of brain injury have been much more accurate in their assessment of the nature of mind than those who just thought about it. For example, the Roman physician Galen (130–200 C.E.), having served as a surgeon to gladiators, vociferously argued for the brain's mental role. However, he believed that the mind resided in the fluid-filled pockets in the middle of the brain and controlled the body by means of ethereal energies. Evidently, ascribing mind to the activity of physical tissue was too great a leap. The French philosopher René Descartes (1596–1650) took a similar tack, arguing that humans have both a physical body and a nonphysical soul (as discussed in Chapter 1). He posited the pineal gland as the seat of the soul; we now know that the pineal gland is mostly involved in regulating the day/night cycle.

PHRENOLOGISTS INTRODUCED A PSEUDOSCIENCE OF LOCALIZATION

Galen's belief in an ethereal substance in the brain called the mind swayed many in the centuries that followed him. Eventually, however, the idea was suggested that not only might the flesh of the brain itself contain mind, but that the mind might not be a unified entity and instead has many components, which might be located in different parts of the brain. This idea was most successfully propounded by Franz Joseph Gall (1758–1828) and Johann Spurzheim (1776–1832), the founders of **phrenology**, the practice of assessing personality traits and mental abilities by measuring bumps on the skull (Figure 4.2).

At the age of nine, Gall noticed that a classmate with bulging eyes had a superior memory. Gall later parlayed this observation into a career, attributing differ-

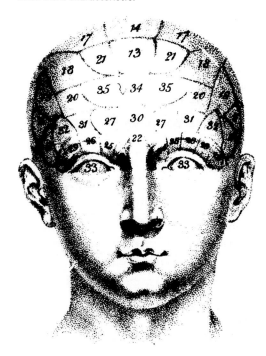

4.2 One of Johann Spurzheim's phrenological maps of the skull. Each numbered region corresponded to a different characteristic.

ent qualities to different regions of the *cerebral cortex*, the convoluted outermost layer that dwarfs the rest of the brain. In this, he was accurate. Furthermore, he correctly noted that the cortex is connected to the spinal cord and can therefore control movement. Yet he went wrong in a couple of ways. The first was the belief that mental characteristics were expressed in the external anatomy of the skull. The second was his ascription of extremely refined psychological attributes to the different regions. Gall and Spurzheim developed elaborate maps of the surface of the skull, indicating the locations of such characteristics as "destructiveness," "acquisitiveness," and "veneration."

It should be noted that the problem with phrenology was not so much that the ideas underlying it were bad, but that its proponents were unwilling to subject them to experimental verification. Phrenology eventually proliferated into absurd quackery and prompted a well-deserved but equally misguided backlash. Marie-Jean-Pierre Flourens (1794–1867), a powerful French scientist, led the charge with an influential theory that all parts of the cortex contributed equally to all mental abilities, a concept known as *equipotentiality*. His methods were far more scientific than Gall's; he systematically removed different parts of animals' brains and observed their subsequent behavior. However, his reliance on experimenting with birds and amphibians caused him to come to erroneous conclusions. Since then, with more sophisticated observation, using the techniques that Flourens himself advocated, the phrenologists' idea of *functional localization* has been accepted as essentially correct.

In the midst of this debate, a construction accident in New England provided a vivid example of selective mental impairment following brain damage. This case is described in "Studying the Mind: Phineas Gage."

SPEECH IMPAIRMENT PROVIDED THE FIRST MODERN LOCALIZATIONS

The controversy between those favoring equipotentiality of the brain and the phrenologists who favored functional localization continued to rage. Jean-Baptiste Bouillard (1796–1881) was influenced by the phrenologists but rejected their skull-measuring methodology; he argued on the basis of clinical observations and animal lesion studies that the centers for speech and vocalization were located in the front of the brain. In a crude experiment typical of the day, he pierced the front of a dog's brain from one side to the other with a pole and found that it regained most of its capacities but lost the ability to bark. In 1848, having accumulated what he clearly viewed as a preponderance of evidence, he laid out the following challenge: "Herewith I offer 500 francs to anyone who will provide me with an example of a deep lesion of the anterior [front] lobules of the brain without a lesion of speech." An example was in fact subsequently provided, and the money duly collected in 1865.

It was in this climate that one of the most famous case studies in neurology was made. In 1861, a Monsieur Leborgne, on his last legs after decades of hospitalization and unable to say anything but the single word "tan," was checked into the surgical ward of the respected physician Paul Broca (1824–1880) and died six days later. Broca examined the patient's brain and found a large lesion from a **stroke**—brain damage caused by a blocked blood vessel—on the left side of the brain, toward the front (Figure 4.3). His finding caused a sensation. This left frontal region became known as **Broca's area**,

phrenology An early method of assessing personality traits and mental abilities by measuring bumps on the skull.

stroke Brain damage caused by a blocked blood vessel.

Broca's area The left frontal region of the brain that is crucial to the production of language.

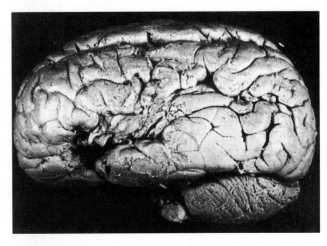

4.3 Monsieur Leborgne's ("Tan's") brain studied by Paul Broca. Broca identified the lesioned area as crucial for speech production.

Studying the Mind

PHINEAS GAGE

Perhaps the most famous historical example of brain damage is the case of Phineas Gage. In 1848, Gage was a 25-year-old foreman on the construction of Vermont's Rutland and Burlington Railroad. One day he dropped his tamping iron on a rock, which ignited some blasting powder. The resulting explosion drove the iron rod—over a yard long and an inch in diameter—into his cheek, through his frontal lobes, and out through the top of his head (Figure 4.4). Gage was still conscious as he was hurried back to town on a cart. Able to walk, with assistance, upstairs to his hotel bed, he wryly remarked to the awaiting physician, "Doctor, here is business enough for you" and said he expected to return to work in a few days. In fact, Gage lapsed into a stupor for two weeks. His condition steadily improved subsequently, though, and he recovered remarkably well.

Unfortunately, the accident had caused some personality changes. Whereas before Gage had been regarded by his employers as "the most efficient and capable" of workers, the new Gage was not. As one of his doctors later wrote: "The equilibrium or balance, so to speak, between his intellectual faculties and animal propensities seems to have been destroyed. He is fitful, irreverent, indulging at times in the grossest profanity . . . impatient of restraint or advice when it conflicts with his desires . . . A child in his intellectual capacity and manifestations, he has the animal passions of a strong man." In sum, Gage was "no longer Gage."

Unable to get his foreman's job back, Gage exhibited himself in various New England towns and at the New York Museum (owned by P. T. Barnum), worked in a stable in New Hampshire, and drove coaches and tended horses in Chile. After a decade, his health began to decline, and in 1860 he began to have epileptic seizures and died a few months later.

Gage's recovery was initially used by opponents of phrenology to

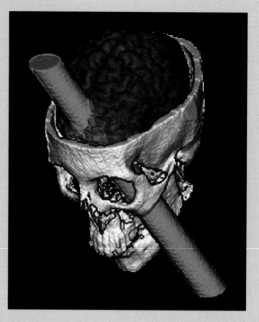

4.4 A computer-generated model of Phineas Gage's skull, with the iron rod that traveled through his head. Analysis of the skull revealed which brain areas had been damaged.

argue for the uniformity of the brain, and the ability of the remaining brain to take over the work of the damaged tissue. His psychological impairments, however, were eventually recognized by the medical community as extremely significant, and they provided the basis for the first modern theories of the roles of the front part of the brain (the *prefrontal cortex*) in personality and self-control.

and it has since been repeatedly confirmed to be crucial for the production of language. This was the first of the nineteenth-century localizations to have survived the test of time.

THE BRAIN IS NOW KNOWN TO BE SPECIALIZED

It is now known that the brain's surface, far from being a uniform structure, is a patchwork of many highly specialized areas. However, instead of being neatly divided into regions corresponding to complex personality traits, as the phrenologists argued, brain areas are actually specialized for far more rudimentary components of perception, behavior, and mental life. A large area of the brain is devoted to different aspects of vision, for example, and another to generating rudimentary movements.

However, the notion that the brain, or at least the *cerebral cortex*, is uniform persisted well into the twentieth century. In the 1920s, physiologist Karl Lashley trained rats to run mazes and then systematically removed pieces of their brains in an effort to determine the location of their maze-navigating memories. To his

Is function distributed throughout the brain or specialized in different regions?

dismay, he found that the rats seemed simply to do worse on the maze in proportion to the amount of brain removed, no matter where the tissue was located. Lashley therefore proposed a "**law of mass action**": that the cortex is basically undifferentiated and participates in all thought equally. He felt that removing pieces of rat cortex merely caused the rat to have less brain power. It is now quite clear, however, that a more likely explanation for his findings is that the rats were able to navigate the mazes by multiple means: the ones that had lost their sight could do it using smell, for example, and vice versa. A similar misconception is embodied in the common myth that we use only a small percentage, say 10 percent, of our brains, with the implication that we would be either smarter or more creative if we used more of the brain, or no worse off if we had less of it. This is absolutely incorrect. Since brain regions are highly specialized, activity in an area at an inappropriate time would be disastrous. Furthermore, the loss of even a small brain region causes the loss of that brain region's function. To some extent we can recover from brain damage, but most often losing a part of the brain leads to deficits, many of which are obvious.

Imaging the brain   Some of the clearest views of the distribution of mental functions come from *functional brain imaging*, the use of technology to generate "maps" of the human brain in action. We will discuss several varieties of these technologies, each with its own relative advantages.

Electroencephalography, or **EEG**, uses electrodes placed on the scalp to "listen to" the electrical activity of the brain region underneath (Figure 4.5). First used in 1929, this is the oldest imaging technique. Using many electrodes, a crude map of brain activity can be obtained. By recording during the performance of various psychological tasks, the researcher can link the relative contributions of different points beneath the skull to those psychological tasks. The real advantage of EEG and its cousin, **magnetoencephalography**, or **MEG** (which records magnetic fields), is not *spatial* but *temporal* resolution; that is, while it is difficult to determine exactly *where* an electrical event comes from, it is very easy to determine exactly *when* it happens. Thus EEG and MEG produce maps of approximate points of origin of the various electrical signals, the relative timing of which is known very well (Figure 4.6). They therefore give insight into how the brain is processing information, on the basis of what regions are activated and when.

Positron emission tomography, or **PET**, was developed in the late 1980s. It is the computer-aided reconstruction of the brain's metabolic activity through the use of a harmless radioactive substance injected into the bloodstream. The research participant lies in a special scanner that detects the radiation, and a three-dimensional map of the density of radioactivity within the participant's brain is produced (Figure 4.7). This is useful because as the brain performs a mental task, blood flow increases to the most active regions, leading to more emitted radiation. The amount of radioactivity emitted by a brain region roughly corresponds to the amount of electrical activity in the local neurons. By scanning participants as they perform some psychological task (for example, reading aloud words on a screen), researchers obtain a map of brain metabolic activity during the task. However, since the entire brain is extremely metabolically active all of the time, scans must also be made while the participant performs another, closely related task (for example, saying words that are antonyms of the words on the screen). By subtracting one image from the other, experimenters obtain a "difference image"

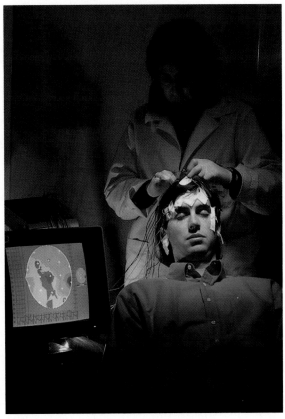

4.5 A subject wearing the apparatus used in EEG.

law of mass action   Karl Lashley's proposition that the cortex is basically undifferentiated and participates equally in psychological activity.

electroencephalography (EEG)   A method for measuring the electrical activity of the brain. Electrodes placed on the scalp are able to detect weak electrical signals produced by neural activity.

magnetoencephalography (MEG)   A technique for examining neural activity that records magnetic fields.

positron emission tomography (PET)   A method of brain imaging that assesses metabolic activity by use of a radioactive substance injected into the bloodstream.

magnetic resonance imaging (MRI)
A method of brain imaging that produces high quality images of the brain.

functional magnetic resonance imaging (fMRI) An imaging technique used to examine changes in the activity of the working human brain.

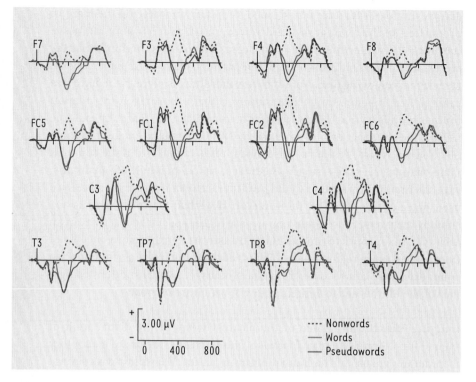

4.6 Electrical activity at different points on the surface of a subject's scalp during exposure to different stimuli. A specific type of response (called the N350) was largest at location T3, on the left temporal hemisphere. This effect occurred only for words or pseudowords, but not for nonwords (strings of consonants).

of which brain regions are most active during the task in question. In this way, regions of the brain can be correlated with specific mental activities.

Magnetic resonance imaging, or **MRI**, is the newest and perhaps most powerful of imaging techniques. It relies on the fact that hydrogen nuclei, also known as *protons*, a major component of water and fat, and therefore of humans, behave like tiny magnets. In MRI, a research participant lies in a scanner that produces a powerful magnetic field, which is not dangerous, but which causes the protons in the participant's body to tend to line up with it, just as a magnetized needle turns to point north. When a pulse of radio waves is delivered, hydrogen nuclei briefly align to a different orientation. As they return to the direction of the MRI scanner, energy is released in the form of radio waves that can be picked up by antennae close to the participant's head. Since the hydrogen nuclei in fat and water give up this energy differently, research can determine the physical location of the protons for different tissues, which results in a high-resolution image of the brain (Figure 4.8).

4.7 A positron emission tomography (PET) scan of blood flow in a subject's brain under different conditions.

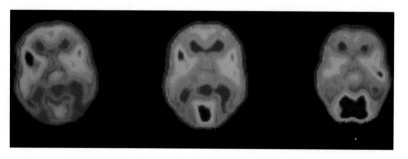

MRI images are extraordinarily valuable for determining the location of brain damage, for example, but they can be even more profitable when used to create an image of the working brain. This is what **functional magnetic resonance imaging**, or **fMRI**, can do; like PET, it makes use of the brain's blood flow to map its activity, scanning the participant during the performance of several tasks. Ideally the tasks differ in only one way, which reflects the particular mental function

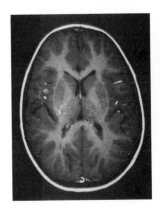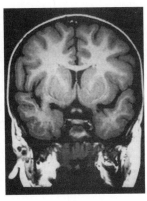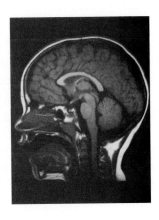

4.8 Magnetic resonance imaging (MRI) provides very high quality images of intact human brains.

of interest. The images are then compared to examine differences in blood flow and therefore brain activity. This produces relatively high-resolution maps of neural activity that can then be superimposed on the anatomical scans to illuminate what brain regions are active during the different tasks (Figure 4.9). All of these brain-imaging techniques make it abundantly clear that the brain is not highly uniform, but rather that specific brain regions are active during different mental functions.

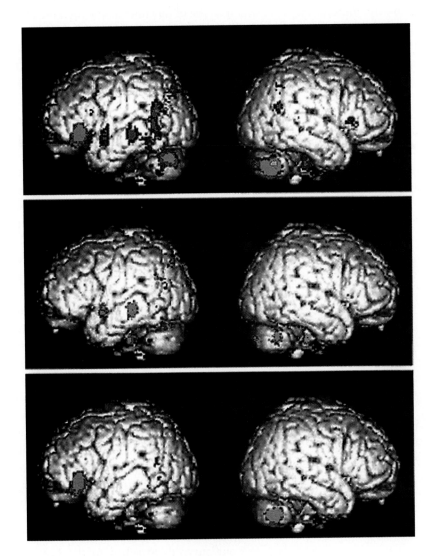

4.9 Activity maps showing changes in blood oxygenation, obtained by functional magnetic resonance imaging (fMRI) while the subject performed some task (and subtracted from another "control" image), superimposed on higher-resolution MRI images taken of the same brain. This allows precise determination of which brain areas are active during different mental activities.

How Have Our Views of the Brain Evolved?

Although the seat of the mind has been ascribed to various body parts, notably the heart, the notion that the brain is somehow involved with the mind is an old one. An issue that captivated early scholars was whether the brain acted as a whole in producing mental experience, or whether there was specialization of function for different brain regions. Examination of the results of head injuries has historically been the most illuminating approach, as in the finding that Broca's area is important for speech. Although the idea of localization of mental function within the nervous system initially reached an absurd apex in phrenology, the resulting discredit was soon overcome. Modern functional brain imaging provides compelling evidence for the specialization of function within the brain.

WHAT ARE THE BASIC BRAIN STRUCTURES AND THEIR FUNCTIONS?

The brain is best viewed as a collection of interacting neuronal circuits that have accumulated and developed throughout human evolution. In this section, we explore how the mind is adaptive, which is one of our four major themes. The first nervous systems were probably little more than a few specialized cells with the capacity for electrical signaling. But, through the process of adapting to the environment, the brain has evolved specialized mechanisms to regulate breathing, food intake, sexual behavior, and bodily fluids, as well as sensory systems to aid in navigation and assist in recognizing friends and foes.

As discussed in Chapter 3, the nervous system is involved in almost every aspect of an organism's maintenance, regulation, and behavior. It is composed of a vast number of interacting brain circuits ranging from those controlling the contractions of the intestines, to those allowing a child to play with a dog, to those allowing college students to choose their majors. All of these are orchestrated by parts of the brain that are as different in their structure and organization as the roles they fulfill. Some of these roles have remained essentially the same throughout our evolution; the neural circuits responsible for such basics as breathing have changed correspondingly little. But although the human nervous system has a fundamental layout shared with all other vertebrates, it has developed an impressive elaboration of structures responsible for our enormous capacities for communication and thought.

Figure 4.10 shows some of the basic structures of the central nervous system. The *spinal cord*, running the length of the vertebral column, contains some basic movement programs and reflex pathways. Above the spinal cord and forming the core of the brain, the *brainstem* houses many of the raw and ancient circuits, such as the *pons* and *medulla*, that are fundamental to our survival. Attached to the back of the

4.10 The human central nervous system.

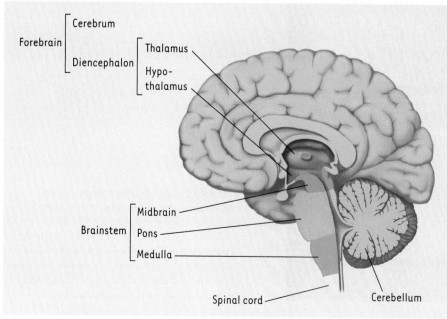

Forebrain
— Cerebrum
— Diencephalon — Thalamus, Hypothalamus

Brainstem
— Midbrain
— Pons
— Medulla

Spinal cord

Cerebellum

brainstem is the *cerebellum*, which is important for controlling movement. The cerebellum, pons, and medulla make up the *hindbrain*. The top of the brain stem, called the *midbrain*, helps integrate motor and sensory information. Above and surrounding the brainstem are the *cerebral hemispheres*, two halves of the *forebrain* that communicate extensively with the brain stem and with each other and are responsible for much of what we think of as our unique selves. The *cerebral cortex*, the prominent and rippled outermost layer of the hemispheres, enables the complex and discriminating abilities of recognition, action, and thought at which humans in particular excel. Beneath the cortex, the *basal ganglia* translate thoughts into action and, probably, more thoughts. Almost all information that gets to the cortex from the senses travels through a way station called the *thalamus*, underneath which is the *hypothalamus*, a cluster of structures vital for regulating basic drives such as hunger and thirst. Finally, the cerebral hemispheres also house the *amygdala* and *hippocampus*, structures important for emotion and memory. We will consider each of these structures in turn.

THE SPINAL CORD IS CAPABLE OF AUTONOMOUS FUNCTION

The **spinal cord** is a rope of neural tissue that runs inside the hollows of the vertebrae, from just above the pelvis up into the base of the skull (Figure 4.11). It is segmented, with each segment marked by its own pair of spinal nerves emerging from the sides of the cord and communicating information to and from the rest of the body. In cross section, the cord is seen to be composed of two distinct tissue types: the **gray matter**, which is dominated by the cell bodies of neurons, and the **white matter**, which consists mostly of axons and the fatty sheaths that surround them. Gray and white matter are clearly distinguishable throughout the brain as well. Sensory information from the body enters the spinal cord and is passed up to the brain. However, as well as relaying information, the spinal cord is able to take action on its own.

Stretch reflex The spinal cord handles one of the simplest behaviors, the *spinal reflex*. This is the conversion of sensation into action by a handful of neurons and the connections between them. As an example, consider the stretch reflex. When the tendon attached to your kneecap is tapped with a rubber hammer, the leg gives a little reflexive kick. This reflex is present throughout the skeletal musculature and functions to maintain the positions of the joints under varying loads. It works by the following very simple neuronal circuit: All muscles have stretch receptors inside them to sense changes in length. These receptors are actually the dendritic tips of receptor neurons whose cell bodies are located in the spinal cord. Stretching the muscle causes the receptor neurons connected to it to fire. The receptor neurons' axons enter the spinal cord and synapse directly on motor neurons,

spinal cord Part of the central nervous system. A rope of neural tissue that runs inside the hollows of the vertebrae from just above the pelvis and into the base of the skull.

gray matter A segment of the spinal cord that is dominated by the cell bodies of neurons.

white matter A segment of the spinal cord that consists mostly of axons and the fatty sheaths.

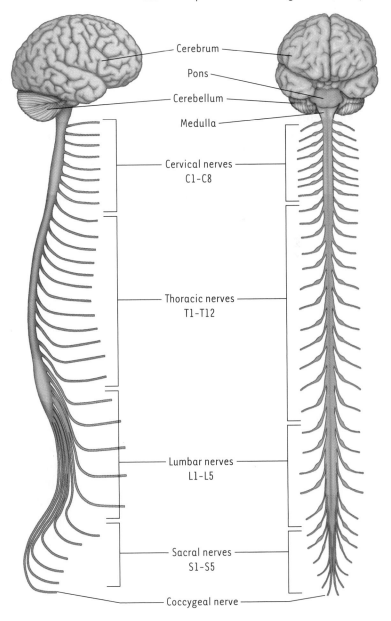

4.11 The spinal cord is organized into segments, each with a pair of nerves leading out to the body.

Cerebrum

Pons

Cerebellum

Medulla

Cervical nerves
C1-C8

Thoracic nerves
T1-T12

Lumbar nerves
L1-L5

Sacral nerves
S1-S5

Coccygeal nerve

central pattern generator A circuit that, once activated, produces a rhythmic, recurring set of movements.

brainstem A section of the bottom of the brain that houses the most basic programs of survival such as breathing, swallowing, vomiting, urination, and orgasm.

reticular formation A large network of neural tissue within the brainstem involved in behavioral arousal and sleep-wake cycles.

tectum Located at the back of the midbrain, this brain structure helps guide orientation towards sounds or moving stimuli.

cerebellum A large convoluted protuberance at the back of the brainstem that is essential for coordinated movement and balance.

hypothalamus A small brain structure that is vital for temperature regulation, emotion, sexual behavior, and motivation.

which lead back out to the same muscle. This closes the loop: stretching the muscle causes the stretch receptor neurons to fire, which causes the motor neurons to increase their firing, which contracts the muscle.

Central pattern generator The spinal cord can execute far more complicated actions than stretch reflexes. Programs for many components of behavior are wired into its circuitry, available for use by higher brain regions to achieve their aims. These components are localized: in animal experiments, electrically stimulating the segment that projects to the hind legs can produce hind leg extension, while farther up the cord stimulation can move the forelegs. The segments communicate through long axons that run vertically through several or all of them, allowing coordinated movement of the entire body.

For example, if a fish's spinal cord is surgically disconnected from the rest of its brain, the isolated spinal cord can still enable the fish to swim. It produces waves of muscular contractions that ripple down the fish's body just as in any other swimming fish. It needs to be induced to start, and this is done experimentally by application of an excitatory neurotransmitter to the neurons, but once begun it keeps going of its own accord. Similarly, a cat's spinal cord can move its legs in coordinated walking movements, even after disconnection from the brain. A circuit that, once activated, produces a rhythmic, recurring set of movements is known as a **central pattern generator**. All vertebrates, including humans, display such spinal autonomy. The headless chicken that continues to run around is a classic case.

THE BRAINSTEM HOUSES THE BASIC PROGRAMS OF SURVIVAL

The spinal cord continues up into base of the skull, thickening and becoming more complex as it transforms into the **brainstem**, which is made up of the hindbrain and midbrain. This is the organism's neural core, housing the most basic programs of survival, such as breathing, swallowing, vomiting, urination, and orgasm. Since the brainstem is also simply the spinal cord continued up into the head, it performs functions for the head similar to those that the spinal cord performs for the rest of the body. A whole complement of reflexes is housed here, analogous to the spinal reflexes; gagging is one example. Just as the spinal cord has nerves that carry information to and from the skin and muscles of the body, the brainstem has nerves that connect it to the skin and muscles of the head, as well as to the specialized sense organs of the head such as eyes and ears. These nerves each have distinct, dedicated clumps of cells within the brainstem that handle their needs.

The brainstem uses the reflexes of the spinal cord to produce useful behavior. For example, electrically stimulating a part of the brainstem can cause an anesthetized animal (or one whose spinal cord and brainstem have been disconnected from the rest of its brain) to begin walking, very much as Wilder Penfield's stimulation of a point on the brain's surface initiated a memory in his patient. Increasing the frequency of the stimulation causes the animal to go from a walk to a trot, and increasing it still more, to a gallop. Stimulating another area will cause the animal to turn to one side.

Reticular formation The brainstem also contains networks of neurons, known collectively as the **reticular formation**, that project up into the cerebral cortex and basal ganglia and affect general arousal. The reticular formation is also involved in inducing and terminating the different stages of sleep. The autonomy of the brain stem can be dramatically illustrated by severing an animal's brain stem from the entire brain above it, including its entire cerebral cortex. Cats that receive this treatment can still walk around and direct attacks at noises; if they then find themselves holding on to food, they will eat it. Some cases have been reported of humans born without cerebral cortices, and their behaviors are extremely basic and reflexive. Such infants tend not to develop normally and also do not tend to survive.

Tectum   On the top of the midbrain sits the **tectum** (Latin, "roof"), an orienting center that receives information from the eyes, ears, and skin and swivels the animal around to face prominent stimuli. The tectum contains a topographic map of space. Attention-grabbing visual displays or noises, or a touch to the skin, activate the point on the tectum map representing that direction in space, causing the torso and neck to twist toward it and the eyes to focus on it. The tectum moves the entire organism in a coordinated response, by commanding the lesser movement centers—such as the twisting and locomoting centers elsewhere in the brain stem and the motor circuits of the eyeballs—to do its bidding. It is quite capable of performing these tasks on its own, but it is subject to descending control by higher regions, including the cerebral cortex.

THE CEREBELLUM IS ESSENTIAL FOR MOVEMENT

The **cerebellum** (Latin, "little brain") is a large protuberance connected to the back of the brain stem (Figure 4.12). Its size and convoluted surface make it look like a supplementary brain. Lesions to different parts of the cerebellum produce very different effects. Its cellular organization, however, appears to be identical throughout. This suggests that the cerebellum is performing identical operations on all of its inputs, with the different effects resulting from the differences in origin, and destination, of the information.

The cerebellum is extremely important for proper motor function. Damage to the little nodes at the very bottom causes head tilt, balance problems, and a loss of smooth compensation of eye position for movement of the head. Damage to the ridge that runs up its back affects walking. Damage to the bulging lobes on either side causes a loss of limb coordination. The most obvious role of the cerebellum is in motor learning. It seems to be "trained" by the rest of the nervous system and operates independently and unconsciously. The cerebellum allows us to ride a bicycle effortlessly while we think about what we'll have for lunch. Functional imaging, however, indicates a broader role for the cerebellum, suggesting that it may be involved in "automatic" psychological activity.

THE HYPOTHALAMUS CONTROLS ELEMENTAL BODILY FUNCTIONS AND DRIVES

The **hypothalamus** is the master regulatory structure of the brain and is indispensable to the organism's survival. It is responsible for regulating the vital functions—body temperature, circadian rhythms, blood

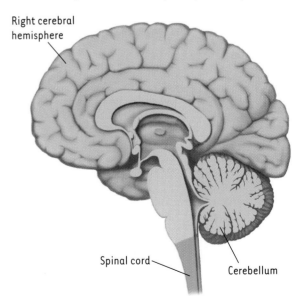

4.12 The cerebellum, at the back of the brain stem, the cerebral hemispheres, and the spinal cord.

Right cerebral hemisphere

Spinal cord

Cerebellum

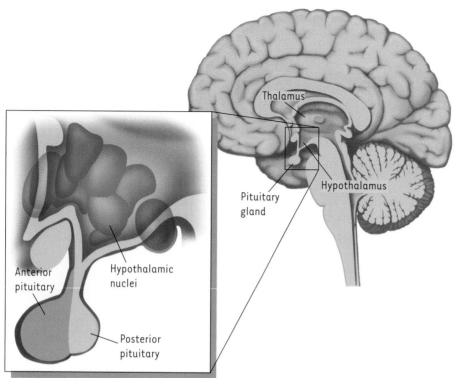

4.13 The hypothalamus and the pituitary gland, the "master gland" of the body.

pressure and glucose level—and, to these ends, impelling the organism by such fundamental drives as thirst, hunger, aggression, and lust (as will be described in Chapter 9).

The hypothalamus is one of the most vital regions of the brain. It receives input from almost everywhere and projects its influence, directly or indirectly, to almost everywhere. Through its projections to the rest of the brain, the hypothalamus induces motivational drives and the behaviors to satisfy them. Through its projections to the spinal cord, it governs much of the function of the internal organs. As discussed in Chapter 3, it controls the *pituitary gland*, the "master gland" of the body, which by releasing hormones into the bloodstream controls all other glands and governs such major processes as development, ovulation, and lactation (Figure 4.13).

The hypothalamus governs sexual and reproductive development and behavior. It is one of the only places in the human brain where clear differences exist between men and women, due to early hormonal influences during nervous system development. Female rats exposed to high levels of testosterone while in the womb develop hypothalamic organization that is more typical of males—so-called *fetal masculinization*. Differences in hypothalamic structure may influence sexual orientation. Using postmortem methods, LeVay (1991) found that the anterior hypothalamus was only half as large in homosexual men as compared to heterosexual men. In fact, the size of this area in homosexual men was comparable to its size in heterosexual women. The implications of this finding are discussed more fully in Chapter 12.

THE CEREBRAL HEMISPHERES UNDERLIE HIGHER COGNITION, MEMORY, AND EMOTION

Above and around the brain stem sits the huge *forebrain*, composed of two symmetrical **cerebral hemispheres**. This is the site of all thoughts, detailed perceptions, and consciousness . . . in short, everything that makes us human. All animals have a forebrain, but in humans it has evolved into a relatively enormous structure that enables our complex culture and communication. Each hemisphere is composed of a *thalamus*, a *hippocampus*, an *amygdala*, *basal ganglia*, and a *cerebral cortex* (Figure 4.14).

Thalamus The **thalamus** is the gateway to the forebrain: almost all incoming sensory information must go through the thalamus before reaching the cortex. The only exception to this rule is the sense of smell, the oldest and most fundamental of the senses; it has a direct route to the cortex, bypassing the thalamus.

During sleep, the thalamus shuts the gate on incoming sensations while the brain rests. The thalamus appears to play a role in attention as well.

Hippocampus and amygdala Two structures within the forebrain are essential for memory and emotions, respectively: the hippocampus (Latin, "sea horse," after its distinctive shape) and the amygdala (Latin, "almond") (Figure 4.14).

The **hippocampus** plays an important role in the storage of new memories. It seems to do this by creating new interconnections with the cerebral cortex with each new experience. We saw earlier that Karl Lashley had failed to find the location of the memory trace by removing parts of rats' cerebral cortices. Had he damaged their hippocampal formations as well, his results would have been quite different.

The **amygdala**, located immediately in front of the hippocampus, serves a vital role in learning to associate things in the world with emotional responses: a new food with its tastiness, for example. To this end, its connections with the cerebral cortex and the hypothalamus allow it to supplement the more primitive emotional pathways with new associations. The amygdala thus enables the organism to overrule instinctive responses by connecting the cortex's memories of things to the emotions they engender. The amygdala also intensifies memory during times of emotional arousal. A frightening experience can be seared into our memories for life.

The amygdala plays a special role in responding to stimuli that elicit fear. Affective processing of frightening stimuli in the amygdala is a hard-wired circuit that has developed over the course of evolution to protect animals from danger. Finally, the amygdala is also involved in evaluating the emotional significance of facial expressions. Studies using fMRI have found that the amygdala activates especially strongly in response to fearful faces.

The basal ganglia The **basal ganglia** are a system of subcortical structures crucial for planning and producing movement. They receive input from the entire cerebral cortex and project to the motor centers of the brain stem and, via the thalamus, back to the cortex's motor-planning area. Damage to the basal ganglia can produce symptoms ranging from the tremors and rigidity of Parkinson's disease to the uncontrollable jerky movements of Huntington's disease. There is evidence that damage can impair the learning of movements as well, because the basal ganglia may be involved in the learning of habits, such as automatically looking for cars before you cross the street. Indeed, Parkinson's patients have trouble learning new tasks that require routine actions.

The basal ganglia may also have a role in producing nonverbal actions and understanding the nonverbal behaviors of other people (Lieberman, 2000). Patients with damage to the basal ganglia often have difficulty producing emotional facial expressions or speaking in an emotional fashion. They also have trouble understanding the emotions expressed in others' faces.

Cerebral cortex The **cerebral cortex** is the outer layer of the cerebral hemispheres. In humans it is relatively enormous—the size of a sheet of newspaper—

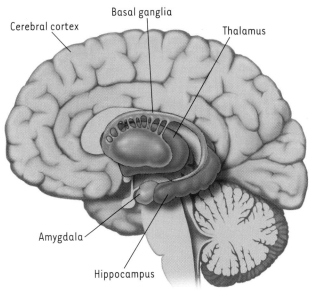

4.14 One of the two cerebral hemispheres, containing the thalamus, hippocampal formation, amygdala, basal ganglia, and cerebral cortex.

cerebral hemispheres The left and right half of the forebrain connected by the corpus collosum.

thalamus The gateway to the brain that receives almost all incoming sensory information before it reaches the cortex.

hippocampus A brain structure important for the formation of certain types of memory.

amygdala A brain structure that serves a vital role in learning to associate things in the world with emotional responses and for processing emotional information.

basal ganglia A system of subcortical structures that are important for the initiation of planned movement.

cerebral cortex The outer layer of brain tissue that forms the convoluted surface of the brain.

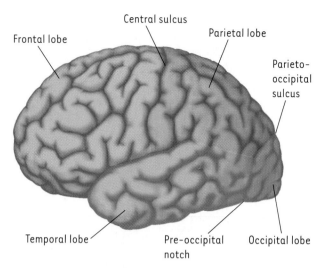

4.15 The lobes of the cerebral hemispheres: parietal, occipital, temporal, and frontal.

occipital lobes A region of the cerebral cortex at the back of the brain that is important for vision.

primary visual cortex The largest area in the occipital lobe, where the thalamus projects the image.

parietal lobes A region of the cerebral cortex lying in front of the occipital lobes and behind the frontal lobes that is important for the sense of touch and the spatial layout of an environment.

temporal lobes The lower region of the cerebral cortex that is important for processing auditory information and also for memory.

primary auditory cortex The region of the temporal lobe concerned with hearing.

and convoluted so as to fit within the skull. The cortex supplements the many functions of the brain stem, allowing us to learn fine distinctions and intricate combinations of attributes of the outside world, as well as enabling complex behaviors and conferring the ability to *think* before we act. Each hemisphere has four "lobes": the *occipital, parietal, temporal,* and *frontal* lobes (Figure 4.15). The two hemispheres are connected by a massive bridge of millions of axons, called the *corpus callosum.*

The **occipital lobe** is almost exclusively devoted to the sense of vision. It is divided into a multitude of different visual areas, of which by far the largest is the **primary visual cortex**. This is the major destination for visual information. Typically for the cerebral cortex, the information is *topographically mapped*, or represented in a way that preserves spatial relationships: that is, the visual image, relayed from the eye through the thalamus, is "projected" more or less faithfully onto the primary visual cortex. Two objects near to each other in a visual image, then, will activate populations of neurons that are near to each other in the primary visual cortex. This is another way of saying that nearby neurons in the cortex tend to have similar jobs. Each hemisphere takes half of the information: the left hemisphere gets the information from the right side of the visual world, the right hemisphere gets that coming from the left side (Figure 4.16). Surrounding the primary visual cortex is a patchwork of secondary visual areas that process various attributes of the visual image, such as its color, motion, and forms.

The **parietal lobe** is partially devoted to the sense of touch: it contains the *primary somatosensory* (Greek, "bodily sense") *cortex*, a strip running from the top of the brain down the side. Again, the labor is divided between the left and right cerebral hemispheres: the left hemisphere receives touch information from the right side of the body; the right hemisphere receives information from the left side of the body. This information is also represented in a topographic map: neurons that respond to sensations on the fingers are near ones that respond to sensations on the palm, and so on. The result is a distorted representation of the entire body covering the primary somatosensory area: the so-called *somatosensory homunculus* (Greek, "little man"; Figure 4.17). The homunculus is distorted because the more sensitive areas of the body, such as the face and fingers, have much more cortical area devoted to them. Similarly, in the primary visual cortex, the center of gaze is represented by a much larger cortical area than are regions in the peripheral visual field.

The parietal cortex is also very important for perceiving the spatial layout of the environment and for effectively moving through it. See "Crossing the Levels of Analysis: Spatial Cognition" for details.

The **temporal lobes** contain the **primary auditory cortex**, an area for hearing analogous to the primary visual and somatosensory cortices, as well as secondary auditory areas that further process what we hear, including, in the left hemisphere, the decoding of words and sentences. The temporal lobes also contain more specialized visual areas for recognizing detailed objects such as faces. Relatedly, the temporal lobes are critical for memory, containing the hippocampal formation and amygdala, discussed earlier; it was the temporal lobes that Dr. Wilder Penfield electrically stimulated to reawaken his patients' past experiences.

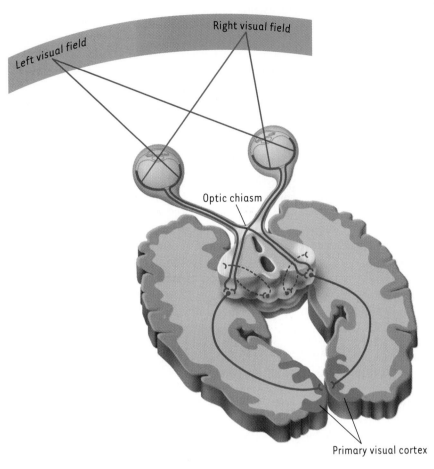

4.16 Input from the eyes is segregated: light coming from the left side goes to the right hemisphere, that coming from the right side goes to the left hemisphere.

frontal lobes The region at the front of the cerebral cortex concerned with planning and movement.

primary motor cortex The region of the frontal lobe concerned with movement.

prefrontal cortex A region of the frontal lobes, especially prominent in humans, important for attention, working memory, decision making, appropriate social behavior, and personality.

The **frontal lobes** are essential for planning and movement. The rearmost portion of the frontal lobes is the **primary motor cortex**. Instead of responding to sensations coming from the body, though, the primary motor cortices send information to it: they project directly to the spinal cord to move the muscles of the body. Just as for the sensory areas, the motor cortex's responsibilities are divided down the middle of the body: the left hemisphere controls the right arm, for example, while the right hemisphere controls the left arm. The primary motor cortex also is supplemented by several auxiliary motor areas responsible for more complex movements.

The rest of the frontal lobes, not directly responsible for movement, is collectively termed the **prefrontal cortex**. The prefrontal cortex, occupying about 30 percent of the brain in humans, is indispensable for rational, directed activity. Parts of the prefrontal cortex are responsible for directing and maintaining attention, keeping ideas in mind while distractions bombard us from the outside world, and developing plans and acting on them. The prefrontal cortex is critical for interpreting social cues and behaving in a socially appropriate manner. The underside and middle surfaces of the prefrontal cortex govern many interpersonal and emotional behaviors. People with damage to the prefrontal cortex

4.17 The somatosensory "homunculus." The cortical representation of the body surface is organized in a strip that runs down the side of the brain. Connected areas of the body tend to be represented next to each other in the cortex, and more sensitive skin regions have more cortical area devoted to them.

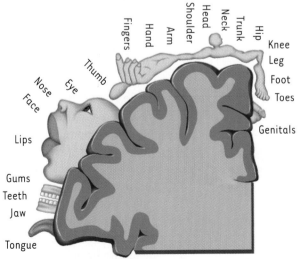

Somatosensory cortex

Crossing the Levels of Analysis

SPATIAL COGNITION

One of the most fundamental jobs of the mind is to represent the spatial relationships between ourselves and objects around us. It has become clear that this is a specialty of the cerebral cortex's parietal lobe. Using a variety of techniques, neuroscientists such as Richard Andersen at CalTech are piecing together how the brain deals with space.

Electrical recording from neurons in the brains of monkeys has provided some of the most valuable insight. Typically, a monkey is trained to perform a task, and then a tiny recording electrode is inserted into its brain to "listen to" the electrical activity of nearby neurons as the monkey performs the task. The results, often surprising, indicate the roles of single neurons in the computations necessary to do the job. Neurons in one area of the parietal lobe have been found to fire only when a visual stimulus appears in one particular location in space, and even then only if the monkey intends to move its eyes to focus on that location. Similarly, a nearby area of the parietal lobe has been found in which neurons again respond only to a visual stimulus at a certain point in space, but this time only if the monkey intends to *reach* toward that point with its arm! The crucial role evidently played in both cases by the *intention to move* indicates that the parietal lobes are critical for allowing us to navigate smoothly through the world. Such experiments allow detailed understanding of how the brain breaks down these computations, information that could not be gained by simply studying humans.

Functional brain imaging provides a high-level look at the activity of the whole brain as it performs spatial tasks. This can illuminate the interaction between brain regions. Maurizio Corbetta and his colleagues at the Washington University School of Medicine used functional magnetic resonance imaging to scan participants viewing a display of moving colored blobs. Some participants were asked to pay attention to the blobs' colors; others had to attend to the blobs' directions of motion; others had to attend to the blobs' shapes. The results showed that different brain regions became active during the different conditions: the parietal lobes became more active when the participants were attending to the blobs' shapes, but not to their colors or motion. Thus, functional imaging reveals that focusing on one aspect of the objects inhibits the brain regions responsible for thinking about their other attributes.

The study of patients with brain injuries shows what can happen when some of the computational components of spatial cognition are missing. A quite common result of a stroke or other damage to the right hemisphere is what is called *hemineglect*; patients' failure to notice anything on their left side. If two objects are held up before them, they will see only the one on the right. Asked to draw a simple object, they will draw only its right half (Figure 4.18). Looking in a mirror, such patients will shave or put makeup on the right side of their face only, not noticing the left side at all. In *The Man Who Mistook His Wife for a Hat,* neurologist Oliver Sacks describes a stroke patient who developed a novel strategy for dealing with her neglect

often are easily distracted and engage in improper social behavior, such as acting on their sexual impulses in inappropriate situations. It is as if these people are oblivious to how they are being evaluated by others. We have already encountered the case of Phineas Gage, the most famous patient with prefrontal damage. In the early part of the twentieth century, deliberately damaging the frontal lobes was established as a means of treating mental patients.

What Are the Basic Brain Structures and Their Functions?

The different parts of the nervous system all have essential roles. The spinal cord is involved in basic movement and reflexes. The brain stem serves survival functions, such as breathing and heart rate. At the back of the brain stem is the cerebellum, a mindless workhorse that learns routine habits of movement and maybe thought. The midbrain integrates motor and sensory information. Beneath the cortex, the thalamus serves as a way station through which sensory information travels; the hypothalamus regulates bodily systems and controls the hormonal system; the basal ganglia aid in motor planning and habit learning; the hippocampus is involved in memory; and the amygdala influences emotional states, especially fear. Finally, the cerebral cortex is the outer surface of the brain, divided into occipital, parietal, temporal, and frontal lobes. Each lobe serves specific functions; the frontal lobe is essential for higher-level thought and social behavior.

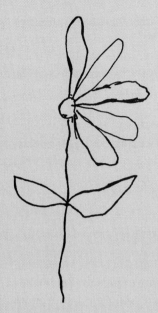

4.18 A drawing made by a neglect patient, omitting the left side of the flower.

at mealtimes. Finding herself hungry after having eaten only the right half of her meal, she would simply rotate her wheelchair around to the right—rotating left was literally unimaginable—until she had undergone almost a complete rotation and the remaining food came into view on her right-hand side. Thus focused on the previously unnoticed food, she would eat as much of it as she could see: of course, only the right half. She would continue to pivot around and eat successively smaller fractions in this manner until she was full.

Neglect of the *right* side of space, incidentally, is almost unheard of, and hemineglect has not been reproduced in experimental animals. A possible explanation for this is that human ancestors, as well as modern nonhuman animals, had complete representations of both sides of space in both cerebral hemispheres. As humans evolved, the language centers of the left hemisphere appear to have crowded the

spatial areas, leaving a representation of only the right side of space in the left hemisphere, while the right hemisphere retained its representation of both sides. Thus, damage to the left hemisphere still leaves a person with maps, in the right hemisphere, of both sides of space, while damage to the right hemisphere wipes out the only existing maps of the left side of space.

Work with stroke patients has also demonstrated that the neglect extends to the inside world: Italian neurologists Eduardo Bisiach and Claudio Luzzatti asked "neglect" patients to close their eyes and imagine themselves standing at one end of Milan's Piazza del Duomo, a public square well known to all of them. Asked to describe the square, the patients talked about the landmarks in great detail, but only those on the right-hand side of their imagined direction of gaze! If they were asked to imagine themselves standing at the other end of the square, they described the landmarks they had previously omitted. Evidently, losing a cortical area that processes a certain kind of information prevents even the imagination or memory of whatever that cortical area was responsible for processing—a conclusion from work with human patients that arguably could not have been reached by any other method.

Modern scientists studying complex issues such as spatial cognition must use a variety of experimental approaches to study the mind. Converging evidence from animal research, brain-damaged humans, and functional brain imaging are all important methods for learning about how the brain enables mind.

HOW IS THE BRAIN DIVIDED?

As we have seen, studying humans whose brains were damaged by accidents or surgically altered has been a rich source of insight into the mechanics of the mind. Many of these surgeries have been attempts to treat epilepsy by specifically removing the part of the brain in which the seizures begin. Another strategy, pioneered in the 1940s and still practiced on occasion today when other interventions have failed, is to cut connections within the brain to try to isolate the site of seizure initiation, so that a seizure that begins there will be less able to spread throughout the cortex.

Does each half of the brain possess the same capacities?

THE HEMISPHERES CAN BE SEPARATED

The only intracortical connections that may readily be cut without damaging the gray matter itself are those that run from one cerebral hemisphere to the other, in the massive fiber bundle called the **corpus callosum** (Figure 4.19). The corpus callosum may be cut only partway through, sparing some of the connecting axons, or it may be completely severed. Most such patients, and all of those on whom the initial operations were performed and who provided the first striking results, have had the corpus callosum completely cut. Apart from a few residual, minor connections, this leaves the two halves of the forebrain almost completely isolated

corpus callosum A fiber of axons that transmits information between the two cerebral hemispheres of the brain.

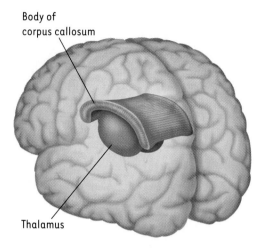

Body of
corpus callosum

Thalamus

4.19 The corpus callosum, a massive bundle of millions of axons connecting the two cerebral hemispheres.

4.20 An experiment with a split-brain subject. The left hemisphere has no knowledge of what was flashed on the left side on the screen, but the right hemisphere can pick the correct object using the left hand.

from one another, and the two hemispheres connected only back to the brainstem, hence only indirectly to each other. This condition is known as the **split-brain**.

Perhaps the most obvious thing about the patients after their operations was how very normal they were. Unlike patients following other types of brain surgery, the split-brain patients had no major problems that were immediately apparent. In fact, some early investigation suggested that the surgery had not affected the patients in any discernable way. They could walk and talk normally, think clearly, and interact socially.

However, work with animals had shown that this could not be the full story. One of the authors (M.S.G.), working with eventual Nobel laureate Roger Sperry, conducted a series of tests on the first split-brain participants. The results were quite stunning: just as the brain had been split in two, so had the mind.

THE SEPARATE HEMISPHERES CAN BE TESTED

Recall from earlier in the chapter that images from the left side of the visual field go to the right hemisphere, and those from the right side go to the left. Remember also that the left hemisphere controls the right hand, and the right hemisphere controls the left hand. These divisions allow researchers to provide information to and get information from only a single hemisphere at a time.

Figure 4.20 shows a typical experimental setup. The split-brain patient sits in front of a screen, staring at a central dot. Two images are flashed simultaneously, one on each side of the dot. Because each hemisphere sees only the contents of the opposite side of the visual field, the right hemisphere would see the image on the left, and the left hemisphere the image on the right.

We have seen that the left hemisphere is dominant for language in most people. If a split-brain patient, having just been flashed two pictures in the manner just described, is asked to report what was shown, he or she will announce that only one picture was shown and will describe the one on the right. Why is this? Because the left hemisphere, with its control over speech, only saw the picture on the right side. The mute right hemisphere (or "right brain"), having seen the picture on the left, is unable to articulate a response. It can be shown, though, that the right brain indeed saw the picture. If the picture on the left was, for example, of a spoon, the right hemisphere can easily pick out an actual spoon from a selection of objects, using, of course, the left hand. The left hemisphere has no knowledge whatsoever of what the right one saw. Splitting the brain, then, produces two half-brains, each with its own independent perceptions, thoughts, and consciousness!

Ring

THE HEMISPHERES ARE SPECIALIZED

Further explorations revealed much more about the division of labor within the brain. In all the patients studied, the left hemisphere was far more competent at language than the right, so much so that in most patients the right hemisphere had no discernable language capacity at all. In some patients, though, the right hemisphere did have some rudimentary language comprehension. Interestingly, such right-hemisphere language capabilities tend to improve in the years following the operation, presumably as the right hemisphere attains communication skills that were unnecessary when the hemisphere was fully connected to the fluent left brain.

The right hemisphere, however, has its own competencies that complement those of the left. The left brain is generally hopeless at spatial relationships. In one experiment, a split-brain participant is given a pile of blocks and a drawing of a simple arrangement in which to put them—for example, a square. If the participant is using his or her left hand, controlled by the right hemisphere, the blocks are arranged effortlessly. If, however, the left brain is doing the arranging, via the right hand, the result is a meandering, incompetent attempt. During such a dismal performance, the idle left hand will attempt to slip in and help out, as the right brain presumably looks on in frustration!

Split-brains have provided insight into not only the functional specializations of the left and right sides, but also the organization within each hemisphere. When the corpus callosum was not cut along its entire length, the relative contributions of its different ends to the transfer of different kinds of information could be explored. Figure 4.21 shows the reaction of one such patient, who had enough right-hemisphere language capability to comprehend words flashed in the left visual field. His operation was done in two parts, with the back half of the corpus callosum cut first. He was tested following the first operation. Since the visual cortex occupies the back of the brain, the cut rear half of the corpus callosum prevented any direct transfer of visual information. The left brain, then, was unable to see the word "knight." Fascinatingly, though, the left brain was nevertheless able to visualize what the right brain was thinking about! Evidently, more "meaningful" information *could* be transferred, through the axons in the front half of the corpus callosum connecting the two front halves of the brain. A phenomenon that seems to be related to the left hemisphere's verbal talents is its tendency to construct an internal narrative that makes sense out of the world, which is the subject of "Using Psychological Science: The Mind is a Subjective Interpreter."

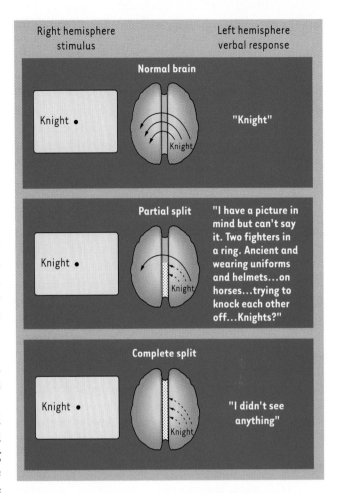

4.21 Different kinds of information are transferred by different parts of the corpus callosum. If the back half is severed but the front half left intact, meaning transfers from one hemisphere to the other, but visual information does not.

split-brain A condition in which the corpus callosum is surgically cut and the two hemispheres of the brain do not receive information directly from each other.

How Is the Brain Divided?

The corpus callosum joins the two cerebral hemispheres. For split-brain patients, the corpus callosum is cut in order to treat epilepsy. Research on split-brain patients shows that the left hemisphere is dominant for language whereas the right hemisphere is dominant for spatial relationships. In split-brain patients both hemispheres seem to have their independent consciousness. The left hemisphere interpreter tries to make sense of the world around us.

THE MIND IS A SUBJECTIVE INTERPRETER

Another interesting dimension to the relationship between the brain's hemispheres is how they work together to reconstruct our experiences. This can be demonstrated by asking a disconnected left hemisphere what it thinks about previous behavior that has been produced by the right hemisphere. In one such experiment, different images are flashed simultaneously to the left and right visual fields and the patient is asked to point *with both hands* to pictures that seem most related to the images on the screen (Figure 4.22). As one example, a picture of a chicken claw was flashed to the left hemisphere and a picture of a snow scene to the right hemisphere. In response, the left hemisphere directed the right hand to point to a picture of a chicken head, and the right hemisphere pointed the left hand at a snow shovel. The participant was then asked why he chose those items. Clearly, the speaking left hemisphere could have no idea what the right hemisphere had seen. However, the patient (or rather his left hemisphere) calmly replied, "Oh, that's simple. The chicken claw goes with the chicken, and you need a shovel to clean out the chicken shed." The left hemisphere had evidently interpreted the left hand's response in a manner consistent with the left brain's knowledge. This left-hemispheric tendency to construct a world that makes sense is called the "interpreter."

This interpreter strongly influences the way we view and remember the world. Shown a series of pictures that form a story and asked later to choose which of another group of pictures had been seen previously, normal participants have a strong tendency to falsely "recognize" pictures that are consistent with the theme of the original series, whereas those that are inconsistent with the theme are easily rejected. The left brain, then, tends to "compress" its experiences into a comprehensible story and reconstructs remembered details on the basis of that story. The right brain seems to simply experience the world and remembers things in a manner less distorted by narrative interpretation. Given the finite capacity of the brain, the advantages of compression seem clear, though it appears that the right brain may check the left brain's unwarranted speculations.

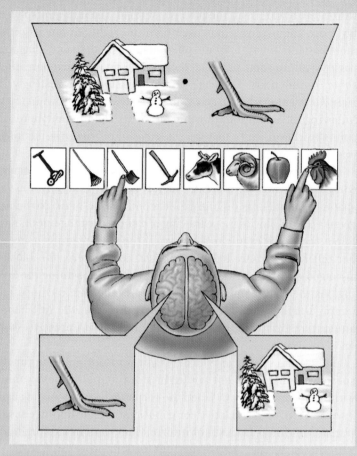

4.22 The left brain interpreter mechanism. The left hemisphere attempts to explain the behavior of the right hemisphere on the basis of limited information.

HOW DOES THE BRAIN CHANGE?

RESEARCH QUESTION

Are there critical periods during brain development?

Despite the great precision and specificity of its connections, the brain is extremely malleable. Over the course of development, after injury, and throughout our constant stream of experience, the brain is continually changing, a property known as **plasticity**. Determining the nature of these changes, and the rules that they follow, is providing major insights into the mind, and is a direct outgrowth of the biological revolution that is energizing the field.

The brain follows a predictable development pattern, with different structures and abilities progressing at different rates and maturing at different points in life. Reptiles hatch from their leathery eggs ready to go; human infants sleep and continue to grow and develop their brains, actively rewiring them, in major ways, for many years. In addition, our brains' connections are refined and retuned with every experience of our lives. Brain plasticity research promises to reveal great insights into the interactive nature of biological and psychological influences on our behavior, drawing on exciting research that crosses all levels of analysis.

plasticity A property of the brain that allows it to change as a result of experience, drugs, or injury.

THE INTERPLAY OF GENES AND THE ENVIRONMENT WIRES THE BRAIN

As you read in Chapter 2, there are complex interactions between genes and the environment. The brain's development follows set sequences encoded in the genes: babies' visual acuity develops before their ability to see in stereo, for example, and the prefrontal cortex is not anatomically fully mature until late adolescence or early adulthood. But even with these meticulously specified genetic instructions, the environment plays a major role. The behavior of the very genes themselves is utterly dependent on their environment. Different genes are "expressed" in different cells, and which genes are expressed, and to what extent, is determined by the environment. The environment does not just affect the products of our DNA's activity; it affects the DNA's activity itself.

Chemical signals guide growing connections In the developing embryo, new cells receive signals from their surroundings that determine what type of cells they will become. Cells release chemical signals to each other that act directly on their genetic material to determine which of the millions of instructions contained in the genetic code will be executed.

If cells from one part of an embryo are surgically transplanted to another part, the result depends on how far along the process has gotten. Tissue that is transplanted early on completely transforms into whatever type is appropriate for its new location. But as time passes, cells become more and more committed to their identities, so that transplanting them results in disfigured organisms. In the case of neural tissue, cells transplanted early take on the identity appropriate to their new location, and the organism develops normally. Cells transplanted later, however, grow connections as if they hadn't been moved; that is, the cells connect to areas that would have been appropriate if they had remained in their old location. Tissue moved from visual areas connects to the visual parts of the thalamus, and so on.

This predestination of connections from cells that have had time to determine their identities exposes the preprogrammed nature of brain wiring. The connections of the brain are produced in large part by the growing axons' detection of particular molecules that tell them where to go, and where not to. The broad brushstrokes of the brain are laid out by this chemical specificity: neurons in one region are looking for particular chemicals, and neurons in another are producing them. Axons from the first region grow steadily toward or away from increasing or decreasing concentrations of these signaling chemicals—so-called *chemical gradients*. Following the gradients of some chemicals guides axons on long trips to their destination areas, whereas the concentration of other chemicals governs their branching patterns once they're there. This method lays down the connections between all brain structures and induces the specific connections between areas within the cerebral cortex.

critical period Time in which certain experiences must occur for normal brain development, such as exposure to visual information during infancy for the normal development of the visual pathways of the brain.

Experience fine-tunes neural connections This is not the whole story, however. Even though the major connections are established by chemical gradients, the detailed connections are governed by experience. If a cat's eyes are sutured closed at birth, depriving it of visual input, the maps in its visual cortex fail to develop properly; when the sutures are removed weeks later, the cat is blind. Evidently the ongoing activity of the visual pathways is necessary to refine the map enough for it to be useful. In general, such plasticity has **critical periods**, times in which certain experiences must occur for development to proceed normally. Adult cats who are similarly deprived do not lose their sight.

A few years ago, it was discovered that rats reared in groups in "enhanced" environments with lots of toys and obstacles grew up to have bigger brains than those reared in normal laboratory conditions (Rosenzweig et al., 1972). However, consider the "normal" conditions: essentially, featureless boxes with bedding in the bottom. The reality may be that the "enhanced" conditions were simply an approximation of rat life in the wild, allowing normal rat development, while the mental deprivation caused by the lab cage environment caused atrophy in the rats' unused brains. Nonetheless, it does demonstrate at a minimum that the environment is important for normal development.

THE BRAIN REWIRES ITSELF THROUGHOUT LIFE

Although plasticity decreases with age, the brain retains the ability to rewire itself throughout life. This is the basis of learning.

4.23 Changes in cortical representations of skin regions in monkeys that were trained or not trained to detect certain touch stimulation. Repeated training led to an increased representation in cortical areas (as shown in **a**). In (**b**), the filled circles indicate where the fingers were touched for the trained (blue) and untrained (green) fingers. The circles show the regions of the finger that became sensitive to the stimulation. More of the finger becomes sensitive to the stimulation after training.

Change in the strength of connections underlies learning With every moment of life, we gain new memories: experiences and knowledge instantaneously acquired that can later be recalled and habits that gradually form. All these forms of memory consist of physical changes in the brain.

It is now widely accepted by psychological scientists that these changes are most likely not in the brain's gross wiring or arrangement, but simply in the strength of preexisting connections. One possibility is that two neurons firing at the same time strengthens the synaptic connection between them, making them more likely to fire together in the future, and that, conversely, *not* firing at the same time tends to weaken two neurons' connection. Known technically as *Hebbian learning* (discussed in Chapter 6), this theory is summarized by the catchphrase "Fire together, wire together," and it is consistent with a great deal of experimental evidence and many theoretical models. It accounts for both the "burning in" of an experience—a pattern of neuronal firing is made more likely to recur, leading us to recall an event—and for the ingraining of habits: merely repeating a behavior makes us tend to perform it automatically.

Another possible method of plasticity is the growth of entirely new connections; this takes much longer but appears to be a major factor in

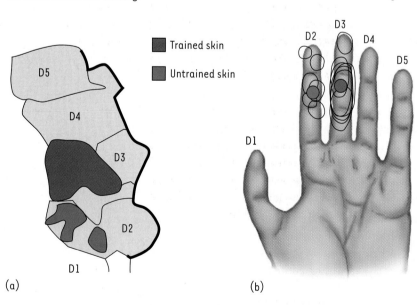

Trained skin

Untrained skin

(a)

(b)

recovery from injury. Until very recently, it was believed that, uniquely among bodily organs, adult brains produced no new cells. This was presumably to avoid obliterating the connections that had been established in response to experience. However, it has now been discovered that new neurons *are* produced in the adult brain. There appears to be fairly heavy turnover in the hippocampus. Recall that memories are retained within (or at least require) this structure initially but are eventually transferred to the cortex, with the hippocampus being continuously overwritten. It may be that lost neurons can be replaced without disrupting memory. New neurons are also produced in the adult cortex itself, but it is not yet known what role this "neurogenesis" plays.

Changes in use distort cortical maps   All the maps in the cerebral cortex shift in response to their activity. Recall the homunculus (Figure 4.17), in which more cortical tissue is devoted to body parts that receive more sensation or that are used more. If a monkey's finger is repetitively stimulated, for example, that finger's cortical representation will expand (Figure 4.23). However, such plasticity apparently does not take place if the brain is not paying attention: *distract* the monkey during the stimulation and this effect will not occur.

Cortical reorganization can also have bizarre results. Amputees are often afflicted with *phantom limbs*, the intense sensation that the amputated body part still exists. Some phantom limbs are experienced as moving normally, being used to gesture in conversation as if they really existed, for example, while some are frozen in position. Unfortunately, phantom limbs are often accompanied by sensations of pain, which may result from the misgrowth of the severed pain nerves at the stump, with the pain being interpreted by the cortex as coming from the place those nerves originally came from (Figure 4.24). This would suggest that the brain had *not* reorganized in response to the injury, and that the cortical representation of the arm was still intact. However, V. S. Ramachandran of the University of California, San Diego, discovered that some of these people, when their eyes were closed, perceived a touch on the cheek as if it were on their missing hand! Apparently, the hand is represented next to the face in our somatosensory homunculus. Following the loss of the limb, the patient's unemployed cortex to some degree assumed the function of the closest group, which was to represent the skin of the face. Touching the face then activated these neurons. Somehow, the rest of the brain had not kept pace with the somatosensory area enough to figure out these neurons' new job.

THE BRAIN CAN RECOVER FROM INJURY

The converse of the brain's reorganization in response to over- or underuse is its reorganization in response to brain damage. Following a lesion in the cortex, the surrounding gray matter assumes the function of the damaged area, with the map distorting everywhere around it to recover the lost capability, like local businesses scrambling to pick up the customers of a newly bankrupt store. Some of this remapping seems to occur immediately and to continue for years. Such plasticity involves all levels of the nervous system, from the cortex down to the spinal cord.

Does the brain rewire itself during learning, aging, and repair?

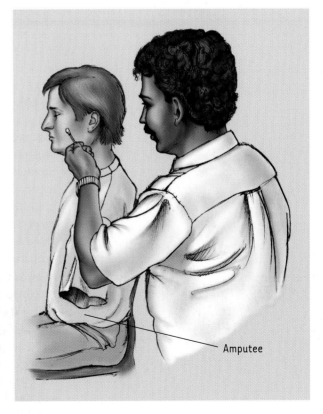

4.24 Cortical remapping following amputation. A cotton swab touching the subject's cheek was felt as touching his missing hand.

Amputee

This reorganization is much greater in children than adults, in accordance with the critical periods of normal development. Young children afflicted with severe and uncontrollable epilepsy sometimes undergo "radical hemispherectomy": the surgical removal of one entire cerebral hemisphere. This procedure is not possible in adults because of the inevitable and permanent paralysis and loss of function that results. Young children, however, eventually regain almost complete use of the initially paralyzed arm and leg, as well as the other functions of the lost hemisphere: these are simply taken up by the remaining one. But even in adults, recovery from brain injury can be quite dramatic. Stroke patients with a paralyzed arm, for example, very often recover its use within a few months.

Finally, one of the most exciting areas of current neurological research is the transplantation of cells into the brain to repair damage. Such an approach, using cells from human fetal tissue, is beginning to be explored as a possible treatment for degenerative diseases such as Parkinson's or Huntington's, and also for strokes. The significant challenge is to get the newly introduced cells to make the proper connections and regrow the damaged circuits. These techniques are still in their earliest days, and they pose obvious ethical dilemmas, but they may well soon become very important treatment methods.

How Does the Brain Change?

Though neural connections are intricate and precise, they are malleable. The human genome is the blueprint for normal development, but it is affected by environmental factors, such as injury or sensory stimulation or deprivation. During development, following injury, and throughout our lifetimes of learning, the circuitry is reworked and updated. Much of this plasticity may require our paying attention. Reorganization occurs following brain injury, with recovery ability far greater in children than in adults.

CONCLUSION

The brain is a unique and remarkable set of structures that have collectively evolved to control the organism as it goes about the business of survival and reproduction. In humans, this evolutionary adaptiveness has enabled the development of complex communication, culture, and thought. Our knowledge about the brain has expanded rapidly and dramatically over the past few decades, drawing on research from all the levels of analysis. For more than 100 years scholars debated whether psychological processes were located in specific parts of the brain or distributed throughout it. Along the way, they also built a formidable base of knowledge and principles. It was not until the 1990s with the results of brain-imaging studies, among other methods, that it became clear that many mental processes are localized to specific regions of the brain that work together to produce behavior and mental activity. Research on the brain has revealed many fascinating phenomena, such as phantom limbs, spit-brains, and a left-brain interpreter that struggles to make sense of the world. Although much remains to be discovered, scientists using the tools of the biological revolution are making great and rapidly accelerating progress in understanding how the circuits of the brain enable the mind.

FURTHER READINGS

Brodal, P. (1998). *The central nervous system.* Oxford, U. K.: Oxford University Press.

Finger, S. (1994). *Origins of neuroscience.* Oxford, U. K.: Oxford University Press.

Gazzaniga, M. S., Ivry, R. B., & Mangun, G. R. (2002). *Cognitive neuroscience: The biology of the mind* (2nd ed.). New York: W. W. Norton.

Kolb, B., & Whishaw, I. Q. (1998). *Fundamentals of human neuropsychology.* New York: Freeman.

Ramachandran, V. S., & Blakeslee, S. (1998). *Phantoms in the brain: Probing the mysteries of the human mind.* New York: William Morrow & Co.

Sacks, O. (1985). *The man who mistook his wife for a hat.* New York: Summit Books.

Zigmond, M. J., Bloom, F. E. Landis, S. C. Roberts, J. L., & Squire, L. R. (1999). *Fundamental neuroscience.* San Diego: Academic Press.

OVERCOMING SENSORY DISABILITIES

Sensation and perception bridge the physical and psychological worlds. A brain-activated video game is a high-tech way to allow disabled children to interact with their peers; similar cutting edge advances now provide some blind and deaf people a certain level of sight or hearing.

TIMELINE

c. 1500

Art and Perception Leon Alberti describes the use of linear perspective and other depth cues to create the impression of depth in representational art.

1672

The Nature of Light Sir Isaac Newton performs his prism experiment, demonstrating that white light is in fact composed of a mixture of the spectral colors.

1709

The Empiricist View of Perception In his *New Theory of Vision* George Berkeley outlines the Empiricist view that perception is learned through experience with the world.

1838

The Stereoscope Charles Wheatstone invents the stereoscope and documents the role of binocular vision in spacial perception.

Sensation, Perception, and Attention

5

OUTLINING THE PRINCIPLES

1860
Psychophysics Gustav Theodor Fechner publishes *Elements of Psychophysics*, laying the foundations for the systematic investigation of sensory processes.

1867
Searching for Biological Foundations Hermann von Helmholtz publishes his seminal *Handbook of Physiological Optics* integrating the physics, physiology, and psychology of visual perception.

1907
Birth of the Gestalt School Max Wertheimer's experiments with Phi motion mark the beginning of the Gestalt movement in perceptual psychology.

1950
Sensation and the Brain Wilder Penfield and Theodore Rasmussen publish *The Cerebral Cortex of Man*, describing cortical stimulation experiments during neurosurgery that evoke sensory experiences.

1961
A Theory of Hearing Georg von Békésy is awarded the Nobel prize for his research into the mechanisms of hearing. His theory articulates how sound waves are transformed into neuronal information.

O n November 28, 1979, Air New Zealand flight 901 crashed into the slopes of Mount Erebus on Ross Island in Antarctica, with the loss of all 257 passengers and crew. Several factors contributed to this disaster. The aircraft's flight computer had been incorrectly programmed, so the plane was badly off course. In addition, the pilot had descended below the minimum altitude allowed for the flight. These factors don't explain, however, why the flight crew failed to notice the 12,000-foot volcano looming in front of them until moments before impact.

Psychologists testifying at the commission of inquiry offered a possible, if startling, explanation—the pilots saw what they expected to see. One of the unique hazards of Antarctic aviation is "white out," in which the sky and the snow-covered terrain appear to merge, and pilots are unable to visually distinguish the ground or the horizon. The pilots believed they were hundreds of miles away, flying over the Ross Ice Shelf, so they had no expectation that there would be mountains anywhere near their flight path. The psychologists argued that the few visual cues available to the pilots were sufficiently consistent with what they expected to see that in their minds their expectations were confirmed. Since there appeared to be no danger, the pilots decided—fatally—to reduce their altitude to give the passengers a better view of the spectacular Antarctic landscape. The combination of an unusually sparse visual environment and the pilots' own beliefs had conspired to fool their visual systems into seeing terrain that wasn't there—and failing to see the mountain that was.

In order to perceive the world, we must rely on information provided by our sense organs—our eyes, ears, skin, nose, and tongue. Each of these organs is sensitive to different physical stimuli, and each contributes different information. Ultimately, our perceptual representation of the environment is limited by the kinds of stimuli to which we are sensitive, and by the limits of our sensory systems in responding to those stimuli. The study of sensation and perception, our focus in this chapter, is the study of those systems and of how the

RESEARCH QUESTIONS

for Studying Sensation, Perception, and Attention

How is information from stimuli in the world transformed into neural activity in the brain?

What do we know about the relationships between neural activity in the brain and our perceptions of the world?

How are we able to perceive space in three dimensions on the basis of two-dimensional inputs from the retina?

How do we know the shapes of objects that we have never seen before?

How does attention influence the way we perceive the world?

1962

Exploring the Neuronal Basis of Vision David Hubel and Torsten Wiesel describe the functional anatomy of the primary visual cortex of cats. They receive a Nobel prize for this work in 1981.

1966

Evolutionary Aspects of Perception James J. Gibson outlines his theory of direct perception proposing that perceptual systems must be understood in terms of the problems they evolved to solve.

1982

Birth of Computational Vision David Marr publishes his monograph *Vision*, emphasizing the computational approach to the study of visual perception.

1987

Feature Integration Theory Anne Treisman investigates aspects of conscious and unconscious visual perception. She articulates the role of attention in perceiving objects.

information they provide is used to create a mental representation of the external world.

Psychological scientists often divide the way we perceive the world into two distinct phases: sensation and perception. The study of **sensation** focuses on how our sense organs respond to external stimuli (lights, sounds, etc.), and how those responses are transmitted to the brain. **Perception** refers to the further processing of sensory signals in the brain that ultimately results in an internal representation of stimuli. For example, a green light emits photons that are detected by specialized neurons in the eyes, which transmit signals to the brain (sensation). The brain processes those neural signals and the observer thinks, "That light is green" (perception). Once again, as we saw in Chapter 1, there are many levels of explanation for psychological processes. Some of the phenomena of sensation and perception are best understood at the physiological level. Other phenomena, especially of perception, cannot be explained in such mechanistic terms and require understanding at the psychological level—at least for the time being.

Psychological scientists have often observed that the way we perceive a stimulus depends on whether or not we are paying attention to it. The study of *attention* focuses on how expectations can influence perception, and how the brain's perceptual resources are allocated to different aspects of the perceptual environment.

HOW CAN WE BEST UNDERSTAND SENSATION AND PERCEPTION?

Sensation and perception bridge the physical and the psychological worlds. Research on these processes grew out of the philosophical quest to understand the nature of human knowledge and is the earliest form of systematic psychological inquiry. The goal was to determine how we know what we know about the various stimuli in our environment. The key question over the years has been whether we are born with knowledge of the world or whether we learn what we know through experience.

Advocates of empiricism (from the Greek *empeiria*, "experience") held that all human knowledge must be acquired through the senses. Seventeenth-century British philosopher John Locke conceived of the mind as a *tabula rasa*, a blank slate on which knowledge is written as a result of experience.

An alternative view to empiricism is *nativism*, which holds that at least some knowledge is innate—an idea that dates back as far as Plato, if not earlier. The eighteenth-century German philosopher Immanuel Kant proposed that our experiences provide sensory input that is then filtered through innate, preexisting mental categories, such as space and time, that organize the information.

The study of perception was a major battleground for the debate between empiricism and nativism. Unfortunately for the seventeenth- and eighteenth-century adherents of these views, however, it was not until the twentieth century that definitive experiments to try to resolve this debate were really possible. Although there are still questions about the extent to which perception is learned or innate, it is clear that at least some perceptual capabilities are present at birth, al-

sensation How sense organs respond to external stimuli and transmit the responses to the brain.

perception The processing, organization, and interpretation of sensory signals that result in an internal representation of the stimulus.

though experience is necessary for normal perception to develop. We will discuss the development of perceptual systems further in Chapter 11.

STIMULI MUST BE CODED TO BE UNDERSTOOD BY THE BRAIN

How does information about the world get to the brain? As you learned in Chapter 3, the brain understands only electrical impulses from neural discharges. The way our sensory organs translate a stimulus's physical properties into neural impulses is called *sensory coding*. Different features of the physical environment are coded by different neural impulses. Thus, a green stoplight will be coded by neurons in the retina of the eye; when the hand touches a hot skillet, other neurons will signal pain. Recall that receptors are specialized neurons in the sense organs that pass impulses to connecting neurons when they receive some sort of physical or chemical stimulation. This process is called **transduction**. After transduction in the receptors, connecting neurons in the sense organs transmit information to the brain in the form of neural impulses. Most sensory information first goes to a structure in the middle of the brain called the thalamus. Connecting neurons in the thalamus then conduct information to the cortex, where the brain interprets the incoming neural impulses as sight, smell, sound, touch, or taste. We will address the issue of how the brain interprets these impulses later in the chapter when we discuss perception. Table 5.1 lists the stimuli, receptors, and pathways for each sense organ.

Sensations are composed of pieces of information that are coded when stimuli are transduced into nerve impulses. Sensory coding can be divided into two categories: quantitative and qualitative. Coding for quantitative factors, such as intensity, brightness, and loudness, is often indexed by the neural firing frequency. The greater the firing frequency, the brighter or louder the stimulus. The number of neurons triggered by the stimulus also contributes to quantitative coding in that more intense stimuli tend to recruit more neurons.

How is information from stimuli in the world transformed into neural activity in the brain?

TABLE 5.1   The Stimuli, Receptors, and Pathways for Each Sense

SENSE	STIMULUS	RECEPTORS	PATHWAY TO THE BRAIN
Hearing	Sound waves	Pressure-sensitive hair cells in cochlea of inner ear	Auditory nerve (8th cranial nerve)
Vision	Light waves	Light-sensitive rods and cones in retina of eye	Optic nerve (2nd cranial nerve)
Touch	Pressure on the skin	Sensitive ends of touch neurons in skin	Trigeminal nerve (5th cranial nerve) for touch above the neck. Spinal nerves for touch elsewhere.
Pain	Wide variety of potentially harmful stimuli	Sensitive ends of pain neurons in skin and other tissues	Trigeminal nerve (5th cranial nerve) for pain above the neck. Spinal nerves for pain elsewhere.
Taste	Molecules dissolved in fluid on the tongue	Taste cells in taste buds on the tongue	Portions of facial, glossopharyngeal, and vagus nerves (7th, 9th, and 10th cranial nerves)
Smell	Molecules dissolved in fluid on mucous membranes in the nose	Sensitive ends of olfactory neurons in the mucous membranes	Olfactory nerve (1st cranial nerve)

While quantitative sensory coding is useful for some dimensions of a sensation, it is less useful for others, such as color or taste. For these tasks, the brain relies on qualitative sensory coding. Qualitative coding is possible because different sensory receptors respond to different qualities of a stimulus. The simplest form of qualitative sensory coding would be to have a dedicated receptor type for every possible stimulus. So, for example, there might be one class of visual receptors that responds only to red light, another class that responds only to purple light, and so on. Obviously, for this to be strictly true there would need to be an enormous number of different receptor types for each sensory modality. In most sensory systems—with the possible exception of olfaction (the sense of smell)—receptors provide what is called *coarse coding*, in which sensory qualities are coded by only a few receptors, each of which responds to a broad range of stimuli. The final percept can be computed only by comparing the activity across the whole range of receptors.

transduction A process by which sensory receptors produce neural impulses when they receive physical or chemical stimulation.

absolute threshold The minimum intensity of stimulation that must occur before one can experience a sensation.

difference threshold The minimum amount of change required in order to detect a difference between intensities of stimuli.

PSYCHOPHYSICS: RELATING STIMULI AND RESPONSES

The scientific effort to understand sensation and perception began in earnest in nineteenth-century Germany, leading to a series of cumulative principles that guide researchers to this day. Gustav Theodor Fechner (1801–1887), a physicist, became interested in the relationship between physical stimuli and the responses of our perceptual systems. Fechner sought to develop equations that related perceptual experience to the intensity of physical stimuli. He coined the term *psychophysics* to describe this endeavor, and he developed most of its early methods, many of which are still used today. Fechner began the exploration of psychophysics by considering thresholds, the physical measurement of how much stimulation sensory organs need before the stimulation is detectable.

Sensory thresholds Fechner defined an **absolute threshold** as the minimum intensity of stimulation that must occur before we can experience a sensation. For instance, the absolute threshold for hearing is the faintest sound a person can hear. How loudly must someone in the next room whisper for you to be able to hear it? In this case the absolute threshold for auditory stimuli would be the quietest whisper that you could hear. As you will see shortly, absolute thresholds can vary considerably from person to person and even for each person depending on the circumstances in which they are measured (Table 5.2 lists some approximate minimum stimuli for various senses).

A **difference threshold** (or differential threshold) is the *just noticeable difference (JND)* between two stimuli—the minimum amount of change required in order to detect a difference. If a friend is watching a television show while you are

TABLE 5.2	Approximate Minimum Stimulus for Each Sense
SENSE	**MINIMUM STIMULUS**
Vision	A candle flame seen at 30 miles on a dark, clear night
Hearing	The tick of a clock at 20 feet under quiet conditions
Taste	One teaspoon of sugar in 2 gallons of water
Smell	One drop of perfume diffused into the entire volume of six rooms
Touch	The wing of a fly falling on your cheek from a distance of 1 centimeter

reading, and the show goes to a commercial that is louder in volume, you might look up, noticing that something has changed. The minimum change in volume required for you to be able to detect a difference would be the difference threshold.

A great deal of work in psychophysics has focused on the measurement of difference thresholds in different experimental conditions. Several psychophysicists have proposed "laws," or equations, aimed at describing the relationships between changes in stimulus intensity and the corresponding changes in the perceptual experience of those stimuli.

Weber's law In 1834 German psychophysicist Ernst Weber made the seemingly simple observation that it is easier to detect a small difference between two light weights than between two heavy weights. Pick up a one-ounce letter and a two-ounce letter, and you will easily detect the difference. But pick up a five-pound package and one weighing one ounce more and the difference is harder to discern. Weber discovered that the difference threshold for a stimulus is a constant proportion of its intensity. Weber's law is expressed as the formula

$$\Delta I/I = k$$

where k is a constant, known as the *Weber fraction*; I is the intensity of the standard stimulus; and ΔI is the JND for the stimulus. For weights, the difference threshold is typically about 2 percent of the weight of the standard. You can probably discriminate between 100 grams and 102 grams (a 2 percent difference) and between 1,000 and 1,020 grams. What is important in determining the difference threshold is the percentage difference between the two weights, not the absolute size of the difference. A similar rule holds for other sensations, such as loudness, pitch, and brightness, though the percentage value varies (see Table 5.3). For loudness, a 15 percent difference is needed; for pitch, only a .3 percent is needed; and for brightness, 1 percent.

Fechner's law Fechner drew a broader relationship between sensation and a stimulus's intensity by combining Weber's law with the daring assumption that every JND represents an equal step in the psychological *magnitude* of a sensation. Fechner's law is expressed by the formula

$$S = k \log I$$

where S is the magnitude of sensory experience, k is a constant, and I is the physical intensity of the stimulus. What this means is that the strength of the sensory experience grows as the logarithm of the stimulus intensity. Fechner's law indicates that when stimulus intensities are high, large increases in physical intensity register as much smaller changes in experienced sensations. Consider a three-way light bulb. Each twist of the switch increases the wattage by the same amount (say 30-60-90), but the difference between 30 and 60 watts seems much larger than the difference between 60 and 90. Although the physical light intensity increases in two equal steps, the room's greater brightness following the first step causes the second step to have a much smaller impact.

Stevens's power law Fechner's law is a theoretical construct. Fechner himself did not think it could be directly tested because he doubted that people could reliably report changes in a sensation's magnitude. It wasn't until the 1950s that the American psychophysicist S. S. Stevens developed a technique in which he asked subjects to assign numbers to sensations of different magnitude. By doing so he

TABLE 5.3	The Weber Fractions for the Senses
STIMULUS DIMENSION	**WEBER'S CONSTANT**
Sound frequency	.003
Sound intensity	.15
Light intensity	.01
Odor concentration	.07
Taste concentration	.20
Pressure intensity	.14

found that people were remarkably consistent in the numbers they assigned, but he discovered that Fechner's logarithm law did not always hold. Instead, he proposed that a power function describes the relation between stimulus intensity and the intensity of sensation. Stevens's power law is expressed by the formula

$$S = kI^p$$

where S is the reported magnitude of a sensory experience, k is a constant, I is the standard stimulus, and p is an exponent that varies according to the sensory modality, so that different exponents are obtained for each sense. Today, Stevens's power law is the accepted equation for describing the relationship between a stimulus's actual and perceived intensity.

Signal detection theory   Imagine standing at an airport gate waiting for an old friend whom you haven't seen for several years. As people stream out of the gateway you scan the crowd hoping to recognize your friend. Your task is complicated by the passage of time—your friend will certainly look somewhat different than the last time you saw her. Taking this into account, you scrutinize each person carefully. Most of the people are easily discounted—they are too old, the wrong sex, too tall. Some people, though, share enough features with her that they *could* be your friend, at least at first glance. Your task is to figure out whether any of them is actually your friend, or whether that initial feeling of recognition is just a false alarm. Your accuracy could be influenced by a number of factors, including how long it has been since you saw your friend, whether you are fatigued, and how many people there are on the plane. In other words, although the stimulus (your friend) is the same, the efficiency with which you detect it can change depending on the situation.

According to classical psychophysics was based on the assumption that any stimulus with sufficient intensity to reach the absolute threshold will be detected. As research progressed, however, it became clear that early psychophysicists had ignored an important variable: human judgment. Researchers began to realize that the concept of an absolute threshold was flawed. Instead, they found that very weak signals could sometimes be detected, and that relatively strong signals were sometimes missed. Observations like these led to the formulation of *signal detection theory*, which maintains that detecting a stimulus requires a judgment about its presence or absence, based on inherently ambiguous information.

According to signal detection theory, there are four critical variables in detecting a stimulus: *signal, response, noise,* and *response bias.* These last two variables reflect the inherent ambiguity of the signal-detection situation. The concept of noise was introduced to account for the variable effect that a stimulus can have on sensory systems. Stimuli are always competing with a changing background of other perceptual and psychological events, so their salience will not always be the same. In our airport example, you are trying to detect a signal—your friend—in a continuously varying background noise—hundreds of disembarking passengers. *Response bias* varies according to how much evidence the observer needs before making the response. In some circumstances, an observer will be strongly biased against making a response and will need a lot of evidence that the signal is present. In other conditions, the same observer will need only a small amount of evidence. For example, if you were a radiologist checking a CAT scan for signs of a brain tumor, you might be extra cautious about accepting any abnormality as a signal (i.e., a tumor), since your response could lead to drastic and dangerous

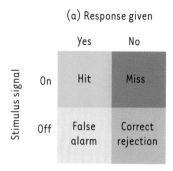
(a) Response given

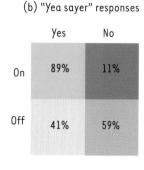
(b) "Yea sayer" responses

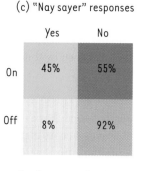
(c) "Nay sayer" responses

5.1 Payoff matrices for signal detection theory. There are four possible outcomes when a subject is asked whether something occurred during a trial (matrix a). Those who are biased toward reporting a signal tend to give the responses in matrix b, those who are biased toward denying that a signal occurred tend to respond according to the percentages in matrix c.

neurosurgery. However, if you were examining an X-ray image for signs of a broken bone, you might be more willing to make a positive diagnosis, since treatment—although it is uncomfortable—doesn't endanger the life of the patient. Figure 5.1 illustrates how bias can influence responses to ambiguous stimuli.

In signal detection theory, any given trial can have one of four outcomes (a trial is an event in which a signal may—or may not—be present). If the signal is present and the observer detects it, the outcome is a *hit*. A failure to detect a true signal is termed a *miss*. If the observer erroneously "detects" a stimulus that wasn't there, the outcome is a *false alarm*. Finally, if the stimulus is not presented, and the observer denies having seen it, the outcome is a *correct rejection*. Signal detection theorists point out that the observer's *sensitivity* to the stimulus can be computed only by comparing the hit rate with the false alarm rate—thus correcting for any bias the observer might bring to the testing situation.

Sensory adaptation Your response to a stimulus changes over time. Imagine you are studying in the library when work suddenly begins at a nearby construction site. When the equipment starts up, the sound seems particularly loud and disturbing. After a few minutes, however, you hardly notice the noise any more; it seems to have faded into the background. This is an example of what researchers call **sensory adaptation**. Researchers have often noticed that observers' sensitivity to stimuli decreases over time. If a stimulus is presented continuously, the responses of the sensory systems that detect it tend to diminish over time. Likewise, if a stimulus is presented repeatedly, the sensory response will tend to decrease with repeated exposures. One way to think about this is to consider that sensory systems are tuned to detect change in the environment. When some aspect of the environment changes, it is important for us to be able to detect it; it is less critical to keep responding to unchanging stimuli. Note that when a continuous stimulus stops, there is usually a large response as well. If the construction noise suddenly halted, you would be very likely to notice the sudden silence. As you will see later in the chapter, researchers often take advantage of sensory adaptation to explore the nature of sensory systems.

sensory adaptation When an observer's sensitivity to stimuli decreases over time.

How Can We Best Understand Sensation and Perception?

The study of sensation focuses on how our sense organs transduce information from external stimuli into neural impulses. Sensory coding for quantitative factors, such as intensity, brightness, and loudness, depends on the neural firing frequency and number of cells firing, while qualitative factors such as color and pitch are coded according to the pattern of activation across an array of fibers. The development of psychophysical methods in the nineteenth century began the effort to quantify how stimuli affect sensations and perceptions. Classical psychophysicists such as Weber, Fechner, and Stevens developed formulas to measure the amount of change needed in stimuli to create changes in subjects' perceptions. Until the development of signal detection theory, psychophysicists had been concerned solely with stimuli and responses. Signal detection theorists recognized that human variables such as motivation and alertness could also contribute to perception.

WHAT ARE THE SENSORY PROCESSES FOR OUR PRIMARY SENSES?

Perceiving a stimulus can be broken down into three parts. First, a physical stimulus impinges upon the receptors of a sense organ. Second, a physiological response in the sense organ transduces the stimulus energy into an electrical code—a neural impulse—that is carried to the brain. Finally, this code is processed in the brain, resulting in a psychological experience: the perception of sight, sound, taste, or smell. Traditionally, the first two parts are thought of as sensation, while the third is perception. To introduce sensation, we will first examine the receptors, transduction, and coding for each sense.

In researching sensation, investigators generally delve into the physiology of the visual, auditory, olfactory, taste, and touch systems: eyes, ears, nose, tongue, skin. In this section we will review how stimuli are detected and sent to the brain for each of the five primary senses, which are often subdivided into two categories: distance senses and close senses. The three distance senses are vision, hearing, and smell. We don't have to be in direct contact with stimuli in order to see, hear, or smell them. The close senses, touch and taste, require direct contact with the stimuli for sensation to occur.

IN VISION, THE EYE DETECTS LIGHT WAVES

If knowledge is acquired through our senses, then vision is by far our most important source of knowledge. Consider how much of what we know comes from what we see. Is a place safe or dangerous? Does that person look friendly or hostile? Even our metaphors for knowledge and understanding are often visual: "I see," "the answer is clear," "I'm fuzzy on that point." It should come as no surprise, then, that most of the scientific study of sensation and perception focuses (so to speak) on vision. The various ways that scientists study sensation and perception are discussed in "Crossing the Levels of Analysis: Converging Evidence in the Study of Perception."

Psychologists refer to the external stimulus as the *distal stimulus* and the stimulus energy that is transduced by sense organs as the *proximal stimulus* ("distal" and "proximal" mean "far" and "near," respectively). In perception the brain uses the information from the proximal stimulus to construct a representation of the distal stimulus. In vision, the proximal stimulus is light waves. Some distal stimuli emit light (stars, lightbulbs, fire), but most objects we see reflect light (chairs, people, grass, and so on). The visual process begins when light is transduced by photoreceptors in the eye into electrical impulses.

The human eye works like a camera, focusing light to form an image on the retina (Figure 5.2). Light first passes through the *cornea*, the transparent outer coating of the eye. Light rays enter and are bent inward by the *lens*, which focuses the light to form an image on the **retina**, the inner surface of the back of the eyeball. The *pupil*, a small hole at the front of the eye, contracts or dilates to alter how much light enters the eye. The *iris*, an opaque, circular muscle, controls the size of the pupil and gives eyes their color. Behind the iris, muscles change the shape of the lens—flattening it to focus on distant objects and thickening it to focus on closer objects. This is called **accommodation**. The lens and cornea work together to collect and focus light rays reflected from an object, and they bring the rays together to form an inverted image of the object on the retina.

retina The thin inner surface of the back of the eyeball. The retina contains the photoreceptors that transduce light into neural signals.

accommodation A process by which muscles change the shape of the lens by flattening it to focus on distant objects or by thickening it to focus on closer objects.

5.2 The eye. The cornea is a clear protective layer covering the lens, which focuses images on the retinal surface. As with a camera, the retinal image is upside down. Receptors in the retina send information to the visual cortex via the optic nerve.

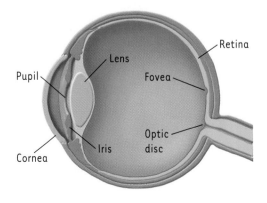

CONVERGING EVIDENCE IN THE STUDY OF PERCEPTION

Although the study of perception is fundamentally psychological in nature, researchers have relied on evidence from many other scientific fields to inform their theories. The effort that began over a century ago with basic psychophysics increasingly draws on innovations in other fields to learn how the brain processes perceptual information.

One of the most influential areas in the study of perception has been *neurophysiology*. Sensory neurophysiologists have relied primarily on single-cell recording experiments on cats, rats, and monkeys to discover how information from the senses is encoded in the brain. As you saw in Chapter 2, microelectrodes inserted into an animal's cortex can record activity in nearby neurons. The animal is then presented with an array of stimuli such as lights or shapes flashed on a screen. Researchers note whether these stimuli cause neurons close to the microelectrode to change their firing rate. This is how researchers discovered that quantitative coding depends on the rate of neural firing; for example, the greater the intensity of the stimulus, the greater the rate of neural firing.

Another influential field in the study of perception is *neuropsychology*. Neuropsychologists study the relationship between brain structures and psychological functions, such as how psychological functions are disrupted when people suffer brain damage. A variety of neuropsychological phenomena are of special interest to perception researchers. For example, damage to one of the areas of the brain that receive sensory input from the receptors—so-called primary sensory areas—results in a disruption of that sensory modality. Thus, damage to the primary visual area in the occipital lobe causes a blind spot, or scotoma, in the patient's visual field.

Neuropsychological evidence has revealed that a myriad of cortical areas are involved in the perceptual process, some of which perform remarkably specific functions. Damage to parts of the occipital, parietal, and temporal lobes can cause seemingly bizarre deficits in visual perception. For example, damage to a region at the junction of the occipital and temporal lobes can result in an inability to recognize certain types of objects. This syndrome, called *object agnosia*, can be amazingly selective; a patient may be unable to recognize animals, for example, but be within the normal range for other types of objects (Caramazza & Shelton, 1998). Similarly, damage to the fusiform gyrus, on the inferior surface of the temporal lobe, sometimes causes a specific deficit in recognizing faces, called *prosopagnosia*. Patients with prosopagnosia can often recognize other objects without difficulty but cannot recognize members of their own families, or even themselves.

One of the main problems with neuropsychological research is that brain damage is seldom restricted to a single brain area, so it is not always easy to draw relationships between brain structure and function. This has led some researchers to create lesions in animal brains that are restricted to a single cortical area so that they can observe the concomitant deficits in perception.

One of the most exciting developments in the last few years has been the introduction of brain-imaging devices such as PET and functional MRI scans that enable scientists to observe the human brain in action noninvasively (i.e., without causing any damage). These techniques have allowed perceptual psychologists to observe which regions of the brain respond to particular stimuli, and to observe how those responses change as the stimulus parameters are varied (Figure 5.3).

Perhaps the most compelling advances in perception research have been the result of converging evidence from two or more fields of research. Such evidence is particularly convincing because it is unlikely that idiosyncrasies or methodological flaws would have the same effect on two entirely independent experiments.

An example of converging evidence in perceptual research comes from studies of the brain regions involved in processing color and motion. As shown in Figure 5.3, visual neuroscientist Semir Zeki and his colleagues have used PET imaging to show that different regions of the visual cortex are activated when subjects process color (in an area called V4) and motion information (in area MT or V5) (Zeki, 1993).

Neuropsychological evidence backs up these findings. Patients with brain damage that includes area V4 are frequently unable to process color. They report that they see the world in black and white—a condition termed *achromatopsia*. Consider also the dramatic case of M.P., a German woman who became blind to motion

Rods and cones   The retina has two types of receptor cells: rods and cones, so called because of their distinctive shapes. Rods respond at extremely low levels of illumination and are primarily responsible for night vision; they do not support color vision, and they are poor at resolving fine detail. Cones, in contrast, are less sensitive to low levels of light; they are primarily responsible for vision under high illumination, and for color and detail. Within the rods and cones, light-sensitive chemicals called *photopigments* initiate the transduction of light waves into electrical neural impulses.

There are approximately 120 million rods and 6 million cones in each retina. Cones are densely packed in a small region near the center of the retina called the **fovea**. Although there are cones spread throughout the remainder of the retina (except in the blind spot, see below), they become increasingly scarce near the

fovea   The center of the retina where cones are densely packed.

following damage to area V5. She saw the world as a series of snapshots rather than as a moving image (Zihl et al., 1983) (Figure 5.4). Pouring tea, M.P. would see the liquid frozen in air and be surprised when her cup overflowed. Before crossing a street, she would spot a car far away, but when she tried to cross it would be right there. M.P.'s unique deficit has been termed *akinetopsia*—the inability to perceive motion.

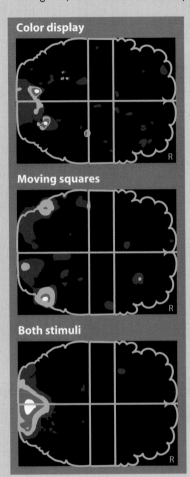

Color display

Moving squares

Both stimuli

5.3 PET scan images show how various sections of the brain are activated by specific visual stimuli.

A second example of how converging evidence helps us understand perception comes from neuropsychologists Leslie Ungerleider and Mortimer Mishkin (1982) at the United States National Institutes of Health. Using single-cell recording in monkeys, they found that outputs from the primary visual cortex follow two parallel processing streams—a ventral pathway that includes occipital and temporal lobe regions, and a dorsal pathway involving occipital and parietal lobe regions. The ventral path appears to be specialized for object perception and recognition, whereas the dorsal path seems to be specialized for spatial perception—determining where an object is and relating it to other objects in a scene. These two pathways

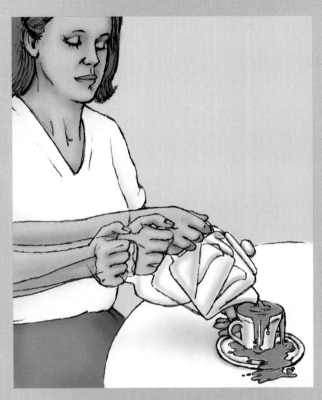

5.4 Patients with motion blindness (akinetopsia) see the world as a series of snapshots, rather than fluid motion. Even pouring a cup of coffee becomes difficult because by the time they see the cup as full, it is overflowing.

therefore are known as the "what" and "where" areas. Subsequent studies using PET and functional MRI scans of humans have confirmed that brain regions in the dorsal pathway are activated by tasks that require decisions about spatial relationships between objects, while regions in the ventral pathway are activated by tasks that require identifying objects.

periphery (Figure 5.5). Rods are all located in the periphery of the retina; none are located in the fovea.

Transmission from the eye to the brain The generation of electrical signals by the photoreceptors in the retina is just the beginning of the visual process. Immediately after light is transduced into neural impulses by the rods and cones, other cells in the retina perform a series of sophisticated computations on those impulses. The outputs from these cells converge on about 1 million retinal **ganglion cells**. Axons from these ganglion cells are gathered into a bundle called the *optic nerve* that exits the eye at the back of each retina. The point at which the optic nerve exits the retina has no rods or cones at all, resulting in a small blind spot in each eye. This blind spot can be isolated, as demonstrated in Figure 5.6, but we

ganglion cells A class of neurons located in the retina that perform a series of sophisticated computations on impulses from the rods and cones. The axons of the ganglion cells form the optic nerve.

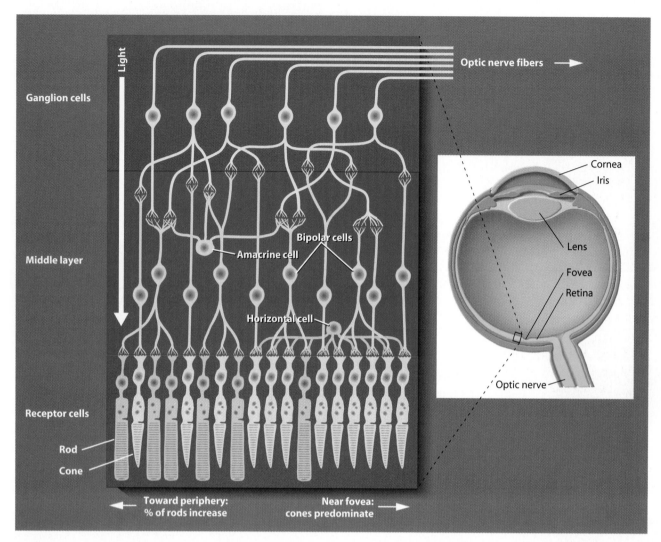

5.5 A schematic cross section of the retina. Light passes through the cornea and is focused on the retina by the lens. It passes through the ganglion cell layer and middle layer before it is transduced into neural impulses by the receptor cells. There are two types of receptors in the retina: rods and cones. The cells in the middle layer transduce the neural impulses, which form a synapse with the ganglion cells. The ganglion cells, in turn, transmit neural impulses to the brain.

are generally not aware of it. Each optic nerve carries information to the central nervous system. Before entering the brain, the optic nerve splits into two parts that cross at the *optic chiasm*, causing all information from the left side of visual space (i.e., left of the point of gaze) to be projected to the right hemisphere of the brain and vice versa, as shown in Figure 5.7. Once in the brain the information first travels to a region of the thalamus called the **lateral geniculate nucleus (LGN)**, and it is then relayed to the visual cortex in the occipital lobe.

The color of light is determined by its wavelength   Visible light consists of electromagnetic waves ranging from about 400 to 700 nanometers (nm) in length. The color of light is determined by the wavelengths of the electromagnetic waves that comprise it. In the simplest terms, each wavelength of light corresponds to a different color (see Figure 5.8). It would be wrong, however, to equate wavelength with color. As you will see, the relationship between wavelength and perceived color is quite complex, and it can only be understood by considering the response of the visual system to different wavelengths. White light, for example, contains the entire range of wavelengths in the visible spectrum.

Human beings can distinguish millions of shades of color, which can be categorized along three dimensions: hue, brightness, and saturation. *Hue* refers to the

lateral geniculate nucleus (LGN)
A region of the thalamus where visual information first travels, and then relays the information to the visual cortex.

distinctive characteristics of a color that place it in the spectrum; hue depends primarily on the light's wavelength when it reaches the eye. *Brightness* relates to the perceived intensity or luminance of a color, which is determined chiefly by the total amount of light, or its intensity. One should be careful not to confuse brightness—a physical dimension—and lightness—a psychological dimension. The *lightness* of an area is determined by its brightness relative to its surroundings. Thus, two grays with the same brightness can differ in lightness, depending on the surrounding levels of brightness. Although lightness is a more important variable than brightness for describing visual appearance, it has no simple physical correlate. The third dimension, *saturation*, refers to the purity of a color. Saturation varies according to the mixture of wavelengths present in a stimulus. Pure spectral colors have only a single wavelength, whereas pastels have a mixture of many wavelengths.

Subtractive and additive mixture of color   Color is determined not just by wavelength, but by the mixture of wavelengths (or spectral pattern) of a stimulus. There are two ways to produce a given spectral pattern: subtractive and additive mixture of wavelengths. In mixing, say, paints, the mixture occurs within the stimulus itself and is a physical process. This is called **subtractive color mixing**. When lights of different wavelengths are mixed, the percept is determined by the interaction of these wavelengths with receptors in the eye and is a psychological process. This is called **additive color mixing**.

5.6 The optic nerve creates the blind spot we all have—a small point at the back of the retina. To find your blind spot, hold this book in front of you and look at the dot, closing your left eye. Move the book toward and away from your face until the rabbit disappears. You can repeat this for your right eye by turning the book upside down.

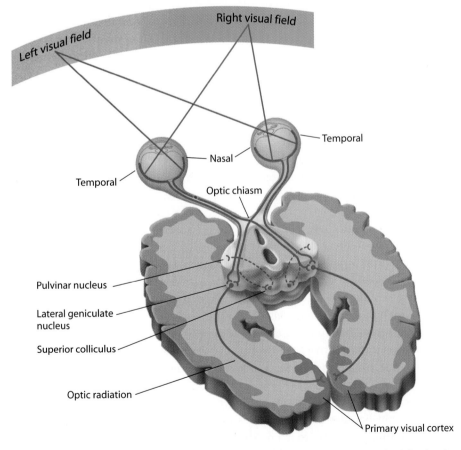

5.7 The pathways along which information from the left visual field projects to the right visual cortex and the information from the right visual field projects to the left visual cortex.

subtractive color mixing A way to produce a given spectral pattern in which the mixture occurs within the stimulus itself and is actually a physical, not psychological, process.

additive color mixing A way to produce a given spectral pattern in which different wavelengths of lights are mixed. The percept is determined by the interaction of these wavelengths with receptors in the eye and is a psychological process.

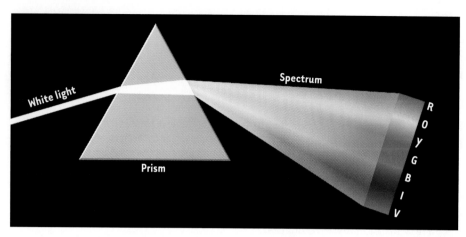

5.8 A prism breaks apart light rays into the spectrum of colors: red, orange, yellow, green, blue, indigo, and violet (ROYGBIV).

Subtractive mixing of paints occurs because colors are determined by pigments—chemicals on objects' surfaces that absorb (or subtract) different wavelengths of light and prevent them from being reflected to the eye. The color of the pigment is determined by the wavelengths that are reflected. Thus blue paint contains pigments that absorb only long wavelengths (yellow and red); the paint appears blue because it reflects the shorter waves. Yellow pigments absorb shorter (blue) and longer (red) wavelengths, but they reflect wavelengths in the central yellow region of the visible spectrum. If we mix blue and yellow paint we get green because the yellow pigment absorbs the blue wavelengths and the blue pigment absorbs the red and yellow wavelengths. What remains is the wavelength corresponding to green. Thus the pigments mix to make green by subtraction. Red, yellow, and blue are the subtractive primary colors. Mix them together and you get black because together these pigments absorb nearly all the colors of the visible spectrum.

Additive color mixing is a technique known to stage lighting designers. For them, red, yellow, and blue are not the primary colors because they can aim a red and green light at the same point on a stage and create a yellow light. In fact, almost any color can be created by combining just three wavelengths, so long as one is from the long-wave end of the spectrum (red), one is from the middle (green-yellow), and one is from the short end of the spectrum (blue-violet). This is called the **three primaries law of color**. Note that the exact colors of the three primaries in additive color mixing are more-or-less arbitrary. However, for reasons that will become clear soon, most psychologists consider the additive primary colors to be red, green, and blue.

Explaining the phenomena of color vision Whether color is created by subtracting hues from white light or mixing colors together, the result is the same: a certain combination of wavelengths striking the retina. However complicated this pattern is, it can often be replaced with light of a single wavelength to yield the same perceived color.

If each wavelength corresponds to one color, how is it that combining multiple wavelengths can create a unique color? This is because of the way light is transduced into neural impulses in the retina. Color vision begins in the retinal cone cells, which transduce light into neural impulses. There are actually three distinct types of cones in the retina, each of which responds best to a different wavelength of light. One type of cone is most sensitive to blue light (short wavelength), another is most sensitive to green light (medium wavelength), and the remaining population is most sensitive to red light (long wavelength). The color of a stimulus is determined by how much of each cone type it activates. Thus, yellow light looks yellow because it stimulates the "red" and "green" cones about equally and hardly stimulates the "blue" cones at all. Similarly, we can create yellow light from red and green light because each stimulates the corresponding cone population. As far as the brain can tell, there is no difference between yellow light and a combination of red and green lights. Physiological research has shown that the three different kinds of cones in the retina each contain photopigments that are most

three primaries law of color Any color can be produced by mixing light of just three wavelengths.

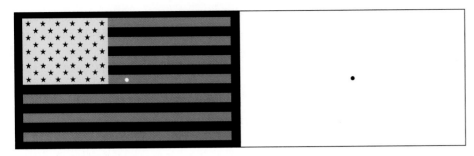

5.9 Stare at the dot in the middle of the flag for at least 30 seconds. Then look at the dot in the blank space to the right. Because your receptors have adapted to the green and yellow in the first image, the afterimage appears in the complementary colors of red and blue.

sensitive to different wavelengths of the visible spectrum. The three cone populations are called "S," "M," and "L" cones because they respond maximally to short, medium, and long wavelengths, respectively (some vision scientists call these cones α, β, and γ, respectively). Ultimately, our perception of different colors is determined by the ratio of activity between the three cone receptors.

The initial coding of color information by just three types of retinal cone cells is one of the most important discoveries in the scientific study of visual perception. It illustrates how an essentially limitless variety of colors can be encoded by a small number of receptors—a ubiquitous principle in neural coding. There are aspects of color vision, however, that are not predicted by the existence of three types of cones in the retina. For example, some colors seem to be "opposites" in some sense (Hering, 1878/1964). When we stare at a red image for some time, we see a green afterimage when we look away (and vice versa). Likewise, when we stare at a blue image for some time, we see a yellow afterimage when we look away (and vice versa) (Figure 5.9). We also have trouble visualizing certain color mixtures. For instance, it is easier to imagine a reddish yellow or a bluish green than a reddish green or a bluish yellow.

These phenomena cannot be explained by the responses of the different cones in the retina. To account for them, we must turn to the next stage of visual processing, in the retinal ganglion cells. As you have seen, the information from the cones converges upon ganglion cells in the retina, some of which are sensitive to the color of a stimulus, and some of which are not. One class of color-sensitive ganglion cells receives excitatory input from L-cones but is inhibited by M-cones (or vice versa). These cells create the perception that red and green are "opposites." Other ganglion cells are excited by input from S-cones, but inhibited by both L- and M-cone activity (or vice versa). These create the perception that blue and yellow are opposites. Similar patterns of excitation and inhibition are repeated in the thalamus and again in the visual cortex.

Lateral inhibition, a retinal process, also influences visual perception

Chances are you are familiar with the phenomenon of *simultaneous contrast*, which makes an object look lighter against a black background than against a white one. We know this effect is caused by the difference in the backgrounds. The physiological mechanism that causes this effect is called *lateral inhibition* (see Figure 5.10).

Single-cell recording experiments in cats' retinae have indicated that cells in neighboring regions of the retina tend to inhibit one another. If a cell is stimulated it sends information up to the brain, but it also sends information to its neighboring neurons inhibiting their activity. The effect of this lateral inhibition is to emphasize changes in visual stimuli, which makes the visual system especially sensitive to edges and contours. This is important because areas of changing

5.10 The Hermann grid is another demonstration of lateral inhibition at work. Look at the figure as a whole and you will immediately see darkened spots at the intersections of the white lines. However, if you look directly at the intersections, or cover all but one row of squares, you see that the dark spots are illusory. What is happening? Receptors coding information from the white lines are inhibited by their neighbors on two sides. Those receptors that code information from the intersections, however, are inhibited from four sides, so they respond less vigorously. This makes it look as though the intersections are darker than the lines.

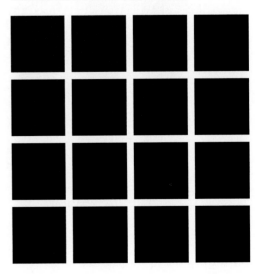

sound wave The pattern of the changes in air pressure through time that results in the percept of a sound.

outer ear The structure of the ear, where the sound wave arrives.

eardrum (tympanic membrane) A thin membrane, which the sound wave vibrates, that marks the beginning of the middle ear.

ossicles Three tiny bones, the incus (hammer), malleus (anvil), and stapes (stirrup), in the middle ear that transfer the vibrations of the eardrum to the oval window.

visual stimulation are likely to correspond to boundaries of objects in the physical world. From a very early stage of processing, then, the circuitry of the visual system is "wired" to make finding the boundaries of objects easier.

IN HEARING, THE EAR IS A SOUND-WAVE DETECTOR

Hearing, or audition, is second only to vision as a source of information about the world. It is not only a mechanism for determining what is happening in the environment, but it also provides a medium for spoken language. Like vision, audition is a distance sense. The proximal stimulus for hearing is *sound*, the displacement of air molecules caused by a change in air pressure. The pattern of the changes in air pressure through time is called a **sound wave** or pressure wave. The simplest sound wave to describe is a regular, sine-wave oscillation that generates compressions and expansions in the air. Such simple sounds are called *pure tones*. The *amplitude* of the wave determines its *loudness*, with higher amplitude perceived as louder. The *frequency* of a sound wave determines its *pitch*, with higher frequencies perceived as higher in pitch. The frequency of sound is measured in vibrations per second, called Hertz (Hz). Humans can detect sound waves with frequencies from about 20 Hz to 20,000 Hz. Most sounds are much more complex than a simple sine wave. However, since the pattern of compression and expansion that describes any complex sound can be represented by a unique combination of simple sine waves with different frequencies and amplitudes, we can usually predict the response of the auditory system to a complex sound from the way it responds to the component pure tones.

Figures 5.11 and 5.12 show the structures of the ear and a cross-section illustrating how these structures convert sound waves to neural signals. Air-pressure changes that produce sound waves arrive at the **outer ear** and travel down the *auditory canal* to the **eardrum**, or *tympanic membrane*. This membrane is stretched tightly across the canal marking the beginning of the *middle ear*. Changes in air pressure make the eardrum vibrate. These vibrations are transferred to three tiny bones called **ossicles**—the *incus* (hammer), *malleus* (anvil), and *stapes* (stirrup). The ossicles transfer the vibrations of the eardrum to the *oval window*, a membrane of the **cochlea**. The cochlea, or *inner ear*, is a fluid-filled tube that curls into a snail-like shape. The ossicles mechanically amplify the vibrations, so that when they reach the oval window from the eardrum these vibrations are about 30 times greater in pressure.

Running through the center of the cochlea is the thin *basilar membrane* that divides the cochlea into three chambers, two outer ducts and an inner duct. The vibrations of the oval window create pressure waves in the fluid of the inner ear, and these waves stimulate the *hair cells* located on the surface of the basilar membrane. These hair cells are primary auditory re-

5.11 The human ear. Sound waves enter the auditory canal, causing the eardrum to vibrate. These vibrations are carried along as waves in the liquid of the inner ear.

ceptors, much like rods and cones are for the visual system. The oscillations of the basilar membrane prompt the hair cells to generate action potentials; thus the mechanical signal of the oscillations is converted into a neural signal that travels down the auditory nerve to the brain.

Time and place coding for pitch   How does the firing of auditory receptors signal different frequencies of sound? In other words, How is pitch coded by the auditory system? Two mechanisms for encoding the frequency of an auditory stimulus operate in parallel in the basilar membrane: temporal coding and place coding.

Temporal coding is used to encode relatively low frequencies. The firing rates of cochlear hair cells match the frequency of the pressure wave, so that a 1,000 Hz tone causes hair cells to fire 1,000 times per second. Physiological research has shown that this strict matching between the frequency of auditory stimulation and firing rate of the hair cells can occur only for relatively low frequencies—up to about 4,000 Hz. At higher frequencies, temporal coding can only be maintained if hair cells fire in volleys. Each cell fires at a lower frequency than the sound, but the overall temporal pattern of firing in the auditory nerve still matches the sound frequency.

The second mechanism for encoding frequency is **place coding**. Hermann von Helmholtz (1821–1894) believed that different cells in the basilar membrane respond to different frequencies, so that low frequencies would activate a whole different set of receptors than high frequencies. Later, perceptual psychologist Georg von Békésy (1899–1972) discovered that Helmholtz's idea was theoretically correct, but wrong in the details. Békésy (1957) discovered that different frequencies do activate different receptors, but their only difference is where they are located on the basilar membrane. This membrane responds to sound waves like a clarinet reed, vibrating in resonance with the sound. Because its stiffness decreases along its length, higher frequencies resonate better at the membrane's base, while lower frequencies vibrate more toward its tip. Thus, hair cells at the base of the cochlea are activated by high-frequency sounds; hair cells at the tip are activated by low-frequency sounds (Culler et al., 1943). The frequency of a sound wave, therefore, is encoded by the receptors on the area of the basilar membrane that vibrates the most.

Both temporal and place coding are involved in our perception of pitch. Most of the sounds we hear—from conversations to concerts—are made up of many frequencies and activate a broad range of hair cells. Individual cells provide only coarse coding of frequencies, whether through their firing rate or location on the basilar membrane. Just as color is encoded by the combined activities of three different types of receptors, our perception of sound relies on the integrated activities of many neurons.

Concurrent processing to locate sounds   Locating the origin of a sound is another significant problem in auditory perception. In audition, the sensory receptors do not code spatial information. Instead, the brain integrates sensory information coming from each of our two ears. Much of our understanding of auditory localization has come from examining barn owls, which use a fine-tuned sense of hearing to locate their prey. These nocturnal animals can locate a mouse in a dark laboratory using their sense of hearing alone. Barn owls use two cues to locate a sound: the difference in timing between its arrival in each ear, and the

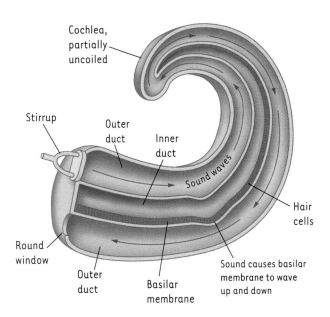

5.12 Path of transduction in the inner ear. When sound waves hit the fluid of the inner ear, the fluid causes the basilar membrane to move up and down, activating electrical potentials in the hair cells (the receptor cells for hearing).

cochlea (inner ear)   A fluid-filled tube that curls into a snail-like shape. The cochlea contains the basilar membrane, which in turn contains auditory receptor cells called hair cells. These transduce the mechanical energy of the sound wave into neural impulses.

temporal coding   A mechanism for encoding low-frequency auditory stimuli in which the frequency of the sound wave is encoded by the frequency of firing of the hair cells.

place coding   A mechanism for encoding high-frequency auditory stimuli in which the frequency of the sound wave is encoded by the location of the hair cells along the basilar membrane.

difference in its intensity in the ears. Unless a sound is coming from a point exactly in front or in back of the owl, it will reach one ear before the other. Likewise, if sound comes from the right, it will be softer on the left because the head acts as a barrier. These differences in timing and magnitude are minute—but not too small for the owl's brain to detect.

Neurobiologist Mark Konishi (1993) has discovered that each cue is processed by separate neural pathways. When auditory nerve signals reach the *cochlear nucleus*, which is composed of two parts, they diverge into two discrete pathways. In one pathway, signals of the time difference it takes a sound to reach each ear determine the stimulus's lateral position, or azimuth, with respect to the owl's head. In the other pathway, the differences in a sound's intensity compute the elevation of the stimulus. Whether there are similar neural mechanisms responsible for sound localization in humans is unknown, but the concept that such functions are likely to be segregated is a key to understanding how and what we perceive.

IN TOUCH, STIMULI ARE CODED FOR PAIN, TEMPERATURE, AND PRESSURE

Pain is a warning system that stops you from continuing activities that may inflict harm. Whether the message is to remove your hand from a hot burner or to stop running when you have damaged a tendon, pain signals that you have to quit doing whatever you are doing. Children born with a rare genetic disorder that leaves them insensitive to pain usually die young, no matter how much they are supervised. They simply do not know how to avoid activities that harm them or to report when they are not feeling well (Melzak & Wall, 1982).

The **haptic** or cutaneous sense, or sense of touch, conveys sensations of pain, temperature, and pressure. Once again, research into how these sensations are coded looks at whether different receptors or brain systems are responsible for different sensations. Receptors for temperature, touch, and pain are sensory neurons that terminate in the outer layer of skin, the epidermis. Their long axons enter the central nervous system by way of spinal or cranial nerves. Some of the receptors for touch and light pressure are nerve fibers at the base of hair follicles that respond to movement in the hair. Other receptors are capsules in the skin that respond to continued vibration, sudden movements, and steady pressure.

5.13 Pain receptors in the skin end in free nerve endings. C fibers carry slow, diffuse pain; A-delta fibers carry fast, sharp pain.

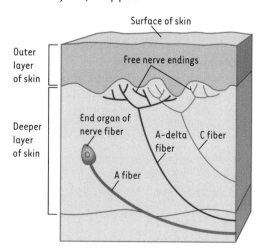

Surface of skin

Outer layer of skin

Free nerve endings

Deeper layer of skin

End organ of nerve fiber

A-delta fiber

C fiber

A fiber

Two types of pain fibers Pain neurons are thinner than neurons for temperature and touch. They do not end in specialized structures. They are just free nerve endings found in all body tissues that sense pain: skin, muscles, membranes around bones and joints, organs, and so on (see Figure 5.13). Two kinds of fibers have been identified for pain: *A-delta fibers*, for sharp, immediate pain, and *C fibers*, for chronic, dull, steady pain. Each type of fiber sends information to a different part of the cortex (Jessell & Kelley, 1991).

A-delta fibers are myelinated, fast-conducting neurons. C fibers are unmyelinated, slow-conducting neurons (see Chapter 4). Think of when you touch a hot pan. You feel two kinds of pain: a sharp, fast, localized pain at the point where your skin touches the pan (conducted by A-delta fibers), followed by a slow, dull, more diffused burning pain (conducted by C fibers). The A-delta fibers are activated by strong physical pressure or temperature extremes. The fibers transmit impulses along the spinal cord to the thalamus, which sends information to the somatosensory area of the cerebral cortex.

The C fibers are activated by chemical changes in tissue when skin is damaged. When C fibers are activated, they send information along the spinal cord to the thalamus; this in turn transmits output to many higher brain areas, including the frontal lobe.

Gate control theory   The brain can prevent us from feeling pain. The *gate control theory* of pain, formulated by Ronald Melzack and Patrick Wall, states that to experience pain, pain receptors must be activated and the neural gate in the spinal cord must allow these signals through to the brain. The gate can be closed by signals sent from the brain to the spinal cord, blocking the reception of pain signals. This explains the influence that mental states can have over pain.

Several observations support the gate control theory. The neural gate involves a region of the midbrain called the **periaqueductal gray** (**PAG**), which has neurons that can inhibit pain receptor cells from carrying their signals to the cortex. Painkillers such as morphine stimulate the PAG, making the gate close and blocking pain (Basbaum & Fields, 1984). Endorphins, painkilling chemicals that humans produce naturally, are believed to act on the PAG in the same way. With rats, if the PAG is stimulated during abdominal surgery, the rats do not seem to feel pain (Reynolds, 1969). This is called *stimulation-induced analgesia*, which occurs with acupuncture therapy.

IN SMELL, THE NASAL CAVITY GATHERS PARTICLES OF ODOR

The sense of smell, or olfaction, has the most direct route to the brain of all of the senses, but it is the least well understood. We know that odorous particles—or *odorants*—pass into the nose and the upper and back portions of the nasal cavity. There they come into contact with the **olfactory epithelium**, a thin layer of tissue embedded with olfactory receptors; the particles dissolve in the solution that surrounds the epithelium and cause a reaction that triggers chemical receptors. These nerve impulses convey information to the **olfactory bulb**, the brain center for smell, just below the frontal lobes. Unlike other sensory information, from here smell signals go directly to olfactory centers in the cerebral cortex, bypassing the thalamus. Researchers have identified thousands of different receptors in the olfactory epithelium, each responsive to a different chemical group. It remains unclear exactly how different smells are encoded by these receptors. One possibility is that each receptor type is uniquely associated with a specific odor, so that there is a receptor that encodes only, for example, the scent of a rose. Another possibility is that odors will each stimulate several receptors, and that the pattern of activation across several receptor types will determine the olfactory percept.

Pheromones are chemicals released by animals—including probably humans—that trigger physiological or behavioral reactions. These chemicals do not elicit "smells" we are conscious of, but they are processed in a similar manner to olfactory stimuli. Specialized receptors in the nasal cavity called *vomeronasal organs* respond to the presence of pheromones. Pheromones play a major role in sexual signaling in many animal species and may affect humans in similar ways. For example, pheromones may explain why the menstrual cycles of women who live together tend to synchronize (McClintock, 1971).

haptic sense The sense of touch.

periaqueductal gray (PAG) A region of the midbrain that has neurons that can inhibit pain receptor cells from carrying their signals to the cortex.

olfactory epithelium A thin layer of tissue embedded with olfactory receptors around which odorants dissolve into solution and cause a reaction, which triggers chemical receptors.

olfactory bulb The brain center for smell, located below the frontal lobes.

pheromones Chemicals released by animals and humans that trigger physiological or behavioral reactions in other members of the same species. Pheromones do not elicit detectable smells but are processed in a similar manner to olfactory stimuli, by specialized receptors in the nasal cavity called vomeronasal organs.

taste buds Structures in the mouth that contain fifty receptor cells. The receptor cells contain structures called microvilli that come into direct contact with saliva. When stimulated, they send electrical impulses that convey information to the medulla and then to the thalamus and cortex.

IN TASTE, STIMULI ARE CODED FOR SWEET, SOUR, SALTY, AND BITTER

The job of our sense of taste, or gustation, is to keep poisons out of our digestive systems while allowing good food in. You know from having a cold that taste relies heavily on the sense of smell—if your nasal passages are blocked, food seems tasteless.

The stimuli for taste are substances that dissolve in saliva (often called *tastants*), though how these stimuli work is still largely a mystery. The taste receptors are part of the **taste buds** of the tongue and mouth. The average person has about 10,000 taste buds, mostly located on the tongue. Each taste bud has about 50 receptor cells. *Microvilli*, short hairlike structures at the tip of each receptor, come into direct contact with saliva. When stimulated, they send electrical signals to a brainstem region called the medulla and from there to the thalamus and cortex.

There are several different kinds of taste receptors. These taste buds each encode one of four "primary" taste sensations: sweet, sour, salty, and bitter. Every taste experience is composed of a mixture of these four qualities. This is analogous to the way a near-infinite variety of colors can be encoded with just three types of receptors. The different varieties of taste buds are not uniformly distributed but instead cluster in regions. You are most sensitive to salty and sweet substances near the front of your tongue, sour substances at the sides of your tongue, and bitterness along the roof of your mouth. Electrical cell recordings from rats and hamsters indicate that some fibers in the taste buds respond to all four substances, though they seem to respond best to one (Nowlis & Frank, 1981).

Beyond the five senses discussed in this section, "Using Psychological Science: Is There a Sixth Sense?" points to additional sensory systems that may be explored.

Using Psychological Science

IS THERE A SIXTH SENSE?

"Sixth sense" is a phrase used to refer to the "unexplainable" feeling that something is about to happen. In actuality, as Dartmouth psychologist Howard Hughes points out, there are several internal human sensory systems in addition to the five primary ones we've discussed (Hughes, 2000). Subtle internal sensory systems send messages to our brains about things like our blood pressure or blood glucose levels. The *kinesthetic* sense, which some group with the touch senses, refers to sensations we gather from receptors in muscles, tendons, and joints that pinpoint the position and movements of our limbs and body in space. This helps us to coordinate voluntary movement and is invaluable in avoiding injury. The *vestibular* or equilibratory senses use data from receptors in the semicircular canals of the inner ear. These canals contain a liquid that moves when the head moves, bending hair cells at the ends of the canal. The bending creates nerve impulses that inform us of the head's rotation and is thus responsible for a sense of balance. It explains why inner-ear infections make you dizzy, and why standing up quickly can give you a "head rush."

Hughes identifies more exotic sensory systems that are only recently being studied in animals as the "7th, 8th, 9th, etc." senses. These include the *sonar* senses and *electroreception* (senses based on electrical fields). Understanding sensory systems that use sonar or electrical fields for navigation comes from studying primarily the sonar systems of bats and dolphins. (SONAR stands for "sound navigation and ranging.") These animals produce a call and then respond to the echoes of that call; the system is actually *biosonar* because the sound waves emanate from the animal. Electroreception operates in a similar way: some fish emit an electrical field and then analyze disruptions in the field to avoid predators or find prey. Others respond to the electrical fields emitted by other fish.

What Are the Sensory Processes for Our Primary Senses?

Each of our sensory systems has receptors that respond to different physical or chemical stimuli by transducing them into some pattern of neural impulses. The selectivity of the receptors in each sensory system determines the kinds of physical stimuli that we are able to perceive. Most sensory systems employ some form of coarse coding, which allows a relatively small number of receptors to encode a wide variety of stimuli. For example, the visual system can represent the entire range of colors with only three cone types. The notable exception to this rule is the olfactory system, which contains thousands of different receptors, each of which responds to different chemical groups in odors. Nature has endowed each of our sensory systems with intricate mechanisms to convert physical stimuli into electrical impulses that are sent to our brain. What our brain does with those impulses, and how they result in our perceptions, is the subject of the remainder of this chapter.

WHAT ARE THE BASIC PERCEPTUAL PROCESSES?

Perceptions are complex. Every minute, our brains make calculations—all in milliseconds—most of which are beyond our conscious awareness. For instance, as you stare at a computer screen, you are aware of one image, not the thousands that dance across your retina to create that constant, static image. What you perceive, then, is vastly different from the pattern of stimulation your retina is taking in. How does the brain extract a stable representation of the world from the information the senses provide? This is what perception research is about.

If we were aware every moment of what our brain was doing we would be paralyzed by the overload of information. Most of the computations the brain performs never reach our conscious awareness—only important new outcomes. Perceptual psychology has drawn on many disciplines to understand how we represent our world. Perceptual psychologists have made many advances by noting how perception is disrupted following some injury to the brain, working backward to infer how the intact brain processes information. In addition, modern psychophysicists have developed clever techniques to describe the perceptual functions of the brain. Areas as diverse as art, computer science, music, philosophy, anatomy, and physiology have also informed our understanding of perception. It is truly an interdisciplinary study that crosses the levels of analysis.

PERCEPTION OCCURS IN THE BRAIN

So far, you have seen how sensory stimuli are transduced into electrical impulses and transmitted to the brain via nerves. These electrical impulses are all that the brain has to work with to create our rich variety of perceptual experiences. With the exception of olfaction, all sensory information is relayed to the brain via the thalamus. From the thalamus, information from each sense is projected to localized regions of the cerebral cortex, called **primary sensory areas**. It is in these areas that the perceptual process begins in earnest.

Cortical processing of vision begins in the occipital lobe By now you are aware that the *primary visual cortex*, also called area **V1** (for first visual area), is in

What do we know about the relationships between neural activity in the brain and our perceptions of the world?

primary sensory areas Localized regions of the cerebral cortex that receive sensory inputs from the thalamus.

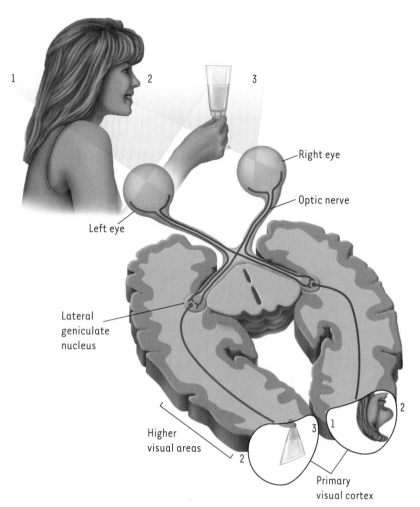

5.14 Schematic view of the visual system, illustrating the contralateral inverted topographic representation of the visual field in the primary visual cortex. The image is also distorted, so that the region corresponding to the fovea is enlarged, and progressively smaller areas of cortex are dedicated to more peripheral areas of the visual field.

the occipital lobe of the brain. The neuronal pathway from the retina to the occipital lobe preserves spatial relationships, so that adjacent areas of the retina correspond to adjacent areas in V1. This remarkably systematic ordering is known as **retinotopic organization.** The fovea of each retina is projected to an area at the very back of the brain called the *occipital pole,* with more peripheral visual areas represented deeper along the V1. Since the retinal image is inverted, as you learned earlier, the visual cortex has a *contralateral* and *inverted* (i.e., backward and upside-down) representation of the visual world (see Figure 5.14).

Beginning in the 1960s, neurophysiologists David Hubel and Torsten Wiesel (1962) began exploring the properties of neurons in V1 using single-cell recording techniques—work for which they were awarded a Nobel prize. They discovered that some neurons in the primary visual cortex respond more to lines of particular orientations; for example, some neurons increase their firing rate when a vertical line segment is presented in their **receptive field** (the region of visual space to which they are sensitive). The firing rate of these cells—termed **simple cells** by Hubel and Wiesel—decreases as the orientation of the line segment is rotated away from the preferred orientation. Further studies by Hubel and Wiesel and others have also found neurons that specialize in detecting the ends of lines, corners, and colors, as well as more complex visual features.

Besides V1, visual information is processed in a cascade of other visual areas, many of which are also organized retinotopically. You have already seen that many of these visual areas appear to process specific aspects of a visual stimulus, such as color or motion. The functions of other visual areas have yet to be discovered. The complexity of visual perception is underscored by the amount of cortical real estate that is dedicated to processing visual information. Some estimates suggest that up to half of the cerebral cortex may participate in visual perception in some way. Damage to visual areas can result in interesting perceptual phenomena, as discussed in "Studying the Mind: Visual Deficits from Brain Injury."

The primary auditory cortex is in the temporal lobe Auditory neurons in the thalamus extend their axons to the *primary auditory cortex* (called *A1*) in a region of the superior temporal lobe known as *Heschl's gyrus.* Single-cell recording experiments have shown that neurons in A1 code the frequency (or pitch) of auditory stimuli. These studies have also revealed that A1 has a *tonotopic organization.* That is, neurons at the rear end of Heschl's gyrus respond best to lower frequencies, whereas neurons at the front end respond best to higher frequencies. Thus, the encoding of frequency in A1 is primarily by location along Heschl's gyrus.

Compared to the wealth of data about the physiology of the visual cortex, the organization of the auditory cortices of primates is relatively unknown—most research has been conducted with birds and cats. Nevertheless, it is known that A1

VISUAL DEFICITS FROM BRAIN INJURY

Patient C.L.T. was 49 when he suffered a right posterior cerebral artery stroke in March 1987 (Fendrich et al., 1992). He awoke one morning disoriented, unable to recognize places or faces. With time, his orientation and face-recognition problems lessened, but he never completely recovered. The stroke also resulted in nearly complete blindness in his left visual field. The right occipital lobe, located in the area of C.L.T.'s stroke, receives information from the left visual field. So damage to the right occipital lobe meant C.L.T. could no longer see anything from his left visual field. Or could he?

C.L.T. didn't believe his left visual field was "completely" blind. He often remarked that that he could "sense" things on his left, which would make him turn his head and see what was going on. By turning his head, things came into view in his right visual field, allowing him to see normally. In fact, by adjusting in this way, C.L.T. still sees fine—the ability to sense things in his left visual field when he shouldn't have been able to see them is a characteristic of *blindsight*. Blindsight is a phenomenon first identified by Lawrence Weiskrantz of Oxford University in 1986. When blindsighted patients have a point of light flashed to their blind visual field, they report seeing nothing, as is expected. But if you ask the patient to point to where the light flashed, they point in the correct direction. What is happening is that they see the light; they just are not aware that they are seeing it.

When this phenomenon was first identified, psychologists, philosophers, and neuroscientists were fascinated. How could our brains see something but not know it? Researchers continue to debate whether blindsight is due to subcortical structures outside the visual cortex that process visual information without our knowing it, or due to tiny areas of intact cortex that allow for residual visual

function (Fendrich et al., 1992). These various explanations are considered in more detail in Chapter 8. What is important to note here is that blindsight highlights a key fact: perception routinely occurs outside our conscious awareness.

Another example of how brain injury helps us understand sensation and perception is the case of D.F. (Goodale & Milner, 1992). When she was 34 years old, D.F. suffered carbon monoxide poisoning that resulted in damage to her visual system. She was no longer able to recognize the faces of her friends and family, common objects, or even a drawing of a square or circle. She could recognize people by hearing their voices, however, and if you placed objects in her hands, she could tell you what they were.

Her condition—*object agnosia*, the inability to recognize objects—is striking in what she can and cannot do. When presented with a drawing of, say, an apple, she cannot identify or reproduce it. But if asked to "draw an apple," she can do so from memory. Despite major deficits in object perception, she can use visual information about the size, shape, and orientation of objects to control visually guided movements. For instance, she can walk across a room and step around things adeptly. She can reach out and shake your hand. Most confounding, in laboratory tests, she can reach out and grasp a block, with the exact right distance between her fingers, even though she cannot tell you what she is going to pick up, or how big it is.

Thus, her conscious perception of objects is impaired—she has no awareness that she is taking in any visual information about objects she sees. However, other aspects of visual processing are unaffected. The intact regions of her visual cortex allow her to use information about the size and location of objects despite her lack of awareness.

---

is surrounded by several secondary auditory areas in the temporal and parietal lobes. Although there is little information about the organization of these secondary areas, it appears that they are also organized tonotopically. There is also some evidence that there are neurons in some of these areas that are maximally sensitive to *phonemes*—the elementary sounds used in speech.

Touch is first processed in the parietal lobe   Touch information from the thalamus is projected to the *primary somatosensory cortex* (called *S1*), in the *postcentral gyrus* in the anterior parietal lobe. In a classic series of studies of patients undergoing brain surgery, described in Chapter 4, the neurosurgeon Wilder Penfield discovered that electrical stimulation of different regions of the postcentral gyrus could evoke the sensation of touch in different regions of the body. Penfield found that neighboring body parts tended to be represented next to one another in the primary somatosensory cortex. That is, S1 has a *somatotopic organization*—the body is effectively mapped out along the postcentral gyrus. Furthermore, more sensitive body parts have relatively larger amounts of S1 dedicated to them.

retinotopic organization The systematic ordering of the neuronal pathway from the retina to the occipital lobe preserves spatial relationships, so that adjacent areas of the retina correspond to adjacent areas in the primary visual cortex.

receptive field The region of visual space to which neurons in the primary visual cortex are sensitive.

simple cells In Hubel and Weisel's 1960s' experiment, the term they used for neurons that preferred certain line orientations over other orientations.

binocular depth cues Cues of depth perception that arise from the fact that people have two eyes.

monocular depth cues Cues of depth perception that are available to each eye alone.

binocular disparity A cue of depth perception that is caused by the distance between a person's two eyes.

The chemical senses The processing of the chemical senses—taste and smell—in the brain remains largely unexplored. Taste information from the thalamus projects to three different regions of the cortex. Two of these regions are at the base of the primary somatosensory cortex—near the area where somatosensory information from the mouth is represented. This has led some researchers to suggest that the sense of taste evolved from the sense of touch. The third area that receives taste information is in an area of the frontal lobe called the *anterior insular cortex*, which is located under the front end of the temporal lobe.

We have already seen that olfactory information bypasses the thalamus on the way to the cortex. Instead, some information from the olfactory bulb projects to a region of the temporal lobe that appears to be the *primary olfactory cortex*. Other olfactory information projects to lower brain centers in the *limbic system*. Limbic structures are associated with emotion and memory, which may partially account for the ease with which olfactory stimuli can evoke powerful memories and feelings.

PERCEPTION IS AN ILL-POSED PROBLEM

The goal of vision research is to understand how we know what objects are where in the visual world. One of the most enduring problems in psychological research is how we are able to reconstruct a three-dimensional mental representation of the visual world on the basis of two-dimensional retinal input. This is what mathematicians call an ill-posed problem; that is, one with many possible solutions. There are an infinite number of possible three-dimensional configurations that would give rise to the same pattern of stimulation on the retina. The fact that we can see depth in a photograph illustrates this point. A three-dimensional array of objects creates exactly the same image on the retina as a photograph of the array of objects. Despite this inherent ambiguity, we seldom have trouble understanding the arrangement of objects in the world. We actually make use of the ambiguous nature of depth perception when we look at photographs, movies, and television images. We are able to perceive depth in these two-dimensional patterns because the brain is able to apply the same rules or mechanisms that it uses to work out the spatial relations between objects in the (three-dimensional) world.

DEPTH PERCEPTION IS IMPORTANT FOR LOCATING OBJECTS

One of the most important tasks for our visual systems is to locate objects in space. Without this capacity we would find it difficult to navigate in and interact with the world. It is obvious that our perception is a much more accurate representation of the distal stimulus—the arrangement of objects in space—than we might expect based on the proximal stimulation alone. To begin to understand this process, let us begin by considering the cues that are available to help the visual system perceive depth. These depth cues can be divided into those that arise from the fact that we have two eyes, called **binocular depth cues**, and those that are available to each eye alone, called **monocular** (or *pictorial*) **depth cues**.

Binocular depth perception One of the most important cues to depth perception is the **binocular disparity** (or *retinal disparity*) caused by the distance between your two eyes. Because each eye has a slightly different view of the world, your brain has access to two different but overlapping retinal images. The brain

How are we able to perceive space in three dimensions on the basis of two-dimensional inputs from the retina?

uses the disparity between these two retinal images to compute distances to nearby objects (see Figure 5.15).

Try this simple demonstration: hold your finger out in front of you and close first one eye and then the other. Your finger appears to move because each eye, due to its position relative to the object in question, has a unique retinal image.

The ability to determine the depth of an object on the basis of its different projections to each eye is called *stereoscopic vision*. In 1838 physicist and inventor Charles Wheatstone devised the *stereoscope*, a device that enables a viewer to perceive depth by presenting a pair of two-dimensional pictures—each taken from a slightly different perspective. Wheatstone used this device to demonstrate that depth perception was influenced by binocular disparity, and thus that stereoscopic vision was an important cue for the depths of objects. In 1849 David Brewster, the Scottish physicist who invented the kaleidoscope, discovered the *autostereogram*—an optical illusion in which you can turn specially designed pairs of two-dimensional images into three-dimensional images by looking at them in an unfocused manner (see Figure 5.16). In recent years the autostereogram has been popularized in the Magic Eye™ book series and related publications.

Monocular depth perception   While binocular disparity is an important cue for depth perception, it is useful only for objects that are relatively close to us. Furthermore, we can still perceive depth with one eye closed. *Monocular depth cues* allow us to do this. Because artists routinely use these cues to create a sense of depth, they are also called *pictorial depth cues*. It was Leonardo da Vinci who first identified many of these cues, which include:

- *occlusion*: a near object occludes (blocks) an object that is farther away;

- *relative size*: far-off objects project a smaller retinal image than close objects;

- *familiar size*: we know how large familiar objects are, so we can tell how far away they are from the size of their retinal images;

- *linear perspective*: parallel lines appear to converge in the distance;

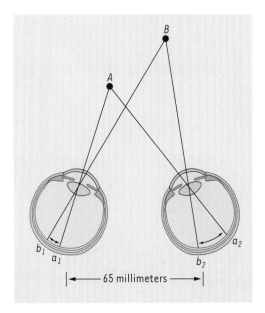

5.15 Binocular disparity. Our two eyes cause us to see every object from two distinct vantage points, resulting in two slightly different retinal images. The distance between the images for objects A and B is different for each eye. This disparity is an important cue for depth.

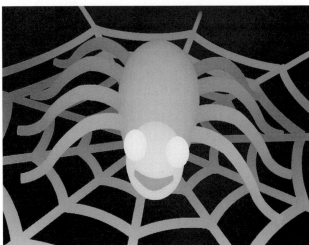

5.16 Autostereogram. Hold the picture on the left close to your eyes and stare straight ahead. Try to relax your eyes and let them look through the book to an imaginary point in the distance. Slowly move the book away from you, still fixating on that imaginary point. Try to allow the doubled images to fall on top of each other and keep them there. The result of superimposing the images should be a three-dimensional effect. The picture on the right is the embedded image. If you don't see it in a few minutes, stop and try again later.

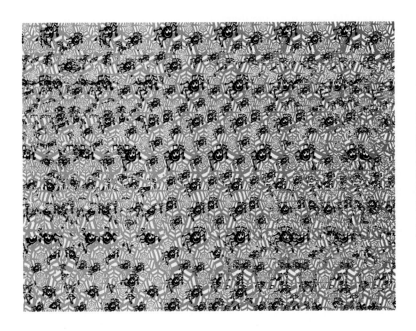

5.17 Texture gradient is another important depth cue. Uniformly textured surfaces appear denser as objects recede. When texture disappears, it indicates a drop-off.

5.18 Motion parallax. Near objects seem to move more quickly in the opposite direction of our movement. Objects farther away seem to move more slowly.

Your direction of motion

- *texture gradient*: there is a continuous change in uniformly textured surfaces. As a surface recedes, its texture becomes denser, as shown in Figure 5.17;

- *position relative to horizon*: All else being equal, objects below the horizon that appear higher in the visual field are perceived as being farther away. Objects above the horizon that appear lower in the visual field are perceived as being farther away.

Motion cues for depth perception Motion is also a cue for depth. *Motion parallax* is the relative movement of objects at varying distances from the observer (Helmholtz, 1866/1909). Imagine sitting in a moving car and watching the scenery. Near objects seem to pass quickly, far objects more slowly (Figure 5.18). If we fixate on a point farther away, such as the moon, it appears to match our speed. If we fixate on an object at an intermediate distance, anything closer moves opposite our direction relative to that object, while anything farther moves in our direction relative to the object. Motion cues such as these help the brain to calculate which objects are closer and which are farther away.

Perceptual psychologist James Gibson (1904–1979) proposed another motion cue for depth, *optic flow*, which is the pattern of movement we see when we move through the environment (Gibson, 1950). If we look in the direction we are moving, the optic flow is the motion of all objects not exactly straight ahead moving outward in our visual field as we advance. Closer objects move outward faster than more distant objects, so the flow pattern indicates distance.

SIZE PERCEPTION DEPENDS ON DISTANCE PERCEPTION

The size of the retinal image of an object depends on the distance of the object from the observer; the farther away it is, the smaller its retinal image. In order to determine the size of an object, then, the visual system needs to know how far away it is. Most of the time there is enough depth information available for the visual system to work out the distances of objects, and thus how big they are. However, there are some circumstances in which size perception fails, and objects look bigger or smaller than they really are. These *optical illusions* arise when normal perceptual processes result in an incorrect representation of the distal stimulus. Optical illusions are some of the favorite tools perceptual scientists have for understanding the way the brain uses information. Researchers rely on these tricks to reveal automatic perceptual systems that, in most circumstances, result in accurate perception. Optical illusions rely on depth cues to fool us into seeing depth when it is not really there. There are many such illusions. We will concentrate on just three: Ames boxes (also called Ames rooms), the Ponzo illusion, and the moon illusion.

Ames boxes Ames boxes, crafted by Adelbert Ames, a painter turned psychologist, are a powerful example of depth illusions. His boxes elaborated on the Victorian trick in which a person looking

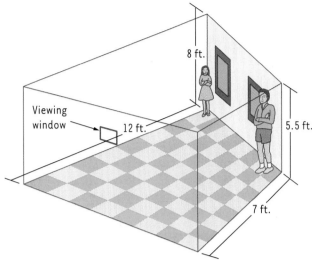

5.19 An example of the Ames box. Ames played with depth cues to create size illusions. He made a diagonally cut room appear rectangular by using crooked windows and floor tiles. When one child stands in a near corner and another (of similar height) stands in a far corner, the room creates the illusion that they are both equidistant from the viewer; therefore the closer child appears as a giant compared to the child farther away.

through a peephole would see a furnished room and then open the door and find the room empty—with a dollhouse room nailed to the door. He built rooms that played with linear perspective and other distance cues. One such perspective illusion was a room that made a far corner appear to be the same distance away as a near corner. Normally, a nearby child projects a larger retinal image than a child farther away but does not appear larger because the perceptual system takes depth into account when assessing size. If the depth cues are wrong, so that the child appears to be farther away than he is, as in the Ames box, the disproportionate size of his image on your retina makes him look huge (see Figure 5.19).

The Ponzo illusion   The *Ponzo illusion*, shown in Figure 5.20, was first described by Mario Ponzo in 1913 and is another classic example of a size-distance illusion. The common explanation for this illusion is that monocular depth cues make the two-dimensional figure seem three-dimensional (Rock, 1984). As noted earlier, parallel lines appear to converge in the distance. Thus the two lines drawn to look like a railroad track receding in the distance trick your brain into thinking that the lines are parallel. Therefore, you perceive the two parallel lines in the center as if they are at different distances, and thus different in size when they actually are the same exact size. This shows how much we rely on depth perception to gauge size—your brain defaults to using depth cues even when there is no depth present.

The moon illusion   You may have noticed that a full moon looks much larger when it is near the horizon than when it is overhead (Figure 5.21). This is an illusion—the moon (obviously) remains the same size and distance from the Earth, and the image of the moon on your retina is the same size whether it is on the horizon or overhead. The most common explanation for this illusion is that when the moon is near the horizon, there are several depth cues to indicate that it is really very far away. When the moon is overhead there are no such cues available, so the moon looks like it is closer to the Earth. The logic of this explanation is similar to that offered for the Ponzo illusion. The horizon moon looks farther away than the overhead moon, yet since they are really the same distance, they create identical images on the retina. The only way for the brain to reconcile this discrepancy is to assume that the horizon moon is larger than the overhead moon.

5.20 The Ponzo illusion. A classic size illusion caused by misleading cues of depth perception. The two parallel lines appear to be different sizes because of the law of perspective that tells us that parallel lines converge in the distance. In fact, the two lines are the same length.

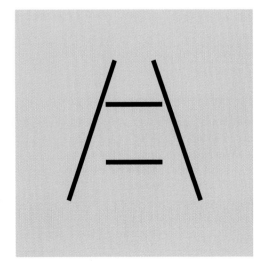

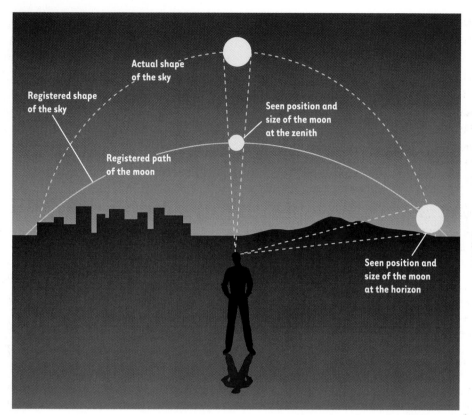

Actual shape of the sky

Registered shape of the sky

Seen position and size of the moon at the zenith

Registered path of the moon

Seen position and size of the moon at the horizon

5.21 The Moon illusion. The moon looks larger when it is near the horizon than when it is overhead, due to various visual cues.

The mechanism responsible for the apparent difference in distance between horizon and overhead moon is still disputed, but all current theories of the moon illusion agree that perceived distance is the source.

Many perceptual psychologists believe that illusions reveal the operation of the mechanisms that help our visual systems determine the sizes and distances of objects in the visual environment. In doing so they illustrate the interdependence of size and distance perception in forming accurate representations of the three-dimensional world.

MOTION PERCEPTION HAS BOTH INTERNAL AND EXTERNAL CUES

Although we know how motion can cue depth perception, how does our brain perceive motion? One answer is that we have neurons that are specialized for detecting movement—they fire when movement occurs. But how does the brain then know what is moving? If you look out a window and see a car driving past a house, how does your brain know that the car is moving and not the house? Unraveling these mysteries is the goal of researchers who study motion perception. We will consider three phenomena that offer some insight into how motion perception is accomplished by the visual system. These are motion aftereffects, compensation for head and eye motion, and stroboscopic motion perception.

Motion aftereffects **Motion aftereffects** occur when you gaze at a moving image for a prolonged period and then look at some stationary scene. You experience a momentary illusion of seeing the new scene moving in the opposite direction from the moving image. This is also called the *waterfall effect*, because if you stare at a waterfall and then turn away, the rocks and trees will seem to move upward for a moment. Aftereffects are strong evidence that motion-sensitive neurons exist in the brain. The theory behind this illusion combines the phenomenon of sensory adaptation with neural specificity. The visual cortex has neurons that respond to movement in a given direction. When you stare at a moving stimulus for long enough, these direction-specific neurons begin to adapt to the motion, becoming less sensitive, or *fatigued*. If the stimulus is suddenly removed, the motion detectors that respond to all the other directions are more active than the fatigued motion detectors. This results in the impression that a new scene is moving in the other direction.

motion aftereffects An effect that occurs when you gaze at a moving image for a prolonged period and then switch to a stationary scene, causing a momentary illusion of seeing the new scene moving in the opposite direction of the previous image.

Compensatory factors The fact that we have motion-sensitive neurons doesn't completely explain motion perception. How do you know, for instance, whether an object is moving or whether you, or your eyes, are moving? Images move across your retina all the time and you don't always perceive them as moving. Each slight blink or movement of the eye creates a new image on the retina. Why is it that every time you move your eye, or your head, the images you see don't jump around?

One explanation is that the brain calculates objects' perceived movement by monitoring the movement of the eyes or head as they track a moving object. In addition, motion detectors track the motion of an image across the retina, receptors in the retina firing one after the other (see Figure 5.22).

Another explanation for movement perception is the *frame of reference effect*: the perceptual system establishes a stable frame of reference and uses it to assess movement of other objects. Suppose you are sitting in the library reading, and around you are dozens of other students studying. While you are watching one student, he rises and moves down two seats. Since you were watching him move, you moved your head, or at least your eyes, prompting an array of images across your retina. However, your brain knows that it was the student who moved, and not the room around him, because it had established a frame of reference.

But when that frame of reference is the wrong one, you can be tricked into thinking that the wrong object is moving. Say you are on a train looking out the window at another stationary train. That train starts to move and you think you are moving. This *induced movement* illusion also happens when you are looking up at the sky on a cloudy night; it seems like the moon is moving through the clouds.

Stroboscopic movement   Movies are made up of still-frame images, presented one after the other to create the illusion of a "motion picture." This phenomenon is based on a perceptual illusion called *stroboscopic movement*, when two or more slightly different images are presented in rapid succession. Perceptual psychologist Max Wertheimer (1880–1943) conducted experiments in 1912 by flashing, at different intervals, two vertical lines placed close together. He discovered that when the interval was less than 30 milliseconds, subjects thought the two lines were flashed simultaneously. When the interval was greater than 200 milliseconds they saw two lines being flashed at different times. Between those times movement illusions occurred. When the interval was about 60 milliseconds the line appeared to jump from one place to another; Wertheimer called this *optimal movement*. At slightly longer intervals, the line appeared to move continuously; this was called *pure movement* (or *phi movement*).

OBJECT RECOGNITION RELIES ON FORM

In visual perception, an object's form (shape) seems to be the most salient cue for the brain to identify it. A square of any size or color is still a square. The ability to recognize objects by their shape develops at an early age. Psychologist Barbara Landau studied three-year-olds and found that when scientists showed the children a shape and told them it was a "dax," the children accepted this definition (Landau, 1994). When they were shown other objects, some with the same shape as the "dax" but made of different materials, sizes, or colors, they still identified each object of the same shape as a "dax." It is perhaps no surprise, then, that we recognize a Granny Smith, a Red Delicious, or a Macintosh as an "apple."

While it is clear that form is the most important cue for object recognition, how we are able to extract an object's form from the image on our retina is still somewhat mysterious. We are able to recognize objects from different perspectives and in unusual orientations. We generally have little trouble telling where one object ends and another begins—consider how we know that a horse and rider

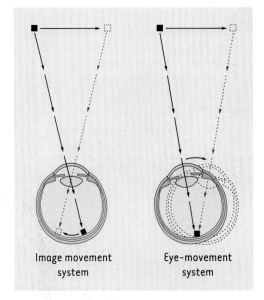

5.22 There are two ways the visual system detects movement of objects: 1) if the eye is fixed, the image moves across the retina; 2) if the eye moves to follow the object, the retinal image stays in place.

How do we know the shapes of objects that we have never seen before?

visual search task An experiment used to study form perception, in which an observer tries to detect a target stimulus among an array of distracter stimuli.

pop-out In Treisman's work, when simple stimuli were used, subjects took the same amount of time to find it, whether there were a few or many distracters.

are two distinct beings, and not some strange animal. We also seldom have trouble recognizing objects that are partially hidden behind other objects.

Features The neural computations required for form perception are extremely complex and are not yet fully understood. It is clear, though, that the process begins very early in visual processing. We have already seen how lateral inhibition between neurons in the retina helps to accentuate areas of changing stimulation—which are likely to correspond to the boundaries of objects. In addition, Hubel and Wiesel's work on the properties of neurons in the primary visual cortex strongly suggests that one of the most important roles for V1 is extracting the contours that define the boundaries of objects. Further studies have revealed that color, motion, and form information are processed in separate—though interconnected—pathways within the visual cortex. Thus it appears that one of the first steps in processing a form is encoding the features that compose it.

Psychologist Anne Treisman and her colleagues developed a clever technique to reveal how these feature detectors can be used (Treisman, 1988). They employed a **visual search task** in which an observer tries to detect a target stimulus among an array of identical distracter stimuli. For example, the display might consist of one vertical line in a crowd of horizontal ones. The observer's job was to respond as soon as he or she saw the target. Treisman and her coworkers found that, for simple stimuli, subjects took no more time to find the target when it was buried in a large number of distracters than when it appeared with only one or two. They termed this phenomenon **pop-out**. The experimenters concluded that these simple scene elements are processed all at once, with oddballs standing out automatically from the crowd. These and other behavioral studies suggest that a vast amount of low-level visual information is automatically detected at the same time.

5.23 Proximity and similarity are two powerful organizing principles identified by Gestalt psychologists.

Gestalt principles of perceptual organization So what do we do with the information we take in about an object's features? How do we organize that information? In the years prior to World War I, psychologists in Germany and the United States began theorizing that perception is more than the result of accumulating sensory data. This *Gestalt school* of perceptual psychology, founded by Max Wertheimer, along with experimental psychologists Wolfgang Kohler and Kurt Koffka, contributed much to the study of perception and other fields of psychology. The Gestalt psychologists believed that our perceptions are more than the sum of their constituent sensations. The German word *gestalt* means "shape" or "form," but as used in psychology it means "organized whole." Gestalt psychology holds that there are certain built-in (innate) organizing principles our brains use to organize sensory information; that is why we perceive, say, "car" as opposed to "metal, tires, glass, door handles, hubcaps, fender." The founders of Gestalt psychology postulated a series of laws to explain how perceived features of a visual scene are grouped into organized wholes.

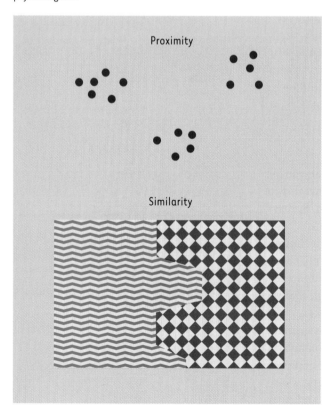

Proximity and similarity Two of the most important Gestalt laws are the principles of proximity and similarity. The *principle of proximity* states that the closer two figures are to one another, the more likely we are to group them together and see them as part of the same object. The *principle of similarity* is illustrated by the Sesame Street song/game "One of these things is not like the others." We tend to group figures according to how closely they resemble each other, whether it be in shape, color, or orientation (Figure 5.23). Both of these principles tend to clump elements of the visual scene into clusters, enabling us to consider them as a whole rather than as their individual parts. For example, we often perceive a flock of birds as a single entity because all the elements—the birds—are similar and in close proximity.

The "best" forms   Other organizing principles of Gestalt psychology describe how we perceive a form's features. *Good continuation* is the tendency to interpret intersecting lines as being continuous, rather than as changing direction radically. *Closure* refers to the tendency to complete figures that have gaps (Figure 5.24).

A phenomenon that illustrates several Gestalt principles is **illusory contours**, which we perceive even though they don't exist. Illusory contours appear when stimulus configurations suggest that contours ought to be present—for example, when depth transitions are implied or useful in interpreting a pattern (Figure 5.25).

Figure and ground   Finally, one of our most basic organizing principles is distinguishing between figure and ground. A classic illustration of this is the *reversible figure* illusion, an example of which is in Chapter 1 (see Figure 1.12). In the figure, we see either a full face or two faces looking at each other—but not both at the same time. This illusion shows that our visual perceptual system divides scenes into *figure and ground*. When we identify a figure, we assign the rest of the scene as the background. In reversible figures, the "correct" assignment of figure and ground is ambiguous, so they periodically switch back and forth as the visual system strives to make sense of the stimulation. This illustrates the dynamic and ongoing nature of visual perception. Even in the face of an unchanging stimulus the visual system is constantly testing and updating its interpretation of the sensory input.

PERCEPTION IS INFORMATION PROCESSING

How do we assemble the information about parts into a perception of a whole object? Most models of pattern recognition are hierarchical, using **bottom-up processing**. This means that data are relayed from lower to higher levels of processing. But perception is actually a combination of both bottom-up and **top-down processing**. This means that information at higher levels of processing can influence lower, "earlier" levels in the processing hierarchy. One illustration of this is the effect of context on perception: what we expect to see influences what we perceive. Consider, for example, the incomplete letter in Figure 5.26; the two lines in the center of each word are perceived as either "H" or "A" depending on which interpretation would make sense in the context of the word.

The plane-crash story that opened this chapter underscores the influence of expectation on perception. Although that is a particularly dramatic example, expectation and context undoubtedly influence our perception all the time. Many perceptual psychologists think of perception as an ongoing process of *hypothesis testing*, in which sensory information, context, and expectation are combined to create a hypothesis about the stimuli. This hypothesis is constantly updated as more sensory information becomes available. The updating process makes use of the current perceptual hypothesis, so that eye movements, for example, tend to be directed at areas of the visual field that will yield the most useful information.

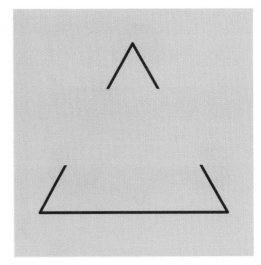

5.24 Closure. We tend to complete figures even when gaps exist.

illusory contours   A phenomenon in which the eyes perceive contours that do not exist that serves as evidence for the Gestalt principles.

bottom-up processing   A hierarchical model of pattern recognition in which data are relayed from one processing level to the next, always moving to a higher level of processing.

top-down processing   A hierarchical model of pattern recognition in which information at higher levels of processing can also influence lower, "earlier" levels in the processing hierarchy.

5.25 Illusory contours. Related to closure, we tend to see contours even when they don't exist.

Theories about visual perception can be tested using computer or robot models. By the same token, advances in artificial intelligence have informed many psychological theories of pattern recognition. Computational models are known as information-processing models of perception and are derived by comparing the brain to a computer. David Marr (1982) proposed perhaps the most influential computational model of vision. It has a hierarchical organization—distinct tasks are carried out at each level of processing, and the output from each level serves as the input to the next higher level. Marr conceived of the visual system as a series of computational algorithms that would be able to perceive the shapes of objects from their retinal images. First it would map out certain visual features—lines and their endpoints, for example—to create what Marr called a *primal sketch* of the scene. From this, the visual system would extract a representation of the surfaces and their distances and orientations present in a scene, which Marr termed the *two-and-a-half-dimensional model*. From this, it would finally construct a *three-dimensional representation* of the objects.

It is important to realize, however, that the step-by-step processing proposed by Marr does not accurately reflect processing in the brain. At nearly every stage of neural processing, what we recognize and what we expect exert a strong influence on the outcome. In the brain each level influences the levels below it as well as those above. Computational models have been devised to incorporate such feedback, allowing, for example, the surface stage to go back and influence the edge extractors, but to date no model has been particularly successful in mimicking the tremendous power and versatility of human vision. Despite this, the models provide useful conceptual guides to researchers, as well as illustrating the complexity of the perceptual process.

PERCEPTUAL CONSTANCIES ARE BASED ON RATIO RELATIONSHIPS

As we discussed earlier, illusions are inaccurate representations of distal stimuli. The opposite situation is called **perceptual constancy**, in which we correctly perceive objects as constant despite raw sensory data that could lead us to think otherwise. How does the brain know that a person is six feet tall when the retinal image of that person changes size according to how near or far he is? How does the brain know that snow is white and a tire is black, even when snow at night or a tire in bright light might send the same luminance cues to the retina? For the most part, changing the angle, distance, or illumination of an object does not change our perception of that object's size, shape, color, or lightness. But to perceive any of these four constancies, we need to understand the relationship between at least two factors. For instance, for *size constancy* we need to know how far away the object is. For *shape constancy* we need to know from what angle we're seeing the object. For *color constancy* we need to compare the wavelengths of light reflected from the object with those from its background. Likewise, for *lightness constancy* we need to know how much light is being reflected from the object and

5.26 Context plays a role in object recognition.

from its background. In each case, the brain is computing a ratio, rather than relying on the absolute magnitude of each sensation. The purpose of these ratios is to allow the visual system to make a relative rather than an absolute judgment about a stimulus. It is the ability of the perceptual system to make relative judgments that allows constancy to be maintained across a variety of perceptual contexts. Although the precise mechanisms of the constancies are unknown, they serve to illustrate that perceptual systems are tuned to detect change from some baseline condition, and not just to respond to sensory inputs.

Gibson's direct-perception theory   Broadly speaking, there are two approaches to the study of how we arrive at these ratio relationships. Classical perceptual theory, which originated with the nineteenth-century works of Hermann von Helmholtz, assumes that perceptual experience provides the information about the ratio relationships that determine constancies. Thus, sensations create impulses to the brain, and the brain then interprets those impulses according to what it has learned in the past. In this view, visual perception was always based on *unconscious inferences*, on mathematical calculations carried out by the brain without our awareness.

Beginning in the 1940s, perceptual psychologist James J. Gibson (1904–1979) offered a different theory, **direct perception** (1966). Gibson approached the study of perception from an evolutionary perspective. He believed that the most important question to ask to understand visual perception is, What is vision good for? In the most basic sense, the function of vision is to identify and locate predators and prey, find mates, avoid cliffs, and so on. The idea that our brains would have to rely on inference, on learning and memory, to form concepts that were basic to survival didn't make sense to him. In his view, the visual system is not built to enable us to see an exact copy of the real world; it is built to interpret cues that maximize its function. His direct-perception theory, then, stated that stimuli already have enough information for us to perceive them—we don't need additional memories or calculations to understand the sensory data.

Gibson himself was uninterested in the brain, so his ideas are often difficult to interpret from a neuroscientific standpoint, but practically speaking they have two main implications. The first is that much of the visual processing performed by the brain is innate rather than learned, since so much of vision depends only on universal perceptual necessities such as distances of obstacles and layout of terrain. This kind of analysis, as opposed to the recognition of useful objects, does not benefit from learning and is probably preprogrammed. The second implication of Gibson's ideas is that these basic visual programs occur in parallel with the more learning-dependent ones, so that while one part of the brain may be recognizing an apple, another part is analyzing the optic flow to keep us out of the way of low branches.

Innate perceptual processes   One consequence of the development of direct-perception theory is the attempt to identify innate perceptual processes in the brain. Studying how illusions work, many perceptual psychologists have come to believe that the brain has built-in assumptions that influence perceptions. The vast majority of visual illusions appear to be beyond our conscious control—we cannot make ourselves *not* see illusions. As an example, look at the two tables in Figure 5.27. Believe it or not, the tops of the tables are the exact same size and shape, and not just the surface area. Our brains will not allow us to accept that fact, however. Even if you trace one and place it on top of the other, your brain still

perceptual constancy   People correctly perceive objects as constant in their shape, size, color, and lightness despite raw sensory data that could mislead perception.

direct perception   A theory of perception that states that the stimulus must already have enough information for us to perceive it, and therefore the visual system is built not to enable us to see an exact copy of the real world, but to interpret cues that maximize its function.

5.27 This unbelievable tabletop illusion of Roger Shepherd's demonstrates the automatic perceptual processes of the brain. Even when we know the two surfaces are the same, we cannot make ourselves "see" it.

cannot see it. The reason is that you have automatic perceptual processes that use perspective cues to tell you the size and shape of the tables are different.

In Chapter 11, when you learn about cognitive development, you will see other evidence that perceptions are the result of innate mechanisms that develop, rather than skills we learn.

What Are the Basic Perceptual Processes?

Perceptual research can be broken down into two questions: How do we know the arrangement of objects in the world? How do we recognize objects from a variety of viewpoints? Both questions are problematic because the visual system is confronted with an ill-posed problem—how to compute a three-dimensional representation of the world on the basis of a two-dimensional retinal image. To solve this problem, the visual system relies on cues present in the stimulus and regularities in the world that help interpret the retinal information. In addition, it has become increasingly clear that many perceptual processes are innately determined, but that normal perceptual experience is necessary for perceptual mechanisms to develop normally.

HOW DOES ATTENTION HELP THE BRAIN MANAGE PERCEPTIONS?

The brain is constantly receiving input from an enormous number of sources. How does the brain combine all this information into coherent, usually correct, perceptions? And how do we manage all of the sensory information that constantly bombards us? The study of **attention** is the study of how the brain selects which sensory stimuli to discard and which to pass along to higher levels of processing.

VISUAL ATTENTION IS SELECTIVE AND SERIAL

As you learned earlier, psychologist Anne Treisman proposed that we identify "primitive" features automatically (color, shape, orientation, etc.). Her theory of the automatic recognition of these features has been a major development in the study of attention. Treisman proposed that different visual features of objects are analyzed by separate systems. These systems process information in parallel (at the same time), and we can attend selectively to one feature by effectively blocking the further processing of the others (Treisman & Gelade, 1980). Recall that in Treisman's visual search tasks (called *feature search* tasks), participants were looking for targets that differed in only one feature, and that these would pop out immediately, regardless of the number of distracters.

A very different picture emerges, however, if the participants are looking for a target that is harder to discriminate from the distracters. In *conjunction search* tasks, observers are asked to search for a target with two or more features. In Figure 5.28, for example, the subject might be asked to search for a green T among red T's and green X's. In this case the target can be distinguished from the distracters only by the conjunction of its features—it shares color with one half of the distracters, and shape with the other half. In contrast to the immediate pop-out found in feature search, participants searching for conjunctions were markedly

How does attention influence the way we perceive the world?

attention The study of how the brain selects which sensory stimuli to discard and which to pass along to higher levels of processing.

binding problem The question considering the issue: if the brain processes features automatically and separately, how does it determine what feature goes with what object?

affected by the presence of distracters. The time it takes to find the target increases linearly with the number of distracters—suggesting that subjects laboriously consider each distracter one by one.

These studies led Treisman to propose a two-stage theory of visual-image processing. According to this theory, visual processing begins with a rapid, parallel extraction of elementary features. At this stage, the visual system is simply mapping the distribution of visual features. Separate maps are created for each feature type—one for color, one for form, and so forth. The second stage of processing is slower and more effortful. In this stage, the features from the various maps are combined to form objects. This stage is not automatic—it requires the deployment of attention. Because of this, only selected regions of the feature maps get bound together. In feature searches, the average time it takes viewers to respond to targets is not affected by the number of distracters. This is the hallmark of *preattentive* searches (searches that do not require attention); the entire array is scanned in parallel, and the critical feature is rapidly registered if it is present. Conjunction searches, however, require attention and are processed serially, so the search time lengthens as more distracters are included.

Segregation of visual functions Other evidence suggests that elementary visual processes proceed in parallel and are integrated relatively late in processing. For example, consider the versions of the Ponzo illusion shown in Figure 5.29. In the left red-on-green version, the illusion remains, but in the version on the right the illusion is much less effective. This is because in the right version the red and green have been set to the same approximate luminance (are "equiluminant"), such that the figure and background are distinguished only by their color; in contrast, the left version has both color and brightness differences. Color and depth are processed in separate pathways in the visual cortex, so the depth information is lost in the right version. Without depth information, the parallel lines appear equidistant and thus equal in length.

Cases in which people suffer visual deficits as a result of brain injuries also support the view that there are distinct perceptual systems for processing different visual features. For instance, color-blind people do not have problems with depth and texture perception—they can still see and recognize objects. The akinetopsia patient described earlier apparently has normal processing of color and form, despite her profound impairment in processing motion.

Binding If the brain processes features automatically and separately, how does it determine what feature goes with what object? This is known as the **binding problem**. Treisman has researched the possibility that attention helps integrate features to correctly perceive objects. When a normal observer is given too many cues to pay attention to, errors in binding occur. For example, in tests in which people are briefly shown red X's and blue O's and are asked to name a digit presented at the same time, they often report that they saw a blue X or red O. These *illusory conjunctions* happen because the observer's attention was divided and overextended between the colored letters and digit-identification task. As a result, features from objects recombine to

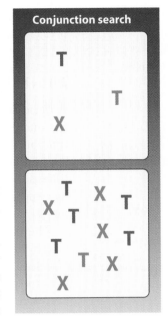
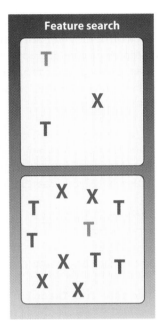

5.28 In visual search tasks, subjects are asked to find the target—the thing unlike the others. In feature searches, in which the target has only one feature (color or shape) that differs from the distracters, this is simple. When the target has more than one feature that differs (for instance, the red T, when there are green and red T's and X's), it takes longer.

5.29 The Ponzo illusion is effective in all but the third panel. When the background and lines are the same brightness, depth cannot be perceived. This indicates that visual processing of brightness and depth are separate.

cocktail party phenomenon A phenomenon of selective attention which refers to the ability to focus on a single conversation in the midst of a chaotic cocktail party.

filter theory A theory that people have a limited capacity for sensory information and thus screen incoming information, only letting in the most important.

early selection theories Theories based on the notion that we can choose the stimuli to which we will we attend before we process their basic features.

late selection theories Theories that assume that people take in sensory information, process it, and then select which aspects of the stimuli should be attended after processing.

form an object that doesn't exist. The automatic feature-recognition system breaks down.

AUDITORY ATTENTION ALLOWS SELECTIVE LISTENING

Because of attention, it is hard to do two tasks at the same time, especially if they rely on the same mechanisms. We easily can listen to music and drive at the same time but find it hard to listen to two conversations at once. The psychologist Steven Pinker points out that even driving and listening to the radio at the same time can be hazardous—depending on what you're listening to. A sports broadcast may engage your visual system to imagine the game in progress, diverting attention away from the visual cues on the road ahead.

The **cocktail party phenomenon**, so called by British psychologist E. C. Cherry (1953), refers to the ability to focus on a single conversation in the midst of a chaotic cocktail party. While proximity and loudness contribute, your selective attention can also determine which conversation you hear. Imagine you are having dinner with a friend at a crowded restaurant. Suddenly the conversation at the next table piques your interest. If you really want to hear that conversation, you can focus your attention on it rather than on what your (closer and therefore louder) friend is saying. When your friend notices the blank look on your face and protests, "You're not listening to me!" chances are you won't be able to tell your friend what he or she said—but you could relate the drama at the next table.

Cherry developed *selective listening* studies to examine this aspect of attention. He used a technique called *shadowing*, in which a participant is presented with two messages in each ear at the same time through, headphones. The person is asked to attend to one message and "shadow" it by repeating it aloud. In this situation, the subject will usually notice the unattended sound (the message given to the other ear) but will have no idea about the content of the message (Figure 5.30).

SELECTIVE ATTENTION CAN OPERATE AT MULTIPLE STAGES OF PROCESSING

Psychologist Donald Broadbent (1958) developed the **filter theory** to explain selective-listening findings. He assumed that we have a limited capacity for sensory information and thus screen incoming information, only letting in the most important. In this model, attention is like a gate we open for important information and close for information we wish to ignore. But can we really close the gate for irrelevant information? When and where is the gate closed?

Broadbent's filter theory is an example of **early selection**, which is the theory that we can choose which stimuli we will attend to even before we process their basic features. In visual processing we could choose to ignore features such as color or form and only process those features that we had decided would be important for the task at hand. Accordingly, attention effectively filters out certain features at an early stage so that they never get processed.

However, some studies revealed that "unattended" visual information is processed to at least some extent. **Late selection** theories of visual attention were proposed to account for these findings. Such

5.30 In shadowing experiments, subjects receive different auditory messages in each ear but are asked to "shadow" or say aloud only one.

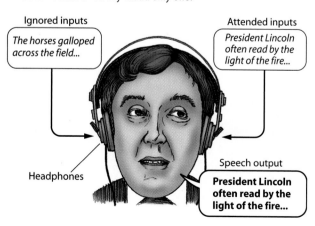

Ignored inputs

The horses galloped across the field...

Attended inputs

President Lincoln often read by the light of the fire...

Headphones

Speech output

President Lincoln often read by the light of the fire...

theories assume that we take in sensory information, process it, and then select which aspects of the stimuli should be attended. The attention stage occurs when the perception enters into our conscious awareness. Several studies of selective listening found that although a subject could not repeat an unattended message, he or she still processed its contents. Fascinating studies by psychologist Donald G. McKay showed that if the unattended message is relevant, we automatically use the information. For instance, subjects attended to the phrase "they threw stones at the bank yesterday," while at the same time either ear was presented with one of two words: "river" or "money." Afterward, subjects could not report which of these two words they heard; however, if they had been presented with "river," they interpreted the sentence to mean that someone had thrown stones at a river-bank. If they had been presented with the word "money," they interpreted the sentence to mean someone had thrown stones at a financial institution. Thus, they extracted meaning from the word even though they were not aware of it.

It now seems clear that attentional selection is not an all-or-none process that eliminates unattended stimuli, as proponents of early-selection theories argued. Nor is unattended information fully processed before selection occurs, as suggested by late-selection theories. Rather, most modern theories of attention suggest that selective attention can operate at multiple stages of perceptual processing. A variety of studies have shown that the processing of attended stimuli is enhanced relative to that of unattended stimuli, but that unattended stimuli are still processed. Treisman proposed that unattended information is not "gated" completely but instead is simply reduced. Broadbent, the major proponent of the filter theory, agreed and amended his view.

How Does Attention Help the Brain Manage Perceptions?

Attention is the study of how the brain selects which sensory stimuli to ignore, and which to pass along to higher levels of perceptual processing. Visual search tasks indicate that we process visual information about primitive features along parallel pathways. Recombining the information from these pathways may require the deployment of attention. A key aspect of attention is that it is selective; we have the ability to choose the stimuli to which we attend (the cocktail party phenomenon). Despite this selectivity, we can still process some information contained in sensory stimuli to which we are not consciously attending. It is now clear that attention can operate on multiple stages of perceptual processing, and that unattended stimuli are reduced rather than eliminated completely from further processing.

CONCLUSION

Perceptual psychologists seek to understand how elementary sensations are translated into conscious perception. As a major part of this effort, researchers have subdivided sensation and perception into their elementary processes in an effort to understand how we are able to create accurate representations of the world.

Our perceptual systems are faced with a challenging problem—that of extracting an accurate representation of the external world based on neural impulses from sensory receptors. Mathematically, this is an ill-posed problem, since there are many (often infinitely) stimuli that could have generated a given pattern of stimulation. Despite this seemingly intractable problem, however, the brain does a remarkably good job of representing the world. After over a century of research, science still cannot state definitely how perception works. No single theory or model has yet successfully accounted for more than a fraction of perceptual phenomena. What we have learned, through an accumulation of evidence from many independent areas of research, is that the perceptual process is tremendously complicated. Some estimates, for example, suggest that over half of the cortex of the primate brain contributes to the process of visual perception.

Despite this mystery, the workings of our perceptual systems have begun to yield to the concerted efforts of psychologists, neurophysiologists, and computational theorists working at many levels of analysis. With the advent of new technologies for studying the brain in action, these efforts have increased in their urgency. Perhaps the new century will finally yield answers to one of history's most enduring questions: How do we know our world?

FURTHER READINGS

Gazzaniga, M. S. (1998). *The mind's past.* Berkeley, CA: University of California Press.

Gazzaniga, M. S., Ivry, R. B., & Mangun, G. R. (2002). *Cognitive neuroscience: The biology of the mind* (2nd ed.). New York: W. W. Norton.

Gibson, J. J. (1979). *The ecological approach to visual perception.* Boston: Houghton Mifflin.

Kandel, E. R., Schwartz, J. H., & Jessell, T. M. (1995). *Essentials of neural science and behavior.* New York: Appleton & Lange.

Marr, D. (1982). *Vision: A Computational investigation into the human representation and processing of visual information.* San Francisco: Freeman.

Pinker, S. (1997). *How the mind works.* New York: W. W. Norton.

Shephard, R. N. (1990). *Mindsights.* New York: W. H. Freeman.

LEARNING THROUGH OBSERVATION

Observation is one of the most powerful forms of learning. Children observe and imitate their parents, which helps them learn many of the behaviors that they will need to function as adults.

TIMELINE

1690

The Mind as a Blank Slate
Building on ideas that can be traced back to Aristotle, philosopher John Locke argues that all knowledge is acquired through contact with the environment.

1898

The Law of Effect Edward Thorndike proposes the Law of Effect, which shows that behaviors that lead to satisfying outcomes are likely to be repeated.

1900–1930

Learning from Association
Russian physiologist Ivan Pavlov provides the first empirical demonstration of simple associative learning, such as a dog associating the sound of a bell with the arrival of food.

1920s

The Rise of Behaviorism
John B. Watson proposes the theory of behaviorism, which emphasizes that all behavior is determined by external forces and that only behaviors that can be manipulated and observed are of value to psychological science.

Learning and Reward

OUTLINING THE PRINCIPLES

1930–1960

Learning from Reinforcement B. F. Skinner develops the theory of operant conditioning, which states that behaviors are controlled by reinforcement or punishment. The widely used method of behavior modification is based on this theory.

1940–1950

Cognitive Learning Approach Edward Tolman, among others, sets the groundwork for the cognitive revolution in psychology by arguing that learning is not the change in behavior as such but is instead the acquisition of new knowledge or cognitions.

1948

Learning by Synaptic Alteration Canadian Psychologist Donald Hebb proposes that learning results from alterations in synaptic connections. Psychological science has since shown the basic tenets of this proposal to be accurate.

1960s

Social Learning Theory Concerned that behaviorism is ignoring the social context of learning, Albert Bandura shows that people learn behaviors by observing whether others are rewarded or punished for performing those behaviors.

1960s–1990s

Learning as an Evolved Mechanism John Garcia argues that certain types of learning involve special mechanisms that have evolved through natural selection.

American soldiers who fought in Vietnam often used drugs to cope with the hellish conditions of war. By the late 1960s, estimates suggested that drug use among American soldiers, including the use of narcotic substances such as heroin and opium, had reached epidemic proportions. The widespread use of drugs was not very surprising—the late 1960s were a time of youthful drug experimentation, the soldiers had easy access to a variety of drugs, and drugs were temporarily effective for helping the soldiers cope with the horrors of war. They used drugs to deal with fear, depression, homesickness, boredom, and the repressiveness of army regulations. The soldiers were also attracted to the euphoric and rewarding qualities of the drugs; they enjoyed getting "high." Although the military was aware of drug use among soldiers, it was mostly ignored, viewed as soldiers blowing off steam.

Beginning in 1971, the military began mandatory drug testing of soldiers in order to identify and detoxify drug users before they returned to the United States. More than 1 in 20 soldiers tested positive for narcotic drugs, even though they knew in advance that they would be tested. With speculation that many of those who were unable to go without drugs even for a short time were addicted to narcotics, concern grew that a flood of addicted soldiers returning from Vietnam would swamp existing treatment facilities. The White House asked a team of behavioral scientists to follow a group of returning soldiers to assess the extent of the addiction problem.

Led by behavioral epidemiologist Lee Robins, the research team examined a random sample of 898 soldiers who were leaving Vietnam in September 1971. Robins and her colleagues found extremely high levels of drug use among U.S. soldiers in Vietnam (Robins et al., 1975). Over 90 percent reported they drank alcohol, nearly three-quarters smoked marijuana, and nearly half used narcotics such as heroin, morphine, and opium. About half of the soldiers who used narcotics either had symptoms of addiction or reported that they believed they would be unable to give up their drug habits. Findings

RESEARCH QUESTIONS ?.?.?

for Studying Learning and Reward

What are the basic mechanisms responsible for learning?

How is behavior shaped by rewards and punishments?

What is learned from observing others?

Why are certain experiences rewarding?

What is the neural basis of learning?

1972

Expectancies and Learning Robert Rescorla and Allan Wagner propose that learning occurs when organisms develop expectancies that allow them to predict future events.

1970–1990s

The Neural Basis of Learning Eric Kandel's studies of the cellular and molecular mechanisms of learning in a type of invertebrate creature earn him a Nobel prize in 2000.

1990s–2000

Computer Models of Neural Networks Superfast modern computers allow psychological scientists to develop neural-network models of learning.

suggested that approximately 1 soldier in 5 returning from Vietnam was an addict. Given the prevailing view that addiction was a biological disorder with a low rate of recovery, these findings indicated that tens of thousands of heroin addicts would soon be inundating American towns and cities. But this didn't happen.

Robins and her colleagues examined drug use among the soldiers after they returned to the United States. Of those who were apparently addicted to narcotics in Vietnam, only half sought out drugs when they returned to the States, and fewer still maintained their narcotic addiction. Approximately 95 percent of the addicts no longer used drugs within months of their return, which is an astonishing quit rate considering that the success rate of the best treatments is typically only 20–30 percent. A long-term follow-up study conducted in the early 1990s confirmed that only a handful of those who were addicts in Vietnam remained addicts.

How is it possible that individuals who were addicted to narcotics could simply give them up when they changed environments? We will find some of the answers in this chapter as we examine the impact of the environment and rewards on learning, including how people develop habits such as drug use and the factors that sustain such behaviors.

Learning is a relatively enduring change in behavior that results from experience. It occurs when organisms benefit from experience so that their future behavior is better adapted to the environment. Learning theorists typically focus on observable behavior rather than on internal states or mental processes, an approach sometimes referred to as *behaviorism*. Learning shares some commonalities with memory (which is discussed in the next chapter), in that both refer to long-lasting changes following environmental exposure. Psychologists, however, have traditionally viewed learning and memory as separate, with learning theorists concentrating on the acquisition of behavior, and memory theorists focusing on the retention and retrieval of knowledge. Moreover, the study of learning has typically relied on nonhuman subjects, especially rats, whereas memory research has been conducted mainly with humans. The distinction between learning and memory is somewhat arbitrary, however, as there is significant overlap in how contemporary psychological scientists view the two processes. Indeed, similar biological mechanisms are involved in learning and memory. The focus in this chapter is on the relation between environmental stimuli and overt behavioral responses.

HOW DID THE BEHAVIORAL STUDY OF LEARNING DEVELOP?

The rise of learning theory in the early twentieth century was due in part to the dissatisfaction among some psychologists with the widespread use of verbal reports to assess mental states. At the time, Freudian ideas were at the heart of

learning An enduring change in behavior that results from experience.

6.1 American John B. Watson was the founder of behaviorism and one of its most ardent supporters.

psychological theorizing. To assess the unconscious mental processes that they believed were the primary determinants of behavior, Freud and his followers used techniques such as dream analysis and free association. American psychologist John B. Watson (1878–1958) (Figure 6.1) was scornful of any form of psychological enterprise that focused on things that could not be observed directly, such as people's mental events. He argued that Freudian theory was unscientific and ultimately meaningless. According to Watson, overt behavior was the only valid indicator of psychological activity. Although he acknowledged that thoughts and beliefs existed, he denied that they could be studied using scientific methods.

Watson founded the school of behaviorism, which was based on the belief that animals and humans are born with the potential to learn anything. Based on philosopher John Locke's idea of *tabula rasa* (Latin, "blank slate"), which states that infants are born knowing nothing and that all knowledge is acquired through sensory experiences, behaviorism stated that the environment and its associated effects on organisms were the sole determinants of learning. Watson felt so strongly about the preeminence of the environment that he issued the following bold challenge: "Give me a dozen healthy infants, well formed, and my own specified world to bring them up in and I'll guarantee to take any one at random and train him to become any type of specialist I might select—doctor, lawyer, artist, merchant-chief, and yes, even beggar-man and thief, regardless of his talents, penchants, tendencies, abilities, vocations and race of his ancestors" (Watson, 1924, p. 82).

BEHAVIORAL RESPONSES ARE CONDITIONED

Watson had an incredible influence on the study of psychology in America. Behaviorism was the dominant psychological paradigm well into the 1960s, and it influenced the methods and theories of every area within psychology. Watson developed his ideas about behaviorism after he read the work of Russian physiologist Ivan Pavlov (1849–1936) (Figure 6.2), a distinguished scientist who had won a Nobel prize for his work on the digestive system. Pavlov was interested in the *salivary reflex*, the automatic and unlearned response that occurs when the stimulus of food is presented to hungry animals. For his work on the digestive system, Pavlov had created an apparatus that collected saliva from dogs (Figure 6.3). He placed various types of food into a dog's mouth and measured differences in salivary output. Like so many major scientific advances, Pavlov's contribution to psychology started with a simple observation. One day he realized that the dogs were salivating well before they tasted the food. Indeed, the dogs started salivating the moment that a lab technician walked into the room, or whenever they saw the bowls that usually contained food. The genius of Pavlov was in recognizing that this behavioral response was a window to the working mind. Unlike inborn reflexes, salivation at the sight of a bowl is not automatic and therefore must have been acquired through experience. The insight that dogs could associate bowls and lab technicians with food led Pavlov to devote the rest of his life to studying the basic principles of learning.

6.2 Ivan Pavlov conducted groundbreaking work on classical conditioning.

Pavlov's experiments In a typical Pavlovian experiment, a *neutral stimulus* unrelated to the salivary reflex, such as a ringing bell, is presented together with a

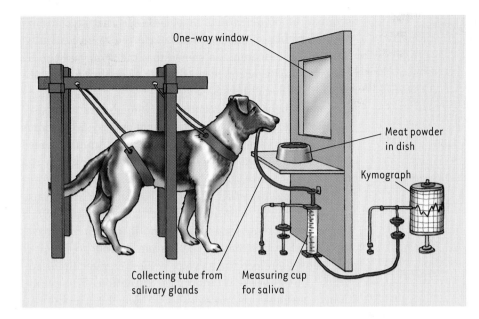

Collecting tube from salivary glands

Measuring cup for saliva

One-way window

Meat powder in dish

Kymograph

6.3 Pavlov's apparatus for collecting saliva. The dog was presented with a bowl containing meat. A tube from the salivary glands carried the saliva to a container that measured the amount of salivation.

stimulus that reliably produces the reflex, such as food. This pairing, known as a *conditioning trial*, is repeated a number of times; then, on *critical trials*, the bell sound is presented alone and the salivary reflex is measured. Pavlov found that under these conditions, the sound of the bell on its own produced salivation. This type of learning is now referred to as *classical conditioning* or *Pavlovian conditioning*. **Classical conditioning** occurs when a neutral object comes to elicit a reflexive response when it is associated with a stimulus that already produces that response.

Pavlov called the salivation elicited by food the **unconditioned response (UR)**, because it occurred without any prior training. Unconditioned responses are unlearned, automatic behaviors, such as any simple reflex. Similarly, the food was referred to as the **unconditioned stimulus (US)**. In the normal reflex response, the food (US) leads to salivation (UR). Because the ringing bell produces salivation only after training, it is called the **conditioned stimulus (CS)**; it stimulates salivation only after learning takes place. The salivary reflex that occurs when only the conditioned stimulus is presented is known as the **conditioned response (CR)**; it is an acquired response that is learned. Note that both the unconditioned and the conditioned response are salivation, but they are not identical: the bell produces less saliva than does the food. The conditioned response usually is less strong than the unconditioned response. The process of conditioning is outlined in Figure 6.4.

Acquisition, extinction, and spontaneous recovery Like many other scientists at the time, Pavlov was greatly influenced by Darwin's *Origin of Species*. Pavlov believed that conditioning was the basis for how animals learn to adapt to their environments. By learning to predict what objects bring pleasure or pain, animals acquire new behaviors that are adaptive to the environment. For instance, let's suppose that each time it rains, a delicious and nutritious plant blooms. An animal that learns this association will seek out this plant each time it rains. **Acquisition**, the initial learning of a behavior, is the gradual formation of an association between the conditioned and unconditioned stimuli. Based on his research, Pavlov concluded that the critical element in the

RESEARCH QUESTION

What are the basic mechanisms responsible for learning?

classical conditioning A type of learned response that occurs when a neutral object comes to elicit a reflexive response when it is associated with a stimulus that already produces that response.

unconditioned response (UR) A response that does not have to be learned, such as a reflex.

unconditioned stimulus (US) A stimulus that elicits a response, such as a reflex, without any prior learning.

conditioned stimulus (CS) A stimulus that elicits a response only after learning has taken place.

conditioned response (CR) A response that has been learned.

acquisition The gradual formation of an association between the conditioned and unconditioned stimuli.

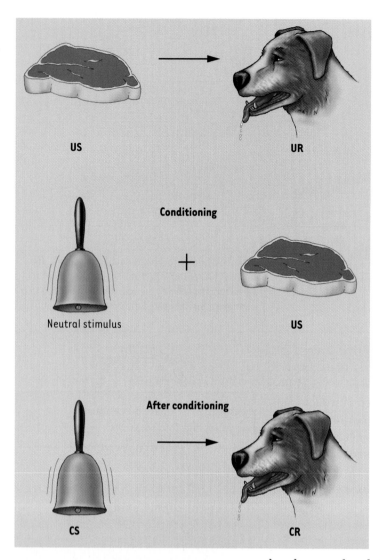

6.4 Initially, the US elicits UR. During acquisition, the formerly neutral CS is paired with the US. Eventually the CS elicits CR. Note that the UR is typically stronger than the CR.

extinction A process in which the conditioned response is weakened when the conditioned stimulus is repeated without the unconditioned stimulus.

spontaneous recovery A process in which a previously extinguished response reemerges following presentation of the conditioned stimulus.

stimulus generalization Occurs when stimuli that are similar but not identical to the conditioned stimulus produce the conditioned response.

acquisition of a learned association is that the stimuli occur together in time, which is referred to as *contiguity*. Subsequent research has shown that the strongest conditioning actually occurs when there is a very brief delay between the CS and the US.

Once a behavior is acquired, how long does it persist? For instance, what if the animal sought out the tasty blooms following rain, but they stopped appearing? Animals sometimes have to *unlearn* previous associations when they are no longer adaptive. Let's look at how this happens. After conditioning, the bell (CS) leads to salivation (CR) because the animal learns to associate the bell with the food (US). If the bell is presented many times and food does not arrive, the animal learns that the bell is not a good predictor of food, and therefore the salivary response gradually disappears. This process is known as **extinction**. The conditioned response is *extinguished* when the conditioned stimulus no longer predicts the unconditioned stimulus (Figure 6.5).

But suppose the delicious plant only blooms during a certain time of the year. The adaptive response is to check back once in a while to see if the plant blooms following rain. In the lab, an analogous situation occurs when the conditioned stimulus is presented a long time after extinction. Sounding the bell will once again produce the conditioned response of salivation (see Figure 6.5). This **spontaneous recovery**, in which the extinguished CS again produces a CR, is temporary and will quickly fade unless the CS is again paired with the US. Even a single pairing of the CS with the US will reestablish the CR, which will then again diminish if CS-US pairings do not continue. Thus, extinction inhibits but does not break the associative bond. It is a new form of learning that overwrites the previous association; what is learned is that the original association no longer holds true (Bouton, 1994).

Generalization, discrimination, and second-order conditioning In any learning situation, there are hundreds of possible stimuli that can be associated with the unconditioned stimulus to produce the conditioned response. How does the brain determine which of these stimuli is relevant? For instance, suppose we classically condition a dog so that it salivates (CR) when it hears a 1000 Hz (Hertz) tone. After the CR is established, tones that are similar to 1000 Hz will also produce it, but the farther the tones are from 1000 Hz, the less the dog will salivate (Figure 6.6). **Stimulus generalization** occurs when stimuli that are similar but not identical to the CS produce the CR. Generalization is adaptive because in nature the CS is seldom experienced repeatedly in an identical fashion. Slight differences in variables such as background noise, temperature, and lighting lead to slightly different perceptions of the CS, so animals learn to respond to variations in the CS.

Of course, there are limits on generalization. Sometimes it is important for animals to distinguish among similar stimuli. For instance, two species of plants may look similar, but one might be poisonous. **Stimulus discrimination** means

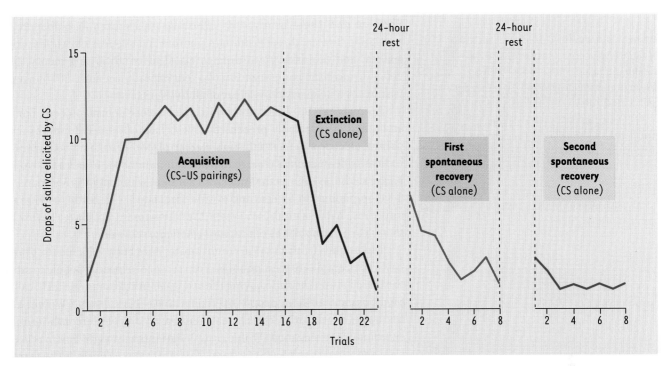

that animals learn to differentiate between two similar stimuli if one is consistently associated with the unconditioned stimulus and the other is not. In various studies, Pavlov and his students demonstrated that dogs could learn to make very fine distinctions between similar stimuli, such as subtle differences in shades of gray.

Sometimes a conditioned stimulus does not become directly associated with an unconditioned stimulus, but rather with other stimuli that themselves are associated with the US, a phenomenon known as *second-order conditioning*. In one of Pavlov's early studies, a CS-US bond was formed between a tone and food so that the tone (CS) led to salivation (CR). Following this conditioning, a second training session was conducted in which a black square was repeatedly presented at the same time as the tone. There was no US during this phase of the study. Following many trials, the black square was presented alone and it also produced salivation. Second-order conditioning helps to account for the complexity of learned associations (Figure 6.7). When some people go to the dentist, they get nervous simply entering the building. This occurs because entering the building (CS$_1$) predicts entering the dentist's office (CS$_2$), which predicts meeting the dentist (CS$_3$), who performs the drilling (US) that leads to a fear response. The association between the office building and the dental drill is many steps removed, but the conditioning is sufficient to produce feelings of nervousness.

PHOBIAS AND ADDICTIONS HAVE LEARNED COMPONENTS

Classical conditioning has helped explain a number of behavioral phenomena, including phobias and addictions.

6.5 During acquisition, the CS-US pairings lead to increased learning such that the CS can produce the CR. However, if the CS is presented without the US, eventually the CR extinguishes. Later, if the CS is presented alone it will produce a weak CR, known as spontaneous recovery. This CR will quickly extinguish if the US does not appear.

6.6 Maximal salivation occurs at the CS of 1000 Hz, but stimuli that are similar to the CS also produce the CR. The strength of the CR diminishes as the tone diverges from 1000 Hz.

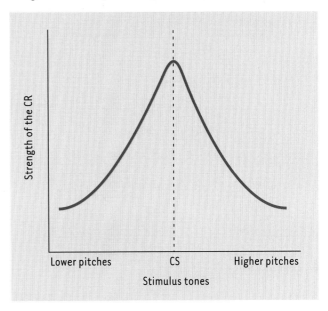

stimulus discrimination A learned tendency to differentiate between two similar stimuli if one is consistently associated with the unconditioned stimulus and the other is not.

phobias Acquired fears that are out of proportion to the real threat of an object.

Phobias and their treatment   **Phobias** are acquired fears that are out of proportion to the real threat. Common phobias include fear of heights, dogs, insects, snakes, and the dark. According to classical-conditioning theory, phobias develop through the generalization of a fear experience, such as when a person who is stung by a wasp develops a fear of all flying insects.

Animals can be classically conditioned to fear neutral objects. For example, if an animal is repeatedly presented with a flash of light followed by a moderately painful electric shock, it will soon display physiological and behavioral responses indicating fear, such as change in heart rate, whenever it sees a flash of light. Similarly, soldiers, such as the American soldiers who fought in Vietnam, sometimes develop phobias to objects and events associated with battle, such as the sight of uniforms, battle sounds, and even the Vietnamese language. Pavlov referred to these learned phobias as *conditioned emotional responses*.

Techniques from classical conditioning have been valuable for developing behavioral therapies to treat phobias. For instance, exposing people to small doses of the feared stimulus while having them engage in a pleasurable task, called *counter-conditioning*, can help people overcome their fears. Joseph Wolpe, a behavioral therapist, developed a formal treatment based on counterconditioning known as *systematic desensitization* (Wolpe, 1997). Patients are taught how to relax their muscles, and when they are able to do so, they are asked to imagine the feared object or situation while continuing to use the relaxation exercises. Eventually the person is exposed to the feared stimulus while relaxing. The general idea is that the CS→CR$_1$ (fear) connection can be broken by developing a new CS→CR$_2$ (relaxation) connection. The behavioral treatment of phobias has proven to be very effective.

6.7 After acquisition, the CS→CR. If another object is paired with the CS, it too will become a CS, and produce the CR. This second-order conditioning helps account for complex learning.

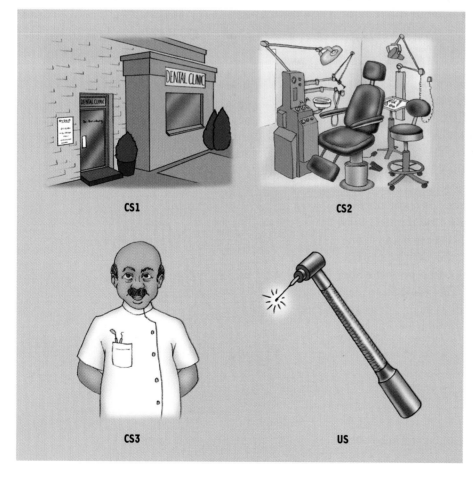

CS1

CS2

CS3

US

Drug addiction   Classical conditioning also plays an important role in drug addiction. Conditioned drug effects are common. For example, the smell of coffee can become a conditioned stimulus, leading coffee drinkers to feel activated and aroused. Likewise, because the needle becomes a CS, heroin addicts will sometimes inject themselves with water, when heroin is not available, to reduce their cravings. These learned associations demonstrate the power of conditioning and the potential for problems. When former heroin addicts are exposed to environmental cues associated with their drug use, they often experience cravings and physiological sensations similar to those they experienced during *withdrawal*, the unpleasant state of tension and anxiety that occurs when addicts stop using drugs. Thus, addicts who quit using drugs in treatment centers often relapse when they return to their old environments. They experience conditioned withdrawal effects. In the laboratory, presenting heroin or cocaine addicts with cues associated with drug ingestion leads to cravings and a variety of physiological responses associated with withdrawal, such as changes in heart rate and blood pressure. In one study of cocaine addicts (Maas et al., 1998), functional MRI found significant activity in the prefrontal cortex and anterior cingulate, part of the limbic system associated with motivation, when the subjects were presented with cocaine-relevant cues. The extent of activation in the anterior cingulate was related to self-reported levels of craving. A recent study using PET imaging found similar limbic-region activations when researchers showed a video of cocaine use to addicts (Figure 6.8, Childress et al., 1999).

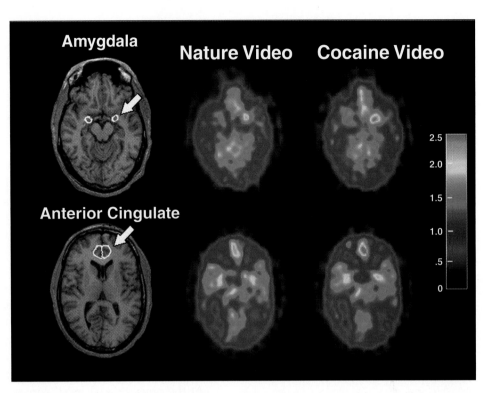

6.8 PET scan showing activation of the amygdala and anterior cingulate for abstinent cocaine addicts who were shown videos of nature scenes or cocaine cues. Areas with greatest activation are shown in red.

Classical-conditioning principles can help us understand how the Vietnam soldiers mentioned at the beginning of this chapter were able to stop taking narcotics when they returned to the United States. For the addicted soldiers, all of the cues for drug use were related to Vietnam and its associated military environment. When they returned home, none of those cues were around, therefore the soldiers did not experience conditioned withdrawal effects.

Another possible scenario is that taking their usual quantity of heroin in the United States might have produced greater drug effects than the soldiers expected, an unpleasant effect that would have discouraged further use.

Learning theorist Shepard Siegel has conducted fascinating research showing that drug tolerance effects are specific to certain situations. *Tolerance* is a process by which addicts need more and more of a drug to experience the same effects. According to research by Siegel, tolerance effects are greatest when the drug is taken in the same location as previous drug use. Tolerance can be so great that addicts regularly use drug doses that would be fatal for the inexperienced user. Conversely, Siegel's findings imply that if addicts take their usual large doses in a novel setting they are more likely to overdose (Siegel et al., 1982; Siegel, 1984).

CLASSICAL CONDITIONING INVOLVES MORE THAN CONTIGUITY

Pavlov's original explanation for classical conditioning was that any two events presented at the same time, in contiguity, would produce a learned association. Pavlov and his followers believed that the strength of the association was determined by factors such as the intensity of the conditioned and unconditioned stimuli, with greater intensity associated with increased learning. In the mid-1960s a number of challenges suggested that some conditioned stimuli were more likely to produce learning than others, and that contiguity was not sufficient to create CS-US associations.

Evolutionary significance According to Pavlov, any object or phenomenon could be converted into a conditioned stimulus during conditioning trials. Thus, a light, tone, color, or odor could be associated with the unconditioned stimulus. The idea that all stimuli are equally capable of producing conditioning is known as *equipotentiality*. However, it appears that not all stimuli are equally potent. Research conducted by psychologist John Garcia and his colleagues showed that certain pairings of stimuli are more likely to become associated than others. For instance, animals that are given poison in their food quickly learn to avoid the tastes or smells associated with the food (Garcia & Koelling, 1966). In these cases, just a few trials are enough to produce a long-lasting avoidance of the food item that was poisoned. These conditioned food aversions are easy to produce with taste or smell, but very difficult to produce with light or sound. This makes sense, since taste and smell are the main cues that guide eating behavior in animals. From an evolutionary viewpoint, animals that quickly associate a certain flavor with illness, and therefore avoid that flavor, are more likely to survive and pass along their genes.

Other research has shown that it is easier to condition monkeys to fear snakes than to fear objects such as flowers or rabbits (Cook & Mineka, 1989). Psychologist Martin Seligman (1970) argued that animals are genetically programmed to fear specific objects, which he refers to as **biological preparedness**. Preparedness helps to explain why phobias tend to be of things that have potential danger (e.g., snakes, fire, heights) rather than objects that pose little threat (e.g., flowers, shoes, babies).

At the most general level, contemporary researchers are interested in how classical conditioning helps animals learn adaptive responses (Hollis, 1997; Shettleworth, 2001). The adaptive value of a particular response varies according to the animal's evolutionary history. For example, taste aversions are easy to condition in rats, but difficult to condition in birds because they rely more on vision than taste to select food. However, birds quickly learn to avoid a visual cue that has been associated with illness. Rats freeze and startle if the CS is auditory, but rise on their hind legs when the CS is a visual cue (Holland, 1977). These differences may reflect the meaning of, and potential danger associated with, auditory and visual stimuli in the environment.

The cognitive perspective Prior to the 1970s, most animal learning theorists were concerned only with observable stimuli and responses. In the past three decades, learning theorists have placed a greater emphasis on trying to understand the mental processes that underlie conditioning. An important principle that has emerged is that classical conditioning is a means by which animals come to *predict* the occurrence of events. This rise in consideration of mental processes, such as prediction and expectancy, is referred to as the cognitive perspective on learning (Hollis, 1997).

Robert Rescorla (1966) conducted one of the first studies highlighting the role of cognition in learning. He argued that for learning to take place, the conditioned stimulus needs to be an accurate predictor of the unconditioned stimulus. For instance, a stimulus that occurs *before* the US is more easily conditioned than one that comes *after* it. Even though the two are both contiguous presentations with the US, the first stimulus is more easily learned because it predicts rather than comes after the US. Indeed, across all conditioning situations, some delay between the CS and the US is optimal for learning. The length of delay varies depending on the nature of the conditioned and unconditioned stimuli. For instance, eyeblink conditioning occurs when a sound (CS) is associated with a puff of air blown into the eye (US), which leads to a blink. Optimal learning for eye-

biological preparedness The idea that animals are biologically programmed to learn to fear specific objects.

blink conditioning is measured in milliseconds. By contrast, conditioned taste aversions often take many hours, since the ill effects of consuming poisons often take time to occur.

Novel stimuli are also more easily associated with the unconditioned stimulus than familiar stimuli. For example, dogs can be conditioned more easily with the novel smell of almonds than with smells more familiar to their environments. Once learned, a conditioned stimulus can prevent the acquisition of a new conditioned stimulus, a phenomenon known as the *blocking effect*. For example, a dog that has acquired the smell of almonds (CS) as a good predictor of food (US) does not need to look for other predictors. Furthermore, a stimulus that is associated with a CS can act as an *occasion setter* or trigger for the CS (Schmajuk et al., 1998). For example, a dog can learn that the smell of almonds predicts food only when the smell is preceded by a sound or a flash of light and not at other times. The smell or light indicates whether or not the association between the smell of almonds and food is active.

In 1972, learning theorists Robert Rescorla and Allan Wagner published a cognitive model of classical conditioning that profoundly changed our understanding of learning (Rescorla & Wagner, 1972). The **Rescorla-Wagner model** states that the strength of the CS-US association is determined by the extent to which the US is unexpected or surprising. According to the model, conditioning is a process by which organisms learn to expect the unconditioned stimulus based on the conditioned stimulus. Your pet wags its tail and runs around in circles when you start to open a can of food because it expects that it will soon be fed. According to Rescorla and Wagner, your pet has developed a mental representation in which the sound of the can opener predicts the appearance of food. When the US occurs unexpectedly, the animal attends to events in the environment that might have produced it. For example, say you use a manual can opener because the electric one is broken. Your pet finds itself presented with the food even though it did not hear the can being opened. Your pet soon will learn to anticipate being fed by the wrist movements you make with the new opener.

According to Rescorla and Wagner, when expectations are contradicted, we automatically search for possible explanations for the unconditioned stimulus. The Rescorla-Wagner model is a mathematical model of conditioning, with a formula that calculates the extent to which current expectations accurately predict the US. Learning involves making adjustments in the expectation of the US until prediction is accurate. The greater the surprise of the US, the more learning is needed for accurate prediction, and therefore the more conditioning occurs. The Rescorla-Wagner model is able to explain a wide range of conditioning phenomena. Consider blocking, in which a new stimulus fails to become associated with the unconditioned stimulus when a well-established conditioned stimulus is present. In this case, because the animal has learned the CS-US association, the US is not a surprise and therefore no association between the novel stimulus and unconditioned stimulus takes place.

Mark Bouton and his colleagues (1999) have demonstrated that background context, in addition to predictiveness, novelty, and expectation, plays an important role in classical conditioning. Consider the process of extinction, in which performance is reduced if the CS is presented many times without the US. According to research by Bouton, if the animal is placed in a new context they produce a CR in response to the CS, as if they forgot extinction. For example, suppose a rat receives fear conditioning, such that each time a CS is presented it receives a shock as the US. Now the rat is placed in a new context and receives the CS without

Rescorla-Wagner model A cognitive model of classical conditioning that states that the strength of the CS-US association is determined by the extent to which the unconditioned stimulus is unexpected.

shock, which eventually extinguishes the fear responses. When the animal is placed back in the original context and presented with the CS, it displays a fear response. This context-change account may be useful for understanding spontaneous recovery of previously extinguished responses in that the passage of time itself reflects a change in context. From the cognitive perspective, context provides important cues about when the CS predicts the US.

How Did the Behavioral Study of Learning Develop?

Behaviorism, led by John B. Watson, focused on observable aspects of learning. Pavlov developed the classical-conditioning theory to account for the learned association between neutral stimuli and reflexive behaviors. Conditioning occurs when the conditioned stimulus becomes associated with the unconditioned stimulus. For learning to occur, the conditioned stimulus needs to be a reliable predictor of the unconditioned stimulus, not simply contiguous. A cognitive model that accounts for most conditioning phenomena is the Rescorla-Wagner model, which states that that the amount of conditioning is determined by the extent to which the unconditioned stimulus is unexpected or surprising.

How is behavior shaped by rewards and punishments?

6.9 Thorndike used a primitive puzzle box such as the one depicted to assess learning in cats.

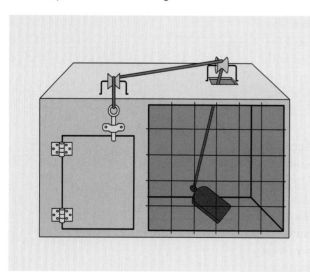

HOW IS OPERANT CONDITIONING DIFFERENT FROM CLASSICAL CONDITIONING?

Classical conditioning is a relatively passive process in which subjects associate events that happen around them. This form of conditioning does not account for the many times that one of the events occurs because of some action on the part of the subject. We don't sit idly waiting for food to be presented to us; we go out and purchase it. Our behaviors often represent a means to an end. We buy food to eat it, we study to get good grades, and we work to receive money. Thus, many of our actions are *instrumental*; they are done for a purpose. We learn to behave in certain ways in order to be rewarded, and we avoid behaving in certain ways in order not to be punished; this is called *instrumental conditioning* or *operant conditioning*.

B. F. Skinner, the psychologist most closely associated with this type of learning, selected the term *operant* to express the idea that animals operate on the environment to produce an effect. **Operant conditioning** is the learning process in which the consequences of an action determine the likelihood that it will be performed in the future.

The study of operant conditioning began in the basement of psychologist William James's house in Cambridge, Massachusetts. A young graduate student working with James, Edward Thorndike, had been influenced by Darwin and was studying whether nonhuman animals showed signs of intelligence. As part of his research, Thorndike built an apparatus called a puzzle box, a small cage with a trap door (Figure 6.9). The trap door would open if the animal performed a specific action, such as pulling a string. Thorndike placed food-deprived animals, usually cats, inside the puzzle box to see if they could figure out how to escape. To motivate the cats, he would place food just outside the box. When a cat was first placed in the box, it usually engaged in a number of nonproductive behaviors in an attempt to escape. After 5–10 minutes of struggling, the cat would *accidentally* pull the string and the door would open. Thorndike would then return the cat to the box and repeat the trial. Thorndike found that the cats would pull the string more quickly on each trial, until they soon learned to escape from the puzzle box within seconds. Based on this line of research Thorndike developed a general theory of learning, known as the **law of effect**, which states that any behavior that leads to a "satisfying state of affairs" is more likely to occur again, and that those that lead to an "annoying state of affairs" are less likely to occur again.

REINFORCEMENT INCREASES BEHAVIOR

Thirty years after Thorndike, another Harvard graduate student in psychology, B. F. Skinner (1904–1990) (Figure 6.10), developed a more formal learning theory based on the law of effect. Skinner had been greatly influenced by John B. Watson and shared his philosophy of behaviorism. He therefore objected to the subjective aspects of Thorndike's law of effect: states of "satisfaction" are not observable empirically. Skinner coined the term *reinforcer* to describe events that produced a learned response. A **reinforcer** is a stimulus that occurs following a response that increases the likelihood that the response will be repeated. Skinner believed that behavior, from studying to eating to driving on the proper side of the road, occurs because it has been reinforced.

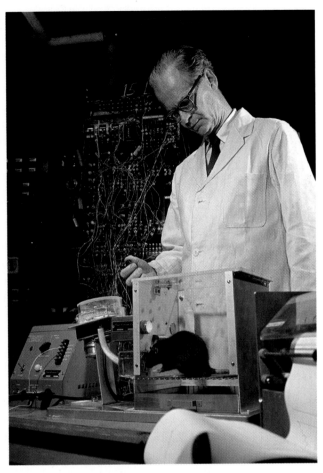

6.10 B. F. Skinner (seen here displaying the Skinner box) was one of the most influential psychologists of all time.

The Skinner box Skinner developed a simple device for assessing operant conditioning called the *Skinner box*, a small chamber or cage in which a lever (or response key) is connected to a food or water supply. An animal, usually a rat or a pigeon, is placed in the box; when it presses the lever, food or water becomes available. Skinner's earlier research used mazes in which a rat had to take a specific turn to get access to the reinforcer. After the rat completed the trial Skinner had to get the rat and return it to the beginning. He developed the Skinner box, or *operant chamber*, as he called it, basically because he got tired of constantly fetching the rats. With the Skinner box, the rats could be exposed to repeated conditioning trials without the experimenter having to do anything but observe. Skinner later built mechanical recording devices that allowed trials to be conducted without the experimenter even being present.

Shaping With little to do in a Skinner box, the animal typically presses the lever sooner rather than later. One of the major problems encountered with operant conditioning outside the Skinner box is that you need to wait until the animal emits an appropriate response before you can provide the reinforcer. Let's say you are trying to teach your dog to roll over. Rather than waiting for your dog to spontaneously perform this action, you can use an operant conditioning technique to teach your dog to do so. The process, called **shaping**, involves reinforcing behaviors that are increasingly similar to the desired behavior. You initially reward your dog for any behavior that even slightly resembles rolling over, such as lying down. Once this behavior is established you become more selective in which behaviors you reinforce. Reinforcing *successive approximations* will eventually

operant conditioning A learning process in which the consequences of an action determine the likelihood that it will be performed in the future.

law of effect Thorndike's general theory of learning, which states that any behavior that leads to a "satisfying state of affairs" is more likely to occur again, and that those that lead to an "annoying state of affairs" are less likely to reoccur.

reinforcer A stimulus following a response that increases the likelihood that the response will be repeated.

shaping A process of operant conditioning that involves reinforcing behaviors that are increasingly similar to the desired behavior.

6.11 The process of shaping can be used to train extraordinary behaviors. Here a trained dog water skis for a boat show.

primary reinforcers Reinforcers that are innately reinforcing, such as those that satisfy biological needs.

secondary reinforcers Events or objects that serve as reinforcers through their repeated pairings with primary reinforcers.

punishment A stimulus following a response that decreases the likelihood that the response will be repeated.

produce the desired behavior, as your dog learns to discriminate which behavior is being reinforced (Figure 6.11). Shaping is a powerful procedure that can condition animals to perform amazing feats, such as pigeons playing ping pong, dogs playing the piano, and pigs doing housework such as picking up clothes and vacuuming. Shaping has also been used to teach mentally ill people appropriate social skills, autistic children language, and mentally retarded individuals basic skills such as dressing themselves. More generally, parents and educators often use subtle forms of shaping to encourage appropriate behavior in children.

Reinforcers can be conditioned   The most obvious reinforcers are those that are necessary for survival, such as food or water. Those that satisfy biological needs are referred to as **primary reinforcers**. From an evolutionary standpoint, the learning value of primary reinforcers makes a great deal of sense, since organisms that repeatedly perform behaviors reinforced by food and water are more likely to survive and pass along their genes. But many apparent reinforcers do not directly satisfy basic biological needs. For instance, money is only pieces of metal or paper, but many people work hard to receive it. Likewise, a compliment, a hug from a friend, or an "A" on a paper can be reinforcing. Events or objects that serve as reinforcers but that do not satisfy biological needs are referred to as **secondary reinforcers**. Secondary reinforcers become established through classical conditioning. We learn to associate a neutral stimulus, such as paper money (CS), with, for example, food (US). Of course, money also takes on other meanings, such as power and security, but the essential point is that a neutral object becomes meaningful through its association with unconditioned stimuli. Animals can be conditioned to perform tasks in order to receive *tokens*, which they can later trade for food. The tokens themselves thus reinforce behavior. Using similar principles, many prisons, mental hospitals, and classrooms have established *token economies* in which people earn tokens for completing certain tasks. These tokens can be saved and later traded for objects or privileges.

Reinforcer potency   Some reinforcers are more powerful than others. An integrative theory of reinforcement was proposed by psychologist David Premack, who theorized that the value of a specific reinforcer could be determined by the amount of time an organism engages in that behavior when free to choose anything. For instance, you could observe that most children choose to spend more time eating ice cream than spinach, indicating that ice cream is more reinforcing. One great advantage of Premack's theory is that it can account for individual differences in values. Undoubtedly some people prefer spinach to ice cream; therefore, spinach serves as a more potent reinforcer for them.

A logical extension of Premack's theory is that a more valued activity can be used to reinforce the performance of a less valued activity, which is referred to as the *Premack principle*. Parents use the Premack principle all the time: "Eat your spinach and then you'll get dessert"; "Finish your homework and then you can go out."

BOTH REINFORCEMENT AND PUNISHMENT CAN BE POSITIVE OR NEGATIVE

Reinforcement and punishment have opposite effects on behavior. Whereas reinforcement increases behavior, punishment decreases behavior. Formally, **punishment** is the process by which the consequences of an action reduce the likelihood that the action will be repeated. For example, giving a rat an electric shock for pressing a lever will decrease the number of times that it presses the lever. Both reinforcement and punishment can be positive or negative.

Positive and negative reinforcement **Positive reinforcement** increases the probability of a behavior being repeated by administering a pleasurable stimulus. Positive reinforcement often is referred to as *reward*. Behaviors that are rewarded increase in frequency, such as working hard because of praise or money. In contrast, **negative reinforcement** increases behavior through the *removal* of an aversive stimulus. For instance, a rat is negatively reinforced when required to press a lever to turn off an electric shock. Note how negative reinforcement is different from punishment, in which the rat receives a shock for pressing the lever. Negative reinforcement is not punishment. Reinforcement—positive or negative—*increases* whereas punishment *decreases* the likelihood of a behavior. Negative reinforcement is quite common in everyday life. You close the door to your room to shut out noise. You change the channel to avoid watching an awful program. In each case, you are trying to escape or avoid an unwanted stimulus, which is the negative reinforcer.

Positive and negative punishment Punishment reduces behavior, but it can do so through positive or negative means. **Positive punishment** decreases the probability of a behavior recurring by administering an averse stimulus. Rats getting a shock for pressing a lever is an example of positive punishment. **Negative punishment** decreases the probability of a behavior by removing a pleasurable stimulus. Youths whose driving privileges are revoked for speeding are less likely to speed the next time they get behind the wheel. Although losing driving privileges is a form of negative punishment, getting a speeding ticket is a form of positive punishment. Figure 6.12 provides an overview of positive and negative reinforcement and punishment.

Effectiveness of parental punishment Punishment is often used by parents who want their children to behave. But many contemporary psychologists believe that punishment is often applied ineffectively and also may have unintended and unwanted consequences. For punishment to be effective, it must be applied immediately so that the relationship between the unwanted behavior and punishment is clear. Also, it must be applied only to unwanted behavior. But there is considerable potential for confusion here. Sometimes punishment is applied following a desired action, as when a student is punished after coming forward to admit cheating on an exam. The student may associate the punishment with being honest rather than with the original offense; the result may be that the student learns *not* to tell the truth.

Punishment can also lead to negative emotions, such as fear or anxiety, which may become associated, through classical conditioning, with the person who administers the punishment. A child may learn to fear a parent or teacher rather than stop the undesired behavior. Another problem with punishment is that it often fails to offset the reinforcing aspects of the behavior. In real life, any behavior is often reinforced in

positive reinforcement The increase in the probability of a behavior being repeated following the administration of a pleasurable stimulus, referred to as a reward.

negative reinforcement The increase in the probability of a behavior being repeated through the removal of an aversive stimulus.

positive punishment Punishment that occurs when administering a stimulus that decreases the probability of a behavior recurring.

negative punishment Punishment that occurs when removing a stimulus that decreases the probability of a behavior recurring.

6.12 Overview of negative and positive reinforcement and punishment.

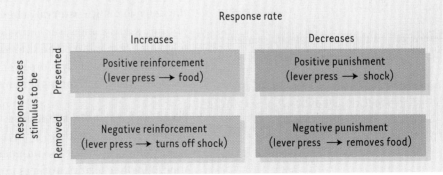

multiple ways. For instance, thumbsucking may be reinforced because it makes a child feel good and provides relief from negative emotions and hunger. The threat of punishment for thumbsucking may not be sufficient to offset the rewards of its use, though it may reinforce secrecy. Finally, the use of physical punishment, such as spanking, teaches the child that violence is appropriate behavior for adults (we consider imitation learning later in this chapter). For these and other reasons, most psychologists recommend that reinforcement be used rather than punishment. A child who receives compliments for being a good student is likely to show better academic performance than one who is punished for doing poorly.

There are occasions, however, when punishment ought to be considered. For instance, a young child who is doing something extremely dangerous needs to be stopped right away. A firm reprimand is appropriate and usually effective at stopping a child from touching a hot stove or running into traffic. For punishment to be effective, it should do three things. First, it should be immediate. Second, it should be unpleasant enough to overcome the reinforcing aspects of the behavior. Finally, it should be followed with reinforcement for appropriate behavior. A common punishment used in day care centers to deal with unruly children is the *time-out*, in which the child is removed from the situation and left to think about the consequences of the offending behavior. The success of the time-out technique depends on the caregiver's willingness to carry out the punishment. One of the most common parenting mistakes is to continually threaten punishment and then fail to take action. Parents who fail to follow through on their threats teach children that the threats can be safely ignored.

OPERANT CONDITIONING IS INFLUENCED BY SCHEDULES OF REINFORCEMENT

How often should a reinforcer be given? For fast learning, you might wish to reinforce the desired behavior each time it occurs, referred to as **continuous reinforcement**. In the real world, behavior is seldom reinforced continuously. Animals do not find food each time they look for it, and people do not receive praise each time they behave in an acceptable fashion. Most behavior is reinforced intermittently, which is referred to as **partial reinforcement**. The effect of partial reinforcement on conditioning depends on the reinforcement schedule.

Ratio and interval schedules   Partial reinforcement can be administered based on the number of behavioral responses or the passage of time. For instance, factory workers can be paid by the piece (behavioral response) or by the hour (passage of time). In a **ratio schedule**, reinforcement is based on the number of times the behavior occurs, such as reinforcing every third or tenth occurrence of the behavior. With **interval schedules**, reinforcement is based on a specific unit of time, such as once every minute or hour. In general, ratio reinforcement leads to greater responding than interval reinforcement. Factory workers who are paid by the piece are usually more productive than those paid by the hour, especially if there are incentives for higher levels of productivity.

Fixed and variable schedules   Partial reinforcement also can be given on a *fixed* or *variable* schedule. With a **fixed schedule**, the reinforcer is consistently given following a specific number of occurrences or after a specific amount of time. Whether factory workers are paid by the piece or by the hour, they usually

continuous reinforcement A type of learning in which the desired behavior is reinforced each time it occurs.

partial reinforcement A type of learning in which behavior is reinforced intermittently.

ratio schedule Reinforcement is based on the number of times the behavior occurs.

interval schedule Reinforcement is based on a specific unit of time.

fixed schedule Reinforcement is consistently provided upon each occurrence.

are paid according to a fixed rate, earning the same for each piece or for each hour. The rate of reinforcement is entirely predictable. In **variable schedules** of reinforcement, the reinforcer is applied at different rates or at different times. The responder does not know how many behaviors need to be performed or how much time needs to pass before reinforcement occurs. An example of variable reinforcement is salespeople who are paid only when a customer agrees to purchase a product.

The influence of reinforcement schedules on behavior can be observed in the study habits of students. Ideally, students will spread their studying out over the entire term, but the reality is that when exams are scheduled at fixed points, students tend to study a great deal just before the exam and not at all afterward. It is typical of *fixed-interval reinforcement* that the behavior is performed only when it is time for the reinforcer to be administered. When exams are on a *variable-interval schedule*, such as having surprise quizzes, students tend to study more often and more consistently. The patterns of behavior typically observed under different schedules of reinforcement can be seen in Figure 6.13.

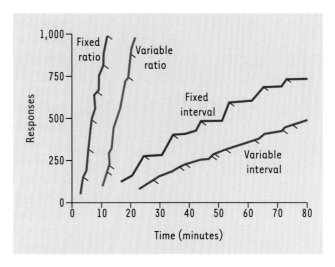

6.13 These curves show typical learning under different schedules of reinforcement. The steeper the line, the higher the response rate. The slash marks on the lines indicate when reinforcement is given. Note that ratio reinforcement leads to the highest rate of response.

Behavioral persistence The schedule of reinforcement also affects the persistence of behavior. Continuous reinforcement is highly effective for acquiring a behavior, but if the reinforcement is stopped, the behavior extinguishes quickly. For instance, typically when you put money in a vending machine it gives you a product. If it fails to do so you will quickly stop giving it your money. In contrast, a slot machine pays out on a *variable-ratio schedule*. People continue to pour money into slot machines even if the machine rarely reinforces their behavior. The **partial-reinforcement extinction effect** describes the greater persistence of behavior under partial reinforcement, due to the difficulty of detecting a lack of reinforcement. During continuous reinforcement, it is easy to detect when reinforcement has ceased. But if the behavior is reinforced only some of the time, the subject needs to repeat the behavior comparatively more times to detect the absence of reinforcement. Thus, the less frequent the reinforcement during training, the greater the resistance to extinction. To condition a behavior that you wish to have persist, reinforce it continuously during early acquisition and then slowly change to partial reinforcement. Parents naturally follow this strategy in teaching their children toilet training and other behaviors.

BIOLOGY AND COGNITION INFLUENCE OPERANT CONDITIONING

Behaviorists such as B. F. Skinner believed that all behavior could be explained by straightforward conditioning principles. Skinner's novel *Walden Two* describes a utopia in which all of society's problems are solved through operant-conditioning principles. In reality, however, there are limits to explaining human behavior through schedules of reinforcement. Biology places constraints on learning, and reinforcement does not always have to be present for learning to take place.

Biological constraints Although behaviorists believed that any behavior could be shaped through reinforcement, it is now apparent that animals have a hard time learning behaviors that run counter to their evolutionary adaptation. A

variable schedule Reinforcement is applied at different rates or at different times.

partial-reinforcement extinction effect The greater persistence of behavior under partial reinforcement than under continuous reinforcement.

good example of biological constraints was obtained by the Brelands, a husband-and-wife team of psychologists who used operant-conditioning techniques to train animals for commercials (Breland & Breland, 1961). They discovered that many of their animals refused to perform certain tasks they had been taught. For instance, they trained a raccoon to place coins in a piggy bank, but, although the raccoon initially learned the task, it eventually refused to deposit the coins. Instead, it stood over the piggy bank and briskly rubbed the coins in its paws. The rubbing behavior was not reinforced; it actually delayed reinforcement. One explanation for the raccoon's behavior is that the task was incompatible with innate adaptive behaviors. The raccoon associated the coin with food and treated it the same way: rubbing food between the paws is hardwired for raccoons. Along similar lines, pigeons can be trained to peck at keys to obtain food or secondary reinforcement, but it is difficult to get them to peck at keys to avoid electric shock. However, they can learn to avoid shock by flapping their wings because it is their natural means of escape. Psychologist Robert Bolles argues that animals have built-in defense reactions to threatening stimuli (Bolles, 1970). Conditioning is most effective when the association between the behavioral response and the reinforcement is similar to the built-in predispositions of the animal.

The evolutionary perspective views the brain as a compilation of different domain-specific modules, each responsible for different cognitive functions. This suggests that learning is the result of many unique mechanisms that solve individual adaptive problems, not the result of general learning mechanisms (Rozin & Kalat, 1971; Shettleworth, 2001). As evolutionary psychologist Randy Gallistel (2000) argues, people readily accept that the lungs are adapted for breathing and the ear is adapted for hearing. No one would argue that the lungs could be used to hear, or the ears to breath. There is no general "sensing organ." Thus, it makes equal sense to postulate that there are a variety of learning mechanisms that have evolved to solve specific problems. Consider an ant that leaves its nest to forage for food. Typically, the ant takes a circuitous and wandering path until it finds food, at which point it takes a direct path back to the nest, even over unfamiliar territory. This differs from what would be expected from traditional models of learning. The ant has never been rewarded for following the path, and there has been no classically conditioned association between the unfamiliar environmental objects and the most direct path back to the nest. Instead, mental processes that compute small changes in distance and direction provide a solution for the most direct path home. Gallistel's point is that learning consists of specialized learning abilities that solve the adaptive problems faced by animals in their environments.

Acquisition-performance distinction   Another challenge to the idea that reinforcement is responsible for all behavior is that learning can take place without reinforcement. Edward Tolman, an early cognitive theorist, argued that reinforcement has more impact on performance than on learning. At the time, Tolman was conducting experiments in which rats had to learn to run through complex mazes to obtain food. Tolman believed that the rats developed **cognitive maps**, spatial representations of the maze that helped them learn to quickly find the food. To test his theory, Tolman and his students studied three groups of rats whose task was to travel through a maze to a "goal box" containing the reinforcer, usually food. The first group did not receive any reinforcement, and their performance was quite poor. With no goal box to find, the rats wandered through the maze. A second group was reinforced on every trial, and they learned to find the goal box quickly. The critical group was the third group, which was not reinforced for the first ten trials but was then reinforced on subsequent trials. Tolman found that this group

cognitive maps A visual/spatial mental representation of the environment.

latent learning Learning that takes place in the absence of reinforcement.

showed an amazingly fast learning curve, so that they immediately caught up to the group that had been continuously reinforced (Figure 6.14). This result implies that the rats had learned a cognitive map of the maze and could use it when reinforcement became available. Tolman used the term **latent learning** to refer to learning that takes place in the absence of reinforcement.

Another form of learning that takes place in the absence of reinforcement is *insight learning*—a form of problem solving (discussed in chapter 8) in which a solution suddenly emerges after a period of inaction or following contemplation of the problem. You probably have had this sort of experience, in which you mull over a problem for a while and then suddenly know the answer. Reinforcement does not provide an adequate account of the process of insight learning, although it does predict whether the behavior is subsequently repeated.

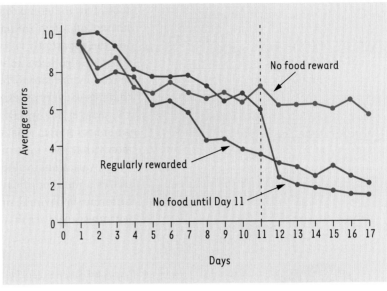

6.14 Rats that were regularly reinforced for correctly running through a maze showed improved performance over time compared to rats that did not receive reinforcement. Rats that were not reinforced for the first ten trials but were then reinforced showed an immediate change in performance, indicating that they had learned a path through the maze, but that their learning was not revealed, or was latent, until it was reinforced.

Behavioral economics of learning   A relatively new approach to understanding operant conditioning considers the value of reinforcement in the context of basic economic principles, such as supply and demand. That which is in short supply is typically valued more, and therefore serves as a more potent reinforcer. Sometimes the economics considerations are more complicated. Which would you prefer, $100 today or $1000 next year? Although it might appear that the larger payment would be more reinforcing, its value is discounted because there is a significant delay before it is received. But, what if you really needed money right now? In that case, waiting has additional costs. Indeed, adults with lower incomes discount future payments more steeply than those with large incomes (Green et al., 1996). At the heart of the behavioral economics approach is the idea that people and other animals often need to make choices between reinforcers. The subjective value of the reinforcer is affected by how long one has to wait to receive it as well as the likelihood that the payoff will actually be received. This approach has provided insights into a variety of behaviors, especially those associated with addiction. Warren Bickel and his colleagues (1999; Madden et al., 1997) found that both smokers and heroin addicts discounted future rewards more greatly than did non-addicts, which may contribute to their problems with impulsivity and self-control. The issue of delaying immediate gratification to obtain long-term rewards is discussed more fully in Chapter 9.

Behavioral choice is also implicated in studies of animal foraging. Where animals choose to eat is dependent on the likelihood that food will be present, the energy costs associated with obtaining the food, and the risks associated with predators (Shettleworth, 2001). Should an animal eat all the berries in one patch and then search for a new patch, or should it save some for later and search for more patches? The new patches might have berries, but they might not. Researchers who study animals in their natural habitats find that animals are highly sensitive to the relative rates of reinforcement between different patches. The time they spend eating in one patch is influenced by the rate of reinforcement, the relative rate of reinforcement in other patches, and the time it takes to travel to those other patches. *Optimal foraging theory* describes how animals in the wild choose to provide their own schedules of reinforcement. It predicts that animals will sometimes act in apparently risky fashion. Consider an animal faced with the choice of feeding from two locations that have the same average amount of food, but one is much more variable, sometimes having no food and sometimes having lots. If an animal is facing starvation, its best chances for survival is to follow the apparently risky strategy of foraging in the more highly variable location. Animals also learn to vary how they eat according to the likelihood of being attacked by predators. Research at the University of Lethbridge in Canada found that rats eat very quickly when in the dark, especially when they are food deprived (Wishaw et al., 1992). Although eating quickly is optimal for consuming large amounts of food, it is not optimal for digestion. When in the light, rats eat more slowly, but they make frequent scans of the environment to check for predators. These variations reflect the fact that even a simple behavior such as eating requires a number of calculations to detect the costs and benefits associated with different behavioral options. The choices made by animals reflect specialized learning capacities that are adaptive to the environment.

How Is Operant Conditioning Different from Classical Conditioning?

Classical conditioning involves the learned association between neutral and reflexive stimuli. Operant conditioning is a form of learning in which the stimuli that follow behaviors determine the likelihood that the behaviors will be repeated. Positive reinforcers increase behavior by providing a reward, whereas negative reinforcers increase behavior by removing an aversive stimulus. Continuous reinforcement is best for the acquisition of novel behavior, whereas partial reinforcement, especially variable-ratio reinforcement, is most resistant to extinction. Punishment is effective only when it is delivered immediately following the undesired behavior. Punishment often is used ineffectively, and it has a number of undesirable outcomes. Biology places constraints on what animals can learn, and animals have difficulty acquiring behaviors that are incompatible with evolutionarily adaptive responses.

HOW DOES WATCHING OTHERS AFFECT LEARNING?

RESEARCH QUESTION

What is learned from observing others?

Suppose that you were trying to teach someone to fly an airplane. How might you apply learning principles discussed in this chapter to accomplish your goal? Reinforcing arbitrary correct behaviors obviously would be a disastrous strategy for training aspiring pilots. Similarly, teaching people to play football, eat with chopsticks, or perform complex dance steps requires more than simply reinforcement. For many behaviors, we learn not by doing, but by observing the actions of others. We learn things such as social etiquette through observation, and we learn whether to be anxious in a situation by watching to see if others are anxious. Similarly, we acquire many of our attitudes about politics, religion, people, and objects from outside sources, such as parents, peers, teachers, and the media. In this section we consider learning that occurs from watching the behavior of others.

LEARNING CAN OCCUR THROUGH OBSERVATION

observational learning Learning that occurs when behaviors are acquired or modified following exposure to others performing the behavior.

Observational learning, which occurs when behaviors are acquired or modified following exposure to others performing the behavior, is a powerful adaptive tool both for humans and for other animals. Animals learn that food is safe by watching what their parents eat, and they learn to fear dangerous objects by watching their parents avoid those objects. Similarly, children acquire beliefs and basic skills by observing their parents and other role models. Any parent will tell you that young children are sponges, absorbing everything that goes on around them. They learn by watching as much as by doing.

Bandura's observational studies The most thorough work on observational learning was conducted by Albert Bandura (Figure 6.15) in the 1960s. In a now-classic series of studies, preschool children were shown a film of an adult playing with a large inflatable doll called Bobo (Figure 6.16). In the film, the adult either played quietly with Bobo or attacked the doll furiously, whacking it with a mallet, socking it in the nose, and kicking it around the room. When the children were later allowed to play with a number of toys, including the Bobo doll, those who had seen the more aggressive display were more than twice as likely to act aggressively toward the doll (Bandura et al., 1961). These results suggest that exposure to media violence may increase the likelihood that children will act aggressively. This possibility is discussed in "Studying the Mind: Media Violence and Aggression."

6.15 Albert Bandura conducted important research showing that people could learn through observation.

Observational learning of fear Observational learning also occurs in animals. For example, psychologist Susan Mineka explored whether rhesus monkeys could develop a phobia of snakes by observing other monkeys react fearfully to them. She had noticed that monkeys raised in the laboratory do not fear snakes, whereas those raised in the wild have an intense fear of them. Mineka and her colleagues set up an experiment with two groups of monkeys, one group reared in the wild and one group reared in the laboratory. The monkeys were required to reach beyond a clear box that contained either a snake or a neutral object to obtain food. When a snake was in the box, not only did the wild-reared monkeys not touch the food, but they showed signs of distress, such as clinging to their cages

6.16 Scenes from the classic Bobo doll studies. After viewing the adult act aggressively (top row), children (bottom two rows) imitated what they had seen.

Studying the Mind

MEDIA VIOLENCE AND AGGRESSION

The average television set in the United States is on for five or six hours per day, and young children often spend more time watching television than doing any other activity, including schoolwork (Roberts, 2000). There is a great deal of violence in television programming. The average child witnesses more than 100,000 violent acts on TV before the end of elementary school; you probably witnessed over 18,000 murders on TV before you started college. More recently, children have also had access to video and cable, where they can observe graphic and sexualized violence in R-rated movies that were never intended for children. What effect does this massive exposure to violence have on aggressive behavior?

Three decades of research have linked viewing violence with imitative violence, aggressive behavior, acceptance of violence as a solution, increased feelings of hostility, and willingness to deliver painful stimuli to others. Some researchers have conducted controlled laboratory studies in which they randomly assign children to watch either violent or neutral film clips and then measure subsequent aggressive behavior. In general, compared to those who watch neutral clips, children exposed to violence are more likely to act in an aggressive manner during subsequent tasks. A study by Leonard Eron and his colleagues found that television viewing habits at age 8 predicted violent behavior and criminal activity at age 30 (Eron, 1987). The average effect size (the magnitude of the association between independent and dependent variables), determined by statistically averaging across the hundreds of studies, is nearly as large as that linking smoking and cancer, and is larger than the effect size for condom non-use and HIV transmission or for lead exposure and IQ in children (Bushman & Anderson, 2001).

There are, however, a number of problems with the studies on this topic. Social psychologist Jonathan Freedman (1984) notes that many of the so-called aggressive behaviors displayed by children could be interpreted as playful behavior rather than aggression. A more serious concern is whether the studies are generalizable to the real world, which refers to their external validity. Exposure to a violent film clip in the lab is unlike watching television in real life. The film clips used in studies are often brief and extremely violent, and the child watches them alone. In the real world violent episodes are interspersed with nonviolent material and children often watch them with others who may buffer the effect.

Even the longitudinal studies that assess childhood television watching and later violent behavior fail to satisfactorily prove that TV caused the behavior. It could easily be that extraneous variables, such as personality, poverty, or parental negligence, have an effect on both television viewing habits and violent tendencies. After all, not all of those who view violence on television become aggressive later in life. Perhaps those who watch excessive amounts of televi-

6.17 Mineka required two sets of monkeys to reach past the clear box to reach food. When the clear box contained a snake, the wild-reared monkeys refused to reach across the box. By observing the actions of those monkeys, the laboratory-reared monkeys who did not originally fear snakes, learned to become afraid of them. This suggests that fears can be learned through observation.

and making threatening faces (Figure 6.17). The laboratory-raised monkeys reached past the box whether it contained a snake or not, and they showed no overt signs of fear. Mineka then showed the laboratory-raised monkeys the fearful response of the wild monkeys to see if it would affect their reaction to the snake. The laboratory monkeys quickly developed a fear of the snakes and this fear was maintained over a three-month period (Mineka et al., 1984).

ANIMALS AND HUMANS IMITATE OTHERS

Animals and humans readily imitate the actions of others. In one study, pigeons observed other pigeons being reinforced at a feeder when they either stepped on a bar or pecked at the feeder directly. When the observing pigeons were themselves placed before the feeder, they tended to use the same technique they had seen (Zentall et al., 1996). Similarly, novel strategies of tool use have been observed in monkey colonies, with infant monkeys imitating the behavior of adults. Within a few days of birth human newborns will imitate facial expressions they observe, and they will continue to imitate gestures and other actions as they mature.

sion, and who therefore have fewer opportunities to develop social skills, act aggressively. Correlation does not prove causation. Only through careful laboratory studies in which participants are randomly assigned to experimental conditions can we determine causality. Obviously, it isn't practical to randomly assign different children to different types of media, and it is ethically questionable to expose any children to watching violence if we think it will make them more aggressive.

In spite of the problems with interpreting specific studies, most scientists believe that there is a direct relation between exposure to violence and aggressive behavior. Indeed, a recent joint statement by the American Academy of Pediatrics, the American Academy of Child and Adolescent Psychiatry, the American Medical Association, the American Academy of Family Physicians, the American Psychological Association, and the American Psychiatric Association concluded that a plethora of studies "point overwhelmingly to a causal connection between media violence and aggressive behavior in some children" (Joint Statement, 2000, p. 1).

How might media violence promote aggression among adolescents? One possibility is that exposure to massive amounts of violence in movies, which misrepresents the prevalence of violence in real life, leads adolescents to believe that violence is both common and inevitable. Because few people are punished for acting violently

in movies, children may come to believe that such behaviors are justified (Bushman & Huesmann, 2001). That is, the portrayal of violence in movies teaches children possible social scripts for solving personal problems. By mentally rehearsing the script, or observing the same script enacted many times in different movies, a child might come to believe that engaging in brutality is an effective way to solve problems and dispense with annoying people (Huesmann, 1998).

Perhaps the most harmful effect of viewing repeated episodes of graphic violence is that it desensitizes viewers, such that witnessing subsequent violent episodes produces a diminished emotional response (Bushman & Anderson, 2001. Just as boot camp systematically inures soldiers to the horrors of combat, movie violence blunts the emotional and cognitive responses that children have to observing graphic violence and gore. Simply put, after watching excruciatingly vivid close-ups of people being maimed, beaten, raped, or tortured, these images eventually do not produce much of a reaction among viewers. In this way, children are perhaps being socialized to be insensitive to the pain and suffering of others. Media exposure to violence may even contribute to violent teenage behaviors, such as recent school shootings. Although it is highly unlikely that media exposure is *the cause* of school shootings, it may be *one factor* that promotes a mental state that is capable of acting on violent urges and impulses.

The imitation of observed behavior is commonly referred to as **modeling**, in that humans or animals reproduce the behaviors of *models*—those being observed. Modeling in humans is influenced by a number of factors. In general, we are more likely to imitate the actions of models who are attractive, have high status, and are somewhat similar to ourselves. In addition, modeling will be effective only if the observer is physically capable of imitating the behavior. Simply watching Tiger Woods blast 300-yard drives does not mean we could do so if handed a golf club.

Vicarious reinforcement Another factor that determines whether observers imitate a model is whether the model is reinforced for performing the behavior. In another study, Bandura and his colleagues showed children a film of an adult aggressively playing with a Bobo doll, but this time the film had one of three different endings (Bandura et al., 1963). A control condition showed no consequences for the model's behavior, while the second film showed the adult being rewarded by being given candy and praise, and the third showed the adult being spanked and verbally reprimanded. When subsequently allowed to play with the Bobo doll, the children who observed the model being rewarded were much more likely to be aggressive toward the doll than those children in the control group. In contrast, those who saw the model being punished were less likely to be aggressive than the control group. Does this mean that those children did not learn the behavior? No. When the children later were offered small gifts to perform the model's actions, all of them could do so reliably. It is important to distinguish between the *acquisition* of a behavior and its *performance*. All of the children learned the behavior, but only

modeling The imitation of behavior through observational learning.

vicarious learning Learning that occurs when people learn the consequences of an action by observing others being rewarded or punished for performing the action.

mirror neurons Neurons in the premotor cortex that are activated during observation of others performing an action.

intracranial self-stimulation (ICSS) A procedure in which animals are able to self-administer electrical shock to specific areas of the brain.

mesolimbic dopamine system The major brain system involved in reward, it connects the ventral tegmental area (VTA) to the nucleus accumbens.

those who saw the model being rewarded actually performed the behavior. **Vicarious learning** occurs when people learn about the consequences of an action by observing others being rewarded or punished for performing the action.

Mirror neurons   What happens in the brain during imitation learning? An intriguing study found that neurons in the premotor cortex called **mirror neurons** become activated when a monkey observes another monkey reaching for an object (Rizzolatti et al., 1996). These mirror neurons are the same neurons that would be activated if the monkey performed the behavior itself. Mirror neurons are especially likely to become activated when monkeys observe a target monkey engaging in movement that has some goal, such as reaching out to grasp an object. Neither the sight of the object on its own nor the mere sight of the target monkey leads to activation of these mirror neurons.

Similar mirror neurons have been identified in humans by using PET imaging and electrical brain recordings (Gallese & Goldman, 1998). Thus, every time you observe another person engaging in an action, similar neural circuits are firing in both your brains. The function of mirror neurons is currently open to debate. This system may serve as the basis of imitation learning, but note that the firing of mirror neurons does not lead to imitative behavior in the observer. This has led some theorists to speculate that mirror neurons help us explain and predict the behavior of others. In other words, they allow us to step into the shoes of those we observe so that we can better understand their actions.

How Does Watching Others Affect Learning?

Much of behavior is learned by observing the behavior of others. Children learn language, social skills, and political attitudes from observing their parents, peers, and teachers, and we teach complex skills, such as surgery and driving, by demonstration. Nonhuman animals also learn through observation, such as which food is safe to eat and which objects should be feared. People imitate models that are attractive, high status, and somewhat similar to themselves. Modeling is more likely to occur when the model has been rewarded for the behavior, and less likely when the model has been punished. Vicarious conditioning influences whether a behavior is performed, but not whether it is learned. It is possible that mirror neurons, which fire when a behavior is observed, may be the neural basis of imitation learning.

WHAT IS THE BIOLOGICAL BASIS OF REWARD?

Although people often use the term "reward" as a synonym for positive reinforcement, Skinner and other traditional behaviorists defined reinforcement strictly in terms of whether it increased behavior. They were relatively uninterested in *why* it increased behavior. Indeed, they carefully avoided any speculation about whether subjective experiences had anything to do with behavior, since they believed that mental states were impossible to study empirically. The biological revolution, however, has begun to provide insights into how we learn. In this section we examine the biological basis of reinforcement and its application to understanding conditioned behaviors such as drug addiction.

SELF-STIMULATION IS A MODEL OF REWARD

One of the earliest discoveries pointing to the role of neural mechanisms in reinforcement came about because of a small surgical error. In the early 1950s, Peter Milner and James Olds were testing whether electrical stimulation to a specific brain region would facilitate learning. To see whether the learning they observed was caused by the activity of the brain or by the aversive qualities of the electrical stimulus, Olds and Milner administered electrical stimulation to the brains of rats only while the rats were in one specific location in the cage. The logic was that if the application of electricity was aversive, the rats would selectively avoid that location. Fortunately for science, they administered the shocks to the wrong part of the brain, and instead of avoiding the area of the cage associated with electrical stimulation, the rats quickly came back, apparently looking for more.

Pleasure centers   Olds and Milner then set up an experiment to see whether rats would press a lever to self-administer shock to specific sites in their brains, a procedure subsequently referred to as **intracranial self-stimulation (ICSS)** (Figure 6.18). The rats self-administered electricity to their brains with gusto, pressing the lever hundreds of times per hour (Olds & Milner, 1954). Olds and Milner referred to brain regions that support ICSS as *pleasure centers*. Although behaviorists might have objected to the term "pleasure," it was clear to everyone that ICSS was a powerful reinforcer. In one experiment, rats that had been on a near-starvation diet for ten days were given a choice between food and the opportunity to administer ICSS. They chose the electrical stimulation more than 80 percent of the time! Deprived rats also chose electrical stimulation over water or receptive sexual partners; they even crossed a painful electrified grid in order to receive ICSS. Rats will continue intracranial self-stimulation until they collapse from exhaustion. Monkeys tested in similar studies have been found to press a bar for electrical stimulation up to 8,000 times per hour (Olds, 1962).

Electrical stimulation and natural reinforcement   Most psychologists believe that ICSS regions are the same as those activated by natural reinforcers, such as food, water, and sex. Electrical stimulation applied to pleasure centers in rats elicits naturally motivated behaviors, such as feeding, drinking, and copulating with an available partner. Also, depriving an animal of food or water leads to increased ICSS, which is taken to indicate that the animal is trying to obtain the subjective state associated with natural reward. Finally, the neural mechanisms underlying ICSS and natural reward appear to use the same neurotransmitter system, namely dopamine. In terms of operant conditioning, this evidence suggests that dopamine serves as the neurochemical basis of positive reinforcement.

DOPAMINE SIGNALS REWARD

Early mapping studies indicated that the strongest and most reliable ICSS occurred in the *medial forebrain bundle* (*MFB*), which consists of a collection, or bundle, of axons that link the midbrain to the forebrain (Figure 6.19). Running through the MFB is the **mesolimbic dopamine system**, which connects the *ventral tegmental area* (*VTA*) to the *nucleus*

Electrode implanted in brain

6.18 A rat will self-administer electricity to pleasure centers in the brain.

6.19 The mesolimbic dopamine pathway connects the ventral tegmental area to the nucleus accumbens. This pathway is involved in reward.

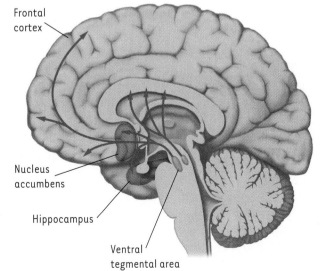

Frontal cortex

Nucleus accumbens

Hippocampus

Ventral tegmental area

Why are certain experiences rewarding?

accumbens. This system is the major brain mechanism underlying reward (Wise & Rompre, 1989). Electrical stimulation of the MFB activates this system and leads to a release of dopamine in the nucleus accumbens. Damage to this pathway interferes with ICSS, as well as other naturally motivated behaviors, such as feeding, drinking, and copulating.

Nucleus accumbens activation   Almost every time you do something pleasurable, the pleasure that you experience results from activation of dopamine neurons in the nucleus accumbens. For example, enjoying food depends on dopamine activity. Hungry rats that are given food have increased release of dopamine in the nucleus accumbens, and the greater the hunger, the greater the release of dopamine (Rolls et al., 1980). Food tastes better when you are hungry and water is more rewarding when you are thirsty because there is a greater release of dopamine under deprived than nondeprived conditions.

In operant conditioning, the release of dopamine sets the value of a reinforcer. Drugs that block the effects of dopamine disrupt operant conditioning. For instance, Jim Stellar and his colleagues taught rats to run a maze in order to receive electrical stimulation, but when they injected a dopamine blocker into the rats, they had to turn up the electrical current in order to get the rats to run the maze (Stellar et al., 1983). The blocker decreased the value of the electrical stimulation reinforcement. As you might expect, drugs that enhance the activation of dopamine, such as cocaine and amphetamine, increase the reward value of stimuli.

Secondary reinforcers also rely on dopamine   Natural reinforcers appear to signal reward directly through the activation of dopamine receptors in the nucleus accumbens. But what about secondary reinforcers, such as money or good grades? Through a process of classical conditioning, neutral stimuli that fail to stimulate a release of dopamine at first do so readily after they are paired with unconditioned stimuli. In one study, monkeys were presented with a trap door that opened occasionally. The door opening did not activate dopamine activity. The experimenters then placed apples in the doorway, such that the door opening was associated with the unconditioned stimulus of food. After many conditioning trials, the door opening led on its own to increased activation of dopamine (Ljungberg et al., 1992). Thus, the sight of a loved one, or getting a good grade or a paycheck, may be conditioned to produce dopamine activation. Drugs that block the effects of dopamine appear to block the rewarding qualities of most activities. Individuals with *Tourette's syndrome*, a disorder of motor control, are given dopamine blockers to control their involuntary body movements. These individuals often have trouble staying on their drug regimens because they feel the drugs rob them of life's enjoyment.

DRUG DEPENDENCE HAS LEARNED AND BIOLOGICAL COMPONENTS

Throughout history, people have discovered that ingesting all sorts of substances can alter their mental state in desirable ways. Societal problems that stem from drug abuse are well known. Even legal drug use, such as cigarette smoking, can be deadly. Why do people risk death or injury to achieve momentary pleasure? Consider the American soldiers described at the beginning of this chapter. Why did they take drugs even when they knew that getting caught could delay their much-desired departure from Vietnam? Research by psychologists has provided a num-

physical dependence   Synonymous with addiction, the physiological state in which failing to ingest a specific substance leads to bodily symptoms of withdrawal.

psychological dependence   Habitual substance use, despite consequences, and a compulsive need to continue using the drug.

psychomotor stimulants   Drugs that activate the sympathetic nervous system and increase behavioral and mental activity.

ber of physiological, behavioral, cognitive, and social explanations for drug use. This section focuses on the rewarding aspects of drug use from learning-theory and biological perspectives.

Physical and psychological dependence   The term **physical dependence** is synonymous with *addiction*, a physiological state in which failing to ingest a substance leads to symptoms of *withdrawal*, which is an unpleasant state characterized by anxiety, tension, and cravings. Physical dependence is often associated with *tolerance*, so that more and more of the drug needs to be consumed to achieve the same subjective effect. **Psychological dependence** refers to habitual and compulsive substance use despite the consequences. Most addictions involve both physiological and psychological factors, and researchers study addiction at multiple levels, as can be seen in "Crossing the Levels of Analysis: Understanding Addiction."

Negative and positive reinforcement   Drug abuse has both negative and positive reinforcement aspects. Addicts habitually abuse drugs to escape the psychological and physical aspects of withdrawal, thereby negatively reinforcing drug use. People also take drugs to forget their problems or to deal with stress, and this too involves negative reinforcement. Recall that one reason our soldiers in Vietnam took narcotics was to escape the horrors of war.

Drug use is also positively reinforced. People take drugs to feel good. The potential for addiction to a specific drug is determined by the speed of its rewarding effects. For instance, heroin enters the brain more easily than morphine, so although heroin and morphine have identical effects on opiate receptors, the greater speed of heroin makes it more addictive than morphine. For the same reason, people are more likely to become addicted to crack cocaine, which they smoke, than powdered cocaine, which they sniff, because smoking increases the speed at which cocaine arrives at the brain.

The mesolimbic dopamine system is the major brain system involved in positive reinforcement of drug use. As is the case with ICSS, food, water, and sex, most drugs that are addicting—including alcohol, nicotine, heroin, cocaine, and cannabis—are associated with increased dopamine activation in the nucleus accumbens. Drugs increase dopamine release or prevent the normal termination of its neural signal. Most researchers have concluded that the release of dopamine is a necessary condition for reinforcement and dependence (Koob, 1999).

Psychomotor stimulants   **Psychomotor stimulants**, including cocaine and amphetamines, are drugs that increase behavioral and mental activity. These drugs activate the sympathetic nervous system (increasing heart rate and blood pressure), improve mood, and disrupt sleep. They are also highly reinforcing. Cocaine is derived from the leaves of the coca bush, found primarily in South America. Cocaine users experience a wave of confidence and good feelings. They are alert, energetic, sociable, and feel little need of sleep. A pharmacist from Georgia, John Pemberton, was so impressed with cocaine that he added it to soda water for easy ingestion, thus creating *Coca-Cola* (Figure 6.20). In 1906, the U.S. Government outlawed cocaine,

6.20   An early ad for Coca Cola.

UNDERSTANDING ADDICTION

Considering only the commonly abused substances, such as illegal drugs, alcohol, and prescription drugs, it is likely that most people know and care about someone who is an addict. If we include nicotine and caffeine, it is likely that addicts are in the majority in most countries in the world. The questions psychological science asks about addiction include, Why do people use drugs? Why do some people become addicts? Why do addicts continue to abuse drugs when it causes such personal turmoil and suffering? To gain a full understanding of addiction it is necessary to address these questions from multiple perspectives, from the genetic level to the neurochemical level to the individual/personality and social/cultural levels.

Many theories related to the initiation of drug or alcohol use among children or adolescents focus on the social/cultural level of analysis. They explore social-learning processes that emphasize the role of parents, peers, and mass media. For example, the Joe Camel advertising campaign of the early 1990s heralded a tenfold increase in market share among adolescents for Camel cigarettes; at one point more young children could identify Joe Camel than Mickey Mouse (Mizerski, 1995). Social-learning theories also emphasize self-identification with high-risk groups (e.g., "stoners" or "druggies") as central to the initiation of drug and alcohol use. Teenagers desire to fit in somewhere, even with groups perceived as deviant by society.

At the individual/personality level, some adolescents are especially likely to experiment with illegal drugs and to abuse alcohol. Children who are high in *sensation-seeking* (a personality trait that involves novelty-seeking and risk-taking) are more likely to associate with deviant peer groups and to use alcohol,

tobacco, and drugs (Wills et al., 1995). These children also tend to have poor relationships with their parents, which, in turn, promotes greater deviant peer group association and so on. So is it the family environment that leads to alcohol and drug use? Some theorists, operating at the genetic level of analysis, turn this around and suggest that an inherited predisposition to sensation-seeking may predict behaviors that increase the risk of substance use, such as affiliating with drug users and watching music videos that glamorize drugs. Indeed, there is some evidence that there are genetic components to addiction, especially for alcoholism. But it is important to point out that there is little direct evidence for a single "alcoholism" or "addiction" gene. Rather, what might be inherited is a cluster of characteristics, including certain personality traits, a reduced concern about personal harm or injury, and a nervous system that is chronically low in arousal. In turn, these factors make some people more likely to explore drugs and to like them.

People continue to use drugs or alcohol because these substances change mental states in a desirable way. At the neurochemical level, scientists are interested in addiction because drugs work on neurotransmitter systems in the brain responsible for motivation and emotion. Some drugs activate reward mechanisms, mostly through their activation of the mesolimbic dopamine pathway. Other drugs reduce anxiety and counteract depression. There has been a recent growing interest in studying the brain centers that are involved with addictive behaviors, such as the nucleus accumbens and various regions of the frontal lobes.

---

so it was removed from the drink. To this day, however, Coca-Cola is made from coca leaves from which the cocaine has been removed. In contrast to the positive effects of cocaine, habitual use of large quantities can lead to paranoia, as well as psychotic and even violent behavior (Ottieger et al., 1992).

Amphetamines are psychomotor stimulants synthesized using simple lab methods that go by street names such as *speed*, *meth*, *ice*, and *crystal*. Amphetamines have a long history of use for weight loss and staying awake. However, amphetamines have a number of negative side effects—such as insomnia, anxiety, and heart problems—and people quickly become addicted to them. They are seldom used for legitimate medical purposes. Psychomotor stimulants generally work by interfering with the normal reuptake of dopamine by the releasing neuron, which allows dopamine to remain in the synapse and thus lengthens its effects. Amphetamines also increase the release of dopamine from relevant neurons. Drugs that block the action of dopamine reduce the reinforcing properties of psychomotor stimulants.

Alcohol Americans have a love-hate relationship with alcohol. On the one hand, moderate drinking is an accepted aspect of normal social interaction. On the other, alcohol is a major source of many of our societal problems, such as spousal abuse and other forms of violence. Alcohol is a factor in over half of all

One of the most fascinating aspects of addiction is that only about 5–10 percent of those who use drugs, other than tobacco or alcohol, become addicted. Indeed, the vast majority of Americans have tried alcohol, and more than 90 million Americans have experimented with illicit drugs. Yet, most either use alcohol or drugs in moderation (especially alcohol) or try them for a while and then give them up completely. In a major longitudinal study, Jonathan Shedler and Jack Block (1990) found that those who had experimented with drugs and alcohol as adolescents were better adjusted in adulthood than those who never tried them at all. Both complete abstainers and heavy drug users had adjustment problems compared to the experimenters. However, this does not mean that everyone should rush out to try drugs and alcohol, or that parents should encourage such behavior. After all, there is no way to know who will become addicted.

Given the seriousness of drug and alcohol problems, great scientific effort has been aimed at treating addiction. A number of early treatments for addiction were based on learning theory. For instance, aversion therapy uses classical-conditioning principles to decrease drug use. Alcoholics are given drugs that make them feel sick when they consume alcohol, and over time they come to associate alcohol with feelings of nausea. Other research has tried to form associative bonds between drug paraphernalia and electric shock. Unfortunately, methods that rely on classical conditioning have had only minimal success. Using techniques from operant conditioning, some behavioral researchers have tried to use reinforcement principles to teach alcoholics moderate drinking. Although these programs have shown some success, their use is highly controversial since some people believe that no amount of alcohol is appropriate for an alcoholic.

More promising are treatments based on pharmacology. For instance, nicotine-replacement therapy (via gum or patches) has been shown to be a great help to those trying to give up smoking. Methadone has long been found to be an effective treatment for those trying to give up heroin. In both of these cases the treatment drugs mimic the effects of the addictive drugs, but in a way that is not as satisfying to the user. Basically, these methods provide sufficient drug effects to stave off withdrawal, but they do not supply the positively reinforcing component of drug use, mostly because their effects are slow and long lasting. There is recent evidence that drugs that enhance the activity of serotonin may be useful in the treatment of addiction. Patients report reduced cravings when given such drugs, which also appear to reduce the reinforcing properties of some addictive substances.

While behavioral neuroscientists are developing treatments for addicts, applied psychologists are trying to prevent addiction in the first place. A number of programs are being tested that help adolescents learn to resist peer pressure and to avoid engaging in behaviors that put them at risk for becoming addicts. Many of these programs teach about the dangers of drug use. At this time there is no single program that has been shown to be consistently effective, especially if effectiveness is measured over the long term (Lynam et al., 1999; White & Pitts, 1998). Nonetheless, a number of interdisciplinary research teams are working to identify the risk factors that lead to addiction, as well as the behavioral and social factors that may prevent addictive behaviors.

fatal car accidents, killing over 20,000 people each year. More Americans are killed by drunk drivers every two years than were killed in the entire Vietnam War (Koshland, 1989). Moreover, one-quarter of suicide victims and one-third of homicide victims have blood-alcohol levels that meet legal criteria for impairment. A recent study found that approximately one-third of college students reported having had sex during a recent drinking binge, and the heaviest drinkers were likely to have had sex with a new or casual partner (Leigh & Shafer, 1993). This places heavy drinkers at great risk for exposure to AIDS. The overall cost of problem drinking, ranging from employee absence to health care, is estimated to be more than 100 billion dollars annually.

Most individuals who drink do so in moderation, although the average American over age 14 consumes the equivalent of 2.5 gallons of pure alcohol per year, which corresponds to nearly 600 12-ounce cans of beer (USDHHS, 1993). It has been estimated that 10 percent of drinkers consume more than 50 percent of the total amount of alcohol consumed, and some 15 million Americans meet criteria for **alcoholism**, defined as abnormal alcohol-seeking with some loss of control over drinking accompanied by physiological effects of tolerance and withdrawal. Some 90 percent of high school seniors have tried alcohol, and in one recent survey almost one-third of seniors reported having had a bout of heavy drinking (five or more drinks) within the preceding two weeks.

alcoholism Abnormal alcohol seeking characterized by loss of control over drinking and accompanied by physiological effects of tolerance and withdrawal.

Using Psychological Science

ALCOHOL AND BEHAVIOR

Alan Marlatt, one of the leading researchers on alcohol and drug abuse, has commented that people view alcohol as the "magic elixir," capable of increasing social skills, sexual pleasure, confidence, power, and aggression. Expectancies about the effects of alcohol are learned very early in life; children see that people who drink have a lot of fun and that drinking is an important aspect of many celebrations (Figure 6.21). Teenagers may view drinkers as sociable and grown-up, two things that they desperately want to be. Thus, through observation, children learn to expect that the consumption of alcohol will have positive effects. It has been shown that children who have very positive expectations about alcohol are more likely to start drinking and to be heavy drinkers than children who do not share those expectations.

According to social psychologists Jay Hull and Charles Bond, expectations have profound effects on behavior. To study the true effects of alcohol, researchers give individuals either tonic water or alcohol and then tell them that they are getting tonic water or alcohol, though not necessarily in correlation to the contents of the actual drink (Figure 6.22). This *balanced-placebo design* allows for a comparison of those who think they are drinking tonic water but are actually drinking alcohol with those who think they are drinking alcohol but are actually drinking tonic water. Researchers thus can separate drug effects from personal beliefs. This research has demonstrated that alcohol truly does impair motor processes, information processing, and mood, independently of whether people think they have consumed alcohol. In contrast, the belief that one has consumed alcohol leads to disinhibition of a variety of social behaviors, such as sexual arousal and aggression, whether or not the person actually consumes alcohol (Hull & Bond, 1986).

Thus, some of people's behaviors when drunk are accounted for by learned beliefs about intoxication rather than by the pharmacological properties of alcohol. Sometimes the pharmacology and learned expectancies work in opposite ways. For instance, alcohol tends to increase sexual arousal, but it interferes with sexual performance.

6.21 Many alcohol and beer companies promote the idea that good times will follow from drinking.

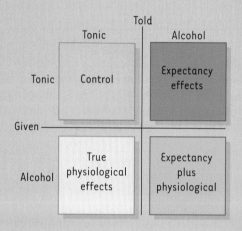

6.22 The consumption of alcohol typically includes both physiological and expectancy effects. The balanced placebo design allows researchers to separately examine these influences on behavior.

One of the reasons people consume alcohol is because of the expected or anticipated effects that alcohol will have on their emotions and behavior. Both light and heavy drinkers believe alcohol can reduce anxiety, and so many people regularly have a drink or two after a difficult day. Unfortunately, the available evidence does not support this belief; although moderate doses of alcohol are associated with increased positive mood, larger doses are associated with a worsening of mood. Also, although alcohol can interfere with cognitive processing of threat cues, such that anxiety-provoking events are less troubling when people are intoxicated, this occurs only if people drink *before* the anxiety-inducing event. According to this research, drinking after a hard day can actually cause people to focus and dwell on their problems more (Sayette, 1993). Further research on the actual and expected effects of alcohol on behavior is discussed in "Using Psychological Science: Alcohol and Behavior."

Alcohol involves a number of different neurotransmitter systems, including activation of receptors for GABA, endogenous opiates, and dopamine (see Chapter 3). A variety of evidence suggests that the reinforcing aspects of alcohol are due to its activation of the mesolimbic dopamine pathway, as is the case with other addictive drugs. Alcohol also interferes with the neurochemical processes involved in memory, which explains why memory loss can follow excessive alcohol intake. Long-term alcohol intake can cause extensive brain damage. *Korsakoff's syndrome* is an alcohol-related disorder characterized by severe memory loss, intellectual deterioration, and disruptions in sensation.

Opiates   One of the drugs used most often by American soldiers in Vietnam was heroin, which along with morphine and codeine is part of the family of drugs known as opiates. These drugs provide enormous reward value by increasing dopamine activation in the nucleus accumbens and binding with opiate receptors, producing feelings of relaxation, analgesia, and euphoria. Prior to the turn of the twentieth century, heroin was widely available without prescription and marketed by the Bayer Aspirin Company. Heroin provides a *rush* of intense pleasure that most addicts describe as similar to orgasm, which then evolves into a pleasant, relaxed stupor. The dual activation of opiate receptors and dopamine receptors may explain why heroin and morphine are so highly addictive.

What Is the Biological Basis of Reward?

Although the behaviorists avoided any reference to internal mental states, it is clear that positive reinforcement generally works because it provides the subjective experience of pleasure. The neural basis of this reinforcement is the release of dopamine in the mesolimbic dopamine pathway. Engaging in naturally motivated behaviors, self-administering electricity to the brain, and taking drugs or alcohol all lead to increased activation of dopamine neurons in the nucleus accumbens, which is associated with the subjective experience of pleasure. Understanding the neural basis of reinforcement helps to explain complex conditioning, such as the development of addiction, which involves both positive and negative reinforcement.

HOW DOES LEARNING OCCUR AT THE NEURONAL LEVEL?

From a biological perspective, scientists have long believed that learning involves relatively permanent changes in the brain that result from exposure to environmental events. The roots of this idea can be traced back to a number of scientists, including the German researcher Richard Semon, who in 1904 proposed that memories are stored through changes in the nervous system. Semon called the storage of learned material an *engram*, a term later popularized by the eminent psychologist Karl Lashley. In 1948, Canadian psychologist Donald Hebb (Figure 6.23) proposed that learning results from alterations in synaptic connections. According to Hebb, when one neuron excites another, some growth process or metabolic change takes place such that the synapse between the two becomes strengthened. Subsequently, the firing of one neuron becomes increasingly likely to cause firing of the other. Although there have been a number of different interpretations of

6.23 Donald Hebb proposed that learning results from changes in synaptic connects: *Cells that fire together, wire together.*

What is the neural basis of learning?

Hebb's postulate, most of them can be summed up as "cells that fire together, wire together." Hebb did not have the technology to examine whether his hypothesis was true or not, but we now know that his basic theory was correct.

According to *Hebb's rule*, the brain is somewhat plastic and new neuronal connections develop as a function of learning. Therefore, learning should be associated with an increased number of synaptic connections in the brain. One experiment supporting this idea was conducted by psychologists Mark Rosenzweig and Edward Bennett. They divided litters of rats into two groups and raised one group in an enriched environment that contained a variety of toys that the animals could explore and play with. The second group was raised in an impoverished setting, a plain cage in a dimly lit room. The brains of the two groups of rats developed very differently. Those raised in the enriched environment had a greater amount of cortex and evidence of a greater number of synapses throughout the brain (Rosenzweig et al., 1972). In addition, the neurochemistry of these rats suggested an enhanced functioning of acetylcholine, a neurotransmitter that has been shown to enhance memory. This and subsequent studies have shown that environmental conditions during formative years have a profound influence on the later capacity for learning.

HABITUATION AND SENSITIZATION ARE SIMPLE MODELS OF LEARNING

What happens at the synapse that leads to learning? One answer is found in research using simple invertebrates such as the *aplysia*, a small marine snail that eats seaweed (Figure 6.24). The aplysia is an excellent species to use to study learning because it has a relatively small number of neurons, some of which are large enough to be seen without a microscope (Kandel et al., 1995). Physiological psychologist Eric Kandel and his colleagues have used the aplysia to study the neural basis of two types of simple learning: *habituation* and *sensitization*. As a result of this research, Kandel received a Nobel prize for medicine in 2000.

Habituation is a decrease in behavioral response following repeated exposure to nonthreatening stimuli. When an animal encounters a novel stimulus, it pays attention to it, which is known as an *orienting response*. If the stimulus is neither harmful nor rewarding, the animal learns to ignore it. We constantly habituate to meaningless events around us. For instance, sit back and listen. Perhaps you can hear a clock, or a computer fan, or your roommates playing music in the next room. You didn't really notice these sounds in the background before because you had habituated to them. Habituation in the aplysia can be demonstrated quite easily by repeatedly touching it. The first few touches cause it to withdraw its gills, but after about 10 touches it quits responding, and this lasts about 2–3 hours. Repeated habituation trials can lead to a state of habituation that lasts several weeks.

Sensitization is an increase in behavioral response following exposure to a threatening stimulus. For instance, imagine that while you are studying you smell burning. You are unlikely to habituate to this smell. You might focus even greater attention on your sense of smell in order to assess the possible threat of fire, and you will be highly vigilant for any indication of smoke or flames. In general, sensitization leads to heightened responsiveness to other stimuli. Giving a strong electrical shock to the tail of the aplysia leads to sensitization. Following the shock, a mild touch anywhere on the body will cause the aplysia to withdraw its gills.

Kandel's research on aplysia has shown that alterations in the functioning of the synapse lead to both habituation and sensitization. For both types of simple learning, neurotransmitter release from presynaptic neurons is altered, with a reduction in neurotransmitter release leading to habituation, and an increase in neurotransmitter release leading to sensitization. Knowing the neural basis of simple learning gives us the building blocks to understand more complex learning processes.

LONG-TERM POTENTIATION IS A CANDIDATE FOR THE CELLULAR BASIS OF LEARNING

To understand learning in the complex mammalian brain, researchers have investigated a phenomenon known as *long-term potentiation*. The word *potentiate* means to strengthen, to make something more potent. **Long-term potentiation (LTP)** is the strengthening of the synaptic connection so that postsynaptic neurons are more easily activated. To demonstrate LTP, researchers first establish the extent to which electrically stimulating one neuron leads to an action potential in a second neuron. They then provide intense electrical stimulation to the first neuron, perhaps giving it a hundred pulses of electricity in five seconds. Finally, a single electrical pulse is readministered to measure the extent of activation of the second neuron. As you can see in Figure 6.25, LTP occurs when the intense electrical stimulation increases the likelihood that stimulating one neuron leads to an action potential in the second neuron. Whereas habituation and sensitization in aplysia are due to changes in neurotransmitter release from the presynaptic neuron, LTP results from changes in the postsynaptic neuron that make it more easily activated.

6.24 The aplysia is a marine invertebrate that is used to study the neurochemical basis of learning.

A number of lines of evidence support the idea that long-term potentiation may be the cellular basis for learning and memory (Beggs et al., 1999). For instance, LTP effects are most easily observed in brain sites known to be involved in learning and memory, such as the hippocampus. Moreover, the same drugs that improve memory also lead to increased LTP, and those that block memory also block LTP. Finally, behavioral conditioning produces neurochemical effects that are nearly identical to LTP.

The process of long-term potentiation also supports Hebb's contention that learning results from a strengthening of synaptic connections that fire together. Hebb's rule can be used to explain a variety of learning phenomena, including classical conditioning. Neurons that signal the unconditioned stimulus are active at the same time as those that signal the conditioned stimulus. Over repeated trials, the synapses that connect these two events become strengthened, so that when one fires the other fires automatically, producing the conditioned response.

Taken together, the evidence suggests that long-term potentiation may be the basic process responsible for complex learning in the brain. However, our knowledge of how LTP works is in its infancy, and there have been some contradictory findings. At this point it is safest to conclude that LTP is a reasonable candidate for the cellular basis of learning.

LEARNING CAN BE SIMULATED BY COMPUTERIZED NEURAL NETWORKS

Working across various levels of analysis, psychological scientists have developed computer models of neural networks to understand how the brain learns. The

habituation A decrease in behavioral response following repeated exposure to nonthreatening stimuli.

sensitization An increase in behavioral response following exposure to a threatening stimulus.

long-term potentiation (LTP) The strengthening of a synaptic connection so that postsynaptic neurons are more easily activated.

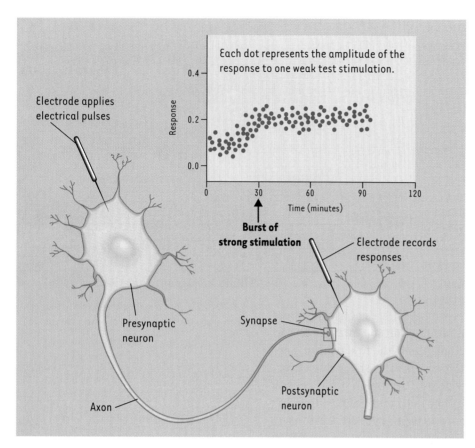

Each dot represents the amplitude of the response to one weak test stimulation.

6.25 A presynaptic neuron is given a brief electric pulse, which causes a slight response in the postsynaptic neuron. Applying intense and frequent electricity leads to a greater response of the postsynaptic neuron. When a single brief pulse is subsequently appplied, it results in a greater effect on the postsynaptic neuron than it did originally.

computer is a widely used metaphor for the working mind. Both the brain and the computer receive information as input, process that information, and create output in the form of actions or behaviors. Computerized models of learning are often referred to as *connectionist models* because they are roughly based on the idea that neurons are connected or associated with each other. Instead of neurons, computer models have units, which are connected with each other in the computerized neural network.

A simple connectionist model is shown in Figure 6.26. Note that this model has three layers of units: it takes in information through the *input units*, processes that information in the *hidden units*, and generates an action through the *output units*. Just as one neuron can pass a message to another neuron to fire or not to fire, the computer units also can be excitatory or inhibitory, and the strength of their connections is modified through learning.

Rules for learning   The rule by which connectionist models operate is based on the degree to which a model's output matches the input. For instance, suppose you are trying to learn someone's name. When you see her face, you want to retrieve the correct name. When the output (i.e., the retrieved name) fails to match the input (i.e., the relevant face), you adjust the strength of association between the units so that the output becomes more similar to what it is supposed to be. For example, perhaps you recall the name as Karen when it is actually Kathy. To rectify the error, your neural network strengthens the association between the person's face and "Kathy" and weakens the association between her face and "Karen." After many trials, you call Kathy by her correct name. Subsequently, the connection between the person's face and the name Kathy is strengthened each time you associate them.

How connectionist models "learn" is similar to the Rescorla-Wagner model of classical conditioning discussed earlier in this chapter. In both models, the greater the deviation from expectancy, the more learning takes place. If Kathy's face triggered an output of the name "Jake," you would need to learn a lot more! However, once the input matches the appropriate output, relatively little further learning would take place.

The parallel-distributed processing model   One of the best-known connectionist models of learning is the *parallel-distributed processing (PDP)* model developed by David Rumelhart and James McClelland. An important feature of the PDP model is that it is based on how neural networks actually operate. For instance, it views neuronal connections as richly distributed throughout the brain and it involves *parallel* processing, in which everything happens at the same time. This represents an advance over serial models, in which learning was thought to occur in a fixed order, like the sequence of operations in a computer program.

The human brain is massively parallel, with millions of synapses within neural networks firing at the same time. In the PDP model, each unit in the network can be connected to all other units, and each is activated or inhibited by other units in the network. Essentially, each unit adds up the various inhibitory and excitatory messages from the other units, and it becomes activated when this sum passes a critical threshold. In this way, units in the PDP model operate as neurons do when they integrate information from other neurons to determine whether they will fire.

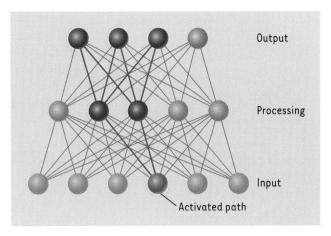

Complex neural networks Connectionist models such as the PDP have proven valuable in conceptualizing complex learning situations, such as the acquisition of abstract concepts and language. Consider, for instance, a Vietnam War veteran who experiences a panic attack during a discussion of whether there should be a military draft. Traditional learning theory has difficulty accounting for the association between discussion of a policy issue and the Vietnam War experience. From a PDP point of view, however, the connect makes perfect sense. The information about drafts and wars is stored in a neural network in which activation of one part of the network leads to activation of the rest.

6.26 A simple network with three layers of units.

How Does Learning Occur at the Neuronal Level?

Researchers are rapidly identifying the neurophysiological basis of learning. Much of what has been learned supports Hebb's theories that neurons that fire together, wire together. Kandel's work on aplysia has shown that habituation and sensitization, two simple forms of learning, occur through alteration in neurotransmitter release. The discovery of long-term potentiation shows that intense stimulation of neurons can strengthen synapses, increasing the likelihood that the activation of one neuron will increase the firing of other neurons in the network. Computerized models of neural networks have helped make predictions about how complex learning takes place.

CONCLUSION

Behaviorism has been a powerful force in psychological science since early in the twentieth century. The shift from subjective to empirical methods established psychology as a science. A renewed interest in mental processes eventually led many to abandon the strict principles of behaviorism, but basic conditioning and learning processes still serve as foundational principles in understanding mind and behavior. Psychological scientists use learning principles in studies across all levels of analysis, from synaptic connections in aplysia to the cultural transmission of morals and values. In fact, the study of learning, itself, has diminished somewhat over the past few decades because psychologists have embraced many learning principles as basic fact and have moved on to other problems. For these reasons, the field of learning serves as an excellent example of how psychological research is based on cumulative principles. The principles of classical and operant conditioning are basic methodologies used by all neuroscientists to study brain mechanisms. In turn, recent advances in neuroscience techniques resulting from the biological revolution have allowed for a more complete understanding of learning processes. Learning occurs in the brain, and our relatively new access to brain-imaging techniques is reigniting interest in basic conditioning processes. Understanding the neurochemical basis of learning may help us to develop more effective treatments for a variety of psychological problems, including phobias and drug addictions.

FURTHER READINGS

Carlson, N. R. (2001). *Physiology of behavior* (7th ed.). Needham Heights, MA: Allyn & Bacon.

Kandel, E. R., Schwartz, J. H., & Jessell, T. M. (2000). *Principles of neural science* (4th ed.). New York: McGraw-Hill.

Lieberman, D. A. (1993). *Learning: Behavior and cognition.* Pacific Grove, CA: Brooks-Cole.

Rescorla, R. A. (1988). Behavioral studies of Pavlovian conditioning. *Annual Reviews of Neuroscience, 11,* 329–352.

Schwartz, B., & Robbin, S. J. (1995). *Psychology of learning and behavior* (4th ed.). New York: W. W. Norton.

Zigmond, M. J., Bloom, F. E. Landis, S. C. Roberts, J. L., & Squire, L. R. (1999). *Fundamental neuroscience.* San Diego, CA: Academic Press.

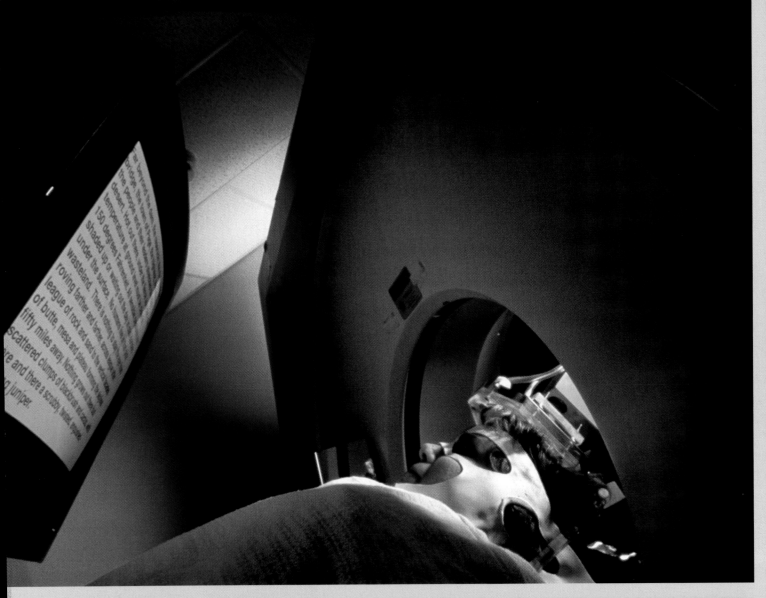

IDENTIFYING THE BRAIN'S MEMORY CENTERS

A volunteer tries to produce synonyms for words displayed on a monitor, as scientists use PET technology to examine her brain activity. It is now well established that memory is stored in multiple, interconnected regions of the brain.

TIMELINE

1885

It Begins with Forgetting
Psychologist Hermann Ebbinghaus studies how quickly people relearn nonsense syllables. He provides compelling evidence that forgetting occurs rapidly at first but then levels off over time.

1932

Reconstructive Memory
Psychologist Frederic Bartlett suggests that human memory involves reconstruction and that people's memories are influenced by prior beliefs, challenging the view that memory is an objective recorder of experience.

1940s

Searching for the Engram
While searching for the physical brain location of memory, called the engram, Karl Lashley concludes that the brain works as a whole to store memories.

1953

Amnesia and the Medial Temporal Lobes Brenda Milner publishes a landmark account of patient H.M., who underwent surgery for epilepsy and afterward experienced profound memory loss.

Memory

OUTLINING THE PRINCIPLES

1956	1960s	1968–70s	1970s	1970s
Memory Span George Miller, one of the intellectual founders of cognitive neuroscience, notes that short-term memory is limited, and he demonstrates that people organize information into meaningful units, or chunks.	**Stage Theories of Memory** A number of memory researchers develop stage theories of memory. Most theories include a brief sensory memory buffer, short-term memory, and long-term memory.	**Neuropsychological Case Studies** Researchers such as Larry Squire, Stuart Zola-Morgan, Lawrence Weiskrantz, Elizabeth Warrington, and Tim Shallice report case studies of individuals with brain injury who have specific memory impairments.	**Levels of Processing** Fergus Craik, Robert Lockhart, and Endel Tulving emphasize that the way people process information determines how memory is stored and later retrieved. The more deeply people process information, the better they remember it.	**Episodic Memory** Endel Tulving introduces an important distinction between semantic memory of facts and knowledge and episodic memory of personal experiences.

Imagine what the world would be like if you lost the ability to remember new experiences. You wouldn't be able to remember meeting people, or what you did last night, or even what you had for breakfast this morning. In a few minutes, you would not even remember having contemplated this problem. Such is the fate of a man who received brain surgery to relieve his epilepsy.

Anticonvulsive drugs had proven ineffective at controlling H.M.'s seizures, and therefore in September 1953 his doctors performed a surgical technique in which they removed parts of his medial temporal lobes, including the hippocampus (Figure 7.1). The idea was to stop the seizures, which originated in the temporal lobes, from spreading throughout the brain. The surgery was successful in quieting the seizures, but it also resulted in a most unfortunate side effect: H.M. lost the ability to form new long-term memories.

H.M.'s memory problems are profound. His world stopped in September 1953 when he was 27 years old. He can tell you about his childhood, explain the rules of baseball, and describe members of his family. According to neuropsychological testing, his IQ is slightly above average. Thus, his thinking abilities are perfectly fine, and he can hold a normal conversation as long as he is not distracted. Yet, he cannot remember new information. Every moment is new and fresh. He never knows the day of the week, what year it is, or even his own age. Canadian psychologist Brenda Milner, who has followed H.M.'s case for more than 40 years, as well as others who work with him, continue to have to introduce themselves to him each time they meet. But, he does seem to learn some new things . . . he just doesn't know it.

Most impressive is H.M.'s ability to learn new motor tasks. For instance, in one task he was required to trace the outline of a star while watching his hand in a mirror. This is a difficult task, and most people do poorly the first time they try it. H.M. was asked to trace the star 10 times on each of 3 consecutive days. As shown in Figure 7.2, H.M.'s performance improved over the 3 days, meaning that he had retained some information about the task; however, H.M. could not recall ever

RESEARCH QUESTIONS ???

for Studying Memory

How are perceptual experiences transformed into memories?

Are there different types of memories, or are all memories essentially the same?

Are memories stored in an organized fashion?

How are people able to retrieve specific memories?

Do people really forget things, and if so, why?

What causes people to have memories that are distorted, false, or inaccurate?

1970s

Animal Models of Memory
Researchers such as Mortimer Mishkin, Patricia Goldman-Rakic, and Howard Eichenbaum develop memory experiments that can be performed by nonhuman animals.

1970s–80s

Spreading Activation Models
Network models suggest that memories emerge from associations between items based on semantic meanings. Activation of one element in the network leads to activation of other elements that share similar meanings.

1978

Ecological Realism   Ulric Neisser emphasizes that researchers need to pay attention to how memory works in the real world, outside of laboratories.

1980s

Multiple Memory Systems
A variety of memory processes are identified that involve separate but interacting brain systems, challenging the view that memory is a unitary entity.

1990s

Imaging and Memory
Researchers such as John Gabrieli, Lars Nyberg, Randy Buckner, Steven Petersen, and Barbara Knowlton use brain imaging to explore the neural basis of memory.

performing the task previously. H.M.'s ability to learn new motor skills allowed him to assume employment at a factory, where he mounted cigarette lighters on cardboard cases. But he cannot give any description of the nature of his job or the place where he works. The case of H.M. has contributed many clues to how memories are stored in the brain, and we will refer to his case throughout the chapter.

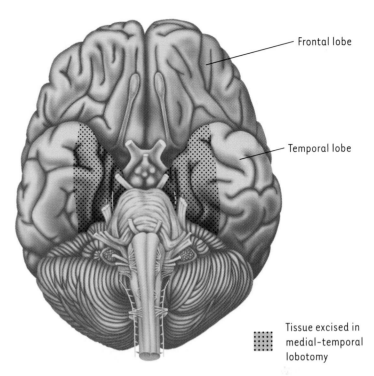

Frontal lobe

Temporal lobe

Tissue excised in medial-temporal lobotomy

7.1 The portions of the medial temporal lobe removed in H.M.

In this chapter we are concerned with **memory,** the capacity of the nervous system to acquire and retain usable skills and knowledge, allowing organisms to benefit from experience. Memory is an amazing capacity. We remember millions of pieces of information, from the trivial to the vital. Our entire sense of self is that which we know from our memories, from our recollection of personal experiences. What kind of person are you? Are you shy or outgoing? To answer such questions we rely upon our memories of past experiences. Yet, as you will see, our memories are often incomplete, biased, and distorted. We are often surprised at how our memories for events differ vastly from those of others who experienced the identical event. There are many sides to every story because each person stores and retrieves memory for the event in distinctive ways. Memory is not like a video camera that faithfully captures objective images. Rather, memory is a story that can be subtly altered through tellings and retellings.

In this chapter we explore the mental processes involved in acquiring and retaining knowledge. Beginning with a discussion of the different stages of memory, we then discuss how different types of information are represented in memories that persist over time. Once we explain the basic processes at the cognitive and behavioral levels, we shift levels of analysis to examine the neurochemical and brain-systems level. There has been a rapid accumulation of knowledge about memory over the last decade through the use of brain-imaging techniques, as well as through case studies of those who have developed memory disorders through brain injury. Finally, we consider the individual and social levels of analysis as we examine how people's memories of past events are selectively distorted.

WHAT ARE THE BASIC STAGES OF MEMORY?

Over the past three decades, most psychologists have viewed memory as a form of information processing, in which memory processes occur in much the same way as they do in a computer. A computer receives information through the keyboard or modem, processes it in software, stores it on the hard disk, and then retrieves that information when requested by the user or another program. From an information-processing perspective, the common way to describe memory is through a three-stage memory system that involves *sensory memory, short-term memory,* and *long-term memory* (Figure 7.3). This general framework is referred to

memory The capacity of the nervous system to acquire and retain usable skills and knowledge, which allows living organisms to benefit from experience.

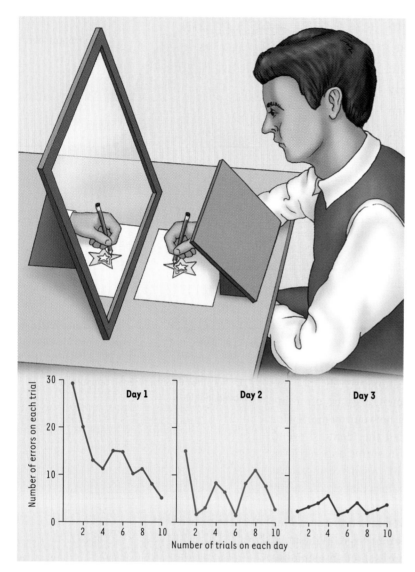

7.2 H.M. was required to trace the star figure while looking in a mirror. This is a difficult task, but H.M. improved in performance over time. However, he had no conscious awareness that he had ever performed the task before.

as the **modal memory model** because it is so widely used; the term "modal" refers to the model being common or standard. Proposed by Richard Atkinson and Richard Shiffrin in 1968, the modal model has dominated psychological thinking about memory, in spite of its being somewhat inaccurate and incomplete. For instance, many psychological scientists now believe that there are multiple memory systems that do not follow the three-stage sequence (and we discuss these alternative views in the next section). However, the modal model is useful for introducing ideas about the memory system, and the vocabulary from this model remains widely used in memory research.

SENSORY MEMORY IS BRIEF

Sensory information, such as lights, smells, and odors, leaves a trace on the nervous system for a split second and then vanishes. For instance, when you look at something and quickly glance away you can briefly picture the image and recall some of its details. When someone angrily proclaims, "you weren't listening to me," you can often repeat back the last few words the person spoke, even if you were thinking about something else. (Of course, this usually irritates the person further.)

This temporary sensory buffer is referred to as **sensory memory.** Visual sensory memory is also called *iconic memory*, whereas auditory sensory memory is also called *echoic memory*. George Sperling (1960) provided initial empirical support for sensory memory. In this classic experiment, three rows of letters were flashed on a screen for one-twentieth of a second, and then following various delay periods participants were asked to recall one of the rows. After very short delays people could perform this task quite well. But their performance became progressively worse with longer delay periods. Sperling concluded that the iconic memory persisted for about one-third of a second, after which the sensory-memory trace faded and was no longer accessible.

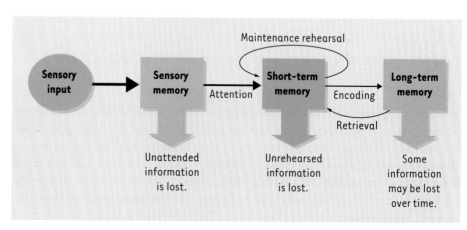

7.3 The modal memory model serves as a useful framework for thinking about the basic stages of memory.

According to many theorists, iconic and echoic memories allow us to experience the world as a continuous stream rather than in discrete sensations, much the same way that a movie projector plays a series of still pictures that follow each other closely enough to look like continuous action. When you turn your head, the scene passes smoothly in front of you rather than in jerky bits.

The idea of iconic memory is somewhat controversial. Most of the evidence for iconic memory is found in laboratory studies, and some researchers question whether it is a useful idea in the real world (Haber, 1983). Other researchers question whether it is a form of memory at all, or simply a perceptual aftereffect, such as the spots that you see after a camera flash goes off. This occurs because of sensory processes rather than because of memory. One related phenomenon is the claim of photographic memory, whereby an individual supposedly can glance at a scene and then later recall it in precise detail. Its possible existence is considered in "Using Psychological Science: Photographic Memory."

SHORT-TERM MEMORY IS ACTIVE

Information that is attended to is passed from sensory stores to **short-term memory (STM)**, a limited-capacity memory system that holds information in awareness for a brief period. Many contemporary researchers use the term *immediate memory*, to capture the idea that this temporary buffer consists of our

RESEARCH QUESTION

How are perceptual experiences transformed into memories?

modal memory model The three-stage memory system that involves sensory memory, short-term memory, and long-term memory.

sensory memory Memory for sensory information that is stored briefly in its original sensory form.

short-term memory (STM) A limited-capacity memory system that holds information in awareness for a brief period of time.

Using Psychological Science

PHOTOGRAPHIC MEMORY

You've probably heard of *photographic memory*, in which some people supposedly can recall an image so vividly that they can provide an accurate report of minor details. Many a student wishes for such an ability when studying. But, does it exist? And if it does, how common is such an ability?

The idea of photographic memory, which psychological scientists call *eidetic imagery*, is based on the supposition that people store information in visual images that faithfully capture the scene in front of them, just like a photograph. As will become obvious throughout this chapter, however, memory is typically not like a video or photographic replay of events. Nonetheless, it is still possible that some people can store and later retrieve individual visual images in a way that simulates mental photography.

It is possible to remember images. Indeed, most people have had the experience of recalling that a test-question answer can be found on a specific page of a textbook, and there is a vague sense of being able to see an image of the page. But what is the fourth word in the second-to-last sentence on the page? The latter is a test of genuine photographic memory. If it truly were a photographic image, you could simply look to the penultimate sentence and count four words. Can people do this? Probably not.

In a study of 150 school children, conducted in the 1960s, Lyn and Ralph Haber found that 12 of the children showed evidence of having better eidetic memory than the others, as evidenced by their apparently holding the image in their mind for a longer period of time, speaking in the present rather than past tense, and scanning their eyes as if across the recalled image. Other surveys of children have found similar rates. Thus, one might conclude that about 8–10 percent of children have some form of eidetic imagery capacity. By contrast, studies of adults have uncovered almost a complete absence of eidetic imagery. Robert Crowder (1992) has concluded that eidetic imagery is a rather poor substitute for a true photographic memory. Indeed, in a mass test published in magazines and newspapers, not a single case of true photographic memory was found. In that study, there were two images, side by side, of dots in an apparently random arrangement. If a person could hold one image in mind while looking at the other image, the two would fuse and a hidden message would be revealed. The fact that no one was able to do this led J. Merrit (1979) to conclude that true photographic memory was a "none-in-a-million phenomenon."

fleeting thoughts, feelings, and impressions of the world. A computer analogy for immediate memory is RAM, which can handle only a small amount of information compared to the vast amount stored in the computer's hard disk. The material in RAM is constantly replaced by new information, and it is lost forever if not saved.

Short-term or immediate memory can hold information for no longer than about 20 seconds; it then disappears unless you actively prevent that from happening by thinking about the information or rehearsing it. For instance, when you call directory assistance for a telephone number, you repeat the number over and over again until you dial it. If the number is busy, or if there is some delay before you can dial it, you may forget the number and have to seek out directory assistance again (and again!). Similarly, suppose you are trying to remember some novel information, such as the three-letter string of consonants X, C, J. As long as you keep repeating the string over and over, you will keep it in short-term memory.

Typically, however, you are bombarded with other events that try to capture your attention, and you may not be able to stay focused. To simulate this, try again to remember X, C, J, but this time as you do it count backward in threes from the number 309. If you are like most people, you will find it difficult to remember the consonants after a few seconds of backward counting. This procedure demonstrates that the longer you spend counting, the less able you are to remember the consonant string (Figure 7.4). By 18 seconds of counting, people have extremely poor recall for the consonants. This occurs because of interference from previous items in STM.

7.4 To test short-term memory, the participant is given a list of consonants and required to remember them while counting backward by threes from a number provided by the experimenter. After periods ranging from 3 to 18 seconds, the participant is asked to recall and repeat aloud the consonant string. Note that the ability to recall the string declines with longer retention intervals.

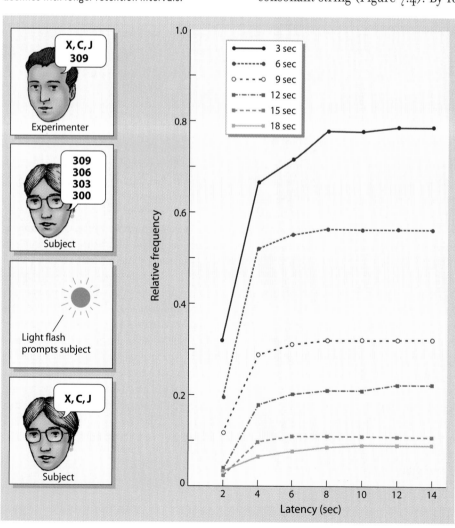

Memory span and chunking Why do new items interfere with the recall of older items? Short-term memory is a limited resource that can hold only so much information. Cognitive psychologist George Miller noted that STM is generally limited to about seven items, plus or minus two, which is commonly referred to as *memory span*. Some recent work suggests that memory span may be limited to as few as four units on average (Cowan, 2001). Memory span also varies among individuals. Indeed, some tests of intelligence use memory span as a measure of IQ.

Because STM is limited, you might expect people to have great difficulty remembering a string of letters such as

OSUPHDNYUMAUCLABAMIT.

These 20 letters would tax even the largest memory span. But, what if we organized the information into smaller, meaningful units? For instance,

OSU-PHD-NYU-MA-UCLA-BA-MIT.

Here we see that the letters can be separated to produce the names of universities or academic degrees. This organization makes them much easier to recall, for two reasons. First, memory span is limited to at most seven items, and probably fewer, but the items can be letters, numbers, words, or even concepts. Second, meaningful units are easier to remember than nonsense units. The process of organizing information into meaningful units is known as *chunking*, as in breaking down the information into chunks. The more efficiently you chunk information, the more you can remember. Master chess players are able to glance at a chess scenario for a few seconds and then later reproduce the exact arrangement of pieces (Chase & Simon, 1973). They are able to do this because they can chunk the board into a number of meaningful subunits based on their past experience with the game. Interestingly, if the game pieces are randomly placed on the chessboard, so that the arrangement makes no "chess sense," experts are no better than novices at reproducing the board. In general, the greater your expertise with the material, the more efficiently you can chunk information, and therefore the more you can remember. The ability to efficiently chunk information relies on our long-term memory system, which will be discussed shortly.

Working memory The initial conception of short-term memory was that it was simply a buffer in which verbal information was rehearsed until it was stored or forgotten. It became apparent, however, that STM is not a single storage system, but rather an active processing unit that deals with multiple types of information, such as sounds, images, and ideas. British psychologist Alan Baddeley and his colleagues developed an influential model of a three-part active memory system that they called working memory (Figure 7.5). **Working memory** is an active processing system that holds information on-line so that it can be used for activities such as problem solving, reasoning, and comprehension. For instance, H.M., from the beginning of this chapter, is able to keep track of a conversation as long as he stays actively involved in it. The three components of working memory are the *central executive*, the *phonological loop*, and the *visuospatial sketchpad*.

The *central executive* presides over the interactions between the subsystems and long-term memory; it's the boss. It encodes information from the sensory systems and then filters information that is sufficiently important to be stored in long-term memory. It also retrieves information from long-term memory as needed. The central executive relies on two subcomponents that temporarily hold auditory or visual information.

The *phonological loop* encodes auditory information and is active whenever you read, speak, or repeat words to yourself in order to remember them. You've probably noticed this "inner voice" that reads along as your eyes process written material. If you haven't, try to read the next sentence without "speaking" the words in your head. It is difficult to obtain meaning simply by scanning your eyes across the text. Evidence for the phonological loop is found in studies in which people are shown lists of consonants and asked to remember them. People tend to make errors with consonants that sound alike rather than those that look alike, for instance, misremembering a G as a T rather than a Q. Recall is also poorer

working memory An active processing system that holds different types of information on-line for current use.

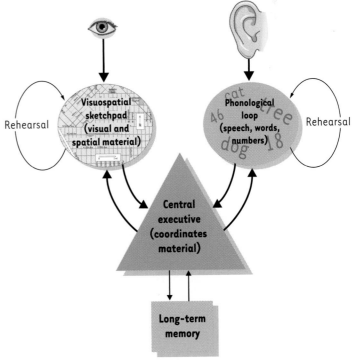

7.5 Working memory system developed by Baddeley. It includes the central executive, phonological loop, and visuospatial sketchpad.

long-term memory (LTM) The relatively permanent storage of information.

serial position effect The ability to recall items from a list depends on order of presentation, with items presented early or late in the list remembered better than those in the middle.

primacy effect In a list, the better memory for items presented first.

recency effect In a list, the better memory for words presented later in the list.

when many words on a list sound the same compared to when they sound dissimilar, even when the latter words are related to each other in meaning. These examples suggest that words are processed in working memory by how they sound rather than by what they mean.

The *visuospatial sketchpad* is used to process visual information, such as objects' features and where they are located. Suppose while walking along you see a dog. The visuospatial sketchpad allows you to keep track of both where the dog is located and whether it is the sort of dog that one needs to be especially careful to track. The distinction between phonological loop and visuospatial sketchpad has been demonstrated by studying patients with specific brain damage. Patients with some types of brain injury might have great difficulty remembering spatial layouts but have little difficulty remembering words, whereas others show the exact opposite pattern. These sorts of research findings demonstrate that short-term memory consists of much more than simply an all-inclusive buffer.

LONG-TERM MEMORY IS RELATIVELY PERMANENT

When people talk about their memories, they are usually referring to the relatively permanent storage of information known as **long-term memory (LTM)**. In the computer analogy, LTM is similar to information stored on a hard disk. Unlike computer storage, however, human LTM is nearly limitless. Long-term memory allows you to remember nursery rhymes from childhood, the meanings and spellings of rarely used words such as *aardvark*, and what you had for lunch yesterday.

7.6 After hearing a list of items, people typically remember more items from the beginning of the list (primacy effect) and the end of the list (recency effect) than from the middle of the list.

Distinguishing long-term memory from short-term memory Long-term memory is distinct from short-term memory in two important ways, duration and capacity. A controversy exists, however, as to whether LTM represents a truly different type of memory storage from STM. Initial evidence that LTM and STM are separate systems came from research that required people to recall long lists of words. The ability to recall items from the list depended on order of presentation, with items presented early or late in the list remembered better than those in the middle. This better recall of early and late items is known as the **serial position effect** (Figure 7.6), which actually involves two separate effects. The **primacy effect** refers to the better memory people have for items presented first, whereas the **recency effect** refers to our better memory for the most recent items.

A common explanation for the serial position effect relies on a distinction between STM and LTM. As people study the long list, they rehearse the earliest items the most, and that information is transferred into LTM. The last few items, by contrast, are in STM. The idea that primacy

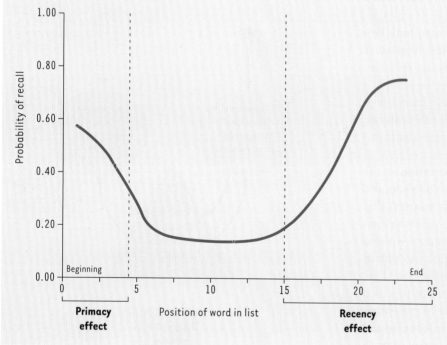

effects are due to LTM whereas recency effects are due to STM is supported by studies in which there is a delay between the presentation of the list and the recall task. Such delays interfere with the recency effect, but not the primacy effect, just as you would expect if the former involves STM. However, it is questionable to attribute the recency effect entirely to STM. After all, you probably remember your most recent class better than the classes held prior to that, even though you are not holding that material in STM. Indeed, studies show that there is a recency effect even for information presented over days and weeks, which makes it unlikely that the material is being maintained in STM. Thus, the recency effect on its own does not prove that STM and LTM are really different types of memory storage.

Perhaps the best support for the distinction between STM and LTM can be found in case studies such as that of H.M., in which his STM system was perfectly normal and much of his LTM system was intact, but he was unable to transfer new information from STM into LTM. In a different case, a 28-year-old accident victim with damage to the left temporal lobe had extremely poor STM, with a span of only one or two items. However, he had perfectly normal LTM—he had a fine memory for day-to-day happenings and reasonable knowledge of past events (Shallice & Warrington, 1969). Somehow, in spite of the bottleneck in his STM, a normal flow of information was getting into LTM. These case studies demonstrate that LTM can be dissociated from STM. However, the two memory systems are highly interdependent. For instance, to chunk information in STM people need to form meaningful connections based on information stored in LTM.

What gets into long-term memory Considering that we are bombarded with so much information and engaged in so many activities, it seems obvious that some type of filtering system or series of rules must constrain what goes into our LTM. Researchers have provided several possible explanations for this process. One possibility is that information enters permanent storage through rehearsal. When you study for exams you often go over the material many times to be sure that you have learned it. Memory researchers have even shown that *overlearning*, in which you keep rehearsing material that you already know pretty well, leads to improved memory, especially over longer periods of time. This is why studying that is spread out over time, known as *distributed practice*, is better remembered than material that is studied in a brief period of time, called *massed practice*, or cramming. The conclusion from many years of research is that studying for shorter periods of time, but spreading your study sessions out over several days or weeks, is the most efficient way to learn.

However, simply repeating or coming into contact with something many times does not mean that we develop long-lasting memory for the event or object. After all, sometimes we have extremely poor memory for objects that are highly familiar. Consider Figure 7.7. Which penny is accurate? Most people have difficulty

7.7 Can you tell which drawing of the penny is correct? See the bottom of the page for the correct answer.*

*Answer to Figure 7.7: The correct penny is (a).

choosing the correct penny, in spite of the fact that we encounter pennies almost every day.

Another possibility is that only information that helps us adapt to the environment is typically transferred from short-term to long-term memory. Out of the billions of sensory experiences and thoughts we have each day, we want to store only information that is useful. Our memory that a penny is money is much more useful to us than remembering its specific features. By storing information that is *meaningful*, organisms can benefit from experience.

Evolutionary theory helps explain how we decide in advance what information will be useful. Memory allows us to use information in a way that assists in reproduction and survival. For instance, organisms that can use past experiences to increase their chances of survival have a selective advantage over organisms that fail to learn from past experiences. Recognizing a predator and remembering the escape route will help an organism avoid being eaten in the future. Accordingly, remembering which objects are edible, which people are friends versus enemies, and how to get home is typically not challenging for those with intact memory systems.

What Are the Basic Stages of Memory?

The informational-processing approach to memory contains three basic stages. Sensory memory consists of brief traces on the nervous system that reflect perceptual processes. Material is passed from sensory memory to short-term memory, a limited buffer that holds information in awareness for a brief period of time. An influential model of STM is working memory, which involves a central executive, a phonological loop, and a visuospatial sketchpad. STM is limited to fewer than seven chunks of information, probably around four. The rules for chunking are determined by the meanings provided from long-term memory. LTM is a limitless, relatively permanent store. Only information that is meaningful in some way is stored in LTM. The distinction between STM and LTM is best established by case studies of those with impairments to one but not the other.

WHAT ARE THE DIFFERENT MEMORY SYSTEMS?

Are there different types of memories or are all memories essentially the same?

Until the last few decades, most cognitive psychologists thought long-term memory was a relatively unitary system. Memories were viewed as differing in terms of strength and accessibility, but generally they were considered to be of the same type. Cognitive psychologists such as Endel Tulving, Dan Schacter, and Larry Squire began to challenge this view in the late 1970s and early 1980s. These researchers argued that memory is not just one monolithic entity, but rather a process that involves a number of interacting systems. Although the systems share a common function, namely, to retain and use information, they encode and store different types of information and they do so in different ways. For instance, there are several obvious distinctions to be made between your memory for being able to ride a bicycle and your ability to recall what you ate for dinner last night or that the capital of Canada is Ottawa. The first task requires a behavioral component, an integration of motor and perceptual skills that you acquired over time during development. You are not consciously aware of your efforts to maintain balance, avoid objects, or follow the basic rules of the road. By contrast, recalling a specific event or bit of knowledge has no behavioral component, and it sometimes requires a conscious effort to retrieve knowledge from long-term memory.

There is not yet agreement on the number of human memory systems. For instance, some researchers have distinguished among memory systems based on how information is stored in memory, such as whether the storage occurs with or without deliberate effort. Other researchers have focused on the types of information stored, such as words and meaning versus particular muscle movements. Because the method of storage often differs based on the type of information being stored, it is important to know whether reference is being made to process or content of memory. Understanding how different memory systems work has provided tremendous insight into memory, such as why it sometimes fails.

EXPLICIT MEMORY INVOLVES CONSCIOUS EFFORT

The most basic distinction between memory systems is between those for which we consciously remember and use information and those for which memory is shown without conscious effort or intention. **Explicit memory** involves the processes used to remember specific information. The information retrieved in explicit memory is known as **declarative memory**, which refers to cognitive information that can be brought to mind, that is, knowledge that can be declared. Many psychological scientists use the terms interchangeably, but explicit memory refers to the *process* of memory whereas declarative memory refers to the *content* of memory.

You use explicit memory when you try to recall what you had for dinner last night or what the word *aardvark* means. Declarative memories can involve words or concepts, visual images, or both. For instance, imagine Earth's satellite. You are probably retrieving both the image and name of the Moon. Most of the examples we have used so far in this chapter refer to explicit memories.

In 1972, Endel Tulving introduced a further distinction in explicit memory between episodic and semantic memory. **Episodic memory** refers to one's personal past experiences. **Semantic memory** represents one's knowledge of trivial or important facts independent of personal experience. For instance, people know the capitals of countries that they've never visited, and even those who have never played baseball know that three strikes means you're out.

Evidence that episodic and semantic explicit-memory systems are separate can be found in cases of brain injury in which semantic memory is intact even though episodic memory is impaired. Such an instance was found in a group of British children who experienced brain damage during infancy or early childhood and developed poor memory for episodic information (Vargha-Khadem et al., 1997). They had trouble reporting what they had for lunch, what they were talking about or watching on television five minutes ago, or what they did during summer vacation. Their parents reported that the children had to be constantly monitored to make sure they remembered things such as to go to school. Remarkably, these children attended mainstream schools and did reasonably well. Moreover, their IQs fell within the normal range. They learned to speak and read, and they could remember a great deal of facts. For instance, when given the question "Who is Martin Luther King Jr.?" one of the children responded, "An American; fought for Black rights, Black rights leader in the 1970 [sic]; got assassinated." These children, then, are capable of encoding and retrieving semantic information, but they do not remember how or when they learned the information.

explicit memory The processes involved when people remember specific information.

declarative memory The cognitive information retrieved from explicit memory; knowledge that can be declared.

episodic memory Memory for one's personal past experiences.

semantic memory Memory for knowledge about the world.

IMPLICIT MEMORY OCCURS WITHOUT DELIBERATE EFFORT

Implicit memory is the process by which people show an enhancement of memory, most often through behavior, without deliberate effort and without any awareness that they are remembering anything. Implicit memory is pervasive throughout daily experiences, such as brushing your teeth, tying your shoes, and remembering how to get to class. Recall the previous chapter in which we described examples of classical conditioning; these are examples of implicit memory. You experience fear as you enter the dentist's office partially because of past associations (implicit memories) with pain.

Implicit memory does not require attention. For instance, you probably have had the experience while driving of realizing at some point that you've been daydreaming and have no episodic memory of the past few seconds or minutes. However, during that time you *remembered* how to drive and where you were going. Implicit memory happens automatically and without deliberate effort.

An example of implicit memory is **procedural memory,** or *motor memory*, which involves motor skills, habits, and other behaviors that you employ to achieve a goal, such as coordinating muscle movements to ride a bicycle or following the rules of the road while driving. You remember to stop when you see a red light because you have learned to do so, and when you drive home, you follow a specific route without even thinking about it. Our procedural memories have an automatic, unconscious aspect to them. For instance, the next time you are walking try to think about each step involved in the process: first you lift your right foot off the ground and slightly bend the knee, then you extend the foot forward while transferring weight to the right leg, etc. Most people find that consciously thinking about automatic behaviors, such as walking, interferes with the smooth production of those behaviors.

Implicit memory influences our lives in subtle ways. Many of our attitudes about objects around us are formed through implicit learning. You might like someone because they remind you of a favorite person, even if you are unaware of the connection. Advertisers rely on implicit memory to influence our purchasing decisions. Constant exposure to brand names makes us more likely to think of them when we go to buy a product.

Implicit attitude formation can even affect our beliefs about whether people are famous. Is Richard Shiffrin famous? Try to think for a second how you know him. You might recall that Richard Shiffrin was one of the psychologists who introduced the modal memory model (which might make him famous in scientific circles), or you might have known that you had read the name before but could not remember where, and therefore you assumed the person was famous. Psychologist Larry Jacoby called this the *false fame effect* (Jacoby et al., 1989). Jacoby had research participants read a list of made-up names as a test of pronunciation. The next day subjects completed an apparently unrelated study in which they were asked to read a list of names and decide whether each person was famous or not. Subjects misjudged some of the made-up names from the previous day as being famous. Why did this happen? Subjects knew they had heard the names before but couldn't remember where. Therefore, the implicit memory led them to assume the name was likely that of a famous person.

Implicit memory is also involved in **repetition priming,** the improvement in identifying or processing a stimulus that has previously been experienced. In a typical priming experiment, participants are exposed to a list of words and asked

implicit memory The process by which people show an enhancement of memory, most often through behavior, without deliberate effort and without any awareness that they are remembering anything.

procedural memory A type of implicit memory, which involves motor skills and behavioral habits.

repetition priming The improvement in identifying or processing a stimulus that has previously been experienced.

to do something, such as count the number of letters in the words. Following some brief delay, the participants are shown word fragments and asked to complete them with the first word that comes to mind. You can try this yourself. Count the letters in the following words: *appearance*, *chestnut*, *patent*. Now, complete the stems app_____, che_____, pat_____, with the first word that comes to mind. The participants in a typical experiment are much more likely to complete the fragments with the words they previously encountered, which were primed and therefore more easily accessible. In our example, you are much more likely to complete the stems as *appearance*, *chestnut*, and *patent* than, say, *application*, *cheese*, or *paternal*. This effect occurs even when participants cannot explicitly recall the words in the first task; even many hours after viewing the primes, participants show implicit memory without explicit recall of the words.

What Are the Different Memory Systems?

Memory researchers reject the idea that memory involves a single process or brain system. They now agree that there is a fundamental distinction between explicit and implicit memory systems. Explicit memory involves the conscious storage and retrieval of declarative memories, such as meanings of words or personal experiences. Implicit memory refers to an enhancement of memory without effort or awareness. Examples of implicit memory included procedural (or motor) memory, attitude formation, and repetition priming.

HOW IS INFORMATION REPRESENTED IN LONG-TERM MEMORY?

Events that are sufficiently important to be remembered permanently need to be represented in a way that allows for later retrieval. Imagine if a video store just put each video onto a shelf, wherever there was empty space. What would happen if you wanted to find a certain movie? You would have to go through the entire inventory one by one until you encountered the right movie. Just as this system does not work for movies, it also does not work for memory. Rather, memories are stored in an organized fashion. In this section we examine the temporal and organizational principles of long-term memory.

Are memories stored in an organized fashion?

LONG-TERM MEMORY IS A TEMPORAL SEQUENCE

Going back to the computer analogy, memory is a process that involves storing new information so that it is available when it is later required. Memory can be divided temporally into three processes: *encoding*, *storage*, and *retrieval*. In **encoding**, our perceptual experiences are transformed into representations, or *codes*, which are then stored. For instance, when your visual system senses a shaggy, four-legged animal and your auditory system senses barking, you perceive a dog. The concept of "dog" is a *mental representation* for a category of animals that share certain features, such as barking and fur. The mental representation for "dog" differs from that for "cat," even though the two are similar in many ways. You also have mental representations for complex things, such as ideas, beliefs, and the feelings of falling in love.

encoding The processing of information so that it can be stored.

Whether simple or complex, information is stored in networks of neurons in the brain. **Storage** refers to the retention of encoded representations over time and corresponds to some change in the nervous system that registers the event. Stored representations are referred to as *memories*. Memories represent many different kinds of information, such as visual images, facts, ideas, tastes, or even muscle movements, such as memory for riding a bicycle. **Retrieval** is the act of recalling or remembering the stored information in order to use it. The act of retrieval often involves an explicit effort to access the contents of memory storage, such as when you try to remember the previous chapter or your fifth birthday. But many times you retrieve information implicitly, without any effort at all, such as when you instantly remember the name of an acquaintance you encounter on the street. Thus, retrieval is involved in both explicit and implicit memory systems.

LONG-TERM STORAGE IS BASED ON MEANING

Books are stored by Library of Congress numbers, video stores tend to organize movies by type, and telephone books are organized alphabetically. Memories, however, are not stored by category, type or number. Memories are stored by meaning. In the early 1970s, psychologists Fergus Craik and Robert Lockhart developed an influential theory of memory based on depth of elaboration. According to their *levels of processing* model, the more deeply an item is encoded, the more meaning it has and the better it is remembered. Craik and Lockhart proposed that different types of rehearsal led to differential encoding. **Maintenance rehearsal** involves simply repeating the item over and over again. **Elaborative rehearsal** involves encoding the information in more meaningful ways, such as thinking about the item conceptually or deciding whether it refers to oneself. In other words, we elaborate on the basic information by linking it to knowledge from long-term memory.

How does this model work? Suppose you showed participants a list of words and then asked them to do one of three things. You could ask them to make simple perceptual judgments, such as, "Is each word printed in capital or small letters?" Or you could ask them to judge the acoustics of the word, such as, "Does the word _____ rhyme with boat?" Or you could ask them about the semantic meaning of the words, such as, "Does the word fit the sentence 'They had to cross the _____ to reach the castle'?" Once they had processed the information, you might later ask them to recall as many words as possible (Figure 7.8). You would find that words that were processed at the deepest level, based on semantic meaning, were remembered the best. Brain-imaging studies have shown that semantic encoding activates more brain regions than shallow encoding (Kapur et al., 1994). This greater brain activity is associated with better memory.

SCHEMAS PROVIDE AN ORGANIZATIONAL FRAMEWORK

People store memories by meaning. But how is meaning determined? We earlier mentioned chunking as a good way to encode groups of items for easy memory. The more meaningful the chunks, the better they are remembered. Decisions about how to chunk information depend upon previous organizational structures in long-term memory. **Schemas** are hypothetical cognitive structures that

7.8 Participants are asked to consider a list of words. They are asked to consider how the words are printed, how they sound, or what they mean. The more deeply the material was processed, the better it was remembered.

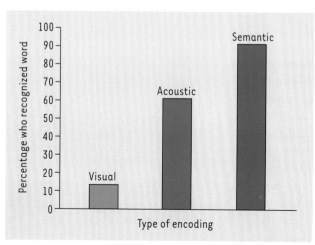

help us perceive, organize, process, and use information. They help us sort out the incoming information and guide our attention to relevant features of the environment. People use their past memories and general knowledge about the world to shape incoming information. By doing so, they construct new memories. They fill in holes, overlook inconsistent information, and interpret meaning based on past experience.

Existing schemas help us make sense of the world, but they can lead to biased encoding. In a classic demonstration conducted in the early 1930s, Frederick Bartlett asked British subjects to listen to a Native American folk tale. After a 15-minute delay, Bartlett asked the subjects to repeat the story exactly as they heard it. Bartlett found that the subjects distorted the story a great deal, and they did so in a consistent way—they altered the story so that it made sense from their own cultural standpoint.

Schemas influence which information is stored in memory. Consider a study in which students read a story about a wild, unruly girl. Some of the subjects were initially told that the girl was Helen Keller, whereas others were told it was "Carol Harris," a made-up name (Sulin & Dooling, 1974). One week later, the subjects who were initially told the girl was Helen Keller were more likely to mistakenly report having seen the sentence "She was deaf, mute, and blind" than those who thought the story was about Carol Harris. Our schema for Helen Keller includes her various disabilities, and when we retrieve information about Helen Keller from memory, everything we know about her is retrieved along with the specific story we are trying to remember.

Read the following paragraph carefully.

The procedure is actually quite simple. First arrange things into different bundles depending on make-up. Don't do too much at once. In the short run this may not seem important, however, complications easily arise. A mistake can be costly. Next, find facilities. Some people must go elsewhere for them. Manipulation of appropriate mechanisms should be self-explanatory. Remember to include all other necessary supplies. Initially the routine will overwhelm you, but soon it will become just another facet of life. Finally, rearrange everything into their initial groups. Return these to their usual places. Eventually they will be used again. Then the whole cycle will have to be repeated. (Bransford & Johnson, 1972)

How easy did you find this to understand? If you had to recall the sentences from this paragraph could you do so? It might surprise you to know that researchers presented this paragraph to college students and that those students found it easy to understand and relatively straightforward to recall. How is that possible? It is easy if you know that the paragraph describes washing clothes! Go back and read the paragraph again. Notice how your schema for doing laundry helps you to understand and remember how the words and sentences are connected to one another.

INFORMATION IS STORED IN ASSOCIATION NETWORKS

One highly influential set of theories of memory organization is based on *networks of associations*. The idea that our knowledge of the world is organized so that things that naturally go together are linked together in storage can be traced back to Aristotle. Network models of memory emphasize the links between semantically related items. In a network model proposed by Allan Collins and Elizabeth

storage The retention of encoded representations over time that corresponds to some change in the nervous system that registers the event.

retrieval The act of recalling or remembering stored information in order to use it.

maintenance rehearsal A type of encoding that involves continually repeating an item.

elaborative rehearsal The encoding of information in a more meaningful fashion, such as linking it to knowledge in long-term memory.

schemas Hypothetical cognitive structures that help us perceive, organize, process, and use information.

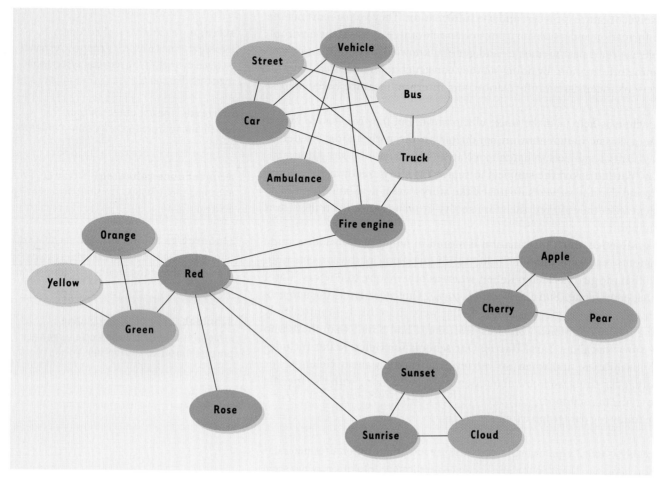

7.9 A semantic network in which similar concepts are connected through their associations.

Loftus (Figure 7.9), distinctive features of an item are linked together in such a way as to identify it. Each unit of information in the network is known as a *node*. Each node is connected to many other nodes. When you look at a fire engine, for example, all of the nodes that represent features of a fire engine are activated, and the resulting pattern of activation gives rise to the knowledge that the object is a fire engine rather than, say, a cat. An important feature of network models is that activating one node increases the likelihood that closely associated nodes will also be activated. In Figure 7.9, the closer the nodes the stronger the association between them and therefore the more likely that activating one will activate the other. Seeing a fire engine activates nodes that indicate other vehicles, so that once your fire engine nodes are activated, you are much quicker to recognize other vehicles than, for instance, fruits or animals. The idea that activating one node increases the likelihood that associated nodes become active is a central tenet of *spreading activation* models of memory. According to these views, stimuli in working memory activate specific nodes in long-term memory, which increases the ease of access to that material, thereby facilitating retrieval.

The overall organization of associative networks is based on categories that are hierarchically structured, providing a clear and explicit blueprint for where to look for needed information. Given the vast amount of material in memory, it is truly amazing how quickly we can search for and obtain needed memories from storage. Each time you hear a sentence, you not only have to remember what all the words mean, but you have to recall all relevant information that helps you understand the meaning. For this to occur, the information needs to be organized in some logical fashion. Imagine trying to find a specific file on a full 40-gigabyte hard disk by opening one file at a time. Such a method would be hopelessly slow. Instead, most computer disks are organized into folders, and within each folder are more-specialized folders, and so on. This hierarchical storage system allows us to find needed files quickly.

As in a computer, the hierarchical structure of memory facilitates efficient retrieval. If we activated memories of your biology professor, for example by asking her name, and we then asked whether she or your casual friend wore glasses, you would probably be able to recall whether she wore glasses more quickly than you would for your friend. This occurs because all of the information about your biology professor is activated at the same time, thereby allowing you to answer quickly. To answer the question for your casual friend, you first have to activate memory for that friend.

RETRIEVAL CUES PROVIDE ACCESS TO LONG-TERM STORAGE

Anything that helps people access information from long-term memory is known as a *retrieval cue*. Retrieval cues help sort through the vast amount of data stored in LTM to identify the right information. The power of retrieval cues explains why it is easier to *recognize* than to *recall* information. For example, What is the capital of Vermont? You probably had to spend a moment or two thinking about this, even if you could retrieve the correct answer. Now consider the question, Is the capital of Vermont Concord, Montpelier, or Pierre? Most people find it easier now to remember that Montpelier is Vermont's capital. Seeing the word helps you to retrieve specific information that allows you to answer the question.

Encoding specificity Almost anything can serve as a retrieval cue, including the smell of turkey, a favorite song from high school, or walking into a familiar building. Encountering these sorts of stimuli often triggers unintended memories. According to psychologist Endel Tulving's **encoding specificity principle**, any stimulus that is encoded along with an experience can later trigger memory for the experience. In an interesting study with provocative findings, Steven Smith and his colleagues had students study 80 words in one of two different rooms. The rooms differed in a number of ways, including size, location, and scent in the room. The students were then tested for recall either in the room in which they studied or the other room. When the study and test sessions were held in the same room, students recalled about 49 words correctly. However, when tested in the room in which they did not study, students recalled only 35 words correctly (Smith et al., 1978). Such enhancement of memory when the recall situation is similar to the encoding situation is known as *context-dependent memory*. Context-dependent memory can be based on such things as odors, background music, and physical location. The most dramatic demonstration showed that scuba divers who learned information underwater later tested better underwater than on land (Godden & Baddeley, 1975; see Figure 7.10).

State-dependent memory Just as physical context can affect memory, so can internal cues, such as mood states or even inebriation.

encoding specificity principle A principle that states that any stimulus that is encoded along with an experience can later trigger memory for the experience.

How are people able to retrieve specific memories?

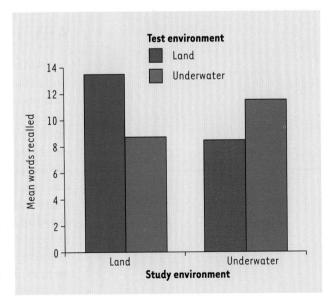

7.10 Mean number of words recalled in the Godden and Baddeley Study (1975). Note that the best memory occurs for words that were studied and tested in the same environment.

Enhancement of memory when there is a match between internal states during encoding and recall is known as *state-dependent memory*. Some of this research was inspired by the observation that alcoholics often misplaced important objects, such as paychecks, because they stored them in a safe place while they were drinking but could not remember where once they were sober. The next time they were drinking, however, they were able to remember where they had hidden the object. Psychological scientist Eric Eich conducted a study of state-dependent memory using marijuana. Subjects studied a test list either sober or high. Eich found that memory was best when subjects were tested in the same state in which they had studied. Note, however, that students recalled the information best when they were sober on both occasions. In a study that used alcohol, the worst performance was for students who studied when intoxicated and took the test sober. They did worse than students who studied sober and took the test intoxicated. Students who studied intoxicated and took the test intoxicated did much worse than students who were sober at both study and test (Goodwin et al., 1969). State-dependent memory works because internal state serves as an additional retrieval cue that can facilitate the recovery of information from long-term memory.

How Is Information Represented in Long-Term Memory?

Memory is composed of a temporal sequence of encoding, storage, and retrieval. Encoding and storage are organized so that information can be quickly retrieved. Human memory is stored according to meaning, and the more that meaning is elaborated at time of storage, the better the later memory will be. Shallow encoding does not lead to long-term storage. Schemas help people perceive, organize, and process information, which is then stored if processed deeply. Hierarchical networks of associated nodes provide semantic links between related items. Activation of a node spreads throughout the rest of its network. Retrieval cues help access stored information. Contextual cues and internal states can serve as retrieval cues.

WHAT BRAIN PROCESSES ARE INVOLVED IN MEMORY?

In the first part of this chapter we focused on the cognitive dimensions of memory, including types of memory and the kinds of information that are stored in memory. Now another fundamental question needs to be asked: What role does biology play in the formulation of our memories? In this section we examine brain structures involved in memory, as well as some of the neurochemical processes that alter memory. As an outgrowth of the biological revolution, there has been tremendous progress over the past two decades in understanding what happens in the brain when we store and retrieve memories. Cognitive-neuroscience approaches are focused on the neural structures that support the encoding, storage, and retrieval of memory. Studies of patients with brain injuries have provided the basic foundations for understanding the neural basis of memory, and brain-imaging techniques have permitted an understanding of memory processes in the healthy brain.

THERE HAS BEEN INTENSIVE EFFORT TO IDENTIFY THE PHYSICAL LOCATION OF MEMORY

Locating where in the brain memories are stored has been one of the central goals of memory researchers during the twentieth century. Harvard University professor Karl Lashley spent much of his career trying to localize memory. He used the term *engram* to refer to the physical site of memory storage. Lashley first trained rats to run a maze. He then removed different areas of their cortices to test how much of the learning they retained. Lashley found that the size of the area removed rather than its location was most important in predicting retention. Thus, he concluded that memory is distributed throughout the brain rather than in any specific location, an idea known as *equipotentiality*. It turns out that Lashley was partially right, but also quite wrong.

It is now well established that memories are not stored in any one specific brain location. Rather, memories are stored in multiple regions of the brain and linked together through memory circuits, as proposed by Donald Hebb's idea that neurons that fire together, wire together (see Chapter 6). This is not to suggest that all areas of the brain are equally involved in memory. As you'll see below, a great deal of neural specialization occurs, with different brain regions responsible for storing different aspects of information. Indeed, different memory systems, such as declarative and procedural memories, use different brain regions. Lashley's failure to find critical brain regions for memory is due to at least two factors. First, the maze task involved multiple sensory systems (such as vision and smell), so the rats could compensate for the loss of one by using the other senses. Second, Lashley did not examine subcortical areas, which are now known to be important for the retention of memories.

THE MEDIAL TEMPORAL LOBES ARE IMPORTANT FOR MEMORY CONSOLIDATION

The one brain area that has been repeatedly identified as important for memory is the middle section of the temporal lobes, which is located right behind your eyes. Recall from Chapter 4 that Wilder Penfield, of the Montreal Neurological Institute, found that stimulating the temporal lobes led to reports of specific memories in some epilepsy patients. The medial temporal lobe consists of a number of struc-

7.11 The major regions of the medial temporal lobe.

tures relevant to memory, including the amygdala, hippocampus, and rhinal cortex, an area located around the front of the hippocampus (Figure 7.11). As was described earlier, H.M.'s brain surgery led to an inability to form new memories. Using brain imaging, Sue Corkin of MIT and her colleagues found that a large portion of H.M.'s hippocampus was removed, as well as a small section of nearby temporal lobe (Corkin et al., 1997). It is now clear that damage to this region causes *anterograde amnesia*, which is the inability to store new explicit memories. However, it is *not* the case that the medial temporal lobes are the final repository of memory. After all, H.M. could remember things from

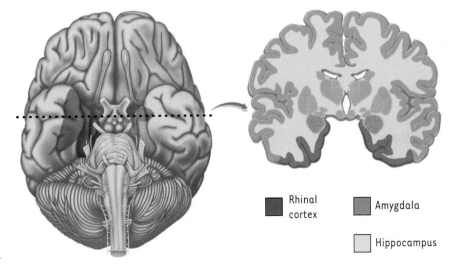

Rhinal cortex

Amygdala

Hippocampus

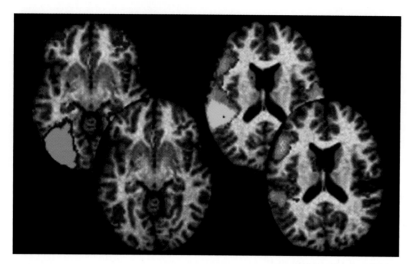

7.12 Four horizontally sliced brain images acquired using magnetic resonance imaging show regions of the brain active during perception of pictures (top left) and sounds (top right), and subsequently during retrieval of the same pictures (bottom left) and sounds (bottom right) from long-term memory. These data indicate that regions of sensory cortex are reactivated when remembering sensory-specific information.

before his surgery. Thus, damage to the medial temporal lobes interrupts storage of new material without impairing access to old material.

The transfer of contents from immediate memory into long-term memory occurs through a hypothetical process known as **consolidation.** Consolidation results from changes in the strength of neural connections that support memory. Current thinking suggests that the medial temporal lobes are responsible for coordinating the strengthening between neuronal activations, but the actual storage most likely occurs in the particular cortical processing systems engaged during perception, processing, and analysis of the material being learned. For instance, visual information is stored in the cortical areas involved in visual perception whereas aural information is stored in those areas involved in auditory perception. In one study, researchers exposed participants either to pictures of common objects (for example, dogs) or to their associated sounds (barking) and asked the participants to become very familiar with the stimuli. Two days later, while the participants were in an MRI, they were re-exposed to the pictures or sounds and then asked to recall the stimuli as vividly as possible. Thus, some participants tried to remember how the objects looked, whereas others tried to remember how they sounded. The same areas that became activated when participants were exposed to the stimuli became reactivated when the participants vividly recollected those stimuli (Figure 7.12; Wheeler et al., 2000). Thus, memory for sensory experiences involves reactivating the cortical circuits involved in perceiving them. The medial temporal lobes form links or pointers between the different sites of storage and direct the gradual strengthening of the connections between these links.

Localizing function within medial temporal lobes   Which parts of the medial temporal lobes are most relevant to memory? Studies of primates with surgical lesions to the medial temporal lobes have given us a pretty good idea. In the 1970s, Mortimer Mishkin at the National Institute of Mental Health developed the first successful animal model of memory. In these studies, monkeys are placed in a box with a retractable door. In the first phase of the study, the monkey learns that a food reward is hidden under an object (Figure 7.13). The door then closes, then opens to reveal two objects: one which previously hid the reward and a new object. The rule is that the food reward is always under the novel object. This provides a good measure of not only learning, since the monkey has to learn the rule, but also memory, since the monkey must remember which of the two objects was presented previously. Research using this task has identified the hippocampus and the surrounding rhinal cortex as the most important areas for consolidation of memory. Lesions to other areas of the medial temporal region, such as the amygdala, do not interfere with this task.

consolidation A hypothetical process that refers to the transfer of contents from immediate memory into long-term memory.

spatial memory Memory for the physical environment that includes such things as location of objects, direction, and cognitive maps.

Spatial memory   For many years it was widely believed that the hippocampus was important for **spatial memory,** which is memory for the physical environment and includes such things as direction, location of objects, and cognitive maps. A good example of this type of learning is the *Morris water maze test,* in which a rat is placed into a circular pool of murky water and learns to swim to an invisible platform that is just below the surface (Figure 7.14). Rats can learn this task quite readily, and they do so by using cues from the environment to remember where to find the platform. Rats with hippocampal damage are severely impaired at this task. The role of the hippocampus in spatial memory is supported by *place cells*, which are neurons that fire only when a rat returns to a specific location, such as one part of a maze. When rats are placed in novel environments, none of the place cells fire. But as the rat becomes familiar with the environment, its hippocampal place cells acquire a link to aspects of the surroundings. This suggests that the hippocampus helps animals to orient and find their way. Indeed, birds that rely on memory to find stored food, such as food-caching chickadees, have larger hippocampal regions than birds who do not store food. Patients with damage to the hippocampus also have trouble remembering the location of objects in pictures (Piggott & Milner, 1993), suggesting that the hippocampus is also important for spatial memory in humans.

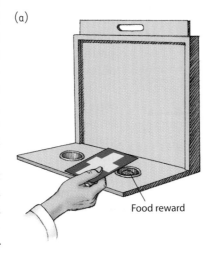
(a)

Food reward

Cue and response

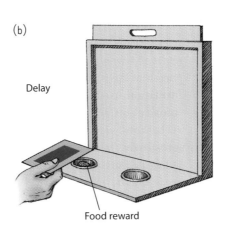
(b)

Delay

Food reward

Cue and response

Right

Wrong

THE FRONTAL LOBES ARE INVOLVED IN MANY ASPECTS OF MEMORY

It has long been known that the frontal lobes are important to many aspects of memory, including episodic memory, working memory, spatial memory, time sequences (see below), and various aspects of encoding and retrieval. There are extensive neural networks connecting the prefrontal cortex with other brain regions involved in memory, such as the medial temporal areas. Thus, the frontal lobes work together with other brain regions to coordinate the encoding, storage, and retrieval of memory.

7.13 (a) The monkey is presented with a sample item, the red and yellow object. (b) After a delay, the monkey is presented with the same object and a new object. The monkey now has to select the new object, which implies it remembers the first object.

Patients with damage to prefrontal regions typically do not develop profound memory loss, but they often have great difficulty remembering the time sequence of events, such as which of two events happened first. Moreover, they often can't tell you where or when they learned information. The inability to recall the circumstances under which learning took place has been reported for elderly individuals, who often experience signs of frontal lobe deficits, as well as young children, who have immature frontal lobes.

Brain-imaging studies have provided compelling evidence that the frontal lobes are crucial for encoding. When people work hard to memorize a list of words, such efforts usually light up the frontal lobes in PET or fMRI studies (Buckner et al., 1999). Moreover, deeper encoding

7.14 A rat is placed in the Morris water maze and must find the hidden platform. After many trials, the animal learns where the platform is hidden and swims directly to it.

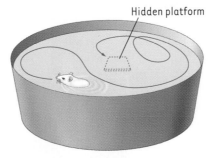

Hidden platform

Before learning

After learning

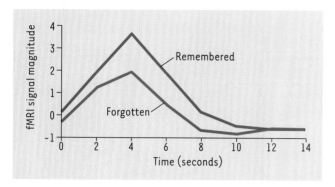

7.15 This graph shows brain activation in the left prefrontal area during a memory task. Words that are later remembered have a larger response than words that are later forgotten.

tasks are more likely to lead to frontal activation than are shallow encoding tasks. The most compelling evidence of frontal lobe involvement in memory formation is that activation of the frontal lobes predicts which events are later remembered or forgotten (Brewer et al., 1998). For instance, during a memory task researchers compared the fMRI frontal response (at the time of encoding) for words that were later remembered with words that were later forgotten. As may be seen in Figure 7.15, words that were later remembered were associated with stronger activation of the frontal lobes (Wagner et al., 1998).

Hemispherical asymmetries in encoding and retrieval There is some evidence that encoding and retrieval occur in different hemispheres. Tulving and his colleagues analyzed a number of studies that used PET imaging to assess the encoding and retrieval of episodic experiences. When they looked at the brain-activation patterns, they found that the left frontal lobes were more active during encoding, whereas the right frontal lobes were more active during episodic retrieval (Tulving et al., 1994). They called this pattern the *hemispherical encoding retrieval asymmetry* or *HERA*. Recently, William Kelley and his colleagues have argued that the pattern of left hemisphere activation might be due to the types of information used in the tasks. They argue that any stimulus that involves verbal information activates the left hemisphere, whereas objects that do not invoke verbal information (such as unfamiliar faces) activate the right hemisphere. Interestingly, nameable objects that contain both visual and verbal information (such as a picture of a frog, see Figure 7.16) activate both left and right frontal areas during encoding (Kelley et al., 1998). Thus, the asymmetry in memory refers more to the type of material studied than to memory processes themselves.

7.16 Frontal regions active during memory formation may depend on the material being memorized. Memorization of verbal material (words) activates the left frontal cortex, whereas memorization of nonverbal, pictorial material (unfamiliar faces) activates the right frontal cortex. Interestingly, memorization of objects (associated with both an image and a name) activates both the right and the left frontal cortex.

Frontal lobes and working memory So what do the frontal lobes do in memory? One hypothesis is that they play a role in working memory. Working memory holds information on-line so that it can be used to solve problems, understand conversations, and follow plans. Patients with damage to the frontal areas often have difficulty following plans and goals, and monkeys given frontal lesions show impaired working memory (Goldman-Rakic et al., 2000). In one task, the monkey watches the experimenter hide a reward under one of two objects. After a delay, the monkey is allowed to reach for the object covering the reward. Monkeys with frontal lesions have difficulty with this task. Interestingly, human infants

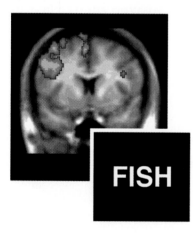

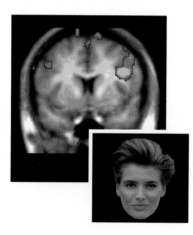

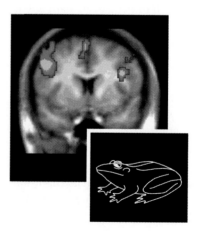

have trouble with a similar task as well, which further implicates the frontal lobes in working memory since the frontal lobes are not fully matured until much later in development (Diamond & Doar, 1989).

Frontal regions become active when information is being either retrieved from long-term memory into working memory or encoded from working memory into long-term memory. For example, when you enter the classroom, the frontal lobes oversee retrieval of stored knowledge from neural networks spread throughout cortical and subcortical locations. This information helps you remember what to do when you enter the room (sit down), who the person is at the front of the class (the professor), and the meaning of the sounds emanating from the professor's mouth. The frontal lobes and medial temporal lobes then work together to consolidate long-term memory storage for the lecture. The hippocampus helps strengthen associations between the events in working memory so that new experiences are processed into permanent storage.

NEUROCHEMISTRY INFLUENCES MEMORY

It is known that memory involves alterations in connections across synapses. As memories are consolidated, distributed networks of neurons become linked together. Research has shown that a variety of neurotransmitters can weaken or enhance memory. Collectively, these neurotransmitters are known as *memory modulators*, because they modulate, or modify, the storage of memory.

Neurochemistry indicates meaningfulness of stimuli   Earlier we pointed out that animals store only information that is meaningful. Memory modulation is the system that evolution has bestowed upon organisms to help determine whether something is important. Important events lead to neurochemical changes that produce emotional experiences. An animal that outruns a predator has experienced a fear reaction that helps to stamp in avoidance of that predator. A child who eats a good-tasting food experiences a rewarding sensation that is easily remembered, as parents who have watched their preverbal children point at cookie jars can readily attest. Events that produce emotional reactions are especially likely to be stored in memory.

So what are the neurochemical signals that indicate that an experience is meaningful? When animals are engaging in minimally arousing tasks, little memory is later shown for those tasks. However, animals injected with epinephrine, which induces a state of arousal, show significant memory enhancement for trivial events. It is as if the jolt of epinephrine gives the message "Remember me!" Of course, epinephrine is in the periphery of the body, not in the brain, and so it does not have a direct effect on memory. Rather, it appears that epinephrine leads to a release of glucose, which then enters the brain and influences memory storage. The role of glucose is also implicated by a study in which elderly individuals were given a memory test after consuming lemonade with either glucose (sugar) or saccharine (a sugar substitute). Those who had glucose had better memory for the studied items the next day (Gold, 1987). Other drugs, such as those that depress neuronal activity, can interfere with memory. Opiates, alcohol, and surgical anesthetics may interfere with memory by reducing arousal.

The amygdala and the neurochemistry of emotion   The amygdala is the prime candidate for the brain structure that controls the modulating effects of neurotransmitters on memory. It is the limbic structure closely tied to fear reactions, and it is located within the medial temporal lobe. Direct stimulation of the amygdala can enhance or impair memory, and damaging the pathways leading to or exiting it eliminates the effects of drugs on memory. In humans, PET studies have shown that the amygdala is activated during recall of emotional film clips but not neutral films clips (Cahill et al., 1996). Interestingly, there appears to be a gender difference in this effect, such that emotional memory activates the right (but not left) amygdala in men and the left (but not right) amygdala in women (Cahill et al., 2001). The basis of this sex difference is currently not known.

Activity within the amygdala provides guidance to other brain structures about which events in the environment are worthy of memory consolidation. Unfortunately, as shown in "Crossing the Levels of Analysis: The Strength of Traumatic and Persistent Memories," such memories may be so strongly consolidated that people cannot forget them even if they want to.

What Brain Processes Are Involved in Memory?

Research during the past thirty years has demonstrated that memories are encoded in distributed networks of neurons in relatively specific brain regions. Lashley failed to uncover the engram, probably because he was looking in the wrong place and not using specific enough tasks. It is now known that damage to the medial temporal lobes, especially the hippocampus or rhinal cortex, causes significant memory disturbances. These medial temporal regions are important for the consolidation of long-term memories into storage. The sites of memory storage are the brain structures involved in perception. The frontal lobes are especially important for working memory, and a variety of neurotransmitters modulate memory storage. Fear causes activation of the amygdala, which is associated with a strengthening of memories.

WHEN DO PEOPLE FORGET?

Up until now we have been focusing on remembering information. But along the way we have noted that failures of memory are extremely common. **Forgetting** is the inability to retrieve memory from long-term storage. Forgetting is an everyday experience that is perfectly normal. Ten minutes after you see a movie you might remember plenty of details, but the next day you probably remember mostly the plot and the main characters. Years later you might remember the gist of the story or you might not remember having seen the movie at all. We forget far more than we ever remember.

Most people bemoan forgetting, wishing that they could better recall information they study for exams, the names of childhood friends, or even the names of all the seven dwarfs. But imagine what life would be like if you couldn't forget. You would walk up to your locker and recall 10 or 20 different combinations. Consider the case of a Russian newspaper reporter who had nearly perfect memory. You could read him a tremendously long list of items, and as long as he could spend a few moments visualizing the items, he could recite them back, even many years later. But he was tortured by his condition and was eventually institutionalized. His memory was so cluttered with information that he had great difficulty functioning in normal society. Paradoxically, not being able to forget is as maladaptive as not being able to remember. It is therefore not surprising that memory tends to be best for meaningful and important points. We remember the forest rather than

forgetting The inability to retrieve memory from long-term storage.

THE STRENGTH OF TRAUMATIC AND PERSISTENT MEMORIES

When people experience severe stress or trauma, such as being in a serious accident, being raped, being in combat, or surviving a natural disaster, they often continue to have negative reactions long after the threat has passed. In severe cases, people develop *post-traumatic stress disorder (PTSD)*, a serious mental-health disorder that involves frequent and recurring unwanted thoughts related to the trauma, including nightmares, intrusive thoughts, and flashbacks. Those with PTSD have chronic tension, anxiety, and health problems, and they may experience memory and attention problems in their daily lives. PTSD affects approximately 1 in 10 individuals at some point in their lives, although obviously the source of trauma differs greatly.

PTSD involves an unusual problem in memory, in that it is the inability to forget that is causing problems. PTSD is associated with an attentional bias, such that people with PTSD are hypervigilant to stimuli associated with their traumatic event. For instance, soldiers with combat-induced PTSD show increased physiological responsiveness to pictures of troops, sounds of gunfire, and even words associated with combat. Richard McNally, an anxiety specialist at Harvard University, notes that soldiers may unintentionally maintain their memory bias by wearing clothes and other memorabilia that serve as constant cues and reminders of the unwanted memories. What causes the memory to be so deeply encoded? There is evidence that highly emotional events are better remembered, possibly due to the action of neurotransmitters and hormones released during stress. Thus, the memory may be "overconsolidated," as if burned into memory.

As might be expected, exposure to stimuli associated with past trauma leads to activation of brain regions, such as the amygdala, involved in emotion (Figure 7.17; Rauch et al., 1996). Some theorists believe there is a strong classically conditioned response that causes people to learn to fear stimuli associated with the traumatic event in one trial. Joseph LeDoux (1996) of New York University, one of the world's leading authorities on the neural basis of fear learning, has argued that emotional memory may be permanent. Thus, cognitive neuroscientists view PTSD as an exaggeration of the way emotional memories are normally formed. Learning to quickly fear dangerous objects and situations has obvious survival value, although perhaps at the cost of permanent unwanted memories.

One of the most serious problems for those with PTSD is constant,

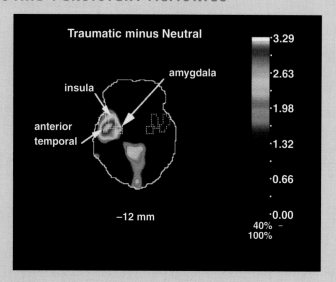

7.17 These findings were obtained using PET imaging with eight PTSD patients. In this task, the patients thought about the traumatic event or a neutral event. The colored areas were more activated for the traumatic thoughts than for neutral thoughts.

recurring unwanted thoughts. Work on thought suppression has been helpful in understanding the cognitive factors involved in trying not to think about things that bother us. Social psychologist Dan Wegner and his colleagues have developed an experiment in which participants attempt not to think about white bears for a five-minute period (Wegner, 1989). Few people are able to avoid thinking of white bears completely, and participants attempt all manner of distraction to vanquish the unwanted thought from their minds. In a follow-up period, the participants are now asked to try to think about white bears. These individuals now display a cognitive rebound effect, thinking much more about white bears than individuals who were not initially asked to suppress their thoughts. In general, any attempt to suppress a thought leads to an increased preoccupation with it. In terms of PTSD, Wegner's group has found that thoughts that are particularly arousing or personally meaningful are more difficult to suppress than are neutral thoughts, with people being hypervigilant to detection of the unwanted thoughts.

the individual trees. Normal forgetting helps us remember and use information that is important.

The study of forgetting has a long history in psychological science. Hermann Ebbinghaus, a German psychologist working in the late nineteenth century, provided compelling evidence that forgetting occurs rapidly over the first few hours and days but then levels off. He used the so-called *methods of savings* to examine how long it took for people to relearn lists of nonsense syllables. Presumably, the more slowly people relearned the list, the greater evidence there was of forgetting.

transience The pattern of forgetting over time.

proactive interference When prior information inhibits the ability to remember new information.

retroactive interference When new information inhibits the ability to remember old information.

TABLE 7.1	**Seven Sins of Memory**	
ERROR	**TYPE**	**EXAMPLE**
Transience	Forgetting	Reduced memory over time, such as forgetting the plot of a movie.
Absentmindedness	Forgetting	Reduced memory due to failing to pay attention, such as losing your keys or forgetting a lunch date.
Blocking	Forgetting	Inability to remember needed information, such as failing to recall the name of a person you meet on the street.
Misattribution	Distortion	Assigning a memory to the wrong source, such as falsely thinking that Richard Shiffrin is famous.
Suggestibility	Distortion	Altering a memory because of misleading information, such as developing false memories for events that did not happen.
Bias	Distortion	Influence of current knowledge on our memory for past events, such as remembering our past attitudes as similar to our current attitudes even though they have changed.
Persistence	Undesired	The resurgence of unwanted or disturbing memories that we would like to forget, such as remembering an embarrassing faux pas.

SOURCE: Based on Schacter (2001).

We've learned a great deal about forgetting over the last century. Harvard psychologist Daniel Schacter identifies what he calls *the seven sins of memory* (Schacter, 1999). These so-called sins are all too familiar for most people (Table 7.1). They are also characteristics that are useful or perhaps even necessary for survival. Schacter argues that the seven sins of memory are by-products of otherwise desirable aspects of human memory. The first three sins are related to forgetting: *transience*, *blocking*, and *absentmindedness* (we will consider some of the other sins later in this chapter).

TRANSIENCE IS CAUSED BY INTERFERENCE

Memory **transience** refers to the pattern of forgetting over time, such as was obtained by Ebbinghaus in his studies of nonsense syllables. What causes transience? Many early theorists argued that forgetting was the result of *decay* of the memory trace in our nervous system. Indeed, there is some evidence that forgetting occurs for memories that are not used. However, research over the last few decades has established that most forgetting occurs because of *interference* from other information. There are two ways that additional information can lead to forgetting. In **proactive interference**, prior information inhibits our ability to remember new information. For instance, if you have a new locker combination each year, you may have difficulty remembering it because you keep recalling the old one. Indeed, the physical context provides retrieval cues for that earlier combination and so it becomes especially difficult to remember the new one while standing in front of your locker. In **retroactive interference**, new information

RESEARCH QUESTION

Do people really forget things, and if so, why?

inhibits our ability to remember old information. Now that you finally know your new locker combination, you may find that you have forgotten the old one. Figure 7.18 shows the typical experimental tests that have been used to demonstrate proactive and retroactive interference. In both cases, we forget because competing information displaces the information we are trying to retrieve.

BLOCKING IS TEMPORARY

Blocking occurs when a person has a temporary inability to remember something that is known. Temporary blockages are common and frustrating, such as forgetting the name of a favorite CD, forgetting lines during a play, or forgetting someone's name when you introduce them. Another good example of blocking is the **tip-of-the-tongue phenomenon,** first described by Roger Brown and David MacNeill, in which people experience great frustration as they try to recall specific words that are somewhat obscure. Researcher Alan Brown (no relation to Roger) has shown that tip-of-the-tongue can be reliably produced in the laboratory (Brown, 1991). For instance, when asked to provide a word that means "patronage bestowed on a relative, in business or politics," people often struggle. Or how about "an astronomical instrument for finding position"? Sometimes people know which letter the word begins with, how many syllables it has, and even what it sounds like, but they can't pull the precise word into working memory. Did you know the words were *nepotism* and *sextant*? Blocking often occurs because of interference from words that are similar in some way, such as in sound or meaning. These similar words often keep recurring as we try to remember the target word.

ABSENTMINDEDNESS RESULTS FROM SHALLOW ENCODING

Absentmindedness describes the inattentive or shallow encoding of events—for instance, forgetting where you left your keys, the name of a person you met five minutes before, or whether you took your vitamins this morning. The major cause of absentmindedness is failing to pay sufficient attention to details. Consider the fascinating phenomenon of "change blindness." Imagine that you are standing around and someone walks up to you and asks directions. While you are answering, two workers, holding a door, cut between you, so you momentarily lose sight of the person asking for directions. Do you think you would notice if the person standing in front of you was switched? When Daniel Simons and Daniel Levin conducted this study, only half the participants noticed the change (Simons & Levin, 1998). Simons and Levin refer to the inability to detect changes to an object or scene as *change blindness*. Interestingly, in the original study, older people were especially likely not to notice a change in the person asking directions; college students were pretty good at noticing the change. Is this because older people are especially inattentive? Or is it that people process the gist of the situation

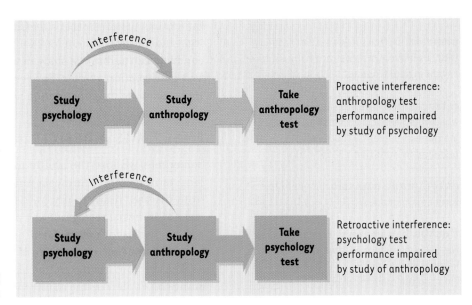

7.18 Proactive interference occurs when material that is already known interferes with the ability to remember new information, whereas retroactive interference occurs when new material interferes with memory for old material.

blocking The temporary inability to remember something that is known.

tip-of-the-tongue phenomenon A phenomenon that occurs when people experience great frustration as they try to recall specific words that are somewhat obscure.

absentmindedness The inattentive or shallow encoding of events.

amnesia Deficits in long-term memory that result from disease, brain injury, or psychological trauma.

retrograde amnesia The condition in which people lose past memories, such as memories for events, facts, people, or even personal information.

anterograde amnesia An inability to form new memories.

flashbulb memories Vivid memories for the circumstances in which one first learned of a surprising, consequential, and emotionally arousing event.

rather than detail? Perhaps the older adults encoded the person as simply "a college student" and did not look for finer detail. To test this idea, Simons and Levin conducted an additional study in which college students were asked for directions by a construction worker. Sure enough, the college students failed to notice the replacement of the construction worker, proving the latter.

AMNESIA IS A DEFICIT IN LONG-TERM MEMORY

Sometimes we lose the ability to retrieve vast quantities of information from long-term memory. **Amnesia** refers to deficits in long-term memory that result from disease, brain injury, or psychological trauma. There are essentially two types of amnesia: retrograde and anterograde. In **retrograde amnesia** people lose past memories for events, facts, people, or even personal information. Most portrayals of amnesia in media are of retrograde amnesia, such as the soap opera star awakening from a coma and not knowing who she is. By contrast, in **anterograde amnesia** people lose the ability to form new memories. H.M. has a classic case of anterograde amnesia. He can remember old information about his past, but since his surgery he has lost the ability to form new memories. Many cases of amnesia, such as H.M.'s, result from damage to the medial temporal lobes. However, damage to other subcortical areas, such as around the thalamus, can also lead to amnesia. A common cause of this type of amnesia is *Korsakoff's syndrome*, a severe form of memory disturbance associated with chronic alcoholism. Long-term alcohol abuse can lead to vitamin deficiency that results in thalamic damage and, subsequently, amnesia.

Amnesia is a fascinating condition that can vary greatly from case to case. For instance, after getting hit in the head or losing blood flow to the brain, some people experience a temporary loss of memory that abates after a day or two. A serious blow to the head can cause a *concussion*, which involves a loss of consciousness that can range from moments to weeks. Trevor Rees-Jones, the private bodyguard for Princess Diana, suffered a concussion during the motor vehicle accident that claimed her life. He later was able to recall getting into the car, but he recalled none of the chase leading up to the crash. This is highly typical of amnesia following concussion. There is often a period of retrograde amnesia for events leading up to the incident and sometimes temporary anterograde amnesia. People visiting such patients in the hospital are often surprised that the person seems lucid during conversation but later fails to remember the visit. This occurs because working memory is not disrupted, but the memories are not consolidated to long-term memory.

When Do People Forget?

Forgetting is the inability to retrieve memory from long-term storage. The ability to forget information is just as important as the ability to remember information. Forgetting that occurs over time is often due to interference from competing stimuli. Blocking is a temporary inability to retrieve specific information, as exemplified by the tip-of-the-tongue phenomenon. It too is caused by interference. Absentmindedness is a result of shallow encoding, which occurs when people fail to pay sufficient attention to details. Amnesia refers to a deficit in long-term memory in which people forget past information (retrograde amnesia) or are unable to store new information (anterograde amnesia). Most amnesia is caused by injury to the brain.

HOW ARE MEMORIES DISTORTED?

Most people believe that human memory is a permanent storage, from which even minute and apparently forgotten details can be retrieved through hypnosis, truth drugs, or other special techniques. Research has clearly shown, however, that human memory is biased, flawed, and distorted. Memory illusions are common and many have been described earlier in this chapter. However, not all memory distortions are so benign. In this section you will learn how the human memory systems provide a less than accurate portrayal of past events. Keep in mind, however, that simply because something doesn't work the way we think it works does not mean it is faulty. As Dan Schacter has argued, many of the seemingly flawed aspects of memory may be byproducts of mechanisms that are beneficial. Let's examine some of the most striking examples of the apparent fallibility of human memory.

What causes people to have memories that are distorted, false, or inaccurate?

FLASHBULB MEMORIES CAN BE WRONG

Do you remember where you were when you found out about the terrorist attacks on the World Trade Center and the Pentagon? Some events cause people to experience what Roger Brown and James Kulik termed **flashbulb memories,** which are vivid memories for the circumstances in which one first learned of a surprising and consequential or emotionally arousing event (Figure 7.19). When Brown and Kulik interviewed people about their memory of the death of President John Kennedy in 1963, they found that people described their memories in highly vivid terms that contained a great deal of detail, such as who they were with, what they were doing or thinking, who told them or how they found out, and what their emotional reaction was to the event.

Do you remember where you were when you heard . . . ? Of course, the question is whether flashbulb memories are accurate. There is an obvious problem in conducting research on flashbulb memories—you have to wait for a "flash" to go off and then immediately conduct your study. The explosion of the space shuttle *Challenger* on January 28, 1986, at 11:38 EST provided a unique opportunity for research on this topic. Ulric Neisser and Nicole Harsch (1993) had 44 psychology students fill out a questionnaire the day the shuttle exploded and then tested their memory three years later. They found that the vast majority of students were incorrect about multiple aspects of the situation, and that only three students had perfect recall. However, other researchers have documented better memory for flashbulb experiences, such as where British subjects were when they heard about Prime Minister Margaret Thatcher's resignation. Martin Conway and his colleagues (1994) showed that better memory for the flashbulb experience occurred among those who found the news surprising and felt that the event was important. Thus, students in the United Kingdom experienced stronger flashbulb memories for the Thatcher resignation than did students in the United States.

Stress and memory revisited Although flashbulb memories are not perfectly accurate, this does not mean that they are less accurate

7.19 Many people report a flashbulb memory for the destruction of the World Trade Center towers.

than any other type of memory. It is indeed possible that flashbulb experiences are recalled more accurately than inconsequential or unsurprising events. To the extent that flashbulb memories contain an unusual number of incidental details, it is possible that this occurs because of the memory modulating effects of stress hormones (Christianson, 1992). Thus, any event that produces a strong emotional response is likely to produce a vivid, although not necessarily accurate, memory. A second explanation is simply based on the well-known finding that distinctive events are recalled more easily than trivial events. This latter finding is known as the *von Restorff effect*, named after the researcher who first described it in 1933.

PEOPLE MAKE SOURCE MISATTRIBUTIONS

Dan Schacter identified source misattributions as one of the "seven sins" of the memory system. **Source misattributions** occur when people misremember the time, place, person, or circumstances involved with a memory. A good example of this is the *false fame effect* described earlier, in which people mistakenly believe that someone is famous simply because they've previously encountered the person's name. Similarly, social psychologists have long known about the *sleeper effect*, in which strong arguments that are initially not very persuasive because they come from questionable sources become more persuasive over time. You would probably disbelieve a weekly tabloid if it claimed that scientists had discovered a way for people to learn calculus while sleeping. Yet over time you might remember the argument but fail to remember that the source was questionable; hence, you later believe that people can learn calculus while sleeping.

Cryptomnesia An intriguing example of source misattribution is **cryptomnesia**, which is when people think they've come up with a new idea, when really they have retrieved an old idea from memory but have failed to attribute the idea to its proper source (Macrae et al., 1999). Students who take verbatim notes while conducting library research sometimes experience the illusion that they've written the sentences, which can later lead to an accusation of plagiarism. Thus students need to be especially vigilant to indicate verbatim notes while they are taking them. George Harrison, the former Beatle, was sued because his song "My Sweet Lord" is strikingly similar to the song "He's So Fine," recorded in 1962 by the Chiffons. Although he acknowledged having heard the song before, he vigorously denied that he plagiarized it. He argued that with a limited number of notes, and an even smaller number of chord sequences in rock and roll, some overlap was inevitable. In a controversial verdict, the judge ruled against Harrison.

PEOPLE MAKE BAD EYEWITNESSES

One of the most powerful forms of evidence is the eyewitness account. Early studies demonstrated that very few jurors are willing to convict an accused individual based on circumstantial evidence alone. But add one person who says "That's the one!" and conviction rates shoot up incredibly, even if it is shown that the witness had poor eyesight or some other condition that raises questions about the accuracy of their testimony. The power of eyewitness testimony is troubling because it is so often in error. Indeed, Gary Wells and his colleagues studied 40 cases in which DNA evidence indicated that a person had been falsely convicted of a crime. In 36 of these cases, the person had been falsely identified by one or more eyewitnesses (Wells et al., 1998). No one knows this story better than William

source misattributions When people misremember the time, place, person, or circumstances involved with a memory.

cryptomnesia A type of misappropriation that occurs when people think they have come up with a new idea, yet have only retrieved a stored idea and failed to attribute the idea to its proper source.

suggestibility The development of biased memories when provided with misleading information.

Jackson (Figure 7.20), who served five years in prison because he was wrongly convicted of a crime based on the testimony of two eyewitnesses. Let's look at some of the memory processes that contribute to eyewitness misidentification.

Cross-ethnic identification   People are particularly bad at accurately identifying individuals of other ethnicities. This effect occurs for Caucasians, Asians, African Americans, and Hispanics. The phrase "they all look alike" appears to be true of all people who are not members of our own ethnic group. One explanation for this problem is that people tend to have less frequent contact with members of other ethnicities; another is that people encode ethnicity according to gist rules of categorization, the way that in the change-blindness experiments older people saw "a college student" and students saw "a construction worker."

Suggestibility and misinformation   Elizabeth Loftus (Figure 7.21) is one of the world's leading specialists in eyewitness memory. During the early 1970s, Loftus and her colleagues conducted a series of important studies demonstrating that people can develop biased memories when provided with misleading information—the "sin" of **suggestibility.** The general methodology of this research involves showing research participants an event and then asking them specific questions about it; the way the questions are worded alters the participants' memories for the event. For instance, in one experiment college students viewed a videotape of a car accident and then were asked, "How fast were the cars going when they _____ each other?" The following words were used in the question: contacted, hit, bumped, collided, or smashed. Loftus and John Palmer (1974) found that students estimated the cars to be traveling faster when the word "smashed" was used than when the other words were used. In a second study, groups of students saw videotapes of car accidents and were then asked about seeing the cars either "smash" into or "hit" each other. One week later they were asked if they had seen broken glass on the ground, an event that did not happen. Nearly one-third of those who heard the term "smashed" falsely recalled having seen the broken glass, whereas very few of those who heard the term "hit" did.

Not only did participants report an altered view of the car accident, in other experiments Loftus and her colleagues demonstrated that people could be induced to report having seen things that did not exist, such as barns, through the use of such questions as "How fast was the white sports car going when it passed the barn while traveling along the country road?" Participants who were asked this question were more likely to report having seen the nonexistent barn than participants who were not asked this question.

You might be wondering whether these sorts of laboratory analogues are appropriate for studying eyewitness accuracy. After all, a real traffic accident has sights and sounds that impress the event on our awareness. Wouldn't our memory be better in the real world? Some evidence supports this idea. A study in Vancou-

7.20 William Jackson (left) served five years in prison because he was wrongly convicted of a crime based on the testimony of two eyewitnesses. The real perpetrator is shown on the right. Do these two men look the same to you?

7.21 Elizabeth Loftus has shown that memory is highly suggestible.

source amnesia A type of amnesia that occurs when a person shows memory for an event but cannot remember where they encountered the information.

ver examined reports of those who had witnessed a fatal shooting (Yuille & Cutshall, 1986). All observers had been interviewed by the police within two days of the shooting. When the researchers went back months later, they found that eyewitness reports were highly stable, including memory for details. Indeed, it makes sense that true eyewitness accounts might be more vivid than those in the laboratory, given the memory modulation effect of stress hormones. However, the real world differs in a number of ways from a controlled laboratory setting, and it is not clear whether the stable memories are accurate. For instance, it could be that by retelling the story over and over again to friends, the eyewitnesses inadvertently developed stronger memories for inaccurate details.

Eyewitness confidence   How good are observers such as jurors at judging whether eyewitnesses are accurate? Gary Wells and his colleagues conducted a number of studies at the University of Alberta and later at Iowa State University, and their general finding was that people cannot differentiate eyewitnesses who are accurate from those who are inaccurate. The problem is that eyewitnesses who are wrong are just as confident, often more confident, than eyewitnesses who are right. Eyewitnesses who report vivid details of all aspects of the scene are probably less credible than those who have poor memory for trivial details. After all, eyewitnesses to real crimes tend to be focused on the weapons or on the action—they fail to pay attention to minor details. Thus, strong confidence for minor details may be a cue that the memory is more likely to be inaccurate or perhaps even false. However, some people are just particularly confident, and whether they are correct or incorrect, jurors find them convincing.

PEOPLE HAVE FALSE MEMORIES

Source amnesia occurs when a person shows memory for an event but cannot remember where they encountered the information. Think back to your earliest childhood memory. Most people cannot remember specific memories before three years of age. The absence of prior memories is known as *childhood amnesia*, and it may be due to an early lack of linguistic capacity as well as immature frontal lobes. But let's consider that first memory. How vivid is it? How do you know you are not remembering something you saw in a photograph, or a story related to you by family members? When people recall childhood events, the memories are often partial and hazy. How do you know if the memory is real?

Creating false recognition   There have recently been some powerful demonstrations that people can be misled to falsely recall or recognize events that did not happen. Read the following list of words, saying each one out loud: sour, candy, sugar, bitter, good, taste, tooth, nice, honey, soda, chocolate, heart, cake, tart, pie. Now put your book aside and try to write down as many of the words as possible.

Henry Roediger and Kathleen McDermott used this experiment to see whether they could create false memories among normal, healthy people (Roediger & McDermott, 1995). For instance, without looking back, which of the following words did you recall? Candy, honey, tooth, sweet, pie. If you recalled "sweet," then you have experienced a false memory. If you look back, you will see that "sweet" was not one of the original words, but note that all of the words are related to the word sweet. This basic paradigm is extremely reliable for producing false recollections.

Moreover, people are often extremely confident in their judgments of previously having seen or heard the critical word.

Mike Miller and George Wolford have recently argued that responses in the Roediger/McDermott task are due to change in the criteria by which people are willing to say they recognize the words, therefore representing a response bias rather than something that could be called a false memory (Miller & Wolford, 1999). They make the important point that errors are common in many memory tasks, and we should be careful before concluding that memory illusions are "false." After all, no one ever said that participants who misjudged made-up names as famous (in the false fame effect discussed earlier) were having a false memory. Nonetheless, there is a growing body of evidence that false memories can be implanted, such as the study described in "Studying the Mind: Lost in the Mall."

Confabulation   Some types of brain injury are associated with the false recollection of episodic memory, which is called **confabulation**. Morris Moscovitch has described confabulating as "honest lying" because there is no intent to deceive and the person is unaware of the falsehood of his or her story. Moscovitch (1995) provides an amazing example of confabulation. H.W. was a 61-year-old

confabulation   The false recollection of episodic memory.

Studying the Mind

LOST IN THE MALL

What if you were to find out that you had been lost in a shopping mall when you were a child? Think back to when you were five. Do you remember getting lost in a mall, and being found by a kind old man who returned you to your family? No? Well, what if your family told you about this incident, including how panicked your parents were when they couldn't find you? According to recent research by Elizabeth Loftus, you may well then remember the incident, even if it didn't happen.

In an initial study, a 14-year-old named Chris was told by his older brother Jim about the "lost in the mall" incident. The context was a game called "Remember when . . . , " and all of the other incidents provided by Jim were true. Two days later, Chris began reporting memories of how he felt during the episode; within two weeks he reported the following:

"I was with you guys for a second and I think I went over to look at the toy store, the Kay-bee toy and uh, we got lost and I was looking around and I thought, 'Uh-oh. I'm in trouble now.' You know. And then I . . . I thought I was never going to see my family again. I was really scared you know. And then this old man, I think he was wearing a blue flannel shirt, came up to me . . . he was kind of old. He was kind of bald on top . . . he had like a ring of gray hair . . . and he had glasses" (Loftus, 1993, p. 532).

You might wonder if Chris was especially gullible, but in a later study, Loftus and her colleagues used the same paradigm to assess whether they could implant false memories in 24 participants. Seven of the participants falsely remembered events that had been implanted by family members who were part of the study. Note that it is unlikely that false memories could be created for truly unusual events, such as receiving an enema (Pezdek & Hodge, 1999). However, a study by Saul Kassin and Katherine Kiechel (1996) found that people could even be induced to make false confessions for minor transgressions that they didn't actually commit. Moreover, it is well established that children are particularly suggestible, and that false memories, such as getting their fingers caught in mousetraps and having to go the hospital, can easily be induced in them. It appears that thinking about whether something happened, and imagining it happening, creates a false image for the event. Later, when thinking about the incident again, people have a source-monitoring problem. Did the event really happen or did they imagine it? For Chris, the memory of being lost in the mall became as real as other events from childhood.

man who was the biological father of four children, all of them now grown. H.W. experienced severe frontal lobe damage following a cerebral hemorrhage. Here is part of the clinical interview:

Q.   Are you married or single?
HW. Married.
Q.   How long have you been married?
HW. About four months.
Q.   How many children do you have?
HW. Four. (He laughs.) Not bad for four months!
Q.   How old are your children?
HW. The eldest is 32, his name is Bob, and the youngest is 22, his name is Joe.
Q.   How did you get those children in four months?
HW. They're adopted.
Q.   Does this all sound strange to you, what you are saying?
HW. (He laughs.) I think it is a little strange.

Patients such as H.W. confabulate for no apparent purpose. They simply recall mistaken facts, and when questioned they try to make sense of their recollections by adding facts that make the story more coherent. Recall from Chapter 4 Gazzaniga's theory of the interpreter and how split-brain patients confabulate to make sense out of discrepant information fed to each cerebral hemisphere. A dramatic example of confabulation occurs in *Capgras syndrome*, in which patients have the delusional belief that their family members have been replaced by impostors. No amount of evidence can convince them that their siblings, parents, spouses, and children are real. Patients with Capgras often have damage to the frontal lobes and limbic brain regions.

REPRESSED MEMORIES ARE CONTROVERSIAL

One of the most vitriolic debates over the past few decades has centered on repressed memories. On one side are some psychotherapists and patients who claim that long-repressed memories for traumatic events can resurface during therapy. Recovered memories of sexual abuse are the most common repressed memories reported, and in the early 1990s there was a rash of celebrity reports of early childhood sexual abuse.

On the other side are memory researchers, such as Elizabeth Loftus, who point out that there is little credible evidence indicating that recovered memories are genuine, or at least sufficiently accurate to be believable. Part of the problem is best summarized by leading memory researcher Daniel Schacter (Figure 7.22): "I know that some traumatic events can be associated with temporary forgetting and subsequent memory recovery. I am convinced that child abuse is a major problem in our society. I have no reason to question the memories of people who have always remembered their abuse, or who have spontaneously recalled previously forgotten abuse on their own. Yet I am deeply concerned by some of the suggestive techniques that have been recommended to recover repressed memories" (Schacter, 1996, p. 251).

Schacter alludes to the frightening possibility that false memories for traumatic events were implanted by well-meaning but misguided therapists. There is convincing evidence that methods such as hypnosis, age regression, and guided recall can implant false memories. Likewise, a growing body of evidence from carefully controlled laboratory studies has demonstrated that children can be induced to remember events that did not occur (Ceci & Bruck, 1995). Indeed, one of the seven sins of memory identified by Schacter is *suggestibility*, which is illustrated by illusory memories that occur when people incorporate information provided by others into their own recollections.

There have been a few infamous examples in which adults have accused their parents of abuse based on memories that they later realize were the products of therapy rather than reality. For instance, Diana Halbrook came to believe not only that she had been abused, but also that she had been involved in satanic ritualistic abuse and that she had herself killed a baby. When she expressed doubts to her therapist about the veracity of these events, the people in her "support" group and her therapist told her she was in denial and not listening to "the little girl" within. After all, all of the other members of the support group had recovered memories that they had been involved in satanic ritualistic abuse. After Diana left her therapy group she came to believe that she was neither abused nor a killer. It is interesting that so many people recover memories of satanic ritualistic abuse, since "though thousands of patients have 'remembered' ritual acts, not a single such case has ever been documented in the United States despite extensive investigative efforts by state and federal law enforcement" (Schacter, 1996, p. 269).

What is a reasonable person to conclude about repressed memories? The repressed-memory debate understandably involves strong and passionate beliefs on both sides. Research shows us that some therapeutic techniques seem especially likely to foster false memories, but it would be a mistake to simply dismiss all adult reports of early abuse. It is certainly possible that abuse occurs and is forgotten until some later period of time, and it is a disservice to actual victims of abuse to ignore their memories. It is interesting to note that in the latter half of the 1990s, the incidence of recovered memories fell dramatically. However, it is not clear whether this was because of less media attention on reports, or because people were less likely to seek therapy to uncover their past memories.

7.22 Daniel Schacter's research has provided numerous insights into the everyday sins of human memory.

PEOPLE RECONSTRUCT EVENTS TO BE CONSISTENT

The final example of memory distortion to consider is memory *bias*, in which people's memories for events are altered over time to be consistent with current beliefs or attitudes. One of psychology's greatest thinkers, Leon Festinger, when writing a tribute to his colleague Stanley Schachter, hit the nail on the head: "I prefer to rely on my memory. I have lived with that memory a long time, I am used to it, and if I have rearranged or distorted anything, surely that was done for my own benefit" (Festinger, 1987, p. 1).

Consider people who take study-skills courses. In spite of only modest evidence that such courses are beneficial, often because students fail to heed the advice they are given, most students who take them describe them as extremely helpful. How can something that often leads to only modest outcomes be so positively endorsed? To understand this, Michael Conway and Michael Ross randomly assigned students to a genuine study-skills course or to a control group that received no special training. Students who took the real course showed few signs of improvement; indeed their final-exam performance was slightly poorer than the control group's. Still they reported the study-skills program as helpful. Why? The experiment had one feature that allows us to understand what is going on. At the beginning of the course, participants were asked to rate their studying skills. At the end of the course they once again rated themselves *and* they were asked to recall how they had originally rated themselves. In describing their earlier ratings, students in the study-skills course recalled themselves as significantly worse than they actually had been at the beginning of the course, thereby "getting what they want by revising what they had "(Conway & Ross, 1984).

People tend to recall their past attitudes and beliefs as being consistent with their current attitudes and beliefs, often revising their memories when they have a change in attitude. People also tend to remember an event so that it casts them in a prominent or favorable light. We tend to exaggerate our contribution to group efforts, to take credit for success and blame failure on others, and to remember our successes more than our failures.

Not only individuals bias their recollection of past events; societies do so as well. The collective memory of groups can seriously distort the past, as expressed in the Orwellian idea that we can change only the past, not the future. Consider that the histories of most societies tend to downplay the unsavory, immoral, and even murderous behaviors of their pasts, and perpetrators' memories are generally shorter than victims'. Is there an objective reality? As Leon Festinger observed, we construct our memories for our own purposes. Our memory for events tends to be highly consistent with our personal beliefs.

How Are Memories Distorted?

Memory is far from a true and faithful recorder of objective facts and events. Rather, memory often includes a number of biases, distortions, and outright lies. People tend to make poor eyewitnesses because human memory is better for gist than for detail. Yet people maintain an unjustified confidence in their personal memories, such as flashbulb memories. Memories can be distorted or even implanted by false information, and there is a general bias toward maintaining consistency in our memories.

CONCLUSION

The brain is a wonderfully evolved instrument that has allowed humans to develop language, build civilizations, and visit the moon. However, we can't always remember where we left our keys, the faces of people whom we've witnessed commit crimes, whether Richard Shiffrin is famous, or details from a book we read last year. It needs to be emphasized that memory has evolved to solve certain problems related to survival, such as remembering our friends and foes. Memory did not evolve to remember phone numbers, textbook definitions, or how to drive a car, but it does a pretty good job at all of these things. Memory is a system that provides an organism with the ability to retain information and skills that are useful to survival. As such, it works pretty well, considering the amount of information that bombards the nervous system. Finally, as one of the most dynamic areas of research in psychological science, memory highlights our four fundamental themes, in particular the way that researchers are working at various levels of analysis to unwrap the mystery of the mind.

FURTHER READINGS

Bjork, E. L., & Bjork, R. A. (1996). *Memory.* San Diego, CA: Academic Press.

Eichenbaum, H. B., Cahil, L., Gluck, M., Hasselmo, M., Keil, F., Martin, A., et al. (1999). Learning and memory: Systems analysis. In M. J. Zigmond, F. E. Bloom, S. C. Landis, J. L. Roberts, & L. R. Squire (Eds.), *Fundamental neuroscience* (pp. 1455–1486). San Diego, CA: Academic Press.

Gazzaniga, M. S. (2000). *The new cognitive neurosciences* (2nd ed.). Cambridge, MA: MIT Press.

Neath, I. (1998). *Human memory: An introduction to research, data, and theory.* Pacific Grove, CA: Brooks-Cole.

Schacter, D. L. (1996). *Searching for memory: The brain, the mind, and the past.* New York: Basic Books.

Schacter, D. L. (2001). *The seven sins of memory: How the mind forgets and remembers.* Boston: Houghton Mifflin.

Squire, L. R., & Kandel, E. R. (1999). *Memory: From mind to molecules.* New York: Scientific American Library.

PUTTING COGNITIVE FUNCTIONS TO THE TEST

Over the decades, standardized tests, such as those given at the International Mathematical Olympiad, have been designed to measure intelligence. However, critics maintain that such tests cannot fully measure intelligence nor predict the abilities of a given individual. Most researchers now agree that intelligence is determined by a combination of genetics and environment, and cannot be understood without considering a person's cultural and social background.

TIMELINE

1600s
The Mind Is a Substance Frenchman René Descartes champions the philosophy of dualism, which develops the view that the mind and brain exist as two separate entities.

1884
Defining Intelligence Sir Francis Galton opens his Anthropometric Laboratory, where people can measure the sensitivity of their sensory systems, the property that Galton proposes is the basis for intelligence.

1890
The Need to Study Consciousness In *The Principles of Psychology*, William James argues that any complete account of the mind must consider the different states of consciousness commonly experienced by humans.

1905
Intelligence Quotient Alfred Binet and Théodore Simon develop the first intelligence test. They later develop the concept of intelligence quotient, or I.Q.

Cognition

OUTLINING THE PRINCIPLES

1931

Problem Solving Involves Insight Wolfgang Köhler reports that after long contemplation, an ape joined two sticks together in order to reach a banana, suggesting that problem solving in animals involves more than random trial and error.

1947

Decisions Are Rational John von Neumann and Oskar Morgenstern publish the seminal book *Theory of Games and Economic Behavior*, which presents the central ideas underlying early utility-based models of rational decision making.

1956

Decisions Are Less Than Optimal Nobel laureate Herbert Simon introduces the notion of *satisficing*, which suggests that human decision making is based on finding approximations to the statistically optimal solutions.

1972

Problems Have "Space" Allen Newell and Herbert Simon, both at Carnegie-Mellon University, publish *Human Problem Solving*, which establishes the idea that problems have a definable solution space.

1973

Mental Representation Through studies of how people mentally rotate objects, Roger Shepard demonstrates that people form mental images, or representations, of objects.

In his book *An Anthropologist on Mars* (1995), neurologist Oliver Sacks tells the story of one of his more remarkable patients, a man in his fifties named Virgil. When Virgil was five years old, he developed a severe case of cataracts, which rendered him blind. Virgil soon adapted to a life without vision, and as the years passed by, his childhood memories of what it had been like to see faded from awareness.

When Virgil was in his fifties, he fell in love and got married. As a wedding gift, Virgil's fiancée offered to pay for corneal transplant surgery to restore his vision. Apprehensive but hopeful, Virgil agreed to the operation.

One of the cataracts was removed, and a new lens was transplanted. A day later the bandages were removed, and for the first time in nearly 45 years, light fell unimpaired upon Virgil's retina. What did he see? How did he react? Sacks tells the story best:

> Virgil told me later that in this first moment he had no idea what he was seeing. There was light, there was movement, there was color, all mixed up, all meaningless, a blur. Then out of the blur came a voice that said, "Well?" Then, and only then, he said, did he finally realize that this chaos of light and shadow was a face—and, indeed, the face of his surgeon. (p. 114)

Virgil saw a kaleidoscope of color and light that had no connection with the world as he had known it. The sudden addition of "vision" felt confusing and awkward, and the joy that he and his wife had hoped for failed to materialize. As time went on, Virgil grew increasingly frustrated by his inability to adapt to this new aspect of his awareness. Only with the return of blindness due to other causes did Virgil find the peace he had had before the operation.

What went wrong? Why did Virgil fail to gain happiness from being able to see? Those who have vision have spent a lifetime learning how to use and understand visual information. We know that

RESEARCH QUESTIONS

for Studying Cognition

Do mental representations exist in different forms?

How do we solve problems?

To what extent is human decision making rational?

How do our decisions deviate from statistically optimal choices?

On what aspects of mind is intelligence based?

To what degree is intelligence influenced by our genes?

What are the elementary properties of consciousness?

How does the brain give rise to phenomenal awareness?

1979

Decisions Are Relative
Daniel Kahneman and Amos Tversky propose prospect theory, which models the tendency of decision makers (1) to use points of reference, and (2) to give more weight to potential losses than to potential gains.

1982

We Try to Avoid Regret
David Bell, Graham Loomes, and Robert Sugden independently propose that making decisions about uncertain events is based on anticipating possible regret regarding the different possibilities.

1983

Multiple Intelligence
Howard Gardner expands the traditional definition of intelligence to recognize that people can excel, or show intelligence, in different ways.

1990s

Evolved Decision Making
Gerd Gigerenzer argues that decision making is best understood by considering how humans have solved problems over the course of evolution.

2000

The Seat of General Intelligence Using brain imaging, researchers led by John Duncan report that "general intelligence" may be tied to the functioning of the frontal cortex.

looming objects are moving toward us and that shrinking objects are moving away, and that people's moods can be gleaned from their faces. Those with vision are so practiced at using it that seeing seems absolutely effortless and automatic.

If Virgil's difficulties stemmed from a lack of knowledge, what does it mean to have this knowledge? How do we represent it in our minds—and in our brains? Moreover, what would it be like to suddenly have an entirely new sensory experience enter our consciousness? This chapter explores such questions, first by considering the nature of mental representations. Building on this foundation, we then ask a series of questions: How do we represent and organize knowledge, and how do we use it in our thinking? Does intelligence stem only from our knowledge-based reasoning, or does it include a broader selection of mental capacities? Finally, what is consciousness? How does the brain give rise to the awareness of the world that we associate with being conscious?

HOW DOES THE MIND REPRESENT INFORMATION?

Cognitive psychology was originally predicated on the notion that the brain *represents* information, and that the act of thinking—that is, *cognition*—is directly associated with manipulating these representations. While these ideas were central to breaking the behaviorist zeitgeist that had dominated American psychology in the first half of the twentieth century, they immediately gave rise to an important new question: What is the nature of these representations? In the following section, we consider the different ways in which mental representations are characterized. The biological revolution has led to the development of new approaches that now allow us to study these representations empirically.

Over the last several decades, one of the more heated debates in cognitive psychology has been over the nature of mental representations: Are they like pictures, or are they based on more verbal-like descriptions? The topic is important because the representation of knowledge in the brain forms the basis of cognition, intelligence, and ultimately consciousness. As is often the case, the opposing views in this debate are not mutually exclusive.

REPRESENTATIONS CAN TAKE DIFFERENT FORMS

The popular view that mental representations are analogous to pictures holds much intuitive appeal in that, in our mind's eye, we often appear to *see* visual images. For instance, it is difficult to think about a "lemon" without having some sort of image come to mind that resembles an actual lemon, with its yellow and somewhat waxy, dimpled skin.

Not surprisingly, several lines of evidence strongly suggest that representations can indeed take on such picturelike qualities. First, in a famous set of

Do mental representations exist in different forms?

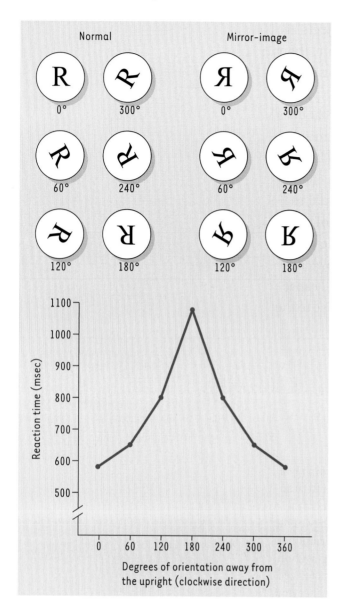

8.1 The time taken to determine whether the "R" is normal or a mirror-image increases with the amount of rotation away from the upright letter.

studies by Roger Shepard and colleagues in the early 1970s, participants were asked to view letters and numbers and to determine whether the given object was in its normal orientation or was a mirror image. The objects were presented in a variety of different rotated positions, such that sometimes the object was upright, sometimes it was upside down, and sometimes it was rotated somewhere in between (Figure 8.1). What Shepard and one of his colleagues found (Cooper & Shepard, 1973) was that the length of time subjects took to determine whether an object was normal or a mirror image depended on its degree of rotation—the further the object was rotated from the upright position, the longer the discrimination took, with the longest reaction time occurring when the object was fully upside down. From this evidence the researchers concluded that, in order to perform the task, participants mentally rotated representations or *pictures* of the objects in their heads in order to "view" the object in its upright position. Presumably, the further the object was from the upright, the longer the task took, because more "rotation" of the representation was required.

A series of related experiments was performed by Stephen Kosslyn and colleagues in the late 1970s (Kosslyn, Ball, & Reiser, 1978). In this case participants were required to scan mental images of maps that they had committed to memory. The maps (of fictitious islands) included a number of different landmarks such as towns, lakes, and mountains. Subjects were asked to visualize a landmark on the island, and then, following a brief interval, to imagine a dot moving from this landmark to a second landmark located elsewhere on the map (Figure 8.2). The results indicated that the time required to imagine the dot moving between landmarks increased proportionately with the actual distance between the landmarks, as measured on the map itself. Consistent with the earlier findings reported by Shepard's group, these data again suggested that people can represent information in a picturelike format.

Propositional representations Although the studies of both Shepard and Kosslyn have been taken as evidence for mental pictures, other researchers have argued that representations are *propositional* in nature. In other words, we are being deceived by our mind's eye. Although it may seem as if we can call up a picture of a lemon in our heads, the representation itself is not really a picture. Rather, it is based on the propositional knowledge that lemons (1) are yellow and (2) have dimpled, waxy skin. From this perspective, representations are based on factual knowledge about the world, and in contrast to the arguments of Shepard and Kosslyn, they have nothing to do with actual pictorial representations of the world itself (Figure 8.3).

The concept of propositional representations is closely linked to the notion of *semantic memory*, which is our memory for factual knowledge (see Chapter 7). As such, there is little argument against the idea that representations *can* be propositional. Instead, debate has centered around the question of whether *all* representations are propositional. Zenon Pylyshyn has argued that evidence in support of picturelike representations can be equally accounted for by propositional theories. In particular, Pylyshyn has stated that the results of the image-scanning experiments of Shepard and Kosslyn are ambiguous and inconclusive.

In a set of experiments addressing this issue, Pylyshyn (1984) found that if participants were asked to imagine shifting their gaze as quickly as possible between two points on an imaginary map instead of imagining a dot moving from one point to the next (as Kosslyn requested), then the distance effect reported by Kosslyn was eliminated. In other words, whether the two points were relatively close or relatively far apart, the time taken by the participants in Pylyshyn's study to "shift their gaze" remained constant. When we shift our gaze in the real world, although the movements are quick, the farther we shift our eyes the longer it takes. Pylyshyn's point was that Kosslyn's data remain open to question as to whether subjects really were using pictorial maps in their mind's eye.

One solution to this debate is that representations can be either picturelike *or* propositional. Developing this view, Phillip Johnson-Laird has suggested that knowledge rests on representations that exist at different hierarchical levels. For example, consider the difference between "machine" language and programming language in computers. Programming language is designed to be a higher-level, easily understood interface between the programmer and the computer, whereas machine language—the code actually used by the computer hardware—is a much lower-level (and unintelligible) platform. Johnson-Laird's main argument can be understood by positing that representations based on visual imagery are much like a higher-level programming language, while representations based on propositional knowledge are more similar to a lower-level machine language. In this sense, we can have representations that share many properties with our perceptual experiences, but that are derived from propositional-based knowledge residing in our memory systems (Figure 8.4). "Studying the Mind: Imagery and the Visual Cortex" presents a more recent, cognitive neuroscience approach to this issue, one that provides strong evidence that representations can indeed take on picturelike qualitites.

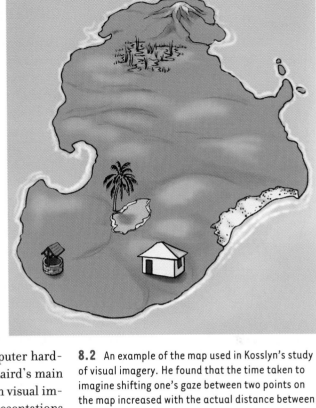

8.2 An example of the map used in Kosslyn's study of visual imagery. He found that the time taken to imagine shifting one's gaze between two points on the map increased with the actual distance between points.

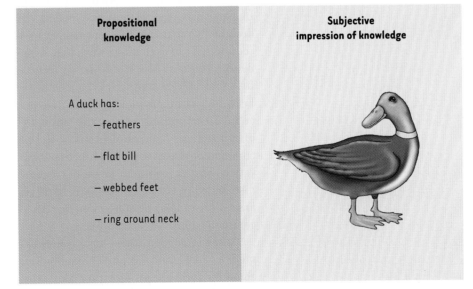

8.3 One theory of visual mental images is that they reflect one's propositional knowledge about how an object appears, rather than actually taking on the form of a picture.

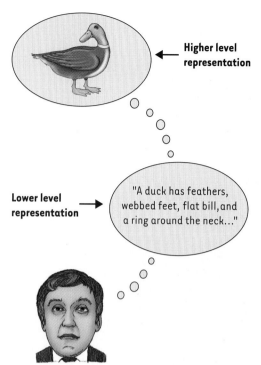

8.4 Johnson-Laird proposed that representations may have a hierarchical organization, thereby accounting for both propositional and pictorial models of mental representation.

8.5 Neural network models attempt to mimic how real neurons interact.

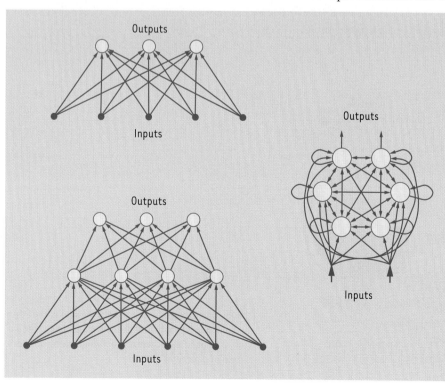

DISTRIBUTED REPRESENTATIONS FOCUS ON NEURAL IMPLEMENTATION

Thus far, our discussion of mental representations has focused on their form—imagery-based or propositional-based. However, another important question concerns how representations are actually implemented in the brain. That is, how does the brain code a representation?

The basic idea is that a representation will be manifest in the activity of a distributed network of neurons. Although the actual number of neurons hosting a representation in the brain is likely on the order of thousands of millions, a *distributed representation* can be understood by considering the behavior of just a few. For example, suppose that our mental representations of different fruits are dependent on the activity of three neurons, and further, that each of these three neurons has three different possible levels of activity (or firing rates): slow, medium, and fast. Given this context, different patterns of activity across these three neurons can be used to represent different fruits—a lemon could be represented when all three neurons are firing quickly, a peach when all three neurons are firing slowly, and a pear when the first neuron is firing slowly and the second and third are firing quickly. In this sense, the mental representation is in the relative pattern of activation across a network of neurons; different activation patterns signal different representations (Figure 8.5).

There are several distinct advantages to thinking about representations from the distributed perspective. First, the basic idea is closely tied to how information is likely represented within the brain, where no single neuron is alone responsible for a representation. If single neurons did in fact code information, we would all be in serious trouble whenever one of these neurons was killed off due to things such as aging and drinking. However, distributed representations allow for loss of neurons while still retaining the ability to represent information. Second, distributed representations can explain how a large but finite number of neurons can represent a potentially infinite number of items. Finally, distributed representations provide a framework for understanding how learning may take place at the neural level, as was discussed in Chapter 6. In particular, neural network models are designed so that the different neurons are "connected" to each other, such that if one neuron starts to fire, it will then affect the firing rate of any neuron it is connected to. Learning is implemented within these *connectionist networks* by varying the "strength" of connections between neurons, such that common or more frequent patterns of activation—that is, common or more frequent distributed representations—are likely to arise more quickly or more often than less-common patterns of activation.

More important, these neural network models make no implicit assumptions about the form a representation takes—that is, whether it's picturelike or propositional.

Studying the Mind

IMAGERY AND THE VISUAL CORTEX

The long-standing debate over whether visual imagery is based on pictorial or propositional representations has taken an interesting turn with the advent of cognitive neuroscience. Stephen Kosslyn, Martha Farah, and others have argued that if visual imagery is indeed based on representations that have picturelike qualities, then visual imagery is probably associated with activity in perception-related areas of the visual cortex. In particular, the initial processing areas in the visual cortex are organized in a topographic manner, such that adjacent groups of neurons have receptive fields in adjacent locations in visual space (see Chapter 4). If so, the argument goes, then these areas would likely be responsible for providing the spatial aspects of pictorial-based visual imagery.

To test this prediction, researchers have relied on functional neuroimaging methods, which reveal what areas of the brain are active during perceptual, cognitive, or motor tasks. In one study, Kosslyn and his colleagues (1995) asked participants to recall images of pictures they had just memorized, while manipulating the size of the visual image being recalled. Specifically, before each block of trials, the subjects were shown a square piece of cardboard that was either small, medium, or large. The task required subjects not only to recall a specific picture that had been memorized, but to recall it in a size that would just fit into the cardboard square. In this study, the prediction was that if visual imagery relies on topographically mapped visual cortex, then the locus of activity in these areas should vary as a function of the size of the recalled image. Consistent with this prediction, Kosslyn and colleagues found that the spatial extent of activation in the primary visual cortex, or area V1, did in fact increase with the size of the image in the mind's eye. These data fit nicely with the position that visual mental imagery is associated with pictorial-based representations.

Converging evidence for the existence of picturelike imagery has come from studies of brain-injury patients. In particular, Farah and her colleagues (1988) examined a patient with damage to the inferior temporal region of cortex, an area of the brain associated with processing the appearance of visual objects. While this damage impaired the patient's ability to recognize and describe visual objects, the patient's ability to locate objects remained intact. The goal of the study was to examine how such damage may have affected the patient's ability to visualize objects and the spatial relationships between them. The patient's tasks included calling up images of animals, common objects, and the shapes of various U.S. states in order to assess object imagery ability. The spatial imagery tasks included imagining object rotations and comparing the relative locations of imaged objects. What Farah and colleagues reported was that, in comparison to normal subjects, the patient was deficient in the object-related imagery tasks, but equal in the spatial-based tasks. As in the Kosslyn study, visual processing areas were implicated in imagery, a finding consistent with picturelike qualities in visual representations.

Given the abundant empirical support for picturelike visual imagery, the focus of debate in the imagery literature has now shifted away from the pictorial-propositional arena to a more empirically tractable question: Exactly what visual areas are activated when one is holding an image in mind? The problem has been that while some research groups—such as Kosslyn's—have reported activation of V1 during imagery, other research groups have not. The question remains of great interest to scientists because if imagery can be shown to activate this cortical region, it would indicate that even the earliest stage of visual processing in the cortex is subject to activation by visual-based memories. The deeper implication would be that areas of the brain traditionally viewed as subserving only sensory-based perception may be allied as well with higher-level cognitive functions. Toward addressing this new version of the "imagery debate," Kosslyn and Thompson (2000) have suggested that whether or not V1 is activated during imagery depends on the properties of the image itself—the more fine-grained detail the image contains, the more likely it is that activation will be observed in V1.

Regardless of whether or not V1 is involved in visual imagery, the results of these studies provide clear support for the position that mental representations can take on picturelike qualities. From a cognitive standpoint, this means that when we decide to retrieve information we have stored in memory, such as recalling a picture we recently saw in a newspaper, the representation of that picture in our mind's eye closely parallels the representation that was in our brain when we were actually observing the picture firsthand.

Indeed, network models do not necessarily require specification of knowledge at that high a level. Rather, they are primarily concerned with how neurons can code or distinguish between different pieces of information. The benefit is that representation in the brain can be studied in a manner that is similar to how the brain works at the individual-neuron level and without having to account for the complex question of the phenomenonological aspects of representation. The downside is that higher-level aspects of cognition remain outside the scope of the models—at least for now.

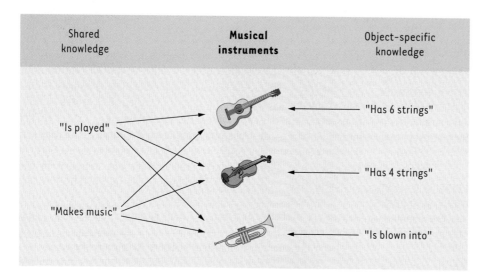

Shared knowledge	**Musical instruments**	Object-specific knowledge
"Is played"		"Has 6 strings"
"Makes music"		"Has 4 strings"
		"Is blown into"

8.6 Cognitive economy is based on the notion of sharing common concepts for different objects whenever possible.

CONCEPT-BASED MODELS ARE ABOUT CLASSIFYING THINGS

We now turn to another question regarding the representation of knowledge: How is it organized? The classic approach to understanding knowledge organization has been based on studying how we classify or group objects into categories. For example, most of us would likely consider baseballs and footballs to fall under the concept of "balls," and guitars and violins to fall under the concept of "musical instruments." It is believed that we do this to promote **cognitive economy,** in that grouping objects together based on shared properties reduces the amount of object knowledge we must hold in memory. For instance, if one understands the category "musical instruments"—something that is played and makes music—this gross definition can be automatically applied to all members of the group. As a result, we don't have to store this same bit of knowledge over and over for each musical instrument that we are aware of (Figure 8.6). However, unique knowledge must also be stored for each member of a group, such as "has six strings" for a guitar and "has four strings" for a violin.

Classification is based on attributes   The initial work of trying to understand how we classify things into groups was done in the early 1950s by Gottlob Frege, who proposed what is now known as the **defining attribute model** of object categorization (see Table 8.1). According to the model, each concept is defined by a list of the necessary attributes or *features* an object must have in order to be categorized under that concept. To be placed in a specific category, an object must have every attribute that is associated with the category in question. Moreover, the concepts are organized hierarchically, such that they can be superordinate or subordinate to each other. For example, a gerbil and a gorilla would both be classified under the concept of mammals (animals that are warm-blooded, have fur, and have mammary glands), but they would be placed in separate cate-

cognitive economy A tendency to group objects together based on shared properties, which reduces the amount of object knowledge we must hold in memory.

defining attribute model A model that defines concepts by the necessary features an object must have in order to be categorized under that concept.

prototype model A model whose premise is that within each category, some members are more representative than others of that category.

TABLE 8.1	Categorization of Memory
MODEL	**DESCRIPTION**
Defining Attribute	Objects are categorized based on whether or not they share common attributes. Based on the idea of cognitive economy, the model assumes that all members of a group are equal.
Prototype	As in the defining attribute model, objects are categorized based on whether or not they share common attributes. However, some category members—exemplars—are considered to be more representative of the category than others.
Script Theory	Knowledge is stored in relation to how we behave or operate within different real-world settings. That is, we have schemas or scripts for deciding what is appropriate in the given situation.

gories subordinate to "mammals," with the gerbil falling under the concept of "rodent" and the gorilla under the concept of "primate" (Figure 8.7).

Although Frege's model has much intuitive appeal, it fails to capture many key aspects of how we organize things in our heads. First, the model suggests that membership within a category is on an all-or-none basis, but in reality we often make exceptions in our categorizations, letting members into groups even if not all attributes are present. For instance, most of us would consider "has legs" as an attribute of the superordinate category "mammals," but most of us would also tend to consider "whales" and "dolphins" as members of the category "mammals." The defining attribute model proposes that we should not consider dolphins and whales to be mammals, or that having legs should not be an attribute associated with mammals. Second, the model posits that all attributes of a category are equally salient in terms of defining the given category. However, research has suggested that not only are some attributes more important for defining membership than others, but that the boundaries between categories are much more fuzzy and indistinct than the defining attribute model allows for.

8.7 A schematic diagram of the defining attribute model.

Categories have exemplars   To address the shortcomings of the defining attribute model, a more flexible—and natural—approach to object categorization has been developed in **prototype models.** The basic premise of this model is that within each category, some members of a particular category are more representative or *prototypical* of that category than other members (Figure 8.8). For example, a dog or a cat would be a more prototypical example of a mammal than, say, a manatee or a platypus. The benefit of recognizing our tendency to view categories as having prototypical exemplars is that it closely resembles how we tend to

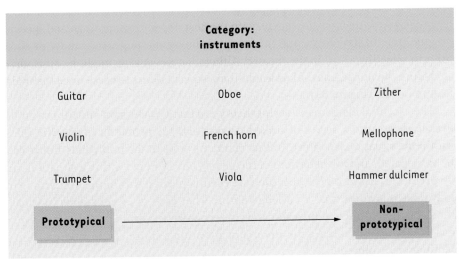

8.8 The prototype model suggests that some items within a group or class are more representative (or prototypical) of that group than other category members.

organize our knowledge of objects. It recognizes that not all members of a category will have the same attributes, meaning that whales and dolphins can remain in the "mammals" category even though they don't have legs. Moreover, prototype models allow the boundaries between categories to be indistinct. If an object contains a critical conjunction of attributes, it may be considered as a member of a certain category, even if its other attributes suggest that it may not be a perfect match. For instance, tomatoes are often classified as a vegetable (e.g., used in salads), even though their attributes are also consistent with the fruit category (e.g., have seeds, are sweet).

Prototype models are useful, but a problem remains: Object categorization is but one small portion of our knowledge base. In what ways are other forms of knowledge organized?

CONTEXTUAL MODELS ARE ABOUT INTERPRETING SCENES

Our discussion of knowledge and its organization has so far centered solely on understanding how we deal with simple concepts and objects. However, our knowledge of the world extends well beyond a simple list of facts about the specific items we encounter every day. Rather, a whole different class of knowledge enables us to interact with our environment. As we find ourselves in different real-world settings, we draw on a knowledge of what behaviors apply to the given setting in order to behave appropriately. For example, at a casino blackjack table it is appropriate to squeeze in between the people already sitting down. However, if a stranger tried to squeeze into a group of people dining together in a restaurant, the reaction of the group would likely be quite negative. Obviously, this kind of knowledge regarding situations and social context is much different from the knowledge associated with object classification.

The basic view of researchers in regard to contextual knowledge is that, over time, we develop *schemas* or *scripts* about the different types of real-life situations that we encounter. One of the more prominent theories in this domain has been Abelson and Schank's **script theory,** which proposes that we develop inferences about the sequences of events that arise in different situations, knowledge that allows us not only to make sense of the behaviors we observe, but also to know how to act appropriately in the situation. For example, "going to the movies" is a script that many people may have in common. First, one would expect to pay a fee to enter the movie, with the cost depending upon age and, possibly, the time of day. Next, one might opt to buy some popcorn, candy, or soda prior to selecting a seat in the theater. Although quiet talking might be appropriate before the movie, most of us would then expect talking to cease once the main feature begins (Figure 8.9).

The essential elements of script theory are that (1) common situations can be broken down into a series of linked events, and (2) people have specific roles within the situational context. In this manner events in the immediate future can be anticipated, and the behaviors of the people encountered within a situation can be predicted, based on the specific role each is playing within the scenario. Not only does this contextual knowledge define what each of us considers "normal" for a situation—which in turn allows us to recognize and avoid unusual or dangerous situations—but it eases the amount of attention required to negotiate within a familiar environment.

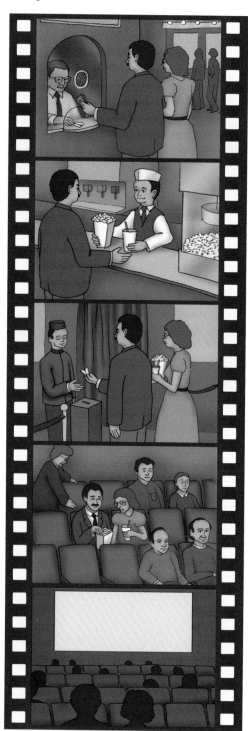

8.9 Script theory suggests that we tend to follow general scripts of how to behave in particular settings.

How Does the Mind Represent Information?

Cognitive psychology is founded on the position that the mind hosts mental representations of information. Some researchers believe that representations take the form of picturelike images and share a number of properties with visual perception. However, others have argued that representations are strictly propositional, in that they are based on factual knowledge of the world. The solution to this debate may be that representations exist on multiple levels, suggesting that both image-based and proposition-based representations can co-exist. In terms of neural implementation in cognition, researchers have described networks of interconnected neurons that signal representations via different patterns of activity across the network. In turn, the organization of knowledge is critically tied to both procedural and declarative memory. Our knowledge of objects is based on categorizing items by their attributes, which reduces the amount of information we need to store on a long-term basis (see Table 8.1). Likewise, our knowledge of situations is based on understanding how events typically unfold in specific scenarios, and the particular roles people play in them.

HOW DO WE SOLVE PROBLEMS AND MAKE DECISIONS?

We have discussed the manner in which knowledge of the world is represented and organized in the mind. We will now consider how knowledge is used to guide our problem solving and decision making. Again, the models discussed here capture some but not all of the critical elements of problem-solving and decision-making behavior (see Table 8.2 for a brief list of the various models we discuss). Although more complete models remain to be developed, exploring the work done so far provides an excellent window into understanding some of the most complex—and capricious—aspects of human cognition and the behaviors it engenders.

THE GESTALT MODEL EMPHASIZES INSIGHT AND STRUCTURE

Although the Gestalt school of psychology is typically associated with issues of visual perception, it has had an important impact on our understanding of human problem solving as well. Work in this domain traces back to the seminal experiments of Wolfgang Köhler in the early part of the twentieth century, who was studying problem solving in monkeys (briefly discussed in chapter 1). Köhler would place a banana out of reach outside the monkey's cage, while providing the monkey with several sticks that, if used properly, could be used to move the banana within grabbing distance. The classic finding reported in 1925 by Köhler was that one of the monkeys under study joined two sticks together in order to move the banana closer to its cage. Moreover, the monkey apparently performed this behavior after much contemplation. Although this finding has proven difficult to replicate, the example introduces two key aspects of human problem solving—*insight* and *problem structure*.

The flash of insight **Insight** is the stereotypical mental lightbulb going on in one's head, a metaphor that is used to capture the phenomenon of suddenly realizing the solution to a problem. In the case of the ape, Kohler argued that, after

How do we solve problems?

script theory People develop inferences about the sequences of events that arise in different situations, which allows them to react appropriately to a situation.

insight The sudden realization of a solution to a problem.

TABLE 8.2 Problem Solving and Decision Making

MODEL	DESCRIPTION
Gestalt	Problem solving requires insight into the nature and structure of a problem.
Information Processing	Problem solving can be broken down into a sequence of steps. In this sense a problem has a "solution space," and the goal is to move sequentially through this space in order to solve the problem.
Heuristic	Problem solving can have shortcuts that minimize the number of steps or the amount of information that must be considered in order to arrive at a solution.
Expected Utility Theory	A normative model in which decision making is based on computing which outcome will maximize personal utility.
Prospect Theory	A descriptive model in which decision making weights, perceived losses more heavily than perceived gains. That is, our aversion to loss is stronger than our desire for gain.
Regret Theory	A descriptive model in which decision making is based on anticipating the remorse or elation that will occur once a particular decision is made.

pondering the problem poised by the distant banana, the ape had eventually had the insight to conjoin the sticks in order to make a tool long enough to reach the banana. Building on the insight perspective, Maier (1931) brought participants, one at a time, into a room that had two strings hanging from the ceiling and a table in the corner. On the table were several random objects, including a pair of pliers. The task given to each participant was to tie the two strings together. However, it was impossible to grab both strings at once—if one string was being held, the other was too far away to grab as well. The solution to the problem was to tie the pliers onto one of the strings, so that the string could be used as a pendulum; one could then hold the nonpendulum string and then grab the pendulum string as it swung by. Although a few participants eventually settled on this solution without any assistance, the key manipulation Maier performed was to brush up against one of the strings after each subject had been pondering the problem for some time. Maier reported that once subjects saw the brushed string swinging back and forth, most immediately solved the problem, as if they had had new insight.

problem structure How people view or conceptualize a problem at hand.

solution space The many different paths to be considered in problem solving, taken collectively, define the space in which the solutions are most probable.

capacity limits The maximum amount of information and operations a system can perform.

The structure of problems Closely related to the concept of insight is the notion of **problem structure**, which concerns how one views or conceptualizes a problem. For example, Maier's "pendulum" experiment is premised on the expectation that most people will fail to see the pliers as a pendulum weight; that is, participants initially structure the problem so as to preclude a solution based on creating a pendulum. Insight into a problem arises when one suddenly *restructures* a problem in a novel way, providing a solution that was not available under the old problem structure. In one now-famous study, Scheerer (1963) gave participants a sheet of paper that had a square of nine dots on it (Figure 8.10). The task was to connect all the dots using only four straight lines, without lifting the pencil off the page. As shown in Figure 8.10, the solution is relatively easy—if one structures the problem such that it is okay to draw the lines beyond the box formed by the dots. The difficulty most people have when first encountering this task is that the problem is structured such that only solutions that keep all lines within the square are considered.

The Gestalt school says that people tend to view problems from narrow perspectives. If our initial perception of the problem allows for a viable solution, then there is no need for insight or restructuring. However, the principles discussed here become important whenever we are faced with a problem that has no immediate solution. If our current view isn't working, are there other, less-obvious ways in which to structure the problem? Although terms such as "thinking out of the box" and "think different[ly]" have become recent clichés in our culture, the ideas they embody have been around for a long time and continue to be of great value.

THE INFORMATION-PROCESSING MODEL IS BASED ON A SOLUTION SPACE

While the Gestalt approach to problem solving centers around understanding the global structure of a problem—and the benefits that can be gained by viewing problems from new perspectives—an alternative view has focused instead on studying the sequential steps people take toward finding a solution to a problem. The idea is that most problems have a number of different paths one can take toward finding an appropriate solution, which, when taken collectively, define the **solution space** of the problem. In turn, each path can be broken down into a series of stages or steps. Researchers focus on understanding how people go from one step to the next, the typical errors people make when tricky or unintuitive steps must be negotiated, and how people converge on more efficient—or, in some cases, less efficient—solution paths with problem-solving experience.

For example, in the classic "Tower of Hanoi" problem, participants are given a board that has a row of three pegs on it, with the peg on one end having three discs stacked on it in a descending order of size, such that the largest disc is on the bottom (Figure 8.11). The task is to move the ordered stack of discs to the peg on the other end, with the following restraints: only one disc can be moved at a time, and a larger disc can never be placed on top of a smaller disc. The reason people have been interested in studying this problem (which can be made more complex by adding more discs and pegs) is that it has well-defined *knowledge states* and *operators*, which describe respectively the different steps and the "legal" moves that can be done to move from step to step in the solution space. In turn, this makes it relatively easy to examine how people approach the task and how they navigate through the solution space.

In many ways the information-processing approach to problem solving has strong analogies to computer programs, which transform an input into an output by going through a series of explicit operations. However, it is clear that human problem solving is not the biological equivalent of an efficient computer program. For one, humans have much lower **capacity limits**, which describe the maximum amount of information and operations a system can handle. Humans can do only so much at once. If we are driving and the traffic gets too heavy, we

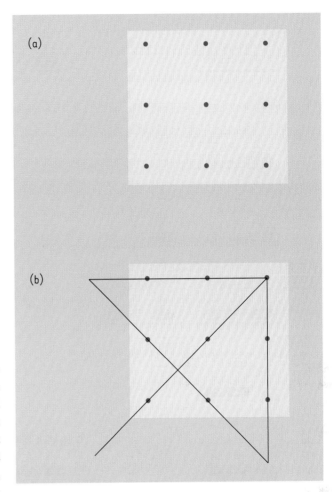

8.10 Scheerer's (1963) nine-dot problem (a) is solved by realizing that the lines can extend beyond the boundary formed by the dots (b).

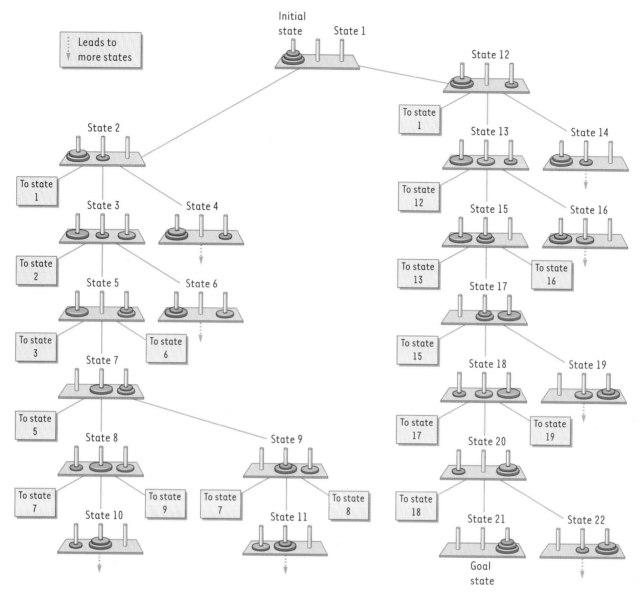

8.11 Solving the Tower of Hanoi problem can be broken down into basic states and the operations that allow transitions between states.

often turn the music down because we need to devote a greater proportion of our "mind" to the task at hand.

One way in which we may deal with these capacity limits is by using **heuristics** in our problem solving, which are essentially shortcuts that minimize the amount of thinking necessary to move from step to step in a solution space. Using an example made popular by Gerd Gigerenzer, How do baseball players know where to run in order to catch a fly ball? A computer-based approach to this problem would likely require a consideration of pitch and bat velocity, wind speeds, ball mass, and the like, information that is of little use to the capacity-limited outfielder who has only a few seconds in which to catch the ball. Rather, as Gigerenzer has argued, if the fielder simply looks up at the ball and keeps his or her direction of gaze at a constant angle between the ball and the ground while running—speeding up or slowing down to keep the angle constant—this should direct the fielder to the approximate location at which the ball will arrive. In this manner, the fielder can literally achieve the solution to the problem on the run, with no dependency on lengthy and time-consuming physics-based computations.

NORMATIVE THEORIES FOCUS ON RATIONAL BEHAVIOR

So far, we have been discussing different approaches to the question of how humans solve problems. We now turn to the related topic of decision making, in which there is a distinction between normative and descriptive theories. Historically speaking, **normative models** of decision making have viewed humans as optimal decision makers, while more recent **descriptive models** have tried to better account for the tendencies humans have to misinterpret and misrepresent the probabilities underlying many decision-making scenarios.

To what extent is human decision making rational?

The goal of normative theories is to describe the decisions people would make if they were to follow the rules of rational, probability-based decision making. If the probabilities associated with a given situation are properly computed, then decisions are based on which option has the highest probability of producing the preferred outcome. For example, if your grandmother is a gambler *and* a rational decision maker in the normative sense, she should always choose to play craps instead of roulette when heading to the casinos, because the odds of winning at craps are more favorable than the odds of winning at roulette. While the shortcomings of normative models are clear—for example, grandma may often choose to play roulette instead of craps because she finds the former is more fun to play or because she is simply an irrational decision maker—they provided the essential foundation from which the contemporary study of human decision making grew.

Expected utility theory describes the optimal decision maker In 1947, John von Neumann and Oskar Morgenstern presented a model of how humans should make decisions if they were to follow pure reason—a model known as **expected utility theory**. The theory breaks down decision making into a computation of utility for each possible outcome in a decision-making scenario, which can be summarized by a set of five basic principles. First, decisions can be condensed to a consideration of possible alternatives, and in turn, the alternatives can be ranked in terms of preferences. Known as the *ordering of alternatives*, each alternative is either more desirable, less desirable, or equally desirable compared to each competing alternative. Second, according to the principle of *dominance*, the rational decision maker will always choose the most desirable—or dominant—alternative, even if the differences between alternatives are small. Third, based on the principle of *cancellation*, decisions between alternatives are based on the differences between them; factors common to both alternatives are ignored, or "cancel out," in the decision process. Fourth, the notion of *transitivity* dictates that if decision B is preferred to decision A, and decision A is preferred to decision C, then decision B will be preferred to decision C (Figure 8.12). Finally, if the outcomes of two different alternatives are equivalent, then the principle of *invariance* indicates that the decision will be invariant to the means by which the outcomes are achieved.

The value of expected utility theory is that it was able to generate testable ideas concerning how humans make decisions. Based on initial experiments, several important adaptations to the theory were soon made. First, it was proposed that preferences for decisions, or the ordering of alternatives, are subject to variability across time. For example, one evening someone may prefer to watch reruns of *The Simpsons* rather than reruns of *The Brady Bunch*, while on the following evening the preference may be reversed. Such variability is still within the bounds of rationality, in that rational decision makers can be expected to have their preferences

heuristics In problem solving, shortcuts that are used to minimize the amount of thinking that must be done when moving from step to step in a solution space.

normative model A model of decision making that views people as rational and optimal decision makers.

descriptive model A model of decision making that accounts for tendencies to misinterpret and misrepresent probabilities underlying many decisions.

expected utility theory A model of how humans should make decisions if they were to follow pure reason in their decision making.

8.12 Expected utility theory is premised on the notion that transitivity applies to all our decision making. In this case if pizza is preferred over hamburgers, and hamburgers are preferred over chicken, then pizza will be preferred over chicken.

change with experience and time. Second, it was suggested that rational decisions are made based not only on **objective probabilities**, or the statistical probabilities that can be computed for a given alternative, but also on **subjective probabilities**. In other words, decisions are often based on a person's subjective impression of probabilities, which may or may not coincide with the true objective probabilities. However, the decision continues to be rational, even though the subjective probabilities underlying the decision may be incorrect.

Bayes' theorem tells us how to update base rates   As expected utility theory suggests, rational decision making in the normative sense demands that we compute the probability of different decision outcomes based on the frequency with which the outcomes have occurred in the past. For example, if a student is living in a dorm and has a friend coming to visit, should the friend be encouraged to park illegally in the dorm parking lot? The answer depends on the frequency with which illegal parking results in having the car towed or getting a ticket. The predicted frequency of an event occurring is known as a **base rate**, and in this example, the decision whether to encourage the friend to park illegally depends on the perceived base rate of a negative outcome; the smaller the predicted base rate of a citation or towing, the more likely it is that the decision will be made to park the car illegally.

As decision makers, humans are fairly accurate at computing the base rates for various events (although we may often ignore base rate information, as will be discussed below). However, we are less proficient at changing our perception of base rates as new information arises. **Bayes' theorem** is a formula used to update the probability of an event, given new information that supplements the preexisting base rate. In the parking example, how should the base rate change if an illegally parked car is towed? The importance of Bayes theorem is that it reveals that humans tend to *underestimate* the impact of new information on updating base rates. That is, if a car is towed, we will tend to maintain a lower base rate for such events happening again than what is predicted statistically. The ideas here closely parallel facets of prejudice toward ethnic and social groups, as it is often easier to see evidence supporting one's beliefs than evidence inconsistent with one's beliefs, a topic we will cover in a later chapter.

objective probabilities In decision making, the statistical probabilities that can be computed for a given alternative.

subjective probabilities In decision making, the personal impression of probabilities, which may or may not coincide with the true objective probabilities.

base rate The predicted frequency of an event occurring.

Bayes' theorem A formula that is used to update the probability of a given event, given new information that supplements the preexisting base rate associated with the event in question.

To better account for biases in human decision making and probability estimations, researchers began to move away from pure probability-based models, developing models that more closely describe the actual idiosyncrasies of human decision making.

DESCRIPTIVE THEORIES DEVELOP THE PSYCHOLOGY OF DECISION MAKING

Whereas normative theories of decision making focus on trying to understand how rational decisions are made, *descriptive theories* of decision making focus on trying to understand how humans actually make decisions in everyday practice—decisions that often fail to comply with the predictions of "rational" behavior. In "Using Psychological Science: An Evolutionary View of Decision Making," we consider two of the alternative theories that have been proposed to account for common decision-making practices.

Losses weigh more heavily than gains In the late 1970s, Daniel Kahneman and Amos Tversky published a paper developing their insight that decision making can be viewed as a calculation of costs and benefits, a model known as **prospect theory**. The importance of moving away from the notion of decision utility is that prospect theory implies that decisions have a reference point from which costs and benefits can be calculated. For example, the decision whether or not to buy a lottery ticket can be viewed as either a potential cost (the price of the ticket) or a potential benefit (winning the lottery). Prospect theory suggests that we tend to estimate the prospects of costs and benefits differently, so that the concern over costs typically has a larger impact on decisions than the hope for potential benefits. This unequal weighting of costs and benefits is known as **loss aversion**. A schematic illustration of this concept is shown in Figure 8.13.

This tendency to view costs and benefits from a differential perspective is exploited by companies that offer people the opportunity to test products on a trial basis before purchasing. These companies are banking on the probability that once their product is being used, the "cost" of giving it up at the end of the trial period will appear to be greater than the cost of actually purchasing it. In this manner, the company has successfully changed the reference point from which the decision to purchase the product has been made—a cost that originally might have been viewed only in terms of dollars has now been juxtaposed with a cost viewed in terms of losing access to the product. If the latter is perceived as the greater cost, people will end up making a purchase they might not have made if only the cost in dollars had been considered.

Decisions involve playing out hypothetical events Another facet of decision making is that we often imagine the different outcomes of a decision, a tendency known as **counterfactual reasoning**. For example, suppose a student has an opportunity to see an up-and-coming band play in a local bar, but the $10 cover charge will use up all the money the student has for the rest of the week. In deciding whether to attend the concert or not, the student will likely consider the different possible outcomes. On the one hand, if the student goes to the concert then not only may a good time be had, but, should the

prospect theory The idea that decision making can be viewed as a calculation of costs and benefits.

loss aversion An unequal weighting of costs and benefits such that potential costs weigh more heavily than potential benefits.

counterfactual reasoning In decision making, a consideration of different hypothetical outcomes for events or decisions.

How do our decisions deviate from statistically optimal choices?

8.13 The critical apect of this figure is that with decision "value" plotted on the vertical axis, potential losses have a bigger impact on perceived value (making it drop more slowly). That is, the potential loss of $500 has a greater effect on our decision making than a potential gain of $500.

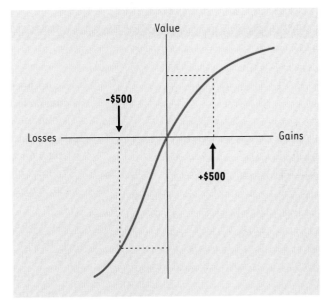

Using Psychological Science

AN EVOLUTIONARY VIEW OF DECISION MAKING

Can human decision making be better understood by considering the ecology in which we evolved? Gerd Gigerenzer and Daniel Goldstein (1996) believe that it can. The classic view of human decision making is premised on the notion that decisions are based upon a multitude of data and follow from intensive calculations concerning objective probabilities and subjective utilities. However, Gigerenzer and Goldstein argue that this classic view fails to capture the ecological reality of most human decisions.

The main premise of their argument stems from the earlier work of Herbert Simon, who proposed that instead of optimizing in our decision making, we actually *satisfice*—a word that combines "satisfy" and "suffice" to convey the idea that we typically choose the first alternative that sufficiently satisfies our needs. For example, in choosing what college or university to apply to, a person certainly doesn't need to consider in detail every available school in the country. Rather, once a sufficient number of schools have been identified, the search can stop and applications can be sent. According to Gigerenzer and Goldstein, we satisfice because we have limited knowledge, time, and mental prowess with which to make most—if not all—of our decisions.

In this sense, decision making is directly constrained by the ecological realities that (1) we rarely if ever have full factual knowledge concerning our decisions; (2) we are usually under strict time constraints when making decisions; and (3) although human brains are remarkable information-processing systems, our computational power to consider available information is far below what the classic view of decision making would suggest; that is, we are capacity limited.

To test their ideas, Gigerenzer and Goldstein used computer modeling to compare decision-making algorithms that were consistent with either normative or "satisficing" models. Both types of algorithms had to decide which of two German cities had a larger population, given a host of variables about each city, such as whether it had a soccer team, a university, a subway, etc. The satis-

ficing model was based on one-reason decision making, in which decisions are based on a consideration of only a single factor. In this manner, a decision can be made with only a small amount of information, which requires less time and relatively little computational ability in comparison to normative models, which would consider all available data. The one-reason decision making was implemented by Gigerenzer and Goldstein in several different variants. For example, a "take the best" algorithm ranked the different variables about each city in order of how well the single variable might reflect the actual population, with the decision about the population then being based solely on the variable ranked the highest, or "best." In comparison, the different algorithms used to model the "classic" view of decision making were allowed to consider all available information and were given a significantly longer amount of time in which to make calculations based on this information.

Interestingly, the "take the best" algorithm matched or outperformed all of the normative-based algorithms, in both the accuracy and the speed of the decisions made. Moreover, several other variations of the one-reason decision making that relied on even less information showed only a small drop in accuracy. Gigerenzer and Goldstein point out that not only do these results indicate that accurate decision making can be made under ecologically valid conditions, but that considerable behavioral evidence suggests humans often do make decisions based on single reasons. Of even greater interest here is that we may continue to gain new insight into human cognition by considering how the environments in which we have evolved have shaped how we think and reason.

However, this doesn't mean that models based on satisficing will win out over normative models in all situations. Decision making is a highly variable process, and we should expect humans to have a number of different strategies. Which one is best will ultimately depend on the nature or context of the particular situation—an adaptive cognitive strategy indeed.

band become very popular, the student could brag about having seen them in a small club. Although these may be positive outcomes, the student would also have no money left to go out with his or her friends later in the week.

Counterfactual reasoning allows us to anticipate how we might feel after making a decision, a concept that forms the core of *regret theory*. According to regret theory, our desire to experience elation and avoid remorse plays a critical role in our decision making. People use counterfactual reasoning to gauge how a decision may feel, basing the actual decision on which imagined outcome produced the greatest elation and least regret. For example, when game-show contestants have to decide whether to keep the winnings they have already earned and quit, or risk losing all in the hopes of gaining an even bigger prize, many will choose to "quit while they're ahead," for fear of experiencing the inevitable regret that would result if they failed to win the bigger prize and ended up with nothing.

How Do We Solve Problems and Make Decisions?

Solving problems can be viewed from several different approaches (see Table 8.2). From a Gestalt perspective, problems have structure, and insight can be gained by restructuring how a problem is understood. From an information-processing perspective, problems can be discussed in relation to a solution space, which describes the different pathways that can be taken toward achieving a solution. Normative theories of decision making suggest that we should act in an "optimal" fashion, based on the most likely outcomes of different decisions. However, we often make errors in our probability estimations, difficulties that are addressed by descriptive theories. As theories of decision making have moved away from normative-based approaches, there has been greater consideration of the feelings—such as regret—that we anticipate a decision may generate.

WHAT DOES INTELLIGENCE REFLECT?

So far, we have considered the manner in which knowledge is represented in the mind and how we use this knowledge to solve problems and make decisions. One of the most hotly debated topics in psychological science concerns how knowledge and its application in everyday life translates into individual intelligence, and the relative degree to which "intelligence" is determined by our genes and our environment. As we will see, **intelligence** is a difficult concept to define, as it can take a number of different forms, but most definitions agree that (1) humans have a range of different abilities, and (2) intelligence can be equated with how a person measures on a particular ability scale. In this section, we first discuss the historical perspective underlying the contemporary idea that human intelligence is context—and culture—dependent. We then turn to several different theories that attempt to explain how intelligence can be described in a context-independent manner. With this background in place, we conclude with an evaluation of the "nature versus nurture" debate over intelligence and its determinants.

> **intelligence** An attribute used to describe a person that is based on the assumptions that (1) a person has a range of different abilities and (2) intelligence can be equated with how a person measures up on a particular ability scale, as valued by a culture.

8.14 Alfred Binet, grandfather of the IQ—and all its problems.

DEFINITIONS AND MEASURES DEPEND ON CONTEXT

The central theme running through the history of scientific research on intelligence has been a quest to define it. The earliest efforts to study intelligence were led by Sir Francis Galton in the late 1800s and were premised on operational definitions that linked intelligence to the speed of neural responses and the sensitivity or *acuity* of sensory/perceptual systems—the quicker our responses and the more acute our perceptions, the smarter Galton believed us to be. Although, as we will see, such factors may underlie aspects of what might be called "intelligence," Alfred Binet (Figure 8.14) soon developed in France a more practical measure of intelligence based on an entirely different definition than Galton's.

Binet proposed that intelligence is best understood as a collection of high-level mental processes—in today's terms, things such as "verbal," "mathematical," and "analytical" abilities. Binet had been commissioned by the French Ministry of Education to identify children in the French school system who needed extra attention and instruction, so he developed a test for measuring children's vocabulary, memory, skill with numbers, and the like—the *Binet-Simon Intelligence Scale*.

mental age A prediction of how advanced or behind a child is relative to peers of the same age, as determined by a comparison of the child's test score against the average score for children of each chronological age.

intelligence quotient The number computed by dividing a child's estimated mental age by the child's chronological age, and then multiplying this number by 100.

The classic view of intelligence The legacy of the Binet scale is twofold. First, it introduced the concept of **mental age**, which is a prediction of how advanced—or behind—a child is relative to peers of the same age. Mental age is determined by comparing a given child's test score with the average score for children of each chronological age. For example, an 8-year-old who reads Shakespeare and performs calculus might score as well as the average 16-year-old, thus giving the 8-year-old a mental age of 16. The infamous **intelligence quotient** or **IQ** is computed by dividing a child's estimated mental age by the child's chronological age and then multiplying this number by 100:

$$\frac{\text{Mental age}}{\text{Chronological}} \times 100 = \text{IQ.}$$

For our child prodigy, this would mean an IQ of 200!

The second legacy of the Binet-Simon Intelligence Scale, along with its later revision known as the *Stanford-Binet Scale*, is that it established the long-held assumption in Western society that intelligence is defined by one's performance on these types of tests. More specifically, tests such as the Stanford-Binet Scale focus on verbal and reasoning skills, posing problems not unlike those discussed earlier in this chapter, such as the Tower of Hanoi and the nine-dot problem. The benefit of defining intelligence in this manner is that tests based on verbal and reasoning abilities are good predictors of academic achievement in children and young adults. Indeed, scores from standardized tests such as the SAT and GRE continue to be used for making admissions decisions in most U.S. colleges and universities. Not surprisingly then, the popular bias in Western culture has been that those of us who perform well on such tests are "intelligent" and those of us who don't perform so well are fated to the "less-intelligent" category.

The limits of the classic view The difficulty with defining intelligence in relation to IQ is that the tests used to estimate IQ are highly context-dependent. What do we mean by this? Suppose a question on an intelligence test concerns two trains—how fast each is traveling and in what direction. Independent of whether or not one is "intelligent," a student who has been exposed to these kinds of questions in school prior to the exam will likely perform much better than a student who hasn't. If so, is the latter student really less intelligent than the former, or do their performance differences simply reflect dissimilar experiences?

Such questions become more complex when one considers the inherent differences between cultures, not only in terms of the schooling students receive, but in the kinds of mental skills that are considered to define "intelligence." In short, although an IQ may continue to be a good predictor of how someone may perform in a U.S. school, whether or not an IQ is a fair measure for comparing two individuals depends on how comparable their backgrounds may be—in terms of things such as culture, education, and socioeconomic class. The problem then isn't that IQ tests are somehow flawed in their design and application. Rather, it is a flawed and narrow view to believe that IQ tests are measuring the gamut of human intellectual capacities.

INTELLIGENCE HAS A MODULAR STRUCTURE

If IQ represents a biased measure of intelligence, what alternatives do we have for gauging and comparing intellectual capacities among people? Perhaps the most fruitful alternative has been to posit that the mental properties underlying intelligence are inherently modular in nature, and that they can be separated into different systems. The roots of the modular view can be found in neuropsychology, in which it has long been known that people can have very specific specialized mental abilities. For example, **savants** are people who develop minimal intellectual capacities in most domains, but who at a very early age show an exceptional ability in some sort of "intelligent" process, such as math, music, or art. The talents of savants can be quite striking. Oliver Sacks (1995) recounts the story of an artistic savant named Stephen, who could reproduce highly accurate drawings of buildings and places years after having only glanced at them (Figure 8.15). Further, his drawings were so remarkable that by the time he was a young teenager, he had a book of his artwork published.

8.15 The artistic savant Stephen Wiltshire.

However, Stephen was *autistic* (see Chapter 16), and it was only with the utmost effort that he was able to acquire language sufficient even for the simplest verbal communication.

The fact that people can be highly proficient in some domains yet terribly inadequate in others lends strong support to the view that intelligence needs to be considered in relation to a host of different capabilities—not just those used to assess IQ. Moreover, to minimize inherent biases, an intelligence measure needs to focus on aspects of intellect that are independent of cultural background and schooling. Below we consider two different models of intelligence that are aimed at addressing these issues—and both are premised on the notion that intelligence can be viewed in relation to dissociable mental qualities.

Intelligence as two factors   Raymond Cattell (1971) proposed that intelligence can be divided into two factors that he labeled fluid intelligence and crystallized intelligence. **Fluid intelligence** is associated with the ability to understand relationships between things in the absence of overt experience or practice with them. For example, consider the following verbal analogy question:

STRING is to GUITAR as REED is to (a) TRUMPET, (b) OBOE, (c) VIOLIN, or (d) TROMBONE?

Without specific knowledge of these different instruments, and in particular an oboe (which would be the correct answer), one would only be able to guess at the correct answer. Cattell argued that fluid intelligence is best measured using items that either (1) no one or (2) everyone has experienced before. In this regard, a better verbal analogy question might be the following (from Horn, 1985):

SOON is to NEVER as NEAR is to (a) NOT FAR, (b) SELDOM, (c) NOWHERE, or (d) WIDELY?

In this case, the assumption is that all adults would understand the meanings of these words (if translated into the appropriate language). As a result, performance on this question can be attributed to the ability to understand the relations between the words. (The correct answer is "c.")

savants People who have minimal intellectual capacities in most domains, but show an exceptional ability in another "intelligent" process, such as math, music, or art.

fluid intelligence The ability to understand relationships between items in the absence of overt experience or practice with the items in question.

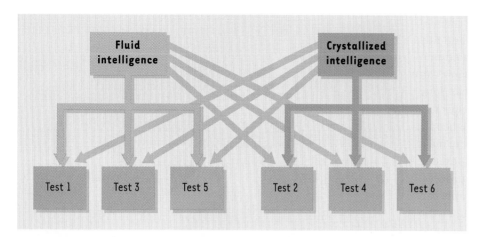

8.16 Cattell hypothesized that we have both crystallized and fluid intelligences.

In contrast, **crystallized intelligence** concerns knowledge that is acquired through experience, on the assumption that people who learn from their experiences are showing a mental capacity that is absent in those who fail to learn from experience. For example, while some people may stop speeding once they get a speeding ticket, others will continue to speed and get more tickets. More important, however, crystallized intelligence makes no distinction regarding what kinds of things are learned, and in this regard, Cattell's model of intelligence can be used to gauge mental abilities independent of context or culture.

Although studies have supported Cattell's distinction between fluid and crystallized intelligence, there has also been consistent evidence of a positive correlation between the two. That is, people who score high on one factor also score high on the other. Not surprisingly, such evidence suggests that a strong crystallized intelligence is likely aided by a strong fluid intelligence (Figure 8.16).

Intelligence as multiple factors Although Cattell's model of intelligence provides a way of accounting for cultural and contextual differences among people, it maintains an emphasis on standard problem-solving questions similar to those in traditional IQ tests. In an attempt to broaden the scope of the debate, Howard Gardner (1983) proposed his **theory of multiple intelligences**, which strives to include practical definitions of what constitutes "intelligence." In particular, Gardner identified seven so-called intelligences: musical, verbal, mathematical/logical, spatial, kinesthetic (or body control), intrapersonal (or self-understanding), and interpersonal (or social understanding) (Figure 8.17). In proposing such a wide range of factors, Gardner's model clearly expands on the traditional IQ model in several important ways.

First, the theory of multiple intelligences recognizes that people can be deficient in some aspects of intelligence and outstanding in others. For example, a person might score low on measures of verbal and mathematical abilities but may nevertheless have high degrees of social and musical skills and be able to perform quite competently in jobs that emphasize these stronger abilities. Second, the theory is consistent with the evidence from neuropsychology—such as studies of savants—suggesting that different mental capacities rely on different underlying neural systems. Third, the theory supports the view that intelligence needs to be defined in relation to many different mental capabilities, and in so doing it provides a framework flexible enough to account for the myriad of differences between cultures and socioeconomic classes in what is valued "intellectually".

GENES AND ENVIRONMENT BOTH INFLUENCE INTELLIGENCE

We conclude this section by addressing what has been perhaps the most heated debate in the psychological sciences over the last several decades: Is intelligence determined by genes or environment? The question has been contentious be-

crystallized intelligence Knowledge that is acquired through experience, on the assumption that people who learn from their experiences are showing a mental capacity that is absent in those who fail to learn from experience.

theory of multiple intelligences A theory that attempts to provide practical definitions of intelligence, including musical, verbal, mathematical/logical, spatial, kinesthetic (or body control), intrapersonal (or self-understanding), and interpersonal (or social understanding).

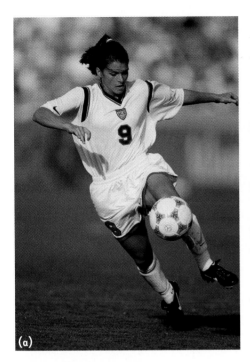

8.17 Gardner suggested that intelligence can take many different forms. Here four different types of intelligence are represented by (a) athlete Mia Hamm, (b) musician Yo Yo Ma, (c) scientist Shirley Jackson, and (d) artist Diego Rivera.

cause the potential implications are dramatic. If genes are the primary factor, does this mean that some people are "biologically smarter" than others, and that the pursuit of education is pointless for "less smart" people? If environment is the primary factor, why aren't we doing more to ensure equal access to quality education for people of all cultures and socioeconomic classes?

Research into this *nature versus nurture* debate has spawned a wealth of fascinating data comparing the intelligence of people with the same genetic makeup—that is, identical twins—who were reared in the same or different households. The idea of these so-called heritability studies is that if identical twins are separated at birth and raised in different families but still correlate highly on intelligence, then it would provide strong evidence that, for the most part, genes are the primary determinant of intelligence (Figure 8.18). In contrast, a related approach has been to compare unrelated people who share no genes, but who were raised in the same familial environment due to adoption. In studies of this sort, a high correlation between intelligence of the nonrelated individuals would suggest that, for the most part, the environment was acting as the primary determinant of intelligence. However, in studies of both sorts, the problem has been that different researchers have produced different results. Indeed, evidence exists to support proponents on each side of the debate.

Taken as a whole, research into the nature versus nurture debate shows that both of these factors play critical roles in how people perform on measures of intelligence such as IQ tests. This "mixed" conclusion should not be surprising—genes cannot be expressed without an environment within which to exist, and likewise, independent of the given environment, people cannot exist without their genes.

Nevertheless, two important conclusions can be drawn from the available evidence. On the one hand, if a researcher is comparing the intelligence of individuals who have been raised in the same culture and socioeconomic class, then genes

Relationship	Rearing	Degree of relatedness	Correlation	Number of pairs
Same individual		1.0	.87	456
Monozygotic twins	Together	1.0	.86	1417
Dizygotic twins	Together	.50	.62	1329
Siblings	Together	.50	.41	5350
Siblings	Apart	.50	.24	203
Parent-child	Together	.50	.35	3973
Parent-child	Apart	.50	.31	345
Adoptive parent-child	Together	0	.16	1594
Unrelated children	Together	0	.25	601
Spouses	Apart	0	.29	5318

Interestingly, the IQ of adoptive parents has little association with the IQ of their adopted children.

The environment appears to have a substantial impact, as dizygotic twins and siblings have the same degree of relatedness but different IQ correlations.

Identical twins score as similarly as the same person taking the test on two occasions.

8.18 Heritability studies compare the degree of relatedness between two people, whether or not they were reared together, and the degree to which they correlate on some measure, such as intelligence.

are probably playing the greater role in any differences that may be found. On the other hand, if a researcher is comparing people across cultures and/or socioeconomic classes, then the environment is likely playing the greater role in observed differences in intelligence. As with deciding how to measure intelligence, it is imperative to consider where and how someone grew up before deciding how to interpret and/or explain that person's intellectual capacities. We consider how recent neurophysiological evidence weighs in on this issue in "Crossing the Levels of Analysis: The Neural Basis of Intelligence."

What Does Intelligence Reflect?

Traditional views of intelligence have defined it in relation to verbal, mathematical, and analytic abilities. However, such measures historically have had inherent biases that favor individuals who have been raised in cultures that promote such skills. In response to these shortcomings, alternative definitions of intelligence have focused on broader views, and models such as Cattell's fluid and crystallized intelligences and Gardner's theory of multiple intelligences have begun to challenge the more narrow, IQ-based definitions. Although a great deal of attention has been paid to the debate over whether genes or the environment play a greater role in determining intelligence, the main conclusion arising from research is that both factors are central to intelligence, and that cultural background needs to be considered when comparing individuals based on how they score on intelligence measures.

Crossing the Levels of Analysis

THE NEURAL BASIS OF INTELLIGENCE

One of the enduring puzzles in intelligence research has centered on the finding first reported early in the twentieth century that individuals tend to perform at consistent levels across a variety of different cognitive tasks.

The finding has led to the idea of a "general intelligence" known as Spearman's g. The enigma surrounding g is whether it reflects a single cognitive process that contributes to a host of different cognitive tasks, or whether it reflects the average efficiency of a collection of distinct cognitive processes. The debate has been of interest because it speaks directly to the manner in which cognitive functioning translates into "intelligent" test performance. Are people good at mental tasks because they have one general process that functions well or because, across the board, their set of domain-specific cognitive processes is exceptional? Moreover, if intelligence can be isolated to a single process in the brain, would this be evidence of the stronger role of genes in determining our intelligence?

Toward answering this question, John Duncan and colleagues (2000) recently used positron emission tomography (PET) to image activity in people's brains as they performed three diverse cognitive tasks, one associated with spatial reasoning, one associated with verbal abilities, and one associated with perceptual-motor abilities. Each of these tasks had two forms or levels, based on prior research: a high correlation with g and a low correlation with g. The idea was to compare activity in the brain between the high-and low-g versions of each task. If g is based on a single, general cognitive process, then this comparison within each type of task should show the same brain region as being more active in the high-versus low-g version. Conversely, if g is based on the average efficiency of domain-specific cognitive processes, then the high-versus low-g comparison within each task type should reveal different areas of increased activation between tasks.

What Duncan and his colleagues found was that despite the diversity of cognitive processes emphasized in the three different tasks, the high-g version of each task produced greater activation in the lateral frontal cortex than the low-g version (Figure 8.19). Accordingly, these results argue that "general intelligence" may be housed in a specific brain area that is recruited by a number of different cognitive tasks.

While this study is a prime example of how modern neuroimaging methods can be used to shed light on long-standing questions of cognitive function, the researchers were quick to point out the limitations of their results. In particular, although the lateral frontal cortex showed increased activation during the high-g version of each cognitive task, this does not necessarily mean that the same general cognitive process was being recruited under the high-g conditions. It is possible that if one could look at activity in this brain region with a finer level of resolution, it might show that different subregions of the lateral frontal cortex are activated in each of the conditions reported by Duncan et al. If so, such evidence would tend to support the position that g is not associated with a single general process, but that g reflects a variety of different cognitive operations. Future research on higher cognitive processes will undoubtedly focus greater and greater attention on the workings of the frontal cortex—the region of the brain that many believe houses the most complex components of cognitive function.

The task now is to investigate the frontal cortex with an eye on what different neural networks are doing in this region. Will we find evidence of divisions among processes in this part of the brain? If so, what would that tell us about the social implications of the debate over genes versus the environment in determining our intelligence? If g reflects a unitary process, teaching strategies for infants and children might require different approaches than if g reflects a variety of processes.

As a fascinating first step toward addressing some of these questions, Claire Rampon of Princeton University and her colleagues (2000) have begun investigating how the expression of genes regulating cellular and subcellular aspects of the cortex are affected by an animal's environment. Genetically identical mice were split into groups that were exposed to different levels of an "enriched" environment—a cage with toys, tunnels, boxes, and the like. Rampon and her colleagues found that the more "enriched" mice displayed evidence of having developed higher levels of neuronal structure, synaptic signaling, and plasticity. Moreover, the evidence suggested that the more-enriched mice had developed a greater capacity for learning and memory as well. These results present a stunning affirmation that our environment can affect properties associated with intelligence, by influencing—at least in part—the expression of our genes. As the popular analogy goes, we are truly seeds that can grow in many different ways, all depending on the nature of the soil, light, and water with which we are provided.

A. Spatial

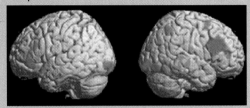

B. Verbal

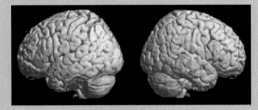

C. Perceptual-Motor

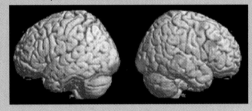

8.19 Neuroimaging data have suggested that "general intelligence" may have a specific seat in the brain.

CAN WE STUDY CONSCIOUSNESS?

Despite our subjective *experience* of being self-aware humans, consciousness has long been a difficult phenomenon to study from a scientific perspective. On the one hand, it is the very mechanism by which we experience and engage in cognitive functioning such as problem solving and decision making. In this sense consciousness is a very tangible thing, as there is a clear delineation for most of us between being "conscious" and being "unconscious." On the other hand, perhaps the greatest unanswered question in the biological sciences today is how neural activity in the brain gives rise to the phenomenal awareness of the world that we associate with the state of being conscious.

Already we see the challenges posed by the scientific study of consiousness, as it can be associated with cognition as well as perception. But the complexity doesn't end there, as consciousness has long been a topic of debate among philosophers as well. Although this is a chapter on cognition, a full discussion of consciousness necessarily requires a consideration of all three of these topics: philosophy, perception, and cognition.

PHILOSOPHERS DEBATE THE NATURE OF MIND-BRAIN RELATIONS

The philosophical debate over the nature of consciousness traces back to René Descartes and his assertion that the mind is a "substance" or "thing" physically distinct from the brain. This view of consciousness, which posits a clear separation between mind and brain, is called *dualism* (see Chapter 1), reflecting the belief that consciousness is linked to two different entities. The logical alternative to dualism, known as *physicalism* or *materialism*, is that the mind and brain are an inseparable, unitary system. Various strains of these competing beliefs have been argued in recent years, presenting some interesting takes on what we may be dealing with when studying consciousness.

Dualism takes a skeptical view of empirical pursuits   Essentially, dualism argues for a separation between what we call mind and where this mind appears to reside in the corporeal world: the brain. The byproduct of this belief is that, if one decides to study consciousness from an empirical perspective, only the brain and its activity can be measured and examined; the mind remains outside the scope of objective, scientific analysis. However, revealing the uncertainty over exactly how the mind is separate from the brain, several different variations on dualism have been proposed. Yet all converge on the assumption that consciousness—the mind, the basis of our cognitive abilities—represents an intractable topic for empirical research.

Materialism sees a more tractable topic   As an alternative to dualism, materialism is founded on the belief that the brain directly enables the mind, and as such, one can study the mind through studying the brain. For those interested in understanding the biological basis of consciousness, materialism is the philosophy of choice because it gives us access to an objective, measurable component of the mind. The view says that it is the activity of neurons in the brain that produces the contents of consciousness, such as cognition and perception. When we drink too much, our decision making becomes impulsive and confused because alcohol

qualia The properties of our subjective, phenomenological awareness.

unconscious Those processes that are outside the realm of conscious awareness.

is affecting the synaptic transmissions between neurons. When we have strokes or traumatic brain injuries, we may lose our ability to solve even the simplest of problems because brain tissue has been damaged. While dualism has difficulty accounting for these effects of brain on mind, materialism also comes in several different varieties, which speaks to our central uncertainty regarding exactly how the brain gives rise to cognition and perception.

Regardless of which of these differing views may ultimately prove correct, we can arrive at a definitive answer only by pursuing consciousness at an empirical level, which necessarily requires us to begin by defining "consciousness." Thus we will move the study of consciousness from the domain of the philosopher to the domain of the scientist.

DEFINITIONS OF CONSCIOUSNESS ALLOW ITS EMPIRICAL STUDY

As discussed in Chapter 2, the methods of psychological science dictate that in order to study a phenomenon, we need to be able to define operationally exactly what it is we're studying. In this regard, consciousness has proven difficult to define in scientifically practical terms. In recent years the solution that researchers have converged on is to break down consciousness into more tractable elements. Foremost among philosophers and scientists working on this front have been Steven Pinker, Thomas Nagel, and John Searle; below we consider several "elements" of consiousness that are directly predicated on their efforts:

Subjectivity or *Sentience*: These terms refer to the unique perspective each of us has on our own conscious experience. What we see, hear, feel, and think can be discussed with other people, but the actual *experience* of these things can never be shared in a manner resembling our own internal awareness of them. How can we explain to others what the color red looks like to us? These aspects of consciousness—the properties of our subjective, phenomenological awareness—are referred to as **qualia,** and perhaps the most difficult aspect of a scientific study of consciousness concerns understanding how qualia arise from neural activity (Figure 8.20).

Access to Information: Mental experience presupposes that we have knowledge of the contents of our consciousness, at least when we are in a normal, nonaltered mind state. However, that content is the by-product of the actions of a number of different underlying processes, of whose workings we have no direct knowledge. We see the products of the visual system, not the computations upon which they are premised. We report what is in our working memory, not the action of the neurons that hold the information in place. What does this mean? Information processing in the brain can be divided into two classes: processes that are accessible to consciousness and processes that are not. The processes that we are not conscious of we label as **unconscious,** or outside our sentient, mental awareness.

A Unitary Experience: Consciousness brings together the fruits of our sensory systems into a unified phenomenal experience that remains continuous over time. Our awareness of the world is based on a melding of these sensations into a single, multimedia event.

What are the elementary properties of consciousness?

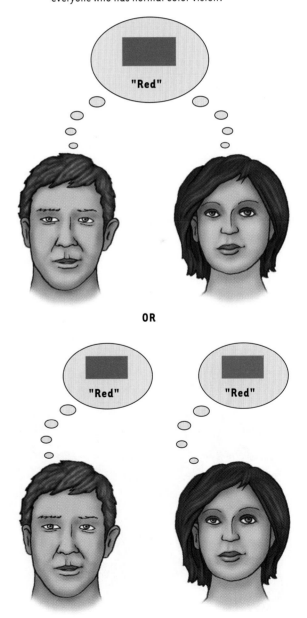

8.20 One of the difficult questions of consciousness is how to account for "qualia," or the phenomenological percepts of the world. For instance, does the color red appear the same to everyone who has normal color vision?

subliminal perception Stimuli that are processed by sensory systems but because of their short duration or subtle form, do not reach the threshold of entering into consciousness.

awareness The notion that to be cognizant of information is to be able to report that the information is being, or has been, perceived.

Self-knowledge: While subjectivity and sentience imply a direct, first-person awareness of consciousness, we can also be detached, third-person observers of our own mental experiences. As Pinker puts it, "I cannot only feel pain and see red, but think to myself, 'Hey, here I am, Steve Pinker, feeling pain and seeing red!'"

Intentionality: Consciousness presupposes that we think about, or interpret, our experiences. As such, our perceptions are giving a meaning beyond the passive impingement of physical stimulation on our sensory systems. For example, a room will appear very different the one-hundredth time you walk into it relative to the first time, even though the room itself may not have changed much if at all. The reason is that experience with the room—or any environment, for that matter—ultimately shapes how it is perceived.

The goal in making these distinctions between different aspects of consciousness is to facilitate empirical study. For instance, now that we have defined qualia, we may be able to design studies that begin to investigate what parts of the brain are active and what parts are inactive when experiencing specific qualia. We now turn to several different definitions of consciousness and the different empirical approaches they have spurred.

UNCONSCIOUS PROCESSING INFLUENCES AWARENESS

One of the properties of consciousness discussed above is "access to information," or the idea that we are aware of some mental processes and unconscious of others. Over the last several decades, one of the more fruitful areas of consciousness research has explored different ways in which unconscious or **subliminal perception** can influence cognition. Subliminal perception refers to stimuli that our sensory systems respond to but that because of their short duration or subtle form, never reach the threshold of entering into consciousness (Figure 8.21).

The case for subliminal perception There is no doubt that stimuli can influence our thoughts and actions even though they stay outside the realm of consciousness. One often-used illustration of this point involves priming test subjects by flashing before them a picture of a boy who appears either mean or kind. Subjects remain unaware that they have been shown the initial picture. For the main test, subjects are shown a picture of the boy wearing a neutral expression on his face, and the subjects are asked whether the boy appears to have a "good" or a "bad" character. Subjects who were previously presented with the kind picture rate the boy's character much higher than those who saw the mean picture (Figure 8.22).

Another example comes from the work of Tony Marcel at Cambridge University in England, who wanted to find out what cognitive systems are being influenced by subliminal stimuli. Marcel presented participants with a set of crosshatched lines on a screen, which was then followed by either a word or a nonword letter string (Figure 8.23). The participants' task was to decide whether a word or a nonword was presented. The critical manipulation in this study, however, was whether an initial word had been presented just prior to the crosshatched lines—half the trials contained this initial word, and half didn't. The brief presentation of the initial word (when present), combined with the crosshatched lines afterward, left the subjects with no awareness of having seen the word. Marcel found that if the subliminal word was semantically related to the

8.21 This design contains a subliminal message that is dramatically obvious when you discover it. Can you find it?

test word, participants were significantly quicker in recognizing that the test word was indeed a word (rather than a letter string). This data suggested that the subliminal words were activating cognitive processes associated with the meanings of words, even though there was no conscious awareness of such an effect.

Free associations and "slips" While experiments in subliminal perception have provided insight into different ways in which unconscious processes can influence cognition, other kinds of effects have been observed as well. In a classic experiment by Richard Nisbett and Timothy Wilson (1977), participants were asked to examine word pairs such as "ocean-moon" that had obvious semantic associations between the words. They were then asked to free associate on other, single words, such as "detergent." Nisbett and Wilson were interested in finding to what degree, if any, the word pairs would influence free associations, and if they did, whether the participants would have any awareness that the pairs had indeed influenced their thoughts. What they found was that when given the word "detergent" after the word pair "ocean-moon," participants' typical free association was the word "Tide." Interestingly, they would usually give reasons such as "My mom used Tide when I was a kid"; they had no awareness that they were being influenced by the word pairs. What this reveals is that we are frequently unaware of the myriad of different things that can affect our decisions about what we say and do. Similar effects underlie the classic *Freudian slip*, in which unconscious thoughts are suddenly expressed at inappropriate times, often to inappropriate people.

AWARENESS HAS MANY SEATS IN THE BRAIN

As we have stated, perhaps the greatest challenge in the psychological sciences today is to understand how neural activity gives rise to the conscious awareness we associate with cognition and perception. However, to approach this issue, we need to ask: What exactly is *awareness*? Although there are a host of definitions, they all converge on the notion that to be aware of information is to be able to report that information is being—or has been—perceived. Based on this general definition, there has been a great deal of research over the last several decades focused on identifying the brain areas involved in **awareness**. By studying awareness in individuals with damage to specific regions of the brain, researchers hope to link selective losses of awareness—that is, awareness for specific forms of information—to the damaged brain areas.

8.22 If asked to judge the character of the boy in panel B, subliminal perception of panel A1 beforehand will bias people to give a negative report. Alternatively, subliminal perception beforehand of panel A2 will bias people toward a positive report.

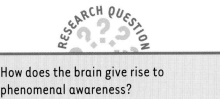

RESEARCH QUESTION

How does the brain give rise to phenomenal awareness?

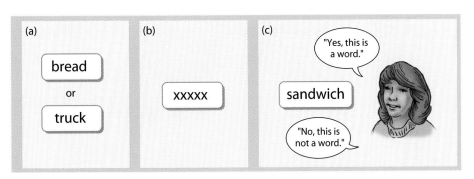

8.23 Subliminal perception of a related word can speed the subsequent decision that a supraliminal word is in fact a word.

blindsight A condition in which people who are blind have some spared visual capacities in the absence of any visual awareness.

One of the more fascinating areas of study in cognitive neuroscience has concerned the neural basis of visual awareness. In particular, researchers have focused on the phenomenon of **blindsight**, a condition in which people suffer blindness due to damage to their primary visual cortex but continue to have some visual capacities in the absence of any visual awareness. Although blindsighted patients are exceedingly rare, they typically have a loss of vision in only a circumscribed portion of their visual field. Researchers have discovered that if these patients are presented with a stimulus in their blind field, they can unconsciously perceive salient aspects of the stimulus. For example, patients might be presented with a moving dot in their blind spot, and their task is to indicate in which direction the dot is moving. The typical scenario will have patients declaring that they have seen nothing and thus have nothing to report. However, when pressed to guess the direction of motion, more often than not patients will guess correctly (Figure 8.24).

Thus, blindsighted patients appear to have some knowledge of what has been presented in their blind field, but without being aware of the stimulation. More specifically, blindsight demonstrates how the functional use of visual information does not necessarily depend on phenomenal awareness of that information.

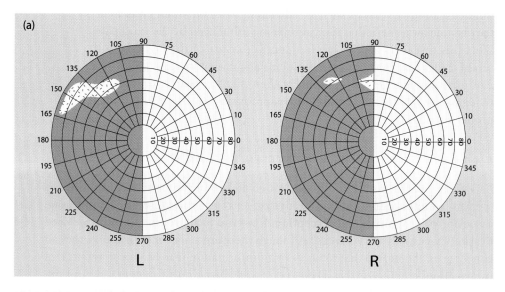

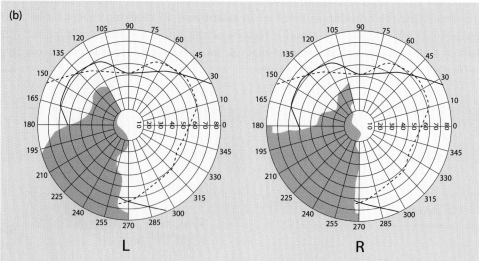

8.24 Blindsight is the ability to respond to visual stimuli in a "blind" portion of the visual field, even though there is no conscious awareness of the stimuli. These are visual field maps for Lawrence Weiskrantz's patient, D.B., who had part of his visual cortex damaged. (a) The purple area shows the region for which D.B. was unable to see (in the left visual field). However, when objects were shown in the crosshatched areas, he was able to guess some of their properties, such as which way a line was oriented, even though he did not consciously see the object. D.B. later recovered vision in part of the left visual field (b). Interestingly, these are the areas in which blindsight was earlier demonstrated.

One of the more popular explanations for blindsight is that although the primary visual pathway from the retina to the cortex is not functioning in these patients, a secondary pathway—going from the superior colliculus in the brainstem to the association cortex—remains intact, providing the functional capacity of blindsight. However, the fact that awareness of this information remains absent suggests that the primary visual cortex may be the key area in providing visual awareness. The goal now is to understand the unique functional properties of the primary visual cortex that give it the property of "awareness." What are the neurons doing in this region of the brain that the neurons in non-awareness-related areas of the brain aren't doing?

The importance of blindsight research is that it demonstrates how awareness of information about our environment depends on access to a variety of different cortical areas. That is, there appears to be no single area in the brain responsible for general "awareness." Rather, different areas of the brain deal with different types of information, and each of these systems in turn is responsible for awareness of that type of information (Figure 8.25). Taken from this perspective, consciousness can be viewed as the mechanism that is "aware" of information, and which serves the important role of prioritizing what information we need or want to deal with at any moment.

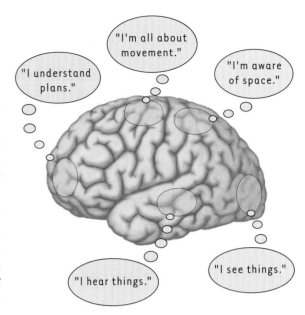

8.25 The central theme emerging from cognitive neuroscience is that awareness of different aspects of the world is associated with functioning in different parts of the brain.

Can We Study Consciousness?

Philosophers have long debated whether the mind and brain are separate entities, a debate between dualist and materialist beliefs. However, a scientific study of consciousness is consistent with the materialist view, and researchers have begun the critical task of defining the different elements of consciousness in order to facilitate empirical investigations into its nature. One of the main areas that has been explored concerns the degree to which unconscious processes influence the contents of consciousness. In a more neuroscientific vein, researchers have also explored how awareness of information changes with damage to the brain, such as with blindsight. Results from this domain of study have converged on the theory that different parts of the brain are responsible for awareness of different types of information, findings that challenge the more traditional idea that awareness has a single center in the brain.

CONCLUSION

Four different aspects of higher cognitive function were considered, and taken in turn they provide important insight into the complexities of the human mind. First, not only can information be represented in the mind, but these representations can take different forms, such as picturelike qualities or simple propositions. Second, we use this representational information to solve problems and make decisions, as well as to form our perceptions of our environment. However, it appears that traditional views of what is "rational" in terms of our knowledge-based thinking fail to appreciate the ecological basis in which human thinking evolved. Third, contemporary ideas on intelligence support the position that logical and verbal thinking are only a subset of a broader spectrum of abilities associated with intelligence. Moreover, the debate over whether intelligence is based on our genetic inheritance or the environment in which we are raised is somewhat unfounded, in that both factors play critical roles. Finally, although some philosophers believe that consciousness cannot be studied empirically, not only have researchers established different ways in which unconscious processes affect consciousness, but they are rapidly uncovering the brain systems underlying phenomenal awareness.

FURTHER READINGS

Ballard, D. H. (1997). *An introduction to natural computation.* Cambridge, MA: MIT Press.

Block, N., Flanagan, O., & Güzeldere, G. (Eds.). (1997). *The nature of consciousness.* Cambridge, MA: MIT Press.

Eysenck, M. W., & Keane, M. T. (1990). *Cognitive psychology: A student's handbook.* Hillsdale, NJ: Erlbaum.

Hameroff, S. R., Kaszniak, A. W., & Scott, A. C. (Eds.). (1996). *Towards a science of consciousness: The first Tucson discussions and debates.* Cambridge, MA: MIT Press.

Kosslyn, S. M. (1994). *Image and brain.* Cambridge, MA: MIT Press.

Neisser, U. (1976). *Cognition and reality: Principles and implications of cognitive psychology.* New York: W. H. Freeman.

Pinker, S. (1997). *How the mind works.* New York: W. W. Norton.

Plous, S. (1993). *The psychology of judgment and decision making.* New York: McGraw-Hill.

OVERCOMING THE CHALLENGES OF LIFE

Three years before Lance Armstrong first won the Tour de France, he was diagnosed with testicular cancer and given only a 50/50 chance of survival. Yet he made a full recovery and went on to achieve four successive victories in the world's premier bicycle race. Key to these impressive feats were Armstrong's powerful motivation to achieve an ambitious personal goal, and an exceptional ability to self-regulate his behavior.

 **TIMELINE**

1890

Instincts as Motives Greatly influenced by Darwin's ideas, William James proposes that human beings are endowed with behavioral instincts that require no experience or education, only environmental triggers to activate them.

1920s

Homeostasis In *The Wisdom of the Body*, Harvard physiologist Walter B. Cannon describes the process by which bodily systems, such as temperature and digestion, are regulated to maintain a steady state.

1940s

Drives Satisfy Needs Clark Hull proposes that states of biological deprivation, or drives, stimulate behaviors to satisfy needs. Drive theory becomes one of the most influential theories in the history of psychological science.

1949

Reticular Formation and Arousal Giuseppe Moruzzi and Horace Magoun discover that stimulating the reticular formation in the brainstem leads to arousal, a state of heightened physical and brain activity.

Motivation

9

OUTLINING THE PRINCIPLES

1953

REM Sleep Nathaniel Kleitman, Eugene Aserinsky, and William Dement note that electrical changes in the brain are associated with rapid eye movements. They believe that these REM periods are the physiological basis of dreaming.

1954

Dual-Center Theory Eliot Stellar proposes that motivated behavior is regulated by excitatory and inhibitory centers in the hypothalamus. The hypothalamus is later found to be crucial for many motivated behaviors.

1960

Plans and Goals George Miller, Eugene Gallanter, and Karl Pribram develop a cognitive model of self-regulation, in which people are motivated by discrepancies between their situation and an ideal state represented as a goal.

1960s

Delay of Gratification Walter Mischel and his students conduct research showing that children who are best able to delay gratification are later able to perform at a superior level in many domains.

1960s

Optimal Arousal Daniel Berlyne proposes that people seek to maintain an optimal level of arousal.

In 1965, 17-year-old Randy Gardner set out to establish a world record for staying awake as a science fair project. To break the prevailing record he would have to deprive himself of sleep for more than 260 hours, or 11 full days. His parents were concerned, since there had been previous reports that sleep deprivation could cause serious psychotic reactions. A New York disc jockey who went 200 hours without sleep as part of a publicity stunt started hallucinating and developed severe paranoia, imagining that he was being poisoned. Gardner's reaction was less severe, but he did become paranoid and irritable and had hallucinations. He also experienced a number of mental difficulties. For instance, on day 11 when he was asked to count backward from 100 by sevens, he stopped at 65 because he forgot what he was supposed to be doing (Ross, 1965).

Gardner did manage to break the record by four hours, but his mental reactions show the difficulties he had in doing so. When he finally went to sleep, he slept for 15 hours the first night and 10 hours the second night. The mental problems that Gardner experienced disappeared after he slept and there did not appear to be any lasting mental or physical problems associated with his stunt. All in all, a quite successful science fair project. By the way, Californian Robert McDonald, who stayed awake for 453 hours and 40 minutes (just under 19 days) in a rocking chair, set the current world record in 1986.

Randy Gardner's record-setting quest involves many ideas central to the concept of motivation. Psychological scientists who study *motives* are interested in the factors that stimulate behavior. These include physical factors such as the need for sleep and food, as well as the psychological factors that inspire people to set goals and try to achieve them. Many times people try to override their biological needs, such as by trying to go without sleep or food, and often they find that doing so is difficult. What determines why people like Randy Gardner set out to break world records? How much can people prevail over their bodies in attempts to reach personal goals? As a

RESEARCH QUESTIONS

for Studying Motivation

How are internal states regulated in the body?

What is the role of instinct in behavior?

What role does pleasure play in motivating behavior?

How do people set and achieve personal goals?

What are the neural correlates of motivation?

Why are people obese?

How is sleep measured?

1974

Undermining Intrinsic Motivation Mark Lepper and his colleagues demonstrate that giving external rewards for behaviors that are enjoyable for their own sake undermines the natural motives to engage in those behaviors.

1975

Restrained Eating Peter Herman and Janet Polivy demonstrate that chronic dieters overeat when they believe they have broken their diets or when they are emotionally upset, ultimately revealing that much of human eating is under cognitive control.

1975

Activation-Synthesis Hypothesis Alan Hobson and Robert McCarley propose that dreams represent the mind's interpretation of random neuronal firing that occurs during REM sleep, concluding that there is no hidden symbolism in dreams.

1990s

Neural Basis of Self-Regulation Neuroscience research reveals that various regions of the prefrontal cortex interact with the limbic system as people develop and use strategies and plans.

student, you probably are highly motivated to succeed, and therefore you spend many of your waking hours reviewing notes, reading textbooks, and writing papers. Although doing well in this course may not aid your immediate survival, it does help you achieve long-term aspirations. This chapter is concerned with the factors that motivate and sustain behavior.

motivation Factors that energize, direct, or sustain behavior.

Motivation (from Latin, "to move") is the area of psychological science that studies the factors that energize, or stimulate, behavior. Specifically, it is concerned with how behavior is initiated, directed, and sustained. Issues of motivation are spread throughout the many levels of analysis of psychological science. For instance, the concepts of reward and reinforcement discussed in Chapter 6 and the physiological mechanisms discussed in Chapter 3 are central to theories of motivation. This chapter explores different conceptions of the basis of motivation and discusses some of the most commonly motivated behaviors. These behaviors relate to immediate biological survival (such as responding to hunger and thirst and the need for sleep), as well as to long-term social needs (such as affiliation, achievement, and play).

HOW DOES MOTIVATION ACTIVATE, DIRECT, AND SUSTAIN ACTION?

Most general theories of motivation emphasize four essential qualities of motivational states. First, motivational states are *energizing* in that they activate or arouse behaviors—they cause animals to do something. For instance, the desire for fitness might motivate you to get out of bed and go for a run on a cold morning. Second, motivational states are *directive* in that they guide behaviors toward satisfying specific goals or needs. Hunger motivates eating, thirst motivates drinking, and pride (or fear or many other things) motivates studying hard for exams. Third, motivational states help people to *persist* in their behavior until goals are achieved or needs are satisfied. Hunger gnaws at you until you find something to eat; persistence drives you to practice foul-line shots until you succeed. Fourth, most theories agree that motives differ in *strength*, depending upon both internal and external factors. We are often faced with competing motives: Should we study (pride) or go out with friends (companionship)? Should we eat pizza (pleasure) or rice cakes (health)? The stronger motive usually wins. Theories of motivation seek to answer questions such as, Where do needs and goals come from? How do needs and goals acquire strength? How are motives converted into action? We will examine several competing theories and their different answers below.

MOTIVATION IS BOTH PURPOSIVE AND REGULATORY

Psychological scientists who study motivation traditionally have followed one of two research emphases. Following the biological revolution in psychology, physiological psychologists study *regulatory motives* in nonhuman animals (especially rats). They focus on internal states and typically view motivation in terms of the underlying neurobiology, such as hormones, neurotransmitters, and brain sites. By contrast, social, personality, and cognitive psychologists focus on *purposive motives*. They examine how people try to satisfy life goals and to exert control over their own and others' behaviors. A **goal** is a desired outcome and is usually associated with some specific object (such as tasty food) or some future behavioral intention (such as getting into medical school). Understanding human motivation requires crossing the levels of analysis to examine both the purposive (cognitive) and regulatory (physiological) bases for human behavior.

Most researchers who study regulatory motivational states, such as thirst or hunger, view motivated behaviors as helping animals maintain a steady internal state, or *equilibrium*. Walter Cannon, a brilliant young physiologist at Harvard in the 1920s, coined the term **homeostasis** to describe the tendency for body functions to maintain equilibrium. For example, in the **negative feedback model**, people respond to deviations from equilibrium. Consider a home heating/cooling system controlled by a thermostat set to some optimal level, which we will call a set-point (see Figure 9.1). A **set-point** is a hypothetical state that indicates homeostasis. If the actual temperature is different from the set-point, the furnace or air conditioner operates to adjust the temperature. Similarly, the human body regulates a set-point of around 37° Celsius (98.6° F). When people are too warm or too cold, brain mechanisms, particularly the hypothalamus, initiate responses such as sweating (to cool the body down) or shivering (to warm the body up). At the same time, purposive behaviors, such as putting on or taking off clothes, also are motivated. Negative feedback models are useful for describing a number of basic biological processes, such as nutrition, fluid regulation, and sleep.

INSTINCTS MOTIVATE BEHAVIOR

In the late nineteenth century, American psychologist William James proposed that much of human behavior was instinctive. **Instincts** are unlearned, automatic actions that are triggered by external cues. For example, if you hear a loud noise you will tend to look toward the source of the noise automatically, perhaps without even realizing you're doing so. James' bold assertion contradicted the beliefs of earlier theorists that human behavior is mainly learned rather than inborn.

Instincts are similar to reflexes in that they produce an immediate impulse to act. Unless something blocks the impulse, the instinct leads to a specific action. Today an instinct is known as a *fixed-action pattern*, an example of which can be found in the three-spined stickleback fish (Tinbergen, 1951). Male sticklebacks develop a distinctive red underbelly during mating season, and they will attack another fish with a red underbelly that comes near. The red underbelly serves as a *releasing stimulus* for the fixed-action pattern of attack. Even a crudely constructed model of a fish painted red on the bottom will elicit this fixed-action pattern. Similarly, male turkeys become aroused simply by observing the head of another turkey, even if there is no body attached to the head or if the head is fake. A host

RESEARCH QUESTION
?·?·?

How are internal states regulated in the body?

9.1 A negative feedback model of homeostasis. When the temperature rises above the set-point (room temperature), a discrepancy is detected and the air conditioning is activated. The air is cooled until the temperature returns to the set-point. Conversely, when the temperature falls below the set-point, the furnace is activated. When the temperature reaches the set-point, the furnace quits working.

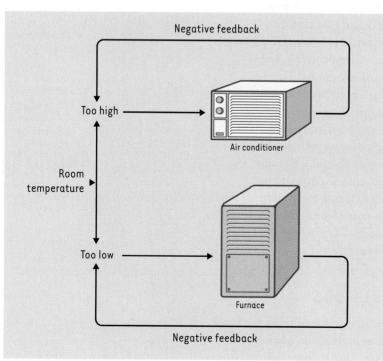

Negative feedback

Too high → Air conditioner

Room temperature

Too low → Furnace

Negative feedback

of other behaviors appear to be instinctive: spiders spin webs, birds fly and sing, dogs chase cats, cats chase mice. Examples of fixed-action patterns in humans are certain facial expressions, which occur universally across cultures and therefore appear to be instinctive.

By the early twentieth century, psychologist William McDougall developed the instinct concept into a general motivational theory. McDougall believed that instincts consist of *cognitive components* (knowing the object or outcome of the instinct), *affective components* (feelings of pleasure or pain), and *strivings* toward or away from a given object. For example, a baby learns that crying brings attention, which engenders feelings of pleasure and a desire to approach the attention giver.

McDougall's conception of instincts excited psychologists, and many researchers and theorists began to catalog behaviors that seemed instinctive. The list grew rapidly to over 6,000 supposedly instinctive behaviors. But critics soon began to attack instinct theory, noting that most of the so-called instinctive behaviors—such as playing, providing sympathy, or learning how to hunt for food— were actually modified through experience. More seriously, critics charged that the whole concept of instinct was based on circular logic and therefore had little explanatory value. One commentator astutely described the situation: "If he goes with his fellows, it is the 'herd instinct'; if he walks alone, it is the 'antisocial instinct'; if he twiddles his thumbs, it is the 'thumb-twiddling instinct'; if he does not twiddle his thumbs, it is the 'thumb-not-twiddling instinct.' Thus, everything is explained with the facility of magic—word magic" (Holt, 1931, p. 4). This circular reasoning led many behaviorists to reject motivational states as meaningless. Instincts were useful at the descriptive level but did not provide much by way of explanation. Interest in the concept of instincts died out in the 1930s, in part because of challenges from behaviorists, who claimed that all behavior is the result of learning. Today, as part of the biological revolution, new understanding of how neural mechanisms translate into behavior has sparked renewed interest in examining behaviors that may be hardwired.

NEEDS, DRIVES, AND REWARDS MOTIVATE BEHAVIOR

Needs are states of deficiency. Physiological psychologists use the term to refer to biological deficiencies, such as a lack of air or food. You *need* air and food to survive. Social psychologists, however, use the term for psychological states and social relations, such as the need for power, achievement, or affiliation. People *need* other people. Needs, however they are defined, lead to goal-directed behaviors. Failure to satisfy the need leads to psychosocial or physical impairment or death. This explanation separates *needs* from *wants*. A young child may claim to *need* a red crayon rather than a blue crayon, but having to use the blue crayon will not in all likelihood cause a lasting problem.

Abraham Maslow proposed an influential need theory of motivation in the 1940s. Maslow's theory is an example of *humanistic psychology*, in which people are viewed as holistic beings who strive toward personal fulfillment. Humanists focus on the *person* in motivation—it is John Smith who desires food, not John Smith's stomach. According to the humanist perspective, human beings are unique among animals because they continually try to improve themselves. A state of **self-actualization** occurs when someone's personal dreams and aspirations are achieved. The self-actualized person has lived up to his or her potential and therefore is truly happy. Maslow writes, "A musician must make music, an

What is the role of instinct in behavior?

goal A desired outcome associated with some specific object of desire or some future behavioral intention.

homeostasis The tendency for bodily functions to maintain equilibrium.

negative feedback model The body's response to deviations from equilibrium.

set-point A hypothetical state that indicates homeostasis.

instincts Unlearned, automatic actions that are triggered by specific cues.

needs States of biological or social deficiencies within the body.

self-actualization A state that is achieved when one's personal dreams and aspirations have been attained.

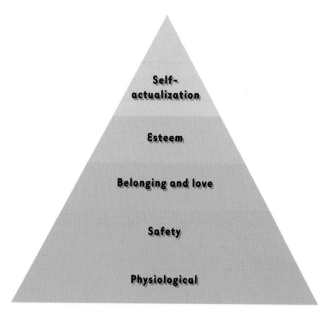

9.2 Maslow's hierarchy of needs indicates that basic needs, such as for food and water, are satisfied before higher needs, such as self-actualization.

artist must paint, a poet must write, if he is ultimately to be at peace with himself. What a man *can* be, he *must* be" (Maslow, 1968, p. 46).

Maslow believed that humans are driven by many needs, which he arranged into a **need hierarchy** (Figure 9.2), in which survival needs (such as hunger and thirst) were lowest and personal growth needs were highest in terms of priority. Maslow believed that satisfaction of lower needs in the hierarchy allowed humans to function at a higher level. People must have their biological needs met, feel safe and secure, feel loved, and have a good opinion of themselves in order to experience personal growth and achieve self-actualization.

Maslow's need hierarchy has long been embraced in education and business, but it is generally lacking in empirical support. Independent of whether one needs to be self-actualized in order to be happy, the ranking of needs is not as simple as Maslow suggests. For instance, some people starve themselves to death to demonstrate the importance of their personal beliefs, whereas others who have satisfied physiological and security needs are loners who do not seek out the companionship of others. Moreover, the concept of self-actualization is difficult to define and measure precisely. Maslow's hierarchy, therefore, is more useful at the descriptive level than at the empirical level.

Drives **Drives** are psychological states activated to satisfy needs. For example, people can be described by their level of sex drive, or characterized as being driven to succeed. Needs create *arousal*, which motivates behaviors that will satisfy these needs (Figure 9.3). **Arousal** is a generic term used to describe physiological activation (such as increased brain activity) or increased autonomic responses (such as quickened heart rate, increased sweating, or muscle tension). Try holding your breath as long as you can. If you continue for more than a minute or two you probably will begin to feel a strong sense of urgency, even anxiety. This state of arousal is drive.

The most influential *drive theory* was proposed in the 1940s by Clark Hull (Figure 9.4), one of the leading behaviorists of his time. Hull proposed that drive states are rooted in biological needs and that behavior can be predicted by environmental factors. Hull proposed that when an animal is deprived of some need (such as water, sleep, or sex), a specific drive increases proportionally. The drive state leads to arousal and behavioral activation, and the animal then acts until one of its behaviors satisfies the drive and reduces arousal. Thus, satisfying needs involves learning. Hull's model proposes that the initial behaviors in which the animal engages are arbitrary. When a behavior satisfies a need the behavior is reinforced and therefore is more likely to occur. Over time, if a behavior consistently reduces a drive, it becomes a *habit*; the likelihood that a behavior will occur is due to both drive and habit.

Hull's theory and his classic book *Principles of Behavior* had a tremendous impact on psychological research. One criticism, however, was that Hull's drive theory could not explain why people choose to engage in behaviors that do not appear to satisfy biological needs. Why, for instance, do people stay up all night studying for an exam? Why do people have a second piece of pumpkin pie at Thanksgiving even though they weren't hungry when they had the first piece?

9.3 Needs create drives that motivate specific behaviors.

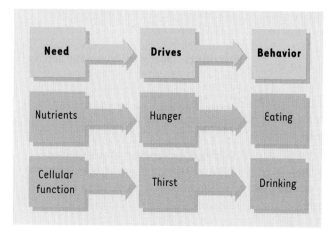

Hedonism and reward Sigmund Freud believed that drives are satisfied according to the *pleasure principle*, which tells organisms to seek pleasure and avoid pain. This idea is central to many theories of motivation. Originating with the ancient Greeks, *hedonism*, as a motivational principle, refers to the human experience of pleasantness and unpleasantness. Freud's pleasure principle and McDougall's instinct theory agree that animals and humans are motivated to seek pleasure and avoid pain. Darwin's contemporary Herbert Spencer wrote, "every animal persists in each act which gives pleasure—and desists from each act which gives pain" (Spencer, 1872, cited in Stellar & Stellar, 1984). Each of these great thinkers has stated an essential truth: pleasure is a primary motivator. We do things that feel good, and if something feels good, we do it again. A prime example of hedonism and adaptiveness is sex. Sex is essential for the survival of the species, and few people need to be persuaded about the pleasurable aspects of sexual behavior, whether or not it leads to reproduction. The scientific study of sexual behavior is discussed in "Crossing the Levels of Analysis: Factors Influencing Sexual Desire."

Recall that one limit of biological drive theories (such as Clark Hull's) is that animals engage in behaviors that do not necessarily satisfy biological needs. This commonly occurs when the behavior is pleasurable. For instance, one classic study examined food preferences in rats (Sheffield & Roby, 1950). One of the substances that produced a strong response was saccharine, which is sweet and therefore pleasurable but does not satisfy any biological need. Often animals even choose pleasure over biological drive reduction. In the classic Olds and Milner study, electrical stimulation applied to certain brain regions was found to be highly rewarding (see Chapter 6). Animals who could self-administer electrical stimulation by pressing a bar did so up to 2,000 times an hour. Male rats would press the bar even when they were food deprived, given access to a sexually receptive female, or had to cross an electrified grid to do so.

9.4 Clark Hull, on of the pioneers of behavioral models of drive reduction. Hull's drive theory of motivation is among the most influential theories in the history of psychological science.

MOTIVATED BEHAVIORS HAVE SURVIVAL VALUE

From an evolutionary perspective, behaviors associated with pleasure are those that promote the animal's survival and reproduction, whereas behaviors associated with pain interfere with survival and reproduction. A good example of this is sweetness, which is preferred by most animals. Infants given sweet solutions seem to find them pleasurable, as revealed by their facial expressions (Steiner, 1977; Figure 9.5). Sweetness usually indicates that food is safe to eat. By contrast, most poisons and toxins taste bitter, so it is not surprising that animals avoid bitter tastes.

Recall from Chapter 6 that the experience of reward is primarily due to activation of dopamine neurons in the nucleus accumbens. Adaptive behaviors also use the dopamine system. Sexual behavior, for example, even the anticipation of sexual behavior, leads to increased dopamine in the nucleus accumbens. Dopamine blockers interfere with the rewarding properties of food, water, and various drugs, such as cocaine or amphetamine, that are usually experienced as rewarding. Thus, dopamine activation may help guide adaptive behaviors by rewarding those that promote survival or reproduction.

Motivation can be viewed as a capability that initiates, directs, and sustains behaviors that promote survival and reproduction. Thus, animals are strongly motivated to repeat adaptive behaviors and to avoid unadaptive behaviors. Motivational states therefore arouse behaviors that solve adaptive problems. Animals need to

What role does pleasure play in motivating behavior?

need hierarchy Maslow's arrangement of needs, in which basic survival needs are lowest, and personal growth needs are highest in terms of priority.

drives Psychological states that motivate an organism to satisfy its needs.

arousal Term to describe physiological activation, such as increased brain activity, autonomic responses, sweating, or muscle tension.

Crossing the Levels of Analysis

FACTORS INFLUENCING SEXUAL DESIRE

Sexual desire has long been recognized as one of humanity's most durable and powerful motivators. The strength of the sex drive varies substantially across individuals and circumstances; still, it is safe to say that most human beings have some significant desire for sex.

Both nature and culture have contributed to shaping patterns of sexual motivation. One of our major themes is that much of behavior is adaptive. In human beings (as in most other species), sexual desire has evolved as a crucial mechanism for propagating the species. Babies are made not (always) because people desperately want babies but because they eagerly engage in sex, which often results in reproduction. Some species have nonsexual means of reproduction, such as cloning. Yet sexual reproduction is superior to nonsexual reproduction in several crucial respects, especially in its ability to mix genes and therefore produce a variety of offspring, making a species more adaptable. Recent advances in evolutionary theory suggest that the precise forms of human sexual desire are the result of natural selection pressures (these findings are discussed in Chapter 14). So how do contemporary psychological scientists study sex?

At the neurochemical and brain-systems levels, most research is conducted on nonhuman animals, especially rats. For instance, studies have examined how hormones, including testosterone and oxytocin, are involved in the production and termination of sexual behaviors (see Chapter 3). One interesting line of research examines the influence of *pheromones*—chemicals transmitted from one animal to another via the sense of smell—on the initiation of sex. Apparently, a protein in pheromones called *aphrodisin* is a sexual attractant. Male hamsters will attempt to mount an anesthetized male hamster if that hamster is spread with aphrodisin (Singer, 1991). Interestingly, pheromones may also affect human social behavior. In one study, female participants who wore a necklace overnight that contained androstenol, a substance found in male underarm sweat, spent more time in social interactions with males the next day than did women who wore necklaces containing inert substances (Cowley & Brooksbank, 1991). This effect did not occur for male participants.

Research is just beginning to examine the neural correlates of human sexual behavior. For instance, in one study using PET imaging men were shown pictures of erotic and neutral video clips. It was found that the erotic clips led to activation of brain areas associated with motivation and reward, such as various limbic structures. The interesting finding was that this effect was greatest for the men who had higher blood levels of testosterone (Stoleru et al., 1999). Whether men and women respond differently to sexual stimuli is currently unknown.

A noticeable and consistent finding in nearly all measures of sexual desire is that men, on average, have a higher level of sexual motivation than women, although there are many individual exceptions. On certain occasions, such as when falling in love, women's sexual desires may match or surpass men's. Research studies also have found that in general men masturbate more frequently than women, want sex earlier in the relationship, think and fantasize about sex more often, spend more time and money (and other resources) in the effort to obtain sex, desire more different sexual activities, initiate sex more and refuse sex less, and rate their own sex drives as stronger than women's (Baumeister et al., 2001). In one study, researchers asked college-age men and women how many sex partners they would ideally like to have in their lives, if they were unconstrained by fears about disease, social pressures, and the like (Miller & Fishkin, 1997). The majority of women wanted one or two, whereas the average answer by the men was several dozen. Still, there were plenty of men who wanted only one sex partner, and women who wanted many.

Women tend to be higher than men in *erotophobia*, which is the disposition to respond to sexual cues negatively. Those high in erotophobia report parental strictness about sex, conservative attitudes, and the avoidance of masturbation (Fisher et al., 1988). Paradoxically, those high in erotophobia may be at greater risk for unwanted pregnancies and sexually transmitted diseases, because they are less likely to carry condoms or take other precautions.

At the social/cultural level, the double standard is a well-known pattern of cultural influence. It stipulates that certain activities (such as premarital or casual sex) are morally and socially acceptable for men but not for women. The sexual revolution of the late twentieth century entailed a large change in sexual behaviors, most of which must be attributed to changing cultural pressures and expectations. Although sexual customs and norms vary to some degree across cultures, all known cultures have some form of sexual morality, which indicates the importance to society of providing some regulation of sexual behavior. Cultures may seek to restrain and control sex for a variety of reasons, including maintaining control over the birth rate, establishing paternity, providing people with a script to follow in courtship and mating, and reducing conflicts.

The relative influence of nature and culture on sexual motivation may vary with gender. Roy Baumeister (2000) used the term *erotic plasticity* to refer to the degree to which the sex drive can be shaped by social, cultural, and situational factors. Evidence suggests that women have higher erotic plasticity than men. A woman's sexuality may evolve and change throughout her adult life, whereas men's desires remain relatively constant (except for the gradual decline with age). Women's sexual desires and behaviors depend significantly on social factors such as education and religion, whereas men's sexuality shows minimal relationship to such influences. For example, in his review of the literature, Baumeister found that highly educated women are much more likely than uneducated women to engage in oral sex, anal sex, homosexual interactions, and experimentation with novel activities, but that educated and uneducated men do not differ much with regard to those forms of sex.

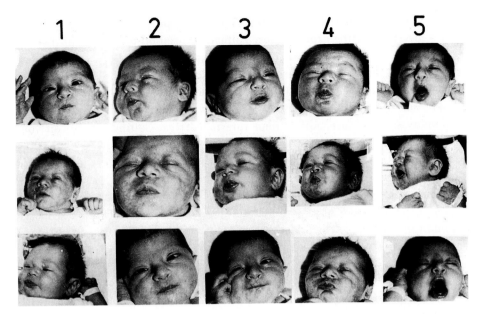

9.5 Even newborns prefer sweet tastes to bitter:
1. resting face, 2. reaction to distilled water,
3. sweet stimuli, 4. sour stimuli, 5. bitter stimuli.

take in oxygen, water, and nutrients, and therefore breathing, drinking, and eating are motivated behaviors. For humans, motivations to perform maternal behaviors promote care of offspring, thereby ensuring that genes are passed on. Breast feeding causes the release of the hormone oxytocin, which promotes bonding and releases endorphins that give rise to feelings of pleasure (Carter, 1998).

How Does Motivation Activate, Direct, and Sustain Action?

Motivational states activate, direct, and sustain behaviors that help satisfy needs or achieve goals. Many theories of motivation are based on the idea that organisms try to maintain homeostasis or equilibrium. Instincts, known as fixed-action patterns, are innate, automatic actions that are triggered by external cues. Drive states develop from need deficiencies and motivate behaviors that satisfy those needs. According to Maslow, needs can be arranged in a hierarchy, in which physiological needs take precedence over personal growth needs. A general motivational principle is hedonism, which directs organisms to repeat behaviors that are pleasurable and avoid behaviors that are painful. Following this principle may assist an organism to survive and reproduce.

HOW DO COGNITIVE, SOCIAL, AND CULTURAL FACTORS INFLUENCE MOTIVATION?

We saw earlier that many motivational researchers focus on the purposive aspects of behavior, on the cognitive and social factors underlying motivation. One of the greatest challenges to behavioristic drive accounts of motivation came from Edward Tolman, a pioneer in cognitive theories of behavior. In the 1920s, Tolman observed that motivated behaviors "reek of purpose"; that is, they are goal directed. Through learning, animals develop expectations about what will lead to the satisfaction of goals. **Expectancies** are mental representations of future outcomes. By emphasizing expectancies, Tolman focused on properties of the goal object rather than on biological needs. For example, you expect that chocolate cake will taste better than sardines, and therefore you choose to eat cake rather than sardines when you are motivated to eat. Focusing on goal objects rather than needs leads to incentive models of motivation. **Incentives** are external objects that motivate behaviors, rather than internal drives. Getting an "A" on your midterm is the incentive for studying hard; the luxurious taste of chocolate is incentive for eating cake; having money to buy the things you want is incentive for working during summer vacation. Tolman's major contribution was to point out that some things are more valuable to us than others, and we are more highly motivated to obtain things of value. What we value, in turn, is determined to a large extent by the culture in which we live.

MOTIVATION IS BOTH EXTRINSIC AND INTRINSIC

Sometimes people are motivated to engage in behaviors simply because they like to do them. People like to draw, listen to music, play chess, read books, and watch their favorite television programs. Psychologists differentiate between two general categories of motives, *extrinsic* and *intrinsic*. **Extrinsic motivation** emphasizes the external goals toward which an activity is directed, such as drive reduction or reward—for example, working to earn a paycheck at the end of the week. **Intrinsic motivation** refers to the value or pleasure that is associated with an activity but that has no apparent biological goal or purpose. Intrinsically motivated behaviors are done for their own sake. Such behaviors are not limited to humans; anyone who has ever had puppies or kittens knows how much of their day is made up of playful behavior.

Play One of the hallmarks of childhood is curiosity, an intrinsically motivated behavior. Children like to seek out new situations and games. When children encounter new objects they become fascinated and tinker with them until the object is fully inspected and all its features are displayed. After the child has thoroughly examined the object, interest diminishes and the child moves on to something new. Playful exploration is characteristic of all mammals and especially primates. For instance, psychologist Harry Harlow and his colleagues showed that monkeys have a strong exploratory drive and will persevere in efforts to solve relatively complex puzzles in the absence of any apparent motivation (Harlow et al., 1950).

What adaptive value might play serve? One obvious function is to learn about objects in the environment; this clearly has survival value. Knowledge of how things work also allows those objects to be used for other tasks. In one study children were given a chance to play with materials involved in a later problem-solving task. The task required the children to join together two sticks to retrieve a piece of chalk. Children who were allowed to play with the various sticks and clamps for ten minutes performed better at the task than children who were not exposed to the materials first or who were shown the solution to the task but not allowed to play (Sylva et al., 1976).

Play also helps animals learn about the social world. Living with others requires the ability to cooperate and follow rules, and play provides the opportunities to learn the rules. Stephen Suomi and Harry Harlow (1972) argued that playing with peers allows monkeys to learn social graces, such as how to behave with those who are dominant and when to curb aggressive impulses.

expectancies Mental representations of potential future outcomes.

incentives External stimuli that motivate behaviors (as opposed to internal drives).

extrinsic motivation Motivation to perform an activity because of the external goals toward which that activity is directed.

intrinsic motivation Motivation to perform an activity because of the value or pleasure associated with that activity, rather than for an apparent biological goal or purpose.

Creativity and problem solving Many intrinsically motivated behaviors allow people to express creativity. **Creativity** is the tendency to generate ideas or alternatives that may be useful in solving problems, communicating, and entertaining ourselves and others (Franken, 1998). Creativity involves constructing novel images, synthesizing two or more disparate ideas or concepts, and applying existing knowledge to solving new problems. The human mind also tries to consolidate information into coherent stories. People are motivated to make sense of the world, and just like split-brain patients who confabulate to make sense of conflicting information arriving in their separate hemispheres (see Chapter 4), people actively develop accounts of how the world works and how causal events are connected. Many theorists have pointed out that creativity is an integral component for solving adaptive problems. Many creative pursuits do not themselves represent adaptive solutions, but they are modern uses of mechanisms that did evolve for such purposes. For instance, we tend to prefer art that has interesting elements that capture our attention. The capacity to notice and attend to features in the environment, such as food or predators, has obvious adaptive value (Pinker, 1997).

Learning and intrinsic motivation Recall that one of the basic principles of learning theory is that rewarded behaviors increase in frequency. You would expect, therefore, that rewarding intrinsically motivated behaviors would reinforce them. Surprisingly, consistent evidence suggests that extrinsic rewards can undermine intrinsic motivation and decrease the likelihood that people will perform the rewarded behavior. In a classic study, social psychologist Mark Lepper and his colleagues allowed children to draw with colored marking pens, an activity that most children find intrinsically motivating (Lepper et al., 1973). One group of children was given an extrinsic motive for drawing by being led to expect a "good player award." Another group of children was unexpectedly rewarded following the task, and a third group was neither rewarded nor given the expectation of reward. During a subsequent free play period, children who had been given the expectation of extrinsic reward spent much less time playing with the pens than did the group of children who were never rewarded or the children who received an unexpected reward.

Control theory and self-perception Why do extrinsic rewards sometimes reduce intrinsic value? Social psychologists Edward Deci and Richard Ryan (1987) argue that feelings of *personal control* and competence make people feel good about themselves and inspire them to do their most creative works. Doing something to gain external rewards does not satisfy our need for autonomy.

Another explanation is based on social psychologist Daryl Bem's (1967) self-perception theory, which states that people are seldom aware of their specific motives and draw inferences about their motivation based on what seems to make the most sense. For example, somebody gives you a big glass of water and you drink the whole thing, exclaiming, "Wow, I must have been thirsty." You believe you were thirsty because you drank the whole glass, even though you were not aware of any physical sensations of thirst. When people are unable to come up with an obvious external explanation for their behavior (such as being rewarded or satisfying a biological drive), they conclude that they simply engage in the behavior because they like it. Rewarding people for engaging in an intrinsic activity, however, gives them an alternative explanation for why they are engaging in it. It is not because the behavior is fun; it is because of the reward. Therefore, in the absence of the reward, there is no reason to engage in the behavior.

> **creativity** The capacity to generate or recognize ideas, alternatives, or possibilities that may be useful in solving problems, communicating with others, or entertaining ourselves and others.

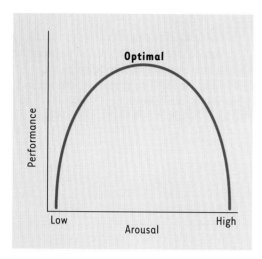

9.6 According to the Yerkes-Dodson law, performance increases with arousal until an optimal point, after which arousal interferes with performance.

9.7 Daniel Berlyne proposed that increased arousal is associated with greater positive affect until an optimal level, after which increasing arousal becomes aversive.

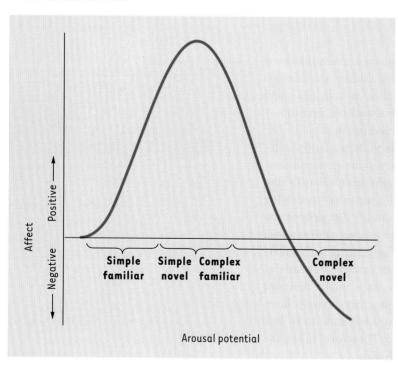

Because school grades reward good performance, you might conclude that we should do away with them in order to preserve young children's curiosity and love of learning. However, Deci and Ryan argue that if the extrinsic reward provides information about how much personal control people have over learning, it will not undermine intrinsic motivation. From this perspective, getting grades in school provides information that you are doing well, and therefore it does not undermine intrinsic motivation. If anything, receiving good grades further reinforces intrinsic motivation: now you know schoolwork is something you like to do and are good at doing. Moreover, extrinsic rewards undermine only behavior that is intrinsically rewarding. Thus, the challenge to educators is to find ways to increase the intrinsic value of schoolwork. Failing this, extrinsic rewards can be used to make an otherwise boring task seem worth pursuing.

NOVELTY AND AROUSAL MOTIVATE

Curiosity, play, and creative endeavors all lead to states of arousal. Arousal is associated with how active and alert you feel throughout the day as well as how you respond to events around you, such as driving in traffic or encountering someone you find attractive. The psychological principle known as the **Yerkes-Dodson law** (named after the two researchers who first studied it in 1908) dictates that behavioral efficiency increases with arousal up to an optimum point, after which it decreases with increasing arousal, thus creating a shape like an inverted U (Figure 9.6). Thus, you perform best on exams when you have a moderate level of anxiety. Too little anxiety can cause you to be inattentive; too much anxiety can paralyze your thinking and interfere with memory.

Interestingly, the increase in arousal that accompanies many desirable behaviors contradicts the original drive theories, which argued that motivation functions to reduce levels of tension and arousal. Instead, it is now well established that animals are motivated to seek out an *optimal level of arousal*, which is the level of arousal associated with maximal hedonic value. In the 1960s, cognitive psychologist Daniel Berlyne proposed that the relation between arousal and hedonic value followed the Yerkes-Dodson law, such that mood increased with increasing complexity and novelty until some optimal level, at which point affect became increasingly negative (Figure 9.7). For instance, people like a good mystery story but become frustrated when the plot is so complex that it is impossible to follow. Berlyne agreed with the basic motivational principle that all organisms should seek positive experiences and avoid negative ones, and therefore a person experiencing a low level of arousal would be motivated to seek out additional stimulation. According to Berlyne, novelty, sudden change, incongruity, complexity, and uncertainty all increase arousal and therefore increase positive affect for those low in arousal. Those who are already aroused, however—such as students studying for exams—experience other arousing events as aversive and will try to reduce stimulation.

Arousal theories of motivation provide an important explanation for many intrinsic behaviors—we perform them because they arouse us and absorb our attention. People like to engage in many activities that are arousing, such as dancing, listening to music, reading exciting books, and watching horror or adventure movies. A number of theorists have noted that music, art, and literature have the power to affect our emotional states. Musical selections are often used in laboratory research to alter people's moods. Liking for new songs follows the inverted U model suggested by Berlyne: as both musicians and listeners become bored with a single style of music, they desire new and fresh sounds. Punk rock, rap, electronica, and other musical styles became popular because they were different and because they aroused the listener, much the way Mozart did for those listening to Bach or Handel in the 1700s.

PEOPLE ARE MOTIVATED TO ACHIEVE GOALS

Purposive motives reflect psychosocial needs for power, self-esteem, and achievement. The study of such motives began with Henry Murray, a personality psychologist at Harvard University. In the 1930s Murray proposed 27 basic psychosocial needs, such as the need for power, autonomy, achievement, sex, and play. The study of psychosocial needs has provided a number of important insights into what motivates human behavior. Chief among these is that people are especially motivated to achieve personal goals. **Self-regulation** of behavior is the process by which people initiate, adjust, or stop actions in order to attain personal goals.

Sometimes when you are up late studying for an exam, you might wonder why you work as hard as you do. For many people, hard work is motivated by their long-term goals. According to an influential theory developed by organizational psychologists Edwin Locke and Gary Latham (1990), goals direct attention and effort, encourage long-term persistence, and help people develop strategies. The types of goals people set influence their efforts at self-regulation. Locke and Latham suggest that goals that are *challenging, difficult,* and *specific* are most productive. Goals that are challenging arouse the greatest effort, persistence, and concentration, whereas goals that are too easy or too hard can undermine motivation and often lead to poor outcomes. Goals that are divisible into specific, concrete steps also foster success. A person interested in running the Boston Marathon must first gain the stamina to run one mile. Once the goal of running a mile is achieved, subsequently more challenging goals can be undertaken to work up to the 26-mile marathon. Focusing on concrete short-term goals facilitates achieving long-term goals.

Feelings of self-efficacy   Albert Bandura (see Chapter 6) has argued that people's personal expectations for success play an important role in motivation. For instance, if you believe that your efforts at studying will lead to a good grade on the exam, you will be motivated to study. **Self-efficacy** represents the expectancy that your efforts will lead to success, and this belief helps to mobilize your energies. If you have low self-efficacy and do not believe that your efforts will pay off, you may be too discouraged to even try to study. People with high self-efficacy tend to set lofty goals and obtain favorable outcomes. However, sometimes people whose self-views are inflated set goals that they cannot possibly achieve. Goals that are challenging but not overwhelming usually are most conducive to success.

Achievement motivation   People differ in the extent to which they pursue challenging goals. The **achievement motive** refers to the desire to do well relative

How do people set and achieve personal goals?

Yerkes-Dodson law A psychological principle that dictates that behavioral efficiency increases with arousal up to an optimum point, after which it decreases with increasing arousal.

self-regulation The process by which people initiate, adjust, or stop actions in order to promote the attainment of personal goals or plans.

self-efficacy The expectancy that one's efforts will lead to success.

achievement motive The desire to do well relative to standards of excellence.

9.8 David McClelland studied the achievement motive in many cultures.

to standards of excellence. One of Henry Murray's students, David McClelland (Figure 9.8), spent most of his career studying people who were high in achievement motivation. In research spanning nearly 50 years McClelland and his students found that the desire to achieve helped people to succeed. Compared to those low in achievement need, high-need students sit closer to the front of classrooms, score higher on exams, and obtain better grades in courses relevant to their career goals (McClelland, 1987). Interestingly, high-achievement-need students tend to be more realistic in their career aspirations than students low in achievement need. They set personal goals that are challenging but attainable, whereas those low in achievement need tend to set goals that are either extremely easy or almost impossible. Parents of students who are high in achievement need tend to set very high goals for their children and they encourage persistence. These parents discourage their children from complaining or making excuses for poor performance, and they encourage them to try novel solutions. The one potential downside for those high in achievement motivation is that they like to achieve personal goals, and therefore in situations in which they have to delegate, such as managerial or political positions, they try to do too much themselves. Indeed, one research team found that need for achievement was inversely related to effectiveness among political leaders (Spangler & House, 1991).

SELF-REGULATION REQUIRES SELF-AWARENESS AND DELAY OF GRATIFICATION

How do people actually control their behavior to achieve their goals? First, people have to have a good idea of what their goals are and what they need to do to achieve them. Consider the goal of becoming an A student. You would first need to recognize that you are currently a B student and that you need to work harder if you are to achieve your goal.

According to cognitive psychologists George Miller, Eugene Galanter, and Karl Pribram (1960), people possess mental representations of their goal states and compare their current standing on relevant dimensions. The cognitive mechanism that directs behavior is based on negative feedback and is similar to the homeostatic models used for regulatory motives. Miller and his colleagues called this mechanism a *TOTE unit*, which stands for test-operate-test-exit (Figure 9.9).

In this model a comparison is made between the person's current state and the goal state. A discrepancy between the two states motivates behavior to minimize the discrepancy, and this process continues until the goal is achieved, at which point the person exits the process. The **TOTE model** requires people to keep track of their goals, and to be self-aware in order to monitor their progress toward achieving those goals. For example, to become an A student you have to pay attention to your performance on class exams and assignments as well as to the scores you need to get an A. If your scores are below the A criteria, you will have to work harder or more efficiently to achieve your goal.

Social psychologists Charles Carver and Michael Scheier (1981; 1998) developed an influential self-

9.9 A TOTE unit is a homeostatic model of self-regulation. Negative feedback from discrepancies between current state and ideal standing motivate efforts to reduce the discrepancy.

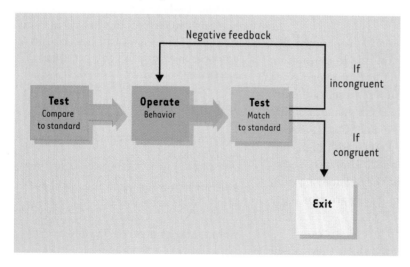

regulatory theory that builds upon the TOTE model by emphasizing the influence of self-awareness. When self-awareness is high, people act in accordance with personal standards; when self-awareness is low their inhibitions disappear and they lose touch with those standards, a mental state known as **deindividuation**. In one study, Edward Diener and his colleagues found that students were less likely to cheat on a test if they were seated in front of a mirror—which presumably increased self-awareness (Diener, 1979). Similarly, Diener found that children who were anonymous stole more candy at Halloween than children who were not anonymous. This is why many gambling casinos are noisy and absent of mirrors. The casinos try to eliminate all self-focusing cues so that people become deindividuated and overcome their inhibitions to gamble away their money.

According to the Carver and Scheier model, self-awareness of discrepancies between ideal and current state lead to either negative or positive affect, which then guides subsequent behavior. When people perform above some standard, they experience positive affect and therefore quit evaluating themselves on that dimension. If you are performing better than your goal you do not adjust your behavior to move back toward the goal (as would be suggested by the TOTE model).

When people are performing below their ideal standards, they experience negative affect, such as feelings of sadness, frustration, and anxiety—negative affect serves as a signal that you are not satisfying personal goals. A key point of the Carver and Scheier model is that future attempts at self-regulation depend on the likelihood of being able to narrow the gap between where you are and where you want to be. If the perceived probability of successfully reducing the discrepancy is high, then the negative affect motivates attempts to reduce the discrepancy. If, however, the perceived probability of success is low, then people may give up trying.

Self-destructive behavior According to Carver and Scheier, one way to reduce negative affect is to avoid self-awareness through *escapism*. Some people drink alcohol or take drugs to help them forget their troubles; others go for a run, read a book, or watch a movie. The selective appeal of escapist entertainment is that it distracts people from reflecting on their failures to live up to their goals, and therefore it helps them to avoid feeling bad about themselves. Unfortunately, evidence suggests that escaping from self-awareness is associated with a variety of self-destructive behaviors, such as binge eating, unsafe sex, and suicide. According to social psychologist Roy Baumeister (1991), these problems occur because people do things when they have low self-awareness that they would never do if self-aware.

Delayed gratification One common challenge in self-regulation is postponing immediate gratification in the pursuit of long-term goals. Students who want to become successful physicians often have to stay in and study rather than go out with their friends. The process of transcending immediate temptations in order to achieve long-term goals is known as **delay of gratification**. In a series of now-classic studies, developmental psychologist Walter Mischel gave children the choice of waiting to receive a preferred toy or food item or having a less preferred toy or food item right away. Mischel found that some children are better at delaying gratification than others, and that the ability to do so is predictive of success in life. Children who were able to delay gratification at age four were rated ten

TOTE model A model of self-regulation in which people evaluate progress towards achieving goals.

deindividuation A mental state of low self-awareness in which people act in an uninhibited manner.

delay of gratification When people transcend immediate temptations to successfully achieve long-term goals.

9.10 Children who are able to turn hot cognitions into cold cognitions have an easier time delaying gratification.

years later as being more socially competent and better able to handle frustration. The ability to delay gratification in childhood has been found to predict higher SAT scores, better school grades, and more positive teacher evaluations (Mischel et al., 1989).

How did some children manage to delay gratification? One strategy was simply ignoring the tempting item rather than looking at it. Older children, who were better at delaying gratification, tried covering their eyes or looking away, whereas very young children tended to look directly at the item they were trying to resist, making the delay especially difficult. A related strategy was self-distraction, through singing songs, playing games, or pretending to sleep. The most successful strategy involved what Mischel and his colleague Janet Metcalfe refer to as turning *hot cognitions* into *cold cognitions*. This sophisticated strategy involves mentally transforming the desired object into something undesired, such as viewing a tempting pretzel as a brown log or viewing marshmallows as clouds (Figure 9.10). Hot cognitions focus on the rewarding, pleasurable aspects of objects, whereas cold cognitions focus on conceptual or symbolic meanings. Metcalfe and Mischel (1999) proposed that this hot/cold distinction is based on how the information is processed in the brain, with the hot system being amygdala-based and the cold system hippocampus-based. According to this theory, the amygdala processes the reward features of biologically significant stimuli, whereas the hippocampus processes plans, strategies, and goals and is therefore responsible for self-control. A theory regarding the limits of self-control is discussed in "Using Psychological Science: Taming the Demands of Everyday Life."

How Do Cognitive, Social, and Cultural Factors Influence Motivation?

People are motivated by extrinsic and intrinsic factors. Extrinsic factors refer to the incentive or reward value of the activity. Intrinsic factors include novelty and motives for play and creativity. Providing extrinsic rewards for intrinsic activities reduces motivation to engage in the intrinsic activity. People are motivated to set and achieve goals and to control their behavior in pursuit of those goals. The best goals are challenging, concrete, and divisible into steps. The process by which people achieve goals is known as self-regulation, which depends on self-awareness of goals and behavior. Self-regulatory strength allows people to delay immediate gratification in the service of long-term goals.

WHAT NEURAL SYSTEMS ARE INVOLVED IN MOTIVATION?

Because early motivation theorists were unable to examine the working brain in action, they focused primarily on observing behavior, and they inferred motivational states from these observations. Now that our knowledge of brain systems has increased, we can study the neural processes involved in motivated behavior. This biological revolution is giving new insight into the neural systems involved in motivation, which include the nucleus accumbens, the hypothalamus, and the frontal lobes (Figure 9.11).

Using Psychological Science

TAMING THE DEMONS OF EVERYDAY LIFE

Humans have the capacity to delay gratification, control appetites and impulses, and persevere in order to attain goals, but many people have difficulties with self-control from time to time. A theory developed by Roy Baumeister and Todd Heatherton (1996) suggests that self-regulation may best be conceptualized as an individual strength. This means that *self-regulatory strength* is a limited resource that is renewable over time and can be increased with practice. It is only by exercising regular self-discipline that people become able to exert self-control when faced with temptations and persevere when goal attainment becomes difficult. Self-regulatory strength also can be depleted by situational demands. The dieter confronted by a party host offering an array of tasty treats may find himself unable to resist. Moreover, people who put a great deal of effort into controlling one aspect of their lives often have problems with self-control in other areas. This may be why New Year's resolutions fail: people vow to give up smoking, drinking, high-calorie foods, and television; and they set for themselves the impossible task of doing all of this at the same time. People only have so much self-regulatory strength, and to spread it too thin is to invite failure in multiple self-regulatory domains (Muraven & Baumeister, 2000).

Recall the discussion in Chapter 6 on the role of the mesolimbic dopamine pathway, which terminates in the nucleus accumbens, in creating reward states. In motivation, objects that satisfy drive states (such as food for hunger, water for thirst, and a partner for sexual arousal) cause release of dopamine in the nucleus accumbens and therefore are experienced as rewarding. At the same time, neurons in the nucleus accumbens communicate with brain regions involved in motor control and planning, thereby guiding behavior toward obtaining objects that will trigger reward.

THE HYPOTHALAMUS IS LINKED TO MOTIVATION

The hypothalamus regulates physiological responses to stimuli and organizes behaviors that maintain homeostasis. As you read in Chapter 3, the hypothalamus controls the autonomic and endocrine systems, which oversee behaviors related to survival and reproduction. In 1954, Eliot Stellar proposed that there are excitatory and inhibitory centers in the hypothalamus that regulate motivated behaviors. This *dual-center theory* of motivation has since been shown to be a bit too simplistic, but it is clear that specific regions within the hypothalamus are involved in many motivated behaviors. For example, damage to the hypothalamus is associated with motivational abnormalities in feeding, aggression, or sexual behavior, depending on which regions are affected; different areas of the hypothalamus are involved in offensive and defensive aggression.

The hypothalamus has many important brain connections that contribute to motivation, including inputs from various brain regions involved in arousal (such as the reticular formation) and projections to the frontal lobes, amygdala, and spinal cord. Through the thalamus, the limbic system receives input from sensory systems. Another limbic structure, the hippocampus, influences motivation primarily through its role in memory. Many motives require people to remember plans, strategies, and personal goals, and these types of memories are associated with the hippocampus.

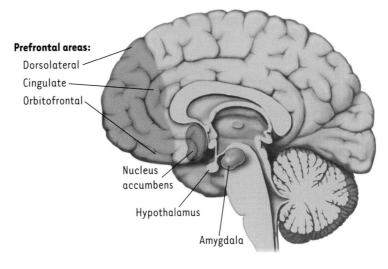

9.11 Major brain regions associated with motivation.

Prefrontal areas:
Dorsolateral
Cingulate
Orbitofrontal

Nucleus accumbens

Hypothalamus

Amygdala

What are the neural correlates of motivation?

THE PREFRONTAL CORTEX IS INVOLVED IN FORMULATING GOALS AND SELF-REGULATION

The frontal lobes, especially the *prefrontal cortex*, are especially important for integrating information from the senses, memory systems, and reward systems via their connections to the thalamus and limbic structures (see Figure 9.11). The prefrontal cortex is also involved in formulating goals, plans, and strategies. Studies using brain imaging have found significant activation of the prefrontal region during difficult tasks but not during simple recall tasks (Schacter & Buckner, 1998). The difficult tasks required effort, which links motivation to the prefrontal cortex. Damage to the prefrontal cortex is associated with difficulties in making plans and executing behavior necessary to achieve goals. Patients with prefrontal damage often have intact intelligence and comprehension but lack the ability to put their knowledge to use. They might be able to tell you how to achieve some goal, but they seem incapable of following their own suggestions and are often unwilling even to try. Scientists believe that people with prefrontal damage have difficulty focusing on a task because they are unable to ignore other stimuli in the environment (Knight & Grabowecky, 1995). For instance, if you sustained damage to your prefrontal region you might be unable to study because you could not tune out background noise or other distractions.

Dorsolateral prefrontal cortex   The *dorsolateral* region of the prefrontal cortex is involved in selecting and initiating actions (Spence & Frith, 1999). For instance, when people have to try to create a random sequence, there is selective increased activity in this prefrontal region. The dorsolateral prefrontal cortex also plays a critical role in working memory (see Chapter 7), which allows people to compare current performance with past standards and future goals. Working memory is important for the temporal organization of memory, which is often required for self-regulatory tasks. Consider the task of cooking a meal, which requires doing things in a certain order. People with frontal lobe dysfunction often have difficulties following plans that require temporal ordering of behaviors. They might be able to tell you all the ingredients for a recipe but be incapable of following the steps of the recipe in the necessary order.

Orbitofrontal cortex   Part of the prefrontal cortex, the *orbitofrontal cortex*, is particularly important for planning and coordinating behaviors designed to achieve goals. Damage to the orbitofrontal region is associated with a lack of self-concern and diminished motivation. It is possible that motivational deficits observed after brain injury occur because of damage to dopamine circuits that link the prefrontal and orbitofrontal cortex to the limbic system. The orbitofrontal cortex is also important for coding the possible reward values of different behavioral outcomes. There is compelling evidence that damage to the orbitofrontal cortex is associated with impaired processing of emotional information that assists judgment and decision making (Bechara et al., 2000). Other research shows that this area of prefrontal cortex is activated during craving for drugs (London et al., 2000). Hence, the overall notion is that the orbitofrontal cortex contributes to self-regulation through its assessment of reward value and its information about emotional responses to situations.

Anterior cingulate   Another brain structure involved in focusing attention on goals is the *anterior cingulate*, which is located in the prefrontal cortex but is sometimes also considered part of the limbic system. PET studies indicate that the anterior cingulate becomes active during novel tasks, difficult divided-attention tasks, and tasks in which participants have to make personal choices. For example, in one study participants were required to perform a working-memory task with increasing levels of difficulty (Bunge et al., 2001). Compared to a condition in which participants had to hold one or four letters in working memory, a condition that required them to hold six letters in working memory produced a significant increase in response time, indicating that it was a difficult task. This increase in response time was correlated with increased activation of the anterior cingulate (Figure 9.12). One fairly consistent conclusion regarding the anterior cingulate is that it is involved in tasks that are demanding (Seidman et al., 1998). The more demanding the task, the more activation is observed (Gevins et al., 1997).

One plausible role for the anterior cingulate is that it acts as an executive attention system by helping other brain regions decide which stimuli require immediate attention. Various emotional states also activate the anterior cingulate, suggesting that it is involved with the processing of mood-relevant information (Lane et al., 1998).

THERE IS A CLOSE CONNECTION BETWEEN MOTIVATION AND EMOTION

Emotional states often motivate specific behaviors. For instance, guilt might motivate you to atone or apologize and fear might motivate you to run away from people or situations that are threatening. Links between the frontal lobes and limbic system, especially the amygdala and orbitofrontal cortex, allow people to anticipate their emotional reactions in different situations, which helps people to regulate their behavior. For instance, thinking about how we would feel if we received a speeding ticket helps us to drive slower.

Neuroscientist Antonio Damasio has suggested that reasoning and decision making are guided by the emotional evaluation of an action's consequences. Damasio developed the **somatic marker theory** in his influential book *Descartes' Error*, in which he proposes that most self-regulatory actions and decisions are affected by the bodily reactions, called *somatic markers*, that arise from contemplating their outcomes. For Damasio, the term "gut feeling" almost can be taken literally. When you contemplate an action you experience an emotional reaction, based in part on your expectation of the action's outcome, which itself is determined by your past history of performing the action or similar actions. To the extent that driving fast has led to speeding tickets in the past, you will be motivated to slow down. Damasio has found that people with damage to the orbitofrontal cortex tend not to use past outcomes to regulate future behavior. For instance, in studies using a gambling task patients continued to follow a risky strategy that had proven faulty in previous trials.

In terms of the adaptiveness explanation for motivation, emotional reactions help us select responses that are likely to promote survival and reproduction. Thus, the anticipation that an event, action, or object will produce a pleasurable emotional state motivates us to approach them, whereas anticipation of negative emotions motivates us to avoid other situations. Hence, somatic markers may guide organisms to engage in adaptive behaviors.

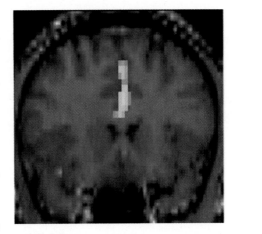
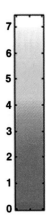
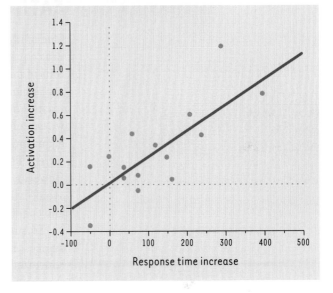

9.12 The graph shows that the increase in response time for the more difficult working-memory task was associated with increased activation of the anterior cingulate. This greater activation is indicated by yellow in the brain picture shown.

somatic marker theory Self-regulatory actions and decisions are affected by the bodily reactions that arise from their contemplation.

WHAT FACTORS MOTIVATE HUMAN EATING BEHAVIOR?

One of life's greatest pleasures is eating, and we do a lot of it—most North Americans consume between 75,000 and 85,000 meals during their lives, more than 40 tons of food! Ingesting food is something everyone needs to do to survive, but eating is much more than simply survival. Special occasions often involve elaborate feasts, and much of the social world revolves around food and eating. With eating we can observe complex interactions between biology and cultural influences on cognition. Common sense dictates that most eating is controlled by hunger and *satiety*. People eat when they feel hungry and quit eating when they become full. However, some people eat a great deal even when they are not hungry while others avoid eating even though they are not full. What are the physiological, cultural, and cognitive determinants of human eating behavior?

To survive and function properly, all living organisms need to take in substances that fuel metabolism. *Metabolism* is the chemical process by which food is converted into energy. This energy is used to run and repair the body. When you eat, food is digested in the gastrointestinal tract and three types of energy are made available to the body to use as fuel: *lipids* (from fat), *amino acids* (from protein), and *glucose*, a form of sugar (from complex carbohydrates). Most foods contain all three.

TIME AND TASTE PLAY A ROLE

Eating is greatly affected by learning. Have you ever noticed that most people get hungry at about the same time each day? This makes little sense, for people differ greatly in metabolic rate, the amount they ate for breakfast, and the amount of fat they have stored for long-term energy needs. Yet, most people eat lunch at approximately the same time. This occurs because people have been classically conditioned to associate eating with regular mealtimes. We eat not because we have deficient energy stores, but because it is time to eat. The clock indicating mealtime is much like Pavlov's bell, in that it leads to a number of anticipatory responses that motivate eating behavior and prepare the body for digestion. For instance, an increase in insulin promotes glucose utilization and increases short-term hunger signals. The sight and smell of tasty foods can have the same effect, and even the mere thought of fresh-baked bread, a favorite pizza, or a decadent dessert may initiate bodily reactions that induce hunger.

One of the main factors that determines eating behavior is flavor; good-tasting food motivates eating. When it comes to flavor, variety really is the spice of life. Animals presented with a variety of foods tend to eat a great deal more than animals presented with only one type. For instance, rats who normally maintain a steady body weight when eating one type of food eat huge amounts and become obese when presented with a variety of high-calorie foods, such as chocolate bars, crackers, and potato chips (Sclafani & Springer, 1976; Figure 9.13). Humans show the same effect, eating much more when several types of foods are available.

EATING IS CONTROLLED BY MULTIPLE NEURAL PROCESSES

The hypothalamus is the brain structure with the greatest influence on eating. Although it does not act alone to produce eating behavior, the hypothalamus integrates the various inhibitory and excitatory feeding messages and organizes behaviors involved in eating. In the first half of the twentieth century it was shown that damage to the hypothalamus leads to dramatic changes in eating behavior and body weight, depending on which specific area is damaged.

One of the first observations occurred in 1939, when researchers discovered that patients with tumors of the hypothalamus developed massive *obesity*, a medical condition of excess body weight. To examine whether obesity could be produced in normal-weight animals, researchers selectively damaged specific hypothalamic regions through lesioning. Experimentally lesioning the middle or *ventromedial* region (*VMH*) of the hypothalamus causes rats to eat great quantities of food, referred to as *hyperphagia*. Rats with VMH lesions grow extremely obese. In contrast to the VMH, lesioning the outer or *lateral* area of the hypothalamus (*LH*) is associated with a condition known as *aphagia*, which is diminished eating behavior that leads to weight loss and eventual death, unless the animal is force-fed. Note that stimulating a region usually has the opposite effects of damaging that region. Indeed, electrical stimulation applied to the VMH inhibits feeding, whereas electrical stimulation of the LH increases feeding.

As part of his dual-center theory of motivation, Eliot Stellar suggested that the LH was the primary hunger center and the VMH was the primary satiety center. Research over the past three decades, however, has shown that the VMH is not a satiety center. Rather, it appears that damage to the VMH causes an increase in blood levels of insulin, which results in increased fat storage; rats with VMH lesions store more fat than control rats even when they are fed the same amount (Woods & Stricker, 1999). Energy is therefore stored rather than used for immediate metabolic requirements, and the animals continue to eat in order to try to satisfy those immediate needs.

Brain structures other than the hypothalamus are also involved in eating behavior. For instance, taste cues such as sweetness or saltiness are processed in the orbitofrontal cortex, but only if the animal is hungry. This suggests that the orbitofrontal cortex processes information about the potential reward value of food. Damage to either the limbic system or right frontal lobes sometimes produces *gourmand syndrome*, in which people become obsessed with fine food and food preparation. One 48-year-old stroke patient who previously showed little interest in food became preoccupied with eating and eventually quit his job as a political correspondent to become a food critic (Regard & Landis, 1997). In spite of their

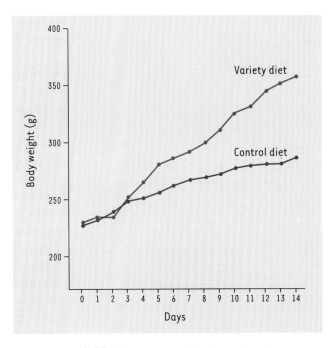

9.13 Rats eat a great deal more when given a variety of food and will become obese if given access to food such as marshmallows, salami, and cookies.

fascination with good-tasting food, those who have gourmand syndrome do not become overweight.

Internal sensations   Earlier you learned how negative feedback processes contribute to homeostasis, and for many years it was believed that eating was a classic homeostatic system. From this perspective, some sort of detector would notice deviations from set-point and would signal an animal to either begin eating or stop eating. But where do hunger signals come from? The search for energy-depletion detectors has led scientists from the stomach to the bloodstream to the brain.

The initial assumption, based on common sense, was that hunger derived from receptors in the stomach. Many people describe the subjective experience of hunger as emanating from their stomachs, and even our common descriptions of not being hungry refer to "feeling full." The first empirical test of the idea that hunger comes from the stomach was conducted by Walter Cannon and his research assistant Arthur Washburn. One day while working in the lab, Cannon noticed that Washburn's stomach was making rumbling sounds. Cannon theorized that perhaps it was doing so because Washburn was hungry, and so he quickly rigged up an experiment to test his hypothesis. Rather than let Washburn eat, Cannon had him swallow an empty balloon and then inflated the balloon so that he could register changes in the stomach walls caused by contractions. At the same time, he asked Washburn to report each time he felt a pang of hunger. Cannon found that Washburn reported feeling hungry at the end of each stomach contraction and therefore proposed that hunger was the subjective feeling associated with stomach contractions. Although these findings were intuitively appealing, it was quickly apparent that stomach contractions are not the only factors that determine hunger. Eating a small amount of food stops stomach contractions but is more likely to lead to additional eating than to terminate eating. Moreover, people who have had their stomachs removed continue to report being hungry. Research over the past few decades has established that stomach contractions and distensions are relatively minor determinants of hunger and eating.

In the 1940s and 1950s a number of researchers postulated the existence of receptors in the bloodstream that monitor levels of vital nutrients. One of the best known of these theories is the *glucostatic theory*, which proposes that specialized glucose receptors, called *glucostats*, monitor the extent to which glucose is taken up into cells so it can be used for energy. Because glucose is the primary fuel for metabolism and is especially crucial for neuronal activity, it makes sense for animals to be sensitive to deficiencies in glucose. Evidence supports the existence of glucoreceptors, and various experiments have demonstrated that injections of glucose in the bloodstream can postpone eating in hungry animals. Similarly, the *lipostatic theory* proposes a set-point for body fat in which deviations from set-point initiate compensatory behaviors to return to homeostasis. So, for instance, when an animal loses body fat, hunger signals motivate eating and a return to set-point.

The recently discovered hormone *leptin* is involved in fat regulation. Leptin is released from fat cells at a rate approximately equal to the amount of fat being stored in those cells. Leptin travels to the hypothalamus, where it acts to inhibit eating behavior. The message from leptin is slow acting and it takes considerable time after eating before leptin levels change in the body. Thus, leptin is more important for long-term body-fat regulation than for short-term eating control. Animals that lack the gene necessary to produce leptin become extremely obese, and injecting leptin into these animals leads to a rapid loss of body fat.

body mass index (BMI)   A ratio of body weight to height used to measure obesity.

OBESITY IS A GENETIC PREDISPOSITION

Because so many people want to lose weight, most research is less concerned with the *motivation to eat* than with understanding the motivation *not to eat*, which is a purposive rather than regulatory motive. Obesity is a major health problem, with both physical and psychological consequences. Although there is no precise definition, people are considered obese if they are approximately 20 percent over ideal body weight, as indicated by various mortality studies. One of the most widely used measures of obesity in research is **body mass index (BMI)**, which computes a ratio of body weight to height. Figure 9.14 shows how to calculate BMI and how to interpret the value obtained. Using standard BMI cutoffs, more than one-third of Americans currently are obese. Researchers have spent the last 60 years trying to understand the causes of obesity. Although we have learned a great deal, it is clear that obesity is a multifaceted problem that is influenced both by genes and the environment.

Genetic influence   A trip to the local mall will immediately reveal one obvious fact about body weight: obesity tends to run in families. Indeed, various family and adoption studies indicate that approximately half of the variability in body weight can be considered the result of genetics. One of the best and largest studies, carried out during the 1980s in Denmark, found that the BMI of adopted children was strongly related to the BMI of the biological parents and *not at all* to the BMI of the adoptive parents (Sorensen et al., 1992). Studies of identical and fraternal twins provide even stronger evidence of genetic control of body weight, with the heritability estimates (see Chapter 3) ranging from 60 to 80 percent. Moreover, the agreement for body weights of identical twins does not differ between twins raised together and twins raised apart, which suggests that environment has little effect on body weight.

If body weight is determined primarily by genes, why has the percentage of Americans who are obese doubled over the past few decades? Albert Stunkard, a leading researcher on human obesity, points out that genetics determine whether a person *can* become obese, but the environment determines whether that person will actually *become* obese (Stunkard, 1996). Consider an important study, conducted by geneticist Claude Bouchard, in which identical twins were overfed by approximately 1,000 calories each day for 100 days. Most of the twins gained some weight, but there was great variability between pairs in how much was gained (ranging from 4.3 to 13.3 kg) (Bouchard et al., 1990). However, there was a striking degree of similarity within the twin pairs in terms of how much weight they gained and in which parts of the body they stored the fat. Some of the twin pairs were especially likely to put on weight. Thus, genetics determine sensitivity to environmental influences. Genes predispose some people to obesity when they are in environments that promote overfeeding, such as contemporary Western societies.

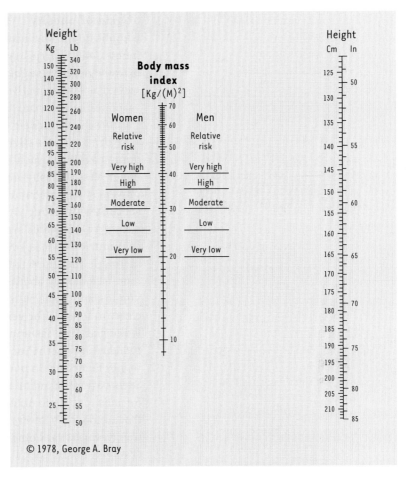

© 1978, George A. Bray

9.14 A nomogram for determining body mass index. You can find your own BMI by drawing a straight line between your height and weight. A BMI under 20 suggests that you are underweight, between 20 and 25 is average, between 25 and 30 is overweight, and 30 and higher is considered obese. According to the latest guidelines from the Centers for Disease Control and Prevention, a healthy BMI for an adult is between 18.5 and 25. Beyond or below this optimal range, the more you are at risk for health problems.

Why are people obese?

Stigma of obesity Obesity is associated with a significant number of medical complications, including heart problems, high blood pressure, and gastric ailments. It also carries a variety of psychological problems, primarily because of the extreme negative stigma associated with being overweight. Obese individuals are viewed as less attractive, less socially adept, less intelligent, and less productive than are their normal-weight peers (Dejong & Kleck, 1986). Moreover, perceiving oneself as overweight is linked to lower self-esteem, depression, and anxiety.

Not all cultures stigmatize obesity (Hebl & Heatherton, 1998). In some developing countries, such as many African nations, being obese is a sign of being upper class. Obesity may be desirable in developing countries because it helps prevent some infectious diseases, reduces the likelihood of starvation, and is associated with having more successful births. Obesity in developing countries may also serve as a status symbol, an indication that one can afford to eat luxuriously. In countries such as Tonga and Fiji, being obese is a source of personal pride and dieting is therefore not particularly common. In most Western cultures, where food is generally abundant, being overweight is associated with lower socioeconomic status, especially for women. The upper classes in Western cultures have a clear preference for very thin body types. These preferences can be verified by looking at high-fashion magazines. The typical woman presented in the glamour industry is 5 feet 11 inches tall and weighs approximately 110 pounds, which is 7 inches taller and 30 pounds lighter than the average woman in the United States. Such extreme standards of thinness reinforce body weight ideals that are difficult for most people to obtain. Indeed, women report holding ideals for body weight that are not only lower than average weight, but also lower than what men find attractive *and* what women think men find attractive, as may be seen in Figure 9.15 (Fallon & Rozin, 1985).

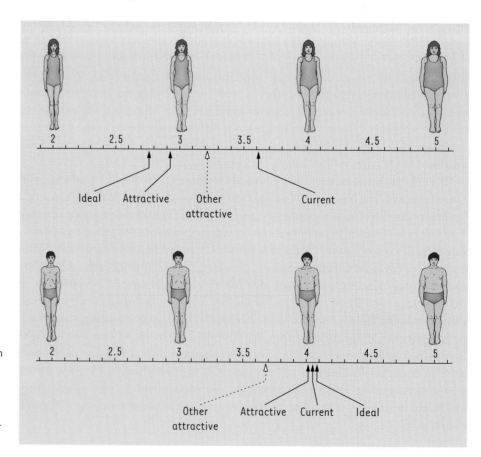

9.15 Men and women were asked to choose which figures represent how they currently view their bodies, what their ideal body shape is, and what they believe is attractive to the opposite sex. Women chose a body-weight ideal that is thinner than what they believe men want and also thinner than what men actually say they want in women. Men chose an ideal that is closer to their current self-rating and close to what they believe women prefer, but heavier than what women say they want in men.

DIETING IS TYPICALLY NOT SUCCESSFUL

Dieting is a notoriously ineffective means of permanent weight loss. Most individuals who lose weight through dieting eventually regain the weight, and very often they gain back *more* than they lost. A review by the National Institutes of Health of all published studies on the efficacy of weight-loss treatments revealed that fewer than 1 percent of those who lost weight managed to maintain weight loss for more than five years (NIH Technology Assessment Conference Panel, 1993). Why are people so bad at dieting?

Body weight set-point   The primary reason that most diets fail has to do with the body's natural defense against weight loss. Body weight is regulated around a set-point that is determined primarily by genetic influence. Although it is possible to alter body weight, the body responds to weight loss by slowing down the metabolism and using less energy. Thus, following food deprivation, it takes less food to maintain a given body weight. This response is described in "Studying the Mind: Understanding Dieting." Likewise, weight gain occurs much faster in previously starved animals than would be expected by caloric intake alone. In addition, repeated alterations between caloric deprivation and overfeeding have been shown to have cumulative metabolic effects, so that weight loss and metabolic functioning are slowed progressively more each time the animal is placed on caloric deprivation, and weight gain occurs more rapidly with each resumption of feeding. Such patterns might explain why "yo-yo dieters" tend to become progressively heavier over time.

Restrained eating   A second reason that diets tend to fail is because of occasional, or not so occasional, bouts of overeating. In important research over the past two decades, psychologists Janet Polivy and Peter Herman (1985) have demonstrated that chronic dieters, whom they call *restrained eaters*, are prone to excessive eating in certain situations. For instance, if restrained eaters believe they have eaten high-calorie foods, they subsequently abandon their diets (see Figure 9.16). The mindset of restrained eaters is, "I've blown my diet, so I might as well just keep eating." Anecdotal reports suggest that this behavior generalizes to the real world, so that restrained eaters diet all week only to have their diets fall apart on the weekends when they are faced with temptations.

Binge eating by restrained eaters depends on their *perception* of whether their diet is broken or not. Dieters can eat 1,000-calorie caesar salads and believe that their diets are fine, but if they eat 200-calorie chocolate bars they feel their diet is ruined and they become disinhibited. The problem for restrained eaters is that they rely on cognitive control of food intake, which is prone to break down when they eat high-calorie foods or feel emotionally distressed. Rather than eating according to internal states of hunger and satiety, restrained eaters eat according to rules, such as time of day, amount of calories, and type of food. Getting restrained eaters back in touch with internal motivational states is one goal of sensible approaches to dieting.

Disordered eating   When dieters fail to lose weight, they often blame their lack of willpower, vowing to redouble their efforts on the next diet. Repeated dietary failures may have harmful and permanent physiological and psychological consequences. Physiologically, weight-loss and weight-gain cycles alter metabolism, which may make future weight loss more difficult. Psychologically, repeated failures diminish body-image satisfaction and damage self-esteem. Over time,

9.16 Chronic dieters (called *restrained eaters*) and nondieters engaged in a supposed taste test, which was described as a test of perception (because the researchers did not want subjects to know that eating was being monitored). Prior to the taste test, some of the participants were asked to drink one or two obviously fattening milkshakes. The participants then were asked to taste and rate flavors of ice cream and were invited to help themselves to as much as they wanted. Nondieters ate sensibly: Those who had drunk one or two milkshakes ate much less ice cream than those who had not. Restrained eaters, however, did just the opposite, eating much more ice cream if they had had the milkshakes. This has been called the "what the hell effect."

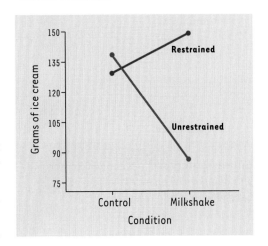

Studying the Mind

UNDERSTANDING DIETING

In 1966, several Vermont prisoners were given an interesting challenge: to try to gain 25 percent more weight (Sims et al., 1968). Sounds easy, right? Compared to the typical prison cuisine, the prison volunteers were plied with good-tasting, high-calorie food—as much as they could eat. For 6 months the average prisoner consumed more than 7,000 calories per day, nearly double their usual intake. Putting on the first few pounds was easy, but very quickly the prisoners found it hard to gain additional weight. Assuming each prisoner was eating about 3,500 extra calories a day (the equivalent of seven large cheeseburgers), simple math suggests each should have gained approximately 170 pounds over the 6 months. In reality, few gained more than 40 pounds. One prisoner stopped gaining weight even while eating more than 10,000 calories a day! The excessive eating was aversive for many of the prisoners, who reported feeling physically ill after eating. When the experiment ended, most of the prisoners quickly returned to their previous weights. Those who did not had family histories of obesity, supporting the view that genetics predispose obesity when people are exposed to overfeeding.

At the other end of the spectrum, how easy would it be for an average-weight person to lose weight? During World War II, more than 100 men volunteered to take part in a scientific study as an alternative to military service (Keys et al., 1950). The researchers were interested in the short- and long-term effects of semistarvation. Over 6 months, the men lost an average of 25 percent of their body weight but most found it very challenging to do and some had great difficulty losing more than ten pounds. The men underwent dramatic changes in emotions, motivation, and attitudes toward food. They became anxious, depressed, and listless; they lost interest in sex and other activities; and they became obsessed with food. Interestingly, many of these outcomes are quite similar to those experienced by people with eating disorders.

These two studies support the idea that body weight is regulated around a genetically determined set-point. Much like the homeostatic models discussed earlier, changes in body weight motivate changes in eating behavior and body functioning to defend against weight change. There is abundant evidence for set-point theory. For instance, most people's weight fluctuates only slightly over long periods of time, in spite of changes in diet and activity. However, set-point theories are controversial, and simple homeostatic models seem to be discredited by the increase in average body weights of Americans over the past few decades. However, physiological psychologist Richard Keesey points out that all homeostatic systems can be readjusted to a new set-point (Keesey, 1995). For this reason, some researchers prefer the term *settling point*. In these models body weight is homeostatic around a given value, but the value can be altered with changes in energy intake or expenditure. For instance, certain drugs are anorectic, meaning that taking them often results in a lowering of the body weight settling point. Researchers are still trying to determine which naturally occurring events lead to changes in settling point.

---

chronic dieters may begin to feel helpless and depressed, and some eventually engage in more extreme behaviors to lose weight, such as taking drugs, fasting, exercising excessively, or purging. For some vulnerable individuals, chronic dieting may promote the development of a clinical eating disorder.

The two best-known eating disorders are anorexia nervosa and bulimia nervosa. Individuals with **anorexia nervosa** have an excessive fear of becoming fat, and as a result they refuse to eat. Anorexia most often begins in early adolescence and mostly affects upper-class Caucasian girls. Although many adolescent girls strive to be thin, fewer than 1 in 100 meet the clinical criteria of anorexia nervosa (Table 9.1). These criteria include both objective measures of thinness and psychological characteristics that indicate an abnormal obsession with food and body weight. Those who have anorexia view themselves as fat in spite of being at least 15–25 percent underweight. Issues of food and weight permeate their lives, controlling not only how they view themselves, but how they view the world. Their self-imposed starvation usually draws favorable comments from others, although as the anorexic approaches her emaciated ideal, family and friends may become quite concerned. In many cases medical attention is required to prevent death from starvation. It is very difficult to treat anorexia, since patients maintain the belief that they are overweight, or not as thin as they would like to be, even when they are severely emaciated. This dangerous disease causes a number of serious health problems, especially a loss of bone density, and about 15–20 percent of

anorexia nervosa An eating disorder characterized by an excessive fear of becoming fat and a refusal to eat.

TABLE 9.1   Diagnostic Criteria for Anorexia Nervosa and Bulimia Nervosa

CRITERIA FOR ANOREXIA NERVOSA	CRITERIA FOR BULIMIA NERVOSA
A. Refusal to maintain body weight at or above a minimum normal for age and height (e.g., weight loss leading to maintenance of body weight less than 85 percent of that expected; or failure to make expected weight gain during period of growth, leading to body weight less than 85 percent of that expected).	A. Recurrent episodes of binge eating. An episode of binge eating is characterized by both of the following: (1) eating, in a discrete period of time (e.g., within any 2-hour period), an amount of food that is definitely larger than most people would eat during a similar period of time and under similar circumstances (2) a sense of lack of control over eating during the episode (e.g., a feeling that one cannot stop eating or control what or how much one is eating)
B. Intense fear of gaining weight or becoming fat, even though underweight.	B. Recurrent inappropriate compensatory behavior in order to prevent weight gain, such as self-induced vomiting; misuse of laxatives, diuretics, enemas, or other medications; fasting; or excessive exercise.
C. Disturbance in the way in which one's body weight or shape is experienced, undue influence of body weight or shape on self-evaluation, or denial of the seriousness of the current low body weight.	C. The binge eating and inappropriate compensatory behaviors both occur, on average, at least twice a week for 3 months.
D. In postmenarcheal females, amenorrhea, i.e., the absence of at least three consecutive menstrual cycles. (A woman is considered to have amenorrhea if her periods occur only following hormone, e.g., estrogen, administration.)	D. Self-evaluation is unduly influenced by body shape and weight.
	E. The disturbance does not occur exclusively during episodes of anorexia nervosa.

SOURCE: Diagnostic and Statistical Manual of the American Psychiatric Association, 1994.

those with anorexia eventually die from the disorder (American Psychiatric Association, 2000).

Individuals with **bulimia nervosa** alternate between dieting and binge eating. Bulimia often develops during late adolescence or early college years. Like anorexia, bulimia is most common among upper-class Caucasian women, but it is more common among minorities and men than is anorexia. Approximately 1–2 percent of women in high school and college meet the definitional criteria for bulimia nervosa. They tend to be average weight, or even slightly overweight, and they regularly binge eat, feel that their eating is out of control, have excessive worries about body weight issues, and engage in one or more compensatory behaviors, such as self-induced vomiting, excessive exercise, or the abuse of laxatives. Unlike anorexia, binge eating behavior tends to occur secretly. Although bulimia is associated with serious health problems, such as dental and cardiac problems, it is seldom fatal (Keel & Mitchell, 1997). A recent variant of bulimia is *binge eating disorder*, a newly identified disorder wherein individuals engage in binge eating but do not purge. Many of those with binge eating disorder are obese.

bulimia nervosa An eating disorder characterized by dieting, binge eating, and purging.

What Factors Motivate Human Eating Behavior?

The consumption of food is necessary for survival. A number of overlapping, redundant physiological systems motivate eating behavior to satisfy nutritional requirements. The motivation for variety helps animals achieve a nutritious diet, whereas fear of new foods and acquired taste aversions help animals avoid potential harm. Obesity results from a genetic predisposition to gain weight when overfed. Because obesity is stigmatized in some societies, many people who believe they are overweight diet. Diets are usually ineffective because of metabolic regulation and a tendency for dieters to binge eat. Long-term dieting is a risk factor for the development of eating disorders.

WHAT IS SLEEP?

The amount of time people spend eating is trivial compared to the amount of time they spend sleeping, a motivated behavior that occupies nearly a third of our lives. The average person sleeps around eight hours per night, although there is tremendous variability, both in terms of individual differences and in terms of age. Infants sleep most of the day, whereas elderly individuals may need only a few hours of sleep per night. Some adults report needing 9 or 10 hours of sleep to feel rested, whereas others report needing only an hour or two a night. One 70-year-old retired nurse, Miss M., reported sleeping only an hour a night. Perhaps, like the researchers who studied Miss M., you find this hard to believe. But after spending two sleepless nights in a sleep laboratory, apparently because of the excitement, she slept for only 99 minutes on the third night, awaking refreshed, cheerful, and full of energy (Meddis, 1977). Imagine having all those extra hours of spare time!

Sleep conforms to the general principles of motivation discussed earlier in this chapter: sleepiness directs a specific action (sleeping); you sleep until you no longer need to; the more deprived of sleep you are, the sleepier you feel. Yet sleep differs from other motivated behaviors in that it directs people to spend time apparently not performing any activity at all. But as you sleep, your brain and other physiological processes are quite active. Sleep is clearly an important behavior, given the amount of time people and other animals devote to it. As discovered by Randy Gardner in the opening to this chapter, you can delay sleep, but you cannot postpone it indefinitely. Given that sleep occurs in all animals, most researchers believe that it serves some biological purpose. However, as you will see, it isn't at all clear at the present time exactly *why* sleep is important.

SLEEP IS AN ALTERED STATE OF CONSCIOUSNESS

When you are asleep your brain is still processing information. People who sleep with pets or children tend not to roll over and smother them. Most people also don't fall out of bed while sleeping, indicating that the brain is still aware of the environment, such as the relative position of the edge of the bed. Indeed, even though you are not conscious when asleep, your mind is at work, analyzing potential dangers, controlling body movements, and shifting body parts to maximize comfort. The difference between sleep and awake states has as much to do with conscious experience as biological processes.

insomnia A sleep disorder characterized by an inability to sleep.

Before the discovery of objective methods to assess brain activity, most people believed that the brain went to sleep along with the rest of the body. However, the invention of the electroencephalogram (EEG), a machine that measures the electrical activity of the nervous system, revealed that there is a great deal going on in the brain during sleep. The fact that there are different psychophysiological states during sleep has been described as one of the first major discoveries of neuroscience (Hobson, 1995). When people are awake, the neurons in their brains are extremely active, as evidenced by short, frequent, desynchronized brain signals known as *beta waves* (Figure 9.17). When people close their eyes and relax, brain activity slows down and becomes more synchronized, a pattern that produces *alpha waves*.

Stages of sleep Sleep occurs in stages, as evidenced by changes in EEG readings. As you drift off to sleep, you enter stage 1, characterized by *theta waves*, from which you can be easily aroused. Indeed, if you are awakened you will probably deny that you were sleeping. In this light sleep you might see fantastical images, such as geometric shapes, or have the sensation that you are falling or that your limbs are jerking. As you progress to stage 2, your breathing becomes more regular and you become less sensitive to external stimulation. You are now really asleep. Interestingly, although the EEG continues to show theta waves, there are occasional bursts of activity known as *sleep spindles* and large waves called *k-complexes*. Some researchers believe that these are signals of brain mechanisms involved with shutting out the external world and keeping people asleep (Steriade, 1992). Abrupt noise can trigger k-complexes, and as people age they show fewer sleep spindles and sleep much more lightly. This is interesting because it suggests that the brain actually has to work to keep you sleeping. For some people, getting to sleep and staying asleep is difficult. **Insomnia** is a sleep disorder in which people's mental health and ability to function is compromised by their inability to sleep. Ways to deal with insomnia are listed in Table 9.2.

The progression to deep sleep occurs through stages 3 and 4, which are marked by large, regular brain patterns referred to as *delta waves*. This period of sleep is often referred to as *slow-wave sleep*, reflecting the presence of delta waves. It is extremely hard to wake someone up if they are in slow-wave sleep, and when they do wake up they are often very disoriented. However, people still process some information in stage 4. Parents can be aroused by crying children but blissfully ignore sirens or traffic noise. The mind continues to evaluate the environment for potential danger.

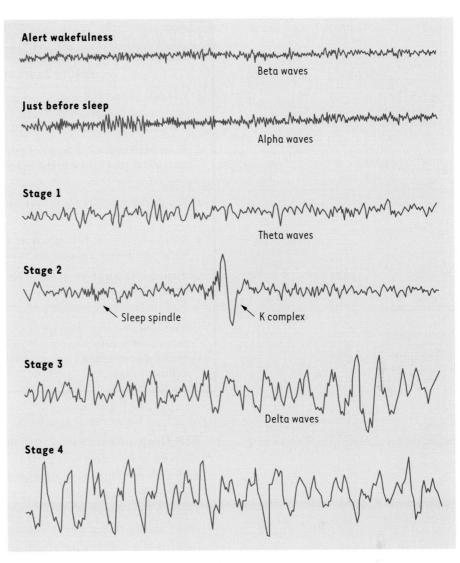

9.17 Patterns of electrical brain activity during different stages of sleep.

How is sleep measured?

TABLE 9.2 Sleeping Through the Night

HOW TO DEVELOP GOOD SLEEPING HABITS

1. Go to bed and wake up at the same time every day, including weekends. Establish a routine to help set your biological clock. Changing the time you wake up each day can alter sleep cycles and disrupt other physiological systems.

2. Never have alcohol or caffeine just before going to bed. Alcohol might help you get to sleep more quickly, but it will interfere with your sleep cycle and cause you to wake up early the next day.

3. Regular exercise will help your sleep cycles, but do not do it immediately before going to sleep.

4. Use your bed only for sleeping and sex. Do not spend time in your bed reading, eating, or watching television. You want your mind to associate your bed with sleeping.

5. Relax. Don't worry about the future. Have a warm bath or listen to soothing music. Learning relaxation techniques, such as imagining you are on the beach, with the sun shining on your back and radiating down your hands, may assist in dealing with chronic stress.

6. If you have trouble sleeping, get up and do something else. Don't force yourself to lie there trying to get to sleep. Remember that one sleepless night won't affect your performance very much and worrying about how you will be affected by not sleeping only makes it more difficult to sleep.

REM sleep   After about 90 minutes of sleep, a very peculiar thing happens. The sleep cycle reverses, returning to stage 3 and then to stage 2. At this point, the EEG suddenly indicates a flurry of beta-wave activity that usually indicates an alert, awake mind. At the same time, the eyes start darting back and forth rapidly beneath closed eyelids. This is called **REM sleep** for the *rapid eye movements* that occur during this stage. It is sometimes called *paradoxical sleep* because of the paradox of a sleeping body with an activated brain. Indeed, some neurons in the brain, especially in the occipital cortex and brainstem regions, are more active during REM sleep than during waking hours. But while the brain is active, most muscles in the limbs and body are paralyzed during REM episodes. At the same time, the body shows signs of arousal in the genitals, with most males of all ages developing an erection and females experiencing clitoral engorgement.

The psychological significance of REM sleep is that about 80 percent of the time that people are awakened during REM sleep they report dreaming, compared to less than half of the time during non-REM sleep (Solms, 2000). As you will see below, the dreams themselves are quite different during the two types of sleep.

Over the course of the night, the sleep cycle repeats, with progression from slow-wave sleep to REM sleep and then back to slow-wave sleep. As morning approaches, the sleep cycle becomes shorter and relatively more time is spent in REM sleep (Figure 9.18). People also briefly awaken many times during the night but do not remember awakening in the morning. As people age, they sometimes have more difficulty falling back to sleep after awakening.

REM sleep The stage of sleep marked by rapid eye movements, dreaming, and paralysis of motor systems.

SLEEP IS AN ADAPTIVE BEHAVIOR

Why do we sleep? It can be dangerous to tune out the external world. If nothing else, it might seem like a huge waste of time that you could spend in more productive ways. But people cannot override indefinitely the desire to sleep; the body shuts down whether we like it or not. Sleep must do something important, because nearly all animals sleep. Some animals have amazing sleeping styles. Some species of dolphins have *unihemispherical sleep*, in which the cerebral hemispheres take turns sleeping! Researchers do not yet know exactly why animals sleep, but there are three general explanations that are used to describe the adaptiveness of sleep: restoration, circadian cycles, and facilitation of learning.

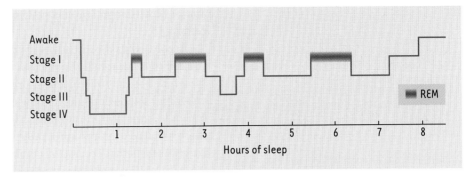

9.18 Stages of sleep over the course of the night.

Restoration and sleep deprivation

The *restorative theory* of sleep emphasizes that the brain and body need to rest and that sleep allows the body to repair itself. Indeed, growth hormone is released during deep sleep, and one of its functions is to facilitate repair of damaged tissue. Additional evidence that sleep is a time of restoration is that people who have engaged in vigorous physical activity, such as running marathons, seem to sleep longer. But people sleep even if they spend the day being physically inactive. In addition, it appears that sleep allows the brain to restore glycogen stores and strengthen the immune system (Hobson, 1999).

Numerous laboratory studies have examined the effects of sleep deprivation on physical and cognitive performance. Surprisingly, most studies find that two or three days of deprivation have little effect on strength, athletic ability, or cognitive performance on complex tasks. Performing boring or mundane tasks when sleep deprived, however, is nearly impossible. A brain-imaging study of sleep-deprived people found increased activation of the prefrontal cortex, suggesting that some brain regions may compensate for the effects of deprivation (Drummond et al., 2000). Over long periods, however, sleep deprivation eventually causes problems with mood and cognitive performance. Indeed, studies using rats have found that extended sleep deprivation compromises the immune system and leads to death.

People who suffer from chronic sleep deprivation, such as many college students, may experience lapses in attention, reduced short-term memory, and **microsleeps**, in which they fall asleep during the day for brief periods of time ranging from a few seconds to as long as a minute. These microsleeps may lead to disastrous results if the person is driving a car or performing a dangerous task.

Interestingly, sleep deprivation might serve one very useful purpose, which is helping people overcome depression. Consistent evidence has emerged over the past decade demonstrating that depriving depressed people of sleep sometimes alleviates their depression. This effect appears to occur because sleep deprivation leads to increased activation of serotonin receptors, as do drugs used to treat depression (Benedetti et al., 1999).

Circadian rhythms

The *circadian rhythm* theory of sleep proposes that sleep has evolved to keep animals quiet and inactive during times of the day when there is greatest danger, which for most is when it is dark. Physiological and brain processes are regulated into regular patterns known as **circadian rhythms** (circadian roughly translates to "about a day"). Body temperature, hormone levels, and sleep-wake cycles are all examples of circadian rhythms, which operate like biological clocks. Circadian rhythms are themselves controlled by cycles of light

microsleeps Brief unintended sleep episodes, ranging from a few seconds to a minute, caused by chronic sleep deprivation.

circadian rhythms The regulation of biological cycles into regular patterns.

and dark, although animals continue to show these rhythms when light cues are removed.

According to the circadian rhythm theory, animals need only so much time in the day to accomplish the necessities of survival, and it is adaptive to spend the remainder of the time inactive, preferably hidden away. Accordingly, the amount an animal sleeps depends on how much time it needs to obtain food, how easily it can hide, and how vulnerable it is to attack. Small animals sleep a great deal, whereas large animals vulnerable to attack, such as cows and deer, sleep little. Large animals that are not vulnerable, such as lions, also sleep a great deal. After a fresh kill, a lion may sleep for days on end. Humans, who depend greatly on vision for survival, adapted to sleeping at night, when the lack of light put them in possible danger.

Facilitation of learning It has been proposed that sleep may be important because it is involved in the strengthening of neuronal connections that serve as the basis of learning. The general idea is that circuits that have been wired together during the waking period are consolidated, or strengthened, during sleep (Wilson & McNaughton, 1994). Robert Stickgold and colleagues (2000) conducted a study in which they required participants to learn a complex visual-discrimination task. They found that participants improved at the task only if they had slept for at least six hours following training. Both slow-wave sleep and REM sleep appeared to be important for learning to take place. The researchers argued that learning the task required neuronal changes that normally occur only during sleep. Although learning certainly can take place in the absence of sleep, sleep seems to be an efficient time for the consolidation of learning. Indeed, some evidence indicates that students have more REM sleep during exam periods, when it might be expected that greater consolidation of information is taking place (Smith & Lapp, 1991).

The argument that sleep, especially REM sleep, promotes development of brain circuits for learning is also supported by the changes in sleep patterns that occur over the life course. Infants and the very young, who learn an incredible amount in a few short years, sleep the most and also spend the most time in REM sleep.

SLEEP AND WAKEFULNESS ARE REGULATED BY MULTIPLE NEURAL MECHANISMS

Multiple neural mechanisms are involved in producing and maintaining circadian rhythms and sleep. For instance, the biological clock is located in the *suprachiasmatic nucleus (SCN)* of the hypothalamus. Light-sensitive photoreceptors in the retina send signals to the SCN. These photoreceptors are different from the rods and cones that provide visual information, and they may even work for people who are otherwise blind. Individual neurons within the SCN seem to be the neural basis of the biological clock, as they show a peak in firing activity about once a day (Welsh et al., 1995). The SCN also signals a tiny structure called the *pineal gland* (Figure 9.19) to secrete melatonin, a hormone that travels through the bloodstream and affects various receptors in the body and the brain. Bright light suppresses production of melatonin, whereas darkness triggers its release. It has recently been noted that taking melatonin can help people cope with jet lag and shift work, both of which interfere with circadian rhythms. Taking melatonin also appears to help people get to sleep, although it is presently unclear why this happens.

Brain stem and arousal   Sleep involves alterations in states of arousal, thereby implicating brain mechanisms that produce aroused states. In 1949, Giuseppe Moruzzi and Horace Magoun found that stimulating the *reticular formation* in the brain stem led to increased arousal in the cerebral cortex. If you cut the fibers from the reticular formation to the cortex, animals fall asleep and stay asleep until they die. Accordingly, Moruzzi and Magoun proposed that low levels of activity in the reticular formation produce sleep, and high levels lead to awakening.

It is now known that multiple regions within the reticular formation participate in the control of sleep-wake cycles. For instance, the *locus coeruleus* sends the neurotransmitter norepinephrine to many regions of the brain, thereby increasing cortical arousal. Research has demonstrated that the locus coeruleus is highly active when animals are awake, less active during non-REM sleep, and almost completely inactive during REM sleep (Figure 9.20). The neurotransmitter serotonin is also involved in sleep. Originating in the *raphe nuclei*, a group of neurons located within the reticular formation, serotonin projects to many areas throughout the cortex. This system is usually most active during strenuous motor activity, such as walking or running. Thus, activation of norepinephrine and serotonin systems produces arousal, and in general, a slowing of activation in the reticular formation appears to be associated with non-REM sleep. This decrease in arousal is associated with a deactivation of many cortical areas, as verified by recent brain-imaging studies (Hobson et al., 2000).

What triggers sleep? There is some evidence that a small area of the basal forebrain just in front of the hypothalamus, called the *preoptic area*, is involved in inducing non-REM sleep. Neurons in this region become more active during non-REM sleep and lesioning this region leads to insomnia. Once the preoptic area is activated, inhibitory signals are sent to the locus coeruleus and raphe nuclei, thereby reducing arousal and triggering sleep.

REM sleep   During REM sleep, various neural processes are activated, of which some lead to paralysis of motor systems whereas others lead to activation of mental circuits related to motivational states. For instance, neurons in the *pons*, a region of the brain stem, send signals to the spinal cord that block movement during REM sleep. Surgical lesioning of the pons causes animals to become very active while in REM sleep, as if they were acting out scenes from their dreams. People who have strokes that damage the brain stem sometimes develop *REM behavior disorder*, in which the normal muscle paralysis that accompanies REM is absent. Unfortunately for their sleeping partners, these individuals can become quite violent

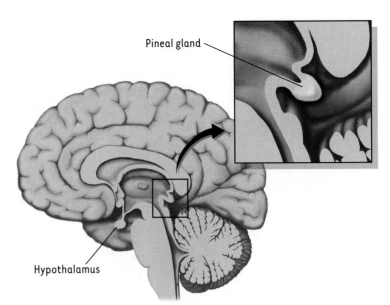

Pineal gland

Hypothalamus

9.19 The pineal gland is a small gland located in front of the cerebellum. It receives signals from the hypothalamus.

9.20 Activity of neurons in the locus coeruleus during wakefulness and stages of sleep.

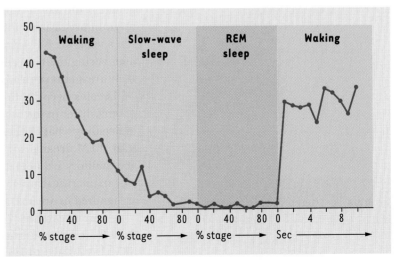

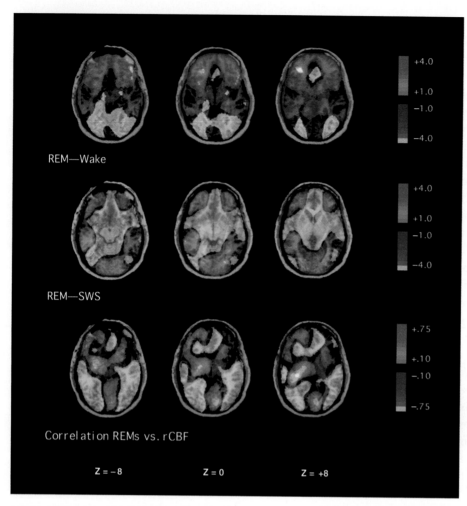

REM—Wake

+4.0
+1.0
−1.0
−4.0

REM—SWS

+4.0
+1.0
−1.0
−4.0

Correlation REMs vs. rCBF

+.75
+.10
−.10
−.75

Z = −8   Z = 0   Z = +8

9.21 Patterns of activation using PET, comparing REM to slow-wave sleep and waking. Note that there is greater activation (indicated by yellow and red) in limbic regions during REM than slow-wave sleep. There is also less activation (indicated by purple) of much of the prefrontal cortex.

during REM episodes. By contrast, people with *cataplexy* experience REM muscle paralysis while awake; their muscles can suddenly become flaccid and they collapse to the floor.

REM sleep is triggered by acetylcholine neurons in the pons. In the minute before REM episodes, these neurons become increasingly active, eventually producing REM. Signals from this region are transmitted to the thalamus and the occipital lobes and also appear to trigger the eye movements that give REM sleep its name.

Brain-imaging studies show activation of limbic structures, such as the amygdala, anterior cingulate, and orbitofrontal cortex, during REM sleep. This activation occurs along with a lessening of activity of the dorsolateral prefrontal cortex, an area typically involved in rational thought and decision making. Surprisingly, the primary visual areas seem to be inhibited during REM sleep, whereas the visual association areas are activated (Braun et al., 1998; Figure 9.21). These patterns of activation may produce one of the hallmark associations of REM sleep, vivid imagery in dreaming.

PEOPLE DREAM WHILE SLEEPING

Dreaming is one of life's great mysteries, as the mind conjures up images and stories that make little sense and sometimes scare the dreamer awake. **Dreams** are an altered state of consciousness in which images and fantasies are confused with reality. Usually, people realize they were dreaming only when they wake up. Some people claim not to remember their dreams, but unless a person has a specific brain injury or is taking medication, everyone dreams. Indeed, the average person spends six full years of his or her life dreaming. People who have trouble remembering their dreams can be taught to do so, mostly by trying to write down their dreams as soon as they wake up.

Dreams occur both in REM and non-REM sleep, although the contents of dreams differ in the two types of sleep. Non-REM dreams are often very dull, such as deciding what clothes to wear or thinking about taking notes in class. By contrast, REM dreams are often very bizarre. They involve intense emotion, visual and auditory hallucinations (but rarely taste, smell, or pain), illogical content, and an uncritical acceptance of events. Rules of time and space and physical laws are ignored in dreams, as when you walk into one room and emerge in another.

When researchers first noticed rapid eye movements in the 1950s, they initially believed that dreams were mainly a product of REM sleep. Initially, non-REM dreams were dismissed as trivial or as based on faulty recollection. However,

dreams An altered state of consciousness in which images and fantasies are confused with reality.

it is now clear that REM sleep can occur without dreaming and dreams can occur without REM sleep. Moreover, REM and dreaming appear to be controlled by different neural signals (Solms, 2000). Activation of different brain regions during REM and non-REM sleep may be responsible for their different types of dreams. The content of REM dreams is a result of the activation of brain structures associated with motivation, emotion, and reward along with the visual association areas. This closed loop allows the brain's emotion centers and visual association areas to interact without self-awareness, reflective thought, or input from the external world.

What do dreams mean?   Sigmund Freud, in one of the first major theories of dreams, argued that dreams contained hidden content that represented unconscious conflicts. According to Freud, the **manifest content** is the dream the way the dreamer remembers it, whereas the **latent content** is what the dream symbolizes, or the material that is disguised to protect the dreamer. However, there is virtually no support for Freud's idea that dreams represent hidden conflicts or that objects in dreams have special symbolic meanings. What is true is that daily life experiences influence the content of dreams. That is, you may be especially likely to have anxiety dreams while studying for exams. The dreams themselves have a thematic structure, in that they unfold as events or stories rather than as jumbles of disconnected images, but there is apparently no secret meaning to the way the story is told.

Activation-synthesis hypothesis   Sleep researcher Alan Hobson proposed an influential theory that has dominated thinking about dreaming for the past two decades. Hobson's **activation-synthesis hypothesis** proposes that neural stimulation from the pons activates mechanisms that normally interpret visual input. The sleeping mind tries to make sense of random neuronal firing by synthesizing apparent activity in visual and motor neurons with stored memories. From this perspective, then, dreams are *epiphenomenal*—they are the experienced side effects of mental processes. Hobson and his colleagues (2000) have recently revised the activation-synthesis model to take into account recent findings in cognitive neuroscience. For instance, they have included amygdala activation as the source of the emotional content of dreams, and they propose that deactivation of the frontal cortices contributes to the delusional and illogical aspect of dreams. By its nature, the activation-synthesis hypothesis is more concerned with REM than non-REM dreams.

Evolved threat-rehearsal strategies   Antti Revonsuo (2000) has proposed an evolutionary account wherein dreams simulate threatening events to allow people to rehearse coping strategies. Although Revonsuo does not believe that all dreams represent this function, he does suggest that dreams that provided people with solutions to adaptive problems helped them to survive and reproduce; thus dreaming is a result of natural selection. That the majority of dreams reported by people involve negative emotions, such as fear and anxiety, supports the evolved threat-rehearsal theory. Dreaming is associated with the activation of limbic structures, such as the amygdala, that are also activated during real threat encounters. Moreover, people tend to dream about real threats in their lives and to have nightmares about past traumas for long periods of time.

manifest content The plot of a dream; the way a dream is remembered.

latent content What a dream symbolizes, or the material that is disguised in a dream to protect the dreamer.

activation-synthesis hypothesis A theory of dreaming that proposes that neural stimulation from the pons activates mechanisms that normally interpret visual input.

What Is Sleep?

All animals experience sleep, an altered state of consciousness in which the sleeper loses most contact with the external world. Sleep has a number of stages that can be identified by different patterns on EEG recordings. There is a basic distinction between non-REM and REM sleep, and different neural mechanisms are responsible for producing each type, although the brainstem figures prominently in the regulation of sleep-wake cycles. Dreams occur in REM and non-REM sleep, although the content of those dreams differs. This may be due to differential activation of brain structures associated with emotion and cognition. Although a number of theories have been proposed to explain sleeping and dreaming, their biological function is currently unclear.

CONCLUSION

Motivation is the area of psychology concerned with determining why people engage in specific behaviors. Although motivational psychologists used to focus exclusively on either regulatory or purposive motives, an increasing emphasis on neuroscience has blurred the distinction between these approaches. For instance, the control of human eating involves both purposive and regulatory mechanisms, and the brain is involved in both types of motivation. Moreover, collaborative efforts across the levels of analysis between neuroscientists and social psychologists have led to new theories of motivation, such as the hot/cold model of delayed gratification, which build as cumulative principles. Neuroscientific approaches have also allowed researchers to reexamine important questions, such as how instincts and drives motivate behavior. Increasing knowledge about the brain may allow for a deeper understanding of important human motives, such as how people set and achieve personal goals, and also of the extent to which people can control or override basic biological processes, such as sleep and eating.

FURTHER READINGS

Brownell, K. D., & Fairburn, C. G. (1995). *Eating disorders and obesity: A comprehensive handbook*. New York: Guilford Press.

Capaldi, E. D. (1996). *Why we eat what we eat*. Washington, DC: American Psychological Association.

Franken, R. E. (1998). *Human motivation*. Pacific Grove, CA: Brooks Cole.

Hobson, J. A. (1995). *Sleep*. New York: Scientific American Library.

Logue, A. W. (1991). *The psychology of eating and drinking*. New York: Freeman.

Mook, D. G. (1987). *Motivation: The organization of action*. New York: W. W. Norton.

Stellar, J. R., & Stellar, E. (1984). *The neurobiology of motivation and reward*. New York: Springer-Verlag.

COPING AS A COMMUNITY

In New York after the September 11 attacks, missing persons posters and individual memorials evolved into collective public shrines for the victims. Strong social support is profoundly important for people trying to cope with all types of emotional stress.

TIMELINE

1872
Emotions Are Adaptive
Charles Darwin publishes *Expression of Emotion in Man and Animals*, in which he argues that for many species emotions are adaptive and are hardwired through the processes of natural selection.

1884
Reactions Cause Emotions
William James and Carl Lange, working separately, assert that physical reactions can cause emotions.

1927
Emotions Cause Bodily Reactions Walter Cannon, in contrast to James, argues that people experience emotional states that subsequently lead to physiological responses.

1930s
General Adaptation Syndrome Endocrinologist Hans Selye proposes that stressors lead to bodily reactions and that prolonged stress could lead to deficiencies in the immune system. Selye's work launches the field of health psychology.

Emotions, Stress, and Coping

OUTLINING THE PRINCIPLES

HOW ARE EMOTIONS ADAPTIVE?

Facial Expressions Communicate Emotion

Emotions Serve Cognitive Functions

Emotions Strengthen Interpersonal Relations

HOW DO PEOPLE EXPERIENCE EMOTIONS?

There Is a Subjective Component

There Is a Physiological Component

There Is a Cognitive Component

People Regulate Their Moods

WHAT IS THE NEUROPHYSIOLOGICAL BASIS OF EMOTION?

Emotions Are Associated With Autonomic Activity

The Amygdala and Orbitofrontal Cortex Are Involved in Emotion

Emotion Systems Are Lateralized in the Brain

HOW DO PEOPLE COPE WITH STRESS?

There Is a General Adaptation Syndrome

There Is Stress in Daily Life

Stress Affects Health

Stress Affects the Immune System

Coping Is a Process

CONCLUSION
FURTHER READINGS

1937

Neural Basis of Emotions
James Papez hypothesizes that emotional expression is mediated by several neural systems that form a circuit (known as the "Papez loop").

1962

Two-Factor Theory Stanley Schachter and Jerome Singer propose that emotions are the result of physical arousal and the attribution, or cognitive explanation, of the source of the arousal.

1963

Facial Feedback Hypothesis Based on Darwin's writings, Silvan Tomkins proposes that facial expressions trigger the experience of emotions.

1970s–1980s

Universal Emotional Expressions Paul Ekman and his colleagues find that people from diverse cultures recognize similar facial expressions. Carroll Izard demonstrates that infants also display basic emotions in their facial expressions.

1980s

Coping Styles Susan Folkman and Richard Lazarus propose that the way people cope with stress determines its impact. They posit a distinction between coping strategies that focus on emotion and those that focus on problem solving.

RESEARCH QUESTIONS
?.?.?

for Studying Emotions, Stress, and Coping

What functions do emotions serve?

What are the components of emotional experience?

How do people control or change their emotions?

Where are emotions located in the body?

What is stress?

What are the effects of stress?

What factors help people deal with stress?

Elliot was in his early thirties when he began to suffer from severe headaches. He was happily married, a good father, and was doing well professionally. His headaches increased until he could no longer concentrate, so he went to see his doctor. Sadly, it turned out Elliot had a tumor the size of a small orange growing behind his eyes. As the tumor grew, it forced his frontal lobes upward into the top of his skull. A group of skilled surgeons removed the benign tumor, but in doing so they could not help but remove some of the surrounding frontal lobe tissue. Although the surgery appeared at first to be a great success—Elliot's physical recovery was quick and he continued to be an intelligent man with a superb memory—Elliot changed in a way that baffled his friends and family. He no longer experienced emotion.

On the surface, Elliot seemed a reasonable, intelligent, and charming man, and yet his life fell apart. He lost his job; entered a doomed business venture with a sleazy character against the advice of his family and lost all his savings; divorced, remarried, and then quickly divorced again; and so on. He was incapable of making even trivial decisions, and he failed to learn from his mistakes. Though he had previously been a caring and compassionate man, he was now detached from his problems, reacting to them as if they had happened to someone else about whom he didn't care that much.

The neurologist Antonio Damasio was asked to examine Elliot to ascertain whether his emotional problems were real and whether they might have been due to the surgery. Damasio noted that Elliot displayed few emotional responses: "I never saw a tinge of emotion in my many hours of conversation with him: no sadness, no impatience, no frustration with my incessant and repetitious questioning" (Damasio, 1994, p. 45). Damasio's research team showed Elliot a series of disturbing pictures, such as severely injured bodies, and found that none of these elicited an emotional reaction from him. Elliot was not oblivious to his loss of emotion. He was able to report that he knew the pictures were disturbing, and that before the

1990s

Interpersonal Functions of Emotions Researchers begin to focus attention on emotions that serve interpersonal functions, such as shame, guilt, and embarrassment, with the idea that emotions evolved to solve adaptive problems.

1990s

The Emotional Brain Researchers such as Joseph LeDoux develop models of how the brain processes emotions. LeDoux's work demonstrates that the amygdala is especially important for the experience and perception of emotion.

2000s

Affective Neuroscience Brain-imaging techniques allow researchers to study the emotional brain in action. Emotions rely on the activity of interrelated brain structures, especially those in the limbic system and prefrontal cortex.

surgery he would have had an emotional response, but now he had none.

Imagine what your life would be like if you did not have any feelings. Like, the android character from *Star Trek: The Next Generation*, Commander Data, you would be a rational being capable of sensation, perception, thought, memory, decision-making, and so on, but you would not have any emotions. What sort of life would that be? For human beings, every action and thought is colored by emotional reactions. As you read in the last chapter, emotions are a primary source of motivation, as people seek objects and activities that make them feel good and avoid doing or saying things that make them feel bad. Emotions permeate human life as people fall in love, achieve success, and enjoy friendships, but they also underlie painful episodes that many would just as soon forget. Sometimes our emotions can overwhelm us, such as when we become stressed by demands on our time. How much control do people have over their emotional states? This chapter explores how emotions influence the human experience, including where they come from and how they are experienced, as well as how people cope with overwhelming negative emotions.

Emotions are a fundamental part of the human experience. They warn of danger, create bonds between people, bring joy to life. However, they can also cause problems. People who feel overly anxious may be too afraid to meet new people or even to leave the house. For thousands of years, people have reflected on why we have emotions and what they do for us. Many scholars have viewed cognition and emotion to be separate, with emotion occasionally overwhelming reason and causing people to act in impulsive or inappropriate ways. It is only recently, that psychological scientists have concentrated on trying to understand emotions. Important research is being conducted across all levels of analysis, and the biological revolution is producing exciting new findings about how neural processes are involved in the experience of emotion. Case studies of people such as Elliot provide ample evidence about the role of various brain regions in producing and regulating emotional responses, as well as how people use emotional information.

Almost everyone has an intuitive sense of what is meant by the term *emotion*, but it has proven to be a difficult concept to define precisely. For psychological scientists, **emotion** (or *affect*) refers to feelings that involve subjective evaluation, physiological processes, and cognitive beliefs. Emotions are immediate responses to environmental events, such as being cut off in traffic or given a nice gift. It is useful to distinguish emotion from mood, since the two are often used equivalently in everyday language. **Moods** are diffuse and long-lasting emotional states that influence rather than interrupt thought and behavior. Many times people who are in good or bad moods have no idea why they feel the way they do. According to some views, mood reflects people's perceptions of whether they have the personal resources necessary to meet environmental demands (Morris,

emotion Feelings that involve subjective evaluation, physiological processes, and cognitive beliefs.

moods Diffuse and long lasting emotional states that influence rather than interrupt thought and behavior.

stress A pattern of behavioral and physiological responses to cope with events that match or exceed an organism's abilities.

1992). As people begin to feel overwhelmed by the demands placed on them, their moods become negative and they experience stress. **Stress** is defined as a pattern of behavioral and physiological responses to events that match or exceed an organism's abilities.

This chapter considers first the functions served by emotion and then how emotion is experienced and regulated. We also examine the implications of emotional processes for daily living. How people deal, or *cope*, with stress has implications for physical and mental health, and these coping strategies are discussed in the final section of the chapter.

HOW ARE EMOTIONS ADAPTIVE?

Our theme that the mind helps to solve adaptive problems is well illustrated by research on emotions. Negative and positive experiences guide behavior that increases the probability of surviving and reproducing. Emotions are adaptive because they prepare and guide motivated behaviors, such as running when you encounter dangerous animals. Emotions provide information about the importance of stimuli to personal goals and then prepare people for actions aimed at helping achieve those goals (Frijda, 1994).

Because humans are social animals, it should not be surprising that many emotions involve interpersonal dynamics. People feel hurt when teased, angry when insulted, happy when loved, proud when complimented, and so on. Moreover, people interpret facial expressions of emotion to predict the behavior of other people. Facial expressions provide many clues about whether our behavior is pleasing to others or whether it is likely to cause them to reject, attack, or cheat us. Thus, both emotions and emotional expressions provide adaptive information.

What functions do emotions serve?

FACIAL EXPRESSIONS COMMUNICATE EMOTION

10.1 Infants display emotions that are distinguishable and similar to facial displays among adults such as (a) joy, (b) disgust, (c) surprise, (d) sadness, (e) anger, and (f) fear.

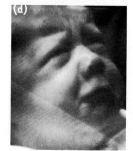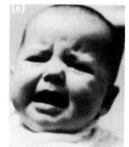

In 1872, Charles Darwin wrote *Expression of Emotion in Man and Animals*, a less famous book than his 1859 work, *On the Origin of Species*, but one with a similar thesis. Darwin argued that expressive characteristics were adaptive in all forms of life, from the dog's hard stare and exposed teeth when defending territory to the redfacedness of humans when preparing to fight. Being able to tell when other people or other species are threatening is of obvious survival value.

Emotional expressions are powerful nonverbal communications. Although there are over 550 words in the English language that refer to emotions (Averill, 1980), humans can communicate emotions quite well without verbal language. Consider human infants. Because infants cannot talk, they must communicate their needs largely through nonverbal action and emotional expressions (Figure 10.1). At birth, an infant is capable of expressing joy, interest, disgust, and pain. By two months of age, infants can express anger and sadness. By six months, they can express fear (Izard & Malatesta, 1987). The social importance of emotional expressions can be seen even in ten-month-old infants, who have been found to smile more while their mothers are watching (Jones et al., 1991). Thus, in the absence of verbal expression, nonverbal displays of emotions signal inner states, moods, and needs. Interestingly, the lower half of the face may be more important than the upper half of the face in communicating emotion. In a classic study conducted in 1927, Dunlap demonstrated that the mouth better conveys emotion than the eyes, especially for positive affect (Figure 10.2).

The display of emotions alters behavior in observers. For instance, people avoid those who look angry and approach those who look happy or in need of comfort. Even among chimpanzees, a smile from a subdominant to a dominant chimp can ward off a potential attack. Hence, emotions provide information to others as to how people are feeling and, in addition, can prompt them to respond in accordance with others' wants and needs.

Facial expressions across cultures   Darwin argued that the face innately communicates emotion to others and that these communications are understandable by all people, regardless of culture. To test this hypothesis, Paul Ekman and Wallace Friesen (1975) went to Argentina, Brazil, Chile, Japan, and the United States and asked people to identify the emotional responses displayed in photographs of posed emotional expressions. They found that people from all of these countries recognized the expressions as anger, fear, disgust, happiness, sadness, and surprise. However, it could be argued that all of the people tested in these countries have extensive exposure to each other's cultures and that learning, not biology, could be responsible for the cross-cultural agreement. So the researchers traveled to a remote area in New Guinea that had little exposure to outside cultures and where the people received only a minimal formal education. The New Guinea natives were able to identify the emotions seen in the photos fairly well, although agreement was not quite as high as in other cultures. The researchers also asked participants in New Guinea to display certain facial expressions and found that these were identified by evaluators from other countries at better than chance level (Figure 10.3; Ekman & Friesen, 1971). Subsequent research finds general support for cross-cultural congruence in identification of some facial expressions, most strongly for happiness and least strongly for fear and disgust (Elfenbein & Ambady, 2002). Some scholars believe that the cross-cultural consistency results may be biased by cultural differences in the use of emotion words and by the way people are asked to identify emotions (Russell, 1994). Overall, however, the evidence is sufficiently consistent to indicate that some facial expressions are universal, and therefore likely to be biologically based.

Display rules and gender   Although basic emotions seem to be expressed similarly across cultures, the situations in which they are displayed differ

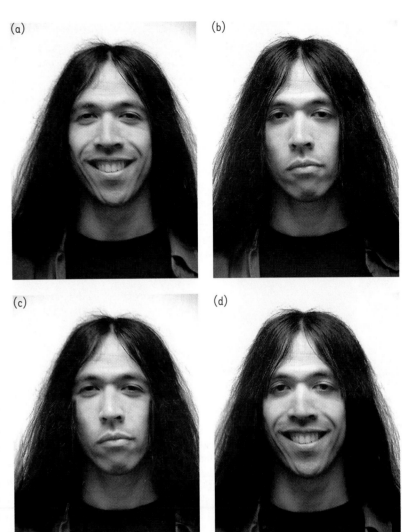

(a)   (b)

(c)   (d)

10.2 Based on Dunlap's classic study of the effects of facial expression, these photos show that the mouth and not the eyes better convey emotion. The two top photos show the original face expressing pleasure (a) and sadness (b). In the bottom photos (c, d) the lower halves of the faces have been interchanged.

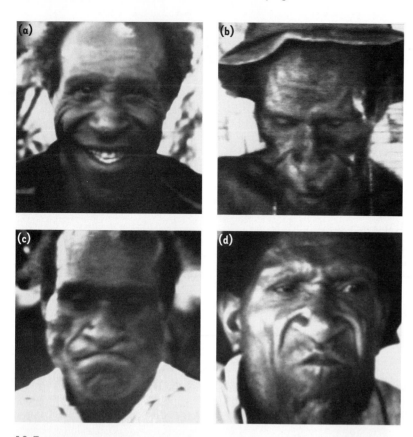

10.3 People across cultures largely agree on the meaning of different facial expressions. These data indicate that recognition of facial expressions may be universal and therefore biologically based. Here the man is expressing (a) happiness, (b) sadness, (c) anger, and (d) disgust.

substantially. **Display rules** govern how and when emotions are exhibited. They are learned via socialization and dictate which emotions are suitable to a given situation. Differences in display rules help to explain cultural stereotypes, such as of Americans as loud and obnoxious, the British as cold and bland, and the French as refined and snobbish. This also may explain why the identification of facial expressions is much better within cultures than between cultures (Elfenbein & Ambady, 2002).

There are gender differences in display rules that guide emotional expression, particularly for smiling and crying. It is generally believed that women more readily, frequently, easily, and intensely display emotions (Plant et al., 2000), and the current evidence suggests that they do, except for perhaps emotions related to dominance (LaFrance & Banaji, 1992). There are evolutionary reasons to think that men and women may vary in their emotional expressiveness: the emotions most closely associated with women are those related to caregiving, nurturance, and interpersonal relationships, whereas emotions associated with men are related to competitiveness, dominance, and defensiveness. But just because women are more likely to display emotion does not mean that they actually experience emotions more intensely. Although the evidence generally indicates that women report more intense emotions, this might reflect societal norms about how women are supposed to feel (Grossman & Wood, 1993). Moreover, in modern Western society, women tend to be better at articulating their emotions than men (Feldman Barrett et al., 2000)—perhaps due to their upbringing—which might account for their more intense descriptions.

EMOTIONS SERVE COGNITIVE FUNCTIONS

Psychological scientists have for many years studied cognitive processes without giving consideration to emotional processes. Studies on decision making, memory, and so on were conducted as if people were evaluating the information from a purely rational perspective. Yet our immediate affective responses arise quickly and automatically, coloring our perceptions at the very instance we notice an object. Robert Zajonc points out, "We do not just see 'a house': We see a *handsome* house, an *ugly* house, or a *pretentious* house" (1980, p. 154). These instantaneous evaluations subsequently guide decision making, memory, and behavior.

Moreover, people's moods can alter ongoing mental processes. When people are in good moods they tend to use heuristic thinking (see Chapter 8), which allows them to make decisions more quickly and efficiently. Positive moods also facilitate creative, elaborate responses to challenging problems and motivate persistence (Isen, 1993). During the pursuit of goals, positive feelings signal that satisfactory progress is being made, thereby encouraging additional effort. One recent theory proposes that increased dopamine levels mediate the effects of positive affect on cognitive tasks (Ashby et al., 1999). According to this view, positive affect leads to higher levels of dopamine production, which subsequently leads to heightened activation of dopamine receptors in other brain areas. Projections to the prefrontal cortex, which regulates behavioral planning, and the anterior cingulate, which coordinates controlled processes, appear to be crucial for the advantageous cognitive effects of positive affect.

display rules Cultural rules that govern how and when emotions are exhibited.

Decision making   Would you rather go rock climbing in the Alps or attend a performance of a small dance troupe in Paris? Anticipated emotional states are an important source of information that guide decision making (see Chapter 8). In the face of complex, multifaceted situations, emotions serve as heuristic guides, providing feedback for making quick decisions (Slovic et al., in press). Moreover, emotion appears to have a direct effect that does not depend upon cognitive processes. For instance, people might decide to cancel air travel shortly after hearing about a plane crash, even if the news did not change their belief about the likelihood of their own plane crashing. Events that are recent or particularly vivid have an especially strong influence on behavior. Thus, risk judgments are strongly influenced by current feelings, and when cognitions and emotions are in conflict, emotions typically have more impact on decisions (Loewenstein et al., 2001).

The *affect-as-information* theory posits that people use their current emotional state to make judgments and appraisals, even if they do not know the source of their moods (Schwarz & Clore, 1983). For instance, the researchers asked people to rate their overall life satisfaction, a question that involves consideration of a lifetime of situations, expectations, personal goals, and accomplishments, as well as a multitude of other factors. Schwarz and Clore note that people do not labor through all these elements to arrive at an answer but instead seem to rely on current mood state. People who are in a good mood rate their lives as satisfactory, whereas people in bad moods give lower overall ratings. People's evaluations of plays, lectures, politicians, and even strangers are influenced by their moods, which themselves are influenced by day of the week, weather, health and the like. Interestingly, if people are made aware of the source of their mood (such as calling attention to the fact that their good mood might be caused by the bright sunshine), their feelings no longer influence judgment.

Likewise recall Damasio's *somatic marker hypothesis*, discussed in the motivation chapter. The *gut feeling* you have as you contemplate an event reflects your body's advice on how to make a decision. As such, somatic markers may be adaptive in directing people toward behaviors that have been associated with successful outcomes. The absence of somatic markers might have been one of the problems that the patient Elliot, described at the beginning of the chapter, had with making decisions.

Emotions captures attention   If emotions truly are adaptive, then people should be especially sensitive to emotional information. Indeed, research has demonstrated that emotional information captures attention. For example, research using the *emotional Stroop task* shows that cognitive processes are biased toward emotional stimuli (Williams et al., 1996). In these studies, participants are asked to name the color of the ink that a word is printed in, which is difficult because it requires overriding a habitual desire to speak the word itself. Typically, words that are emotionally arousing (such as "anger") are more difficult to override than are neutral words (such as "pencil"), suggesting that there is an attentional bias for encoding affective stimuli.

Emotions aid memory People have improved memory for emotion-producing events or stimuli. Think back to your childhood. What memories come to mind most rapidly? Research has found that important, clear personal memories are typically those that are highly emotional. Moreover, considerable research shows that increased arousal enhances memory across a variety of tasks for many species. For instance, creating stress or administering drugs that produce arousal in rats leads to enhanced memory formation (as described in Chapter 6).

The link between emotionality and memory was tested directly in an experiment using the *remember/know* procedure, in which participants are asked about their recognition of an item from a previous trial. Participants state whether they have a feeling that the item is familiar, which is a *know* judgment, or whether their recollection of the item is accompanied by sensory, semantic, or emotional detail, which is a *remember* judgment. This study found that highly negative photographs were more likely to be identified as "remember" items than were neutral or positive photos (Ochsner, 2000).

EMOTIONS STRENGTHEN INTERPERSONAL RELATIONS

For most of the past century, psychologists paid little attention to interpersonal emotions. Guilt, shame, and the like were associated with Freudian thinking and therefore not studied in mainstream psychological science. However, recent theories have reconsidered interpersonal emotions based on the evolutionary need of humans to belong to social groups. Given that survival was enhanced for those who lived in groups, those who were expelled would have been less likely to survive and pass along their genes. According to this view, people were rejected primarily because they drained group resources or threatened group stability. Thus, those who tried to cheat others, steal mates, or freeload were rejected. Accordingly, people feel anxious when engaging in behaviors that could lead them to be expelled from groups. Hence, anxiety serves as an alarm function that motivates people to behave according to group norms (Baumeister & Tice, 1990). This new approach views interpersonal emotions as evolved mechanisms that facilitate interpersonal interaction, such as helping to appease and repair interpersonal transgressions.

Guilt strengthens social bonds Guilt is a negative emotional state associated with anxiety, tension, and agitation. The experience of guilt, including its initiation, maintenance, and avoidance, rarely makes sense outside of the context of interpersonal interaction. For instance, the prototypical guilt experience occurs when someone feels responsibility for another person's negative affective state. Thus, when people believe that something they did either directly or indirectly caused another person harm, they experience feelings of anxiety, tension, and remorse, which can be labeled guilt. Guilt can occasionally arise even when individuals do not feel personally responsible for others' negative situations (such as survivor guilt).

A recent theoretical model of guilt outlines its benefits to close relationships. Roy Baumeister and colleagues (1994) contend that guilt protects and strengthens interpersonal relationships through three mechanisms. First, feelings of guilt keep people from doing things that would harm their relationships, such as cheating on their partners, while encouraging behaviors that strengthen relationships, such as phoning their mothers on Sundays. Second, displays of guilt demonstrate that people care about their relationship partners, thereby affirming

guilt A negative emotional state associated with an internal experience of anxiety, tension, and agitation.

social bonds. Third, guilt is an influence tactic that can be used to manipulate the behavior of others. For instance, you might try to make your boss feel guilty so that you don't have to work overtime.

Socialization is crucial for interpersonal emotions   Recent evidence indicates that socialization is more important than biology for the specific manner in which children experience guilt. One longitudinal study examined the impact of socialization on the development of a variety of negative emotions, including guilt, in monozygotic and dizygotic twins at 14, 20, and 24 months (Zahn-Waxler & Robinson, 1995). The study found that all the negative emotions showed considerable genetic influence (as evidenced by higher concordance rates for identical twins), but guilt was unique in being highly influenced by the social environment. With age, the influence on guilt of a shared environment became stronger, while the evidence for genetic influences disappeared. These findings support the hypothesis that socialization is the predominant influence on moral emotions such as guilt. Perhaps surprisingly, parental warmth is associated with greater guilt in children, suggesting that feelings of guilt arise in healthy and happy relationships. Thus, as children become citizens in a social world they develop the capacity to empathize, and they subsequently experience feelings of guilt when they transgress against others.

Embarrassment and blushing   Embarrassment is a naturally occurring, ecologically based state that usually occurs following social events such as violations of cultural norms, loss of physical poise, teasing, and self-image threats (Miller, 1996). Some theories of embarrassment suggest that it rectifies interpersonal awkwardness and restores social bonds after a transgression. Embarrassment represents submission to and affiliation with the social group and a recognition of the unintentional social error. Research supports these propositions in showing that individuals who look embarrassed after a transgression elicit more sympathy, forgiveness, amusement, and laughter from onlookers (Cupach & Metts, 1990). Hence, like guilt, embarrassment may serve to reaffirm close relationships after a transgression.

Mark Twain once said, "Man is the only animal that blushes. Or needs to." Darwin, in his 1872 book, called blushing the "most peculiar and the most human of all expressions," thereby separating it from emotional responses he deemed necessary for survival. Recent theory and research suggests that blushing occurs when people believe that others view them negatively, and that blushing communicates a realization of interpersonal errors. This nonverbal apology is an appeasement that elicits forgiveness in others, which repairs and maintains relationships (Keltner & Anderson, 2000).

Jealousy   In his book *The Dangerous Passion: Why Jealousy Is as Necessary as Love and Sex*, David Buss (2000) argues that jealousy serves adaptive functions. Although no one enjoys feeling jealous and threatened, Buss contends that jealousy is an indispensable component of long-term relationships because it keeps mates together by sparking passion and commitment. Buss theorizes that when faced with the possibility of a sexual rival, a person feels and displays jealousy as a sign of commitment to the relationship. This hypothesis is supported by research showing that people who are more invested in the relationship often purposely provoke jealousy as a test of their partners' commitment. Buss also proposes that jealousy revives sexual passion in the threatened partner. Of course, there are negative sides to jealousy. Jealousy is one of the most common reasons for spousal/partner abuse and homicide, and when unfounded it can ruin a relationship by exposing a lack of trust. Sexual jealousy is considered in greater detail in Chapter 14.

How Are Emotions Adaptive?

Emotions are adaptive because they bring about a state of behavioral readiness. The evolutionary basis for emotions is supported by research on the cross-cultural recognition of emotional displays. Facial expressions communicate meaning to others and enhance emotional states. Emotions aid in memory processes by garnering increased attention and deeper encoding of emotionally relevant events. Positive and negative emotions serve as guides for action. Emotions also serve to repair and maintain close interpersonal relationships.

HOW DO PEOPLE EXPERIENCE EMOTIONS?

Emotions are difficult to define because they defy language. Imagine trying to describe the concept of emotions to an alien from another planet. What would you say? You might say that emotions make you "feel," but the alien doesn't understand the word "feel." You could demonstrate the behaviors that accompany certain emotions, such as smiling, frowning, or crying, but the alien doesn't understand how water spouting from the eyes is associated with this thing we call "emotions." In the end it would be akin to trying to describe color to someone who is blind.

Psychologists generally agree that emotions consist of three components. There is the feeling state that accompanies emotions—the *subjective experience* that psychologists and laypeople alike refer to when they ask "How are you feeling?" Psychologists also consider *physical changes*, such as increased heart rate, skin temperature, or brain activation, to be an integral part of what makes an emotion. A third component, *cognitive appraisals*, involves people's beliefs and understandings about why they feel the way they feel.

THERE IS A SUBJECTIVE COMPONENT

What are the components of emotional experience?

Emotions are *phenomenological*, meaning that they are subjectively experienced. You know when you're experiencing an emotion because you *feel* it. The intensity of emotional reactions varies; some people report many distinct emotions every day, whereas others report only infrequent and minor emotional reactions. People who are either over- or under-emotional tend to have psychological problems. Among the former are people with *mood disorders* such as severe depression or panic attacks. People with mood disorders experience such strong emotions that they can become immobilized.

At the other extreme are those who suffer from **alexithymia**, a disorder in which people do not experience the subjective component of emotions. Elliot, considered at the beginning of this chapter, suffered from alexithymia. The explanation for the disorder is that the physiological messages associated with emotions do not reach the brain centers that interpret emotion. Damage to certain brain regions, especially the prefrontal cortex, is associated with a loss of the subjective component of mood.

Self-reports   The most direct way to study emotions is simply to ask people how they feel. Psychological scientists use both *trait* and *state* self-reports, in which people are asked to report how they feel *in general* or how they feel *right now*, respectively. Questionnaires are the most popular self-report method because they require no special training or skills and can be given quickly to many people at once. Interviews are another form of self-reports. Interviews are often conducted in clinical settings because they allow for a deeper analysis of a person's emotional status. They are most useful when the total sample to be assessed is small and when the emotional reports are obtained for a specific purpose (such as to assess the possibility that a person is suicidal).

Distinguishing among types of emotions   How many emotions does a person experience and how do they relate to each other? Many emotion theorists distinguish between primary and secondary emotions, an approach conceptually similar to viewing color as consisting of primary and secondary hues. Basic or **primary emotions** are evolutionarily adaptive, shared across cultures, and associated with specific biological and physical states. These include anger, fear, sadness, disgust, and happiness, as well as possibly surprise and contempt. **Secondary emotions** are blends of primary emotions; they include remorse, guilt, submission, and anticipation.

One approach to understanding the experience of emotion is the **circumplex model**, in which two basic factors of emotion are arranged in a circle around the intersections of the core dimensions of affect (Russell, 1980). James Russell and Lisa Feldman Barrett (1999) developed one such model that posits that emotions can be mapped according to their *valence*, or degree of pleasantness or unpleasantness, and their *activation*, which is the level of arousal or mobilization of energy (Figure 10.4). Thus, "excited" is an affective state that includes pleasure and arousal, whereas "depressed" describes a state of low arousal and negative affect. There has been some debate about naming the dimensions, but circumplex models have proven useful for providing a basic taxonomy of mood states.

Psychological scientists David Watson, Lee Anna Clark, and Auke Tellegen make a distinction between *positive activation* (pleasant affect) and *negative activation* (unpleasant affect), which can be plotted on a circumplex. They also propose that negative and positive affect are independent, such that people can experience both simultaneously. For example, people sometimes take pleasure in others' downfalls. When this occurs, people may experience "mixed feelings," such as happiness (a positive affect) combined with guilt (a negative affect). Neurochemical evidence suggests

alexithymia   A disorder that leads to a lack of the subjective experience of emotion.

primary emotions   Evolutionarily adaptive emotions that are shared across cultures and associated with specific biological and physical states.

secondary emotions   Blends of primary emotions, including states such as remorse, guilt, submission, and anticipation.

circumplex model   An approach to understanding emotion, in which two basic factors of emotion are spatially arranged in a circle, formed around the intersections of the core dimensions of affect.

10.4 James Russell and Lisa Feldman Barrett's model of emotion. The figure depicts a circumplex map of the structure of emotions.

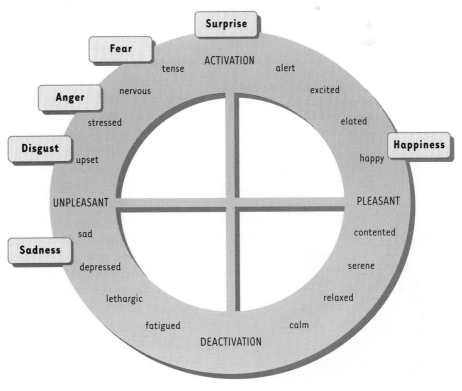

10.5 Alteration of facial expressions can lead to changes in the subjective experience of emotions. The person on the left (pen in mouth) is more likely to report feeling happy than the person on the right (pencil on lip).

James-Lange theory of emotion A theory that suggests that the experience of emotion is elicited by a physiological response to a particular stimuli or situation.

facial feedback hypothesis The idea that facial expressions trigger the experience of emotion.

10.6 Water Cannon, a physiologist at Harvard University, formulated the regulatory idea of homeostasis, the role of the body in emotion, and the flight-or-fight autonomic response.

that positive activation states are associated with an increase in dopamine and that negative activation states are associated with an increase in norepinephrine, which supports the likelihood that positive and negative affect are independent. Furthermore, Watson and colleagues argue that the distinction between positive and negative activation is adaptive. For instance, they link affect to motivational states of approach and avoidance—the motivation to seek out food, sex, and companionship is typically associated with pleasure, whereas the motivation to avoid dangerous animals is associated with pain (Watson et al., 1999).

THERE IS A PHYSIOLOGICAL COMPONENT

A clumsy mistake causes most people to feel embarrassed and brings a rush of blood to the face that warms the cheeks. Indeed, emotions are associated with physical changes. But, which causes which? Common sense suggests that the emotion leads to the physical change. But in 1884, William James argued that it was just the opposite. In a proposal similar to one made by Descartes in the 1600s, James asserted that it is how people interpret the physical changes in a situation that leads to the feeling of an emotion. In James's words, "we feel sorry because we cry, angry because we strike, afraid because we tremble, and not that we cry, strike, or tremble because we are sorry, angry, or fearful." James believed that physical changes occur in distinct patterns that translate directly into a specific emotion. Around the same time, a similar theory was independently proposed by a Danish psychologist named Carl Lange. Thus, the idea that felt emotion is the result of perceiving specific patterns of bodily responses is called the **James-Lange theory of emotion**.

One implication of the James-Lange theory is that if you mold the facial muscles to mimic an emotional state, you activate the associated emotion. According to the **facial feedback hypothesis**, first proposed by Silvan Tomkins in 1963, facial expressions trigger the experience of emotions, not the other way around. James Laird tested this idea in 1974 by having people hold a pencil between their teeth in a way that produced a smile or a frown (see Figure 10.5). When participants rated cartoons, those in a posed smile found the cartoons funniest. Further support comes from the results of studies by Paul Ekman and colleagues (1983), who asked professional actors to relive feelings of anger, distress, fear, disgust, joy, and surprise. Physiological changes recorded during the actors' portrayals were in fact different for various emotions. Heart rate changed little with surprise, joy, and disgust, but it increased with distress, fear, and anger. Anger was also associated with higher skin temperature, whereas the other emotions resulted in little change in skin temperature. Thus, these results give some support to James' theory that specific patterns of physical changes are the basis for emotional states. However, subsequent evidence suggests that there is not sufficient specificity of emotional reactions to fully explain the subjective experience of emotions.

The counterintuitive James-Lange theory quickly attracted criticism. In 1927, Harvard University's Walter Cannon (Figure 10.6) noted that although humans are quick to experience emotions, the body is much slower, taking at least a second or two to respond. Cannon also noted that many emotions produced similar visceral responses, making it too difficult for people to quickly determine which emotion they were experiencing. For instance, anger, excitement, and sexual interest all produce similar changes in heart rate and blood pressure. Cannon, along with Philip Bard, proposed instead that the mind and body operate independently in experiencing emotions. According to the **Cannon-Bard theory**, the information from an emotion-producing stimulus is processed in subcortical structures, causing the experience of two separate things at roughly the same time: an emotion and a physical reaction. When you see a grizzly bear you simultaneously feel afraid, begin to sweat, experience a pounding heart, and run (Figure 10.7). Everything happens together. As you will see later, recent evidence from brain research

Cannon-Bard theory A theory of emotion that asserts that emotion-producing stimuli from the environment elicit both an emotional and a physical reaction.

10.7 The three major theories of emotion differ not only in their relative emphasis on physiology and cognition, but also in terms of when emotional state is determined.

Three theories of emotion

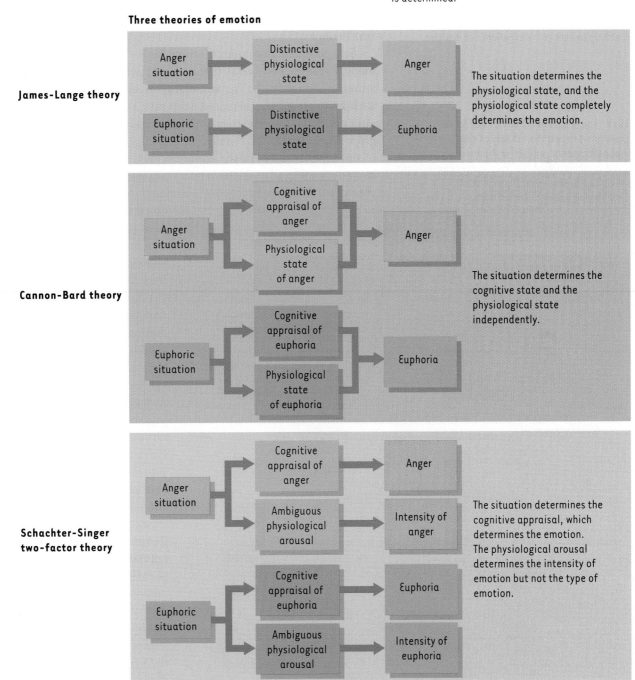

10.8 Stanley Schachter emphasized the role of cognitive beliefs in the experience of emotion.

10.9 The results of Schachter and Singer's experiment to test their theory of emotion showed that participants' subjective experience of emotion was a combination of the situation they were in, the physiological arousal of the stimulant pill, and whether they knew the purported effects of the pill.

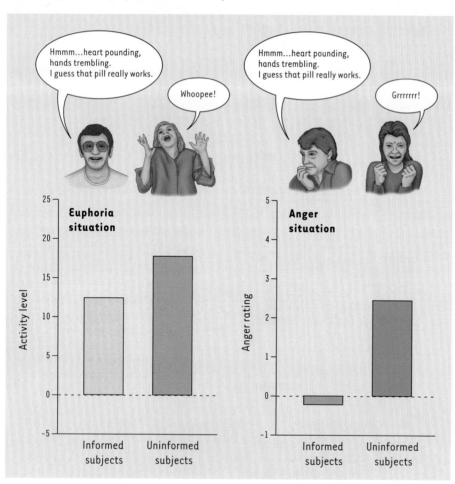

provides support for the idea that there are separate pathways for the processing of emotional information. As such, there is generally more support for the Cannon-Bard theory than for the James-Lange theory.

THERE IS A COGNITIVE COMPONENT

Stanley Schachter (Figure 10.8) developed the hypothesis that emotions are the interaction of physiological arousal and cognitive appraisals. His **two-factor theory of emotion** proposed that a situation evokes both a physiological response, such as arousal, and a cognitive interpretation, or *emotion label*. When people experience arousal they initiate a search for its source. Although the search for a cognitive explanation is often quick and straightforward, as people generally recognize what event led to their emotional state, sometimes people are incorrect in their conclusions.

Schachter and his student Jerome Singer (1962) devised an ingenious experiment to test the two-factor theory. First, participants were injected with either a stimulant or a placebo. The stimulant was adrenaline, which produced symptoms such as sweaty palms, increased heart rate, and the shakes. Participants were then either told that the drug they took would make them feel aroused or they were not given any information. Finally, the participant was left to wait with a confederate of the experimenter. In the euphoric condition, participants were exposed to a confederate who played with a hula hoop and made paper airplanes. In the angry condition, they were exposed to a confederate who asked them very intimate, personal questions, such as "With how many men (other than your father) has your mother had extramarital relationships?" (Making the question even more insulting were the three choices: (a) four or fewer, (b) five to nine, or (c) ten or more!) Note that those participants who received the adrenaline but were told what to expect would have an easy explanation for their arousal. However, those participants who received adrenaline but were not given information would be aroused but would not know why. Thus, they would look to the environment to explain or label their mood. Participants in the uninformed condition reported being happy with the euphoric confederate but less happy with the angry confederate (Figure 10.9).

People can misattribute the source of emotional states One interesting implication of the Schachter theory is that emotion can be mistakenly attributed to something that actually did not cause the arousal. *Misattribution of arousal* is a term used when an emotion label is derived from the wrong source. In one of the most amazing demonstrations of this phenomenon, researchers tried to see whether people could fall in love through misattribution (Dutton & Aron, 1974). Male participants were asked to meet an interviewer on one of two bridges over the Capilano River in British Columbia. One was a narrow suspension bridge with a low rail that swayed 230 feet above raging, rocky rapids (see Figure 10.10); the other was a sturdy modern bridge just above the river. An attractive female research assistant approached the men and interviewed them in the middle of the bridge. She gave them her phone number and offered to explain the results of the study to them at a later date. According to the two-factor theory of emotion, the scary bridge would produce arousal that could possibly be misattributed to the interviewer. Indeed, this is what happened, as men who were interviewed on the scary bridge were more likely to call the interviewer and ask her for a date.

A similar form of misattribution is called **excitation transfer**, during which residual physiological arousal caused by one event is transferred to a new stimulus. In the period after exercise, for example, there is a slow return to baseline during which the person continues to have residual arousal such as an elevated heart rate. Of course, after a few minutes people have caught their breath and do not realize their bodies are still aroused. If a second event occurs in this interim period, the residual excitation from the first event is transferred to the second event. This has an important practical application. It is perhaps best to take a date out to a movie that produces arousal, perhaps a strong tearjerker or action adventure. There is always the possibility that residual arousal will be misattributed to you.

10.10 Men who walked across a narrow and scary bridge (like the Capilano Bridge) displayed more attraction to a female experimenter than those who walked across a stable bridge.

Emotions are affected by cognitive framing Emotions do not happen in a vacuum; they are part of a psychological system that includes other emotions, cognitions, and behaviors. **Cognitive framing**, or the way in which we think about an event, can contribute to the intensity of an emotional response as well as influence what label we place on it. Craig Smith and Phoebe Ellsworth (1985) concluded that emotional states vary along at least six dimensions: (a) desirability of the outcome, (b) level of effort that was anticipated within a given situation, (c) certainty of the outcome, (d) attention devoted to the situation, (e) personal control over the situation, and (f) control attributed to external forces. As an example, if the roof of your house is blown off during a storm and you attribute the situation to external forces, you will likely feel sad. However, if you see the outcome as having been under your personal control because you failed to replace what you knew to be a faulty roof, you will instead feel guilty and angry.

Counterfactuals People devote years of their lives to compete in the Olympics, and every Olympic athlete dreams of winning a gold medal. It is no surprise that those who win gold medals are pretty happy about it. But who do you think would be next happiest, the silver- or the bronze-medal winner? Perhaps surprisingly, bronze-medal winners look happier than silver-medal winners (Medvec et al., 1995). The difference in medalists' emotional responses can be explained by *counterfactual thinking*, which is the act of imagining a possible alternative outcome that didn't happen. For instance, asking the question "What would the

two-factor theory of emotion A theory that proposes that a situation evokes both a physiological response, such as arousal, and a cognitive interpretation.

excitation transfer A form of misattribution where residual physiological arousal caused by one event is transferred to a new stimulus.

cognitive framing The way people think about events can contribute to the intensity of emotional responses and shape the labels they place on emotions.

United States be like if President Kennedy had not been killed?" is a counterfactual, in that it rests on the assumption of something happening that did not. For the bronze medalists, the most salient alternative outcome was not winning any medal, so compared to that situation, they are pretty happy. By contrast, the silver medalists are focused on having just missed the gold medal, not on having just beaten the bronze-medal winner. In general, people use counterfactual thinking to account for the negative emotions that result when things do not work out favorably.

PEOPLE REGULATE THEIR MOODS

How do people control or change their emotions?

There are a variety of emotion-regulation processes that people use multiple times every day. Self-control processes, as a whole, enable individuals to better adjust to their environment. James Gross (1999) has organized emotion-regulation strategies into five categories. The first four, which are labeled *situation selection*, *situation modification*, *attentional deployment*, and *cognitive change*, are antecedent-focused methods that occur prior to an emotion-provoking event. The last, *response modulation*, occurs after the reaction has been initiated. Gross's research shows that the effectiveness of each method depends on the situational demands and the individual's personality traits.

Situation selection involves knowing the types of people, places, and objects that alter your emotional state and choosing to either approach or avoid them. Imagine that you want to have a nice night out with your romantic partner. You might choose a restaurant in which you had previous good dining experiences. *Situation modification* refers to active efforts to alter a situation in an attempt to change its emotional effects. Using the same example, if you want a quiet meal but find conversation impossible because of an adjacent party of nine, you might ask to be moved to another table. The use of *attentional deployment* allows people to isolate certain aspects of the situation that will manage their emotional state. People who are scared of flying may distract themselves from their anxiety by watching the in-flight movie. *Cognitive change* is a method of mood regulation that is useful when none of the other processes are applicable, as it involves reconstructing the situation in alternative ways. For example, if the restaurant is a disaster you might choose to recast the situation as funny. *Response modulation* refers to directly controlling emotional responses after they are initiated. You may try to amplify your happiness and dampen your disappointment if the romantic evening didn't turn out as planned.

Humor Humor is a simple and effective method of regulating negative emotions, one that has numerous mental and physical health benefits. Most obviously, humor increases positive affect. When we find something humorous, we smile, laugh, and are in a state of pleasurable, relaxed excitation. Research shows that laughter stimulates endocrine secretion; an improved immune system; and the release of hormones, catecholamines, and endorphins. When people laugh, they experience a rise in circulation, blood pressure, skin temperature, and heart rate, along with a reduction in perception of pain. All these responses are similar to those resulting from physical exercise, and they are considered beneficial to both short-term and long-term health.

People sometimes laugh in situations that do not seem very funny, such as at funerals or wakes. According to one theory, laughing in these situations helps people distance themselves from their negative emotions and strengthens their interpersonal connections to other people. Dacher Keltner and George Bonanno (1997) interviewed 40 people who had recently lost a spouse. They found that genuine laughter during the interview was associated with positive mental health and fewer negative feelings, such as grief.

Suppression and rumination   There are two common mistakes that people make when trying to regulate mood. The first is *thought suppression*, in which they attempt not to respond or feel the emotion at all. Research by Daniel Wegner and his colleagues has demonstrated that suppressing any thought is extremely difficult and often leads to a *rebound effect* in which people think more about something after suppression than before. Thus, for example, those who try not to think of a white bear end up obsessed with thoughts of white bears (Wegner et al., 1990). **Rumination**, the second mistake, involves thinking about, elaborating, and focusing on the undesired thoughts or feelings, which prolongs the mood. Moreover, rumination impedes successful mood-regulation strategies, such as focused problem solving or distraction (Lyubomirsky & Nolen-Hoeksema, 1995).

Overall, distraction is the best way to avoid the problems of suppression or rumination, since it absorbs attention and temporarily helps people to stop thinking about their problems. But some distractions backfire, such as thinking about other problems or engaging in maladaptive behaviors. Watching a movie that captures your attention helps you to escape your problems, but watching a movie that reminds you of your troubled situation may lead you to wallow in mental anguish.

rumination Thinking about, elaborating, and focusing on undesired thoughts or feelings, which prolongs, rather than alleviates, a negative mood.

How Do People Experience Emotions?

Emotions are comprised of a subjective experience, physiological changes, and cognitive interpretation. There are three main theories of emotion, which differ in their relative emphasis on these components. The James-Lange theory states that specific patterns of physical changes give rise to the perception of associated emotions. The Cannon-Bard theory states that there are two separate pathways of emotion. Schachter's two-factor theory emphasizes the combination of generalized physiological arousal and cognitive appraisals in determining specific emotions. People also use a number of strategies to alter their moods. The best methods for regulating negative affect include humor and distraction.

WHAT IS THE NEUROPHYSIOLOGICAL BASIS OF EMOTION?

As was apparent in the three major theories discussed in the preceding section, the body plays an important role in emotional experience. People who have spinal cord injuries report feeling less intense emotions than prior to injury, which occurs because the messages have difficulty reaching the brain. This provides some support for the James-Lange theory. The closer the damage is to the brain, the greater the loss of sensation, and consequently, the greater the decrease in emotional intensity. As you will recall from Chapter 3, various hormones, neurotransmitters, and drugs affect mood states. For instance, drugs that increase the activity of serotonin receptors lead to a reduction in depressed mood; drugs that activate dopamine receptors lead to feelings of euphoria.

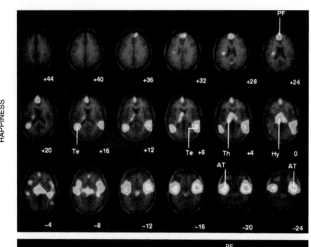

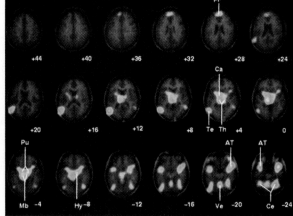

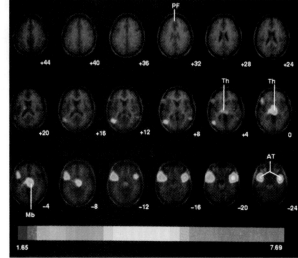

10.11 Significant increases in regional brain activity occur during happiness, sadness, and disgust. Note that these emotions produce different patterns of brain activation.

During the biological revolution over the past decade, researchers have found that specific emotional states are associated with unique patterns of brain activation, although many of the same brain structures are involved in multiple emotional experiences. For instance, PET studies have shown that disgust, sadness, and happiness all activate the thalamus and prefrontal cortex. However, differential activation in surrounding structures can be distinguished among these three emotions; for example, happiness and sadness cause increased activation in the hypothalamus, whereas disgust does not (Lane et al., 1997; Figure 10.11). Similarly, processing of faces showing fear and disgust may lead to differential patterns of brain activity, with fear activating the amygdala and disgust activating the insula. The insula has previously been related to gustatory reactions to unpleasant tastes and smells (Phillips et al., 1997). We understand much about the neurophysiology of emotion, but we have a great deal still to learn. In this section we will examine several key issues regarding the link between physiology and emotion.

EMOTIONS ARE ASSOCIATED WITH AUTONOMIC ACTIVITY

Emotions tend to overlap in their pattern of autonomic nervous system (ANS) activity, although there are some differences between emotional states. For instance, when a person is aroused, whether because of anger or sexual attraction, the face becomes flushed, but the pupils constrict during anger and dilate during sexual arousal. As mentioned, actors who portrayed particular emotions showed differential heart rate and blood pressure patterns. These findings have been replicated with the Minangkabau people of West Sumatra (Levenson et al., 1992), in spite of dramatic differences in culture, religion, lifestyles, and display rules. The Minangkabau people showed patterns of ANS arousal similar to those of American actors: heart rate increases with distress, fear, and anger, the last of which was also accompanied by higher skin temperature. However, the overlap in autonomic activity between emotions is so great that in most cases it is difficult to distinguish emotions based solely on autonomic responses (Cacioppo et al., 1993).

The fact that ANS activity is associated with emotional states is the basis of polygraphy. As discussed in "Using Psychological Science: Lie Detection," the general idea is that lying causes anxiety, which can be detected through changes in ANS activity.

Robert Zajonc and colleagues described another link between physiological states and emotion. Zajonc hypothesized that facial expressions, through facial musculature, control the directional flow of air into the brain, resulting in warming or cooling of the hypothalamus. This in turn affects the release of neurotransmitters that influence emotions. According to Zajonc, cooling the brain produces positive emotions, whereas warming the brain produces negative emotions. To test his theory, participants allowed air to be blown into their nasal passages. In support of his predictions, Zajonc found that people reported more negative emotions when the air was warm and more pleasant emotions when the air was cool (Zajonc et al., 1989).

LIE DETECTION

As part of the normal interview process for certain types of jobs, people are asked to take a polygraph test, known informally as a lie detector test. A *polygraph* is an electronic instrument that assesses the body's physiological response to questions. It records numerous aspects of arousal such as breathing rate, heart rate, and so on (Figure 10.12). The use of polygraphs is highly controversial. Most courts don't allow them as evidence and most people have little appreciation for what a lie detector can and cannot do.

The goal of polygraphy is to determine a person's level of emotionality when confronted with certain questions. For instance, criminals might be asked about specific illegal activities, whereas job applicants might be asked about previous drug use or job performance. Psychologists have long known that lying is stressful. Thus, autonomic arousal should be higher when a person is lying than when they are telling the truth. Accordingly, intense emotional responses to incriminating questions supposedly indicate that a person is lying.

There is no absolute measure of autonomic arousal that indicates the presence or absence of a lie, because each person's level of autonomic arousal is different. Thus, polygraphers employ a *control question* technique to assess physiological arousal. The examiner asks a variety of questions, some of which are relevant to the critical information and some of which are not. Examples of control questions are "What is your home address?" and "Have you ever been in jail before?" Control questions are usually those unlikely to lead to a strong emotional response. Critical questions are those of specific interest to the investigators. The difference in the physiological response between the control and critical questions is the measure used to determine whether the person is lying.

What is the success rate of polygraphs? Two researchers chose 50 criminal investigations in which a polygraph was administered to two suspects and then later one suspect confessed to the crime (Kleinmuntz & Szucko, 1984). When comparing the polygraph results to the suspects' true guilt or innocence, the researchers found that the polygraph correctly identified the guilty person 76 percent of the time but also wrongly accused someone of lying 37 percent of the time. Thus, they are far from infallible.

Not only can the test falsely accuse people of lying, but for those who do not feel anxious about lying, the polygraph is totally useless. There are also ways to cheat the test. One well-known method is to inflate one's physiological arousal on the control questions and to try to relax on the critical questions, thus making it more difficult to find a physiological difference between the two. Some ways of increasing arousal include biting the tongue, pressing fingernails into the palms, or tightening the sphincter muscle for several seconds to increase blood pressure. Studies of college students who were taught to use these techniques found that they avoided detection by two expert polygraphers 50 percent of the time.

As you might expect, researchers are currently seeking new strategies to uncover deception. For instance, researchers using event-related brain potentials have found that a brain wave pattern typically associated with rare, meaningful stimuli may indicate deception (Rosenfield, 2001). In a recent study using fMRI, deceptive responses were associated with increased activation of specific frontal lobe regions, including the anterior cingulate (Langleban et al., 2002). However, the deception task in this study was relatively trivial and the participants did not report feeling anxious about being deceptive. Whether these findings indicate genuine deception or simply reflect general inhibitory responses during the experimental task remains to be determined.

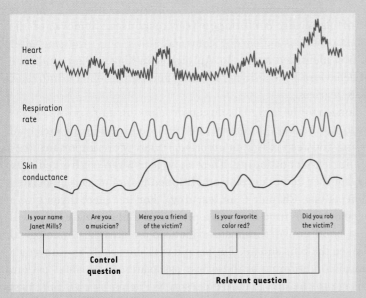

10.12 A polygraph measures autonomic systems such as respiration, skin conductance from sweating, and heart rate. Differences in autonomic reactions to critical questions, compared to control questions, indicate arousal, which in turn may indicate nervousness as a result of lying. Unfortunately, the arousal might be due to general nervousness and may falsely indicate that the person is lying.

THE AMYGDALA AND ORBITOFRONTAL CORTEX ARE INVOLVED IN EMOTION

In 1937, James Papez proposed that emotion is mediated by several neural systems, including the hypothalamus, thalamus, cingulate gyrus, and hippocampus. In 1952, Paul MacLean expanded this list to include the amygdala, orbitofrontal

Where are emotions located in the body?

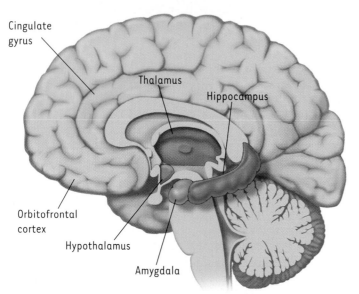

Cingulate gyrus

Thalamus

Hippocampus

Orbitofrontal cortex

Hypothalamus

Amygdala

10.13 The limbic system is important for assessing and responding to emotionally relevant stimuli. The two most important structures are the amygdala and orbitofrontal cortex.

10.14 Joseph LeDoux has conducted important work showing that the amygdala is important for emotional learning.

cortex, and portions of the basal ganglia. He called this extended neural circuit of emotion the *limbic system*. It is now known that many brain structures that are not part of MacLean's limbic system are involved in emotion, and many of his limbic structures do not seem central to emotion per se. For instance, it is now known that the hippocampus is mostly important for memory and the hypothalamus for motivation. Thus, the term *limbic system* is generally used in a rough descriptive way rather than directly linking brain areas to specific emotional functions (Figure 10.13). In an ironic twist, the two brain areas now known to be most crucial to emotion were not considered to be very important by Papez or MacLean. These are the amygdala and the orbitofrontal cortex.

Amygdala The amygdala processes the emotional significance of stimuli and generates immediate emotional and behavioral reactions. According to Joseph LeDoux (Figure 10.14), affective processing in the amygdala is a circuit that has developed over the course of evolution to protect animals from danger. LeDoux (1996) has established the amygdala as the brain structure most important for emotional learning, such as the development of classically conditioned fear responses. Removal of the amygdala in animals produces a disorder known as *Kluver-Bucy syndrome*, after the scientists who first identified it in 1939. Animals with Kluver-Bucy syndrome engage in unusual behaviors, such as hypersexuality and putting objects into their mouths, and they are fearless.

Humans with damage to the amygdala do not develop the more severe symptoms associated with Kluver-Bucy syndrome, but they do experience a variety of deficits in processing and responding to emotional cues. More important, they show impairments in fear conditioning. They show fear when confronted with dangerous objects, but they do not develop conditioned fear of objects associated with dangerous objects (see Chapter 6 on learning). For instance, if you give a person an electric shock each time they see a picture of a blue square, they will normally develop a conditioned response, evidenced by greater physiological arousal, when they see the blue square. But people with damage to the amygdala do not show classical conditioning of these fear associations. Consider patient S.P., who had damage to the amygdala (Anderson & Phelps, 2000). S.P. first showed signs of neurological impairment around age three and was later diagnosed with epilepsy. At age 48, she had her right amygdala removed to reduce the frequency of the seizures. The surgery was reasonably successful, and S.P. retained most of her intellectual faculties. She has normal IQ, has taken college courses, and performs well on standardized tasks of visual attention. However, she does not show fear conditioning. Strangely, S.P. can tell you that the blue square is associated with shock, but her body shows no physiological evidence of having acquired the fear response.

Information reaches the amygdala along two separate pathways. The first path is a quick and dirty system that processes sensory information nearly instantaneously. Sensory information travels quickly through the thalamus to the amygdala for priority processing. The second pathway is somewhat slower, but it leads to evaluations that are more deliberate and thorough. Sensory material travels from the thalamus to the sensory cortex, where the information is scrutinized in greater depth before it is passed along to the amygdala. Contemporary thinking is that the fast system prepares the animal to respond should the slower pathway confirm the threat.

Recall from the earlier discussion that emotional events are especially likely to be stored in memory. Larry Cahill and his colleagues argue that this occurs because the amygdala interacts with stress hormones released during emotional events to facilitate memory storage. Brain-imaging studies indeed demonstrate that increased activity of the amygdala during an emotional event is associated with improved long-term memory for the event. However, there is an interesting sex difference in this pattern. Cahill and colleagues (2001) confirmed that enhanced memory for emotional films leads to greater activation of the left amygdala for women and right amygdala for men (Figure 10.15). Interestingly, sex differences are beginning to be observed in a number of imaging studies that assess the neurobiology of cognition. The reason that men and women differ in brain activation during emotional and cognitive tasks is currently unknown.

Another role of the amygdala in emotion processing is its involvement in perceiving social stimuli, such as deciphering the affective meaning of facial expressions. For instance, fMRI studies demonstrate that the amygdala is especially sensitive to the intensity of fearful faces (Dolan, 2000; Figure 10.16). This effect occurs even if the participants are unaware that they have seen a face at all (Whalen et al., 1998).

Given that the amygdala is involved in processing the emotional content of facial expressions, it is not surprising that damage to the amygdala leads to social impairments. Those with damage to the amygdala often have difficulty evaluating the intensity of fearful faces even though they do not show impairments in judging the intensity of other facial expressions, such as happiness. One interesting study suggests that those with damage to the amygdala fail to use information contained within facial expressions to make accurate interpersonal judgments (Adolphs et al., 1998).

The orbitofrontal cortex Recall from the motivation chapter that the orbitofrontal cortex is involved in assessing the potential reward value of situations and objects. It is also involved in the processing of emotional cues, especially those related to interpersonal interactions. People with damage to this region often act inappropriately and are generally insensitive to the emotional expressions of others. Moreover, orbitofrontal damage is sometimes associated with excessive aggression and violence, suggesting difficulties with emotional control.

Antonio Damasio has found that patients with damage to the orbitofrontal region often fail to use somatic markers. When these regions are damaged, people still can recall information, but it has lost most of its affective meaning. They might be able to describe their current problems or talk about the death of a loved one, but they do so without experiencing any of the emotional pain that normally accompanies such thoughts.

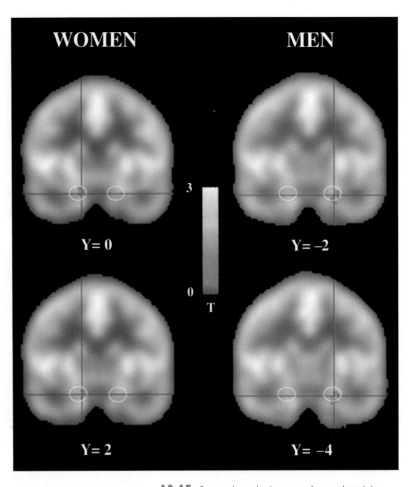

10.15 Scans show the increased neural activity that accompanies increased recall of emotional versus neutral films in both men and women. The white circle indicates the approximate amygdala region. Note that women show greater activation of the left amygdala whereas men show greater activation of the right.

cerebral asymmetry An emotional pattern associated with unequal activation of the left and right frontal lobes.

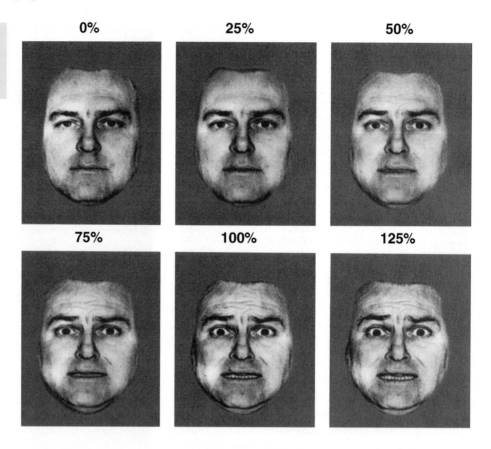

| 0% | 25% | 50% |
| 75% | 100% | 125% |

10.16 As participants view these faces, the amygdala becomes more activated as the face displays more fear.

10.17 Richard Davidson has proposed that affective style is influenced by cerebral asymmetry, with the right hemisphere being associated with negative moods and the left hemisphere associated with positive moods.

EMOTION SYSTEMS ARE LATERALIZED IN THE BRAIN

Psychological scientist Richard Davidson (Figure 10.17) has shown that unequal activation of the left and right frontal lobes is associated with specific emotional states, a pattern known as **cerebral asymmetry**. In a series of studies, Davidson and his colleagues found that greater activation of the right prefrontal cortex is associated with negative affect, whereas greater activation of the left hemisphere is associated with positive affect. A study of responses to film clips found that people who were left-hemisphere dominant showed the most positive response to pleasant scenes, whereas those who were right-hemisphere dominant showed the most negative response to unpleasant scenes. Another study found that those who reported the strongest negative emotion showed the greatest activation of the right amygdala in response to unpleasant pictures (Davidson, 2000a; Figure 10.18).

Cerebral asymmetry is associated with general motivation (Davidson, 2000b). For instance, greater activation of the left hemisphere is associated with increased confidence and effort to achieve goals. A greater activation of the right hemisphere is associated with lack of motivation, a symptom of clinical depression. PET studies have shown diminished left-hemisphere activation among depressed patients, and depression is more common among those who have brain injuries to the left hemisphere. Remarkably, as early as three months of age, children of depressed mothers also show asymmetrical brain activation (Field et al., 1995). Although the functional significance of cerebral asymmetry is not known, recent work by Davidson and his colleagues suggests it may have to do with the

(a)

(b)

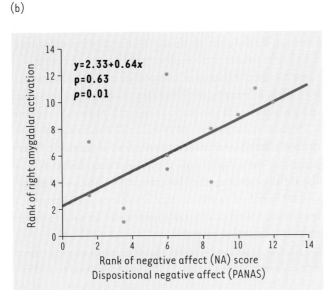

$y = 2.33 + 0.64x$
$p = 0.63$
$p = 0.01$

Rank of right amygdalar activation (y-axis)

Rank of negative affect (NA) score
Dispositional negative affect (PANAS) (x-axis)

10.18 (a) The amygdala region is magnified in the bottom image and shows the greater activation of the right amygdala (on the left side of the image) during viewing of unpleasant pictures. (b) This activation corresponds with greater negative affect.

regulation of emotional states. For instance, anti-anxiety drugs decrease fearful behavior and increase left frontal activation in infant monkeys, suggesting that negative affective states such as anxiety may suppress the left frontal lobe and thus reduce motivation.

Research has demonstrated that the right hemisphere is more involved than the left in the interpretation and comprehension of emotional material. Neuroimaging studies have found that although emotional stimulation activates both hemispheres, activation is much greater on the right side. The right hemisphere is also more accurate at detecting the emotional tone of speech (such as whether the voice sounds sad or happy), whereas the left hemisphere is more accurate at decoding semantic content. As an example, consider that when we look at facial expressions, the left half of the face is projected to the right hemisphere and the right half of the face is projected to the left hemisphere. Researchers who create divided faces, such as in Figure 10.19, have found that the emotion "seen" by the right hemisphere heavily influences the interpretation of an emotional expression. Which face looks sadder to you? Which face looks happier?

10.19 Divided faces have enabled psychologists to determine that the right hemisphere interprets the meaning of facial expressions.

What Is the Neurophysiological Basis of Emotion?

Emotions lead to specific autonomic reactions, but there is considerable overlap between emotions. A number of brain structures, especially the amygdala and orbitofrontal cortex, are involved in emotion and social judgment. Research indicates that left-hemisphere activity is related to positive emotions and right-hemisphere activity to negative emotions.

stressor An environmental event or stimulus that threatens an organism.

coping response Any response made by an organism to avoid, escape from, or minimize an aversive stimulus.

fight-or-flight response A term used to describe the physiological preparedness of animals to deal with danger.

tend and befriend The argument that females are more likely to protect and care for their offspring and form social alliances than flee or fight in response to threat.

general adaptation syndrome (GAS) A consistent pattern of responses to stress that consists of three stages; alarm stage, resistance stage, and exhaustion stage.

RESEARCH QUESTION

What is stress?

10.20 Hans Selye popularized the term *stress* and demonstrated that stress could affect physical health. Although Hungarian, he spent most of his career in Montreal, Canada.

HOW DO PEOPLE COPE WITH STRESS?

Stress is a common component of everyday emotional life, and it consists of a number of emotional responses. Although the term stress has negative connotations, a moderate level of stress is beneficial. Different levels of stress are optimal for different people, and learning how much stress you can handle is essential for recognizing its effects on your mental, physical, and emotional well-being.

Stress involves both physical and psychological factors. It has direct effects on the body, but how stressed people feel depends on factors such as how people perceive the stressful event, their tolerance for stress, and their personal beliefs about the resources they have to cope with the stressor. A **stressor** is an environmental event or stimulus that threatens an organism and that leads to a **coping response**, which is any response made by an organism to avoid, escape from, or minimize an aversive stimulus.

As makes sense from an adaptive point of view, the physiological response that accompanies stress helps mobilize resources to either fight or flee from danger, thereby facilitating survival and reproduction. Harvard physiologist Walter Cannon coined the term **fight-or-flight response** to describe the physiological preparation of animals to deal with any attack. This physical reaction includes increased heart rate, contraction of the spleen, redistribution of the blood supply from skin and viscera to muscles and brain, deepening of respiration, dilation of the pupils, inhibition of gastric secretions, and an increase in release of glucose from the liver. This response to a stressor occurs within seconds or minutes and allows an organism to direct all energy to dealing with the threat at hand while postponing less critical autonomic activities. One important analysis of responses to stress suggests that females may be more likely to "**tend and befriend**" than fight or flee. This research is featured in "Crossing the Levels of Analysis: Sex and Stress: Making Friends or Fighting Foes."

THERE IS A GENERAL ADAPTATION SYNDROME

In the early 1930s, Hans Selye (Figure 10.20) began studying the physiological effects of sex hormones by injecting rats with samples from other animals. When he examined the rats, he found enlarged adrenal glands, decreased levels of lymphocytes in the blood, and stomach ulcers. Selye surmised that the foreign hormones must have been the cause of these changes, so he conducted further tests, using different types of chemicals and even physically restraining the animals. He found slight variations in some physiological effects, but each manipulation produced this tripartite pattern of bloated adrenal glands, atrophied lymphatic structures, and stomach ulcers. He concluded that these three responses were the hallmarks of *nonspecific stress response*. But these changes reduce the organism's potential ability to resist additional stressors. Selye borrowed the term *stress* from engineering, in which it is used to describe a force applied against resistance. Walter Cannon had earlier used the term as part of his model of homeostasis, but it was Selye who popularized the term and contributed most to our early knowledge of the stress response.

The **general adaptation syndrome (GAS)**, a consistent pattern of responses identified by Selye, consists of three stages: *alarm stage, resistance stage*, and *exhaustion stage* (Figure 10.22). GAS occurs in addition to specific physiological responses to particular stressors. The first stage is the *alarm stage*, an emergency

SEX AND STRESS: MAKING FRIENDS OR FIGHTING FOES

In 1932 Walter Cannon proposed that the human stress response follows a fight-or-flight pattern, in which energies are directed toward either confronting and combating rivals and predators or fleeing from them. This idea has been central to the study of stress, both in human and nonhuman research. However, Shelley Taylor (Figure 10.21) and her colleagues have recently pointed out that the vast majority of both human and nonhuman animal research has been conducted using males, which has distorted the scientific understanding of responses to stress. Most rat studies use male rats to avoid hormonal cycles such as estrus. Although the reasons are unclear, a similar sex inequality exists for human studies, with women representing fewer than 1 in 5 participants in laboratory stress studies.

Taylor and her colleagues suggest that females respond to stress by protecting and caring for their offspring, as well as by forming aliances with social groups to reduce individual risk. They refer to this pattern as *tending and befriending*. Such responses make great sense from an evolutionary point of view. Females typically bore a greater responsibility for the care of offspring, and responses that protected offspring as well as the self were maximally adaptive. When threat appears, quieting the offspring and hiding may be an effective means of avoiding harm. In contrast, trying to flee while pregnant, nursing, or with a clinging infant may not have been particularly successful. Furthermore, those females who selectively affiliate with others, especially other females, might acquire additional protection and

10.21 Shelley Taylor has conducted important research in health psychology. She and her colleagues have revolutionized thinking about how animals respond to threat.

support. Thus, Taylor's group proposes that women respond adaptively to stress by becoming more nurturing and by seeking out friendships.

A wide variety of evidence supports the tend-and-befriend hypothesis. At the neuroendocrine level, females lack androgens that, in many species, are involved in aggressive behavior, such as that necessary to fight predators or rivals. By contrast, females tend to show a greater oxytocin response to stress, and estrogens seem to further enhance its behavioral properties. The neuropeptide oxytocin has received a great deal of attention for its role in maternal behavior, enhancing sedation and relaxation, and promoting feelings of social acceptance and interpersonal bonding (Panksepp, 1992). Thus, a large release of oxytocin during stress may calm females as well as promote affiliative behavior toward offspring. At the behavioral level, mothers who are stressed by their jobs tend to pay *more* attention to their children, whereas stressed fathers tend to withdraw from their families. Indeed, children report receiving the most love and nurturance from their mothers on the days that their mothers report the highest levels of stress (Repetti, 1997, cited in Taylor et al., 2000).

Women are much more affiliative under stress than men, in that they are more likely to seek out social support, to receive social support, and to be satisfied with the social support they receive. Interestingly, when stressed, women are especially likely to seek out other women. Thus, women are more connected to their social networks than are men. According to Roy Baumeister and Kristin Sommer (1997), women generally are friendlier with each other. Compared to men, they disclose more, smile more, and pay more attention to their same-sex interaction partners. Female-female networks are especially common among nonhuman primates. These female-female groups may be useful for controlling food resources and protecting individual females from aggressive males. The tend-and-befriend stress response provides an excellent example of how thinking about psychological mechanisms in terms of their evolutionary significance leads us to question long-standing assumptions about how the mind works. Females who responded to stress by nurturing and protecting their young and by forming alliances with other females apparently had a selective advantage over those who tried to fight or flee.

reaction that prepares the body to fight or flee. In this stage, physiological responses are aimed at boosting physical abilities while reducing activities that make the organism vulnerable to infection after injury. This is the stage in which the body might be exposed to infection and disease. Thus, the immune system kicks in and the body begins to fight back. During the *resistance stage*, the defenses are prepared for a longer, sustained attack against the stressor; immunity to disease continues to increase somewhat as the body maximizes its defenses. However, the body eventually hits the *exhaustion stage*, in which a variety of

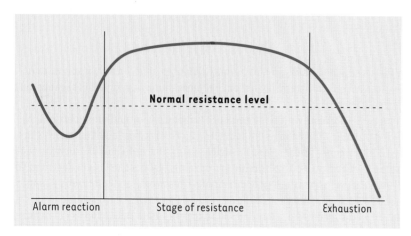

10.22 Selye's general adaption syndrome describes the three stages of physiological response to stress. Initially, resistance is reduced as the body prepares to fight or flee. However, the body eventually adapts and resistance increases. Eventually, the system becomes exhausted and resistance plummets.

hypothalamic-pituitary-adrenal axis (HPA) A bodily system that is activated in response to stress.

adrenocorticotropic hormone (ACTH) A hormone secreted by the pituitary gland in response to stress.

glucocorticoids A type of steroid hormone, often called cortisol, released by the adrenal glands during a stress response, that produces many of the physical effects of stress.

physiological and immune systems fail. Bodily organs that were already weak before the stress are the first to fail. The general principles of the GAS theory have been confirmed by scientific research.

It is now generally agreed that a stressor leads to activation of the **hypothalamic-pituitary-adrenal (HPA) axis** (Figure 10.23). During a stress response, the hypothalamus (H) secretes a hormone called *corticotropin-releasing factor* (*CRF*), which triggers the pituitary (P) to release **adrenocorticotropic hormone (ACTH)** into the bloodstream. ACTH acts on the adrenal cortex (A) to release **glucocorticoids** (often referred to as *cortisol*), a type of steroid hormone, from the adrenal glands. It is the glucocorticoids that produce many of the bodily effects of stress, such as breaking down protein and converting it to glucose, which helps meet immediate energy needs. When glucocorticoid levels are sufficiently high, the central nervous system shuts down the process that releases ACTH. But, because it takes from 15 minutes to an hour before the glucocorticoids reach a sufficient level to signal the termination of ACTH, the continued presence of glucocorticoids in the bloodstream sustains their effects for a considerable time after the occurrence of the stressor. In addition to glucocorticoids, the adrenal glands also release norepinephrine and epinephrine, due to activation of the sympathetic nervous system (see Chapter 3).

THERE IS STRESS IN DAILY LIFE

Stress occurs when aspects of the environment overwhelm people. That is, people feel stressed when too much is expected of them, or when events seem scary or worrisome. Stress occurs when there is a perceived discrepancy—whether real or not—between the demands of the situation and the resources of the person's biological, psychological, and social systems. Psychologists typically think of stressors as falling into two categories: major life stressors and daily hassles. *Major life stressors* are changes or disruptions that strain central areas of people's lives. Positive events can be as stressful or even more stressful than negative events; for instance, some parents report that having their first child is one of the most joyful—but also one of the most taxing—experiences of their lives. Major life stressors can be choices made by individuals, not just things that happen to them. Nonetheless, research has shown that catastrophic events that are unpredictable and uncontrollable (such as an earthquake) are especially stressful. In general, life changes are stressful, whether it is moving to a new college or job, getting married, being fired, losing a parent, or winning a major award. The greater the number of changes, the greater the stress, and the more likely stress is to have an impact on physiological state.

Daily hassles are small day-to-day irritations and annoyances, such as driving in traffic, dealing with unfair bosses or teachers, or having to wait in line. Daily hassles are stressful and their effects can be comparable to those of major life changes. These low-level irritations are ubiquitous and, most important, pose a threat to coping responses by slowly wearing down personal resources. Studies that ask people to keep diaries of their daily activities consistently find that the more intense and frequent the hassles, the poorer the physical and mental health of the participant. People appear to habituate to daily problems, but some types seem to have a cumulative effect on health, such as interpersonal difficulties. Living or working in a crowded city or in an area with noise or environmental pollution can also have detrimental effects on emotional well-being.

STRESS AFFECTS HEALTH

One of Selye's central points was that the prolonged action of glucocorticoids, such as occurs during chronic stress, has a negative impact on health. Indeed, although glucocorticoids are essential to normal health, over the long term they are associated with increased blood pressure, cardiac disease, diabetes, declining sexual interest, dwarfism, and so on. People who have stressful jobs—air-traffic controllers, combat soldiers, firefighters—have numerous health problems, presumably in part due to the effects of chronic stress. Robert Sapolsky (1994) chronicles the multiple health problems attributable to chronic stress, especially psychosocial stress. He notes that chronic stress can even lead to memory impairments because glucocorticoids damage neurons in the hippocampus. Recall from Chapter 7 on memory that the hippocampus is the brain structure involved in the consolidation of memory.

There is overwhelming evidence that stress is associated with the initiation and progression of a wide variety of diseases, from cancer to AIDS to cardiac disease. Not only does stress lead to specific physiological responses that affect health, but many people cope with stress by engaging in damaging behaviors. For instance, the number one reason that problem drinkers give for abusing alcohol is to cope with negative stress in their lives. When people are stressed they smoke cigarettes, eat junk food, use drugs, and so on. Most of the major health problems in Western society are attributable to unhealthful behaviors, many of which occur when people are stressed.

Challenge versus threat James Blascovich and his colleagues have drawn a central distinction between challenging and threatening situations (Blascovich et al., 1999). *Threat* and *challenge* are motivational states relevant to achieving goals; they result from cognitive and affective evaluations of situational demands and personal resources. *Threat* occurs when demands are perceived to outweigh resources, whereas *challenge* results when resources are perceived to approximate or exceed demands. For example, you would feel threatened playing chess with someone who was better than you, but challenged if the person was as good or slightly worse. Gross imbalances, such as competing against a grand master or an inexperienced child, do not provide information that is personally meaningful and therefore do not lead to challenge or threat.

Blascovich and his colleagues have shown that there are cardiac and vascular differences associated with challenge and threat. Challenge mimics aerobic exercise, producing increased heart rate and decreased vascular resistance. This pattern represents the efficient mobilization of energy for coping. Threat, however, increases heart rate but does not decrease vascular resistance, with the result that blood pressure increases. Threat, therefore, may produce health problems over the long run.

Personality differences related to heart disease We tend to see a link between anger and health, saying things such as "I'm going to burst a blood vessel" and "He was boiling over with rage." Indeed, cardiologists have long considered people who are hostile, easily irritated, and aggressive to be at risk for a heart at-

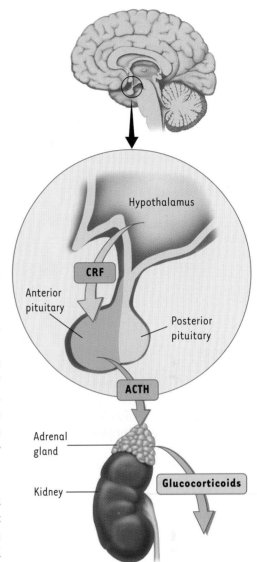

10.23 HPA axis and neuroendocrine response. CRF is secreted by the hypothalamus into the pituitaries, which then release ACTH into the bloodstream. Receptors in the adrenal cortex, in the adrenal glands near the kidney, release glucocorticoids, norepinephrine, and epinephrine.

RESEARCH QUESTION

What are the effects of stress?

Type A personality A pattern of personality traits characterized by competitiveness, achievement orientation, aggressiveness, hostility, time urgency, restlessness, inability to relax, and impatience with others.

Type B personality A pattern of personality traits characterized by relaxed, non-competitive, easy-going, and accommodative behavior.

psychoneuroimmunology The study of the body's immune system in response to psychological variables.

immune system The body's mechanism for dealing with invading microorganisms, such as allergens, bacteria, and viruses.

lymphocytes Specialized white blood cells known as B cells, T cells, and natural killer cells that make up the immune system.

antibodies Protein molecules that attach themselves to foreign agents and mark them for destruction.

tack. This assumption was first put to the test in 1960 when the Western Collaborative Group began what was to be an eight-and-a-half-year study to examine the effects of personality on coronary heart disease. Physicians recruited 3,500 men from northern California who were initially free of heart disease symptoms and screened them annually for blood pressure, heart rate, cholesterol, and overall health practices. Personal details such as level of education, medical and family history, income, and personality traits were also assessed. The study results indicated that, adjusting for the presence of established risk factors (such as high blood pressure or high cholesterol), a pattern of personality traits predicted heart disease. This pattern, called **Type A personality**, includes competitiveness, being achievement oriented, aggressiveness, hostility, time urgency (constantly feeling hurried, restless, unable to relax), and being impatient and confrontational with others. Men who exhibited these traits were much more likely to develop coronary heart disease than were their peers who were labeled **Type B personality**, which describes a relaxed, noncompetitive, accommodative person. In fact, this study found that Type A personality was as strong a predictor of heart disease as was smoking or high cholesterol or blood pressure (Krantz et al., 1987).

The effect of Type A personality was called into question by later researchers. Some investigators failed to find a predictive effect of Type A behavior, others showed a small effect, while still other investigators showed a strong effect. There are several reasons for these mixed results, but the consensus among researchers and physicians is that one component of the Type A personality pattern is especially harmful. High levels of hostility—both toward others and toward oneself—appear to lead to poor health.

STRESS AFFECTS THE IMMUNE SYSTEM

Stress alters the functions of the neuroendocrine and immune systems. As Esther Sternberg (2000) has noted, "stress *can* make you sick because the hormones and nerve pathways activated by stress change the way the immune system responds, making it less able to fight invaders" (p. 131). The field of **psychoneuroimmunology** studies the response of the body's immune system to psychological variables. The **immune system** is the body's mechanism for dealing with invading microorganisms, such as allergens, bacteria, and viruses. Sometimes the immune system attacks its own body, as occurs with autoimmune disorders.

The immune system is made up of three types of specialized white blood cells known as **lymphocytes**: B cells, T cells, and natural killer cells. *B cells* produce **antibodies**, protein molecules that attach themselves to foreign agents and mark them for destruction. There are also *memory B cells* that remember specific invaders, making for easier identification in the future. This is why you have lifelong immunity to some diseases once you've been exposed to them naturally or through inoculation. The *T cells* often are involved in attacking the intruders; they also sometimes act as helper cells by increasing the activation of the immune response. *Natural killer cells* are especially potent in killing viruses and also help attack tumors. The detrimental effects of both immediate and long-term stress on physical health are due, in part, to decreased lymphocyte production, which renders the body less capable of warding off foreign substances. One recent idea is that the immune system functions as a sensory system, which is discussed in "Studying the Mind: Is the Immune System a Sensory System?"

Psychoneuroimmunology research has found that a variety of factors moderate the effects of stress, including intensity, novelty, and predictability. *Intensity* of the

Studying the Mind

IS THE IMMUNE SYSTEM A SENSORY SYSTEM?

Steven Maier and Linda Watkins (2000) have argued that the immune system operates as a sensory system, in that it communicates information to the brain about infection and injury. In turn, the brain uses this information to launch a coordinated attack on potentially dangerous intruders. The important point is that the pathway between the brain and the immune system is bidirectional, so that processes within the immune system influence psychological functioning, and mental state alters immune functioning.

When you are infected with a virus, approximately 1 to 3 hours later a variety of actions occur within the brain to affect cognition, mood, and behavior. As people become sick they feel depressed and fatigued, they want to be left alone, and they want to lie down. These responses make sense from an evolutionary standpoint. To fight infection, the body needs to direct energy toward the fight, and therefore activity is limited to conserve energy. How does this occur?

When people are infected, substances known as interleukins (which communicate signals between white blood cells, known as leukocytes) transmit a message to the brain that essentially says "I am sick." Injections of certain interleukins cause fatigue, negative mood, and confused mental activity.

Interestingly, many of the mental and physical changes caused by infection are similar to those due to environmental stressors. For instance, certain neurotransmitters are released in the hypothalamus and hippocampus. Maier and Watkins propose that stress may activate the same system that is used to fight infection. The link between the immune and stress responses can be seen in the reports of depression among those with autoimmune diseases such as arthritis. Understanding potential links between the immune system and the brain may help scientists to understand the connection between stress and illness.

---

stressor is positively related to glucocorticosteroid and autonomic responses, indicators of immune response. *Novelty* is related to physiological reactions: first-time parachutists show increased glucocorticosteroid and catecholamines on the first jump, but these physiological reactions rapidly diminish on subsequent jumps. *Predictability* increases adaptive responses to stress. For instance, aversive noise is less tolerable when it is administered unpredictably (Glass & Singer, 1972).

In a particularly clear demonstration that stress affects health, Sheldon Cohen and his colleagues (1991) paid healthy volunteers to be exposed to the common cold virus. Those who had reported the highest levels of stress in a questionnaire had worse cold symptoms and higher viral counts than those who reported being less stressed (Figure 10.24). In another study, participants kept a daily diary for up to 12 weeks in which they recorded their moods and events in their lives. The participants also rated these events as desirable or undesirable. Each day, the participants took a novel protein to challenge their secretory immune systems and provided a saliva sample so that researchers could examine antibody responses. The study revealed that the more desirable events a participant reported, the greater the antibody production. Similarly, the more undesirable events reported, the weaker the antibody production. The effect of a desirable event on antibodies lasted for two days (Stone et al., 1994). These and subsequent findings provide substantial evidence that perceived stress influences the immune system. As more research is conducted on the bidirectional nature of mental and physical well-being, the field of psychoneuroimmunology will continue to flourish.

COPING IS A PROCESS

Cognitive appraisals affect people's perception of and reactions to potential stressors. Coping that occurs before the onset of a future stressor is called *anticipatory coping*, such as when parents rehearse

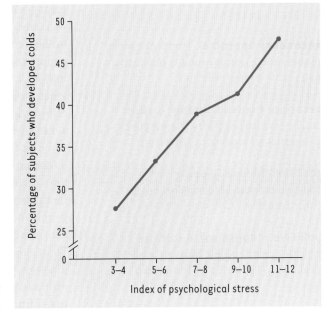

10.24 People who reported the greatest levels of stress were the most likely to catch colds.

RESEARCH QUESTION

What factors help people deal with stress?

what they will say when telling their children about plans to divorce. Psychologist Richard Lazarus (1993) conceptualized a two-part appraisal process. **Primary appraisals** are used to decide whether the stimulus is stressful, benign, or irrelevant. If the stimulus is deemed stressful, **secondary appraisals** are used to evaluate response options and choose coping behaviors.

Types of coping   A taxonomy of coping strategies developed by Folkman and Lazarus suggests that there are two general categories of coping style. **Emotion-focused coping** involves trying to prevent having an emotional response to the stressor. It includes strategies such as avoidance, minimizing the problem, trying to distance oneself from the outcomes of the problem, or doing things such as eating or drinking. These are often passive strategies that are used to numb the pain. They do nothing to solve the problem or prevent it from reoccurring in the future. By contrast, **problem-focused coping** involves taking direct steps to solve the problem. People generate alternative solutions, weigh them in terms of costs and benefits, and choose between them. Problem-focused behaviors are used when the stressor is perceived as controllable and there is only a moderate level of stress. Conversely, emotion-focused behaviors enable people to continue functioning in the face of an uncontrollable stressor or a high level of stress.

Most people report using both problem- and emotion-focused coping. Usually, emotion-based strategies are effective only in the short run. For example, if someone in a bad mood is giving you a hard time, just ignoring him can be the best option. Yet ignoring your partner's drinking problem won't make it go away, and eventually you'll need a better coping strategy. However, for problem-focused coping strategies to work, people need to be able to do something about the situation. A fascinating study tested the best way to cope with an extremely threatening situation (Strentz & Auerbach, 1988). In this study, 57 airline workers were taken hostage by five "terrorists," who were actually FBI agents. Even though the participants volunteered to be hostages with full knowledge, the situation was very realistic and they were extremely stressed over the four days of the study. Half of the people were trained to use emotion-based coping whereas the other half were trained to use problem-based coping. Which strategy worked better? The emotion-based group experienced less stress because there was nothing the hostages could do that would not put them in greater danger. However, this study was done in 1988, and following the World Trade Center and Pentagon tragedies on September 11, 2001, it is no longer clear that a passive response would help people cope. The previous assumption that it is safer to cooperate with hijackers may no longer be true. Thus, the best way to cope with stress depends on personal resources and on the situation. Although problem-focused coping is usually more effective over the long run, emotion-focused coping might be a useful strategy in some circumstances over the short term, especially when people have little control over the situation.

Susan Folkman and Judith Moskowitz (2000) have demonstrated that in addition to problem-focused coping, two strategies can help people use positive thoughts to deal with stress. **Positive reappraisal** is a cognitive process in which people focus on possible good things in their current situation, the proverbial silver lining, such as when people compare themselves to those who are worse off. These *downward comparisons* have been shown to help people coping with serious illnesses. *Creation of positive events* refers to a strategy of infusing ordinary events with positive meaning. Doing such things as taking note of a beautiful sunset, trying to find humor in a situation, or simply taking satisfaction in a recent compli-

primary appraisals   Part of the coping process that involves making decisions about whether a stimulus is stressful, benign, or irrelevant.

secondary appraisal   Part of the coping process where people evaluate their options and choose coping behaviors.

emotion-focused coping   A type of coping in which people try to prevent having an emotional response to a stressor.

problem-focused coping   A type of coping that involves taking direct steps to solve a problem.

positive reappraisal   A cognitive process in which people focus on possible good things in their current situation.

ment allows people to focus on the positive aspects of their lives, which helps them deal with their negative stress. For instance, caregivers of those with AIDS are under enormous stress. Folkman and Moskowitz have found that positive appraisal, creation of positive events, and problem-focused coping—which gave the caregivers some sense of control—were instrumental in successful coping.

Individual differences in coping   People differ widely in the degree to which they perceive life events as being stressful. Some people could be termed "stress-resistant individuals" for their ability to adapt to life changes by viewing the events constructively. An idea that captures this personality characteristic is **hardiness**, developed by Suzanne Kobasa (1979), which has three components: *commitment*, *challenge*, and *control*. People who are high in hardiness are committed to their daily activities, view threats as challenges or opportunities for growth, and see themselves as being in control of their lives. People who are low in hardiness are typically alienated, view events as under external control, and fear or resist change. Numerous studies have found that people high in hardiness report fewer negative responses to stressful events. In a laboratory experiment in which participants were given difficult cognitive tasks, people high in hardiness exhibited higher blood pressure during the task, a physiological indicator of active coping. Moreover, a questionnaire completed immediately after the task revealed that participants high in hardiness boosted the number of positive thoughts about themselves in response to the stressor.

Social support   One of the most important factors for whether people effectively cope with stress is the level of social support they receive. **Social support** refers to having other people who can provide help, encouragement, and advice. Having social support is an essential component of positive mental and physical health. Ill people who are socially isolated are much more likely to die than those who are well connected to others (House et al., 1988), in part because isolation itself is associated with numerous health problems. Conversely, a recent review of more than 80 studies found strong evidence linking social support to fewer health problems (Uchino et al., 1996). For example, Janice Kiecolt-Glaser and Ronald Glaser (1988) found that people with troubled marriages and people going through divorce or bereavement all had compromised immune systems. In a study that categorized newlyweds based on observed interactions, couples that fought more and showed more hostility toward each other exhibited decreased natural-killer-cell activity in the 24 hours after the interaction (Kiecolt-Glaser et al., 1993).

Social support is important for people of all ages. Studies of children who seem *resilient*, meaning they have good outcomes in spite of being raised in deprived or chaotic situations, show the presence of parental or family support to be especially important (Masten, 2001). The elderly are particularly prone to social isolation, therefore the effects of social support on health are particularly strong for this group.

Social support helps people cope with stress in two basic ways. First, people with social support experience less stress overall. Consider single parents who have to deal with job and family demands in isolation. Not having a partner places more demands on them, which increases the likelihood that they will feel stressed. Second, social support aids coping because other people lessen the negative effects of the stress that occurs. The **buffering hypothesis** (Cohen & Wills, 1985) proposes that others can provide direct support in helping people cope with

hardiness   A personality trait that enables people to perceive stressors as controllable challenges.

social support   A network of other people who can provide help, encouragement, and advice.

buffering hypothesis   Proposes that other people can provide direct support in helping individuals cope with stressful events.

stressful events. Receiving emotional support is more important than just having others who provide information. Emotional support includes expressions of caring and willingness to listen to another person's problems. Social support can also take more tangible forms, such as providing material help or assisting with daily chores. But, to be effective, social support needs to imply that people *care* about the recipient of the support.

How Do People Cope With Stress?

Stress occurs when people feel overwhelmed by the challenges they face, such as when major change happens in their lives. Hans Selye proposed the general adaptation theory to conceptualize the stages of physiological coping. The stress of daily life includes both major life changes and daily hassles. Psychoneuroimmunology is uncovering the links between stress and health, such as the risks of a hostile personality. However, cognitive appraisals, such as determining the relevancy of the stressor or adopting a problem- versus emotion-focused approach, can alleviate stress or minimize its harmful effects. Perhaps the most important way people cope with stress is through their interactions with others who provide social support.

CONCLUSION

For many years scientists likened the brain to an information-processing device such as a computer. Humans are hardly like this. They react to environmental input with physiological reactions and cognitions, which together produce mental states that are perceived to be positive or negative, or shades in between. This response is known as emotion, and it is a primary force that motivates adaptive behaviors and discourages maladaptive behaviors. Thinking about emotions and stress from an evolutionary viewpoint provides novel perspectives for understanding them. For instance, emotions such as shame and guilt are often viewed as unnecessary emotional baggage. But guilt, embarrassment, and the like help to maintain and affirm social bonds and thereby serve adaptive functions. Similarly, the assumption that fight or flight was a uniform response to stress does not make sense from an evolutionary perspective. Scholars have recently shown that females of many species behave in a completely different manner—tending and befriending—that makes more adaptive sense. The biological revolution has produced research building on the cumulative knowledge about emotions. This research has provided ample evidence about how the brain processes threatening information and produces adaptive responses. As psychological scientists take a more functional approach to understanding stress and emotion, new insights will continue to emerge.

FURTHER READINGS

Damasio, A. R. (1999). *The feeling of what happens*. New York: Harcourt Brace.

Ekman, P., & Davidson, R. J. (1994). *The nature of emotion: Fundamental questions*. New York: Oxford University Press.

Glaser, R., & Kiecolt-Glaser, J. K. (1994). *Handbook of human stress and immunity*. San Diego: Academic Press.

Jenkins, J. M., Oatley, K., & Stein, N. L. (1998). *Human emotions: A reader.* Malden, MA: Blackwell Publishers.

Lane, R. D., Nadel, L., & Ahern, G. (1999). *Cognitive neuroscience of emotion.* New York: Oxford University Press.

LeDoux, J. E. (1996). *The emotional brain: The mysterious underpinnings of emotional life.* New York: Simon & Schuster.

Lewis, M., & Haviland, J. M. (1993). *Handbook of emotions.* New York: Guilford.

Panksepp, J. (1998). *Affective neuroscience: The foundations of human and animal emotions.* New York: Oxford University Press.

Sapolsky, R. M. (1994). *Why zebras don't get ulcers.* New York: Freeman.

Sternberg, E. M. (2000). *The balance within.* New York: Freeman.

MYSTERIES OF COGNITIVE DEVELOPMENT

Five-year-old Jordan Adams, a child prodigy, is able to play the piano as well or better than much older, more experienced students. Cases such as Jordan's challenge traditional notions about cognitive development. Although we do not fully understand the mechanisms involved, most scientists maintain cognitive development is usually governed by constraints related to chronological age.

TIMELINE

1900–1910

Babies Are Built By Experience William James states that an infant's world is a "blooming, buzzing confusion." James' uncharacteristically wrong observation leads scientists to believe perception and cognition come about through learning.

1920–1970

Cognitive Development View Introduced Swiss psychologist Jean Piaget proposes four distinct stages of how "thinking" develops in the brain.

1920s

Cultural Context and Cognition Russian psychologist Lev Vygotsky develops the first major theory of how cultural and social context influences cognitive and language development.

1950–1960

The Psycholinguistic Revolution Noam Chomsky transforms linguistics by noting that language must be governed by a universal grammar, a set of rules and principles built into the brain.

Cognitive and Language Development

OUTLINING THE PRINCIPLES

1960–1970
Fundamental Mental Properties Pioneering researchers such as Robert Fantz, Peter Eimas, Jacques Mehler, and Tom Bever demonstrate that many concepts are built in to the human brain.

1960s
Teaching Language to Apes Researchers, including Allen and Beatrice Gardner, Duane Rumbaugh, David Premack, and Herb Terrace attempt to teach apes human language, with limited success.

1970–1980
Development and Brain Maturation Jerome Kagan argues that so-called learned responses based on sensory experiences in young children actually reflect ongoing brain maturation.

1980–1990
Higher-Order Concepts Are Built-In As Well Rochel Gelman, Dan Osherson, Susan Carey, Renee Baillargeon, Elizabeth Spelke, and others propose that from birth, a child develops skills independently rather than as part of a progression.

1980s–1990s
Social Context Shapes Development Researchers such as Michael Tomasello demonstrate that social and cultural context contributes to language development.

for Studying Cognitive and Language Development

What methods do developmental psychologists use to study perception in infants?

What is the relationship between physical development and learning?

What skills do infants have that indicate Piaget's stage theory of development may be incorrect?

What evidence suggests that the mind develops cognitive skills, independent of each other, rather than as an integrated whole?

How do children's memory systems develop?

How do culture and other social factors affect cognitive development?

What suggests that language is innate?

What cognitive functions decline with age?

Wolfgang Amadeus Mozart (Figure 11.1) was born in Salzburg, Austria, in 1756. Before the age of four, he had exhibited such extraordinary powers of musical memory and ear-sophistication that his father, Leopold (a highly esteemed violinist and composer in his own right), decided to sign young Wolfgang up for harpsichord lessons. It took all of thirty minutes for the boy to master his first musical composition. The scherzo had been copied by his father into his older sister's notebook. Below it Mozart's father jotted: "This piece was learnt by Wolfgangerl on 24 January 1761, 3 days before his 5th birthday, between 9 and 9:30 in the evening."

Wolfgang's achievement was followed in rapid succession by others: a minuet and trio "learned within a half an hour" on January 26, a march learned on February 4, another scherzo on February 6. It wasn't long before the little boy entered a composition of his own into the notebook.

From that time on, young Mozart was constantly performing and writing music. He composed concertos before he was able to write words. He became the toast of Austria and gave many concerts of prepared works and improvisation. Wherever he appeared, people gaped in awe at his incredible talent. By his early teens, he had mastered the piano, violin, and harpsichord, and he was writing keyboard pieces, oratorios, symphonies, and operas. His first major opera, *Mitridate*, was performed in Milan in 1770 (when he was still only 14), to such unqualified raves that critics compared him to Handel. At 15, Mozart was installed as the concertmaster in the orchestra of the archbishop of Salzburg.

The story of Mozart illustrates the life of a child prodigy. Children who exhibit skills equal to (or in many cases far above) adults challenge traditional notions about cognitive development. As we shall see in this chapter, cognitive development is thought to be sequential, and bound in some ways by biological constraints related to chronological age. It is clear, though, that we still do not completely

---

1990–2000

Setting Conditions on Innateness Critical questions center around how many cognitive skills or abilities a child is born with, and what they are.

1995–2000

The Overreach of Brain Science Theorists and researchers attempt to relate developmental psychology to developmental neurobiology, an effort that mostly fails.

2001

Human Neurobiology and Brain Development A major research agenda, led by Michael Posner, seeks to understand human development using new brain-imaging knowledge.

understand the precise mechanisms of cognitive development. This chapter examines what is currently known about the development of the human mind.

11.1 A portrait of Mozart as a young boy (seated at the piano) with his father and sister.

Despite the fact that you were once an infant and have since learned how to walk, talk, read, reason, and do countless other things, you most likely have very little knowledge about how you acquired those skills. Most of us can remember learning how to swim or to play a particular game and can offer insight on how we went about learning the new skill, but this is not the case with early development. Infancy is one of the few phenomena in psychology that we all have experienced, but none of us remember. In fact, scientists know more about the entire life cycle of the fruit fly than about the way infants and children develop cognition.

The study of **cognitive development** is concerned with how humans acquire knowledge and understanding about the world during the course of their lives. To study this, scientists have focused on age-related changes in thinking, reasoning, and language. We will see that the mind develops in a way that is adaptive, as new useful skills appear at appropriate times, even in the absence of specific training. For years, the study of developmental psychology was largely based on Jean Piaget's theory of development, which states that children learn in stages that are qualitatively different from one another, with each stage building on the previous one. In recent decades, however, scholars have been asking new questions that have fundamentally reshaped the research in this field and ultimately our understanding about the way that we develop. The cumulative findings have convinced most psychological scientists now that development does not occur through a building-block progression in which skill A must be acquired before skill B, and so on. Research that crosses the levels of analysis suggests that humans are born with more built-in abilities than was previously believed. This new approach to cognitive development has grown out of the careful study of perception and motor skills in infants, much of it informed by the recent biological revolution in our understanding of how the mind works. These experiments have revealed that many skills previously believed to develop later are actually present early in development. In fact, some of the precursors to these behaviors appear to be present from birth. In this chapter we will review astonishing findings that suggest that even very young infants seem to have some basic knowledge about the laws of physics and mathematics.

HOW DOES COGNITION DEVELOP IN INFANCY?

Studying cognitive development is like trying to hit a moving target. Because human beings change so rapidly in the first two decades of life, scientists have to constantly modify their methods to study developing processes. Two types of studies have been most commonly used in developmental research.

cognitive development The way in which individuals acquire knowledge and understanding about the world around them over the life course.

Cross-sectional studies examine change over time by examining subjects of different ages. Cross-sectional studies are very good at describing differences between age groups, but are not very good at assessing change in an individual. Longitudinal studies follow changes in the same individuals over time. They can be used to compare how changes occur among individuals.

Studying cognitive processes in children is often very different from studying them in adults. First, very young children are not able to tell researchers what they see, hear, or think because children younger that 12 months do not generally speak very well. This makes it very difficult to accurately assess what they know. To get around this problem, researchers have begun to take advantage of techniques that rely on different types of information to assess infant knowledge.

INFANTS LOOK LONGER AT NOVEL THAN FAMILIAR STIMULI

In recent years, scientists have devised clever experiments for gauging what babies know about objects in their environments. These experimental techniques are based on two simple observations of infant behavior: first, that infants tend to look more at stimuli that interest them, and second, that they will look longer at novel (new) stimuli than at familiar stimuli. The *preferential looking technique* is used in many perceptual tests. In these tests, an infant is shown two things. If he looks longer at one, researchers know the infant distinguishes between the two things and prefers one. Thus, experiments can be designed to measure whether or not an infant treats two stimuli as different and if so which stimulus an infant "chooses."

The **orienting reflex** is the tendency of humans, even from birth, to pay more attention to novel stimuli than to stimuli to which they have become habituated, or grown accustomed (Fantz, 1966). This means that if you time the number of seconds an infant looks at something, you find that the infant will look away more quickly from something familiar than from something unfamiliar or puzzling. So researchers developed a technique that allows them to create a preference for one stimulus over another. The technique is known as **habituation**. An infant is shown a picture or object until the infant is familiar enough with it that the amount of time she looks at it declines (the infant gets bored by or adapts to the stimulus). Once the infant is habituated to the stimulus, researchers can measure whether she has a reaction to a change in the stimulus: If a new stimulus is now shown, does the infant look longer at the novel stimulus? If so, this indicates that she notices a difference between the two stimuli. Looking longer at the novel stimulus is called *dishabituation*. If the amount of time the infant looks at the new stimulus does not change, it is assumed that she does not distinguish between the two. These techniques are used to gauge everything from infants' perceptual abilities—how and when they can perceive color, depth, and movement, for instance—to their understanding of words, faces, numbers, and laws of physics.

Because psychological scientists believe that the brain largely regulates human behavior, developmental psychologists have sought to relate maturational changes in the brain to age-related changes in behavior. Methods that have been used to investigate the relationship between brain and behavior in adults (CAT, PET, MRI), however, are often unsuitable for infants and children because they use potentially harmful agents, or because they require the subject to remain still for long periods of time. Some methods, such as EEG, have been adapted for use in very young subjects, but this is more the exception than the rule (Figure 11.2).

What methods do developmental psychologists use to study perception in infants?

cross-sectional studies A research design that compares people across different samples or ages.

longitudinal studies A research design that examines the same individuals over time.

orienting reflex The tendency for humans to pay more attention to novel stimuli.

habituation A decrease in response due to repeated exposure to a stimulus.

However, scientists have made great strides in understanding how the brain develops, and in turn how this influences behavior.

THE BRAIN IS HIGHLY COMPLEX BY BIRTH

For the most part, human physical development follows a predictable progression. Humans all do certain things, such as physically grow and mature at about the same period in the life span. No babies are born and start talking immediately, nor do any babies walk before they can sit up. Virtually all normal human babies learn to roll over, sit up, crawl, stand, walk, and talk in that order (occasionally a step may be skipped or reversed) within a predictable range of ages (Figure 11.3). The consistency of this pattern suggests that it is set by our genes. However, our environments can influence what happens throughout the development process. In essence, individuals act on the environment, which in turn acts on the individuals.

Prenatal development   The prenatal development of the human nervous system is determined by a careful plan governed by genes. Most of the brain's nerve cells develop within the first seven months of gestation (Rakic, 2000). The first two trimesters are critical to the development of the central nervous system. The forebrain, midbrain, and hindbrain areas begin to form by week 4. The cells that will form the cortex are visible by week 7; the thalamus and hypothalamus are visible by week 10; the basal ganglia and the left and right hemispheres, by week 12. *Myelination* begins on the spinal cord during the first trimester and on the brain's

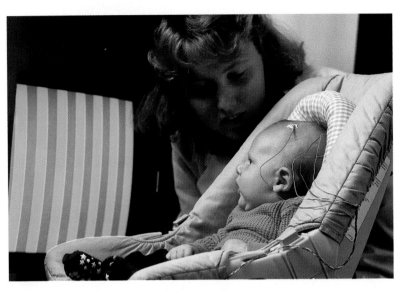

11.2 This baby is wearing electrodes that measure electrical activity of the brain.

11.3 A baby learns to walk without formal teaching. Learning to walk progresses along a fixed time-ordered sequence characteristic of all humans.

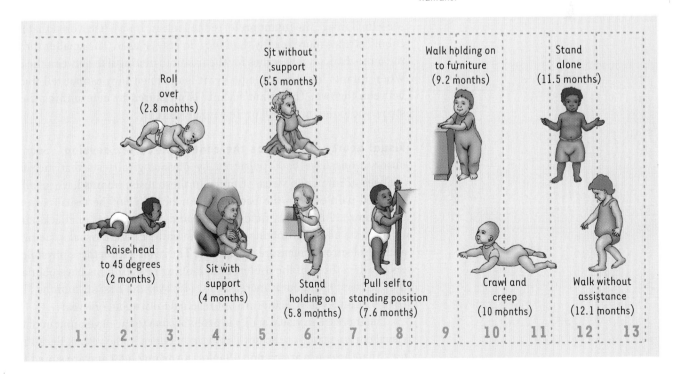

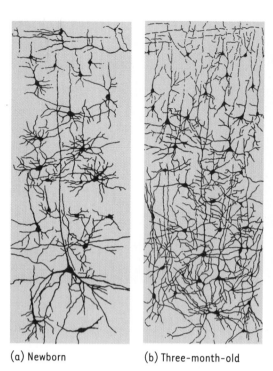

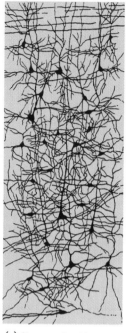

(a) Newborn   (b) Three-month-old   (c) Six-month-old

11.4 The development of the human brain is represented through drawings of neurons in the visual cortex of (a) a newborn, (b) a three-month-old, and (c) a six-month-old.

neurons during the second trimester. Recall from Chapter 3 that myelination is the brain's way of insulating its "wires": fibers are wrapped with a fatty sheath, a lot like the plastic coating around electrical wire, to increase the speed with which they are able to transmit signals. Myelination occurs in different brain regions at different stages of development and is believed to reflect the maturation of the fibers (Figure 11.4). Hearing and balance areas are fully myelinated at birth; areas involved in abstract thinking may not become fully myelinated until the individual is more than 20 years old. By the seventh month, the fetus has a working nervous system. By birth, the brain is complex: it has cortical layers, neuronal connectivity, and myelination.

PERCEPTION DEVELOPS IN INFANCY

The ability to distinguish differences among shapes, patterns, and colors begins early in infancy. The preferential looking technique is used to determine infants' visual acuity. Have you ever wondered why mobiles and other playthings for infants are made of bold black-and-white patterns rather than the colorful images we associate with children's toys and books? This is because developmental psychologists have discovered that infants respond more to these kinds of bold patterns than to other stimuli (Figure 11.5). In the early 1960s Robert Fantz and other developmental psychologists showed infants patterns of black-and-white stripes as well as patches of gray. Making sure the two images reflected the same amount of light, they observed the infants' reactions. They would ask the mother to hold the infant in front of a display of the two images (Figure 11.6). The experimenter, not knowing which image was where, would look through a peephole to see which image the infant preferred to look at. It was discovered that infants look at bold stripes more readily than they do gray images. The smaller the stripes get, the more difficult it becomes for the infant to distinguish between the two images. When infants look at both equally, it is assumed they cannot tell the difference between the two. The infant's acuity is measured by determining the narrowest stripe width the infant will preferentially look at.

Visual acuity develops as the cones and cortex develop Such behavioral observations have been bolstered by physiological tests that measure the responses of infants to visual stimuli. In these tests, infants have small electrodes attached painlessly to the backs of their heads near the visual cortex. They are then shown either a gray field or black-and-white stripes or checks such as those in the tests above. If infants can see the pattern, their visual system is activated and the electrodes measure a response. The results from these physiological studies confirm those of the preferential looking tests: infants have poor acuity when they are first born, but it increases rapidly over the first six months (Teller et al., 1974). Adult levels of acuity are not reached until about one year.

The increase in visual acuity is probably due to the development of the infant's visual cortex as well as the development of cones in the retina. Recall from Chapter 5 that the cones are responsible for absorbing light and are suited to detecting detail. Thus, as the cortex and cones develop over the first six months, the infant's vision becomes more capable of attending to visual detail.

Depth perception and binocular disparity   The development of depth perception in infants is tied to the development of binocular disparity. By three months, infants can binocularly fixate (that is, direct both eyes to the same place). But just because they can fixate both eyes on one spot does not mean they use the binocular disparity information to perceive depth. To assess when depth perception emerges in infancy, perceptual psychologist Robert Fox and his colleagues showed infants stereograms (Fox et al., 1980). Recall that stereograms work because we see one view of an image with one eye and another view with the other and convert this information into depth perception. If infants cannot use the disparity information to perceive depth, they will see only a random collection of dots. To determine whether infants are seeing stereograms, Fox devised an experiment in which a baby wearing special viewing glasses is seated on the parent's lap, looking at a screen. If the baby has binocular disparity he should see a three-dimensional rectangle moving back and forth, and he would presumably follow the movement of the rectangle with his eyes. If there were no binocular disparity he would see only dots and would not be able to follow the rectangle's movement (Figure 11.7). Fox's results indicate that the ability to use disparity information to perceive depth develops between 3½ months and 6 months of age. Other studies have supported this finding. Researchers believe that maturation of the visual cortex at three to four months enables the sudden ability to use binocular disparity to perceive depth.

Auditory perception in infants   Newborns can hear and appear capable of locating a sound's general source. When infants are presented with rattle sounds in either their right or left ears they will turn in the direction of the sound, indicating that they have perceived it. Detailed analysis of the tone levels that infants can hear indicates that by six months babies have nearly adult levels of auditory function (DeCasper and Spence, 1986).

Infants also seem to have some memory for sounds. Using habituation techniques, researchers have determined that infants can recognize sounds they have heard before. By measuring the infant's rate of sucking on a rubber nipple, researchers are able to determine if an infant is aroused in response to a specific sound. In an experiment by Anthony DeCasper and William Fifer (1980), two-day-old infants wore earphones and were given a nipple linked to recordings of their mother's voices and a stranger's voice. If they paused longer between their sucking bursts, the mother's voice played. If they paused for a shorter time, the stranger's voice played. Even at this young age, the newborns altered their sucking patterns to hear their mother's voices more often. In a similar vein, researchers had one group of pregnant women read *The Cat in the Hat* aloud. A second group read the book aloud but replaced the words "cat" and "hat" with "dog" and "fog." In subsequent tests, the women's newborns changed their sucking patterns to hear the version they had heard in the womb. These experiments, along with others, provide compelling evidence

11.5 Robert Fantz was the first to determine that infants prefer bold patterns. A more thorough understanding of infants' visual abilities has led parents to buy mobiles and toys that use some of Fantz's testing patterns.

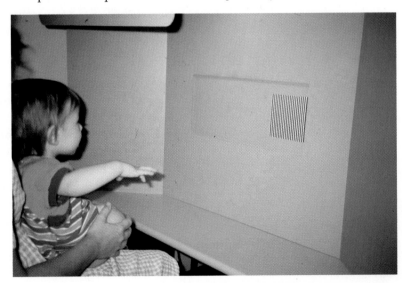

11.6 An infant's visual acuity being tested by the preferential looking procedure. The mother holds the infant in front of the display. An experimenter, who does not know which side the grating is on in any trial, looks through a peephole (barely visible between the two stimuli) and judges whether the infant is looking to the right or to the left.

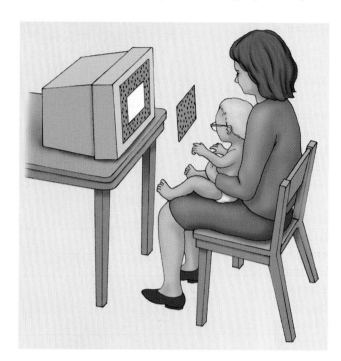

11.7 Fox's experiment for binocular disparity. If the infant can use disparity information to see depth, he sees a rectangle moving back and forth in front of the screen and will respond by visually tracking it.

that infants learn their mothers' voices in the womb. As we shall see, though, even these very early perceptual abilities undergo a great deal of change as the brain continues to develop.

LEARNING IS CONSTRAINED BY BRAIN DEVELOPMENT

In the past 25 years, many developmental psychologists have become cognitive scientists, looking to the brain to understand development. One critical question for cognitive scientists is whether it is possible to compare universal behavioral stages of development to actual physical stages of change in the developing brain. For instance, if learning math begins to happen at a certain age, is there a specific brain structure or set of neurons that develop at that time to take charge of mathematical learning? The answer seems to be yes; there is a correlation between neural changes and cognitive development. Neural correlates of cognitive changes have been investigated in perception, attention, memory, language, motor skills, and mental processes such as reasoning. It is important to remember, though, that simply observing a correlation between neural and cognitive development does not necessarily mean that brain changes *caused* changes in behavior. After all, there is also a correlation between children's height and behavior, but it is unlikely that physical size is responsible for cognitive development. Nonetheless, these experiments provide convergent evidence that is consistent with a causal link.

There are two important goals of early brain growth. The first is for specific areas within the brain to mature and become functional, and the second is for regions of the brain to learn to communicate with each other through synaptic connections. Synaptic connections are like wires connecting a string of lights (in this case different brain regions), only the human brain is more like a web than a string. The infant brain grows far more of these connections than it will ever use. Then something remarkable happens—the brain adopts a very strict "use or lose" policy. The connections that are frequently used are preserved, while those that are not are removed. This process is called **synaptic pruning**, and it occurs in different areas of the brain at different times. Once these connections are established, the brain sets about making them more permanent. One way this is accomplished is through myelination, as described above. Some developmental psychologists believe that it is not until certain brain connections are made that infants develop specific cognitive skills. This idea that learning is constrained by, or at least closely tied to, brain development is a new and exciting concept that is energized by the biological revolution in psychological science.

Reflexes at birth shape later learning Infants have basic reflexes that are present at birth. Perhaps you observed the grasping reflex when a baby held your finger. Some believe this is a survival reflex that remains from our primate ancestors, since young apes grasp their mothers. Another innate reflex is the *rooting reflex*, the automatic sucking that infants engage in when a nipple or similar object is near their mouths. Some theorists believe that these reflexes pave the way for learning more complicated behavior patterns. Infants may first respond reflexively to a finger or a nipple, and those reflexive responses help them develop more complex behavior patterns in response to stimuli. These patterns, then, allow infants to begin to control their motor responses rather than to react reflexively.

synaptic pruning A process whereby the synaptic connections in the brain that are frequently used are preserved, and those that are not are lost.

Jerome Kagan and his colleagues have a different explanation. They have looked at what is known about physical development and what has been observed in the behavioral development of infants, and Kagan has drawn some likely correlations between brain maturation and behavior. He divides first-year development into milestones at two ages: two months and seven to ten months. At two months children lose or decrease reflexive actions that are well recognized in the newborn, including the grasp reflex, and spontaneous smiling and crying. At the same point in development, their recognition memory—the ability to know, for example, that this face belongs to mom and the other belongs to dad—begins to improve. Also during this period, the cortex goes through major changes as the brainstem (which controls motor functions) develops cortical control. An infant's spontaneous smiling is probably controlled by the brainstem. So when neurons in the motor cortex develop, they now can control the brainstem and, by extension, spontaneous smiling. Kagan argues that this is not because the infant has "learned" certain complex behaviors. Rather, it is because of brain development. While this correlation suggests that the brain's maturation is critical for the development of cognitive skills, it is not yet conclusive.

Kagan argues that changes in the brain happen again at around ten months. These brain changes are responsible for behavioral events at this age: improved retrieval memory, self-initiated locomotion, and emotional responses such as fear during novel events (the appearance of strangers, separation from mother in a strange environment). Thus, Kagan argues that the emergence of certain behaviors actually reflects ongoing brain maturation—yet another example of how learning is constrained by brain development.

In addition to predictable ("planned") growth, the brain is also an amazingly "plastic" organ: part of its hardwiring includes the brain's ability to adapt to different environments. The most extreme example of this is that the brain is prepared to compensate for damage. Cognitive scientists believe that what allows for this *plasticity*, the brain's ability to rewire itself when one part is damaged, is its ability to make new neuronal connections. Though most neurons are already formed at birth, the brain's physical development continues through the growth of neurons and the new connections they make. The brain grows from about 350 grams to about 1,250 grams (about 80 percent of the adult size) by age four. This size increase is due to myelination and to new synaptic connections between neurons. This plasticity in the developing brain has also led researchers to some remarkable findings about the influence of early environment on the physical architecture of the brain.

Critical learning periods   A *critical period* is a development stage during which young animals are able to acquire specific skills or knowledge. If these skills or knowledge are not acquired during the critical period for some reason, the knowledge cannot be acquired at a later point in development. Cognitive scientists believe that the key to learning is creating connections among certain neurons, and that critical learning periods may exist because brain development goes through periods when certain connections are most easily made, assuming the right stimulus is provided.

One example of a critical period is the development of birdsong. Peter Marler has shown that sparrows must learn their adult song pattern at a critical point in their development by listening to an adult male of the same species. If the young white-crowned sparrow is not exposed to any song, or only to the song of sparrows of other species, it will never learn to sing a fully developed song as an adult. This is true even if it is exposed to white-crowned sparrow songs later in development

RESEARCH QUESTION

What is the relationship between physical development and learning?

assimilation The process through which a new experience is placed into an existing schema.

accommodation The process through which a schema is adapted or expanded to incorporate a new experience that does not easily fit into an existing schema.

sensorimotor stage The first stage in Piaget's theory of cognitive development in which infants acquire information about the world through their senses and respond reflexively.

(Marler, 1970). Thus environment and development have a crucial interaction: If an organism is not exposed to the correct stimulus at the correct time, normal development can be hindered.

Whether or not human development goes through critical periods is more controversial. In humans, the primary evidence for a critical period in cognitive development is found in language development, a debate we will examine later. In general, humans appear to have sensitive periods when the brain is primed to acquire certain skills or knowledge. These periods do not seem critical, however, as learning is still possible later, though it may not be as efficient or successful. Environmental influences may also affect development during these periods. For instance, in the prenatal environment, drugs, alcohol, or malnutrition can all impair physical and future development. Excessive consumption of alcohol during pregnancy can lead to *fetal alcohol syndrome*, which consists of low birth weight, face and head abnormalities, slight mental retardation, and later behavioral and cognitive problems. Smoking cigarettes during pregnancy can also lead to low birth weight as well as spontaneous abortion or birth defects. While some prenatal complications result in physical abnormalities that are apparent at birth, language or reasoning disorders may not become apparent until the child is older. The paradoxical resilience and fragility of the developing brain is something that continues to puzzle developmental psychologists. By increasing their understanding of how the brain develops and how this is related to behavior, scientists and health practitioners can design methods to correct problems and maximize healthy development.

PIAGET EMPHASIZED STAGES OF DEVELOPMENT

Obviously, infants differ from adults. But are infants merely inexperienced humans who have not yet learned the skills they will develop over time? Or do infants not yet possess the neural or cognitive abilities that will enable them to acquire these skills? Jean Piaget (Figure 11.8) was the first to link cognitive development to biological development. By observing infant and child behavior, he devised a theory of how "thinking" developed in the brain. He suggested that by closely examining infant behavior we could trace developmental stages and make assumptions about how the brain was developing. He believed that, up to the age of two, children acquire information about the world through their senses. Piaget believed that children were not able to reason or use language until later in their development. For Piaget it was pointless to try, say, to teach a child to walk before the age of one because she had not yet developed the physical capabilities to learn that skill. Ultimately Piaget experimentally demonstrated how children perceive the world differently from the way that adults do, and he sketched out the notion of developmental stages.

Piaget proposed four distinct stages of development (Figure 11.9), each characterized by a different way of thinking—a new set of schemas. *Schemas* was Piaget's term for mental patterns that children form at each stage of development. Piaget believed each stage builds on the previous ones through learning by assimilation and accommodation. **Assimilation** is the process through which a new experience is placed into an existing schema; **accommodation** is the process through which a schema is adapted or expanded to incorporate the new experience.

Sensorimotor stage (birth to two years) The first stage Piaget identified was the **sensorimotor stage**. Piaget's theory was that from birth until about age two, infants acquire information about the world only through their senses—they react reflexively to objects. "Intelligence" at this stage consists of motor actions toward

11.8 Jean Piaget introduced the idea that cognitive development occurs in stages.

objects and the sensory feedback gained from those actions. Thus, infants understand objects only when they reflexively react to their sensory input—such as when they suck on a nipple, grasp a finger, or recognize a face. As they begin to control their movements, they develop their first schemas—the mental representations of the kinds of actions that can be performed on certain kinds of objects. For instance, consider the sucking reflex. This begins as a reaction to the sensory input from the nipple: the infant simply responds reflexively by sucking. Soon the child realizes it can suck other things—a bottle, a finger, a toy, a blanket. Piaget explained that sucking other objects is an example of assimilation, in that other objects are now understood as suckable. But sucking a toy or a blanket does not result in the same experience as the reflexive sucking of a nipple. This leads to accommodation with respect to the sucking schema—the child must adjust her understanding of sucking. Piaget believed that all of the sensory-motor schemas eventually merge into an exploratory schema. In other words, infants learn they can act on objects—manipulate them in order to understand them—rather than simply react.

One of the cognitive concepts that Piaget explored in this stage was **object permanence**, the notion that an object continues to exist even when it is hidden from view. Piaget noted it was not until nine months of age that most infants will search for objects that they have seen being hidden, even though the motor skills to do so are developed by four months of age. Even at nine months, when infants will begin to snatch a blanket away to find a hidden toy, the infants' search skills still have limits. For instance, suppose a child is given several trials in which an experimenter hides a toy under a blanket while the child watches and then finds the toy. If the hiding place is changed to under a different blanket, in full view of the child, the child will still look for the toy in the first hiding place. Piaget concluded that infants do not fully understand that an object continues to exist once it is hidden, and that they still view an object's existence in relation to their own action. Full comprehension of object permanence was, for Piaget, one of the key accomplishments of the sensory-motor period.

Preoperational period (two to seven years)

Piaget argued that in the **preoperational period** (two to seven years), children can think about objects that are not in their immediate view. They begin to think symbolically. For example, at this stage children will take a stick and pretend it is a gun. Piaget believed that what they cannot do yet is think "operationally"—they cannot imagine the logical

Stage	Characterization
Sensorimotor (birth–2 years)	Differentiates self from objects
	Recognizes self as agent of action and begins to act intentionally; for example, pulls a string to set a mobile in motion or shakes a rattle to make a noise
	Achieves object permanence: realizes that things continue to exist even when no longer present to the senses
Preoperational (2–7 years)	Learns to use language and to represent objects by images and words
	Thinking is still egocentric: has difficulty taking the viewpoint of others
	Classifies objects by a single feature; for example, groups together all the red blocks regardless of shape or all the square blocks regardless of color
Concrete operational (7–11 years)	Can think logically about objects and events
	Achieves conservation of number (age 6), mass (age 7), and weight (age 9)
	Classifies objects according to several features and can order them in series along a single dimension, such as size
Formal operational (11 years and up)	Can think logically about abstract propositions and test hypotheses systematically
	Becomes concerned with the hypothetical, the future, and ideological problems

11.9 Piaget's stages of cognitive development.

object permanence The understanding that an object continues to exist even when it cannot be seen.

preoperational period The second stage in Piaget's theory of cognitive development in which children think symbolically about objects, but reason based on appearance rather than logic.

11.10 In the preoperational stage children cannot yet understand conservation tests. In this example a six-year-old understands that the two short glasses contain the same amount of water (a). She carefully pours the water from one of the short glasses into a taller glass (b). Yet when asked "which has more," she points to the taller glass (c).

outcome of certain actions on objects. They base their reasoning on immediate appearance, rather than logic. For instance, children at this stage have no understanding of the law of conservation of quantity: that the quantity of a substance remains unchanged, even if its appearance changes. For instance, if you pour a short, fat glass of water into a tall, thin glass, we all know that the amount of water has not changed. However, if you do this and ask a child in the preoperational stage which glass has more, they will pick the tall, thin glass because the water is at a higher level. Children make this error even when they have seen someone (even themselves) pour the same amount of water into each glass (Figure 11.10).

Children in this stage may ask "how" but not "why"; they like to act on the things in their environment, turn things on and off, but they do not yet ask why their actions have the effect they do. Piaget characterized children in the preoperational stage as egocentric: they are not able to see another person's point of view, only their own. Later we will show how the idea that young children don't understand other people's points of view has been challenged.

Concrete operational stage (7 to 12 years) Next, according to Piaget, children enter the **concrete operational stage** (about 7 to 12 years). He believed that humans do not develop logic until they begin to think about and understand operations, which he defined as actions that can be undone: a light can be turned on and off; a stick can be moved across the table and then moved back. He suggested that the ability to understand that an action is reversible enabled children to begin to understand concepts such as conservation. While this is the beginning of logic, Piaget believed children at this stage reason only about concrete things—objects they could act on in the world—they do not yet have the ability to reason abstractly, or hypothetically, about what might be possible.

Formal operational stage (12 to adulthood) The **formal operational stage** (12 to adulthood) is Piaget's final stage. This involves abstract thinking, characterized by what he called hypothetic-deductive reasoning, the ability to form a hypothesis about something and test the theory through deductive logic. For instance, at this stage teens can systematically begin to test a theory or solve a problem. Piaget used the example of providing students with four flasks of colorless liquid and a fifth flask with colored liquid. He told them that by combining two of the colorless liquids, they could obtain the colored liquid. Adolescents were able to try different combinations in a systematic fashion and obtain the correct result. Younger children, who just randomly combined liquids, could not. If you think back to your school curricula, you will recall that subjects that require abstract reasoning, such as algebra or the scientific method, are not usually taught until around eighth grade.

Critique of Piaget There have been many challenges to Piaget's views of how cognition develops. A key criticism disputes the idea that every person goes through the stages of development in the same order. Piaget believed that as children progress through each stage they all use the same kind of logic to solve problems. This leaves little room for differing cognitive strategies or skills among individuals—or cultures. More recently, developmental psychologists who call themselves "neo-Piagetians" have revised many of Piaget's theories, while preserving a great number of his basic ideas. They agree with Piaget that children actively structure their understanding, that knowledge progresses from preconcrete to concrete and then to abstract, and that this all occurs in roughly the order and ages reported by Piaget (Bidell & Fischer, 1995; Case, 1992; Fischer, 1980). Unlike Piaget, the neo-Piagetians believe that the brain has different modules responsible for different skills, and that the development of different skills can therefore be distinct.

Another substantial challenge to Piaget has arisen from those who have modified the response criteria for his tasks. Many researchers believe that by insisting that an infant plan and execute a complex motor task (as was required in many of the preoperational tasks), Piaget obscured the fact that infants possess a great deal of knowledge regarding objects and how they behave in the world. As we will see, tests that have made use of preferential-looking techniques have revealed that infants as young as three months are able to discern an object's existence, even when it is no longer in plain sight, which seemingly contradicts Piaget's ideas about object permanence. It is also clear from these tests that infants do not need to act on objects in the world in order to demonstrate cognitive skills.

Many of the experiments that have led to modifications in Piaget's theory have been designed to present infants with novel stimuli rather than familiar ones. For example, an infant is shown a card with three dots on it. Once the infant is habituated to that image, the card is changed to one with two dots. If the baby looks at the two-dot card longer than she looked at the three-dot card, it is assumed she is able to distinguish between two and three.

A slightly more complex version of the habituation technique involves showing infants from 2½ to 3½ months old "magic tricks," or events that transpire behind a hidden screen. If you show infants events that are magic (that is, that do not make rational sense), they will stare at the result longer than if you show them something that does make sense. For instance, suppose you show an infant an apple and then lower a screen. When you raise the screen again the infant sees one of two situations: a possible event (one apple is still there) or an impossible event (no apple, or more than one apple). If an infant looks longer at the impossible event, the experimenter deduces that the infant can tell the difference between the two scenes (Baillargeon, 1995).

By responding differently to possible and impossible events, infants demonstrate some understanding that an object continues to exist when it is out of sight, even though they may not pursue a hidden object on Piaget's object permanence test. While current thinking has revised many of Piaget's original ideas, his contribution to developmental psychology is immeasurable. He was one of the first to study how children develop cognition. Following his work, many other scientists have begun studying how children develop their knowledge about the world; we will now examine some of their work.

concrete operational stage The third stage in Piaget's theory of cognitive development in which children begin to think about and understand operations in ways that are reversible.

formal operational stage The final stage in Piaget's theory of cognitive development, it involves the ability to think abstractly and to formulate and test hypotheses through deductive logic.

What skills do infants have that indicate Piaget's stage theory of development may be incorrect?

How Does Cognition Develop in Infancy?

Scientists have begun to understand that some aspects of learning are constrained by brain development. This means that there are some behaviors that do not emerge until specific milestones in neurophysiological maturity are reached. Piaget was the first to link biology with development. He carefully observed the behavior of infants and children and mapped out the consistent stages of how cognitive processes emerge. His theory suggested that each stage of learning is built, in large part, on the previous one. Recently, using ingenious tests based on the fact that infants look longer at novel than familiar stimuli, developmental researchers have learned that young infants have very early, perhaps even "hardwired" knowledge about objects in the world. The looking-time tests also have provided compelling evidence that infants have advanced sensory systems from birth.

DOES OBJECT KNOWLEDGE DEVELOP IN INFANCY OR IS IT INNATE?

Knowledge about objects and how they move is measurable within the first few months of life. Furthermore, this knowledge appears to have constraints—a particular content and organization—that suggest that perceptual "rules" are built into the brain. Hence, infants are able to demonstrate use of very basic concepts about objects and how they move in the physical world very early on in infancy.

INFANTS HAVE INNATE KNOWLEDGE ABOUT PHYSICS

Developmental psychologist Elizabeth Spelke at MIT has conducted numerous object-perception studies that have suggested that infants have a primitive understanding of basic physical laws. Many of the studies focus on how infants acquire knowledge of their surroundings (object perception) and put that knowledge to use (object-directed or object-motivated action).

We are born with the ability to perceive movement: newborns will follow moving stimuli with their eyes and head and prefer to look at a moving stimulus over a stationary one. Experiments by Spelke and Philip Kellman (Kellman et al., 1986) indicate that as infants get older, they use movement information to help identify if an object is continuous. In one such experiment, the researchers showed four-month-old infants a rod moving back and forth behind a block. Once habituated, the infants were shown two scenes—one in which the block was removed and there was a single rod, and another in which the block was removed and there were two small rods (Figure 11.11). The infants looked longer at the scene with two smaller rods. This indicated that they expected the rod moving behind the block to be one continuous object rather than two smaller ones. If the experiment is conducted with the rod remaining stationary, the infants do not look longer at the two small rods. So infants appear to use movement to infer that objects that move together are continuous, whereas two stationary objects may or may not be continuous. This perception entails basic concept formation. It involves the ability to see the rod as an object separate from the block, and to surmise that since the two ends are moving together, they must be part of the same whole rod, even though it is hidden from view. Thus infants as young as four months appear to have rudimentary cognitive skills in concept formation.

Spelke went on to conduct several more studies with collaborator Renee Baillargeon. Their experiments have further elucidated infants' intuitive knowledge regarding the laws of physics. The physical concepts that infants seem to understand include: objects cannot pass through another object; objects move along continuous trajectories; objects are cohesive (as described above); objects can move each other only if they come into contact. The three-to-four-month-old infants in these studies are clearly too young to have used sensory motor experience to "learn" the laws of physics they appear to understand. In fact, the data suggest that certain concepts are either built into the brain or that infants are predisposed to learn them very quickly and efficiently.

INFANTS ARE INTUITIVE MATHEMATICIANS

Recent research over the past 25 years has shown that we are born with certain numerical abilities, such as the ability to understand

11.11 The perceptual effect of occlusions in early infancy. Four-month-olds were shown a rod that moved back and forth behind an occluding block as shown in (a). After being habituated to this stimuli they were shown two events, one in which a solid rod (b) moved behind the occluding block, another in which two separate rods (c) moved back and forth behind the block. The infants spent much more time looking at the unexpected event (c).

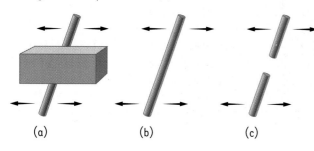

(a)   (b)   (c)

quantity. Piaget surmised initially from his experiments that young children do not understand numbers, and that counting and other number-related skills must therefore be done by rote memorization. His experiments consisted of showing children four to five years old two rows of marbles (Figure 11.12). He found that if the marbles were arranged side by side so that the rows were the same length, children said the rows contained the same number of marbles. However, if one of the rows was spread out, then the child would usually say that the longer row had more marbles in it. Piaget concluded that children had no inherent sense of number—rather, their understanding of "more than" had to do with their perception of the length of the rows. Not until children were seven or eight did they get Piaget's task right.

This view was challenged by Jacques Mehler and Tom Bever (1967), who argued that children as young as 2½ years old could understand the concept of more than or less than without using perceptual information. They repeated Piaget's experiment, only they used M&Ms (Figure 11.13). They presented the two rows of four M&Ms each and asked if they were the same. When the children said yes, the researchers then transformed the rows. For instance, they would add two candies to the second row, but they would compress that row so it was shorter in length than the row with fewer candies. Then they would tell the children to pick the row they wanted to eat. More than 80 percent picked the row with more M&Ms, even though it was the visually shorter row. Thus children do appear to understand the concepts of more than or less than, when properly motivated. Amazingly, infants seem to have the ability to do a wide range of simple math tasks. Infants can add and subtract small quantities. Psychologist Karen Wynn has shown that infants as young as five months can do simple math (Wynn, 1992). She showed babies a Mickey Mouse doll until they became habituated. Then a screen came up and covered the doll, and a hand visibly placed a second doll behind the screen. When the screen was removed, babies were bored if there were two dolls, but they looked longer if there was only one or if there were three. This indicates that they understood that one doll plus one doll should equal two dolls.

Other experiments showed they also understood that $2 - 1 = 1$. Wynn habituated the babies to two dolls, and when the screen hid the dolls, the hand made a big show of taking one of the dolls away. Again, babies looked longer at the unexpected result of two dolls still being there than they did if there was just one doll when the screen was removed.

INFANTS CAN REASON AND SOLVE PROBLEMS

Is the physics and math that infants can do the result of knowledge about objects and numbers that we are born with, as Spelke and others suggest? Baillargeon argues that we are born with what are actually highly constrained "mechanisms" that guide infants' reasoning about objects. These rules help us to figure out things about the physical world. In other words, the important finding in these studies is the way that genes prepare infants to understand their environment. Baillargeon's research identified two ways in which infants reason about the physical world. First, infants form an "all-or-none" concept about a physical phenomenon that captures a general rule but not specifics. They then build on the general concept and refine it. Second, infants begin to reason about a variable in a qualitative way before they do so quantitatively.

To illustrate her theory of how infants reason, Baillargeon ran experiments to find out about infants' knowledge of support phenomena. Working with infants of

11.12 Piaget's marble test.

11.13 The M&M version of Piaget's marble test. Children who did not succeed on Piaget's marble test were able to choose the row that contained more items when those items were M&Ms and the test question was phrased as "Which row would you like to eat?"

Possible event

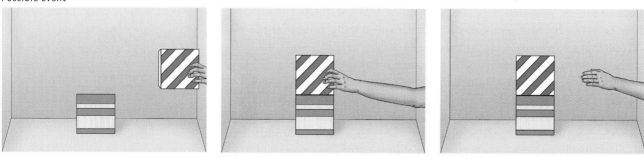

Impossible event

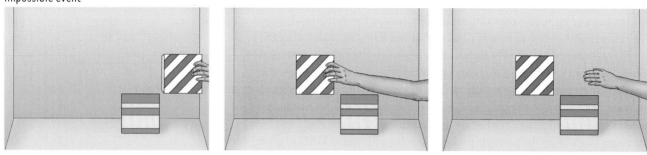

11.14 In Baillargeon's tests, infants looked longer during the impossible event in which the box was placed in midair without any contact support, but did not fall.

different ages, the experimenters determined how well infants understand whether a box will be stable when it is released on a platform versus off the platform (Figure 11.14). They found that by three months of age, infants expect the box to be stable if it is released on the platform, but not if it is released off the platform.

Next they tested whether infants understood what type of contact the box required to be stable. They showed a hand placing a small square box against the side of a large open platform, and on top of a smaller closed platform. The impossible event was the same except that the closed box was much shorter; the added box now hovered above it without touching (Figure 11.15). Thus by 4½ months in-

11.15 In these tests, infants showed a beginning understanding of the type of contact needed to support an object.

Possible event

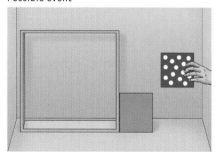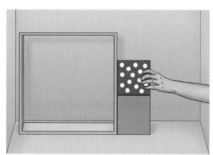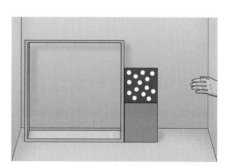

Impossible event

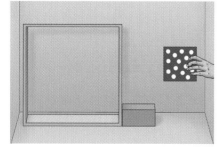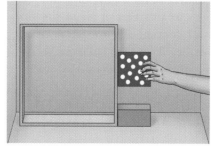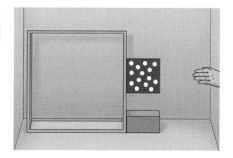

fants are beginning to understand the type of contact needed to support another object.

Finally, researchers examined at what age infants begin to understand not just the type but the amount of contact needed to support a box. To do this they habituated infants to a scenario of a hand pushing a box across the top of a platform and onto another platform, so that the box is always supported (Figure 11.16). Next they showed the infants a possible event in which the box's leading edge is pushed to the end of the platform and stops there, and an impossible event in which the box is pushed way past the edge, until only a fraction of its bottom surface is still touching the platform. They found that by 6½ months, infants looked longer at the impossible event, suggesting they were surprised the box did not fall.

Based on these tests, Baillargeon concluded that by three months any contact is deemed sufficient for the box to remain stable—infants expect the box to fall if it loses contact with the platform and to remain stable otherwise. By 4½ months, they understand that only contact at the bottom will stabilize the box, though they believe that only a small portion of the bottom surface need be supported by the platform. By 6½ months, they seem to understand that the box will fall unless a large portion of the bottom is supported by the surface of the platform.

What is the basic developmental sequence underlying an infant's ability to reason about the physical world? Baillargeon suggests that when infants are learning about the support relation between two objects, they first form an initial concept centered on a contact/no contact distinction. With further experience, this initial concept is progressively revised. Infants identify first a discrete (type of contact) and later a continuous (amount of contact) variable and incorporate these variables into their initial concept, resulting in more successful predictions over time.

Habituation events

1

2

Test events

Possible event

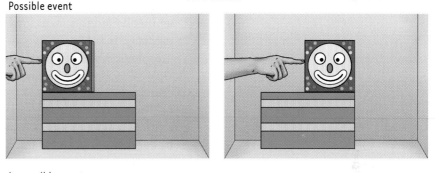

Impossible event

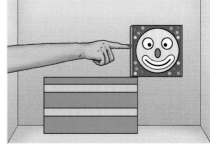

11.16 At 6½ months, infants begin to understand the amount of contact needed to support an object.

CHILDREN HAVE THEORIES OF MIND

Theory of mind (TOM) is a term coined by experimental psychologist David Premack to describe the unique human ability to explain and predict behavior in terms of people's mental states—such as wanting, believing, or pretending. For the past 15 years, researchers have been looking at how the brain acquires these

theory of mind (TOM) The term used to describe the ability to explain and predict behavior in terms of other people's mental states.

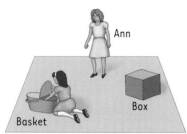

Ann

Box

Basket

Sally puts her marble in the basket.

Sally goes away.

Ann moves the marble.

?

"Where will Sally look for her marble?"

11.17 An example of a child's theory of mind. When a child acquires TOM, she is able to understand that different individuals have different perspectives and different knowledge based on their individual experiences.

RESEARCH QUESTION ?????

What evidence suggests that the mind develops cognitive skills, independent of each other, rather than as an integrated whole?

kinds of abstract concepts. Studies indicate that even very young children seem to have this capacity, as do children with limited intellectual ability. Psychologist Alan Leslie illustrates the theory with the following example. Sally places a marble in a basket and then leaves. Ann comes in, removes the marble from the basket, and places it in a box instead. A child who has watched both actions take place is asked to guess where Sally will look for the marble when she comes back in the room. In order to do this correctly, the child must develop a theory—Sally put the marble in the basket, Sally doesn't know Ann moved the marble, so Sally will still look in the basket (Figure 11.17). Normally, developing children are able to solve this by age four.

Leslie believes that the key mechanism at work with TOM is the ability to make inferences about people's mental states by observing their behavior. "How is the young brain able to attend to mental states when the states cannot be seen, heard, or felt?" Leslie asks. He suggests that children note a person's behavior and infer the mental state from which the behavior arises. For instance, a young child who sees his mother holding a banana to her ear and talking assumes, "Mom must be pretending that banana is a telephone." Leslie has found that normal two-year-olds are capable of this (Leslie, 2000). Even very young children can lie, which requires TOM. This ability is discussed in "Crossing the Levels of Analysis: Why Do Children Lie?"

There is evidence that TOM, like math or physics or the ability to form concepts, is a domain-specific cognitive skill, meaning it develops independently from other brain functions such as the ability to reason or general intelligence. Evidence for this comes from the study of autistic children, who are not able to solve the Sally/Ann problems. Autistic children are unable to form correct theories of other people's behavior. By contrast, children with Down's syndrome can solve this problem, indicating that it is not a general intelligence or reasoning mechanism that governs TOM, since Down's children are impaired in these areas.

REVIEWING THE PRINCIPLE

Does Object Knowledge Develop in Infancy or Is It Innate?

Perception, action, and reasoning all appear early in infancy and appear to be built-in abilities that develop together over time. Research suggests that the development of cognitive skills reflects a process in which abilities built in to the brain are activated and mature as the developing child interacts with the environment, rather than being exclusively "taught" by caregivers or through trial and error. The brain is primed to acquire knowledge and understand it within a set of predesigned constraints, but we still need to be taught or exposed to ideas such as algebra, physics, grammar, and logic problems to develop those inborn skills. In short, the infant brain may be able to recognize numbers and form theories about other people's behavior, but the brain will continue to refine those skills with exposure to the world and formal teaching.

WHY DO CHILDREN LIE?

It is Christopher's third birthday. He eagerly unwraps a present from his grandmother, hoping that it is the new racetrack he had asked for several times during the past year. Upon opening the gift he sees that he has been given a bright green sweater—not exactly what he had hoped for. Christopher looks at the sweater, smiles broadly at his grandmother, and says, "Oh thank you, it is exactly what I wanted, I like it so much that I am going to put it on right this minute." At the young age of three, Christopher has learned to lie.

Lying, or more politely, deceiving, is something that has origins in our neurochemistry, our culture, and several levels between the two. Until recently methodological obstacles have hampered the systematic examination of how children learn to lie. Michael Lewis and his colleagues have come up with an ingenious technique for studying deceptive behavior in young children. In these studies young children are brought into a room where, unknowingly, they are videotaped. While the child is seated at a table, the experimenter, positioned behind the child, unpacks and constructs an elaborate and complex toy. The experimenter tells the child not to turn around and informs the child that he will be able to look at and play with the toy shortly. After the toy is constructed, the experimenter informs the child that she must leave the room for a few minutes. The experimenter tells the child not to look at the toy while she is gone. The experimenter leaves and the child is left alone in the room—for five minutes if he does not look at the toy or until he turns around and looks. As soon as the child looks, the experimenter returns to the room and looks at the child. This is called the stare condition, which lasts for five to ten seconds. Then the experimenter asks the child, "Did you peek?" The child's verbal response, as well as his facial and bodily behavior, are recorded and scored from the videotapes.

This simple experiment allows the scientists to observe what children do in a real-life situation in which they have violated an adult-imposed rule. It also can be used with very young children because of its limited verbal complexity.

Using this technique, Lewis and his colleagues have discovered some pretty amazing things about the development of lying in children. First, they found that 90 percent of children between the ages of $2\frac{1}{2}$ and $3\frac{1}{2}$ looked at the toy when left alone in the room. Second, of the 90 percent that "peeked," 77 percent told the experimenter that they did not. This percentage increased with age, with 100 percent of children 5 years or older lying about the fact that they peeked. What are the causes of this?

The researchers describe several things that are necessary for a child to be capable of deception. The child must (1) understand what is expected, (2) compare what is expected to what he has done, (3) consider the consequence of the violation, and (4) know what behaviors are likely to be successful in "fooling" the other into thinking he is not lying. Clearly, these four factors are reliant upon the acquisition of specific cognitive skills. We have seen that there are strong relations between neurobiological maturation and the emergence of specific cognitive abilities. Does this imply that we are hardwired to be deceptive? This is not likely; it is more plausible that the development of certain cognitive abilities (including TOM—which not coincidentally emerges at the same age as lying) enables humans to lie.

According to Lewis, children most often lie to avoid punishment for violating an authority figure's expectation. He argues that while this is morally wrong, it is adaptive and highly advantageous to the young child who does not enjoy being in trouble. This type of lie, however, is somewhat different from that committed by Christopher, the boy who pretended to love the sweater his grandmother gave him for his birthday. This type of lying, to spare the feelings of another, is usually classified as a separate type of deception, one that is influenced to a greater degree by social or cultural values. A group of researchers led by Kang Lee has compared Canadian and Chinese children's views on telling the truth versus lying. Overall, Chinese children rated truth telling less positively and lie telling more positively in social settings than did Canadian children. This implies that the emphasis on self-effacement and modesty in Chinese culture influences Chinese children's evaluations of lying in some situations. The researchers concluded that in the realm of lying and truth telling, a close relation between sociocultural practices and moral judgment exists (Lee et al., 1999). Specific social and cultural norms, as well as age and experience, have an impact on children's developing moral judgments.

DO CHILDREN HAVE GOOD MEMORY SYSTEMS?

Understanding the development of memory helps us to understand cognitive development. For instance, at age five or six children can distinguish memories of real events from imagined events; younger children have lots of trouble with this. Interestingly, a three- or four-year-old can tell you about events from the previous week or even a few months back, but these same memories are nearly impossible for the individual to recall in adulthood. Researchers are interested

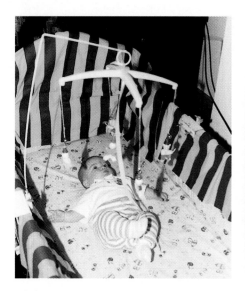
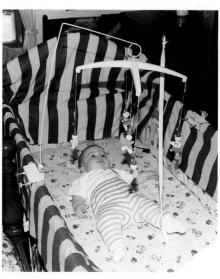
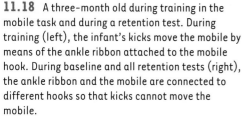

11.18 A three-month old during training in the mobile task and during a retention test. During training (left), the infant's kicks move the mobile by means of the ankle ribbon attached to the mobile hook. During baseline and all retention tests (right), the ankle ribbon and the mobile are connected to different hooks so that kicks cannot move the mobile.

in determining at what age children develop a sense of memory that is similar to adults.

The question of whether infants possess memory is a tricky one. It is difficult to devise experiments that test infant memory because we cannot ask infants what they remember. For years it was believed that infants did not remember anything. *Infantile amnesia*, a term first introduced by Freud, referred to the theory that since adults cannot recall memories of their childhood prior to about age three, infants must not have developed memory skills prior to this age. But, once again, clever experiments have revealed that infants do possess some types of memory from an early age—though that memory is quite rudimentary.

Carolyn Rovee-Collier and her colleagues devised two such experiments. In one, infants learn to move a mobile hanging over the crib by kicking. During the task, a ribbon attaches their ankle to the mobile so the infants learn that the mobile moves when they kick (Figure 11.18). The rate at which an infant kicks when the mobile is not attached serves as the baseline. Then, when the infant is tested later, the ribbon is attached to the ankle but not to the mobile (so now the kicks do not move the mobile). If the baby recognizes the mobile, it will presumably kick faster than the baseline rate to try to make the mobile move. If the infant does not recognize it, the kicking rate will not increase. Infants ranging in age from 2 to 18 months have been trained for two days on the mobile and then tested after different lengths of time have passed. Findings indicate that infants remember longer as they get older. By 18 months, they can remember the event for several weeks (Rovee-Collier, 1999).

Although young children can form the types of memories described above, a memory for a learned behavior is not the same as the ability to recall facts and events. Some psychologists believe that we have memories from before age three, but if the memories are cued by a different context we attribute them to the later event. Others think that memories are retained only when we have the ability to create autobiographical memory based on personal references—for instance, recalling that "a cat scratched me" versus the fact that "cats scratch." Still other psychologists suggest that childhood memory development increases with the acquisition of language because the ability to create a causal narrative aids in memory retention. Nevertheless, no one agrees on why adults cannot recall their earliest memories (Eacott, 1999). One theory has posited that young children lack the brain structures, or "hardware," to create memories this early in life, while another suggests that early memories are overwritten by later experience.

THERE ARE LIMITS TO EARLY MEMORY

A different type of amnesia studied in relation to childhood memory is called source amnesia, which occurs when people can remember a fact or something that happened in the past but not the source of their knowledge. This is quite common in young children. Even when tested immediately after being presented with information, young children (age three) forget the source of the information faster than do older children (age five) (Gopnik and Graf, 1988). Evidence from investigations of source amnesia suggests that many of your earliest memories may come from watching home movies or hearing stories from your parents—not from an actual memory you have of the events.

Anyone who has spent time with young children knows that they confabulate—inaccurately recount events. In Chapter 7 we learned about confabulation in adults and how it is often associated with damage to the frontal lobes. The fact that children have underdeveloped frontal lobes may explain why they are more likely than adults to engage in this behavior. Confabulation happens most when children are asked about personal experiences rather than general knowledge. Psychologist Morris Moscovitch has dubbed this "honest lying" because children believe that what they are saying is true. In studies, researchers have found that children create such false narratives if they are cued with leading or suggestive questions or strong stereotypes, or if they are asked to visualize the event (Schacter et al., 1995).

In one study preschool children were interviewed repeatedly and asked to think hard if they had ever gotten their fingers caught in a mousetrap. Children were asked to visualize this event, including thinking about the scene (who was with you, what you were wearing, etc.). After ten weeks of thinking hard the children were interviewed by a new adult who asked them if they had ever gotten their fingers caught in a mousetrap. Sixty percent of the children provided false narratives, telling a story about this happening to them and behaving as if it really had. Many of the children developed very elaborate stories with numerous details about why it had happened and how it felt (Bruck and Ceci, 1993).

How do these memory errors occur? Research suggests that children's memories can be influenced by previous stereotypes and by repeated suggestive questioning. This phenomenon is illustrated in "Using Psychological Science: The Sam Stone Study."

MEMORY IS INFLUENCED BY BRAIN DEVELOPMENT

As previously described, some researchers think that younger children are more prone to memory errors, due to immature frontal lobes. Studies of adult subjects with frontal lobe damage have established a clear relationship between frontal lobe integrity and specific types of memory function. These patients have similar memory problems; they also tend to have problems with source amnesia, confabulation, and false recognition. Consistent with the idea that frontal lobe functionality contributes to children's memory errors is the fact that the frontal lobes are slower to mature than other brain regions. Indeed, the frontal lobes do not fully mature until early adulthood.

Other possible explanations include Jerome Kagan's findings that the ability to distinguish the source of a memory and a true versus a false memory may be related to the later development of other cognitive skills. Kagan (1984, 1994) has suggested that early memory errors may be related to impulsivity, Piaget's concrete-operational stage, or temperamental factors. Younger children tend to be more impulsive and so may not take the time to reflect on an answer, which could explain why they are so susceptible to suggestive or leading questions. Younger children have also not yet achieved Piaget's concrete-operations skills—they fail conservation tasks, for instance, when asked whether two equal balls of clay are still equal after one has been elongated and the other has not. This reflects an inability to relate an earlier event to a later event, which may explain why

RESEARCH QUESTION

How do children's memory systems develop?

Using Psychological Science

THE SAM STONE STUDY

Nearly 200 preschoolers were divided into four groups: control, stereotype, suggestion, and stereotype plus suggestion. In each condition, a stranger named Sam Stone came into the daycare class while the teacher was reading a story. He said hello, was introduced by the teacher, commented that he liked the story they were reading, walked around the room, said good-bye, and left. The whole event lasted only two minutes. Following the visit the children were asked for details of Sam's visit during four interviews over a ten-week period.

The control group received no information about Sam before or after the visit. In the stereotype group, the teacher told stories about Sam Stone before he visited. Each week, beginning a month prior to the visit, the children were told a story in which the character Sam Stone was depicted as very clumsy: "You'll never guess who visited me last night. That's right, Sam Stone. And guess what he did this time? He asked to borrow my doll and when he was carrying it down the stairs he tripped and fell and broke her arm. That Sam Stone is always getting into accidents and breaking things!" In their four interviews afterward, the children in this group were simply asked what Sam Stone had done when he came to visit.

The suggestion group did not get the above priming, but each of their four follow-up interviews contained two erroneous suggestions, one having to do with ripping a book and the other with soiling a bear. The questions were misleading: "Remember the time Sam Stone visited and spilled chocolate on the bear? Did he do it on purpose or by accident?"

The fourth group, stereotype plus suggestion, received both the stereotyped stories of the clumsy Sam Stone before his visit and the leading questions in the four interviews afterward.

All groups went through a fifth and final interview. In this, a new interviewer began with an open question about what happened the day Sam Stone came to visit. Then they were asked whether they had "heard something" about the two events that never happened: soiling the bear and ripping the book.

The results of that fifth interview are striking (Figure 11.19). The control group had practically no errors. Children in the stereotype group had more errors, with the three- to four-year-olds having twice as many errors as those five to six years old, but when they were gently challenged by the interviewers about whether they'd really seen Sam soil the bear or rip the book, most retracted their stories. The suggestion group had even more errors (53 percent of the younger children and 38 percent of the older children indicated that Sam had done one or both misdeeds) and more of them stuck to their story when challenged. The stereotype plus suggestion group had the highest level of errors. In this case, 72 percent of the younger chil-

dren claimed Sam Stone both soiled the bear and ripped the book. Even after repeated questioning, 21 percent maintained their conviction that their story was correct. Among the older children, close to 40 percent reported that Sam Stone did the behaviors, whereas only 11 percent stuck to their story after repeated questioning.

What purpose could such an easily misled memory system serve in young children? It actually is quite functional, if you consider the vulnerability of a young child. For example, it may be essential for children not to wander away from their parents into the woods, and so having a memory system that incorporates warning information from more experienced adults without a great deal of resistance is quite handy. While there may not be actual "monsters" in the woods, there very well may be other harmful things, and until the child is able to adequately reason about when and how to handle a trip into the woods, it may be more functional to believe in monsters (Leichtman & Ceci, 1995).

11.19 Results from the "Sam Stone" study. In all graphs (a–d) the percentage of preschoolers' erroneous answers is expressed. The red bars indicate that the child asserted that an incorrect event occurred; the green bars indicate that the child claimed to have observed the nonevent; the blue bars indicate that the child insisted on having witnessed the event, despite a mild attempt at dissuading them.

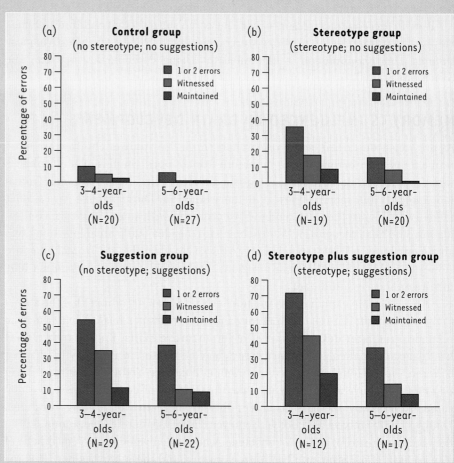

young children have trouble with false memories: they may not be relating the real event to the one being suggested. Finally, a child's temperament may come into play. Children's responses to authority vary. Children who are unwilling to question authority or give a response that they sense is unwanted may be more prone to false memories.

Do Children Have Good Memory Systems?

Few people have memories of events that occurred before three years of age. And often our earliest memories are the result of stories we have been told or pictures we have seen of ourselves at a young age. Because of this, it was historically assumed that memory did not develop in the young brain until after age three. New research has revealed that children are able to create memories as early as 18 months. One thing is clear, however: even after age three, young children are more prone to specific types of memory errors. The precise reasons for this are still debated by psychologists.

HOW DOES LANGUAGE DEVELOP?

In 1970, a 13-year-old girl known as "Genie" walked into a welfare office in Los Angeles with her mother, who came seeking help after escaping an abusive husband. When a social worker saw Genie, she reported the young girl to her supervisor, thinking she suffered from autism. Upon closer examination they discovered that the girl was actually a teenager, although at 4'6" and 59 pounds she appeared much younger. Her physical state revealed she had been severely neglected and abused. She could not hop, skip, climb, or do anything requiring the full extension of her limbs (Curtiss, 1977; Rymer, 1993). She was admitted to the hospital and then taken from her parents and placed in foster care.

Scientists were drawn to the case of this young girl because she had been deprived of normal exposure to language early in life and had no apparent language skills when she was discovered (Figure 11.20). Her father, who was mentally ill, had kept her in a tiny dark bedroom, tied to a chair, and caged in a crib at night. She had been beaten, poorly fed, and isolated from the world—there was no one to talk to and nothing to listen to or even look at in her barren room. She had been raised with essentially no stimulation. She could speak only a few words, such as "Stop it" and "No more." She understood a few words but was unable to form even simple sentences—she had learned no language. In her new foster home, she was exposed to English. Linguists and psychologists studied her deficits and her learning patterns as she was tutored over the years.

While Genie did learn to speak and acquired a large vocabulary, after four years of intensive training her language skills were similar to those of a typical five-year-old. Although she was capable of combining these words to express her ideas in semantically varied ways, her ability to use adult grammar fell far behind in both production and comprehension. Genie's sentences remained "telegraphic"; sometimes the words were oddly arranged, and they often lacked grammatical parts (such as "ed" to mark tense or "s" to mark plurals). Genie's incomplete grammar was evident in sentences such as "At school scratch face," which lacks a subject as well as the past tense marker "ed." Genie also did not comprehend passive construction, for example, that "The dog was bitten by the cat," is equivalent in meaning to "The cat bit the dog."

11.20 Genie as a young women in 1971.

The case of Genie is a tragic story and we will never know what role her social and physical abuse played in the enduring difficulties that she had in acquiring language after age 13. Yet one factor about her brain's organization provided a tantalizing demonstration that innate biological factors contribute to our species' acquisition of language and its cerebral organization. Rather than having her language functions occur in the left hemisphere, Genie's appeared largely in the right hemisphere. This fact intrigued scientists because her language profile bore striking similarities to the grammatical patterns seen in patients whose language was subsumed by the right hemisphere after the left hemisphere was surgically removed for medial reasons. In such cases the right hemisphere is not always as good at language processing as is the left. Thus, Genie's case suggested that exposure to language in very early life is essential in order to develop the normal left hemisphere cerebral specialization for language, and thus for normal language development.

The idea that there are biologically determined time periods when a child must be exposed to language in order to achieve normal brain development was first termed "the critical period hypothesis" by Eric Lenneberg (1967). The theory states that environmental input is important, but biology determines when an organism needs to receive particular input in order to make use of it. Genie taught us that the critical period noted by Lenneberg (generally thought to be before age 12) is not as rigid as originally thought because she was able to learn some aspects of language later. The phenomenon is now referred to as "sensitive periods" to reflect the fact that nature permits some aspects of development to occur beyond age 12.

Genie also taught us that biology alone will not result in a child learning language. Instead, innate aspects of language interact with environmental triggers. If language were entirely built in, Genie would have begun to speak regardless of the amount of language she was exposed to. Yet although she was eventually exposed to language, she never developed the proficiency of a native speaker, despite intensive tutoring. It seems that if you don't use language in childhood, your brain loses a good deal of the ability to learn it. (This also explains why children who are exposed to many languages early on can easily acquire several, but those of us who wait until high school to learn a new language have to struggle through years of study only to be proficient.)

Language may be the most complex wonder of the human brain. While many species communicate, language represents a quantum leap from other forms of communication. Think of what humans can do with language: speak, read, and write over 4,000 languages, communicating basic information as well as the subtle nuances of great literature and complex emotions. Language is what sets us apart from other species. But how do we learn language? There are clearly things that can be taught, such as the standard rules of grammar or a foreign language. But there are ways humans acquire language that do not rely on formal teaching. Every fluent speaker has extensive implicit knowledge of grammar even if he or she cannot explicitly explain the rules. In addition, simple observation reveals that babies begin speaking without a great deal of formal teaching. Further, children who are exposed to several languages somehow learn all of them and keep them straight. They know that one set of words is English, one is Spanish, and another is French.

What is innate and what is learned about language? Consider that children cannot learn to produce spoken words before about age one. It is pointless to try to teach them to do so any earlier. Is this because it takes a year for a baby to learn to say "mama" and "dada" (in spite of parents who incessantly repeat these words to them)? No. It is because the brain circuitry that enables speaking has not formed until this age. In other words, we don't talk until our brain is able to say something. A person such as Genie suggests that simple brain maturation is not sufficient, however.

Genie was able to learn to produce and understand words and to combine these words to convey basic meanings, but the sentence structure of her word combinations remained idiosyncratic. This suggests that there is a basic dichotomy between words and the grammatical ways in which we combine words into phrases and sentences. Once Genie was exposed to language, she was able quickly to learn to associate strings of sounds with specific events and objects. As psychologist Steven Pinker says, "The word 'duck' does not look like a duck, walk like a duck, or quack like a duck, but refers to a duck all the same because the members of a language community, as children, all memorized the pairing." However, Genie was never able to learn the rules that govern the way we combine words to convey complex thoughts. The case of Genie illustrates the levels of complexity involved in comprehension and production of language.

LANGUAGE IS BASED ON GRAMMATICAL RULES

The grammar of a language is the system of rules that characterizes the structure of a given language. Grammar consists of a number of components of increasing complexity. At the lowest level, **phonology** is the study of the set of meaningless sounds and the rules by which people combine them to make all the words and sentences in language (Figure 11.21). The units of phonology are phones and phonemes. *Phones* are the set of speech sounds that we actually say when we move our mouths to form words and sentences. The set of mouth articulations and the rules that govern how speech sounds are combined and vary depending on their position in utterances constitute the phonetic level of language.

Still deeper is the phonemic level of language organization. Every natural language is derived from a highly restricted set of sounds, called its "phonemic inventory," a fact intriguing in itself because the human vocal tract has the capacity to make many more sounds than any language uses. A language's phonemic inventory is comprised of *phonemes*, speech sounds that signal a difference in meaning between words. For example, we recognize "pat" and "bat" as having different

phonology The study of the set of meaningless sounds and the rules by which we combine them to make words and sentences.

11.21 The units of language.

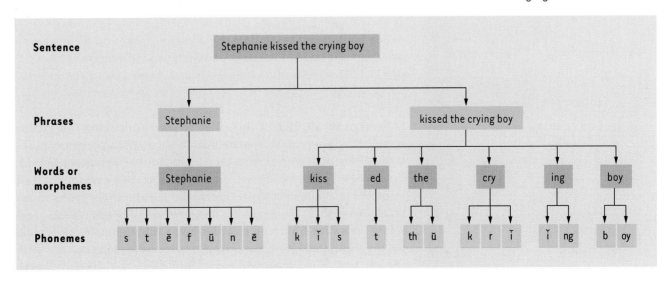

morphology   The system of rules for combining the smallest meaningful units of language into words.

morpheme   The smallest unit of speech that has meaning.

syntax   The system of rules by which words are combined into phrases and phrases into sentences.

semantics   The study of the system of meanings that underlie words, phrases, and sentences.

pragmatics   The way people use language to get what they want and to influence their listeners.

discourse   The systematic ways by which people engage in conversations.

meanings although /p/ and /b/ carry no meanings in themselves. Although both are stop consonants formed by pressing the lips together and releasing, the larynx vibrates to make the consonant /b/ voiced, but not when producing the unvoiced consonant /p/. Phonemes constitute the basic building blocks of language.

The next level of complexity is **morphology**, which is the system of rules of combining the smallest meaningful units of language into words. A **morpheme** is the smallest unit of speech that has meaning. It can consist of free morphemes—freestanding words such as "cup"—or bound morphemes such as prefixes and suffixes. The word "unendingly" consists of four morphemes: the bound prefix "un-," the free stem "end," and the bound suffixes "-ing" and "-ly." The morpheme "-s" is another example of a bound morpheme as it cannot stand alone in English; it carries meaning and grammatical information only when attached to another morpheme (or word). For example, when the "-s" morpheme is added to a noun it can make it plural (as in the word "pills"); when it is added to a verb it marks the third person singular ("He eats"). When added to nouns it can also be a possessive pronoun marker ("John's book"). However, note that in the word "spill," the /s/ is a phoneme and not a morpheme because it does not have meaning in and of itself but only in combination with the other phonemes of the word. As can be seen from these examples, some morphemes represent concepts (they are words) while others modify the meaning of words or provide grammatical information.

The system of rules by which words are combined into phrases and phrases are combined to make sentences is the **syntax** of a language. English belongs to the class of languages with "analytic" structure, which rely heavily on word order to signal changes in meaning. For example, "Mary hit John" versus "John hit Mary." By contrast, languages with "synthetic" structure mark grammatical relations (such as the sentence's subject and object) through morphological inflections, which are most often affixed to the language's verbs and nouns. Both structures can equally express the full range of meanings that is the hallmark of language.

The study of the system of meanings that underlie words, phrases, and sentences is called **semantics**. The study of the way we use language to get what we want and to influence our listeners is called **pragmatics**. Finally, the study of the systematic ways by which we engage in conversations (introduce a new topic, interrupt, take and yield the floor, and the like) is called **discourse**.

LANGUAGE DEVELOPS IN AN ORDERLY FASHION

As the brain develops, so does the ability to speak and form sentences. For the most part, the stages of language development are remarkably uniform across individuals, though the time frame of language acquisition may vary up to a year or more.

From zero to 60,000   Babies may not be born talking, but experiments have revealed that they are born understanding the difference between their parents' language and another language, and can distinguish between different phonemes. Psychologists Peter Eimas and Peter Jusczyk devised a version of the habituation technique that allows experimenters to study when very young infants prefer to listen to one thing over another, or note a difference between sounds. They inserted the switch for a tape recorder into a rubber nipple; when infants suck on the nipple, the sucking turns on the tape recorder, which plays a syllable such as "ba" each time the sucking occurs. Once babies get tired of the syllable, their sucking rate decreases. Once the infants are habituated, the researchers change the syllable, to "pa," for instance. The sucking rate increases when the babies hear the new sound (Eimas et al., 1971). Researchers used this same technique to show that French babies as young as four days old sucked more in response to French than to Russian, indicating that they had learned the sound of their native language in the womb or in the first days outside the womb (Mehler et al., 1988).

There are over 40 phonemes in English and each phoneme has a distinct sound. For example, the distinction between "r" and "l" is important in English: "read" means something quite different than "lead." However, Japanese does not distinguish those two sounds and instead makes other distinctions that English does not make. If babies are tested young enough, they are capable of making phonemic distinctions from all languages. However, after several months of exposure to their own language, infants lose the ability to make distinctions that do not matter in their language and gain an increased ability to discriminate among the sounds that will prove to be most key in their native language. The development of language-specific phoneme distinctions supports the theory that language potential is innate but shaped by experience: an infant is born with the ability to understand any language, but soon the brain begins to selectively respond to the language that the baby is exposed to. This ability to efficiently attend to specific linguistic units and their patterns of arrangement in their own languages may be what makes infants so efficient at language learning.

Given that babies can hear the difference between sounds immediately after birth and continue to learn the sounds of their own languages, how does this affect the development of spoken words? A normal adult knows about 60,000 words. Humans appear to go from babbling as babies to a full adult vocabulary without working very hard at it. Speech production follows a distinct path. During the first months of life, newborns' actions generate all of their sounds: crying, fussing, eating, and breathing. The sounds are cries, gurgles, or grunts. Cooing and laughing are added from three to five months. From five to seven months babies begin babbling using consonants and vowels. From seven to eight months they babble in syllables (ba-ba-ba, dee-dee-dee), and by one year, the syllables are mixed (ba-dee, dah-dee) and those babbles begin to take on the sounds and rhythms of the infant's native language.

A recent study by Siobhan Holowka and Laura Ann Petitto (2001) provides a new glimpse at the inner workings of the brain when young babies babble and suggests that babbling is a biologically controlled component of acquiring a language. Although there is universal agreement that babbling occurs prior to the onset of young babies' first words, there is controversy over whether the neural determinants of the behavior are fundamentally linguistic or reflect only oral-motor developments. If babbling is fundamentally linguistic, then left hemispheric specialization should be reflected in right mouth asymmetry while babies are babbling. If babbling is fundamentally motoric, then equal hemispheric participation should be reflected in equal mouth opening while babbling. Two groups of babies acquiring two distinct spoken languages were studied (English and French). Holowka and Petitto discovered that all babies had significantly greater right mouth asymmetry while babbling as compared to their left or equal mouth opening during nonbabble productions (such as crying). This discovery is among the earliest demonstrations of left hemisphere lateralization for language in humans. Moreover, the crosslinguistic findings suggest that left cerebral laterality for babbling is a universal phenomenon. Holowka and Petitto thus concluded that babbling represents the onset of the productive language capacity in humans.

The fact that babbling is a universal development milestone is reinforced by two fascinating observations. First, in the early months of babbling (around 6–7 months) babbles tend to have the same content across all languages; only later (around 10–11 months) do babbles begin to contain phonological features of specific languages. Second, if a deaf baby's parents use sign language, the baby makes hand movements that are fundamentally identical to vocal babbling (Petitto & Marentette, 1991). Deaf babies' manual babbling contained the three defining features of vocal babbling. Their forms were (1) produced with a subset of the possible phonetic units (in sign) and organized into well-formed syllables (rhythmically alternating opening/closing movements), (2) reduplicated with the prosody (timing) of a signed sentence, and (3) used without apparent meaning or reference. Thus, the hands of deaf babies reveal the biological underpinnings of this monumental milestone previously associated exclusively with speech. The similarities between manual and vocal babbling teach us that babbling must be fundamentally tied to the core organization of language, providing a baby with a means to discover the basic phonetic units and their syllabic patterning from which the language will be built.

Single words   Babbling may be an infant's way of testing the system—checking that the basic parts exist and how they get tossed together. The onset of language is marked by the first words that a baby utters and appears to understand. First words tend to appear around age one. There are two types of words that babies most often first utter. One type is known as *performatives*, wordlike sounds that are learned in a context, and that a baby may not be using to represent a meaning. For instance, a baby says "hello" or something that sounds like it when holding a phone. Does the baby know that "hello" is a greeting used to talk to someone on the other end of the line? Or is the baby simply imitating what it sees people do when they pick up the phone? Chances are it is the latter if the baby does not say "hello" in other appropriate settings. *True words*, in contrast, are clearly meant to represent concepts. For instance, "cat" names the family pet, "book" a bedtime story. When babies develop single words, they are often used to identify things present in the immediate environment, but they can also refer to things that are not physically present, such as when a baby points to the cookie jar and says "cookie." It is curious that first words tend to be the same throughout the world. Most first words identify objects ("cat," "sky," "nose," "book"), the rest tend to be simple action words ("go," "up," "sit"), quantifiers ("all gone!" "more!"), qualities or adjectives ("hot"), socially interactive words ("bye," "hello," "yes," "no"), and even internal states ("booboo" after being hurt; Petitto, 1988; Pinker, 1984). Interestingly, as you might guess from these words, even very young children freely use early words to express a wide range of communicative functions, including naming, commenting, and requesting.

Two words, sentences, grammar   By about 18 months children begin to put words together and their vocabularies start to grow rapidly. Rudimentary sentences of roughly two words or more emerge. The fascinating thing is that these minisentences, though missing words and grammatical markings, actually have a logic or "syntax." Typically the order of the words indicates what has happened or should happen: "Throw ball. All gone" roughly translates as "I threw the ball and now it's gone." In fact, psychologist Roger Brown, often referred to as the father of child language for his pioneering research on the language of three children, first termed this phase **telegraphic speech** because children speak as if they are sending a telegram—just bare-bones words without any frills.

As children's vocabularies grow and they get better at expressing ideas with words, they begin to have fluent conversations. Sentences become longer and the syntax in the sentences becomes more complex. Young children acquire and apply grammatical rules so fast that no linguist has been able to explain fully how it happens.

Overlapping rules of grammar As children begin to use language in more sophisticated ways, they make interesting errors in word formation and syntax. Sometimes children start to make mistakes at ages three to five with words they previously used correctly at age two or three. Psycholinguists believe this occurs because when children learn a new grammar rule, they tend to overapply it. For example, they learn that adding "ed" to a verb in English makes something past tense. They then add "ed" to every verb, including irregular verbs that do not follow that rule. For instance, they will say "runned" or "holded" even though they may have said "ran" or "held" at an earlier age. A similar pattern of errors is found with plurals. The rule to add "s" leads to errors such as "mouses" and "mans" when the rule is overapplied. Children do this despite having used the correct irregular plural at a younger age.

While overgeneralizations are relatively infrequent in children's speech, they reflect an important aspect of language acquisition. Children are not simply repeating what they have heard others say, as they most likely have not heard anyone say "runned." Instead, these errors occur because children are able to use language in a generative way. Simply, children have discovered a general rule of grammar, but they have not yet discovered that there are exceptions to the rule. Children make more errors with words that are used less frequently (such as "drank" and "knew") because they have heard the irregular form less often. Adults tend to do the same thing; we are more likely to make errors on the past tenses of words such as "trod," "strove," or "slew" (saying "treaded," "strived," or "slayed") because those are words we do not use often (Pinker, 1994).

THERE IS A UNIVERSAL GRAMMAR

Much of the research by linguists and psycholinguists is aimed at breaking down language production and comprehension into detailed steps to understand how language is assembled, produced, and understood. Linguist Noam Chomsky (Figure 11.22) transformed the field when he observed that language was too complex to be governed by rules learned entirely through intensive reinforcement of environmental input. Prior to this, behaviorists, most notably B. F. Skinner, had argued that language was a learned behavior rather than an innate ability. By contrast, Chomsky maintained that language must be governed by "universal grammar," or innate knowledge of a set of universal and specifically linguistic elements and relations that form the heart of all human languages.

Until Chomsky came on the scene in the late 1950s, linguists had focused on analyzing language and identifying basic components of grammar. In his early work, Chomsky argued that the way people combine these elements to form sentences and convey meaning is only the surface structure of a language. He introduced the concept of deep structure: the implicit meanings of sentences. For instance, "The fat cat chased the rat" implies that there is a cat, it is fat, and it

11.22 Noam Chomsky, the father of modern linguistic theory.

chased the rat. "The rat was chased by the fat cat" implies the same idea even though on the surface it is a different sentence. Chomsky believed that we automatically and unconsciously transform surface structure to deep structure. Research has shown that the underlying meaning of a sentence is what we remember, not its surface structure. For example, in studies in which subjects are shown sentences with similar meanings but different syntax, as in the examples above, they can remember the point of the sentences, but not which version they saw (Sachs, 1967).

But Chomsky's theory went even further. He offered what was a breathtaking hypothesis for its time: that babies are born with a "language acquisition device" ("LAD"). Starting from his hypothesized universal grammar, Chomsky proposed that the LAD provided young babies with the means to (1) narrow the range of possible grammars consistent with a partial (and often defective) set of sentences that is typical of spontaneous conversations (called "the primary linguistic data") and (2) "fix" or deduce a theory (a grammar) for the specific native language to which the baby is being exposed (a now-famous idea called "parameter setting"). This was a most daring idea for its time because at its core was the assumption that aspects of language were part of our biological makeup, and housed in the human brain. Although Chomsky based his theories exclusively on logical analysis (as he did not do research with babies), his proposal sent shockwaves through the scientific world. It inspired decades of research with children in pursuit of the biological foundations of language, which in turn has yielded surprising ways in which a child's biological makeup contributes to her or his ability to learn language.

LANGUAGE IS ALSO INFLUENCED BY SOCIAL CONTEXT

How do culture and other social factors affect cognitive development?

There is little doubt that the environment has a great deal of influence on a child's acquisition of language. However, the specific nature of this influence is still under debate. Lev Vygotsky, a Russian psychologist interested in applying Marxist social theory to individual psychology, developed the first major theory that emphasized the role of social and cultural context on cognition and language development. At the time, in the 1920s, most psychological theories were behaviorist or gestalt in orientation. Vygotsky believed that these theories failed to explain the development of higher cognitive processes in ways that made sense given what was known about genetics and biological development. According to Vygotsky, humans are unique because they use symbols and psychological tools, such as speech, writing, maps, art, and so on, through which they create culture. Culture, in turn, dictates what people need to learn and the sorts of skills that need to be developed. For example, some cultures might value science and rational thinking whereas others might emphasize supernatural and mystical forces. Some cultures emphasize keeping social distance whereas others encourage people to be in close proximity. These cultural values shape how people think about and relate to the world around them. Vygotsky made a distinction between elementary mental functions, such as innate sensory experiences, and higher mental functions, such as language, perception, abstraction, and memory. As children develop, their elementary capacities are gradually transformed, primarily through the influence of culture.

Central to Vygotsky's theories is the idea that social context influences language development, which in turn influences cognitive development. Children start off directing their speech towards specific communications with others, such as asking for food or toys. As children develop, they begin directing speech towards themselves, such as by giving themselves directions or talking to themselves while they play. Eventually, children internalize their words into *inner speech*, which comprises verbal thoughts that direct behavior and cognition. Your thoughts are based on the language that you acquire through your culture, and this ongoing inner speech reflects higher-order cognitive processes.

Vygotsky's emphasis on culture continues to influence research in cognitive development. For instance, a series of clever studies by Michael Tomasello and his colleagues (Tomasello, 1998) have convincingly outlined the importance of precise and well-timed interactions between mothers and infants. These researchers videotaped children ages 1¼ to 2 years old and their mothers with the hope of cataloging the exact moment at which the mothers made reference to objects in the infants' environments. It was found that mothers largely talked about objects that were already a part of the children's ongoing actions and the objects of joint attention. It is believed that this strategy, called **joint attentional engagement**, significantly improves a child's chance of recognizing and learning the referent object. Research has found that the more joint attentional engagement children receive after about nine months of age, the faster their comprehension and production of language becomes. In order to understand these findings more thoroughly, the same group of scientists conducted a second study in which they deliberately varied the ways in which they taught children new words. Half of the time the adult labeled an object that was not the focus of the child's attention in an effort to direct the child's attention to it. The other half of the time, the adult labeled the object after the child had focused his or her attention on it. The scientists discovered that labeling an object that was already the focus of the child's attention was significantly more effective than using labels to direct the child's attention to an object.

Theorists such as Tomasello believe that the explicit rewards behaviorists have cited as the motivation for learning language are unnecessary. Instead, it is thought that the reinforcement for language acquisition comes from the child's increased mastery at communicating and the increased agency and autonomy that language enables. Another important difference between the work of Tomasello and other language acquisition theorists is the exact mechanism that enables acquisition. Though Chomsky and others have suggested that a module in the human brain mutated in the relatively recent past to allow for language and a universal grammar, Tomasello believes that humans inherit a special ability to identify with other human beings, and that this is the cornerstone of joint attentional engagement.

But are humans truly unique in their ability to speak? This is the subject of "Studying the Mind: Can Chimps Be Taught to Speak?"

THERE IS A SENSITIVE PERIOD FOR LANGUAGE ACQUISITION

As we noted earlier in the chapter, there are critical learning periods for certain cognitive skills. But for humans, these periods are not rigid or inflexible but rather represent *sensitive periods* in which skills such as language are most easy to learn. Cases such as those of Genie and other children raised in deprived environments indicate that humans are best able to acquire language prior to puberty.

Multilinguals and creoles The extent to which postadolescent individuals are able to become multilingual also supports a sensitive learning period. People who

joint attentional engagement A process whereby caregivers make reference to objects that are part of a child's ongoing actions.

are truly bilingual or multilingual have generally acquired the multilanguages before the age of 12. Adults who move to a new country rarely become as fluent as their children (Zatorre, 1989).

Creole describes a language that evolves over time from the mixing of existing languages. Creole languages develop, for example, when several different cultures colonize a new place, such as occurred when the French established themselves in southern Louisiana and acquired slaves who were not native French speakers. Populations that speak several different languages develop a new means for communicating, often mixing words from each group's native language, which is called a *pidgin*. Linguist Derek Bickerton has found that the pidgin is then fully developed by the children of the colonists into its own language—a creole language—as the children hear the pidgin spoken by their parents and impose rules on it. Bickerton argues that this is evidence for built-in, universal grammar: The brain takes a nonconforming language, applies rules to it, and changes it.

Studying the Mind

CAN CHIMPS BE TAUGHT TO SPEAK?

We know that animals have ways of communicating with each other. But no other animal uses language the way humans do. Scientists have tried for years to teach language to chimpanzees, one of our nearest living relatives (along with bonobos). Chimps lack the vocal abilities to speak aloud, so studies have used sign language or visual cues to determine whether they understand words or concepts such as causation. While chimpanzees can learn some words and have some sense of causation, the idea that this means they have innate language abilities has been challenged. Consider the work of psychologists Herbert Terrace, Laura Ann Petitto, and Tom Bever, who set out to test Noam Chomsky's assertion that language was a uniquely human trait by attempting to teach a chimpanzee language. Hopeful of success, they named the chimp Neam Chimpsky (nicknamed Nim) (Figure 11.23). Petitto became Nim's surrogate mother and raised the chimp just like a child, wrapping him in a rich social, emotional, and linguistic world. But after years of teaching Nim American Sign Language, or ASL, the team had to admit that Chomsky might be right.

11.23 "Nim" Chimpsky.

Nim, like all other language-trained chimps, consistently failed to master key components of human language syntax. While Nim was quite adept at communicating with a small set of basic signs ("eat," "play," "more"), he never acquired the ability to generate creative rule-governed sentences; he was like a broken record, talking about the same thing over and over again in the same old way. Crucially, unlike even the young child who names, comments, requests, and more with his or her first words, all the chimps used ASL almost exclusively to get something, to request. What the chimps seemed to appreciate was the power of language to obtain outcomes, mentioned above as the "pragmatics" of language. In the end, the chimps could use bits and pieces of language only to get something from their caretakers (food, more food) rather than to truly express meanings, thoughts, and ideas by generating language (Petitto & Seidenberg, 1979).

More recently, evolutionary psychologists have argued that this apparent inability to teach chimps human language also shows that language is indeed an innate ability that has been selected for in humans (Pinker & Bloom, 1990).

Bickerton also found that creole languages formed in different parts of the world, with different combinations of languages, are more similar to each other in grammatical structure than long-lived languages. He suggests this is also evidence for built-in grammar, arguing that older languages have evolved away from the grammatical constructions most natural for the brain to impose, whereas creole languages have not been around long enough to do this yet. Thus creole languages may be similar because the brain imposes the same basic rules on a new language (Bickerton, 1998).

Acquiring language on the hands   Most prevailing accounts about how very young babies acquire language assert that the maturation of the speech production and perception mechanisms in the brain wholly determines the time course, structure, and content of early language acquisition. But what would happen if we stripped the human brain of sound and speech? If sound perception and production are the key neurological determinants of early language acquisition, then babies exposed to signed languages should acquire these languages in fundamentally different ways. If, however, what makes human language special is its highly systematic patterns and the human brain's sensitivity to them, then signing and speaking babies should acquire their respective languages in highly similar ways.

To test this hypothesis, Laura Ann Petitto and her students videotaped deaf babies of deaf parents in households using two entirely different signed languages—American Sign Language (ASL) and the signed language of Quebec, Langue des Signes Quebecoise (LSQ). They found that deaf babies exposed to signed languages from birth acquire these languages on an identical maturational time table as hearing babies acquire spoken languages, including the (a) syllabic babbling stage (ages 7–11 months), (b) first-word stage (11–14 months), (c) first two-word stage (16–22 months), and (d) grammatical and semantic developments beyond (Petitto, 2000). This research teaches us that the development of speech perception and production mechanisms cannot alone be driving all of human language acquisition. The research provides an exciting glimpse into language and the brain by showing us that humans must possess biologically endowed sensitivity to aspects of the patterns of language—a sensitivity that launches a baby into the course of acquiring language.

ASPECTS OF LANGUAGE ARE INNATE

The most fundamental question debated by scientists who study human language acquisition is whether language is innate. In order to answer this we need to define more carefully what we mean by language. When speakers are fluent in a language, they know a comprehensive set of words as well as how to put those words together to communicate ideas. Each child must learn the vocabulary of her own language as well as the rules of grammar. Certainly there is some learning that is necessary for this accomplishment. There is, however, compelling evidence that some aspects of language are innate—specifically, the ability or drive to develop language.

Several characteristics help determine whether behavior is innate. First, innate abilities generally exist in all normal members of a population, though this is not a necessary requirement. There are examples, such as color blindness, in which innate genetic defects produce abnormalities. Second, the development of an innate ability should be uniform and automatic. In other words, it should naturally develop in individuals at about the same age and in the same series of stages. Take walking as an example. All normal humans learn to walk at roughly one year

RESEARCH QUESTION

What suggests that language is innate?

of age, and they do not need any formal training to do so. Another indicator that a skill is innate is if there is a sensitive period for acquiring it, which indicates that the acquisition of the skill correlates with a biological development stage (Lenneberg, 1967; Stromswold, 2000).

Determining whether language adheres to these characteristics can be deceptively difficult. All normal humans acquire language, and language does appear to develop in a common fashion across individuals. However, there are specific aspects of language that are taught, and this is where the controversy arose. Behaviorists such as B. F. Skinner suggested that language is not innate and that children learn language through a system of repetition and imitation: Adults speak to children and the children imitate what they hear. When parents speak to children, they generally use simple sentences and repeat words. This way of speaking has been dubbed "motherese:"

"Hello there! HELLO! How's the BABY? You want a BOTTLE? Baby wants a BOTTLE? YES! Yes, that's right. BABY wants a BOTTLE."

The sing-song nature of motherese has been likened to the way that some species of adult birds simplify their birdsong to their chicks in the nest. Together, this suggests that there is some biological tuning at work between adults and the young of their species that may help launch communication-skills learning. Precisely which aspects of the adults' signals a baby is most sensitive to, how this sensitivity changes over time, and what a baby does with this information are presently being pursued. The first challenge to such a strong behaviorist view is that some studies reveal that most parents do not correct young children's grammatical errors when they are learning to speak. Parents correct children if the content of what they say is wrong, but not if the grammar is wrong. Further, it has been shown that if parents do try to correct grammar at too young an age, it is of no use—the child will continue to make the same mistake (Brown & Hanlon, 1970). Finally, language is productive, meaning that children do not simply repeat sentences that they have heard before, but generate new sentences in creative ways.

A second challenge to this strong behaviorist view of language acquisition is that there can be tremendous variability in the input a child receives and language will still emerge. In some cultures parents do not speak to their children until they have acquired enough language to have a meaningful conversation. These children still acquire language normally. These examples and others already mentioned suggest a strong innate drive to communicate using language, a drive most definitely shaped and facilitated by experience.

How Does Language Develop?

Research supports the theories that aspects of our capacity for language are innate, that language is unique to humans, and that its development is relatively uniform across individuals. While at first glance it may seem that language is taught to children, studies have revealed that this is not exactly what is happening. Rather, the brain appears to have built-in methods of acquiring words and forming them into grammatical sentences. We cannot, however, learn language in a vacuum; language input is needed. Children raised in language-deprived environments who are later exposed to conventional language never acquire completely normal language, implying that there is a sensitive learning period during which language must be acquired in order to develop normally. So while universal grammar may be innate, we must still learn the things specific to individual languages, such as the phonological properties, the lexicon, and other rules of grammar.

HOW DOES COGNITION CHANGE AFTER CHILDHOOD?

For decades, developmental psychologists adamantly believed that humans were fully developed physically and cognitively by their early twenties, and that abilities then leveled off and remained fairly unchanged until the inevitable decline in the last decade or two before death. However, researcher Paul Baltes, among others, has argued that human beings and their brains continue to develop and change across the lifespan. Recent research has revealed that plasticity does indeed remain a common attribute of the adult brain. Our brains are subject to change due to causes ranging from disease, drug use, and positive and negative emotions to new experiences and the creation of memories. At this point, however, developmental psychologists know more about human beings in their childhood than in old age. In this section we consider what is known about cognitive development beyond childhood.

COGNITION CHANGES DURING ADOLESCENCE

Recall from earlier sections that Piaget had several ideas about the ways in which adolescent thought differs from that of younger children. Piaget attributed the changes in adolescent thinking to the emergence of formal operations. Daniel Keating (1980) has expanded some of Piaget's ideas and has identified five basic qualities that differentiate adolescent thought:

1. Thinking about possibilities: This basic form of abstract thought distinguishes adolescents from younger children, in that younger children tend to think exclusively about that which is directly observable.
2. Thinking ahead: Adolescents tend to spend more time thinking about the future than do younger children. While younger children do consider future events, they are not as likely to do so systematically or realistically. Adolescents are more likely to make effective use of past experience when contemplating the future.
3. Thinking through hypotheses: During adolescence individuals become capable of generating and testing hypotheses about situations. For example, an adolescent thinking about going to a party might reason, "What if there's alcohol at the party? I guess I can always leave, but people might think I'm a loser. Well, better that than do something I don't really want to." Prior to adolescence, children rarely consider many different scenarios that may take place.
4. Thinking about thought: As children mature, they become increasingly capable of engaging in metacognition. Adolescents also gain the ability to utilize second-order thinking, which enables them to hold different (even disparate) ideas in mind as they reason about them. During adolescence, individuals also begin to think in a more complex way about other people's thoughts.
5. Thinking beyond conventional limits: All of the changes described above culminate in adolescents challenging established ideals and the behavior of the people around them. They begin to consider issues such as morality, politics, and religion. During adolescence, individuals become highly interested in "doing the right thing," something that researchers have used to explain youth's idealism and search for heroes.

While these five characteristics describe some aspects of cognitive change in adolescence, researchers also emphasize the importance of environment. Current thinking argues that the way in which adolescent thought develops is largely dependent on the content of the problems teenagers encounter and the contexts in which they encounter them.

There is gowing evidence that the way cognition changes during adolescence may be due in part to brain maturation, particularly in the growth of synaptic connections in the frontal lobes. For many years it was believed that the frontal lobes were developed by late childhood. However, recent studies using brain imaging have shown that there is continued maturation of the prefrontal cortex well into early adulthood, primarily as a result of increasing myelination, which indicates more axons and therefore neural connections (Giedd et al., 1999; Sowell et al., 2002). Thus, there is further wiring of frontal circuits throughout adolescence. As these circuits mature, they may support the development of new cognitive abilities. For instance, an increased efficiency in memory during adolescence may be related to maturation of the frontal lobes (Sowell et al., 2001).

Much of the cognitive development observed during adolescence is related to an increased capacity for cognitive control, such as the ability to filter out irrelevant information and to inhibit unwanted or maladaptive behavioral responses. In a recent study, Sylvia Bunge and her colleagues (2002) used fMRI to compare how brain activity differs in cognitive control between adults and children aged 8 to 12. In contrast to the typical pattern of right frontal activation during cognitive control for adults, Bunge et al. found that age-related increases in cognitive control among children were associated with the activation of posterior brain regions. Moreover, children failed to recruit the right frontal regions during cognitive control tasks that are most strongly activated for adults. Thus, it is possible that the capacity for cognitive control strengthens as the frontal lobes mature and relevant circuits become active. The increase in the efficiency of cognitive control continues throughout adolescence and coincides with biological changes in brain development.

AGING AFFECTS COGNITION AND MEMORY

What cognitive functions decline with age?

With the "graying" of the population in Western societies, more resources are being dedicated to research on cohorts over the age of 60. Public opinion regarding the effects of aging on cognition differs greatly among cultures. Just think of the mixed messages that we see reflected in American popular culture. For example, films and television often depict older Native Americans as wise and knowing, while Anglo-American grandparents are often shown as doddering and senile.

The messages are confusing because the data are confusing. Many studies have demonstrated that cognitive function does appear to decline with age, but it is difficult to pinpoint what exactly causes the decline. Some sensory-perceptual changes occur with age and may account for some of the observed decline. For instance, as we age we have a reduced sensitivity to contrasts, thus activities such as climbing stairs or driving at night may become more difficult and more dangerous. Sensitivity to sound also decreases with age. This change may make older people seem unaware or forgetful, when they simply are not able to hear adequately.

It is difficult to determine exactly which functions slow during advanced aging. Are the changes attributable to a decline in memory function? If so, what is it specifically about memory that declines—encoding or retrieval? Perhaps it is the ability—or desire—to focus attention that underlies a general decline in cognition. Or is it the speed of mental processing? Further, are these declines due to aging brain connections, or are they a result of elderly people simply growing less interested in things over time?

Here is a statistic that violates the TV grandparent stereotype: only about 5 percent of the population actually suffer incurable dementia, defined as a progressive disturbance of mental function characterized by loss of memory, personality changes, and lack of judgment. An additional 10–15 percent experience mild to moderate memory loss. Vascular problems (such as stroke) can cause dementia by reducing the amount of blood going to the brain. Neurological problems brought on by alcohol or exposure to other toxins can also cause some forms of dementia. More than half the cases of senile dementia are the result of Alzheimer's disease, which destroys neurons in the brain and leads to impaired memory, language, reasoning, perception, and behavior (Figure 11.24). As we saw in Chapter 7, the causes of Alzheimer's are unknown in spite of a great deal of research. One reason that so little is known about dementia is that although about 25 percent of those over 85 have Alzheimer's disease, most people die before the age of 85.

What, then, characterizes the memory loss of aging? There are no universal answers, but older people have difficulty with memory tasks that require the ability to juggle multiple pieces of information at the same time. Tasks in which attention is divided also prove difficult. These are all short-term memory tasks, and some scientists believe these deficits reflect a decreased ability to store multiple pieces of information in working memory simultaneously (Salthouse, 1992).

Generally speaking, long-term memory is less affected by aging than short-term memory, although certain aspects of long-term memory do appear to suffer in advanced age. Older people often need more time to learn new information, but once it is learned, they perform as well as younger subjects. Long-term memory tasks that divide attention or require the retrieval of memories are often more difficult for older people. It is also clear that elderly subjects are better at recognition than retrieval tasks. For example, they have no trouble recognizing words that have been shown to them if they are asked, "Did you see the word 'cat'?" But if they are asked what word they saw, or if they saw an animal name, they do not do as well.

In an intriguing study, Logan and colleagues (2002) used fMRI to examine memory processes in younger (age 20s) and older adults (age 70s and 80s). The older adults performed worse than young adults, and in terms of brain processes, they had less activation in left hemisphere brain areas known to support memory and greater activation in right hemisphere areas that do not aid memory. Next, these researchers sought to determine whether the memory deficit could be reduced if they gave the older subjects a strategy to improve memorization. Recall from Chapter 7 that the more deeply items are encoded, the better they are remembered. Accordingly, in a second study the researchers asked older participants to classify words as concrete or abstract, a strategy that leads to deeper encoding. This strategy produced better memory and greater activation of left frontal regions. These findings suggest that one reason for the

11.24 (top) A wife helps her husband, who is an Alzheimer's patient. (bottom) PET scans comparing the brain of an Alzheimer's patient with a healthy brain.

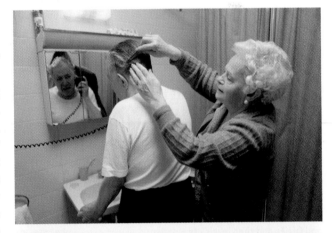

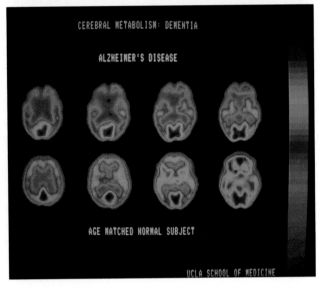

CEREBRAL METABOLISM: DEMENTIA

ALZHEIMER'S DISEASE

AGE MATCHED NORMAL SUBJECT

UCLA SCHOOL OF MEDICINE

decline in memory observed with aging is that older adults tend to under recruit strategies that facilitate memory, which indicates that cognitive training might provide useful for preventing age-related memory deficits.

Researchers are still trying to understand what causes these changes. While exact causes have yet to be pinpointed, processing speed, along with other basic mechanisms such as attention and working memory, appear to be responsible for the ways memory changes with age (Light, 1990).

SPEED OF MENTAL PROCESSING DECLINES WITH AGE

While there are differences in how cultures view the aging individual and in how individuals' cognitive capacities are influenced by age, one thing is clear: Aging does affect cognition. One of the most consistent and identifiable changes is a slowing of mental processing speed. Experiments that test the time it takes to process a sensory input and react with a motor response show a decline in response time as early as an individual's mid-twenties (Era et al., 1986). This decline continues at a more rapid rate as the individual ages. Psychologists still do not know why processing speed declines. One theory, the parallel distributed processing model, suggests that if mental processes are distributed across a series of parallel neurons that form a circuit, then as these connections weaken or are broken with age, the brain has to work harder and longer to find an alternative neuronal route (Cerella, 1990). This is consistent with evidence from examinations of the aging brain. We know that the neuropathology that occurs with aging is distributed across the entire cortex: There is no focal point, no particular area that gets knocked out with aging. Thus it seems likely that this kind of neural weakening accounts for the declines we see with age.

INTELLIGENCE NEED NOT DECLINE WITH AGE

One of the main difficulties with studying the effects of aging on cognition is determining what cognitive process is responsible for general cognitive decline. This is particularly true of intelligence. Research has consistently indicated that IQ, as measured with standard psychometric tests, declines with advanced age. As we age, do we really lose IQ points? Or do older people just have a shorter attention span or lack the motivation to complete such tests? Perhaps the issues we touched on above—memory decline and decreased speed of mental processing—are what cause lower scores.

Some researchers have identified a distinction between different forms of intelligence: fluid intelligence and crystallized intelligence (Horn & Hofer, 1992). As you will recall from Chapter 8, fluid intelligence is the ability to process new general information that requires no specific knowledge. Many standardized tests measure this kind of intelligence: the ability to recognize an analogy or to arrange blocks to match a picture. This type of intelligence is associated with speed of mental processing. Fluid intelligence tends to peak in early adulthood and decline steadily as we age. Crystallized intelligence refers to more specific knowledge that must be learned or memorized, such as vocabulary, or to knowledge of specialized information or reasoning strategies. This type of intelligence usually increases throughout life and breaks down only when declines in other cognitive abilities prevent new information from being processed (Figure 11.25).

11.25 Fluid and crystallized intelligence throughout the life span. Unlike fluid intelligence, which shows a steady decline with age, crystallized intelligence increases through at least the forties and fifties and then levels off.

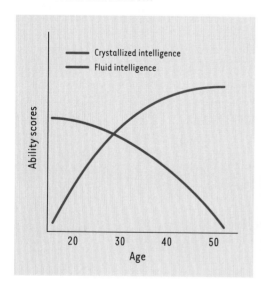

These two different types of intelligence also seem to reflect the two different cultural views of aging. The decline in fluid intelligence is in keeping with the stereotype of the doddering old grandparent, whereas the continued increase in crystallized intelligence represents the respected elder who is turned to for guidance. So which is it? The Seattle Longitudinal Study, published by Schaie in 1990, tracked adults from age 25 to 81 over 7 years, administering tests of cognitive abilities such as verbal and mathematical skills. They found that intellectual decline does not actually occur until the sixties or seventies. Further, people who were healthy and remained mentally active demonstrated less decline. Thus, while there may be declines in memory and the speed of processing, the continued ability to learn new information may outweigh those losses. Further, if we know that memory and speed of processing declines, there are ways to compensate by using alternative cognitive strategies. As with any muscle, so long as the brain stays exercised it stays in shape.

How Does Cognition Change After Childhood?

Early adulthood is marked by the emergence of an individual's ability to reason abstractly about his or her own thoughts, the future, and the surrounding environment. While many studies have shown that some types of memory and information processing slow with advanced age, other studies have emphasized that intellectual decline is not a certainty. Through continued use, the brain's plasticity enables individuals to maintain their cognitive abilities.

CONCLUSION

From the very beginning of developmental research, people such as Piaget emphasized the importance of the reciprocal relationship between an individual's neurological mechanisms and the influence of the environment. While Piaget believed that interaction with the environment was essential for the development of certain behaviors, more recently researchers building on cumulative principles have discovered that infants possess a great deal of knowledge about objects and the physical laws that govern them. The results from research that crosses levels of analysis demonstrate that there are certain aspects of object knowledge that may be hardwired in the infant brain. It also appears that the infant brain is born ready for the acquisition of language, a demonstration of the adaptiveness of the human mind. Linguist Noam Chomsky posited that humans have a language acquisition device that uniquely enables infants to acquire language, and that barring complete deprivation, the brain is hardwired to acquire the language of the child's environment. Finally, while as adults we may have trouble remembering events from our very early childhoods, this does not mean that children have no ability to create memories. Some types of memories, such as the relationship of an action and an object, as demonstrated by the work of Rovee-Collier, are very functional at an early age. However, it is also believed that an immature brain limits certain types of memory function and therefore makes children more susceptible to suggestion and stereotypes. While much has been learned about how the brain and behavior develop, the question for the present and future is how the relation between the two can be better understood. Developmental psychologists will seek to build a bridge between neurobiology and behavioral studies and continue to look for causal relations between brain and behavior.

FURTHER READINGS

Birren, J. E., & Schaie, K. W. (Eds.). (1991). *Handbook of the psychology of aging* (3rd ed.). New York: C. Van Nostrand Reinhold.

Ceci, S. J., & Bruck, M. (1995). *Jeopardy in the courtroom: A scientific analysis of children's testimony*. Washington, DC: American Psychological Association.

Flavell, J. H. (1999). Cognitive development: Children's knowledge about the mind. *Annual Review of Psychology, 50*, 21–45.

Gazzaniga, M. (Ed.). (2000). *The cognitive neurosciences* (2nd ed.). Cambridge, MA: MIT Press.

Geary, D. C. (1994). *Children's mathematical development*. Washington, DC: American Psychological Association.

Goldstein, B. E. (1996). *Sensation and perception* (4th ed.). Pacific Grove, CA: Brooks/Cole Publishing.

Kellman, P. J., & Arterberry, M. E. (1998). *The cradle of knowledge: Development of perception in infancy*. Cambridge, MA: MIT Press.

Pinker, S. (1994). *The language instinct*. New York: Morrow.

Tomasello, M. (1999). *The cultural origins of human cognition*. Cambridge, MA: Harvard University Press.

EXPLORING GENDER IDENTITY

The 1999 film *Boys Don't Cry* was based on the life story of Brandon Teena (played by Hilary Swank, at left), who was raised as a girl but adopted a male identity. Males and females, though physically different, are psychologically similar in many ways; gender roles are determined by cultural norms.

TIMELINE

1935

Imprinting Ethologist Konrad Lorenz demonstrates that animals tend to follow or form an attachment to other animals if exposed to them during a critical stage of development.

1950s

Motherless Monkeys Harry Harlow demonstrates that, when raised with artificial surrogate mothers, infant rhesus monkeys far prefer a mother made of soft cloth to one that is made of wire and gives milk.

1960s

Attachment John Bowlby proposes that infants are born with proximity-seeking behaviors that act to increase survival odds by keeping the child close to its mother.

1968

Stages of Identity Erik Erikson proposes an eight-stage theory of identity development that considers identity from infancy to old age.

Social Development and Gender

OUTLINING THE PRINCIPLES

WHAT IS ATTACHMENT?

Attachment Is Adaptive

Attachment Occurs in Many Species

Human Infants Differ in Attachment Style

Attachment Has a Chemical Basis

WHO INFLUENCES SOCIAL DEVELOPMENT?

Importance of Parental Style Depends on Infant
    Temperament

Friendships Change with Age

Parents and Peers Are Both Important

Childhood Rejection Is Associated with Negative
    Consequences

Gender Differences Exist in Adult Friendships

Cross-Sex Friendships Can Be Difficult

HOW DOES MORAL BEHAVIOR DEVELOP?

Moral Reasoning Follows Stages

Moral Emotions Emerge Early in Life

Parental Practices Relate to Children's
    Prosocial Behavior

There Are Physiological Aspects of Morality

WHAT INFLUENCES GENDER DEVELOPMENT
AND IDENTITY?

There Are Biological Sex Differences

Gender Roles Are Determined by Cultural Norms

There Are Stages of Identity Development

Ethnic Identity Develops Early

CONCLUSION

FURTHER READINGS

1969

Moral Reasoning Lawrence Kohlberg uses dilemmas to examine moral reasoning. His stage model is later criticized for not applying equally across genders and cultures.

1970s

Strange Situation Mary Ainsworth tests Bowlby's attachment ideas using the Strange Situation Test. Ainsworth's research identifies three attachment styles that characterize most children.

1970s–1980s

Child-Caregiver Interaction Theorists discover there is a bidirectional influence between a child and a caregiver, which provides new insights into this dynamic relationship.

1982

Gender and Morality Carol Gilligan proposes that care-based reasoning and justice-based reasoning are equally sophisticated levels of moral development.

1985

Self-Conscious Emotions Emotions such as empathy, sympathy, guilt, and shame are shown to be strong predictors of moral behavior.

On April 27, 1966, two seven-month-old twin boys named Bruce and Brian Reimer were brought to St. Boniface Hospital in Winnepeg, Canada, for routine circumcision. Unfortunately, during the first operation, Bruce's penis was badly damaged by a faulty cautery machine. Its condition deteriorated over the next several days, and within the week it shriveled up and disappeared. (It should be noted that after what happened to Bruce, no attempt was made to circumcise Brian.) The accident and the events that followed changed not only the lives of the Reimer family but also psychologists' beliefs about the concept of gender.

As recounted in John Colapinto's book *As Nature Made Him: The Boy Who Was Raised As A Girl*, Bruce's parents, Janet and Ron, decided to investigate whether he should undergo sexual reassignment and be raised as a girl. The process had never been attempted on a child born with normal genitalia; sexual reassignment cases had previously been conducted on hermaphrodite children, who were born with ambiguous genitalia. They contacted world-renowned (and controversial) sexologist John Money at Johns Hopkins University, who convinced the Reimers that sexual reassignment was the best course of action for Bruce's psychological well-being. Bruce was castrated when he was 22 months old, renamed Brenda, and was raised as a girl (Figure 12.1). Throughout the 1970s and 1980s, media accounts and psychology textbooks recounted the story as a successful demonstration that gender was the result of socialization rather than biology. Whether one was a boy or a girl was the result of how one was treated, not because of genes or biology. Unfortunately, a recent analysis indicates that Brenda's sexual reassignment was a failure from the start.

Brenda's life can be described as tumultuous at best, hellish at worst. Although her parents let her hair grow long, dressed her in feminine colors and clothing styles, and encouraged her to play with other girls, by all accounts, Brenda was not comfortable or happy being a girl. She was teased incessantly for her rough and aggressive

RESEARCH QUESTIONS for Studying Social Development and Gender

- How do people become attached to others?
- Are parents or peers more important for a child's social development?
- How does a person's gender or age affect his or her friendships?
- How do children learn social rules and develop morals?
- How do physiological and neurological factors influence gender development?
- What factors shape personal identity throughout the life span?

1995

Importance of Peers
Judith Rich Harris argues that peers are more important than parents to a child's social development. This controversial theory invigorates the nature-nurture debate.

1980s

Gender Roles and Schema
A variety of researchers demonstrate that many assumed differences between males and females are the result of gender stereotypes that are transmitted through socialization.

ways. It got worse when Brenda was given hormones at age 11 to initiate development of secondary sexual characteristics. The development of breasts was a source of intense embarrassment and horror for Brenda that did not fade with time.

As the years passed, Janet and Ron were finally forced to consider that Brenda was not—nor would ever truly be—a girl. After 15 years of familial and peer problems and intense psychological troubles, Brenda was told the truth about what had happened. A flood of emotions welled up within Brenda, but the most overwhelming feeling was relief. In her own words, Brenda recalled that day: "I was *relieved*. Suddenly it all made sense why I felt the way I did. I wasn't some sort of weirdo. I wasn't *crazy*" (p. 180).

Brenda immediately decided to return to being male. She stopped hormone therapy. She changed her name to David, which she chose because of the legendary biblical story of David and Goliath. Although there were serious adjustment problems for a few years, David eventually sorted them out. New techniques in surgery allowed physicians to provide David with a functional artificial penis that could be used for sexual intercourse. At the age of 23, he met a woman with three children. Jane and David fell in love. David is now a healthy, happy man with a beautiful wife and family (Figure 12.2).

The case of David (Bruce/Brenda) Reimer is fascinating and horrific on many levels. For ethicists and researchers it highlights the need for full disclosure of all research findings in addition to other complex issues focusing on how good research should be conducted. For psychologists, the case is remarkable because it addresses many of the central issues in the unending debate of nature versus nurture. As David's transformations illustrate, the effects of nature and nurture on gender development are complex and multifaceted. His story provides the backdrop for research on gender, identity, friendships, and social development.

12.1 Brian (at left) and Bruce (Brenda) Reimer as children. The fact that they were identical twins was ideal for understanding the effects of culture on gender identity.

12.2 David (Bruce) Reimer as an adult.

Historically, psychological science paid minimal attention to children or their social development. Over the last 40 years, however, a growing number of researchers have investigated the forces that shape people's interactions with their social worlds from childhood through adulthood and old age. **Social development** refers to the maturation of skills or abilities that enable people to interact. In all cultures and across all time periods, every person's life is touched by the lives of others. Infants innately form bonds with others, an adaptive trait that provides protection and facilitates survival. As children grow, they are taught how to communicate with and behave appropriately around others, and how to establish and maintain relationships. Social development is studied on many levels of analysis—from the "chemistry" (actual chemicals exchanged) in some social relationships to the differences between cultures. This chapter explores the early attachments that children develop to their caregivers as well as the relationships children have with their friends. We consider how socialization affects human characteristics such as morality and gender. Finally, we consider change in social identity across the life span.

WHAT IS ATTACHMENT?

Like all primates, human infants need nurturance and care from adults to survive. Unlike horses and deer, who can walk and find food within hours after birth, humans are born profoundly immature, unable even to hold up their own heads or roll over. But they are far from helpless or passive. From minutes after birth, the cries of infants cause psychological, physiological, and behavioral reactions in caregivers that compel the offering of food and comfort to the newborns. As you read in the previous chapter, infants also possess a variety of cognitive and perceptual abilities that allow them to interact with their caregivers. Between six and eight weeks of age most infants display their first social smile, which typically leads to powerful feelings of love and bonding between caregiver and child. Psychological scientists refer to this bond as an **attachment**, a strong, intimate emotional connection between people that persists over time and across circumstances. Infant attachment leads to heightened feelings of safety and security. Even young infants have highly interactive social relationships; for example, infants are profoundly affected by the facial expressions of their caregivers within ten weeks after birth, and young infants become very upset when their mothers fail to display emotional reactions.

ATTACHMENT IS ADAPTIVE

According to John Bowlby (1907–1990), who popularized its importance, attachment serves to motivate infants and caregivers to stay in close contact. Bowlby argued that infants have an innate repertoire of attachment behaviors that motivate adult attention. For instance, infants put out their arms to be lifted, they smile when they see their caregivers, and they express distress when they feel abandoned. Adults also seem to have innate predispositions to respond to infants, such as picking up a crying child and rocking him gently. Adults also automatically respond to infants in a way that infants can understand. They make exaggerated facial expressions and pitch their voices higher. Bowlby argues that these behaviors motivate both infants and caregivers to stay in proximity. Staying close to caregivers, acting distressed when they leave, and rejoicing when they return are all aimed at securing caregivers' attention and, ultimately, their protection. Thus, attachment is adaptive, as infants who exhibit attachment behaviors have a higher chance of survival and consequently are more likely to pass along their genes to future generations.

How do people become attached to others?

social development The maturation of skills or abilities that enable people to live in a world with other people.

attachment A strong emotional connection that persists over time and across circumstances.

imprinting An instinctual tendency in some animals that produces a strong attachment to a nearby adult.

contact comfort A phenomenon whereby social development is facilitated when an infant is allowed to touch something that is soothing.

ATTACHMENT OCCURS IN MANY SPECIES

The idea that attachment is important for survival applies not only to humans but also to many other species. For instance, infant birds communicate hunger through crying, thereby triggering actions on the part of caregivers. For some birds, there appears to be a critical period in which they develop a strong attachment to whichever adult is nearby, even if that adult is not a member of their species! This pattern, first noticed in the nineteenth century, occurs for birds such as chickens, geese, and ducks, which are able to walk right after hatching and are therefore at risk for straying from their mother's care. Within about 18 hours after hatching, these birds will attach themselves, usually to their mothers, and then follow the object of their attachment. Noted ethologist Konrad Lorenz (1903–1989) called such behavior **imprinting** and noted that goslings that became imprinted on him did not go back to their biological mothers when later given access to them (Figure 12.3). However, such birds preferentially imprint on a female of their species if one is available.

12.3 Konrad Lorenz shown walking with goslings that had imprinted themselves on him. These little geese followed Lorenz as if he was their mother.

In the early 1960s, Harry Harlow (1905–1981) provided one of the most striking examples of nonhuman attachment. At that time, psychologists generally believed that infants needed their mothers because the mother was the primary source of food. For Freudians, the mother was the source of libidinal pleasures. From the behaviorist perspective, the mother was valued as the result of secondary reinforcement, given her role as the provider of food. An explanation based on either Freudian thinking or learning theory was unsatisfactory to Harlow, who recognized that, in addition to food, infants needed comfort and security.

In a now-famous series of experiments, Harlow placed infant rhesus monkeys in a cage with two different "mothers." One surrogate mother was made of bare wire and could give milk through an attached bottle. The second surrogate mother was made of soft terry cloth and had a monkeylike head (rudimentary eyes, nose, mouth, and ears attached to a flat circle) but could not give milk. The monkeys'

12.4 Harlow's monkeys and their "mothers." The infant rhesus monkey is shown clinging to its cloth mother, which it uses for contact comfort and security (left). The monkey still clings to the cloth mother while it takes milk from the wire mother (right).

responses were unmistakable: they clung to the cloth mother most of the day and went to it for comfort in times of threat; the monkeys only approached the wire mother when they were hungry (Figure 12.4). Harlow tried various manipulations, such as the introduction of a strange object, to test the monkeys' attachment to the mother. He repeatedly found that the infants were calmer, braver, and overall better adjusted when the cloth mother was near. Hence, the mother-as-food theory of mother-child attachment was debunked. Harlow's findings established the importance of **contact comfort**—allowing an infant to cling to and hold something soft—in social development.

There is more to social development, however, than the presence of a secure base. In follow-up investigations, Harlow's monkeys failed to show normal sexual and social behaviors in adulthood, and they were terrible mothers. They ignored or physically abused their offspring. But, despite this treatment, the infants of monkeys raised by surrogates developed attachments to their abusive mothers. As Harlow stated, "it was a case of the baby adopting the mother, not the mother adopting the baby" (Harlow, 1965, p. 259). Interestingly, if other monkeys were around to serve as peers, the monkeys raised by surrogates did not display abnormal behaviors. The monkeys' peers acted as a substitute for the mother in teaching the "motherless" monkeys how to act.

HUMAN INFANTS DIFFER IN ATTACHMENT STYLE

Attachment behaviors begin during the first months of life and have been observed in children around the world. If Bowlby was correct that attachment serves to encourage proximity between infant and caregiver, then one might expect attachment responses to increase at around the age children naturally become mobile. Indeed, at around six to eight months, just as children are starting to crawl, they typically display **separation anxiety**, in which they become very upset and distressed when they can't see or are separated from their attachment figure. This pattern occurs in all human cultures.

Bowlby focused on the role of exploration and security in social development. He conceptualized the mother as the *secure base* to which the child can go if afraid. He characterized attachment as the infant's attempt to balance proximity-seeking and exploratory behaviors in a homeostatic fashion. Thus, under low-stress conditions, the presence of the caregiver encourages exploration of the environment. As the situation becomes more stressful, the presence of the caregiver encourages more proximity-seeking and affiliative behaviors. Indeed, it can be readily observed that many children play happily on their own until they realize they haven't seen their attachment figure recently. After they look around to find the attachment figure, they will often return to quiet play.

Mary Ainsworth (Figure 12.5) translated Bowlby's ideas into a 20-minute evaluation of attachment called the **Strange Situation Test**. The procedure involves observing the infant, caregiver, and a friendly but unfamiliar adult in a series of eight semistructured episodes in a laboratory playroom. The crux of the procedure is a standard sequence of separations and reunions between the infant and each of the two adults. Over the course of the eight episodes, the child experiences increasing distress and a greater need for caregiver proximity. The extent to which children cope with these needs and the strategies they use to do so are considered to indicate the quality of attachment. During these events, the child is observed through a one-way mirror, and actions such as crying, playing, level of activity, and attention to the mother and stranger are recorded. Using the Strange Situation Test, Ainsworth originally identified three types of child attachment:

Secure attachment describes the majority of children (approximately 65 percent). A secure child is happy to play alone and is friendly to the stranger while the attachment figure is present. When the attachment figure leaves, the child is distressed, whines or cries, and shows signs of looking for the attachment figure. When the attachment figure returns, the child is happy and quickly comforted (Figure 12.6), often wanting to be held or hugged. The child then returns to playing.

12.5 (a) Mary Ainsworth and (b) John Bowlby. These developmental researchers' studies of the bond between children and their caregivers set the groundwork for decades of systematic research in the area of attachment.

(a)

(b)

Avoidant attachment describes approximately 20–25 percent of children. Avoidant children do not appear distressed or upset by the attachment figure's departure. If upset, many of them can be comforted by the stranger. When the attachment figure returns, the child does not want a reunion but rather ignores or snubs the attachment figure. If the child approaches the attachment figure, it is often in a tentative manner.

Anxious-ambivalent attachment describes approximately 10–15 percent of a given sample. A child with an anxious-ambivalent style is anxious throughout the test. The child clings to the attachment figure after first entering the room; when the attachment figure leaves, the child becomes inconsolably upset. When the attachment figure returns, the child will both elicit and reject caring contact; for instance, the child may want to be held but then fight to be released.

Other researchers have identified variants on these attachment styles. For instance, some children show inconsistent or contradictory behaviors, such as smiling when seeing the caregiver but then displaying fear or avoidance. These children have been described as having *disorganized attachment* (Main & Solomon, 1986).

Researchers examining the role of the child's personality or temperament in determining attachment style have found that children with behavioral problems, such as those who rarely smile, who are disruptive, or who are generally fussy, are more likely to be insecurely attached (that is, anxious-ambivalent or avoidant). The caregiver's personality also contributes to the child's attachment style. Caregivers who are emotionally or behaviorally inconsistent tend to have children with an anxious-ambivalent attachment style, whereas those who are rejecting tend to have children with an avoidant attachment style. The influence of caregiving on attachment style is considered in greater detail in "Using Psychological Science: Maternal Care Versus Day Care."

ATTACHMENT HAS A CHEMICAL BASIS

Scientists have recently discovered that the hormone oxytocin is related to affiliative behaviors, including infant-caregiver attachment. **Oxytocin** plays a role in maternal tendencies, feelings of social acceptance and bonding, and sexual grati-

12.6 Scenes from the Strange Situation Test. In (a), the caregiver engages in solitary activity while the child plays. In (b), the child is crying and distressed because the caregiver has left. In (c), the child touches and clings to the caregiver after her return.

separation anxiety The distress and anxiety displayed by infants when separated from their primary attachment figure.

Strange Situation Test A test of infant-caregiver attachment that involves observing how infants respond to separation from their caregivers.

oxytocin A hormone that plays a role in maternal behavior and infant-caregiver attachment.

fication. In maternal behaviors, oxytocin affects both the mother and the infant. Oxytocin promotes maternal behaviors that seek to ensure the survival of the young. For instance, in both animal and human studies, the release of oxytocin during infant suckling leads to biological processes that pump milk from the breast so the infant can nurse. Oxytocin also facilitates infant attachment to the mother. Research using rat pups that have been separated from their mothers and later reunited with them has found that pups who formed an association between a specific odor and maternal reunion show a preference for that smell. However, the odor is not preferred among pups that have been given an oxytocin inhibitor, indicating that oxytocin is integral to attachment associations.

There is also evidence that oxytocin strengthens social memories. In a recent study, researchers found that male mice mutant for the oxytocin gene (meaning that they were unable to produce oxytocin) failed to form normal social memories (Ferguson et al., 2000). The researchers repeatedly paired normal and oxytocin-lacking male mice with the same ovariectomized mouse, a female that cannot reproduce, which is a state that can be detected by male mice through olfactory cues. In mice with normal oxytocin genes, repeated pairings led to decreased time spent exploring the female, evidence that those mice "remembered" her ovariectomized state. Oxytocin-lacking mice, however, showed the same level of interest in the female over all pairings. Further tests established that these mice were not deficient in olfactory detection. The researchers concluded that the lack of oxytocin rendered the mice "socially amnesic."

Using Psychological Science

MATERNAL CARE VERSUS DAY CARE

Not long ago, the word "mother" brought to mind a woman who had one or more children and whose role was to stay at home to raise them. Not anymore. Mothers are working outside the home more than ever before; researchers estimated that by 1995, 66 percent of preschool children and 75 percent of elementary school children would have mothers working outside the home. Frequently, both parents working outside the home means that the children must attend day care, which led researchers and laypeople alike to question whether there are negative consequences of nonmaternal care.

To answer the question of whether children are affected by day care, researchers used a technique called meta-analysis to examine the overall effects of day care versus maternal care across 59 studies (Erel et al., 2000). The quantitative review of the data revealed no significant differences between children attending day care and those not attending day care. More specific analyses revealed some findings that qualified the overall effect. For instance, the researchers found that studies published more recently were more likely to find that day care is associated with higher rates of secure attachment. This finding may reflect changes over time in the types of families who use day care. Perhaps an increased emphasis on "quality" time improved children's attachment style during the limited time they are with their parents. Or perhaps rising standards for day care centers over the years have had positive effects on attachment style.

This study also found that the older the child is at entry into day care, the more likely it is that the child will show an insecure attachment. This finding suggests that there may be a window of time before the child has fully attached to the parents, in which it is less disruptive to start day care. If the child starts day care after two and a half years old, when the child's attachment behaviors are well established, this separation may be more traumatic and require more adjustment.

In sum, there is no overall difference between day care and maternal care on a variety of development outcomes, although there is evidence of a limited detrimental effect of day care on attachment style if day care is initiated after 30 months of age. Mothers and fathers may rest easier knowing that the combined results of almost 60 studies on day care reveal no ill effects on child development.

What Is Attachment?

Harlow's studies demonstrated that the need for comfort is vitally important to an infant's development, even more so than the need for nourishment. The type of bond between a caregiver and a child is known as attachment. Research by Ainsworth provided a method of testing qualitatively different mother-child bonds and described differences among attachment styles. The biological basis of attachment involves oxytocin. Oxytocin research connects neural responses to behavior and also relates findings from animal and human studies.

WHO INFLUENCES SOCIAL DEVELOPMENT?

How important are the behaviors of caregivers in determining the well-being of children? Most parents believe that their actions have a significant effect on how their children turn out, and indeed, you can imagine how your parents would react if they were told nothing that they did had much influence on you. What might you be like if you had been raised by different people? This section considers the evidence for how caregivers influence social development.

Outside of the family, peers and friends form the majority of children's interactions. In cultures all over the world and across historical periods, children's lives are filled with other children. Regardless of context, most children spend their time together playing. Play exists in numerous forms and helps children learn and practice skills that will be valuable in adulthood. Developmentally, attention to peers begins at the end of the first year of life, when infants begin to imitate other children and to smile and make vocalizations and other specific social signals to their peers (Brownell & Brown, 1992). Children of all ages learn how to behave from their friends, in part because they receive social rewards or punishments for behaving appropriately or inappropriately. Thus, early friends are both playmates and teachers. This section reviews what is known about the social influences in the developing child's environment, focusing on the importance of parents, the nature of friendship at differing ages, the effects of being "popular" or "rejected" among one's peers, and gender-related factors.

IMPORTANCE OF PARENTAL STYLE DEPENDS ON INFANT TEMPERAMENT

One of the first major studies of the importance of the child-parent interaction is the New York Longitudinal Study started in 1956 by pediatric psychiatrists Stella Chess and Alexander Thomas. The study continued over a six-year time span, assessing 141 children from 85 middle- to upper-middle-class families. Thomas and Chess focused on children's biologically based temperament as the most important aspect of the parent-child interaction (see Chess & Thomas, 1984). *Temperament* can be characterized as the *how* of behavior, the way in which it is expressed, separate from the content of or the motivation for the behavior. Thus, the frequency of fussiness is not necessarily a signal of a child's temperament type; instead, the intensity of the fussiness and how easily it can be controlled are better indicators (the concept of temperament is explored more fully in Chapter 15).

parallel play The type of play characteristic of two year olds, usually limited to sitting side-by-side and playing independently.

Chess and Thomas found that the "fit" between the child's temperament and the parents' behaviors is most important in determining social development. For instance, consider *difficult children*, who tend to have negative moods and difficulty adapting to new situations. Most parents find it frustrating to raise these types of children. Parents who openly demonstrate their frustration or insist on exposing the child to conflict are often met with negative behavioral outcomes. For example, if the child is unsure about entering a new setting, pushing or forcing the child can lead to behavioral problems. If the child is very distractible, forcing the child to concentrate for long periods of time may lead to emotional upset. In the study, parents of difficult children who responded in a calm, firm, patient, and consistent style tended to have the most positive outcomes. These parents did not engage in a lot of self-blame for their children's negative behaviors, and they managed to cope with their own negative feelings. Chess and Thomas also noted that overprotective parents can encourage a child's anxiety in response to a new situation, thereby escalating the child's distress. Ultimately, then, the best method of parenting takes into account the parent's own personality, the child's temperament, and the situation; thus, it is a dynamic style that emphasizes flexibility.

FRIENDSHIPS CHANGE WITH AGE

There are differences in what makes someone "a friend" at different stages of development. Children's first rudimentary friendships develop before age two, but friendship at this age is usually limited to **parallel play**, sitting side-by-side and playing independently. Around age three, interactive friendships emerge that are mainly characterized by physical proximity and shared activities. For example, if you ask a child if Tim is her friend, the child may say, "Yes because we just played with the truck." At late preschool age, children begin to engage in sharing and reciprocity and to show commitment to their friends, tending to stay friends unless one of them moves away (Collins & Gunnar, 1990). Similarity appears to engender friendship, as friends are more similar in gender, appearance, age, attitudes, size, physical maturity, academics, and intelligence than are nonfriends (Kupersmidt et al., 1995).

John Gottman (1983) has carefully studied the process by which young children become friends. He had pairs of children, between the ages of three and nine, meet for the first time and play together. The play sessions were recorded, and Gottman compared the interactions of those who became friends with those who did not. There were five factors that emerged as being essential to the formation of friendship:

1. *Common-ground activity*. The children who became friends were those who quickly found something they could do together. In addition, they explored their similarities and differences.

2. *Clear communication*. Children who became friends were less likely to engage in what Jean Piaget termed "collective monologues"—a type of speech that occurs when children are playing near each other and speaking, but not directing their speech at any individual. Children who became friends listened to each other, requested clarification when they did not understand, and spoke in ways that were relevant to the task at hand.

3. *Exchange of information*. Children who became friends both asked for and provided information relevant to their partners.

4. *Resolution of conflicts*. Children who became friends gave good reasons when they disagreed and were able to bring conflicts to a quick resolution.

5. *Reciprocity*. Children who became friends were likely to respond to their partner's positive behaviors with appropriate positive contributions of their own. Videotapes of pairs of sixth-grade friends and acquaintances found that friends were more attentive, emotionally positive, vocal, active, involved, relaxed, and playful with each other. They were also more likely to share the same mood than were acquaintances.

Around puberty, adolescents begin confiding their fears and secrets to friends, and as a result they become especially vulnerable to being hurt. Adolescents are also more concerned with shared preferences and attitudes than with similarity in basic properties, such as attractiveness. An interesting extension of how friendship changes at adolescence can be seen in "Studying the Mind: Why Do Adolescents Socialize So Much and Take So Many Risks?"

PARENTS AND PEERS ARE BOTH IMPORTANT

A controversial topic in the area of developmental psychology is the importance of peers versus parents. People often describe individuals as "coming from a good home" or as having "fallen in with the wrong crowd"; these clichés reflect the

Studying the Mind

WHY DO ADOLESCENTS SOCIALIZE SO MUCH AND TAKE SO MANY RISKS?

When children become adolescents, they start rejecting parental involvement and begin spending most of their social time with friends. Moreover, adolescence is also a time of risk-taking. This occurs worldwide and is even seen among a variety of animals, such as rats. Why is this pattern so common? Are the two behaviors related? A recent review of animal and human studies concerning the behavioral patterns of adolescents led Linda Patia Spear (2000) to propose that increased sociability with peers and heightened risk-taking are two different consequences of one set of changes. She posits that neurological development at this period is responsible for these behaviors and, further, that both the behavioral and neurological changes are evolutionarily based. According to this model, risky behaviors allow the adolescent to acquire skills necessary for surviving in adulthood, and increased sociability far from home prevents inbreeding.

Adolescents engage in risky behaviors, such as drug use, at a higher rate than other age groups. Importantly, Spear does not consider adolescents to be merely acting out against authority or being risky because of peer pressure. Rather, she believes that risk-taking behaviors occur in response to increased stress, sensitivity to which also changes during adolescence. Stressors have greater effects—both psychologically and physiologically—in adolescents than they do in adults or children. An example of the psychological effects of stress can be seen in the relative greater incidence of depression among adolescents (Petersen et al., 1993).

Researchers claim that a modest amount of riskiness in adolescents is "developmentally appropriate experimentation" (Shedler & Block, 1990), and note that teens who engage in a moderate amount of risk-taking have been shown to have better social skills than their peers who engage in little or excessive amounts of risk. Thus, riskiness and sociability during adolescence aren't behaviors that are performed solely to irritate one's parents or to rebel against society. Rather, these are changes that mark normal development.

Are parents or peers more important for a child's social development?

group socialization theory The idea that children are socialized by their peers.

clique A small group that serves as the primary peer group.

crowds Large groups of people who may or may not spend a lot of time together but who share a common social identity.

sociometric analysis A method for assessing the social hierarchy among members of groups.

importance that is placed on both parents and peers when it comes to influencing an individual. In 1995, Judith Rich Harris suggested that beyond choosing where to live and to what schools to send their children, parents contribute little to a child's social development. Harris reviewed a number of psychological studies and concluded that parents have "no important long-term effects on the development of their child's personality" (p. 458). Further, she posited that a child's peers are the most important influence when it comes to socialization. Harris's work is based largely on her **group socialization theory**, in which children learn two sets of behaviors, one for inside the home and one for outside. The behaviors and responses learned inside the home, such as those typically taught by the parents early in life, are not useful to the child in outside social contexts. According to Harris, only those behaviors learned outside the home have long-term effects on personality and adult behavioral outcomes. While this theoretical stance has received a great deal of criticism, it stimulated a fresh look at the social lives of children and the importance of their peers.

In contrast to Harris's theory, there has been a substantial amount of research that has affirmed the influence of parents throughout the individual's life. Significantly, researchers have emphasized that neither the peer group nor the family can be assigned the primary role in this process. Instead, the two social contexts play complementary roles. B. Bradford Brown and his colleagues (1993) argue that the influence of parents is actually multifaceted. Parents not only contribute to specific individual behaviors but also affect social development indirectly by influencing the choices the child makes about what kind of crowd to join. In observations of 695 young people from childhood through adolescence, Robert and Beverly Cairns (1994) found that parents and teachers played a major role in realigning social groups so that they were consistent with family norms.

In the actual mechanics of peer influence, friendships, defined as a group of two, are the smallest unit of interaction. In many Western countries, as children move into adolescence, cliques and crowds, both more expansive social groupings, become central fixtures in the social world. A **clique** is a group that remains small enough to enable the members to be in regular interaction with one another and to serve as the primary peer group (Brown, 1990). Cliques consist of the people adolescents interact with on a regular basis. Dexter Dunphy (1963) has remarked that cliques are about the size of a two-child family with the grandparents present. "Their similarity in size to a family," Dunphy wrote, "facilitated the transference of the individual's allegiance to them and allows them to provide an alternative center of security" (p. 233).

Although cliques are like families in size, they have one very important difference. Cliques are voluntary groups that adolescents are free to leave. The fact that adolescents actively choose clique membership reflects the increased autonomy with which adolescents make decisions about their social settings, their friends and acquaintances, and their activities.

As children enter high school, cliques often become part of a larger social unit, called a crowd. **Crowds** are larger groupings of people, organized by social persona, who may or may not spend a great deal of time together. Brown (1990) describes crowds as "reputation-based collectives" of people who are similarly stereotyped by their peers. The interests, activities, abilities, and attitudes that their members have in common are most often the factors that differentiate crowds. Interestingly, despite wide differences in geographic regions, crowds tend to be described by a fairly small set of stereotypic names: jocks, brains, loners, druggies, nerds, and other not-so-flattering designations.

CHILDHOOD REJECTION IS ASSOCIATED WITH NEGATIVE CONSEQUENCES

Years and even decades after finishing school, adults can usually remember where they fit into the social hierarchy. Today researchers measure social hierarchies in the classroom using a technique called **sociometric analysis**, in which children select the classmates they most like or dislike. From these nominations, researchers classify children into four categories: 1) *popular* children are those who get many "like" nominations and few "dislike" nominations; 2) *rejected* children get many "dislike" nominations and few "like" nominations; 3) *neglected* children get few votes at all; and 4) *controversial* children get many "like" and "dislike" nominations.

Research on consequences and correlates of early sociometric status has emphasized rejected children. During childhood, these children tend to be withdrawn, disobedient, and aggressive, even in the absence of provocation, and they tend to have difficulties in schoolwork. They make lower grades, score lower on tests, and are inattentive in school (Newcomb et al., 1993). Even among their friends they show low levels of interaction, which may result from their disruptive behaviors upon entering a social group. Higher levels of anxiety and depression have been directly related to being rejected. High levels of depression also have been associated with rejection by roommates among college students (Joiner & Metalsky, 1995). Theorists believe that rejected children are sometimes caught in a negative spiral of inappropriate behaviors leading to rejection and rejection prompting further inappropriate behaviors (Hodges & Perry, 1999). Because peer rejection has been identified as a possible cause of school violence, a number of researchers are currently examining whether social-skills training will forestall negative outcomes. Although some evidence suggests that these programs are useful, they have obtained limited success in changing the sociometric ratings given by classmates.

GENDER DIFFERENCES EXIST IN ADULT FRIENDSHIPS

From childhood through adulthood, men's and women's friendships differ. This is especially true during adolescence, when girls and boys are at different developmental stages. Girls mature earlier than boys, which may be why they express more sensitivity and subtlety when describing others and are more likely to talk about their feelings. Early maturity plus a more interpersonal orientation may be one reason why women are more likely, in general, to express and desire intimacy in their relationships.

Intimacy is an area in which men's and women's friendships differ greatly. Women tend to reveal more personal information to both their same-sex friends and their opposite-sex romantic partners than do men (Dindia & Allen, 1992). When a man does disclose personal information, the recipient is very likely a woman; men are not likely to disclose to other men. The differences in self-disclosure mirror differences in activities that friends share. Typically, women's same-sex friendships revolve around conversation and discussing personal issues, whereas men's involve participation in sports or other games. A role-playing study of men and women talking with their friends found that women expressed twice as many feelings as men and were more likely to ask about a friend's feelings (almost 40 percent of women inquired about the friend's feelings, whereas none of the men did). Men talked about private issues, such as the

RESEARCH QUESTION

How does a person's gender or age affect his or her friendships?

effects of a romantic breakup, by generally avoiding a personal discussion, whereas women were more open about their true feelings (Caldwell & Pepau, 1982).

On the whole, women spend more time with their friends than do men, although both sexes report an equivalent number of friends (Wright, 1999). This finding may be explained by the fact that women tend to spend time with their friends in pairs, whereas men tend to spend time with their friends in groups (see Eder & Hallinan, 1978). Another dimension on which same-sex friendships differ is physical contact. Same-sex female friends touch most often, cross-sex friends touch less often, and male friends avoid physical contact, except for that which occurs during athletic activity (Val Derlega et al., 1989). Thus, the same-sex friendships of men and women vary in numerous ways, perhaps because each type of relationship has different needs and, hence, requires different responses to satisfy an individual's need to belong.

CROSS-SEX FRIENDSHIPS CAN BE DIFFICULT

After preschool, during which time boys and girls often engage in parallel play together, boys and girls overwhelmingly prefer same-sex friends. Studies have found that at 6 years of age, 68 percent of children report a same-sex "best friend," and by 12 years of age this number swells to 90 percent (Daniels-Beirness, 1989). Even after maturity, women and men tend to have a greater number of same-sex friends. Donald O'Meara (1989) has studied the dynamics and difficulties of cross-sex friendships and has determined that they are associated with a number of unique challenges, such as how to define the emotional bond. The friends must strike a balance between the norms of women's friendships, in which intimacy is valued, and the norms of men's friendships, in which intimacy is discouraged and shared activities are valued.

There are positive aspects to cross-sex friendships. The few studies conducted have found that cross-sex friendships provide a vehicle for self-expression, companionship, and intimacy (Monsour, 1992) and that cross-sex friends provide each other with validation as attractive members of the opposite sex. Unfortunately, there are also possible drawbacks to cross-sex friendships, the forerunner being the potential for sexual attraction (among heterosexual cross-sex friends). Most cross-sex friends maintain a purely platonic relationship; some, however, engage in a variety of sexual activities, though doing so often makes it difficult to maintain just a friendship. A substantial number of cross-sex friendships end because of failed attempts at romance (Werking, 1994).

In a study conducted by Bleske-Rechek and Buss (2000), men and women were asked about the benefits and costs of their cross-sex friendships. Perceptions varied by gender. For men, a major benefit was having sex or the potential of having sex with their friend. Women were more varied. Some women reported as a benefit feeling protected by their male friends, while others cited long- and short-term mate potential. Both genders agreed that becoming more informed about how to attract potential mates was a significant benefit to having a cross-sex friend. The researchers also found that there were many commonalities between same-sex and cross-sex friendships. For instance, both men and women reported initiating cross-sex friendships because they provide companionship, good times, conversation, and laughter. As with same-sex friendships, both men and women prefer cross-sex friends who are honest, intelligent, sensitive, funny, and dependable.

Who Influences Social Development?

Parents can have both a positive and a negative influence on their children. The unique interaction between the caregiver and child is crucial when considering the importance of the caregiver to the child's development. Peers are also a major influence during development. Early friends are both playmates and teachers because playing encourages the development of many important social skills. Characteristics of children's friendships change with the age of the child, with younger children focusing on exchange and older children emphasizing emotional ties. Men's and women's same-sex friendships differ mainly because of differential emphasis on shared activities versus disclosure, respectively. These differences in self-disclosure among same-sex friends are also reflected in cross-sex friendships.

HOW DOES MORAL BEHAVIOR DEVELOP?

Morality is an important component of social development because it involves choices people make that affect the lives of others, such as whether to take actions that may result in harm to another or that may break implicit or explicit social contracts. Thus, **moral development** concerns the way in which people learn to decide between behaviors with competing social outcomes.

Typically, morality has been divided into *moral reasoning*, which rests on cognitive processes, and *moral emotions*. Of course, cognition and affect are intertwined: research has shown that if people lack adequate cognitive abilities, their moral emotions may not translate into moral behaviors; similarly, moral reasoning is enhanced by moral emotions. This section reviews the development of the cognitive and affective components of morality.

How do children learn social rules and develop morals?

MORAL REASONING FOLLOWS STAGES

Psychologists who study the cognitive processes of moral behavior have focused largely on Lawrence Kohlberg's stage theory. Kohlberg (1927–1987) tested moral reasoning skills by asking people to respond to hypothetical situations in which a main character is faced with a moral dilemma. Kohlberg's most famous example (see Kohlberg, 1984) is a story about a man named Heinz and a local druggist:

> In Europe a woman was near death from a special kind of cancer. There was one drug that the doctors thought might save her. It was a form of radium that a druggist in the same town had recently discovered. The drug was expensive to make, but the druggist was charging ten times what the drug cost him to make. He paid $200 for the radium and charged $2,000 for a small dose of the drug. The sick woman's husband, Heinz, went to everyone he knew to borrow the money, but he could only get together about $1,000, which is half of what it cost. He told the druggist that his wife was dying and asked him to sell it cheaper or let him pay later. But the druggist said, "No, I discovered the drug and I'm going to make money from it." So Heinz got desperate and broke into the man's store to steal the drug for his wife. Should the husband have done that?

Kohlberg was not concerned with the "yes" or "no" answer that the person gave, but rather the reasons for the answer. Kohlberg devised a theory of moral judgment that involved three levels of moral reasoning, with two stages within

moral development Concerns the way in which people decide between behaviors with competing social outcomes.

preconventional level Moral reasoning that is based on personal benefits, self-interest, or hedonistic advantages.

conventional level The stage of moral reasoning that reflects conformity to rules of law and order that are learned from others.

postconventional level The highest level of moral reasoning, reflects complex reasoning skills that take into account abstract principles and values.

each level. The level and stage are determined by the participant's thoughts about why Heinz should or should not have broken into the drugstore.

Kohlberg classified answers pertaining to self-interest or hedonistic advantages at the **preconventional level**. For example, a child at this level may say, "Heinz should steal the drug if he really likes his wife." He classified at the **conventional level** responses that conform to rules of law and order or focus on others' disapproval, such as "He shouldn't take the drug because it is wrong to steal, so everyone will think he is a bad person." **Postconventional level** responses center around complex reasoning about abstract principles and values, such as "Sometimes people have to break the law if the law is unjust."

Kohlberg's theory and subsequent empirical data (Colby et al., 1983) indicate that people advance through the levels and stages of moral reasoning with age. That is, children tend to score at Stages 1 and 2 of the preconventional level, whereas most 13-year-olds will score at least at Stage 1 of the conventional level. However, not all people progress through all the stages, and some stages are associated with specific life outcomes. For instance, researchers have found that juvenile delinquents typically are still within the preconventional level characterized by motivation to obtain individual rewards (Trevethan & Walker, 1989). In addition, very few adults achieve Kohlberg's final level, postconventional (Kurtines & Gewirtz, 1991).

There have been a number of challenges to Kohlberg. The best known came from Carol Gilligan (1982), who criticized his theory as valuing men's moral orientations over women's. Gilligan was motivated by early studies showing that adult women were mainly "stuck" at Kohlberg's first stage of the conventional level, which focuses on gaining approval from others. Gilligan proposed that there were two types of high-level reasoning: one that involved justice (as in Kohlberg's theory) and another that involved relationships. Gilligan's theory has received mixed support, with some studies showing that women around the world are more interpersonally focused than are men, and other studies showing that there is no difference in stages achieved as a function of gender (see Wark & Krebs, 1996). Moreover, there are more general criticisms of stage theories—some research indicates that moral reasoning is fluid and that responses to real-life moral dilemmas cannot be categorized by stage (Krebs et al., 1991).

Moral reasoning theories have been faulted for emphasizing the cognitive aspects of morality. Some theorists contend that moral reasoning, as such, fails to predict moral behavior. These psychological scientists believe that moral actions, such as helping others in need, are influenced more by emotions than by cognitive processes.

MORAL EMOTIONS EMERGE EARLY IN LIFE

Research on the emotional components of moral behavior has focused largely on empathy, sympathy, guilt, and shame. These are called moral emotions because they relate to moral *behaviors* (as opposed to the cognitive processes that predict moral *reasoning*). Along with embarrassment, they are considered "self-conscious" emotions, because they require comprehension of the self as a causal agent and an evaluation of one's own responses. Moral emotions form early in life, though they emerge later than primary emotions (such as happiness or anger), which is why they are also called secondary emotions.

Developmental psychologists differentiate between empathy and sympathy. *Empathy* is an emotional state that arises from understanding another's emotional state in a manner similar to what the other person is feeling or would be expected to feel in a given situation. In contrast, *sympathy* arises from feelings of concern, pity, or sorrow for another (Eisenberg, 2000). When someone feels empathy, they feel *with* the other person, whereas when someone feels sympathy, they feel *for* the other person. Similarly, a distinction is made between guilt and shame. *Guilt* is an emotional state involving negative feelings about a specific event or action, whereas *shame* involves negative feelings about the entire self and one's identity. Guilt and shame differ on numerous dimensions, including degree of distress and the feelings associated with each emotion.

Role of cognitive development   Some researchers contend that the fundamental components of empathy are present at birth. Hoffman (1998) has shown that infants as young as one day old respond to another infant's cries with distress that is intense, powerful, and indistinguishable (physiologically and, from what researchers can tell, psychologically) from responses emitted under true distress—a response called *empathetic distress*. However, most psychological scientists believe that moral emotions require cognitive development, such as the recognition that behaviors are chosen (Kagan, 1984), which occurs around age four.

Prosocial behavior   Moral emotions are associated with moral behaviors, which have been studied by examining *prosocial* responses—such as being helpful or taking reparative actions. Psychologist Nancy Eisenberg has conducted extensive investigations of children's prosocial behaviors and has proposed that they also follow a developmental course. She uses scenarios in her experiments, but the scenarios differ from Kohlberg's in that they describe more realistic dilemmas that young people may encounter. For instance, children choose whether they would alert an injured child's parent or whether they would go to a party; adolescents are asked to weigh the merits of donating a rare type of blood versus the resultant costs to the self (see Eisenberg et al., 1991).

In her studies of actual helping behavior, Eisenberg has found that around age four children show prosocial responses that are hedonistic and self-centered. For instance, by the time toddlers are 18 to 20 months, they commonly respond prosocially to seeing another's distress (by bringing them a teddy bear, for example), but they do not respond prosocially when they have caused another's distress. As they reach grade school, children show responses that are other-oriented, focusing on how the distressed person and others will think of them. These children often want to behave in ways consistent with their ideas of what is stereotypically "good." In adolescence, prosocial responses have matured to the point where they are internally generated and include taking another's perspective and being mindful of social responsibility. Eisenberg's research has shown that the type of prosocial reasoning predicts the type and degree of prosocial behavior (Eisenberg et al., 1995).

PARENTAL PRACTICES RELATE TO CHILDREN'S PROSOCIAL BEHAVIOR

Recent research has asked whether parents' behaviors influence their children's level of moral emotions or prosocial behavior. Parents of sympathetic children tend to be high in sympathy themselves, to allow their children to express negative emotions in a manner that does not harm others, to not express hostility in the home, to help their children cope with negative emotions, and to promote an understanding of and focus on others. By contrast, parents whose children were high in shame tended to show frequent anger, to be lax in discipline, and to not respond positively to appropriate behavior in the child (Ferguson & Stegge, 1995).

The interaction between the child and the parents is important in the development of moral emotions. Research has shown the value of reasoning with the child about his or her behavior, which involves *inductive reasoning*, as exemplified by the statements, "You made Chris cry. It's not nice to hit." Inductive reasoning on the part of the parents promotes sympathetic attitudes, feelings of guilt, and an awareness of others' feelings. One study reported that when mothers of four-year-olds commented on emotions and intentions ("you didn't mean to hurt him"), and made evaluative statements ("you were good to do that for her"), their children were more likely to show appropriate forms of guilt and regret after misbehavior (Laible & Thompson, cited in Eisenberg, 2000). Attachment styles, too, have been linked to the presence of moral emotions. A secure attachment style between the mother and child has been shown to promote appropriate guilt, empathy, and sympathy.

Sociologist Samuel Oliner describes being 12 years old in Nazi-occupied Poland and having to flee his village because he was a Jew. Oliner escaped to a nearby village where his father's friend, Balwina Piecuch, who was not Jewish, took him in. The Piecuchs gave him food, clothing, and shelter and taught him to pass for a non-Jew. They did these kind acts despite their knowledge that if Oliner were found in their house, all of them would be killed. Later, as an adult living in California, Oliner and his wife, Pearl, studied over 400 rescuers of Jews during World War II (Oliner & Oliner, 1988) to examine their personalities. The Oliners noted that the rescuers' prosocial behaviors were perhaps the result of their parents' positive prosocial role modeling, as many people said that they learned kindness and generosity from their parents. Thus, parental practices can leave a lifelong impression on a child, which may someday lead to the benefit of many other individuals.

THERE ARE PHYSIOLOGICAL ASPECTS OF MORALITY

Some evidence indicates that moral emotions are based in physiological mechanisms that help people make decisions. Recall from Chapter 10 that Damasio's somatic-marker hypothesis states that people have a visceral response to real or imagined outcomes and that this response aids decision making. Damasio found that patients with damage to the prefrontal cortex fail to become emotionally involved in decision making because their somatic markers are not engaged. Damasio and colleagues (Anderson et al., 1999) recently studied two people who experienced prefrontal damage during infancy. Both of these individuals showed serious deficiencies in moral and social reasoning. When given Kohlberg's moral dilemma task, both patients scored at the preconventional level. These patients also neglected social and emotional factors in their life decisions. Both failed to express empathy, remorse, or guilt for wrongdoing, and neither had particularly good parenting skills. One engaged in petty thievery, was verbally and physically threatening (once to the point of physical assault), and frequently lied for no obvious reason.

In contrast to these two patients, people who experience frontal lobe injuries as adults score in the normal adult range on the Kohlberg task. Thus, there may be a critical time during brain development for the acquisition of moral and social knowledge. Some researchers believe that it is the *experience* of emotions produced by rewards and punishments that establishes moral behaviors, and that those with prefrontal damage in early childhood do not develop these learned associations.

A team of social psychologists applied Damasio's theory to see if people use information about their physiological state when making value judgments. In this study, participants listened to two stories, one about justice and the other about equality. In the stories, these values were threatened or violated (for example, participants heard about a law proposing that police could stop any driver younger than 30 without cause [a freedom violation] and a case of clear racial bias in management practices of several companies [an equity violation]). Participants were given false feedback about their physiological arousal during the two stories. The researchers found that although participants drew upon their preconceived ideas about the importance of each value, their judgments were also influenced by the false arousal feedback. That is, people who were told they became more aroused during the equity violation story than during the freedom story later rated equity as more important than freedom. This study shows that moral decisions can be the result of both cognitive and emotional components. Further, these results are consistent with the suggestion that moral emotions involve physiological components (Batson et al., 1999).

In keeping with the biological revolution in psychological science, researchers have begun to examine the regions that are active in people's brains when they are engaged in moral decision making. Joshua Greene and his colleagues at Princeton University collected fMRI data while subjects were making moral decisions. The study focused on a classic set of problems that have fascinated moral philosophers for years because of the difficulty in identifying moral principles that agree with the way people react. One dilemma, known as the trolley problem, involves a runaway train that is about to kill five people. The question is whether it is appropriate for a bystander to throw a switch to divert the trolley onto a spur on which it will kill one person and allow the five to survive. Philosophers compare this problem to a second scenario, sometimes called the footbridge problem, in which a train is again heading toward five people, but there is no spur. Two bystanders are on a bridge above the tracks, and the only way to save the five people is for one bystander to push the other in front of the train.

Both cases involve killing one person to save five, but they evoke very different responses. People tend to agree that it is permissible to flip the switch, but it is not permissible to push a person off the bridge. This decision has puzzled philosophers, who have not been able to find a hard and fast rule to explain why one is right and the other is wrong. For each potential principle, there seems to be another scenario that undermines it. The researchers believe that one reason for the different responses is that the two scenarios engage different psychological processes, with different levels of emotionality, that rely on different parts of the brain. Envisioning flipping a switch and envisioning pushing a human being to his or her death elicit very different levels of emotion, patterns that were observed in the brain activation of the study subjects (see Figure 12.7). The researchers emphasized that there is

12.7 Brain activation during the trolley and footbridge dilemmas. Areas of the brain known to be associated with emotion were significantly more active during personal moral dilemmas than impersonal moral dilemmas, or nonmoral decisions (top). The brain scans show the location of these activations (bottom).

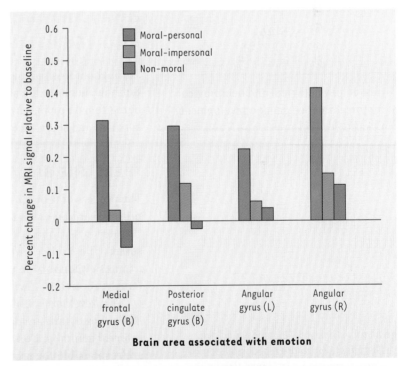

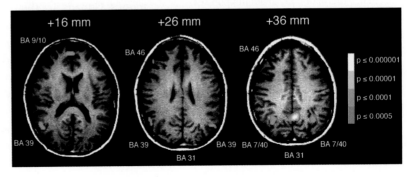

not a single region of the brain exclusively responsible for "moral thought." Instead, it is more likely that in making moral decisions we engage a number of different mental processes, including memory of personally and socially relevant standards or previous experience with similar situations, and abstract thinking in terms of predicting how we might emotionally respond to the outcome of the decision.

How Does Moral Behavior Develop?

Moral development comprises cognitive and emotional components. The cognitive component is known as moral reasoning and was studied by Kohlberg, who used hypothetical scenarios to establish how people think about moral dilemmas. Kohlberg's theory has been criticized for being rigid and gender-biased. The other component of morality, emotions, includes feelings of sympathy, empathy, guilt, and shame. Empathy appears to be the first moral emotion to emerge, while the others develop within the first several years of life. Moral emotions and decisions appear to have a neurological component, as evidenced by studies that have tested the somatic-marker hypothesis.

How do physiological and neurological factors influence gender development?

WHAT INFLUENCES GENDER DEVELOPMENT AND IDENTITY?

Throughout this book we have discussed differences between males and females. But how much do the sexes really differ? How do we develop our conceptions of being female or male? This section addresses the biological, neurological, personality, and social factors that influence gender development.

THERE ARE BIOLOGICAL SEX DIFFERENCES

The process of reproduction begins with approximately 300 million sperm swimming toward an ovum that has been released by the woman's ovary. Recall from Chapter 3 that one's status as a male or female is determined by sex chromosomes. The mother always contributes an X chromosome whereas the father contributes either an X or a Y. Receiving an X from the father will make the offspring female, receiving a Y will make the offspring male.

The development of sex organs is the primary way in which men and women differ. Sex organs are divided into three classes: gonads, internal sex organs, and external genitalia. **Gonads** are the testes (in males) and ovaries (in females) that are responsible for producing sperm or ova, respectively, and for secreting hormones. Gonads are the first sex organs to develop; through the first four weeks of development, the gonads of all fetuses are identical and undifferentiated. The presence or absence of the Y chromosome determines sex, because it activates an enzyme that turns the undifferentiated gonads into testes. The *internal sex organs* are bisexual—they contain elements of both male and female sex organs—until the third month of pregnancy. At this time, the precursor of the female sex organs is called the *Müllerian system* and the precursor of the male sex organs is called the *Wolffian system*. In the absence of androgen, a male sex hormone, the Müllerian system develops. Thus, female internal sex organs are the "default" system because they do not require androgen to develop (Figure 12.8).

gonads The testes (in males) and ovaries (in females), which are responsible for producing sperm or ova, depending on sex, and for secreting hormones.

gender A term that refers to the culturally constructed differences between males and females.

gender roles The characteristics associated with men and women because of cultural influence or learning.

The *external sex organs* are the visible genitalia, including the penis and scrotum in males and the labia, clitoris, and outer vagina in females. Female genitalia do not need additional hormones to develop. Male genitalia, in contrast, require androgen to develop. An interesting condition known as *androgen insensitivity syndrome* occurs when the receptors for androgen fail to function. Thus, in spite of the genes being male, the body develops as if it were female. This has led to shocking discoveries by some women that the reason for their infertility is that they are biologically men. Note, however, that this was not the case for David Reimer, whom we met in the opening vignette. David was exposed to androgens while in the womb and therefore would have naturally developed as a male. Feminizing hormones can be used to develop breasts in a male, but they do not change his sex. Although for many years it was believed that socialization was the major determinant of whether one's *gender identity* was male or female, current evidence suggests that gender identity and development is a complex combination of biological, social, and cultural influences. The debate on whether homosexuality is biologically or socially based is discussed in "Crossing the Levels of Analysis: The Origins of Homosexuality."

GENDER ROLES ARE DETERMINED BY CULTURAL NORMS

How different are men and women? Although there are obvious physical differences, such as in height and weight, what people really want to know is how women and men differ in psychological terms. Indeed, there are some differences in cognition, with men being more spatially oriented and women being more verbally oriented, and there are also differences in behaviors such as aggression and intimacy that generally conform to stereotypes. But in most ways men and women are pretty similar. According to evolutionary theory, sex differences ought to reflect different adaptive problems faced by men and women, and this is generally supported by research. But since men and women faced similar adaptive problems, for the most part, they are similar on most dimensions.

"Sex" refers to biological differences between males and females. The term **gender** is used for differences between males and females that result from socialization. **Gender roles** are behaviors that differ between men and women because of cultural influence or learning. For instance, you may believe that it is more appropriate for men to initiate sexual encounters or to work on automobiles for a living. Although many people now object to such beliefs, their existence is easy to observe. When young children are asked to draw a picture of a scientist, most draw a man. Children develop their expectations about gender through observing their parents, peers, and teachers, as well as through media. Cultural norms and media have a strong influence on the development of gender roles. Most news

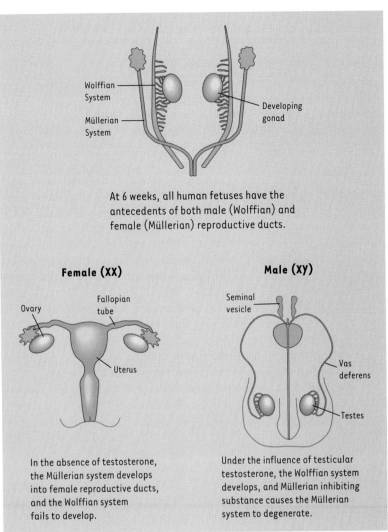

At 6 weeks, all human fetuses have the antecedents of both male (Wolffian) and female (Müllerian) reproductive ducts.

Female (XX)

In the absence of testosterone, the Müllerian system develops into female reproductive ducts, and the Wolffian system fails to develop.

Male (XY)

Under the influence of testicular testosterone, the Wolffian system develops, and Müllerian inhibiting substance causes the Müllerian system to degenerate.

12.8 Early developmental depictions of internal sex organs. At six weeks, the gonads of biological males and females are identical, but soon differentiate. If there is no Y chromosome, the primordial gonad develops into an ovary. Under the influence of the Y chromosome, it develops into a testis. The figure represents the development of the Wolffian and Müllerian reproductive systems. Note that the "default" reproductive system is female.

Crossing the Levels of Analysis

THE ORIGINS OF HOMOSEXUALITY

People have long questioned the origins or causes of homosexuality. Early theories of homosexuality regarded it as deviant, abnormal, and a psychological disorder. Classic psychoanalytic theories emphasized the importance of parenting practices. Families with a domineering mother and a submissive father were thought to cause the children to identify with the opposite-sex parent, which would translate into a sexual attraction toward the gender opposite of their identification—that is, a same-sex attraction. However, the overwhelming majority of studies testing the link between parental personalities, self-identification, and sexual orientation failed to find any relation. Now, most researchers and theorists believe that homosexuality is not under the control of the individual or due to family variables. The most compelling evidence on the origins of homosexuality comes from biological studies and social psychological models.

Twin studies have shown a high similarity in sexual orientation among monozygotic (identical) twins. Studies of homosexuals and family members of varying degrees (such as twins versus siblings) have found a genetic component for both men and women (Hamer, 1993). Finding a genetic basis for a behavior or attitude does not explain what biological variables are responsible for the difference. However, researchers have identified a gene that may determine the development of sexual orientation. In 1993, biologist Dean Hamer announced that he had found a link between a marker on the X chromosome and sexual orientation in males, which was quickly dubbed "the gay gene" by the media. In this study, 33 out of 40 pairs of siblings showed inherited genetic information in this region. It is important to note that Hamer's study used male homosexuals only. Some theorists believe that male sexual orientation is determined more by genetics than is female sexual orientation, which is seen as more influenced by the environment (Baumeister, 2000).

One area in which a more precise biological explanation has been advanced is in investigations of brain structure as related to sexual orientation. In postmortem examinations, neuroscientist Simon LeVay (1991) found that the brains of heterosexual and homosexual men differed. An area of the anterior hypothalamus was only half as large in homosexual men as compared to heterosexual men. In fact, the size of this area in homosexual men was comparable to its size in heterosexual women. This now-famous study was heralded as a scientific breakthrough by some, and heavily criticized by others. The main criticism is that correlation does not equal causation. That is, a size difference in a part of the brain cannot establish whether development of this area *causes* sexual orientation, whether being heterosexual or homosexual *results in* changes to brain structures, or whether a third variable is responsible for both effects. For instance, some researchers believe that the size of the anterior hypothalamus is determined by prenatal exposure to androgens. Level of prenatal androgen is also thought to be a possible mechanism for the established link between homosexual orientation and being left-handed (Lalumiere et al., 2000). Thus, there is currently insufficient evidence for establishing a causal connection between size of brain regions and sexual orientation.

A social psychological theory of sexual orientation by Daryl Bem (1996) posits that feeling different from opposite- or same-sex peers predicts later sexual orientation. Note that Bem's theory begins with the idea that there are biological differences among children that lead to different social experiences. His model, called "the exotic becomes erotic," states that people are attracted to that which is initially different. Many homosexuals report childhood and adolescent feelings of being different from or not fitting in with same-sex peers. During adolescence and early adulthood, "feeling different" is translated into a high state of arousal associated with same-sex peers, which is subsequently eroticized. Thus, what is different becomes what is attractive. Bem's model similarly accounts for heterosexual attraction. It is the interaction of biology and the social environment that determines sexual orientation.

---

anchors are male, most fighter fighters are male, most nurses portrayed in films and television are female, and so on. These portrayals help to develop *gender stereotypes*, which refer to commonly held beliefs about men and women. There are many examples of stereotyping in children's toys (Figure 12.9).

Whether you think of yourself as a man or a woman determines your *gender identity*. Children as young as one or two years old can tell you whether they are a boy or a girl. However, they sometimes have trouble identifying other people's sex because they rely on physical appearance cues, such as clothing style and hair length. For instance, if a young boy wore a dress, a two-year-old might mistakenly think he was a girl. The idea that one's sex stays the same throughout life does not become solidified until age four or five. Once boys and girls discover that they are boys or girls, they seek out activities that are culturally sex-appropriate. In North American culture, parents and teachers discourage girls from playing too roughly and boys from crying. The separation of boys and girls into different playgroups also serves as a powerful socializing force.

Gender schemas are cognitive structures that influence how people perceive the behaviors of men and women. A gender schema acts as a lens through which people see the world. People raised in environments in which there are clear distinctions between men and women become **sex typed**; that is, they believe there are strong differences between males and females. Sandra Bem measures the degree to which people are sex typed by administering a questionnaire that asks people to what extent traits that are typical of men and women describe them. People who rate themselves high on stereotypically masculine traits (e.g., competitiveness) and low on stereotypically feminine traits (e.g., tenderness) are labeled *masculine*, those who rate themselves high on feminine and low on masculine traits are labeled *feminine*, and those who rate themselves equally on both types of traits are **androgynous**. Bem believes that being androgynous is advantageous because it allows for more flexibility in one's social behavior. Conversely, her studies show that being sex typed can be cognitively efficient during tasks that benefit from encoding by gender, such as predicting whether a mechanic is likely to be male or female (Bem, 1975; Bem et al., 1976).

12.9 Many children's toys may promote gender stereotyping.

Situational factors also contribute to gender differences. According to a theory by social psychologists Kay Deaux and Brenda Major (1987), the interaction between people and a specific situation "creates" gender-related behaviors. Deaux and Major incorporate the idea that people have beliefs and expectations about how men and women differ, but they emphasize that people of both sexes act differently depending on the situation. For instance, men may talk about football and cars around their male friends, but they are likely to change the topic when women are around.

A study of young women talking to either their boyfriends or casual male friends on the telephone illustrates how the situation alters gender-related responses. When the women talked to their boyfriends, their voices changed to a higher pitch and became more soft and relaxed, relative to the way they talked to their male friends. The way they spoke to their boyfriends was also more babylike, feminine, and absentminded, as rated by objective judges. When asked, the women said they knew they had taken on a different manner of speaking to their boyfriends relative to their male friends. The women reported doing this in order to communicate affection for their boyfriends (Montepare & Vega, 1988). Likewise, experiments have shown that heterosexual young men behave more masculinely when they think they are talking to a homosexual man versus a heterosexual man (Kite & Deaux, 1986).

THERE ARE STAGES OF IDENTITY DEVELOPMENT

People often look back and think about the various periods of their lives in terms of their identity. For instance, a person might say about their youth, "I was a different person then" or "I really didn't know who I was during those times." These statements reflect the idea that identity is a dynamic construct. Psychologist Erik

gender schemas Cognitive structures that influence how people perceive the behaviors of men and women.

sex-typed To have the view that there are clear distinctions between males and females, which usually fall along the lines of perceived gender differences.

androgynous Those who have both masculine and feminine traits.

12.10 Erik Erikson proposed a stage theory of identity development. Here he is pictured with his wife Joan in 1988.

RESEARCH QUESTION

What factors shape personal identity throughout the life span?

Erikson (Figure 12.10) was the foremost researcher and theoretician of identity formation. Erikson was both Danish and Jewish. He was raised by his mother as a Jew but because of his Nordic appearance was seen as "not quite" a Jew by those at temple and "not quite" a Gentile by his Danish peers. These experiences may have contributed to Erikson's interest in identity and conflict.

Erikson's **psychosocial theory of development** emphasizes age-related psychological processes and their effects on social functioning. Erikson thought of development as composed of eight stages, ranging from an infant's first year to old age. Further, he conceptualized each stage as having a developmental "crisis" to be confronted. Each crisis provides an opportunity for psychological progression, but if progress is not made, further psychosocial development is impaired.

Erikson's first stage focused on how infants' needs are met by their parents, which is why it is called *trust versus mistrust*. Infants up to 18 months old seek to develop strong ties with their caregivers. At the second stage, around age two, *autonomy versus doubt*, children try to establish self-reliance and exploration skills. Caregivers are particularly important at this stage, too, as they can promote or hinder investigative behaviors. Stage three, around age three to five, is called *initiative versus guilt* because it highlights the importance of self-control and planning, which lead to personal responsibility. Failure to resolve this crisis usually involves the child's growing conscience punishing him or her for having "bad" impulses. The fourth stage, *industry versus inferiority*, refers to the formation of efficacy as children enter their grade-school years.

The fifth stage, *identity versus confusion*, has been a primary focus of subsequent tests of Erikson's model. *Identity* refers to a solid sense of one's ideologies, philosophies, values, and beliefs. The sixth, seventh, and eighth stages take place during adulthood. The sixth stage involves close relationships and the crisis of *intimacy versus isolation*, which means the formation and maintenance of committed friendships and romantic relationships. The seventh stage takes place during middle life. Termed *generativity versus stagnation*, this stage refers to producing or giving back to society, and usually involves parenthood or engaging in activities, such as volunteering, that bring meaning to life. Erikson's last stage, *integrity versus despair*, takes place in old age. In this stage, older adults reflect on their lives and respond either positively to having had a worthwhile life or with regret and sadness at what has passed.

Adolescence Erikson saw adolescence as a time of struggle to establish a clear identity (see Erikson, 1968), which is how the phrase "identity crisis" came about. The most important question in an adolescent's life is, "Who am I, and where am I going?" It is thought that adolescents often question who they are because of three changes: 1) changing physical appearance, which leads to examining self-image, 2) more sophisticated cognitive abilities, which prompt increased introspection, and 3) heightened pressure to prepare for the future and, in particular, to make career choices. Erikson noted that these changes all signal the movement from dependent child to independent adult, which is a difficult transition for most adolescents. One extension of this period of intense self-scrutiny is that adolescents often have a sense of *egocentrism*, exemplified by the adolescent's anxiety over wearing the "right" clothes, as if everyone will notice exactly what he or she is wearing.

Identity status Erikson's "identity versus confusion" stage was further developed by psychologist James Marcia (1966), who proposed a theory of patterns of

12.11 James Marcia's model of identity includes four statuses that combine a person's level of commitment and the presence or absence of a crisis.

identity development that can occur at any point in life. According to Marcia, identity formation involves crisis and commitment. Marcia defined a crisis as a period of conscious decision making, which for adolescents means breaking away from childhood beliefs by questioning and challenging parental and societal ideas. Adolescents might explore alternative belief systems and wonder what they would be like if they were raised in other cultures or in other times. The crisis is the search for an identity that "fits." The person resolves the crisis by making a commitment to a particular ideology and set of beliefs. The process of dealing with an identity crisis can lead to four possible outcomes, known as *identity statuses* (Figure 12.11):

Identity achievement is a status in which a complete identity is obtained. A person who has reached this stage has usually investigated a number of philosophies and chosen a clear identity. However, identity achievement is not necessarily permanent, as circumstances may prompt another identity search in the future.

Identity foreclosure is a status in which a person is committed to a set of values, beliefs, and roles because they are the values they were taught when growing up. A person in foreclosure is not faced with an identity crisis but is also not acting in accordance with his or her own chosen goals and values (for example, the majority of children are in a state of foreclosure). People in foreclosure may act defensive or intolerant when questioned by others about their belief system. Those who stay in foreclosure through early adulthood may be more likely to face a midlife identity crisis, as they have effectively postponed their search for identity.

Identity moratorium is a status in which a person explores and experiments with varying philosophies and vocations. No single alternative is seen as more viable than the others, and a person in this state may seem confused and anxious. Typically, those in moratorium eventually reach identity achievement.

Identity diffusion is characterized by apathy and passivity. A person in diffusion does not challenge his or her sense of identity and fails to commit to an ideology. Thus, people in this stage avoid confrontation, but at a cost, as they have not resolved a former identity crisis.

psychosocial theory of development Erikson's theory that emphasizes age-related psychological processes and their effects on social functioning.

ETHNIC IDENTITY DEVELOPS EARLY

There are approximately six billion people on Earth. Given that these people fall into a variety of groups, how individuals develop a sense of their own and others' racial or ethnic identities is an important component of social development. Researchers have studied how children acquire the racial and ethnic categories prevalent in their community, identify their own race or ethnic group, and form stable attitudes toward their own and others' groups (Spencer & Markstrom-Adams, 1990).

Several studies have demonstrated that by the time children are four years old, they can sort dolls and pictures into racial categories (Bigler & Liben, 1993). These results, however, do not reveal how this ability contributes to the way a child develops ethnic stereotypes or self-concepts. Understanding how children come to form categories about race and ethnicity has been a controversial topic in social psychology. The majority opinion to date is that shortly after children acquire the ability to make categorical distinctions about ethnicity and race, they become aware of their own ethnicity and form judgments about it. Their attitudes toward their own and other people's ethnicity depend on both the attitudes of their adult caregivers and their perceptions of the power and wealth of their own group in relation to others.

The process of identity formation in a country like the United States, where people of so many ethnicities live together, is particularly complicated. Due to prejudice and discrimination and the accompanying barriers to economic opportunities, children of ethnic minorities often have challenges with regard to the development of their ethnic identity. The factors that influence this process vary widely among individuals and groups. For example, Spencer and Markstrom-Adams (1990) have reported that skin color is more central to ethnic identity among African Americans and Native Americans than among Hispanic Americans. Children entering middle childhood have acquired an awareness of their ethnic identity to the extent that they know the label and attributes that the culture applies to their ethnic group. Many researchers believe that during middle childhood and adolescence, children in ethnic minority groups often engage in additional processes aimed at ethnic identity formation.

Ethnic identity refers to the psychological association of a member of an ethnic or racial group with that group, along with awareness of the group as part of a larger society (Phinney, 1990). Jean Phinney proposed an ethnic identity theory that shares many features with other theories of identity development. She outlined three stages of ethnic identity: unexamined, exploration, and achieved. The *unexamined* stage is similar to both the diffusion and foreclosure subtypes of Marcia's identity theory. Someone belonging to an ethnic minority in the unexamined stage may show a preference for the dominant culture or apathy toward his or her ethnicity (diffusion), or the person may have simply adopted their parents' views of ethnicity (foreclosure). The *exploration* stage involves an awareness of one's ethnicity as part of one's self-concept and is similar to Marcia's moratorium stage. Movement into this stage may be the result of a significant experience and may develop into intense involvement in one's ethnic culture and sometimes a devaluation of the dominant culture. The last stage, *achievement*, represents an intricate understanding of one's ethnicity, acknowledging differences between one's culture and the dominant culture. Being in the achievement stage does not necessarily mean a more intense involvement with one's culture; it simply means that the person recognizes his or her ethnicity as a part of the larger society. Thus, a person does not have to wear ethnic dress or speak a certain dialect or language to be ethnically achieved.

ethnic identity The psychological association between people and their own ethnic or racial group.

What Influences Gender Development and Identity?

Although there are differences between the sexes, males and females are more similar than different. Gender is socialized through a variety of forces, including caregivers, teachers, media, and peers, and there are stereotypes about how men and women behave. Males and females respond to situations by acting in ways that conform to stereotypes. People who act in gender-inappropriate ways are often punished for doing so. These various cultural influences lead men and women to behave differently in many social contexts. Erik Erikson proposed a model of identity development that focuses on how people view themselves throughout their lives, and how various challenges lead to different crises. The search for identity is particularly strong during adolescence and often involves reflecting on one's ethnic identity.

CONCLUSION

People are influenced by their social worlds, which help to shape and mold them over the life course. Humans are socialized to act and to treat others in certain ways and to believe certain things. Most of this socialization helps people to navigate the social world and to get along with others. Evolutionary forces have produced attachment behaviors that bond us to significant others, such as caregivers. Psychological science has also confirmed the importance of relationships in social development, and that peers are especially important for identity issues related to gender. At the same time, it is clear that gender identity is not simply a matter of socialization, but a combination of biological, social, and cultural influences. Research that crosses the levels of analysis shows how culture molds the way people come to identify themselves throughout social development.

FURTHER READINGS

Bybee, J. (1998). *Guilt and children*. San Diego, CA: Academic Press.

Chess, S., & Thomas, A. (1996). *Temperament: Theory and practice*. New York: Brunner/Mazel, Inc.

Colapinto, J. (2000). *As nature made him: The boy who was raised as a girl*. New York: HarperCollins Publishers.

Goldberg, S., Muir, R., & Kerr, J. (1997). *Attachment theory: Social, developmental, and clinical perspectives*. Hillsdale, NJ: Analytic Press, Inc.

Gottman, J., & Declaire, J. (1997). *The heart of parenting: Raising an emotionally intelligent child*. New York: Simon & Schuster.

Harris, J. R. (1998). *The Nurture assumption: Why children turn out the way they do*. New York: The Free Press.

Hoffman, M. L. (2000). *Empathy and moral development: Implications for caring and justice*. New York: Cambridge University Press.

Maccoby, E. E. (1998). *The two sexes: Growing up apart, coming together*. Cambridge, MA: Belknap Press/Harvard University Press.

TRANSFORMING SOCIETY

People use persuasion when they intend to change the attitudes of others. After decades of political struggle, anti-apartheid activists around the world convinced South Africa's ruling minority to allow free and open elections. Nelson Mandela's victory over F. W. de Klerk in the 1994 presidential election marked the end of apartheid, and provided reason to hope for widespread change of popular attitudes in that country.

1890s

The Self in Psychology
William James differentiates the self as the knower ("I") from the self as the object that is known ("me"). James also notes that people's selves change according to social context.

1930s

Attitude Measurement
L. L. Thurstone and Rensis Likert develop attitude scales based on principles of psychophysics. Carl Hovland at Yale University studies how attitudes are changed.

1945

Field Theory Kurt Lewin's influential field theory, based on physics, proposes that behavior is a function of the person interacting with the environment.

1950s

People as Intuitive Scientists Fritz Heider argues that social psychologists need to understand "commonsense psychology." Heider's ideas form the basis of attribution theory.

Self and Social Cognition

OUTLINING THE PRINCIPLES

WHAT IS THE NATURE OF SELF?

The Symbolic Self Is Uniquely Human

Self-Awareness Develops in Infancy

The Frontal Lobes Are Involved in Self-Awareness

The Self-Concept Is a Cognitive Knowledge Structure

WHAT IS SELF-ESTEEM AND WHAT IS IT GOOD FOR?

Self-Esteem Is Influenced by Perceived Social Regard

Most Views of Self Are Favorable

People Use Strategies to Maintain Self-Esteem

HOW DO ATTITUDES GUIDE BEHAVIOR?

Attitudes Develop Through Experience and Learning

Attitudes Predict Behavior in Certain Circumstances

Discrepancies Between Attitudes and Behavior Lead to Cognitive Dissonance

Attitudes Can Be Changed Through Persuasion

HOW DO PEOPLE FORM ATTITUDES ABOUT OTHERS?

People Make Attributions

Social Information Processing Is Biased

Stereotypes Are Based on Automatic Categorization

Prejudice and Stigma Have an Evolutionary Basis

Stereotypes Can Be Self-Fulfilling

Prejudice and Discrimination Can Be Reduced

CONCLUSION

FURTHER READINGS

1954

The Nature of Prejudice
Gordon Allport provides a comprehensive review of the nature of stereotyping and prejudice. Allport points out that prejudice arises out of normal cognitive processes.

1957

Cognitive Dissonance
Leon Festinger argues that people want to maintain consistency between their attitudes and their behaviors, and that discrepancies create unpleasant tension that needs to be resolved.

1961

Cooperation Reduces Intergroup Hostility
Muzafer Sherif demonstrates that competition creates hostility and that cooperation reduces it, contradicting the assumption that simple contact between the races reduces prejudice.

1960s

Correspondence Bias and Attributions Edward Jones demonstrates that people overemphasize the importance of personal factors when explaining others' behaviors, which has been called the fundamental attribution error.

1977

Social Cognition and the Self-Schema Hazel Markus, heavily influenced by cognitive psychology, conducts research on the self-schema. Her findings contribute to increased interest in social cognition.

A
ubrey Gibbons moved his family from their native Barbados to England in late 1963. At the time, he was the father of four children, including two young twins, June and Jennifer (Figure 13.1). As toddlers, the twins had speech problems that made them difficult to understand. This might have contributed to the teasing they received from their schoolmates. However, the major reason they were taunted mercilessly was because they were the only black children in their school. When they entered a new school at age 11, the bullying was so severe that the twins had to be dismissed early so that they could get a head start on their tormentors. Around this time, the twins made a pact to refuse to communicate with anyone else. They did not speak or make eye contact with teachers, schoolmates, or even the other members of their family. But they did speak to one another, in a language largely unintelligible to others that they made up to serve as a special code between them.

A succession of educators, psychologists, and physicians tried unsuccessfully to get the girls to speak. As a drastic measure, the girls were sent at age 14 to different residential schools. This led to disaster. Their self-imposed isolation had fused their identities; the two had become one, and separating them did little to facilitate their rehabilitation. After they were reunited the twins committed a series of crimes, including vandalism and arson, and they were sentenced to a maximum-security prison for the criminally insane, where they remained for 14 years. Tragically, Jennifer died within hours after release from an undetected heart problem. June now lives in a halfway house, still traumatized by her childhood experiences, though at least now she communicates with others (Als, 2000).

The case of June and Jennifer Gibbons raises a number of psychological issues related to self, identity, and social perception. The merging of the twins' identities poses intriguing questions about identity development in general. Our feelings of having a unique sense of self, of being separate from others, are challenged by their story. At the same time, it is clear that the way people are treated by

RESEARCH QUESTIONS ?.?.?

for Studying the Self and Social Cognition

Is the sense of self limited to humans?

How is information about the self processed?

What is the role of self-esteem?

How do our attitudes develop?

How are attitudes related to behavior?

What factors influence how we perceive others?

How do stereotypes influence our treatment of others?

1978

Jigsaw Classroom Eliot Aronson develops the jigsaw classroom, which emphasizes cooperation among interracial groups in classroom settings. More than 800 studies have shown that it reduces prejudice and discrimination.

1980–1990s

Self-Serving Biases and Positive Illusions Social psychologists such as Shelley Taylor, Anthony Greenwald, and Roy Baumeister describe a variety of cognitive biases and illusions that people use to maintain a positive self-image.

2000

Social Cognitive Neuroscience Social psychologists begin to examine the neural correlates of social cognition and behavior.

others, such as being ridiculed and abused, can profoundly affect development. Racism was present throughout the Gibbons' medical treatment, in which many of their problems were dismissed as "cultural differences."

The way people process information about others has a profound impact on their social lives. The mind allows us to judge and categorize people quickly and efficiently. Phenomena such as racism and stereotyping are the result of cognitive shortcuts that allow people to make quick decisions about others based on physical characteristics and behavior. Yet this cognitive processing can lead to prejudice and mistreatment. In this chapter you will learn how people process information about themselves and about others. You will see that there are significant biases in information processing that favor the self and things associated with the self, and that this favoritism occurs automatically and without effort. These cognitive processes have important implications for how we understand ourselves and those around us.

13.1 Twins June and Jennifer Gibbons developed their own form of communication and refused to speak with others.

Humans are social animals. Some six billion people are right now busily talking with friends, forming impressions of strangers, arguing with family members, even falling in love with potential mates. Our regular interactions with others—even imagined others—shape who we are and how we understand the world. **Social psychology** is concerned with how others influence how we think, feel, and act. Because almost every human activity has some social dimension, research in social psychology covers expansive and varied territory: how we perceive ourselves and others, how we function in groups, why we hurt or help people, why we fall in love, why we stigmatize and discriminate against certain people. This chapter is concerned with how we process information relevant to self and others. The next chapter considers how people interact with each other, especially in terms of how people are influenced by and form relationships with others.

Social cognition concerns the mental processes by which we make sense of ourselves, other people, and our social situations. One of the central ideas in social cognition is that a great deal of mental activity occurs automatically and without conscious awareness or intent (Bargh & Ferguson, 2000; Wegner & Bargh, 1998). Within a fraction of a second, we automatically evaluate people and objects we encounter. We are cognitive "misers" who because of limited mental resources do not always carefully analyze and scrutinize all of our attitudes and behaviors; we make snap judgments about others based on very little information. Such judgments typically influence our actions without our knowledge. We also automatically process information regarding the self and engage in a number of strategies to protect our self-esteem, often without our awareness.

In this chapter you will see that these automatic processes work efficiently to maintain our personal sense of identity as well as to assist us in navigating

social psychology The branch of psychology concerned with how others influence the way a person thinks, feels, and acts.

social cognition The mental processes by which people make sense of themselves, others, and their social situations.

through our social world. One topic that appears throughout the chapter is *racism*, the mistreatment of people based on their appearance or ethnic origins. To understand racism, we need first to understand the nature of self, and of self-esteem. We need to understand attitudes—what they are, how they are formed and maintained, and when they predict behavior. We also need to understand the basis of stereotypes and prejudice, as well as how beliefs are translated into behavior. Understanding social cognition requires crossing multiple levels of analysis, from imaging the brain in action to assessing beliefs, motives, behaviors, and cognitive responses. It also requires us to examine the cultural and adaptive contexts that influence our attitudes about self and others.

WHAT IS THE NATURE OF SELF?

Sit back for a second and think about your self. What is it that you are visualizing? Although the word "self" is probably spoken by nearly everyone every day, it is quite difficult to define. At a general level, the **self** involves the mental representation of personal experience and includes thought processes, a physical body, and a conscious experience that one is separate and unique from others. This sense of self is a unitary experience that is continuous over time and space. When you wake up in the morning, you don't have to figure out who you are, even if you sometimes do have to figure out where you are, such as when you are on vacation.

THE SYMBOLIC SELF IS UNIQUELY HUMAN

Psychological scientists distinguish among many levels of self. The basic, primitive sense of self, called the *minimal self*, is the conscious experience of self in the here and now, as it is shaped by, but separate from, the immediate environment. Accordingly, insects, fish, birds, and most other animals experience this minimal self. A higher level of self, called the *objectified self*, is the cognitive capacity to serve as the object of one's own attention, such as being aware of one's own state of mind. There is some evidence that certain nonhuman primates, such as chimpanzees and orangutans, have an objectified sense of self. At the highest level is the *symbolic self* (also called the *narrative self*), which is the uniquely human capacity to form an abstract mental representation of oneself through language. It refers to the sense of self extended in time and abstractly represented; it includes sense of identity, autobiographical memories of the past, and expectations and beliefs about the future. It is our own life story that defines who we are, where we have been, and where we are going.

Recall that a major theme of this text is that the mind is adaptive. From an evolutionary perspective, the symbolic self is a relatively recent adaptation to selective pressures, such as the need to hunt for food and the challenge of living in social groups. Constantine Sedikides and John Skowronski (1997) argue that the symbolic self is a widely shared human trait that leads to more efficient mental processing of personal and contextual information, thereby increasing the likelihood of survival and reproduction. They include in the symbolic self the ability to be self-reflective and introspective, to have sexual fantasies, to create narrative descriptions using language, to make long-term plans, to have a sense of one's own mortality, to develop moral arguments, and to form governments and coali-

self The mental representation of personal experience, including thought processes, a physical body, and a conscious experience of individuality.

self-awareness A state in which the sense of self is the object of attention.

tions beyond boundaries (such as the United Nations). Of course, the symbolic self also allows people to develop racist beliefs.

SELF-AWARENESS DEVELOPS IN INFANCY

Among the first to consider the nature of self, both psychologist William James and sociologist George Herbert Mead differentiated between the self as the knower ("I") and the self as the object that is known ("me")—now known as the objectified self. In the former sense, the self is the subject doing the thinking, feeling, and acting. The "I" is involved in executive functions, such as choosing, planning, and exerting control. In the latter sense, the self is the knowledge that you hold about yourself, such as when you think about your best and worst qualities. The sense of self as the object of attention is the psychological state known as **self-awareness**. This occurs when the "I" thinks about the "me."

Both James and Mead noted that infants are born with a minimal sense of self that develops through social interaction. Important contributors to self-awareness are *reflected appraisals*, the views we believe others have of us. For instance, we believe we are generous because we think that other people view us as generous. Imagining how others would view certain behaviors produces emotional states that help guide our actions. The anticipation of negative reactions encourages behaviors that enhance social bonds, such as honesty and faithfulness. These reflected appraisals determine how we view and evaluate ourselves, as will be discussed shortly.

Self-recognition Developmental psychologists have shown that the initial sense of self typically develops at some point between 18 months and 2 years of age. How does one study the sense of self among children who cannot speak? One way is to study *self-recognition*. For instance, if you look in the mirror or see a picture of yourself, you know that it is you. In a series of studies, Michael Lewis and Jeanne Brooks-Gunn (1979) observed infants (5 to 24 months of age) in front of mirrors or as they watched themselves on videotapes. They found that at around 18 months, children show evidence that they recognize a mirror or video image as their own. How did the researchers demonstrate this? They had mothers covertly put some rouge on their childrens' noses and then tested to see if the children would notice the rouge. When shown their image in a mirror, infants younger than 16 months saw the red spot, but they did not appear to recognize it as an alteration of their usual face. They treated the face as if it belonged to someone else. Older children, however, typically made funny expressions and tried to rub off the rouge (Figure 13.2). The children now understood that the nose in the mirror belonged to them and was located in the middle of their face. There is some evidence, discussed in "Studying the Mind: Do Animals Have a Self?" that some primates also display self-recognition.

Personal reference and the symbolic self At about age two, after they can recognize themselves in mirrors and pictures, children come to use personal pronouns to acknowledge the self, proudly proclaiming "me!" and pointing to their images in photographs. This is when children begin to show an understanding of the self as existing across time, recognizing themselves in pictures taken earlier in their lives, for example. At about age three, children begin to play with their

Is the sense of self limited to humans?

13.2 Sometime around 18 months, children will reach for a spot of unscented rouge placed on their noses, indicating that they know it is their reflection in the mirror. Younger children either ignore the dot or point at the mirror.

Studying the Mind

DO ANIMALS HAVE A SELF?

If the symbolic self is a result of evolution, then mental representations of self might be expected to exist in animals closely related to humans, such as other primates. When researchers first began teaching sign language to apes, there was great excitement. Imagine being able to ask a gorilla what it felt like to be a gorilla! Unfortunately, it appears that most nonhuman primates are incapable of answering such questions. But, is it possible that they have some rudimentary sense of self that allows them to complete a task such as self-recognition?

To find out, George Gallup Jr. conducted a series of studies in the 1960s that examined the ability of primates to recognize themselves in mirrors. When the chimpanzees first saw their images in a mirror, they reacted as if they were suddenly confronted by another chimpanzee, screeching at it and making threatening gestures. But over time they began using the mirror to explore body parts that they could not otherwise see, such as their teeth, ears, tongue, and genital region. In order to directly test the hypothesis that chimpanzees could recognize themselves, Gallup anesthetized the chimpanzees, and while they were unconscious, he marked their eyebrows or ears with a brightly colored dye. The chimpanzees had no sensory knowledge (e.g., feel, smell) that the body parts had been marked. Then they were shown their mirror image. If, as Gallup reasoned, the chimps really had a sense of self, then they would notice the marked body parts and attend to them. This is precisely what happened (Figure 13.3). In contrast to humans, however, chimpanzees do not appear to recognize themselves in mirrors until they are six to eight years old (Povinelli et al., 1997).

Interestingly, although chimpanzees and orangutans have been shown to demonstrate self-recognition, there has been little success in obtaining self-recognition in other animals. Although the reports of one gorilla (named Koko) seem to indicate reasonable self-recognition, many other attempts to induce self-recognition in gorillas have failed. Occasional claims are also made for self-recognition in monkeys and dolphins, but the evidence for such claims is ambiguous.

If chimpanzees and orangutans have self-recognition, does this mean that they have a sense of self similar to the human sense of self? Probably not. When human infants develop self-recognition, they also show an increase in self-conscious emotions and an understanding that other people have intentional mental states; that is,

they develop a *theory of mind*. Sometimes chimps appear to try to deceive other chimps, which suggests the possibility of a rudimentary theory of mind. But researchers such as Daniel Povinelli have concluded that nonhuman primates have limited self-concepts and minimal knowledge of the mental states of others.

13.3 This chimpanzee appears to recognize itself in the mirror (top). In the bottom photo, the chimpanzee uses a towel to wipe off a mark applied by the experimenter before the mirror exposure.

shadows, which they realize are caused by their bodies. The emergence of the self-conscious emotions of embarrassment, shame, and guilt occurs at about the same age. The basis of these social emotions is the recognition that the self is being evaluated by others, which requires that children understand that others have minds capable of evaluating people. Finally, by about age four—as episodic memory for personal experiences develops—children begin to tell stories about themselves, describing incidents from the past or projecting themselves into the future. This ability to mentally represent the self's past and future is called *auto-noetic consciousness* (Wheeler et al., 1997).

Self-awareness guides behavior   Social psychologists have long been interested in the consequences of self-awareness. In 1972, Shelley Duval and Robert Wicklund introduced an important theory that self-awareness produces a comparison of self against relevant standards, which inevitably leads to emotional motivation to act in accordance with personal values, attitudes, and beliefs. For instance, college students are less likely to cheat, when given the opportunity, if they are sitting in front of mirrors. Recall from our earlier discussion (Chapter 9) that discrepancies between personal standards and goals motivate behaviors that reduce the discrepancy. According to social psychologist Tory Higgins' *self-discrepancy theory*, awareness of differences between personal standards leads to strong emotions (1987). For instance, discrepancies between how we see ourselves and how we would like to see ourselves lead to disappointment, frustration, and depression; discrepancies between how we see ourselves and how we believe we ought to seem to others produce anxiety and guilt.

THE FRONTAL LOBES ARE INVOLVED IN SELF-AWARENESS

The biological revolution in psychological science has provided new insights for understanding the sense of self. A growing body of evidence suggests that the awareness of self depends largely on the frontal lobes of the brain, which are important for memory and for interpreting ongoing events. This is consistent with the fact that the frontal lobes are a recent evolutionary adaptation especially prominent in human brains. Moreover, the frontal lobes are poorly developed in infancy; they mature following birth and do not become fully formed until early adulthood. Thus, the absence of symbolic self-awareness in nonhuman animals and young infants supports the idea that our sense of self develops with the frontal lobes.

Executive function of the self   The frontal lobes are associated with the selection and use of controllable mental operations, called *executive functions*, which help the self achieve its goals. People with lesions to the frontal lobes show impairments in tasks that involve self-awareness. For instance, they have difficulty remembering where they learned specific information, though they know they know the information. It has long been recognized that such patients are not self-reflective and seldom report daydreaming or other types of introspection. They also often show a surprising lack of interest or knowledge about their disorders. Such individuals are not completely unaware of themselves following frontal lobe damage, but they don't find information about the self personally significant. They are casual observers of themselves, in the way that children under age 16 months view themselves in mirrors. Surprisingly, these patients can identify impairments in others, but they don't seem to notice that they themselves have similar impairments.

Neuropsychologist Donald Stuss (1991) reported a highly intelligent patient who had a tumor removed from his frontal lobes. Subsequently, even though his intelligence and knowledge about the world were intact, he had difficulty at work and became extremely unproductive. Despite 18 months of therapy, the patient continued to do poorly at work, but he could not recognize that he had a problem. When asked to role-play the situation as if he were the boss, thereby evaluating his objective self, he quickly and clearly recognized the problem and made appropriate recommendations—that the worker be put on a disability pension. However, when he was asked to evaluate himself from his personal, subjective perspective, he failed to agree with the recommendations he had just made. This dramatic example—and others like it—shows that the patient couldn't internalize knowledge about his situation.

Self-recognition and the right hemisphere The ability to recognize oneself in a mirror or photograph may involve the right hemisphere frontal lobe. Researchers have conducted studies in which they morph a famous face (e.g., Bill Clinton's) with the participant's face or the face of someone familiar to the participant. The morphs are presented as a series that starts with the famous face and slowly morphs into the participant's or the familiar face, with the participant instructed to press a button when the face becomes the self or familiar. Participants identified the self morph faster when using the left hand to push the button than when using the right hand (Keenan et al., 2000). No significant time differences occurred when the famous face was morphed with the familiar face. These findings implicate the right hemisphere in self-recognition because each hemisphere controls the motor actions of the opposite side of the body. In a follow-up study, the same researchers used a group of patients who were undergoing a neurological exam to prepare for possible brain surgery to treat epilepsy. To test for psychological functioning, neurologists used a *Wada test* in which they anaesthetized each hemisphere individually. While one hemisphere was anaesthetized, the patients were shown a morph of their face and a famous person's (e.g., Marilyn Monroe's). After the test, patients were asked whether they had been shown a picture of themselves or of someone famous. If the left hemisphere had been anaesthetized, the patients reported that they had observed their own face, whereas the opposite effect occurred for the right hemisphere (Figure 13.4; Keenan et al., 2001).

13.4 Wada test of self-recognition. While each of their hemispheres was anaesthetized in turn, patients were shown a picture of their face morphed with that of a famous person. When the anaesthesia wore off, patients were asked whether they had been shown a famous person or their own face. When the left hemisphere had been anaesthetized they selected their own face, whereas they selected the famous person when their right hemisphere had been anaesthetized.

THE SELF-CONCEPT IS A COGNITIVE KNOWLEDGE STRUCTURE

Write down 20 answers to the question "Who am I?" What sorts of items did you choose? The answers that you provided are part of your **self-concept**, which is everything that you know about yourself. For example, common answers by college students include gender, age, student status, interpersonal style (shy, friendly), interpersonal characteristics (moody, optimistic), and body image. Many social psychologists view the self-concept as a cognitive knowledge structure that guides our attention to information that is relevant to us and that helps us adjust to the environment.

Self-schema   Have you ever been at a crowded, noisy party in which you could barely hear yourself speak, but when someone across the room mentioned your name, you heard it clearly above the din? The *cocktail party effect* occurs because information about the self is processed deeply and thoroughly. According to Hazel Markus (1977), the **self-schema** is the cognitive aspect of the self-concept, consisting of an integrated set of memories, beliefs, and generalizations about the self. Your self-schema consists of those aspects of your behavior and personality that are important to you. For instance, being a good athlete or a good student may be an important component of your self-schema, while having few cavities probably is not. The self-schema helps us perceive, organize, interpret, and use information about the self; it can be viewed as a network of interconnected knowledge about the self (Figure 13.5). Thus, when asked "Are you ambitious?" we do not have to sort through all occasions in which we acted ambitiously or not to come up with an answer. Rather, self-schemas summarize past information so we can provide an answer automatically.

Self-schemas may lead to enhanced memory for information that is processed in a self-referential manner. Tim Rogers and colleagues (Rogers et al., 1977), showed that trait adjectives that were processed with reference to the self (e.g., "Does the word *honest* describe you?" were better recalled than comparable items that were processed only for their general meaning (e.g. "Does the word *honest* mean the same as *trustworthy*?") Researchers have sought to examine the neural correlates of self-referential processing. In one study, researchers used PET brain imaging to examine frontal lobe activation when people were answering questions that were self-relevant or not. In addition to the typical left frontal activation observed during memory encoding tasks, the researchers found increased activation in the midline of the frontal lobes when participants answered self-relevant questions (Craik et al., 1999). A recent study using fMRI also found medial frontal lobe activation for self-relevant processing (Kelley et al., in press.) These findings are consistent with evidence reviewed earlier that patients with damage to this area show deficits in self-awareness and self-understanding. Considered together, the available evidence points to the medial frontal lobes as the region in which information about the self is processed.

Working self-concept   The immediate experience of self is limited to the amount of personal information

self-concept The full store of knowledge that people have about themselves.

self-schema The cognitive aspect of the self-concept, consisting of an integrated set of memories, beliefs, and generalizations about the self.

RESEARCH QUESTION ???

How is information about the self processed?

13.5 The self-schema consists of interrelated knowledge about the self.

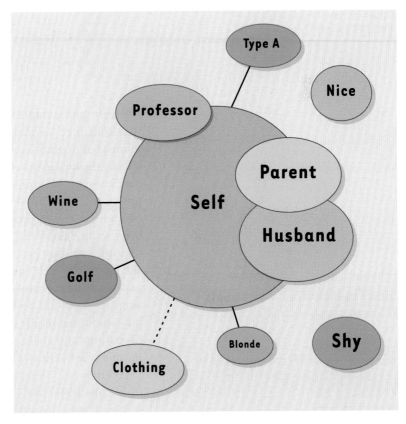

(a) Who am I?

I am male.

(b) Who am I?

I am African American.

13.6 When answering the question "Who am I?" people are especially likely to mention characteristics that are distinctive.

that can be processed cognitively at any given time. Because this *working self-concept* contains only part of the vast array of self-knowledge about experiences and relationships, the sense of self varies from situation to situation. For instance, at a party you might think of yourself as fun-loving rather than as intelligent, even though both are aspects of your self-concept. Thus, your personal self-descriptions vary as a function of which memories you retrieve, which can be affected by the situation you are in, the people you are with, and your role in that situation.

When people are considering who they are, they often emphasize things that make them distinct from others. For instance, think back to your 20 responses to "Who am I?" People are especially likely to mention things such as ethnicity, gender, or age if they differ from other people around them at the time (Figure 13.6). Thus, Canadians would be more likely to note their nationality if they were in Boston than if they were in Toronto. Because beliefs about the self guide behavior, this implies that they are also more likely to feel and act like Canadians in Boston than in Toronto. There is, of course, an optimal level of distinctiveness, since most people also avoid standing out too much; teenagers especially want to fit in with the crowd.

interdependent self-construals When self-concepts are determined largely by social roles and personal relationships.

independent self-construals A view of the self as separate from others, emphasizing self-reliance and the pursuit of personal success.

Multiple and complex selves People differ not only in the types of information contained in their self-schemas, but also in their *self-complexity*, or the number of distinct aspects that they use to define themselves. According to Patricia Linville (1985), having a complex and differentiated sense of self helps people cope with stressful events. Consider two students, Bill and Linda. Bill is pre-med and all his activities center around his studies. His relationships with his parents and girlfriend center on his dreams of being a physician. His hobbies, leisure activities, and indeed most of his spare time, focus on activities that will help him get into the best medical schools. Linda is also pre-med, but she defines herself in multiple ways. She is a skilled musician, an enthusiastic golfer, politically active on environmental issues, and so on. Now consider what happens when Bill and Linda fail a chemistry exam. Bill is devastated because his failure has implications for *all* aspects of his life, including disappointing his parents and girlfriend. Linda can deal with the failure more easily by thinking about her skill as a musician or her love of the environment.

Do these different aspects of self mean that a person has many distinct selves inside one body? No, it just means that different aspects of self are activated in different social contexts. William James claimed that we have as many social selves as there are people who know us, since people tend to act differently depending on who is around. You might notice that your behavior is different when speaking to your professors than when speaking to your roommates or friends, which is again different from how you speak to your parents. Indeed, interacting with mixed audiences, such as with your friends and parents at the same time, can be difficult because of the discrepancy.

Independent and interdependent selves An important way that people differ in their self-concepts is whether they view themselves as fundamentally separate from, or as inherently connected to, other people. Harry Triandis (1989) notes that some cultures (such as in Japan, Greece, mid-Africa, Pakistan, and China) place greater emphasis on the collective self than on the personal self. The *collective self* emphasizes connections to family, social groups, and ethnic groups and conformity to societal norms and group cohesiveness. Individualist cultures (such as in Northern and Western Europe, Australia, Canada, New Zealand, and the United States) place greater emphasis on the *personal self*, which emphasizes personal rights and freedoms, self-expression, and diversity. For example, in the United States people dress differently, are concerned with personal interests, and often enjoy standing out from the crowd. In Japan, people tend to dress more similarly and to respect situational norms. When an American family goes to a restaurant, each person orders what he or she prefers. In China, when a family goes to a restaurant, multiple dishes are shared by the entire table.

Hazel Markus and Shinobu Kitayama (1991) noted that people in collectivist cultures tend to have **interdependent self-construals**, in which their self-concepts are determined to a large extent by their social roles and personal relationships (Figure 13.7). As children, they are raised to follow group norms and to be obedient to parents, teachers, and other people in authority. They are expected to find their proper place in society and not to challenge or complain about their status. Friendships in collectivist cultures are difficult to initiate but long-lasting once they are formed. By contrast, those in individualist cultures tend to have **independent self-construals**; children are encouraged by parents and teachers to be self-reliant and to pursue personal success, even at the expense of interpersonal relationships. Their sense of self is based on their feelings of being distinct from others. It is important to note, however, that these are broad and general patterns, and that there is variability in terms of independent/interdependent self-construals within both individualist and collectivist cultures.

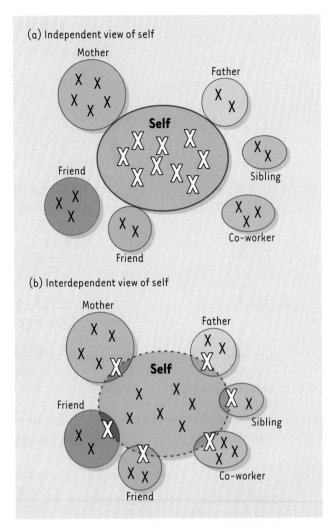

13.7 Self-construals in (a) individualist and (b) collectivist cultures.

What Is the Nature of Self?
Through the course of evolution, humans have developed a symbolic self, in which they are able to represent themselves mentally. Self-awareness develops during early childhood and depends on maturation of the frontal lobes. Information about the self is processed efficiently and quickly through a self-schema. How people describe themselves can vary across situations. Cross-cultural differences in how the self is construed exist, with collectivist cultures emphasizing the interdependent self and individualist cultures emphasizing the independent self.

self-esteem The evaluative aspect of the self-concept.

sociometer An internal monitor of social acceptance or rejection.

WHAT IS SELF-ESTEEM AND WHAT IS IT GOOD FOR?

North American culture has been obsessed with self-esteem for the past two decades. At a basic level, **self-esteem** is the evaluative aspect of the self-concept, referring to whether people perceive themselves to be worthy or unworthy, good or bad. It is people's emotional response as they contemplate and evaluate different characteristics about themselves. Although self-esteem is related to the self-concept, it is possible for people to believe objectively positive things about themselves without really liking themselves very much. Conversely, it is possible for people to like themselves very much, and therefore have high self-esteem, even when objective indicators don't support such positive self-views. In this section, we will consider the affective aspects of processing information about the self.

SELF-ESTEEM IS INFLUENCED BY PERCEIVED SOCIAL REGARD

Social cognition involves making sense of other people's actions, such as how they behave toward us. Many theories assume that people's self-esteem is based on how they believe others perceive them, known as *reflected appraisals*. According to this view, people internalize the values and beliefs expressed by important people in their lives. They do this by observing the attitudes and actions of others and adopting these attitudes and behaviors as their own. In effect, people come to respond to themselves in a manner consistent with the ways others respond to them. From this perspective, when important figures reject, ignore, demean or devalue a person, low self-esteem is likely to result.

This social view of self-esteem led some theorists to promote *unconditional acceptance* of children by their parents, meaning that parents should love their children no matter what the children do. Later theorists have noted, however, that unconditional acceptance needs to occur in the context of relatively strict parenting, in which parents clearly define limits and enforce those limits by providing positive reinforcement for behaviors within those limits and punishment for behaviors outside those limits (Coopersmith, 1967). Children are accepted and loved no matter what they do, but inappropriate behaviors are corrected through punishment.

Sociometer theory   A novel and important social account of self-esteem has been proposed by Mark Leary and colleagues (1995). Leary assumes that humans have a fundamental need to belong that is adaptive. For most of human evolution, those who belonged to social groups were more likely to survive and reproduce than those who were excluded and left to survive on their own. According to Leary, self-esteem monitors the likelihood of social exclusion. When people behave in ways that increase the likelihood they will be rejected, they experience a reduction in self-esteem. Thus, self-esteem serves as a **sociometer**, an internal monitor of social acceptance/rejection (Figure 13.8). Those with high self-esteem have sociometers that indicate a low probability of rejection, and therefore such individuals do not worry about how they are being perceived by others. By contrast, those with low self-esteem have sociometers that indicate the imminent possibility of rejection, and therefore they are highly motivated to manage their public impres-

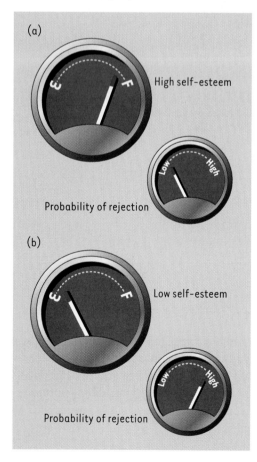

13.8 According to sociometer theory, self-esteem is the gauge that measures the extent to which people are being included (a) in or excluded (b) from their social groups.

(a)

High self-esteem

Probability of rejection

(b)

Low self-esteem

Probability of rejection

maintain their self-esteem (Baumeister, 1998). The sociometer theory of self-esteem suggests that people are using these strategies not to maintain positive self-feelings per se, but rather to avoid being rejected by the group.

Self-evaluative maintenance   Abraham Tesser (1988) notes that self-esteem can be affected not only by how people perform, but by how relevant their performances are to their self-concepts and how their performances compare to those of significant people around them. According to the theory of *self-evaluative maintenance*, people can be threatened when someone close to them outperforms them on a task that is personally relevant. If you had a twin brother who shared your aspiration to be a world-class chef, his brilliant success at cooking would have important implications for how you felt about yourself. To maintain your sense of self-esteem, Tesser argues that you would either distance yourself from the relationship or select a different aspiration. Of course, if your twin brother excels at something you don't find personally relevant, then you might *bask in the glow of reflected glory* and experience a boost in self-esteem based on your relationship. Similarly, if you had a friend who was a gold medalist in track and field, you would likely experience a boost in self-esteem simply by knowing her. Self-evaluation maintenance causes people to exaggerate or publicize their connections to winners and to minimize or hide their relations to losers.

Biased comparisons   Social comparison occurs when people evaluate their own actions, abilities, and beliefs by contrasting them with other people's. Especially when there are no objective criteria, such as knowing how thin one ought to be or how much money represents a good income, people compare themselves to others to see where they stand. Obviously, who is chosen as a standard of comparison will have a great influence on self-esteem. In general, people with high self-esteem make *downward comparisons*, contrasting themselves with people who are deficient to them on relevant dimensions. People with low self-esteem tend to make *upward comparisons* with those who are superior to them. When thinking about the future, however, people with high self-esteem also tend to make upward comparisons, looking to highly successful role models to inspire them.

Interestingly, people also use a form of downward comparison when they recall their own past. That is, people often view their current selves as being better than their former selves (Figure 13.11; Wilson & Ross, 2001). For example, people remember themselves as being awkward and shy as adolescents. Happiness is relative, and people can maintain positive self-feelings by focusing on how much better off they are now than they were in the past.

Self-serving biases   People with high self-esteem tend to take credit for success but blame failure on outside factors, which is referred to as a **self-serving bias**. For instance, students who do extremely well on exams often explain their performance by referring to personal skills or hard work. Those who do poorly often note that the test was an arbitrary examination of trivial details. People with high self-esteem also assume that criticism is motivated by envy or prejudice. Indeed, members of groups that are prone to discrimination (such as the disabled and ethnic minorities) may have high self-esteem. One elegant theory proposed by Jennifer Crocker and

positive illusions   Overly favorable and unrealistic beliefs about one's skills, abilities, and competencies.

social comparison   Occurs when people evaluate their own actions, abilities, and beliefs by contrasting them with other people.

self-serving bias   The tendency for people to take personal credit for success but blame failure on external factors.

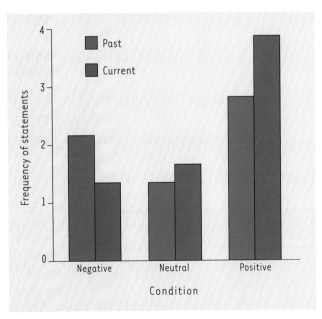

13.11 College students rated their past selves as having had more negative features than their current selves, which were rated as having more positive features.

Brenda Major (1989) suggests that members of these groups maintain positive self-esteem by taking credit for success and blaming negative feedback on prejudice. So, if you succeed, you succeed due to personal strengths and despite the odds. If you fail, you fail because of external factors and unfair obstacles. Imagine how this might be useful in maintaining self-esteem for those who regularly face discrimination.

What Is Self-Esteem and What Is It Good For?

Self-esteem is the evaluative aspect of the self-concept that corresponds to an overall view of the self as worthy or unworthy. Most theories of self-esteem have focused on the role of reflected appraisals, or the subjective perception of whether the self is valued by others. Sociometer theory views self-esteem as an adaptive monitor used to avoid social rejection. Most people have moderate to high levels of self-esteem, viewing themselves as better than average on a number of dimensions. These and other strategies help people maintain positive self-esteem.

HOW DO ATTITUDES GUIDE BEHAVIOR?

attitude The evaluation of objects or ideas to indicate like or dislike toward them.

Up to this point in the chapter we have considered the basic nature of the self, and how people evaluate themselves. Social psychologists are also interested in how people evaluate other objects, including other people, within their environments.

One of the central concepts in social cognition is **attitude**, which refers to the evaluation of an object or idea. Attitudes, like many variables in social psychology, are not observable entities. You generally have to ask people whether they like something or not, or how much they like or dislike it. Attitudes consist of three components—affect, cognition, and behavior—that become linked. This *tricomponent model* of attitudes indicates that how people feel about an object, what they believe about that object, and how they behave toward that object correlate. For instance, Breckler (1984) found that people who held negative attitudes about snakes reported being anxious around them, believed negative things about them, and didn't want to touch them. Some attitudes are more complex. You might eat ice cream and enjoy doing so while believing it is bad for your health. It is the unique combination of affect, cognition, and behavioral tendencies that forms the basis of your attitudes.

ATTITUDES DEVELOP THROUGH EXPERIENCE AND LEARNING

How do our attitudes develop?

Attitudes develop through many sources. Direct experience or exposure to items provides information that shapes attitudes. For example, you might know you like ice cream and don't like liver because you've tasted them. Typically, the more that people are exposed to an item the more they tend to like it. Robert Zajonc, in a classic set of studies, exposed people to unfamiliar items a few times or many times. Greater exposure to the item, and therefore greater familiarity, caused people to have more positive attitudes about the item; this is known as the *mere exposure effect*. For example, when people are presented with a normal and a reversed photograph of themselves, they tend to prefer the reversed images, which correspond to what they see when they look in the mirror (Figure 13.12). Friends and family prefer the true photograph, which corresponds to how they perceive the person.

Conditioning   Attitudes can be conditioned. Following *classical conditioning*, a formerly neutral stimulus leads to the same attitude response as the paired object. Advertisers often use classical conditioning; seeing an attractive celebrity paired with a brand of toilet-bowl cleaner leads to more positive attitudes about that product. *Operant conditioning* also shapes attitudes. If each time you study you are rewarded with good grades, you will develop a more positive attitude toward studying.

Attitudes are also shaped through socialization. Caretakers, media, teachers, religious leaders, and politicians guide attitudes about many things. For instance, Hindus are taught to eat pork but not beef, while Jews are taught to eat beef but not pork. Society socializes many of our attitudes, including which things are edible. Would you eat a worm? Most Westerners would find this disgusting. But in some cultures worms are a delicacy.

13.12   If he is like most people, George W. Bush will prefer his mirror-image (right), with which he is most familiar, to his photographic image (left).

Heritability of attitudes   Although most attitudes are shaped through exposure and learning, some people may be genetically predisposed to acquire specific attitudes. Research by Nicholas Martin, Lindon Eaves, and their colleagues reveals that attitudes toward the death penalty, jazz, censorship, and apartheid have high heritability components whereas attitudes toward coeducation, straightjackets, and flogging do not (Eaves et al., 1989). Tesser (1993) has shown that highly heritable attitudes elicit faster responses, are more resistant to change, and have a stronger impact on attractiveness ratings than less heritable attitudes. Tesser argues that attitudes are not inherited in the sense that eye color is; rather, people inherit physiological characteristics that lead to certain responses. Thus, for instance, people may inherit a nervous system that predisposes them to find certain types of music, such as jazz, interesting or irritating.

ATTITUDES PREDICT BEHAVIOR IN CERTAIN CIRCUMSTANCES

To the extent that attitudes are adaptive, they should guide behavior. So when do attitudes predict behavior? In general, the stronger, more personally relevant the attitude, the more likely it is to predict behavior, to be consistent over time, and to be resistant to change. For instance, a vegan may be unlikely to buy leather shoes and someone who really hates mushrooms is more likely to avoid them than someone who simply doesn't care for them that much. Moreover, the more specific the attitude, the more predictive it is. For instance, your attitudes toward recycling are more predictive of whether you take your soda cans to a recycling bin than are your general environmental beliefs. Attitudes that are formed through direct experience also tend to predict behavior better. No matter what you think you would do if confronted by a mugger holding a gun, once you've been in that situation and acted, your attitude about what you would do next time becomes very strong.

How are attitudes related to behavior?

Implicit attitudes   Greenwald and Banaji (1995) noted that many attitudes influence our feelings and behavior at an unconscious level, and they refer to these

implicit attitudes Attitudes that influence our feelings and behavior at an unconscious level.

as **implicit attitudes**. Implicit attitudes are accessed from memory quickly with little conscious effort or control. The ease with which memories related to an attitude are retrieved—known as *attitude accessibility*—predicts behavior consistent with the attitude. Russell Fazio (1995) has shown that attitudes that are easily activated are more stable, predictive of behavior, and resistant to change. Thus, the more quickly you recall that you like caviar, the more likely it is that you will eat it when given the opportunity.

Just as implicit memory allows us to ride a bicycle without thinking about it, implicit attitudes shape behavior without our awareness. Some evidence suggests that implicit attitudes involve the basal ganglia, brain regions associated with implicit learning in general (Lieberman, 2000). Also like implicit memory, implicit attitudes are assessed through indirect means, such as through behavior rather than through self-report. The fact that people prefer the letters of their own names is an example of an implicit attitude about the self.

One way to assess implicit attitudes is through a reaction-time test, in which people are asked to associate pairs of objects (such as flowers and insects) with evaluative labels (such as hope and death). The *implicit attitudes test* (IAT; Greenwald et al., 1998) demonstrates that people generally find it easier to associate positive objects with positive labels (flowers and hope) than positive objects with negative labels (flowers and death). The opposite is also true. It is easier to pair insects and death than insects and hope. Interestingly, scores on the IAT tend to correlate poorly with explicit self-reports of attitudes. Recall from Chapter 1 that the IAT can be used to assess racial attitudes, and that scores on the IAT predict amygdala activation (indicating fear) when viewing black faces whereas explicit measures of racism do not. This suggests that people may possess dual attitudes about many objects: one is automatic and unconscious, the other is explicit and comes to mind when people contemplate their attitudes (Wilson et al., 2000). Dual attitudes may occur when people have a change of heart, such as after a falling out with a sibling. Even if they state explicitly that they do not care for their sibling, they still might show concern and offer aid if the sibling is in trouble. The new explicit attitude does not wipe out the implicit attitude that developed over the course of childhood. You will see later that implicit attitudes are important for understanding racial stereotypes.

13.13 Whether or not they were accompanied by their Caucasian friend, the young Chinese couple received either a normal or better than expected reception (top). This was surprising because of the rampant negative attitudes toward Asians at the time in California (bottom).

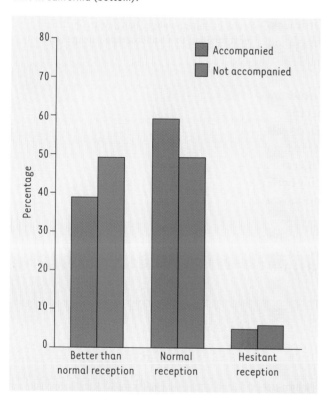

Discrepancies between attitudes and behavior Most people expect attitudes to guide behavior. People should vote for candidates they like, and they should avoid eating foods they don't like. However, sometimes attitudes seem unrelated to behavior. In the 1930s in California, researcher Richard LaPiere conducted a study while traveling with two Chinese friends. At the time, prejudice against Asians was rampant in California, due to a perception that Asians were taking all the good jobs. At a series of hotels and restaurants, LaPiere had the Chinese couple enter first in order to see how they were treated. It turned out that they received excellent treatment at the more than 250 places they visited (Figure 13.13). This was a surprise to LaPiere because the newspapers were full of accounts of negative attitudes toward Asians. To test whether white Californians actually had negative attitudes about the Chinese, LaPiere sent out a questionnaire to hotels and restaurants in the region that the threesome had visited. The questionnaire included the question "Will you accept members of the Chinese race as guests in your establishment?" The responses he received indicated vast and profound prejudice: 92 percent said they would not serve Chinese. What is most surprising is that of the responses he received, 128 were from places that had treated his Chinese companions extremely well, revealing that privately held attitudes may not predict behavior when they contradict normative social values or when their expression would lead to embarrassing interpersonal encounters.

DISCREPANCIES BETWEEN ATTITUDES AND BEHAVIOR LEAD TO COGNITIVE DISSONANCE

In 1957, Leon Festinger (Figure 13.14) proposed an elegant theory that was to become one of the most important catalysts of research in experimental social psychology. Festinger was interested in how people resolved situations in which they held conflicting attitudes. He proposed that **cognitive dissonance** occurs when there is a contradiction between two attitudes or between an attitude and behavior. People who smoke in spite of knowing that smoking may kill them experience cognitive dissonance. A basic assumption of dissonance theory is that dissonance causes anxiety and tension and therefore motivates people to reduce it and relieve displeasure. Generally, people reduce dissonance by changing their attitudes or behaviors; they also rationalize or trivialize the discrepancy. Moreover, cognitive dissonance shapes behavior and perceptions so that people maintain cognitive constancy. We ignore information that refutes or contradicts our beliefs and accept uncritically information that confirms them. Consider a 1950s study by Edward Jones and Rika Kohler of people who were either strongly for or against racial segregation. They asked their participants to read a number of statements and arguments supporting each side of the issue. Some of these arguments made a great deal of sense, whereas others were simply ludicrous or clearly wrong. If people were purely rational, they would remember the plausible arguments for both sides (after all, you would want to know what the opposition really believed). Dissonance theory predicts, however, that people would remember the plausible arguments supporting their position but the ridiculous arguments supporting the other side. This is exactly the pattern the researchers found.

Attitude change In one of the original dissonance studies, Leon Festinger and Merrill Carlsmith (1959) had students perform an incredibly boring task for an hour. The experimenter then told each student that some participants in the study were being told that the experiment was really interesting, and that the next participant was supposed to be given this misinformation. The experimenter asked the student to tell the next participant that the experiment was really interesting, educational, and worthwhile. The experimenter then offered to pay the student either $1 or $20. Nearly all of the participants agreed to help and they subsequently provided the false information. Later, under the guise of a different survey, the same participants were asked how worthwhile and enjoyable the actual task had been. You might think that those paid $20 remembered the task as more enjoyable, but just the opposite happened. Participants who had been paid $1 rated the task much more highly than those who had been paid $20. According to Festinger, this effect occurred because those in the $1 group had *insufficient justification* for lying. Therefore, in order to justify why they went along with the lie,

cognitive dissonance When there is a contradiction between two attitudes or between some attitude and behavior.

13.14 Leon Festinger developed the influential theory of cognitive dissonance.

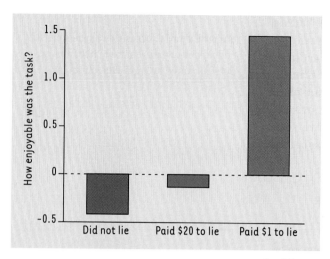

13.15 Those who were paid only $1 to mislead a fellow student experienced cognitive dissonance, which led them to alter their attitudes about how pleasurable the task had been.

they changed their attitude about performing the dull experimental task. The group who was paid $20 had plenty of justification for lying since $20 was a large amount of money. Thus, they did not experience dissonance and their attitudes about the task were unchanged (Figure 13.15).

If people are forced to perform an action that is inconsistent with their beliefs, they experience minimal dissonance. But, if they *choose* to perform a counter-attitudinal behavior, dissonance is aroused and needs to be resolved. Consider a study in which participants were told that they had been randomly assigned to eat a large dead worm (Comer & Laird, 1975). The experimenter reminded people that they were free to leave the study and that they didn't have to participate. The participants were then left alone to contemplate the situation. The experimenter returned and informed the participants that there had been a mistake, and that they were actually assigned to a different condition in which they could choose to eat the worm or perform a neutral task. According to Festinger, the participants would have already resolved the dissonance by having a more favorable attitude toward eating worms. Believe it or not, 80 percent of the participants chose to eat the worm. One participant was so resigned to his fate that he had cut up the worm into bite-size pieces while waiting for the experimenter.

Postdecisional dissonance   Many people find it difficult to choose which college to attend. They narrow down their choice to two or three alternatives and then they have to decide. According to cognitive dissonance theory, holding positive attitudes about two schools, and selecting one of them, causes dissonance. *Postdecisional dissonance* then motivates the person to focus on the positive characteristics of the school chosen and the negative aspects of the school not chosen. Similarly, when people choose to purchase a truck rather than a car they suddenly think of a million reasons why owning a truck is better than owning a car. Car owners do just the opposite. This effect occurs automatically and apparently without awareness. Indeed, even patients with long-term memory loss show a postdecisional effect for past choices, although they cannot consciously recall which object they chose (Lieberman et al., 2001). Thus, dissonance requires minimal cognitive processing to occur.

Selective exposure and denial   After a decision is made and people develop more positive attitudes about the chosen alternative, they maintain their new attitude through *selective exposure*; they seek out information that supports their decision and avoid information that suggests they made a poor choice. Selective exposure is a form of denial in which people avoid thinking about the negative implications of their actions. Denial is clearly important when people are engaging in behaviors that they know are unhealthy. Smokers tend to avoid news reports about the consequences of smoking. A recent study found that smokers with high self-esteem who failed in their efforts to quit smoking subsequently reported that they did not believe that smoking was all that bad (Gibbons et al., 1997).

Justifying effort   Hazing and other initiation rites are a serious problem on college campuses. Administrators pass laws and impose penalties to discourage hazing, and yet it continues to occur. What function does hazing serve for the group that makes it so resistant to change? Why don't fraternities and sororities simply select new members and let them in without initiation? It turns out that requiring people to undergo an embarrassing or difficult initiation makes the group seem much more valuable. Eliot Aronson and Judson Mills (1959) required women to undergo an embarrassing test to see if they qualified to take part in a study of human sexuality. The women were required to read a list of obscene words and sexually explicit passages in front of the male experimenter, whereas a control group read a list of very mild words (such as "prostitute"). The women then listened to an incredibly boring and technical presentation about mating rituals in lower animals. Women who underwent the embarrassing initiation reported that the presentation was much more interesting, stimulating, and important than the women who underwent the mild initiation. When people put themselves through pain, embarrassment, or discomfort to join a group, they experience a great deal of dissonance. They resolve the dissonance by increasing the importance of the group and their commitment to it. This *effort justification* may explain why people who give up connections to families and friends to join cults or follow enigmatic leaders are willing to die rather than leave the group. If they have sacrificed so much to join the group, the group must be extraordinarily important.

persuasion The active and conscious effort to change attitudes through the transmission of a message.

elaboration likelihood model A theory of how persuasive messages lead to attitude change.

13.16 When people are motivated to carefully consider information, it is processed by the central route, and attitudes are changed accordingly. Otherwise, people process information at a shallow level and are persuaded by peripheral cues.

ATTITUDES CAN BE CHANGED THROUGH PERSUASION

A number of forces other than dissonance conspire to change attitudes. People are bombarded by television advertisements; lectures from parents, teachers, and physicians; public service announcements; politicians appealing for our votes; and so on. **Persuasion** is the active and conscious effort to change attitudes through the transmission of a message. The earliest scientific work on persuasion was conducted by Carl Hovland (1912–1961) and his colleagues at Yale University, who emphasized that persuasion was most likely to occur when people attended to the message, understood it and found it convincing, and when the message was memorable so that its impact lasted over time.

A number of researchers have noted that there are two fundamental ways in which persuasion leads to attitude change (Figure 13.16). According to Richard Petty and John Cacioppo's **elaboration likelihood model** (1986), the *central route* to persuasion is one in which people pay attention to arguments, consider all the

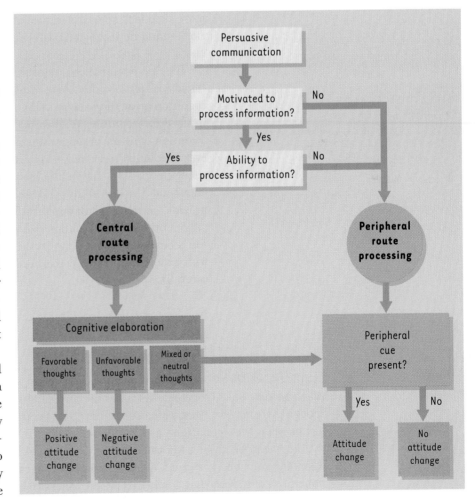

information, and use rational cognitive processes; it leads to strong attitudes that last over time and are resistant to change. By contrast, the *peripheral route* to persuasion is one in which people minimally process the message, such as deciding to purchase a new type of bottled water because an advertisement for it featured their favorite soap star.

A number of cues influence the extent to which a message is persuasive. These include the *source* (who says it), the *content* (what the message says), and the *receiver* (who is processing the message). Sources who are credible and attractive are most persuasive. This is why television ads feature unusually attractive people playing the roles of physicians to encourage people to purchase a certain brand of antacid. The message is effective because of peripheral processing. In addition, people who are perceived as similar to the receiver are liked better and viewed as more credible and therefore are also persuasive.

The arguments contained in the message are clearly important for persuasion. Strong arguments that appeal to our emotions are most persuasive. Advertisers also use the mere exposure effect, repeating their messages over and over in the hopes that repeated exposure will lead to increased persuasiveness. As the old saying goes, "If you repeat a lie often enough people will believe it." This is why politicians often espouse the same statements over and over during campaigns. Also, those who want to persuade have to decide whether to deliver a one-sided argument or to consider both sides. One-sided arguments are best if the audience is on the speaker's side or is gullible. When speaking to a crowd that is more skeptical, speakers who acknowledge both sides but argue that one is superior tend to be more persuasive than those who completely ignore the opposing view.

The one personal characteristic that seems to be important in persuasion is called *need for cognition*. According to Petty and Cacioppo, those high in need for cognition pride themselves on being thoughtful and reflective, whereas those low in need for cognition tend to make decisions quickly. People high in need for cognition typically process information centrally rather than peripherally. However, the ability to make fast decisions can be highly adaptive when situations are changing quickly. Indeed, sometimes thinking too much can lead to inferior judgments. In one study, researchers found that people who were required to provide a verbal explanation for why they liked certain kinds of jam made inferior judgments compared to those who rated the jam based on their first tastes (Wilson & Schooler, 1991). That is, the immediate ratings corresponded more highly with expert taste ratings than did the ratings made by those induced to think carefully.

How Do Attitudes Guide Behavior?

Attitudes, which are evaluations of objects or ideas, consist of affect, cognition, and behavior, which become linked together. Attitudes are formed through socialization and direct experience, although there may be genetic predispositions to form certain specific attitudes. Attitudes predict behavior when they are strong and easily accessible. Discrepancies between attitudes, or between attitudes and behavior, lead to cognitive dissonance. Dissonance theory can be used to explain a wide range of human behavior. Attitudes can be changed by persuasion, either through central or peripheral means, depending on whether people think carefully about the issues or not.

HOW DO PEOPLE FORM ATTITUDES ABOUT OTHERS?

Over the course of human evolution, one fact has remained constant: people are social animals who live in groups. Groups provide security from predators and competing groups, as well as mating opportunities and assistance in hunting and gathering food. At the same time, members within a group are essentially competitors for the same food and mates. Hence, mechanisms have evolved for distinguishing members of one's own group from other groups, as well as for detecting dangers from within the group, such as deception, coercion, and infidelity. People are constantly required to make social judgments, assessing whether a person is friend or foe, potential mate or potential challenger, honest or dishonest, trustworthy or unreliable, and so on.

Over the years, social psychology has confirmed the importance of first impressions on long-term evaluations of people, a process known as *impression formation*. For instance, if a professor begins a course full of enthusiasm, humor, and energy, students will forgive the odd boring lecture later in the term. However, professors who give a monotonous, dry, and dull lecture on the first day are unlikely to be viewed more positively as the course progresses. In a now classic study conducted in the 1940s, Solomon Asch presented participants with a list of terms describing a person: intelligent, industrious, impulsive, critical, stubborn, and envious. This person was rated more positively than a person described as envious, stubborn, critical, impulsive, industrious, and intelligent, even though the words are identical, just presented in the opposite order. This *primacy effect* in impression formation occurs because the initial information alters the way that the subsequent information is interpreted. Many factors influence impression formation, ranging from the observer's initial expectations and attitudes to what the observed person says, as well as his or her nonverbal gestures and physical appearance. In this chapter on social cognition we will focus on the observer's expectations and attitudes; in Chapter 14 we will consider what the observed person brings to impression formation.

RESEARCH QUESTION

What factors influence how we perceive others?

PEOPLE MAKE ATTRIBUTIONS

People constantly try to explain other people's motives, traits, and preferences. Why did she say that? Why is he crying? Why does she study so hard? and so on. *Attributions* are people's causal explanations for why events or actions occur. People are motivated to draw inferences in part by a basic need for order and predictability in their lives. The world can be a dangerous place in which unexpected things happen. People prefer to think that things happen for a reason, and therefore that they can anticipate future events. For instance, they might believe that people become overweight from eating too much. Therefore, if they just avoid overeating, they will not become overweight. Indeed, when events occur that don't seem to make any sense, such as when a person is brutally raped or murdered, people often make attributions about the victim, such as "she deserved it" or "he provoked it." Such attributions are part of what is referred to as the *just world hypothesis*. From this perspective, victims must have done something to justify what happened to them.

Attributional dimensions In any situation, there are dozens of plausible explanations for specific outcomes. Doing well on a test could be due to brillance,

personal attributions Explanations that refer to internal characteristics, such as abilities, traits, moods, and effort.

situational attributions Explanations that refer to external events, such as the weather, luck, accidents, or the actions of other people.

correspondence bias The tendency to expect people's behavior to agree with their dispositions.

luck, intensive studying, or an easy test. Fritz Heider, the originator of attribution theory, drew the essential distinction between *personal* and *situational* attributions. **Personal attributions**, also known as *internal* or *dispositional attributions*, are explanations that refer to something within a person, such as abilities, traits, moods, and effort. By contrast, **situational attributions**, also known as *external attributions*, refer to outside events, such as the weather, luck, accidents, or the actions of other people. Bernie Weiner later noted that attributions can vary on other dimensions, such as whether they are stable over time versus variable, or controllable versus uncontrollable. For instance, weather is situational, variable, and uncontrollable. Good study habits are personal, stable, and controllable. Weiner's theory has also been used to explain psychological states such as depression. People who are depressed tend to attribute their failure to personal, stable, yet uncontrollable attributes. Depressed people attribute their failures to their incompetence, which they believe is permanent.

Theory of mind and intentions When people make attributions about the intentions of others, they are trying figuratively to "get in the head" of the other person to determine that person's motives or thought processes. Recall from Chapter 11 that the basic capacity to wonder about the mental states of others requires that people possess *theory of mind (TOM)*. Understanding why someone is crying requires understanding and empathizing with that person's emotional state. There is currently a debate over whether TOM is essentially a cognitive belief system about other people's belief systems, or whether it is the ability to simulate the mental and emotional states of others. This latter perspective suggests that people actively imagine themselves in the other person's situation to experience what the other person feels. Research on TOM has implications for many areas of psychology, as can be found in "Crossing the Levels of Analysis: Understanding Theory of Mind."

SOCIAL INFORMATION PROCESSING IS BIASED

Theorists such as Fritz Heider and Harold Kelly described people as *intuitive scientists*, trying to draw inferences about others and make attributions about events. However, unlike the metaphorical objective scientist, people tend to be systematically biased in their social-information processing. They make attributions that are self-serving and consistent with preexisting beliefs, and they fail to take into account that other people are influenced by social circumstances.

Correspondence bias Most of us realize that we are deeply affected by our social situations, and yet we often fail to recognize the degree to which others are influenced by their situations. In a classic 1967 study, Edward Jones and Victor Davis had participants listen to a debater either support or attack Fidel Castro. The participants were told either that the debater had freely chosen which side to argue or that the experimenter had assigned the person to the position. Irrespective of whether the person had had a choice, those who gave a speech supporting Castro were viewed as liking Castro more than those who gave a speech attacking Castro. Jones and his colleagues called this the **correspondence bias**, meaning we expect people's behavior to *correspond* with their beliefs and personality. People tend to assume that others are the way they behave, even if they know those people are acting. Consider Alex Trebeck, host of *Jeopardy*, who is considered by many to be extremely smart. Most people fail to take into account that he is given the an-

UNDERSTANDING THEORY OF MIND

People need to be aware of the intentions of other people. For example, defensive driving is based on the idea that you can predict the potential erratic actions of others. When people are deciding whether to go on a date or begin a physical relationship, they often want to know what the other person has in mind. The ability to predict what another person is feeling or thinking is known as having theory of mind (TOM). Developmental psychologists have studied the emergence of TOM in young children. This research, discussed in Chapter 11, shows that children initially infer mental states in others based on desires, such as thinking that their siblings want to eat pizza rather than noodles. It isn't until they are four or five years old that children grasp the idea that other people have belief systems and engage in problem solving and reasoning. For instance, a younger child has difficulty with the concept that people can hold beliefs that are false or that are different from hers. Moreover, studies show that very young children are egocentric and can't take the perspective of others. Thus, the ability to perceive the social significance of other people's mental states develops around age four. Interestingly, this is approximately the same time that children can project themselves into the future. Apparently, there is a large growth in mental activity around age four or five associated with both an increase in self-knowledge and the development of TOM.

Children's development of TOM coincides with the frontal lobes becoming relatively mature. This would imply that TOM is related to activity in frontal lobe brain regions. Indeed, lesion and fMRI studies have shown that the frontal lobes, and more precisely the orbitofrontal region of the prefrontal cortex, may be especially important for TOM. Prefrontal brain regions become active when people are asked to think about others' mental states, and people with damage to the orbitofrontal region have difficulty attributing mental states to others in stories (Stone et al., 1998). The area of the brain involved in inferring the emotional states of others is the amygdala. Recall from Chapter 10 that the amygdala is activated during the processing of facial expressions. Moreover, Simon Baron-Cohen found that the amygdala is activated when people have to judge the mental states of others by looking at their eyes (Baron-Cohen et al., 1997). Taken together, these studies suggest that the frontal lobes and the amygdala are important for TOM.

Knowing whether others are trustworthy or not is an important aspect of social cognition and impression formation. A variety of evidence suggests that people with either high-functioning autism or with damage to the amygdala have difficulty in judging whether peo-

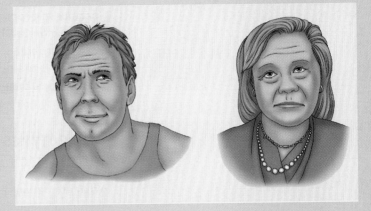

13.17 People with damage to the amygdala can tell a smiling from a frowning face, but they have difficulty judging whether the people smiling or frowning are trustworthy. Which of these people would you trust?

ple should be trusted based on pictures, a task that most people can do without any trouble (Figure 13.17). People with amygdala damage can tell a smile from a frown, but they do not seem to use this information in making social judgments (Adolphs et al., 2001). People with amygdala damage also tend to be unusually friendly toward others, which may mean they lack the normal mechanisms that lead to cautiousness around strangers and the feeling that some people should be avoided. Interestingly, impairment in the social domain may be associated with strength in nonsocial domains, such as knowledge of intuitive physics.

Finally, social psychologists have been studying the related idea of empathic accuracy, or everyday mind-reading. William Ickes and Jeffrey Simpson have participants watch videotapes of others over time and assess the other people's mental states as they watch. Researchers have found that empathic accuracy increases as people get to know each other, although some people are simply better at judging others, and some people seem to be easier to read. Interestingly, couples who have been together shorter lengths of time may have greater empathic accuracy than couples together for long periods of time, perhaps reflecting the fact that the former are more motivated to understand one another (Ickes & Simpson, 1997). Indeed, only those who truly want to know what others are thinking show high levels of empathic accuracy. Thus, motives for understanding others' mental states influence the operation of TOM.

swers in advance. Similarly, many people view actors as similar to the characters they portray, even though at some level people know that actors follow a script and are paid to do so.

Although initial studies indicated that the correspondence bias was so common that it is sometimes called the *fundamental attribution error*, some research has indicated that it is more common in Western cultures than in Eastern cultures. Moreover, when people are making attributions about themselves, they tend to focus on situations rather than on their personal dispositions, which in concert with the correspondence bias leads to the *actor-observer discrepancy*. For instance, if people are explaining why they are late, they tend to attribute it to external factors, such as traffic or competing demands. When others are late, people tend to attribute it to personal characteristics, such as laziness. Hence, people are biased toward situational factors when explaining their own behavior, but toward dispositional factors when explaining the behavior of others.

STEREOTYPES ARE BASED ON AUTOMATIC CATEGORIZATION

What are Italians like? How about Canadians—do they all like hockey? Can white men jump? People possess attitudes and beliefs about groups that allow them to answer these sorts of questions. These attitudes and beliefs are **stereotypes**, cognitive schemas that organize information about people based on their membership in certain groups. Stereotypes are mental shortcuts that allow for easy, fast processing of social information. They occur automatically and, in most cases, outside of awareness. In and of themselves, stereotypes are neutral and simply reflect efficient cognitive processes. Indeed, some stereotypes are true, such as that women are generally more emotionally expressive and men more violent. **Prejudice** refers to the affective or attitudinal responses associated with stereotypes, and it usually involves negative judgments about people based on their group memberships. Often, prejudice leads people to engage in **discrimination**, which is the unjustified and inappropriate treatment of people based solely on their group memberships. Prejudice and discrimination are major problems, responsible for much of the conflict and warfare around the world. Within nearly all cultures, some classes of people are treated negatively based on prejudice. Social psychologists have spent the last half-century studying the determinants and consequences of prejudice as well as trying to find ways to reduce its pernicious effects.

People construct and use categories to streamline the process of impression formation in order to deal with the limitations inherent in mental processing. Rather than considering each person as unique and unpredictable, we categorize people as belonging to a group, a group about which we hold knowledge in long-term memory. These stereotypes then affect how we view and treat others. Consider a study in which participants are asked to judge whether a person is famous or not. Those who have seen the person's name in a prior task are likely to falsely remember the name as that of a famous person, which is known as the *false fame effect*. However, this is much more likely to happen for male names than for female names, apparently because of the stereotype that men are more likely to be famous than are women (Banaji & Greenwald, 1995).

We began Chapter 1 by describing the killing of Amadou Diallo by New York police officers. How can social cognition help us understand this tragedy? Recall from Chapter 1 that for white people high in *implicit racism*, viewing black faces leads to activation of the amygdala, associated with fear. Crossing levels of analysis, these implicit social attitudes can also influence basic perceptual processes. In two experiments that demonstrated this, Payne (2001) showed pictures of guns or tools to white participants and asked them to classify the objects as quickly as possible (Figure 13.18). Just prior to seeing an object, the participants were

stereotypes Cognitive schemas that allow for easy and efficient organization of information about people based on their membership in certain groups.

prejudice The affective or attitudinal responses associated with stereotypes.

discrimination The inappropriate and unjustified treatment of people based solely on their group membership.

primed by a brief presentation of either a white or a black face. Priming by black faces led participants to more quickly identify guns and to mistake tools for guns. These findings suggest that implicit racism may have been involved in the Diallo shooting. The officers were looking for individuals who fit a specific racial profile and when faced with a split-second decision, mistook Diallo's wallet for a weapon.

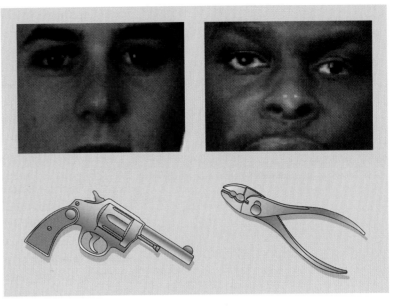

Whether a particular category is used depends on how salient it is in a given situation. Imagine meeting a very short African American male dentist. Which category would you use? According to Neil Macrae and Galen Bodenhausen (2000), although all categories are activated in parallel, only one category comes to dominate mental resources. Which category becomes dominant depends on the salience of the category, the extent to which the categories are chronically used, and the goals and motivations of the person forming the impressions. In an interesting demonstration of the selective activation of categories, Lisa Sinclair and Ziva Kunda (1999) presented white participants with a black physician who either praised them or gave them negative feedback. Following praise, which presumably motivated the participants to think highly of the doctor, negative stereotypes of blacks were inhibited while positive stereotypes of physicians became activated. Following criticism, the opposite occurred. In another study, the researchers found that black managers who criticized the white participants' interpersonal skills were evaluated more negatively in return than were critical white managers.

13.18 After being primed by black or white faces, white participants had to quickly classify pictures as tools or guns. Participants misidentified tools as guns when primed with black faces, suggesting that stereotypes alter perceptual processes.

Overriding and suppressing stereotypes Most people do not consider themselves prejudiced, and many are motivated to avoid stereotyping others. Yet according to many researchers in social cognition, categorization and stereotyping occur automatically, without awareness or intent (Bargh & Ferguson, 2000). However, Patricia Devine (1989) made the important point that people could override their stereotypes and act in a nondiscriminatory fashion. For instance, most people in North America know the negative stereotypes associated with African Americans, and when a nonblack person encounters a black person, the information in the stereotypes becomes cognitively available. According to Devine, people who are low in prejudice override this automatic activation and act in a nondiscriminatory fashion.

One problem with suppressing activated stereotypes is that doing so is difficult and can even backfire. Active effort to suppress a thought typically leads to a subsequent obsession with that very thought. As might be expected, research has demonstrated that people who actively try to suppress stereotypes experience a *cognitive rebound effect*, increasing their use of the stereotype in subsequent evaluations and behavioral actions. For instance, Neil Macrae and his colleagues (1994) asked participants to write about a typical day in the life of a "skinhead." Those warned to avoid stereotypical preconceptions subsequently rated skinheads more negatively and chose to sit farther away from a skinhead they encountered.

Maintaining stereotypes Once formed, stereotypes are maintained by a number of processes. As schematic structures, stereotypes guide attention toward in-

outgroup homogeneity effect The tendency for people to view outgroup members as more similar to each other than ingroup members.

ingroup favoritism The tendency for people to evaluate favorably and privilege members of the ingroup more than members of the outgroup.

formation that confirms the stereotypes and away from disconfirming evidence. People's memories are also biased to match stereotypes. These biases lead to an *illusory correlation*, in which people believe that a relationship exists when it actually does not. The professor who notices that a black student performs poorly but fails to notice other black students who do well will confirm a false belief relating race to performance. Similarly, the meaning of a behavior can be altered so that it is consistent with the stereotype. A white man's success may be attributed to his hard work and determination, whereas a black man's success may be attributed to outside factors, such as luck or affirmative action. A lawyer described as aggressive conjures up different images than a construction worker described as aggressive. Moreover, when people encounter someone who does not fit the stereotype, rather than alter the stereotype they put that person in a special category, a process known as *subtyping*. Thus, a racist who believes that blacks are lazy categorizes Michael Jordan as an exception to the rule rather than as evidence for the invalidity of the stereotype. Forming a subtype that includes successful blacks helps racists maintain the stereotype that most blacks are unsuccessful.

PREJUDICE AND STIGMA HAVE AN EVOLUTIONARY BASIS

Why do stereotypes so often lead to prejudice and discrimination? A variety of theories have been proposed over the years, including that only certain types of people are prejudiced, that people treat others as scapegoats to relieve the tensions of daily living, and that people discriminate to protect their self-esteem. An explanation consistent with our theme that the mind is adaptive is that evolution has led to two processes that produce prejudice and discrimination. First, there is a tendency to favor our own groups over other groups. Second, there is a tendency to stigmatize those who pose threats to our groups.

Ingroup-outgroup bias We are powerfully connected to the groups to which we belong. We cheer them on, we fight for them, and sometimes we are even willing to die for them. Those groups to which we belong are called *ingroups* and those to which we do not belong are called *outgroups*. People treat ingroup members much differently than outgroup members. For instance, people tend to view outgroup members as less varied than ingroup members, which is called the **outgroup homogeneity effect**. Stanford students may think Harvard students are all alike, but when they think about Stanford students they can't help but notice the wide diversity of different student types. Of course, the reverse is true as well.

The consequence of categorizing people as ingroup and outgroup is **ingroup favoritism**, in which people are more likely to distribute resources to members of the ingroup than to the outgroup. People are more willing to do favors, forgive mistakes or errors, and give tangible resources to ingroup members. The power of group membership is so strong that people will even exhibit ingroup favoritism if the groups are determined by arbitrary processes. British psychologist Henri Tajfel and his American collaborator John Turner (1979) randomly assigned volunteers into one of two groups, based on totally meaningless criteria, such as flipping a coin. Participants were then given a task in which they divided up money. Not surprisingly, they gave more money to their ingroup members. But they also tried to prevent the outgroup members from getting any money, even when they were told that the basis of group membership was arbitrary and that giving money to the outgroup would not affect how much money their group obtained!

Why do people value members of their own groups? Over the course of human evolution, personal survival has depended upon group survival. Especially when there was competition over scarce resources, those who worked together to keep resources within their group and deny resources to outgroup members had a selective advantage over those willing to share. Throughout human history, the ingroup has also been more likely to contain people who share genes. Because the group is so central to individual survival, it is not surprising that people show favoritism to their own groups. Indeed, our group memberships are an important part of our social identity and contribute to our overall sense of self-esteem.

Stigma **Stigma** is a very strong devaluation that extends to a person's entire character; typically, the person is viewed as deviant and perhaps even less than human. Stigmatized people are defined by their "flaws," such as being disabled, a member of a certain racial minority, obese (in Western cultures), a drug addict, homosexual, and so on. Often, stigmatized people are scorned, especially if they are perceived to have control over their stigmatizing conditions (such as with obesity or alcoholism). Interacting with stigmatized people may be awkward and people may try to avoid doing so.

Those who pose threats to the self or to the social group are most likely to be stigmatized (Neuberg et al., 2000). The sharing of resources is one of the most tangible benefits of group membership, but it relies on reciprocation. Those who do not reciprocate, such as those who lie, cheat, or steal, are stigmatized as liars, cheaters, and thieves. They are socially ostracized and avoided. Evolutionary psychologists Leda Cosmides and John Tooby (2000) believe that humans may have evolved *cheater detectors* to identify those unlikely to reciprocate resources. In addition, those who are physically disabled drain group resources, and therefore in prehistoric times they may have been perceived as undue burdens on the group. Indeed, there is substantial evidence of stigmatization of those who are physically or emotionally handicapped. Similarly, people who are ill might spread disease and are a direct danger to others within the group. Therefore, it is not surprising that many disease victims (such as those with AIDS or leprosy) are stigmatized (Kurzban & Leary, 2001). Support for the idea that stigma represents a threat can be found in studies that have assessed brain activation patterns associated with prejudice. For instance, recall the finding that unfamiliar but not familiar black faces activated the amygdala in white participants (Phelps et al., 2000).

STEREOTYPES CAN BE SELF-FULFILLING

Stereotypes that are initially untrue can become true through the process of **self-fulfilling prophecy**, in which people come to behave in ways that confirm their own or others' expectations.

Let's consider the general process of the self-fulfilling prophecy. One of the most impressive early demonstrations was conducted in the 1960s by Robert Rosenthal with school principal Lenore Jacobsen. In this study, elementary-school students took a test that supposedly identified some of them as being especially likely to show large increases in IQ during the school year. Teachers were given a list of these "bloomers" in their classes. At the end of the year, standardized testing revealed that the "bloomers" actually did show a large increase in IQ. As you might have guessed, students were chosen at random rather than through any test, and therefore the increase in IQ was attributed to the extra attention provided by the teachers. In effect, the teachers paid more attention to the

stigma A very strong devaluation that extends to a person's entire character.

self-fulfilling prophecy People come to behave in ways that confirm their own or other's expectations.

How do stereotypes influence our treatment of others?

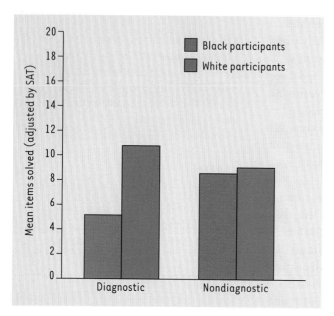

13.19 When the test was described as diagnostic, stereotype threat led the black students to perform poorly.

"bloomers," perhaps giving them extra encouragement. Thus, teacher expectations turned into reality. Of course, not only can positive stereotypes become self-fulfilling, but so can negative stereotypes. Thus, teachers who expect certain students to fail—for example, minority students—might do things to subtly undermine students' self-confidence or motivation. For instance, offering unwanted help—even with the best of intentions—can send the message that the teacher does not believe the student has what it takes to succeed.

Recent studies have demonstrated that students who feel that their behavior may confirm a negative stereotype are especially likely to do poorly, a phenomenon known as **stereotype threat** (Steele, 1997). For instance, when men and women take a test for which they are told there are typically no sex differences, no sex differences emerge in the actual test performance. However, if women are told that men typically do better, then women do significantly worse than men (Spencer et al., 1999). The same pattern was obtained when equally intelligent (as assessed by SAT scores) black and white Stanford students took a difficult test of verbal skills. When told that the test was unrelated to intelligence, black and white students performed at the same level. However, when the students were told the test was a measure of intelligence, black students did quite poorly (Figure 13.19; Steele & Aronson, 1995). According to the researchers, worries about confirming the negative stereotypes led the women and black students to become anxious and preoccupied. This cognitive load and anxiety interfered with their performances. In an especially intriguing example of stereotype threat, researchers found that Asian American women did well on a math test when the "Asians are good at math" stereotype was primed and poorly when the "women are bad at math" stereotype was primed (Shih et al., 1999).

Self-fulfilling prophecy effects are powerful moderators of behavior. Expectancies influence outcomes through a four-step process. First, expectancies influence others' evaluations of the person through illusory correlation and the confirmation bias. Second, others behave toward the person in a manner consistent with their expectations, for instance by discouraging the person from pursuing high goals. Third, the person's behavior changes in the direction of others' expectations, such as occurs with stereotype threat. Finally, the person internalizes and therefore acts in a way consistent with the expectation.

PREJUDICE AND DISCRIMINATION CAN BE REDUCED

Over the past 50 years, a number of strategies for reducing prejudice have been attempted. Most have failed completely. It is extraordinarily difficult to change culture, and attitudes toward ethnic groups are embedded deeply in culture. Around the world, groups clash based on disputes that predate the births of most of the combatants, and sometimes people can't even remember the original source of conflict. Can prejudice be eliminated? Probably not.

There is some good news, however. Social psychologists have uncovered a variety of strategies that are effective in producing greater tolerance for and liking of outgroup members. The first efforts to reduce prejudice were based on the **contact hypothesis** that prejudice comes from a lack of familiarity with outgroup members and that getting to know the outgroup better would reduce negative attitudes. Such ideas were behind efforts to desegregate schools. Although most so-

stereotype threat A phenomenon in which individuals who feel that their behavior may confirm or verify a negative stereotype perform poorly in a given test.

contact hypothesis The idea that increasing contact and familiarity with outgroup members will reduce negative attitudes towards them.

superordinate goals Goals that require people to cooperate in order to succeed.

cial scientists expected desegregation to reduce racial tension, they found instead that it led to increased tension and hostility. Social psychologists now know simple contact is not enough. A study conducted by Muzafer Sherif (1906–1988) and his colleagues in the late 1950s provided some evidence for what needs to be done to effectively combat racism. This study is described in "Using Psychological Science: Overcoming Intergroup Hostility Through Cooperation."

Research over the past four decades has indicated that only certain types of contact between hostile groups are likely to reduce prejudice and discrimination. Based on Sherif's study, it is clear that having shared **superordinate goals**, those that require people to cooperate to succeed, reduces hostility between groups. Research has shown that people who work together to achieve a common goal often break down subgroup distinctions as they become one larger group. Athletes on multi-ethnic teams often have positive attitudes toward other ethnicities. Programs that require cooperation are most effective when they include members who challenge or defy the negative stereotypes of their groups. In addition, everyone should have equal status in the cooperative task. If white professors tried to

Using Psychological Science

OVERCOMING INTERGROUP HOSTILITY THROUGH COOPERATION

In the late 1950s, before the turbulent sixties and the recognition of tremendous racial problems in the United States, social psychologist Muzafer Sherif was trying to understand how conflict over resources could lead to discrimination. To study this, he conducted what has become one of the best-known and most provocative field studies in psychological history. Sherif arranged for 22 well-adjusted and intelligent white fifth-grade boys from Oklahoma City to attend a summer camp. None of the boys knew each other before that summer. Prior to arriving at camp, the boys were divided into two groups that were essentially the same. During the first week, the boys lived in separate camps, unaware that a similar group of boys was across the lake.

Once the groups were established, Sherif started the experiment by having the groups compete in a number of athletic competitions over a four-day period, such as tug-of-war, football, and softball. Group pride was extremely strong, with the groups naming themselves the Rattlers and the Eagles. The stakes in the competition were high. The winning team would get a trophy, individual medals, and appealing prizes. The losers were to receive nothing. Animosity between the two groups quickly escalated. The Eagles burned the Rattlers' flag, and the Rattlers retaliated by trashing the Eagles' cabin. When the Eagles finally won the competition, the Rattlers again raided the Eagles' cabin, this time making off with their winning prizes. This led to a confrontation and physical fights, which had to be broken up by the experimenters. After a cooling-off period, the boys were asked to rate their own group's members versus the other group's members. All of the signs of prejudice emerged, including the outgroup homogeneity bias and ingroup favoritism. Phase 1 of the study was complete. Sherif showed how easy it was to get people to hate each other. Simply divide them into groups and then have the groups compete over limited resources, and prejudice and mistreatment would result. The question in Phase 2 of the study was, could it be undone?

Sherif first tried what made sense at the time, simply having the groups come into contact with one another. This failed miserably. The hostilities were too strong and skirmishes continued. Sherif reasoned that if competition led to hostility, then cooperation should reduce hostility. Thus, the experimenters created situations in which members of both groups had to cooperate in order to achieve their goals. For instance, the experimenters rigged a truck to break down. Getting the truck moving required all the boys pulling together, ironically on the same rope used earlier in the tug-of-war. Upon success there was a great cheer from all and plenty of backslapping all around. After a series of tasks that required cooperation, the walls between the two sides broke down and the boys became friends across the groups. From strangers, competition and isolation created enemies. From enemies, cooperation created friends. Subsequent research has demonstrated that putting people into situations that require them to work together to achieve larger goals reduces prejudice and hostility.

cooperate with a black-students group, the initial status differences might prevent meaningful change in attitudes or stereotypes.

The programs that are most successful involve person-to-person interaction. A good example is Eliot Aronson's *jigsaw classroom*. In this program, students work together in mixed-race or mixed-sex groups in which each member of the group is an expert on one aspect of the assignment. For instance, when studying Mexico, one group member might study its geography, another its history, and so on. The various geography experts from each group get together and master the material. They then return to their own groups and teach the material to their team members. Thus, cooperation is twofold: each group member cooperates not only with members of other groups, but within the group as well. More than 800 studies of the jigsaw classroom have demonstrated that not only does it lead to more positive attitudes toward other ethnicities, but students also learn the material better and perform at a higher level. According to Aronson, children in jigsaw classrooms grow to like each other more and develop higher self-esteem than do children in traditional classrooms. The lesson is clear: communal activities working toward superordinate goals can reduce prejudice.

How Do People Form Attitudes About Others?

Humans have evolved mechanisms to try to figure out what causes other people to behave the way they do. People make attributions about others, which are often biased. They tend to attribute other people's behavior to dispositions rather than to situations, and they use heuristic processing that biases social judgment. Stereotypes result from the normal cognitive process of categorization. However, negative stereotypes and prejudice lead to discrimination. There is some evidence that stereotypes are activated automatically, although people can control their behavioral responses to them. There is a natural tendency to discriminate against those who are threatening, such as outgroup members or those who bear stigmatizing conditions. Competition can lead to intergroup hostility, although cooperation can reduce that hostility. This principle has been used to develop the jigsaw classroom, which reduces prejudice.

CONCLUSION

Consistent throughout the discussion of social cognition is the idea that humans make automatic judgments about self and others based on minimal information. These judgments are often biased in ways that make people feel good about the self, often at the expense of others. The sense of self, which develops in early childhood, is adaptive in that it places the person at the center of its attention, interpreting the world in ways that benefit the person and thereby possibly enhance survival. Evidence indicates that people typically have false positive illusions about the self that are resistant to change when confronted with contradictory evidence. Research that is informed by the biological revolution and that crosses levels of analysis has shown that stereotypes alter the way people perceive and process information about others. Many times the brain reveals what people themselves do not report, or perhaps even know, such as negative attitudes about ethnic minorities. Human minds automatically categorize others using limited mental resources, with the outcome that people fail to treat others individually and with respect. It is all too easy for people to develop ingroups and outgroups;

all it takes is three people. Social psychologists have discovered that cooperative learning systems can lead to benefits for both the self and society. The challenge now is to adapt these techniques to larger groups in society, and then to motivate these groups to use them.

FURTHER READINGS

Baumeister, R. F. (1998). The self. In D. T. Gilbert, S. T. Fiske, & G. Lindzey (Eds.), *The handbook of social psychology* (4th ed.), (pp. 680–740). Boston, MA: McGraw Hill.

Franzoi, S. (2000). *Social psychology.* Boston, MA: McGraw Hill.

Heatherton, T. F., Kleck, R. E., Hebl, M., & Hull, J. G. (2000). *The social psychology of stigma.* New York: Guilford Press.

Higgins, E. T., & Kruglanski, A. W. (1996). *Social psychology: Handbook of basic principles.* New York: Guilford Press.

Kunda, Z. (2000). *Social cognition.* Cambridge, MA: MIT Press.

Macrae, C. N., & Bodenhausen, G. V. (2000). Social cognition: Thinking categorically about others. *Annual Review of Psychology, 5,* 93–120.

Parker, S. T., Mitchell, R. W., & Boccia, M. L. (1994). *Self-awareness in animals and humans.* New York: Cambridge University Press.

"FITTING IN" WITH A GROUP
Children in computer costumes rehearse for the Carnival in Rio de Janeiro. People often underestimate the powerful influence of group norms on individual behavior.

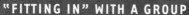

TIMELINE

1897

Social Facilitation Norman Triplett conducts the first social psychology experiment by demonstrating that people ride their bicycles more quickly in the presence of others.

1939

Frustration-Aggression Hypothesis John Dollard, Neil Miller, and their colleagues publish *Frustration and Aggression*, in which they propose that not attaining goals produces aggression.

1955

Conformity to Group Norms Solomon Asch demonstrates that people will conform to a group standard by giving an answer that they know is incorrect.

1959

Affiliation Stanley Schachter publishes a monograph on the determinants of affiliation. His research demonstrates that people seek the presence of others when they are anxious.

Interpersonal Processes

OUTLINING THE PRINCIPLES

HOW SOCIAL ARE HUMANS?

Humans Have a Fundamental Need to Belong

Anxiety Increases Affiliation

People Detect and Reject Cheaters

WHAT INFORMATION IS CONTAINED IN NONVERBAL BEHAVIOR?

Facial Expressions Communicate Meaning

Body Language Is Meaningful

Detecting Deception Is Difficult

The Need for Personal Space Varies Across Situations and Cultures

HOW DO PEOPLE MANAGE THEIR PUBLIC IMPRESSIONS?

There Are Many Self-Presentational Goals

There Are Individual Differences in Impression Management

WHEN DOES SOCIAL POWER INFLUENCE OTHERS?

Groups Influence Individual Behavior

People Conform to Social Norms

People Are Compliant

People Are Obedient to Authority

WHEN DO PEOPLE HARM OR HELP OTHERS?

Biological Factors Influence Aggression

Negative Affect Can Produce Aggression

Learned and Cultural Aspects Factor into Aggression

Multiple Factors May Influence Helping Behavior

Some Situations Lead to Bystander Apathy

WHAT DETERMINES THE QUALITY OF RELATIONSHIPS?

Many Factors Influence Affiliative Choice

There Are Sex Differences in Mating Strategies

Love Is an Important Component of Human Relationships

Making Love Last Is Difficult

CONCLUSION

FURTHER READINGS

1962

The Risky Shift An initial finding on how group membership alters decision-making processes shows that members make riskier decisions; but later research suggests that groups tend to polarize and reinforce the initial opinions of members.

1964

Ingratiation and Impression Management Edward Jones describes various strategies of impression management, which involve altering self-presentation to achieve goals.

1965

Obedience to Authority Stanley Milgram shows that people will administer painful electric shocks when ordered to do so by an authority figure.

1970

Bystander Apathy Social psychologists Bibb Latané and John Darley propose that people are unlikely to help a person in need if there is a diffusion of responsibility among the observers.

1972

Stanford Prison Study Researcher Philip Zimbardo "jails" Stanford undergraduates and assigns other students to act as guards. Within a short time, the students assume the social roles of guards and prisoners.

Canadians are by reputation a polite and gentle people, who live in safe and clean cities and are recognized internationally for their efforts to promote world peace. Perhaps this is why the sordid crimes committed by Karla Homolka and Paul Bernardo were so shocking. Their story begins in the early 1990s. Paul was an extremely handsome young accountant who was making a good wage, and Karla was an attractive, intelligent young woman who worked at a veterinary clinic. From all appearances, the couple had it all—they were beautiful, young, vigorous, healthy, and in love (Figure 14.1). Who could have known the dark secrets running through Paul's mind? They certainly weren't obvious when he was young.

In *Lethal Marriage* Nick Pron describes Paul as a little boy: "He was always happy. A young boy who smiled a lot. And he was so cute, with his dimpled good looks and sweet smile, that many of the mothers just wanted to pinch him on the cheek whenever they saw him. He was the perfect child they all wanted: polite, well-mannered, doing well in school, so sweet in his Boy Scout uniform." As a young man, Paul continued to be involved in scouting, was adored by girls, and was a successful student at the University of Toronto. He was also a serial rapist. But that was just the beginning.

Karla fell deeply in love with Paul, so much so that she was willing to go along with his perverse sexual interests. As a Christmas gift to Paul, she drugged her virgin teenage sister so that Paul could sexually assault her. Tragically, the girl died due to Karla's incompetence at administering the anesthetic she had stolen from the veterinary clinic. Paul remained obsessed with raping young virgins, and so Karla helped him kidnap, rape, torture, and kill two other teenager girls. They even made videotapes of the killings, which show Karla's willing participation in many of the sadistic acts.

When it was clear that they were about to be caught, Karla confessed and claimed that because Paul had battered her, she was unable to disobey him when he forced her to participate in his brutal crimes. When Karla received a light sentence for her part in one of

RESEARCH QUESTIONS

for Studying Interpersonal Processes

When do people affiliate with each other?

How much do people infer from nonverbal behaviors and body cues?

How do people manage the way they present themselves to others?

How are people influenced by others?

When do people help or hurt others?

What determines how much people like others?

What is love and what makes it last?

1972

What Is Beautiful Is Good Karen Dion and her colleagues propose the existence of a physical attractiveness stereotype, in which good-looking people are viewed as possessing a wide variety of positive characteristics.

1980s

Evolutionary Social Psychology Led by David Buss and Doug Kenrick, social psychologists begin to recognize the importance of evolutionary theory in understanding social behavior, especially human mating.

1984

The Power of Influence Robert Cialdini conducts undercover research that reveals the power of influence strategies such as those used in car sales, cult recruitment, and political lobbying.

1995

Need to Belong Roy Baumeister and Mark Leary propose that humans have a fundamental need to belong that has evolved for adaptive purposes.

the most horrible crime sprees in Canadian history, the media and many Canadian citizens were outraged. Many felt that it was impossible to accept her claim that she was forced to comply with Paul's sadistic fantasies. She had also initially claimed that she assisted Paul because she was so in love that she would do anything for him. Is love's power really so strong?

If the Canadian people were outraged by Karla's excuses, they were completely baffled by Paul's behavior. How could this angelic-looking young man hold such disturbed thoughts? Nothing in his earlier life foreshadowed his evil actions. Paul challenges many commonsense notions about human nature and forces us to consider questions about the dark side of humanity. People beat, rape, torture, and murder others. What explains the violent side of human nature? Why did soldiers in Milosevic's Serbian army slaughter ethnic Albanians? Why did terrorists fly airplanes into the World Trade Center towers in New York? Sometimes it seems as if humans are inherently evil.

Yet many people are kind, compassionate, generous, and loving. Some people risk their personal safety to help those in danger. Most people seek out positive relationships, wanting the loving companionship of friends and family. Even some of those who engage in barbarous acts are otherwise gentle people. In this chapter, you will learn how human beings interact. You will learn how people interpret the actions of others and, in turn, how people manage the impressions they wish to convey. You will also discover how psychological scientists, working across the levels of analysis, study why people help each other, why they hurt each other, and why they fall in love. One of the major lessons of social psychology is that humans have an incredible ability to influence others, and that much of human behavior can be understood by recognizing that humans have evolved a profound and basic need to belong to social groups.

14.1 By all appearances, Karla Homolka and Paul Bernardo were an attractive and happy young couple.

Most humans spend about 75 percent of their waking time with other people. People crave companionship and love and they seek social support when they feel anxious or alone. In Chapter 13, we noted that social psychology was concerned with how other people influence the way we think, feel, and act. That chapter was concerned with how we process information relevant to the self and others. This chapter focuses on the interaction between the self and others, such as personal relationships and **social influence**, which is how other people shape our actions.

Throughout this book, we have emphasized that the brain has evolved to solve adaptive problems. What has been the greatest adaptive challenge facing humans through all of history? Other humans, of course. As noted by evolutionary

social influence The ways in which other people shape our actions.

psychologists David Buss and Douglas Kenrick (1998), the large brain of our species may be dedicated largely to solving adaptive social problems. One of the essential findings of social psychology over the past century is that humans are highly sensitive to *social context*, the norms, standards, and values of other people in a particular situation.

HOW SOCIAL ARE HUMANS?

Suppose you are offered a sizeable amount of money to remain alone in a room. The longer you stay, the more money you make. The room has no windows and only a limited number of amenities, such as a bed, chair, table, and toilet. You will not have contact with other people, and you will not have access to newspapers, books, television, or the Internet. How long could you last? To understand **affiliation**, the tendency to be in social contact with others, Stanley Schachter (1959) found five men who were willing to try living under such isolated conditions. Most of the men found it very difficult. Indeed, the first was unable to remain in the room for more than 20 minutes before experiencing an uncontrollable desire to leave. Three of the volunteers lasted two uneasy days but then wanted out. Even the fifth man, who lasted eight days, started to feel nervous while alone. The evidence from this and other studies indicates that people feel anxious when socially isolated. Although you may often wish to find a nice quiet place where you can get away from other people, human nature requires us to have frequent and close contacts with other people. Understanding any behavior requires a consideration of the interpersonal context in which that behavior occurs. Psychological scientists have provided substantial documentation that the nature of social relationships has far-reaching implications for emotion, cognition, and mental well-being (Reis et al., 2000).

HUMANS HAVE A FUNDAMENTAL NEED TO BELONG

Roy Baumeister and Mark Leary (1995) formulated the **need to belong theory**, which says that the need for interpersonal attachments is a fundamental motive that has evolved for adaptive purposes. Over the course of human evolution, those who lived with others were more likely to survive and pass along their genes. Children who stayed with adults (and who resisted being left alone) were more likely to survive until their reproductive years because the group would provide protection and nurturance. Similarly, adults who were capable of developing long-term committed relationships were more likely to reproduce, and also more likely to have their offspring survive to reproduce. Effective groups shared food, provided mates, and helped care for offspring (including orphans). Some survival tasks (such as hunting large mammals or looking out for predatory enemies) were best accomplished by group cooperation. It therefore makes great sense that, over the millennia, humans have committed to living in groups.

Baumeister and Leary argue that the need to belong is a basic motive that activates behavior and influences cognition and emotion, and that it leads to ill effects when not satisfied. Their theory highlights the ease and frequency with which people form social bonds. Consider the classic study from Chapter 13, in which boys were randomly assigned to groups and quickly developed a strong sense of group identity. Societies differ in their types of groups, but all societies have some form of group membership (Brewer & Caporael, 1990). Not belonging

affiliation The tendency to be in social contact with others.

need to belong theory The need for interpersonal attachments is a fundamental motive that has evolved for adaptive purposes.

to a group increases a person's risk for a number of adverse consequences, such as illnesses and premature death (Cacioppo et al., 2000).

The need to belong theory is supported by evidence that people feel anxious when they face exclusion from their social groups. According to *social exclusion theory*, anxiety warns individuals that they may be facing rejection from their group (Baumeister & Tice, 1990). People are socially excluded for reasons of immorality, incompetence, or unattractiveness. Breaking group norms and rules, which is the essence of immorality, threatens group structure; incompetence provides a drain on group resources; being unattractive or having a stigmatizing condition (see Chapter 13) may suggest inferior genes. People who feel incompetent, unworthy, or unattractive experience anxiety, which leads them to behave in ways that enhance their value to the group, such as contributing additional effort. People who are rejected show increased social sensitivity, as evidenced by increased memory for social events (Gardner et al., 2000). This sensitivity means that those who fear rejection are especially aware of others' reactions to them. When people are unable to alter what is causing their anxiety, such as their appearance, they may avoid contact with group members or seek less evaluative groups.

ANXIETY INCREASES AFFILIATION

In the study described earlier, Schachter found that isolation caused anxiety. He reasoned that the opposite might also be true, that anxiety could increase the desire for company. To test this, he manipulated anxiety levels and then measured how much the participants preferred to be around others (Schachter, 1959). The participants, all women in these studies, thought they were taking part in a routine psychological study. They were greeted at the lab by a serious-looking man named Dr. Zilstein, who had a cold look about him and spoke with a vaguely European accent. He told them that he was from the neurology and psychiatric school and that the study involved measuring "the physiological effects of electric shock." Zilstein told the participants that he would hook them up to some electrical equipment and would administer some electric current to their skin. Those in the low-anxiety condition were told that the shocks would be painless, no more than a tickle. Those in the high-anxiety condition were told, "These shocks will hurt, they will be painful. As you can guess, if we're to learn anything that will really help humanity, it is necessary that our shocks be intense. These shocks will be quite painful, but, of course, they will do no permanent damage." As you might imagine, those who heard this speech were quite fearful and anxious.

Zilstein then said he needed time to set up his equipment so there would be a ten-minute period before the shocks would begin. At this point the participants were offered a choice: they could spend the waiting time alone or with others. This was the critical dependent measure, and after the choice was made, the experiment was over. Schachter found that increased anxiety did indeed lead to increased affiliative tendencies. As can be seen in Figure 14.2, those in the high-anxiety condition were much more likely to want to wait with other people. Hence, it appears that misery loves company. But, does misery love just any company? A further study revealed that high-anxiety participants wanted to wait only with other high-anxiety participants, not with people who supposedly were just waiting to see their research supervisors. So, misery loves miserable company, not just any company.

Why do anxious people prefer to be around other anxious people? According to Schachter, others provide information that helps people to evaluate whether they are acting appropriately. According to Leon Festinger's *social comparison the-*

When do people affiliate with each other?

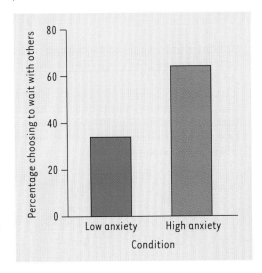

14.2 People who were told they would receive either a painful or a harmless shock were given the choice to wait alone or with others. People preferred to spend time with others when they were expecting painful shocks.

social dilemma When there is a motivational conflict both to cooperate and to be selfish.

ory (1954), people have a strong desire to have accurate information about themselves and others. People compare themselves to those around them in order to test and validate personal beliefs and emotional responses, especially when the situation is ambiguous and they can compare themselves to people who are relatively similar to them. For instance, if you receive an exam score of 75 percent, you might not know whether it is a good score unless you compare it to the class average.

PEOPLE DETECT AND REJECT CHEATERS

We noted earlier that people feel anxious when they face possible group exclusion, such as when they act immorally. However, there is a clear and powerful dilemma facing members of groups, which is whether to primarily give or take resources. On one hand, the group survives only if members contribute. On the other hand, individuals who get more than they give will have a tremendous advantage. A **social dilemma** exists when there is a motivational conflict both to cooperate and to be selfish; typically, being selfish maximizes short-term interests, whereas cooperating maximizes long-term interests. Social psychologists generally find that people act for individual short-term interests in social dilemmas, especially if they believe that others are doing so as well. But much of this research occurs when strangers are used as research participants. If this happened within groups, more and more group members would start being selfish, which would eventually threaten the stability of the group. Therefore, group members are vigilant to detect those who cheat and they punish these individuals accordingly.

There are a number of methods for detecting and dealing with cheaters. Leda Cosmides and John Tooby (2000) have provided compelling evidence that people have specialized *cheater detectors*. They have found that people are especially good at solving logical problems that represent cheating in a social exchange. For instance, the standard *Wason selection task* (Figure 14.3) typically results in only one in four people choosing the correct response. In the first problem, most people choose the cards that say *Boston* and *subway* even though the subway card provides no useful information. Even people with training in logical thinking often make this error. In contrast, when the task involves a social contract, such as in the second problem, nearly three out of four people answer correctly, and no training is required. Indeed, even people with serious mental impairments, such as those with schizophrenia, are able to solve this problem.

The finding that people are better at solving the social version of the Wason task implies that humans have an inference

14.3 In this task, only cards A and D provide useful information about whether the person violated the rule. Most people find the second problem (b) to be much easier than the first (a).

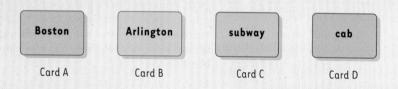

(a) Part of your new job for the City of Cambridge is to study the demographics of transportation. You read a previous study on the habits of Cambridge residents that says, "If a person goes into Boston, then that person takes the subway."

The cards below have information on four Cambridge residents. Each card represents one person. One side of the card tells where a person went, and the other side of the card tells how that person got there. Indicate only the card(s) you definitely need to turn over **to see if any of these people violate the rule.**

Boston	Arlington	subway	cab
Card A	Card B	Card C	Card D

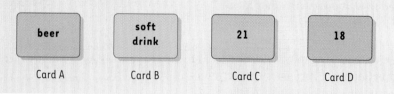

(b) Part of your new job as bar manager requires you to check whether the bartender is properly checking proof of age. The rule says, "If a person drinks beer, then that person must be 21 or over."

The cards below have information on four bar patrons. Each card represents one person. One side of the card tells what the person is drinking, and the other side of the card tells the person's age. Indicate only the card(s) you definitely need to turn over **to see if any of these people violate the rule.**

beer	soft drink	21	18
Card A	Card B	Card C	Card D

mechanism for detecting cheating specific to the social domain. A variety of other evidence supports the general idea that people are sensitive to cheaters. For instance, in one very large study of romantic couples, a partner who suspected the other of infidelity was accurate more than 90 percent of the time (Blumstein & Schwartz, 1983).

What happens when cheaters are detected? People who violate norms of trust, reciprocity, honesty, and morality are stigmatized and socially excluded by group members (Neuberg et al., 2000). Indeed, the deepest and most horrific circle of hell in Dante's *Inferno* was reserved for those who had betrayed their kin or countries. Traitors are often punished severely and seldom given a second chance. Of course, the stigmatization of behaviors such as cheating, stealing, or betrayal refer to ingroup behaviors—stealing from or cheating outgroups can lead to great advantages for the group doing the stealing and cheating. The important point is that people are rejected for violating ingroup reciprocity norms.

Although people generally expect reciprocation from ingroup members, this depends in part on the type of relationship. Margaret Clark and Judd Mills (1993) distinguish between exchange and communal relationships to understand how people react to reciprocation. *Exchange relationships*, which are typical of how people interact with coworkers or casual acquaintances, are ruled by the expectation of immediate repayment for benefits given. People keep track of plusses and minuses in exchange relationships, and they desire a balance in which costs are quickly offset by rewards. In contrast, *communal relationships* involve friends, lovers, and family members and are ruled by the expectation that there is a mutual interdependency and care for each other's needs. People's expectations differ depending on the type of relationship.

How Social Are Humans?

The human need to belong is a fundamental motive that drives social affiliation. People who behave in ways that could lead them to be excluded from their social groups feel anxiety, which can influence them to change their behavior. Indeed, there is evidence that groups will ostracize and reject members who are disloyal or who try to cheat other members. Most people who feel anxious prefer to affiliate with other people, especially those who are also anxious, since they allow for social comparisons.

WHAT INFORMATION IS CONTAINED IN NONVERBAL BEHAVIOR?

Living in a social world requires that people understand and predict the behavior of others. Suppose someone is walking toward you. You make a number of quick judgments, such as whether you know the person, whether the person poses danger, or whether you might like to know the person better. How people feel about others is often based on first impressions, which are made quickly and determined mostly by nonverbal behaviors. Facial expressions, gestures, walking style, and fidgeting are all examples of **nonverbal behavior**, sometimes referred to as *body language*.

nonverbal behavior Communication based on gestures, expressions, vocal cues, and body movements rather than words.

RESEARCH QUESTION

How much do people infer from nonverbal behaviors and body cues?

Throughout the course of human evolution, being able to identify potential adversaries or allies quickly was of importance, obviously. Being sensitive to subtle differences in nonverbal behavior allows people to predict the intentions and future actions of others. Although we do not often consciously evaluate people's physical actions for their communication value, we are influenced by those actions. Whether we believe someone is telling the truth or lying depends more on how they say something than on what they say, and the snap judgments we make about people guide our future interactions with them. These various sources of nonverbal information are referred to as *channels* and include facial expression, gestures, and tone of voice.

FACIAL EXPRESSIONS COMMUNICATE MEANING

The first thing people notice about others is usually the face. Human newborns within one hour of birth prefer to look at and will track a picture of a human face over a drawing of a blank outline of a head (Morton & Johnson, 1991). The face communicates a great deal, such as emotional state, interest, and distrust. People use their eyes to indicate anger, to flirt, and to catch the attention of a passing waiter. When people won't meet our eyes we assume, perhaps incorrectly, that they are embarrassed, ashamed, or lying, whereas people who look us in the eye are viewed as truthful and friendly. Social interactions can even be awkward when we can't see someone's eyes. Wearing sunglasses leads people to be described as cold and aloof, and police officers sometimes wear sunglasses partially to seem intimidating.

Physical appearance also influences social interaction. As you will read later, people respond much more positively to attractive than unattractive faces. Moreover, some facial characteristics lead people to make judgments about personality. For instance, people with small eyes and thin lips may be viewed as less trustworthy. Research by Leslie Zebrowitz and Diane Berry has shown that people who have "baby" faces, consisting of large round eyes, a narrow chin, high eyebrows, and a sloping forehead, are perceived to be more honest, naïve, warm, and kind than those with more mature faces, but they are also viewed as weak and submissive. In one study, people with babyfaces were judged as much less likely to be guilty of crimes of which they'd been accused than those with mature faces, even though the putative jurists were given identical information (Berry & Zebrowitz-McArthur, 1988). According to Zebrowitz (1997), people's faces affect how they are perceived in a variety of ways. For instance, people with atypical faces are often rated as less intelligent, perhaps in part because unusual facial structures often accompany mental deficiency.

Given the importance of recognizing other people, it should come as no surprise that the brain appears to contain specialized areas that are especially receptive to faces. Indeed, psychological scientists have conducted research across multiple levels of analysis that examines the processing of facial cues, as described in "Crossing the Levels of Analysis: Perceiving Faces."

BODY LANGUAGE IS MEANINGFUL

How much can be learned from nonverbal behavior? Nalini Ambady and Robert Rosenthal (1993) have found that people can make very accurate judgments based on only a few seconds of observation, what they refer to as *thin slices of behavior*. For instance, research has found that the level of confidence in a mother's tone of voice predicts how well her child behaves in public. Videotapes of judges giving instructions to juries reveal that the nonverbal actions of the judge can predict whether the jury finds a person guilty. The judges, perhaps unconsciously, indicated their beliefs about guilt or innocence through their facial expressions, tone of voice, and physical gestures. In another study, participants were asked to view 30-second clips of college teachers in which the sound was removed. Based solely on nonverbal behaviors, the participants' ratings corresponded very highly with the ratings given by the instructor's actual students (Ambady & Rosenthal, 1993).

One important nonverbal cue is how people walk, known as *gait*. For instance, gait provides information about affective state. People with a bounce in their steps, who walk along swinging their arms, are seen as happy. By contrast, people who scurry along, taking short steps while stooped over, are perceived as hostile, while those taking long strides with heavy steps are perceived to be angry. In an intriguing study, researchers found that participants accurately judged sexual orientation at a better-than-chance rate after watching a ten-second silent video or a dynamic figural outline (Figure 14.4; Ambady et al., 1999). These thin slices of behavior are powerful cues to impression formation.

Nonverbal behavior also guides social interaction. People who maintain a closed posture, in which they keep their feet close together, cross their arms on their chests, and lean away, are viewed as cold, unfriendly, and nervous. When people like someone, they lean toward the person with a more open posture. More telling are *gestures*, which can be equivalent to verbal language. Gestures that have specific meanings (such as the peace sign) are referred to as *emblems*, whereas those that expand upon or explain verbal communication (such as indicating direction by pointing) are known as *illustrators*. The use and meanings of specific gestures vary across cultures—it is wise to be careful making hand gestures in foreign countries.

Vocal cues also communicate meaning independently of language. For instance, people who are talking to babies tend to use a very high pitched voice, whereas people who are angry tend to change the emphasis in their sentences ("Come here *now*"). Vocal cues are often referred to as *paralanguage* and include stress, intonation, pitch, and nonwords (such as grumbling and sighs). Women generally are better than men at reading nonverbal behaviors.

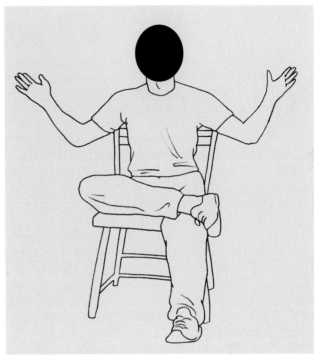

14.4 This is an example of a figural outline. In the study, participants watched a ten second dynamic clip. Observers correctly guessed the person's sexual orientation at a better-than-chance rate.

DETECTING DECEPTION IS DIFFICULT

Social psychologists study paralanguage and other nonverbal cues to see how people determine whether others are lying. **Deception** is an important part of smooth human social interactions. We tell "white lies" to avoid hurting people, we pretend to be surprised by gifts that we knew were coming, and we lie to cover up minor transgressions. We also need to disguise our nonverbal behaviors in some situations, such as looking relaxed during a job interview or happy for friends who obtain things we wanted for ourselves. Bella DePaulo and Deborah Kashy (1998) found that people reported telling small lies almost every day, and that people lie to about 30 percent of the people they know each week. For college students, the person they lie to most often is their mothers.

How good are people at detecting deception? Not very good. Almost no one can unerringly tell the difference between someone who is lying and someone

deception The act of making others believe something that is not true.

PERCEIVING FACES

The ability to perceive faces is critical for social interaction. Not only must people be able to recognize friends and enemies and to detect attributes such as sex, age, and genetic fitness, but they also need to be sensitive to subtle changes in facial expression that indicate others' emotions and intentions. As highly social animals, humans have a well-developed ability to perceive and interpret facial expressions. Psychological scientists working from the brain-systems level to the social/cultural level have explored how people perceive faces.

There appear to be brain regions, and even specific neurons, that are specialized to perceive faces. Scottish psychologist David Perrett and his colleagues found that neurons in the superior temporal sulcus (STS) of monkeys became active when the monkeys were looking at faces (Perrett et al., 1987). A number of imaging studies using either PET or fMRI have identified an area of the right hemisphere that seems particularly active during the observation of faces. Researchers such as Gregory McCarthy, James Haxby, and Nancy Kanwisher, working in separate laboratories, have found that the fusiform gyrus may be specialized for perceiving faces (Figure 14.5; McCarthy et al., 1997). Indeed, this brain area responds most strongly to upright faces, such as would be perceived in the normal environment (Kanwisher et al., 1998). By contrast, the perception of nonface objects leads to greater activation of the left hemisphere.

Although some have argued that faces are simply a specialized category of object, Martha Farah (1996) has found people who have selected deficits in the ability to recognize faces (a condition known as *prosopagnosia*) but not in the ability to recognize other objects. In general, it appears that some areas of the brain, especially the fusiform gyrus, are important for the identification of faces whereas other areas, especially STS, are sensitive to changes in faces, such as in facial expression and gaze direction. The emotional significance of a face appears to activate the amygdala, which is involved in calculating the potential danger of objects. The recognition of familiar or

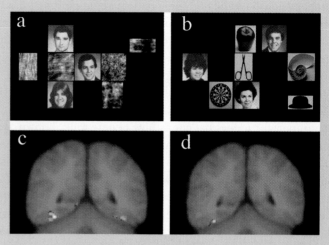

14.5 Faces presented within an array of (a) nonobjects or (b) objects activated the fusiform gyrus. This occurred more strongly for the right hemisphere (c and d), especially when faces were presented among objects (d). Note that the right side of the brain (c and d) is presented on the left side of the image.

famous faces activates areas of the temporal lobes involved in memory. Overall, the evidence suggests that there is a distributed neural system for perception of faces.

Interestingly, people have a surprisingly hard time recognizing faces that are upside down. We are much worse at this than we are at recognizing other inverted objects. People have difficulty with inverted faces, especially unknown faces, because they interfere with how people perceive the relations between various facial features (Hancock et al., 2000). For instance, if one feature of the face is changed, such as if the eyebrows are bushier, the change is obvious if the face is upright, but not detectable when the face is inverted. One interesting example of the perceptual difficulties associated with inverted faces is evident in the Thatcher illusion (Thompson,

who is telling the truth. Studies of people who have no special training suggest that they can detect lies at a rate only slightly better than chance, and even those who make deception judgments for a living, such as police officers, judges, and customs inspectors, are no more accurate than chance. However, Secret Service agents can detect deception about 70 percent of the time. Some strategies people use to increase their ability to detect deception are discussed in "Using Psychological Science: How to Catch a Lie."

The inability of people to detect deception appears at odds with the idea that humans have evolved cheater detectors that are sensitive to violations of social contracts. It needs to be recognized that humans have simultaneously evolved mechanisms to avoid being detected during deception. The ability to deceive observers increases with age. Of course, since most lies are small lies and many are made for another's benefit, not being able to detect deception can be a good thing.

14.6 These two inverted pictures of former British prime minister Margaret Thatcher look normal. But, turn your book upside down to reveal a different perspective.

1980). When you view the faces upside down (see Figure 14.6), they both look pretty normal. However, if you turn your textbook upside down you will notice that one of the faces looks grotesque. Inversion of the whole face interferes with the perception of the inversion of individual components.

At the social level, people are better at recognizing members of their own ethnic group than members of other ethnic groups. There is some truth to the old saying "They all look alike," but the saying applies to all groups. This may occur because people have more exposure to members of their own ethnicity. Indeed, in the United States, where whites greatly outnumber blacks, whites were much better at recognizing white faces than black faces (Brigham

& Malpass, 1985). An interdisciplinary team of social and cognitive psychologists from Stanford University sought to examine the neural correlates of this same-race effect (Golby et al., 2001). They asked white and black participants to remember pictures from both groups along with pictures of objects (antique clocks) as a control comparison. They found that there was a significantly greater activation of the fusiform gyrus for same-race faces compared to other-race faces, especially for whites, and that these activations were associated with better recognition of those faces (Figure 14.7). Thus, differential activation of the fusiform gyrus may contribute to the same-race recognition effect. One possible explanation for why this effect appears to be smaller for blacks is that they are in the minority and therefore have more outgroup exposure than do whites. Thus, cultural context may affect the perception of faces.

14.7 Both whites and blacks showed better memory for same-race faces than for other-race faces, but this effect was only significant for whites. In both groups, there was greater activation of the fusiform gyrus for same-race faces than for other-race faces. This response might indicate greater exposure to same-race faces, especially for whites.

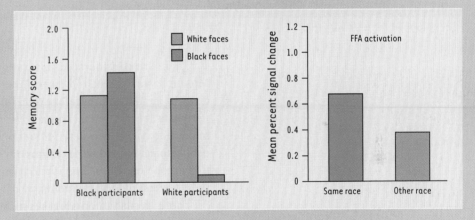

THE NEED FOR PERSONAL SPACE VARIES ACROSS SITUATIONS AND CULTURES

Anthropologist Edward T. Hall proposed that a major form of nonverbal communication is **personal space**, the physical distance that people maintain between themselves and others. People walk along with an invisible bubble of personal territory that they feel is their own. Working in the 1960s, Hall found that the degree of personal space required by people changed according to the social context. For instance, close friends are allowed into the *intimate zone*, which is within about 18 inches, whereas most casual conversations take place in the *personal zone*, which extends several feet. Casual acquaintances or strangers who crowd personal space make people uncomfortable. Conversely, people who are romantically interested in each other tend to move closer and lean in toward each other.

personal space The distance that people routinely maintain from others.

HOW TO CATCH A LIE

Researcher Paul Ekman (1992) has studied deception for many years and has concluded that it can be detected at a better-than-chance level if people know which cues to look for. For instance, people seldom have genuine smiles when they lie, so the eyes reveal a lie more than the words people say (Figure 14.8). A genuine smile of enjoyment wrinkles the skin around the eyes. Because the muscles that cause puckering around the eyes are more difficult to control, a smile with the absence of eye puckering may indicate deception. People also need to watch for what are called *microexpressions*, fleeting facial expressions that are instantaneous and nearly impossible to control, such as when hearing someone say something foolish causes you to roll your eyes a bit.

To detect deception, people should also listen for unexpected changes in voice tone and quality, such as someone talking more slowly and carefully, perhaps hesitating to plan a lie. In terms of nonverbal cues, casual liars are typically aroused and therefore have dilated pupils and often blink a lot; but these can also be signs of nervousness among the innocent. Discrepancies between nonverbal channels can also indicate attempted deception, such as nervous tapping of feet with a totally calm face. According to Ekman, the

14.8 The smile on the right is genuine.

feet and lower body are leakier channels, and are therefore likely to be more indicative of the truth than the more secure nonverbal channels, such as tone of voice.

There are considerable cultural differences in personal space. People in the Middle East, France, and Latin America have small personal space zones, especially in public, and therefore tend to stand close to each other while talking, with perhaps a lot of physical contact. People in the United States, England, and Germany more vigorously defend their personal space and are typically annoyed when people touch them during casual conversation. These differences may lead to conflict among travelers. English tourists in the Middle East may feel threatened by the closeness of local residents, who in turn find the English standoffish and rude.

There are also interesting sex differences in the use of personal space. Generally, women have smaller personal space zones. They allow others to get closer to them and they approach other people more closely. Women also take up smaller amounts of personal space, typically sitting with their legs crossed and their arms close to their bodies. By contrast, men sprawl onto chairs, assuming more expansive territory. The result is that they keep others at bay and claim larger personal space zones.

What Information Is Contained in Nonverbal Behavior?

Human social interaction requires that people be able to form impressions of others based on both verbal and nonverbal information. People are highly sensitive to nonverbal information and can develop accurate impressions based on very thin slices of behavior. At the same time, people are not very good at detecting deception, perhaps in part because they pay too much attention to channels that do not provide meaningful information. One form of nonverbal behavior is the regulation of personal space, which varies widely across cultures.

HOW DO PEOPLE MANAGE THEIR PUBLIC IMPRESSIONS?

William James claimed that we have as many social selves as people who know us. We might act one way with our parents, another way with our friends (perhaps even very differently with same-sex friends and cross-sex friends), and yet another way when we are trying to impress a job interviewer. In the 1950s, anthropologist Erving Goffman analyzed the strategic presentation of self in everyday life, leading to his theory of **impression management**. According to Goffman, a person who receives social approval is "in face"; one whose image fails is "out of face." Maintaining face is important for successful social relations. When circumstances threaten the face of an interaction participant, a process referred to as *face-work* is initiated to smooth over the rough spot. For instance, we sometimes overlook other people's embarrassing slips or social blunders. Impression management is often referred to as *self-presentation*, for it refers to how we exhibit our personal characteristics before an audience.

> **impression management** The tendency for people to strategically alter how they present themselves in order to achieve interpersonal goals.

THERE ARE MANY SELF-PRESENTATIONAL GOALS

In 1982, Edward Jones and Thane Pittman proposed a taxonomy of goals that people pursue through *strategic self-presentation* (Table 14.1). Although each strategy can lead to success, each has potential risks, and therefore self-presentation can backfire. In general terms, people tend to use self-presentational strategies more with strangers than with friends, since strangers form their impressions during initial interactions (Tice et al., 1995).

Perhaps the most important strategic goal of self-presentation is *ingratiation*, or convincing others that you are likeable. Although the term has a pejorative meaning, Jones and Pittman used it to reflect the idea that most people have a strong desire to be liked by others. There are many ways to be liked, such as providing compliments, doing favors, being supportive and caring, or being funny. In his best-selling book *How to Win Friends and Influence People*, Dale Carnegie advises that the best way to make a positive impression is to smile. Seeking people's advice can also be viewed as an ingratiation strategy since it implies respect and admiration for another person's knowledge.

People who inappropriately use flattery or other ingratiation tactics can be perceived as manipulative and deceitful. Jones' *ingratiator's dilemma* states that the more a person needs to be liked (and therefore, needs to ingratiate him- or

RESEARCH QUESTION

How do people manage the way they present themselves to others?

TABLE 14.1 Strategies That People Use to Manage Their Public Impressions

STRATEGY	IMPRESSION	TACTICS	RISKS
Ingratiation	"I am likeable"	Gives compliments, favors; is smiling and attentive	Being perceived as a sycophant
Self-promotion	"I am competent"	Makes positive claims about one's self or one's performance	Being perceived as conceited or boastful
Intimidation	"I am powerful"	Makes threats, displays of dominance, and aggression	Being perceived as a bully
Exemplification	"I am worthy"	Makes claims of moral superiority, self-denial, and suffering	Being perceived as self-righteous
Supplication	"I am weak"	Offers submission, pleading, and self-deprecation	Being perceived as overly needy

SOURCE: Based on Jones & Pittman, 1982; Forsyth, 1995.

herself), the more sensitized the target person will be to any cues suggesting deceit or ulterior motives. To avoid the ingratiator's dilemma, it is important to be sincere and to be careful giving compliments to people on whom you are too dependent, such as bosses or professors.

People not only want to be liked, but they want to be viewed as competent and moral. *Self-promotion* is showing one's competence and aptitude in order to gain others' respect. According to research, people seem to present themselves as favorably as they can get away with. Especially with strangers, people are likely to describe themselves in very positive terms. We are less likely to do so around friends and family, since they already know us well and we could be perceived as boastful (Tice et al., 1995). The risk of too much self-promotion is being seen as arrogant and conceited. Indeed, in collectivist cultures, such as Japan and Korea, self-promotion is considered rude in most circumstances.

Exemplification refers to convincing people that you are, by example, a morally virtuous person. The major risk for the exemplifier is the appearance of hypocrisy, such as with the preacher who is caught having an affair. Research demonstrates that exemplifiers who fall from grace are viewed much more negatively than are those who never claimed the moral high ground (Gilbert & Jones, 1986).

People also use self-presentational strategies to achieve other goals. *Intimidation* refers to demonstrating personal importance and power over others through words and actions. People may argue, confront, demand, and even threaten while they glare at their adversaries. They may dress in powerful clothes, invade body space, and grip a person's hand like a vise while they forcefully introduce themselves. These signs of confidence discourage challenges and occasionally terrorize others.

Finally, people sometimes use *supplication*, in which they stress their weaknesses and rely on others' reluctance to kick a person who is down. The use of supplication is a very risky strategy, since it may induce feelings of disgust in others, even as they provide assistance. Although it might be useful in specific situations, it is a bad strategy to use over the long term. Consider research that examines friendship patterns among college roommates. Those who engage in *negative reassurance seeking*, in which they constantly look to their roommates for compliments (such as asking, "I'm not fat, am I?" or "People like me, don't they?") become disliked as people get tired of providing constant reassurance (Joiner et al., 1992).

THERE ARE INDIVIDUAL DIFFERENCES IN IMPRESSION MANAGEMENT

Some people are much more likely to closely monitor and regulate the image they present to the public. People who are high in **self-monitoring** are very sensitive to cues of situational appropriateness and use these cues as guidelines for regulating self-presentations. Psychologist Mark Snyder, who coined the term, has conducted research on the trait of self-monitoring since the 1970s. According to his research, people high in self-monitoring are flexible and adaptive to situations, so that they can seem like very different people in different situations. They are gifted in social interaction and are especially likely to initiate and sustain conversation. People high in self-monitoring also are skilled in using and reading nonverbal behavior. They have excellent control over their emotional expressions

self-monitoring A personality characteristic that describes the extent to which people monitor and alter their behavior according to situational cues.

and can read subtle changes in other people. Nearly by definition, a successful diplomat would be extremely high in self-monitoring.

By contrast, people low in self-monitoring are less attentive to their surroundings and are not particularly good at altering their self-presentation to fit the setting. They have trouble smiling if they are truly unhappy. If you asked them what they thought of your dreadful haircut, they just might tell you, oblivious to social norms of being polite. Those low in self-monitoring prefer not to compromise who they are just because of circumstances. They tend to have a small number of very close friends and they avoid social situations in which they would feel pressured to behave in ways that were not true to themselves.

How Do People Manage Their Public Impressions?

Human social interaction requires people to regulate the impressions that they are giving to others. People regulate their self-presentations in order to influence others and achieve strategic goals. Perhaps the most important goal is to be liked, and people ingratiate themselves in order to make a good impression. Other self-presentational strategies are used to intimidate people or to earn their pity. Those who are high in self-monitoring are more pragmatic in managing their public presentations.

WHEN DOES SOCIAL POWER INFLUENCE OTHERS?

An overriding human motivation is to *fit in* with the group. One way people do this is through strategic self-presentation. But people also conform to group norms, obey direct commands by authorities, and are easily influenced by others in their social group. The desire to fit in with the group and avoid being ostracized is so great that under some circumstances people willingly engage in behaviors they would otherwise condemn. The power of the social situation is much greater than most people believe, which may be the single most important lesson from social psychology.

GROUPS INFLUENCE INDIVIDUAL BEHAVIOR

The first social psychology experiment was conducted by Norman Triplett in 1897 when he showed that bicyclists pedalled faster when with other people than when alone. This is due to **social facilitation**, in which the mere presence of others enhances performance. Social facilitation also occurs in other animals, including dogs, rats, birds, fish, and even cockroaches. Robert Zajonc (1965) proposed a model of social facilitation that involves three basic steps (Figure 14.9). First, Zajonc proposed that all animals are genetically predisposed to become aroused by the *mere presence* of others of their own species, because conspecifics are associated with most of life's rewards and punishments. Zajonc then invoked Clark Hull's well-known learning principle that arousal leads animals to emit a *dominant response*, that is, the one that is best learned. Interestingly, Zajonc's model predicts that social facilitation can lead to either enhancement or impairment in performance, depending on whether the dominant response is the correct

social facilitation When the mere presence of others enhances performance.

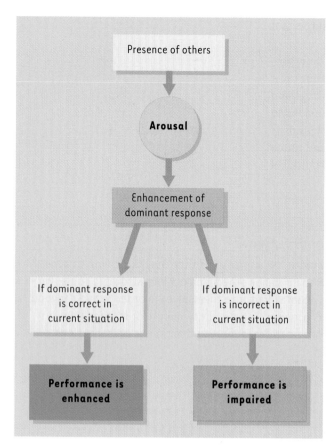

14.9 The mere presence of other people leads to increased arousal, which in turn favors the dominant response. If this is the correct response, performance is enhanced, but if it is the incorrect response, performance suffers.

social loafing The tendency for people to work less hard in a group than when working alone.

deindividuation A phenomenon of low self-awareness in which people lose their individuality and fail to attend to personal standards.

group polarization A process where group members conform to the initial attitudes of other members who already agree.

social norms Expected standards of conduct that influence behavior.

conformity The altering of one's opinions or behavior to match those of others.

response. The presence of others improves simple tasks for which the dominant response is well learned, such as adding single digits, but it interferes with complex tasks for which the correct answer requires greater thought, such as differential calculus.

Social loafing In some cases, people work less hard when in a group than when working alone. This **social loafing** occurs when people's efforts are pooled so that no one individual is accountable or feels personally responsible for the group's outcome. In a classic study, six blindfolded people wearing headphones yelled as loudly as they could under the expectation that they were shouting either alone or with other people. Participants did not shout as loudly when they believed others were shouting as well (Latane et al., 1979). Of course, making it clear that individual efforts can be monitored wipes out social loafing. Thus, if you are part of a group working on a class project, it is important to make each person feel personally responsible for some component of the project if you want her or him to exert maximum effort.

Deindividuation Sometimes people lose their individuality when they become part of a group. **Deindividuation** occurs when people are not *self-aware* and therefore are not paying attention to their personal standards. Deindividuated people often do things they would not do if they were alone. A good example is crowd behavior. Most of us like to think that we would try to help a person who was threatening suicide. But people in crowds often not only fail to intercede, they sometimes egg the person on, such as by yelling "jump, jump" to a person on a ledge.

People are especially likely to become deindividuated when they are aroused and anonymous, and when there is a diffusion of responsibility. Rioting by fans, looting following disasters, and other mob behaviors are the products of deindividuation. In a famous study conducted at Stanford University, researchers randomly assigned students to be either guards or prisoners in a makeshift prison set up in the basement of the psychology department. The study had to be halted after six days because the students became so immersed in their roles that many guards acted brutally and many prisoners became listless and apathetic (Figure 14.10; Haney et al., 1973). The situation was sufficiently powerful to radically alter people's behavior through a process of deindividuation. Not all deindividuated behavior is violent, of course. Gamblers in crowded casinos, fans doing the wave, and people dancing the funky chicken while inebriated in nightclubs are most likely in deindividuated states, and accordingly they act in ways that they would not if they were self-aware.

Group decision making It has been said that the intelligence of a group can be determined by averaging the IQs of its members and then dividing by the number of people in the group. In other words, groups are known for making bad decisions. Social psychologists have shown that being in a group does influence decision making, but in curious ways. For instance, you might think that group decisions would be especially cautious. However, when James Stoner set out to study this assumption in the 1960s, he found that groups often made riskier decisions than individuals did, which is known as the *risky-shift* effect. Subsequent research has demonstrated that groups are sometimes riskier and sometimes more cautious, as groups tend to enhance the initial attitudes of members who already agree, a process known as **group polarization**. In juries, for example, discussion tends to make people believe more strongly in their initial opinions about guilt or innocence. When groups make risky decisions, it is usually because the individuals initially favor a risky course of action, and through mutual persuasion they come to agreement.

Sometimes group members are particularly concerned with maintaining the cohesiveness of the group, and so for the sake of cordiality, groups make bad decisions. Irving Janis coined the term *groupthink* to describe this extreme form of group polarization. Examples of groupthink include the decision to launch the space shuttle *Challenger* and decisions made by President Clinton and his advisers following the allegations of his affair, which ultimately led to his impeachment. Groupthink typically occurs when the group is under intense pressure, is facing external threats, and is biased in a particular direction. The group does not carefully process all of the information, dissension is discouraged, and group members assure each other that they are doing the right thing.

PEOPLE CONFORM TO SOCIAL NORMS

Society needs rules. It would cause a lot of problems if you woke up one morning and decided that you would henceforth drive on the wrong side of the road. **Social norms**, expected standards of conduct, influence behavior in multiple ways, such as indicating which behavior is appropriate in a given situation. Standing in line is a social norm, and people who try to violate that norm by cutting the line are treated rudely and often directed to the back of the line. Muzafer Sherif was one of the first researchers to demonstrate the power of norms in social judgment. His studies, conducted in the 1930s, relied on a perceptual phenomenon known as the *autokinetic effect*, in which a stationary point of light appears to move when viewed in a totally dark environment. This effect occurs because there is no frame of reference and therefore people cannot correct for small eye movements. Sherif had participants who were alone in a room estimate how far the light moved. Individual differences were considerable; some participants saw the light move only an inch or two whereas others saw it move eight inches or more. In the second part of the study, Sherif put two or more participants in the room and had them call out their estimates. Although there were initial differences, participants very quickly revised their estimates until they agreed.

Conformity, the altering of one's behavior or opinions to match those of others, is a powerful form of social influence. In an interesting variant of Sherif's procedure, Robert Jacobs and Donald Campbell (1961) placed one participant in a group with three confederates (who exaggerated distances); the group ultimately established a norm of 16 inches for how far the light had moved, a full foot longer than most participants had guessed initially. Following the establishment of the norm, the researchers had a new naïve participant replace a confederate. After four generations of replacement, all the confederates had been replaced. However, the confederate-influenced norm continued to determine the group's estimates. Thus, once established, a social norm continues to have power. This may explain why the norms of past generations continue to influence new generations.

A few years later, Solomon Asch (1955) speculated that Sherif's effect probably occurred because the autokinetic effect is a subjective visual illusion. If there were objective perceptions, Asch thought, then participants would not conform. To test

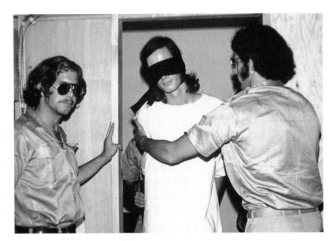

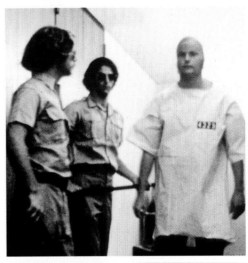

14.10 The basement of the psychology department at Stanford University was turned into a mock prison, with students randomly assigned to be guards or prisoners. The participants took on their roles with such vigor that the situation became overwhelming for many. The study was terminated early because of concerns for the well-being of the students.

RESEARCH QUESTION

How are people influenced by others?

14.11 In the Asch task, participants were shown a standard line (left) and then three comparison lines. Their task was simply to say which of the three lines matched the standard. When confederates gave false answers first, three-quarters of participants conformed by giving the wrong answer.

his hypothesis, Asch assembled a group of seven men to take part in a study of visual acuity. He had the seven look at a reference line and then judge which of three other lines matched it (Figure 14.11). There were 18 trials and each member of the group said his answer aloud. This is an easy task and normally people are able to do it with a high level of accuracy. But then Asch had a naïve participant join a group of six confederates. In these trials, the participant always went sixth, giving his answer after five of the confederates gave theirs. On 12 of the 18 trials, the confederates deliberately gave the same wrong answer. After hearing five wrong answers, the participant then had to state his answer. Because the answer was obvious, Asch speculated that the participant would give the correct answer, but about one-third of the time, the participant went along with the confederates. More surprisingly, in repeated trials, three out of four people conformed to the incorrect response at least once (Figure 14.12).

Research has consistently demonstrated that people tend to conform to social norms. This can be seen outside the laboratory as well: groups dress alike and listen to the same music; jury members go along with the group rather than state their own opinions; people at parties do things they might not do on their own. In fact, you might be wondering when people fail to conform to social norms. In a series of follow-up studies, Asch and others have identified factors that mitigate conformity. One factor is group size. If there are only one or two confederates, usually the participant does not conform. But as soon as the confederates number three or more, conformity occurs. Interestingly there seems to be a limit to conformity. Subsequent research has found that even groups of 16 do not lead to greater conformity than groups of 7.

Asch found that another factor that diminishes conformity is a lack of unanimity. If even one of the confederates gave the correct answer, then conformity to the group norm decreased a great deal. Any dissent from the majority opinion can diminish the influence of social norms. But dissenters are typically not treated well by groups. In 1951, Stanley Schachter conducted a study in which a group debated the fate of a juvenile delinquent, Johnny Rocco. A confederate deviated from the group judgment of how Johnny should be treated. The group began to ostracize the confederate when it became clear he would not be persuaded by the group sentiment. When group members were subsequently given the opportunity to reduce group size, they consistently rejected the "deviant" confederate. The bottom line is that groups enforce conformity, and those who fail to go along are rejected. The need to belong, and the anxiety associated with the fear of social exclusion, gives a group powerful influence over its members.

14.12 The only true participant is number 6 (in the middle of each photo with glasses). He can't believe his eyes as the other participants, actually confederates of the experimenter, give incorrect answers.

PEOPLE ARE COMPLIANT

Many times people influence the behavior of others simply by asking them to do something. When people agree to do things requested by others, they are exhibit-

ing **compliance**. There are a number of factors that increase compliance. For instance, Australian psychologist Joseph Forgas (1998) has demonstrated that people are especially likely to comply when they are in good moods. This may be why people try to "butter up" others when they want something from them. According to psychologist Robert Cialdini, many times people are influenced by others because they fail to pay attention and respond without fully considering their options. For instance, if you simply give people a reason for a request, they are much more likely to comply, even if the request makes little sense. According to Cialdini, people often comply with requests because they really aren't thinking—they are simply following a standard mental shortcut to avoid conflict.

A number of powerful strategies can be used to influence people to comply. For instance, in the *foot-in-the-door effect*, people are more likely to comply with a large and undesirable request if they have earlier agreed to a small request. In 1962, Jonathan Freedman and Scott Fraser asked homeowners to allow a large, unattractive DRIVE CAREFULLY sign to be placed on their front lawns. As you might imagine, fewer than one in five people agreed to do so. However, another group of homeowners was initially asked to sign a petition to support legislation that would reduce traffic accidents. A few weeks later, these same people were approached about having the large sign placed on their lawns, and more than half of them agreed. Once people are committed to a course of action they subsequently behave in ways consistent with that course.

The opposite influence technique is the *door in the face*, in which people are more likely to agree to a small request after they have refused a large request, because the second request seems modest in comparison, and people want to seem reasonable. Sales people often use influence techniques such as these. One of their favorites is the *low-balling* strategy, which begins when a salesperson offers a product—for example, a car—for a very low price. Once the customer agrees, the salesperson may claim the manager didn't approve the price or that there are additional costs. Whatever the reason, once people are committed to buying the car, they often agree to pay the increased costs.

PEOPLE ARE OBEDIENT TO AUTHORITY

One of the most famous and disturbing psychology experiments was conducted by Stanley Milgram (Figure 14.13), who wanted to understand how apparently normal German citizens would willingly obey orders to injure or kill innocent people during World War II. Milgram was interested in the determinants of **obedience**, why people follow orders given by an authority. Try to imagine yourself as a participant in his experiment. You have agreed to take part in a study of learning, and upon arrival at the laboratory, you meet another participant, a 50-year-old grandfatherly type (Figure 14.14). The study is described as one in which a teacher will administer electric shocks to a learner during a simple memory task in which word pairs are learned. Your role as the teacher is determined by an apparently random drawing of your name from a hat. Upon hearing that he may receive electric shocks, the learner reveals that he has a heart condition and expresses minor reservations. The experimenter says

14.13 Stanley Milgram, pictured here with his infamous shock generator, demonstrated that average people will obey even hideous orders given by an authority figure.

14.14 (a) The Milgram experiment required participants to "shock" the confederate learner (seated). The research participant (left) helped apply the electrodes that would be used to shock the learner. (b) An obedient participant shocks the learner in the "touch" condition. Fewer than one-third obeyed the experimenter in this condition. (c) After the experiment, all of the participants were introduced to the confederate learner so they could see he was not actually harmed.

14.15 Psychiatrists, college students, and middle-class adults predicted that fewer than one-tenth of one percent of participants in the Milgram experiment would be completely obedient and provide the maximum level of shock (each level = 15 volts). They believed that fewer than 10 percent of people would go beyond level 15 (225 volts). In fact, all of the participants were obedient at this level, and 65 percent were obedient to the highest level of shock.

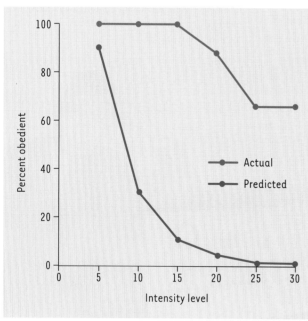

that although the shocks will be painful, they will not cause permanent tissue damage. You help as the experimenter takes the learner to a small room and hooks him up to the electric shock machine. You are then seated at a table in front of a large shock generator that has switches from 15 to 450 volts. Each voltage level has a label attached, such as DANGER—SEVERE SHOCK and finally, an ominous XXX.

During the task, you are to give the learner a shock each time he makes a mistake, increasing the voltage with each subsequent error. So, you dutifully begin to administer shocks whenever the learner makes a mistake. When you reach 75 volts, the man yelps with pain, which you can hear through an intercom. At 150 volts, the man starts screaming in pain, banging on the wall, and demanding that the experiment be stopped. The man is clearly in agony as you apply additional stronger shocks, and at 300 volts he refuses to answer any additional questions. After 330 volts, the learner is silent. All along you have wanted to quit the study, and you severely regret ever agreeing to participate. You might have killed the man for all you know. Indeed, you have tried to stop the experiment, but each time you said you were quitting, the experimenter told you, "The experiment requires that you continue"; "It is essential that you go on"; "There is no other choice, you must go on!" So you do.

Does this sound simply crazy to you? How high do you think you would go in terms of shocking the learner? Do you think you would go as high as 450 volts or do you think you would quit as soon as the man started to complain? A group of psychiatrists Milgram asked predicted that people would go no higher than 135 volts and that less than one in a thousand people would administer the highest level of shock. But that's not what happened. What happened was to change forever how people viewed the power of authority.

Milgram found that although almost all the participants tried to quit the experiment, nearly two-thirds obeyed the directives of the experimenter completely (Figure 14.15), believing they were administering 450 volts to a nice old man with a heart condition (actually a confederate). These findings have been replicated by Milgram and others in countries around the world. The conclusion of these studies is that ordinary people can be coerced into obedience by insistent authorities.

You may wonder about the ethics of Milgram's study. It is important to recognize that Milgram was surprised by the results of the study. Once he found that people were obedient, he then set out to study how to reduce obedience. Milgram did find that some situations produced less compliance. For instance, if participants could physically see or had to touch the learner who was being shocked, then obedience decreased. When the authority was more removed from the situation, giving the orders over the telephone, obedience dropped dramatically.

Throughout his study, Milgram was highly concerned with the mental state of his participants. He carefully revealed the true nature of the experiment to the participants in a systematic debriefing, and he made sure that they met the confederate learner and could see that he was not hurt in any way. Milgram also followed his participants over time to ensure that they experienced no long-term negative effects. Actually, many people were glad they had participated, in that they learned something about themselves and about human nature. Most of us assume that only sadistic miscreants would willingly inflict injury on others when given an order. Milgram's research, and that which followed, demonstrated that ordinary people will do horrible things when ordered to do so by an authority.

When Does Social Power Influence Others?

For the most part, people follow group norms, are influenced by others' opinions, and are obedient to authority. These effects are powerful, although most people underestimate their importance or do not believe they themselves would be affected by social influence. Yet the evidence is overwhelming that in many situations people will engage in behaviors quite inconsistent with their personal standards. This sometimes occurs because people fail to attend to their internal beliefs and values, such as when they are in a state of deindividuation. Those who are aware of the power of social influence often employ specific strategies to manipulate the behavior of others, such as foot-in-the-door, door-in-the-face, and low-balling techniques.

WHEN DO PEOPLE HARM OR HELP OTHERS?

The events of September 11, 2001, provide ample testimony to the different ways that humans interact. Hijackers who seized control of four airplanes were willing to give up their lives in order to take the lives of others, whereas airplane passengers, police officers, and firefighters were willing to give up their lives to save the lives of others. This section describes the accumulated findings of psychological scientists working across the levels of analysis to provide insight into when people harm or help others.

Aggression refers to a variety of different behaviors, but basically it is any behavior or action that involves the intention to harm someone else. Aggression in animals often occurs in the context of fighting over mates or defending territory from intruders. Sometimes just the threat of aggressive action is sufficient to dissuade invaders; at other times animals will fight to defend their turf. Physical aggression, although common among young children, is relatively rare among adult humans; their aggressive acts more likely involve words or actions designed to threaten, intimidate, or hurt others. Aggression needs to be considered across the levels of analysis, from basic biology to cultural context.

BIOLOGICAL FACTORS INFLUENCE AGGRESSION

Several brain structures have been implicated in aggressive behaviors, including the septum, the amygdala, and the hypothalamus. Stimulating or damaging these

When do people help or hurt others?

aggression Any behavior or action that involves the intention to harm someone else.

regions leads to corresponding changes in the level of aggression displayed by animals. For example, stimulating the amygdala with an electric probe causes cats to attack, whereas damaging the amygdala leads to passive behavior. In 1937, researchers Heinrich Kluver and Paul Bucy produced a striking behavioral change by removing the amygdalas of normally very aggressive rhesus monkeys. Following the surgery, the monkeys were tame, friendly, and easy to handle. They began to approach and explore normally feared objects, such as snakes. They also showed unusual oral behavior. They would put anything within their reach into their mouths, including snakes, matches, nails, dirt, and feces. The behavior associated with damage to this region is now referred to as *Kluver-Bucy syndrome*.

Frontal lobe damage is also associated with increased aggression, although it is possible that this occurs because frontal injuries are associated with a loss of self-control, including control over aggressive impulses. That is, frontal injuries may not cause increased aggression, they may just lead to a reduction in the ability to control aggressive tendencies. Neurologist Jonathan Pincus (1999) has examined more than 100 violent criminals, many of whom are on death row. He has found a combination of early childhood abuse, psychiatric disorders such as paranoia, and frontal lobe dysfunction evident in more than 90 percent of these violent killers. None of these problems appears to be sufficient on its own, but when all three are combined in an individual, serious trouble results.

Serotonin and aggression   In terms of neurochemistry, several lines of evidence suggest that serotonin is especially important in the control of aggressive behavior. Luigi Valzelli (1973) found that mice with low levels of serotonin were much more aggressive. Drugs that enhance the activity of serotonin lower aggression, whereas those that interfere with serotonin increase aggressive behaviors (Figure 14.16; Raleigh et al., 1991). In humans, low levels of serotonin have been associated with reports of aggression in adults and hostility and disruptive behavior in children (Kruesi et al., 1992). In a large sample of men from New Zealand, low levels of serotonin were associated with violence, but not with criminal acts in general (Moffitt et al., 1998). In addition, postmortem examinations of suicide victims have revealed extremely low levels of serotonin. Obviously, suicide is not the same as aggression, but many psychiatrists believe that suicide and violence toward others are manifestations of the same aggressive tendencies. Indeed, low serotonin levels were found among those who had killed themselves using violent means (such as shooting themselves or jumping from buildings) but not among those using nonviolent means (such as taking a drug overdose) (Asberg et al., 1987).

Serotonin levels possibly interfere with good decision making in the face of danger or social threat. For instance, monkeys with the lowest levels of serotonin are apt to pick fights with much larger monkeys. They also are the least socially skilled (Higley et al., 1996). This lack of social competence often leads them to be attacked and killed by the other monkeys. Do these findings have implications for humans? Possibly. In one study, participants given a drug that enhances serotonin activity were found to be less hostile and more cooperative over time compared to the control group (Knutson et al., 1998).

Sex differences in aggression   It is generally believed that men are much more aggressive than women. It is clear that men are much

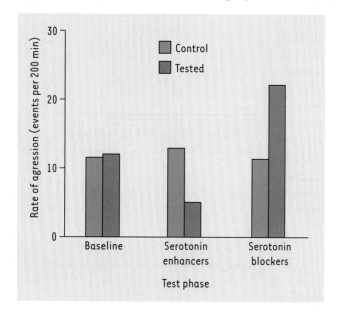

14.16 Male vervet monkeys were given either serotonin enhancers or serotonin blockers, and a corresponding change occurred in the number of aggressive acts against other members of the group.

more violent than women, committing more than 80 percent of murders and the vast majority of rapes, assaults, and so on. Indeed, more than 90 percent of those arrested for violence are men; violent acts by women are rare (and almost never involve strangers). But although men are much more physically aggressive than women, men and women show similar levels of verbal aggression, such as in expressing anger, hurling insults, talking behind someone's back, or revealing secrets. The choice of social rather than physical aggression by women may reflect societal discouragement of the latter among young girls, or it may reflect the relative physical strengths of the sexes.

NEGATIVE AFFECT CAN PRODUCE AGGRESSION

John Dollard and his colleagues proposed the first major psychological model of aggression in the 1930s. According to their **frustration-aggression hypothesis**, the extent to which people feel frustrated predicts the likelihood that they will be aggressive. The more that goals are blocked, the greater the frustration and therefore the greater the aggression. Thus, slow traffic is frustrating, and to the extent that it is impeding you from getting somewhere you really want to go, such as making you late for a concert you have been looking forward to attending, you may feel especially frustrated. If someone were to cut in front of you, you might feel especially angry and perhaps make some aggressive hand gesture. Indeed, road rage is most likely to occur where traffic is heavy and people feel frustrated.

According to Leonard Berkowitz's *cognitive-neoassociationistic model* (1990), frustration leads to aggression because it elicits negative affect. Thus, any situation that induces negative affect, such as being insulted, afraid, overly hot, or in pain, can trigger physical aggression even if it does not induce frustration. Berkowitz proposed that negative affect leads to aggression because it primes cognitive knowledge associated with aggression. From this perspective, negative events activate thoughts related to escaping or fighting, which prepare people to act in aggressive ways. Whether someone behaves aggressively depends on the situational context. If the situation also cues violence, such as if the person has recently watched a violent movie or been in the presence of weapons, then the person is more likely to act in an aggressive fashion.

LEARNED AND CULTURAL ASPECTS FACTOR INTO AGGRESSION

An evolutionary approach to aggression would dictate that similar patterns of aggressive behavior should exist in all human societies. After all, if aggression provided a selective advantage for human ancestors, then it should have done so for all humans. But an examination of the data shows us that violence varies dramatically across cultures and even within cultures at different points in time. For example, over the course of 300 years, Sweden went from being one of the most violent nations to one of the most peaceable, which certainly did not correspond with a change in the gene pool. Moreover, murder rates in some countries are far higher than in others (Figure 14.17). In the United States, physical violence is much more common in the South than in the North. Hence, although human nature might be aggressive, it is clear that culture exerts a strong influence on the actual commission of physical violence.

Some cultures are more violent because they subscribe to a *culture of honor*, a belief system in which men are primed to protect their reputations through phys-

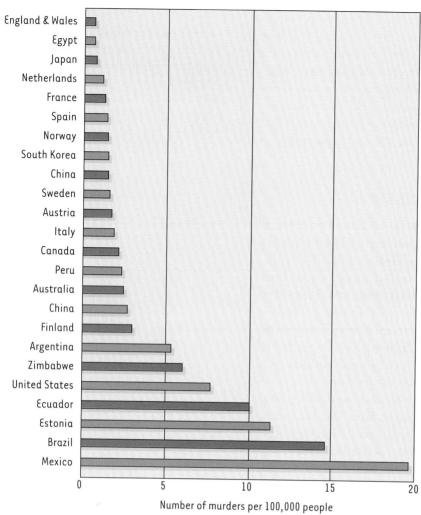

14.17 Murder rates vary dramatically in different countries.

ical aggression. Men in the Southern United States, for example, are traditionally raised to be ready to fight for their honor and to respond aggressively to personal threats. To determine whether Southern males are more likely to be aggressive than Northern males, researchers conducted a series of studies at the University of Michigan (Cohen et al., 1996). In each study, male participants walking down a narrow hallway had to pass a male confederate who was blocking the hallway at a filing cabinet. This man responded angrily and insulted the passing participant. Compared to participants raised in the North, those raised in the South were more upset, more likely to feel personally challenged, more physiologically aroused (measured by cortisol and testosterone increases), more cognitively primed for aggression, and more likely to act in an aggressive and dominant manner for the rest of the experiment, such as by vigorously shaking the experimenter's hand (Figure 14.18). The culture-of-honor theory of violence supports Bandura's social-learning theory (discussed in Chapter 6) that much aggressive behavior is learned through social observation of vicarious reward and punishment. People are rewarded for defending their honor in the South and young men are taught that violence is an acceptable way to do so. Presumably, attitudes about the acceptability of aggression are determined by cultural norms throughout the world.

MULTIPLE FACTORS MAY INFLUENCE HELPING BEHAVIOR

Although there are many situations in which people inflict harm on one another, the opposite is true as well; people often behave in ways that are **prosocial**, meaning that someone benefits from another's actions. Prosocial behaviors include doing favors, offering assistance, paying compliments, subjugating our egocentric desires or needs, resisting the temptation to insult or throttle, or simply being pleasant and cooperative. By providing benefits to those around us, prosocial behaviors promote positive interpersonal relationships. Group living, in which people share and cooperate, may be a central human survival strategy. After all, a group that works well together is a strong group, and belonging to a strong group benefits the individual members.

There are multiple theories about why humans are prosocial, which range from the selfless to the selfish, and from the biological to the philosophical. For instance, Daniel Batson and his colleagues argue that prosocial behaviors are motivated by empathy, in which people value the welfare of the other person. Conversely, Robert Cialdini and his colleagues have argued that most prosocial behaviors have selfish motives, such as wanting to manage one's public impres-

prosocial Tending to benefit others.

altruism To provide help when it is needed, without any apparent reward for doing so.

kin selection The tendency to be altruistic toward those who share a genetic bond.

reciprocal helping The tendency to help another because the recipient may return the favor.

sion or relieve a negative mood. Others have proposed that people have an inborn disposition to help others. Young infants become distressed when they see other infants crying, and although their early attempts to soothe other children are generally ineffective (for instance, they tend initially to comfort themselves rather than the other children), this empathic response to the suffering of others suggests that prosocial behavior is hardwired.

Altruism is the providing of help when it is needed, without any apparent reward for doing so. The fact that people help others, and even risk personal safety to do so, may seem contrary to evolutionary principles; after all, those who protect themselves first would appear to have an advantage over those who risk their lives to help others. In the 1960s geneticist William Hamilton offered an answer to the riddle; he proposed that natural selection occurs at the level of the gene rather than at the level of the individual. Thus, the "fittest" animals are those that pass along the most genes to future generations, through the survival of their offspring. Hamilton introduced the concept of *inclusive fitness* to describe the adaptive benefits of considering the passing along of genes rather than individual survival. According to this model, people are altruistic toward those with whom they share genes, a process known as **kin selection**. A good example of kin selection occurs among insects such as ants and bees whose workers feed and protect the egg-laying queen but never reproduce themselves. By protecting the eggs, they maximize the number of their common genes that will survive into future generations.

Of course, sometimes animals help nonrelatives: for example, dolphins and lions will look after orphans. Similarly, a person who jumps into a lake to save a stranger is probably not acting for the sake of genetic transmission. Robert Trivers proposed the idea of **reciprocal helping** to explain altruism toward nonrelatives. According to Trivers, one animal helps another because the other can return the favor in the future. Consider grooming, in which primates take turns cleaning each other's fur: "You scratch my back, and I'll scratch yours." For reciprocal helping to be adaptive, benefits must outweigh costs, and indeed people are less likely to help when the costs of doing so are high. Reciprocal helping is also much more likely to occur among animals that live in social groups, such as humans, in which species survival depends on cooperation. This suggests that people will be more likely to help members of their ingroups than those of outgroups, and indeed this is generally supported by the data. From an evolutionary perspective, then, altruism does confer benefits, either by increasing the transmission of genes or by increasing the likelihood that others in the social group will reciprocate when needed.

SOME SITUATIONS LEAD TO BYSTANDER APATHY

In 1964, a young woman named Kitty Genovese (Figure 14.19) was walking home from work in a relatively safe area of New York City. An assailant savagely attacked her, eventually killing her during a 30-minute beating. There were 38 witnesses to the crime, who watched it happen from their windows. How many called the police or tried to intervene? None. In fact, it is reported that one of the couples

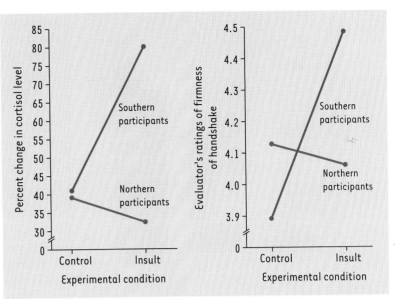

14.18 When insulted, men from the Southern United States had increased cortisol responses and shook hands more vigorously than Northern men.

14.19 Kitty Genovese was attacked and killed while 38 of her neighbors listened but did not try to stop the attack or even phone the police.

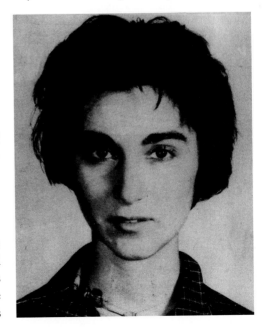

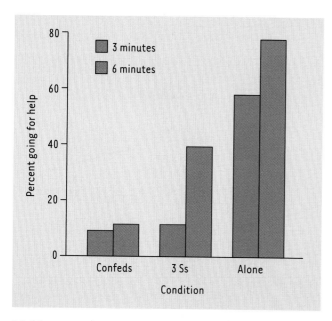

14.20 Research participants waited alone, with two other naïve participants, or with two apathetic confederates. When smoke started to fill the room, those who were on their own went for help quickly. Those with the apathetic confederates did not seek out assistance.

bystander intervention effect The failure to offer help by those who observe someone in need.

pulled up chairs and turned out the lights so they could better observe the action. As you might have guessed, the next day most people were outraged that 38 people could sit by and watch a brutal murder.

Why didn't these people help? Shortly after the Genovese murder, social psychologists Bibb Latané and John Darley conducted important research uncovering the situations that produce the **bystander intervention effect**, or the failure to offer help by those who observe someone in need. Although common sense might suggest that more people available to help would make it more likely that a person was helped, Latané and Darley made the paradoxical claim that a person was less likely to help if there were other bystanders around. To test their theory, they conducted studies in which people were placed in situations that indicated that they should seek help. In one of their first studies (Latané & Darley, 1968), male college students in a room filling out questionnaires were exposed to pungent smoke puffing in through the heating vents. Participants were either alone, with two other naïve participants, or with two confederates who noticed the smoke, shrugged, and continued filling out the questionnaire. As can be seen in Figure 14.20, when participants were on their own, most went for help. However, when three participants were in the situation, few initially went for help. In the condition with the calm confederates, only 10 percent of participants went for help in the first six minutes. The other 90 percent "coughed, rubbed their eyes, and opened the window—but they did not report the smoke." Similar results were obtained in subsequent studies in which people were confronted with mock crimes, apparent heart attack victims in subway cars, and people passed out in public spaces. The bystander intervention effect has been shown to occur in a wide variety of contexts—even among divinity students who while rushing to give a lecture on the Good Samaritan failed to help a person in apparent need of medical attention (Darley & Batson, 1973).

Years of research have indicated four major reasons for the bystander intervention effect. First, there is a *diffusion of responsibility*, in which people expect that others who are also around will offer help. Thus, the more people that witness the need for help, the less likely it is that someone will actually step forward. Second, people fear making social blunders in an ambiguous situation. In all of the laboratory studies, there was some degree of ambiguity and people may have felt constrained from seeking out help that was not needed, thereby maybe seeming foolish. There is some evidence that helping increases as the need for help becomes clear. Third, people are less likely to help when they are not identifiable. If people are not anonymous, they are much more likely to help. Thus, if you need help in a situation, it is often wise to point to a specific person and request his or her help.

Fourth, there is a cost-benefit trade-off that involves how much harm people risk by helping, or what benefits they would have to forego if they stopped to help. Imagine walking to a potentially really dull class on a sunny warm day and somebody falls down, twists an ankle, and needs help to get to the nearest clinic. You probably would be willing to help. Now imagine you are trying to get to a final exam on time, and you are almost late, and the exam counts for 90 percent of your grade. In this case you probably would be much less likely to offer assistance.

When Do People Harm or Help Others?

Humans engage in aggressive acts in all cultures. Whereas men are usually more physically aggressive, women tend to be aggressive in verbal and indirect ways. Being frustrated can lead to aggression, as can other factors that lead to negative affect. This may occur because negative affect primes aggressive mental representations. Cultural norms and beliefs can alter the expression of aggressive behavior. People are likely to offer help to others in many situations, especially if the person needing help is a relative. However, people are less likely to help when there are personal risks to doing so and there is a diffusion of responsibility.

WHAT DETERMINES THE QUALITY OF RELATIONSHIPS?

Given the fundamental human need to belong and desire for social contacts, how do people select their friends and relationship partners? You might expect that studying relationships would be a high priority for psychological scientists. But until the last decade or so the topic was given little attention, perhaps due to the difficulty of developing operational definitions for complex and fuzzy concepts such as *love*, a mysterious state that some think more appropriate for consideration by poets than by scientists. However, researchers have made considerable progress in identifying the factors that lead us to form friendships and close relationships. Many of these findings consider the adaptiveness of forming lasting affiliative bonds with others. This section considers the factors that determine the quality of human relationships. We will first discuss the factors that promote friendships and then we will turn our attention to why people fall in love and why love relationships sometimes fail. As you will see, many of the same principles are involved in choosing our friends and choosing our lovers.

MANY FACTORS INFLUENCE AFFILIATIVE CHOICE

Think for a second about your best friend. How is it that you came to be friends? Psychological scientists have discovered a number of factors that promote friendships. In 1950, Leon Festinger, Stanley Schachter, and Kurt Back examined people who lived in a college dorm. Because people were assigned to rooms at random, the researchers were able to examine the effects of **proximity**, or how often people come into contact, on friendship. They found that the more often students came into contact, the more likely they were to become friends. Indeed, it is commonplace for friendships to form among those who sit by each other in classrooms or are members of the same groups or clubs.

Proximity might have its effects because of *familiarity*. People like things with which they are familiar more than what is strange. Humans have a general fear of anything novel, also known as *neophobia*. As discussed in Chapter 13, simply being exposed to something repeatedly leads to increased liking, which is called the *mere exposure effect*. This effect has been demonstrated in hundreds of studies using a variety of objects, including faces, geometric shapes, Chinese letters, and nonsense words. The effect appears to be strongest when people are not aware that they are being exposed to the objects.

What determines how much people like others?

proximity The frequency with which individuals come into contact.

what is beautiful is good stereotype
To attribute a variety of positive characteristics to people simply based on their physical attractiveness.

Birds of a feather flock together Another factor that increases liking is *similarity*. Birds of a feather really do flock together. People who are similar in attitudes, values, interests, backgrounds, and personalities tend to like each other. Roommates who are most similar at the beginning of the year are most likely to become good friends. Studies of high school friendships have found that people tend to be friends with those of the same sex, race, age, and year in school; also, the most successful romantic couples tend to be the most physically similar, which is called the *matching principle* (Bentler & Newcomb, 1978; Caspi & Herbener, 1990).

Occasionally people have friends and lovers who appear to be opposites in many ways. This is also captured by a popular notion that people are attracted when sparks fly. Although similarity is an important determinant of liking, people who complement each other's strengths and weaknesses can be mutually satisfied. For instance, a person who is very dominant might prefer friends who are willing to be submissive. An outgoing person might help a shy person engage in desirable behavior, and so on. Thus, people who are generally similar, but who complement each other, are perhaps especially likely to be friends or lovers.

Personal characteristics People tend especially to like those who have admirable personality characteristics and who are physically attractive, both for friends and lovers. In a now classic study conducted in the 1960s, Norman Anderson asked college students to rate 555 trait descriptions by how much people would like others who possessed those traits. Based on the earlier discussion of who is rejected from social groups, you might expect that people dislike cheaters and others who drain group resources. Indeed, as can be seen in Table 14.2, the least likeable characteristics are those that indicate dishonesty, insincerity, or lack of personal warmth. Conversely, people especially like those who are kind, dependable, and trustworthy. People like those who are competent much more than those perceived to be incompetent or unreliable, perhaps because competent people make valuable group members. However, people who are overly competent or too perfect make others feel uncomfortable or inadequate. In one study, a person who was highly competent but who spilled a cup of coffee on himself was rated more highly than an equally competent person who did not perform this clumsy act (Helmreich et al., 1970). Making small mistakes makes people human, and therefore more likeable. Generally, people like those who have personal characteristics valuable to the group.

Most people are also drawn to those who are physically attractive. Attractive people are typically judged to be happier; more intelligent, sociable, and successful; and less socially deviant. Taken together, these findings point to what Karen Dion and her colleagues dubbed the **what is beautiful is good stereotype**. People who are physically attractive are less likely to be perceived as criminals, are given lighter sentences when convicted of crimes, are rated more intelligent by teachers, are paid more for doing the same work, and have greater career opportunities. The preference for physical attractiveness begins early. Children as young as six months prefer to look at attractive faces, and young children prefer attractive over unattractive playmates (Rubenstein et al., 1999).

Even mothers treat attractive children differently from unattractive children. In one study, researchers examined mothers of over 100 infants feeding and playing with their newborns just after birth (while the mothers were in the hospital) and then again three months later (Langlois et al., 1995). Mothers of attractive children were much more affectionate and playful than mothers of unattractive

TABLE 14.2	The Ten Most Positive and Most Negative Personal Characteristics	
MOST POSITIVE	**MOST NEGATIVE**
Sincere	Unkind
Honest	Untrustworthy
Understanding	Malicious
Loyal	Obnoxious
Truthful	Untruthful
Trustworthy	Dishonest
Intelligent	Cruel
Dependable	Mean
Thoughtful	Phony
Considerate	Liar

Studying the Mind

THE DETERMINANTS AND CONSEQUENCES OF PHYSICAL ATTRACTIVENESS

What determines physical attractiveness? Although some standards for beauty appear to change over time and across cultures, such as preferences for body type, how people rate attractiveness is generally consistent across all cultures (Cunningham et al., 1995). In terms of facial attractiveness, most people prefer symmetrical faces. This may be adaptive, in that a lack of symmetry could indicate poor health or a genetic defect. In a cleverly designed study of what people find attractive, Langlois and Roggman (1990) used a computer program to combine (or "average") a variety of faces. They found that as more faces were combined together, participants rated the "average" as more attractive (Figure 14.21). Such "average" faces may be viewed as attractive due to the mere exposure effect, in that they may be more familiar to people than unusual faces. However, other researchers contend that although average faces might be attractive, averaged attractive faces are rated more favorably than averaged unattractive faces (Perrett et al., 1994). These faces may be rated more attractive because they enhance feminine features, resulting in larger eyes, a smaller nose, plumper lips, and a smaller chin (Figure 14.22).

You might wonder, given this preferential treatment, whether people who are physically attractive actually possess characteristics consistent with the "what is beautiful is good" stereotype. The evidence on this question is mixed. Among studies of college students, the correlation between objective ratings of attractiveness and other characteristics appears small. In one study that examined physical attractiveness, objectively rated by multiple judges, the researchers did not find any relation between appearance and self-esteem, grades, number of personal relationships, financial resources, or just about anything (Diener et al., 1995). However, evidence obtained from more diverse settings indicates a robust effect of attractiveness on many outcomes. A meta-analysis of research studies examined the effects of attractiveness on interpersonal evaluation and behavioral outcomes and found that being attractive confers a number of benefits (Langlois et al., 2000). Attractive people not only are considered especially capable and gifted, but they enjoy greater school and occupational success, and they are more popular, socially skilled, and healthy. At the same time, they are similar to less attractive people in intelligence, life satisfaction, and self-esteem. Why does having all the benefits of attractiveness not lead to greater happiness? It is possible that attractive people learn to distrust attention from others, and especially from the opposite sex, because they assume that people like them simply for their looks. Believing that good things happen to them primarily because they are good-looking may leave people feeling insecure, in that looks can fade or change with age.

(a) (b) (c)
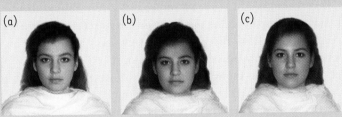
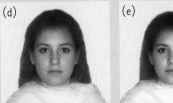

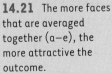

14.21 The more faces that are averaged together (a–e), the more attractive the outcome.

(a)

(b)

(c)

14.22 Which of these faces do you prefer? Image (a) represents the averaging of 60 women. Image (b) is the composite of the 15 most attractive faces. Given a choice between image (a) and (b), the vast majority of people prefer image (b). Image (c) exaggerates the subtle differences between images (a) and (b). Given a choice between image (b) and (c), 7 out of 10 participants prefer image (c).

children, who attended to other people more than to their infants. Mothers of attractive infants expressed slightly more positive attitudes about their children as well. Given the importance of physical attractiveness, you may wonder what makes people physically attractive. This is discussed in "Studying the Mind: The Determinants and Consequences of Physical Attractiveness."

14.23 David Buss uses evolutionary theory to examine mating strategies. His research shows that there is great cross-cultural consistency in what men and women desire as mates, and that mating strategies are adaptive.

THERE ARE SEX DIFFERENCES IN MATING STRATEGIES

All humans desire to enter into romantic relationships. However, men and women look for different qualities in relationship partners. According to the **sexual strategies theory** of evolutionary psychologist David Buss (Figure 14.23), these differences are due to the different adaptive problems that have faced men and women throughout human history (Buss & Schmitt, 1993). From this perspective, women differ from men in how to best maximize their chances that their genes will be passed along to future generations. Women's basic strategy is intensive care of a relatively small number of infants. Their commitment is to nurture rather than to simply maximize production. Once a women is pregnant, additional matings are of no use, and once she has a small child, an additional pregnancy can put her current offspring at risk. Thus, biological mechanisms, such as nursing typically preventing ovulation, ensure spacing between children. On purely reproductive grounds, men have no such interludes. For them, all additional matings may have a reproductive payoff, since they bear few of the personal costs of pregnancy.

Because having offspring is a much more intensive commitment for women, it is likely that they will be much more cautious about having sex. Indeed, there is evidence that women are much less willing to have sex with someone they don't know well. In one study, an attractive stranger approached people of the opposite sex and said, "I have been noticing you around campus. I find you attractive. Would you go to bed with me tonight?" Although not one woman said yes, perhaps because of potential danger, three-quarters of the men agreed to the request (Figure 14.24). Indeed, the men were less likely to agree to go out on a date with the attractive woman than they were willing to have sex with her (Clark & Hatfield, 1989). In another study, people were asked to state how long a couple should be together before it is okay to engage in sexual intercourse, given mutual desire. Women tend to think that couples should be together for a month or so before sex is appropriate, whereas males believe that even relatively short periods of acquaintanceship make having sex okay (Buss & Schmitt, 1993).

14.24 When men and women were propositioned by an attractive stranger, men were much more willing than women to agree to have sex or to go home with the stranger. Note that not a single woman agreed to have sex.

Although men and women value many of the same things in a relationship partner, such as physical attractiveness, kindness, and intelligence, men and women diverge in terms of which features they emphasize. Strictly in terms of maximizing reproduction, men primarily need to be concerned with whether a woman looks like she could bear healthy children. Conversely, women are better able to maximize reproduction by seeking mates who are likely to provide resources and assistance to help nurture offspring. In one study, Buss asked 92 married couples about which characteristics they valued in their spouse. Women preferred the following characteristics: considerate, honest, dependable, kind, understanding, fond of children, well-liked by others, good earning capacity, ambitious, career-oriented, good family background, and fairly tall. Men tended to value good looks, cooking skills, and sexual faithfulness. In general, men rate physical attractiveness as much more important than do women, who demonstrate a preference for education and good earning capacity—in other words, status. Across some 37 cultures studied, females valued a good financial prospect to a greater extent than did men (Buss, 1989). In addition, women in all 37 cultures tended to marry older

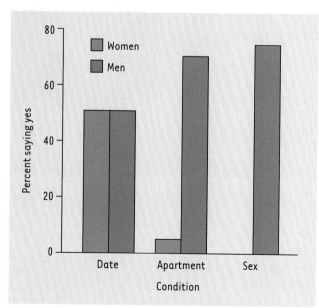

men, who are often more settled and financially stable. The relative male preference for attractiveness and the female preference for status can be observed in studies of newspaper personal ads, in which males tend to seek out good looks and females tend to seek out maturity and financial stability. Recall, however, that both men and women seek mates who are roughly similar in attractiveness, and that physical attractiveness does affect how both sexes judge other people. It is the relative emphases that conform to evolutionary predictions.

The evolutionary account of human mating is controversial. Some researchers believe that behaviors shaped by evolution have little impact on contemporary relationships. There are two important factors to consider. First, the modern era is only a tiny fraction of human evolutionary history, and the modern mind resides in a Stone Age brain, solving adaptive problems that have faced our species for millions of years. Thus, remnants of behaviors that were adaptive in prehistoric times may still exist even if they are not adaptive in contemporary society. More important, however, natural selection not only bestows biological urges, it also bestows a strong sensitivity to cultural and group norms, so that instinctive behaviors are constrained by social context. The frontal lobes work to inhibit people from breaking social rules, which are determined to a great extent by the culture in which they live. The current social context differs greatly from that of many millions of years ago and human mating strategies are indeed influenced by these contemporary norms. For example, from a biological view, it might seem advantageous for humans to reproduce as soon as they are able. But many contemporary cultures discourage sexual behavior until people are older and better able to care for their offspring. The critical point is that human behavior emerges to solve adaptive problems, and to some degree the modern era introduces new adaptive challenges based on societal standards of conduct. These standards shape the context in which both men and women view sexual behavior as desirable and appropriate.

sexual strategies theory Evolutionary theory that suggests men and women look for different qualities in relationship partners due to the gender-specific adaptive problems they've faced throughout human history.

LOVE IS AN IMPORTANT COMPONENT OF HUMAN RELATIONSHIPS

As noted earlier, psychological scientists have long neglected the study of *love*, in part because it seems a mysterious state that defies sensible comprehension. Thanks to the pioneering work of Elaine Hatfield and Ellen Berscheid (Figure 14.25), it is now clear that researchers can use scientific methods to examine this

14.25 Elaine Hatfield (left) and Ellen Berscheid (right) are pioneers in the study of human relationships.

What is love and what makes it last?

important interpersonal bond. Hatfield and Berscheid drew an important distinction between passionate love and companionate love. **Passionate love** is a state of intense longing and sexual desire. This is how love is often portrayed in the movies. In passionate love people fall head over heels for each other, feel an overwhelming urge to be together, and are constantly sexually aroused. **Companionate love** is a strong commitment to care for and support a partner that develops slowly over time. It is based on friendship, trust, respect, and intimacy.

Robert Sternberg (1986) developed a more complex model to account for the subtleties of love. His **triangular theory of love** proposes that love is made up of three components—passion, intimacy, and commitment—that can vary in intensity. Sternberg uses these three dimensions to describe seven basic types of love (Figure 14.26). For instance, typical friendships feature intimacy without passion or commitment, whereas infatuation is passion without intimacy or commitment. In the center of the triangle is the sort of love that most people seek, a consummate love that includes passion, intimacy, and commitment.

MAKING LOVE LAST IS DIFFICULT

An unfortunate aspect of contemporary marriages is that most of them fail. In North America, approximately half to two-thirds of marriages end in divorce or separation, many within the first few years. In addition, many couples who do not get divorced are unhappy and live together in a constant state of fighting or as strangers sharing a house. Social psychologist Rowland Miller notes, "married people are meaner to each other than they are to total strangers" (1997, p. 12). People often take their relationship partners for granted, openly criticize them, and take out their frustrations on them by being cruel or cold. It is perhaps no surprise then that relatively few marriages meet the blissful ideals that newlyweds expect. What factors cause such dissatisfaction in relationships?

Passion fades In the first stages of most romantic relationships, people are passionately attracted to one another. The long-term pattern of sexual activity within relationships shows a rise and then a decline. When first dating, people often limit their physical affection to kissing and holding hands. If love begins to blossom, people go further, and at some point they may commence having sex.

14.26 Sternberg's triangular theory describes love as being comprised of different combinations of passion, intimacy, and commitment.

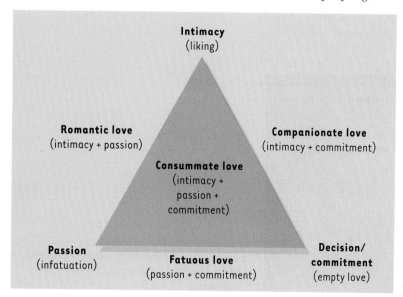

There is typically a period of months or even years when the two people experience frequent, intense desire for each other and have sex as often as they can arrange it. Past that peak, however, their interest in sex with each other wanes. Frequency of sex declines by about half from the first year of marriage to the second, and it continues to decline, although more gradually, thereafter. Not only does frequency of sex decline, but people typically experience less passion for their partners over time. Unless people develop other forms of satisfaction in their romantic relationships, such as friendship, social support, and intimacy, the loss of passion leads to dissatisfaction and often to the eventual dissolution of the relationship.

Jealousy and possessiveness Even when people lose some of their sexual desire for each other, however, they generally do not want their mates to have sex with anyone else. Some degree of sexual possessiveness and jealousy is found in all cultures, although there is variation as to what makes people jealous and how they express it. Although people may disapprove of sexual infidelity in general, many engage in it sooner or later. Even so, these occurrences are far less frequent than one might think. The best estimates are that one out of four husbands and one out of ten wives have had extramarital sex. Earlier estimates suggesting that half of married men and almost as many women were unfaithful may have reflected the more permissive patterns during the "sexual revolution," and people may well be more faithful now than they were a couple of decades ago.

Couples are more likely to break up if either partner has sex with someone else. This is true even of "open marriages," in which the partners agree to allow each other to have sex with others. It does not appear, however, that these marriages break up because one person decides to get a divorce in order to marry the adulterous lover, although certainly that happens in some cases. In fact, extramarital sex is better described as a "risk factor" than as an actual cause of breaking up. People who are dissatisfied with their marriages are probably more likely to take a new sex partner, and so the dissatisfaction with the marriage may be the cause rather than the consequence of the infidelity.

Dealing with conflict   Even in the best relationships, some conflict is inevitable, and couples need to constantly resolve strife. Confronting and discussing important issues is clearly an important aspect of any relationship. The way a couple deals with conflict often determines whether the relationship will last. John Gottman (1994) describes four interpersonal styles that typically lead to marital discord and dissolution. These maladaptive strategies include being overly critical, holding the partner in contempt, being defensive, and mentally withdrawing from the relationship. When one partner launches a complaint, the other responds with his or her own complaints and often raises the stakes by recalling all of the other person's failings. Inevitably, any disagreement, no matter how small, escalates into a major fight over the core marital problems, which often center around a lack of money or sex or both. Couples who are more satisfied tend to express concern for each other, even while disagreeing, try to see each other's point of view, and manage to stay relatively calm.

Attributional style and accommodation   Unhappy couples also differ from happy couples in attributional style, which refers to how one person explains another's behavior (Bradbury & Fincham, 1990). Unhappy couples make *distress-maintaining attributions* in which they view each other in the most negative way possible. In contrast, happy couples make *partner-enhancing attributions* in which they overlook bad behavior or respond constructively, a process referred to as *accommodation* (Rusbult & Van Lange, 1996). Essentially, happy couples attribute good outcomes to each other and bad outcomes to situations, whereas distressed couples do the opposite—if their partners bring them flowers, they wonder what ill deed their partners committed rather than thinking about what sweethearts they married.

Can anything be done to save marriages? Social psychologists have found that people who tend to be happiest in their relationships are those who see their partners in the most positive ways, perhaps even exaggerating their partners' positive features (Murray et al., 1996). This may surprise you, since you might expect that people would be happiest with someone who knows them very well, including

passionate love   A state of intense longing and sexual desire.

companionate love   A strong commitment based on friendship, trust, respect, and intimacy that strengthens over time.

triangular theory of love   Proposes that love is made up of differing combinations of passion, intimacy, and commitment.

both their strengths and weaknesses. However, research indicates that people who ignore their partners' weaknesses while valuing their strengths have the most enduring relationships. In addition, people who believe that their relationships are better than average, in effect using downward comparisons, have more stable marriages (Rusbult et al., 2000). Thinking positively about the relationship, giving occasional compliments, and continuing to court the partner's affections are key ingredients in relationships that endure.

What Determines the Quality of Relationships?

People form friendships based on proximity, familiarity, similarity, and personal characteristics such as personality and attractiveness. Men and women look for different qualities in potential partners, which may be due in part to the different adaptive problems faced by the sexes over the course of human evolution. Sexual behavior is an important component of romantic relationships, especially in the beginning, although relationships based solely on passion may fail when it starts to wane. How a couple deals with conflict is an important determinant of whether the relationship will endure.

CONCLUSION

The human need to belong exerts a powerful force on human behavior. Those who act in ways that place them at risk for group exclusion become anxious, and this anxiety causes them to conform to group norms. People reject those who lie, cheat, steal, or violate group standards. This may occur because those individuals who lived in well-functioning groups had a decided evolutionary advantage over those who lived in discordant groups. However, the pressures to conform to the group leave people susceptible to social influence and cause them to act in ways that conflict with their personal standards. Learning about the power of social situations allows a partial understanding of the long and tragic history of inhumane acts, such as genocide and other organized forms of brutality.

FURTHER READINGS

Baumeister, R. F. (1997). *Evil: Inside human violence and cruelty*. New York: W. H. Freeman.

Berscheid, E., & Reis, H. T. (1998). Attraction and close relationships. In D. T. Gilbert, S. T. Fiske, & L. Gardner (Eds.), *Handbook of social psychology*. Vol. 2. (pp. 193–281). New York: Oxford University Press.

Buss, D. M., & Kenrick, D. T. (1998). Evolutionary social psychology. In D. T. Gilbert, S. T. Fiske, & L. Gardner (Eds.), *Handbook of social psychology*. Vol 2. (pp. 982–1026). New York: Oxford University Press.

Cialdini, R. (2001). *Influence: Science and practice*. Boston: Allyn & Bacon.

Gottman, J. (1994). *Why marriages succeed or fail*. New York: Simon & Schuster.

Zebrowitz, L. A. (1997). *Reading faces: Window to the soul?* Boulder, CO: Westview Press.

IDENTIFYING INFLUENCES ON PERSONALITY

Rock musician Steven Tyler (left) is the father of actress Liv Tyler (right), but Liv didn't know that until she was 12 years old. This case and others like it interest psychological scientists, who want to know to what extent human personality is inherited, and to what extent it is subject to cultural and social influences. Recent evidence suggests that biological processes play an important role in determining personality.

TIMELINE

200 C.E.
Humoral Theory of Temperament The physician Galen formalizes Hippocrates' idea that personality is rooted in the body, arguing that it is determined by the relative amounts of different humors, or fluids.

1890s–1930s
Freudian Psychodynamics Sigmund Freud proposes that unconscious processes that originate in early childhood experiences determine much of human personality.

1930s
Study of Lives Henry Murray uses projective measures to examine unconscious needs and champions the scientific study of whole persons.

1937
Allport Defines Personality Gordon Allport publishes the first major textbook in personality psychology, helping to shape personality as the scientific study of the individual.

Personality

OUTLINING THE PRINCIPLES

1950s–1960s

Humanism and Phenomenology Dissatisfied with deterministic views of personality, a number of psychologists emphasize personal experience and belief systems, focusing on the potential for individual growth.

1950s–1960s

Biological Basis of Personality Hans Eysenck demonstrates physiological differences between introverts and extraverts, setting the foundation for contemporary research on the biological basis of personality.

1968

Trait Consistency Is Overrated Walter Mischel charges that personality traits are not predictive of behavior across different situations, which launches the person-situation debate.

1982

Inhibition and Approach Jeffrey Gray at Oxford University proposes that approach and inhibition motives, residing in distinct brain structures and processes, are the neural underpinnings of introversion and extraversion.

1980s–1990s

The Big Five Building on earlier work by Warren Norman, researchers such as Lewis Goldberg, Paul Costa, Robert McCrae, and Oliver John argue that the universe of personality traits can be reduced to five basic factors.

They were a happy couple in their early thirties, with three healthy young children. When their infant son died during a routine surgical procedure they understandably were devastated. Although many people in this situation might have wanted to have another child, this couple did not; they wanted to bring their dead son back to life. To do so, they decided to finance—using money from a malpractice settlement with the hospital where he died—an attempt to clone their son. Welcome to the twenty-first century.

The idea of human cloning moved from the realm of science fiction to plausibility with the announcement in 1997 that Scottish researchers had created a successful sheep clone named *Dolly*. If sheep could be cloned, why not humans? Aghast at the idea, many governments around the world banned research on human cloning. At a conference in August 2001, however, separate teams of researchers confirmed that they were actively attempting to clone a person using the methods pioneered in Scotland. Ethicists, religious leaders, and scientists are locked in debate about whether human cloning is viable and ethical. In the midst of this debate, psychological scientists can't help but wonder what cloning might tell us about human personality and identity.

Nature already clones people, in the form of monozygotic twins who share identical genes. Recall from Chapter 3 that there are many remarkable similarities among identical twins, even if they are raised apart. But will "clones" be as similar to their gene donors as monozygotic twins are to each other? There are many reasons to believe they will not. Consider the infant boy that the young couple wants to revive. Among other things, his clone will have a different uterine environment, will be raised by parents who previously lost a child and therefore might be overprotective, and will be interacting with siblings who are older. Moreover, even though identical twins grow up to be quite similar in many respects, they still differ from each other in multiple ways. The evidence from behavioral genetics suggests that a cloned child would share many similarities in personality with

RESEARCH QUESTIONS

for Studying Personality

What is personality?

How much is personality influenced by unconscious processes?

How is personality measured?

How stable is personality across situations?

What does personality predict?

What roles do biology and environment play in shaping personality?

Can personality change?

1990s
Behavioral Genetics
Beginning with studies of twins, researchers demonstrate that personality traits are determined more by inheritance than by family environment.

1990s
Personology Led by Dan McAdams, researchers focus on how people's personal stories form coherent life narratives.

1990s
The Return of Temperaments
Converging evidence indicates that basic temperaments, which can be observed in infancy and throughout childhood, are biologically based and have consequential impact on personality and behavior.

the first child, including some unusual quirks, but these might simply haunt the parents as painful reminders of their dead child and their failure to exactly reproduce him through cloning.

Human cloning raises a number of issues of great interest to psychological scientists. Will the cloned child develop at the same rate as the first child, or might he be affected by the parents' expectations? What role does parental treatment play in the development of personality? How much of who you are, your personality, is determined by your genes and how much by the environment? If two clones were raised in different cultures, how different might they be? What if they were raised ten years apart, and therefore exposed to different cultural environments? Every person you know is unique. What determines this uniqueness? A great deal has been learned about human personality through research that crosses levels of analysis. This chapter is concerned with the scientific understanding of human personality.

personality Characteristics, emotional responses, thoughts, and behaviors that are relatively stable over time and across circumstances.

personality trait A characteristic; a dispositional tendency to act in a certain way over time and across circumstances.

Understanding personality may be among the oldest quests in psychology. Since antiquity, an incredibly wide array of grand theories have been proposed to explain basic differences between individuals. **Personality** refers to an individual's characteristics, emotional responses, thoughts, and behaviors that are relatively stable over time and across circumstances. Personality psychologists study the basic processes that influence the development of personality on a number of different levels of analysis, such as the influence of culture, learning, biology, and cognitive factors. At the same time, those who study personality are most interested in understanding *whole persons*. That is, they try to understand what makes each person unique. People differ greatly in many ways, as you have no doubt noticed. Some are hostile, some are loving, and others are withdrawn. Each of these characteristics is a **personality trait**, a dispositional tendency to act in a certain way over time and across circumstances. What sort of person are you? More to the point, Why are you who you are?

What is personality?

15.1 Dan McAdams believes that to know people well, we need to know everything about them, including their personal narratives of their whole lives.

HOW HAS PERSONALITY BEEN STUDIED?

Dan McAdams (Figure 15.1), a leading personality researcher, has posed the interesting question, What must we know to know a person well? The specific way that psychologists try to answer this question varies greatly, often depending on their overall theoretical approach. Some psychological scientists emphasize the biological and genetic factors that predispose behaviors. Others might emphasize culture, patterns of reinforcement, or mental and unconscious processes. To really understand people is to understand everything about them, from their biological makeups, to their early childhood experiences, to the way they think, to the cultures in which they were raised. All of these factors work together to shape a person in a unique way. Thus, personality psychologists approach the study of personality on many levels.

15.2 Gordon Allport published the first major textbook of personality psychology, which defined the field. He also championed the study of individuals and established traits as a central concept in personality research.

Gordon Allport (Figure 15.2), who published the first major textbook on personality in 1937, gave perhaps the best working definition of personality: "the dynamic organization within the individual of those psychophysical systems that determine his characteristic behavior and thought" (1961, p. 28). This definition includes many of the concepts most important to a contemporary understanding of personality. The notion of *organization* indicates that personality is not just a list of traits, but that there is a coherent whole. Moreover, this organized whole is *dynamic*, in that it is goal seeking, sensitive to context, and adaptive to the environment. By emphasizing *psychophysical systems*, Allport highlights the psychological nature of personality, while clearly recognizing that personality arises from basic biological processes. Finally, Allport's definition stresses that personality *causes* people to think, behave, and feel in relatively consistent ways over time. Personality researchers use diverse approaches to explore different aspects of Allport's definition.

PSYCHODYNAMIC THEORIES EMPHASIZE UNCONSCIOUS AND DYNAMIC PROCESSES

Sigmund Freud, an Austrian physician whose theories dominated psychological thinking for many decades, developed one of the most influential theories of human personality. Freud developed many of his ideas about personality by observing people he was treating for various psychological disturbances, such as patients who experienced paralysis without any apparent physical cause. The central premise of Freud's **psychodynamic theory** of personality is that unconscious forces, such as wishes and motives, influence behavior. Freud referred to these psychic forces as *instincts* (although he used the term in a way slightly different from its contemporary use), defining them as mental representations arising out of biological or physical need. For instance, Freud proposed that people have a *life instinct* that is satisfied by following the *pleasure principle*, which directs people to seek pleasure and avoid pain. The energy that drives the pleasure principle is called *libido*; although nowadays the term has a strong sexual connotation, Freud used it to refer more generally to the energy that promotes pleasure seeking. Instincts can be viewed as wishes or desires to satisfy libidinal urges for pleasure. These psychological forces can be in conflict, which was what Freud viewed as the essential cause of mental illness.

How much is personality influenced by unconscious processes?

A topographical model of mind Freud believed that most of the conflict between various psychological forces occurred below the level of conscious awareness. In his *topographical model* (Figure 15.3), Freud proposed that the structure of the mind, the topography as it were, was divided into three different zones of mental awareness. At the *conscious* level, people are aware of their thoughts. The *preconscious* consists of content that is not currently in awareness but could be brought to awareness; it is roughly analogous to long-term memory. The *unconscious* contains material that the mind cannot easily retrieve. According to Freud, the unconscious mind contains wishes, desires, and motives that are associated with conflict, anxiety, or pain and are therefore not accessible to protect the person from distress. Sometimes, however, this information leaks into consciousness, such as occurs during a *Freudian slip*, in which a person accidentally reveals a hidden motive, such as the person who introduces her- or himself to someone attractive by saying "Excuse me, I don't think we've been properly seduced."

Development of sexual instincts An important component of Freudian thinking was the idea that early childhood experiences had a major impact on the development of personality. Freud believed that children went through developmental stages that corresponded to their pursuit of satisfaction of libidinal urges. At each **psychosexual stage**, libido is focused on one of the *erogenous zones*: the mouth, anus, and genitals. The *oral stage* lasts from birth to approximately 18 months, during which time pleasure is sought through the mouth. Hungry infants experience relief when they breastfeed and come to associate pleasure with sucking. When children are two to three years old, toilet training leads them to focus on the anus; therefore mastery of controlling the bowels is the key focus of the *anal phase*. From three to five, children enter the *phallic stage*, during which libidinal energies are directed toward the genitals. Children often discover the pleasure of rubbing their genitals during this time, although there is no sexual intent per se.

One of the most controversial Freudian theories applies to children in the phallic stage. According to Freud, children desire an exclusive relationship with the opposite-sex parent. Because the same-sex parent is therefore a rival, children develop hostility toward the same-sex parent, which for boys is known as the *Oedipus complex*, after a Greek tragedy in which Oedipus accidentally kills his father and marries his mother. Freud believed that children develop unconscious wishes to kill the one parent in order to claim the other, and that they resolve this conflict through identification with the same-sex parent, taking on many of their values and ideals. This theory was mostly applicable for boys. Freud's theory for girls was more complex and even less convincing.

Following the phallic stage, children enter a brief *latency stage*, in which libidinal urges are suppressed or channeled into schoolwork or building friendships. Finally, in the *genital stage*, adolescents and adults work to attain mature attitudes about sexuality and adulthood. Libidinal urges are centered on the capacity to reproduce and contribute to society.

According to Freud, progression through these psychosexual stages has a profound impact on personality. For example, some people become *fixated* at a stage during which they have received excessive parental restriction or indulgence. Those fixated at the oral stage develop *oral personalities*; they continue to seek out pleasure via the mouth, such as by smoking, and they are excessively needy. Those fixated at the anal phase may have *anal-retentive* personalities, meaning they are stubborn and overly regulating. The latter may be due to overly strict toilet training, or overly rule-based rearing more generally.

Structural model of personality Freud proposed an integrated model of how the mind is organized, which consists of three theoretical structures that vary across the levels of consciousness. At the most basic level, and completely submerged in the unconscious, is the **id**, which operates according to the pleasure principle, acting on impulses and desires. The innate forces driving the id are sex and aggression. Acting as a brake on the id is the **superego**, which is the internalization of societal and parental standards of conduct. Developing during the phallic phase, the superego is a rigid structure of morality, or human conscience. Mediating between superego and id is the **ego**, which tries to satisfy the wishes of the id while being responsive to the dictates of the superego. The ego operates according to the *reality principle*, which involves rational thought and problem solving.

Conflicts between the id and superego lead to anxiety, which the ego copes with by employing a variety of **defense mechanisms**, unconscious mental

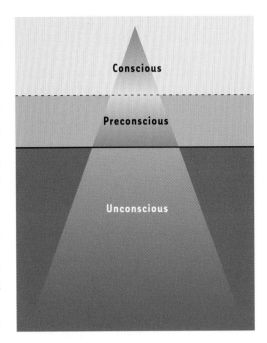

15.3 Freud differentiated levels of consciousness into three zones. He believed that much of human behavior was influenced by unconscious processes.

psychodynamic theory Freudian theory that unconscious forces, such as wishes and motives, influence behavior.

psychosexual stage According to Freud, the developmental stages that correspond to the pursuit of satisfaction of libidinal urges.

id In psychodynamic theory, the component of personality that is completely submerged in the unconscious and operates according to the pleasure principle.

superego In psychodynamic theory, the internalization of societal and parental standards of conduct.

ego In psychodynamic theory, the component of personality that tries to satisfy the wishes of the id while being responsive to the dictates of the superego.

defense mechanisms Unconscious mental strategies used to protect the mind from conflict and distress.

strategies that the mind uses to protect itself from distress. For instance, people often *rationalize* their behavior by blaming situational factors over which they have little control, such as explaining that you didn't call your parents because you were too busy studying for an exam. Much of the theoretical work on defense mechanisms can be credited to Sigmund's daughter, Anna Freud. Several common defense mechanisms are listed in Table 15.1. Research in psychology over the past 40 years has provided considerable support for the existence of many of these defense mechanisms (Baumeister et al., 1998), although contemporary researchers believe that these mechanisms protect self-esteem rather than relieve unconscious conflict over libidinal desires. For instance, *reaction formation* occurs when people ward off an uncomfortable thought about the self by embracing its opposite. In one study of homophobic men, those who expressed the most negative views of homosexuality showed greater physiological arousal when showed video depictions of homosexual sex than did men who were more accepting of homosexuality (Adams et al., 1996).

Psychodynamic theory since Freud Although Freud is most closely identified with psychodynamic theory, a number of scholars, while rejecting certain aspects of Freudian thinking, embraced the notion of unconscious conflict. These *neo-Freudians* include Carl Jung, Alfred Adler, and Karen Horney, each of whom modified Freud through the development of their own psychodynamic theories. For instance, Adler and Horney strongly criticized Freud's view of women, believing many of his theories to be misogynistic. Many neo-Freudians rejected Freud's emphasis on sexual forces and instead focused on social interactions, especially the emotional attachments that children develop to their parents. This focus is

TABLE 15.1 Common Defense Mechanisms

MECHANISM	DEFINITION	EXAMPLE
Denial	Refusing to acknowledge source of anxiety	Ill person ignores medical advice
Repression	Excluding source of anxiety from awareness	Person fails to remember an unpleasant event
Projection	Attributing unacceptable qualities of the self to someone else	Competitive person describes others as supercompetitive
Reaction Formation	Warding off an uncomfortable thought by overemphasizing its opposite	Person with unacknowledged homosexual desires makes homophobic remarks
Rationalization	Concocting a seemingly logical reason or excuse for behavior that might otherwise be shameful	Person cheats on taxes because "everyone does it"
Displacement	Shifting the attention of emotion from one object to another	Person yells at children after a bad day at work
Sublimation	Channeling socially unacceptable impulses into constructive, even admirable, behavior	Sadist becomes a surgeon or dentist

embodied in *object relations* theory, in which the object of attachment is another person, such as a parent or spouse (Westen, 1991). In addition, some neo-Freudians, including Horney and Erik Erikson, emphasized the influence of culture, which Freud saw monolithically as "civilization."

Psychological scientists have largely abandoned psychodynamic theories because of the lack of scientific evidence for Freud's central premises, since many of the ideas have not been amenable to empirical examination. However, Freud has to be understood in the context of the time in which he was working and the methods he had at his disposal. He was an astute observer of behavior and an amazingly creative theorist. His observations and ideas continue to have an important impact on personality psychology and have framed much of the research in personality over the last century (Westen, 1998).

humanistic approaches Approaches to studying personality that emphasize personal experience and belief systems, and propose that people seek personal growth to fulfill their human potential.

HUMANISTIC APPROACHES EMPHASIZE INTEGRATED PERSONAL EXPERIENCE

By the early 1950s, most psychological theories of personality were heavily deterministic; that is, personality and its associated behavioral characteristics were considered to be caused by forces beyond the person's control. As we have seen, Freud believed that personality was determined by unconscious conflicts. In a different vein, behaviorists such as B. F. Skinner argued that patterns of reinforcement determined response tendencies, which were the basis of personality. Against this backdrop emerged a view of personality that emphasized the uniqueness of the human condition. **Humanistic approaches** to personality emphasized personal experience and belief systems and proposed that people sought to fulfill their human potential. At its core, humanism emphasizes subjective human experience, or *phenomenology*, and views each person as inherently good. Humanistic approaches to personality encourage people to fulfill their individual potential for personal growth through greater self-understanding; this process is referred to as *self-actualization*. Maslow's theory of motivation, discussed in Chapter 9, is an example of a humanistic approach to personality. Maslow believed that the desire to become self-actualized was the ultimate and most important human motive.

The most prominent humanistic psychologist was Carl Rogers (Figure 15.4), whose *person-centered* approach to personality emphasized people's personal understandings or phenomenology. As a therapeutic technique, Rogers focused on the need for the therapist to create a warm, supportive, and accepting environment and to deal with clients' problems and concerns as clients understood them.

Rogers' theory highlights the importance of how parents show affection for their children and how parental treatment affects personality development. Rogers speculated that although most parents provide love and support, it is often conditional. That is, parents love their children as long as the children do what the parent wants them to do. Parents who do not approve of their children's behavior often behave in ways that indicate they may withhold their love from the child. As a result, children quickly abandon their true feelings, dreams, and desires and accept only those parts of themselves that elicit parental love and support. Thus, people lose touch with their true selves in their pursuit of positive regard from others. By contrast, Rogers encouraged parents to raise their children with *unconditional positive regard*, in which children are accepted, loved, and prized no matter how they behave. Parents are to express disapproval with bad

15.4 Carl Rogers emphasized people's subjective understandings of their whole lives.

behavior, but in a context that ensures that children feel loved, as epitomized in the saying "Love the sinner, hate the sin." According to Rogers, children raised with unconditional positive regard will develop a healthy sense of self-esteem and will be able to become, in Rogers' term, a *fully functioning person*.

By its nature, humanistic psychology has not been overly concerned with the scientific study of personality, since it emphasizes subjective personal experience. Recently, however, psychologists have begun to use the methods of science to study the positive aspects of humanity. The *positive psychology movement* was launched by clinical psychologist Martin Seligman when he was president of the American Psychological Association (Seligman & Csikszentmihalyi, 2000). Seligman and others have encouraged the scientific study of qualities such as faith, values, creativity, courage, and hope. For instance, Ed Diener (2000) has conducted more than three decades of research on *subjective well-being*, a general term for how much happiness and satisfaction people have in their lives. He has found that well-being varies across cultures such that the wealthiest countries often have higher levels of satisfaction, a finding that fits in well with Maslow's proposal that people need to satisfy basic needs (such as food, shelter, and safety) before they are able to focus on self-esteem needs.

TYPE AND TRAIT APPROACHES DESCRIBE BEHAVIORAL DISPOSITIONS

Psychodynamic and humanistic approaches focus on explaining the mental processes that shape personality. The same underlying processes are thought to occur within each person, but people differ because they experience different conflicts, situations, parental treatment, and so forth. Other approaches to personality focus more on description than explanation, which is actually similar to the way most people intuitively view personality. For example, if asked to describe a friend, you would probably not delve into unconscious conflicts; rather, you would describe the person as a certain type, such as an *introvert* or an *extravert*. **Personality types** are discrete categories into which we place people. Subsequently, we fill in gaps in our knowledge with our beliefs about what behaviors and dispositions are associated with these types. Our tendency to assume that personality characteristics go together, and therefore to make predictions about people based on minimal evidence, is referred to as *implicit personality theory*. For example, we think that introverts don't like to go to parties, that they like to read books, and that they are sensitive.

In addition to typologies, many personality psychologists are concerned with *traits*, defined earlier as behavioral dispositions that endure over time and across situations. Traits are on a continuum, with most people toward the middle and relatively few at the extreme ends. Thus, people range from being very unfriendly to very friendly, but most people are moderately friendly. The **trait approach** to personality provides a method for assessing the extent to which individuals differ in personality dispositions, such as sociability, cheerfulness, and aggressiveness (Funder, 2001).

How many traits are there? In the earliest stages of his career, Gordon Allport, along with colleague Henry Odbert of Dartmouth College, went through the dictionary to count the number of words that could be used as personality traits. They counted nearly 18,000. Even weeding out synonyms and archaic words left 4,500 apparent traits.

personality types Discrete categories based on global personality characteristics.

trait approach An approach to studying personality that focuses on the extent to which individuals differ in personality dispositions.

Raymond Cattell set out in the 1950s to ascertain the basic elements of personality. Cattell believed that by using statistical procedures he could take the scientific study of personality to a higher level and perhaps uncover the basic structure of personality. Cattell had participants fill out personality questionnaires containing many trait items, which he reduced from the larger set produced by Allport and Odbert. Cattell then performed *factor analysis*, grouping items based on their similarities. For instance, all the terms that referred to friendliness ("nice," "pleasant," "cooperative," and so on) were grouped together. Through this procedure Cattell came to believe that there were 16 basic dimensions of personality, one of which was intelligence. The others were given rather unusual names to avoid confusion with everyday language; most personality psychologists no longer use these terms.

Eysenck's hierarchical model   Reducing the number of basic traits even further was British psychologist Hans Eysenck, who in the 1960s proposed a hierarchical model of personality. As may be seen in Figure 15.5, the basic structure begins at the *specific response level*, which consists of observed behaviors. For instance, a person buys an item because it is on sale. A person might then repeat the behavior on different occasions, which is the *habitual response level*. Some people find it hard to pass up sale items, whether they need them or not. If people are observed on many occasions to behave in same way, they are characterized as possessing a *trait*. Traits such as impulsiveness and sociability can then be viewed as components of *superordinate traits*, of which Eysenck proposed there were three: *introversion-extraversion*, *emotional stability*, and *psychoticism*.

The dimension of *introversion-extraversion*, terms originally coined by psychoanalyst Carl Jung, refers to the extent that people are shy, reserved, and quiet versus sociable, outgoing, and bold. As you will see later in this chapter, Eysenck believed that this dimension reflects differences in biological functioning. *Emotional stability* refers to the extent that people's moods and emotions change; people who are *neurotic* experience frequent and dramatic mood swings, especially toward negative emotions, relative to those who are more stable. People who are high in neuroticism report often feeling anxious, moody, and depressed, and they also tend to hold very low opinions of themselves. Finally, *psychoticism* describes a

15.5 Eysenck hierarchical model of personality. Extraversion is a superordinate trait made up of sociability, dominance, assertiveness, activity, and liveliness at the trait level. Each trait is made up of habitual and specific responses.

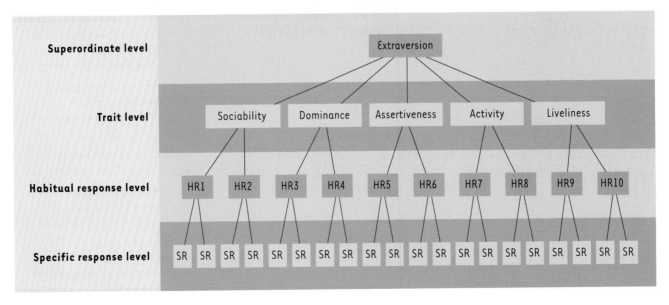

five factor theory The idea that personality can be described using five traits: openness to experience, conscientiousness, extraversion, agreeableness, and neuroticism.

mix of impulse control, empathy, and aggression, with those who are high in psychoticism being more aggressive, impulsive, and self-centered than those low in psychoticism. The term "psychoticism" was perhaps not a wise choice, as it implies a level of psychopathology that Eysenck did not intend. More recent conceptions of this superordinate trait call it *constraint*, with people ranging from restrained to disinhibited (Watson & Clark, 1997).

The Big Five In the last 20 years many personality psychologists have agreed that there are five basic personality traits, which is referred to as the **five factor theory** (McCrae & Costa, 1999). The *Big Five*, as they are known, consist of *extraversion*, *neuroticism* (similar to Eysenck's model), *conscientiousness*, *agreeableness*, and *openness to experience*. A good way to remember the five is that they can be arranged to spell the acronym OCEAN. Each of these five factors is a higher-order trait comprised of lower-order traits that are related to each other. For instance, as can be seen in Table 15.2, conscientiousness is determined by how careful and organized someone is, while agreeableness refers to the extent that a person is or is not trusting and helpful. Those high in openness to experience are imaginative and independent whereas those low in this basic trait are down-to-earth and conformist.

There is considerable evidence supporting the five factor theory (John, 1990). The Big Five emerge cross-culturally, among adults and children, even when vastly different questionnaires are used to assess traits, and the same five traits appear whether people rate themselves or are rated by others. Nonetheless, some researchers have questioned whether the five factor solution really helps us understand personality, since the trait terms are descriptive rather than explanatory, and because reducing all of human personality to five descriptions inevitably ignores human subtleties. For instance, there is evidence that many of these traits apply to animals as well as humans, as discussed in "Studying the Mind: Do Animals Have Personality?" However, one value of the five factor theory is that it serves as an organizational structure for the vast number of traits that can be used to describe personality; by providing a common descriptive framework, the the-

TABLE 15.2 The Big Five	
OPENNESS TO EXPERIENCE	Imaginative vs. down to earth Variety vs. routine Independent vs. conforming
CONSCIENTIOUSNESS	Organized vs. disorganized Careful vs. careless Self-disciplined vs. weak-willed
EXTRAVERSION	Social vs. retiring Fun-loving vs. sober Affectionate vs. reserved
AGREEABLENESS	Softhearted vs. ruthless Trusting vs. suspicious Helpful vs. uncooperative
NEUROTICISM	Worried vs. calm Insecure vs. secure Self-pitying vs. self-satisfied

DO ANIMALS HAVE PERSONALITY?

If you've ever owned a pet such as a dog or cat, you probably had the intuitive feeling that your pet had a personality of its own. For most of the history of psychological science, your intuition would have been treated with skepticism, with the assumption that you were *anthropomorphizing*, or humanizing, your pet by projecting your own sense of personality onto it. But if we are to take the principles of evolution seriously, there is continuity across species, raising the possibility that animals might display consistent behaviors across circumstances that reflect an underlying personality. Indeed, evidence has grown over the past few years that identifiable patterns of personality traits occur in animals in somewhat similar ways as they do in humans (Gosling, 2001). How do psychologists determine the personality of animals?

Sam Gosling studied the behavior of a group of spotted hyenas (Gosling, 1998). He created a personality scale consisting of 44 traits, applicable to humans and hyenas, that four observers who knew the hyenas well independently used to rate the animals. It turned out that the agreement among the raters was as high as is typically found in personality studies of humans, suggesting that the raters could assess the hyenas reliably. Using factor analysis, Gosling found that the traits clustered into five factors, albeit not exactly the same five factors found for humans. Although there were rough similarities between humans and hyenas in traits related to agreeableness, neuroticism, and openness to experience, hyenas showed no evidence of a conscientiousness factor, and extraversion seemed

to exist more in the form of assertiveness, which makes sense given that hyenas are a species that form dominance hierarchies.

What about other animals? Gosling and John (1999) summarized the findings of 19 studies that assessed multiple personality traits in modestly large samples of nonhuman animals, ranging from household pets to monkeys and other primates, to pigs and donkeys, and even to aquatic animals. They found evidence that traits similar to extraversion, neuroticism, and agreeableness could be found in most species. Extraversion reflected different levels of energy, approach, and sociability. Neuroticism indicated differences in emotional reactivity, fearfulness, and excitability, whereas agreeableness reflected differences in aggression, hostility, and affinity for mates. What about openness and conscientiousness? In about half of the species, animals did display individual differences in curiosity and play, and Gosling and John thought that openness in animals may be similar to behaviors one might observe in young children. Conscientiousness, a core human trait, was found in a narrow form only among chimpanzees, with some showing more unpredictability and disorganized behavior. The finding that only chimpanzees showed any signs of conscientiousness is perhaps not surprising, since they are humans' closest relatives. Gosling and John hope that their classification of animal traits according to the five factor theory may allow for greater understanding of the biological foundations and evolutionary significance of human personality.

ory has helped integrate and invigorate the trait approach to personality (John & Srivastava, 1999). In addition, there is now substantial evidence that personality traits have genetic components and are related to underlying neurophysiology. Thus, traits do exist at more than a descriptive level. Working across levels of analysis provides new ways to understand the basic traits (Clark & Watson, 1999), as will be discussed later in this chapter.

PERSONALITY REFLECTS LEARNING AND COGNITIVE PROCESSES

In contrast to those who saw personality as a result of internal processes, behaviorists such as B. F. Skinner viewed personality as little more than learned responses to patterns of reinforcement. However, growing dissatisfaction with strict models of learning theory led researchers to incorporate cognition into the understanding of personality. For instance, early cognitive theorist George Kelly emphasized the importance of people's understandings, or *personal constructs*, of their circumstances. According to Kelly, personal constructs develop through people's experiences and represent their interpretations and explanations for events in their social worlds. Building further on the cognitive approach was Julian Rotter, who in the 1950s introduced the idea that behavior was a function of people's *expectancies* for reinforcement, as well as the *value* they ascribed to the reinforcer. Thus, if a person is deciding whether to study for an exam or go to a party, the likelihood that studying will lead to a good grade, as well as how much that grade matters, is weighed against the likelihood that the party will be fun and the extent to which the person values having fun. Rotter proposed that people differ in the belief that their efforts will lead to positive outcomes, which he referred to as *locus of control*. People with an internal locus of control believe that they bring about their own rewards, whereas those with an external locus of control believe that rewards, and therefore their personal fate, are the result of forces beyond their control. These generalized beliefs have been shown to have a powerful effect on psychological adjustment.

The incorporation of cognition into learning theories led to the development of *cognitive-social theories* of personality, which emphasize how personal beliefs, expectancies, and interpretations of social situations shape behavior and personality. For instance, Albert Bandura (1977) accepts many of the tenets of learning theory but argues that humans possess mental capacities, such as beliefs, thoughts, and expectations, that interact with the environment to influence behavior. For Bandura, the extent to which people believe they can achieve specific outcomes, called *self-efficacy*, is an important determinant of behavior. Moreover, as discussed in Chapter 6, Bandura has proposed that people develop expectancies in part through *observational learning*, such as by noticing whether others are rewarded or punished for acting in certain ways.

One of the most influential cognitive-social theorists is Walter Mischel. As you will read later in the chapter, Mischel sparked controversy by proposing that personality traits often fail to predict behavior across different circumstances. According to Mischel's *Cognitive-Affective Personality System* (*CAPS*) (Mischel & Shoda, 1995), people's responses in a given situation are influenced by how they encode or perceive the situation, their affective (emotional) response to the situation, the skills and competencies they have to deal with challenges, and their anticipation of the outcomes that their behavior will produce.

Imagine, for instance, a person who walks into a party with an expectation of making a good impression, based on having done so many times in the past. This person will act very differently from a person whose past experiences of awkwardness, discomfort, and shyness lead to the expectation of rejection. Consider the personality style of *defensive pessimism*, studied by Julie Norem and Nancy Cantor. Defensive pessimists expect to fail and therefore enter test situations with dread. By contrast, optimists enter test situations with great expectations. You have probably encountered both of these types at your exams, with the pessimists predicting their imminent academic demise. And yet, both pessimists and optimists tend to perform similarly on exams (Norem, 1989). These two personality styles reflect different motivational strategies, with pessimists expecting the worst so they can be relieved when they succeed, and optimists focusing on positive outcomes.

The CAPS model also emphasizes *self-regulatory capacities*, in which people set personal goals, evaluate their progress, and adjust their ongoing behavior in pursuit of those goals. In addition, the values that people attach to goals, such as the importance of obtaining good grades, is part of the dynamic system. The pursuit of personal goals is an important component of cognitive-social theories of personality. Indeed, many personality psychologists believe that personal motives and strivings, such as those for achievement, power, or intimacy, are an essential aspect of personality (Snyder & Cantor, 1998). Personality, then, represents behavior that emerges from how people interpret their social worlds, and from the beliefs that they have about how they will affect and be affected by their social situations.

How Has Personality Been Studied?

According to the psychodynamic approach, unconscious motives and conflicts that are experienced throughout life, but especially in childhood, shape personality. Humanists believe that each person is unique and capable of fulfilling great potential. Trait theorists describe the behavior of people based on trait dispositions. Cognitive-social theorists focus on how cognitive interpretations and beliefs affect people's perceptions of their social environments. These varied approaches are not necessarily in opposition to each other. They share the common goal of trying to understand the ways in which people are similar to and different from one another.

HOW IS PERSONALITY ASSESSED AND WHAT DOES IT PREDICT?

Personality researchers have yet to agree on the best method for assessing various aspects of personality. To understand people you need to examine them in some way. But, unlike behavior or biological responses, personality cannot be directly assessed or observed. Psychological scientists measure personality by asking people to report on themselves, by asking people's friends or relatives to describe them, or by watching how people behave. Each of these methods has strengths and limitations that are important to understand. This section considers how psychological scientists assess personality, and how these different methods of assessment influence how we understand individuals.

How is personality measured?

PERSONALITY REFERS TO BOTH UNIQUE AND COMMON CHARACTERISTICS

As differentiated by Allport, there are two approaches to studying personality: idiographic and nomothetic. **Idiographic approaches** are *person-centered* in that they focus on individual lives and how various characteristics are integrated into unique persons. If your classmates were to write down 10 personality traits that described them, although there would be some overlap, each person would probably have a unique list of traits. People like to be distinctive, and therefore they tend to choose traits that are particularly descriptive of them as compared to other people. These *central traits* are especially important for how individuals define themselves. In contrast, *secondary traits* are those that people consider less personally descriptive or not applicable at all. In general, central traits are more predictive of behavior than are secondary traits.

Researchers who use idiographic approaches often examine case studies of individuals, perhaps through interviews or biographical information. For example, many scholars have tried to account for Adolph Hitler's behavior in Nazi Germany by asking questions about his early childhood experiences, his physical stature,

idiographic approaches Person-centered approaches to studying personality that focus on individual lives and how various characteristics are integrated into unique persons.

and his personal motivations. Henry Murray pioneered this approach at Harvard University. The study of people's lives emphasizes the idea that personality unfolds over the life course, as people react to their circumstances and come to define themselves.

There has recently been a resurgence of interest in the narrative approach to understanding human lives (McAdams, 1999, 2001). According to McAdams, humans weave a *life story* that integrates self-knowledge into a coherent whole. Life stories help bring meaning to life and help people make sense of the world. Like all good stories, the ones people tell about their lives contain characters, settings, acts, plot twists, and themes. The life story is a reconstructive and imaginative process in which people link together personal motives, goals, and beliefs with the events, people, and circumstances in which they find themselves. People define themselves by creating *personal myths* that bind together past events and future possibilities. To study personality, then, one needs to pay attention to the stories that people tell about their lives. The method of *psychobiography* uses personal life stories to develop and test theories about human personality.

Nomothetic approaches differ from idiographic approaches in that they focus on characteristics that are common among all people, but on which people vary—in other words, traits. For instance, every human can be rated along a continuum from very disagreeable to very agreeable. Researchers who follow this tradition tend to compare people by using common trait measures, such as questionnaires or other objective data. For instance, they might give participants a list of 100 personality traits and ask them to rate themselves on each, on a scale from 1 to 10. From the nomothetic perspective, individuals are unique because of their unique combinations of common traits.

THERE ARE OBJECTIVE AND PROJECTIVE WAYS TO ASSESS PERSONALITY

There are numerous methods for assessing personality, ranging from self-reports to clinical interviews to observer reports. Aside from the manner by which the data are collected, how researchers choose to measure personality depends to a great extent on their theoretical orientations. For instance, trait researchers use personality descriptions to predict specific behaviors, whereas humanistic psychologists use more holistic approaches. At the broadest level, assessment procedures can be grouped into *projective* and *objective* measures.

Projective measures According to psychodynamic theory, personality is influenced by conflicts that people aren't aware of. So, how can they tell you about something they don't know? **Projective measures** are tools that attempt to delve into the realm of the unconscious by presenting people with ambiguous stimuli and asking them to describe the stimulus items or tell stories about them. The general idea is that people will *project* their mental contents onto the ambiguous items, thereby revealing otherwise hidden aspects of personality, such as motives, wishes, and unconscious conflicts. Many of these procedures, such as *inkblot tests*, are used to assess psychopathology.

One classic projective measure used by personality psychologists is the **Thematic Apperception Test**, or **TAT**, developed by Henry Murray and Christiana Morgan, who used the TAT to study achievement motivation. In the TAT, a person

---

nomothetic approaches Approaches to studying personality that focus on characteristics that are common to all people, although there is individual variation.

projective measures Personality tests that examine unconscious processes by having people interpret ambiguous stimuli.

TAT (Thematic Apperception Test) A projective measure of personality where a person is shown an ambiguous picture and asked to tell a story about the picture.

objective measures Relatively unbiased assessments of personality usually administered through self-report questionnaires or through observer ratings.

is shown an ambiguous picture (Figure 15.6) and asked to tell a story about it. The story is then scored based on the motivational schemes that emerge, which are assumed to reflect the storyteller's personal motives. Many projective measures have been criticized for being too subjective and poorly validated. The TAT, however, has been shown to be useful for measuring motivational states, especially those related to achievement, power, and affiliation, and therefore continues to be used in contemporary research (McClelland et al., 1989). Indeed, evidence exists that projective tests, if used properly, are reliably predictive of behavior (Bornstein, 1999).

Objective measures   **Objective measures** of personality are straightforward assessments usually made by self-report questionnaires or observer ratings. For instance, the *NEO Personality Inventory* consists of 240 items designed to assess the Big Five personality traits (Costa & McCrae, 1992). Although called objective, the tests require people to make subjective judgments, and self-reports can be affected both by desires to avoid looking bad and by biases in self-perception that arise through self-relevant motives.

It can be difficult to directly compare self-reported objective measures because individuals do not have objective standards against which to rate themselves. Just because two individuals report a "5" on a 7-point shyness scale does not mean they are equally shy. After all, the term can mean different things to different people.

One technique that assesses personal meanings of traits is the *California Q-sort*, which requires people to sort 100 statements printed on cards into nine piles according to what extent the statement is descriptive of them. These piles represent categories ranging from "not at all descriptive" to "extremely descriptive." A person is allowed to place only so many cards in each pile, usually with fewer cards allowed for the extreme ends of the scale. Because most of the cards must be piled in the moderately descriptive categories, the Q-sort has a built-in procedure for getting at central dispositions. The Q-sort, like most objective measures, can also be used by observers, such as parents, teachers, therapists, and friends.

Objective tests make no pretense of uncovering hidden conflicts or secret information. They only measure what the raters believe or observe. Personality researchers use them to compare people's responses and assess the extent to which the answers predict behavior. In addition to large personality inventories, personal researchers often use self-report questionnaires that target specific traits, such as how much excitement you seek out of life, a trait known as *sensation seeking*.

15.6 A picture similar to those shown in a typical TAT card.

OBSERVERS SHOW ACCURACY IN TRAIT JUDGMENTS

Do you think other people know you pretty well? Imagine that you often feel a bit shy in new situations, as many people do. Would others know that shyness is part of your personality? Some shy people force themselves to act in an outgoing manner in order to mask their inner feelings. Their friends might have no indication that they feel shy. Others react to the fear of social situations by remaining quiet and aloof. Observers might believe them to be cold, arrogant, and unfriendly. People are judged by others throughout their lives. How accurate are those judgments? That is, how well do the personality judgments people make predict the behavior of others?

An important paper by personality psychologist David Funder (1995) found a surprising degree of accuracy for trait judgments, at least under certain circumstances. For instance, it turns out that your close acquaintances may be more accurate at predicting your behavior than you are. In one study, ratings of assertiveness made by friends predicted assertive behavior in the lab better than did the person's own ratings (Kolar et al., 1996). The same was true for a variety of other traits. This may occur because friends observe how you behave in situations while in turn you may be preoccupied with evaluating other people. In other words, you may pay more attention to others than to yourself, and therefore you may fail to notice how you actually behave. Another possibility is that your subjective perception may diverge from your objective behavior. In either case, the study implies that there is some disconnect between how people view themselves and how they behave.

PEOPLE SOMETIMES ARE INCONSISTENT

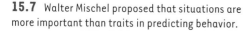
How stable is personality across situations?

Imagine again that you are a shy person. Are you shy in all situations? Probably not. Shy people tend to be most uncomfortable in new situations in which they are being evaluated; they tend not to be shy around family and close friends. Walter Mischel (Figure 15.7) dropped a bombshell on the field of personality in 1968 by proposing that behaviors are determined to a much greater extent by situations than by personality traits, a theory referred to as **situationism**. As evidence, he referred to studies in which people who are dishonest in one situation are completely honest in another. For instance, the student who is not totally honest with a professor in explaining why a paper is late is probably no more likely to steal from classmates or cheat on her taxes than is the student who admits he overslept. Mischel's critique of personality traits affected the field for more than a decade and caused considerable rifts between social psychologists, who tended to emphasize situational forces, and personality psychologists, who focused on individual dispositions. After all, the most basic definition of personality is that it is relatively stable across situations and circumstances. If Mischel was correct and there was relatively little stability, then the whole concept of personality seemed empty.

15.7 Walter Mischel proposed that situations are more important than traits in predicting behavior.

As you might expect, there was a rather vigorous response to Mischel's critique. The basic argument made by personality researchers in the *person-situation debate* is that the extent to which traits predict behavior depends on the *centrality* of the trait, the *aggregation* of behaviors over time, and the type of trait being evaluated. People tend to be more consistent for central traits than for secondary traits, since the former are most relevant to them. In addition, if behaviors are averaged across many situations, then personality traits are more predictive of behavior. A shy person may not be shy all the time, but on average they are shy more often than not. Moreover, people who report being shy in college continue to report being shy many years later, which indicates that there is stability to the trait of shyness. Finally, some people may be more consistent than others. Consider the trait of self-monitoring, in which some people are highly sensitive to cues of situational appropriateness (see Chapter 14). Those who are high in self-monitoring alter their behavior to match the situation, so that they exhibit low levels of consistency. By contrast, those low in self-monitoring are less able to alter their self-presentations to match situational demands, and they tend to be much more consistent across situations.

BEHAVIOR IS INFLUENCED BY THE INTERACTION OF PERSONALITY AND SITUATIONS

Considerable evidence now exists that personality traits are predictive of behavior. For instance, people who are high in neuroticism tend to be more depressed and have more illness, are more likely to have a midlife crisis, and so on. Indeed, being highly neurotic is the single best predictor of marital dissatisfaction and divorce (Karney & Bradbury, 1995). Likewise, those high in sensation seeking are more likely to smoke, use drugs, have sex, be impulsive, watch erotic movies, begin conversations, and engage in physically risky activities such as mountain climbing. The past two decades have found strong and compelling evidence that personality dispositions are meaningful constructs that predict people's behavior over time and across many circumstances. Yet people are also highly sensitive to social context and most conform to situational norms. Few people would break the law right in front of a police officer or drive on the wrong side of the road just because they felt like it. The situation dictates behavior irrespective of personality.

Situational influences can be subtle. Consider your own behavior. Do you behave in the exact same way around your family, friends, and teachers? Although you remain the same person, you may reveal different aspects of your personality during your interactions with different people. Your goals for social interaction change, as do the potential consequences of your actions. For example, your family may be more tolerant of your bad moods than are your friends. Thus, you may feel more free to express your bad moods around your family.

Situations themselves differ in the extent to which they constrain the expression of personality (Kenrick & Funder, 1991). Consider two people, one highly extraverted, aggressive, and boisterous and the other shy, thoughtful, and restrained. At a funeral, it would be hard to tell them apart based on their behavior. But at a party there would be obvious differences between them. Personality psychologists differentiate between *strong* situations (elevators, religious services, job interviews) and *weak* situations (parks, bars, your house); the former tend to mask differences in personality because of the power of the social environment. Most trait theorists are **interactionists**, in that they believe that behavior is jointly determined by situations and underlying dispositions. In other words, you need to know something about both the person and the environment to predict behavior.

However, it is important to point out that people also have an impact on their environments. First, people choose their situations. Introverts tend to avoid parties or other situations in which they would feel anxious, whereas extraverts seek out social opportunities. Moreover, once in the situation, the behavior of introverts and extraverts affects those around them. Some extraverts may draw people out and encourage them to have fun, whereas others might act aggressively and turn people off. Some introverts might create an intimate atmosphere and encourage people to open up and reveal personal concerns, whereas others might make people uncomfortable and anxious as both actors try to fill awkward gaps in the conversation. There is a reciprocal interaction between the person and the environment so that they simultaneously influence each other. The important point is that personality is a dynamic system that reflects both underlying dispositions and the activation of goals and affective responses in given situations.

RESEARCH QUESTION

What does personality predict?

situationism The theory that proposes that behavior is determined to a much greater extent by situations than by personality traits.

interactionists Theorists who believe that behavior is jointly determined by underlying dispositions and situations.

How Is Personality Assessed and What Does It Predict?
Personality is assessed through either projective or objective measures, depending on the goals of the researcher. Sometimes personality psychologists examine individuals, such as by examining personal myths that people use to explain their lives. Other times they examine many people using a common measure to assess whether individual differences in those measures predict behavior. People are relatively good at assessing personality traits in others, and some evidence suggests that observers might even be better at predicting people's behavior than are the people themselves. This occurs when observers are sensitive to environmental cues that might shape behavior. Indeed, traits interact with environments, such that situations sometimes constrain behavior, and personality sometimes influences situations.

WHAT IS THE BIOLOGICAL BASIS OF PERSONALITY?

Where does personality come from? Why are you the person that you are? Freud emphasized early childhood experiences in his theory of psychosexual stages. Certainly most people assume that the way parents treat their children will have a substantial impact on personality, such as Rogers' belief that unconditional positive regard leads to positive mental health. But what role does biology play? Are you born with certain predispositions? How do the workings of your body and brain affect the sort of person you are?

Over the past few decades, evidence has emerged indicating that biological processes—such as genes, brain structures, and neurochemistry—do play an important role in determining personality. This is not to say that these processes are insensitive to experience, but rather that they serve as a blueprint for psychological processes that interact with the environment, such as how people are socialized or the situational demands that they face.

PERSONALITY IS ROOTED IN GENETICS

The evidence is overwhelming that nearly all personality traits have a genetic component (Plomin & Caspi, 1999). One of the earliest studies to document the heritability of personality was conducted by James Loehlin and Robert Nichols (1976). They looked at similarities in personality between more than 800 pairs of twins. Across a wide variety of traits they found that monozygotic twins were much more similar than dizygotic twins. Recall from Chapter 3 that this pattern reflects the actions of genes, since monozygotic twins share the same genes whereas dizygotic twins do not. Numerous twin studies have subsequently found that genetic influence accounts for approximately half of the variance (40–60 percent) in personality traits, including the Big Five (Figure 15.8). These genetic patterns can be found whether the twins rate themselves or whether friends, family, or trained observers rate them.

Of course, you might wonder whether identical twins are treated more similarly than other siblings and if that explains the similarities in personality. The best evidence refuting this idea was obtained by Thomas Bouchard and his colleagues from the University of Minnesota. Their studies of twins raised apart (such as the twins described in Chapter 3) reveal that twins raised apart are often as similar, or even more similar, than twins raised together. Why might twins raised apart be more similar than twins raised together? One possibility is that parents strive to bring out individual strengths in each twin so that each feels unique and special. Thus, parenting style may foster differences rather than similarities. If this were true, one might expect that the correlations between personality traits would be stronger for older twins than for younger twins, since the effects of parenting would diminish over time. And indeed, identical twins become more alike as they grow older. By contrast, siblings and dizygotic twins do not.

Adoption studies Further evidence for the genetic basis of personality can be found in adoption studies, although such studies usually yield lower estimates of gene influence than do twin studies. Siblings who are adopted (and not biologically related) and raised in the same household are no more alike in personality than any two strangers randomly plucked off the street (Plomin & Caspi, 1999). Moreover, the personalities of adopted children bear no significant relationship to those of the adoptive parents who raised them. These findings suggest that parenting style may have relatively little impact on personality. Is that true? The current evidence suggests that parental style has much less impact than has long been assumed. For instance, studies typically find only small correlations in personality between biological siblings or between children and their biological parents. Although small, however, these correlations are larger than for adopted children, suggesting that the similarities have a genetic component. Why are children raised together in the same household (who are not monozygotic twins) so different? One explanation is that the lives of siblings diverge as they establish friendships outside the home. Thus, siblings' personalities slowly grow apart as their initial differences become magnified through their interactions with the world. One given difference between siblings is birth order, which itself has been shown to influence personality (see "Using Psychological Science: What Is the Effect of Birth Order on Personality?") and therefore may be part of the reason that siblings are different.

Although the small correlations in personality between siblings might imply that parenting style has little effect, there are reasons to believe that caretakers matter a great deal. David Lykken (2000), a leading behavioral genetics researcher, has argued that children who are raised with inadequate parenting, such as those raised in poverty by single parents who are not able to spend time parenting, are not socialized properly and are therefore much more likely to become delinquent or display antisocial behavior. Thus, a minimum level of parenting is crucial, but the particular style of parenting does not appear to have a major impact on shaping personality.

Are there specific genes for personality? Research has revealed genetic components for particular behaviors such as television viewing and getting divorced, and even for specific attitudes, such as feelings about capital punishment and appreciation of jazz music. This does not mean, of course, that there is a gene

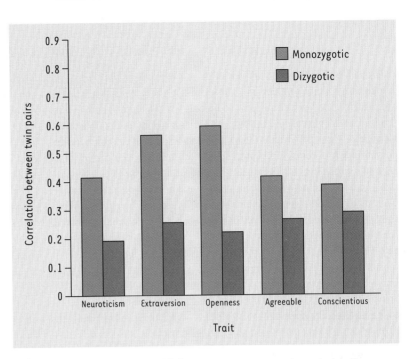

15.8 Researchers examined correlations between 123 pairs of identical twins (monozygotic) and 127 pairs of fraternal twins (dizygotic) in Vancouver, Canada. For each Big Five trait, the correlations for monozygotic twins were higher than for dizygotic twins, resulting in heritability estimates of 41%, 53%, 61%, 41%, and 44% of the variance in neuroticism, extraversion, openness, agreeableness, and conscientiousness.

Using Psychological Science

WHAT IS THE EFFECT OF BIRTH ORDER ON PERSONALITY?

It is commonly believed that whether you were born first, last, or somewhere in between has a big influence on the type of person you are. Is this true? Alfred Adler, a colleague of Sigmund Freud's, was the first to propose a role for birth order in personality development. He believed that parents pampered first- and lastborns, which led to personality problems. Firstborns being dethroned by the arrival of a second child faced a special burden, according to Adler, and were likely to become "neurotics, criminals, drunkards, or perverts." However, he also acknowledged some positive effects of being born first, such as the independence that might result from being responsible for the care of younger siblings. Middle children, such as Adler himself, he predicted would be competitive, rebellious, and skeptical of authority, constantly striving to become superior to their older siblings. Stanley Schachter found some support for Adler in his well-known studies of social affiliation (discussed in Chapter 14). In these studies, he found that firstborns were much more likely to choose to affiliate with someone when anxious than were later-borns. He later found that firstborns were much less likely to pursue dangerous activities, such as skydiving, and more likely to seek therapy.

More recently, historian Frank Sulloway proposed that differences in personality that result from birth order represent competition among siblings as they fight to find their special niche within the family, which is an adaptive strategy that has developed over the course of human evolution. Sulloway (1996) organized the many studies of birth order according to the Big Five factors of personality. He found that firstborns tended to be more conscientious, extraverted, and neurotic, as well as less agreeable and open to experience. Firstborns are generally assertive, dominant, responsible, and achievement-oriented, but they are also anxious and jealous. This same pattern has been demonstrated by Paulhus and his colleagues with over 1,000 research participants in the United States and Canada (Paulhus et al. 1999). They found that firstborns overall were viewed by their family members as the most achievement-focused, and that this occurred whether or not the research participants knew that birth order was relevant. It should be noted that only children appear to have personality characteristics that are similar to firstborns.

For later-borns, the consensus appears to be that they are more prone to rebellion, as suggested by Adler, and that they are also more liberal (Paulhus et al., 1999). Sulloway noted that later-borns are much more accepting of new ideas than are firstborns. For instance, Sulloway looked at the reactions of scientists to the theories of Darwin, Copernicus, Bacon, Einstein, and Freud. He found that firstborn contemporaries of these great theorists tended to dismiss their ideas, whereas later-borns embraced them. Unlike their older siblings, later-borns are more likely to resist authority, including that wielded by parents. Indeed, some evidence indicates that middle children are not even particularly close to their families. Evolutionary psychologists Catherine Salmon and Martin Daly have shown that middleborns are much less connected to family than either first- or lastborns. They are less likely to report turning to their parents when stressed, less likely to report feeling loved, less likely to pursue genealogical information about their family tree, and less likely to refer to themselves by the family name (Salmon, 1999; Salmon & Daly, 1998). Although the impact of birth order on personality was dismissed many years ago as unimportant, this recent evidence suggests that each birth changes family dynamics in such a way that siblings experience the family environment differently, which may explain why people who grow up in the same house are often no more similar than strangers.

lurking in your DNA that determines the amount or type of television that you watch. Rather, genes predispose certain personality traits that are associated with behavioral tendencies. In most cases researchers are referring to the influence of multiple genes that each independently interact with the environment to produce general dispositions, such as a preference for quiet and passive activities over active outdoor pursuits. These *polygenetic* effects, as discussed in Chapter 3, are typically involved in the genetic transmission of complex behaviors.

Yet, there is growing evidence that genes can be linked with some specificity to personality traits. For instance, a gene that regulates one particular dopamine receptor has been associated with novelty seeking in a number of studies (Cloninger et al., 1996; Ekelund et al., 1999). The theory is that people with one form of this gene are deficient in dopamine and seek out novel experiences to increase the release of dopamine. Research on the traits of neuroticism and agreeableness implicates a particular gene that regulates serotonin, although the effect is not large (Jang et al., 2001). With the completion of the first stage of the Human Genome

Project, it is likely that researchers will identify additional genes that are associated with specific personality dispositions.

TEMPERAMENTS ARE EVIDENT IN INFANCY

Genes work by affecting biological processes. Thus, to the extent that genes influence personality, there ought to be corresponding biological differences, referred to as **temperaments**, in personality. Temperaments are considered much broader than traits, referring to general tendencies to feel or act in certain ways. Most of the research on temperaments focuses on infants, in that personality differences that exist very early in life indicate the actions of biological mechanisms. Although life experiences may alter personality traits, temperaments represent the basic innate biological structure of personality.

Arnold Buss and Robert Plomin (1984) argue that there are essentially three personality traits that can be considered temperaments. *Activity level* refers to the overall amount of energy and behavior exhibited by a person. For example, some children zoom around the house at great speeds whereas others are less vigorous and still others slow-paced. *Emotionality* describes the intensity of emotional reactions, or how easily and frequently people become aroused or upset. Children who cry often or become easily frightened and adults who are quickly angered are likely to be high in emotionality. Finally, *sociability* refers to the general tendency to affiliate with others. Those high in this temperament prefer to be with others rather than to be alone. According to Buss and Plomin, these three temperamental styles are the main personality factors influenced by genes. Indeed, evidence from twin studies, adoption studies, and family studies indicates a powerful effect of heredity on these core temperaments.

A somewhat different approach to temperament has been pursued by Mary Rothbart and her colleagues (Rothbart et al., 2000). According to Rothbart, the two central dimensions relevant to temperament are *reactivity* and *self-regulation*. Some children are more reactive than others, both in terms of behavior and emotion, but children develop the capacity to control or modulate these reactions. Rothbart and her colleagues study the neural and behavioral correlates of attention and self-regulation, such as the ability to focus on a task for extended periods of time, and how the development of brain systems related to these processes influences social development and the emergence of personality.

Personality types according to temperament Some researchers have attempted to cluster individuals into personality types based on temperament. The first major contemporary study to use this approach was conducted in the 1970s by Stella Chess and Alexander Thomas, who assessed 141 children from 85 middle- to upper-middle-class families over a six-year period. From their careful observations, they concluded that about 60 percent of children can be grouped into one of three temperament styles. *Easy children* exhibit regular cycles of eating and sleeping, approach novel situations positively, and adapt to change quickly with few if any problems. *Difficult children* display irregular sleep and eating patterns, have an overall negative response to most situations, especially new situations, and have a tendency to withdraw from others; as they grow older, they develop problems dealing with the expectations of parents, teachers, and peers. *Slow-to-warm-up children* are initially cautious and anxious in new situations but generally adjust well over time; they lack the overall positive emotionality of easy children. The remaining 40 percent of children do not possess a dominant tem-

temperaments Biologically based tendencies to feel or act in certain ways.

perament style but usually display a combination of two. For Chess and Thomas, these early temperamental styles were associated with the development of different types of personality. Throughout this chapter we have referred to the trait of shyness. Many researchers believe that shyness is rooted in temperament, as can be seen in "Crossing the Levels of Analysis: Shyness and Social Inhibition."

Long-term implications of temperaments   To what extent do infant temperaments predict adult personality? If you were a fussy child, are you now a fussy adult? The early evidence suggested that the direct correlation between childhood temperaments and adult personalities was only modest. For instance, follow-ups of the original children in the Chess and Thomas study revealed that tempera-

Crossing the Levels of Analysis

SHYNESS AND SOCIAL INHIBITION

Throughout this chapter we have used the example of shyness, which refers to feelings of discomfort and inhibition during interpersonal situations (Henderson & Zimbardo, 1998). People who are shy are excessively self-focused and spend a great deal of time worrying about what others think of them. As such, they feel most shy when being evaluated. Shyness involves genetic, physiological, behavioral, cognitive, affective, and social factors. Although most people feel shy at some point in their lives, chronically shy people, who make up around 40 percent of the population, are those who suffer impairments in pursuing life goals, making friends, or entering relationships.

Shy people show cognitive biases in how they process information. They tend to have low self-esteem, to blame themselves for failures over which they had no control, to remember negative feedback more than positive feedback, and to overestimate the likelihood that they will be socially rejected. They have a pessimistic coping style in which they ruminate about their negative feelings and physical reactions. Shy people are socially awkward because they tend to focus much more on themselves than on the people with whom they are interacting. Their constant concerns about how they are being evaluated can operate in a self-fulfilling way to produce negative evaluations, although these often aren't nearly as bad as the shy person believes them to be.

Shyness is strongly determined by genetic components and is among the most heritable of traits. Research conducted at Harvard University by Jerome Kagan, Nancy Snidman, and their colleagues has shown that children as young as six weeks of age can be identified as likely to be shy (Kagan & Snidman, 1991). Approximately 15–20 percent of newborns react to new situations or strange objects by becoming startled and distressed, crying, and vigorously moving their arms and legs. Kagan refers to these children as *inhibited*,

which he views as being biologically determined. Children with blue eyes, fair skin, and allergies are more likely to be inhibited. Showing signs of inhibition at two months of age predicts later parental reports that the children are shy at four years of age, and such children are likely to be shy well into their teenage years. Indeed, measures of brain stem reactivity at age 10–12 correspond to ratings made of these children when they were four months old (Woodward et al., 2001), with inhibited children showing greater reactivity. Similar genetic findings for inhibited behavior have been found in a variety of species, including dogs and monkeys. The biological evidence suggests that the amygdala is involved in shyness. For instance, in one study people who were *socially phobic*, extremely shy, showed much greater amygdala activation when shown unfamiliar faces than did control participants (Birbaumer et al., 1998).

Although shyness has a biological component, it clearly has a social component as well: approximately one-quarter of behaviorally inhibited children are not shy later in childhood. This development typically occurs when parents create supportive and calm environments in which children are able to deal with stress and novelty at their own pace. At the same time, these parents do not completely shelter their children from stress, so that the children learn to deal with their negative feelings in novel situations. Moreover, shyness is related to being highly feminine in sex-role orientation and varies across cultures; it is quite common in Japan and less common in Israel.

A number of effective treatments exist for shyness in children and adults. Some programs focus on the development of social skills and on assertiveness training, which provide shy people with the tools necessary to deal with their social worlds. Drug therapy, especially with selective serotonin reuptake inhibitors such as Prozac, is also highly effective in the treatment of severe shyness, especially when combined with cognitive behavioral therapies.

mental style did not correspond particularly well with personality outcomes in young adulthood. Yet recent research using more sophisticated methods has documented compelling evidence that early childhood temperaments have a pervasive and powerful influence over behavior and personality structure throughout development (Caspi, 2000). In a particularly impressive study, a team of researchers in Dunedin, New Zealand, investigated the health, development, and personality of over 1,000 children born during a one-year period. These individuals were examined approximately every two years, with an impressive 97 percent remaining in the study through their twenty-first birthdays (Silva & Stanton, 1996). Children were classified at three years of age into temperamental types based on examiners' ratings. The researchers found five temperament types, three of which were remarkably similar to those described by Chess and Thomas, although renamed "well-adjusted" (easy), "undercontrolled" (difficult), and "inhibited" (slow-to-warm-up). The classification of children at age three predicted personality structure and a variety of behaviors in early adulthood. For instance, those judged undercontrolled at age three were later more likely to have alcohol problems, to be criminals or unemployed, to attempt suicide, to be antisocial and anxious, and to have less social support (see Figure 15.9). Inhibited children were much more likely to become depressed.

PERSONALITY IS LINKED TO SPECIFIC NEUROPHYSIOLOGICAL MECHANISMS

Genes act to produce temperaments, which affect how children respond to and shape their environments, which in turn interact with temperament to shape personality. But how do these genetic predispositions produce personality? That is, what neurophysiological mechanisms are linked to personality? Some theories focus on the underlying biological processes that produce the thoughts, emotions, and behaviors that make up personality. From this perspective, personality differences may reflect differences in the relative activation of different biological systems. Most research on the neurobiological underpinnings of personality has focused on the dimension of extraversion/introversion, and it is there that we focus as well.

Arousal and extraversion/introversion　The intellectual founder of the modern biological approach to personality was Hans Eysenck (Figure 15.10). Eysenck believed that underlying differences in cortical arousal produced the observed behavioral differences between extraverts and introverts. Cortical arousal, or alertness, is regulated by the *ascending reticular activating system (ARAS)*, and Eysenck proposed that this system differed between extraverts and introverts. Eysenck noted that extraverts seem to be constantly trying to seek out additional arousal—for example, by attending parties or seeking out new people. By contrast, introverts seem to avoid arousal by preferring solitary, quiet activities, such as reading. According to earlier psychological theories, each person prefers to operate, and

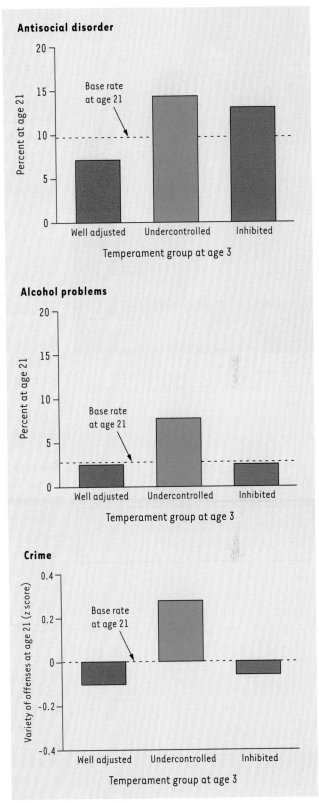

15.9 Temperament group at age 3 predicts antisocial personality disorder, alcohol problems, and criminal activity at age 21.

15.10 Hans Eysenck was one of the leading proponents of the idea that personality is rooted in biology.

What roles do biology and environment play in shaping personality?

operates best, at some *optimal level of arousal* (see Chapter 9). Eysenck proposed that the resting levels of the ARAS are higher for introverts than for extraverts, which places them above their optimal levels. In contrast, extraverts are typically below their optimal levels, which means that they are chronically underaroused. To operate efficiently, extraverts have to find arousal. Thus, they impulsively seek out new situations and new emotional experiences. Introverts don't want any additional arousal. They prefer quiet solitude with few incoming stimuli. So, if you are an introvert, a noisy environment will distract you, whereas if you are an extravert, quiet places are boring. Consistent with Eysenck's theory, research has demonstrated that extraverts prefer to perform, and actually do perform better, in noisy settings (Geen, 1984).

If introverts are chronically more aroused than extraverts, they ought to be more sensitive to stimuli at all levels of intensity. This appears to be generally true. For instance, introverts are more sensitive to pain and they salivate more than extraverts do if you place a drop of lemon juice on their tongues. However, evidence for baseline differences in arousal has been more difficult to produce. Thus, it appears that what differentiates introverts from extraverts is level of *arousability*, or reactivity to stimuli, with introverts being more arousable.

Psychologist Marvin Zuckerman describes the arousal-based trait of **sensation seeking** as similar to extraversion, but with an impulsive element that more closely matches Eysenck's psychoticism superordinate trait. According to Zuckerman, sensation seekers have a neurochemical deficiency that motivates them to seek arousal through adventures and new experiences. Moreover, those who are high in sensation seeking are easily bored and escape boredom through the use of drugs and alcohol.

Neurophysiology of extraversion/introversion Since Eysenck's initial work on the biological underpinnings of personality, a number of theorists have offered refinements that reflect more recent understandings of functional neuroanatomy. Although a variety of theories have been proposed, they share common features, including a basic differentiation between approach and avoidance learning. Jeffrey Gray of Oxford University incorporated this distinction in his approach/inhibition model of learning and personality. Gray proposed that personality was rooted in motivational functions that had evolved to help organisms efficiently respond to reinforcement and punishment. In Gray's model, the **behavioral approach system (BAS)** consists of the brain structures that lead organisms to approach stimuli in pursuit of rewards. It's the *Go* system. There is also a *Stop* system, known as the **behavioral inhibition system (BIS)**, which is sensitive to punishment and therefore inhibits behavior that might lead to danger or pain (Figure 15.11). According to Gray, extraverts have a stronger BAS than BIS, so they are more influenced by rewards than punishments. Indeed, extraverts tend to act impulsively in the face of strong rewards, even following punishment (Patterson & Newman, 1993). By contrast, introverts have a more active BIS. Their chronic anxiety often leads them to avoid social situations in which they anticipate possible negative outcomes.

The BIS is associated with activity in the frontal lobes, which are known to help inhibit inappropriate social behavior. Those with injury to the frontal lobes, especially the ventromedial region of the prefrontal cortex, exhibit social incompetence, disinhibition, impaired social judgment, and a lack of sensitivity to social cues. A study using PET found that introversion was associated with greater activation of the frontal lobes (Johnson et al., 1999), which supports Gray's model of BIS. The amygdala is another brain region involved in both social sensitivity and processing of cues related to possible punishment. Some researchers believe that personality traits such as fearfulness, anxiousness, and shyness are associated with excessive activation of the amygdala (Zuckerman, 1991).

Studies of the neurochemistry of the behavioral activation system implicate heightened activation of dopamine circuits for extraverts compared to introverts. The mesolimbic dopamine pathway is involved in reward (as you will recall from Chapter 6), and extraversion appears to be associated with greater activation of this pathway, especially of dopamine receptors in the nucleus accumbens. Links between the mesolimbic dopamine pathway and the orbitofrontal region of the prefrontal cortex, an area that helps process information about the reward value of objects, also seem to be involved in extraversion (Depue & Collins, 1999). A second line of evidence for the role of dopamine in extraversion is that they are both associated with positive affect (Ashby et al., 1999). Extraverts report high levels of energy, desire, and self-confidence. Indeed, the experience of positive affect may be the fundamental feature of extraversion (Lucas et al., 2000). Finally, the link between dopamine and extraversion is also supported by the finding that a gene involved in dopamine reception is an indicator for novelty seeking, which itself is related to the greater willingness of extraverts to approach novel stimuli.

There is still a lot to be learned about the biological bases of personality. As recently as two decades ago personality psychologists largely ignored the question of biology. It is only with recent advances in technology that researchers have started to explore the genetic and neurophysiological correlates of personality. It can be anticipated that many exciting new discoveries relevant to personality and temperament will emerge as the biological revolution spreads throughout psychological science.

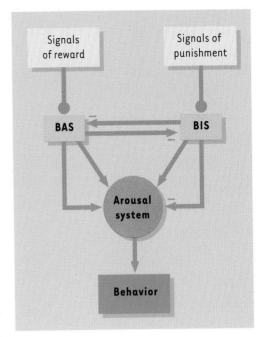

15.11 Signals of potential reward and punishment are processed by the BIS and the BAS. This information affects behavioral responses, with the BAS activating behavior and the BIS inhibiting behavior.

PERSONALITY IS ADAPTIVE

Natural selection has shaped the human genome over the course of evolution. Adaptive characteristics were likely to have spread through the gene pool and been passed along to increasing numbers in future generations. Thus, in terms of personality, one might expect that traits that were useful for survival and reproduction would have been favored. It is easy to imagine how being competitive might lead a person to obtain great rewards, or how being cooperative might increase a person's value to the group. But traits also provide important information about desirable and undesirable qualities in mates, such as whether a person is conscientious and agreeable or neurotic. David Buss (1999a) has argued that the Big Five personality traits emerged as foundational traits because they each provide important information regarding mate selection.

But if traits are adaptive, why are there such great individual differences among people? Natural selection ought to make people more similar rather than more different. After all, if a trait increased survival and reproduction, that trait should predominate in future generations. One possibility is that individual differences reflect characteristics that were of trivial importance over the course of evolution, perhaps resulting from random processes (Tooby & Cosmides, 1990). However, Buss and Greiling (1999a) have proposed that individual differences may reflect the inheritance of alternative strategies that become activated depending on situational context. For instance, consider a situation in which most people are honest and cooperative and therefore routinely trust others to be

sensation seekers Individuals who routinely seek out novel, complex situations and are willing to take physical and social risks in order to achieve thrills.

behavioral approach system (BAS) The brain system involved in the pursuit of incentives or rewards.

behavioral inhibition system (BIS) The brain system that is sensitive to punishment and therefore inhibits behavior that might lead to danger or pain.

honest and cooperative as well. A dishonest person in such a system could do well by exploiting the basic trust of others. Of course, if too many people did this, then the system would change or collapse. However, the important point is that evolution has bestowed multiple strategies that are differentially adaptive depending on the environment, and that there is a built-in calibration system that is sensitive to environmental demands. According to Buss and Greiling, the *early experiential calibration* system locks a person into the strategy chosen, to the exclusion of others that might have been pursued under different circumstances.

Another possible explanation for individual differences is that human groups whose members possess diverse skills have a selective advantage over other groups (Caporael, 2001). Members of successful groups and their relatives would all benefit from being members of a strong group, since they would be more likely to survive and reproduce. Consider the trait of novelty seeking. Having group members who seek out and explore new territory might lead to the discovery of new resources, such as an abundant food supply. At the same time, novelty seekers expose themselves to greater risks, and the group would suffer if all its members followed this strategy. Therefore it is to the advantage of the group to have cautious members in addition to bold members; these individuals may enhance the group in other ways, such as being more thoughtful or providing social support.

What Is the Biological Basis of Personality?

Evidence from behavioral genetics has demonstrated that personality has a substantial genetic component explaining approximately half of the variance in most traits. Temperaments, the biological bases of traits, are evident in early childhood and have long-term implications for adult behavior. Temperamental styles reflect underlying differences in biological processes, suggesting that people are different, in part, because they have different underlying neurophysiology. Such differences may reflect adaptive advantages over the course of human evolution.

CAN PERSONALITY CHANGE?

Can personality change?

The Jesuit maxim "Give me a child until he is seven, and I will show you the man" is the thesis of Michael Apted's well-known documentary series of films (called *7Up*, *14Up*, *21Up*, etc.) which follows the development of a group of British school children through interviews at ages 7, 14, 21, 28, 35, and 42. A striking aspect of these films is the apparent stability of personality over time. The child interested in the stars and science becomes a professor of physics; the boy who finds his childhood troubling and confusing develops an apparent schizo-affective personality; the reserved, well-mannered, upper-class girl at age 7 grows into the reserved, well-mannered woman in her pastoral retreat at age 35; a second-grader successfully predicts not only his future career, but the schools that he will eventually attend. Are people really so stable? Is personality at age 70 preordained at age 7?

From a functional perspective, it makes sense that personality should remain relatively stable over time. People need to predict the behavior of those they care about or rely upon. When people choose friends or relationship partners, they do so with the general expectation that their interactions with these people will be somewhat predictable across time and situations. Yet, people sometimes expect others to be able to change. Marital partners often hope that unfaithful spouses will change their wandering ways, and the penal system releases prisoners with the expectation that they will adopt less deviant roles in society. Are these expectations realistic?

Earlier you learned that childhood temperaments predict behavioral outcomes in early adulthood. But what about change during adulthood? If you are shy now, are you doomed to be shy forever? Indeed, the foundation of clinical psychology is the belief that people can and do change important aspects of their lives, and people exert considerable energy trying to change—they attend self-help groups, read self-help books, buy time with therapists, and struggle with themselves and others. But how much do people really change over the course of their lives?

TRAITS REMAIN STABLE OVER TIME

How one defines the essential features of personality has tremendous implications for whether it is fixed or changeable. Continuity over time and across situations is inherent in the definition of "trait," and accordingly it is not surprising that most research finds personality traits to be remarkably stable over the adult life span (Heatherton & Weinberger, 1994). For instance, over many years the relative rankings of individuals on each of the Big Five personality traits remain stable (McCrae & Costa, 1990). People who are very extraverted tend to stay very extraverted and people who are very introverted tend to remain that way as well. A recent meta-analysis of 150 studies consisting of nearly 50,000 participants who had been followed for at least one year found strong evidence for stability in personality (Roberts & Friend-DelVecchio, 2000). The rank orderings of individuals on any personality trait were quite stable over long periods of time across all age ranges. However, stability was lowest for young children and highest for those over age 50 (Figure 15.12). This suggests that personality does change somewhat in childhood, but that it becomes more stable by middle age. Such findings tend to support the contention of William James, who stated in 1890, "for most of us, by age 30, the character has set like plaster and will never soften again." According to the meta-analysis, James was right that personality becomes set, but this appears to happen a little later than age 30.

Stability in rank ordering means that individuals stay the same compared to others. However, is it possible that all people change in personality as they age, while retaining their relative rankings? For instance, stereotypes exist that people become wiser and more cautious as they get older. Is this true? In general, people do become less neurotic, less extraverted, and less open to new experiences as they get older. People also tend to become more agreeable and much more conscientious with age. These effects are not large, but they are consistent. What is most amazing is that the pattern holds in different cultures (Figure 15.13; McCrae et al., 2000).

15.12 This graph shows consistency across time measures for personality at different ages. Consistency is smallest in childhood and greatest after age 50.

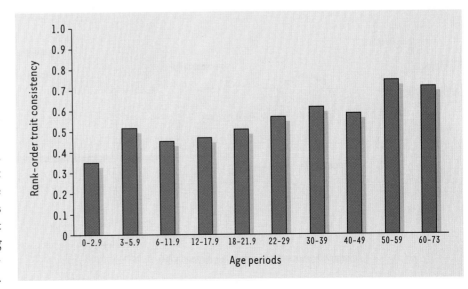

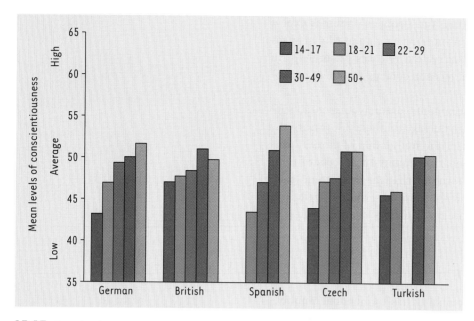

15.13 Mean levels of conscientiousness at different ages in five cultures. Note that conscientiousness increases as people age, in all five cultures.

This suggests that age-related changes in personality occur independent of environmental influences, and therefore that personality change itself may be based in human physiology. Indeed, there is some evidence that personality change has a genetic component, such that the extent of change is more similar in monozygotic twins than dizygotic twins (McGue et al., 1993).

The reason personality is so stable, especially among adults, appears to be due to a number of factors. If personality is determined in part by biological mechanisms, then changes are expected only to the extent that there are changes in biological makeup. The fact that the brain develops well into early adulthood may explain the greater evidence of personality change before age 30. Perhaps more important, environments tend to be relatively stable, especially after early adulthood. People tend to marry those who are similar in attitudes and personality, and people tend to have successive jobs that have the same level of status. It seems likely that the stability of situations contributes to the stability of personality.

CHARACTERISTIC ADAPTATIONS CHANGE ACROSS TIME AND CIRCUMSTANCES

In their research on potential change in personality, Robert McCrae and Paul Costa (1999) emphasize an important distinction between basic tendencies of personality and characteristic adaptations (Figure 15.14). *Basic tendencies* are dispositional traits that are determined to a great extent by biological processes. As such, they are very stable. *Characteristic adaptations* are the adjustments people

15.14 McCrae and Costa's model of personality. Basic tendencies are biologically based, but characteristic adaptations are influenced by the situation and how the person behaves. The lines with arrows indicate some of the ways in which the different components interact. The important point is that basic tendencies do not change across situations, but observable behavior (objective biography) does because it is influenced by personal goals and motives as well as by the situation.

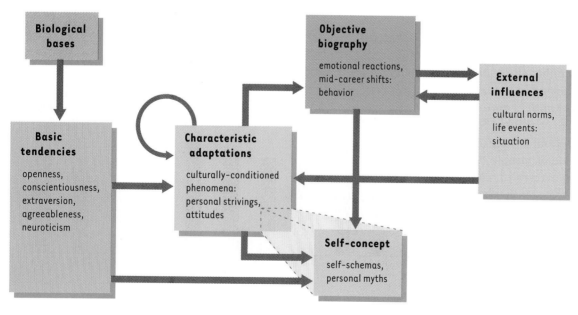

make to situational demands, which tend to be consistent because they are based on skills, habits, roles, and so forth. These changes in behavior do not indicate changes in the underlying core disposition. For instance, consider a young adult who is high in extraversion. She may go to a lot of parties, be a thrill seeker, and have multiple sexual partners. As she approaches 90, she is less likely to do these things, but she may still have many friends and enjoy traveling. Although the behaviors are different, they continue to reflect the underlying trait of extraversion.

Dan McAdams (1999; 2001) has proposed that some aspects of personality do change, depending on how you define personality. According to McAdams, personality can be examined at three levels (Table 15.3). At the basic level are *dispositional traits*, such as the Big Five, which by their nature are relatively stable. At the second level are *personal concerns*, which include goals, motives, and social roles; these reflect the tasks and challenges that people face within specific contexts or situations. Unlike dispositional traits, McAdams argues, personal concerns ebb and flow as people mature into new roles (such as career and family) and encounter new challenges. For instance, as people grow older they may express more concern with the well-being of future generations, such as by making plans to educate their children or donating to environmental charities. At the third level are *life narratives*, the personal myths and stories that people use to define their lives and identities. McAdams argues that life narratives evolve as people develop coherent stories from the different places, opportunities, and positions they encounter.

Indeed, some people tell stories of sudden, dramatic changes in personality, much like the transformation of Ebenezer Scrooge in Charles Dickens' *A Christmas Carol*. William Miller and Janet C'de Baca (2001) describe a type of story they

TABLE 15.3 Three Levels of Personality

LEVEL	DEFINITION	EXAMPLES
Dispositional traits	Broad dimensions of personality that describe assumedly internal, global, and stable individual differences in behavior, thought, and feeling. Traits account for consistency in individual functioning across different situations and over time.	Friendliness Dominance Tendency toward depression Punctuality
Characteristic adaptations	More particular facets of personality that describe personal adaptations to motivational, cognitive, and developmental challenges and tasks. Characteristic adaptations are usually contextualized in time, place, situation, or social role.	Goals, motives, and life plans Religious values and beliefs Cognitive schemas Relational modes Psychosocial stages Developmental tasks
Life stories	Internalized and evolving narratives of the self that people construct to integrate the past, present, and future and provide life with some sense of unity, purpose, and meaning. Life stories address the problems of identity and integration in personality—problems especially characteristic of modern adulthood.	Earliest memory Reconstruction of childhood Perceptions of future self "Rags to riches" stories Imagery and theme in story

quantum change A transformation of personality that is sudden, profound, enduring, and affects a wide range of behaviors.

refer to as **quantum change**, which is a transformation of personality that is sudden, profound, and enduring. The people telling the stories claimed to remember the episodes vividly, down to the date and time of day when the change occurred. The quantum change experiences tended to be unexpected, often originating from some external source or event. The specific antecedents were amazingly varied and ranged from taking a walk to cleaning a toilet to having an abortion. Those who reported quantum change emphasized that everything about them changed, including their temperaments, perceptual styles, goals, and values. After the change, most people reported an increased sense of meaning and happiness, an increased sense of spirituality, and increased overall satisfaction. Of course, without an objective measure of personality before the experience it is hard to know whether the reported changes are accurate, but family members and friends substantiated the stories, which gives them some credence.

Quantum change appears to happen without effort. What about those who try to make major changes in their lives, such as changes in personality? There is currently limited evidence available as to whether such change is possible. Heatherton and Nichols (1994) examined narrative accounts from people who had succeeded at making major life changes versus accounts from people who had tried and failed. The successful and unsuccessful change stories differed in substantial and predictable ways. Individuals who reported making changes described having suffered extreme negative affect before the change was made. One common theme in the successful change stories was the occurrence of a trigger event, such as the woman who decided to leave her husband after taking a class that changed her entire outlook on life.

BRAIN INJURY AND PHARMACOLOGICAL INTERVENTIONS AFFECT PERSONALITY

To the extent that biological processes determine personality, it might be anticipated that physical changes would produce personality changes. Indeed, damage to specific regions of the brain is associated with dramatic changes in personality. For example, damage to the frontal lobes, such as in the case of railroad worker Phineas Gage described in Chapter 4, has been found to produce a variety of changes in personality, including causing people to become more extraverted, impulsive, socially inappropriate, and moody (Stuss et al., 1992). Patients with temporal lobe damage also experience personality change, often becoming humorless, obsessive, paranoid, and rule bound. One sign of a possible brain tumor is a sudden and profound change in personality. Indeed, the whole point of psychosurgery, which was popular in the 1950s, was to surgically alter the brain to change abnormal aspects of personality (see Chapter 4). Some diseases that cause damage to the brain, such as Alzheimer's disease, also produce changes in personality that can be dramatic and surprising to family members.

Neurochemistry and personality change In his 1993 book, *Listening to Prozac*, Peter Kramer claimed that a drug used to treat depression could lead to dramatic changes in personality. His book includes stories of patients who underwent dramatic transformations after taking Prozac, a drug used to treat depression that enhances the activity of the neurotransmitter serotonin by selectively blocking its reuptake into the presynaptic neuron, thereby prolonging its effects in the synapse. In one story, a dour, shy, pessimistic woman suddenly became outgoing and sociable after she took Prozac. Her bubbly new personality, Kramer claimed, is a result of her altered serotonin levels.

Research has demonstrated that serotonin is related to some aspects of personality. For instance, low levels of serotonin are associated with hostility, aggressiveness, and criminality. Low levels of serotonin have also been linked to impulsivity and sensation seeking (Depue & Collins, 1999; Zuckerman, 1993). Thus, it might be expected that drugs that enhance the activity of this neurotransmitter would lead to decreased impulsiveness. Indeed, evidence has been found that serotonin-enhancing drugs do cause significant changes in personality, such as increased social dominance and decreased hostility (Brody et al., 2000). One research team found that use of drugs that enhanced serotonin led to changes in two of the Big Five personality traits: neuroticism decreased and extraversion increased (Bagby et al., 1999). This effect apparently occurs independent of changes in mood or depression (Ekselius & von Knorring, 1999). That is, the personality change does not appear to occur simply because depression is lifted.

In perhaps the best empirical test of the effects of serotonin-based drugs, researchers had normal volunteers take a selective serotonin reuptake inhibitor (SSRI) and assessed its effects on social behavior and personality (Knutson et al., 1998). Animal research had previously shown that SSRIs led to decreased aggression and increased social affiliation among monkeys, and the researchers sought to examine whether it would produce similar effects in nondepressed humans. Following a careful screening for any psychiatric disorders, volunteers received either an SSRI or a placebo for four weeks. The results indicated that administration of the SSRI led to reductions in hostility and increases in cooperative behavior. Thus, altering brain neurochemistry can change personality even among normal, nondepressed individuals.

Can Personality Change?

There is considerable evidence that personality is generally stable over the life course, especially for basic dispositions such as traits. People adapt to novel situations by altering behavior, but they tend to do so in ways that are consistent with their basic personalities. As evidenced by their life stories, people believe that they change, and such change narratives might help predict motives and behavior. Indeed, the story of change is itself a part of personality whether or not change occurs. Although it isn't clear whether people can purposefully change, brain injury or disease and alterations in neurochemistry can alter personality. This supports the general idea that biological processes are important to personality.

CONCLUSION

Studying personality is complex because each person is unique. Researchers have contributed to the accumulated principles underlying personality by examining cognitive processes, both conscious and unconscious; behavioral dispositions; and people's own life narratives. Knowing a person well requires knowing a great deal about him or her. At the same time, it is now apparent—based on research that crosses levels of analysis—that the basic blueprint for personality is genetically determined and is manifest through biologically based temperaments. Yet these temperaments do not predetermine personality; interaction between people and their social worlds creates unique individuals, perhaps by influencing brain processes that determine personality. What is clear is that personality is coherent and stable. Although people change jobs, relationships, and living circumstances, the fundamental core of their personalities stays with them throughout their lives.

FURTHER READINGS

Funder, D. C. (2000). *The personality puzzle*. New York: W. W. Norton.

Heatherton, T. F., & Weinberger, J. L. (1994). *Can personality change?* Washington, DC: American Psychological Association.

Hogan, R., Johnson, J. & Briggs, S. (1997). *Handbook of personality psychology*. San Diego, CA: Academic Press.

McAdams, D. P. (2000). *The person: An integrated introduction to personality psychology*. (3rd ed.). Fort Worth, TX: Harcourt.

Pervin, L. A., & John, O. P. (1999). *Handbook of personality: Theory and research*. New York: Guilford Press.

LIVING WITH SCHIZOPHRENIA

In the 2001 film *A Beautiful Mind* (which was based on a true story), Russell Crowe played the part of John Nash, a Princeton University mathematician whose life and career were nearly destroyed by schizophrenia. Nash overcame his disease after a long struggle, and eventually won a Nobel prize in 1994 for his work on game theory (which he completed before suffering the symptoms of the disease). Biological factors are now widely believed to play a critical role in the development of schizophrenia and other mental disorders.

TIMELINE

460–377 B.C.E.
Humoral Imbalance
Hippocrates explains abnormal behavior as the result of imbalances of four bodily fluids: blood, phlegm, black bile, and yellow bile.

130–200 C.E.
Psychological Factors
Galen postulates that abnormal behavior could be due to imbalances in bodily fluids but also suggests psychological origins.

1400s
Demonic Possession   In the Middle Ages, abnormal behavior is attributed to demonic possession.

1831
Unacceptable Impulses
Johann Christian Heinroth states that mental disorders are the result of unconscious conflict arising from unacceptable impulses.

Disorders of Mind and Body

16

OUTLINING THE PRINCIPLES

HOW ARE MENTAL DISORDERS CONCEPTUALIZED AND CLASSIFIED?

Mental Disorders Are Classified into Categories

There Are Multiple Causes of Mental Disorders

There Is a Stigma of Mental Illness

The Legal System Has Its Own Definition of Psychopathology

CAN ANXIETY BE THE ROOT OF SEEMINGLY DIFFERENT DISORDERS?

There Are Different Types of Anxiety Disorders

There Are Cognitive, Situational, and Biological Components to Anxiety Disorders

ARE MOOD DISORDERS EXTREME MANIFESTATIONS OF NORMAL MOODS?

There Are Different Types of Mood Disorders

There Are Cognitive, Situational, and Biological Components to Mood Disorders

IS SCHIZOPHRENIA A DISORDER OF MIND OR BODY?

Schizophrenia Has Positive and Negative Symptoms

Schizophrenia Is Primarily a Biological Disorder

ARE PERSONALITY DISORDERS TRULY MENTAL DISORDERS?

Personality Disorders Are Maladaptive Ways of Relating to the World

Borderline Personality Disorder Is Associated with Poor Self-Control

Antisocial Personality Disorder Is Associated with a Lack of Empathy

SHOULD CHILDHOOD DISORDERS BE CONSIDERED A UNIQUE CATEGORY?

Autism Is a Lack of Awareness of Others

Attention-Deficit/Hyperactivity Disorder Is a Disruptive Behavior Disorder

CONCLUSION
FURTHER READINGS

1867

Brain Diseases Wilhelm Griesinger argues that "mental diseases are brain diseases," in that mental disorders result from brain dysfunction.

1883

Classifying Mental Illness Emil Kraepelin suggests a classification system based on a biological conception of abnormal behavior.

1893

The Unconscious Sigmund Freud and Josef Breuer develop the psychoanalytic approach, emphasizing that mental disorders result from unsatisfied drives and unconscious wishes.

1925

Behaviorism John B. Watson argues that mental illness results from basic principles of conditioning.

1952

The DSM The first edition of the *Diagnostic and Statistical Manual of Mental Disorders (DSM)* is published.

RESEARCH QUESTIONS ???

for Studying Disorders of Mind and Body

What is psychopathology?

How can we best describe and categorize mental illness?

Are there problems with labeling someone as mentally ill?

How do the mind and body interact in the development of mental illness?

How are personality disorders defined?

Can children have mental disorders?

Gertrude and Henry met in the 1930s. She found him annoying but eventually agreed to marry him after he threatened suicide. Gertrude became pregnant after three years of marriage, and in the fifth month of pregnancy, Gertrude's doctor predicted that she would have twins. In fact, she had quadruplets: Nora, Iris, Myra, and Hester. (Their names have been changed to protect their privacy.) Henry was frequently unemployed, so they could not afford to raise four babies. A local newspaper raised money, and a house was donated to them. There was a steady stream of visitors who wanted to see the babies, and Henry began charging admission. After a while, however, he became worried about the safety of his family and barred all visitors. At one point, he fired a pistol at his wife, mistaking her for an intruder.

Henry and Gertrude both believed that the four girls really represented one person split into four. They consistently preferred the two larger babies, Nora and Myra, to the other two, and Gertrude took a particular dislike to Hester, especially after she caught her masturbating. Gertrude continued to worry excessively about masturbation. After she caught Hester and Iris engaging in mutual masturbation, she had a doctor amputate their clitorises. As the girls got older, Henry insisted on watching them dress and undress, and he even watched them changing their sanitary pads. In high school, Hester became irritable and depressed; her behavior was at times destructive and bizarre. She "admitted" to a series of sexual activities dating back to elementary school. Rather than fully exploring the causes for this behavior, her parents concluded that masturbation had made her mentally retarded. She was heavily sedated and kept at home. Although the other girls graduated from high school and even held jobs for a while, they all had psychotic episodes resulting in hospitalization. All four women were eventually diagnosed with schizophrenia. The National Institute of Mental Health offered free care in return for the opportunity to study them. To preserve their anonymity, the NIMH dubbed them the Genain quadruplets and assigned them first

1970s	**1980**	**1990**	**2001**
Cognitions and Beliefs	**Multiaxial Diagnoses**	**Decade of the Brain**	**Genes and Behavior**
The cognitive perspective focuses on the ways in which distorted thought processes can contribute to mental disorders.	The third edition of the *DSM* introduces a new classification system emphasizing description of mental disorders.	The National Institutes of Health sponsors programs and publications aimed at introducing the general public to cutting-edge research on the brain.	The Human Genome Project has the potential to contribute greatly to the search for genetic contributions to mental illness.

names beginning with the initials of NIMH (Figure 16.1; information from Rosenthal, 1963).

Although in modern times the Genains are recognized as being mentally ill and receive appropriate treatment, the mentally ill have not always been viewed in a humane manner. In the Middle Ages, the Genain quadruplets might have been thought to be possessed by demons and been persecuted. In the 1700s, they would likely have languished in understaffed, overcrowded mental institutions. There would have been little attempt to understand their disorders and even less of an attempt to treat them. In the 1800s, the focus would have been on the environmental factors contributing to their illness, such as the physical abuse they suffered and their father's bizarre and inappropriate behavior. Although psychological factors probably contributed to the development of the quadruplets' mental disorders, we now understand that biological factors play a critical role in schizophrenia. Advances in research have demonstrated that most mental disorders are ultimately disorders of both mind and body.

16.1 The Genain quadruplets as adults.

Over the course of human history, people have struggled with how best to understand **psychopathology**—literally, sickness or disorder of the mind. The prevailing view in the twenty-first century is that psychopathology has its origins in psychological turmoil and biological dysfunction. Philosophers as early as Plato and Aristotle suggested that mental illness might be the result of conflicts between thought and emotion. Sigmund Freud was the first to develop a theory of psychopathology and to propose specific treatment techniques based on his theory.

Understanding the role of both psychological and biological factors in the genesis of mental disorders is now known to be critical. The willingness of those who are afflicted with mental illness, such as the Genain sisters, to participate in scientific investigations has allowed researchers to make significant strides in understanding mental disorders. Advances in medical technology such as structural and functional neuroimaging have given us a window into the workings of the human brain. Our increased understanding of the effects of genes, neurotransmitters, and hormones on brain and behavior has resulted in remarkable advances in understanding both normal and abnormal human behavior. This chapter examines how we think about mental illness and how mind and body interact in the development of mental disorders.

HOW ARE MENTAL DISORDERS CONCEPTUALIZED AND CLASSIFIED?

Whereas physical illness can often be detected by medical tests, such as blood tests or biopsies, there are few diagnostic instruments for mental illness. Indeed, the whole concept of psychopathology is rather fuzzy and depends on cultural

psychopathology A disorder of the mind.

context. Many behaviors that are considered normal in one setting may be considered deviant in other settings. Some tribes in Africa spread feces in their hair as part of rituals. You can predict how this same behavior would be received in an industrialized society. In some Native American and Far Eastern cultures, having spirits talk to you is considered a great honor. In urban America, this would be taken as evidence of auditory hallucinations. There are, however, some criteria that are important to consider in determining whether behavior represents psychopathology: Does the behavior deviate from cultural norms? Is the behavior maladaptive? Is the behavior causing the individual personal distress?

Because the line between normal and abnormal is hard to draw, there is an increasing trend toward defining psychopathology as thoughts and behaviors that are maladaptive rather than deviant. Excessive hand-washing can be deviant but adaptive—after all, it is the single best way of avoiding contagious disease. The same behavior, however, can be maladaptive when people cannot stop from washing their hands raw. The diagnostic criteria for all of the major disorder categories include the stipulation that the symptoms of the disorder must interfere with at least one aspect of the person's life, such as work, social relations, or self-care. This is a critical component in determining whether a given behavior or set of behaviors represents a mental disorder or is simply unusual.

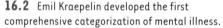

What is psychopathology?

MENTAL DISORDERS ARE CLASSIFIED INTO CATEGORIES

Despite the problems in conceptualizing mental disorders, there are clear advantages to categorizing them. Diagnosing someone with a particular mental disorder provides a starting point for therapy. Most treatments, whether biological or psychological, are specific for given disorders. The course and probable outcome, or *prognosis*, of different mental disorders is different as well, and the correct diagnosis can help the patient and family understand what the future might bring. Differentiating among different mental disorders is also critical for researchers. In order to investigate the etiology (factors that contribute to the development) and possible treatments of mental disorders, there must be a way of grouping these disorders into meaningful categories.

Researchers and clinicians have struggled for many years with how best to categorize mental disorders. Emil Kraepelin (Figure 16.2) was one of the first to propose a classification system for mental disorders. He recognized that not all patients with mental illness suffered from the same disorder, and he identified mental disorders based on groups of symptoms that occurred together.

The idea of categorizing mental disorders in a systematic manner was not officially adopted until the first edition of the ***Diagnostic and Statistical Manual of Mental Disorders (DSM)*** was published in 1952. Although it has undergone several revisions over the years, it remains the standard in the fields of psychology and psychiatry. Although the earlier versions focused on the presumed causes of mental illness, beginning with the *DSM III* (1980) there was a return to Kraepelin's approach of classifying psychopathology based on description. In the current fourth edition, disorders are described in terms of observable symptoms, and patients must meet specific criteria in order to be given a particular diagnosis. In addition, patients are not given a single label but rather are classified in terms of a set of clinically important factors (see Table 16.1). This **multiaxial system** is based on the growing realization that mental health is affected by a variety

16.2 Emil Kraepelin developed the first comprehensive categorization of mental illness.

TABLE 16.1 DSM-IV Multiaxial Classification System

Axis I   Clinical disorders and other conditions that may be a focus of clinical attention (schizophrenia, mood disorders, anxiety disorders, sexual and gender disorders, sleep disorders, eating disorders).

Axis II   Mental retardation and personality disorders (antisocial personality disorder, paranoid personality disorder, borderline personality disorder).

Axis III   General medical conditions that may be relevant to mental disorders (cancer, epilepsy, obesity, Parkinson's disease, Alzheimer's disease).

Axis IV   Psychosocial and environmental problems that might affect the diagnosis, treatment, and prognosis of mental disorders (unemployment, divorce, legal problems, homelessness, poverty, parental overprotection).

Axis V   Global assessment of functioning (social, psychological, and occupational). Rated on a scale from 1 to 100, with 1 representing danger of hurting self or others and 100 meaning superior functioning in a wide range of areas.

SOURCE: Diagnostic and Statistical Manual of the American Psychiatric Association, 1994.

of factors. Diagnosing a patient on all five axes provides a more complete picture of the person.

THERE ARE MULTIPLE CAUSES OF MENTAL DISORDERS

Although there is not complete agreement for the causes of most mental disorders, there are some factors that are thought to play important developmental roles.

Psychological factors   The first edition of the *DSM* was heavily influenced by Freudian psychoanalytic theory. Freud believed that mental disorders were due to mostly unconscious conflicts, often sexual in nature, that dated back to childhood. Later life experiences trigger the emotions and unresolved conflicts associated with these early events. Consistent with this perspective, many disorders in the first edition of the *DSM* were described as reactions to environmental conditions or as involving various defense mechanisms. Symptoms were described more in terms of inner causes than external behaviors.

Psychological factors play an important role in the manifestation and treatment of mental disorders. Thoughts and emotions are shaped by the environment and can profoundly influence behavior, including abnormal behavior. Not only traumatic events but also less extreme circumstances can have long-lasting effects. The **family systems model** is based on the idea that the behavior of an individual must be considered within a social context, in particular the family. Problems that arise within an individual are manifestations of problems within the family. Developing a profile of an individual's family interactions can be important not only in understanding possible factors contributing to the disorder, but also in determining whether the family is likely to be helpful or detrimental to the client's progress in therapy. Similarly, the **sociocultural model** views psychopathology as the result of the interaction between individuals and their cultures. Some disorders, such as schizophrenia, are more common among the lower socioeconomic classes, whereas disorders such as anorexia nervosa are more

RESEARCH QUESTION

How can we best describe and categorize mental illness?

Diagnostic and Statistical Manual of Mental Disorders (DSM) A handbook of clinical disorders used for diagnosing psychopathology.

multiaxial system The system used in the *DSM* that provides assessment along five axes describing important mental health factors.

family systems model Considers symptoms within an individual as indicating problems within the family.

sociocultural model Views psychopathology as the result of the interaction between individuals and their cultures.

common among the middle and upper classes. From the sociocultural perspective, these differences in prevalence are due to differences in lifestyles, expectations, and opportunities among the classes of society. Note, however, that it is possible that there are cultural biases in the willingness to ascribe disorders to different social classes.

Cognitive-behavioral factors The central principle of the **cognitive-behavioral approach** is that abnormal behavior is learned. Whereas the psychoanalytic approach focuses on unconscious internal factors, the behavioral approach is based on observable variables. As you recall from Chapter 6, in classical conditioning, an unconditioned stimulus produces an unconditioned response. For example, a loud noise produces a startle response. If a neutral stimulus is paired with this unconditioned stimulus, it can eventually by itself produce a similar response. For example, if a child is playing with a fluffy white rat and is frightened by a loud noise, the white rat alone can later cause fear in the child. In fact, this is how John B. Watson, the founder of behaviorism, demonstrated that many fears are learned rather than innate.

Proponents of strict behaviorism argue that mental disorders are the result of classical and operant conditioning. Behavior was defined as only overt observable actions, but this view was later challenged. The revised cognitive-behavioral perspective includes the idea that thoughts and beliefs should be considered as another type of behavior that can be studied empirically. The premise of this approach is that thoughts can become distorted and produce maladaptive behaviors and emotions. In contrast to the psychoanalytical perspective, thought processes are believed to be available to the conscious mind. Individuals are aware of, or can be easily made aware of, the thought processes that give rise to maladaptive behavior.

Biological factors The biological perspective on mental disorders focuses on how physiological factors, such as genetics, contribute to mental illness. Chapter 3 described how comparing the rates of mental illness between identical and fraternal twins and studying individuals who have been adopted have revealed the importance of genetic factors to the development of mental illness. Other biological factors also influence the development and course of mental illness. The fetus is particularly vulnerable, and there is evidence that some mental disorders may arise from prenatal problems such as maternal illness, malnutrition, and exposure to toxins. Environmental toxins and malnutrition during childhood and adolescence can also put the individual at risk for mental illness. All of these biological factors are thought to contribute to mental disorders because of their effects on the central nervous system. There is emerging evidence that neurological dysfunction contributes to the manifestation of many mental disorders, although a causal link has not been proven.

The recent use of brain imaging, such as PET and fMRI, to identify brain regions associated with the manifestation of mental disorders has allowed researchers to generate hypotheses about the types of subtle deficits that might be associated with different mental disorders. Structural imaging has revealed neuroanatomical differences, perhaps due to genetics, between those with mental disorders and those without, but it is functional neuroimaging that is currently at the forefront of research into the neurological correlates of mental disorder. PET and fMRI have revealed brain regions that may function differently in those with mental illnesses (Figure 16.3). Another source of insights into neural dysfunction has been research

cognitive-behavioral approach Views psychopathology as the result of learned, maladaptive cognitions.

diathesis-stress model Proposes that a disorder may develop when an underlying vulnerability is coupled with a precipitating event.

on the role of neurotransmitters in mental disorders. In some cases, medications have been developed based on what is known about the neurochemistry of mental illness. In other cases, however, it is the unexpected effects of medications that have led to discoveries about the neurotransmitters involved in mental disorders.

Integrating the factors involved in mental disorders Perhaps the most useful way to think about the causes of mental disorders is as an interaction among multiple factors. The **diathesis-stress model** provides one such way of thinking about the onset of mental disorders. In this model, an individual can have an underlying vulnerability or predisposition (diathesis) to a mental disorder. This can be biological, such as a genetic predisposition to a specific disorder, or environmental, such as childhood trauma. The vulnerability by itself may not be sufficient to trigger mental illness, but the addition of stressful circumstances can tip the scales. If the stress level exceeds an individual's ability to cope, the symptoms of mental illness will manifest. In this way of thinking, a family history of mental illness suggests vulnerability rather than destiny.

16.3 Although these men are twins, the one on the right has schizophrenia. Compared to his normal twin, he has larger ventricles, as revealed through MRI. This same pattern has emerged in the study of other twin pairs in which one has schizophrenia and the other does not.

THERE IS A STIGMA OF MENTAL ILLNESS

Given the difficulties in defining mental illness, it is inevitable that there will be errors in diagnosing. Some people who are mentally ill may not be identified as such, while others who are not mentally ill may nevertheless be labeled as ill. People with undiagnosed mental illness do not have treatment options available to them, and they may feel isolated and desperate, with no explanation for what they are feeling. This can be life threatening, since suicide is a frequent consequence of untreated mental illness. People who are labeled as mentally ill when they are not can face different problems.

A dramatic illustration of labeling was published in the journal *Science* by David Rosenhan (1973). Eight research participants presented themselves at 12 different psychiatric hospitals saying that they had been hearing voices that said such things as "thud," "empty," and "hollow." These symptoms were chosen because they have never been reported in the psychiatric literature. Aside from the voices, the "patients" reported no other symptoms and did not alter any aspect of their personal or medical histories. All 12 of the hospitals admitted the patients for treatment. Once admitted, they stopped reporting any symptoms. The staff interpreted all of their normal behavior in the hospital, such as waiting in line at the cafeteria, as further evidence of their mental illness, and none of the staff at any of the hospitals realized that these pseudo-patients were in fact sane. (Interestingly, some of the real patients did!) It took between 7 and 52 days for the "patients" to be released, and each of them was given the label of "schizophrenia in remission." Critics of this study noted that it is unusual for healthy people to show up at a psychiatric hospital seeking admission, and therefore it is difficult to assess the extent to which misdiagnosis occurs for those truly seeking help. It is important to keep in mind that the diagnosis refers to the behavior displayed rather than to the people themselves.

Are there problems with labeling someone as mentally ill?

THE LEGAL SYSTEM HAS ITS OWN DEFINITION OF PSYCHOPATHOLOGY

In clinical psychology, the *DSM* provides the structure for conceptualizing and categorizing mental disorders. The legal system, however, has a fundamentally different approach. Whereas clinical psychologists are concerned with diagnosing and treating mental illness, the legal profession is focused on the issue of personal responsibility for one's actions.

The insanity defense In England in the 1840s, a Scotsman named Daniel M'Naughten assassinated the secretary to the British prime minister (Figure 16.4). After the crime, it was discovered that M'Naughten suffered from delusions and hallucinations, and that he thought the voice of God had told him to kill the prime minister (he mistakenly shot the secretary instead). Because it was determined that he did not know that what he was doing was wrong, he was acquitted. This case resulted in the *M'Naughten* (or *McNaughten*) *rule*, which stipulated that a person was considered to be insane and therefore not responsible for his actions if he did not know right from wrong. In the 1950s, this rule was modified; the new *Durham rule* said that a person was not responsible for criminal behavior if the behavior was the result of mental illness or mental defect. The current rule is the *American Law Institute rule*, which states that a person is not responsible if, at the time of the crime, a mental illness or defect led to a lack of capacity to appreciate the criminality of the act or to an inability to conform to the requirements of law. The notion of insanity is therefore a legal term, not a psychological one.

Contrary to public perception, the *insanity defense* is not used often (Table 16.2), but its use in high-profile trials such as that of John Hinckley Jr. has caused public outcry (Figure 16.5). In an attempt to assassinate President Ronald Reagan in 1980, Hinckley shot Reagan in the lung and Reagan's press secretary, James Brady, through the head. Both survived, but Brady sustained permanent severe physical and cognitive impairments. There was no doubt that Hinckley planned and committed the crime. The only question at the trial was whether he was legally insane at the time. After many hours of testimony, it became clear that Hinckley had psychological problems beginning in early childhood. The two sides disagreed, however, about the severity of those problems and whether they met the criteria for legal insanity. According to the law at the time, the burden was on the prosecution to prove that the defendant was sane if the defense claimed he was not. The jury concluded that there was reasonable doubt about his sanity at the time of the crime and returned a verdict of "not guilty by reason of insanity."

As a result of the public outrage following the verdict, the law was revised so that the burden of proof now falls on the defense, which must prove that the defendant was not sane at the time of the crime. Although the insanity defense has received a great deal of attention in the media, an issue that more commonly arises is whether a defendant is competent to stand trial. "Using Psychological Science: Legal Competency" discusses the relevance of competency in other aspects of the legal system.

16.4 A rendering of the M'Naughten trial. The rule for determining insanity was based on the crimes of Daniel M'Naughten.

CENTRAL CRIMINAL COURT, OLD BAILEY—M'NAUGHTEN'S TRIAL.

TABLE 16.2 Perceptions of the Use of the Insanity Defense Compared with Actual Frequency

	PUBLIC PERCEPTION	REALITY
Percentage of felony indictments for which an insanity plea is made	37%	1%
Percentage of insanity pleas resulting in "not guilty by reason of insanity"	44%	26%
Percentage of persons "not guilty by reason of insanity" sent to mental hospitals	51%	85%
Percentage of persons "not guilty by reason of insanity" set free	26%	15%
Conditional release		12%
Outpatient treatment		3%
Unconditional release		1%
Length of confinement of persons "not guilty by reason of insanity" (in months)		
All crimes	21.8	32.5
Murder		76.4

SOURCE: Data from Silver et al., 1994.

Predicting violent behavior In the 1950s and 1960s, people could be involuntarily committed to mental institutions if the state deemed them to be mentally ill. A 1979 Supreme Court decision, however, was instrumental in tightening the standards for *civil commitment*. This court decision and subsequent state regulations specify that people cannot be involuntarily committed to mental institutions just because they are mentally ill. Currently, many states require that people be judged dangerous to themselves or others in order to be committed. However, determining whether a person is dangerous is fraught with ethical, legal, and clinical difficulties. Although a great deal of effort has been expended on trying to predict violent behavior, it remains virtually impossible to accurately do so.

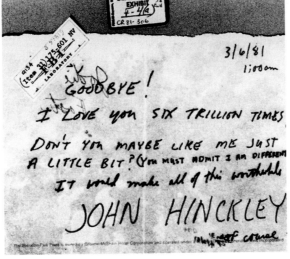

16.5 John Hinckley Jr. and a letter he wrote to actress Jodie Foster, with whom he was obsessed.

LEGAL COMPETENCY

Whether someone is competent to stand trial is not a judgment about the person's responsibility for the crime. It is simply a question of whether the defendant can understand the legal proceedings and contribute to his or her own defense. If a defendant is judged incompetent, that person is generally placed in a mental institution without bail. More than 90 percent of these defendants are eventually judged to be competent and do stand trial. In some cases, however, the amount of time defendants are held before they are judged competent can be longer than the amount of jail time they would have served if they had been found guilty.

The case of Theodore Kaczynski, referred to in the media as the Unabomber, hinged on his competence to stand trial (Figure 16.6). Kaczynski's lawyers planned to argue that he was insane at the time of the crimes, but Kaczynski refused to consider this approach. Kaczynski then requested permission to act as his own attorney, but this request was denied. A court-appointed psychiatrist evaluated Kaczynski and determined that he met the *DSM* criteria for paranoid schizophrenia, but that he was competent to stand trial despite his mental illness. Faced with the choice of having his lawyers present a case for insanity or pleading guilty, Kaczynski pled guilty.

Sometimes competency does not become an issue until after a person is convicted. The judgment of a person's competency to be punished is illustrated by the case of Alvin Bernard Ford, a convicted murderer who was sentenced to death in 1974. At the time of the crime, and during the trial and the sentencing, Ford did not exhibit any symptoms of mental disorder. In 1982, however, he began to have odd ideas and perceptions. His condition slowly worsened until he became convinced that he was the target of a complex conspiracy aimed at trying to force him to commit suicide. He believed that the prison guards were killing people and hiding the bodies inside the prison. He became convinced that his relatives had been taken hostage and were being tortured and sexually abused, and that only he could save them. Ford continued to regress until he spoke entirely in a code characterized by the use of the word "one," making statements such as "Hands one, face one. Mafia one. God one, father one, Pope one. Leader one."

A number of psychiatrists evaluated Ford and came to different conclusions. Because most of these specialists judged him to be insane but competent, the Governor of Florida signed his death warrant. Ford's lawyer appealed on the grounds that it was not clear that Ford understood the death penalty and why he was to be executed. The uncertainty about his competency resulted in a number of appeals. The Supreme Court eventually held that the Eighth Amendment to the Constitution prohibits execution of a prisoner who is insane. They ordered that Ford be given a new hearing as to his competency to be executed. The Court's decision created an ethical dilemma for mental health professionals: should they treat death row inmates who have been judged insane, knowing that therapeutic success will result in the death of the patient?

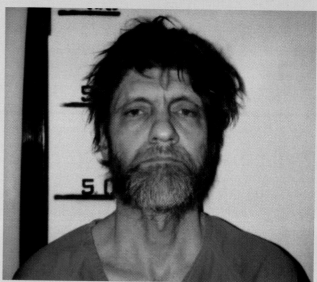

16.6 Theodore Kaczynski, known as the Unabomber, shown here (top) as a young professor and (bottom) after his arrrest. Kaczynski pled guilty rather than use the insanity defense.

Edmund E. Kemper III murdered his grandparents in 1964. At his trial, he was found not guilty by reason of insanity and was committed to a mental institution. Five years later, he was judged to be "cured" and was released. He then murdered six college students, his mother, and one of her friends. This time, the jury found him sane and guilty. As Kemper's case illustrates, patients who are mistakenly judged to be not dangerous can wreak havoc on the lives of others.

Conversely, patients who are mistakenly judged to be dangerous can languish for many years in mental institutions. One study of clinicians' ability to assess a patient's risk of future violence found the clinicians to be only modestly more accurate than chance for male patients, and no better than chance for female patients (Lidz et al.,1993).

If a clinician believes a patient to be dangerous to someone else, the clinician has the obligation to warn that person. This *duty to warn* is one of few situations in which clinicians are required to violate patient confidentiality. The rule was created in response to the case of Prosenjit Poddar, who was undergoing outpatient psychotherapy at the University of California student health facility. Poddar told the therapist that he intended to kill his former girlfriend Tatiana Tarasoff when she returned from a trip outside the country. The therapist and the health facility supervisors agreed that Poddar was dangerous and should be committed for observation and treatment. They contacted the campus police, who picked him up but released him since he seemed rational and promised to leave Tarasoff alone. He terminated therapy and when Tarasoff returned from her trip, he killed her. Tarasoff's parents subsequently sued all parties. The case went to the California Supreme Court, which ruled that the university was not liable for failing to hospitalize Poddar, but it was liable for the therapist's failure to warn Tarasoff that she might be in danger. The duty to warn has been upheld by other courts, and it was the first time therapists were deemed to have a responsibility to persons other than their patients (Anfang & Appelbaum, 1996). Although the rule seems clear, it can be very difficult for therapists to decide when to violate a patient's confidentiality.

REVIEWING THE PRINCIPLE

How Are Mental Disorders Conceptualized and Classified?

Psychopathology takes many forms, and mental disorders are consequently difficult to define and categorize. Although the behavioral manifestations of mental disorders vary widely, those who are diagnosed with these disorders have two things in common: their behavior is maladaptive and it interferes with some important aspect of their lives. Diagnoses of specific mental disorders are based on the checklist system of the DSM. The specific cause of most mental disorders is unknown and may arise from a complex interaction of psychological, biological, and cognitive-behavioral factors. Psychopathology is conceptualized differently in the legal system than in the medical field: the former focuses on responsibility for one's actions, the latter on understanding and treating the disorder.

CAN ANXIETY BE THE ROOT OF SEEMINGLY DIFFERENT DISORDERS?

What does the fear of spiders have in common with the need to repeatedly check that the stove is turned off? They are both manifestations of anxiety disorders. Anxiety itself is normal and even useful. It can prepare us for upcoming events and motivate us to learn new ways of coping with life's challenges. For some people, however, anxiety can become debilitating and can interfere with every aspect of life. **Anxiety disorders** are characterized by excessive anxiety in the absence of true danger. It is normal to be anxious in stressful or threatening situations. It is abnormal to feel strong chronic anxiety without cause.

anxiety disorders Characterized by the experience of excessive anxiety in the absence of true danger.

THERE ARE DIFFERENT TYPES OF ANXIETY DISORDERS

People suffering from anxiety disorders feel tense, anxious, and apprehensive. They are often depressed and irritable because they cannot see any solution to the anxiety they feel. Constant worry can make falling asleep and staying asleep difficult, and attention span and concentration can be impaired. Problem solving and judgment may suffer as well. Chronic anxiety also causes a variety of somatic symptoms, due to the arousal of the autonomic nervous system. Sweating, dry mouth, rapid pulse, shallow breathing, increased blood pressure, and increased muscular tension are all consequences of autonomic arousal. Chronic arousal can also result in hypertension, headaches, and intestinal problems and can even cause illness or tissue damage. Because of their high levels of autonomic arousal, those who suffer from anxiety disorders also exhibit restless and pointless motor behaviors. Exaggerated startle response is typical and behaviors such as toe tapping and excessive fidgeting are common. Recent research has shown that chronic stress can produce atrophy in the hippocampus, a brain structure involved in learning and memory (McEwen, 2000). It is not yet known whether the damage is reversible, or if there are functional implications of hippocampal atrophy. The fact that chronic stress can damage the body and brain, however, indicates the importance of identification and effective treatment of disorders that involve chronic anxiety. Although different anxiety disorders share some emotional, cognitive, somatic, and motor symptoms, the behavioral manifestations of these disorders are quite different.

Phobic disorder   A **phobia** is a fear of a specific object or situation. Fear can be adaptive, as it can lead us to avoid potential danger, such as poisonous snakes and rickety bridges. In phobias, however, the fear is exaggerated and out of proportion to the actual danger. Phobias are classified based on the object of the fear. *Specific phobias* (formerly known as simple phobias) are to particular objects and situations, such as snakes (ophidiophobia), enclosed spaces (claustrophobia), and heights (acrophobia). *Social phobia* is a fear of being negatively evaluated by others and includes fear of public speaking and of eating in front of others. Specific phobias are more common than social phobia, affecting about 10 percent of the population versus 2–5 percent for social phobia (Robins & Regier, 1991). Women are diagnosed with specific phobias at least twice as often as men, but with social phobia only slightly more often.

Generalized anxiety disorder   Whereas the anxiety in phobic disorders has a specific focus, the anxiety in **generalized anxiety disorder** is diffuse and omnipresent. People with this disorder are constantly anxious and worry incessantly about even minor matters (Sanderson & Barlow, 1990). Because the anxiety is not focused, it can occur in response to almost anything, and so the sufferer is constantly on the alert for problems. This hypervigilance results in distractibility, fatigue, irritability, and sleep problems, as well as headaches, restlessness, and muscle pain. Probably 3–4 percent of the population is affected by this disorder, with women more likely to be diagnosed than men (Kessler et al., 1994).

Panic disorder   It has been estimated that panic disorder affects about 3 percent of the population, with women twice as likely to be diagnosed as men (Kessler et al., 1994). **Panic disorder** sufferers experience attacks of terror that are sudden and overwhelming. The terror can seemingly come out of nowhere or

phobias Irrational fears of specific objects or situations.

generalized anxiety disorder Diffuse state of constant anxiety not associated with any specific object or event.

panic disorder An anxiety disorder characterized by sudden overwhelming attacks of terror.

can be cued by external stimuli or internal thought processes. Panic attacks typically last for several minutes. The victim of such an attack begins to sweat and tremble; her heart races and she begins to feel short of breath and her chest hurts; she can feel dizzy and light-headed with numbness and tingling in her hands and feet. People experiencing panic attacks often feel that they are going crazy or that they are dying, and people who suffer from persistent panic attacks attempt suicide much more frequently than those in the general population (Fawcett, 1992; Korn et al., 1992; Noyes, 1991). A related disorder is **agoraphobia**, a fear of being in situations in which escape is difficult or impossible, such as a crowded shopping mall. Being in those situations causes panic attacks.

Obsessive-compulsive disorder   Obsessive-compulsive disorder (OCD) involves frequent intrusive thoughts and compulsive actions, and affects 2–3 percent of the population. It is more common in women than men and generally begins in early adulthood (Robins & Regier, 1991; Weissman et al., 1994). Obsessions and compulsions plague sufferers of this disorder. *Obsessions* are recurrent, intrusive, and unwanted thoughts, ideas, or images. They often include fear of contamination, accidents, or one's own aggression. *Compulsions* are particular acts that the OCD patient feels driven to perform over and over again. The most common compulsive behaviors are cleaning, checking, and counting. For instance, people may constantly check to make sure they locked the door because of their obsession that their home may be invaded, or they may engage in superstitious counting to protect against accidents. Those with OCD anticipate catastrophe and loss of control. However, as opposed to those who suffer from other anxiety disorders, who fear what might happen to them, those who suffer from OCD often fear what they might do or might have done:

> While in reality no one is on the road, I'm intruded with the heinous thought that I *might* have hit someone . . . a human being! God knows where such a fantasy comes from. . . . I try to make reality chase away this fantasy. I reason, "Well, if I hit someone while driving, I would have *felt* it." This brief trip into reality helps the pain dissipate . . . but only for a second. . . . I start ruminating, "Maybe I did hit someone and didn't realize it. . . . Oh my God! I might have killed somebody! I have to go back and check." Checking is the only way to calm the anxiety. (Rapoport, 1990, pp. 22–27)

THERE ARE COGNITIVE, SITUATIONAL, AND BIOLOGICAL COMPONENTS TO ANXIETY DISORDERS

Although the behavioral manifestations of anxiety disorders can be quite different, they share some causal factors. When presented with ambiguous or neutral situations, anxious individuals tend to perceive them as threatening, whereas nonanxious individuals assume them to be nonthreatening (Eysenck et al., 1991). The ambiguous sentence "The doctor examined little Emma's growth" is interpreted by anxious individuals as "The doctor looked at little Emma's cancer" and by nonanxious individuals as "The doctor measured little Emma's height." Anxious individuals also tend to focus excessive amounts of attention on perceived threats. Threatening events are thus more easily recalled than nonthreatening events, increasing their perceived magnitude and frequency. In addition to cognitive components, situational factors also may play a role in the development of anxiety disorders. In Chapter 6 you learned that monkeys will develop a fear of

agoraphobia An anxiety disorder marked by fear of being in situations in which escape may be difficult or impossible.

obsessive-compulsive disorder (OCD) An anxiety disorder characterized by frequent intrusive thoughts and compulsive actions.

snakes if they observe other monkeys responding to snakes in a fearful way. Similarly, a person could develop a fear of elevators by observing another person's reaction to the closing of the elevator doors. Such a fear might then generalize to other enclosed spaces, resulting in claustrophobia. Biological factors also seem to play an important role in the development of anxiety disorders; recent investigations have resulted in a number of exciting findings. Next we will consider some of the ways these three factors interact in the development of two anxiety disorders.

The causes of obsessive-compulsive disorder   A paradoxical aspect of OCD is that people are aware that their obsessions and compulsions are irrational and yet they are unable to stop them. One explanation is that the disorder results from operant conditioning. Anxiety is somehow paired to a specific event, and the person engages in behavior that reduces anxiety. This reduction of anxiety is reinforcing and increases the chance of engaging in that behavior again. For example, say you are forced to shake hands with someone who has a bad cold, and you have just seen that person wiping his nose with his right hand. Shaking that hand might cause you to be anxious or uncomfortable because you don't want to get sick yourself. As soon as the pleasantries are over, you run to the bathroom and wash your hands. You feel relieved. You have just paired hand washing with a reduction in anxiety, thus increasing the chances of hand washing in the future.

There is good evidence that the etiology of OCD is at least in part genetic (Crowe, 2000). Recently, it has been demonstrated that the caudate nucleus is dysfunctional in people with OCD (Baxter, 2000). The caudate is part of the basal ganglia, a region that helps to suppress impulses. In patients with OCD, the caudate is smaller and has structural abnormalities (Figure 16.7). In addition, patients with basal ganglia disease often manifest symptoms of OCD. Because this region is involved in impulse suppression, it is thought that dysfunction in this region results in the leak of impulses into consciousness. The prefrontal cortex then becomes overactive in an effort to compensate. It has been demonstrated that there are alterations in brain waves over the prefrontal cortex in OCD patients; severing the connections between the prefrontal cortex and the caudate can often result in dramatic improvement in the symptoms of the disorder.

It may be that biological and cognitive-behavioral factors interact to produce the symptoms of OCD. A dysfunctional caudate nucleus allows impulses to enter consciousness, and these impulses may give rise to the obsessions of OCD. The prefrontal cortex becomes overactive in an attempt to compensate, and this overactivity can establish associations between obsessions and behaviors that reduce the anxiety arising from the obsessions. These behaviors thus become compulsions through conditioning.

The link between panic disorder and agoraphobia   People who suffer from agoraphobia avoid going into open spaces or to places where there might be crowds. Specifically, they seem to fear being in places from which escape might be difficult or embarrassing. In extreme cases, sufferers of this type of phobia may feel unable to leave their homes:

> Ms. Watson began to dread going out of the house alone. She feared that while out she would have an attack and would be stranded and helpless. She stopped riding the subway to work out of fear she might be trapped in a car between stops when an attack struck, preferring instead to walk the

How do the mind and body interact in the development of mental illness?

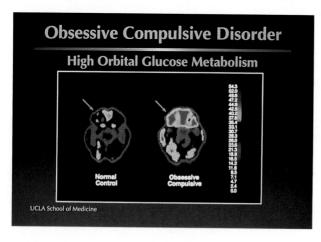

16.7 PET scans of people with OCD show greater activity in the frontal lobes, basal ganglia, and thalamus than do those of normal controls.

20 blocks between her home and work. She also severely curtailed her social and recreational activities—previously frequent and enjoyed—because an attack might occur, necessitating an abrupt and embarrassing flight from the scene. (Spitzer et al., 1983)

This sort of description is typical of those with agoraphobia, and such descriptions have led many to explore the relationship between panic attacks and agoraphobia. The symptoms of sympathetic nervous system arousal that occur during a panic attack often lead victims to believe that they are having a heart attack. From a cognitive-behavioral perspective, a tendency to catastrophize (to expect the worst) paired with some kind of trigger stimulus can produce a panic attack. It has been speculated that agoraphobia is the result of untreated panic attacks (Barlow, 1988). People who have had panic attacks begin to fear having them again. This fear results in avoidance of situations in which it might be embarrassing to have an attack and difficult to escape. The fear then develops into a phobia.

Although agoraphobic symptoms are thought to arise from learned associations, panic attacks themselves seem more influenced by biological factors. Research suggests that panic disorder is in part genetic and linked to abnormalities in the locus coeruleus (Crowe, 2000). The abnormalities result in increased arousal of the central nervous system. Studies show that infusions of lactate and inhalation of carbon dioxide, which heighten arousal, can produce panic attacks in those with a family history of panic disorder, but not in those without a family history (Figure 16.8). Interestingly, although medication can be quite effective in reducing or eliminating panic attacks, it has no effect on agoraphobia. The fear of open places has been learned and treating the neural basis for the fear has no effect. The conditioned response must be unlearned via cognitive-behavioral therapy.

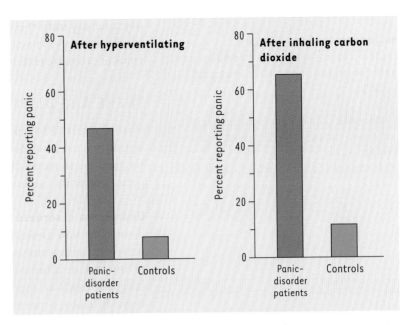

16.8 Research participants prone to panic attacks are more likely than normal controls to have a panic attack after hyperventilating or inhaling carbon dioxide.

Can Anxiety Be the Root of Seemingly Different Disorders?

On the surface, many of the anxiety disorders seem to be quite different. However, they share many of the same emotional, cognitive, somatic, and motor symptoms. All of the disorders in this category are associated with anxiety that is out of proportion with reality. This anxiety may arise from biological factors, but many of the behavioral and cognitive manifestations of the disorders are strongly influenced by psychological and environmental factors.

ARE MOOD DISORDERS EXTREME MANIFESTATIONS OF NORMAL MOODS?

Our moods color every aspect of our lives. When we are happy, the world seems like a wonderful place and we are filled with boundless energy. When we are sad, we view the world in a decidedly less rosy light. Feelings of sadness, hopelessness, and isolation are all too common. Few of us, however, experience these symptoms

major depression A disorder characterized by severe negative moods and a lack of interest in normally pleasurable activities.

dysthymia A form of depression that is not severe enough to be diagnosed as major depression.

day after day until they disrupt our ability to work, learn, and play. In addition, while it is easy to imagine how periods of sadness can interfere with daily life, periods of excessive elation can be equally devastating.

THERE ARE DIFFERENT TYPES OF MOOD DISORDERS

Mood disorders reflect extreme emotions, with depressive disorders featuring persistent and pervasive feelings of sadness, and bipolar disorders involving radical fluctuations in mood. While some of their characteristics overlap, the two categories represent fundamentally different disorders.

Depressive disorders Within the category of depressive disorders are major depression and dysthymia. In order to be diagnosed with **major depression**, a person must have one of two symptoms: depressed (often irritable) mood or loss of interest in pleasurable activities. In addition, the person must have other symptoms such as appetite and weight changes, sleep disturbances, loss of energy, difficulty concentrating, feelings of self-reproach or guilt, and frequent thoughts of death and suicide. The following case study is of a 56-year-old woman diagnosed with depression:

> She described herself as overwhelmed with feelings of guilt, worthlessness, and hopelessness. She twisted her hands almost continuously and played nervously with her hair. She stated that her family would be better off without her and that she had considered taking her life by hanging herself. She felt that after death she would go to hell, where she would experience eternal torment, but that this would be a just punishment. . . .(Andreasen, 1984, p. 39)

Episodes of depression can last from a few weeks to many years. On average, depressive episodes last approximately six months. In many cases, the episodes are self-limiting and resolve without intervention. Although 90 percent of sufferers will recover from depression, they have a 50 percent chance of experiencing another depressive episode in the future (Keller et al., 1982).

Unlike major depression, **dysthymia** is of mild to moderate severity. Those diagnosed with dysthymia must have a depressed mood most of the day, more days than not, for at least two years. The depression is not, however, severe enough to merit a diagnosis of major depression. Periods of dysthymia last from 2 to 20 or more years, although the typical duration is about 5–10 years. Because the depressed mood is so long-lasting, some psychological scientists consider it to be a personality disorder rather than a mood disorder. In fact, earlier editions of the *DSM* included a category of "affective personality" in the personality disorders section. In later editions, this term was dropped and dysthymia was added to the mood disorders category. The distinction between a depressive personality, dysthymic disorder, and major depression is unclear. They may be points along a continuum rather than distinct disorders. In support of this view, it has been found that dysthymia often precedes major depression (Lewinsohn et al., 1991, 1999).

Estimates of the likelihood of developing major depression in one's lifetime vary from as low as 7 percent to as high as 20 percent. One study found the lifetime prevalence of depression to be 13 percent in men and 21 percent in women (Kessler et al., 1994). These statistics are for major depression; the number of persons affected by less severe depression is much higher. A recent survey found that as many as 48 percent of Americans have experienced some form of depressive disorder.

Bipolar disorders   Although we have all experienced variations in our moods, normal fluctuations from sadness to exuberance seem miniscule in comparison to the extremes experienced by those with bipolar disorder. Bipolar disorder was previously known as manic-depression, a term that captured the essence of the disorder. Those who are diagnosed with **bipolar disorder** have periods of major depression but also experience episodes of mania. *Manic episodes* are characterized by elevated mood, increased activity, diminished need for sleep, grandiose ideas, racing thoughts, and extreme distractibility. Kay Redfield Jamison, a well-known author and professor of psychiatry, describes one of her own episodes of mania:

> With vibrissae twinging, antennae perked, eyes fast-forwarding and fly faceted, I took in everything around me. I was on the run. Not just on the run but fast and furious on the run, darting back and forth across the hospital parking lot, trying to use up a boundless, restless, manic energy. I was running fast, but slowly going mad. (Jamison, 1995, p. 3)

During episodes of mania, the heightened levels of activity and euphoria often result in excessive involvement in pleasurable but foolish activities—such as sexual indiscretions, buying sprees, and risky business ventures—that the individual will come to regret once the mania has subsided. Whereas some sufferers of bipolar disorder experience true manic episodes, others may experience less extreme mood elevations. These *hypomanic episodes* are often characterized by heightened creativity and productivity and can be extremely pleasurable and rewarding. People experiencing episodes of major depression and mania are diagnosed with *bipolar I* disorder, whereas people fluctuating between major depression and hypomania are diagnosed with *bipolar II*. A third category of bipolar disorder is **cyclothymia**, in which individuals experience hypomania and mild depression. Bipolar disorder is much less common than depression; the lifetime prevalence is estimated at 1 percent. In addition, whereas depression is more common in women, the prevalence of bipolar disorder is equal in women and men.

THERE ARE COGNITIVE, SITUATIONAL, AND BIOLOGICAL COMPONENTS TO MOOD DISORDERS

Mood disorders can be extremely devastating. The sadness, hopelessness, and inability to concentrate that characterize major depression can result in the loss of jobs, friends, and family relationships. Because of the profound effects of this disorder, and the danger of suicide, a great deal of research has been focused on understanding the causes of and treating major depression. Suicide is also a risk with those with bipolar disorder. In addition, errors in judgment during manic episodes can have devastating effects on the lives of those who suffer from the disorder as well as on their families and friends.

Depression is caused by a combination of factors   Studies of twins, families, and adoptions support the notion that there is a genetic component to depression. Although there is some variability among studies, concordance rates

bipolar disorder A mood disorder characterized by alternating periods of depression and mania.

cyclothymia A less extreme form of bipolar disorder.

seasonal affective disorder (SAD)
Periods of depression that are linked to the times of year with minimal sunlight.

learned helplessness model A cognitive model of depression in which people feel unable to control events around them.

between identical twins are generally around four times higher than rates between fraternal twins (Gershon et al., 1989). The existence of a genetic component implies that there are biological factors involved in depression, but there is as yet no consensus as to what these factors are. We know that medications that increase the availability of norepinephrine alleviate depression, whereas those that decrease levels of this neurotransmitter can cause depression. More recent medications, such as Prozac, selectively increase serotonin, so there is increased interest in understanding the role of this neurotransmitter in modulation of mood. Studies of brain function have suggested neural structures that may be involved in mood disorders. Damage to the left anterior or prefrontal cortex often leads to depression, but this is not true of damage to the right hemisphere. The brain waves of depressed persons show low activity in these same regions in the left hemisphere. Interestingly, this pattern persists in patients who have been depressed but are currently in remission. It therefore may be a kind of biological marker of predisposition to depression.

Biological rhythms have also been implicated in depression. Depressed patients enter REM sleep more quickly and have more of it. There is also evidence for abnormalities in a number of other biological rhythms, such as body temperature. Many people show a cyclical pattern of depression depending on the season. This disorder, known as **seasonal affective disorder** (SAD), results in periods of depression corresponding to the shorter days of winter in northern latitudes (Figure 16.9). Treatment with an artificial light source seems to alleviate the depression, possibly by resetting biological rhythms.

Although biological factors may play a role in depression, situational factors are also important. A number of studies have implicated life stressors in many cases of depression (Figure 16.10). One study estimated that in 50 percent of depressed subjects, stressful life events were a causal factor in the development of their depression. Another study found that depressed patients had more negative life events during the year before the onset of their depression (Dohrenwend et al., 1986). How an individual reacts to stress, however, can be influenced by interpersonal relationships. A person who has a close friend or group of friends is less likely to become depressed when faced with stress. This protective factor is not related to the number of friends, but to the quality of the friendships. One good friend is more protective than a large number of casual acquaintances.

Cognitive and behavioral factors may also play a role in depression. Depressed people take a negative view of their interactions with others, and others report having negative impressions of depressed people. This may be due to poor social skills in depressed people that result in a downward spiral (Dykman et al., 1991). More important than behavioral aspects, however, may be cognitive factors. Aaron T. Beck proposed that depressed people think about themselves, their situation, and the future in a negative manner, which he refers to as the *cognitive triad* (Beck, 1967, 1976; Beck et al., 1979, 1987). Misfortunes are blamed on personal defects whereas positive occurrences are seen as the result of luck. Nondepressed people tend to do the opposite. Beck also notes that depressed people make

16.9 For some people, there is a direct correspondence between the amount of sunlight and their levels of depression.

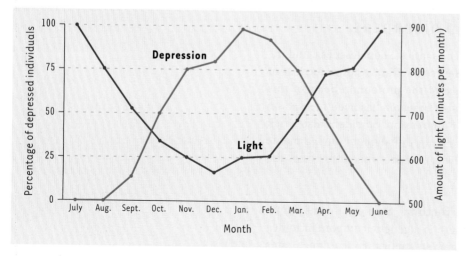

errors in logic, such as overgeneralizing based on single events, magnifying the seriousness of bad events, and personalizing, or taking responsibility for, bad events in the world that have little to do with them.

A second cognitive model of depression is the **learned helplessness model** (Seligman, 1974, 1975), in which people see themselves as unable to have any effect on events in their lives. Seligman's model is based on years of research demonstrating that animals placed in aversive situations that they cannot escape eventually become passive and unresponsive, lacking the motivation to try new methods of escape when given the opportunity. People suffering from learned helplessness come to expect that bad things will happen over which they will have little control. The attributions, or explanations, they make for negative events tend to refer to personal factors that are stable and global, rather than to situational factors that are temporary and specific. This attributional pattern leads people to feel hopeless about making positive changes in their lives (Abramson et al., 1989). The accumulation of evidence suggests that dysfunctional cognitive patterns are a cause rather than a consequence of depression.

Bipolar disorder is a biological disorder Although depression may arise from a variety of factors, there is strong evidence that bipolar disorder is predominantly a biological disorder. Twin studies reveal that the concordance for bipolar disorder in identical twins is upward of 70 percent, versus only 20 percent in fraternal or dizygotic twins (Nurnberger et al., 1994). In the 1980s, a genetic research study was carried out on the Amish, an ideal population because they keep good genealogical records and few outsiders marry into the community. In addition, substance abuse is virtually nonexistent, so mental illness is easier to detect. The results revealed that bipolar disorder ran in a limited number of families and that all of those afflicted had a similar genetic defect (Egeland et al., 1987).

Genetic research suggests that the hereditary nature of bipolar disorder is complex, and not linked to a single gene. Current research is focusing on identifying genes that may be involved. In addition, it appears that in families with bipolar disorder, successive generations tend to have more severe illness and earlier age of onset (McInnis et al., 1993; Petronis & Kennedy, 1995). This may be due to a particular type of genetic transmission, known as trinucleotide repeat expansion. Focus on this pattern of transmission may help to reveal the genetics of the disorder, but the specific nature of the heritability of bipolar disorder remains to be discovered.

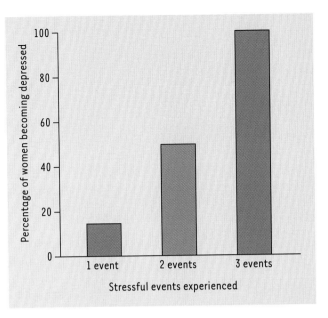

16.10 In this study, the greater the number of stressors, the more likely it was that people felt depressed.

Are Mood Disorders Extreme Manifestations of Normal Moods?

Although all people experience extreme moods and fluctuations in mood, mood disorders are qualitatively different from normal variations in emotion. Mood disorders disrupt the person's ability to function for significant lengths of time, and they are accompanied by a number of psychological and physiological elements. Depressive and bipolar disorders are included in the same DSM category and share some behavioral characteristics, but they are distinctly different disorders. Depressive disorders seem to result from a variety of psychological, cognitive, and biological factors, whereas bipolar disorders seem to arise from predominantly biological factors.

schizophrenia A mental disorder characterized by alterations in perceptions, emotions, thoughts, or consciousness.

positive symptoms Symptoms of schizophrenia, such as delusions and hallucinations, that are excesses in behavior.

negative symptoms Symptoms of schizophrenia marked by deficits in functioning such as apathy, lack of emotion, and slowed speech and movement.

IS SCHIZOPHRENIA A DISORDER OF MIND OR BODY?

Schizophrenia literally means "splitting of the mind" and refers to a split between thought and emotion. **Schizophrenia** is a *psychotic disorder*, which means that it is characterized by alterations in thoughts, perceptions, or consciousness. Currently, it is estimated that about 1 percent of the population has schizophrenia (Keith et al., 1991). In the 1940s and 1950s, researchers and clinicians broadened the definition of schizophrenia by proposing new subtypes and suggesting that schizophrenia could sometimes masquerade as other disorders. Because of these changes, by 1952, 80 percent of the patients in the New York Psychiatric Institute were diagnosed with schizophrenia, up from 20 percent in the 1930s. With more specific guidelines described in the recent editions of the *DSM*, the rate of schizophrenia diagnoses has stabilized (Manderscheid et al., 1985). Clinicians and researchers now rely on lists of symptoms to diagnose various subtypes of schizophrenia (Table 16.3).

SCHIZOPHRENIA HAS POSITIVE AND NEGATIVE SYMPTOMS

Schizophrenia is arguably the most devastating of the mental disorders for the victim and for the family. It is characterized by a combination of motor, cognitive, behavioral, and perceptual abnormalities that result in impaired social, personal, and/or vocational functioning. Some researchers have grouped these characteristics into two categories: **positive symptoms** are excesses whereas **negative symptoms** are deficits in functioning.

TABLE 16.3 DSM-IV Subtypes of Schizophrenia

SUBTYPE	CHARACTERISTICS
Paranoid type	Preoccupation with delusion(s) or auditory hallucinations. Little or no disorganized speech, disorganized or catatonic behavior, or inappropriate or flat affect.
Disorganized type	All the following—disorganized speech, disorganized behavior, and inappropriate or flat affect—are prominent in behavior, but catatonic-type criteria are not met. Delusions or hallucinations may be present, but only in fragmentary or noncoherent form.
Catatonic type	At least two of the following: extreme motor immobility; purposeless excessive motor activity; extreme negativism (motionless resistance to all instructions) or mutism (refusing to speak); peculiar or bizarre voluntary movement; echolalia.
Undifferentiated type	Does not fit any of the subtypes above, but meets the symptom criteria for schizophrenia.
Residual type	Has experienced at least one episode of schizophrenia, but currently does not have prominent positive symptoms (delusions, hallucinations, disorganized speech or behavior). However, continues to show negative symptoms and a milder variation of positive symptoms (odd beliefs, eccentric behavior).

SOURCE: Diagnostic and Statistical Manual of the American Psychiatric Association, 1994.

TABLE 16.4 Delusions and Associated Beliefs

Persecution	Belief that others are persecuting, spying on, or trying to harm them.
Reference	Belief that objects, events, or other people have particular significance to them.
Grandeur	Belief that they have great power, knowledge, or talent.
Identity	Belief that they are someone else, such as Jesus Christ or the President of the United States.
Guilt	Belief that they have committed a terrible sin.
Control	Belief that their thoughts and behaviors are being controlled by external forces.

Positive symptoms of schizophrenia   Delusions and hallucinations are the symptoms most commonly associated with schizophrenia. **Delusions** are false personal beliefs based on incorrect inferences about external reality (Table 16.4). Delusional people will persist in their beliefs in spite of evidence to the contrary. An example of a *paranoid delusion* arose in response to the Domino's Pizza advertising campaign "Avoid the Noid." The Noid was depicted as an elflike creature who turned pizzas cold. In 1989, Kenneth Noid, a 22-year-old Georgia man, concluded that this ad campaign was directed at him, and in retaliation he took two Domino's employees hostage. The hostages escaped and Kenneth Noid surrendered to the police.

Although delusions are characteristic of schizophrenia regardless of the culture, the type of delusion can be influenced by cultural factors (Tateyama et al., 1993). When the delusions of German and Japanese schizophrenia patients were compared, the two groups had similar rates of *delusions of grandeur*. However, there were significant differences between the two groups for other types of delusions. The German patients had delusions involving guilt and sin, particularly as these concepts related to religion. They also suffered from *delusions of persecution*, whereas the Japanese patients had delusions of harassment, such as the belief that they were being slandered by others.

Hallucinations, the other hallmark of schizophrenia, are perceptions with no clear external cause. Hallucinations are frequently auditory, although they can also be visual, olfactory, or somatosensory:

> I was afraid to go outside and when I looked out of the window, it seemed that everyone outside was yelling, "kill her, kill her." . . . Things continued to get worse. I imagined that I had a foul body odor and I sometimes took up to six showers a day. I recall going to the grocery store one day, and I imagined that the people in the store were saying "Get saved, Jesus is the answer." (O'Neal, 1984)

Auditory hallucinations are often voices giving a running commentary of what a person is doing. They can be accusatory, telling the person he is evil or inept, or they can command the person to do dangerous things. Sometimes the person hears a cacophony of environmental sounds with voices intermingled. Although the cause of hallucinations remains unclear, recent neuroimaging studies suggest that hallucinations are associated with activation in cortical areas that process external sensory stimuli. For example, auditory hallucinations accompany increased

delusions False personal beliefs based on incorrect inferences about reality.

hallucinations False sensory perceptions that are experienced without an external source.

loosening of associations A speech pattern among schizophrenic patients in which their thoughts are disorganized or meaningless.

activation in brain areas that are also activated in normal subjects when they engage in inner speech (Stein & Richardson, 1999). This has led to speculation that auditory hallucinations might be caused by a difficulty in distinguishing inner speech from external sounds.

Loosening of associations is another characteristic associated with schizophrenia, in which patients shift between seemingly unrelated topics as they speak, making it difficult or impossible for the listener to follow their train of thought:

> "They're destroying too many cattle and oil just to make soap. If we need soap when you can jump into a pool of water, and then when you go to buy your gasoline, my folks always thought they could get pop, but the best thing to get is motor oil, and money. May as well go there and trade in some pop caps and, uh, tires, and tractors to car garages, so they can pull cars away from wrecks, is what I believed in." (Andreasen, 1984)

In more extreme cases, *clang associations* become apparent—the stringing together of words that rhyme but that have no other apparent link.

Negative symptoms of schizophrenia A number of behavioral deficits associated with schizophrenia result in patients becoming isolated and withdrawn. People with schizophrenia often avoid eye contact and seem apathetic. They do not express emotion even when discussing emotional subjects, and they tend to use slowed speech, reduced speech output, and a monotonous tone of voice. This is characterized by such things as long pauses before answering, failing to respond to a question, or being unable to complete an utterance after it has been initiated. There is often a similar reduction in overt behavior; a patient's movements may be slowed and overall amount of movement reduced, with little initiation of behavior and no interest in social participation. These symptoms, while less dramatic than delusions and hallucinations, can be equally serious. Negative symptoms are more common in men than women (Raesaenen et al., 2000) and are associated with a poorer prognosis.

Interestingly, although the positive symptoms of schizophrenia can be dramatically reduced or eliminated with antipsychotic medications, the negative symptoms often persist. The fact that negative symptoms are often intractable to medications has led researchers to speculate that positive and negative symptoms may result from different organic causes. Since positive symptoms do respond to antipsychotic medications that act on neurotransmitter systems, these symptoms are thought to be the result of neurotransmitter dysfunction. In contrast, it has been speculated that negative symptoms are associated with neuroanatomical factors, since structural brain deficits are not affected by changes in neurochemistry.

SCHIZOPHRENIA IS PRIMARILY A BIOLOGICAL DISORDER

Although schizophrenia runs in families, the etiology of the disorder is complex and not well understood. It has been established that genetics plays a role in the development of schizophrenia (Figure 16.11). If one twin develops schizophrenia, the likelihood of the other also succumbing is almost 50 percent if the twins are identical, but only 14 percent if the twins are fraternal. If one parent has schizophrenia, the risk of the child developing the disease is 13 percent. If, however,

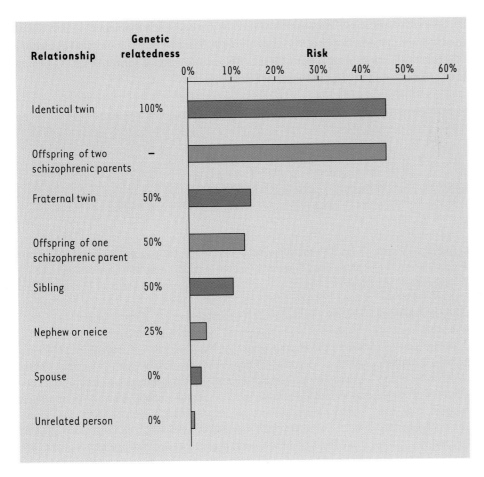

Relationship	Genetic relatedness	Risk
Identical twin	100%	
Offspring of two schizophrenic parents	–	
Fraternal twin	50%	
Offspring of one schizophrenic parent	50%	
Sibling	50%	
Nephew or neice	25%	
Spouse	0%	
Unrelated person	0%	

16.11 The more closely someone is genetically related to a person with schizophrenia, the greater is the risk that he or she will develop schizophrenia.

both parents have schizophrenia, the risk jumps to almost 50 percent (Gottesman, 1991). However, the genetic component of schizophrenia represents a predisposition rather than destiny. In 89 percent of those diagnosed with schizophrenia, there is no known relative with the disorder (Cromwell, 1993). In addition, if schizophrenia was caused solely by genetic factors, concordance in identical twins would approach 100 percent. Although this is true of the Genains, the identical quadruplets introduced at the beginning of the chapter, there is a marked difference in the severity of the disorder among the four sisters (Mirsky et al., 2000). Because they are identical genetically, the difference in severity of the disorder cannot be accounted for by genetic factors.

Since genetics does not fully account for the onset and severity of schizophrenia, there must be other factors at work. The rate of schizophrenia tends to be similar across cultures, suggesting that cultural influences play a relatively minor role. However, being born or raised in an urban area approximately doubles the risk of developing schizophrenia later in life (Torrey, 1999). Some have theorized that urban environments are more stressful and that the increased stress can trigger the onset of the disorder. Others have speculated that there may be some kind of *schizovirus*, and that living in the close quarters of a big city increases the likelihood of spreading the virus. In support of the virus hypothesis, some researchers have reported finding antibodies in the blood of schizophrenics that are not found in the blood of those without the disorder (Waltrip et al., 1997). In those at risk for schizophrenia, environmental stress does seem to contribute to its development. In a study of adopted children whose biological mothers were diagnosed with schizophrenia, it was found that if the adoptive families were psychologically healthy, none of the children became psychotic, but if the adoptive families were severely disturbed, 11 percent of the children became psychotic and 41 percent had severe psychological disorders (Tienari et al., 1990, 1994). For a further discussion of schizophrenia see "Crossing the Levels of Analysis: Understanding Schizophrenia."

Crossing the Levels of Analysis

UNDERSTANDING SCHIZOPHRENIA

Consider the following two epidemiological observations: First, those diagnosed with schizophrenia are more likely to be born during the late winter and early spring (Torrey et al., 1977; Mednick et al., 1994). Second, in the western Netherlands in 1945, there was a severe famine resulting from a Nazi blockade, and babies born in the few months following the famine grew up to have twice the rate of schizophrenia as other Netherlanders (Susser et al., 1996). Taken together, these two seemingly disparate findings may help us understand the etiology of schizophrenia. Mothers of children born in the late winter and early spring are in their second trimester of pregnancy during flu season. Retrospective studies suggest that the mothers of those with schizophrenia are more likely than other mothers to have contracted influenza during this critical period. In the second group of subjects described above, malnutrition caused by the famine may have similarly damaged the fetuses during the second trimester of pregnancy.

Why is the second trimester so important? The answer comes from neuroembryology. During the second trimester a great deal of fetal brain development occurs. New cells are being created and are migrating to the cortical plate where they orient themselves and establish connections with other nerve cells. Thus the cortical plate is critical to the formation of proper neuronal connectivity in the brain. It has been demonstrated that abnormalities in the brains of those with schizophrenia are related to problems in the development of the cortical plate. Trauma or pathogens in the second trimester have the potential to interfere with neuronal migration, resulting in disordered connectivity in these critical brain regions.

Studies of identical twins provide yet another piece of the puzzle. In identical twins, the embryo splits in two any time up until the fifteenth day after conception. If the embryo splits by day four, the twins are identical genetically and in every physical way. If the embryo splits later, the twins are more likely to be mirror images of each other, with opposite handedness. Early splitters have separate placentas, whereas late-splitting twins usually share the same placenta, which means they share the same blood supply as well as any viruses that pass through that blood supply. Therefore, if prenatal exposure to viruses does play a role in the etiology of schizophrenia, then late-splitting twins should be more likely to be concordant for schizophrenia than early splitters. There is evidence that this is true. For twins who have the same hand preference, the concordance rate for schizophrenia is 32 percent. In contrast, for twins who have opposite handedness, the rate is 60 percent. This shows not only that there is a strong genetic component to schizophrenia, but that the prenatal environment plays a role in the development of the disorder.

Twin studies have also helped to pinpoint the critical period within the second trimester. The formation of fingerprints is largely genetic. Identical twins, therefore, have virtually identical fingerprints. If there are differences in fingerprints between twins, it is due to external factors. The number and shape of fingerprint ridges, loops, whorls, and arches are created at different points during prenatal development. Fingerprints at the tips of the fingers develop from the eleventh to the thirteenth week. The fingerprints at the base of the fingers do not develop until the fifteenth week. Researchers examining the fingerprints of identical twins discordant for schizophrenia have found differences at the base of the index and third fingers. This suggests that one of the twins sustained some kind of prenatal insult during the early part of the second trimester.

Some have proposed that these early neurological insults are a kind of "second hit." For those who have a genetic predisposition to schizophrenia, abnormal neural circuitry or structural damage interacts with genetic vulnerability to increase the likelihood of developing the disorder, or perhaps increases the severity of the disorder if it is expressed.

Although neurological dysfunction may occur early in life, schizophrenic symptoms do not develop until late adolescence or early adulthood. How can brain damage present at or before birth cause the onset of schizophrenia many years later? Exciting new research in brain development provides a possible explanation. Until recently it was believed that the brain was fully developed long before children reached puberty. A combination of postmortem analyses and *in vivo* brain-imaging studies has conclusively shown this to be false. During adolescence, many neural circuits are being reorganized and consolidated, resulting in more efficient circuitry and more rapid neural transmission. This process is not complete until people reach their early twenties, when schizophrenic symptoms are most likely to emerge. The combination of more efficient circuitry and more rapid neural transmission could overload defective brain structures and result in the onset of schizophrenia.

Is Schizophrenia a Disorder of Mind or Body?

Schizophrenia consists of negative and positive symptoms, and it is at least in part a biological disorder. Twin and adoption studies have highlighted the critical role of genetics in the development of schizophrenia, and recent advances in genetic analysis have begun to yield more insights into the complexities of this disorder. In addition, research suggests that there are neurochemical and neuroanatomical anomalies in the brains of those afflicted with schizophrenia. Despite all of this evidence, however, the specific ways in which genetics, neurochemistry, and neuroanatomy contribute to this disorder remain unclear. Also, most researchers would agree that environmental factors play a role in the development of schizophrenia, but little is known about how the environment interacts with biological factors.

ARE PERSONALITY DISORDERS TRULY MENTAL DISORDERS?

Personality is each person's unique way of responding to the environment. Although people do change somewhat over time, the ways we interact with the world and cope with events tend to be fairly fixed by the end of adolescence. Some people interact with the world in ways that are maladaptive and inflexible. When this style of interaction is long-lasting and causes problems in work and social situations, it becomes a **personality disorder**. All of us at some point have likely exhibited at least some of the symptoms of personality disorders. We might be indecisive, self-absorbed, or emotionally unstable. Why isn't everyone diagnosed with a personality disorder? In general, those with true personality disorders consistently behave in maladaptive ways, whereas most people do so only on occasion. In addition, those with personality disorders show a more extreme level of maladaptive behavior and consequently experience more personal distress and more problems as a result of their behavior.

PERSONALITY DISORDERS ARE MALADAPTIVE WAYS OF RELATING TO THE WORLD

While the other disorders discussed in this chapter are classified on Axis I (see Table 16.1), the personality disorders are classified on Axis II, along with mental retardation. The personality disorders and mental retardation are grouped together because they both usually last throughout the life span with no expectation of significant change.

The personality disorders are generally divided into three groups, as listed in Table 16.5. People with the first group of disorders display odd or eccentric behavior. *Paranoid, schizoid,* and *schizotypal* personality disorders are included in this group. People with these personality disorders are often reclusive and suspicious. They have difficulty forming personal relationships because of their strange behavior and aloofness. The second group—*histrionic, narcissistic, borderline,* and *antisocial* personality disorders—is characterized by dramatic, emotional, and erratic behaviors. Borderline and antisocial personality disorders have been the focus of a great deal of research, and they are considered in more detail in the following sections. The third group of personality disorders—*avoidant, dependent,* and *obsessive-compulsive*—involves anxious or fearful behaviors.

How are personality disorders defined?

personality disorder A class of mental disorders marked by inflexible and maladaptive ways of interacting with the world.

TABLE 16.5 Personality Disorders and Associated Characteristics

ODD OR ECCENTRIC BEHAVIOR

Paranoid	Tense, guarded, suspicious; holds grudges.
Schizoid	Socially isolated, with restricted emotional expression.
Schizotypal	Peculiarities of thought, appearance, and behavior that are disconcerting to others; emotionally detached and isolated.

DRAMATIC, EMOTIONAL, OR ERRATIC BEHAVIOR

Histrionic	Seductive behavior; needs immediate gratification and constant reassurance; rapidly changing moods; shallow emotions.
Narcissistic	Self-absorbed; expects special treatment and adulation; envious of attention to others.
Borderline	Cannot stand to be alone; intense, unstable moods and personal relationships; chronic anger; drug and alcohol abuse.
Antisocial	Manipulative, exploitive; dishonest; disloyal; lacking in guilt; habitually breaks social rules; childhood history of such behavior; often in trouble with the law.

ANXIOUS OR FEARFUL BEHAVIOR

Avoidant	Easily hurt and embarrassed; few close friends; sticks to routines to avoid new and possibly stressful experiences.
Dependent	Wants others to make decisions; needs constant advice and reassurance; fears being abandoned.
Obsessive-compulsive	Perfectionistic; overconscientious; indecisive; preoccupied with details; stiff; unable to express affection.

Personality disorders remain controversial in modern clinical practice for a variety of reasons. First, personality disorders appear to be extreme or exaggerated versions of normal personality traits. For example, indecisiveness is characteristic of obsessive-compulsive personality disorder, but the *DSM* does not define the degree to which someone must be indecisive in order to be diagnosed as obsessive-compulsive. Second, there is overlap among the traits listed as characteristic of different personality disorders, so that the majority of people who are diagnosed with one personality disorder also meet the criteria for another personality disorder. This suggests that the categories may not be mutually exclusive and that there actually may be fewer types of personality disorders than are listed in the *DSM*.

It may seem that personality disorders do not have as large an impact on daily life as do some of the Axis I disorders discussed in this chapter. However, although people with personality disorders do not hallucinate or have radical mood swings, their ways of interacting with the world can have serious consequences. An in-depth consideration of borderline personality disorder and antisocial personality disorder will illustrate the devastating effect these disorders can have on the individual, family and friends, and society in general.

BORDERLINE PERSONALITY DISORDER IS ASSOCIATED WITH POOR SELF-CONTROL

Borderline personality disorder, characterized by identity, affective, and impulse disturbances, was officially recognized as a diagnosis in 1980. The term "borderline" was initially used because these patients were considered to be on the border between normal and psychotic (Knight, 1953). The wide variety of clinical features of this disorder reflects its complexity (see Table 16.6).

People with borderline personality disorder do not seem to have a strong sense of self. They cannot tolerate being alone and have an intense fear of abandonment. Because they desperately need an exclusive and dependent relationship with another person, they can be very manipulative in their attempts to control relationships.

> A borderline patient periodically rented a motel room and, with a stockpile of pills nearby, would call her therapist's home with an urgent message. He would respond by engaging in long conversations in which he "talked her down." Even as he told her that she could not count on his always being available, he became more wary of going out evenings without detailed instructions about how he could be reached. One night the patient couldn't reach him due to a bad phone connection. She fatally overdosed from what was probably a miscalculated manipulation. (Gunderson, 1984, p. 93)

In addition to problems with identity, borderline individuals also have affective disturbances. Emotional instability is paramount, with episodes of depression, anxiety, anger, and irritability that are often sudden and last from a few hours to a few days. Shifts from one mood to another usually occur with no clear precipitating cause.

borderline personality disorder A personality disorder characterized by identity, affective, and impulse disturbances.

TABLE 16.6 Clinical Features of Borderline Personality Disorder

A person having at least five of these characteristics might be considered to have a borderline personality disorder.

1. Employment of frantic efforts to avoid real or imagined abandonment.

2. Unstable and intense interpersonal relationships.

3. Persistent and markedly disturbed, distorted, or unstable sense of self (e.g., a feeling that one doesn't exist or that one embodies evil).

4. Impulsiveness in such areas as sex, substance use, crime, and reckless driving.

5. Recurrent suicidal thoughts, gestures, or behavior.

6. Emotional instability, with periods of extreme depression, irritability, or anxiety.

7. Chronic feelings of emptiness.

8. Inappropriate intense anger or lack of control of anger (e.g., loss of temper, recurrent physical fights).

9. Transient, stress-related paranoid thoughts or severe dissociative symptoms.

SOURCE: Diagnostic and Statistical Manual of the American Psychiatric Association, 1994.

Impulsivity is the third hallmark of borderline personality disorder. Impulsive behaviors can include sexual promiscuity, physical fighting, and binge eating and purging. The impulsive behavior most commonly associated with this disorder, however, is self-mutilation. Cutting and burning of the skin are typical behaviors for those with the disorder, who are also at high risk for suicide.

Although a few studies have been done on the genetics of borderline personality disorder, it remains unclear whether heredity is involved. There tend to be high rates of mood disorders in the families of borderline patients, and these patients often show sleep abnormalities characteristic of depression. One possible reason that borderline personality disorder and affective disorders such as depression may be linked is that both appear to involve the neurotransmitter serotonin. Evidence has linked low serotonin levels to the impulsive behavior seen in borderline personality disorder.

A strong relationship exists between borderline personality disorder and trauma or abuse. Some studies have reported that 70–80 percent of patients with borderline personality disorder have experienced physical or sexual abuse or observed some kind of extreme violence. Consider the following case of a young woman with borderline personality disorder:

> [When Roberta was in fourth grade, her] oldest brother, Sam, turned fifteen and began babysitting his younger siblings two evenings a week while his mother went to Bingo and his father was out with "the boys." On one of these evenings, a few weeks after he'd started babysitting, Sam decided to "help" Roberta with her bath. Overriding her protests with the statement that he was in charge while their parents were gone, he demanded that she stand naked in front of him so that he could "make sure I was clean." Gradually, over the next several months, Sam's demands escalated. He watched her undress. He watched her urinate. By spring he had begun to masturbate as he watched her. (Bernheim, 1997, pp. 257–58)

Other theories implicate early interactions with caretakers. It has been suggested that borderline patients had caretakers who were not accepting of them, reliable, or available. The constant rejection and criticism made it difficult for the individual to learn to regulate emotions and understand emotional reactions to events (Linehan, 1987). An alternative theory is that caregivers may have encouraged dependence, and therefore individuals do not adequately develop a sense of self. They become extremely sensitive to the reactions of others, and if they are rejected, they reject themselves.

ANTISOCIAL PERSONALITY DISORDER IS ASSOCIATED WITH A LACK OF EMPATHY

In the 1800s, the term "psychopath" was coined to describe people who seem willing to take advantage of and hurt others without any evidence of concern or remorse (Koch, 1891). The *DSM* dropped this pejorative label and adopted the term **antisocial personality disorder**. This disorder is distinguished not so much by particular behaviors as by an approach to life, the most salient feature being a lack of remorse. Those with antisocial personality disorder tend to be hedonistic, seeking immediate gratification of wants and needs without any thought of others. Because they lack empathy, their interpersonal relationships tend to be shallow at best. They are very impulsive and engage in sensation-seeking behavior, as is

antisocial personality disorder A personality disorder marked by a lack of empathy and remorse.

illustrated in the following case of Gary Gilmore (Figure 16.12), who was sentenced to death for the murder he describes here.

"I went in and told the guy to give me the money. I told him to lay on the floor and then I shot him. I then walked out and was carrying the cash drawer with me. I took the money and threw the cash drawer in a bush and I tried to push the gun in the bush, too. But as I was pushing it in the bush, it went off and that's how come I was shot in the arm. It seems like things have always gone bad for me. It seems like I've always done dumb things that just caused trouble for me. I remember when I was a boy I would feel like I had to do things like sit on a railroad track until just before the train came and then I would dash off. Or I would put my finger over the end of a BB gun and pull the trigger to see if a BB was really in it. Sometimes I would stick my finger in water and then put my finger in a light socket to see if it would really shock me." (Spitzer et al., 1983, pp. 66–68)

Characteristics of antisocial personality disorder Antisocial personality disorder is surprisingly common, with an estimated lifetime prevalence of 4.5 percent in men and 0.8 percent in women (Robins & Regier, 1991). Interestingly, the disorder is most apparent in late adolescence and early adulthood, and it appears to remit around age 40 (Hare et al., 1988). A diagnosis of antisocial personality disorder cannot be made before age 18, but the person must have displayed antisocial conduct before age 15. This stipulation ensures that only those with a lifetime history of antisocial behaviors can be diagnosed with antisocial personality disorder. The individual must also meet criteria such as repeatedly performing illegal acts, repeated lying or use of aliases, and reckless disregard for their own safety or the safety of others. Many of these individuals can be quite bright and highly verbal, and as a result many can talk their way out of bad situations. In any event, punishment seems to have very little effect on them (Lykken, 1957, 1995), and they often repeat the problem behavior a short time later.

16.12 Gary Gilmore after his arrest. He would have been given the diagnosis of antisocial personality disorder under the *DSM-IV*.

It has been estimated that 40–75 percent of the prison population meet the criteria for antisocial personality disorder (Hare, 1993; Widiger & Corbitt, 1995), but not everyone with this disorder engages in criminal behavior. Because of the prevalence of the disorder in the prison population, much of the research on antisocial personality disorder has been conducted in this setting. One researcher, however, came up with an ingenious way of finding research participants outside of prison. She put the following advertisement in a counterculture newspaper:

Wanted: charming, aggressive, carefree people who are impulsively irresponsible but are good at handling people and at looking after number one. Send name, address, phone, and short biography proving how interesting you are to . . . (Widom, 1978, p. 72)

Seventy-three people responded to the ad, about one-third of whom met the criteria for antisocial personality disorder. These individuals were then interviewed and given a battery of psychological tests. It was found that their characteristics were very similar to those of prisoners diagnosed with antisocial personality disorder, except that the group who responded to the ad had been able to avoid imprisonment.

The causes of antisocial personality disorder In 1957, David Lykken reported that psychopaths did not become anxious when subjected to aversive stimuli. He and other investigators have continued this line of work, showing that psychopathic individuals do not seem to feel fear or anxiety (Lykken, 1995). EEG examinations have demonstrated that criminals who meet the criteria for antisocial personality disorder have slower alpha-wave activity (Raine, 1989). This indicates a lower overall level of arousal and may explain why these people often engage in sensation-seeking behavior. It also may explain why they do not learn from punishment—because of their low arousal, they do not experience punishment as particularly aversive. Deficits in frontal lobe functioning have also been found and may account for the lack of forethought and the inability to consider the implications of actions characteristic of antisocial personality disorder.

To what can we attribute these biological correlates of antisocial personality disorder? There is good evidence for both genetics and the environment. Identical twins have a higher concordance of criminal behavior than do fraternal twins (Lykken, 1995), although this research did not rule out the role of shared environment. A large study of 14,000 adoptions (Mednick et al., 1987) found that adopted male children had a higher rate of crime if their biological fathers had criminal records. In addition, the more entrenched the criminal behavior of the biological father, the more likely it was that the adopted son had engaged in criminal behavior. Although genetics may be at the root of antisocial behaviors, such factors as low socioeconomic status, dysfunctional families, and childhood abuse may also play important roles.

Are Personality Disorders Truly Mental Disorders?

Personality disorders are diagnosed along a different axis than are the other mental disorders discussed thus far. Personality disorders are not considered clinical disorders, yet they can have devastating effects on the individual, the family, and society. Borderline personality disorder is characterized by identity, affective, and impulse disturbances. Those with the disorder often have a history of abuse or rejection by caregivers. Those with antisocial personality disorder are hedonistic and sensation seeking, and they lack empathy for others. Although the outward symptoms of these disorders are not as severe as those of some of the clinical disorders, they are highly resistant to change, and the ways these individuals interact with others cause significant personal and societal problems.

SHOULD CHILDHOOD DISORDERS BE CONSIDERED A UNIQUE CATEGORY?

When Emil Kraepelin published his classic text on the classification of mental disorders in 1883, no mention was made of childhood disorders. The first edition of the *DSM*, published 70 years later, also considered children to be essentially mini versions of adults, and consequently disorders of childhood were not considered separately from disorders of adulthood. Currently, in response to the belief that cognitive, emotional, and social abilities should be considered in the context of the individual's developmental state, the *DSM* has a category in Axis I called "disorders usually first diagnosed in infancy, childhood, or adolescence." This category includes a wide range of disorders, from those affecting only circumscribed areas of a child's world, such as reading disorders and stuttering, to those affecting every aspect of a child's life, such as autism and attention-deficit/

Can children have mental disorders?

TABLE 16.7 Childhood Disorders

DISORDER	DESCRIPTION
Attention-Deficit/Hyperactivity Disorder	A pattern of hyperactive, inattentive, and impulsive behavior that causes social or academic impairment.
Autism	Characterized by unresponsiveness; impaired language, social, and cognitive development; and restricted and repetitive behavior.
Elimination Disorders	The repeated passing of feces or urination in inappropriate places by children from whom continence should be expected.
Learning Disorders	Marked by substantially low performance in reading, mathematics, or written expression with regard to what is expected for age, amount of education, and intelligence.
Mental Retardation	Characterized by below average intellectual functioning (IQ less than 70) and limited adaptive functioning that begins before age 18.
Rumination Disorder	The repeated regurgitation and re-chewing of partially digested food, not related to nausea or gastrointestinal disorder.
Selective Mutism	Failure to speak in certain social situations, despite the ability to speak in other situations; interferes with social or academic achievement.
Tourette's Disorder	Recurrent motor and vocal tics that cause marked distress or impairment and are not related to a general medical condition.

hyperactivity disorder (see Table 16.7). Despite the variety of disorders in this category, all should be considered within the context of knowledge about normal childhood development. Some symptoms of childhood mental disorders represent extreme manifestations of normal behavior or actually are normal behaviors for children at an earlier developmental stage. Bedwetting, for example, is normal for two-year-olds but not for ten-year-olds. Other behaviors, however, deviate significantly from normal development. Two disorders of childhood, autism and attention-deficit/hyperactivity disorder, will be explored to illustrate this issue.

AUTISM IS A LACK OF AWARENESS OF OTHERS

Autism is characterized by deficits in social interaction, impaired communication, and restricted interests. Autism was first described in 1943 by Leo Kanner, who was struck by the profound isolation of some children and coined the term "early infantile autism." Kanner described the syndrome in the following way: "There is from the start an extreme autistic aloneness that, whenever possible, disregards, ignores, shuts out anything that comes to the child from the outside." When people think of autism, they often imagine a beautiful, graceful child who seems tragically shut off from the world. Some autistic children are beautiful, and there is a tendency for autistics to walk on their toes, which might have given rise to the myth of gracefulness. However, autistic children usually look the same as

autism A developmental disorder involving deficits in social interaction, impaired communication, and restricted interests.

IDIOT SAVANTS

Autistic individuals who have an area of great ability are sometimes referred to as "idiot savants," a label that suggests an oasis of brilliance in an otherwise bleak cognitive profile. Some savants are talented artists and musicians. Their artistry, however, is generally characterized by an amazing ability to mimic what they see or hear, rather than a capacity for creativity. Another area of brilliance typical in savants is calculation. The ability to tell almost instantly what day of the week a particular date fell on in the distant past or future is mind-boggling to most of us. Some have concluded that idiot savants who are able to do this type of calculation are resorting to some type of calendrical algorithm. Oliver Sacks, in *The Man Who Mistook His Wife for a Hat*, questions this conclusion. He describes autistic twins who seem to have numerical abilities that defy explanation:

> A box of matches on their table fell, and discharged its contents on the floor: "111," they both cried simultaneously; and then, in a murmur, John said "37." Michael repeated this, John said it a third time and stopped. I counted the matches—it took me some time—and there were 111.
>
> "How could you count the matches so quickly?" I asked. "We didn't count," they said. "We *saw* the 111." (Sacks, 1985, p. 188)

Pursuing the conversation further, Sacks realized the reason behind the three repetitions of the number 37: $37+37+37=111$. They had factored 111 into three equal parts. More astonishingly, he observed the twins later in a more complex numerical "game":

They seemed to be locked in a singular, purely numerical, converse. John would say a number—a six-figure number. Michael would catch the number, nod, smile and seem to savour it. Then he, in turn, would say another six-figure number, and now it was John who received, and appreciated it richly. They looked, at first, like two connoisseurs wine-tasting, sharing rare tastes, rare appreciations.

What were they doing? . . . I already had a hunch. . . . *All the numbers, the six-figure numbers, which the twins had exchanged, were primes*—i.e., numbers that could be evenly divided by no other whole number than itself or one. . . . Were they, in some unimaginable way, themselves "seeing" primes, in somewhat the same way as they had "seen" 111-ness, or triple 37-ness? Certainly they could not be *calculating* them—they could calculate nothing. (Sacks, 1985, pp. 191–192)

The way in which the twins were generating these prime numbers remains mysterious, as do the mechanisms behind many of the talents possessed by idiot savants. The relation of these exceptional abilities to brain function has been the source of much speculation. Some researchers argue that processes such as attention are at the root of savant abilities, proposing that autistics tend to process the physical characteristics of stimuli exclusively without attending to meaningful aspects. Other researchers invoke neural explanations, suggesting that perhaps cortical space usually devoted to language is reallocated to other functions. This is an intriguing idea that suggests how our brains might be organized. As yet, however, the reasons for savant abilities remain unknown.

---

any other children, and they are often clumsier than normal children. Another misconception about autistic children is that they often have some area of great skill. These remarkable children are the subject of "Studying the Mind: Idiot Savants." But whereas some autistics do have such talents, most do not.

Core symptoms of autism   Autistic children are seemingly unaware of others. As babies, they do not smile at their caregivers, they do not respond to vocalizations, and they often actively reject physical contact with others. Autistic children do not establish eye contact and do not use gaze to either gain or direct the attention of those around them. One group of researchers had participants view video footage of autistic children's first birthdays to see if autistic characteristics could be detected before the child was diagnosed with autism (Osterling & Dawson, 1994). By considering only the number of times a child looked at another person's face, the participants correctly classified the children as either autistic or normal 77 percent of the time (see Figure 16.13).

Deficits in communication are the second major cluster of behaviors characteristic of autism. Autistic children show severe impairments in both verbal and nonverbal communication. Even if they do vocalize, it is often not with any intent to communicate. Autistics who develop language often exhibit odd speech patterns, such as **echolalia** and *pronoun reversal*. Echolalia is the repetition of words or phrases, sometimes including an imitation of the intonation and sometimes using a high-pitched monotone. Pronoun reversal, in which autistic children may replace "I" with "you," may be related to echolalia. Even if a child ceases being echolalic, pronoun confusion often persists. Autistic children who develop functional language also often interpret words in a literal manner, use language inappropriately, and lack verbal spontaneity.

A third category of deficits is restricted activities and interests. Although autistic children appear to be oblivious to the people around them, they are acutely aware of their surroundings. Any changes in the daily routine or in the placement of furniture or toys is very upsetting and can result in extreme agitation and tantrums. Autistic children also do not play in the same way as other children. Their play tends to be stereotyped and obsessive, and the focus is often on the sensory aspects of objects. They may smell and taste objects, or spin and flick them for the visual stimulation. Similarly, their own behavior tends to be stereotyped, with ritualistic hand movements, body rocking, and hand flapping. Self-abuse is common, and in some cases children must be forcibly restrained to keep them from hurting themselves.

Autism is a biological disorder   Kanner believed autism was an innate disorder that was exacerbated by cold and unresponsive mothers, whom he called "ice box mothers" or "refrigerator mothers." He described the parents of autistic children as insensitive, meticulous, introverted, and highly intellectual. This view is given little credence today, as it is now well established that autism is the result of biological factors, the specific nature of which is still undetermined. Genetic studies of autism have been hampered by the rarity of the disorder and by the fact that autistic persons rarely marry and almost never have children. Despite the limited genetic research, there are indications that the disorder has a hereditary component. If one child in a family is autistic, the probability of a second also being diagnosed is anywhere from 2 to 9 percent (Szatzmari et al., 1993; Jorde et al., 1990). Although this risk is relatively low, it is significantly higher than the estimated 0.4 percent prevalence of the disorder in the population at large. If two siblings are autistic, the chances of a third sharing the same diagnosis jumps to 35 percent. A number of studies have found concordance rates in twins to be 70–90 percent for monozygotic twins and 10 percent for dizygotic twins (Steffenburg et al., 1989; Bailey et al., 1995).

Research into the causes of autism points to prenatal and/or neonatal events that may result in brain dysfunction. In some cases, mothers of autistic children have experienced significant bleeding during the second trimester of pregnancy, suggesting some kind of insult during the critical period for neuronal development. Autistic children also have a higher rate of neonatal complications such as apnea, seizures, and delay in breathing. Moreover, autistic children are more likely to have minor physical anomalies, to be the product of a first pregnancy, and to be born to older mothers (Gilberg, 1980).

Two exciting new research developments may help to focus the future of autism research. A deficit in oxytocin, a neuropeptide involved in social behavior, may be related to some of the behavioral manifestations of autism. It has been demonstrated that mice lacking oxytocin behave normally, except that they cannot recognize other mice or their mother's scent. A single dose of oxytocin cured them (Ferguson et al., 2000). In a preliminary study, autistic adults who received injections of oxytocin showed a dramatic improvement in their symptoms

16.13 Scenes from videotapes of children's birthday parties. The child in (a) focused more on objects than on people and was later diagnosed with autism. The child in (b) developed normally.

echolalia The repetition of words or phrases that is characteristic of children with autism.

(Novotny et al., 2000). A second recent finding suggests that levels of four proteins in the blood are elevated in 97 percent of autistic children and 92 percent of retarded children, but in none of the healthy controls. These elevated protein levels were found in blood samples taken at birth, and all four proteins are involved in brain development (Nelson et al., 2001). The cause of these elevated protein levels and the role they play in the development of autism are matters for future research.

ATTENTION-DEFICIT/HYPERACTIVITY DISORDER IS A DISRUPTIVE BEHAVIOR DISORDER

A hyperactive child's mother might report that he has difficulty remembering not to trail his dirty hand along the clean wall as he runs from the front door to the kitchen. His peers may find that he spontaneously changes the rules while playing Monopoly or soccer. His teacher notes that he asks what he is supposed to do immediately after detailed instructions were presented to the entire class. He may make warbling noises or other strange sounds that inadvertently disturb anyone nearby. He may seem to have more than his share of accidents—knocking over the tower his classmates are erecting, spilling his cranberry juice on the linen tablecloth, or tripping over the television cord while retrieving the family cat—and thereby disconnecting the set in the middle of the Super Bowl game. (Whalen, 1989)

We can laugh at this description, yet most of us have come into contact with children like this. Although the symptoms can seem humorous in the retelling, the reality is a different story. Children with **attention-deficit/hyperactivity disorder (ADHD)** are restless, inattentive, and impulsive. They need to have directions repeated and rules explained over and over. Although these children are often friendly and talkative, they can have trouble making and keeping friends because they miss subtle social cues and make unintentional social mistakes. Note that many of these symptoms are exaggerations of the typical behavior of toddlers. This makes the line between normal and abnormal behavior hard to draw—as many as 50 percent of mothers of four-year-old boys believe their sons are hyperactive (Varley, 1984).

The etiology of (ADHD)   The American Psychiatric Association (1994) estimates that 3–5 percent of children have ADHD, although estimates from other sources vary widely, with some estimates as high as 20 percent (Gillis et al., 1992). The causes of the disorder are unknown; one of the difficulties in pinpointing the etiology is that ADHD is most likely a heterogeneous disorder. In other words, the behavioral profiles of children with ADHD vary, so it is likely that the causes of the disorder vary as well. There is some suggestion that children with ADHD are more likely than other children to grow up in disturbed families. This finding has led researchers to speculate that there may be a psychological component to the disorder. Factors such as poor parenting and social disadvantage may contribute to the onset of symptoms. Whether psychological factors are the cause or effect of the disorder, however, is not always clear. Most current research is focused on biological factors contributing to the development of ADHD.

There is clearly a genetic component to ADHD, with a 10–35 percent incidence of the disorder in families of those diagnosed with ADHD (Biederman et al., 1990, 1992). Concordance is estimated at 55 percent in monozygotic twins and

attention-deficit/hyperactivity disorder (ADHD) A disorder characterized by restless, inattentive, and impulsive behaviors.

32 percent in dizygotic twins (Goodman & Stevenson, 1989; Sherman et al., 1997). Although it is clear that something is inherited in ADHD, the question is what. In a positron-emission study, Zametkin and his colleagues (1990) found that adults who had been diagnosed with ADHD in childhood had reduced metabolism in brain regions involved in self-regulation of motor functions and attentional systems (Figure 16.14). He postulated that the frontolimbic system was impaired in ADHD patients. The symptoms of ADHD are similar to those seen in patients with frontal lobe damage: problems with planning, sustaining concentration, using feedback, and thinking flexibly. Current research continues to focus on underarousal of the frontal lobes (Barkely, 1997; Neidemeyer & Naidu, 1997) but also implicates subcortical structures. In particular, researchers have demonstrated differences in the basal ganglia, and specifically the caudate nucleus, in the brains of some ADHD patients (Aylward et al., 1996; Castellanos et al., 1998; Fillipek et al., 1997; Hynd et al., 1993). These regions are involved in regulation of motor behavior and impulse control, and dysfunction in these structures could contribute to the hyperactivity characteristic of ADHD.

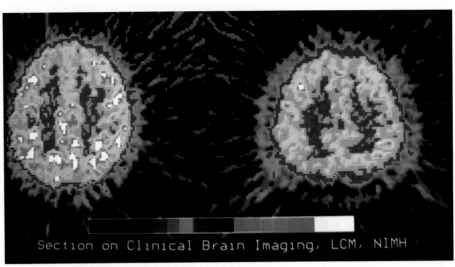

Section on Clinical Brain Imaging, LCM, NIMH

16.14 During PET scanning, the brain of the person on the right, who has a history of ADHD, shows lesser overall activation, especially in frontal and limbic regions.

ADHD across the life span   Children are not generally given a diagnosis of ADHD until they enter a structured setting in which they are expected to conform to rules, get along with peers, and sit in a seat for long periods of time. In the past, this happened when children entered school, between the ages of five and seven. Now, with the increasing prevalence of structured day-care settings, the demands on children to conform are occurring much earlier. While it is not unreasonable to expect a six-year-old to sit quietly and share crayons, it is probably unrealistic to expect the same of a three-year-old. Many preschoolers who are considered inattentive and overactive by their parents and teachers are simply going through a normal developmental stage that will not become the persistent pattern of ADHD. There are some characteristics that discriminate between children who go on to develop ADHD and those who do not. Infants who are later diagnosed with ADHD have difficulty establishing regular patterns for eating and sleeping (Ross & Ross, 1982). Toddlers exhibit excessive activity and temperamental behavior quite early in life (Hartsough & Lambert, 1985). They are very curious and engage in vigorous play, and consequently they tend to be quite accident-prone. Older children do not generally demonstrate excess motor activity but are instead restless and fidgety (Pelham & Bender, 1982).

It was previously thought that children outgrew ADHD by the time they entered adulthood. More recent longitudinal studies, however, dispute this notion. Between 30 and 80 percent of those with ADHD in childhood continued to show symptoms of this disorder in adulthood (Weiss & Hechtman, 1993). Adults with ADHD symptoms may struggle both academically and vocationally. They generally reach a lower-than-expected socioeconomic level and change jobs more frequently (Bellak & Black, 1992; Mannuzza et al., 1991). The impact of ADHD on society is apparently greater than previously believed. However, some ADHD patients do learn to adapt and are successful in their personal and vocational lives.

Should Childhood Disorders Be Considered a Unique Category?

Until recently, children were considered to be mini versions of adults, and mental disorders in children were classified using adult categories. Currently, it is understood that disorders in children should be considered in the context of normal development. In some cases, mental disorders identified in childhood have a lasting impact on the individual, and the problems apparent early in life continue throughout maturation. This is clearly the case for autism, in which the social and cognitive characteristics of the disorder deviate significantly from normal childhood development and continue to have a major impact throughout the life span. The impact of childhood ADHD on adult functioning is less certain.

CONCLUSION

Mental disorders are ultimately disorders of both mind and body. Although the specific factors that cause these disorders are still under investigation, exciting new research that crosses the levels of analysis continues to bring us closer to an understanding of mental disorders and of the ways in which psychological and physiological factors interact to produce normal and deviant behavior. In this chapter, we have explored the nature and causes of psychopathology. In the following chapter, we will consider the ways in which this knowledge can be used to develop treatment strategies for these devastating disorders.

FURTHER READINGS

Grandin, T., & Scariano, M. M. (1986). *Emergence: Labeled autistic*. Novato, CA: Arena Press.

Jamison, K. R. (1995). *An unquiet mind*. New York: Vintage Books.

Kaysen, S. (1948). *Girl, interrupted*. New York: Turtle Bay Books.

Lachenmeyer, N. (1969). *The outsider: A journey into my father's struggle with madness*. New York: Broadway Books.

Lezak, M. D. (1995). *Neuropsychological assessment* (3rd ed.). New York: Oxford University Press.

Rapoport, J. (1990). *The boy who couldn't stop washing: The experience and treatment of obsessive-compulsive disorder*. New York: Penguin Books.

Sacks, O. (1985). *The man who mistook his wife for a hat*. New York: Harper & Row.

Styron, W. (1990). *Darkness visible: A memoir of madness*. New York: Random House.

USING A GROUP APPROACH

Group therapy was originally developed as a way to stretch resources and reduce costs, but therapists soon realized the method had its own unique therapeutic merits. Therapy groups can be highly structured or loosely organized; they can help modify thought and behavior, or just provide needed social support.

 **TIMELINE**

460–377 B.C.E.

Trepanning Fossil evidence indicates that holes were drilled into human skulls, possibly to cure mental illness.

1700s

Humane Treatment
Phillipe Pinel in France is among the first to release supposedly dangerous and violent mental patients from chains and manacles.

1800s

Reform in the United States
Dorothea Dix promotes reform of mental institutions in the United States, leading to the establishment of the state hospital system.

1900

Dreams in Therapy
Sigmund Freud advocates dream interpretation as part of psychoanalytic therapy.

Treating Disorders of Mind and Body

17

OUTLINING THE PRINCIPLES

1940s
Treatment of Mental Illness Loses Ground Many overcrowded mental hospitals return to the use of physical restraints, creating barbaric conditions.

1948
Behaviorism as Therapy B. F. Skinner pioneers behavior modification as a treatment for mental disorders.

1949
Lobotomies as Treatment Egas Moniz receives a Nobel prize for his work on prefrontal lobotomies as a treatment for mental disorders, a technique later shown to cause further problems.

1950s
Drugs for Depression Antidepressant medications are discovered and revolutionize the treatment of depression, as their benefits outweigh some side effects.

1960s
The Cognitive Approach Aaron T. Beck and Albert Ellis develop cognitive therapy to treat dysfunctional thoughts and beliefs.

RESEARCH QUESTIONS

for Studying the Treatment of Disorders of Mind and Body

What determines the type of treatment?

How do drugs affect mental disorders?

How can you tell if therapy is successful?

What are effective treatments for anxiety disorders?

What are effective treatments for depression?

What are effective treatments for schizophrenia?

Can children be treated for mental disorders?

Dennis was a 31-year-old insurance salesman. One day while shopping in a mall with his fiancée, Dennis suddenly felt very sick. His hands began to shake, his vision became blurred, and he felt a great deal of pressure in his chest. He began to gasp and felt weak all over. All of this was accompanied by a feeling of overwhelming terror. Without stopping to tell his fiancée what was happening, he ran from the store and sought refuge in the car. He opened the windows and lay down, and he started to feel better in about ten minutes. Later, Dennis explained to his fiancée what had happened and revealed that he had experienced this sort of attack before. Because of this, he would often avoid places like shopping malls. At the urging of his fiancée, Dennis agreed to see a psychologist. During his first several treatment sessions, Dennis downplayed his problems, clearly concerned that others might think him crazy. He was also reluctant to rely on medications because of the stigma attached. He had read about cognitive-behavioral therapy and was interested in trying this approach to address his problem.

His therapist explained that Dennis was experiencing panic attacks combined with agoraphobia. The therapist believed Dennis's problems were the result of vulnerability to stress combined with thoughts and behaviors that exacerbated anxiety. The first step in treatment was therefore relaxation training, to give Dennis a strategy to use when he became anxious and tense. The next step was to modify his maladaptive thought patterns. Dennis kept a diary for several weeks to identify situations in which distorted thoughts might be producing anxiety, such as meeting with prospective clients. Before meeting with a client, Dennis would become extremely anxious because he felt that it would be catastrophic if he was unable to make the sale. With the help of his therapist, Dennis came to recognize that being turned down by a client was difficult but manageable, and that it was unlikely to have any long-term impact on his career. The final phase of treatment was to address Dennis's avoidance of situations that he associated with panic attacks. Dennis and his therapist con-

---

1970s

Focus on Interaction
Interpersonal psychotherapy is used to identify and modify interpersonal problems.

1980s

The Era of Deinstitutionalization
With the advent of psychotropic medications, patients are discharged from mental hospitals in large numbers and cared for through community-based treatment.

1987

Therapy on the Border
Marsha Linehan introduces dialectical behavior therapy for the treatment of borderline personality disorder.

1990s

The Failure of Deinstitutionalization?
Inadequate support for those released from mental hospitals results in patients not taking their medications, an increase in unemployment, and a surge in the homeless population.

1990s

Prozac and Beyond
Researchers pursue new drugs to treat mental illness that have increasing specificity and fewer side effects.

structed a hierarchy of increasingly stressful situations. The first was an easy situation, involving a short visit to a department store on a lightly crowded weekday morning. Dennis's fiancée accompanied him so that he would feel less vulnerable. After completing this task, Dennis moved on to increasingly difficult situations, using relaxation techniques as necessary to control his anxiety. After six months, therapy was discontinued. Dennis's anxiety levels were significantly reduced and he was able to make himself relax when he did become tense. In addition, he had not experienced a panic attack during that period and was no longer avoiding situations that he previously found stressful (Oltmans et al., 1999).

There are two essential methods used to treat mental illness, psychological and biological, and research findings show that there is more than one way to treat most mental disorders. The generic name given to formal psychological treatment is **psychotherapy**, although the particular techniques and methods used depend on the theoretical orientation of the practitioner. **Biological therapies** reflect the medical approach to illness and disease. For example, *psychopharmacology*, the use of medications that affect brain or bodily functions, has proven to be very effective in treating many mental disorders. The success of medication in the treatment of mental illness is largely responsible for the era of deinstitutionalization, in which scores of patients were discharged from mental hospitals and treated with drugs as outpatients. In California in the 1980s, the number of hospital beds for mentally ill patients decreased from 40,000 to 5,000. The smaller number of inpatients meant that many institutions could better care for those still under their care.

Both psychotherapy and biological therapies have proven to be beneficial to many of those who suffer from mental illness. The case of Dennis illustrates the effectiveness of cognitive-behavioral therapy, a form of psychotherapy. Recent focus has been on combining biological therapies with other therapeutic approaches to optimize treatment for each patient. This chapter explores the basic principles of therapy and describes the various treatment approaches to specific mental disorders.

HOW IS MENTAL ILLNESS TREATED?

As outlined in Chapter 16, a number of theories have been proposed to account for psychopathology. These approaches propose treatment strategies based on assumptions about the causes of mental disorders. However, even if we gain more understanding into the etiology of a mental disorder, this does not always give us further insights into how best to treat it. It is becoming clear that autism, for example, is caused by biological factors. While this knowledge has helped parents accept that they are not responsible for their children's problems, it has not led to any significant advances in therapies for the disorder. In fact, the best available treatment at this point is based on behavioral, not biological, principles.

psychotherapy The generic name given to formal psychological treatment.

biological therapies Treatment based on the medical approach to illness and disease.

insight A goal of some types of therapy; a patient's understanding of his or her own psychological processes.

client-centered therapy An empathic approach to therapy that encourages personal growth through greater self-understanding.

What determines the type of treatment?

PSYCHOTHERAPY IS BASED ON PSYCHOLOGICAL PRINCIPLES

Psychotherapy, regardless of the theoretical perspective of the treatment provider, is generally aimed at changing patterns of thought or behavior, though the way in which such changes are effected can differ dramatically. It has been estimated that there are over 400 approaches to treatment (Kazdin, 1994). The discussion that follows highlights the major components of the most widely used approaches and describes how therapists use these methods to treat specific mental disorders. Today, many practitioners use an eclectic mix of techniques based on what they believe is best for the client's particular condition.

Psychodynamic therapy focuses on insight Sigmund Freud believed that mental disorders were caused by prior experiences, particularly early traumatic experiences. Along with Josef Breuer, he developed the method of psychoanalysis. During early forms of psychoanalysis, patients typically lay on a couch with therapists sitting out of view, in order to reduce patients' inhibitions and allow freer access to unconscious thought processes (Figure 17.1). Treatment was based on uncovering unconscious feelings and drives thought to give rise to maladaptive thoughts and behaviors, using techniques such as *free association*, in which the patient says whatever comes to mind, and *dream analysis*, in which the therapist interprets the hidden meaning of dreams. The general goal of psychoanalysis is to increase patients' awareness of these unconscious processes and how they affect daily functioning. With this **insight**, or personal understanding of their own psychological processes, patients are freed of these unconscious influences and symptoms disappear. Some of Freud's ideas have since been reformulated; these later adaptations are collectively known as *psychodynamic approaches*. Although the couch was replaced with a chair, proponents of the psychodynamic perspective continue to embrace Freud's "talking therapy," in more of a conversational format.

17.1 Freud sat behind his desk while his patients lay on the couch facing away from him, in order to reduce their inhibitions about revealing their unconscious beliefs and wishes.

Humanistic therapies focus on the whole person Recall from Chapter 15 that the humanistic approach to personality emphasizes personal experience and belief systems and the phenomenology of individuals. The goal of humanistic therapy is to treat the person as a whole, not as a collection of behaviors or a repository of repressed and unconscious thoughts. One of the best-known humanistic therapies is **client-centered therapy**, developed by Carl Rogers, which encourages people to fulfill their individual potentials for personal growth through greater self-understanding. A key ingredient of client-centered therapy is a safe and comforting setting for clients to access their true feelings. Therapists strive to be empathic, to take the client's perspective, and to accept the client through unconditional positive regard. Rather than directing the client's behavior or passing judgment on the client's actions or thoughts, the therapist helps the client focus on his or her subjective experience, often by using *reflective listening*, in which the therapist repeats the client's concerns in order to help the person clarify his or her feelings. One current treatment for problem drinkers, known as *motivational interviewing*, uses a client-centered approach over a very short period of time (such as one or two interviews). William Miller (2000) attributes the outstanding success of this brief form of empathic therapy to the warmth expressed by the therapist toward the client. Although relatively few practitioners follow strictly the tenets of humanistic theory, many of the techniques advocated by Rogers currently are used to establish a good therapeutic relationship between practitioner and client.

Behavioral therapy focuses on observable behavior Whereas insight-based therapies consider maladaptive behavior to be the result of an underlying problem, behavioral therapists see the behavior itself as the problem and directly target this in therapy. The basic premise is that behavior is learned and therefore can be unlearned using the principles of classical and operant conditioning (see Chapter 6). **Behavior modification**, based on operant conditioning, rewards desired behaviors and ignores or punishes unwanted behaviors. In order for desired behavior to be rewarded, however, the client must exhibit this behavior. **Social-skills training** is an effective way to elicit desired behavior. When clients have particular interpersonal difficulties, such as with initiating a conversation, they are taught appropriate ways of responding in specific social situations. The first step is often *modeling*, in which the therapist acts out appropriate behavior. The client is encouraged to imitate this behavior, rehearse it in therapy, and later apply the learned behavior to real-world situations. An approach that integrates insight therapy with behavioral therapy is *interpersonal therapy* (Markowitz & Weissman, 1995), which focuses on relationships that the patient attempts to avoid. Because interpersonal functioning is seen as critical to psychological adjustment, treatment is focused on helping patients express their emotions and explore interpersonal experiences (Blagys & Hilsenroth, 2000).

Many behavioral therapies for phobia include **exposure**, in which the client is repeatedly exposed directly to the anxiety-producing stimulus or situation (Figure 17.2). The theory, based on classical conditioning, is that when clients avoid the feared stimuli or situations, they experience reductions in anxiety that reinforce avoidance behavior. Repeated exposure to a feared stimulus increases the client's anxiety, but if the client is not permitted to avoid the stimulus, the avoidance response is eventually extinguished. Exposure methods vary in intensity. A gradual form of exposure therapy, known as **systematic desensitization**, uses relaxation techniques to allow the client to imagine anxiety-producing situations while maintaining relaxation. Relaxation is therefore paired with the feared situation via classical conditioning, gradually weakening or replacing the learned anxiety response.

behavior modification Principles of operant conditioning are used to reinforce desired behaviors and ignore or punish unwanted behaviors.

social-skills training Treatment designed to teach and reinforce appropriate interpersonal behavior.

exposure A behavioral therapy technique that involves repeated exposure to an anxiety-producing stimulus or situation.

systematic desensitization An exposure technique that pairs the anxiety-producing stimulus with relaxation techniques.

17.2 A child is encouraged to approach a dog that scares her. This mild form of exposure teaches the girl that the dog is not dangerous, and she overcomes her fear.

17.3 Aaron T. Beck is one of the pioneers of cognitive therapy for mental disorders, especially depression.

Cognitive-behavioral therapy focuses on faulty cognitions Cognitive therapy is based on the theory that distorted thoughts can produce maladaptive behaviors and emotions. Modifying these thought patterns via specific treatment strategies should eliminate the maladaptive behaviors and emotions. A number of approaches to cognitive therapy have been proposed. Aaron Beck (Figure 17.3), a leader in cognitive therapy, advocated **cognitive restructuring**, in which clinicians help their patients recognize maladaptive thought patterns and replace them with ways of viewing the world that are more in tune with reality. Albert Ellis, another major thinker in this area, introduced *rational-emotive therapy*, in which therapists act as teachers who explain and demonstrate more adaptive ways of thinking and behaving. In both types of therapies, maladaptive behavior is assumed to result from individual belief systems and ways of thinking rather than from objective conditions.

Perhaps the most widely used version of cognitive therapy is **cognitive-behavioral therapy (CBT)**, which incorporates techniques from behavioral therapy and cognitive therapy. CBT tries both to correct faulty cognitions and to train clients to engage in new behaviors. For instance, people with social phobia, who fear negative evaluation, might be taught social skills while at the same time the therapist helps them understand how their appraisals of other peoples' reactions to them might be inaccurate. CBT has proven to be one of the most effective forms of psychotherapy for many types of mental illness, especially anxiety disorders and mood disorders.

Group therapy builds social support Group therapy rose in popularity after World War II, when there were more people needing therapy than there were therapists available to treat them. Subsequently it was realized that group therapy offers advantages that make it preferable to individual therapy in some instances. The most obvious benefit is cost, as group therapy is often significantly less expensive than individual treatment. In addition, the group setting provides an opportunity for members to improve their social skills and to learn from each others' experiences. Group therapies vary widely in the types of patients enrolled in the group, the duration of the treatment, and the theoretical perspective of the therapist running the group. The size of the group also varies, although it is believed by some that eight patients is the ideal number. Many groups are organized around a particular type of problem (such as sexual abuse) or around a particular type of client (such as adolescents). Often, groups continue over long periods of time, with some members leaving and others joining the group at various intervals. Depending on the orientation of the therapist, the group may be highly structured or may be a more loosely organized forum for discussion. Behavioral and cognitive-behavioral groups are often highly structured, with specific goals and techniques designed to modify thought and behavior patterns of group members. This type of group has been effective for disorders such as bulimia and obsessive-compulsive disorder. In contrast, less structured groups are often more focused on increasing insight and providing social support. The social support that group members can provide each other is one of the most beneficial aspects of group therapy, and attendance at group therapy is often used to augment individual psychotherapy.

Family therapy focuses on the family context Although the therapy a patient receives is an important element in treating mental disorders, the patient's family plays an almost equally important role. According to a *systems approach*, an

cognitive therapy Treatment based on the idea that distorted thoughts produce maladaptive behaviors and emotions.

cognitive restructuring A therapy that strives to help patients recognize maladaptive thought patterns and replace them with ways of viewing the world that are more in tune with reality.

cognitive-behavioral therapy (CBT) Incorporates techniques from behavioral therapy and cognitive therapy to correct faulty thinking and change maladaptive behaviors.

individual is part of a larger context and any change in individual behavior will affect the whole system. This is often most clear at the family level. Within the family context, each person plays a particular role and interacts with the other members in specific ways. In the course of therapy, the way the individual thinks, behaves, and interacts with others may change, and this change could have profound effects on family dynamics.

Family members can have a tremendous impact on client outcomes. For instance, the importance of the family to the long-term prognosis of schizophrenia patients has been documented in studies of the attitudes expressed by family members toward the patient. Negative **expressed emotion** includes making critical comments about the patient, being hostile toward him or her, and being emotionally overinvolved. A number of studies have shown that families' levels of negative expressed emotion correspond to the relapse rate for patients with schizophrenia (Hooley & Gotlib, 2000). Schizophrenia patients released from the hospital to families with high levels of negative expressed emotion have high relapse rates, and the relapse rates are highest if the patient has a great deal of contact with the family (more than 35 hours per week) (Figure 17.4). Because family attitudes are often critical to long-term prognoses, some therapists insist that family members be involved in therapy. Indeed, evidence suggests that helping families provide social support leads to better therapy outcomes and reduces relapses.

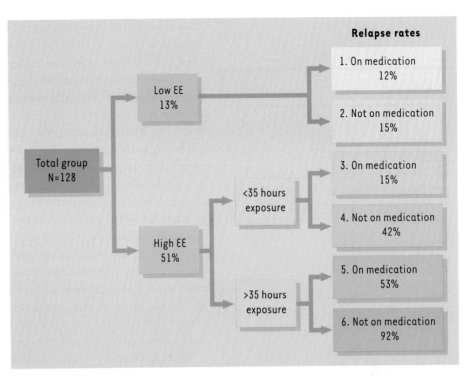

17.4 After nine months, schizophrenia patients who were most exposed to family members high in negative expressed emotion were most likely to relapse, particularly if they were not on medication.

BIOLOGICAL THERAPIES ARE NECESSARY FOR SOME DISORDERS

Biological therapies are based on the notion that mental illness results from abnormalities in neural and bodily processes, such as imbalances in specific neurotransmitters or malfunctions in certain brain regions. Treatments range from drugs, to electrical stimulation of brain regions, to surgical interventions. In this section we will focus on the most widely used biological treatment. Drugs have proven to be quite effective for treating many mental disorders. Those that act on the brain to affect mental processes are known as **psychotropic medications**. They act by changing brain neurochemistry, such as by inhibiting action potentials or by altering synaptic transmission to increase or decrease the action of particular neurotransmitters.

Although there are numerous drugs available, most psychotropic medications fall into three categories. **Anti-anxiety drugs**, commonly called tranquilizers, are used for the short-term treatment of anxiety. Benzodiazepines, such as Valium, increase activity of GABA, an inhibitory neurotransmitter (see Chapter 3). Although these drugs reduce anxiety and promote relaxation, they also induce drowsiness and are highly addictive. A newer anti-anxiety medication, buspirone,

expressed emotion A pattern of interactions that includes emotional overinvolvement, critical comments, and hostility directed toward a patient by family members.

psychotropic medications Drugs that affect mental processes.

anti-anxiety drugs A class of psychotropic medications used for the treatment of anxiety.

How do drugs affect mental disorders?

has fewer side effects and does not appear to have the addictive potential of the benzodiazepines.

A second class of psychotropic medications is the **antidepressants**, which as the name implies are used to treat depression. Monoamine oxidase (MAO) inhibitors were the first antidepressants to be discovered. *Monoamine oxidase* is an enzyme that converts serotonin into another chemical form. **MAO inhibitors** therefore result in more serotonin being available in the synapses of the brain. These drugs also raise levels of norepinephrine and dopamine. A second category of antidepressant medications is the **tricyclic antidepressants**, named after their core molecular structure of three rings. These drugs inhibit reuptake of a number of different neurotransmitters, and this inhibition results in more of each neurotransmitter being available in the synapse. More recently, **selective serotonin reuptake inhibitors (SSRIs)** have been introduced. Although these drugs do act by inhibiting the reuptake of serotonin, contrary to their name, they also act on other neurotransmitters, to a significantly lesser extent (Figure 17.5). One of the most widely prescribed SSRIs is Prozac, though some people criticize the widespread use of drugs such as Prozac to treat people who are sad and have low self-esteem, but who are not clinically depressed. This is a problem because all drugs have some side effects and SSRIs can cause sexual dysfunction.

Antipsychotics, also known as *neuroleptics*, are used to treat schizophrenia and other disorders that involve psychosis. These drugs reduce symptoms such as delusions and hallucinations. Traditional antipsychotics bind to dopamine receptors without activating them, which blocks the effects of dopamine. Antipsychotics are not always effective, however, and they have significant side effects that can be irreversible, such as *tardive dyskinesia*, the involuntary twitching of muscles, especially in the neck and face. Moreover, these drugs are not useful for treating the negative symptoms of schizophrenia (see Chapter 16). *Clozapine*, one of the more recently developed antipsychotics, is significantly different in that it acts not only on dopamine receptors but also on serotonin, norepinephrine, acetylcholine, and histamine. Many patients who do not respond to the other neuroleptics improve on clozapine.

17.5 Selective serotonin reuptake inhibitors (SSRIs), such as Prozac, work by blocking reuptake into the presynaptic neuron, thereby allowing serotonin to remain in the synapse, where its effects on postsynaptic receptors are prolonged.

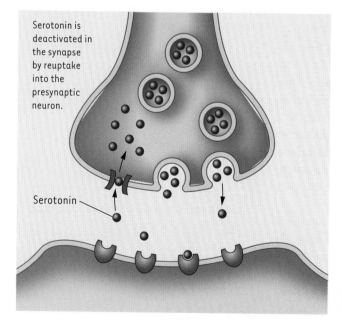

Serotonin is deactivated in the synapse by reuptake into the presynaptic neuron.

Serotonin

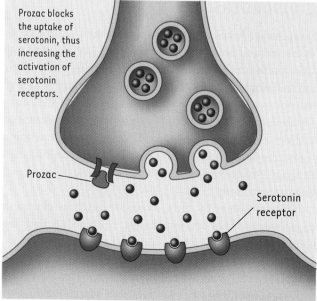

Prozac blocks the uptake of serotonin, thus increasing the activation of serotonin receptors.

Prozac

Serotonin receptor

Other drugs used to treat mental illness do not fall into traditional categories. *Lithium* is the most effective treatment for bipolar disorder, although the neural mechanisms of how it works are currently unknown. Drugs that work to prevent seizures, called *anticonvulsants*, are also used to treat symptoms of mania.

THERE ARE COMMON FACTORS THAT ENHANCE TREATMENT

Although the basic goals of all psychotherapeutic approaches are similar, the paths to these goals vary dramatically. Are some approaches better than others? Which approaches are more effective for specific types of clients or disorders? Perhaps most important, do psychotherapeutic approaches really do any good? These questions have been the focus of research and debate for many years.

Evaluating the effectiveness of therapy   How can we determine if therapy is effective? One way is to ask people who have received therapy if they felt it helped them. In 1994, *Consumer Reports* magazine asked readers to evaluate their mental health treatments. Seven thousand readers responded. Of these, 2,900 sought treatment from mental health professionals, 1,300 joined self-help groups, and 1,000 consulted a family physician. The majority of respondents felt that intervention had helped them, and those who sought help from mental health professionals reported more positive results than those who consulted with a family doctor. No specific type of therapy yielded more positive results than any other, but duration of therapy did make a difference, with longer duration associated with better results. Patients whose choice of therapists or duration of treatment were limited for insurance reasons had the poorest outcome. Note, however, that there are many problems with this type of survey. People are motivated to justify their actions, and few people who go to the trouble of spending many years in therapy will want to admit to possibly wasting their time and money. Moreover, it is possible that only those people who had positive outcomes chose to respond to the survey. In addition, readers of *Consumer Reports* may differ from the general population in meaningful ways, so it is impossible to know whether these results generalize to most people.

What does the empirical literature tell us about the success of psychotherapy? In 1952, Hans Eysenck, a British psychologist, claimed that 75 percent of all neurotic patients improved whether or not they were in therapy. All people have ups and downs, and people tend to enter therapy during low points in their lives. Left on their own, Eysenck claimed, these people might improve just as much without ever having therapy. As you can imagine, this theory created a furor and sparked numerous studies to determine whether therapy for mental disorders did make a difference. The accumulated evidence suggests that Eysenck was much too critical of psychotherapy. Indeed, subsequent studies found that the average patient or client receiving therapy was better off than those suffering from mental disorders who did not receive treatment.

In the 1970s, a number of landmark studies addressed the issue of treatment efficacy. One study followed college students who sought therapy at an outpatient psychiatric facility (Sloane et al., 1977). Some students received either behavioral therapy or psychodynamic therapy, while the rest were placed on a waiting list for four months. After four months, both treatment groups had improved equally and both more than the control group. After one year, the group receiving behavioral

antidepressants A class of psychotropic medications used to treat depression.

MAO inhibitors A category of antidepressant drugs that inhibit the action of monoamine oxidase.

tricyclic antidepressants A category of antidepressant medications that inhibit the reuptake of a number of different neurotransmitters.

selective serotonin reuptake inhibitors (SSRIs) A category of antidepressant medications that prolong the effects of serotonin in the synapse.

antipsychotics A class of drugs used to treat schizophrenia and other disorders that involve psychosis.

RESEARCH QUESTION
? ? ?

How can you tell if therapy is successful?

therapy showed more improvement in the specific problem for which they had initially sought therapy, but students in both types of therapies demonstrated the same level of social adjustment. The conclusion from this study was that therapy helps, but the type does not matter. One year after the start of the study, the students were asked what factors they considered most important to the success of their treatment. Regardless of the type of therapy they had undergone, the responses all focused on the same factors: the insight gained into the problem, the relationship with the therapist, the opportunity to vent emotions, and the development of self-confidence. The critical role of the therapist is underscored in a study of 240 patients being seen by 25 therapists at 4 different treatment centers (Luborsky et al., 1986). Surprisingly, it was found that who performed the therapy was more important than the type of therapy. At all of the centers, there were a few therapists who had better success rates than others regardless of the type of treatment or patient. However, as you will see throughout the remainder of this chapter, other research has shown that certain types of treatments are particularly effective for specific types of mental illness. Although the effectiveness of these treatments is not due simply to the qualities of the therapist, there are *common factors* in therapy that might facilitate positive outcomes regardless of the type of therapy used.

A caring therapist   One factor known to affect the outcome of therapy is the relationship between the therapist and patient. This is not limited to mental illness, however—a good relationship with a service provider is important for any aspect of physical or mental health. A good relationship may be important to therapy in part because it can foster an expectation of receiving help (Miller, 2000; Talley et al., 1990). Most people in the mental health field use the curative power of patient expectation to help their patients achieve success in therapy. The issue of selecting a particular type of therapist is discussed in "Using Psychological Science: Choosing a Mental Health Practitioner."

17.6 James Pennebaker has demonstrated that talking about personal traumas and secrets is beneficial to physical and mental health.

Confession is good for the spirit   Aristotle coined the term "catharsis" to describe the way certain messages evoke powerful emotional reactions and subsequent relief. Freud later incorporated this idea into his psychoanalytic approach to the treatment of mental disorders. He believed that uncovering unconscious material and talking about it would bring about catharsis and therefore relief from symptoms. Although other therapeutic approaches do not explicitly rely on this process, the opportunity to talk about one's problems to someone who will listen plays a role in all therapeutic relationships. Just the act of telling someone about your problems can have healing power. James Pennebaker (Figure 17.6) has explored this theory extensively in the laboratory. He finds that when people reveal intimate and highly emotional material, they go into an almost trancelike state. The pitch of their voices goes down and their rate of speech speeds up. In this seemingly hypnotic state, they lose track of time and place. Subsequent research has revealed the far-reaching effects of confession. Talking or writing about emotionally charged events reduces blood pressure, muscle tension, and skin conduction during the disclosure and immediately after (Pennebaker, 1990, 1995). In addition to these short-term benefits, there is evidence for improved immune function, better performance in work and school, and improved memory and cognition. In

CHOOSING A MENTAL HEALTH PRACTITIONER

In 1999, the surgeon general of the United States reported that approximately one in five Americans has some form of diagnosable mental illness in a given year, and that about 15 percent seek mental health treatment of some kind. Treating mental illnesses costs more than 100 billion dollars each year. Treatment for mental disorders is offered by a dizzying array of providers, ranging from those with limited training (such as former addicts who provide peer counseling) to those with advanced degrees in psychopathology and its treatment. In addition to mental health specialists, regular health care providers (e.g., internists, pediatricians), human-service workers (e.g., school counselors), and volunteers (e.g., self-help groups) also provide assistance to those with mental problems. The major types of specialized mental practitioners include:

Clinical psychologists typically have a doctoral degree. The graduate training for a Ph.D. takes four to six years and emphasizes research design and analysis. Many clinical psychologists work in academic or hospital settings where they conduct research in addition to providing treatment. A relatively new training program in clinical psychology leads to the Psy.D. This program tends to emphasize clinical skills over research and is meant for those who intend primarily to provide direct mental health services. Clinical psychologists typically are not able to prescribe medications, although efforts are underway to give them prescription privileges. New Mexico passed legislation to allow clinical psychologists to prescribe drugs in March 2002, provided they receive appropriate training.

Psychiatrists have a medical degree (M.D.) and three to four additional years of specialized training in residency programs. They often work in hospitals or private practice. Psychiatrists are the only mental health practitioners legally authorized to prescribe drugs in most states.

Psychiatric social workers most often have a master's degree in social work (M.S.W.), followed by specialized training in mental health care. They commonly visit people in their homes and deal with problems that arise from that environment. This might include helping the client receive appropriate resources from social and community agencies.

Psychiatric nurses typically have a bachelor's degree (R.N.) in nursing and special training in the care of mentally ill patients. They often work in hospitals or treatment centers that specialize in serious mental illness.

Counseling psychologists often have a Ph.D. in counseling psychology. They typically deal with problems of adjustment and life stress, such as that related to school, marital, and occupational problems that do not involve mental illness. Most colleges have staff who specialize in problems common to students, such as test anxiety, learning disorders, sleep problems, and family issues.

Paraprofessionals have limited advanced training and usually work under supervision. They assist those with mental health problems in the challenges of daily living. For example, they may work in crisis intervention, pastoral counseling, community outreach programs, or may supervise clients of residential treatment centers.

The World Wide Web provides a growing number of resources for those trying to adjust to life problems on their own. These self-help programs are meant for minor stresses associated with daily living rather than for more serious mental disorders. The websites of the American Psychological Association (www.apa.org) and the National Institute of Mental Health (www.nimh.nih.gov) provide additional information for choosing mental health practitioners.

---

addition, the opportunity to talk about troubling events may help clients reinterpret the events in less threatening ways, which is a central component of many cognitive therapies.

How Is Mental Illness Treated?

There are many ways to treat mental disorders. Psychotherapy uses psychological methods that are based on the practitioner's theoretical orientation. Some therapies help people gain insight into why they think, behave, and interact in certain ways. Other psychotherapy methods are more concerned with action than insight and may try to correct faulty or biased thinking or to teach new behaviors. Psychopharmacology is based on the idea that maladaptive behavior results from neurological dysfunction, and psychotropic medications are therefore aimed at correcting imbalances of neurotransmitters in the brain. Treatment of mental illness is often effective, perhaps in part because of commonalities among therapies, such as the client-practitioner relationship.

WHAT ARE THE MOST EFFECTIVE TREATMENTS?

Earlier we mentioned that certain types of treatments are particularly effective for specific types of mental illness. This conclusion is based on research that crosses the levels of analysis to examine treatment outcomes. Because outcomes are influenced by the interaction of client and therapist, it is difficult to make comparisons across disorders and therapists. Nonetheless, the accumulated evidence obtained by psychological scientists indicates that some treatments for specific disorders have empirical support for their use and others do not. Moreover, the scientific study of treatment indicates that although some mental disorders are quite easily treated, others are not. For instance, there are highly effective treatments for anxiety disorders, mood disorders, and sexual dysfunction, but there are few treatments for alcoholism that are superior to the natural course of recovery that occurs without treatment (Seligman et al., 2001). As with all other areas of psychological science, the only way to know whether a treatment is valid is to conduct empirical research.

TREATMENTS THAT FOCUS ON BEHAVIOR AND COGNITION ARE SUPERIOR FOR ANXIETY DISORDERS

Over the years, a variety of treatment approaches to anxiety disorders have met with mixed success. In the era when the classification of mental disorders was based on Freudian psychoanalytic theory, anxiety disorders were thought to be the result of repressed sexual and aggressive impulses. It was the underlying cause, rather than the specific symptoms, that was of interest to the therapist. Ultimately, psychoanalytic theory did not prove useful for treating anxiety disorders. The accumulated evidence suggests that cognitive and behavioral techniques work best to treat most anxiety disorders. The use of anxiety-reducing drugs is also beneficial in some cases, although there are risks of side effects as well as relapse after drug treatment is terminated. For instance, tranquilizers work for generalized anxiety disorder as long as the drug is taken, but they do little to alleviate the source of anxiety. By contrast, the effects of cognitive-behavioral therapy persist long after treatment.

Specific phobias   Specific phobias are characterized by fear and avoidance of particular stimuli, such as heights, blood, and spiders. Learning theory suggests that these fears are acquired either through experiencing a traumatic personal encounter or by observing similar fear in others. As discussed in the preceding chapter, however, most phobias seem to develop in the absence of any particular precipitating event. Although the development of phobias cannot be completely explained by learning theory, behavioral techniques are the treatment of choice. In systematic desensitization therapy, the client first makes a *fear hierarchy*, a list of situations in which fear is aroused, in ascending order. The next step is relaxation training, in which clients learn to contrast muscular tension with muscular relaxation and to use relaxation techniques. Once the client has learned to relax, exposure therapy is often the next step. While the client is relaxed, he is asked to imagine or enact scenarios that become progressively more upsetting (Figure 17.7). New scenarios are not presented until the client is able to maintain relax-

What are effective treatments for anxiety disorders?

Degree of fear	Anxiety hierarchy
5	I'm standing on the balcony of the top floor of an apartment tower.
10	I'm standing on a stepladder in the kitchen to change a lightbulb.
15	I'm walking on a ridge. The edge is hidden by shrubs and treetops.
20	I'm sitting on the slope of a mountain, looking out over the horizon.
25	I'm crossing a bridge 6 feet above a creek. The bridge consists of an 18-inch-wide board with a handrail on one side.
30	I'm riding a ski lift 8 feet above the ground.
35	I'm crossing a shallow, wide creek on an 18-inch-wide board, 3 feet above water level.
40	I'm climbing a ladder outside the house to reach a second-story window.
45	I'm pulling myself up a 30-degree wet, slippery slope on a steel cable.
50	I'm scrambling up a rock, 8 feet high.
55	I'm walking 10 feet on a resilient, 18-inch-wide board, which spans an 8-foot-deep gulch.
60	I'm walking on a wide plateau, 2 feet from the edge of a cliff.
65	I'm skiing an intermediate hill. The snow is packed.
70	I'm walking over a railway trestle.
75	I'm walking on the side of an embankment. The path slopes to the outside.
80	I'm riding a chair lift 15 feet above the ground.
85	I'm walking up a long, steep slope.
90	I'm walking up (or down) a 15-degree slope on a 3-foot-wide trail. On one side of the trail the terrain drops down sharply; on the other side is a steep upward slope.
95	I'm walking on a 3-foot-wide ridge. The slopes on both sides are long and more than 25 degrees steep.
100	I'm walking on a 3-foot-wide ridge. The trail slopes on one side. The drop on either side of the trail is more than 25 degrees.

17.7 In systematic desensitization, the client creates a fear hierarchy, in which specific fears are graded from least to most threatening. This woman is in therapy to conquer her fear of heights in order to go mountain climbing.

ation at the previous levels. The theory behind this technique is that the relaxation response competes with and eventually replaces the previously exhibited fear response. The available evidence indicates that it is exposure to the feared object rather than the relaxation that extinguishes the phobic response. One way to expose people without putting them in danger is to use *virtual environments*, sometimes called virtual reality. Computers can simulate the environments and objects that are feared, such as by having a person *virtually* stand on the edge of a very tall building or fly in an aircraft (Figure 17.8). There is impressive evidence that exposure to these virtual environments can reduce fear responses (Rothbaum et al., 1999).

Used along with the behavioral methods, some cognitive strategies have also proven useful for the treatment of phobia. If clients are not aware that their fears are irrational, therapy would likely begin by increasing their awareness of the thought processes that maintain the fear of a particular stimulus. Tranquilizers

17.8 Computer-generated images can simulate feared environments, such as heights, flying, or social interactions. Clients can conquer these virtual environments before taking on the fear object in real life.

can help people handle immediate fear, but they are not the treatment of choice for most phobias because as soon as the drug wears off, the phobia returns. Some recent studies have suggested that SSRIs (such as Prozac) might be useful for social phobia, but the long-term prognosis remains better for behavioral therapies.

Panic disorder Although many of us at some point experience some of the symptoms of a panic attack, we react to these symptoms in different ways. Some shrug off the symptoms while others interpret heart palpitations as the beginnings of a heart attack, or hyperventilation as a sign of suffocation. Panic disorder is the result of multiple components, each of which may require a different treatment approach.

This clinical observation is supported by the finding that *imipramine*, a tricyclic antidepressant, prevents panic attacks but does nothing to reduce the anticipatory anxiety that clients have when they fear they might have a panic attack. In order to break the learned association between the physical symptoms and the feeling of impending doom, cognitive-behavioral therapy can be effective, as was illustrated in the opening case study of Dennis.

The most important psychotherapeutic methods for treating panic disorder are based on cognitive therapy. Cognitive restructuring addresses the ways the client reacts to the symptoms of panic attack. First, clients are asked to identify the specific fears they have. Often, people having a panic attack are convinced they are having a heart attack or that they are going to pass out. Clients are then asked to estimate how many panic attacks they have had, and the therapist helps them to assign percentages to specific fears and then to compare these numbers to the actual number of times these fears have been realized. When people are feeling anxious, they tend to overestimate the probability of danger and this can contribute to rising feelings of panic. For example, a client might estimate that she fears a heart attack during 90 percent of her panic attacks and passing out during 85 percent of attacks. The therapist can then point out that the actual rate that these occurred was zero. In fact, people do not pass out during panic attacks; the physical symptoms of panic attack are the reverse of passing out.

Even if clients recognize the irrationality of their belief systems, however, they often still suffer panic attacks. From a cognitive-behavioral perspective, the panic attacks continue because of a conditioned response to the trigger, whether it is shortness of breath or some other factor. The goal of therapy is to break the connection between the trigger symptom and the resulting panic. This can be done by exposure treatment, which induces feelings of panic, perhaps by asking the client to breathe in and out through a straw to induce hyperventilation or by spinning the client rapidly in a chair. Whatever the method, it is done repeatedly to induce habituation and then extinction. Cognitive-behavioral therapy appears to be as effective or perhaps more effective than medication in the treatment of panic attacks. Intriguingly, there is also evidence that cognitive-behavioral therapy produces changes in the patterns of brain activation similar to those produced by psychotropic medication.

So, what is the treatment of choice for panic disorder? Both drugs and cognitive-behavioral therapy are effective, especially in the short term, but psychotherapy has the advantage because it does not require continued administration. For those who have panic disorder with agoraphobia, the combination of CBT and drugs is significantly better than either treatment alone.

Obsessive-compulsive disorder Obsessive-compulsive disorder (OCD) is a combination of recurrent intrusive thoughts (obsessions) and behaviors that the client feels compelled to perform over and over (compulsions). Evidence that OCD is at least in part genetic and appears to be related to Tourette's syndrome, a neurological disorder characterized by motor and vocal tics, convinced many that OCD was a biological disorder that should have a biological treatment. However, traditional antianxiety drugs are completely ineffective for OCD. When SSRIs began to be used to treat depression, it was found that they were particularly effective in reducing the obsessional components of some depressions, such as constant feelings of worthlessness. Because of this, SSRIs were tried with clients suffering from OCD and found to be effective (Rapoport, 1989, 1991). The drug of choice for OCD is the potent serotonin reuptake inhibitor *Clomipramine*. It is not a true SSRI since it also blocks reuptake of other neurotransmitters, but its strong enhancement of the effects of serotonin appears to make it effective for OCD. A further discussion of the biological basis of treatment for OCD can be found in "Crossing the Levels of Analysis: Lessons from the Treatment of OCD."

Cognitive-behavioral therapy is also effective for OCD and is especially valuable for those who do not benefit from or who do not want to rely on medication. Behavioral therapy for OCD differs from therapy for panic disorder in that relaxation training is not typically part of treatment. The two most important components of behavioral therapy for OCD are exposure and response prevention. Clients are directly exposed to the stimuli that trigger compulsive behavior, but are prevented from engaging in the behavior. This treatment is based on the theory that a particular stimulus triggers anxiety, and performing the compulsive behavior reduces that anxiety (see hand-washing example in Chapter 16). For example, a client might compulsively wash his hands after touching a door knob, using a public telephone, or shaking hands with someone. In exposure and response-prevention therapy, the client would be required to touch a door knob and then would be instructed not to wash his hands afterward. As with exposure therapy for panic disorder, the goal is to break the conditioned link between particular stimuli and compulsive behavior. Some cognitive therapies are also useful for OCD, such as helping the client learn that most people experience unwanted thoughts and compulsions from time to time. The goal is to help clients recognize that having unwanted negative thoughts is not a catastrophe but rather a normal part of human experience.

THERE ARE MULTIPLE EFFECTIVE TREATMENTS FOR DEPRESSION

Depression, characterized by depressed mood and loss of interest in pleasurable activities, is one of the most widespread mental disorders among adolescents and adults, and it has become more common over the past few decades. Fortunately, there are a number of effective treatments that have been validated through scientific research. There is no "best" way to treat depression; many treatment approaches are available to the depressed patient, and ongoing research is determining which type of therapy works best for individual clients.

Pharmacological treatment In the 1950s, tuberculosis was a major health problem in the United States, particularly in urban areas. A common treatment was *iproniazid*, a drug that reduced tubercule bacilli in the sputum of patients. It

What are effective treatments for depression?

Crossing the Levels of Analysis

LESSONS FROM THE TREATMENT OF OCD

Researchers can learn much about the neural processes underlying mental disorders by studying treatments. Findings from a variety of disciplines can provide insights into the etiology of mental disorders. In the case of obsessive-compulsive disorder, the effectiveness of SSRIs implicates the serotonin system in OCD. Despite the effectiveness of SSRIs, however, clinical studies have shown that 40–60 percent of patients with OCD do not improve when treated with these medications. For some of these patients, combining SSRIs with dopamine receptor antagonists, which block the action of dopamine, has been effective. Interestingly, the patients who benefit from this combination are those who also suffer from tics or who have a family history of tic disorders. Tic disorders, such as Tourette's syndrome, are thought to be linked to dopamine dysfunction; medications that block dopamine receptors are effective in suppressing tics (Shapiro et al., 1989). In addition, neuropathological (Singer et al., 1991) and neuroimaging (Malison et al., 1995) studies have revealed changes in dopamine pathways in the basal ganglia of patients with Tourette's syndrome. The basal ganglia help regulate motor behavior, and dysfunction in this region would be consistent with the development of motor tics. Genetic studies have hinted at a link between OCD and Tourette's syndrome, and it has been clinically observed that half to two-thirds of Tourette's patients also have OCD symptoms.

Investigation of neuropeptides has also provided insights into the link between OCD and tic disorders. Neuropeptides are derived from proteins and can act as neurotransmitters or can modulate the effects of neurotransmitters. The levels of oxytocin, a neuropeptide, are elevated in the cerebral spinal fluid of people with OCD (Leckman et al., 1994), but only those with no history of tic disorders. Patients with tic-related OCD have normal oxytocin levels. Oxytocin receptors are found in a number of brain regions, many of which have been implicated in OCD (Insel, 1992). Oxytocin aids in memory consolidation and retrieval, as well as in maternal and grooming behavior. Levels of oxytocin peak during the third trimester of pregnancy and remain high in breastfeeding women. Since higher levels of oxytocin are related to OCD, it might be expected that pregnant and breastfeeding women might be prone to developing obsessive and compulsive symptoms. Anecdotal reports suggest that women are more likely to develop OCD during these times, and for those who already have OCD, the higher levels of oxytocin during pregnancy and nursing can exacerbate the symptoms (Epperson et al., 1995).

Taken together, the findings on the roles of dopamine and oxytocin in OCD have an intriguing implication. There may be two distinct types of OCD: one tic-related and one non-tic-related. OCD patients with no history of tics show increased levels of oxytocin. Those with a personal or family history of tics do not show elevated

also stimulated patients' appetites, increased their energy levels, and gave them an overall sense of well-being. In 1957, researchers who had noted the drug's effect on mood reported preliminary success in using it to treat depression. In the following year, nearly half a million depressed patients were given iproniazid, which is a MAO inhibitor. Although they can relieve depression, MAO inhibitors can be toxic because of their effects on a variety of physiological systems. Patients taking this drug must avoid ingesting any substances containing tyramine, including red wine and aged cheeses, because they can experience severe, sometimes lethal elevations in blood pressure. Interactions with both prescription and over-the-counter medications can also be fatal, so MAO inhibitors are generally reserved for patients who do not respond to other antidepressants.

Another type of antidepressant, *tricyclics*, was also identified in the 1950s. The first tricyclic to be identified, imipramine, a drug developed as an antihistamine, was found to be effective in relieving clinical depression. This drug and others like it act on neurotransmitters as well as on the histamine system. Tricyclics are extremely effective antidepressants. However, as a result of their broad-based action, they have a number of unpleasant side effects. Because of their effect on the histamine system, patients often experience sedation and weight gain. Sweating, constipation, heart palpitations, and dry mouth can result from the effects of tricyclics on acetylcholine.

The discovery of these early antidepressants was largely serendipitous, but subsequently researchers began to search for antidepressants that did not affect multiple physiological and neurological systems and so would not have such trou-

oxytocin levels but do seem to have dysfunction in the dopamine system. These two subtypes may well have different neural underpinnings, and their differential reactions to psychotropic medications suggest that this is true. Although the neurochemistry seems to be different in the two groups of OCD patients, the neuroanatomical regions involved in the two groups are similar. There is evidence that dysfunction of the basal ganglia may be at the root of OCD.

Altering levels of serotonin and sometimes dopamine with medication can result in a reduction of OCD symptoms. In addition, cognitive-behavioral therapy has been found to be very effective in treating OCD, although it was unclear until recently how such therapy affects thoughts and actions. In the 1990s, researchers used PET scanning to examine the brains of patients with OCD who were treated either with Prozac or with cognitive-behavioral therapy. As Figure 17.9 illustrates, patients in both treatment groups showed the same changes in neural activity in the thalamus and basal ganglia (Baxter et al., 1992; Schwartz et al., 1996). This study provides striking evidence that non-pharmacological therapies can indeed change brain function. Cognitive-behavioral therapy may thus be a more effective way of treating OCD than medication. Presumably, medication changes brain function only while it is being taken, whereas the brain changes induced by cognitive-behavioral therapy can potentially be much longer lasting.

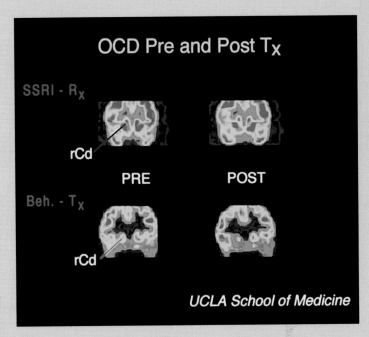

17.9 In these PET scans of OCD patients, arrows point to locations in the basal ganglia that showed similar changes with psychotherapy and drug therapy.

blesome side effects. In the 1980s, researchers discovered fluoxetine hydrochloride, better known as Prozac, which is an SSRI. Because this drug does not affect histamine or cholinergic systems it has none of the side effects associated with the tricyclic antidepressants, although it can occasionally cause insomnia, headache, weight loss, and sexual dysfunction. Because they have fewer serious side effects than MAO inhibitors, Prozac and other SSRIs began to be prescribed more frequently. A number of other drug treatments for depression have also been validated, such as *bupropion* (e.g., Wellbutrin), which affects many neurotransmitter systems but has far less serious side effects for most people than other drugs. For instance, unlike most antidepressants, bupropion does not cause sexual dysfunction. Interestingly, unlike SSRIs, bupropion is an ineffective treatment for panic disorder and OCD.

Approximately 60–70 percent of clients who take antidepressants will experience relief from their symptoms, compared to approximately 30 percent who respond to placebos. This indicates that drugs are quite effective, since placebo effects are a component of all therapeutic outcomes. Indeed, there is recent evidence that placebo treatment for depression leads to changes in brain activity (Leuchter et al., 2002). In this study, 38 percent of those given placebos showed improvement in depressive symptoms. For those who responded to placebos, there was increased activity in the prefrontal cortex. This was a different pattern of brain activation than that observed for patients receiving antidepressants, but it does suggest that placebo treatments are associated with changes in neurochemistry, which supports the findings that they do alleviate symptoms for some people. Placebos may work by giving people hope that they will feel better, and these positive expectancies may alter brain activity.

Despite attempts to predict patient response to antidepressants, physicians must often resort to a trial-and-error approach in treating depressed patients. At this time no single drug stands out as being most efficacious. The decision of which drug to use often depends on the client's overall medical health and the possible side effects of each medication. Once the depressive episode has ended, should patients continue taking medication? Research has shown that patients who continue taking medication for at least a year have only a 20 percent relapse rate, whereas those who are maintained on a placebo have an 80 percent relapse rate (Frank et al., 1990).

Cognitive-behavioral treatment of depression Despite the success of antidepressant medications, not all patients benefit from these drugs. Moreover, others cannot or will not tolerate the side effects associated with drug therapy. Fortunately, the available evidence indicates that cognitive-behavioral therapy is just as effective in treating depression as biological therapies. From a cognitive perspective, people who become depressed do so because of automatic, irrational thoughts. According to the cognitive distortion model of Aaron Beck, one of the most influential thinkers in this area, depression is the result of a cognitive triad of negative thoughts about oneself, the situation, and the future. The thought patterns of depressed patients are different from those of people with anxiety disorders. Whereas patients with anxiety disorders worry about the future, depressed people think about how they have failed in the past, how poorly they are dealing with the present situation, and how terrible the future will be.

The goal of the cognitive-behavioral treatment of depression is to help the patient think more adaptively, which in turn should improve mood and behavior. Although the specific nature of the treatment will be adapted to each individual patient, there are some general principles of this type of therapy for depression. Patients may be asked to recognize and record negative thoughts (Figure 17.10). Thinking about situations in a negative manner can become automatic and recognizing these thought patterns can be difficult. Once the patterns are identified and monitored, the clinician can help the patient recognize that there are other ways of viewing the same situation—ways of thinking that are not as dysfunctional.

Although cognitive-behavioral therapy can be effective on its own, research shows that combining it with antidepressant medication is significantly more effective than either one of these approaches alone (McCullough, 2000). In addition, the response and remission rates of the combined-treatment approach were higher than any ever reported for depression (Keller et al., 2000). The issue is not drugs versus psychotherapy, but rather identifying the specific treatments from the avail-

17.10 A record of automatic thoughts used in cognitive-behavioral therapy for depression.

Date	Event	Emotion	Automatic thoughts
April 4	Boss seemed annoyed.	Sad, anxious, worried	Oh, what have I done now? If I keep making him mad, I'm going to get fired.
April 5	Husband didn't want to make love.	Sad	I'm so fat and ugly.
April 7	Boss yelled at another employee.	Anxious	I'm next.
April 9	Husband said he's taking a long business trip next month.	Sad, defeated	He's probably got a mistress somewhere. My marriage is falling apart.
April 10	Neighbor brought over some cookies.	A little happy, mostly sad	She probably thinks I can't cook. I look like such a mess all the time. And my house was a disaster when she came in!

able options that provide relief for individual clients. For instance, for clients who are suicidal, in acute distress, or unable to commit to regular attendance with a therapist, drug treatment may be most effective. For many others, especially those who have physical problems, psychotherapy may be the treatment of choice because it is long-lasting and does not have the side effects associated with medications.

Alternative treatments In some patients, episodes of depression occur during the winter. The rate of this disorder, known as seasonal affective disorder (SAD), increases with latitude, with rates highest in regions with the fewest hours of daylight during the winter (Figure 17.11). Many of these patients respond favorably to phototherapy, in which patients are exposed to a high-intensity light source for a period of time each day (Figure 17.12). Patients who crave carbohydrates and sleep a great deal in the winter seem to respond better to phototherapy than do SAD patients who do not exhibit these symptoms.

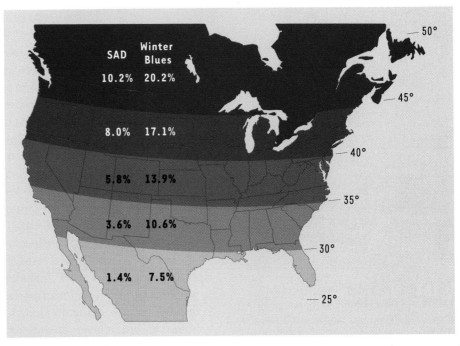

For some depressed patients, regular aerobic exercise can reduce depression and prevent recurrence. It has been speculated that aerobic exercise reduces depression because it releases endorphins, which are chemically related to norepinephrine, a neurotransmitter implicated in depression. Release of endorphins can result in an overall feeling of well-being, which marathoners may recognize as "runner's high." Aerobic exercise may also serve to regularize bodily rhythms, improve self-esteem, and provide social support if people exercise with others. For depressed patients, however, it may be difficult to find the energy and motivation to begin an exercise regime.

17.11 The incidence of seasonal affective disorder (SAD) varies by latitude, being much more common in areas that receive less sunlight during the winter.

In addition to these somewhat benign interventions, there are more drastic treatments that may be warranted for some depressed patients. In the 1930s, **electroconvulsive therapy (ECT)** was developed in Europe and tried on the first human in 1938. ECT involves placing electrodes on the patient's head and administering an electrical current strong enough to produce a seizure (Figure 17.13). Although ECT frequently results in an amelioration of depressed mood, the mechanism by which this occurs is unknown (Fink, 2001). ECT may affect neurotransmitters or the neuroendocrine system; it has been shown to increase levels of acetylcholine, and drugs that block the action of acetylcholine reverse the beneficial effects of ECT. ECT also causes the release and production of peptides, and the higher levels of peptides may lead to an elevation of mood.

17.12 This woman sits in front of strong lighting for several hours each day to reduce her symptoms of SAD.

The general public views ECT in a predominately negative manner. The 1975 film *One Flew over the Cuckoo's Nest* did a great deal to expose the abuses in mental health care and graphically depicted ECT as well as the tragic effects of lobotomy. Although the care of the mentally ill is still far from perfect, many reforms have been implemented. ECT is now generally done under anesthesia with powerful muscle relaxants. This essentially eliminates the motor convulsions

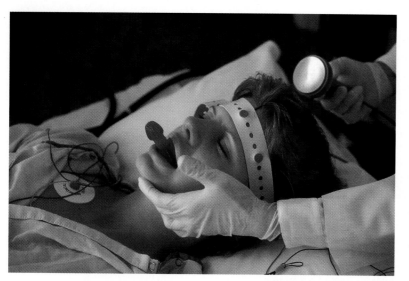

17.13 This woman is being prepared for electroconvulsive therapy. To prevent her from possibly swallowing her tongue, a soft object is placed between her teeth.

and confines the seizure to the brain. There are a number of reasons why ECT might be preferable to other treatments for depression. Antidepressant medication takes about six weeks to be effective whereas ECT works quickly. In a suicidal patient, waiting six weeks for relief can literally be deadly. In addition, ECT may be the treatment of choice for depression in pregnant women, since there is no evidence that the seizures harm the developing fetus. Many psychotropic medications, on the other hand, can cause birth defects. Most important, ECT has proven effective in clients for whom other treatments have failed, providing an effective last resort for those who would otherwise continue to suffer.

ECT does, however, have some serious limitations, including a high relapse rate, often necessitating repeated treatments, and memory impairments (Fink, 2001). In most cases, memory loss is transient and is limited to the day of ECT treatment. Some patients, however, experience substantial memory loss that can be permanent (Donahue, 2000). Some centers perform unilateral ECT over only the hemisphere that is not dominant for language since this seems to reduce any memory disruption (Papadimitrious et al., 2001). New research suggests that the degree of memory and cognitive impairment resulting from ECT may be related to levels of cortisol, a steroid hormone released in response to physical and psychological stress. Depressed patients with higher levels of cortisol show greater impairments in memory and cognitive functions (Neylan et al., 2001). This research may help to identify patients at risk for memory and cognitive losses due to ECT, and these potentially serious side effects can be weighed against the benefits of the treatment.

Recently, research has begun to explore whether **transcranial magnetic stimulation (TMS)** can reduce depressive symptoms. In this procedure, an electromagnetic coil is placed on the scalp and transmits pulses of high-intensity magnetism. The rapid buildup and collapse of the magnetic field induces a momentary electrical current in the brain. The net result is that normal brain activity is disrupted in the brain region beneath the coil. In effect, the coil creates a brief transient brain lesion. A series of studies have demonstrated that TMS over the left frontal regions results in a significant reduction in depression (George et al., 1995; Pascual-Leone et al., 1996; George et al., 1999; Klein et al., 1999). Because TMS does not involve anesthesia and does not have any major side effects (other than headache), it can be administered outside of hospital settings. It is not likely, however, that TMS will ever completely replace ECT, since the two methods may act via different mechanisms and may therefore be appropriate for different types of patients. TMS seems to be more effective for nonpsychotic depression, whereas ECT seems to be more effective for psychotic depression (George et al., 1999).

electroconvulsive therapy (ECT) A procedure used to treat depression that involves administering a strong electrical current to the patient's brain.

transcranial magnetic stimulation (TMS) A procedure that transmits pulses of high-intensity magnetism to the brain.

LITHIUM IS MOST EFFECTIVE FOR BIPOLAR DISORDER

Although major depression and bipolar disorder are both disorders of mood, they are fundamentally different and require different treatments. Bipolar disorder, in which mood cycles between mania and depression, is one of the few mental disorders for which there is a clear optimal treatment. Psychotropic medications have been found to be the most effective way to treat this disorder, especially **lithium**. Only about 20 percent of patients maintained on lithium experience relapses (Keller & Baker, 1991). The mechanisms by which lithium stabilizes mood are not well understood, but the drug seems to modulate neurotransmitter levels, balancing excitatory and inhibitory activities (Jope, 1999). As with other psychotropic drugs, the discovery of lithium for the treatment of bipolar disorder was serendipitous. In 1949, an Australian named John Cade found that the urine of manic patients was toxic to guinea pigs. He postulated that this effect might be due to uric acid. When he gave lithium urate, a salt in uric acid, to the guinea pigs, however, it was not toxic. To his surprise, it protected them against the toxic effects of the manic patients' urine and also sedated them. He next tried lithium salts on himself. When he was assured of their safety, he gave the salts to ten hospitalized manic patients, all of whom recovered rapidly. Lithium does, however, have unpleasant side effects, including thirst, hand tremors, excessive urination, and memory problems. These side effects often diminish after several weeks on the drug.

Although lithium is effective in stabilizing mood, it works better on mania than on depression, and patients are often treated both with lithium and with an antidepressant. Compliance with drug therapy can be a problem for a variety of reasons. Patients may skip doses or stop taking the medications completely in an effort to reduce the side effects of the drugs. Cognitive-behavioral therapy can be an effective way to increase compliance with medication regimes (Miller et al, 1989). Patients with bipolar disorder also may stop taking their medications because they miss the "highs" of their hypomanic and manic phases. Psychological therapy can help patients accept their need for medication and understand the impact their disorder has on them and on those around them.

> **lithium** A psychotropic medication used to treat bipolar disorder.

PHARMACOLOGICAL TREATMENTS ARE SUPERIOR FOR SCHIZOPHRENIA

Freud's psychoanalytic theory and treatment were widely touted as the answer to many mental disorders in the early 1900s. Even Freud, however, admitted that his techniques were only effective for what he termed "neuroses" and were unlikely to be of any benefit to patients with more severe psychotic disorders such as schizophrenia. Because psychotic patients were difficult to handle and even more difficult to treat, they were generally institutionalized in large mental hospitals. By 1934, it was estimated that the physician-to-patient ratio in such institutions was more than 1 to 200 in the state of New York. This set up a situation in which the staff and administration of mental hospitals were willing to try any treatment that was inexpensive and had a chance of decreasing the patient population, or that at the very least might make the inmates more manageable.

Brain surgery was considered to be a viable option in the management of patients with severe mental illness. Although some brain surgeries were performed in the early 1880s, Egas Moniz is generally credited with bringing the practice to the attention of the medical world in the 1930s. His surgical procedure, later known as lobotomy, severed nerve-fiber pathways in the prefrontal cortex. Although Moniz initially reported that the operation was frequently successful it soon became evident to him that the patients who benefited most from the surgery were those who were anxious or depressed. Schizophrenia patients did not seem to improve following the operation. With the introduction of psychotropic medications in the 1950s, lobotomies were virtually discontinued.

What are effective treatments for schizophrenia?

tardive dyskinesia A side effect of some antipsychotic medications that produces involuntary movements of the lips, tongue, face, legs, or other parts of the body.

clozapine An antipsychotic medication that acts on multiple neurotransmitter receptors and is beneficial in treating both the negative and positive symptoms of schizophrenia.

Pharmacological treatment It had been known since the sixteenth century that extracts from dogbane, a toxic herb, could calm highly agitated patients. The critical ingredient was isolated in the 1950s and was named reserpine. When given to schizophrenia patients, it not only had a sedative effect, it also was an effective antipsychotic, reducing the positive symptoms of schizophrenia, such as delusions and hallucinations. Shortly afterward, a synthetic version of reserpine was created that had fewer side effects. This drug, called *chlorpromazine*, is a neuroleptic, or major tranquilizer. It reduces anxiety, sedates without causing sleep, and decreases the severity and frequency of the positive symptoms of schizophrenia. Later, another antipsychotic, *haloperidol*, was developed that was chemically different and had less of a sedating effect than chlorpromazine.

Haloperidol and chlorpromazine revolutionized the treatment of schizophrenia and became the most frequently used therapy for the disorder. Schizophrenia patients who had been hospitalized for years were able to walk out of mental institutions and live independently. These antipsychotics are not without drawbacks, however. The medications have little or no impact on the negative symptoms of schizophrenia, such as apathy and social withdrawal. In addition, they have significant side effects. Chlorpromazine sedates patients, can cause constipation and weight gain, and causes cardiovascular damage. Although haloperidol does not cause these symptoms, both drugs have significant motor side effects that resemble Parkinson's disease. Immobility of facial muscles, trembling of extremities, muscle spasms, uncontrollable salivation, and a shuffling walk can all occur as a result of antipsychotic medication. **Tardive dyskinesia**, involuntary movements of the lips, tongue, face, legs, or other parts of the body, is another devastating side effect of neuroleptic medications and is irreversible once it appears. Despite these debilitating side effects, chlorpromazine and haloperidol were essentially the only medications available to schizophrenia patients for many years.

In the late 1980s, clozapine was introduced. **Clozapine** was significantly different from the previous antipsychotic medications in a number of ways. First, it acted not only on dopamine receptors, but also on those for serotonin, norepinephrine, acetylcholine, and histamine. Second, it was beneficial in treating the negative symptoms of schizophrenia as well as the positive symptoms. Many patients who had not responded to the previously available neuroleptics improved on clozapine (Figure 17.14). Third, there was no evidence of Parkinsonian symptoms or of tardive dyskinesia in any of the patients taking the drug. Clozapine has fewer side effects than either chlorpromazine or haloperidol, but its side effects are serious. Clozapine is associated with seizures, heart arrhythmias, and substantial weight gain. Of even greater concern, clozapine can cause a fatal reduction in white blood cells. Although the risk of this is low, frequent blood tests are required for patients taking the drug. The cost of the blood tests in addition to the high cost of the medication itself has made this drug treatment prohibitively expensive for many patients. More recently, other medications similar to

17.14 Clozapine is more effective than previously available neuroleptics in treating both the positive and negative symptoms of schizophrenia.

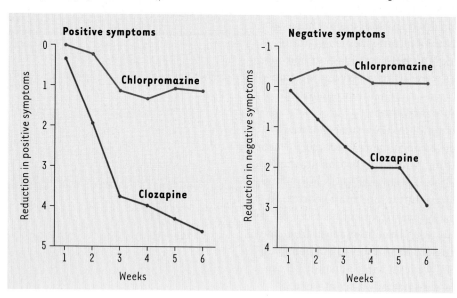

clozapine in structure and pharmacology have been introduced. These medications appear to be as effective as clozapine but do not reduce white blood cell counts. Researchers continue to pursue new medications based on findings in the areas of receptor affinities and other new discoveries about the nervous system. The possibility that individuals with schizophrenia might inadvertently give themselves psychopharmacological treatment is considered in "Studying the Mind: Smoking as Self-medication?"

Psychosocial treatments   It is well established that medication is essential in the treatment of schizophrenia. Without it, patients may deteriorate, experiencing more frequent and more severe psychotic episodes. When antipsychotic drugs became available, other types of therapies for schizophrenia were virtually dismissed. It became clear over time, however, that although medication is effective in reducing delusions and hallucinations, it does not have a substantial impact on patients' social functioning. A study of the clinical outcome of schizophrenia treatments over a 100-year period demonstrated that antipsychotic drugs improved the

Studying the Mind

SMOKING AS SELF-MEDICATION?

Patients who have schizophrenia smoke tobacco more than patients diagnosed with any other mental illness. Between 74 and 92 percent of schizophrenia patients smoke, whereas the prevalence of smoking is 35–54 percent for all psychiatric patients and 30 percent for the general population (Lohr & Flynn, 1992). Schizophrenia patients who smoke also tend to use high-nicotine cigarettes and to extract more nicotine from their cigarettes when compared to other smokers (Olincy et al., 1997). Those with schizophrenia generally start smoking before their first psychotic episode (McEvoy & Brown, 1999).

Intriguing new research suggests why individuals with schizophrenia smoke. When a stimulus is presented to a subject in a laboratory experiment, the change in brain activity that results can be measured using EEG. When neurologically normal subjects hear pairs of clicks, each click results in a distinct brain wave 50ms after the click. The wave is called the P50 because of its valence and timing. In normal subjects, the P50 to the second click in the pair is significantly smaller than to the first click. In those with schizophrenia, however, the P50 to the second click is nearly as large as to the first (Adler et al., 1982). Immediately after unrestricted smoking, however, the second P50 of schizophrenia subjects is smaller, similar to that seen with normal subjects. The effect lasts for about 30 minutes after smoking. In neurologically normal subjects who smoke, unrestricted smoking results in bigger P50s. This suggests that the effect of smoking is significantly different for those with schizophrenia. Equally telling is that high doses of nicotine have the same effect on

the brains of about half the nonaffected relatives of schizophrenia patients as on the brains of those with schizophrenia themselves (Siegel et al., 1984).

It seems that there may be some neurological dysfunction that makes individuals susceptible to schizophrenia. Adler and his colleagues (1998) have speculated that it is a deficit in the alpha7-nicotinic acetylcholine receptor. This receptor seems to be involved in filtering incoming sensory information. A deficit in the alpha7 receptor could thus be responsible for difficulty in processing sensory information. This could account for some of the sensory abnormalities in schizophrenia, such as auditory hallucinations. Genetic analysis of schizophrenics' families suggests that it may be possible to link the P50 deficit with a specific chromosome. Research in this area is ongoing and may one day reveal a genetic risk factor for schizophrenia.

One last finding is worth mentioning. Although people with schizophrenia tend to smoke heavily, they have a lower incidence of lung cancer than other heavy smokers. The alpha7-nicotinic acetylcholine receptor may be the reason. Nicotine is known to promote the growth of neuroendocrine cells in the lungs, which may be a factor in the development of lung cancer in smokers. The alpha7-nicotinic acetylcholine receptor mediates the growth of neuroendocrine cells; therefore, a deficit in these receptors in schizophrenia patients might result in less abnormal growth of neuroendocrine cells in the lungs.

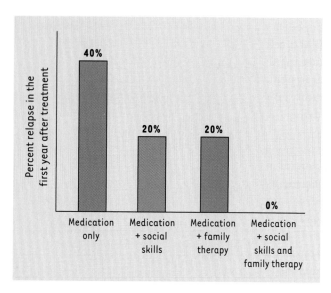

17.15 Medication is the most effective way to reduce the rate of relapse for patients with schizophrenia, but adding psychosocial interventions, such as family therapy and social-skills training, improves outcome.

outcome for schizophrenia patients from just under 40 percent to about 50 percent (Hegarty et al., 1994). While this is an improvement, it falls far short of a cure.

Antipsychotic medication is most effective when used in combination with other treatment approaches. Social-skills training has been an effective way to address some of the deficits shown by those with schizophrenia. Schizophrenia patients can benefit from intensive training on regulating affect, recognizing social cues, and predicting the effects of their behavior in social situations (Figure 17.15). With intensive long-term training, schizophrenia patients can generalize the skills learned in therapy to other social environments. Self-care skills can be another area in which schizophrenia patients are deficient. Behavioral interventions can be focused on such areas as grooming and bathing, management of medications, and financial planning. Training in specific cognitive skills, such as modifying thinking patterns and coping with auditory hallucinations, has been less effective.

Prognosis in schizophrenia Most patients diagnosed with schizophrenia experience multiple psychotic episodes over the course of the illness. In some patients the disorder seems to be progressive, with each schizophrenic episode laying the groundwork for increasingly severe symptoms in the future. For this reason, it is thought to be in the patient's best interest to treat the disorder early and aggressively. Usually, physicians prefer to start with less expensive medications and move to more recent drugs only if the traditional medications are not effective. However, despite the cost and potential problems with the newer medications, some researchers argue that they should be the drugs of choice for most schizophrenia patients. These drugs control more symptoms of schizophrenia and are effective for a larger percentage of patients than the earlier neuroleptics.

Although the disorder becomes progressively more severe in some affected individuals, this is not true for a majority of those diagnosed with schizophrenia. In fact, most schizophrenia patients improve over time. One long-term study that followed schizophrenia subjects for an average of 32 years showed that between half and two-thirds were recovered or had had considerable improvement in functioning on follow-up (Harding et al., 1987). No one knows why most of those with schizophrenia seem to improve as they grow older. It may be that the patients who improve have found the treatment regimen that is most effective for them. Another theory is that the changes in the brain that occur with aging somehow result in fewer psychotic episodes. Dopamine levels may decrease with age and this may be related to the improvement in schizophrenic symptoms.

Prognosis for schizophrenia patients depends on a variety of factors, including age of onset, gender, and culture. Those diagnosed with schizophrenia later in life tend to have a more favorable prognosis than those who experience their first symptoms during childhood or adolescence (McGlashan, 1988). Women tend to have a better prognosis than men (Hambrecht et al., 1992), perhaps because the onset of schizophrenia in women tends to be later than in men. Interestingly, culture also plays a role in prognosis. Schizophrenia in developing countries is often not as severe as in developed countries (Jablensky, 1989; Leff et al., 1992). More extensive family networks in developing countries may provide more support in caring for schizophrenia patients.

What Are the Most Effective Treatments?

Psychotherapy and biological therapy are used to treat mental disorders. When the two are equally effective, psychotherapy may be preferred because it has fewer side effects and persists beyond treatment. Cognitive and behavioral therapies, especially exposure and response prevention, are particularly useful for anxiety disorders, although drug treatments are also used for panic disorder and OCD. There are a number of treatment strategies for mood disorders, including exercise, antidepressants, cognitive-behavioral therapy, electroconvulsive therapy, and transcranial magnetic stimulation. For mania, however, only lithium appears to be effective. Psychopharmacology is the recommended treatment for schizophrenia. Clozapine is effective for many patients who have not responded to other medications and works for negative as well as positive symptoms of the disorder. Pharmacological interventions for schizophrenia are most effective when used in combination with other treatment approaches. Training in social and self-care skills can help patients improve their ability to interact with others and to take care of themselves. Behavioral interventions can also help in improving self-care and in increasing compliance with medication.

CAN PERSONALITY DISORDERS BE TREATED?

Just as not much is known about the causes of personality disorders, little is known about how best to treat them. There is a growing literature of case studies describing treatment approaches for personality disorders, but there are few large well-controlled studies. The one thing about personality disorders that most therapists agree on is that they are notoriously difficult to treat. Individuals with personality disorders who are in therapy are usually also being treated for an Axis I disorder, which typically is the problem for which they sought therapy in the first place. People rarely seek therapy for personality disorders because one of the hallmarks of these disorders is that patients tend to see the environment rather than their own behavior as the cause of their problems. Individuals with personality disorders can be very difficult to engage in therapy since they do not see their behavior as a problem. We now consider two of the better-researched personality disorders.

DIALECTICAL BEHAVIOR THERAPY IS MOST SUCCESSFUL FOR BORDERLINE PERSONALITY DISORDER

The impulsivity, affective disturbances, and identity disturbances that are characteristic of borderline personality disorder make therapy with these individuals very challenging. Traditional psychotherapy approaches have been largely unsuccessful, so there have been efforts to develop approaches specific to borderline personality disorder.

The most successful treatment approach to date for borderline personality disorder was developed by Marsha Linehan (Figure 17.16) in the 1980s. **Dialectical behavior therapy** (**DBT**) combines elements of the behavioral, cognitive, and psychodynamic approaches. Clients are seen in both group and individual sessions, and the responsibilities of both the client and the therapist are made

dialectical behavior therapy (DBT)
A treatment for borderline personality disorder that combines elements of behavioral, cognitive, and psychodynamic approaches.

17.16 Marsha Linehan developed dialectical behavior therapy, one of the few effective treatments for borderline personality disorder.

explicit. Therapy proceeds in three stages. In the first stage, the therapist targets the client's most extreme and dysfunctional behaviors. Often these are self-cutting and suicidal threats or attempts. The focus is on replacing these behaviors with ones that are more appropriate. Clients are taught problem-solving techniques and more effective and acceptable ways of coping with emotions. In the second stage of the treatment, the therapist helps the client explore past traumatic experiences that may be at the root of emotional problems. In the third stage, the therapist helps the patient develop self-respect and independent problem-solving. This is a crucial stage in therapy. Borderline patients are very dependent on others for support and validation, and they must be able to generate these things themselves or they will likely revert to their previous patterns of behavior.

Because of the depressive and sometimes psychotic-like symptoms experienced by individuals with borderline personality disorder, it was previously believed that they would develop an Axis I disorder such as schizophrenia or depression. Studies that have followed these individuals over time, however, have demonstrated that this is not the case. Instead, they continue with their symptoms relatively unchanged over time (Plakun et al., 1985). The only group that does seem to show some improvement in the long term is borderline patients of a high socioeconomic level who receive intensive treatment. These individuals show improvement in interpersonal relationships and often achieve full-time employment (Stone et al., 1987). In the remainder of borderline patients, however, interpersonal and occupational problems are the norm. Substance abuse is not uncommon, and many attempt suicide multiple times.

Therapeutic approaches specifically targeted at borderline personality disorder, such as DBT, may improve the prognosis for these patients. Studies have demonstrated that clients undergoing DBT are more likely to remain in treatment and less likely to be suicidal than are clients in other types of therapy (Linehan et al., 1991; Linehan et al., 1993; Koons, 2001). Although DBT was initially developed as an outpatient therapy, it has recently been adapted for use in an inpatient setting (Swenson et al., 2001). Because borderline patients thrive on attention, inpatient settings that are not specifically designed for these patients can inadvertently reinforce dysfunctional behavior that brings them attention, such as self-injury and suicide attempts. The result is often a worsening of symptoms and long-term hospitalization (Rosenbluth & Silver, 1992). The DBT program begins with a three-month inpatient stay followed by long-term outpatient therapy, and it has been found to be very effective in reducing depression, anxiety, and suicidal gestures (Bohus et al., 2000).

ANTISOCIAL PERSONALITY DISORDER IS DIFFICULT TO TREAT

Although treating borderline patients may be very difficult, treating those with antisocial personality disorder often seems impossible. These patients lie without thinking twice about it, care little for the feelings of others, and live for the present without consideration of the future. All of these make development of a therapeutic relationship and motivation for change remote possibilities at best. Antisocial individuals are often more interested in manipulating their therapists than in changing their behavior. Therapists working with these patients must be constantly on guard.

Therapeutic approaches for antisocial personality disorder A number of treatment approaches have been tried for antisocial personality disorder. Because antisocial individuals have been reported to have diminished cortical arousal, stimulants have been prescribed to normalize arousal levels. There is evidence that these drugs are beneficial in the short term, but they are not a long-term solution. Antianxiety drugs may lower hostility levels somewhat, and lithium has shown some promise in treating the aggressive, impulsive behavior of violent criminals. Overall, however, psychotropic medications have not proven effective in treating this disorder.

Similarly, traditional psychotherapeutic approaches have proved to be of little use in treating antisocial personality disorder. Behavioral and cognitive approaches have met with somewhat more success. Behavioral approaches reinforce appropriate behavior and ignore or punish inappropriate behavior in an attempt to replace maladaptive behavior patterns with more socially appropriate behavior. This approach seems to work best when the therapist controls reinforcement, the client cannot leave treatment, and the client is part of a group. Individual therapy sessions rarely result in any change in antisocial behavior. Clearly, the behavioral approach cannot be implemented on an outpatient basis, since the client will receive reinforcement for his behavior outside of therapy and can leave treatment at any time. For these reasons, therapy for this disorder is most effective in a residential treatment center or correctional facility.

More recently, cognitive approaches have been tried for antisocial personality disorder. Beck and his colleagues (1990) have conceptualized this disorder as a series of faulty cognitions. The antisocial individual believes that his desire for something justifies any actions he takes to attain it. He believes his actions will not have negative consequences, or if they do that these consequences are not important. He also believes he is always right and that what others think is unimportant. Therapy is therefore focused on making the client aware of these beliefs and challenging their validity. Therapists try to demonstrate that the client's goals can be met more easily by following the rules of society than by trying to get around them, as in the following example:

> Therapist: How well has the "beat-the-system" approach actually worked out for you over time?
>
> Brett: It works great . . . until someone catches on or starts to catch on. Then you have to scrap that plan and come up with a new one.
>
> Therapist: How difficult was it, you know, to cover up one scheme and come up with a new one?
>
> Brett: Sometimes it was really easy. There are some real pigeons out there.
>
> Therapist: Was it always easy?
>
> Brett: Well, no. Sometimes it was a real bitch . . . . Seems like I'm always needing a good plan to beat the system.
>
> Therapist: Do you think it's ever easier to go with the system instead of trying to beat it in some way?
>
> Brett: Well, after all that I have been through, I would have to say yes, there have been times that going with the system would have been easier in the long run. . . . But . . . it's such a challenge to beat the system. It feels exciting when I come up with a new plan and think I can make it work. (Beck et al., 1990)

This dialogue illustrates both the cognitive approach and why these patients are so difficult to work with. Even if they can understand that what they are doing

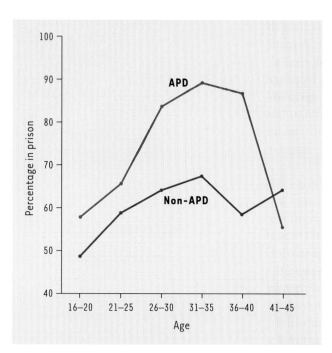

17.17 Of 521 prisoners studied by Robert Hare and his colleagues, those with antisocial personality disorder were more likely than other criminals to spend time in jail before age 40. After age 40 they were less likely.

is wrong, they don't care. They live for the thrill of getting away with something.

Prognosis for antisocial personality disorder   The prognosis that antisocial patients will change their behavior as a result of therapy is poor. Some of the more recently developed cognitive techniques show promise, but as yet there is no good evidence that the changes they produce are long-lasting or even real. Fortunately for society, however, most antisocial individuals improve after age 40 (Figure 17.17). The reasons for this are not known, but the improvement may be due to a reduction in biological drives. Alternative theories suggest that these individuals may gain insight into their self-defeating behaviors or may just get worn out and be unable to continue their manipulative ways. This improvement, however, is only in the realm of antisocial behavior. The egocentricity, callousness, and manipulativeness remain unchanged (Harpur & Hare, 1994). In fact, although criminal acts decrease among those with antisocial personality disorder after age 40, over 50 percent of these individuals continue to be arrested after age 40 (Hare et al., 1988).

Because of the limited effectiveness of therapy for this disorder, time and effort may be better spent in prevention. Conduct disorder is a childhood condition known to be a precursor to antisocial personality disorder. Some of the environmental and developmental risk factors for conduct disorder have been identified, and focusing on these may reduce the likelihood that a child with conduct disorder will grow up to have antisocial personality disorder.

Can Personality Disorders Be Treated?

Personality disorders are characterized by long-standing maladaptive ways of interacting with the world, and they are notoriously difficult to treat. Efforts have been made to develop treatment programs for both borderline and antisocial personality disorders because they can have devastating effects on the individual, the family, and society. Dialectical behavior therapy is the most successful method of treating borderline personality disorder. At this point, there is no treatment approach that appears to be particularly successful in treating antisocial personality disorder.

HOW SHOULD CHILDHOOD DISORDERS BE TREATED?

It is estimated that more than 12 percent of children and adolescents in the United States suffer from mental disorders (Leckman et al., 1995). In 1990, the National Advisory Mental Health Council recommended that funding for research in childhood and adolescent mental disorders increase from $92 million to $283 million by 1995. The stated purpose of this increase was to "hasten the day when no child or adolescent need be too hard to handle, too sad to survive, too strange and angry to live among us, too ill to laugh, play and love." The recommendation reflected growing awareness of the scope and persistence of mental disorders in children. Childhood experience and development are critically important to adult mental health. Problems not addressed during childhood will still be there in adulthood and are likely to be more significant and more difficult to treat. Most theories of human development regard children as more malleable than adults and therefore more amenable to treatment. That would suggest that childhood disorders should be the focus of research into etiology, prevention, and treatment. To illustrate the issues involved in treating childhood disorders, we will consider treatment approaches for two of these disorders.

RESEARCH QUESTION
???

> Can children be treated for mental disorders?

AUTISTIC CHILDREN BENEFIT FROM A STRUCTURED TREATMENT APPROACH

The treatment of autistic children presents unique challenges to mental health professionals. The core symptoms of autism—impaired communication, restricted interests, and deficits in social interaction—make these children particularly difficult to work with. They often exhibit extreme behaviors as well as public self-stimulation. Although these behaviors must be reduced or eliminated before progress can be made in other areas, elimination is difficult because it is hard to find effective reinforcers. Although normal children respond positively to social praise and small prizes, autistic children are often oblivious to these things. In some cases, food is the only effective reinforcement in the initial stages of treatment. Another characteristic of autistic children is an overselectivity of attention. This tendency to focus on specific details while ignoring others interferes with generalizing learned behavior to other stimuli and situations. A child who learns to set the table with plates may be completely stymied when presented with bowls instead. Generalization of skills must be explicitly taught. For this reason, structured therapies are more effective for these children than unstructured interventions such as play therapy.

Behavioral treatment for autism   One of the best known and perhaps most effective treatments for autistic children was developed by Ivar Lovaas and his colleagues at the University of California at Los Angeles. The program is based on principles of operant conditioning. Behaviors that are reinforced should increase in frequency while behaviors that are not reinforced should be extinguished. This very intensive approach requires a minimum of 40 hours of treatment per week. Preschool-age children with autism were treated by teachers and by their parents, who were given specific training. After more than two years of treatment, the children had gained about 20 IQ points on average and most of them were able to enter a normal kindergarten program (Lovaas, 1987). In contrast, there was no change in IQ in a comparable control group of children who did not receive any treatment. A group of children who received ten hours of treatment per week fared no better than the control group. Initiating treatment at a younger age was also shown to yield better results, as did involving the parents and having at least a portion of the therapy take place in the home. Children with better language skills before entering treatment had better outcomes than those who were mute or echolalic.

Although Lovaas's program has been demonstrated to be effective, it has its drawbacks. The most obvious is the time commitment. The therapy must be very intensive and last for years. Parents essentially become full-time teachers for their autistic children. The financial and emotional drains on the family can be substantial. If the family has other children, they may feel neglected or jealous because of the amount of time and energy expended on the disabled child.

Biological treatment for autism   Because there is good evidence that autism is caused by brain dysfunction, there have been many attempts to use this knowledge to treat the disorder. It is easy to find reports of children who benefited from alternative treatment approaches. These case studies are compelling, but when the treatments are assessed in controlled studies, there is little or no evidence that most of them are effective. However, a few biologically based treatment approaches have shown some promise.

In the 1990s, it was noted that some autistic children had increased levels of peptides in their urine. These peptides were derived from gluten and were thought to have a negative pharmacological effect on learning, attention, brain maturation, and social interaction. Autistic children with elevated peptide levels were put on a special diet and their progress was monitored for several years (Reichelt et al., 1991). After one year, the level of peptides in their urine was normal. The children demonstrated reductions in odd behavior and improvements in social, cognitive, and communicative abilities. Four years later, they continued to improve, but their development lagged behind that of their neurologically normal peers. Findings like this are exciting and can provide hope to families with autistic children. However, this treatment was only effective for a subgroup of autistic children, and even within that group it was clearly not a cure.

Another approach to the treatment of autism involves serotonin. SSRIs such as Prozac have been found to reduce compulsions in patients diagnosed with obsessive-compulsive disorder. Because autism involves compulsive and stereotyped behavior, and because there is some evidence of abnormal serotonin metabolism in autistic children, SSRIs have been tried as a treatment for autism. It has been reported that in some autistic children the drug reduces stereotyped motor behavior and self-abuse and improves social interactions (McDougle, 1997). There is also evidence that medications that block the action of dopamine have similar effects. Still, at this point, the neurobiology of autism is not well understood, and although attempts to use psychopharmacology to treat the disorder have resulted in some improvements in behavior, they have not yielded dramatic results.

Prognosis for children with autism   Although there are a few reports of remarkable recovery from autism, the long-term prognosis is considered poor. A recent follow-up study of men in their early twenties revealed that they continued to show the ritualistic behavior typical of autism. In addition, nearly three-quarters had severe social difficulties and were unable to live and work independently (Howlin et al., 2000). There are several factors that affect prognosis for autistic individuals. The prognosis is particularly poor for children whose symptoms are apparent before age two (Hoshino et al., 1980). Early language ability is associated with better outcome (Howlin et al., 2000), as is higher IQ. Autistic children have difficulty generalizing from the therapeutic setting to the real world, and this severely limits their social functioning (Handleman et al., 1988). A higher IQ may mean a better ability to generalize learning and therefore a better overall prognosis.

CHILDREN WITH ADHD CAN BENEFIT FROM A VARIETY OF APPROACHES

Although no one disputes the validity of the classification of autism, there are many who continue to question whether attention-deficit/hyperactivity disorder is a mental disorder or simply a troublesome behavior pattern that children will eventually outgrow. Some children diagnosed with ADHD do grow out of it. Many more, however, continue to suffer from the disorder throughout adolescence and adulthood. Longitudinal studies show that 70 percent of individuals diagnosed with ADHD during childhood still meet the criteria for the disorder in adolescence. These individuals are more likely to drop out of school and to reach a lower socioeconomic level than expected. They continue to show a pattern of inattention, impulsivity, and hyperactivity, and they are at increased risk for other psychiatric disorders. Because of this somewhat bleak long-term prognosis, it is clear that effective treatment early in life is of great importance.

Pharmacological treatment of ADHD Currently, the most common treatment for ADHD is a central nervous system stimulant such as **methylphenidate** (*ritalin*). The effects of this drug are similar to those of caffeine and amphetamines, but it is more potent than the former and less potent than the latter. Although the actions of methylphenidate are not fully understood, it is thought to act on multiple neurotransmitters, in particular dopamine. Based on the external behavior of children with ADHD, one might conclude that their brains are overly active, and it may seem surprising that a stimulant would improve their symptoms. In fact, functional brain imaging shows that children with ADHD have underactive brains; their hyperactivity may be a way of raising their arousal levels.

At appropriate doses, central nervous system stimulants decrease overactivity and distractibility and increase attention and the ability to concentrate. Children on stimulants are able to work more effectively on a task without interruption and are more academically productive. Even their handwriting seems to improve. They are less disruptive and noisy, and this likely has contributed to the large number of children who take this medication (Figure 17.18). Parents often feel pressured by the school system to medicate children who are an ongoing behavior problem in the classroom. Parents themselves can pressure physicians to prescribe the drug because it can make home life much more manageable. One study measured the effects of methylphenidate on the behavior of children during a baseball game (Pelham et al., 1990). Those children with ADHD who were taking the medication would assume the ready position in the outfield and could keep track of the game. Children with ADHD who were not taking the drug would often throw or kick their mitts even while the pitch was in progress.

Studies have shown that children taking methylphenidate are happier, more socially adept, and more academically successful. They also interact more positively with their parents, perhaps because they are more likely to comply with requests. The medication has its drawbacks, however. There is evidence that although stimulants are beneficial in the short term, their benefits do not seem to be maintained over the long term. In addition, there is a very real risk of abuse, and there have been

methylphenidate A central nervous system stimulant medication used to treat ADHD.

17.18 The use of methylphenidate (ritalin) for children with ADHD dramatically reduces negative behaviors while only slightly increasing the amount of positive behavior.

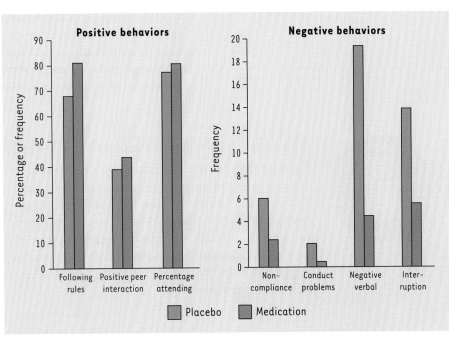

numerous cases of children and adolescents buying and selling these stimulants. There are also side effects, including sleep problems, reduced appetite, bodily twitches, and temporary growth suppression. Perhaps most important, some children on medication may see their problem as beyond their control. They may not feel responsible for their behavior and may not learn coping strategies that they will need later if they discontinue their medication or if it ceases to be effective. Most therapists believe that medication should be supplemented by psychological therapies such as behavior modification, and some even urge that medication be replaced by other treatment approaches when possible. Nonetheless, the data are clear that treatment progresses much better if drugs are part of the overall treatment plan.

Behavioral treatment of ADHD Behavioral treatment of ADHD aims to reinforce positive behaviors and ignore or punish problem behaviors. The difficulties with this treatment approach are similar to those discussed in the section on autism. Treatment is very intensive and time-consuming. In addition, although it is often not difficult to improve behavior in a structured setting, the effects of therapy do not necessarily generalize beyond the clinic or classroom. Many therapists advocate combining behavioral approaches with medication. The medication is used to gain control over the behavior, and then behavioral modification techniques can be taught and the medication slowly phased out. Others argue that medication should be used only if behavioral techniques do not reduce inappropriate behaviors. Although this controversy is ongoing, recent research has shown that medication plus behavioral therapy is more effective than either approach alone.

The National Institute of Mental Health in collaboration with teams of investigators began the Multimodal Treatment of Attention-Deficit Hyperactivity Disorder (MTA) in 1992. The study involved 579 children who were randomly assigned to community care or to one of three treatment groups, each lasting 14 months. The treatment groups were: medical management (usually treatment with a stimulant such as methylphenidate), intensive behavioral treatment, and a combination of the two. Follow-up studies reveal that the children receiving medication and those receiving a combination of medication and behavioral therapy had greater improvement in their ADHD symptoms than did those in the other two groups (Jensen et al., 2001). Children who received both medication and behavioral therapy showed a slight advantage over those who received only medication in areas such as social skills, academics, and parent-child relations.

How Should Childhood Disorders Be Treated?

The most effective treatment for autism currently is structured and intensive behavioral therapy. Biological interventions, such as medication and restricted diet, have shown some promise in subgroups of children with autism but have been largely ineffective. In contrast, medications such as methylphenidate can be quite effective in treating children with ADHD. However, there are side effects associated with this type of medication, as well as ethical concerns. For these reasons, many parents and clinicians have turned to other approaches, such as behavioral therapy. Recent research suggests that the most effective management strategy for ADHD may be a combination of medication and behavioral therapy.

CONCLUSION

Although great strides have been made in identifying the etiology of mental disorders, this growing knowledge has not always given rise to new treatment approaches. Treatment of mental disorders is aimed at helping the individual think and behave in more adaptive ways, but the approaches can vary tremendously. For some disorders, several approaches are equally effective. For other disorders, some approaches are more effective than others. New understanding of the ways in which mental disorders affect neural functioning may lead to the discovery of more effective psychotropic medications. History teaches us, however, that medication is not the magic bullet for mental illness. Even with the creation of more effective medications, other interventions remain crucial. A pill may help relieve the symptoms of mental illness, but it cannot help the patient cope with the effects of the disorder, interact with others, or think and behave in more adaptive ways. Psychological, cognitive, and behavioral interventions can address these issues more effectively than any medication. Further research may help identify and implement the treatment approaches or combinations of approaches that are best for each disorder and for each individual.

FURTHER READINGS

Dawes, R. M. (1994). *House of cards: Psychology and psychotherapy built on myth*. New York: Maxwell Macmillan International.

Endler, N. (1982). *Holiday of darkness: A psychologist's personal journey out of his depression*. New York: John Wiley & Sons.

Kramer, P. D. (1993). *Listening to Prozac: A psychiatrist explores antidepressant drugs and the remaking of the self*. New York: Viking Penguin.

Linehan, M. M. (1993). *Cognitive-behavioral treatment of borderline personality disorders*. New York: Guilford Publications.

Maurice, C. (1994). *Let me hear your voice: A family's triumph over autism*. New York: Knopf.

Pennebaker, J. W. (1990). *Opening up: The healing power of confiding in others*. New York: William Morrow & Co., Inc.

Rosen, L. E., & Amador, X. F. (1996). *When someone you love is depressed: How to help your loved one without losing yourself*. New York: Free Press.

Seligman, M. E. P., Walker, E. F., & Rosenhan, D. L. (2001). *Abnormal psychology*. New York: W. W. Norton.

GLOSSARY

absentmindedness   The inattentive or shallow encoding of events.

absolute threshold   The minimum intensity of stimulation that must occur before one can experience a sensation.

accommodation   (1) A process by which muscles change the shape of the lens by flattening it to focus on distant objects or by thickening it to focus on closer objects. (2) The process through which a schema is adapted or expanded to incorporate a new experience that does not easily fit into an existing schema.

accuracy   The extent to which an experimental measure is free from error.

acetylcholine (ACh)   The neurotransmitter responsible for motor control at the junction between nerves and muscles and are also involved in mental processes such as learning, memory, sleeping, and dreaming.

achievement motive   The desire to do well relative to standards of excellence.

acquisition   The gradual formation of an association between the conditioned and unconditioned stimuli.

action potential   The neural impulse that passes along the axon and subsequently causes the release of chemicals from the terminal buttons.

activation-synthesis hypothesis   A theory of dreaming that proposes that neural stimulation from the pons activates mechanisms that normally interpret visual input.

adaptations   In evolutionary theory, the physical characteristics, skills, or abilities that increase the chances of reproduction or survival and are therefore likely to be passed along to future generations.

additive color mixing   A way to produce a given spectral pattern in which different wavelengths of lights are mixed. The percept is determined by the interaction of these wavelengths with receptors in the eye and is a psychological process.

adrenocorticotropic hormone (ACTH)   A hormone secreted by the pituitary gland in response to stress.

affiliation   The tendency to be in social contact with others.

aggression   Any behavior or action that involves the intention to harm someone else.

agonist   Any drug that enhances the actions of a specific neurotransmitter.

agoraphobia   An anxiety disorder marked by fear of being in situations in which escape may be difficult or impossible.

alcoholism   Abnormal alcohol seeking characterized by loss of control over drinking and accompanied by physiological effects of tolerance and withdrawal.

alexithymia   A disorder that leads to a lack of the subjective experience of emotion.

all-or-none principle   A neuron fires with the same potency each time, although frequency can vary; it either fires or not, it cannot partially fire.

altruism   To provide help when it is needed, without any apparent reward for doing so.

amnesia   Deficits in long-term memory that result from disease, brain injury, or psychological trauma.

amygdala   A brain structure that serves a vital role in learning to associate things in the world with emotional responses and for processing emotional information.

androgynous   Those who have both masculine and feminine traits.

anorexia nervosa   An eating disorder characterized by an excessive fear of becoming fat and a refusal to eat.

antagonist   Any drug that inhibits the action of a specific neurotransmitter.

anterograde amnesia   An inability to form new memories.

anti-anxiety drugs   A class of psychotropic medications used for the treatment of anxiety.

antibodies   Protein molecules that attach themselves to foreign agents and mark them for destruction.

antidepressants   A class of psychotropic medications used to treat depression.

antipsychotics   A class of drugs used to treat schizophrenia and other disorders that involve psychosis.

antisocial personality disorder   A personality disorder marked by a lack of empathy and remorse.

anxiety disorders   Characterized by the experience of excessive anxiety in the absence of true danger.

arousal   Term to describe physiological activation, such as increased brain activity, autonomic responses, sweating, or muscle tension.

assimilation   The process through which a new experience is placed into an existing schema.

attachment   A strong emotional connection that persists over time and across circumstances.

attention   The study of how the brain selects which sensory stimuli to discard and which to pass along to higher levels of processing.

attention-deficit/hyperactivity disorder (ADHD)   A disorder characterized by restless, inattentive, and impulsive behaviors.

attitude   The evaluation of objects or ideas to indicate like or dislike toward them.

autism   A developmental disorder involving deficits in social interaction, impaired communication, and restricted interests.

autonomic nervous system (ANS)   A major component of the peripheral nervous system, which regulates the body's internal environment by stimulating glands and by maintaining internal organs such as the heart, gall bladder, and stomach.

autoreceptors   A neuron's own neurotransmitter receptors, which regulate the release of the neurotransmitters.

awareness   The notion that to be cognizant of information is to be able to report that the information is being, or has been, perceived.

axon   A long narrow outgrowth of a neuron by which information is transmitted to other neurons.

basal ganglia   A system of subcortical structures that are important for the initiation of planned movement.

base rate   The predicted frequency of an event occurring.

Bayes' theorem   A formula that is used to update the probability of a given event, given new information that supplements the preexisting base rate associated with the event in question.

behavior   Any observable action or response.

behavior modification   Principles of operant conditioning are used to reinforce desired behaviors and ignore or punish unwanted behaviors.

behavioral approach system (BAS)   The brain system involved in the pursuit of incentives, or rewards.

behavioral inhibition system (BIS)   The brain system that is sensitive to punishment and therefore inhibits behavior that might lead to danger or pain.

behaviorism   A psychological approach that emphasizes the role of environmental forces in producing behavior.

binding problem   The question considering the issue: if the brain processes features automatically and separately, how does it determine what feature goes with what object?

binocular depth cues   Cues of depth perception that arise from the fact that people have two eyes.

binocular disparity   A cue of depth perception that is caused by the distance between a person's two eyes.

biological preparedness   The idea that animals are biologically programmed to learn to fear specific objects.

biological therapies   Treatment based on the medical approach to illness and disease.

bipolar disorder   A mood disorder characterized by alternating periods of depression and mania.

blindsight   A condition in which people who are blind have some spared visual capacities in the absence of any visual awareness.

blocking   The temporary inability to remember something that is known.

body mass index (BMI)   A ratio of body weight to height used to measure obesity.

borderline personality disorder   A personality disorder characterized by identity, affective, and impulse disturbances.

bottom-up processing   A hierarchical model of pattern in which data are relayed from one processing level to the next, always moving to a higher level of processing.

brain   An organ located in the skull that produces mental activity.

brainstem   A section of the bottom of the brain that houses the most basic programs of survival such as breathing, swallowing, vomiting, urination, and orgasm.

Broca's area   The left frontal region of the brain that is crucial to the production of language.

buffering hypothesis   Proposes that other people can provide direct support in helping individuals cope with stressful events.

bulimia nervosa   An eating disorder characterized by dieting, binge eating, and purging.

bystander intervention effect   The failure to offer help by those who observe someone in need.

Cannon-Bard theory   A theory of emotion that asserts that emotion-producing stimuli from the environment elicit both an emotional and a physical reaction.

capacity limits   The maximum amount of information and operations a system can perform.

case study   A research method that involves the intensive examination of one person.

cell body   The region of the neuron where information from thousands of other neurons is collected and processed.

central nervous system (CNS)   The brain and spinal cord.

central pattern generator   A circuit that, once activated, produces a rhythmic, recurring set of movements.

central tendency   A measure that represents the typical behavior of the group as a whole.

cerebellum   A large convoluted protuberance at the back of the brainstem that is essential for coordinated movement and balance.

cerebral asymmetry   An emotional pattern associated with unequal activation of the left and right frontal lobes.

cerebral cortex   The outer layer of brain tissue that forms the convoluted surface of the brain.

cerebral hemispheres   The left and right half of the forebrain connected by the corpus collosum.

cholecystokinin (CCK)   The peptide found in highest concentration in the cerebral cortex and plays a role in learning and memory, pain transmission, and exploratory behavior.

chromosomes   Structures within the cell body made up of genes.

circadian rhythms   The regulation of biological cycles into regular patterns.

circumplex model   An approach to understanding emotion, in which two basic factors of emotion are spatially arranged in a circle, formed around the intersections of the core dimensions of affect.

classical conditioning   A type of learned response that occurs when a neutral object comes to elicit a reflexive response when it is associated with a stimulus that already produces that response.

client-centered therapy   An empathic approach to therapy that encourages personal growth through greater self-understanding.

clique   A small group that serves as the primary peer group.

clozapine   An antipsychotic medication that acts on multiple neurotransmitter receptors and is beneficial in treating both the negative and positive symptoms of schizophrenia.

cochlea (inner ear)   A fluid-filled tube that curls into a snail-like shape. The cochlea contains the basilar membrane, which in turn contains auditory receptor cells called hair cells. These transduce the mechanical energy of the sound wave into neural impulses.

cocktail party phenomenon   A phenomenon of selective attention which refers to the ability to focus on a single conversation in the midst of a chaotic cocktail party.

cognitive-behavioral approach Views psychopathology as the result of learned, maladaptive cognitions.

cognitive-behavioral therapy (CBT) Incorporates techniques from behavioral therapy and cognitive therapy to correct faulty thinking and change maladaptive behaviors.

cognitive development The way in which individuals acquire knowledge and understanding about the world around them over the life course.

cognitive dissonance When there is a contradiction between two attitudes or between some attitude and behavior.

cognitive economy A tendency to group objects together based on shared properties, which reduces the amount of object knowledge we must hold in memory.

cognitive framing The way people think about events can contribute to the intensity of emotional responses and shape the labels they place on emotions.

cognitive maps A visual/spatial mental representation of the environment.

cognitive restructuring A therapy that strives to help patients recognize maladaptive thought patterns and replace them with ways of viewing the world that are more in tune with reality.

cognitive therapy Treatment based on the idea that distorted thoughts produce maladaptive behaviors and emotions.

companionate love A strong commitment based on friendship, trust, respect, and intimacy that strengthens over time.

compliance The tendency to agree to do things requested by others.

concrete operational stage The third stage in Piaget's theory of cognitive development in which children begin to think about and understand operations in ways that are reversible.

conditioned response (CR) A response that has been learned.

conditioned stimulus (CS) A stimulus that elicits a response only after learning has taken place.

confabulation The false recollection of episodic memory.

conformity The altering of one's opinions or behavior to match those of others.

confounds Anything that affects a dependent variable that may unintentionally vary between the different experimental conditions of a study.

consolidation A hypothetical process that refers to the transfer of contents from immediate memory into long-term memory.

contact comfort A phenomenon whereby social development is facilitated when an infant is allowed to touch something that is soothing.

contact hypothesis The idea that increasing contact and familiarity with outgroup members will reduce negative attitudes towards them.

continuous reinforcement A type of learning in which the desired behavior is reinforced each time it occurs.

conventional level The stage of moral reasoning that reflects conformity to rules of law and order that are learned from others.

coping response Any response made by an organism to avoid, escape from, or minimize an aversive stimulus.

corpus callosum A fiber of axons that transmits information between the two cerebral hemispheres of the brain.

correlation A statistical procedure that provides a numerical value, between +1 and −1, indicating the strength and direction of the relation between two variables.

correlational study A research method that examines how variables are naturally related in the real world, without any attempt by the researcher to alter or change them.

correspondence bias The tendency for humans to expect people's behavior to agree with their dispositions.

counterfactual reasoning In decision making, a consideration of different hypothetical outcomes for events or decisions.

creativity The capacity to generate or recognize ideas, alternatives, or possibilities that may be useful in solving problems, communicating with others, or entertaining ourselves and others.

critical period Time in which certain experiences must occur for normal brain development, such as exposure to visual information during infancy for the normal development of the visual pathways of the brain.

cross-sectional studies A research design that compares people across different samples or ages.

crowds Large groups of people who may or may not spend a lot of time together but who share a common social identity.

cryptomnesia A type of misappropriation that occurs when people think they have come up with a new idea, yet have only retrieved a stored idea and failed to attribute the idea to its proper source.

crystallized intelligence Knowledge that is acquired through experience, on the assumption that people who learn from their experiences are showing a mental capacity that is absent in those who fail to learn from experience.

culture The beliefs, values, rules, and customs that exist within a group of people who share a common language and environment, that are transmitted through learning from one generation to the next.

cyclothymia A less extreme form of bipolar disorder.

data Objective observations or measurements.

deception The act of making others believe something that is not true.

declarative memory The cognitive information retrieved from explicit memory, knowledge that can be declared.

defense mechanisms Unconscious mental strategies used to protect the mind from conflict and distress.

defining attribute model A model that defines concepts by the necessary features an object must have in order to be categorized under that concept.

deindividuation A phenomenon of low self-awareness in which people lose their individuality and fail to attend to personal standards.

delay of gratification When people transcend immediate temptations to successfully achieve long-term goals.

delusions False personal beliefs based on incorrect inferences about reality.

dendrites Branchlike extensions of the neuron that detect information from other neurons.

dependent variable In an experiment, the measure that is affected by manipulation of the independent variable.

descriptive model A model of decision making that accounts for tendencies to misinterpret and misrepresent probabilities underlying many decisions.

descriptive studies A research method that involves observing and noting the behavior of people or other animals in order to provide a systematic and objective analysis of behavior.

***Diagnostic and Statistical Manual of Mental Disorders* (DSM)** A handbook of clinical disorders used for diagnosing psychopathology.

dialectical behavior therapy (DBT) A treatment for borderline personality disorder that combines elements of behavioral, cognitive, and psychodynamic approaches.

diathesis-stress model Proposes that a disorder may develop when an underlying vulnerability is coupled with a precipitating event.

difference threshold The minimum amount of change required in order to detect a difference between intensities of stimuli.

direct perception   A theory of perception that states that the stimulus must already have enough information for us to perceive it, and therefore the visual system is built not to enable us to see an exact copy of the real world, but to interpret cues that maximize its function.

discourse   The systematic ways by which people engage in conversations.

discrimination   The inappropriate and unjustified treatment of people based solely on their group membership.

display rules   Cultural rules that govern how and when emotions are exhibited.

dizygotic twins   Twin siblings who result from two separately fertilized eggs (i.e., fraternal twins).

dominant gene   A gene that is expressed in the offspring whenever it is present.

dopamine   A monoamine neurotransmitter that is involved in reward, motivation, and motor control.

dreams   An altered state of consciousness in which images and fantasies are confused with reality.

drives   Psychological states that motivate an organism to satisfy its needs.

dualism   The philosophical idea that the mind exists separately from the physical body.

dysthymia   A form of depression that is not severe enough to be diagnosed as major depression.

eardrum (tympanic membrane)   A thin membrane, which the sound wave vibrates, that marks the beginning of the middle ear.

early selection theories   Theories based on the notion that we can choose the stimuli to which we will attend before we process their basic features.

echolalia   The repetition of words or phrases that is characteristic of children with autism.

ego   In psychodynamic theory, the component of personality that tries to satisfy the wishes of the id while being responsive to the dictates of the superego.

elaboration likelihood model   A theory of how persuasive messages lead to attitude change.

elaborative rehearsal   The encoding of information in a more meaningful fashion, such as linking it to knowledge in long-term memory.

electroconvulsive therapy (ECT)   A procedure used to treat depression that involves administering a strong electrical current to the patient's brain.

electroencephalography (EEG)   A method for measuring the electrical activity of the brain. Electrodes placed on the scalp are able to detect weak electrical signals produced by neural activity.

electrophysiology   A method of data collection that measures electrical activity in the brain.

emotion   Feelings that involve subjective evaluation, physiological processes, and cognitive beliefs.

emotion-focused coping   A type of coping in which people try to prevent having an emotional response to a stressor.

encoding   The processing of information so that it can be stored.

encoding specificity principle   A principle that states that any stimulus that is encoded along with an experience can later trigger memory for the experience.

endocrine system   A communication system that uses hormones.

endorphins   Peptides involved in natural pain reduction and reward.

enzyme deactivation   The process whereby the neurotransmitter is destroyed by an enzyme, thereby terminating its activity.

epinephrine   A monoamine, found primarily in the body, which causes a burst of energy after an exciting event.

episodic memory   Memory for one's personal past experiences.

ethnic identity   The psychological association between people and their own ethnic or racial group.

evolutionary theory   An approach to psychological science that emphasizes the inherited, adaptive value of behavior and mental activity throughout the entire history of a species.

excitation transfer   A form of misattribution where residual physiological arousal caused by one event is transferred to a new stimulus.

expectancies   Mental representations of potential future outcomes.

expected utility theory   A model of how humans should make decisions if they were to follow pure reason in their decision making.

experiment   A research method for testing causal hypotheses in which variables are both measured and manipulated.

experimenter expectancy effects   When observer bias leads to actual changes in the behavior of the people or animals being observed.

explicit memory   The processes involved when people remember specific information.

exposure   A behavioral therapy technique that involves repeated exposure to an anxiety-producing stimulus or situation.

expressed emotion   A pattern of interactions that includes emotional over-involvement, critical comments, and hostility directed toward a patient by family members.

extinction   A process in which the conditioned response is weakened when the conditioned stimulus is repeated without the unconditioned stimulus.

extrinsic motivation   Motivation to perform an activity because of the external goals toward which that activity is directed.

facial feedback hypothesis   The idea that facial expressions trigger the experience of emotion.

family systems model   Considers symptoms within an individual as indicating problems within the family.

fight-or-flight response   A term used to describe the physiological preparedness of animals to deal with danger.

filter theory   A theory that people have a limited capacity for sensory information and thus screen incoming information, only letting in the most important.

five factor theory   The idea that personality can be described using five traits: openness to experience, conscientiousness, extraversion, agreeableness, and neuroticism.

fixed schedule   Reinforcement is consistently provided upon each occurrence.

flashbulb memories   Vivid memories for the circumstances in which one first learned of a surprising, consequential, and emotionally arousing event.

fluid intelligence   The ability to understand relationships between items in the absence of overt experience or practice with the items in question.

forgetting   The inability to retrieve memory from long-term storage.

formal operational stage   The final stage in Piaget's theory of cognitive development, it involves the ability to think abstractly and to formulate and test hypotheses through deductive logic.

fovea   The center of the retina where cones are densely packed.

frontal lobes   The region at the front of the cerebral cortex concerned with planning and movement.

frustration-aggression hypothesis   The extent to which people feel frustrated predicts the likelihood that they will act aggressively.

functional magnetic resonance imaging (fMRI)   An imaging technique used to examine changes in the activity of the working human brain.

functionalism   An approach to psychology concerned with the adaptive purpose, or function, of mind and behavior.

GABA (gamma-aminobutyric acid) The primary inhibitory transmitter in the nervous system.

ganglion cells A class of neurons located in the retina that perform a series of sophisticated computations on impulses from the rods and cones. The axons of the ganglion cells form the optic nerve.

gender A term that refers to the culturally constructed differences between males and females.

gender roles The characteristics associated with men and women because of cultural influence or learning.

gender schemas Cognitive structures that influence how people perceive the behaviors of men and women.

general adaptation syndrome (GAS) A consistent pattern of responses to stress that consists of three stages; alarm stage, resistance stage, and exhaustion stage.

generalized anxiety disorder Diffuse state of constant anxiety not associated with any specific object or event.

genes The units of heredity that determine a particular characteristic in an organism.

genotype The genetic constitution determined at the moment of conception.

Gestalt theory A theory based on the idea that the whole of personal experience is much greater than simply the sum of its constituent elements.

glucocorticoids A type of steroid hormone, often called cortisol, released by the adrenal glands during a stress response, that produces many of the physical effects of stress.

glutamate The primary excitatory transmitter in the nervous system.

goal A desired outcome associated with some specific object of desire or some future behavioral intention.

gonads The main endocrine glands involved in sexual behavior: in males, the testes, in females, the ovaries.

gray matter A segment of the spinal cord that is dominated by the cell bodies of neurons.

group polarization A process where group members conform to the initial attitudes of other members who already agree.

group socialization theory The idea that children are socialized by their peers.

guilt A negative emotional state associated with an internal experience of anxiety, tension, and agitation.

habituation A decrease in behavioral response following repeated exposure to nonthreatening stimuli.

hallucinations False sensory perceptions that are experienced without an external source.

haptic sense The sense of touch.

hardiness A personality trait that enables people to perceive stressors as controllable challenges.

heritability A statistical estimate of the fraction of observed measure of the overall amount of difference among people in a population that is caused by differences in heredity.

heuristics In problem solving, shortcuts that are used to minimize the amount of thinking that must be done when moving from step to step in a solution space.

hippocampus A brain structure important for the formation of certain types of memory.

homeostasis The tendency for bodily functions to maintain equilibrium.

hormones Chemical substances typically released from endocrine glands, which travel through the bloodstream to targeted tissues, which are subsequently influenced by the hormone.

humanistic approaches Approaches to studying personality that emphasize personal experience and belief systems, and propose that people seek personal growth to fulfill their human potential.

hypothalamic-pituitary-adrenal (HPA) axis A bodily system that is activated in response to stress.

hypothalamus A small brain structure that is vital for temperature regulation, emotion, sexual behavior, and motivation.

hypothesis A specific prediction of what should be observed in the world if a theory is correct.

id In psychodynamic theory, the component of personality that is completely submerged in the unconscious and operates according to the pleasure principle.

idiographic approaches Person-centered approaches to studying personality that focus on individual lives and how various characteristics are integrated into unique persons

illusory contours A phenomenon in which the eyes perceive contours that do not exist that serves as evidence for the Gestalt principles.

immune system The body's mechanism for dealing with invading microorganisms, such as allergens, bacteria, and viruses.

implicit attitudes Attitudes that influence our feelings and behavior at an unconscious level.

implicit memory The process by which people show an enhancement of memory, most often through behavior, without deliberate effort and without any awareness that they are remembering anything.

impression management The tendency for people to strategically alter how they present themselves in order to achieve interpersonal goals.

imprinting An instinctual tendency in some animals that produces a strong attachment to a nearby adult.

incentives External stimuli that motivate behaviors (as opposed to internal drives).

independent self-construals A view of the self as separate from others, emphasizing self-reliance and the pursuit of personal success.

independent variable In an experiment, the condition that is manipulated by the experimenter to examine its impact on the dependent variable.

inferential statistics A set of procedures used to make judgments about whether differences actually exist between sets of numbers.

informed consent A process in which people are given full information about a study, which allows them to make a knowledgeable decision about whether to participate.

ingroup favoritism The tendency for people to evaluate favorably and privilege members of the ingroup more than members of the outgroup.

insight (1) The sudden realization of a solution to a problem. (2) A goal of some types of therapy; a patient's understanding of his or her own psychological processes.

insomnia A sleep disorder characterized by an inability to sleep.

instincts Unlearned, automatic actions that are triggered by specific cues or external stimuli.

Institutional Review Boards (IRBs) Groups of people responsible for reviewing proposed research to ensure that it meets the accepted standards of science and provides for the physical and emotional well being of research participants.

intelligence An attribute used to describe a person that is based on the assumptions that (1) a person has a range of different abilities and

(2) intelligence can be equated with how a person measures up on a particular ability scale, as valued by a culture.

intelligence quotient The number computed by dividing a child's estimated mental age by the child's chronological age, and then multiplying this number by 100.

interactionists Theorists who believe that behavior is jointly determined by underlying dispositions and situations.

interdependent self-construals When self-concepts are determined largely by social roles and personal relationships.

interneurons One of the three types of neurons, these neurons communicate only with other neurons, typically within a specific brain region.

interval schedule Reinforcement is based on a specific unit of time.

intracranial self-stimulation (ICSS) A procedure in which animals are able to self-administer electrical shock to specific areas of the brain.

intrinsic motivation Motivation to perform an activity because of the value or pleasure associated with that activity, rather than for an apparent biological goal or purpose.

introspection A systematic examination of subjective mental experiences that requires people to inspect and report on the content of their thoughts.

James-Lange theory of emotion A theory that suggests that the experience of emotion is elicited by a physiological response to a particular stimuli or situation.

joint attentional engagement A process whereby caregivers make reference to objects that are part of a child's ongoing actions.

kin selection The tendency to be altruistic toward those who share a genetic bond.

late selection theories Theories that assume that people take in sensory information, process it, and then select which aspects of the stimuli should be attended after processing.

latent content What a dream symbolizes, or the material that is disguised in a dream to protect the dreamer.

latent learning Learning that takes place in the absence of reinforcement.

lateral geniculate nucleus (LGN) A region of the thalamus where visual information first travels, and then relays the information to the visual cortex.

law of effect Thorndike's general theory of learning, which states that any behavior that leads to a "satisfying state of affairs" is more likely to occur again, and that those that lead to an "annoying state of affairs" are less likely to reoccur.

law of mass action Karl Lashley's proposition that the cortex is basically undifferentiated and participates equally in psychological activity.

learned helplessness model A cognitive model of depression in which people feel unable to control events around them.

learning An enduring change in behavior that results from experience.

lithium A psychotropic medication used to treat bipolar disorder.

longitudinal studies A research design that examines the same individuals over time.

long-term memory (LTM) The relatively permanent storage of information.

long-term potentiation (LTP) The strengthening of a synaptic connection so that postsynaptic neurons are more easily activated.

loosening of associations A speech pattern among schizophrenic patients in which their thoughts are disorganized or meaningless.

loss aversion An unequal weighting of costs and benefits such that potential costs weigh more heavily than potential benefits.

lymphocytes Specialized white blood cells known as, B cells, T cells, and natural killer cells that make up the immune system.

magnetic resonance imaging (MRI) A method of brain imaging that produces high quality images of the brain.

magnetoencephalography (MEG) A technique for examining neural activity that records magnetic fields.

maintenance rehearsal A type of encoding that involves continually repeating an item.

major depression A disorder characterized by severe negative moods and a lack of interest in normally pleasurable activities.

manifest content The plot of a dream; the way a dream is remembered.

MAO inhibitors A category of antidepressant drugs that inhibit the action of monoamine oxidase.

mean A measure of central tendency that is the arithmetic average of a set of numbers.

median A measure of central tendency that is the value in a set of numbers that falls exactly in the half-way point between the lowest and highest values.

meiosis After fertilization, a process of cell division in which the chromosome pairs are split within each cell and then joined in a random fashion.

memory The capacity of the nervous system to acquire and retain usable skills and knowledge, which allows living organisms to benefit from experience.

mental age A prediction of how advanced or behind a child is relative to peers of the same age, as determined by a comparison of the child's test score against the average score for children of each chronological age.

mesolimbic dopamine system The major brain system involved in reward, it connects the ventral tegmental area (VTA) to the nucleus accumbens.

methylphenidate A central nervous system stimulant medication used to treat ADHD.

microsleeps Brief unintended sleep episodes, ranging from a few seconds to a minute, caused by chronic sleep deprivation.

mind Mental activity, such as thoughts, feelings, and subjective experience.

mind-body problem A fundamental psychological issue that considers whether mind and body are separate and distinct or whether the mind is simply the subjective experience of the physical brain.

mirror neurons Neurons in the premotor cortex that are activated during observation of others performing an action.

mitosis After a zygote is created, a process in which a cell duplicates its chromosome structure and then divides into two new cells that have an identical chromosome structure.

modal memory model The three-stage memory system that involves sensory memory, short-term memory, and long-term memory.

mode A measure of central tendency that is the most frequent score or value in a set of numbers.

modeling The imitation of behavior through observational learning.

monoamines A group of neurotransmitters synthesized from a single amino acid that are involved in a variety of psychological activities.

monocular depth cues Cues of depth perception that are available to each eye alone.

monozygotic twins Twin siblings who result from one zygote splitting in two, and therefore contain the same genes (i.e., identical twins).

moods Diffuse and long lasting emotional states that influence rather than interrupt thought and behavior.

moral development Concerns the way in which people decide between behaviors with competing social outcomes.

morpheme The smallest unit of speech that has meaning.

morphology The system of rules for combining the smallest meaningful units of language into words.

motion aftereffects An effect that occurs when you gaze at a moving image for a prolonged period and then switch to a stationary scene, causing a momentary illusion of seeing the new scene moving in the opposite direction of the previous image.

motivation Factors that energize, direct, or sustain behavior.

motor neurons One of the three types of neurons, these efferent neurons direct muscles to contract or relax, thereby producing movement.

multiaxial system The system used in the *DSM* that provides assessment along five axes describing important mental health factors.

myelin sheath A fatty material, made up of glial cells, that insulates the axon and allows for the rapid movement of electrical impulses along the axon.

natural selection Darwin's theory that those who inherit characteristics that help them adapt to their particular environment have a selective advantage over those who do not.

naturalistic observation A passive descriptive study in which observers do not change or alter ongoing behavior.

nature-nurture debate The arguments concerning whether psychological activity is biologically innate or acquired through education, experience, and culture.

need hierarchy Maslow's arrangement of needs, in which basic survival needs are lowest, and personal growth needs are highest in terms of priority.

need to belong theory The need for interpersonal attachments is a fundamental motive that has evolved for adaptive purposes.

needs States of biological or social deficiencies within the body.

negative feedback model The body's response to deviations from equilibrium.

negative punishment Punishment that occurs when removing a stimulus that decreases the probability of a behavior recurring.

negative reinforcement The increase in the probability of a behavior being repeated through the removal of an aversive stimulus.

negative symptoms Symptoms of schizophrenia marked by deficits in functioning such as apathy, lack of emotion, and slowed speech and movement.

neurons Basic units of the nervous system that operate through electrical impulses, which communicate with other neurons through chemical signals. They receive, integrate, and transmit information in the nervous system.

neurotransmitter Chemical substances that carry signals from one neuron to another.

nodes of Ranvier Small gaps of exposed axon, between the segments of myelin sheath, where action potentials are transmitted.

nomothetic approaches Approaches to studying personality that focus on characteristics that are common to all people, although there is individual variation.

nonverbal behavior Communication based on gestures, expressions, vocal cues, and body movements rather than words.

norepinephrine A monoamine neurotransmitter involved in states of arousal and vigilance.

normative model A model of decision making that views people as rational and optimal decision makers.

obedience The willingness to follow an order given by an authority.

object permanence The understanding that an object continues to exist even when it cannot be seen.

objective measures Relatively unbiased assessments of personality usually administered through self-report questionnaires or through observer ratings.

objective probabilities In decision making, the statistical probabilities that can be computed for a given alternative.

observational learning Learning that occurs when behaviors are acquired or modified following exposure to others performing the behavior.

observational techniques A research method of careful and systematic assessment and coding of overt behavior.

observer bias Systematic errors in observation that occur due to an observer's expectations.

obsessive-compulsive disorder (OCD) An anxiety disorder characterized by frequent intrusive thoughts and compulsive actions.

occipital lobes A region of the cerebral cortex at the back of the brain that is important for vision.

olfactory bulb The brain center for smell, located below the frontal lobes.

olfactory epithelium A thin layer of tissue embedded with olfactory receptors around which odorants dissolve into solution and cause a reaction, which triggers chemical receptors.

operant conditioning A learning process in which the consequences of an action determine the likelihood that it will be performed in the future.

operational definitions The method by which researchers quantify the variables of interest in order to measure them.

orienting reflex The tendency for humans to pay more attention to novel stimuli.

ossicles Three tiny bones, the incus (hammer), malleus (anvil), and stapes (stirrup), in the middle ear that transfer the vibrations of the eardrum to the oval window.

outer ear The structure of the ear, where the sound wave arrives.

outgroup homogeneity effect The tendency for people to view outgroup members as more similar to each other than ingroup members.

oxytocin A hormone that plays a role in maternal behavior and infant-caregiver attachment.

panic disorder An anxiety disorder characterized by sudden overwhelming attacks of terror.

parallel play The type of play characteristic of two year olds, usually limited to sitting side-by-side and playing independently.

parasympathetic division of ANS A division of the autonomic nervous system that returns the body to its resting state.

parietal lobes A region of the cerebral cortex lying in front of the occipital lobes and behind the frontal lobes that is important for the sense of touch and the spatial layout of an environment.

Parkinson's disease A neurological disorder marked by muscular rigidity, tremors, and difficulty initiating voluntary action, which seems to be caused by dopamine depletion.

partial reinforcement A type of learning in which behavior is reinforced intermittently.

partial-reinforcement extinction effect The greater persistence of behavior under partial reinforcement than under continuous reinforcement.

participant observation A type of descriptive study in which the researcher is actively involved in the situation.

passionate love A state of intense longing and sexual desire.

peptides Chains of two or more amino acids that exist in the brain and the body that can act like classic neurotransmitters or modify the quality of the neurotransmitter with which they are released.

perception The processing, organization, and interpretation of sensory signals that result in an internal representation of the stimulus.

perceptual constancy People correctly perceive objects as constant in their shape, size, color, and lightness despite raw sensory data that could mislead perception.

periaqueductal gray (PAG) A region of the midbrain that has neurons that can inhibit pain receptor cells from carrying their signals to the cortex.

peripheral nervous system (PNS) All nerve cells in the body that are not part of the central nervous system. The PNA includes the somatic and autonomic nervous systems.

personal attributions Explanations that refer to internal characteristics, such as abilities, traits, moods, and effort.

personal space The distance that people routinely maintain from others.

personality Characteristics, emotional responses, thoughts, and behaviors that are relatively stable over time and across circumstances.

personality disorder A class of mental disorders marked by inflexible and maladaptive ways of interacting with the world.

personality trait A characteristic; a dispositional tendency to act in a certain way over time and across circumstances.

personality types Discrete categories based on global personality characteristics.

persuasion The active and conscious effort to change attitudes through the transmission of a message.

phenotype Observable physical characteristics that result from both genetic and environmental influences.

pheromones Chemicals released by animals and humans that trigger physiological or behavioral reactions in other members of the same species. Pheromones do not elicit detectable smells but are processed in a similar manner to olfactory stimuli, by specialized receptors in the nasal cavity called vomeronasal organs.

phobias Acquired fears that are out of proportion to the real threat of an object or situation.

phonology The study of the set of meaningless sounds and the rules by which we combine them to make words and sentences.

phrenology An early method of assessing personality traits and mental abilities by measuring bumps on the skull.

physical dependence Synonymous with addiction, the physiological state in which failing to ingest a specific substance leads to bodily symptoms of withdrawal.

pituitary gland Located at the base of the hypothalamus, the gland that sends hormonal signals that control the release of hormones from endocrine glands.

place coding A mechanism for encoding high-frequency auditory stimuli in which the frequency of the sound wave is encoded by the location of the hair cells along the basilar membrane.

plasticity A property of the brain that allows it to change as a result of experience, drugs, or injury.

pop-out In Treisman's work, when simple stimuli were used, subjects took the same amount of time to find it, whether or not there were a few or many distracters.

positive illusions Overly favorable and unrealistic beliefs about one's skills, abilities, and competencies.

positive punishment Punishment that occurs when administering a stimulus that decreases the probability of a behavior recurring.

positive reappraisal A cognitive process in which people focus on possible good things in their current situation.

positive reinforcement The increase in the probability of a behavior being repeated following the administration of a pleasurable stimulus, referred to as a reward.

positive symptoms Symptoms of schizophrenia, such as delusions and hallucinations, that are excesses in behavior.

positron emission tomography (PET) A method of brain imaging that assesses metabolic activity by use of a radioactive substance injected into the bloodstream.

postconventional level The highest level of moral reasoning, reflects complex reasoning skills that take into account abstract principles and values.

pragmatics The way people use language to get what they want and to influence their listeners.

preconventional level Moral reasoning that is based on personal benefits, self-interest, or hedonistic advantages.

prefrontal cortex A region of the frontal lobes, especially prominent in humans, important for attention, working memory, decision making, appropriate social behavior, and personality.

prejudice The affective or attitudinal responses associated with stereotypes.

preoperational period The second stage in Piaget's theory of cognitive development in which children think symbolically about objects, but reason based on appearance rather than logic.

primacy effect In a list, the better memory for items presented first.

primary appraisals Part of the coping process that involves making decisions about whether a stimulus is stressful, benign, or irrelevant.

primary auditory cortex The region of the temporal lobe concerned with hearing.

primary emotions Evolutionarily adaptive emotions that are shared across cultures and associated with specific biological and physical states.

primary motor cortex The region of the frontal lobe concerned with movement.

primary reinforcers Reinforcers that are innately reinforcing, such as those that satisfy biological needs.

primary sensory areas Localized regions of the cerebral cortex that receive sensory inputs from the thalamus.

primary visual cortex The largest area in the occipital lobe, where the thalamus projects the image.

proactive interference When prior information inhibits the ability to remember new information.

problem-focused coping A type of coping that involves taking direct steps to solve a problem.

problem structure How people view or conceptualize a problem at hand.

procedural memory A type of implicit memory, which involves motor skills and behavioral habits.

projective measures Personality tests that examine unconscious processes by having people interpret ambiguous stimuli.

prosocial Tending to benefit others.

prospect theory The idea that decision making can be viewed as a calculation of costs and benefits.

prototype model A model whose premise is that within each category, some members are more representative than others of that category.

proximity The frequency with which individuals come into contact.

psychoanalysis A method developed by Sigmund Freud that attempts to bring the contents of the unconscious into conscious awareness so that conflicts can be revealed.

psychodynamic theory Freudian theory that unconscious forces, such as wishes and motives, influence behavior.

psychological dependence Habitual substance use, despite consequences, and a compulsive need to continue using the drug.

psychological practitioners Refers to those who apply the findings from psychological science in order to assist people in their daily lives.

psychological science The study of mind, brain, and behavior.

psychological scientist Refers to those who use the methods of science to study the interplay between brain, mind, and behavior and how the social environment impacts these processes.

psychomotor stimulants Drugs that activate the sympathetic nervous system and increase behavioral and mental activity.

psychoneuroimmunology The study of the body's immune system in response to psychological variables.

psychopathology A disorder of the mind.

psychophysiological assessment A research method that examines how changes in bodily functions are associated with behavior or mental state.

psychosexual stage According to Freud, the developmental stages that correspond to the pursuit of satisfaction of libidinal urges.

psychosocial theory of development Erikson's theory that emphasizes age-related psychological processes and their effects on social functioning.

psychotherapy The generic name given to formal psychological treatment.

psychotropic medications Drugs that affect mental processes.

punishment A stimulus following a response that decreases the likelihood that the response will be repeated.

qualia The properties of our subjective, phenomenological awareness.

quantum change A transformation of personality that is sudden, profound, enduring, and affects a wide range of behaviors.

random assignment The procedure for placing research participants into the conditions of an experiment in which each participant has an equal chance of being assigned to any level of the independent variable.

ratio schedule Reinforcement is based on the number of times the behavior occurs.

reaction time A quantification of performance behavior that measures the speed of a response.

reactivity The knowledge that one is being observed alters the behavior being observed.

recency effect In a list, the better memory for words presented later in the list.

receptive field The region of visual space to which neurons in the primary visual cortex are sensitive.

receptors In neurons, specialized protein molecules on the postsynaptic membrane that neurotransmitters bind to after passing across the synaptic cleft.

recessive gene A gene that is expressed only when it is matched with a similar gene from the other parent.

reciprocal helping The tendency to help another because the recipient may return the favor.

reinforcer A stimulus following a response that increases the likelihood that the response will be repeated.

relative risk An important component of the ethical review in which the potential for possible harm to the participant is considered.

reliability The extent to which a measure is stable and consistent over time in similar conditions.

REM sleep The stage of sleep marked by rapid eye movements, dreaming, and paralysis of motor systems.

repetition priming The improvement in identifying or processing a stimulus that has previously been experienced.

replication Studies that are properly designed and conducted can be repeated and produce the same findings.

Rescorla-Wagner model A cognitive model of classical conditioning that states that the strength of the CS-US association is determined by the extent to which the unconditioned stimulus is unexpected.

research Scientific process that involves the systematic and careful collection of data.

response performance A research method in which researchers quantify perceptual or cognitive processes in response to a specific stimulus.

resting membrane potential The electrical charge of a neuron when it is not active.

reticular formation A large network of neural tissue within the brainstem involved in behavioral arousal and sleep-wake cycles.

retina The thin inner surface of the back of the eyeball. The retina contains the photoreceptors that transduce light into neural signals.

retinotopic organization The systematic ordering of the neuronal pathway from the retina to the occipital lobe preserves spatial relationships, so that adjacent areas of the retina correspond to adjacent areas in the primary visual cortex.

retrieval The act of recalling or remembering the stored information in order to use it.

retroactive interference When new information inhibits the ability to remember old information.

retrograde amnesia The condition in which people lose past memories, such as memories for events, facts, people, or even personal information.

reuptake The process whereby the neurotransmitter is taken back into the presynaptic terminal buttons and repackaged in the vesicles, thereby stopping its activity.

rumination Thinking about, elaborating, and focusing on undesired thoughts or feelings, which prolongs, rather than alleviates, a negative mood.

savants People who have minimal intellectual capacities in most domains, but show an exceptional ability in another "intelligent" process, such as math, music, or art.

schemas Hypothetical cognitive structures that help us perceive, organize, process, and use information.

schizophrenia A mental disorder characterized by alterations in perceptions, emotions, thoughts, or consciousness.

script theory People develop inferences about the sequences of events that arise in different situations, which allows them to react appropriately to a situation.

seasonal affective disorder (SAD) Periods of depression that are linked to the times of year with minimal sunlight.

secondary appraisal Part of the coping process where people evaluate their options and choose coping behaviors.

secondary emotions Blends of primary emotions, including states such as remorse, guilt, submission, and anticipation.

secondary reinforcers Events or objects that serve as reinforcers through their repeated pairings with primary reinforcers.

selective serotonin reuptake inhibitors (SSRIs) A category of antidepressant medications that prolong the effects of serotonin in the synapse.

self The mental representation of personal experience, including thought processes, a physical body, and a conscious experience of individuality.

self-actualization A state that is achieved when one's personal dreams and aspirations have been attained.

self-awareness A state in which the sense of self is the object of attention.

self-concept The full store of knowledge that people have about themselves.

self-efficacy The expectancy that one's efforts will lead to success.

self-esteem The evaluative aspect of the self-concept.

self-fulfilling prophecy People come to behave in ways that confirm their own or other's expectations.

self-monitoring A personality characteristic that describes the extent to which people monitor and alter their behavior according to situational cues.

self-regulation The process by which people initiate, adjust, or stop actions in order to promote the attainment of personal goals or plans.

self-report method A method of data collection in which people are asked to provide information about themselves, such as in questionnaires or surveys.

self-schema The cognitive aspect of the self-concept, consisting of an integrated set of memories, beliefs, and generalizations about the self.

self-serving bias The tendency for people to take personal credit for success but blame failure on external factors.

semantic memory Memory for knowledge about the world.

semantics The study of the system of meanings that underlie words, phrases, and sentences.

sensation How sense organs respond to external stimuli and transmit the responses to the brain.

sensation seekers Individuals who routinely seek out novel, complex situations and are willing to take physical and social risks in order to achieve thrills.

sensitization An increase in behavioral response following exposure to a threatening stimulus.

sensorimotor stage The first stage in Piaget's theory of cognitive development in which infants acquire information about the world through their senses and respond reflexively.

sensory adaptation When an observer's sensitivity to stimuli decreases over time.

sensory memory Memory for sensory information that is stored briefly in its original sensory form.

sensory neurons One of the three types of neurons, these afferent neurons detect information from the physical world and pass that information along to the brain.

separation anxiety The distress and anxiety displayed by infants when separated from their primary attachment figure.

serial position effect The ability to recall items from a list depends on order of presentation, with items presented early or late in the list remembered better than those in the middle.

serotonin A monoamine neurotransmitter that is important for a wide range of psychological activity, including emotional states, impulse control, and dreaming.

set-point A hypothetical state that indicates homeostasis.

sex-typed To have the view that there are clear distinctions between males and females, which usually fall along the lines of perceived gender differences.

sexual strategies theory Evolutionary theory that suggests men and women look for different qualities in relationship partners due to the gender-specific adaptive problems they've faced throughout human history.

shaping A process of operant conditioning that involves reinforcing behaviors that are increasingly similar to the desired behavior.

short-term memory (STM) A limited-capacity memory system that holds information in awareness for a brief period of time.

simple cells In Hubel and Weisel's 1960s experiment, the term they used for neurons that preferred certain line orientations over other orientations.

situational attributions Explanations that refer to external events, such as the weather, luck, accidents, or the actions of other people.

situationism The theory that proposes that behavior is determined to a much greater extent by situations than by personality traits.

social cognition The mental processes by which people make sense of themselves, others, and their social situations.

social comparison Occurs when people evaluate their own actions, abilities, and beliefs by contrasting them with other people.

social development The maturation of skills or abilities that enable people to live in a world with other people.

social dilemma When there is a motivational conflict both to cooperate and to be selfish.

social facilitation When the mere presence of others enhances performance.

social influence The ways in which other people shape our actions.

social loafing The tendency for people to work less hard in a group than when working alone.

social norms Expected standards of conduct that influence behavior.

social psychology The branch of psychology concerned with how others influence the way a person thinks, feels, and acts.

social support A network of other people who can provide help, encouragement, and advice.

socially desirable responding When people respond to a question in a way that is most socially acceptable or that makes them look good.

social-skills training Treatment designed to teach and reinforce appropriate interpersonal behavior.

sociocultural model Views psychopathology as the result of the interaction between individuals and their cultures.

sociometer An internal monitor of social acceptance or rejection.

sociometric analysis A nomination method for assessing the social hierarchy among members of groups.

sodium-potassium pump A mechanism of the neuron that keeps the resting membrane potential at a constant -70 mV, which sets the stage for electrical action.

solution space The many different paths to be considered in problem solving, taken collectively, define the space in which the solutions are most probable.

somatic marker theory Self-regulatory actions and decisions are affected by the bodily reactions that arise from their contemplation.

somatic nervous system A major component of the peripheral nervous system, which transmits sensory signals to the CNS via nerves.

sound wave The pattern of the changes in air pressure through time that results in the percept of a sound.

source amnesia A type of amnesia that occurs when a person shows memory for an event but cannot remember where they encountered the information.

source misattributions When people misremember the time, place, person, or circumstances involved with a memory.

spatial memory Memory for the physical environment and includes such things as location of objects, direction, and cognitive maps.

spinal cord   Part of the central nervous system. A rope of neural tissue that runs inside the hollows of the vertebrae from just above the pelvis and into the base of the skull.

split-brain   A condition in which the corpus callosum is surgically cut and the two hemispheres of the brain do not receive information directly from each other.

spontaneous recovery   A process in which a previously extinguished response reemerges following presentation of the conditioned stimulus.

standard deviation   A statistical measure of how far away each value is on average from the mean.

stereotype threat   A phenomenon in which individuals who feel that their behavior may confirm or verify a negative stereotype perform poorly in a given test.

stereotypes   Cognitive schemas that allow for easy and efficient organization of information about people based on their membership in certain groups.

stigma   A very strong devaluation that extends to a person's entire character.

stimulus discrimination   A learned tendency to differentiate between two similar stimuli if one is consistently associated with the unconditioned stimulus and the other is not.

stimulus generalization   Occurs when stimuli that are similar but not identical to the conditioned stimulus produce the conditioned response.

storage   The retention of encoded representations over time that corresponds to some change in the nervous system that registers the event.

Strange Situation Test   A test of infant-caregiver attachment that involves observing how infants respond to separation from their caregivers.

stream of consciousness   A phrase coined by William James to describe one's continuous series of ever-changing thoughts.

stress   A pattern of behavioral and physiological responses to cope with events that match or exceed an organism's abilities.

stressor   An environmental event or stimulus that threatens an organism.

stroke   Brain damage caused by a blocked blood vessel.

structuralism   An approach to psychology based on the idea that conscious experience can be broken down into its basic underlying components or elements.

subjective probabilities   In decision making, the personal impression of probabilities, which may or may not coincide with the true objective probabilities.

subliminal perception   Stimuli that are processed by sensory systems but because of their short duration or subtle form, do not reach the threshold of entering into consciousness.

substance P   A Peptide that acts as a neurotransmitter and is involved in pain perception.

subtractive color mixing   A way to produce a given spectral pattern in which the mixture occurs within the stimulus itself and is actually a physical, not psychological, process.

suggestibility   The development of biased memories when provided with misleading information.

superego   In psychodynamic theory, the internalization of societal and parental standards of conduct.

superordinate goals   Goals that require people to cooperate in order to succeed.

sympathetic division of ANS   A division of the autonomic nervous system that prepares the body for action.

synapse   The site for chemical communication between neurons.

synaptic cleft   The small space that exists between neurons that contains extracellular fluid.

synaptic pruning   A process whereby the synaptic connections in the brain that are frequently used are preserved, and those that are not are lost.

syntax   The system of rules by which words are combined into phrases and phrases into sentences.

systematic desensitization   An exposure technique that pairs the anxiety-producing stimulus with relaxation techniques.

tardive dyskinesia   A side effect of some antipsychotic medications that produces involuntary movements of the lips, tongue, face, legs, or other parts of the body.

taste buds   Structures in the mouth that contain fifty receptor cells. The receptor cells contain structures called microvilli that come into direct contact with saliva. When stimulated, they send electrical impulses that convey information to the medulla and then to the thalamus and cortex.

TAT (Thematic Apperception Test)   A projective measure of personality where a person is shown an ambiguous picture and asked to tell a story about the picture.

tectum   Located at the back of the midbrain, this brain structure helps guide orientation towards sounds or moving stimuli.

telegraphic speech   The tendency for children to speak using rudimentary sentences that are missing words and grammatical markings but follow a logical syntax.

temperaments   Biologically based tendencies to feel or act in certain ways.

temporal coding   A mechanism for encoding the low-frequency auditory stimuli in which the frequency of the sound wave is encoded by the frequency of firing of the hair cells.

temporal lobes   The lower region of the cerebral cortex that is important for processing auditory information and also for memory.

tend and befriend   The argument that females are more likely to protect and care for their offspring and form social alliances than flee or fight in response to threat.

terminal buttons   Small nodules at the ends of axons, that release chemical signals from the neuron to an area called the synapse.

thalamus   The gateway to the brain that receives almost all incoming sensory information before it reaches the cortex.

theory   An idea or model of how something in the world works, which can be used to make predictions.

theory of mind (TOM)   The term used to describe the ability to explain and predict behavior in terms of other people's mental states.

theory of multiple intelligences   A theory that attempts to provide practical definitions of intelligence, including musical, verbal, mathematical/logical, spatial, kinesthetic (or body control), intrapersonal (or self-understanding), and interpersonal (or social understanding).

third-variable problem   When the experimenter cannot directly manipulate the independent variable and therefore cannot be confident that another, unmeasured variable is not the actual cause of differences in the dependent variable.

three primaries law of color   Any color can be produced by mixing light of just three wavelengths.

tip-of-the-tongue phenomenon   A phenomenon that occurs when people experience great frustration as they try to recall specific words that are somewhat obscure.

top-down processing   A hierarchical model of pattern recognition in which information at higher levels of processing can also influence lower, "earlier" levels in the processing hierarchy.

TOTE model A model of self-regulation in which people evaluate progress towards achieving goals.

trait approach An approach to studying personality that focuses on the extent to which individuals differ in personality dispositions.

transcranial magnetic stimulation (TMS) A procedure that transmits pulses of high-intensity magnetism to the brain.

transduction A process by which sensory receptors produce neural impulses when they receive physical or chemical stimulation.

transience The pattern of forgetting over time.

triangular theory of love Proposes that love is made up of differing combinations of passion, intimacy, and commitment.

tricyclic antidepressants A category of antidepressant medications that inhibit the reuptake of a number of different neurotransmitters.

two-factor theory of emotion A theory that proposes that a situation evokes both a physiological response, such as arousal, and a cognitive interpretation.

Type A personality A pattern of personality traits characterized by competitiveness, achievement orientation, aggressiveness, hostility, time urgency, restlessness, inability to relax, and impatience with others.

Type B personality A pattern of personality traits characterized by relaxed, non-competitive, easy-going, and accommodative behavior.

unconditioned response (UR) A response that does not have to be learned, such as a reflex.

unconditioned stimulus (US) A stimulus that elicits a response, such as a reflex, without any prior learning.

unconscious A term that identifies mental processes that operate below the level of conscious awareness.

validity The extent to which the data collected address the research hypothesis in the way they were intended.

variability In a set of numbers, how widely dispersed the values are from each other and from the mean.

variable schedule Reinforcement is applied at different rates or at different times.

variables Refers to things in the world that can be measured and that can vary.

vicarious learning Learning that occurs when people learn the consequences of an action by observing others being rewarded or punished for performing the action.

visual search task An experiment used to study form perception, in which an observer tries to detect a target stimulus amongst an array of distracter stimuli.

what is beautiful is good stereotype To attribute a variety of positive characteristics to people simply based on their physical attractiveness.

white matter A segment of the spinal cord that consists mostly of axons and the fatty sheaths.

working memory An active processing system that holds different types of information on-line for current use.

Yerkes-Dodson law A psychological principle that dictates that behavioral efficiency increases with arousal up to an optimum point, after which it decreases with increasing arousal.

REFERENCES

Abramson, L. Y., Metalsky, G., & Alloy, L. (1989). Hopelessness depression: A theory-based subtype of depression. *Psychological Review, 96*, 358–372.

Adams, H. E., Wright, L. W., & Lohr, B. A. (1996). Is homophobia associated with homosexual arousal? *Journal of Abnormal Psychology, 105*, 440–445.

Adler, L. E., Olincy, A., Waldo, M., Harris, J. G., Griffith, J., Stevens, K., et al. (1998). Schizophrenia, sensory gating, and nicotinic receptors. *Schizophrenia Bulletin, 24*(2), 189–202.

Adler, L. E., Pachtman, E., Franks, R., Pecevich, M., Waldo, M. C., & Freedman, R. (1982). Neurophysiological evidence for a defect in neuronal mechanisms involved in sensory gating in schizophrenia. *Biological Psychiatry, 17*, 639–654.

Adolphs, R., Sears, L., & Piven, J. (2001). Abnormal processing of social information from faces in autism. *Journal of Cognitive Neuroscience, 13*, 232–240.

Adolphs, R., Tranel, D., & Damasio, A. R. (1998). The human amygdala in social judgement. *Nature, 393*, 470–474.

Alicke, M. D., Klotz, M. L., Breitenbecher, D. L., Yurak, T. J., & Vredenburg, D. S. (1995). Personal contact, individuation, and the better-than-average effect. *Journal of Personality and Social Psychology, 68*, 804–825.

Allport, G. W. (1961). *Pattern and growth in personality*. New York: Holt, Rinehart & Winston.

Als, H. (2000, December 4). We two made one. *The New Yorker* (p. 72).

Ambady, N., Hallahan, M., & Conner, B. (1999). Accuracy of judgments of sexual orientation from thin slices of behavior. *Journal of Personality and Social Psychology, 77*, 538–547.

Ambady, N., & Rosenthal, R. (1992). Thin slices of expressive behavior as predictors of interpersonal consequences: A meta-analysis. *Psychological Bulletin, 111*, 256–274.

Ambady, N., & Rosenthal, R. (1993). Half a minute: Predicting teacher evaluations from thin slices of nonverbal behavior and physical attractiveness. *Journal of Personality and Social Psychology, 64*, 431–441.

American Psychiatric Association. (1994). *Diagnostic and statistical manual of mental disorders* (4th ed.). Washington, DC: Author.

American Psychiatric Association. (2000). Practice guidelines for the treatment of patients with eating disorders (revised). *American Journal of Psychiatry, 157* (Suppl.), 1–39.

Anderson, A. K., & Phelps, E. A. (2000). Expression without recognition: Contributions of the human amygdala to emotional communication. *Psychological Science, 11*, 106–111.

Anderson, S. W., Bechara, A., Damasio, H., Tranel, D., & Damasio, A. R. (1999). Impairment of social and moral behavior related to early damage in human prefrontal cortex. *Nature Neuroscience, 2*, 1032–1037.

Andreasen, N. C. (1984). *The broken brain: The biological revolution in psychiatry*. New York: Harper & Row.

Anfang, S. A., & Appelbaum, P. S. (1996). Twenty years after Tarasoff: Reviewing the duty to protect. *Harvard Review of Psychiatry, 4*(2), 67–76.

Antell, S. E., & Keating, D. P. (1983). Perception of numerical invariance in neonates. *Child Development, 54*, 695–701.

Aronson, E. (1999). Dissonance, hypocrisy, and the self concept. In E. Harmon-Jones & J. Mills (Eds.), *Cognitive dissonance theory: Revival, revisions and controversies* (pp. 103–126). Washington, DC: American Psychological Association.

Aronson, E., & Mills, J. (1959). The effects of severity of initiation on liking for a group. *Journal of Abnormal and Social Psychology, 59*, 177–181.

Asberg, M., Shalling, D., Traskman-Bendz, L., & Wagner, A. (1987). Psychobiology of suicide, impulsivity, and related phenomena. In H. Y. Melzer (Ed.), *Psychopharmacology: The third generation of progress* (pp. 655–668). New York: Raven Press.

Asch, S. E. (1955). Opinions and social pressure. *Scientific American, 193*, 31–35 (offprint 450).

Ashby, F. G., Isen, A. M., & Turken, A. U. (1999). A neuropsychological theory of positive affect and its influence on cognition. *Psychological Review, 106*, 529–550.

Averill, J. R. (1980). A constructivist view of emotion. In R. Plutchik & H. Kellerman, (Eds.), *Theories of emotion* (pp. 305–339). New York: Academic Press.

Aylward, E. H., Reiss, A. L., Reader, M. J., & Singer, H. S. (1996). Basal ganglia volumes in children with attention-deficit hyperactivity disorder. *Journal of Child Neurology, 11*(2), 112–115.

Bagby, R. M., Levitan, R. D., Kennedy, S. H., Levitt, A. J., & Joffe, R. T. (1999). Selective alteration of personality in response to noradrenergic and serotonergic antidepressant medication in a depressed sample: Evidence of non-specificity. *Psychiatry Research, 86,* 211–216.

Bailey, A., Le Couteur, A., Gottesman, I., Bolton, P., Simonoff, E., Yuzda, E., et al. (1995). Autism as a strongly genetic disorder: Evidence from a British twin study. *Psychological Medicine, 25,* 63–78.

Baillargeon, R. (1987). Object permanence in 3½- and 4½-month-old infants. *Developmental Psychology, 23,* 655–664.

Baillargeon, R. (1995). Physical reasoning in infancy. In M. S. Gazzaniga (Ed.), *The cognitive neurosciences* (pp. 181–204). Cambridge, MA: MIT Press.

Baillargeon, R., Needham, A., & DeVos, J. (1992). The development of young infants' intuitions about support. *Early Development and Parenting, 1*(2), 69–78.

Baltimore, D. (2001). Our genome unveiled. *Nature, 409,* 814–816.

Banaji, M. R., & Greenwald, A. G. (1995). Implicit gender stereotyping in judgments of fame. *Journal of Personality and Social Psychology, 68,* 181–198.

Bandura, A. (1977). *Social learning theory.* Englewood Cliffs, NJ: Prentice-Hall.

Bandura, A., Ross, D., & Ross, S. (1961). Transmission of aggression through imitation of aggressive models. *Journal of Abnormal and Social Psychology, 66,* 3–11.

Bandura, A., Ross, D., & Ross, S. (1963). Vicarious reinforcement and imitative learning. *Journal of Abnormal and Social Psychology, 67,* 601–607.

Bargh, J. A., & Ferguson, M. J. (2000). Beyond behaviorism: On the automaticity of higher mental processes. *Psychological Bulletin, 126,* 925–945.

Barkley, R. A. (1997). *ADHD and the nature of self-control.* New York: Guilford Press.

Barlow, D. H. (1988). *Anxiety and its disorders: The nature and treatment of anxiety and panic.* New York: Guilford Press.

Baron-Cohen, S., Leslie, A. M., & Frith, U. (1985). Does the autistic child have a "theory of mind"? *Cognition, 21,* 37–46.

Baron-Cohen, S., Wheelwright, S., & Jolliffe, T. (1997). Is there a "language of the eyes"?: Evidence from normal adults and adults with autism or Asperger Syndrome. *Visual Cognition, 4,* 311–332.

Basbaum, A. I., & Fields, H. L. (1984). Endogenous pain control systems: Brainstem spinal pathways and endorphin circuitry. *Annual Review of Neuroscience, 7,* 309–338.

Batson, C. D., Engel, C. L., & Fridell, S. R. (1999). Value judgments: Testing the somatic marker hypothesis using false physiological feedback. *Personality and Social Psychology Bulletin, 25,* 1021–1032.

Baumeister, R. F. (1991). *Escaping the self: Alcoholism, spirituality, masochism, and other flights from the burden of selfhood.* New York: Basic Books.

Baumeister, R. F. (1991a). *Meanings of life.* New York: Guilford Press.

Baumeister, R. F. (1998). The self. In D. T. Gilbert, S. T. Fiske, & L. Gardner (Eds.), *Handbook of social psychology* (pp. 680–740). New York: Oxford University Press.

Baumeister, R. F. (2000). Gender differences in erotic plasticity: The female sex drive as socially flexible and responsive. *Psychological Bulletin, 126,* 347–374.

Baumeister, R. F., Catanese, K. R., & Vohs, K. D. (2001). Is there a gender difference in strength of sex drive? Theoretical views, conceptual distinctions, and a review of the relevant literature. *Personality and Social Psychology Review, 5,* 242–273.

Baumeister, R. F., Dale, K., & Sommers, K. L. (1998). Freudian defense mechanisms and empirical findings in modern social psychology: Reaction formation, projection, displacement, undoing, isolation, sublimation, and denial. *Journal of Personality, 66,* 1081–1124.

Baumeister, R. F., & Heatherton, T. F. (1996). Self-regulation failure: An overview. *Psychological Inquiry, 7,* 1–15.

Baumeister, R. F., Heatherton, T. F., & Tice, D. M. (1993). When ego threats lead to self-regulation failure: Negative consequences of high self-esteem. *Journal of Personality and Social Psychology, 64,* 141–156.

Baumeister, R. F., & Leary, M. R. (1995). The need to belong: Desire for interpersonal attachments as a fundamental human motivation. *Psychological Bulletin, 117,* 497–529.

Baumeister, R. F., Shapiro, J. P., & Tice, D. M. (1985). Two kinds of identity crisis. *Journal of Personality, 53,* 407–424.

Baumeister, R. F., & Sommer, K. L. (1997). What do men want? Gender differences and two spheres of belongingness: Comment on Cross and Madson (1997). *Psychological Bulletin, 22,* 38–44.

Baumeister, R. F., Stillwell, A. M., & Heatherton, T. F. (1994). Guilt: An interpersonal approach. *Psychological Bulletin, 115,* 243–267.

Baumeister, R. F., & Tice, D. M. (1990). Anxiety and social exclusion. *Journal of Social and Clinical Psychology, 9,* 165–195.

Baxter, L. R. (2000). Functional imaging of brain systems mediating obsessive-compulsive disorder. In D. S. Charney, E. J. Nestler, & B. S. Bunney (Eds.), *Neurobiology of mental illness* (pp. 534–547). New York: Oxford University Press.

Baxter, L. R., Schwartz, J. M., Bergman, K. S., Szuba, M. P., Guze, B., Mazziota, J. C., et al. (1992). Caudate glucose metabolic rate changes with both drug and behavior therapy for obsessive-compulsive disorder. *Archives of General Psychiatry, 49,* 681–689.

Bechara, A., Damasio, H., & Damasio, A. (2000). Emotion, decision making, and the orbitofrontal cortex. *Cerebral Cortex, 10,* 295–307.

Beck, A. T. (1967). *Depression: Clinical, experimental and theoretical aspects.* New York: Harper & Row.

Beck, A. T. (1976). *Cognitive therapy and the emotional disorders.* New York: International Universities Press.

Beck, A. T., Brown, G., Seer, R. A., Eidelson, J. L., & Riskind, J. H. (1987). Differentiating anxiety and depression: A test of the cognitive content-specificity hypothesis. *Journal of Abnormal Psychology, 96,* 179–183.

Beck, A. T., Freeman, A., & Associates (1990). *Cognitive Therapy of Personality Disorders.* New York: Guilford Press.

Beck, A. T., Rush, A. J., Shaw, B., & Emery, G. (1979). *Cognitive therapy of depression.* New York: Guilford Press.

Beggan, J. K. (1992). On the social nature of nonsocial perception: The mere ownership effect. *Journal of Personality and Social Psychology, 62,* 229–237.

Beggs, J. M., Brown, T. H., Byrne, J. H., Crow, T., LeDoux, J. E., LeBar, K., et al. (1999). Learning and memory: Basic mechanisms. In M. J. Zigmond, F. E. Bloom, S. C. Landis, J. L. Roberts, & L. R. Squire (Eds.), *Fundamentals of neuroscience* (pp. 1411–1454). San Diego, CA: Academic Press.

Békésy, G. Von. (1957). The ear. *Scientific American, 197,* 66–78.

Bellak, L., & Black, R. B. (1992). Attention-deficit hyperactivity disorder in adults. *Clinical Therapeutics, 14,* 138–147.

Bem, D. (1967). Self-perception: An alternative explanation of cognitive dissonance phenomena. *Psychological Review, 74,* 183–200.

Bem, D. J. (1996). Exotic becomes erotic: A developmental theory of sexual orientation. *Psychological Review, 103,* 320–335.

Bem, S. L. (1975). Sex role adaptability: One consequence of psychological androgyny. *Journal of Personality and Social Psychology, 31,* 634–643.

Bem, S. L., Martyna, W., & Watson, C. (1976). Sex typing and androgyny: Further explorations of the expressive domain. *Journal of Personality and Social Psychology, 34,* 1016–1023.

Benedetti, F., Serretti, A., Colombo, C., Campori, E., Barbini, B., di Bella, D., et al. (1999). Influence of a functional polymorphism within the promoter of the serotonin transporter gene on the effects of total sleep deprivation in bipolar depression. *American Journal of Psychiatry, 156*, 1450–1452.

Bentler, P. M., & Newcomb, M. D. (1978). Longitudinal study of marital success and failure. *Journal of Consulting and Clinical Psychology, 46*, 1053–1070.

Berkowitz, L. (1990). On the formation and regulation of anger and aggression: A cognitive-neoassociationistic analysis. *American Psychologist, 45*, 494–503.

Bernheim, K. F. (Ed.). (1997). *The Lanahan cases and readings in abnormal behavior.* Baltimore: Lanahan Publishers.

Bickel, W. K., Odum, A. L., & Madden, G. J. (1999). Impulsivity and cigarette smoking: Delay discounting in current, never, and ex-smokers. *Psychopharmacology, 146*, 447–454.

Bickerton, D. (1998). The creation and re-creation of language. In C. B. Crawford & D. L. Krebs (Eds.), *Handbook of evolutionary psychology: Ideas, issues, and applications* (pp. 613–634). Mahwah, NJ: Lawrence Erlbaum Associates, Inc.

Bidell, T. R., & Fischer, K. W. (1995). Between nature and nurture: The role of agency in the epigenesis of intelligence. In R. Sternberg & E. Grigorenko (Eds.), *Intelligence: Heredity and environment.* New York: Cambridge University Press.

Biederman, J., Faraone, S. V., Keenan, K., Knee, D., & Tsuang, M. T. (1990). Family-genetic and psychosocial risk factors, in DSM-III attention deficit disorder. *Journal of the American Academy of Child and Adolescent Psychiatry, 29*, 526–633.

Biederman, J., Faraone, S. V., & Lapey, K. (1992). Comorbidity of diagnosis in attention-deficit hyperactivity disorder. In G. Weiss (Ed.), *Child and adolescent psychiatry clinics of North America: Attention deficit hyperactivity disorder* (pp. 335–360). Philadelphia: Saunders.

Bigler, R. S., & Liben, L. S. (1993). A cognitive-development approach to racial stereotyping and reconstructive memory in Euro-American children. *Child Development, 64*, 1507–1518.

Birbaumer, N., Grodd, W., Diedrich, O., Klose, U., Erb, M., Lotze, M., et al. (1998). fMRI reveals amygdala activation to human faces in social phobics. *Neuroreport, 9*, 1223–1226.

Blagys, M. D., & Hilsenroth, M. J. (2000). Distinctive feature of short-term psychodynamic-interpersonal psychotherapy: A review of the comparative psychotherapy process literature. *Clinical Psychology: Science and Practice, 7*(2), 167–188.

Blakemore, C. (1983). *Mechanics of the mind.* Cambridge, UK: Cambridge University Press.

Blascovich, J., Mendes, W. B., Hunter, S. B., & Salomon, K. (1999). Social "facilitation" as challenge and threat. *Journal of Personality and Social Psychology, 77*, 68–77.

Bleske-Rechek, A. L., & Buss, D. M. (2000). Can men and women be just friends? *Personal Relationships, 21*, 131–151.

Blumstein, P., & Schwartz, P. (1983). *American couples.* New York: Simon & Schuster.

Bohus, M., Haaf, B., Stiglmayr, C., Pohl, U., Boehme, R., & Linehan, M. M. (2000). Evaluation of inpatient dialectical-behavioral therapy for borderline personality disorder—A prospective study. *Behaviour Research and Therapy, 38*(9), 875–887.

Bolles, R. C. (1970). Species-specific defense reactions and avoidance learning. *Psychological Review, 77*, 32–48.

Bornstein, R. F. (1999). Criterion validity of objective and projective dependency tests: A meta-analytic assessment of behavioral prediction. *Psychological Assessment, 11*, 48–57.

Bouchard Jr., T. J., Lykken, D. T., McGue, M., Segal, N. L., & Tellegen, A. (1990). Sources of human psychological differences: The Minnesota study of twins reared apart. *Science, 250*, 223–228.

Bouchard, C., Tremblay, A., Despres, J. P., Nadeau, A., Lupien, J. P., Theriault, G., et al. (1990). The response to long-term overfeeding in identical twins. *New England Journal of Medicine, 322*, 1477–1482.

Bourin, M., Baker, G. B., & Bradwejn, J. (1998). Neurobiology of panic disorder. *Journal of Psychosomatic Research, 44*, 163–180.

Bouton, M. E. (1994). Context, ambiguity, and classical conditioning. *Current Directions in Psychological Science, 3*, 49–53.

Bouton, M. E., Nelson, J. B., & Rosas, J. M. (1999). Stimulus generalization, context change, and forgetting. *Psychological Bulletin, 125*, 171–186.

Bradbury, T. N., & Fincham, F. D. (1990). Attributions in marriage: Review and critique. *Psychological Bulletin, 107*, 3–33.

Bransford, J. D., & Johnson, M. K. (1972). Contextual prerequisites for understanding: Some investigations of comprehension and recall. *Journal of Verbal Learning and Verbal Behavior, 11*, 717–726. Modified by E. B. Zechmeister & S. E. Nyberg, 1982. *Human memory* (p. 305). Pacific Grove, CA: Brooks Cole.

Braun, A. R., Balkin, T. J., Wesensten, N. J., Gwadry, F., Carson, R. E., Varga, M., et al. (1998). Dissociated pattern of activity in visual cortices and their projections during human rapid eye movement sleep. *Science, 279*, 91–95.

Breckler, S. J. (1984). Empirical validation of affect, behavior, and cognition as distinct components of attitude. *Journal of Personality and Social Psychology, 47*, 1191–1205.

Breland, K., & Breland, M. (1961). The misbehavior of organisms. *American Psychologist, 16*, 681–684.

Brewer, J. B., Zhao, Z., Glover, G. H., & Gabrieli, J. D. E. (1998). Making memories: Brain activity that predicts how well visual experiences will be remembered. *Science, 281*, 1185–1187.

Brewer, M. B., & Brown, R. J. (1998). Intergroup relations. In D. T. Gilbert, S. T. Fiske, & G. Lindzey (Eds.), *The handbook of social psychology* (4th ed., Vol. 2, pp. 554–594). New York: McGraw-Hill.

Brewer, M. B., & Caporael, L. R. (1990). Selfish genes vs. selfish people: Sociobiology as origin myth. *Motivation and Emotion, 14*, 237–243.

Brigham, J. C., & Malpass, R. S. (1985). The role of experience and contact in the recognition of faces of own- and other-races persons. *Journal of Social Issues, 41*, 139–155.

Broadbent, D. A. (1958). *Perception and communication.* New York: Pergamon.

Brody, A. L., Saxena, S., Fairbanks, L. A., Alborzian, S., Demaree, H. A., Maidment, K. M., et al. (2000). Personality changes in adult subjects with major depressive disorder or obsessive-compulsive disorder treated with paroxetine. *Journal of Clinical Psychiatry, 61*, 349–355.

Brown, A. S. (1991). A review of the tip-of-the-tongue phenomenon. *Psychological Bulletin, 109*, 204–223.

Brown, A. S., & Murphy, D. R. (1989). Cryptomnesia: Delineating inadvertent plagiarism. *Journal of Experimental Psychology: Learning, Memory, and Cognition, 15*, 432–442.

Brown, B. B. (1990). Peer groups and peer culture. In S. S. Feldman & G. R. Elliot, (Eds.), *At the threshold: The developing adolescent.* Cambridge, MA: Harvard University Press.

Brown, B. B., Mounts, N., Lamborn, S. D., & Steinberg, L. (1993). Parenting practices and peer group affiliations in adolescence. *Child Development, 64*, 467–482.

Brown, G. W., & Harris, T. O. (1978). *Social origins of depression: A study of psychiatric disorders in women.* New York: The Free Press.

Brown, R. (1973). *A first language: The early stages*. Cambridge, MA: Harvard University Press.

Brown, R., & Hanlon, C. (1970). Derivational complexity and order of acquisition in child speech. In J. R. Hayes (Ed.), *Cognition and the development of language* (pp. 11–53). New York: Wiley.

Brownell, C. A., & Brown, E. (1992). Peers and play in infants and toddlers. In V. Van Hasselt & M. Hersen (Eds.), *Handbook of social development: A lifespan perspective* (pp. 183–200). New York: Plenum.

Bruck, M. L., & Ceci, S. (1993). Amicus brief for the case of State of New Jersey v. Michaels. Presented by Committee of Concerned Social Scientists. Supreme Court of New Jersey docket no. 36,633. (Reprinted from *Psychology, Public Policy and Law 1*, 1995, 272–322.)

Buckner, R. L., Kelley, W. M., & Petersen, S. E. (1999). Frontal cortex contributes to human memory formation. *Nature Neuroscience, 2*, 311–314.

Bunge, S. A., Dudukovic, N. M., Thomason, M. E., Vaidya, C. J., & Gabrielli, E. J. D. (2002). Immature frontal lobe contributions to cognitive control in children: Evidence from fMRI. *Neuron, 33*, 301–311.

Bunge, S. A., Ochsner, K. N., Desmond, J. E., Glover, G. H., & Gabrieli, J. D. (2001). Prefrontal regions involved in keeping information in and out of mind. *Brain, 124*, 2074–2086.

Bushman, B. J., & Anderson, C. A. (2001). Media violence and the American public: Scientific facts versus media misinformation. *American Psychologist, 56*, 477–489.

Bushman, B. J., & Huesmann, L. R. (2001). Effects of televised violence on aggression. In D. G. Singer & J. L. Singer (Eds.), *Handbook of children and the media* (pp. 223–254). Thousand Oaks, CA: Sage.

Buss, A. H., & Plomin, R. (1984). *Temperament: Early developing personality traits*. Hillsdale, NJ: Erlbaum.

Buss, D. M. (1989). Sex differences in human mate preferences: Evolutionary hypotheses tested in 37 cultures. *Behavioral and Brain Sciences, 12*, 1–49.

Buss, D. M. (1995). Evolutionary psychology: A new paradigm for psychological science. *Psychological Inquiry, 6*, 1–30.

Buss, D. M. (1999). *Evolutionary psychology: The new science of mind*. Boston, MA: Allyn & Bacon.

Buss, D. M. (1999a). Human nature and individual differences: The evolution of human personality. In L. A. Pervin & O. P. John (Eds.), *Handbook of personality: Theory and research* (pp. 31–56). New York: Guilford.

Buss, D. M., & Greiling, H. (1999). Adaptive individual differences. *Journal of Personality, 67*, 209–243.

Buss, D. M., & Kenrick, D. T. (1998). Evolutionary social psychology. In D. T. Gilbert, S. T. Fiske, & L. Gardner (Eds.), *Handbook of social psychology* (pp. 982–1026). New York: Oxford University Press.

Buss, D. M., & Schmitt, D. P. (1993). Sexual strategies theory: An evolutionary perspective on human mating. *Psychological Review, 100*, 204–232.

Cacioppo, J. T., Berntson, G. G., Sheridan, J. F., & McClintock, M. K. (2000). Multilevel integrative analyses of human behavior: Social neuroscience and the complementing nature of social and biological approaches. *Psychology Bulletin, 126*, 829–843.

Cacioppo, J. T., Klein, D. J., Berntson, G. C., & Hatfield, E. (1993). The psychophysiology of emotion. In M. Lewis & J. M. Haviland (Eds.), *Handbook of emotions* (pp. 119–142). New York: Guilford Press.

Cahill, L., Haier, R. J., Fallon, J., Alkire, M. T., Tang, C., Keator, D., et al. (1996). Amygdala activity at encoding correlated with long-term, free recall of emotional information. *Proceedings of the National Academy of Sciences of the United States of America, 93*, 8016–8021.

Cahill, L., Haier, R. J., White, N. S., Fallon, J., Kilpatrick, L., Lawrence, C., et al. (2001). Sex-related difference in amygdala activity during emotionally influenced memory storage. *Neurobiology of Learning and Memory, 75*, 1–9.

Cairns, R. B., & Cairns, B. D. (1994). *Lifelines and risks: Pathways of youth in our times*. Cambridge: Cambridge University Press.

Caldwell, M. A., & Pepau, L. A. (1982). Sex differences in same-sex friendship. *Sex Roles, 7*, 721–732.

Caporael, L. R. (2001). Evolutionary psychology: Toward a unifying theory and a hybrid science. *Annual Review of Psychology, 52*, 607–628.

Caramazza, A., & Shelton, J. R. (1998). Domain specific knowledge systems in the brain: The animate-inanimate distinction. *Journal of Cognitive Neuroscience, 10*, 1–34.

Carey, S., & Hauser, M. (2000). The representation of number: A case study of evolution and development. In M. S. Gazzaniga (Ed.), *The cognitive neurosciences* (2nd ed.). Cambridge, MA: MIT Press.

Carter, C. S. (1998). Neuroendocrine perspectives on social attachment and love. *Psychoneuroendocrinology, 23*, 779–819.

Carver, C. S., & Scheier, M. F. (1981). *Attention and self-regulation: A control theory approach to human behavior*. New York: Springer-Verlag.

Carver, C. S., & Scheier, M. F. (1998). *On the self-regulation of behavior*. New York: Cambridge University Press.

Case, R. (1992). The role of the frontal lobes in development. *Brain and Cognition, 20*(1), 51–73.

Caspi, A. (2000). The child is father of the man: Personality continuities from childhood to adulthood. *Journal of Personality and Social Psychology, 78*, 158–172.

Caspi, A., & Herbener, E. S. (1990). Continuity and change: Assortative marriage and the consistency of personality in adulthood. *Journal of Personality and Social Psychology, 58*, 250–258.

Castellanos, F. X., Giedd, J. N., Eckberg, P., & Marsh, W. L. (1998). Quantitative morphology of the caudate nucleus in attention deficit hyperactivity disorder. *American Journal of Psychiatry, 151*(12), 1791–1796.

Cattell, R. B. (1971). *Abilities: Their structure, growth, and action*. Boston: Houghton Mifflin.

Ceci, S. J., & Bruck, M. (1995). *Jeopardy in the courtroom: A scientific analysis of children's testimony*. Washington, DC: American Psychological Association.

Cerella, J. (1990). Aging and information processing rate. In J. E. Birren & K. W. Schaie, (Eds.), *Handbook of the psychology of aging* (3rd ed). New York: Van Nostrand Reinhold.

Chabris, C. F. (1999). Prelude or requiem for the "Mozart effect." *Nature, 26*, 826–827.

Chase, W. G., & Simon, H. A. (1973). Perception in chess. *Cognitive Psychology, 4*, 55–81.

Cherry, E. C. (1953). Some experiments on the recognition of speech, with one and two ears. *Journal of the Acoustic Society of America, 25*, 975–979.

Chess, S., & Thomas, A. (1984). *Origins and evolution of behavior disorders: From infancy to early adult life*. Cambridge, MA: Harvard University Press.

Childress, A. R., Mozley, D., McElgin, W., Fitzgerald, J., Reivich, M., & O'Brien, P. C. (1999). Limbic activation during cue-induced cocaine craving. *American Journal of Psychiatry, 156*, 11–18.

Chomsky, N. (1975). *Reflections on language*. New York: Pantheon Books.

Christianson, S. (1992). Emotional stress and eyewitness memory: A critical review. *Psychological Bulletin, 112*, 284–309.

Clark, A. C., & Watson, D. (1999). Temperament: A new paradigm for trait psychology. In L. A. Pervin & O. P. John (Eds.), *Handbook of personality: Theory and research* (pp. 399–423). New York: Guilford.

Clark, M. S., & Mills, J. (1993). The difference between communal and exchange relationships: What it is and is not. *Personality and Social Psychology Bulletin, 19,* 684–691.

Clark, R. D., & Hatfield, E. (1989). Gender differences in receptivity to sexual offers. *Journal of Psychology and Human Sexuality, 2,* 39–55.

Cloninger, C., Adolfsson, R., & Svrakic, N. (1996). Mapping genes for human personality. *Nature and Genetics, 12,* 3–4.

Cohen, D., Nisbett, R. E., Bowdle, B. F., & Schwarz, N. (1996). Insult, aggression, and the southern culture of honor: An "experimental ethnography." *Journal of Personality and Social Psychology, 70,* 945–960.

Cohen, S., Tyrrell, D. A. J., & Smith, A. P. (1991). Psychological stress and susceptibility to the common cold. *The New England Journal of Medicine, 325,* 606–612.

Cohen, S., & Wills, T. A. (1985). Stress, social support, and the buffering hypothesis. *Psychological Bulletin, 98,* 310–357.

Coie, J. D., & Krehbiel, G. (1984). Effects of academic tutoring on the social status of low-achieving, socially rejected children. *Child Development, 55,* 1465–1478.

Colby, A., Kohlberg, L., Gibbs, J., & Lieberman, M. (1983). A longitudinal study of moral judgment. *Monographs of the Society for Research in Child Development, 48,* 1–124.

Collins, A. M., & Loftus, E. F. (1975). A spreading-activation theory of semantic processing. *Psychological Review, 82,* 407–428.

Collins, W. A., & Gunnar, M. R. (1990). Social and personality development. *Annual Review of Psychology, 41,* 387–416.

Comer, R., & Laird, J. D. (1975). Choosing to suffer as a consequence of expecting to suffer: Why do people do it? *Journal of Personality and Social Psychology, 32,* 92–101.

Conway, M. A., Anderson, S. J., Larsen, S. F., Donnelly, C. M., McDaniel, M. A., McClelland, A. G. R., et al. (1994). The formation of flashbulb memories. *Memory and Cognition, 22,* 326–343.

Conway, M., & Ross, M. (1984). Getting what you want by revising what you had. *Journal of Personality and Social Psychology, 47,* 738–748.

Cook, M., & Mineka, S. (1989). Observational conditioning of fear to fear-relevant versus fear-irrelevant stimuli in rhesus monkeys. *Journal of Abnormal Psychology, 98,* 448–459.

Cooper, L. A., & Shepard, R. N. (1973). Chronometric studies of the rotation of mental images. In W. G. Chase (Ed.), *Visual information processing* (pp. 75–176). New York: Academic Press.

Cooper, R. G., Jr. (1984). Early number development: Discovering number space with addition and subtraction. In C. Sophian (Ed.), *Origins of cognitive skills: The eighteenth annual Carnegie symposium on cognition* (pp. 157–192). Hillsdale, NJ: Erlbaum.

Coopersmith, S. (1967). *The antecedents of self-esteem.* San Francisco: Freeman.

Corkin, S., Amaral, D. G., Gonzalez, R. G., Johnson, K. A., & Hyman, B. T. (1997). H. M.'s medial temporal lobe lesion: Findings from magnetic resonance imaging. *Journal of Neuroscience, 17,* 3964–3979.

Cosmides, L., & Tooby, J. (2000). The cognitive neuroscience of social reasoning. In M. S. Gazzaniga (Ed.), *The new cognitive neurosciences* (pp. 1259–1270). Cambridge, MA: MIT Press.

Cosmides, L., & Tooby, J. (2001). Evolutionary psychology: A primer. Retrieved May 24, 2002 from University of California at Santa Barbara, Center for Evolutionary Psychology Web site: http://www.psych.ucsb.edu/research/cep/primer.html

Costa, P. T., & McCrae, R. R. (1992). *Revised NEO Personality Inventory (NEO-PI-R) and NEO Five-Factor Inventory (NEO-FFI) professional manual.* Odessa, FL: Psychological Assessment Resources.

Cowan, N. (2001). The magical number 4 in short-term memory: A reconsideration of mental storage capacity. *Behavioral and Brain Sciences, 24*(1), 87–114.

Cowley, J. J., & Brooksbank, L. B. W. (1991). Human exposure to putative pheromones and changes in aspects of social behavior. *Journal of Steroid Biochemistry and Molecular Biology, 39,* 647–659.

Craik, F. I. M., & Tulving, E. (1975). Depth of processing and the retention of words in episodic memory. *Journal of Experimental Psychology: General, 104,* 268–294.

Craik, F. I. M, Moroz, T. M., Moscovitch, M., Stuss, D. T., Winocur, G., Tulving, E., et al. (1999). In search of the self: A positron emission tomography study. *Psychological Science, 10,* 26–34.

Crocker, J., & Major, B. (1989). Social stigma and self-esteem: The self-protective properties of stigma. *Psychological Review, 96*(4), 608–630.

Cromwell, R. L. (1993). Searching for the origins of schizophrenia. *Psychological Science, 4,* 276–279.

Crowder, R. G. (1992). Eidetic imagery. In L. R. Squire (Ed.), *Encyclopedia of learning and memory* (pp. 154–156). New York: Macmillan.

Crowe, R. R. (2000). Molecular genetics of anxiety disorders. In D. S. Charney, E. J. Nestler, & B. S. Bunney (Eds.), *Neurobiology of mental illness* (pp. 451–462). New York: Oxford University Press.

Culler, E. A., Coakley, J. D., Lowy, K., & Gross, N. (1943). A revised frequency-map of the Guinea-pig cochlea. *American Journal of Psychology, 56,* 475–500.

Cupach, W. R., & Metts, S. (1990). Remedial processes in embarrassing predicaments. In J. Anderson (Ed.), *Communication yearbook* (pp. 323–352). Newbury Park, CA: Sage.

Curtiss, S. (1977). *Genie: a psycholinguistic study of a modern day "wild child."* New York: Academic Press.

Damasio, A. R. (1994). *Descartes' error.* New York: Avon Books.

Darley, J. M., & Batson, C. D. (1973). "From Jerusalem to Jericho": A study of situational and dispositional variables in helping behavior. *Journal of Personality and Social Psychology, 27,* 100–108.

Davidson, R. J. (2000a). Affective style, psychopathology, and resilience: Brain mechanisms and plasticity. *American Psychologist, 55,* 1196–1214.

Davidson, R. J. (2000b). The functional neuroanatomy of affective style. In R. D. Lane & L. Nadel (Eds.), *Cognitive neuroscience of emotion* (pp. 371–388). New York: Oxford University Press.

Davison, K., & Pennebaker, J. (1996). Social psychosomatics. In E. T. Higgins & A. W. Kruglanski (Eds.), *Social psychology: Handbook of basic principles* (pp. 102–130). New York: Guilford.

Deaux, K., & Major, B. (1987). Putting gender into context: An interactive model of gender-related behavior. *Psychological Review, 94,* 369–389.

DeCasper, A. J., & Fifer, W. P. (1980). Of human bonding: Newborns prefer their mothers' voices. *Science, 208,* 1174–1176.

DeCasper, A. J., & Spence, M. J. (1986). Prenatal maternal speech influences newborn's perception of speech sounds. *Infant Behavior and Development, 9,* 133–150.

Deci, E. L., & Ryan, R. M. (1987). The support of autonomy and the control of behavior. *Journal of Personality and Social Psychology, 53,* 1024–1037.

Dejong, W., & Kleck, R. E. (1986). The social psychological effects of overweight. In C. P. Herman, M. P. Zanna, & E. T. Higgins (Eds.), *Physical appearance, stigma and social behavior: The Ontario Symposium* (pp. 65–87). Hillsdale, NJ: Erlbaum.

Dennerstein, L., & Burrows, G. D. (1982). Hormone replacement therapy and sexuality in women. *Clinics in Endocrinology and Metabolism, 11,* 661–679.

DePaulo, B. M., & Kashy, D. A. (1998). Everyday lies in close and casual relationships. *Journal of Personality and Social Psychology, 74,* 63–79.

Depue, R. A., & Collins, P. F. (1999). Neurobiology of the structure of personality: Dopamine, facilitation of incentive motivation, and extraversion. *Behavioral and Brain Sciences, 22,* 491–569.

Devine, P. G. (1989). Stereotypes and prejudice: Their automatic and controlled components. *Journal of Personality and Social Psychology, 56,* 5–18.

Diamond, A., & Doar, B. (1989). The performance of human infants on a measure of frontal cortex function, delayed response task. *Developmental Psychobiology, 22,* 271–294.

Dickson, P. R., & Vaccarino, F. J. (1994). GRF-induced feeding: Evidence for protein selectivity and opiate involvement. *Peptides, 15,* 1343–1352.

Diener, E. (1979). Deindividuation, self-awareness, and disinhibition. *Journal of Personality and Social Psychology, 37,* 1160–1171.

Diener, E. (2000). Subjective well-being: The science of happiness and a proposal for a national index. *American Psychologist, 55,* 34–43.

Diener, E., Wolsic, B., & Fujita, F. (1995). Physical attractiveness and subjective well-being. *Journal of Personality and Social Psychology, 69,* 120–129.

Dindia, K., & Allen, M. (1992). Sex differences in self-disclosure: A meta-analysis. *Psychological Bulletin, 112,* 106–124.

Dohrenwend, B. P., Shrout, P. E., Link, B. G., Skodol, A. E., & Martin, J. L. (1986). Overview and initial results from a risk factor study of depression and schizophrenia. In J. E. Barrett (Ed.), *Mental disorders in the community: Progress and challenge.* New York: Guilford Press.

Dolan, R. J. (1999). On the neurology of morals. *Nature Neuroscience, 2,* 927–929.

Dolan, R. J. (2000). Emotion processing in the human brain revealed through functional neuroimaging. In M. S. Gazzaniga (Ed.), *The new cognitive neurosciences* (pp. 115–131). Cambridge, MA: MIT Press.

Donahue, A. B. (2000). Electroconvulsive therapy and memory loss: A personal journey. *Journal of ECT, 16,* 133–143.

Drummond, S. P., Brown, G. G., Gillin, J. C., Stricker, J. L., Wong, E. C., & Buxton, R. B. (2000). Altered brain response to verbal learning following sleep deprivation. *Nature, 403,* 655–657.

Duncan, J., Seitz, R. J., Kolodny, J., Bor, D., Herzog, H., Ahmed, A., et al. (2000). A neural basis for general intelligence. *Science, 289,* 457–460.

Dunphy, D. C. (1963). The social structure of urban adolescent peer groups. *Sociometry, 26,* 230–246.

Dutton, D. G., & Aron, A. P. (1974). Some evidence for heightened sexual attraction under conditions of high anxiety. *Journal of Personality and Social Psychology, 30,* 510–517.

Dykman, B. M., Horowitz, L. M., Abramson, L. Y., & Usher, M. (1991). Schematic and situational determinants of depressed and nondepressed students' interpretation of feedback. *Journal of Abnormal Psychology, 100,* 45–55.

Eacott, M. J. (1999). Memory for the events of early childhood. *Current Directions in Psychological Science, 8*(2), 46–49.

Eaves, L. J., Eysenck, H. J., & Martin, N. G. (1989). *Genes, culture and personality: An empirical approach.* San Diego, CA: Academic Press.

Eder, D., & Hallinan, M. T. (1978). Sex differences in children's friendships. *American Sociological Review, 43,* 237–250.

Egeland, J. A., Gerhard, D. S., Pauls, D. L., Sussex, J. N., Kidd, K. K., Allen, C. R., et al. (1987). Bipolar affective disorders linked to DNA markers on chromosome 11. *Nature, 325,* 783–787.

Eich, J. E., Weingartner, H., Stillman, R. C., & Gillin, J. C. (1975). State-dependent accessibility of retrieval cues in the retention of a cate-gorized list. *Journal of Verbal Learning and Verbal Behavior, 14,* 408–417.

Eimas, P. D., Siqueland, E. R., Jusczyk, P., & Vigorito, J. (1971). Speech perception in infants. *Science, 171,* 303–306.

Eisenberg, N. (2000). Emotion, regulation, and moral development. *Annual Review of Psychology, 51,* 665–697.

Eisenberg, N., & Fabes, R. A. (1998). Prosocial development. In W. Damon & N. Eisenberg (Eds.), *Handbook of child psychology: Social, emotional, and personality development* (pp. 701–778). New York: Wiley and Sons.

Eisenberg, N., Fabes, R. A., Murphy, M., Maszk, P., Smith, M., & Karbon, M. (1995). The role of emotionality and regulation in children's social functioning: A longitudinal study. *Child Development, 66,* 1239–1261.

Eisenberg, N., Miller, P. A., Shell, R., McNalley, S., & Shea, C. (1991). Prosocial development in adolescence: A longitudinal study. *Developmental Psychology, 27,* 849–857.

Ekelund, J., Lichtermann, D., Jaervelin, M., & Peltonen, L. (1999). Association between novelty seeking and type 4 dopamine receptor gene in a large Finnish cohort sample. *American Journal of Psychiatry, 156,* 1453–1455.

Ekman, P. (1977). Biological and cultural contributions to body and facial movement. In J. Blacking (Ed.), *The anthropology of the body* (pp. 58–84). A. S. A. Monograph 15. London: Academic Press.

Ekman, P. (1992). *Telling lies: Clues to deceit in the marketplace, marriage, and politics.* New York: W. W. Norton.

Ekman, P., & Friesen, W. V. (1971). Constants across cultures in the face and emotion. *Journal of Personality and Social Psychology, 17,* 124–129.

Ekman, P., & Friesen, W. V. (1975). *Unmasking the face: A guide to recognizing emotions from facial clues.* Englewood Cliffs, NJ: Prentice Hall.

Ekman, P., Levenson, R. W., & Friesen, W. V. (1983). Autonomic nervous system activity distinguishes among emotions. *Science, 221,* 1208–1210.

Ekselius, L., & von Knorring, L. (1999). Changes in personality traits during treatment with sertraline or citalopram. *British Journal of Psychiatry, 174,* 444–448.

Elfenbein, H. A., & Ambady, N. (2002). On the universality of cultural specificity of emotion recognition: A meta-analysis. *Psychological Bulletin, 128,* 203–235.

Epperson, C. N., McDougle, C. J., Brown, R. M., Leckman, J. F., Goodman, W. K., & Price, L. H. (1995). OCD during pregnancy and the puerperium [Abstract]. *American Psychiatric Association New Research Abstracts, 84,* NR112.

Era, P., Jokela, J., & Heikkinen, E. (1986). Reaction and movement times in men of different ages: A population study. *Perceptual and Motor Skills, 63,* 111–130.

Erel, O., Oberman, Y., & Yirmiya, N. (2000). Maternal versus nonmaternal care and seven domains of children's development. *Psychological Bulletin, 126,* 727–747.

Erikson, E. H. (1968). *Identity: Youth and crisis.* New York: W. W. Norton.

Eron, L. D. (1987). The development of aggressive behavior from the perspective of a developing behaviorism. *American Psychologist, 42,* 435–442.

Evers, S., & Suhr, B. (2000). Changes of the neurotransmitter serotonin but not of hormones during short time music perception. *European Archives of Psychiatry and Clinical Neuroscience, 250,* 144–147.

Eysenck, M. W., Mogg, K., May, J., Richards, A., & Matthews, A. (1991). Bias in interpretation of ambiguous sentences related to threat in anxiety. *Journal of Abnormal Psychology, 100,* 144–150.

Fallon, A. E., & Rozin, P. (1985). Sex differences in perceptions of desirable body shape. *Journal of Abnormal Psychology, 94*, 102–105.

Fantz, R. L. (1966). Pattern discrimination and selective attention as determinants of perceptual development from birth. In A. H. Kidd & L. J. Rivoire (Eds.), *Perceptual development in children*. New York: International Universities Press.

Farah, M. J. (1996). Is face recognition "special"? Evidence from neuropsychology. *Behavioural Brain Research, 76*, 181–189.

Farah, M. J., Levine, D. N., & Calvanio, R. (1988). A case study of mental imagery deficit. *Brain and Cognition, 8*, 147–164.

Fawcett, J. (1992). Suicide risk factors in depressive disorders and in panic disorders. *Journal of Clinical Psychiatry, 53*, 9–13.

Fazio, R. H. (1995). Attitudes as object-evaluation associations: Determinants, consequences, and correlates of attitude accessibility. In R. E. Petty & J. A. Krosnick (Eds.), *Attitude strength: Antecedents and consequences* (pp. 247–282). Hillsdale, NJ: Erlbaum.

Feldman Barrett, L., Lane, R. D., Sechrest, L., & Schwartz, G. E. (2000). Sex differences in emotional awareness. *Personality and Social Psychology Bulletin, 26*, 1027–1035.

Fendrich, R., Wessinger, C. M., & Gazzaniga, M. S. (1992). Residual vision in a scotoma: Implications for blindsight. *Science, 258*, 1489–1491.

Ferguson, J. N., Young, L. J., Hearn, E. F., Matzuk, M. M., Insel, T. R., & Winslow, J. T. (2000). Social amnesia in mice lacking the oxytocin gene. *Nature Neuroscience, 25*, 284–288.

Ferguson, T. J., & Stegge, H. (1995). Emotional states and traits in children: The case of guilt and shame. In J. P. Tangney & K. W. Fischer (Eds.), *Self-conscious emotions* (pp. 174–197). New York: Guilford.

Festinger, L. (1954). A theory of social comparison processes. *Human Relations, 7*, 117–140.

Festinger, L. (1987). A personal memory. In N. E. Grunberg, R. E. Nisbett, J. Rodin, & J. E. Singer (Eds.), *A distinctive approach to psychological research: The influence of Stanley Schachter* (pp. 1–9). New York: Erlbaum.

Festinger, L., & Carlsmith, J. M. (1959). Cognitive consequences of forced compliance. *Journal of Abnormal and Social Psychology, 58*, 203–210.

Field, T., Fox, N. A., Pickens, J., & Nawrocki, T. (1995). Relative right frontal EEG activation in 3- to 6-month-old infants of "depressed" mothers. *Developmental Psychology, 31*, 358–363.

Fillipek, P. A., Semrud-Clikeman, M., Steingard, R. J., Renshaw, P. F., Kennedy, D. N., & Biederman, J. (1997). Volumetric MRI analysis comparing subjects having attention deficit hyperactivity disorder with normal controls. *Neurology, 48*, 589–600.

Fink, M. (2001). Convulsive therapy: A review of the first 55 years. *Journal of Affective Disorders, 63*(1–3), 1–15.

Fischer, K. (1980). A theory of cognitive development: The control and construction of hierarchies of skills. *Psychological Review, 87*, 477–531.

Fisher, A. (1993). Sex differences in emotionality: Fact or stereotype. *Feminism and Psychology, 3*, 303–318.

Fisher, W. A., Byrne, D., White, L. A., & Kelley, K. (1988). Erotophobia-erotophilia as a dimension of personality. *Journal of Sex Research, 25*, 123–151.

Foley, K. M. (1993). Opioids. *Neurologic Clinics, 11*, 503–522.

Folkman, S., Lazarus, R. S., Dunkelschetter, C., Delongis, A., & Gruen, R. (1986). Dynamics of a stressful encounter: Cognitive appraisal, coping, and encounter outcomes. *Journal of Personality and Social Psychology, 50*, 992–1003.

Forgas, J. P. (1998). Asking nicely: Mood effects on responding to more or less polite requests. *Personality and Social Psychology Bulletin, 24*, 173–185.

Forsyth, D. R. (1995). *Our social world*. Pacific Grove, CA: Brooks Cole.

Fox, R., Aslin, R. N., Shea, S. L., & Dumais, S. T. (1980). Stereopsis in human infants. *Science, 207*, 323–324.

Frank, E., Kupfer, D., Perel, I., Comes, C., Jarret, D., Mallinger, A., et al. (1990). Three-year outcomes for maintenance therapies in recurrent depression. *Archives of General Psychiatry, 47*, 1093–1099.

Franken, R. E. (1998). *Human motivation*. Pacific Grove, CA: Brooks Cole.

Freedman, J. L. (1984). Effects of television violence on aggression. *Psychological Bulletin, 96*, 227–246.

Frijda, N. H. (1994). Emotions are functional, most of the time. In P. Ekman & R. J. Davidson (Eds.), *The nature of emotion: Fundamental questions. Series in affective science* (pp. 112–122). New York: Oxford University Press.

Frith, C. D., Friston, K., Liddle, P. F., & Frackowiak, R. (1991). Willed action and the prefrontal region cortex in man: A study with PET. *Proceedings of the Royal Society of London, Biological Sciences, 244*, 241–246.

Fromkin, V., Krashen, S., Curtiss, S., Rigler, D., & Riler, M. (1974). The development of language in Genie: A case of language acquisition beyond the "critical period." *Brain and Language, 1*, 81–107.

Funder, D. C. (1995). On the accuracy of personality judgment: A realistic approach. *Psychological Review, 102*, 652–670.

Funder, D. C. (2001). Personality. *Annual Review of Psychology, 52*, 197–221.

Gallese, V., & Goldman, A. (1998). Mirror neurons and the simulation theory of mind-reading. *Trends in Cognitive Sciences, 2*, 493–501.

Gallistel, C. R. (2000). The replacement of general-purpose learning models with adaptively specialized learning modules. In M. S. Gazzaniga (Ed.), *The new cognitive neurosciences* (pp. 1179–1191). Cambridge, MA: MIT Press.

Garcia, J., & Koelling, R. A. (1966). Relation of cue to consequence in avoidance learning. *Psychonomic Science, 4*, 123–124.

Gardner, H. (1983). *Frames of mind: The theory of multiple intelligences*. New York: Basic Books.

Gardner, W. L., Pickett, C. L., & Brewer, M. B. (2000). Social exclusion and selective memory: How the need to belong affects memory for social information. *Personality and Social Psychology Bulletin, 26*, 486–496.

Gazzaniga, M. S., Ivry, R. B., & Mangun, G. R. (1998). *Cognitive neuroscience: The biology of the mind*. New York: W. W. Norton.

Geen, R. G. (1984). Preferred stimulation levels in introverts and extraverts: Effects on arousal and performance. *Journal of Personality and Social Psychology, 46*, 1303–1312.

George, M. S., Lisanby, S. H., & Sackheim, H. A. (1999). Transcranial Magnetic Stimulation: Applications in neuropsychiatry. *Archives of General Psychiatry, 56*, 300–311.

George, M. S., Wassermann, E. M., Williams, W. A., Callahan, A., Ketter, T. A., Basser, P., et al. (1995). Daily repetitive transcranial magnetic stimulation (rTMS) improves mood in depression. *Neuroreport, 6*, 1853–1856.

Gershon, E. S., Berrettini, W. H., & Goldin, L. R. (1989). Mood disorders: Genetic aspects. In H. I. Kaplan & B. J. Sadock (Eds.), *Comprehensive textbook of psychiatry* (5th ed). Baltimore: Williams & Wilkins.

Geula, C., & Mesulam, M. (1994). Cholinergic systems and related neuropathological predilection patterns in Alzheimer disease. In R. D. Terry, R. Katzman, & K. Bick (Eds.), *Alzheimer disease* (pp. 263–291). New York: Raven Press.

Gevins, A., Smith, M. E., McEvoy, L., Yu, D. (1997). High-resolution EEG mapping of cortical activation related to working memory: Effects of task difficulty, type of processing, and practice. *Cerebral Cortex, 7,* 374–385.

Gibbons, F. X., Eggleston, T. J., & Benthin, A. C. (1997). Cognitive reactions to smoking relapse: The reciprocal relation between dissonance and self-esteem. *Journal of Personality and Social Psychology, 72,* 184–195.

Gibson, J. J. (1950). *The perception of the visual world.* Boston: Houghton Mifflin.

Gibson, J. J. (1966). *The senses considered as perceptual systems.* Boston: Houghton Mifflin.

Giedd, J. N., Blumental, J., Jeffries, N. O., Castellanos, F. X., Liu, H., Zijdenbos, A., et al. (1999). Brain development during childhood and adolescence: A longitudinal MRI study. *Nature Neuroscience, 2,* 861–863.

Gigerenzer, G., & Goldstein, D. G. (1996). Reasoning the fast and frugal way: Models of bounded rationality. *Psychological Review, 103,* 650–669.

Gilberg, C. (1980). Maternal age and infantile autism. *Journal of Autism and Developmental Disorders, 10,* 293–297.

Gilbert, D. T., & Jones, E. E. (1986). Exemplification: The self-presentation of moral character. *Journal of Personality, 54,* 593–615.

Gilligan, C. (1982). *In a different voice.* Cambridge, MA: Harvard University Press.

Gillis, J. J., Gilger, J. W., Pennington, B. F., & DeFries, J. C. (1992). Attention deficit disorder in reading-disabled twins: Evidence for a genetic etiology. *Journal of Abnormal Child Psychology, 20*(3), 303–315.

Gilovich, T. (1991). *How we know what isn't so: The fallibility of human reason in everyday life.* New York: The Free Press.

Glass, D. C., & Singer, J. E. (1972). *Urban stress.* New York: Academic Press.

Godden, D. R., & Baddeley, A. D. (1975). Context-dependent memory in two natural environments: On land and underwater. *British Journal of Psychology, 66,* 325–331.

Golby, A. J., Gabrieli, J. D. E., Chiao, J. Y., & Eberhardt, J. L. (2001). Differential responses in the fusiform region to same-race and other-race faces. *Nature Neuroscience, 4,* 845–850.

Gold, P. E. (1987). Sweet memories. *American Scientist, 75,* 151–155.

Goldenberg, J. L., McCoy, S. K., Pyszczynski, T., Greenberg, J., & Solomon, S. (2000). The body as a source of self-esteem: The effects of mortality salience on identification with one's body, interest in sex, and appearance monitoring. *Journal of Personality and Social Psychology, 79,* 118–130.

Goldman-Rakic, P. S., Scalaidhe, S., & Chafee, M. (2000). Domain specificity in cognitive systems. In M. S. Gazzaniga (Ed.), *The new cognitive neurosciences* (pp. 733–742). Cambridge, MA: MIT Press.

Goodale, M. A., & Milner, A. D. (1992). Separate visual pathways for perception and action. *Trends in Neuroscience, 15,* 22–25.

Goodman, R., & Stevenson, J. (1989). A twin study of hyperactivity-II. The aetiological role of genes, family relationships, and perinatal adversity. *Journal of Child Psychology and Psychiatry, 30*(5), 691–709.

Goodwin, D. W., Powell, B., Bremer, D., Hoine, H., & Stern, J. (1969). Alcohol and recall: State dependent effects in man. *Science, 163,* 1358.

Gopnik, A., & Graf, O. (1988). Knowing how you know: Young children's ability to identify and remember the sources of their beliefs. *Child Development, 59,* 1366–1371.

Gosling, S. D. (1998). Personality dimensions in spotted hyenas (Crocuta crocuta). *Journal of Comparative Psychology, 112,* 107–118.

Gosling, S. D. (2001). From mice to men: What can we learn about personality from animal research? *Psychological Bulletin, 127,* 45–86.

Gosling, S. D., & John, O. P. (1999). Personality dimension in nonhuman animals: A cross-species review. *Current Directions in Psychological Science, 8,* 69–75.

Gottesman, I. I. (1991). *Schizophrenia genesis: The origins of madness.* New York: Freeman.

Gottman, J. (1994). *Why marriages succeed or fail.* New York: Simon & Schuster.

Gottman, J. M. (1983). How children become friends. *Monographs of the Society for Research in Child Development 48*(3, Serial No. 201).

Green, L., Myerson, J., Lichtman, D., Rosen, S., & Fry, A. (1996). Temporal discounting in choice between delayed rewards: The role of age and income. *Psychological Science, 11,* 79–94.

Greenberg, J., Solomon, S., & Pyszczynski, T. (1997). Terror management theory of self-esteem and cultural worldviews: Empirical assessments and conceptual refinements. In M. P. Zanna (Ed.), *Advances in Experimental Social Psychology* (Vol. 29, pp. 61–136). New York: Academic Press.

Greenwald, A. G. (1980). The totalitarian ego: Fabrication and revision of personal history. *American Psychologist, 35,* 603–618.

Greenwald, A. G., & Banaji, M. R. (1995). Implicit social cognition: Attitudes, self-esteem, and stereotypes. *Psychological Review, 102,* 4–27.

Greenwald, A. G., McGhee, D., & Schwartz, J. (1998). Measuring individual differences in implicit cognition: The implicit association test. *Journal of Personality and Social Psychology, 74,* 1464–1480.

Gregory, A. H., Worrall, L., & Sarge, A. (1996). The development of emotional responses to music in young children. *Motivation and Emotion, 20,* 341–348.

Gross, J. J. (1999). Emotion and emotion regulation. In L. A. Pervin & O. P. John (Eds.), *Handbook of personality: Theory and research* (2nd ed., pp. 525–552). New York: Guilford Press.

Grossman, M., & Wood, W. (1993). Sex differences in intensity of emotional experience: A social role interpretation. *Journal of Personality and Social Psychology, 65,* 1010–1022.

Guerin, B. (1994). What do people think about the risks of driving? Implications for traffic safety interventions. *Journal of Applied Social Psychology, 24,* 994–1021.

Gunderson, J. G. (1984). *Borderline personality disorder.* Washington, DC: American Psychiatric Press.

Haber, R. N. (1983). The impending demise of the icon: A critique of the concept of iconic storage in visual information processing. *Behavioral and Brain Sciences, 6,* 1–54.

Hall, D. E., Eubanks, L., Meyyazhagan, S., Kenney, R. D., & Johnson, S. C. (2000). Evaluation of covert video surveillance in the diagnosis of Munchausen Syndrome by Proxy: Lessons from 41 cases. *Pediatrics, 105,* 1305–1312.

Hambrecht, M., Maurer, K., Hafner, H., & Sartorius, N. (1992). Transnational stability of gender differences in schizophrenia: Recent findings on social skills training and family psychoeducation. *Clinical Psychology Review, 11,* 23–44.

Hamer, D. H., Hu, S., Magnuson, V. L., Hu, N., & Pattatucci, A. M. L. (1993). A linkage between DNA markers on the X chromosome and male sexual orientation. *Science, 261,* 321–327.

Hancock, P. J., Bruce, V. V., & Burton, A. M. (2000). Recognition of unfamiliar faces. *Trends in Cognitive Sciences, 4,* 330–337.

Handleman, J. S., Gill, M. J., & Alessandri, M. (1988). Generalization by severely developmentally disabled children: Issues, advances, and future directions. *Behavior Therapist, 11,* 221–223.

Haney, C., Banks, C., & Zimbardo, P. (1973). Interpersonal dynamics in a simulated prison. *International Journal of Criminology and Penology, 1,* 69–97.

Harding, C. M., Zubin, J., & Strauss, J. S. (1987). Chronicity in schizophrenia: Fact, partial fact, or artifact? *Hospital and Community Psychiatry, 38,* 477–486.

Hare, R. D. (1993). *Without conscience: The disturbing world of the psychopaths among us.* New York: Pocket Books.

Hare, R. D., McPherson, L. M., & Forth, A. E. (1988). Male psychopaths and their criminal careers. *Journal of Consulting and Clinical Psychology, 56,* 710–714.

Harlow, H. F., & Harlow, M. K. (1962). Social deprivation in monkeys. *Scientific American, 207,* 136–146.

Harlow, H. F., Harlow, M. K., & Meyer, D. R. (1950). Learning motivated by a manipulation drive. *Journal of Experimental Psychology, 40,* 228–234.

Harmer, C. J., Thilo, K. V., Rothwell, J. C., & Goodwin, G. M. (2001). Transcranial magnetic stimulation of medial-frontal cortex impairs the processing of angry facial expressions. *Nature Neuroscience, 4,* 17–18.

Harpur, T. J., & Hare, R. D. (1994). Assessment of psychopathy as a function of age. *Journal of Abnormal Psychology, 103*(4), 604–609.

Harris, J. R. (1995). Where is the child's environment? A group socialization theory of development. *Psychological Review, 102,* 458–489.

Hartsough, C. S., & Lambert, N. M. (1985). Medical factors in hyperactive and normal children: Prenatal, developmental, and health history findings. *American Journal of Orthopsychiatry, 55,* 190–201.

Hartup, W. W. (1989). Social relationships and their developmental significance. *American Psychologist, 44,* 120–126.

Haydon, P. G. (2001). Glia: Listening and talking to the synapse. *Nature Reviews: Neuroscience, 2,* 185–193.

Heatherton, T. F., & Nichols, P. A. (1994). Personal accounts of successful versus failed attempts at life change. *Personality and Social Psychology Bulletin, 20,* 664–675.

Heatherton, T. F., & Polivy, J. (1991). Development and validation of a scale for measuring state self-esteem. *Journal of Personality and Social Psychology, 60,* 895–910.

Heatherton, T. F., & Weinberger, J. L. (1994). *Can personality change?* Washington, DC: American Psychological Association.

Hebl, M. R., & Heatherton, T. F. (1998). The stigma of obesity in women: The difference is black and white. *Personality and Social Psychology Bulletin, 24,* 417–426.

Hegarty, J., Baldessarini, R., Tohen, M., Waternaux, C., & Oepen, G. (1994). One hundred years of schizophrenia: A meta-analysis of the outcome literature. *American Journal of Psychiatry, 151,* 1409–1416.

Heishman, S. J., Taylor, R. C., & Henningfield, J. E. (1994). Nicotine and smoking: A review of effects on human performance. *Experimental and Clinical Psychopharmacology, 2,* 345–395.

Helmholtz, H. von. (1909–1911). *Treatise on physiological optics* (3rd ed., vols. 2–3, J. P. Southall, Ed. and Trans.). Rochester, NY: Optical Society of America. (Original work published 1866)

Helmreich, R., Aronson, E., & LeFan, J. (1970). To err is humanizing sometimes: Effects of self-esteem, competence, and a pratfall on interpersonal attraction. *Journal of Personality and Social Psychology, 16,* 259–264.

Helms, J. (1990). *Black and white racial identity: Theory, research, and practice.* New York: Greenwood.

Henderson, L., & Zimbardo, P. G. (1998). Shyness. *Encyclopedia of Mental Health, 3,* 497–509.

Hering, E. (1964). *Outlines of a theory of the light sense* (L. M. Hurvich & D. Jameson, Trans.). Cambridge, MA: Harvard University Press. (Original work published 1878)

Herschkowitz, N., Kagan, J., & Zilles, K. (1997). Neurobiological bases of behavioral development in the first year. *Neuropediatrics, 28,* 296–306.

Hibscher, J., & Herman, C. P. (1977). Obesity, dieting, and the expression of "obese" characteristics. *Journal of Comparative and Physiological Psychology, 91,* 374–380.

Higgins, E. T. (1987). Self-discrepancy: A theory relating self and affect. *Psychological Review, 94,* 319–340.

Higley, J. D., Mehlman, P. T., Higley, S. B., Fernald, B., Vickers, J., Lindell, et al. (1996). Excessive mortality in young free-ranging male nonhuman primates with low cerebrospinal fluid 5-hydroxyindoleacetic acid concentrations. *Archives of General Psychiatry, 53,* 537–543.

Hobson, J. A. (1995). *Sleep.* New York: Scientific American Library.

Hobson, J. A. (1999). Sleep and dreaming. In M. J. Zigmond, F. E. Bloom, S. C. Landis, J. L. Roberts, & L. R. Squire (Eds.), *Fundamentals of neuroscience* (pp. 1207–1225). San Diego, CA: Academic Press.

Hobson, J. A., Pace-Schott, E. F., & Stickgold, R. (2000). Consciousness: Its vicissitudes in waking and sleep. In M. S. Gazzaniga (Ed.), *The new cognitive neurosciences* (pp. 1341–1354). Cambridge, MA: MIT Press.

Hodges, E. E. V., & Perry, D. G. (1999). Personal and interpersonal antecedents and consequences of victimization by peers. *Journal of Personality and Social Psychology, 76,* 677–685.

Hoffman, M. L. (1998). Varieties of empathy-based guilt. In J. Bybee (Ed.), *Guilt and children* (pp. 90–111). San Diego: Academic Press.

Hogarty, G. E., Anderson, C. M., Reiss, D. J., Kornbith, S. J., Greenwald, D. P., Jaund, C. D., et al. (1986). Family psychoeducation, social skills training, and maintenance chemotherapy in the aftercare treatment of schizophrenia: One-year effects of a controlled study on relapse and expressed emotion. *Archives of General Psychiatry, 43,* 633–642.

Holland, P. C. (1977). Conditioned stimulus as a determinant of the form of the Pavlovian conditioned response. *Journal of Experimental Psychology: Animal Behavior Processes, 3,* 77–104.

Hollis, K. L. (1997). Contemporary research on Pavlovian conditioning: A "new" functional analysis. *American Psychologist, 52,* 956–965.

Holowka, S., & Petitto, L. A. (2001). Left hemisphere cerebral specialization for babies while babbling [Abstract]. *Abstracts of the 31st Annual Meeting Society for Neuroscience* (no. 529.5).

Holt, E. B. (1931). *Animal drive and the learning process.* New York: Holt.

Hooley, J. M., & Gotlib, I. H. (2000). A diathesis-stress conceptualization of expressed emotion and clinical outcome. *Applied and Preventive Psychology, 9,* 135–152.

Horn, J. L. (1985). Remodeling old models of intelligence. In B. B. Wolman (Ed.), *Handbook of intelligence: Theories, measurements, and applications* (pp. 267–300). New York: Wiley.

Horn, J. L., & Hofer, S. M. (1992). Major abilities and development in the adult period. In R. J. Sternberg & C. A. Berg (Eds.), *Intellectual development* (pp. 44–99). New York: Cambridge University Press.

Hoshino, Y., Kumashiro, H., Yashima, Y., Tachibana, R., Watanabe, M., & Furukawa, H. (1980). Early symptoms of autism in children and their diagnostic significance. *Japanese Journal of Child and Adolescent Psychiatry, 21*(5), 284–299.

Hothersall, D. (1995). *History of psychology.* New York: McGraw-Hill.

House, J. S., Landis, K. R., & Umberson, D. (1988). Social relationships and health. *Science, 241,* 540–545.

Howlin, P., Mawhood, L., & Rutter, M. (2000). Autism and developmental receptive language disorder—A follow-up comparison in early adult life. II: Social, behavioural, and psychiatric outcomes. *Journal of Child Psychology and Psychiatry and Allied Disciplines, 41*(5), 561–578.

Hubel, D. H., & Wiesel, T. N. (1962). Receptive fields, binocular interaction, and functional architecture in the cat's visual cortex. *Journal of Physiology (London), 160*, 106–154.

Huesmann, L. R. (1998). The role of social information processing and cognitive schemas in the acquisition and maintenance of habitual aggressive behavior. In R. G. Geen & E. Donnerstein (Eds.), *Human aggression: Theories, research, and implications for policy* (pp. 73–109). New York: Academic Press.

Hughes, H. C. (2000). *Sensory exotica*. Cambridge, MA: MIT Press.

Hull, J. G., & Bond, C. F. (1986). Social and behavioral consequences of alcohol consumption and expectancy: A meta-analysis. *Psychological Bulletin, 99*, 347–360.

Hynd, G. W., Hern, K., & Novey, E. S. (1993). Attention deficit-hyperactivity disorder and asymmetry of the caudate nucleus. *Journal of Child Neurology, 8*(4), 339–347.

Ickes, W., & Simpson, J. A. (1997). Managing empathic accuracy in close relationships. In W. Ickes (Ed.), *Empathic accuracy* (pp. 218–250). New York: Guilford.

Insel, T. R. (1992). Oxytocin and the neurobiology of attachment. *Behavioral and Brain Sciences, 15*(3), 515–516.

Isen, A. M. (1993). Positive affect and decision making. In M. Lewis & J. M. Haviland (Eds.), *Handbook of emotions* (pp. 261–277). New York: Guilford Press.

Izard, C. E., & Malatesta, C. Z. (1987). Perspectives on emotional development. In J. Osofsky (Ed.), *Handbook of infant development* (pp. 494–554). New York: Wiley.

Jablensky, A. (1989). Epidemiology and cross-cultural aspects of schizophrenia. *Psychiatric Annals, 19*, 516–524.

Jacobs, R. C., & Campbell, D. T. (1961). The perpetuation of arbitrary tradition through several generations of a laboratory microculture. *Journal of Abnormal and Social Psychology, 62*, 649–658.

Jacoby, L. L., Kelley, C., Brown, J., & Jasechko, J. (1989). Becoming famous overnight: Limits on the ability to avoid unconscious influences of the past. *Journal of Personality and Social Psychology, 56*, 326–338.

Jamison, K. R. (1995). *An unquiet mind*. New York: Vintage Books.

Jang, K. L., Hu, S., Livesly, W. J., Angleitner, A., Riemann, R., Ando, J., et al. (2001). Covariance structure of neuroticism and agreeableness: A twin and molecular genetic analysis of the role of the serotonin transporter gene. *Journal of Personality and Social Psychology, 81*, 295–304.

Jensen, P. S., Hinshaw, S. P., Swanson, J. M., Greenhill, L. L., Conners, C. K., Arnold, L. E., et al. (2001). Findings from the NIMH Multimodal Treatment Study of ADHD (MTA): Implications and applications for primary care providers. *Journal of Developmental and Behavioral Pediatrics: Special Issue, 22*(1), 60–73.

Jessell, T. M., & Kelley, D. D. (1991). Pain and analgesia. In E. R. Kandel, J. H. Schwartz, & T. M. Jessell (Eds.), *Principles of neural science* (3rd ed., pp. 385–399). New York: Elsevier.

John, O. P. (1990). The "Big Five" factor taxonomy: Dimensions of personality in the natural language and in questionnaires. In L. A. Pervin & O. P. John (Eds.), *Handbook of personality: Theory and research* (pp. 66–100). New York: Guilford Press.

John, O. P., & Srivastava, S. (1999). The Big Five trait taxonomy: History, measurement, and theoretical perspectives. In L. A. Pervin & O. P. John (Eds.), *Handbook of personality: Theory and research* (2nd ed., pp. 102–138). New York: Guilford Press.

Johnson, D. L., Wiebe, J. S., Gold, S. M., Andreasen, N. C., Hichwa, R. D., Watkins, G. L., et al. (1999). Cerebral blood flow and personality: A positron emission tomography study. *American Journal of Psychiatry, 156*, 252–257.

Johnson, M. M. S. (1986). *The initial letter effect: Ego-attachment or mere exposure?* Unpublished doctoral dissertation, Ohio State University. (Reported in A. G. Greenwald & M. R. Banaji. 1995. Implicit social cognition: Attitudes, self-esteem, and stereotypes. *Psychological Review, 102*, 4–27).

Joiner, T. E., Alfano, M. S., & Metalsky, G. (1992). When depression breeds contempt: Reassurance seeking, self-esteem, and rejection of depressed college students by their roommates. *Journal of Abnormal Psychology, 101*, 165–173.

Joiner, T. E., & Metalsky, G. I. (1995). A prospective test of an integrative interpersonal theory of depression: A naturalistic study of college roommates. *Journal of Personality and Social Psychology, 69*, 778–788.

Joint Statement. (2000). *Joint statement on the impact of entertainment violence on children*. Congressional Public Health Summit. July 26, 2000.

Jones, E. E., & Pittman, T. S. (1982). Toward a general theory of strategic self-presentation. In J. Suls (Ed.), *Psychological perspectives on the self* (Vol. 1, pp. 231–262). Hillsdale, NJ: Erlbaum.

Jones, R. A., & Ellis, G. D. (1996). Effect of variation in perceived risk on the secretion of beta-endorphin. *Leisure Sciences, 18*, 277–291.

Jones, S. S., Collins, K., & Hong, H. (1991). An audience effect on smile production in 10-month-old infants. *Psychological Science, 2*, 45–49.

Jope, R. S. (1999). Anti-bipolar therapy: Mechanism of action of lithium. *Molecular Psychiatry, 4*(2), 117–128.

Jorde, L. B., Mason-Brothers, A., Waldman, R., Ritvo, E. R., Freeman, B. J., Pingree, C., et al. (1990). The UCLA-University of Utah epidemiologic survey of autism: Genealogical analysis of familial aggregation. *American Journal of Medical Genetics, 36*, 85–88.

Kagan, J. (1984). *The nature of the child*. New York: Basic Books.

Kagan, J. (1994). *Galen's prophecy*. New York: Basic Books.

Kagan, J. (1997). Temperament and the reactions to unfamiliarity. *Child Development, 68*, 139–143.

Kagan, J., & Snidman, N. (1991). Infant predictors of inhibited and uninhibited profiles. *Psychological Science, 2*, 40–44.

Kandel, E. R., Schwartz, J. H., & Jessell, T. M. (1995). *Essentials of neural science and behavior*. Norwalk, CT: Appleton & Lange.

Kane, J. M., Honigfield, G., Singer, J., & Meltzer, N. (1988). Clozapine for the treatment-resistant schizophrenic. *Archives of General Psychiatry, 45*, 789–796.

Kanwisher, N., Tong, F., & Nakayama, K. (1998). The effect of face inversion on the human fusiform face area. *Cognition, 68*, 1–11.

Kapur, S. E., Craik, F. I. M., Tulving, E., Wilson, A. A., Houle, S., & Brown, G. R. (1994). Neuroanatomical correlates of encoding in episodic memory: Levels of processing effects. *Proceedings of the National Academy of Sciences, 91*, 2008–2011.

Karney, B. R., & Bradbury, T. N. (1995). The longitudinal course of marital quality and stability: A review of theory, methods, and research. *Psychological Bulletin, 118*, 3–34.

Kassin, S. M., & Kiechel, K. L. (1996). The social psychology of false confessions: Compliance, internalization, and confabulation. *Psychological Science, 7*, 125–128.

Kazdin, A. E. (1994). Methodology, design, and evaluation in psychotherapy research. In A. E. Bergin & S. L. Garfield (Eds.), *International handbook of behavior modification and behavior change* (4th ed., pp. 19–71). New York: Wiley.

Keating, D. (1980). Thinking processes in adolescence. In J. Adelson (Ed.), *Handbook of adolescent psychology*. New York: Wiley.

Keel, P. K., & Mitchell, J. E. (1997). Outcome in bulimia nervosa. *American Journal of Psychiatry, 154*, 313–321.

Keenan, J. P., Freund, S., Hamilton, R. H., Ganis, G., & Pascual-Leone, A. (2000). Hand response differences in a self-face identification task. *Neuropsychologia, 38*, 1047–1053.

Keenan, J. P., Nelson, A., O'Connor, M., & Pascual-Leone, A. (2001). Self-recognition and the right hemisphere. *Nature, 409*, 305.

Keesey, R. (1995). A set-point model of body weight regulation. In K. D. Brownell & C. Fairburn (Eds.), *Eating disorders and obesity: A comprehensive handbook* (pp. 46–50). New York: Guilford.

Keith, S. J., Regier, D. A., & Rae, D. S. (1991). Schizophrenic disorders. In L. N. Robins & D. A. Regier (Eds.), *Psychiatric disorders in America: The epidemiological catchment areas study*. New York: The Free Press.

Keller, M. B., & Baker, L. A. (1991). Bipolar disorder: Epidemiology, course, diagnosis, and treatment. *Bulletin of the Menninger Clinic, 55*, 172–181.

Keller, M. B., McCullough, J. P., Klein, D. N., Arnow, B., Dunner, D. L., Gelenberg, A. J., et al. (2000). A comparison of nefazodone, a cognitive behavioral analysis system of psychotherapy, and their combination for the treatment of chronic depression. *New England Journal of Medicine, 342*, 1462–1470.

Keller, M. B., Shapiro, R. W., Lavori, P. W., & Wolfe, N. (1982). Recovery in major depressive disorder. *Archives of General Psychiatry, 39*, 905–910.

Kellerman, J. (1989). *Silent Partner*. New York: Bantam Books.

Kelley, W. M., Miezin, F. M., McDermott, K. B., Buckner, R. L., Raichle, M. E., Cohen, N. J., et al. (1998). Hemispheric specialization in human dorsal frontal cortex and medial temporal lobe for verbal and nonverbal memory encoding. *Neuron, 20*, 927–936.

Kelley, W. T., Macrae, C. N., Wyland, C., Caglar, S., Inati, S., & Heatherton, T. F. (In press). Finding the self? An event-related fMRI study. *Journal of Cognitive Neuroscience*.

Kellman, P. J., Spelke, E. S., & Short, K. R. (1986). Infant perception of object unity from translatory motion in depth and vertical translation. *Child Development, 57*(1), 72–86.

Keltner, D., & Anderson, C. (2000). Saving face for Darwin: The functions and uses of embarrassment. *Current Directions in Psychological Science, 9*, 187–192.

Keltner, D., & Bonanno, G. A. (1997). A study of laughter and dissociation: Distinct correlates of laughter and smiling during bereavement. *Journal of Personality and Social Psychology, 73*, 687–702.

Kendler, K. S., Gardner, C. O., & Prescott, C. A. (1998). A population-based twin study of self-esteem and gender. *Psychological Medicine, 28*, 1403–1409.

Kenrick, D. T., & Funder, D. C. (1991). The person-situation debate: Do personality traits really exist? In V. J. Derlega, B. A. Winstead, & W. H. Jones (Eds.), *Personality: Contemporary theory and research* (pp. 149–174). Chicago, IL: Nelson Hall.

Kessler, R. C., McGonagle, K. A., Zhao, S., Nelson, C. B., Hugh, M., Eshleman, S. et al. (1994). Lifetime and 12-month prevalence of DSM-III-R psychiatric disorders in the United States: Results from the National Comorbidity Study. *Archives of General Psychiatry, 51*(1), 8–19.

Keys, A., Brozek, J., Henschel, A. L., Mickelsen, O., & Taylor, H. L. (1950). *The biology of human starvation*. Minneapolis: University of Minnesota Press.

Kiecolt-Glaser, J. K., & Glaser, R. (1988). Immunological competence. In E. A. Blechman & K. D. Brownell (Eds.), *Handbook of behavioral medicine for women* (Vol. 149, pp. 195–205). Elmsford, NY: Pergamon Press.

Kiecolt-Glaser, J. K., Malarkey, W. B., Chee, M., & Newton, T. (1993). Negative behavior during marital conflict is associated with immunological down-regulation. *Psychosomatic Medicine, 55*, 395–409.

Kite, M. E., & Deaux, K. (1986). Attitudes toward homosexuality: Assessment and behavioral consequences. *Basic and Applied Social Psychology, 7*, 137–162.

Klein, E., Kreinin, I., Chistyakov, A., Koren, D., Mecz, L., Marmur, S., et al. (1999). Therapeutic efficacy of right prefrontal slow repetitive transcranial magnetic stimulation in major depression: A double-blind controlled study. *Archives of General Psychiatry, 56*, 315–320.

Kleinmuntz, B., & Szucko, J. J. (1984). Lie detection in ancient and modern times: A call for contemporary scientific study. *American Psychologist, 39*, 766–776.

Knight, R. (1953). Borderline states. *Bulletin of the Menninger Clinic, 17*, 1–12.

Knight, R. T., & Grabowecky, M. (1995). Escape from linear time: Prefrontal cortex and conscious experience. In M. S. Gazzaniga (Ed.), *The cognitive neurosciences* (pp. 1357–1371). Cambridge, MA: MIT Press.

Knutson, B., Wolkowitz, O. M., Cole, S. W., Chan, T., Moore, E. A., Johnson, R. C., et al. (1998). Selective alteration of personality and social behavior by serotonergic intervention. *American Journal of Psychiatry, 155*, 373–379.

Kobasa, S. C. (1979). Personality and resistance to illness. *American Journal of Community Psychology, 7*, 413–423.

Koch, J. L. (1891). *Die psychopathischen Minderwertigkeiten*. Ravensburg, Germany: Maier.

Kohlberg, L. (1984). *Essays on moral development. Vol. 2, The psychology of moral development*. New York: Harper & Row.

Kolar, D. W., Funder, D. C., & Colvin, C. R. (1996). Comparing the accuracy of personality judgments by the self and knowledgeable others. *Journal of Personality, 64*, 311–337.

Kolb, B., & Wishaw, I. (1990). *Fundamentals of human neuropsychology*. New York: W. H. Freeman.

Konishi, M. (1993). Listening with two ears. *Scientific American, 268*, 66–73.

Koob, G. F. (1999). Drug reward and addiction. In M. J. Zigmond, F. E. Bloom, S. C. Landis, J. L. Roberts, & L. R. Squire (Eds.), *Fundamentals of neuroscience* (pp. 1261–1279). San Diego, CA: Academic Press.

Koole, S. L., Dijksterhuis, A., & van Knippenberg, A. (2001). What's in a name: Implicit self-esteem and the automatic self. *Journal of Personality and Social Psychology, 80*, 669–685.

Koons, C. R., Robins, C. J., Tweed, J. L., Lynch, T. R., Gonzalez, A. M., Morse, J. Q., et al. (2001). Efficacy of dialectical behavior therapy in women veterans with borderline personality disorder. *Behavior Therapy, 32*(2), 371–390.

Korn, M. L., Kotler, M., Molcho, A., Botsis, A. J., Grosz, D., Chen, C., et al. (1992). Suicide and violence associated with panic attacks. *Biological Psychiatry, 31*, 607–612.

Koshland, D. E. (1989). Drunk driving and statistical mortality. *Science, 244*, 513.

Kosslyn, S., & Koenig, O. (1995). *Wet mind: The new cognitive neuroscience*. New York: Free Press.

Kosslyn, S. M., & Thompson, W. L. (2000). Shared mechanisms in visual imagery and visual perception: Insights from cognitive neuroscience. In M. S. Gazzaniga (Ed.), *The new cognitive neurosciences* (pp. 975–985). Cambridge, MA: MIT Press.

Kosslyn, S. M., Thompson, W. L., Kim, I. J., & Alpert, N. M. (1995). Topographical representations of mental images in primary visual cortex. *Nature, 378,* 496–498.

Kraepelin, E. (1921). *Manic-depressive insanity and paranoia.* Edinburgh, Scotland: E. & S. Livingstone.

Krantz, D. S., Lundberg, U., & Frankenhaeuser, M. (1987). Stress and type A behavior: Interactions between environmental and biological factors. In A. Baum & J. E. Singer (Eds.), *Handbook of psychology and health: Stress* (Vol. 5, pp. 203–228). Hillsdale, NJ: Lawrence Erlbaum.

Krebs, D. L., Vermeulen, S. C., & Denton, K. L. (1991). Competence and performance in moral judgment: From the idea to the real. *Moral Education Forum, 16,* 7–22.

Kruesi, M. J., Hibbs, E. D., Zahn, T. P., Keysor, C. S., Hamburger, S. D., Bartko, J. J., et al. (1992). A 2-year prospective follow-up study of children and adolescents with disruptive behavior disorders. Prediction by cerebrospinal fluid 5-hydroxyindoleacetic acid, homovanillic acid, and autonomic measures. *Archives of General Psychiatry, 49,* 429–435.

Kupersmidt, J. B., DeRosier, M. E., & Patterson, C. P. (1995). Similarity as the basis for children's friendships: The roles of sociometric status, aggressive and withdrawn behavior, academic achievement and demographic characteristics. *Journal of Social and Personal Relationships, 12,* 439–452.

Kurtines, W. M., & Gewirtz, J. L. (1991). *Handbook of moral behavior and development* (vols. 1–3). Hillsdale, NJ: Lawrence Erlbaum.

Kurzban, R., & Leary, M. R. (2001). Evolutionary origins of stigmatization: The functions of social exclusion. *Psychological Bulletin, 127,* 187–208.

LaFrance, M., & Banaji, M. (1992). Toward a reconsideration of the gender-emotion relationship. In M. Clarke (Ed.) *Review of personality and social psychology* (pp. 178–201). Beverly Hills, CA: Sage.

Laible, D. J., & Thompson, R. A. (2000). Attachment and self-organization. In M. D. Lewis & I. Granic (Eds.), *Emotion, development, and self-organization: Dynamic systems approaches to emotional development* (pp. 298–323). New York: Cambridge University Press.

Laird, J. D. (1974). Self-attribution of emotion: The effects of expressive behavior on the quality of emotional experience. *Journal of Personality and Social Psychology, 29,* 475–486.

Lalumiere, M. L., Blanchard, R., & Zucker, K. J. (2000). *Psychological Bulletin, 126,* 575–592.

Landau, B. (1994). Where's what and what's where: The language of objects in space. In L. E. Gleitman and B. Landau (Eds.), [special issue] *Lexical acquisition, Lingua, 92,* 259–296.

Lane, R. D. (2000). Neural correlates of conscious emotional experiences. In R. D. Lane & L. Nadel (Eds.), *Cognitive neuroscience of emotion* (pp. 345–370). New York: Oxford University Press.

Lane, R. D., Reiman, E. M., Ahern, G. L., & Schwartz, G. E. (1997). Neuroanatomical correlates of happiness, sadness, and disgust. *American Journal of Psychiatry, 154,* 926–933.

Lane, R. D., Reiman, E. M., Axelrod, B., Yun, L. S., Holmes, A., & Schwartz, G. E. (1998). Neural correlates of levels of emotional awareness. Evidence of an interaction between emotion and attention in the anterior cingulate cortex. *Journal of Cognitive Neuroscience, 10,* 525–535.

Langer, E. (1975). The illusion of control. *Journal of Personality and Social Psychology, 32,* 311–328.

Langleben, D. D., Schroeder, L., Maldjian, J. A., Gur, R. C., McDonald, S., Ragland, J. D., et al. (2002). Brain activity during simulated deception: An event-related functional magnetic resonance study. *Neuroimage, 15,* 727–732.

Langlois, J. H., Kalakanis, L., Rubenstein, A. J., Larson, A., Hallam, M., & Smoot, M. (2000). Maxims or myths of beauty? A meta-analytic and theoretical review. *Psychological Bulletin, 126,* 390–423.

Langlois, J. H., Ritter, J. M., Casey, R. J., & Sawin, D. B. (1995). Infant attractiveness predicts maternal behaviors and attitudes. *Developmental Psychology, 31,* 464–472.

Langlois, J. H., & Roggman, L. A. (1990). Attractive faces are only average. *Psychological Science, 1,* 115–121.

Lasagna, L., Mosteller, F., von Felsinger, J., & Beecher, H. (1954). A study of the placebo response. *American Journal of Medicine, 16,* 770–779.

Latané, B., & Darley, J. M. (1968). Group inhibition of bystander intervention in emergencies. *Journal of Personality and Social Psychology, 10,* 215–221.

Latané, B., Williams, K., & Harkins, S. G. (1979). Many hands make light work: The causes and consequences of social loafing. *Journal of Personality and Social Psychology, 37,* 822–832.

Lazarus, R. S. (1993). From psychological stress to the emotions: A history of changing outlooks. *Annual Review of Psychology, 44,* 1–21.

Leary, M. R., Tambor, E. S., Terdal, S. K., & Downs, D. L. (1995) Self-esteem as an interpersonal monitor: The sociometer hypothesis. *Journal of Personality and Social Psychology, 68,* 518–530.

Leckman, J. F., Elliott, G. R., Bromet, E. J., Campbell, M., Cicchetti, D., Cohen, D. J., et al. (1995). Report card on the National Plan for Research on Child and Adolescent Mental Disorders: The midway point. *Archives of General Psychiatry, 34,* 715–723.

Leckman, J. F., Goodman, W. K., North, W. G., Chappell, P. B., Price, L. H., Pauls, D. L., et al. (1994). The role of central oxytocin in obsessive compulsive disorder and related behavior. *Psychoneuroendocrinology, 19*(8), 723–749.

LeDoux, J. E. (1996). *The emotional brain: The mysterious underpinnings of emotional life.* New York: Simon & Schuster.

Lee, K., Cameron, C., Xu, F., Fu, G., & Board, J. (1999). Chinese and Canadian children's evaluations of lying and truth telling: Similarities and differences in the context of pro- and antisocial behaviors. In A. Slater & D. Muir (Eds.), *The Blackwell reader in developmental psychology* (pp. 402–420). Oxford: Blackwell.

Leff, J., Sartorius, N., Jablensky, A., Korten, A., & Ernberg, G. (1992). The International Pilot Study of Schizophrenia: Five-year follow-up findings. *Psychological Medicine, 22,* 131–145.

Leibowitz, S. F. (1992). Neurochemical-neuroendocrine systems in the brain controlling macronutrient intake and metabolism. *Trends in Neuroscience, 15,* 491–497.

Leichtman, M. D., & Ceci, S. J. (1995). The effects of stereotypes and suggestions on preschoolers' reports. *Developmental Psychology, 31*(4), 568–578.

Leigh, B. C., & Schafer, J. C. (1993). Heavy drinking occasions and the occurrence of sexual activity. *Psychology of Addictive Behaviors, 7,* 197–200.

Lenneberg, E. (1967). *The biological foundations of language.* New York: Wiley.

Lenneberg, E. H., Rebelsky, F. G., & Nichols, I. A. (1965). The vocalizations of infants born to hearing and deaf parents. *Human Development, 8,* 23–27.

Lepper, M. R., Greene, D., & Nisbett, R. E. (1973). Undermining children's intrinsic interest with extrinsic reward: A test of the "overjustification" hypothesis. *Journal of Personality and Social Psychology, 28,* 129–137.

Leslie, A. (2000). "Theory of mind" as a mechanism of selective attention. In M. S. Gazzaniga (Ed.), *The cognitive neurosciences* (2nd ed.). Cambridge, MA: MIT Press.

Leuchter, A. F., Cook, I. A., Witte, E. A., Morgan, M., & Abrams, M. (2002). Changes in brain function of depressed subjects during treatment with placebo. *American Journal of Psychiatry, 159,* 122–129.

LeVay, S. (1991). A difference in hypothalamic structure between heterosexual and homosexual men. *Science, 253,* 1034–1037.

Levenson, R. W., Ekman, P., Heider, K., & Friesen, W. V. (1992). Emotion and autonomic nervous system activity in the Minangkabau of West Sumatra. *Journal of Personality and Social Psychology, 62,* 972–988.

Levine, J. D., Gordon, N. C., & Fields, H. L. (1979). Naloxone dose dependently produces analgesia and hyperalgesia in postoperative pain. *Nature, 278,* 740–741.

Lewinsohn, P. M., Allen, N. B., Seeley, J. R., & Gotlib, I. H. (1999). First onset versus recurrence of depression: Differential processes of psychosocial risk. *Journal of Abnormal Psychology, 108*(3), 483–489.

Lewinsohn, P. M., Rodhe, P. D., Seeley, J. R., & Hops, H. (1991). Comorbidity of unipolar depression: I. Major depression with dysthymia. *Journal of Abnormal Psychology, 98,* 107–116.

Lewis, M. (1993). The development of deception. In M. Lewis & C. Saarni (Eds.), *Lying and deception in everyday life* (pp. 90–106). New York: Guilford Press.

Lewis, M., & Brooks-Gunn, J. (1979). *Social cognition and the acquisition of self.* New York: Plenum.

Lidz, C. W., Mulvey, E. P., & Gardner, W. (1993). The accuracy of predictions of violence to others. *Journal of the American Medical Association, 269,* 1007–1011.

Lieberman, M. D. (2000). Intuition: A social cognitive neuroscience approach. *Psychological Bulletin, 126,* 109–137.

Lieberman, M. D., Ochsner, K. N., Gilbert, D. T., & Schacter, D. L. (2001). Do amnesics exhibit cognitive dissonance reduction? The role of explicit memory and attention in attitude change. *Psychological Science, 121,* 135–140.

Light, L. (1990). Interactions between memory and language in old age. In J. E. Birren & K. W. Schaie (Eds.), *Handbook of the psychology of aging* (3rd ed.). New York: Van Nostrand Reinhold.

Linehan, M. M. (1987). Dialectical behavior therapy for borderline personality disorder: Theory and method. *Bulletin of the Menninger Clinic, 51*(3), 261–276.

Linehan, M. M., Armstrong, H. E., Suarez, A., Allmon, D., & Heard, H. (1991). Cognitive behavioral treatment of chronically parasuicidal borderline patients. *Archives of General Psychiatry, 48,* 1060–1064.

Linehan, M. M., Heard, H., & Armstrong, H. E. (1993). Naturalistic follow-up of a behavioral treatment for chronically parasuicidal borderline patients. *Archives of General Psychiatry, 50*(12), 971–974.

Linville, P. W. (1985). Self-complexity and affectivity: Don't put all your eggs into one cognitive basket. *Social Cognition, 3,* 94–120.

Lippa, R. A., Martin, L. R., & Friedman, H. S. (2000). Gender-related individual differences and mortality in the Terman Longitudinal Study: Is masculinity hazardous to your health? *Personality and Social Psychology Bulletin, 26,* 1560–1570.

Ljungberg, T., Apicella, P., & Schultz, W. (1992). Responses of monkey dopamine neurons during learning of behavioral reactions. *Journal of Neurophysiology, 67,* 145–163.

Locke, E. A., & Latham, G. P. (1990). *A theory of goal setting and task performance.* Englewood Cliffs, NJ: Prentice-Hall.

Loehlin, J. C., & Nichols, R. C. (1976). *Heredity, environment, and personality: A study of 850 sets of twins.* Austin, TX: University of Texas Press.

Loewenstein, G. F., Weber, E. U., Hsee, C. K., & Welch, N. (2001). Risk as feelings. *Psychological Bulletin, 127,* 267–286.

Loftus, E. (1993). The reality of repressed memories. *American Psychologist, 48,* 518–537.

Logan, J. M., Sanders, A. L., Snyder, A. Z., Morris, J. C., & Buckner, R. L. (2002). Under-recruitment and nonselective recruitment: Dissociable neural mechanisms associated with aging. *Neuron, 33,* 1–20.

Lohr, J. B., & Flynn, K. (1992). Smoking and schizophrenia. *Schizophrenia Research, 8*(2), 93–102.

London, E. D., Ernst, M., Grant, S., Bonson, K., & Weinstein, A. (2000). Orbitofrontal cortex and human drug abuse: Functional imaging. *Cerebral Cortex, 10,* 334–342.

Lord, C. G., & Saenz, D. S. (1985). Memory deficits and memory surfeits: Differential cognitive consequences of tokenism for tokens and observers. *Journal of Personality and Social Psychology, 49,* 918–926.

Lovaas, O. I. (1987). Behavioral treatment and normal educational and intellectual functioning in young autistic children. *Journal of Consulting & Clinical Psychology, 55*(1), 3–9.

Luborsky, L., Crits-Christoph, P., McLellan, T., Woody, G., Piper, W., Liberman, B., et al. (1986). Do therapists vary much in their success? Findings from four outcome studies. *American Journal of Orthopsychiatry, 56*(4), 501–512.

Lucas, R. E., Diener, E., Grob, A., Suh, E., & Shao, L. (2000). Cross-cultural evidence for the fundamental features of extraversion. *Journal of Personality and Social Psychology, 79,* 452–468.

Lykken, D. T. (1957). A study of anxiety in the sociopathic personality. *Journal of Abnormal Social Psychology, 55*(1), 6–10.

Lykken, D. T. (1995). *The antisocial personalities.* Hillsdale, NJ: Erlbaum.

Lykken, D. T. (2000). The causes and costs of crime and a controversial cure. *Journal of Personality, 68,* 559–605.

Lynam, D. R., Milich, R., Zimmerman, R., Novak, S. P., Logan, T. K., Martin, C., et al. (1999). Project DARE: No effects at 10-year follow-up. *Journal of Consulting and Clinical Psychology, 67,* 590–593.

Lyubomirsky, S., & Nolen-Hoeksema, S. (1995). Effects of self-focused rumination on negative thinking and interpersonal problem solving. *Journal of Personality and Social Psychology, 69,* 176–190.

Maas, L. C., Lukas, S. E., Kaufman, M. J., Weiss, R. D., Daniels, S. L., Rogers, et al. (1998). Functional magnetic resonance imaging of human brain activation during cue-induced cocaine craving. *American Journal of Psychiatry, 155,* 124–126.

Macrae, C. N., & Bodenhausen, G. V. (2000). Social cognition: Thinking categorically about others. *Annual Review of Psychology, 51,* 93–120.

Macrae, C. N., Bodenhausen, G. V., & Calvini, G. (1999). Contexts of cryptomnesia: May the source be with you. *Social Cognition, 17,* 273–297.

Macrae, C. N., Bodenhausen, G. V., Milne, A. B., & Jetten, J. (1994). Out of mind but back in sight: Stereotypes on the rebound. *Journal of Personality and Social Psychology, 67,* 808–817.

Madden, G. J., Petry, N. M., Badger, G. J., & Bickel, W. K. (1997). Impulsivity and self-control choices in opioid-dependent patients and non-drug-using control participants: Drug and monetary rewards. *Experimental and Clinical Psychopharmacology, 5,* 256–262.

Maier, N. R. F. (1931). Reasoning in humans II: The solution of a problem and its appearance in consciousness. *Journal of Comparative Psychology, 12,* 181–194.

Maier, S. F., & Watkins, L. R. (2000). The immune system as a sensory system: Implications for psychology. *Current Directions in Psychological Science, 9,* 98–102.

Main, M., & Solomon, J. (1986). Discovery of a new, insecure-disorganized/disoriented attachment pattern. In T. B. Brazelton & M. Yogman (Eds.), *Affective development in infancy* (pp. 95–124). Norwood, NJ: Ablex.

Malison, R. T., McDougle, C. J., van Dyck, C. H., Scahill, L., Baldwin, R. M., Seibyl, J. P., et al. (1995). [123I]B-CIT SPECT imaging demonstrates increased striatal dopamine transporter binding in Tourette's syndrome. *American Journal of Psychiatry, 152,* 1359–1361.

Mananuzza, S., Klein, R. G., Bonagura, N., Malloy, P., Giampino, T. L., & Addalli, K. A. (1991). Hyperactive boys almost grown up. Replications of psychiatric status. *Archives of General Psychiatry, 48,* 77–83.

Manderscheid, R. W., Witkin, M. J., Rosenstein, M. J., Milazzo-Sayre, L. J., Bethel, H. E., & MacAskill, R. L. (1985). In C. A. Taube & S. A. Barrett (Eds.), *Mental health, United States, 1985.* Washington DC: National Institute of Mental Health.

Marcel, A. (1983). Conscious and unconscious perception: Experiments on visual masking and word recognition. *Cognitive Psychology, 15,* 238–300.

Marcia, J. E. (1966). Development and validation of ego-identity status. *Journal of Personality and Social Psychology, 3,* 551–558.

Markowitz, J. C., & Weissman, M. M. (1995). Interpersonal psychotherapy. In E. E. Beckham & W. R. Leber (Eds.), Handbook of depression (2nd ed., pp. 376–390). New York: Guilford Press.

Markus, H. R. (1977). Self-schemata and processing information about the self. *Journal of Personality and Social Psychology, 35,* 63–78.

Markus, H. R., & Kitayama, S. (1991). Culture and the self: Implications for cognition, emotion, and motivation. *Psychological Review, 98,* 224–253.

Marler, P. (1970). A comparative approach to vocal learning: Song development in white-crowned sparrows. *Journal of Comparative and Physiological Psychology, 71,* 1–25.

Marr, D. (1982). *Vision: A computational investigation into the human representation and processing of visual information.* San Francisco: Freeman.

Martin, N. G., Eaves, L. J., Heath, A. R., Jardine, R., Feingold, L. M., & Eysenck, H. J. (1986). Transmission of social attitudes. *Proceedings of the National Academy of Science, 83,* 4364–4368.

Maslow, A. (1968). *Toward a psychology of being.* New York: Van Nostrand.

Masten, A. S. (2001). Ordinary magic: Resilience processes in development. *American Psychologist, 56,* 227–238.

McAdams, D. P. (1999). Personal narratives and the life story. In L. A. Pervin & O. P. John (Eds.), *Handbook of personality: Theory and research* (2nd ed., pp. 478–500). New York: Guilford Press.

McAdams, D. P. (2000). *The person: An integrated introduction to personality psychology.* New York: Harcourt.

McAdams, D. P. (2001). The psychology of life stories. *Review of General Psychology, 5,* 100–122.

McCarthy, G., Puce, A., Gore, J. C., & Allison, T. (1997). Face-specific processing in the human fusiform gyrus. *Journal of Cognitive Neuroscience, 9,* 605–610.

McClelland, D. C. (1987). *Human motivation.* New York: Cambridge University Press.

McClelland, D. C., Koestner, R., & Weinberger, J. (1989). How do self-attributed and implicit motives differ? *Psychological Review, 96,* 690–702.

McClintock, M. K. (1971). Menstrual synchrony and suppression. *Nature, 229,* 244–245.

McCormick, D. A. (1999). Membrane potential and action potential. In M. J. Zigmond, F. E. Bloom, S. C. Landis, J. L. Roberts, & L. R. Squire (Eds.), *Fundamentals of neuroscience* (pp. 129–154). San Diego, CA: Academic Press.

McCrae, R. R., & Costa, P. T., Jr. (1982). Self-concept and the stability of personality: Cross-sectional comparisons of self-reports and ratings. *Journal of Personality and Social Psychology, 43,* 1282–1292.

McCrae, R. R., & Costa, P. T., Jr. (1990). *Personality in adulthood.* New York: Guilford Press.

McCrae, R. R., & Costa, P. T., Jr. (1999). A five-factor theory of personality. In L. A. Pervin & O. P. John (Eds.), *Handbook of personality: Theory and research* (2nd ed., pp. 139–153). New York: Guilford Press.

McCrae, R. R., Costa, P. T., Ostendorf, F., Angleitner, A., Hrebickova, M., Avia, M. D., et al. (2000). Nature over nurture: Temperament, personality, and life span development. *Journal of Personality and Social Psychology, 78,* 173–186.

McCullough, J. P. (2000). *Treatment for chronic depression: Cognitive Behavioral Analysis System of Psychotherapy (CBASP).* New York: The Guilford Press.

McDougle, C. (1997). Psychopharmacology. In D. Cohen & R. Volkmar (Eds.), *Handbook of autism and pervasive developmental disorders* (2nd ed., pp. 707–729). New York: Wiley.

McEvoy, J. P., & Brown, S. (1999). Smoking in first-episode patients with schizophrenia. *American Journal of Psychiatry, 156*(7), 1120–1121.

McEwen, B. S. (2000). The effects of stress on structural and functional plasticity in the hippocampus. In D. S. Charney, E. J. Nestler, & B. S. Bunney (Eds.), *Neurobiology of mental illness* (pp. 475–493). New York: Oxford University Press.

McGlashan, T. H. (1988). A selective review of recent North American long-term follow-up studies of schizophrenia. *Schizophrenia Bulletin, 14,* 515–542.

McGue, M., Bacon, S., & Lykken, D. T. (1993). Personality stability and change in early adulthood: A behavioral genetic analysis. *Developmental Psychology, 29,* 96–109.

McInnis, M. G., McMahon, F. J., Chase, G. A., Simpson, S. G., Ross, C. A., & DePaulo, J. R. (1993). Anticipation in bipolar affective disorder. *American Journal of Human Genetics, 53,* 385–390.

Meddis, R. (1977). *The sleep instinct.* London: Routledge & Kegan Paul.

Mednick, S. A., Gabrielli, W. F., & Hutchings, B. (1987). Genetic factors in the etiology of criminal behavior. In S. A. Mednick, T. E. Moffitt, & S. A. Stacks (Eds.), *The causes of crime: New biological approaches* (pp. 267–291). Cambridge, MA: Cambridge University Press.

Mednick, S. A., Huttunen, M. O., & Machon, R. A. (1994). Prenatal influenza infections and adult schizophrenia. *Schizophrenia Bulletin, 20*(2), 263–267.

Medvec, V. H., Madey, S. F., & Gilovich, T. (1995). When less is more: Counterfactual thinking and satisfaction among Olympic medalists. *Journal of Personality and Social Psychology, 69,* 603–610.

Mehler, J., Jusczyk, P. W., Lambertz, G., Halsted, N., Bertoncini, J., & Amiel-Tison, C. (1988). A precursor of language acquisition in young infants. *Cognition, 29,* 143–178.

Melzack, R., & Wall, P. D. (1982). *The Challenge of pain.* New York: Basic Books.

Merrit, J. (1979). None in a million: Results of mass screening for eidetic ability using object tests published in newspapers and magazines. *Behavioral and Brain Sciences, 2*, 612.

Metcalfe, J., & Mischel, W. (1999). A hot/cool-system analysis of delay of gratification: Dynamics of willpower. *Psychological Review, 106*, 3–19.

Milgram, S. (1974). *Obedience to authority: An experimental view.* New York: Harper & Row.

Miller, G. A., Galanter, E., & Pribram, K. H. (1960). *Plans and the structure of behavior.* New York: Holt.

Miller, I. W., Norman, W. H., & Keitner, G. I. (1989). Cognitive-behavioral treatment of depressed inpatients: Six- and twelve-month follow-up. *American Journal of Psychiatry, 146*(10), 1274–1279.

Miller, L. C., & Fishkin, S. A. (1997). On the dynamics of human bonding and reproductive success: Seeking windows on the adapted-for human-environmental interface. In J. Simpson & D. T. Kenrick (Eds.), *Evolutionary social psychology* (pp. 197–236). Mahwah, NJ: Lawrence Erlbaum.

Miller, M. B., & Wolford, G. L. (1999). Theoretical commentary: The role of criterion shift in false memory. *Psychological Review, 106*, 398–405.

Miller, R. S. (1996). *Embarrassment: Poise and peril in everyday life.* New York: Guilford Press.

Miller, R. S. (1997). We always hurt the ones we love: Aversive interactions in close relationships. In R. M. Kowalski (Ed.), *Aversive interpersonal behaviors* (pp. 11–29). New York: Plenum Press.

Miller, W. R., & C'de Baca, J. (2001). *Quantum changes: When epiphanies and sudden insights transform ordinary lives.* New York: Guilford Press.

Miller, W. T. (2000). Rediscovering fire: Small interventions, large effects. *Psychology of Addictive Behaviors, 14*, 6–18.

Mineka, S., Davidson, M., Cook, M., & Keir, R. (1984). Observational conditioning of snake fear in rhesus monkeys. *Journal of Abnormal Psychology, 93*, 355–372.

Mirsky, A. F., Bieliauskas, L. A., French, L. M., Van Kammen, D. P., Jonsson, E., & Sedvall, G. (2000). A 39-year followup of the Genain quadruplets. *Schizophrenia Bulletin, 26*(3), 699–708.

Mischel, W. (1984). Convergences and challenges in the search for consistency. *American Psychologist, 39*, 351–364.

Mischel, W., & Shoda, Y. (1995). A cognitive-affective system theory of personality: Reconceptualizing situations, dispositions, dynamics, and invariance in personality structure. *Psychological Review, 102*, 246–268.

Mischel, W., Shoda, Y., & Rodriguez, M. L. (1989). Delay of gratification in children. *Science, 244*, 933–938.

Mishkin, M. (1978). Memory in monkeys severely impaired by combined but not by separate removal of amygdala and hippocampus. *Nature, 273*, 297–298.

Mizerski, R. (1995). The relationship between cartoon trade character recognition and attitude toward product category in young children. *Journal of Marketing, 59*, 58–70.

Moffitt, T. E., Brammer, G. L., Caspi, A., Fawcett, J. P., Raleigh, M., Yuwiler, A., et al. (1998). Whole blood serotonin relates to violence in an epidemiological study. *Biological Psychiatry, 43*, 446–457.

Monsour, M. (1992). Meanings of intimacy in cross-sex and same-sex friendships. *Journal of Social and Personal Relationships, 9*, 277–295.

Montepare, J. M., & Vega, C. (1988). Women's vocal reactions to intimate and casual male friends. *Personality and Social Psychology Bulletin, 14*, 103–113.

Morris, K. A., & Swann, W. B., Jr. (1996). Denial and the AIDS crisis: On wishing away the threat of AIDS. In S. Oskamp & S. Thompson (Eds.), *Safer sex in the 90's: Understanding and preventing HIV risk behavior.* New York: Sage Publications.

Morris, N. M., Udry, J. R., Khan-Dawood, F., & Dawood, M. Y. (1987). Marital sex frequency and midcycle female testosterone. *Archives of Sexual Behavior, 16*, 27–37.

Morris, W. N. (1992). A functional analysis of the role of mood in affective systems. In M. S. Clark (Ed.), *Emotion: Review of personality and social psychology* (Vol. 13, pp. 256–293). Newbury Park, CA: Sage.

Morton, J., & Johnson, M. H. (1991). CONSPEC and CONLERN: A two-process theory of infant face recognition. *Psychological Review, 98*, 164–181.

Moscovitch, M. (1995). Confabulation. In D. L. Schacter (Ed.), *Memory distortions: How minds, brains, and societies reconstruct the past* (pp. 226–251). Cambridge, MA: Harvard University Press.

Muraven, M., & Baumeister, R. F. (2000). Self-regulation and depletion of limited resources: Does self-control resemble a muscle? *Psychological Bulletin, 126*, 247–259.

Murray, S. L., Holmes, J. G., & Griffin, D. W. (1996). The benefits of positive illusions: Idealization and the construction of satisfaction in close relationships. *Journal of Personality and Social Psychology, 70*, 79–98.

Needham, A., & Baillargeon, R. (1993). Intuitions about support in 4-5-month-old infants. *Cognition, 47*(2), 121–148.

Neidemeyer, E., & Naidu, S. B. (1997). Attention deficit hyperactivity disorder (ADHD) and frontal-motor cortex disconnection. *Clinical Electroencephalography, 28*(3), 130–135.

Neisser, U., & Harsch, N. (1993). Phantom flashbulbs: False recollections of hearing the news about Challenger. In E. Winograd & U. Neisser (Eds.), *Affect and accuracy in recall: Studies of "flashbulb" memories* (pp. 9–31). New York: Cambridge University Press.

Nelson, K. B., Grether, J. K., Croen, L. A., Dambrosia, J. M., Dickens, B. F., Jelliffe, L. L., et al. (2001). Neuropeptides and neurotrophins in neonatal blood of children with autism or mental retardation. *Annals of Neurology, 49*(5), 597–606.

Neuberg, S. L., Smith, D. M., & Asher, T. (2000). Why people stigmatize: Toward a biocultural framework. In T. F. Heatherton, R. E. Kleck, M. Hebl, & J. G. Hull (Eds.), *The social psychology of stigma* (pp. 31–61). New York: Guilford.

Newcomb, A. F., Bukowski, W. M., & Pattee, L. (1993). Children's peer relations: A meta-analytic review of popular, rejected, neglected, controversial, and average sociometric status. *Psychological Bulletin, 113*, 99–128.

Newport, E. L. (1990). Maturational constraints on language learning. *Cognitive Science, 14*, 11–28.

Neylan, T. C., Canick, J. D., Hall, S. E., Reus, V. I., Spolosky, R. M., & Wolkowitz, O. M. (2001). Cortisol levels predict cognitive impairment induced by electroconvulsive therapy. *Biological Psychiatry, 50*(5), 331–336.

NIH Technology Assessment Conference Panel. (1993). Methods for voluntary weight loss and control. *Annals of Internal Medicine, 199*, 764–770.

Nisbett, R. E., & Wilson, T. D. (1977). Telling more than we can know: Verbal reports on mental processes. *Psychological Review, 84*, 231–259.

Nolen-Hoeksema, S. (1998). *Abnormal psychology.* Boston: McGraw Hill.

Norem, J. K. (1989). Cognitive strategies as personality: Effectiveness, specificity, flexibility and change. In D. M. Buss & N. Cantor (Eds.),

Personality psychology: Recent trends and emerging issues (pp. 45–60). New York: Springer-Verlag.

North, A. C., Hargreaves, D. J., & O'Neill, S. A. (2000). The importance of music to adolescents. *British Journal of Educational Psychology, 70,* 255–272.

Novotny, S. L., Hollander, E., Allen, A., Aronowitz, B. R., DeCaria, C., Cartwright, C., et al. (2000). Behavioral response to oxytocin challenge in adult autistic disorders. *Biological Psychiatry, 47*(8), 523.

Nowlis, G. H., & Frank, M. E. (1981). Quality coding in gustatory systems of rats and hamsters. In D. M. Norris (Ed.), *Perception of behavioral chemicals* (pp. 58–80). Amsterdam: Elsevier.

Noyes, R. (1991). Suicide and panic disorder: A review. *Journal of Affective Disorders, 22,* 1–11.

Nurnberger, J. J., Goldin, L. R., & Gershon, E. S. (1994). Genetics of psychiatric disorders. In G. Winokur & P. M. Clayton (Eds.), *The medical basis of psychiatry* (pp. 459–492). Philadelphia: W. B. Saunders.

Ochsner, K. N. (2000). Are affective events richly recollected or simply familiar? The experience and process of recognizing feelings past. *Journal of Experimental Psychology: General, 129,* 242–261.

Olds, J. (1962). Hypothalamic substrates of reward. *Psychological Review, 42,* 554–604.

Olds, J., & Milner, P. (1954). Positive reinforcement produced by electrical stimulation of the septal area and other regions of the rat brain. *Journal of Comparative and Physiological Psychology, 47,* 419–428.

O'Leary, S. G. (1995). Parental discipline mistakes. *Current Directions in Psychological Science, 4,* 11–13.

Olincy, A., Young, D. A., & Freedman, R. (1997). Increased levels of the nicotine metabolite cotinine in schizophrenic smokers compared to other smokers. *Biological Psychiatry, 42*(1), 1–5.

Oliner, S. P., & Oliner, P. M. (1988). *The altruistic personality: Rescuers of Jews in Nazi Europe.* London: Free Press.

Oltmans, T. F., Neale, J. M., Davison, G. C. (Eds.). (1999). *Case studies in abnormal psychology.* New York: John Wiley & Sons, Inc.

O'Meara, J. D. (1989). Cross-sex friendship: Four basic challenges of an ignored relationship. *Sex Roles, 21,* 525–543.

O'Neal, J. M. (1984). First person account: Finding myself and loving it. *Schizophrenia Bulletin, 10,* 109–110.

Osterling, J., & Dawson, G. (1994). Early recognition of children with autism: A study of first birthday home videotapes. *Journal of Autism and Developmental Disorders, 24,* 247–257.

Ottieger, A. E., Tressell, P. A., Inciardi, J. A., & Rosales, T. A. (1992). Cocaine use patterns and overdose. *Journal of Psychoactive Drugs, 24,* 399–410.

Panksepp, J. (1992). Oxytocin effects on emotional processes: Separation distress, social bonding, and relationships to psychiatric disorders. *Annals of the New York Academy of Sciences, 652,* 243–252.

Papadimitrious, G. N., Zervas, I. M., & Papakostas, Y. G. (2001). Unilateral ECT for prophylaxis in affective illness. *Journal of ECT, 17*(3), 229–231.

Pascual-Leone, A. Catala, M. D., & Pascual-Leone, P. A. (1996). Lateralized effect of rapid-rate transcranial magnetic stimulation of the prefrontal cortex on mood. *Neurology, 46*(2), 499–502.

Patterson, C. M., & Newman, J. P. (1993). Reflectivity and learning from aversive events: Toward a psychological mechanism for the syndromes of disinhibition. *Psychological Review, 100,* 716–736.

Paulhus, D. L., Trapnell, P. D., & Chen, D. (1999). Birth order effects on personality and achievement within families. *Psychological Science, 10,* 482–488.

Paunonen, S. V., Ewan, K., Earthy, J., Lefave, S., & Goldberg, H. (1999). Facial features as personality cues. *Journal of Personality, 67,* 555–583.

Payne, B. K. (2001). Prejudice and perception: The role of automatic and controlled processes in misperceiving a weapon. *Journal of Personality and Social Psychology, 81,* 181–192.

Pelham, W., & Bender, M. E. (1982). Peer relationships in hyperactive children: Description and treatment. In K. D. Gadow & I. Bailer (Eds.), *Advances in learning and behavioral disabilities: A research annual.* Greenwich, CT: JAI Press.

Pelham, W. E., Jr. (1993). Pharmacotherapy for children with attention-deficit hyperactivity disorder. *School Psychology Review, 22,* 199–227.

Pelham, W. E., McBurnett, K., Harper, G. W., Milich, R., Murphy, D. A., Clinton, J., et al. (1990). Methylphenidate and baseball playing in ADHD children: Who's on first? *Journal of Consulting and Clinical Psychology, 58*(1), 130–133.

Pennebaker, J. W. (1990). *Opening up: the healing power of confiding in others.* New York: William Morrow & Co., Inc.

Pennebaker, J. W. (1995). *Emotion, Disclosure, & Health.* Washington, DC: American Psychological Association.

Peretz, I. (1996). Can we lose memory for music? A case of music agnosia in a nonmusician. *Journal of Cognitive Neuroscience, 8,* 481–496.

Perrett, D. I., May, K. A., & Yoshikawa, S. (1994). Facial shape and judgments of female attractiveness. *Nature, 368,* 239–242.

Perrett, D. I., Mistlin, A. J., & Chitty, A. J. (1987). Visual neurons responsive to faces. *Trends in Neurosciences, 10,* 358–364.

Petersen, A. C., Compas, B. E., Brooks-Gunn, J., Stemmler, M., Ey, S., & Grant, K. E. (1993). Depression in adolescence. *American Psychologist, 48,* 155–168.

Petitto, J. A., & Marentette, P. (1991). Babbling in the manual mode: Evidence for the ontogeny of language. *Science, 251,* 1483–1496.

Petitto, L. A. (1988). "Language" in the pre-linguistic child. In F. Kessel (Ed.), *Development of Language and Language Researchers: Essays in Honor of Roger Brown* (pp. 187–221). Hillsdale, NJ: Lawrence Erlbaum Associates.

Petitto, L. A. (2000). On the biological foundations of human language. In H. Lane & K. Emmorey (Eds.), *The signs of language revisited* (pp. 447–471). Mahwah, NJ: Lawrence Erlbaum Associates.

Petitto, L. A., Holowka, S., Sergio, L., & Ostry, D. (2001). Language rhythms in babies' hand movements. *Nature, 413,* 35–36.

Petitto, L. A., & Seidenberg, M. S. (1979). On the evidence for linguistic abilities in signing apes. *Brain and Language, 8,* 72–88.

Petronis, A., & Kennedy, J. L. (1995). Unstable genes—Unstable mind? *American Journal of Psychiatry, 152,* 164–172.

Petty, R. E., & Cacioppo, J. T. (1986). *Communication and persuasion: Central and peripheral routes to attitude change.* New York: Springer-Verlag.

Pezdek, K., & Hodge, D. (1999). Planting false childhood memories in children: The role of event plausibility. *Child Development, 70,* 887–895.

Phelps, E., & Gazzaniga, M. S. (1992). Hemispheric differences in mnemonic processing: The effects of left hemisphere interpretation. *Neuropsychologia, 30,* 293–297.

Phelps, E. A., O'Connor, K. J., Cunningham, W. A., Funayama, E. S., Gatenby, J. C., Gore, J. C., et al. (2000). Performance on indirect measures of race evaluation predicts amygdala activation. *Journal of Cognitive Neuroscience, 12,* 729–738.

Phillips, M. L., Young, A. W., Senior, C., Brammer, M., Andrew, C., Calder, A. J., et al. (1997). A specific neural substrate for perceiving facial expressions of disgust. *Nature, 398,* 495–498.

Phinney, J. S. (1990). Ethnic identity in adolescents and adults: *Review of research*. *Psychological Bulletin, 108*, 499–514.

Piggott, S., & Milner, B. (1993). Memory for different aspects of complex visual scenes after unilateral temporal- or frontal-lobe resection. *Neuropsychologia, 31*, 1–15.

Pincus, J. H. (1999). Aggression, criminality, and the frontal lobes. In B. L. Miller & J. L. Cummings (Eds.), *The human frontal lobes* (pp. 547–556). New York: Guilford Press.

Pinker, S. (1984). *Language learnability and language development*. Cambridge, MA: Harvard University Press.

Pinker, S. (1994). *The language instinct*. New York: William Morrow and Company.

Pinker, S. (1997). *How the mind works*. New York: W. W. Norton.

Pinker, S., & Bloom, P. (1990). Natural language and natural selection. *Behavioral and Brain Sciences, 13*, 707–784.

Plakun, E. M., Burkhardt, P. E., & Muller, A. P. (1985). Fourteen-year follow-up of borderline and schizotypal personality disorders. *Comprehensive Psychiatry, 26*, 448–455.

Plant, E. A., Hyde, J. S., Keltner, D., & Devine, P. G. (2000). The gender stereotyping of emotions. *Psychology of Women Quarterly, 24*, 81–92.

Plomin, R., & Caspi, A. (1999). Behavioral genetics and personaliity. In L. A. Pervin & O. P. John (Eds.), *Handbook of personality: Theory and research* (2nd ed., pp. 251–276). New York: Guilford Press.

Polivy, J., & Herman, C. P. (1985). Dieting and bingeing: A causal analysis. *American Psychologist, 40*, 193–201.

Posner, M. I., & DiGirolamo, G. J. (2000). Cognitive neuroscience: Origins and promise. *Psychological Bulletin, 126*, 873–889.

Povinelli, D. J., Gallup, G. G., Jr., Eddy, T. J., Bierschwale, D. T., Engstrom, M. C., Perilloux, H. K., et al. (1997). Chimpanzees recognize themselves in mirrors. *Animal Behaviour, 53*, 1083–1088.

Premack, D., & Premack, A. J. (1983). *The mind of an ape*. New York: W. W. Norton.

Pylyshyn, Z. (1984). *Computation and cognition*. Cambridge, MA: MIT Press.

Raesaenen, S., Pakaslahti, A., Syvaelahti, E., Jones, P. B., & Isohanni, M. (2000). Sex differences in schizophrenia: A review. *Nordic Journal of Psychiatry, 54*(1), 37–45.

Raine, A. (1989). Evoked potentials and psychopathy. *International Journal of Psychopathology, 8*(1), 1–16.

Rakic, P. (2000). Molecular and cellular mechanisms of neuronal migration: Relevance to cortical epilepsies. *Advances in Neurology, 84*, 1–14.

Raleigh, M. J., McGuire, M. T., Brammer, G. L., Pollack, D. B., & Yuwiler, A. (1991). Serotonergic mechanisms promote dominance in adult male vervet monkeys. *Brain Research, 559*, 181–190.

Rampon, C., Jiang, C. H., Dong, H., Tang, Y., Lockhart, D. J., Schultz, P. G., et al. (2000). Effects of environmental enrichment on gene expression in the brain. *Proceedings of the National Academy of Sciences, 97*, 12880–12884.

Rapee, R. M., Brown, T. A., Antony, M. M., & Barlow, D. H. (1992). Response to hyperventilation and inhalation of 5.5% carbon dioxide-enriched air across the DSM III-R anxiety disorders. *Journal of Abnormal Psychology, 101*, 538–552.

Rapoport, J. (1990). *The boy who couldn't stop washing: The experience and treatment of obsessive-compulsive disorder*. New York: Penguin Books.

Rapoport, J. L. (1989). The biology of obsessions and compulsions. *Scientific American, 260*(3), 83–89.

Rapoport, J. L. (1991). Recent advances in obsessive-compulsive disorder. *Neuropsychopharmacology, 5*, 1–10.

Rauch, S. L., van der Kolk, B. A., Fisler, R. E., & Alpert, N. M. (1996). A symptom provocation study of posttraumatic stress disorder using positron emission tomography and script-driven imagery. *Archives of General Psychiatry, 53*, 380–387.

Regard, M., & Landis, T. (1997). "Gourmand syndrome": Eating passion associated with right anterior lesions. *Neurology, 48*, 1185–1190.

Reichelt, K. L., Knivsberg, A. M., Lind, G., & Nodland, M. (1991). Probable etiology and possible treatment of childhood autism. *Brain Dysfunction, 4*(6), 308–319.

Reis, H. T., Collins, W. A., & Berscheid, E. (2000). The relationship context of human behavior and development. *Psychological Bulletin, 126*, 844–872.

Rescorla, R. (1966). Predictability and number of pairings in Pavlovian fear conditioning. *Psychonomic Science, 4*, 383–384.

Rescorla, R. A. (1988). Behavioral studies of Pavlovian conditioning. *Annual Review of Neuroscience, 11*, 329–352.

Rescorla, R. A., & Wagner, A. R. (1972). A theory of Pavlovian conditioning: Variations in the effectiveness of reinforcement and nonreinforcement. In A. H. Black & W. F. Prokosy (Eds.), *Classical conditioning II: Current research and theory* (pp. 64–99). New York: Appleton-Century-Crofts.

Revonsuo, A. (2000). The reinterpretation of dreams: An evolutionary hypothesis of the function of dreaming. *Behavioral and Brain Sciences, 23*, 6.

Reynolds, D. V. (1969). Surgery in the rat during electrical analgesia induced by focal brain stimulation. *Science, 164*, 444–445.

Rizzolatti, G., Fadiga, L., Gallese, V., & Fogassi, L. (1996). Premotor cortex and the recognition of motor actions. *Cognitive Brain Research, 3*, 131–141.

Roberts, B. W., & Friend-DelVecchio, W. (2000). The rank-order consistency of personality traits from childhood to old age: A quantitative review of longitudinal studies. *Psychological Bulletin, 126*, 3–25.

Roberts, D. F. (2000). Media and youth: Access, exposure, and privatization. *Journal of Adolescent Health 27*(Suppl.), 8–14.

Robins, L. N., Helzer, J. E., & Davis, D. H. (1975). Narcotic use in Southeast Asia and afterward: An interview study of 898 Vietnam returnees. *Archives of General Psychiatry, 32*, 955–961.

Robins, L. N., & Regier, D. A. (1991). *Psychiatric disorders in America: The epidemiological catchment areas study*. New York: The Free Press.

Rodgers, J. L., Cleveland, H. H., van den Oord, E., & Rowe, D. C. (2000). Resolving the debate over birth order, family size, and intelligence. *American Psychologist, 55*, 599–612.

Roediger, H. L., & McDermott, K. B. (1995). Creating false memories: Remembering words not presented in lists. *Journal of Experimental Psychology: Learning, Memory, and Cognition, 21*, 803–814.

Rogers, T. B., Kuiper, N. A., & Kirker, W. S. (1977). Self-reference and the encoding of personal information. *Journal of Personality and Social Psychology, 35*, 677–688.

Rolls, E. T., Burton, M. J., & Mora, F. (1980). Neurophysiological analysis of brain-stimulation reward in the monkey. *Brain Research, 194*, 339–357.

Rolls, E. T., Murzi, E., Yaxley, S., Thorpe, S. J., & Simpson, S. J. (1986). Sensory-specific satiety: Food-specific reduction in responsiveness of ventral forebrain neurons after feeding in the monkey. *Brain Research, 368*, 79–86.

Rosenberg, S. (1965). *Society and the adolescent self-image*. Princeton, NJ: University Press.

Rosenbluth, M., & Silver, D. (1992). The inpatient treatment of borderline personality disorder. In D. Silver & M. Rosenbluth, *Handbook of borderline disorders*. Madison, CT: International Universities Press.

Rosenfeld, J. P. (2001). Event-related potentials in detection of deception. In M. Kleiner (Ed.), *Handbook of Polygraph* (pp. 265–286). New York: Academic Press.

Rosenhan, D. (1973). On being sane in insane places. *Science, 179*, 250–258.

Rosenthal, D., (Ed). (1963). *The Genain quadruplets*. New York: Basic Books.

Rosenthal, N. E., Sack, D. A., Gillin, J. C., Lewy, A. J., Goodwin, F. K., Davenport, Y., et al. (1984). Seasonal affective disorder: A description of the syndrome and preliminary findings with light therapy. *Archives of General Psychiatry, 41*, 72–80.

Rosenzweig, M. R., Bennett, E. L., & Diamond, M. C. (1972). Brain changes in response to experience. *Scientific American, 226*, 22–29.

Ross, D. M., & Ross, S. A. (1982). *Hyperactivity: Research, theory, and action*. New York: Wiley.

Ross, J. J. (1965). Neurological findings after prolonged sleep deprivation. *Archives of Neurology, 12*, 399–403.

Rothbart, M. K., Ahadi, S. A., & Evans, D. E. (2000). Temperament and personality: Origins and outcomes. *Journal of Personality and Social Psychology, 78*, 122–135.

Rothbaum, B. O., Hodges, L., Alarcon, R., Ready, D., Shahar, F., Graap, K., et al. (1999). Virtual reality exposure therapy for PTSD Vietnam veterans: A case study. *Journal of Traumatic Stress, 12*, 263–271.

Rovee-Collier, C. (1999). The development of infant memory. *Current Directions in Psychological Science, 8*(3), 80–85.

Rozin, P., & Kalat, J. W. (1971). Specific hungers and poison avoidance as adaptive specializations of learning. *Psychological Review, 78*, 459–486.

Rubenstein, A. J., Kalakanis, L., Langlois, J. H. (1999). Infant preferences for attractive faces: A cognitive explanation. *Developmental Psychology, 35*, 848–855.

Rubin, L. (1985). *Just friends*. New York: Harper & Row.

Rumelhart, D., & McClelland, J., and the PDP Research Group. (1986). *Parallel distributed processing: Explorations in the microstructure of cognition*. Cambridge, MA: MIT Press.

Rusbult, C. E., & Van Lange, P. A. M. (1996). Interdependence processes. In E. T. Higgins & A. Kruglanski (Eds.), *Social psychology: Handbook of basic principles* (pp. 564–596). New York: Guilford Press.

Rusbult, C. E., Van Lange, P. A. M., Wildschut, T., Yovetich, N. A., & Verette, J. (2000). Perceived superiority in close relationships: Why it exists and persists. *Journal of Personality and Social Psychology, 79*,:521–545.

Russell, J. A. (1980). A circumplex model of affect. *Journal of Personality and Social Psychology, 39*, 1161–1178.

Russell, J. A. (1994). Is there universal recognition of emotion from facial expressions? A review of the cross-cultural studies. *Psychological Bulletin, 115*, 102–141.

Russell, J. A., & L. Feldman Barrett. (1999). Core affect, prototypical emotional episodes, and other things called emotion: Dissecting the elephant. *Journal of Personality and Social Psychology, 76*, 805–819.

Rymer, R. (1993). *Genie: A scientific tragedy*. New York: Harper-Collins.

Sachs, J. (1967). Recognition memory for syntactic and semantic aspects of connected discourse. *Perception and Psychophysics, 2*, 437–442.

Sacks, O. (1985). *The man who mistook his wife for a hat*. New York: Harper & Row.

Sacks, O. (1995). *An anthropologist on Mars: Seven paradoxical tales*. New York: Knopf.

Salmon, C. A. (1999). On the impact of sex and birth order on contact with kin. *Human Nature, 10*, 183–197.

Salmon, C. A., & Daly, M. (1998). Birth order and familial sentiment: Middleborns are different. *Evolution and Human Behavior, 19*, 299–312.

Salthouse, T. (1992). The information-processing perspective on cognitive aging. In R. Sternberg & C. Berg (Eds.), *Intellectual development*. Cambridge, MA: Cambridge University Press.

Sanderson, W. C., & Barlow, D. H. (1990). A description of patients diagnosed with DSM-III-R generalized anxiety disorder. *The Journal of Nervous and Mental Disease, 178*, 588–591.

Sapolsky, R. M. (1994). *Why zebras don't get ulcers*. New York: Freeman.

Sayette, M. A. (1993). An appraisal-disruption model of alcohol's effects on stress responses in social drinkers. *Psychological Bulletin, 114*, 459–476.

Scarr, S., & McCarthy, K. (1983). How people make their own environments: A theory of genotype l environment effects. *Child Development, 54*, 424–435.

Schachter, S. (1959). *The psychology of affiliation*. Stanford, CA: Stanford University Press.

Schachter, S., & Singer, J. (1962). Cognitive, social, and physiological determinants of emotional state. *Psychological Review, 69*, 379–399.

Schacter, D. L. (1996). *Searching for memory: The brain, the mind, and the past*. New York: Basic Books.

Schacter, D. L. (1999). The seven sins of memory: Insights from psychology and cognitive neuroscience. *American Psychologist, 54*, 182–203.

Schacter, D. L., & Buckner, R. L. (1998). On the relations among priming, conscious recollection, and intentional retrieval: Evidence from neuroimaging research. *Neurobiology of Learning and Memory, 70*, 284–303.

Schacter, D. L., Kagan, J. L., & Leichtman, M. D. (1995). True and false memories in children and adults: A cognitive neuroscience perspective. *Psychology, Public Policy and Law, 1*(2), 411–428.

Schaie, K. W. (1990). Intellectual development in adulthood. In J. E. Birren & K. W. Schaie (Eds.), *Handbook of the psychology of aging* (3rd ed.). New York: Van Nostrand Reinhold.

Scheerer, M. (1963). Problem-solving. *Scientific American, 208*, 118–128.

Schmajuk, N. A., Lamoureux, J. A., & Holland, P. C. (1998). Occasion setting: A neural network approach. *Psychological Review, 105*, 3–32.

Schwartz, J. M., Stoessel, P. W., Baxter, L. R., Martin, K. M., & Phelps, M. E. (1996). Systematic changes in cerebral glucose metabolic rate after successful behavior modification treatment of obsessive-compulsive disorder. *Archives of General Psychiatry, 53*, 109–113.

Schwarz, N., & Clore, G. L. (1983). Mood, misattribution, and judgments of well-being: Informative and directive functions of affective states. *Journal of Personality and Social Psychology, 45*, 513–523.

Sclafani, A., & Springer, D. (1976). Dietary obesity in adult rats: Similarities to hypothalamic and human obesity syndromes. *Physiology and Behavior, 17*, 461–471.

Sedikides, C., & Skowronski, J. J. (1997). The symbolic self in evolutionary context. *Personality and Social Psychology Review, 1*, 80–102.

Seidman, L. J., Breiter, H. C., Goodman, J. M., Goldstein, J. M., Woodruff, P. W., O'Craven, K. et al. (1998). A functional magnetic resonance imaging study of auditory vigilance with low and high information processing demands. *Neuropsychology, 12*(4), 505–518.

Seligman, M. (1970). On the generality of the laws of learning. *Psychological Review, 77*, 406–418.

Seligman, M. E. P. (1974). Depression and learned helplessness. In R. J. Friedman & M. M. Katz (Eds.), *The psychology of depression: Contemporary theory and research*. Washington, DC: V. H. Winston.

Seligman, M. E. P. (1975). *Helplessness: On depression, development, and death*. San Francisco: W. H. Freeman.

Seligman, M. E. P., & Csikszentmihalyi, M. (2000). Positive psychology: An introduction. *American Psychologist, 55*, 5–14.

Seligman, M. E. P., Walker, E. F., & Rosenhan, D. L. (2001). *Abnormal psychology*. New York: W. W. Norton.

Shapiro, E., Shapiro, A. K., Fulop, G., Hubbard, M., Mandell, J., Nordlie, J., et al. (1989). Controlled study of haloperidol, pimozide, and placebo for the treatment of Gilles de la Tourette's syndrome. *Archives of General Psychiatry, 46*, 722–730.

Shedler, J., & Block, J. (1990). Adolescent drug use and psychological health: A longitudinal inquiry. *American Psychologist, 45*, 612–630.

Sheffield, F. D., & Roby, T. B. (1950). Reward value of a non-nutritive sweet taste. *Journal of Comparative and Physiological Psychology, 43*, 471–481.

Sherman, D. K., McGue, M. K., & Iacono, W. G. (1997). Twin concordance for attention deficit hyperactivity disorder: A comparison of teacher's and mother's reports. *American Journal of Psychiatry, 154*(4), 532–535.

Sherwin, B. B. (1988). A comparative analysis of the role of androgen in human male and female sexual behavior: Behavioral specificity, critical thresholds, and sensitivity. *Psychobiology, 16*, 416–425.

Sherwin, B. B. (1994). Sex hormones and psychological functioning in postmenopausal women. *Experimental Gerontology, 29*, 423–430.

Shettleworth, S. J. (2001). Animal cognition and animal behaviour. *Animal Behaviour, 61*, 277–286.

Shih, M., Pittinsky, T. L., & Ambady, N. (1999). Stereotype susceptibility: Identity salience and shifts in quantitative performance. *Psychological Science, 10*, 80–83.

Siegel, C., Waldo, M., Mizner, G., Adler, L. E., & Freedman, R. (1984). Deficits in sensory gating in schizophrenic patients and their relatives. *Archives of General Psychiatry, 41*, 607–612,

Siegel, J. M. (1990). Stressful life events and use of physician services among the elderly: The moderating role of pet ownership. *Journal of Personality and Social Psychology, 58*, 1081–1086.

Siegel, S. (1984). Pavlovian conditioning and heroin overdose: Reports by overdose victims. *Bulletin of the Psychonomic Society, 22*, 428–430.

Siegel, S., Hinson, R. E., Krank, M. D., & McCully, J. (1982). Heroin "overdose" death: Contribution of drug-associated environmental cues. *Science, 216*, 436–437.

Silva, P. A., & Stanton, W. (1996). *From child to adult: The Dunedin study*. Oxford, UK: Oxford University Press.

Silver, R. L., Cirincione, C., & Steadman, H. J. (1994). Demythologizing inaccurate perceptions of the insanity defense. *Law and Human Behavior, 18*, 63–70.

Simons, D. J., & Levin, D. T. (1998). Failure to detect changes to people during a real-world interaction. *Psychonomic Bulletin and Review, 5*, 644–649.

Sims, H. E. A., Goldman, R. F., Gluck, C. M., Horton, E., Kelleher, P., & Rowe, D. (1968). Experimental obesity in man. *Transactions of the Association of American Physicians, 81*, 153–170.

Sinclair, L., & Kunda, Z. (1999). Reactions to a Black professional: Motivated inhibition and activation of conflicting stereotypes. *Journal of Personality and Social Psychology, 77*, 885–904.

Singer, A. G. (1991). A chemistry of mammalian pheromones. *Journal of Steroid Biochemistry and Molecular Biology, 39*, 627–632.

Singer, H. S., Hahn, I. H., & Moran, T. H. (1991). Abnormal dopamine uptake sites in post-mortem striatum from patients with Tourette's syndrome. *Annals of Neurology, 30*, 558–562.

Sloane, R. B., Staples, F. R., Whipple, K., & Cristol, A. H. (1977). Patients' attitudes toward behavior therapy and psychotherapy. *American Journal of Psychiatry, 134*(2), 134–137.

Slovic, P., Finucane, M., Peters, E., & MacGregor, D. (In press). The affect heuristic. In T. Gilovich, D. Griffin, & D. Kahneman (Eds.), *Intuitive judgment: Heuristics and biases*. Cambridge, U.K.: Cambridge University Press.

Smith, C., & Lapp, L. (1991). Increases in number of REMs and REM density in humans following an intensive learning period. *Sleep, 14*, 325–330.

Smith, C. A., & Ellsworth, P. C. (1985). Patterns of cognitive appraisal in emotion. *Journal of Personality and Social Psychology, 48*, 813–838.

Smith, S. M., Glenberg, A. M., & Bjork, R. A. (1978). Environmental context and human memory. *Memory and Cognition, 6*, 342–353.

Snyder, M. (1987). *Public appearances, private realities: The psychology of self-monitoring*. New York: Freeman.

Snyder, M., & Cantor, N. (1998). Understanding personality and personal behavior: A functionalist strategy. In D. T. Gilbert, S. T. Fiske, & G. Lindzey (Eds.), *Handbook of social psychology* (pp. 635–679). New York: McGraw-Hill.

Solms, M. (2000). Dreaming and REM sleep are controlled by different brain mechanisms. *Behavioral and Brain Sciences, 23*(6), 793.

Sorensen, T., Holst, C., Stunkard, A. J., & Skovgaard, L. T. (1992). Correlations of body mass index of adult adoptees and their biological and adoptive relatives. *International Journal of Obesity and Related Metabolic Disorders, 16*, 227–236.

Sowell, E. R., Delis, D., Stiles, J., & Jernigan, T. L. (2001). Improved memory functioning and frontal lobe maturation between childhood and adolescence: A structural MRI study. *Journal of the International Neuropsychological Society, 7*, 312–322.

Sowell, E. R., Trauner, D. A., Gamst, A., & Jernigan, T. L. (2002). Development of cortical and subcortical brain structures in childhood and adolescence: A structural MRI study. *Developmental Medicine and Child Neurology, 44*, 4–16.

Spangler, W. D., & House, R. J. (1991). Presidential effectiveness and the leadership motive profile. *Journal of Personality and Social Psychology, 60*, 439–455.

Spear, L. P. (2000). Neurobehavioral changes in adolescence. *Current Directions in Psychological Science, 9*, 111–114.

Spelke, E. S., Vishton, P., & Von hofsten, C. (1995). Object perception, object-directed action, and physical knowledge in infancy. In M. S. Gazzaniga (Ed.), *The cognitive neurosciences* (pp. 1612–1680). Cambridge, MA: MIT Press.

Spence, S. A., & Frith, C. D. (1999). Towards a functional anatomy of volition. *Journal of Consciousness Studies, 6*, 11–29.

Spencer, M. B., & Markstrom-Adams, C. (1990). Identity processes among racial and ethnic minority children in America. *Child Development, 56*, 564–572.

Spencer, S. J., Steele, C. M., & Quinn, D. M. (1999). Stereotype threat and women's math performance. *Journal of Experimental Social Psychology, 35*, 4–28.

Sperling, G. (1960). The information available in brief visual presentations. *Psychological Monographs, 74*, 1–29.

Spitzer, R. L., Skodol, A. E., Gibbon, M., & Williams, J. B. W. (1983). *Psychopathology, a case book*. New York: McGraw-Hill.

Steele, C. M. (1988). The psychology of self-affirmation: Sustaining the integrity of the self. In L. Berkowitz (Ed.), *Advances in experimental social psychology* (Vol. 21, pp. 261–302). New York: Academic Press.

Steele, C. M. (1997). A threat in the air: How stereotypes shape intellectual identity and performance. *American Psychologist, 52*, 613–629.

Steele, C. M., & Aronson, J. (1995). Stereotype threat and the intellectual test performance of African Americans. *Journal of Personality and Social Psychology, 69*, 797–811.

Steffenburg, S., Gillberg, C., Helgren, L., Anderson, L., Gillberg, L., Jakobsson, G., et al. (1989). A twin study of autism in Denmark, Finland, Iceland, Norway, and Sweden. *Journal of Child Psychological Psychiatry, 30*, 405–416.

Stein, J., & Richardson, A. (1999). Cognitive disorders: A question of misattribution. *Current Biology, 9*(10), R374-R376.

Steiner, J. E. (1977). Facial expressions of the neonate infant indicating the hedonics of food-related chemical stimuli. In J. M. Weiffenbach (Ed.), *Taste and development* (pp. 173–189). Bethesda, MD: U.S. Department of Health, Education, and Welfare.

Stellar, J. R., Kelley, A. E., & Corbett, D. (1983). Effects of peripheral and central dopamine blockade on lateral hypothalamic self-stimulation: Evidence for both reward and motor deficits. *Pharmacology, Biochemistry, and Behavior, 18*, 433–442.

Stellar, J. R., & Stellar, E. (1984). *The neurobiology of motivation and reward*. New York: Springer-Verlag.

Steriade, M. (1992). Basic mechanisms of sleep generation. *Neurology, 42*(Suppl.), 9–18.

Sternberg, E. M. (2000). *The balance within*. New York: Freeman.

Sternberg, R. J. (1986). A triangular theory of love. *Psychological Review, 93*, 119–135.

Stickgold, R., Whidbee, D., Schirmer, B., Patel, V., & Hobson, J. A. (2000). Visual discrimination task improvement: A multi-step process occurring during sleep. *Journal of Cognitive Neuroscience, 12*, 246–254.

Stoleru, S., Gregoire, M. C., Gerard, D., Decety, J., Lafarge, E., Cinotti, L., et al. (1999). Neuroanatomical correlates of visually evoked sexual arousal in human males. *Archives of Sexual Behavior, 28*, 1–21.

Stone, A. A., Neale, J. M., Cox, D. S., & Napoli, A. (1994). Daily events are associated with a secretory immune response to an oral antigen in men. *Health Psychology, 13*, 440–446.

Stone, M. H., Stone, D. K., & Hurt, S. W. (1987). The natural history of borderline patients treated by intensive hospitalization. *Psychiatric Clinics of North America, 10*, 185–206.

Stone, V. E., Baron-Cohen, S., & Knight, R. T. (1998). Frontal lobe contributions to theory of mind. *Journal of Cognitive Neuroscience, 10*, 640–656.

Strentz, T., & Auerbach, S. M. (1988). Adjustment to the stress of simulated captivity: Effects of emotion-focused versus problem-focused preparation on hostages differing in locus of control. *Journal of Personality and Social Psychology, 55*, 652–660.

Stromswold, K. (2000). The cognitive neuroscience of language acquisition. In M. S. Gazzaniga (Ed.), *The cognitive neurosciences* (2nd ed.). Cambridge, MA: M.I.T. Press.

Stunkard, A. J. (1996). Current views on obesity. *American Journal of Medicine, 100*, 230–236.

Stuss, D. T. (1991). Self, awareness, and the frontal lobes: A neuropsychological perspective. In J. Strauss & G. R. Goethals (Eds.), *The self: Interdisciplinary approaches* (pp. 255–278). New York: Springer-Verlag.

Stuss, D. T., Gow, C. A., & Hetherington, C. R. (1992). "No longer Gage": Frontal lobe dysfunction and emotional changes. *Journal of Consulting and Clinical Psychology, 60*, 349–359.

Sulin, R. A., & Dooling, D. J. (1974). Intrusion of a thematic idea in retention of prose. *Journal of Experimental Psychology, 103*, 255–262.

Sulloway, F. J. (1996). *Born to rebel*. New York: Vintage.

Suomi, S. J., & Harlow, H. F. (1972). Social rehabilitation of isolate-reared monkeys. *Developmental Psychology, 6*, 487–496.

Susser, E., Neugebauer, R., Hoek, H. W., Brown, A. S., Lin, S., Labovitz, D., et al. (1996). Schizophrenia after prenatal famine: Further evidence. *Archives of General Psychiatry, 53*(1), 25–31.

Svenson, O. (1981). Are we all less risky and more skillful than our fellow drivers? *Acta Psychologica, 47*, 143–148.

Swenson, C. R., Sanderson, C., Dulie, R. A., & Linehan, M. M. (2001). The application of dialectical behavior therapy for patients with borderline personality disorder on inpatient units [special issue]. *Psychiatric Quarterly, 72*(4), 307–324.

Sylva, K., Bruner, J. S., & Genova, P. (1976). The role of play in the problem-solving of children 3–5 years old. In J. S. Bruner, A. Jolly, & K. Sylva (Eds.), *Play: Its role in development and evolution* (pp. 244–257). New York: Penguin.

Szatzmari, P., Jones, M. B., Tuff, L., Bartolucci, G., Fisman, S., & Mahoney, W. (1993). Lack of cognitive impairment in first-degree relatives of children with pervasive developmental disorders. *Journal of the American Academy of Child and Adolescent Psychiatry, 32*, 1264–1273.

Tajfel, H., & Turner, J. C. (1979). An integrative theory of intergroup conflict. In W. G. Austin & S. Worchel (Eds.), *The social psychology of intergroup relations* (pp. 33–47). Monterey, CA: Brooks/Cole.

Talley, P. R., Strupp, H. H., & Morey, L. C. (1990). Matchmaking in psychotherapy: Patient-therapist dimensions and their impact on outcome. *Journal of Consulting & Clinical Psychology, 58*, 182–188.

Tangney, J. P. (1998). How does guilt differ from shame? In J. Bybee (Ed.), *Guilt and children* (pp. 1–16). San Diego, CA: Academic Press.

Tateyama, M., Asai, M., Kamisada, M., Hashimoto, M., Bartels, M., & Heimann, H. (1993). Comparison of schizophrenic delusions between Japan and Germany. *Psychopathology, 26*(3–4), 151–158.

Taylor, S. E., & Brown, J. D. (1988). Illusion and well-being: A social psychological perspective on mental health. *Psychological Bulletin, 103*, 193–210.

Taylor, S. E., Klein, L. C., Lewis, B. P., Gruenewald, T. L., Gurung, R. A., & Updegraff, J. A. (2000). Biobehavioral responses to stress in females: Tend-and-befriend, not fight-or-flight. *Psychological Review, 107*, 411–429.

Teller, D. Y., Morse, R., Borton, R., & Regal, C. (1974). Visual acuity for vertical and diagonal gratings in human infants. *Vision Research, 14*, 1433–1439.

Terrace, H. (1979). *Nim*. New York: Knopf.

Tesser, A. (1988). Toward a self-evaluation maintenance model of social behavior. *Advances in Experimental Social Psychology, 21*, 181–227.

Tesser, A. (1993). The importance of heritability in psychological research: The case of attitudes. *Psychological Review, 100*, 129–142.

Thompson, P. (1980). Margaret Thatcher: A new illusion. *Perception, 9*, 483–484.

Tice, D. M., Butler, J. L., Muraven, M. B., Stillwell, A. M. (1995). When modesty prevails: Differential favorability of self-presentation to friends and strangers. *Journal of Personality and Social Psychology, 69*, 1120–1138.

Tienari, P., Lahti, I., Sorri, A., Naarala, M., Moring, J., Kaleva, M., et al. (1990). Adopted-away offspring of schizophrenics and controls: The Finnish adoptive family study of schizophrenia. In L. Robins & M. Rutter (Eds.), *Straight and devious pathways from childhood to adulthood*. New York: Cambridge University Press.

Tienari, P., Wynne, L. C., Moring, J., Lahti, I., Naarala, M., Sorri, A., et al. (1994). The Finnish adoptive family study of schizophrenia: Implications for family research. *British Journal of Psychiatry Supplement, 23*, 20–26.

Tinbergen, N. (1951). *The study of instinct*. New York: Oxford University Press.

Tollesfson, G. D. (1995). Selective serotonin reuptake inhibitors. In A. F. Schatzberg & C. B. Nemeroff (Eds.), *The American psychiatric press textbook of psychopharmacology* (pp. 161–182). Washington, DC: American Psychiatric Press.

Tooby, J., & Cosmides, L. (1990). On the universality of human nature and the uniqueness of the individual: The role of genetics and adaptation. *Journal of Personality, 58*, 17–68.

Torrey, E. F. (1999). Epidemiological comparison of schizophrenia and bipolar disorder. *Schizophrenia Research, 39*(2), 101–06.

Torrey, E. F., Torrey, B. B., & Peterson, M. R. (1977). Seasonality of schizophrenic births in the United States. *Archives of General Psychiatry, 34*(9), 1065–1070.

Treisman, A. (1988). Features and objects: The Fourteenth Bartlett Memorial Lecture. *Quarterly Journal of Experimental Psychology, 40A*, 201–237.

Treisman, A., & Gelade, G. (1980). A feature-integration theory of attention. *Cognitive Psychology, 12*, 97–136.

Trevethan, S. D., & Walker, L. J. (1989). Hypothetical versus real-life moral reasoning among psychopathic and delinquent youth. *Development and Psychopathology, 1*, 91–103.

Triandis, H. C. (1989). The self and social behavior in differing cultural contexts. *Psychological Review, 96*, 506–520.

Tulving, E. T., Kapur, S., Craik, F. I. M., Moscovitch, M., & Houle, S. (1994). Hemispheric encoding/retrieval asymmetry in episodic memory: Positron emission tomography findings. *Proceedings of the National Academy of Sciences, 91*, 2016–2020.

Uchino, B. N., Cacioppo, J. T., & Kiecolt-Glaser, J. K. (1996). The relationship between social support and physiological processes: A review with emphasis on underlying mechanisms and implications for health. *Psychological Bulletin, 119*, 488–531.

Ungerleider, L. G., & Mishkin, M. (1982). Two cortical visual systems. In D. J. Engle, M. A. Goodale, & R. J. Mansfield (Eds.), *Analysis of visual behavior* (pp. 549–586). Cambridge, MA: MIT Press.

United States Department of Health and Human Services. (1993). *Alcohol and health*. Washington, DC: U.S. Government Printing Office.

Upton, N. (1994). Mechanisms of action of new antiepileptic drugs: Rational design and serendipitous findings. *Trends in Pharmacological Sciences, 15*, 456–463.

Val Derlega, V. J., Lewis, R. J., Harrison, S., & Winstead, B. A. (1989). Gender differences in the initiation and attribution of tactile intimacy. *Journal of Nonverbal Behavior, 13*, 83–96.

Valzelli, L. (1973). The "isolation syndrome" in mice. *Psychopharmacologia, 31*, 305–320.

Van Goozen, M. S. H., Cohen-Kettenis, P. T., Gooren, L. J. G., Frijda, N. H., & Can de Poll, N. E. (1995). Gender differences in behaviour: Activating effects of cross-sex hormones. *Psychoneuroendocrinology, 20*, 343–363.

Vanzetti, N., & Duck, S. (1996). *A lifetime of relationships*. Pacific Grove, CA: Brooks Cole.

Vargha-Khadem, F., Gadian, D. G., Watkinds, K., Connelly, A., Can Paesschen, W., & Mishkin, M. (1997). Differential effects of early hippocampal pathology on episodic and semantic memory. *Science, 277*, 376–380.

Varley, C. K. (1984). Attention deficit disorder (the hyperactivity syndrome): A review of selected issues. *Developmental and Behavioral Pediatrics, 5*, 254–258.

Vaugh, E. E., & Leff, J. P. (1976). The influence of family and social factors on the course of psychiatric illness. *British Journal of Psychiatry, 129*, 125–137.

von Neumann, J., & Morgenstern, O. (1947). *Theory of games and economic behavior*. Princeton, NJ: Princeton University Press.

Wagner, A. D., Schacter, D. L., Rotte, M., Koutstaal, W., Maril, A., Dale, A. M., et al. (1998). Building memories: Remembering and forgetting of verbal experiences as predicted by brain activity. *Science, 281*, 1188–1191.

Wallach, H. (1948). Brightness constancy and the nature of achromatic colors. *Journal of Experimental Psychology, 38*, 310–324.

Waltrip, R. W., Buchanan, R. W., Carpenter, W. T., Kirkpatrick, B., Summerfelt, A., Breier, A., et al. (1997). Borna disease virus antibodies and the deficit syndrome of schizophrenia. *Schizophrenia Research, 23*(3), 253–257.

Warburton, D. M. (1992). Nicotine as a cognitive enhancer. *Progress in Neuro-Psychopharmacology and Biological Psychiatry, 16*, 181–191.

Wark, G. R., & Krebs, D. L. (1996). Gender and dilemma differences in real-life moral judgment. *Developmental Psychology, 32*, 220–230.

Watson, D., & Clark, L. A. (1997). Extraversion and its positive emotional core. In R. Hogan, J. Johnson, & S. Briggs (Eds.), *Handbook of personality psychology* (pp. 767–793). San Diego, CA: Academic Press.

Watson, D., Wiese, D., Vaidya, J., & Tellegen, A. (1999). The two general activation systems of affect: Structural findings, evolutionary considerations, and psychobiological evidence. *Journal of Personality and Social Psychology, 76*, 820–838.

Watson, J. B. (1924). *Behaviorism*. New York: W. W. Norton.

Wegner, D. M. (1989). *White bears and other unwanted thoughts*. New York: Penguin USA.

Wegner, D. M., & Bargh, J. A. (1998). Control and automaticity in social life. In D. T. Gilbert, S. T. Fiske, & L. Gardner (Eds.), *Handbook of social psychology* (pp. 446–496). New York: Oxford University Press.

Wegner, D. M., Schneider, D. J., Carter, S., & White, L. (1987). Paradoxical effects of thought suppression. *Journal of Personality and Social Psychology, 53*, 5–13.

Wegner, D., Shortt, J., Blake, A., & Page, M. (1990). The suppression of exciting thoughts. *Journal of Personality and Social Psychology, 58*, 409–418.

Weiskrantz, L. (1986). *Blindsight: A case study and implications*. Oxford, UK: Oxford University Press.

Weiss, G., & Hechtman, L. T. (1993). *Hyperactive children grown up*. New York: Guilford Press.

Weissman, M. M., Bland, R. C., Canino, G. J., Greenwald, S., Hwu, H. G., Lee, C. K., et al. (1994). The cross national epidemiology of obsessive compulsive disorder. The Cross National Collaborative Group. *Journal of Clinical Psychiatry, 55*, 5–10.

Wells, G. L., Small, M., Penrod, S., Malpass, R. S., Fulero, S. M., & Brimacombe, C. A. E. (1998). Eyewitness identification procedures: Recommendations for lineups and photospreads. *Law and Human Behavior, 22*, 603–647.

Welsh, D. K., Logothetis, D. E., Meister, M., & Reppert, S. M. (1995). Individual neurons dissociated from rat suprachiasmatic nucleus express independently phased circadian firing rhythms. *Neuron, 14*, 697–706.

Werking, K. J. (1994). *Dissolving cross-sex friendships*. Paper presented at the Speech Communication Association Convention, New Orleans, LA.

Werner, L. A., & Bargones, J. Y. (1992). Psychoacoustic development of human infants. In C. Rovee-Collier & L. Lipsett (Eds.), *Advances in infancy research* (Vol. 7, pp. 103–145). Norwood, NJ: Ablex.

Wertheimer, M. (1912). Experimentelle studien über das Sehen von Bewegung. *Zeitschrift Psychologie, 61,* 161–265.

Westen, D. (1991). Social cognition and object relations. *Psychological Bulletin, 109,* 429–455.

Westen, D. (1998). The scientific legacy of Sigmund Freud: Toward a psychodynamically informed psychological science. *Psychological Bulletin, 124,* 333–371.

Whalen, C. K. (1989). Attention deficit and hyperactivity disorders. In T. H. Ollendick & M. Herson (Eds.), *Handbook of child psychopathology* (2nd ed., pp. 131–169). New York: Plenum.

Whalen, P. J., Rauch, S. L., Etcoff, N. L., McInerney, N. L., Lee, M. B., & Jenike, M. A. (1998). Masked presentations of emotional facial expressions modulate amygdala activity without explicit knowledge. *Journal of Neuroscience, 18,* 411–418.

Wheeler, M. A., Stuss, D. T., & Tulving, E. (1997). Toward a theory of episodic memory: The frontal lobes and autonoetic consciousness. *Psychological Bulletin, 121,* 331–354.

Wheeler, M. E., Petersen, S. E., & Buckner, R. L. (2000). Memory's echo: Vivid remembering reactivates sensory-specific cortex. *Proceedings of the National Academy of Sciences, 97,* 11125–11129.

White, D., & Pitts, M. (1998). Educating young people about drugs: A systematic review. *Addiction, 93,* 1475–1487.

Widiger, T. A., & Corbitt, E. M. (1995). Are personality disorders well-classified in DSM-IV? In W. J. Lively (Ed.), *The DSM-IV personality disorders* (pp. 103–126). New York: Guilford Press.

Widom, C. S. (1978). A methodology for studying noninstitutionalized psychopaths. In R. D. Hare & D. A. Schalling (Eds.), *Psychopathic behavior: Approaches to research* (pp. 72ff). Chichester, England: John Wiley.

Williams, J. M. G., Mathews, A., & MacLeod, C. (1996). The emotional Stroop task and psychopathology. *Psychological Bulletin, 120,* 3–24.

Wills, T. A., DuHamel, K., & Vaccaro, D. (1995). Activity and mood temperament as predictors of adolescent substance use: Test of a self-regulation mediational model. *Journal of Personality and Social Psychology, 68,* 901–916.

Wilson, A. E., & Ross, M. (2001). From chump to champ: People's appraisals of their earlier and present selves. *Journal of Personality and Social Psychology, 80,* 572–584.

Wilson, M. A., & McNaughton, B. L. (1994). Reactivation of hippocampal ensemble memories during sleep. *Science, 265,* 676–679.

Wilson, T. D., Lindsey, S., & Schooler, T. Y. (2000). A model of dual attitudes. *Psychological Review, 107,* 101–126.

Wilson, T. D., & Schooler, J. W. (1991). Thinking too much: Introspection can reduce the quality of preferences and decisions. *Journal of Personality and Social Psychology, 60,* 181–192.

Wilson, T. W., & Grim, C. E. (1991). Biohistory of slavery and blood pressure differences in Blacks today. *Hypertension, 17*(Suppl. 1), I122–I128.

Wise, R. A., & Rompre, P. P. (1989). Brain dopamine and reward. *Annual Review of Psychology, 40,* 191–225.

Wishaw, I. Q., Drigenberg, H. C., & Comery, T. A. (1992). Rats (rattus norvegicus) modulate eating speed and vigilance to optimize food consumption: Effects of cover, circadian rhythm, food deprivation, and individual differences. *Journal of Comparative Psychology, 106,* 411–419.

Wolpe, J. (1997). Thirty years of behavior therapy. *Behavior Therapy, 28,* 633–635.

Woodruff, G. N., & Hughes, J. (1991). Cholecystokinin antagonists. *Annual Review of Pharmacology & Toxicology, 31,* 469–501.

Woods, S. C., & Stricker, E. M. (1999). Food intake and metabolism. In M. J. Zigmond, F. E. Bloom, S. C. Landis, J. L. Roberts, & L. R. Squire (Eds.), *Fundamentals of neuroscience* (pp. 1091–1109). San Diego, CA: Academic Press.

Woodward, S. A., McManis, M. H., Kagan, J., Deldin, P., Snidman, N., Lewis, M., et al. (2001). Infant temperament and the brainstem auditory evoked response in later childhood. *Developmental Psychology, 37,* 533–538.

Wright, D. E. (1999). *Personal relationships.* Mountain View, CA: Mayfield Publishing Co.

Wynn, K. (1992). Addition and subtraction by human infants. *Nature, 358,* 749–750.

Wynn, K. (1998). Numerical competence in human infants. In C. Donlan (Ed.), *The development of mathematical skills* (pp. 3–25). Hove, UK: Psychology Press/Taylor & Francis.

Yuille, J. C., & Cutshall, J. L. (1986). A case study of eyewitness memory of a crime. *Journal of Applied Psychology, 71,* 291–301.

Zahn-Waxler, C., & Robinson, J. (1995). Empathy and guilt: Early origins of feelings of responsibility. In J. P. Tangney & K. W. Fischer (Eds.), *Self-conscious emotions: The psychology of shame, guilt, embarrassment, and pride* (pp. 143–173). New York: Guilford.

Zajonc, R. B. (1965). Social facilitation. *Science 149,* 269–274.

Zajonc, R. B. (1980). Feeling and thinking: Preferences need no inferences. *American Psychologist, 35,* 151–175.

Zajonc, R. B., Murphy, S. T., & Inglehart, M. (1989). Feeling and facial efference: Implications of the vascular theory of emotions. *Psychological Review, 96,* 395–416.

Zametkin, A. J., Nordahl, T. E., Gross, M., King, A. C., Stemple, W. E., Rumsey, J., et al. (1990). Cerebral glucose metabolism in adults with hyperactivity of childhood onset. *New England Journal of Medicine, 323,* 1361–1366.

Zatorre, R. J. (1989). On the representation of multiple languages in the brain: Old problems and new directions. *Brain and Language, 36*(1), 127–147.

Zebrowitz, L. A. (1997). *Reading faces: Window to the soul?* Boulder, CO: Westview Press.

Zeki, S. (1993). *A vision of the brain.* Oxford, UK: Blackwell Scientific.

Zentall, S. S., Sutton, J. E., & Sherburne, L. M. (1996). True imitative learning in pigeons. *Psychological Science, 7,* 343–346.

Zihl, J., von Cramon, D., & Mai, N. (1983). Selective disturbance of movement vision after bilateral brain damage. *Brain, 106,* 313–340.

ACKNOWLEDGMENTS AND CREDITS

Every effort has been made to contact the copyright holders of the material used in *Psychological Science*. Rights holders of any material not credited should contact W. W. Norton & Company, Inc., 500 5th Avenue, New York, NY 10110 for a correction to be made in the next reprinting of our work.

PHOTOS

CHAPTER OPENERS: p. 2: Photo by Dennis Hallinan/Getty Images. **p. 30:** Chris Lisle/Corbis. **p. 58:** Bob Collier & Sion Touhig/Corbis Sygma. **p. 94:** Reuters NewMedia Inc./Corbis. **p. 122:** Mauro Fermariello/Photo Researchers, Inc. **p. 162:** Tony Stone/Getty Images. **p. 200:** S. Elleringmann/Bilderberg/Aurora. **p. 238:** Kenneth Dickerman. **p. 272:** Doug Pensinger/Allsport/Getty Images. **p. 310:** AFP/Corbis. **p. 344:** Robert A. Reeder/© The Washington Post. **p. 386:** Photofest. **p. 414:** David Turnley/Corbis. **p. 448:** AFP/Corbis. **p. 484:** (left) Rufus F. Folkks/Corbis; (right) Marshall John/Corbis Sygma. **p. 518:** Unimedia International/Corbis Sygma. **p. 556:** Bob Krist/Corbis.

CHAPTER 1: Figure 1.1: AP/Wide World Photos. **Figure 1.2:** From Phelps, E. A., O'Connor, K. J., Cunningham, W. A., Funayama, E. S., Gatenby, J. C., Gore, J. C., Banji, M. R. (2000). Performance on indirect measures of race evaluation predicts amygdala activation. *Journal of Cognitive Neuroscience, 12,* 729–738. Images courtesy Elizabeth A. Phelps, Phelps Lab. **Figure 1.3:** Courtesy Professor Joseph J. Campos, University of California, Berkeley. **Figure 1.5:** The Granger Collection, New York. **Figure 1.6:** Bettmann/Corbis. **Figure 1.7:** Bettmann/Corbis. **Figure 1.9:** Archives of the History of American Psychology, University of Akron. **Figure 1.10:** Archives of the History of American Psychology, University of Akron. **Figure 1.11:** From *American Journal of Psychology.* Copyright 1974 by the Board of Trustees of the University of Illinois. Used with permission of the University of Illinois Press. **Figure 1.12:** From *Mind sights,* by Roger N. Shepard. © 1990 by Roger N. Shepard. Henry Holt and Company, LLC. **Figure 1.13:** Corbis. **Figure 1.14:** Archives of the History of American Psychology, The University of Akron. **Figure 1.15:** Courtesy George Miller, Princeton University.

© 2001, Pryde Brown Photographs, Princeton, NJ. **Figure 1.16:** Archives of the History of American Psychology, University of Akron.

CHAPTER 2: Figure 2.3: Karl Ammann/Corbis. **Figure 2.4:** Courtesy Robert Rosenthal, University of California, Riverside.

CHAPTER 3: Figure 3.1: Courtesy Hereditary Disease Foundation. **Figure 3.2:** CNRI/Science Photo Library/Photo Researchers, Inc. **Figure 3.4:** (top row, second from the left) Harry B. Clay, Jr., photographer, Bernardsville, N.J. **Figure 3.5:** Bob Sacha. **Figure 3.8:** (b) Fritz Goro/TimePix. **Figure 3.13:** James Stevenson/Science Photo Library/Photo Researchers, Inc. **Figure 3.16:** Color plates 2 and 4 from Greenberg, J. O., and Adams, R. D. (Eds.), *Neuroimaging: A companion to Adams and Victor's principles of neurology.* New York: McGraw-Hill, Inc., 1995. **Figure 3.17:** From Jon Palfreman and J. William Langston, *The case of the frozen addicts.* New York: Pantheon Books, 1995. Photograph by Russ Lee, © Pantheon Books, 1995. **Figure 3.18:** From Widner, H., Rehncrona, S., Snow, B., Brudin, P., Gustavii, B., Bjorklund, A., Lindvall, O., Langston, J. W. (1992). Bilateral fetal mesencephalic grafting in two patients with parkinsonism induced by 1-methyl-4-phenyl-1,2,3,6 tetrahydropyridine (MPTP). *The New England Journal of Medicine, 327,* (22). Copyright © 1992 Massachusetts Medical Society. All rights reserved.

CHAPTER 4: Figure 4.1: From Penfield, Wilder (1958). *The excitable cortex in conscious man.* Liverpool University Press. **Figure 4.2:** From Spurzheim, J. 1825. *Phrenology, or, the doctrine of the mind; and the relations between its manifestations and the body.* London: C. Knight. **Figure 4.3:** From the Musée Dupuytren. Courtesy Assistance Publique, Hopitaux de Paris. **Figure 4.4:** Damasio, H., Grabowski, T., Frank, R., Galaburda, A. M., Damasio, A. R. (1994). The return of Phineas Gage: Clues about the brain from a famous patient. *Science, 264,* 1102–1105.

Department of Neurology and Image Analysis Facility, University of Iowa. **Figure 4.5:** © Richard T. Nowitz/Photo Researchers, Inc. **Figure 4.7:** Photo Researchers, Inc. **Figure 4.8:** Fig. 1–1 (B), (C), and (D), Greenberg, J. O., and Adams, R. D. (Eds.), *Neuroimaging: A companion to Adams and Victor's principles of neurology.* New York: McGraw-Hill, Inc., 1995. **Figure 4.9:** Courtesy Cathy J. Price, Institute of Neurology, University College, London. From Delineating necessary and sufficient neural systems with functional imaging studies of neuropsychological patients. *Journal of Cognitive Neuroscience.* (1999). 11(4): 377, Figure 2.

CHAPTER 5: **Figure 5.16:** © 2002 Magic Eye Inc. (www.magiceye.com). **Figure 5.17:** David Muench/Corbis. **Figure 5.19:** (left) © Exploratorium, www.exploratorium.edu.

CHAPTER 6: **Figure 6.1:** Culver Pictures. **Figure 6.2:** Bettmann/Corbis. **Figure 6.8:** From Childress, A. R., Mozey, P. D., McElgin, W., Fitzgerald, J. Reivich, M., O'Brien, C. P. (1999). Limbic activation during cue-induced cocaine craving. *American Journal of Psychiatry, 156,* 11–18. Copyright © 1999 by American Psychiatric Association. Images courtesy Anna Rose Childress, University of Pennsylvania. **Figure 6.10:** Nina Leen/TimePix. **Figure 6.11:** AP/Wide World Photos. **Figure 6.15:** Albert Bandura, Department of Psychology, Stanford University. **Figure 6.16:** Albert Bandura, Department of Psychology, Stanford University. **Figure 6.17:** Susan Mineka, Northwestern University. **Figure 6.20:** Bettmann/Corbis. **Figure 6.21:** AP/Wide World Photos. **Figure 6.23:** McGill Reporter, PR050904. **Figure 6.24:** © Biophoto Associates/Photo Researchers, Inc.

CHAPTER 7: **Figure 7.12:** From Wheeler, M. E., Petersen, S. E., & Buckner, R. L. (2000). Memory's echo: Vivid remembering reactivates sensory-specific cortex. *Proceedings of the National Academy of Sciences, 97,* 11125–11129. **Figure 7.17:** Rauch, S. L. et al. (1996); reprinted with permission from *Archives of General Psychiatry,* vol. 53, no. 5, May 1996, p. 385; Copyrighted 2002, American Medical Association. **Figure 7.19:** AP/Wide World Photos. **Figure 7.20:** AP/Wide World Photos. **Figure 7.21:** Courtesy Elizabeth Loftus, University of Washington. **Figure 7.22:** Courtesy Daniel Schacter, Harvard University.

CHAPTER 8: **Figure 8.14:** The Granger Collection, New York. **Figure 8.15:** © BBC Picture Archives. **Figure 8.17:** (a) Duomo/Corbis; (b) Reuters NewMedia Inc./Corbis; (c) AP/Wide World Photos; (d) AP/Wide World Photos. **Figure 8.19:** From Duncan, J., Seitz, R. J., Kolodny, J. Bor, D., Herzog, H., Ahmed, A., Newell, F. N., Emslie, H. (2000). A neural basis for general intelligence. *Science, 289,* 457–460. Images courtesy John Duncan, MRC Cognition and Brain Sciences Unit, Cambridge. **Figure 8.21:** © August Bullock. SubliminalSex.com. All Rights Reserved.

CHAPTER 9: **Figure 9.4:** Archives of the History of American Psychology, University of Akron. **Figure 9.5:** Jacob E. Steiner, PhD, Laboratory of Oral Physiology, The Hebrew University. **Figure 9.8:** Photo Services, Harvard University. **Figure 9.12:** (top) Sylvia Bunge. **Figure 9.21:** From Braun, A. R., Balkin, T. J., Wesensten, N. J., Gwadry, F., Carson, R. E., Varga, M., Baldwin, P., Belenky, G., & Herscovitch, P. (1998). Dissociated pattern of activity in visual cortices and their projections during human rapid eye movement sleep. *Science, 279,* 91–95. Images courtesy Allen R. Braun, NIH.

CHAPTER 10: **Figure 10.1:** From Izard, C. E., Fantauzzo, C. A., Castle, J. M., Haynes, O. M., Rayias, M. F., Putnam, P. H. (1995). The ontogeny and significance of infants' facial expressions in the first nine months of life. *Developmental Psychology, 31,* 997–1013. Photographs courtesy

Carroll Izard, University of Delaware. **Figure 10.3:** Paul Ekman. **Figure 10.6:** Edgar Fahs Smith Collection, University of Pennsylvania Library. **Figure 10.8:** Photo by Bill Apple. **Figure 10.10:** Chris Lisle/Corbis. **Figure 10.11:** From Lane, R. D., Reiman, E. M., Ahern, G. L., Schwartz, G. E., Davidson, R. J. (1997). neuroanatomical correlates of happiness, sadness, and disgust. *American Journal of Psychiatry, 154,* 926–933. Copyright © 1997 by American Psychiatric Association. **Figure 10.14:** Photo by James Prince. **Figure 10.15:** From Cahill, L., Haier, R. J., White, N. S., Fallon, J. Kilpatrick, L., Lawrence, C., Potkin, S. G., Alkire, M. T. (2001). Sex related differences in amygdala activity during emotionally influenced memory storage. *Neurobiology of Learning and Memory, 75,* 1–9. Images courtesy Larry Cahill, University of California, Irvine. **Figure 10.16:** From Dolan, R. J. Emotion processing in the human brain revealed through functional neuroimaging. In M. S. Gazzaniga (Ed.) *The new cognitive neurosciences.* Cambridge, MA: MIT Press. **Figure 10.17:** Courtesy Richard J. Davidson, University of Wisconsin. **Figure 10.18:** (a) American Psychological Association. **Figure 10.20:** Archives of the History of American Psychology, University of Akron. **Figure 10.21:** Courtesy Shelley Taylor, UCLA.

CHAPTER 11: **Figure 11.1:** © National Gallery Collection; By kind permission of the Trustees of the National Gallery, London/Corbis. **Figure 11.2:** Stock Boston, LLC/Lawrence Migdale. **Figure 11.5:** Stock Boston, LLC/Spencer Grant. **Figure 11.6:** Courtesy Velma Dobson, University of Arizona. **Figure 11.8:** Bettmann/Corbis. **Figure 11.10:** Michael Newman/PhotoEdit. **Figure 11.18:** © Dr. Carolyn Rovee-Collier, Director, Rutgers Early Learning Project. **Figure 11.20:** Courtesy HarperCollins Publishers Inc. **Figure 11.22:** AFP/Corbis. **Figure 11.23:** Herbert S. Terrace. **Figure 11.24:** (top) Stephanie Maze/Corbis; (bottom) Roger Ressmeyer/Corbis.

CHAPTER 12: **Figure 12.1:** Photograph courtesy David Reimer. From Colapinto, John, *As nature made him: The boy who was raised as a girl,* (2000), HarperCollins Publishers Inc. **Figure 12.2:** Reuters Newsmedia Inc./Corbis. **Figure 12.3:** Nina Leen/Life Magazine © Time Inc. from Westen. **Figure 12.4:** Harlow Primate Laboratory, University of Wisconsin. **Figure 12.5:** (a, b) Robert Marvin, Estate of Mary Ainsworth. **Figure 12.9:** Corbis/Sygma. **Figure 12.10:** Sarah Putnam/Index Stock Imagery, Inc.

CHAPTER 13: **Figure 13.1:** From Wallace, Marjorie, *Silent twins,* Prentice Hall Press. Copyright © 1986 by Marjorie Wallace. With permission of the author. **Figure 13.2:** From *Introduction to Psychology with InfoTrac, 6th edition,* by © 2002 Reprinted with permission of Brooks/Cole, an imprint of the Wadsworth Group, a division of Thomson Learning. Fax 800-730-2215. **Figure 13.3:** Photo courtesy Cognitive Evolution Group, University of Louisiana at Lafayette. **Figure 13.4:** Reprinted by permission from *Nature,* January 18, 2001, vol. 409, #6818, copyright 2002 Macmillan Publishers Ltd. Image courtesy Julian Paul Keenan, Montclair State University. **Figure 13.12:** Najlah Feanny/Corbis. **Figure 13.13:** (bottom) Bettmann/Corbis. **Figure 13.14:** © 1982 Karen Zebuion, Courtesy New School Public Relations Department. **Figure 13.18:** Courtesy Keith Payne, Washington University.

CHAPTER 14: **Figure 14.1:** © Toronto Sun. **Figure 14.5:** From McCarthy, G., Price, A., Allison, T. (1997). Face specific processing in the human fusiform gyrus. *Journal of Cognitive Neuroscience, 9,* 605–610. Images courtesy Dr. Gregory McCarthy, The Duke-UNC Brain Imaging and Analysis Center. **Figure 14.6:** Courtesy Peter Thompson, University of York. **Figure 14.10:** © Philip G. Zimbardo, Ph.D. **Figure 14.12:** Photos by William Vandivert. **Figure 14.13:** Courtesy Alexandra Milgram. **Figure 14.14: Courtesy Alexandra Milgram. **Figure 14.19:** New York Times Pictures. **Figure 14.21:** From Langlois, J. H., Ruggerman, L. A. (1990). Attractive faces are only average. *Psychological Science 1*, 115–121. Photographs courtesy Judith Hall Langlois, University of Texas at Austin. **Figure 14.22:** From Perrett, D. I., May, K. A., Yoshikawa, S. (1994). Facial shape and judgments of female attractiveness. Reprinted by permission from *Nature*, 1994, vol. 368, 239–242, Copyright 2002 Macmillan Publishers Ltd. Images courtesy D. I. Perrett, University of St. Andrews. **Figure 14.23:** Courtesy David Buss, University of Texas at Austin. **Figure 14.25:** (left) Courtesy Elaine Hatfield, University of Hawaii at Manoa; (right) Courtesy Ellen Berscheid, University of Minnesota.

CHAPTER 15: **Figure 15.1:** Dan McAdams, Northwestern University. **Figure 15.2:** Bettmann/Corbis. **Figure 15.4:** Courtesy Carl Rogers Memorial Library. **Figure 15.6:** Adapted from Norman, W. T. (1963). Toward an adequate taxonomy of personality attributes: replicated factor structure in peer nomination personality rating. *Journal of Abnormal and Social Psychology*, 66, 5770. **Figure 15.7:** Columbia University. **Figure 15.10:** Hulton Archive/Getty Images.

CHAPTER 16: **Figure 16.1:** Edna Morlok. **Figure 16.2:** The Granger Collection, New York. **Figure 16.3:** Joe McNally. **Figure 16.4:** The Granger Collection, New York. **Figure 16.5:** Bettmann/Corbis. **Figure 16.6:** (top) Manchester Scott/Corbis Sygma; (b) Denver Post/Kent Meireis/Corbis Sygma. **Figure 16.7:** Courtesy Dr. Lewis Baxter, UAB. **Figure 16.12:** Peter Aprahamian/Corbis. **Figure 16.13:** From Osterling, J., & Dawson, G. (1994). Early recognition of children with autism. A study of first birthday home videotapes. *Journal of Autism and Developmental Disorders*, 24, 247–257. Photographs courtesy Geraldine Dawson. **Figure 16.14:** From Zametkin, A. J., Nordhal, T. E., Gross, M. et al. (1990). Cerebral glucose metabolism in adults with hyperactivity of childhood onset. *New England Journal of Medicine*, 323(20), 1361–1366. Images courtesy Alan Zametkin, NIH.

CHAPTER 17: **Figure 17.1:** Bettmann/Corbis. **Figure 17.2:** © 1983 Erika Stone. **Figure 17.3:** Courtesy Barbara A. Marinelli. **Figure 17.6:** Courtesy James Pennebaker, University of Texas at Austin. **Figure 17.8:** AP/Wide World Photos. **Figure 17.9:** From Baxter, L. R., et al. (1992). Caudate glucose metabolic rate changes with both drug and behavior therapy for obsessive-compulsive disorder, reprinted with permission from Archives of General Psychiatry, vol. 49, 681–689, Copyright © American Medical Association. Images courtesy Dr. Lewis Baxter, UAB. **Figure 17.12:** © Pascal Goetheluck/Science Photo Library/Photo Researchers, Inc. **Figure 17.13:** © Will McIntyre/Photo Researchers, Inc. **Figure 17.16:** Courtesy Marsha Linehan, University of Washington.

FIGURES

CHAPTER 1: **Figure 1.8:** Grant, Peter R., Darwin's Finches, *Ecology and evolution of Darwin's finches*. Copyright © 1986 by Princeton University Press. Reprinted by permission of Princeton University Press. **Figure 1.17:** "Some of the Subfields of Psychology." Copyright by the American Psychological Association. Reprinted with permission.

CHAPTER 2: **Figure 2.7:** From *Cognitive neuroscience: The biology of the mind* by Michael S. Gazzaniga, Richard Ivry, and George R. Mangun. Copyright © 1998 by W. W. Norton & Company, Inc. Used by permission of W. W. Norton & Company, Inc. **Figure 2.8:** From *Cognitive neuroscience: The biology of the mind* by Michael S. Gazzaniga, Richard Ivry,

and George R. Mangun. Copyright © 1998 by W. W. Norton & Company, Inc. Used by permission of W. W. Norton & Company, Inc.

CHAPTER 3: **Figure 3.11:** From Pinel, John P. J., figure 4.8, *Biopsychology*, 4th Edition. Copyright © 2000 by Pearson Education. Reprinted by permission by Allyn & Bacon.

CHAPTER 4: **Figure 4.6:** Bentin, S., Mouchetant-Rostaing, Y., Giard, M. H., Echailler, J. F., and Pernier, J, ERP manifestations of processing printed words at different psycholinguistic levels: Time course and scalp distribution, *Journal of Cognitive Neuroscience*, 11:3 (May, 1999), 235–260. Copyright © 1999 by the Massachusetts Institute of Technology. **Figure 4.18:** Ramachandran, V. S. and Blakeslee, Sandra, Fig. 6.1, Drawing made by a neglect patient, from *Phantoms in the brain*. Copyright © 1998 by V. S. Ramachandran and Sandra Blakeslee. Reprinted by permission of HarperCollins Publishers Inc. **Figure 4.17:** From *Cognitive neuroscience: The biology of the mind* by Michael S. Gazzaniga, Richard Ivry, and George R. Mangun. Copyright © 1998 by W. W. Norton & Company, Inc. Used by permission of W. W. Norton & Company, Inc. **Figure 4.20:** From *Cognitive neuroscience: The biology of the mind* by Michael S. Gazzaniga, Richard Ivry, and George R. Mangun. Copyright © 1998 by W. W. Norton & Company, Inc. Used by permission of W. W. Norton & Company, Inc.

CHAPTER 5: **Figure 5.1:** From Zimbardo, Philip G. and Gerrig, Richard J., figure 3.2, The theory of signal detection, *Psychology and life*, 15th Edition. Copyright © 1999. Adapted by permission by Allyn & Bacon. **Figure 5.4:** From *Cognitive neuroscience: The biology of the mind* by Michael S. Gazzaniga, Richard Ivry, and George R. Mangun. Copyright © 1998 by W. W. Norton & Company, Inc. Used by permission of W. W. Norton & Company, Inc. **Figure 5.5:** From *Cognitive neuroscience: The biology of the mind* by Michael S. Gazzaniga, Richard Ivry, and George R. Mangun. Copyright © 1998 by W. W. Norton & Company, Inc. Used by permission of W. W. Norton & Company, Inc. **Figure 5.7:** From *Cognitive neuroscience: The biology of the mind* by Michael S. Gazzaniga, Richard Ivry, and George R. Mangun. Copyright © 1998 by W. W. Norton & Company, Inc. Used by permission of W. W. Norton & Company, Inc. **Figure 5.9:** From Zimbardo, Philip G. and Gerrig, Richard J., figure 3.11, Color afterimages, *Psychology and life*, 15th Edition. Copyright © 1999. Reprinted by permission by Allyn & Bacon. **Figure 5.23:** From *Psychology* by Peter Gray © 1991, 1994, 1999 by Worth Publishers. Used with permission. **Figure 5.24:** From *Psychology*, Fourth Edition by Henry Gleitman. Copyright © 1995, 1991, 1986, 1981 by W. W. Norton & Company, Inc. Used by permission of W. W. Norton & Company, Inc. **Figure 5.25:** Kuhl, Jerome, Subjective contours, *Scientific American* 234 (1976), 44–52. Reprinted by permission of Jerome Kuhl. **Figure 5.27:** Turning the tables diagram from *Mind Sights* by Roger N. Shepard, © 1990 by Roger N. Shepard. Reprinted by permission of Henry Holt and Company, LLC. **Figure 5.28:** From *Cognitive neuroscience: The biology of the mind* by Michael S. Gazzaniga, Richard Ivry, and George R. Mangun. Copyright © 1998 by W. W. Norton & Company, Inc. Used by permission of W. W. Norton & Company, Inc. **Figure 5.29:** From *Cognitive neuroscience: The biology of the mind* by Michael S. Gazzaniga, Richard Ivry, and George R. Mangun. Copyright © 1998 by W. W. Norton & Company, Inc. Used by permission of W. W. Norton & Company, Inc. **Figure 5.30:** From *Cognitive neuroscience: The biology of the mind* by Michael S. Gazzaniga, Richard Ivry, and George R. Mangun. Copyright © 1998 by W. W. Norton & Company, Inc. Used by permission of W. W. Norton & Company, Inc.

CHAPTER 6: **Figure 6.12:** From *Psychology* by Peter Gray © 1991, 1994, 1999 by Worth Publishers. Used with permission.

CHAPTER 7: **Figure 7.8:** Adapted from Craik, F. I. M., & Tulving, E. (1975). Depth of processing and the retention of words in episodic memory. *Journal of Experimental Psychology: General, 104,* 268–294. **Figure 7.9:** Adapted from Collins, A. M., & Loftus, E. F. (1975). A spreading-activation theory of semantic processing. *Psychological Review, 82,* 407–428. **Figure 7.10:** Adapted from Godden, D. R., & Baddeley, A. D. (1975). Context-dependent memory in two natural environments: On land and underwater. *British Journal of Psychology, 66,* 325–331. **Figure 7.13:** From *Cognitive neuroscience: The biology of the mind* by Michael S. Gazzaniga, Richard Ivry, and George R. Mangun. Copyright © 1998 by W. W. Norton & Company, Inc. Used by permission of W. W. Norton & Company, Inc. **Figure 7.15:** Adapted from Wagner, A. D., Schacter, D. L., Rotte, M., Koutstaal, W., Maril, A., Dale, A. M., et al. (1998). Building memories: remembering and forgetting of verbal experiences as predicted by brain activity. *Science, 281,* 1188–1191.

CHAPTER 8: **Figure 8.1:** Eysenck, M. W., figures 7.6 and 7.7, *Cognitive psychology: A student's handbook,* 2nd Edition, Lawrence Erlbaum Associates. Copyright © 1990. **Figure 8.7:** Eysenck, M. W., figure 8.3, *Cognitive psychology: A student's handbook,* 2nd Edition, Lawrence Erlbaum Associates. Copyright © 1990. **Figure 8.13:** Plous, S., figure 9.1, *Psychology of judgement and decision making.* Copyright © 1993 by The McGraw-Hill Companies. Reprinted by permission of The McGraw-Hill Companies. **Figure 8.22:** From *Cognitive neuroscience: The biology of the mind* by Michael S. Gazzaniga, Richard Ivry, and George R. Mangun. Copyright © 1998 by W. W. Norton & Company, Inc. Used by permission of W. W. Norton & Company, Inc. **Figure 8.23:** From *Cognitive neuroscience: The biology of the mind* by Michael S. Gazzaniga, Richard Ivry, and George R. Mangun. Copyright © 1998 by W. W. Norton & Company, Inc. Used by permission of W. W. Norton & Company, Inc. **Figure 8.24:** From *Cognitive neuroscience: The biology of the mind* by Michael S. Gazzaniga, Richard Ivry, and George R. Mangun. Copyright © 1998 by W. W. Norton & Company, Inc. Used by permission of W. W. Norton & Company, Inc.

CHAPTER 9: **Figure 9.7:** Berlyne, D. E., Novelty, complexity and hedonic value. *Perception and psychophysics.* Copyright © 1970. Reprinted by permission of Psychonomic Society Publications. **Figure 9.9:** Adapted from Miller, G. A., Galanter, E., & Pribram, K. H. (1960). *Plans and the structure of behavior.* New York: Holt. **Figure 9.12:** Adapted from Bunge, S. A., Ochsner, K. N., Desmond, J. E., Glover, G. H., & Gabrieli, J. D. (2001). Prefrontal regions involved in keeping information in and out of mind. *Brain, 124,* 2074–2086. **Figure 9.14:** Bray, George A., Nomogram for determining body mass index. Copyright © 1978 George A. Bray. **Figure 9.15:** Fallon, A. E., Sex differences in perceptions of desirable body shape, *Journal of Abnormal Psychology,* 94 [1985]: 102–105. **Figure 9.16:** Adapted from Hibscher, J., & Herman, C. P. (1977). Obesity, dieting, and the expression of "obese" characteristics. *Journal of Comparative and Physiological Psychology, 91,* 374–380. **Figure 9.20:** Aston-Jones, G. and Bloom, F. E., *The Journal of Neuroscience,* 1981, 1, 876–886. Copyright © 1981 by The Society for Neuroscience.

CHAPTER 10: **Figure 10.4:** Adapted from Russell, J. A., & Feldman Barrett, L. (1999). Core affect, prototypical emotional episodes, and other things called emotion: Dissecting the elephant. *Journal of Personality and Social Psychology, 76,* 805–819. **Figure 10.7:** Kalat, James W., Three theories of emotion, table 12.1, from *Introduction to psychology,* 5th Edition, Wadsworth Group.

CHAPTER 11: **Figure 11.14:** Reprinted from *Cognition,* vol. 47 (2) May 1993, Needham, Amy, and Baillargeon, Renee, Intuitions about support in 4.5 month-old infants, 121–148, Copyright © 1993, with permission from Elsevier Science. **Figure 11.15:** Baillargeon, Renee, Physical reasoning in infancy, from *The cognitive neurosciences,* edited by M. S. Gazzaniga, MIT Press. Copyright © 1995. **Figure 11.16:** Baillargeon, Renee, The development of young infants' intuitions about support, *Early Development and Parenting,* vol. 1 (2), July 1992, 69–78. Copyright © 1992 John Wiley & Sons, Ltd. Reproduced with permission. **Figure 11.21:** Nairne, J. S., figure 9.2 from *Psychology: The adaptive mind,* Wadsworth Group. **Figure 11.25:** Sternberg, Robert J., Major abilities and development in the adult period, *Intellectual development.* Reprinted with the permission of Cambridge University Press.

CHAPTER 12: **Figure 12.8:** From Pinel, John P. J., figure 11.7, *Biopsychology,* 4th Edition. Copyright © 2000 by Pearson Education. Reprinted by permission by Allyn & Bacon.

CHAPTER 13: **Figure 13.9:** Adapted from Johnson, M. M. S. (1986). The initial letter effect: Ego-attachment or mere exposure? Unpublished doctoral dissertation, Ohio State University. Reported in Greenwald, A. G., & Banaji, M. R., (1995). Implicit social cognition: Attitudes, self-esteem, and stereotypes. *Psychological Review, 102,* 4–27.

CHAPTER 14: **Figure 14.2:** Adapted from Schachter, S. (1959). *The psychology of affiliation.* Stanford, CA: Stanford University Press. **Figure 14.9:** Adapted from Zajonc, R. B. (1965). Social facilitation. *Science, 149,* 269–274. **Figure 14.11:** Adapted from Asch, S. E. (1955). Opinions and social pressure. *Scientific American, 193,* 31–35 (offprint 450). **Figure 14.15:** Adapted from Milgram, S. (1974). *Obedience to authority: An experimental view.* New York: Harper & Row. **Figure 14.16:** Adapted from Raleigh, M. J., McGuire, M. T., Brammer, G. L., Pollack, D. B., & Yuwiler, A. (1991). Serotonergic mechanisms promote dominance in adult male vervet monkeys. *Brain Research, 559,* 181–190. **Figure 14.17:** Data from United Nations, 1991. **Figure 14.18:** Adapted from Cohen, D., Nisbett, R. E., Bowdle, B. F., & Schwartz, N. (1996). Insult, aggression, and the southern culture of honor: An "experimental ethnography." *Journal of Personality and Social Psychology, 70,* 945–960. **Figure 14.20:** Adapted from Latané, B., & Darley, J. M. (1968). Group inhibition of bystander intervention in emergencies. *Journal of Personality and Social Psychology, 10,* 215–221. **Figure 14.24:** Adapted from Clark, R. D., & Hatfield, E. (1989). Gender differences in receptivity to sexual offers. *Journal of Psychology and Human Sexuality, 2,* 39–55.

CHAPTER 15: **Figure 15.8:** Adapted from Jang, K. L., Lively, W. J., & Vernon, P. A. (1996). Heritability of the Big Five personality dimensions and their facets: A twin study. *Journal of Personality, 64,* 577–591. **Figure 15.9:** Adapted from Caspi, A. (2000). The child is father of the man: Personality continuities from childhood to adulthood. *Journal of Personality and Social Psychology, 78,* 158–172. **Figure 15.12:** Adapted from Roberts, B. W., & Friend-Del Vecchio, W. (2000). The rank-order consistency of personality traits from childhood to old age: A quantitative review of longitudinal studies. *Psychological Bulletin, 126,* 3–25. **Figure 15.13:** Adapted from McCrae, R. R., Costa, P. T., Ostendorf, F., Angleitner, A., Hrebickova, M., Avia, M. D., et al. (2000). Nature over nurture: Temperament, personality, and life span development. *Journal of Personality and Social Psychology, 78,* 173–186. **Figure 15.14:** Adapted from McCrae, R. R., & Costa, P. T., Jr. (1999). A five-factor theory of personality. In L. A. Pervin and O. P. John (Eds.), *Handbook of personality: Theory and research* (2nd ed.). (pp. 139–153). New York: Guilford Press.

CHAPTER 16: Figure 16.8: Adapted from Rapee, R. M., Brown, T. A., Antony, M. M., & Barlow, D. H. (1992a). Response to hyperventilation and inhalation of 5.5% carbon dioxide enriched air across the DSM-III-R anxiety disorders. *Journal of Abnormal Psychology, 101*, 538–552. **Figure 16.9:** Rosenthal, Sack, Gillin, Lewy, Goodwin, Davenport, Mueller, Newsome, Wehr, Depression and length of daylight in seasonal affective disorder, *Archives of General Psychiatry, 41*, [1984], 72–80. **Figure 16.10:** Adapted from Brown & Harris, 1978, *Social origins of depression: A study of psychiatric disorders in women.* New York: The Free Press. **Figure 16.11:** Gottesman, *Schizophrenia genesis: The origins of madness,* W. H. Freeman. Copyright © 1991.

CHAPTER 17: Figure 17.4: Vaughn, C. E., Relapse rates in schizophrenia patients, *British Journal of Psychiatry,* 129 (1976). **Figure 17.7:** Rudestam, Kjell Erik, Anxiety Hierarchy, *Methods of Self-Change: An ABC Primer,* 1980, Monterrey, CA: Brooks/Cole. **Figure 17.10:** Nolen-Hoeksema, S., figure 5.16 from *Abnormal psychology* (1998), The McGraw-Hill Companies. **Figure 17.14:** Adapted from Kane, J. M., Honingfield, G., Singer, J., & Meltzer, N. (1988). Clozapine for the treatment-resistant schizophrenic. *Archives of General Psychiatry, 45*, 789–796. **Figure 17.15:** Adapted from Hogarty, G. E., Anderson, D. M., Reiss, D., J., Kornblith, S. J., Greenwald, D. P. Jaund, D. D. et al. (1986). Family psychoeducation, social skills training, and maintenance chemotherapy in the aftercare treatment of schizophrenia: One-year effects of a controlled study on relapse and expressed emotion. *Archives of General Psychiatry, 43*, 633–642. **Figure 17.17:** Adapted from Hare, R. D., McPherson, L. M., & Forth, A. E. (1988). Male psychopaths and their criminal careers. *Journal of Consulting and Clinical Psychology, 56(5)*, 710–714. **Figure 17.18:** Adapted from Pelham, W. E., Jr. (1993). Pharmacotherapy for children with attention-deficit hyperactivity disorder. *School Psychology Review, 22*, 199–227.

TABLES

Table 7.1: Adapted from Schacter, D. L. (2001). *The seven sins of memory: How the mind forgets and remembers.* Boston: Houghton Mifflin. **Table 9.1:** Adapted from *Diagnostic and Statistical Manual of Mental Disorders DSM-IV,* American Psychiatric Association, 1994. **Table 14.1:** Adapted from Jones, E. E., & Pittman, T. S. (1982). Toward a general theory of strategic self-presentation. In J. Suls (Ed.), *Psychological perspectives on the self* (Vol. 1, pp. 231–262). Hillsdale, NJ: Erlbaum. And Forsyth, D. R. (1995). Our social world. Pacific Grove, CA: Brooks/Cole. **Table 15.3:** Adapted from McAdams. (2000). *The person: an integrated introduction to personality psychology.* Orlando, FL: Harcourt. **Table 16.1:** Adapted from *Diagnostic and Statistical Manual of Mental Disorders DSM-IV,* American Psychiatric Association, 1994. **Table 16.2:** Adapted from Silver, E., Cirincione, C., & Steadman, H. J. (1994). Demythologizing inaccurate perceptions of the insanity defense. *Law & Human Behavior, 18*, 63–70. **Table 16.3:** Adapted from *Diagnostic and Statistical Manual of Mental Disorders DSM-IV,* American Psychiatric Association, 1994. **Table 16.6:** Adapted from *Diagnostic and Statistical Manual of Mental Disorders DSM-IV,* American Psychiatric Association, 1994.

NAME INDEX

SUBJECT INDEX

absentmindedness, 226, 227–28
absolute refractory periods, 74–75
absolute threshold, 127, 129
abuse, 367–68, 546, 548, 551
accommodation, 131, 354, 355, 481–82
acetylcholine (ACh), 80–81, 84, 86, 194, 306, 564, 572, 575, 578, 579
achievement,
    identity, 411
    and motivation, 285–86
    and personality, 496–97, 498–99, 504
achromatopsia, 132–33
acquisition-performance distinction, 180–81
action potentials, 59, 71–73, 74–76, 77, 78, 79, 86, 92, 118, 274, 563
actions, 73–74, 88–89
activation-synthesis hypothesis, 274, 307
actor-observer discrepancy, 440
adaptations, characteristic, 512–14
adaptiveness,
    characteristic, 512–14
    definition of, 9
    and evolutionary theory, 9–10
    and foundations of psychological science, 20
    and functions of behavior, 2
    and influence of neurotransmitters, 81, 93
    and integration of neural messages into communication systems, 92, 93
    and origins of psychological science, 17
    and self-esteem, 426, 428, 430
    and themes of psychological science, 9, 14
    See also specific topic
addiction, 8, 82–83, 86, 163–64, 169–71, 181, 186, 188–93, 198, 563, 564
additive color mixing, 135–36
A-delta fibers, 140
adolescence,
    cognition changes during, 379–80
    depression during, 397
    and gender, 411

and identity, 410, 411, 412, 413
    memory during, 380
    and morality, 403
    and personality disorders, 547
    risks-taking by, 397
    and schizophrenia, 542
    and social development, 397, 399, 403, 410, 411, 412, 413
    and treatments for childhood disorders, 584–88
    and treatments for mental illness, 580
adoption studies, 66, 67, 69, 503, 505, 535–36, 541–42, 548
adrenal glands, 334, 336
adrenaline, 81, 324
adrenocorticotropic hormone (ACTH), 336
affect. *See* emotions
affect-as-information theory, 317
affective neuroscience, 312
afferent neurons, 70–71
affiliation, 448, 452, 453–54, 455, 475–77. *See also* attachment
African Americans, 65, 68, 412, 441, 443, 444. *See also* racism
age,
    and behavior, 348
    and brain, 348, 380–82
    and cognition, 346, 348, 363, 380–83
    and cross-sectional studies, 348
    and culture, 383
    and hearing, 380
    and intelligence, 382–83
    and interpersonal process, 458
    and memory, 380–82, 383
    mental, 258
    and mental processes, 382
    and perception, 380
    and sensory, 380
    and social development, 409–10, 411
    and stress, 341
    and treatments for personality disorders, 584
aggression,
    biological factors influencing, 469–71

and brain, 289, 331
    and culture, 471–72
    definition of, 469
    and frustration-aggression hypothesis, 448, 471, 472
    and gender, 407, 470–71
    and heart disease, 337–38
    and identity, 407
    and interpersonal process, 448, 469–72, 475
    learning, 183, 184–85, 471–72
    and motivation, 282, 289
    and neurotransmitters, 84
    and personality, 489, 494, 495, 515
    and social development, 407
    and stress, 335
agonists, 78, 79, 83, 85, 86
agoraphobia, 531, 532–33, 558–59, 570
agreeability, 494, 495, 504
Air New Zealand crash, 124
akinetopsia, 133, 157
alcohol, 84, 190–93, 218, 223, 228, 354, 508
alcoholism, 191, 337, 568
alexithymia, 320–21
alleles, 63
all-or-none principle, 75, 78
alpha waves, 301, 548
alternative treatment approaches, 575–76, 586
altruism, 472, 473
Alzheimer's disease, 8, 80–81, 381, 514
American Academy of Child and Adolescent Psychiatry, 185
American Academy of Family Physicians, 185
American Academy of Pediatrics, 185
American Law Institute rule, 526
American Medical Association, 185
American Psychiatric Association, 185, 299, 552
American Psychological Association, 185, 299, 552
Ames boxes, 148–49
amino acids, 80, 81, 84–85, 86, 90, 292
amnesia, 80–81, 200, 219, 228, 232, 364–65
amphetamines, 190, 279

amygdala,
    and attitude formation, 432, 439, 440, 443
    and brain structure and functions, 105, 108, 109, 110, 112
    and emotions, 223–24, 291, 312, 328, 329–32, 333
    functions of, 330, 331
    and interpersonal process, 458, 469, 470
    and memory, 219, 220, 223–24, 225
    and motivation, 288, 289, 291, 306, 307
    and personality, 506, 509
    and racial attitudes, 5, 9
    and sleep, 306, 307
anal phase, 489
anal-retentive personalities, 489
analysis, 50–55. *See also* levels of analysis
androgen, 91, 335, 406, 407, 408
androgen insensitivity syndrome, 407
androgynous, 409
anger, 321, 322, 324, 325, 328, 545
animals,
    and attachment, 386, 391–92
    and emotions, 315
    and ethical issues in research methodology, 49–50
    influence of groups on individual, 463
    and learning, 182–83, 184–86
    and memory, 202
    personality of, 494, 495
    and research methodology, 49–50
    self of, 418, 419, 420
    social development among, 395
Anna O. (case study), 30
anorexia nervosa, 298–99, 523–24
antagonists, 78, 79, 86, 572
anterior cingulate, 171, 290–91, 306, 317, 329
antianxiety drugs, 333, 563–64, 571, 583. *See also specific drug*
antibodies, 338, 339
anticipatory coping, 339–40
anticonvulsants, 565